SUPPLEMENT XIII
Edward Abbey to William Jay Smith

American Writers
A Collection of Literary Biographies

JAY PARINI
Editor in Chief

SUPPLEMENT XIII
Edward Abbey to William Jay Smith

Charles Scribner's Sons
an imprint of the Gale Group
New York • Detroit • San Francisco • London • Boston • Woodbridge, CT

American Writers, Supplement XIII
Jay Parini, Editor in Chief

Copyright © 2003 Charles Scribner's Sons
Charles Scribner's Sons is an imprint of
The Gale Group, Inc., a division of
Thomson Learning.

Charles Scribner's Sons™ and Thomson
Learning™ are trademarks used herein under
license.

For more information, contact
Charles Scribner's Sons
An imprint of The Gale Group
300 Park Avenue South, 9th Floor
New York, NY 10010
Or visit our Internet site at
http://www.gale.com

ALL RIGHTS RESERVED
No part of this work covered by the copyright hereon may be reproduced or used in any form or by any means—graphic, electronic, or mechanical, including photocopying, recording, taping, Web distribution, or information storage retrieval systems—without the written permission of the publisher.

For permission to use material from this product, submit your request via Web at http://www.gale-edit.com/permissions, or you may download our Permissions Request form and submit your request by fax or mail to:

Permissions Department
The Gale Group, Inc.
27500 Drake Rd.
Farmington Hills, MI 48331-3535
Permissions hotline:
248 699-8006 or 800 877-4253, ext. 8006
Fax: 248 699-8074 or 800 762-4058

Since this page cannot legibly accommodate all copyright notices, the acknowledgments constitute an extension of the copyright notice.

LIBRARY OF CONGRESS CATALOGING-IN-PUBLICATION DATA

American writers : a collection of literary biographies / Leonard Unger, editor in chief.
    p. cm.
    The 4-vol. main set consists of 97 of the pamphlets originally published as the University of Minnesota pamphlets on American writers; some have been rev. and updated. The supplements cover writers not included in the original series.
    Supplement 2, has editor in chief, A. Walton Litz; Retrospective suppl. 1, c1998, was edited by A. Walton Litz & Molly Weigel; Suppl. 5–7 have as editor-in-chief, Jay Parini.
    Includes bibliographies and index.
    Contents: v. 1. Henry Adams to T.S. Eliot — v. 2. Ralph Waldo Emerson to Carson McCullers — v. 3. Archibald MacLeish to George Santayana — v. 4. Isaac Bashevis Singer to Richard Wright — Supplement[s]: 1, pt. 1. Jane Addams to Sidney Lanier. 1, pt. 2. Vachel Lindsay to Elinor Wylie. 2, pt. 1. W.H. Auden to O. Henry. 2, pt. 2. Robinson Jeffers to Yvor Winters. — 4, pt. 1. Maya Angelou to Linda Hogan. 4, pt. 2. Susan Howe to Gore Vidal — Suppl. 5. Russell Banks to Charles Wright — Suppl. 6. Don DeLillo to W. D. Snodgrass — Suppl. 7. Julia Alvarez to Tobias Wolff — Suppl. 8. T.C. Boyle to August Wilson. — Suppl. 9. Nelson Algren to David Wagoner. — Suppl. 10. Madison Smartt Bell to John Edgar Wideman. — Suppl. 11. Toni Cade Bambara to Richard Yates.
    ISBN 0-684-19785-5 (set) — ISBN 0-684-13662-7
    1. American literature—History and criticism. 2. American literature—Bio-bibliography. 3. Authors, American—Biography. I. Unger, Leonard. II. Litz, A. Walton. III. Weigel, Molly. IV. Parini, Jay. V. University of Minnesota pamphlets on American writers.

PS129 .A55
810'.9
[B]   73-001759

ISBN: 0-684-31233-6

Printed in the United States of America
10 9 8 7 6 5 4 3 2 1

Editorial and Production Staff

Project Editor
ALJA KOOISTRA COLLAR

Assisting Editor
MARK DROUILLARD

Copyeditors
JANET L. BADGLEY
LISA DIXON
MELISSA A. DOBSON
GRETCHEN GORDON
MARCIA MERRYMAN MEANS
ANNA NESBITT

Proofreader
CAROL HOLMES

Permission Researchers
DEBRA FREITAS
JULIE VAN PELT

Indexer
KATHARYN DUNHAM

Compositor
GARY LEACH

Publisher
FRANK MENCHACA

Acknowledgments

Acknowledgment is gratefully made to those publishers and individuals who have permitted the use of the following material in copyright. Every effort has been made to secure permission to reprint copyrighted material.

EDWARD ABBEY Excerpts from an introduction by Charles Bowden in *Black Sun*, by Edward Abbey. Capra Press, 1990. Copyright © 1990 by Capra Press. All rights reserved. Reproduced by permission. Excerpts from "A Writer's Credo," by Edward Abeey. In *One Life at a Time, Please*. Henry Holt and Company, Inc., 1988. Copyright © 1988 by Henry Holt and Company, Inc. All rights reserved. Reproduced by permission. Excerpts from "Hallelujah on the Bum" and "Introduction," by Edward Abbey. In *The Journey Home: Some Words in Defense of the American West*. E. P. Dutton, 1977. Copyright © 1977 by Edward Abbey. All rights reserved. Reproduced by permission by the author.

MARGARET ATWOOD Excerpts from "A Bus Along St. Clair: December," by Margaret Atwood. In *The Journals of Susanna Moodie: Poems*. Oxford University Press, 1970. Copyright © 1970 by Oxford University Press. All rights reserved. Reproduced by permission. Excerpts from "Untitled Epigraph," by Margaret Atwood. In *Power Politics*. House of Anansi Press Limited, 1971. Copyright © 1971 by Margaret Atwood. All rights reserved. Reproduced by permission of the author. In the USA by permission of the Houghton Mifflin Company. In Canada by permission of Oxford University Press, Canada. Excerpts from "Dreams of Animals" and "Procedures for Underground," by Margaret Atwood. In *Procedures for Underground*. Oxford University Press, 1970. Copyright © 1970 by Oxford University Press. All rights reserved. Reproduced by permission. Excerpts from "There Is Only One of Everything" and "You Are Happy," by Margaret Atwood. In *You Are Happy*. Harper & Row Publishers, Inc., 1974. Copyright © 1974 by Margaret Atwood. All rights reserved. Reproduced by permission of the author. In the USA by permission of the Houghton Mifflin Company. In Canada by permission of Oxford University Press, Canada. Excerpts from "You Begin," by Margaret Atwood. In *Two-Headed Poems*. Oxford University Press, 1978. Copyright © 1978 by Margaret Atwood. All rights reserved. Reproduced by permission of the author. In the USA by permission of the Houghton Mifflin Company. In Canada by permission of Oxford University Press, Canada. Excerpts from "Notes Towards a Poem That Could Never Be Written" and "True Stories," by Margaret Atwood. In *True Stories*. Oxford University Press, 1981. Copyright © 1981 by Margaret Atwood. All rights reserved. Reproduced by permission of the author. In the USA by permission of the Houghton Mifflin Company. In Canada by permission of Oxford University Press, Canada.

NICHOLSON BAKER Excerpts from "Inner Space: Changes of Mind," by Nicholson Baker. *The Atlantic* 250 (November 1982). Reproduced by permission of the author's agent. Excerpts from "He Knows What You've Been Reading," by Laura Miller. Salon.com. Reprinted by permission. (http://archive.salon.com/media/1998/04/03mediab.htm). Excerpts from "Annals of Scholarship: Discards," by Nicholson Baker. *The New Yorker Magazine*, April 4, 1994. Reproduced by permission of the author's agent. Excerpts from *The Fermata*, by Nicholson Baker. Random House, Inc., 1994. Copyright © 1994 by Nicholson Baker. All rights reserved. Reproduced by permission of the author's agent. Excerpts from *The Mezzanine*, by Nicholson Baker. Weidenfeld & Nicolson, 1988. Copyright © 1988. All rights reserved. Reproduced by permission. Excerpts from "Lumber," by Nicholson Baker. In *The Size of Thoughts: Essays and Other Lumber*. Random House, 1996. Copyright © 1996 by Nicholson Baker. All rights reserved. Reproduced by permission.

STEPHEN DOBYNS Excerpts from "A Bach Partita," by Stephen Dobyns. In *The Porcupine's Kisses*. Penguin, 2002. Copyright © 2002 by Penguin. All rights reserved. Reproduced by permission. Excerpts from "The Gun," by Stephen Dobyns. *Antaeus* 47 (autumn 1982). Reproduced by permission of the author. Excerpts from "Black Dog, Red Dog," by Stephen Dobyns. *American Poetry Review* 11 (July/August 1982). Reproduced by permission of the author. Excerpts from "The Body's Weight," by Stephen Dobyns. *American Poetry Review* 19 (July/August 1990). Reproduced by permission of the author. Excerpts from "How To Like It," by Stephen Dobyns. *Ploughshares* (spring 1985). Reproduced by permission of the author. Excerpts from "Tenderly," by Stephen Dobyns. *Ploughshares* (winter 1993/94). Reproduced by permission of the author.

LESLIE FIEDLER Excerpts from *From Tyranny of the Normal: Essays on Bioethics, Theology & Myth*, by Leslie Fiedler. David R. Godine, Publisher, Inc., 1996. Copyright © 1996 by Leslie Fiedler. All rights reserved. Reproduced by permission of the author. Excerpts from a review by Kenneth Lynn of *What Was Literature?* by Leslie Fiedler. *Commentary* 75 (January 1983). Reproduced by permission of the publisher and the author. Excerpts from "Fiedler's Utopian Vision," by David Gates. *Newsweek*, January 9, 1984. Reproduced by permission. Excerpts from "Montana; or, the End of Jean-Jacques Rousseau," by Leslie Fiedler. *Partisan Review* 16 (December 1949). Reproduced by permission.

YUSEF KOMUNYAKAA Excerpts from "Lines of Tempered Steel," by Vince Gotera. *Callaloo* 13, no. 2 (1990). Reproduced by permission. Excerpts from "Control Is the Mainspring," by Yusef

Komunyakaa. *Hayden's Ferry Review* 10 (spring–summer 1992). Reproduced by permission. Excerpts from "Still Negotiating with Yusek Komunyakaa," by William Baer. *The Kenyon Review* 20 (summer/fall 1998). Reproduced by permission of the author. Excerpts from "An Interview with Yusef Komunyakaa," by Muna Asali. *New England Review* 16, no. 1 (1994). Reproduced by permission of Yusef Komunyakaa and Muna Asali. Excerpts from "Conversation with Yusef Komunyakaa," by Alan Fox. *Rattle* 4 (summer 1998). Reproduced by permission. Excerpts from "The Body Is Our First Music," by Tony Barnstone and Michael Garabedian. *Poetry Flash* (June–July 1998). Reproduced by permission. Excerpts from "Notations in Blue," by Radiclani Clytus. In *Blue Notes: Essays, Interviews, and Commentaries.* Edited by Radiclani Clytus. The University of Michigan Press, 2000. Copyright © 2000 by the University of Michigan. All rights reserved. Reproduced by permission. Excerpts from "Kit and Caboodle," by Yusef Komunyakaa. In *The Eye of the Poet: Six Views of the Art and Craft of Poetry.* Edited by David Citino. Oxford University Press, 2002. Copyright © 2002 by Oxford University Press. All rights reserved. Reproduced by permission. Excerpts from "After the Heart's Interrogation," "Ambush," "Anodyne," "The Beast & Burden," "Blue Light Lounge Sutra for the Performance Poets at Harold Park Hotel," "Blues Chant Hoodoo Rival," "The Brain to the Heart," "Camouflaging the Chimera," "Corrigenda," "Dog Act," "Everybody's Reading Li Po' Silkscreened on a Purple T-Shirt," "Facing It," "False Leads," "Family Tree," "February in Sydney," "Floor Plans," "For the Walking Dead," "Fragging," "I Apologize," "Landscape for the Disappeared," "Legacy," "Leper's Bell," "Lightshow," "Missing in Action," "Moonshine," "My Father's Love Letters," "No-Good Blues," "Nothing Big," "Reflections," "Returning (1975)," "Returning to the Borrowed Road," "Roll Call," "Safe Subjects," "Sitting in a Rocking Chair, Going Blind," "Soliloquy," "Somewhere Near Phu Bai," "Songs for My Father," "Starlight Scope Myopia," "Sunday Afternoons," "The Thorn Merchant," "The Tongue Is," "Tour Guide," "Unnatural State of the Unicorn," "Untitled Blues," "Urban Renewal," "Venus's-flytraps," "Water Buffalo," "The Way the Cards Fall," "When In Rome–Apologia," and "The Whistle," by Yusef Komunyakaa. In *Pleasure Dome: New and Collected Poems.* Wesleyan University Press, 2001. Copyright © 2001 by Yusef Komunyakaa. All rights reserved. Reproduced by permission. Excerpts from "Ecstatic," "The Four Evangelists," "Happenstance," "Infidelity," "Meditations in a Swine Yard," and "Negative Capability," by Yusef Komunyakaa. In *Talking Dirty to the Gods.* Farrar, Straus and Giroux, 2000. Copyright © 2000 by Yusef Komunyakaa. All rights reserved. Reproduced by permission.

HORACE MCCOY Excerpts from a review by Robert Van Gelder of *They Shoot Horses, Don't They,* by Horace McCoy. *New York Times,* July 25, 1935. Reproduced by permission.

TERRENCE MCNALLY Excerpts from "The Muses of Terrence McNally," by Toby Silverman Zinman. *American Theatre* 12 (March 1995). Reproduced by permission. Excerpts from "What I Know about Being a Playwright," by Terrence McNally. *American Theatre* 15 (November 1998). Reproduced by permission. Excerpts from "Terrence McNally," by Steven Drukman. In *Speaking on Stage: Interviews with Contemporary American Playwrights.* Edited by Philip C. Kolin and Colby H. Kullman. University of Alabama Press, 1996. Copyright © 1996 by The University of Alabama Press. All rights reserved. Reproduced by permission. Excerpts from "Terrence McNally," by David Savran. In *The Playwright's Voice: American Dramatists on Memory, Writing, and the Politics of Cultures.* Theatre Communications Group, Inc., 1999. Copyright © 1999 by Theatre Communications Group, Inc. All rights reserved. Reproduced by permission. Excerpts from "The Three Branches," by Marc A. Scorca. (http://www.operaam.org/3balla.htm). Published by operaam.org. Reprinted by permission.

PAT MORA Excerpts from "Coatlicue's Rules: Advice from an Aztec Goddess," "Consejos de Nuestra Señora de Guadalupe: Counsel from the Brown Virgin," "Llantos de La Llorona: Warnings from the Wailer," and "Malinche's Tips: Pique from Mexico's Mother," by Pat Mora. In *Agua Santa/Holy Water.* Beacon Press, 1995. Copyright © 1995 by Pat Mora. All rights reserved. Reproduced by permission. Excerpts from "Bilingual Christmas," "Sonrisas," and "Tomas Rivera," by Pat Mora. In *Borders.* Arte Publico Press, 1986. Copyright © 1986 by Pat Mora. All rights reserved. Reproduced by permission. Excerpts from "Gentle Communion" and "My Word-house," by Pat Mora. In *Communion.* Arte Publico Press, 1991. Copyright © 1991 by Pat Mora. All rights reserved. Reproduced by permission.

WALTER MOSLEY Excerpts from "Equal Opportunity," by Walter Mosley. In *Always Outnumbered, Always Outgunned.* W. W. Norton & Company, 1998. Copyright © 1998 by Walter Mosley. All rights reserved. Reproduced by permission. Excerpts from "Walter Mosley," by Thulani Davis. *Bomb* 44 (summer 1993). Reproduced by permission. Excerpts from "The Clues to the City of L.A.; Walter Mosley's Gumshoe Tracks Decades of Despair," by David Streitfeld. *Washington Post,* November 10, 1992. Reproduced by permission.

JOHN NICHOLS Excerpts from *An American Child Supreme: The Education of a Liberation Ecologist,* by John Nichols. Milkweed Editions, 2001. Copyright © 2001, Essay by John Nichols. Copyright © 2001, Bibliography by John Nichols and Patrick Barron. All rights reserved. Reproduced by permission. Excerpts from "My Sentimental Education," by John Nichols. In *Dancing on the Stones.* University of New Mexico Press, 2000. Copyright © 2000 by John Nichols. All rights reserved. Reproduced by permission. Excerpts from "John (Treadwell) Nichols." (www.galenet.com). Published by Contemporary Authors Online. Reprinted with permission.

NAOMI SHIHAB NYE Excerpts from "Things Don't Stop," by Naomi Shihab Nye. In *19 Gazelles: Poems of the Middle East.* Greenwillow Books, A Imprint of Harper Collins Publishers, 2002. Copyright © 1994, 1995, 1998, 2002 by Naomi Shihab Nye. All rights reserved. Reproduced by permission. Excerpts from "Different Ways to Pray," by Naomi Shihab Nye. In *Different Ways to Pray.* Breitenbush Publications, 1980. Copyright © 1980 by Naomi Shihab Nye. All rights reserved. Reproduced by permission. Excerpts from "Fuel," "Hidden," and "Steps," by Naomi Shihab Nye. In *Fuel.* BOA Editions, 1998. Copyright © 1998 by Naomi Shihab Nye. All rights reserved. Reproduced by permission. Excerpts from "Thank You in Arabic," by Naomi Shihab Nye. In *Going Where I'm Coming From.* Edited by Anne Mazer. Persea, 1995. Copyright © 1995 by Persea. Reprinted in *Never in a Hurry: Essays on People and Places*. University of South Carolina Press 1996. Copyright © 1996 by University of South Carolina. All rights reserved. Reproduced by permission. Excerpts from "Jerusalem," by Naomi Shihab Nye. In *Red Suitcase*. BOA Editions, 1994. Copyright © 1994 by Naomi Shihab Nye. All rights reserved. Reproduced by permission. Excerpts from "To Any Would-Be Terrorists," by Naomi Shihab Nye. In *September 11, 2001: American Writers Respond*. Edited William Heyen. Etruscan Press, 2002. Copyright © 2002 by William Heyen. All rights reserved. Reproduced by permission.

TILLIE OLSEN Excerpts from "Tell Me a Riddle," by Tillie Olsen. In *New World Writing, Volume 16*. Edited by Stewart Richardson and Corlies M. Smith. J. B. Lippincott Company, 1960. Copyright © 1960 by J. B. Lippincott Company. All rights reserved. Reproduced by permission. Excerpts from "Requa," by Tillie Olsen. *Iowa Review* 1 (summer 1970). Reproduced by permission of the author. Excerpts from "Obstacle Course," by Margaret Atwood. *New York Times Book Review,* July 30, 1978. Reproduced by permission. Excerpts from "Help Her To Believe," by Tillie Olsen. *Pacific Spectator* 10 (winter 1956). Reproduced by permission. Excerpts from "Baptism," by Tillie Olsen. *Prairie Schooner* 31 (spring 1957). Reproduced by permission.

LUIS OMAR SALINAS Excerpts from "Going North," "Magnificent Little Gift," "Ode to the Mexican Experience," "Olivia," "Salinas Is on His way," and "Salinas Sends Messengers to the Stars," by Luis Omar Salinas. In *Afternoon of the Unreal*. Abramas, 1980. Copyright © 1980 by Abramas. All rights reserved. Reproduced by permission. Excerpts from "Aztec Angel," "Death in Viet Nam" "Saturday," and "Title Poem," by Luis Omar Salinas. In *Crazy Gypsy*. Origines, 1970. Copyright © 1970 by Luis Omar Salinas. All rights reserved. Reproduced by permission. Excerpts from "A Clever Magician Carrying My Heart," "Darkness under the Trees" "Fragments for Fall," "I'm on My Way," "I'm Walking behind the Spanish," "My Father Is a Simple Man," "Ode to Cervantes" "The Odds," "Someone Is Buried" "Soto Thinking of the Ocean," "This Is What I Said," and "When We Have To," by Luis Omar Salinas. In *Darkness under the Trees/Walking behind the Spanish*. Chicano Studies Library Publications, University of California, 1982. Copyright © 1982 by Luis Omar Salinas. All rights reserved. Reproduced by permission. Excerpts from *Luis Omar Salinas: Greatest Hits 1969–1996,* by Luis Omar Salinas. Pudding House, 2002. Copyright © 2002 by Pudding House. All rights reserved. Reproduced by permission. Excerpts from "As Evening Lays Dying," "I Sigh in the Afternoon," "Last Tango in Fresno," "Prelude to Darkness," and "Visitors," by Luis Omar Salinas. In *Prelude to Darkness*. Mango, 1981. Copyright © 1981 by Mango. All rights reserved. Reproduced by permission. Excerpts from "After a Party," "The Beginning of Enthusiasm," "Love Rushes By," "My 50 Plus Years Celebrate Spring," "Prayer to the Child of Prague," and "Sometimes Mysteriously," by Luis Omar Salinas. In *Sometimes Mysteriously*. Salmon Run, 1997. Copyright © 1997 by Salmon Run. All rights reserved. Reproduced by permission. Excerpts from "Beyond the Sea," "How Much Are You Worth," "Letter to Soto," "On a Visit to a Halfway House after a Long Absence," and "Sadness of Days," by Luis Omar Salinas. In *The Sadness of Days: Selected and New Poems*. Arte Publico, 1987. Copyright © 1987 by Luis Omar Salinas. All rights reserved. Reproduced by permission. Excerpts from "Mexican-American Literature: An Overview," by Raymund A. Paredes. In *Recovering the U.S. Hispanic Literary*. Edited by Ramón Gutiérrez and Genaro Padilla. Arte Publico, 1993. Copyright © 1993 by Arte Publico Press. All rights reserved. Reproduced by permission. Excerpts from "Strange Hours of the Day," by Donald Wolff. *Berkeley Poetry Review* 14, no. 1 (1982). Reproduced by permission. Excerpts from "Luis Omar Salinas: Chicano Poet," by Gary Soto. *MELUS* 9 (summer 1982). Reproduced by permission. Excerpts from "Any Good Fortune," by Christopher Buckley. *Quarterly West* 55 (fall/winter 2002/2003). Reproduced by permission. Excerpts from A Life Charmed and Haunted," by Donald Wolff. *SOLO* 3 (1999). Reproduced by permission.

WILLIAM JAY SMITH Excerpts from "The Closing of the Rodeo," by William Jay Smith. In *Celebration at Dark*. Farrar, Straus and Company, 1950. Copyright © 1950 by Farrar, Straus and Company. All rights reserved. Reproduced by permission of Johns Hopkins University Press. Excerpts from "The Floor to Ceiling," "Journey to the Interior," and "The Players," by William Jay Smith. In *Collected Poems 1939–1989*. Scribners, 1990. Copyright © 1990 by William Jay Smith. Copyright © 1989 by William Jay Smith. All rights reserved. Reproduced by permission. Excerpts from "Quail in Autumn," by William Jay Smith. In *L'Arbre du voyageur*. Translated by Sonja Haussmann. Sud, 1990. Copyright © 1990 by Sud. All rights reserved. Reproduced by permission. Excerpts from "A Pavane for the Nusery," by William Jay Smith. In *The Girl in Glass: Love Poems*. Books & Co., 2002. Copyright © 2002 by Books & Co. All rights reserved. Reproduced by permission. Excerpts from "Moon Solo," by William Jay Smith. In *Selected Writings of Jules Laforgue*. Edited and translated by William Jay Smith. Grove Press, 1956. Copyright © 1956 by William Jay Smith. All rights reserved. Reproduced by permission. Excerpts from "American Primitive" and "Death of a Jazz Musician," by William Jay Smith. In *Poems 1947–1957*. Seymour Lawrence–Little, Brown, 1957. Copyright © 1957 by William Jay Smith. All rights reserved. Reproduced by permission. Excerpts from "Children and Poetry," "A Frame for Poetry," "In Praise in Childhood," "The Makers of Poems," and "1966," by William Jay Smith. In *The Streaks of the Tulip: Selected Criticism*. Seymour Lawrence–Delacorte Press, 1972. Copyright © 1972 by William Jay Smith. All rights reserved. Reproduced by permission. Excerpts from "Morels," "Quail in Autumn," and "The Tin Can," by William Jay Smith. In *The Tin Can, and Other Poems*. Seymour Lawrence–Delacorte Press, 1966. Copyright © 1966 by William Jay Smith. All rights reserved. Reproduced by permission. Excerpts from "The Cherokee Lottery," "The Eagle Warrior: An Invocation," "Full Circle: The Connecticut Casino," "The Pumpkin Field," "The Trail," and acknowledgments and notes, by William Jay Smith. In *The Cherokee Lottery: A Sequence of Poems*. Curbstone Press, 2002. Copyright © 1998, 2000 by William Jay Smith. All rights reserved. Reproduced by permission. Excerpts from "The Journey of William Jay Smith," by Dana Gioia. *Cumberland Poetry Review* 2 (spring 1983). Reproduced by permission. Excerpts from "The Dark Train and the Green Place: The Poetry of William Jay Smith," by Josephine Jacobsen. *The Hollins*

Critic 12 (February 1975). Reproduced by permission. Excerpts from "William Jay Smith: Enter the Dark Horse," by William Taylor. *Michigan Quarterly Review* 30 (fall 1991). Reproduced by permission. Excerpts from "William Jay Smith at Eighty: An Interview," by Robert Phillips. *New Letters* 65, no. 3 (1999). Reproduced by permission.

List of Subjects

Introduction	*xiii*	TERRY McMILLAN *Kathy Heininge*	179
List of Contributors	*xv*	TERRENCE McNALLY *Karma Waltonen*	195
EDWARD ABBEY *Donna Seaman*	1	PAT MORA *Bert Almon*	213
MARGARET ATWOOD *Joy Arbor*	19	WALTER MOSLEY *Rebecca Berg*	233
NICHOLSON BAKER *D. Quentin Miller*	41	JOHN NICHOLS *Charles R. Baker*	253
OCTAVIA BUTLER *Stefanie K. Dunning*	59	NAOMI SHIHAB NYE *Bert Almon*	273
STEPHEN DOBYNS *Janna King*	73	TILLIE OLSEN *Jennifer M. Hoofard*	291
LESLIE FIEDLER *Sanford Pinsker*	93	LUIS OMAR SALINAS *Christopher Buckley*	311
YUSEF KOMUNYAKAA *Joyce Sutphen*	111	WILLIAM JAY SMITH *David R. Slavitt*	331
LUCY LARCOM *Karen L. Kilcup*	137	*Cumulative Index*	*351*
HORACE McCOY *Robert Niemi*	159		

Introduction

This supplement of American Writers, our thirteenth, is largely concerned with contemporary writers, poets and novelists, many of whom have won a wide and sympathetic audience for their work, although the critics have yet to catch up with them. One of the things this series does is provide substantial, full-length readings of many fine American authors in different genres who have not been afforded this kind of attention to date. As such, these essays provide a starting point, a place where interested readers can find straightforward, intelligent, provocative accounts of the careers of the writers under consideration.

American Writers had its origin in a series of monographs that appeared between 1959 and 1972. The Minnesota Pamphlets on American Writers made a considerable impact at the time. Written by well-known critics, they were incisive and informative, treating ninety-seven American writers in a format and style that attracted a devoted following of readers. The series proved invaluable to a generation of students and teachers, who could depend on these reliable and interesting readings of the lives and works of major figures. The idea of reprinting these essays occurred to Charles Scribner Jr. (1921–1995). The series, in its new package, appeared in four volumes entitled *American Writers: A Collection of Literary Biographies* (1974).

Since then, a dozen supplements have appeared, treating well over two hundred American writers: poets, novelists, playwrights, essayists, and autobiographers. The idea has been consistent with the original series: to provide clear, informative essays aimed at the general reader. These essays often rise to a high level of craft and critical vision, but they are meant to introduce a writer of some importance in the history of American literature, and to provide a sense of the scope and nature of the career under review. In each case, the critics are asked to avoid using jargon and to write clearly and without pretense. In an age when critical writing has increasingly become opaque and jargon-ridden, these essays provide a refuge for readers who crave a subtle, well-informed reading not intended for a specialist or a tenure committee. The essays also try to provide as much background information as readers will need to interpret the work at hand.

The authors of these essays are mostly college teachers, scholars, and writers. Most have published books and articles in their field, and several are well-known writers of poetry or fiction as well as critics. As anyone glancing through this volume will see, they are held to the highest standards of good writing and sound scholarship, and their arguments are expected to make sense. The essays each conclude with a select bibliography meant to provide an overall view of the subject's achievement and to direct the reading of those who want to pursue the work of a given author further.

The subjects of these essays have on the whole received little sustained attention from critics. They have been written about in the review pages of newspapers and magazines, and their writing has acquired a substantial readership in many cases, but their work has yet to attract sustained and significant scholarship. That kind of scholarly reading will certainly follow, but the essays included here constitute a beginning.

The poets included here are Stephen Dobyns, Yusef Komunyakaa, Lucy Larcom (a writer from the nineteenth century who once had a huge following), Luis Omar Salinas, William Jay Smith, Pat Mora, and Naomi Shihab Nye (the latter three are also well known as writers for children). These writers are well known in the poetry world, and their work has in each case been honored with prizes and fellowships. Their poetry has been widely anthologized as well. Nevertheless, the real work of assimilation, of discovering the true place of each poet in the larger traditions of American poetry, has only begun. In some cases, these poets are written about by critics who are themselves poets, and the depth and eloquence of their essays should be obvious even to casual readers.

In the area of nonfiction, this volume includes an essay on Edward Abbey, one of the great nature writers of the twentieth century. The fiction writers treated here range from the Canadian Margaret Atwood (who is also a poet of considerable fame) and Nicholson Baker to Tillie Olsen and John Nichols, who has had many of his novels turned into films. As in previous volumes, we attempt to look at popular writers as well as those who might be considered more literary, although these distinctions are often less than helpful. Certainly Terry McMillan is one of the most popular African American novelists, and she is discussed in this supplement, as are Walter Mosley, a sophisticated novelist who has focused on the genre of the detective story, and Horace McCoy, who writes in the hard-boiled genre. Science fiction writer Octavia Butler is also considered.

The only dramatist considered in this supplement is Terrence McNally, a contemporary playwright who has made a huge career on Broadway by writing popular plays that treat serious themes. He has also won acclaim for his sensitive writing in the area of gay literature. The single critic discussed here is Leslie Fiedler, an influential scholar of American literature and a memoirist.

The critics who contributed to this volume of *American Writers* represent a wide range of backgrounds and critical approaches, although the baseline for inclusion was that each essay should be accessible to the non-specialist reader or beginning student. The creation of culture involves the continuous reassessment of major texts produced by its writers, and my belief is that this supplement performs a useful service here, providing substantial introductions to American writers who matter, and it will assist readers in the difficult but rewarding work of close reading.

—*JAY PARINI*

Contributors

Bert Almon. Professor of English at the University of Alberta. Author of a book on William Humphrey and a study of autobiography, *This Stubborn Self: Texas Autobiographies 1925–2001*, as well as eight collections of poetry. Born in Port Arthur, Texas. PAT MORA, NAOMI SHIHAB NYE

Joy Arbor. Teaches at the University of Nebraska–Lincoln. She has written for Women Writers (www.womenwriters.net) and the *Oxford Encyclopedia of American Literature*. She has poems in *Crab Orchard Review, Hayden's Ferry Review*, and others. MARGARET ATWOOD

Charles R. Baker. Poet, short story writer, and essayist. Latest published work of fiction is a 2002 Christmas story, "The Harp." A frequent contributor to *American Writers, British Writers*, and *American Writers Classics*, Mr. Baker has also written for the upcoming *Oxford Encyclopedia of American Literature* and is curator of "Mark Twain: Father of Modern American Literature" at Bridwell Library, Southern Methodist University. JOHN NICHOLS

Rebecca Berg. Freelance writer and editor. Her publications include the short stories "A History of Song," which appeared in the *Five Fingers Review*, and "The Shriek of a Heron," which appeared in the *Talus Review*. Recently she has completed work on a novel. She earned her Ph.D. in English from Cornell University. WALTER MOSLEY

Christopher Buckley. Teaches in the creative writing department at the University of California Riverside. His most recent books of poetry are *Star Apocrypha* and *Closer to Home: Poems of Santa Barbara, 1975–1995*. A letter-press chapbook, *Cloud Journal*, has been published by Aureole Press in 2003. LUIS OMAR SALINAS

Stefanie K. Dunning. Assistant Professor of English at Miami University of Ohio. Her essay "Parallel Perversions: Interracial and Same-Sex Desire in James Baldwin's *Another Country*" has been published in *MELUS*; "Vegetarianism and Dreadlocks: The Politics of 'Consciousness' and Cultural Identification" has been published in *Black Renaissance/Renaissance Noire*; her latest work of fiction, "Bus Stop," is published at ExittheApple.com. She has also published several essays in the *Stanford Black Arts Quarterly*. OCTAVIA BUTLER

Kathy Heininge. Teaches English at the University of California, Davis. Her publications include an essay on Stephen King for the *Oxford Encyclopedia of American Writers* and "Observe the Sons of Ulster Talking Themselves to Death." Her research focus is primarily Irish drama. TERRY MCMILLAN

Jennifer M. Hoofard. Ph.D. candidate in English at the University of California, Davis specializing in literature by women. She is an associate in English at University of California, Davis, teaching composition and comparative literature classes, and has published poetry in the journals *Fireweed, Samsara, Psychopoetica*, among others. She also works with California Poets in the Schools. TILLIE OLSEN

Karen L. Kilcup. Professor of American literature at the University of North Carolina at Greensboro and recently named Davidson Eminent Scholar Chair at Florida International University. Her books include *Native American Women's Writing, c. 1800–1924: An Anthology*;

Soft Canons: American Women Writers and Masculine Tradition; and *Robert Frost and Feminine Literary Tradition.* LUCY LARCOM

Janna King. Freelance writer and editor who has published poetry, short stories, essays, and interviews in various periodicals. STEPHEN DOBYNS

D. Quentin Miller. Assistant Professor of English at Suffolk University. Author of *Re-Viewing James Baldwin: Things Not Seen* and *John Updike and the Cold War: Drawing the Iron Curtain.* He has published on a wide variety of American authors and is a member of the editorial board of the *Heath Anthology of American Literature.* NICHOLSON BAKER

Robert Niemi. Associate Professor of English, St. Michael's College. Author of books on Russell Banks and Weldon Kees and numerous articles on literature and popular culture. HORACE MCCOY

Sanford Pinsker. Shadek Professor of Humanities at Franklin and Marshall College. Writes widely about American literature for journals, such as the *Virginia Quarterly, Sewanee Review, Georgia Review,* and *Partisan Review.* Author of *The Comedy That "Hoits": An Essay on the Fiction of Philip Roth.* LESLIE FIEDLER

Donna Seaman. Selected and introduced the short story anthology *In Our Nature: Stories of Wilderness.* An editor for *Booklist,* she also writes essays, reviews, and articles for a variety of publications, including the *Chicago Tribune, Newsday,* the *Ruminator Review,* and *TriQuarterly.* EDWARD ABBEY

David R. Slavitt. Author and translator who has taught at Columbia University, University of Pennsylvania, Princeton University, and Bennington. His recent and forthcoming books include *Propertius in Love: The Elegies of Sextus Propertius; Selected Poems of Manuel Bandeira; Aspects of the Novel: A Novel;* and *New and Selected Poems.* WILLIAM JAY SMITH

Joyce Sutphen. Associate Professor of English at Gustavus Adolphus College in St. Peter, Minnesota. Her first collection of poems, *Straight Out of View,* won the Barnard New Women Poets Prize. Her second book, *Coming Back to the Body,* was a Minnesota Book Award finalist, and her third book is *Naming the Stars.* Some of her poems are included in *33 Minnesota Poets; Boomer Girls; The POETRY Anthology, 1912–2002;* and Garrison Keillor's *Good Poems.* YUSEF KOMUNYAKAA

Karma Waltonen. Ph.D. candidate in English Literature at the University of California, Davis. She teaches at American River College and Sacramento City College. She has published an essay on Margaret Atwood in *Identity and Alterity in Canadian Literature* and an essay on George Bernard Shaw in *Shaw: The Annual of Bernard Shaw Studies,* both forthcoming. TERRENCE MCNALLY

SUPPLEMENT XIII
Edward Abbey to William Jay Smith

Edward Abbey

1927–1989

EDWARD ABBEY BELIEVED in freedom and wilderness, honesty and art. A man of profound convictions and complicated contradictions, a romantic and a skeptic, he fit no category and towed no line, and confounded friend and foe alike. A philosopher, he nonetheless distrusted abstractions. An acute and exacting observer of the natural world, he objected to being called a nature writer and was highly critical of science's reductiveness. Driven by an innate faith in the soul and a preacher's impulse to testify and sermonize, he disdained religion. Born in the Allegheny Mountains, he fell madly in love with the desert of the Southwest. A genuine nature lover who believed that all life is sacred, Abbey decried humanity's hubristic and destructive notion of its own supremacy. Wildly inventive and unflaggingly energetic in his protest against America's rampant governmental-industrial-consumer culture on the one hand, and the hypocrisy and triteness of political correctness on the other, Abbey appalled readers who shared his environmental convictions by making disparaging remarks about non-Anglo cultures and advocating the practice of monkey-wrenching, acts such as torching highway billboards and disabling bulldozers.

Abbey has been revered as a naturalist and maligned as a racist. He has been recognized as a major twentieth-century writer—albeit "one of the most underrated in American literature," according to his biographer James Cahalan—and been dismissed as a vulgarian and curmudgeon. A man who adored and needed women, he came across as a blatant misogynist. All but ignored by the Eastern literati, who were impervious to the wily humor that spikes his satirical fiction and blazing essays, Abbey persevered in spite of critical neglect, writing with undiminished passion and discipline until he achieved a place in the pantheon of his heroes: Walt Whitman, Mark Twain, Henry Thoreau, and John Steinbeck, not to mention Henry Miller and Hunter S. Thompson.

In "A Writer's Credo" (collected in *One Life at a Time, Please,* 1988), Abbey reflects on the writer's duties and responsibilities: "The task of the honest writer—the writer as potential hero—is to seek out, write down, and publish forth those truths which are *not* self-evident, not universally agreed upon, not allowed to determine public feeling and official policy." This pursuit of truth, this commitment to voicing uncompromising opinions and observations that people do not want to hear, can earn a writer more resentment than admiration, and Abbey came to accept the fact that he made numerous enemies. But he was also revered by legions of appreciative readers for his extraordinary literary gifts and his uncompromising and prescient defense of the earth.

Jack Loeffler, a close friend of Abbey's who shared his passion for music and love of the desert (he estimates that they hiked thousands of miles together), describes his much-missed buddy as a "born anarchist" and "a revolutionary with a sense of humor" in his intimate and incisive tribute to Abbey, *Adventures with Ed* (2002). In *Epitaph for a Desert Anarchist* (1994), James Bishop Jr. declares, "Abbey was a genuine rebel who simply did not believe in the modern industrial way of life. He wrote against the grain, always choosing the path of the greatest resistance." Wendell Berry praises

Abbey as a "cultivated man" and a "splendid writer" in the 1985 collection *Resist Much, Obey Little*, even as he avers that Abbey was a perpetual "horse of another color, and one that requires care to appreciate." David Petersen, a friend and ardent admirer who edited Abbey's substantial journals to create the powerful volume, *Confessions of a Barbarian* (1994; the title is Abbey's), describes Abbey as a "great soulful intellect." And Abbey himself relished the role of *vox clamantis in deserto,* a voice crying in the wilderness.

APPALACHIAN SPRING

Born on January 29, 1927, Edward Abbey was the first of five children raised by Paul Revere Abbey, the son of a farmer, and Mildred Postlewaite Abbey, the daughter of a principal and schoolteacher. As part of his habitual and often misleading self-mythologizing, Abbey liked to say that he was born in tiny Home, Pennsylvania, relishing the sound of it, but in fact he entered the world in Indiana, Pennsylvania, the county seat. Legend also has it that Abbey grew up on a farm, but it was not until Abbey turned fourteen that his parents were able to buy a home and some land of their own. Nonetheless, his love for the Allegheny Mountains and their lush woods was already in full flower by then, an indelible connection to place that became intrinsic to his writings.

Abbey pays tribute to his parents in the dedication to his essay collection *The Journey Home* (1977): "This book is for Mildred Postlewaite Abbey, my wise, enduring and beautiful mother; and for Paul Revere Abbey, my father, who taught me to hate injustice, to defy the powerful, and to speak for the voiceless." Mildred was a remarkable woman for any time, but especially for her era, when few country women attained the level of education she did. Small yet dynamic and indefatigable, she was wife, mother, schoolteacher, pianist, organist, church choir leader, active in volunteer work, a journal-keeper, and famous for taking long walks, a habit passed down to her oldest son. Some of Abbey's most precious memories were of listening to Mildred play the piano. Classical music became an essential element of Abbey's rich inner life, and music is as constant a presence in his books as evocative landscapes.

Abbey inherited his height, strength, free-spiritedness, and defiance from his self-educated jack-of-all-trades, hunter, logger, farmer father, who loved to quote the advice of his favorite poet, Whitman, who intoned "Resist much, obey little," words to live by for both father and son. Paul Abbey was a rare creature in his neck of the woods, a lifelong socialist, and because Edward Abbey was as opinionated and independent-minded as his willful father, the two often crossed swords.

Young Abbey loved to read and draw (many of his books feature his sketches), and he frequently angered his father and siblings by slipping off with a book instead of helping with the chores. He began writing early on with "verve and imagination," according to Cahalan and, in spite of his love of baseball, was essentially a loner. As Cahalan observes, "Erudite learning and hillbilly grit would combine to form Abbey's distinctive voice."

LEAVING HOME

As Abbey writes in a seminal essay, "Hallelujah on the Bum" (collected in *The Journey Home*), he "hitchhiked from Pennsylvania to Seattle by way of Chicago and Yellowstone National Park; from Seattle down the coast to San Francisco; and from there by way of Barstow and Needles via boxcar, thumb, and bus through the Southwest back home" during the summer of 1944 between his junior and senior years of high school. He wanted to see his country before being sent to war, and what he saw set the course for the rest of his life. He describes his young self as "wise, brown, ugly, shy, poetical; a bold, stupid, sun-dazzled kid," but one who possessed a great sense of adventure, keen observational skills, and a ready talent for improvisation when it came to sizing up strangers, earning just enough money to get by, and finding a safe place, preferably under the stars, to bed down for the night. His instant affinity with the glorious and inhospitable West, a land that filled him with "strange excitement," is key to his work, but before he could call the place that nurtured his imagination home, he had to journey across the Atlantic and back.

Abbey describes his cushy army experience in an essay (collected in *Abbey's Road,* 1979) bearing one of his typically needling titles: "My Life as a P.I.G., or the True Adventures of Smokey the Cop." Abbey is writing primarily about his many gigs as a ranger and fire lookout for the National Park Service and the Forest Service, but his life in uniform began with his induction into the army. Drafted right out of high school and sent to Naples, Italy, he was selected to serve in the military police by virtue of his height. He cheated his way into becoming the most coveted of all brands of MP, a motorcycle cop, a position that enabled him to sample many pleasures. As Cahalan writes, "As antimilitaristic as Abbey would become after his tour of duty, he nonetheless clearly enjoyed his army adventures," most notably his initiation into sex, a realm that would claim a great deal of his attention and energy throughout his promiscuous life.

The GI bill made college possible for Abbey, and he expressed his gratitude in a characteristically uncompromising fashion by writing a vehement letter against the draft that brought him to the attention of the FBI, which subsequently kept a file on him for many years. After a spell at a community college near his Pennsylvania home, he was thrilled to get into the University of New Mexico at Albuquerque, land of his dreams. But Abbey was one of many outsiders who came to the Southwest during the postwar boom, and his witnessing of and vociferous objections to the environmental and social havoc wrought by hectic growth in the region became the primary impetus and theme of his writing. His view of this sort of precipitous change is encapsulated in what became his best-known aphorism (a master of the form, Abbey completed a collection of his venomous one-liners just before he died): "Growth for the sake of growth is the ideology of the cancer cell."

While Abbey's official education included courses in English, music, and philosophy (his specialty was anarchism), he taught himself the survival skills necessary for enjoying the extended, devil-may-care desert sojourns that became as intrinsic to his life as writing. Abbey's wry and feisty temperament and tremendous vigor engendered contradictory hungers for both solitude and camaraderie, for the quiet and stillness of desk hours and the physical challenges and sensual pleasures of hiking and camping in the desert, climbing mountains, floating down rivers, and driving across rugged terrain, all of which he enjoyed whenever possible, imbibing plenty of beer and bourbon along the way. These adventures and the revelations they kindled became the subject of his peppery essays, of which he wrote dozens.

As both student and writing teacher Abbey had a love-hate relationship with the academy, alternately impressing and outraging professors and students. No one could deny his intelligence or gift for language, however, qualities that earned him a Fulbright scholarship to Scotland's Edinburgh University in 1951, ostensibly to continue his studies of the Scottish poet Robert Burns. As Jack Loeffler recounts, "Abbey identified with Burns," the son of a poor farmer who "rebelled against the existing social order." So captivated was Abbey by this Scottish free thinker and artist, he paid tribute to him by naming "the most heroic of his literary characters" Jack Burns.

Abbey married a fellow student, Jean Schmechel, during his senior year, but by the time the not-so-happy couple traveled to Edinburgh he was already passionately in love with another University of New Mexico student, the painter Rita Deanin. Abbey began keeping a journal in 1946 during his stint in the military, but because several of his earliest journals were lost in a flood in the Abbey family home, *Confessions of a Barbarian: Selections from the Journals of Edward Abbey, 1951–1989* begins in November 1951 as Abbey takes measure of Edinburgh, his problematic love life, and his burning desire to write. Here he begins to find his voice, exploring his propensity for rants and detailed and dramatic responses to place, and evincing a startling candor regarding his lust for women. He was also feeling his way into his fiction, noting that he might write "a novel vindicating the philosophy of adventure & disorder, soaked in the democratic popular culture of contemporary U.S.A. (A modern *Huckleberry Finn*?)" Abbey eventually did emulate Twain in his use of satire and in his ability to spike exuberant tales of adventure, romance, and melodrama with piquant moral and social commentary. Always ahead of his time and even of himself, Abbey has already identified the motif he later elaborated on in his renegade novels: "My favorite melodramatic theme: the harried anarchist, a wounded wolf, struggling toward the green hills, or the black-white alpine mountains, or the purple-golden desert range and liberty. Will he make it? Or will the FBI shoot him down on the very threshold of wilderness and freedom?"

THREE EARLY NOVELS

Abbey's first novel, *Jonathan Troy,* published in 1954, was the only book he later hoped would be forgotten, although he did include an excerpt in *Slumgullion Stew: An Edward Abbey Reader,* published thirty years later, a two-page sentence that hints at both the flaws and promise of this bravado if derivative debut about a self-centered nineteen-year-old. Ann Ronald, a professor at the University of Nevada and author of *The New West of Edward Abbey* (1982), characterizes *Jonathan Troy* as "a fictional morass of adolescent hopes and fears." The novel does, however, offer "an early glimpse of Abbey's greatest strength—the power of his prose," as well as nascent glimmerings of his anarchist beliefs and environmental concerns. (Ronald's volume of criticism won Abbey's typically forked-tongue approval when he wrote in his journal that it was "a good sympathetic scrutiny of my books, though she takes 'em all much too seriously.")

Abbey knew that his first novel fell short of his intentions. He reports in his journal in December 1953 that proofreading the galleys "was a discouraging task. The book seems even worse than I had thought. Very juvenile, naive, clumsy, pretentious. I tried to do everything at once, and succeeded in almost nothing." He wisely concludes, "I must be patient. Between the conception and the creation falls the shadow."

A quick study, Abbey created a far more structured, entertaining, and memorable book in his second novel, *The Brave Cowboy* (1956), although he admitted it was not as much fun to write. Cahalan notes that Abbey "was happiest, and eventually most successful, in writing about himself," and, indeed, Abbey's two favorite novels, the tragic romance, *Black Sun* (1971), and his magnum opus, *The Fool's Progress* (1988), as well as the best of his essays, are basically autobiographical.

The Brave Cowboy is not entirely devoid of self-portraiture, but the model for Jack Burns, Abbey's Don Quixote–like hero, was a friend named Ralph Newcomb, who hugely impressed the cowboy-struck author by riding his horse from Wyoming to Utah, then through both Utah and Arizona. As to the story, Jack Burns's mission is to bust his buddy, Paul, out of an Albuquerque jail where he is serving time for refusing to register for the draft. (Abbey himself had spent a few miserable days behind bars for reckless driving, a harrowing experience he quickly transformed into "field work.") Burns gets himself arrested, but once inside discovers that his principled friend won't join him in a jailbreak: Paul insists on seeing his protest through to the end. So Burns escapes on his own, and ends up on the run from the authorities in the Sandia Mountains, a situation tailor-made for suspenseful chase scenes that culminate in what becomes a quintessential Abbey showdown: man (and horse) against machine, be it helicopter, airplane, tractor-trailer, or earthmover.

The Brave Cowboy seems to fit the mold of the traditional Western, but Abbey, simultaneously mischievous and poetic, was sharply attuned to the resonance of archetypes and profoundly concerned with the relationship between the individual and society. Consequently, he deliberately subverted the popular form used so successfully by Zane Grey, Louis L'Amour, and countless Hollywood screenwriters. James Bishop writes that by the time young Abbey recognized that "the true dream of the anarchist was the Western frontier—its deserts, mountains, and rivers—with dependence on space and wilderness, courage, self-reliance, and self-rule," this very paradise was rapidly being destroyed by highways, billboards, dams, and uranium mines. Abbey therefore felt "trapped in a crossfire between the Hollywood-created nineteenth-century myth and shocking twentieth-century reality. Exposing the existence of that gap, and trying to close it, would be the basis for his lifework."

Ann Ronald observes that Abbey did more than explode the stereotypes perpetuated by clichéd Westerns; he went back to the medieval world to retrieve an "appropriate mythos" and "designed *The Brave Cowboy* not like a romantic Western but like a formal romance." Ronald's definition of the form and function of the romance, the armature Abbey used with such fluency and creativity, is worth quoting. (Other critics missed this ploy altogether, although it is the key to all of Abbey's fiction.) She writes:

> By definition and by practice, a romance opens its audience's eyes to a unique way of looking at the immediate world. Its purpose is twofold—a celebration of life, of freedom and survival, and a celebration of life's possibilities, of dreams both marvelous and visionary. To achieve those ends, the romancer must first create a self-sustaining world, isolated from tangible reality but still suggestive of it. He must populate his microcosm with figures whose stylized behavior patterns remind us of our own less predictable modes but whose actions would nevertheless be extraordinary in conventional society. . . . By exaggerating [his characters'] behavior traits, by intensifying their experiences, and by relying on sensory impressions to heighten their tale, the author fabricates the world of the romance. Such a creation must not be mistaken for fantasy, however, because the romancer also calls into question the ethical, social, and moral assumptions of his age.

At least one reviewer evinced some understanding of what Abbey hoped to convey. Lewis Nordyke wrote in the September 9, 1956, *New York Times,* "The idea of a romantic cowboy riding an almost locoed mare named Whisky in the speed, the noise and the civilization of the atomic age is a fascinating one and it is cleverly and engagingly handled."

So striking was the juxtaposition between the old and the new, so compelling was Jack Burns, the first of Abbey's Davids who faces the Goliath of twentieth-century life, that Kirk Douglas "knew he had to make the film" as soon as he read the book, according to James Bishop. The studio, Janus Films, had rejected other books

Douglas suggested, and now declined this one, too, says Bishop, but "Douglas didn't give up. He remembered a clause in his contract allowing him to make a 'disapproved' picture if it did not exceed a budget of three million dollars. That was it." Fittingly, then, "The Abbey project would be a 'disapproved' picture."

Neither Douglas nor Abbey liked the title the studio insisted on, *Lonely Are the Brave,* but at least Abbey approved of Dalton Trumbo's screenplay. This was an especially hard time for Abbey and his wife, Rita, and he was grateful for the money the sale of the film rights brought, however modest, and for pay as a location scout in New Mexico and a bit part as a cop. Douglas loved the film, touting it as his favorite picture and best role, but the studio was vindictive, releasing it with no publicity whatsoever. When their deliberate neglect backfired and the film became a critical and box office success, the studio chiefs pulled it. Bishop quotes Douglas musing years later, "The egos of the studio heads wouldn't let them admit they had made a mistake, and capitalize on the publicity. They just dropped the picture flat." *Lonely Are the Brave* remains a Western classic.

In the six years between publication of *The Brave Cowboy* and his third novel, *Fire on the Mountain* (1962), Abbey struggled with money and marital problems, conflicts and responsibilities acerbated by Rita's need to live near her family in Hoboken. Abbey left his beloved bright desert for sooty New Jersey and the dark, dank canyons of Manhattan, and he was miserable. His gloom was unrelieved by the birth of his and Rita's second son, and it was compounded by the suffering of his ill father-in-law. He soon broke free from domestic discord and the crush and squalor of urban life, especially the overwhelming hopelessness he witnessed as a Welfare Department worker, and gratefully returned to his meditative life as a ranger, taking a job in Arizona at the Petrified Forest National Monument in 1961.

In spite of the tumult of his peripatetic, emotionally volatile, cash-poor existence, he wrote nonstop and soon completed his third novel, *Fire on the Mountain.* Like *The Brave Cowboy,* it was inspired by a true life story of a determined individual Abbey admired, in this case New Mexican cattleman John Prather, who in the 1950s, when he was in his eighties, successfully thwarted the U.S. government's attempt to commandeer his land as part of the White Sands Missile Range. Abbey transforms Prather into John Vogelin, whose standoff with the government ends tragically rather than triumphantly as Prather's did.

The book is narrated by its beleaguered hero's young and innocent grandson, Billy, and as Ann Ronald writes, "it is tempting to discuss *Fire on the Mountain* as a novel of initiation, a Western *Bildungsroman* in which a youth learns what it means to be a man." She believes, however, that Abbey "deliberately picked a naive point of view because through it he can manipulate his audience. Billy reports what he sees and reproduces what he hears, but Abbey makes the selections."

James Bishop approaches *Fire on the Mountain* by way of Abbey's master's thesis on anarchy, tracing Abbey's intellectual and spiritual struggle to conceive of a way to defend the wild without resorting to mere propaganda or, much worse, violence. Bishop writes that in his third novel Abbey also "fully develops the theme that would dominate his later work: in a rapidly urbanizing America, it is humans who are in the greatest jeopardy, not the environment; the planet will heal itself through fire and flood and vulcanism as it always has."

Fire on the Mountain received a smattering of positive reviews, but it did nothing to alleviate Abbey's personal woes, the dire consequences of his inability to be monogamous or hold a steady job and earn enough money to keep his family together. So, as always, he returned to the desert for solace.

DESERT SOLITAIRE

Published in 1968 and read with ardor ever since, *Desert Solitaire,* a highly imaginative nonfictional work based on Abbey's stints as a ranger primarily in Arches National Monument, near Moab, Utah, made Abbey famous, and will stand forevermore, as Ronald claims, as "the cornerstone of his creative output." Anecdotal, lyrical, philosophical, and wickedly caustic, it traces a season in the wilderness and in a man's life, running from April Fool's Day (the fool is a cherished figure of Abbey's) to September. Here Abbey transmutes the cogitations of his journals into a meticulously crafted narrative in which he muses at length on nature and mankind's place within its mesh. He celebrates the majestic if forbidding beauty of the fantastic slickrock and canyon landscape he loves and longs to protect, and he expresses his fury over its abuse by government, business, and tourists alike.

Desert Solitaire is a weave of many strands: radiant veins of natural history; fiery social critique; poetic metaphors (Abbey wrote poetry all the time, mostly for himself); allegedly true but no doubt much-embellished tales of adventure, including one about a "moon-eyed" horse and another about a uranium prospector; an activist's strongly stated recommendations for averting social and ecological catastrophe; and arresting musings on death. Here are some memorable Abbeyisms:

> No more cars in national parks. Let the people walk. Or ride horses, bicycles, mules, wild pigs—anything—but keep the automobiles and the motorcycles and all their motorized relatives out. We have agreed not to drive our automobiles into cathedrals, concert halls, art museums, legislative assemblies, private bedrooms and other sanctums of our culture; we should treat our national parks with the same deference, for they, too, are holy places.

> But the love of wilderness is more than a hunger for what is always beyond reach; it is also an expression of loyalty to the earth, the earth which bore us and sustains us, the only home we shall ever know, the only paradise we ever need—if only we had the eyes to see. Original sin, the true original sin, is the blind destruction for the sake of greed of this natural paradise which lies all around us—if only we were worthy of it.

> Under the desert sun, in that dogmatic clarity, the fables of theology and the myths of classical philosophy dissolve like mist. The air is clean, the rock cuts cruelly into flesh; shatter the rock and the odor of flint rises to your nostrils, bitter and sharp. Whirlwinds dance across the salt flats, a pillar of dust by day; the thornbush breaks into flame at night. What does it mean? It means nothing. It is as it is and has no need for meaning. The desert lies beneath and soars beyond any possible human qualification. Therefore, sublime.

And finally: "I am not an atheist but an earthiest. Be true to the earth."

The famed naturalist Edwin Way Teale praised the book's verisimilitude, humor, and sheer nerve in the *New York Times Book Review,* and he was not alone in his admiration. The southwestern poet and essayist Richard Shelton homed in on the intriguing and significant conflicts inherent in *Desert Solitaire,* stating that it "was written by an arch-romantic trying desperately not to be romantic" (in Hepworth and McNamee, eds., *Resist Much, Obey Little*). Further, Shelton discerns that the book's captivating power is generated by the tension between two facets of Abbey's complex personality, "the realist who sees the hopeless condition of contemporary society with its hideous impact on nature and the lyric lover who wants only to sing about the beauties of the natural world."

James Bishop notes that reviewers viewed Abbey as "a kind of ecological Ezekiel, raging against the attack on the planet by the forces of mindless growth." For his part, Bishop feels that "overall, *Desert Solitaire* is a spicy, complex work, containing enough contradictions to provide a lifetime of challenge for any psychologist."

Not only does Abbey shift abruptly on the page from sage to bigot; in life he was by turns wise, gentlemanly, generous, even shy, as well as cynical, offensive, and self-indulgent. He wrote and spoke about the holiness of the land, yet he tossed empty beer cans out the window of his pickup truck. He abhorred war and bloodshed and believed in peaceful protest and civil disobedience, yet he supported gun rights and orchestrated bloody confrontations in his novels. He treasured justice, yet railed against immigrants and the urban poor. But no one was more aware of his paradoxical nature than Abbey, and he wrote, in part, to redeem himself and his readers by exposing all his confusions and contradictions in order to render them emblematic of our muddled species. Abbey wanted us to see ourselves clearly, to recognize the consequences of our often irrational assumptions and actions. And his provocative and infuriating, rhapsodic and profound, sardonic and spiritual books do just that.

LOVE AND LOSS: *BLACK SUN*

Naturally, much was going on in Abbey's life behind the selectively edited scenes of the seemingly autobiographical *Desert Solitaire*. Abbey's love life was turbulent, often derailed by the lust for young women he wrote about with boastfulness and despair in his journals: "Lust rides me like a monkey, panting in my ear continually; hardly ever a moment's rest." Abbey finally gave up on the pretense his marriage had become and left Rita and their two sons, Joshua and Aaron, in July 1965. He married Judy Pepper, with whom he was already in love, only forty-six days later. Judy gave birth to their daughter, Susannah, in August 1968. She and Abbey loved each other, but he strayed. Then Judy became ill, diagnosed with acute leukemia. Abbey spent two weeks with Judy in Mount Sinai Hospital in New York, watching her suffer, and feeling both agony and guilt over the "repulsive degradations of the hospital routine." Judy died at age twenty-seven on July 4, 1970. Abbey was forty-three, their daughter a tender twenty-two months.

Abbey was by all accounts devastated by Judy's death, although the self-described "satyr-maniac" was already involved with another woman. Three weeks after he buried his third wife he wrote in his journal, "What now is the aim of my life? To sit on a rock in the desert and stare at the sun until the sun goes black." These dramatic words are drawn from a recurring image in his work and echo the reigning symbol of his fourth novel, *Black Sun,* a pastoral and tragic love story about a divorced, thirty-seven-year-old Forest Service fire lookout, Will Gatlin, who falls in love with Sandy, a beautiful, vibrant, virginal, and strong-willed nineteen-year-old student. In the spring of 1968, Abbey's journal records that he had a fight with Judy over some "discarded" love letters just as he was trying to finish the novel that became *Black Sun.* He writes, "An excellent little novel in my opinion. Very romantic. In fact, I think I'll call it 'a romantic novel,' or maybe simply 'a romance.' Judy hates it, of course, thinking it the story of one of my old love affairs."

Certainly it is romantic in its depiction of a man's utter infatuation with an elusive woman, but for all its celebration of natural beauty and life at its most fecund, it is in fact a brooding fairy tale about isolation and loss, and it does not have a happy ending. In a reversal of the classic "maiden in a tower waiting to be rescued" scenario, Abbey sequesters his isolated hero in a fire tower. Will has taken himself out of the fray of everyday human life, much to the irritation of his much more down-to-earth buddy, Art Ballantine, who tries to lure him away from his anchorite's perch. Will ignores Art's call to return to the pleasures of human society, then falls hard for Sandy, who is described as a wood nymph: lithe, sensuous, enchanting, and free. In their brief but intense erotic idyll, Will knows absolute ecstasy, but Sandy knows better than to get trapped in his malaise; for that matter, she also knows better than to follow through on her plans to marry her fiancé, an air force cadet. Enigmatic and independent, Sandy is the first of Abbey's invincible heroines: good-looking and sexy women as physically tough, courageous, and daring as the men who love them, and a whole lot smarter.

Once again, most reviewers missed the deeper levels Abbey so slyly accessed, responding only to the novel's shimmery surface, distracted and perhaps made uncomfortable by explicit sex scenes (sweet and humorous as they are) and the crudeness of Will and Art's banter (exchanges that serve to disclose two sides of the male psyche, the wild and the civilized, the predator and the pacifist). But the perceptive critic Ann Ronald sees the skillfully wrought *Black Sun* as "an allegorical tapestry, a modern man's ascent into heaven and descent into hell, his fictive journey there and back ending in an existential nothingness peculiarly Abbey's own."

ANARCHY AND ECOTAGE: *THE MONKEY WRENCH GANG*

After the concentrated introspection of *Black Sun* and the shock and grief of Judy's death, Abbey pushed himself to work on a novel he had long been contemplating, a comedic, even madcap tale that would channel his anger over the abuse of the land he loved into a wily dramatization of a highly controversial form of environmental defense. The antic *The Monkey Wrench Gang* (1975) was the end result, and it earned him his most avid followers and most infuriated detractors. Abbey's outrage over every assault on the desert spurred him to write, but the source of his deepest despair and most subversive creativity was the ill-conceived, horrendously expensive, ecosystem-killing, habitat-obliterating Glen Canyon Dam, a horror erected in 1962 without public debate and with the backroom collusion of the Sierra Club.

This monstrosity flooded Glen Canyon, one of the most spectacularly beautiful and mysterious landscapes on earth, a place rich not only in natural wonders but also in archaeological treasures and a beloved mecca for Abbey and his friends who were some of the last people to explore the canyon before it was flooded. James Bishop observes that to Abbey its destruction "was nothing less than a great—and unnecessary—holocaust that insulted his soul and also moved the anarchist within him to action." In Douglas Brinkley's introduction to the twenty-fifth anniversary edition of *The Monkey Wrench Gang*, he observes that Abbey wrote his most famous novel with a "bellyful of bile over Glen Canyon Dam." And sure enough, the book begins with a seething description of that very abomination:

> Great river—greater dam. Seen from the bridge the dam presents a gray sheer concave face of concrete aggregate, implacable and mute. A gravity dam, eight hundred thousand tons of solidarity, countersunk in the sandstone Navajo formation, fifty millions years emplaced, of the bedrock and canyon walls. A plug, a block, a fat wedge, the dam diverts through penstocks and turbines the force of the puzzled river.

Dedicated to Ned Ludd, the legendary early-nineteenth-century British weaver who rallied his peers to destroy the machines that threatened their livelihood (thus the designation "Luddite"), *The Monkey Wrench Gang* is an ecological caper that transmutes tragedy into rowdy comedy and fury into mischief with the intent to incite revolt. At the center of this riotous caper is Abbey's eccentric band of monkey wrenchers (Webster's defines "monkey wrench" both as a tool and as "something that disrupts"), or ecosaboteurs (those who practice sabotage in defense of the earth), a group loosely based on Abbey's desert rat, river-running friends.

Doc Sarvis, the most soulful of the gang, is an Albuquerque heart specialist who saves lives by day and burns down billboards at night with the able-bodied assistance of his sexy nurse and lover Bonnie Abbzug, an escapee from the Bronx and an avid desert convert. They meet Seldom Seen Smith, a jack Mormon river guide with three content wives, when they embark on a raft trip down the Colorado, a mighty river that Smith remembers in its magnificent, undammed, "unchained and unchanneled" natural state. He has just hired an assistant, George Washington Hayduke, a former Green Beret Vietnam vet who has returned home angry over the war and who becomes increasingly enraged by what is being done to his cherished West. In his journal Abbey explains the origin of his hero's name: "Hayduke, of course, is a *hajduk, heiduk:* a Magyar, Serbian, Turkish word meaning 'brigand' or 'robber' or Balkan bandit-resister (*Oxford English Dictionary*); or (thanks to Katie Lee [the singer, author, and fellow Glen Canyon mourner]), in Hungarian, 'foot soldier.'"

This quirky quartet soon comes together in the recognition that they are kindred spirits, and before long they are concocting elaborate plans for performing various modes of monkey wrenching. Abbey is gleefully specific in his accounts of their risky endeavors, which range from pulling up survey stakes to the disabling of bulldozers and the demolition of a railroad bridge. This procedural precision led to charges that the book was essentially a how-to manual for ecoextremists, and, in fact, Abbey's friends and biographers attest to Abbey's "night work," or monkey wrenching. Yet in spite of the author's practice and support of ecotage, and his delight in writing scenes of kinetic physicality, much of the novel actually grapples with difficult moral questions about the parameters of civil disobedience and the rights of other living entities to exist unmolested by human beings.

The Monkey Wrench Gang is spiked with witty dialogue, provocative cultural allusions, keen philosophizing, and a prescient sense of just how bad things would get as the twentieth century ground on to its bitter end. Abbey once again stages David versus Goliath showdowns, as well as jousting-at-windmill scenes à la Don Quixote, and he cannily subverts such Western icons as Jesse James, the Lone Ranger, John Wayne, and even Bonnie and Clyde. One would expect the novel's craft and farcical humor to garner critical praise, and it did, but Abbey's achievement was all but ignored by critics east of the Mississippi, and a number of reviewers professed to be appalled by the militant actions of Abbey's characters.

While predictably riling the establishment, Abbey also ticked off members of the counterculture. Although *The Monkey Wrench Gang* helped inspire the radical arm of the environmental movement, most notably the group Earth First! founded by Dave Foreman, Abbey offended many environmentalists and potential fans with his seemingly sexist attitudes, raucous praise for redneck ways, and over-the-top social commentary that reeked of racism. Older than most hippies, he detested rock and roll, found pot and LSD debilitating, considered New Age mysticism half-baked and escapist, and had no compunction about mocking the superficialities of the "alternative" scene.

In the essay "Telluride Blues—A Hatchet Job," for instance, he decries the infiltration of a western haven: "In came the hippies then, the trust funders, the freaks, the rootless ones, the middle-class proletariat with their beards and unisex ponytails, all of them, male and female, wearing the same bib overalls, Goodwill workshirts and waffle-stomper boots, all trying to look different in the same way." He even mocks his own alluring creation, Bonnie Abbzug, for her hippie ways, making fun of her geodesic dome and "teenybopper intellectual's standard library of the period," which included the *I Ching,* Carlos Castaneda, Richard Brautigan, and Hermann Hesse. While Tom Robbins charmed just this sort of reader with his silly and hugely popular Western fable, *Even Cowgirls Get the Blues,* Abbey, a far more thorny, frank, intellectual, conflicted, and literary writer, was aggressively abrasive, demanding the sort of rigorous self-critiques he subjected himself to from his readers, not all of whom could take his strong medicine. Yet *The Monkey Wrench Gang* has always found its audience, staying in print and attaining what publishers love to call cult status.

GOOD NEWS, SORT OF

Good News (1980), Abbey's sixth novel, is a futuristic, somewhat Orwellian but all-the-way Abbeyesque Western. He kicks things off with a grim overture that is unnervingly prophetic in its detailed description of an overpopulated world in the not-too-distant future in which war is a constant and resources are scarce. He writes, "Religious fanaticism joined with nationalism and secular ideologies to destroy and sometimes self-destroy the sources of power on which the overindustrialized nations depended. Invisible poisons spread through the atmosphere, borne by the winds from the guilty to the innocent. But all were innocent, all were guilty." The governmental-industrial complex has collapsed, and a totalitarian paramilitary regime now rules a sprawling and devastated urban landscape and its dazed and cowed population, sending out its bloodthirsty, black-uniformed motorcycle patrols to raid the countryside for food, supplies, and recruits.

As the story gets under way, two men sit beside a campfire. One-eyed Jack Burns, having survived what seemed like certain death at the conclusion of *The Brave Cowboy* only to be resurrected in true cliffhanger fashion in *The Monkey Wrench Gang,* is now an old man heading across the blasted desert on horseback to search the shattered city for his son, whom he has not seen in many years. Sam Banyaca is his loyal companion. A Hopi trained in the shamanic arts, Sam also holds a Ph.D. from Harvard. Back in the saddle, the "the searcher and the researcher" acquire a third companion, young Arthur, whose father has just been murdered by marauding soldiers.

As the trio travels on, Jack and Sam argue over the deplorable state of their world, giving Abbey ample opportunity to air his views on a slew of prickly social topics. Once they reach the city, the action accelerates in a nonstop sequence of gun battles, arrests, imprisonment, romance under fire, torture, executions, chases, escapes, and confrontations involving a motley underground resistance movement. Abbey's women characters are resilient and resourceful, and the demented powers-that-be include the cartoonish Chief, whom Bishop describes as a "satanic melange of Adolf Hitler, Darth Vader, and Richard Nixon."

Because Abbey was envisioning a world in which man, to quote a passage from his journal, had become "a scourge and a pestilence upon the Earth, a threat to all life, including his own," he offers no descriptions of the splendor of nature in *Good News,* which has the most indoor scenes of any of his novels and is therefore distressingly claustrophobic. Add to that the lack of the renegade humor that gives *The Monkey Wrench Gang* its zing, and the fact that its wisecracking characters fail to achieve full dimensionality, and the news about *Good News* was mostly bad. Smothered by thumbs-down reviews, it was not even embraced by readers who recognized the significance of Abbey's vision of a poisoned and bereft future. Even Ronald, Abbey's most discerning critic, writes that "romance becomes irony" in this "parody of his previous writing." The good news Abbey meant to impart in this absurd and disjointed fable is his conviction that the military-industrial state cannot be sustained, but his message is unclear, his story unconvincing.

ESSAYIST EXTRAORDINAIRE

Few modern writers have spent so much time outdoors, walked so many wild miles, floated down so many rivers, spent so many nights beneath starry skies, or brewed so many pots of cowboy coffee as Abbey. He traveled the countryside with friends and lovers, books and notebooks, booze and flute, and loved the wild as a place of communion and bliss. The undomesticated landscapes of desert and river canyon were proving grounds for his friendships with the novelists William Eastlake, Jack Loeffler, Doug Peacock, Ralph Newcomb, Ken Sleight, and the painter John De Puy; all steadfast supporters of Abbey's writing, who appear in one guise or another in all his books. In his journal Abbey writes, "Friendship's a rare and elusive gift in this shattered, chaotic, frantically moving society of ours," and his gratitude for the munificence of friendship surfaces as a significant theme in both his novels and essays.

The success of *Desert Solitaire* inspired Abbey to perfect his writing methods so that he could make the most of his travels and ranger experiences. He composed vinegary articles for a slew of magazines, including *American West, Audubon, National Geographic, Outside, Harper's, Field and Stream, Slickrock, Natural History, Playboy* (Abbey agreed that *Playboy* and *Penthouse* were sexist: they exploited men), *Mountain Gazette,* and *High Country News.* He then meticulously reworked his favorite pieces to create the polished and potent essays that were eventually collected in five stellar and seminal volumes.

As he writes in the introduction to *The Journey Home,* which Cahalan believes is Abbey's "single best collection of essays":

If certain ideas and emotions are expressed in these pages with what seems an extreme intransigence, it is not merely because I love an argument and wish to provoke (though I do), but because I am—really am—an extremist, one who lives and loves by choice far out on the very verge of things, on the edge of the abyss, where this world falls off into the depths of another. That's the way I like it.

Wild pigs, retirees in Winnebagos, Australian aborigines, and a coral reef (what a kick it is to witness this desert rat snorkeling in the south Pacific) all appear in *Abbey's Road* (1979), an impassioned and intelligent assemblage of vivid travel pieces, prickly "polemics and sermons," and glinting autobiographical essays. Sadly, reviewers could not get beyond their reactions to Abbey's self-caricatures and therefore overlooked the cogency and value of his keen insights into the limitations and menace of corporate science, distrust of mysticism, praise of reason, and understanding that environmentalism is nothing less than the "conscience of our race," which is "trying to tell us that we must offer to all forms of life and to the planet itself the same generosity and tolerance we require from our fellow humans."

Stephen Chapman was harsh in *The New Republic,* citing Abbey's various "poses," such as the "harddrinking rounder thumbing his nose at respectability" and the "visionary liberal," as excuses merely for "self-congratulation." Writing in the *New York Times Book Review,* Lucinda Franks also detects different Abbey personas, but she understands the source of his self-portraits: "a rather pouty swaggerer and a much wiser, sorrier man; perhaps both are the result of his inability to save his beloved wilderness."

Down the River (1982) was a favorite of Abbey's, and, indeed, the writing is exceptionally tight, the ideas sparkling. "Down the River with Henry Thoreau" is a masterful reading of the works of his mentor, a fluent homage to Thoreau's ecological perspective and belief in civil disobedience that forges a crucial link in the chain of American environmental sensibility and thought. Abbey notes that although he was nearly forgotten after his death at age forty-five in 1862,

> [Thoreau] becomes more significant with each passing decade. The deeper our United States sinks into industrialism, urbanism, militarism—with the rest of the world doing its best to emulate America—the more poignant, strong, and appealing becomes Thoreau's demand for the right of every man, every woman, every child, every dog, every tree, every snail darter, every lousewort, every living thing, to live its own life in its own way at its own pace in its own square mile of home.

In a *New York Times* review, Tim Cahill recognizes that Abbey, "like Thoreau, has been chipping away at the pyramids of power for most of his adult life," but notes that he prefers writing about "sweeter, funnier themes . . . and about the most simple outdoor pleasures: planting a tree, seeing a bear, watching hawks in flight, getting drunk." Dennis Drabelle, writing for *The Nation,* is not as charmed. He duns Abbey for his "arrogance and xenophobia" and writes that "Abbey will no doubt be unmoved by the observation that many of his attitudes give aid and comfort to the enemies of conservation by inviting them to apply the label of elitism." Clearly, Abbey's strategy of provocation frequently backfired.

The ten essays collected in *Beyond the Wall: Essays from the Outside* (1984) chronicle various in-the-wild adventures, particularly such long, thirst-inducing, bone-wearying walks as Abbey's arduous, solitary hike across one hundred and ten miles of the Sonoran Desert, including the U.S. Air Force Bombing and Gunnery Range. Walking for the sake of walking, a time-honored endeavor beloved by poets and pilgrims alike, stimulates the mind and clarifies convictions, and for Abbey that meant annealing his piercing meditations on our need for open, undefiled land and "authentic experience." Reviewing the collection for the *New York Times,* Alice Hoffman writes,

> The author is the voice of all that is ornery and honorable. He's a prospector for truth, an exile from the city, a desert rat who "cannot breathe properly without at least a cubic mile of unshared space." It is his aim, in every one of these essays, to advise us of what we stand to lose if we lose our wilderness.

One Life at a Time, Please is the last of Abbey's brilliant and curmudgeonly essay collections, and it contains some of his most deliberately taunting declarations about the touchiest of topics: the myth of the cowboy versus the harsh reality of the government-subsidized cattle industry, the "fungoid growth" of people and industry in Arizona, anarchy's role in democracy, ecodefense ("illegal but ethically imperative"), immigration (he was against an open-door policy and scathing on the subject of Mexico), overpopulation, and poverty. As he wryly intones in his introduction, "If there's anyone still present whom I've failed to insult, I apologize." Abbey raised difficult questions and readers' hackles in the belief that controversy and debate are essential to the health of society and the preservation of justice and freedom. And the attention his cantankerousness aroused wasn't bad either.

THE FOOL'S PROGRESS

Abbey often referred to the "fat masterpiece" he struggled for years to write, a great American novel that would link his Appalachian youth to his fruitful years in the Southwest. James Cahalan traces the slow gestation of Abbey's tour de force, *The Fool's Progress: An Honest Novel,* which was released in late 1988, barely six months before his death, all the way back to Abbey's flawed first novel, *Jonathan Troy,* published thirty-four years earlier: "If *Troy* had been his failed *Iliad,* then he was determined to make *The Fool's Progress* his successful *Odyssey.*" After numerous false starts, extensive research, many variations on the novel's focus and point of view, and myriad interruptions, Abbey began work on what became the final incarnation in 1982.

Abbey had married for the fourth time in 1974. Renee Downing was only sixteen when they met, and all of eighteen when she married Abbey, who was in his prime at age forty-seven. Their union lasted six years. Abbey then tied the knot for the last time, with Clarke Cartwright. Jack Loeffler observes that Abbey's marriage to Clarke coincided with the "most prolific years of his literary career. It was as though for the first time he had committed himself to marriage, and with that commitment came the freedom of intellect and spirit to pursue his art." But there was another goad to the muse: Abbey's brush with mortality, a cancer scare that proved inaccurate but was merely premature. Abbey began a race with death, and so did his hero, the "fool" Henry Lightcap.

By writing *The Fool's Progress* late in life, Abbey brought a lifetime's worth of experience and wisdom to the story of one man's journey back home after a long exile, an odyssey knowingly undertaken in the face of death. By turns comic and lyrical, frenetic and contemplative, this lengthy and picaresque novel flows robustly within its Homeric framework like a river through a canyon. Henry's journey begins with the violent implosion of his latest marriage and the discovery that his cancer is terminal. He throws his belongings into his battered old Dodge pickup truck—his "old steel horse," his "Rosinante" (Homer's *Odyssey* may be Abbey's model here, but everything he wrote pays tribute to Cervantes' *Don Quixote*)—settles his old dying dog, Solstice, by his side; and leaves Tucson heading east for the family farm in Stump Creek, West Virginia.

Henry Holyoak Lightcap's outward odyssey, a series of mishaps and escapades, is paralleled with an inner journey rife with romance and regrets. As his hero revisits his past, Abbey widens the circumference of one man's life to embrace the vicissitudes of his besieged environment and out-of-whack social milieu. Flinty and churlishly erudite as always, Abbey namedrops those he reveres and reviles (Thomas Paine, Virginia Woolf) and pokes fun at literary convention. His narrator's memories, for instance, are not triggered by anything so civilized as the madeleine that awakens Marcel Proust's protagonist. No, beer-guzzling Henry's recollections get a jump-start when he pulls off the road to pee. Just as he is about to relieve himself he notices a boy's baseball glove amid the garbage that is strewn all over the ground. Suddenly he is carried back to an Allegheny Mountain spring when he was fifteen and crazy for baseball:

> He loved the lament of the mourning doves, echoing his own heartache, when they returned each spring from wherever they went in winter. He loved the soft green of the linwood trees, the bright green of the Osage orange against the morning sun. He loved the red-dog dirt road that meandered through the smoky hills beside the sulfur-colored creek, into and through the covered bridge and up the hollow that led, beyond the last split-rail fence, toward the barn, the forge, the pigpen, the wagon shed, the icehouse, the springhouse and the gray good gothic two-story clapboard farmhouse that remained, after a century, still the Lightcap family home.
>
> . . . But most of all and above all and always in April Henry loved the sound of a hardball smacking into leather. The WHACK! of a fat bat connecting with ball.

Abbey is liberated in *The Fool's Progress.* He has no specific environmental or political agenda in mind. On leave from the desert, he brings fresh eyes to greener and homier, if just as ravaged, terrain. His characters are more complex and psychologically authentic because he is working from life, not from a schematic designed to lampoon and subvert romantic conventions. Rather than assuming a spectrum of personas calculated to rile readers, he is honestly trying to understand himself—where he has been and where he ended up, and why. To that noble end he offers imaginative and cathartic portraits of his parents; writes for the first time with true emotional depth about his abhorrence of war; ponders different paths to wisdom; dramatizes the dire consequences of lost intimacy with the land; wrestles with the infinitely mysterious states of lust, love, and marriage; questions the tenets of religion and the power of faith; confronts the paradoxes of American life; and, most wrenchingly of all, faces death.

Many powerful scenes emerge in *The Fool's Progress,* some hilarious, others tragic. One memorable episode involves Henry's detour to find his old friend Morton Bildad, Morton the Mystic, whose long fasts and meditations seem to have put an end to his earthly existence. Also memorable is Henry's vehement account of the surreal tragedies he witnessed as a New York welfare worker, and likewise, Henry's ludicrous interview for work as a national park ranger. Dark romance surrounds the story of Claire, the greatest love of Henry's life (he's amazed that such a fine woman could love a "hillbilly redneck pseudointellectual"), and her harrowing demise. And in every scene Abbey is riveting, his prose spangled, fast-moving, and redemptive.

The Fool's Progress is damn near the masterpiece Abbey hoped it would be. Henry Lightcap, rough-edged and loud-mouthed, feral and brave in his own crusty way, foolishly romantic and unabashedly conflicted and alive, is a compelling and mythic character who spans America's West and East, the industrial present and the agrarian past, the crude and the sensitive. As always with Abbey's fiction, squeamish reviewers had a hard time seeing past the red flags of his characters' political incorrectness, but most recognized the novel's indisputably evocative power. Howard Coale objected to the "harpings of a slightly malevolent and self-indulgent voice" in the *New York Times Book Review,* but he also wrote that "everything takes on a treasured glow in the sections that deal with Henry's past, and for all their sentimentality, they are the best parts of the book. . . . Mr. Abbey can attain a kind of glory in his writing."

James Bishop writes,

Almost every aspect of Abbey's life is contained in *The Fool's Progress:* birth and death, loves and lost loves, prejudices and dreams. Funny, touching, outrageous, it is a tumultuous look at twentieth-century America and a man's soul. . . . Abbey draws word pictures of a paradise lost, the decomposing, damaged face of America, whose people are losing touch with the land, with the goals of the Founding Fathers, and are becoming either greed-addicted opportunists, or, worse yet, subjects of same.

Sadly, *The Fool's Progress* remains neglected and overlooked, but surely it will eventually be recognized as one link in the golden chain that comprises such quintessential American odysseys as Mark Twain's *Huckleberry Finn,* John Steinbeck's *Grapes of Wrath,* Jack Kerouac's *On the Road,* and another woefully overlooked tale of pilgrimage across the governmental-corporate landscape, Stanley Elkin's *The Franchiser.*

HAYDUKE LIVES!

In late 1979 Abbey wrote in his journal, "I fear dying, pain, suffering, but I do not fear death. The earth has fed me for half a century; I owe the earth a meal—that is, my body." Abbey had to affirm this profound perspective during the cancer scare of 1982 and then affirm it again, for real, six years later. Happily married to Clarke, crazy about their two very young children, and finally receiving some of the accolades he deserved, Abbey became ill, sensed that he truly was dying, and set himself the tough task of writing his last novel as quickly and efficiently as possible so as to leave his family in relative financial security.

He sequestered himself and somehow managed to write the entertaining, satirically funny, and triumphant sequel to *The Monkey Wrench Gang, Hayduke Lives!* (1990). At the conclusion of the first novel, Hayduke's death seemed certain, yet, just like trusty Jack Burns, he magically reappears, every bit as rascally and more determined than ever to fight the forces of industrial development. While he has been evading the authorities by donning hilarious disguises, his fellow ecodefenders have all been maintaining low profiles, but he rousts them out, insisting that it is time to reunite and go after Goliath, a seven-story uranium-excavating machine that is stomping and chewing its way across the magnificent Utah-Arizona canyon country.

Razzmatazz action gives way to smart-aleck philosophizing and wicked caricatures of everyone from the sort of staid environmentalists who hated *The Monkey Wrench Gang* to daring protesters (some flaky, some sexy), corrupt politicians, law enforcement officials, mine owners, and even the author himself. Under the gun, Abbey pushed his buffoonish characters and preposterous plot to the limit, and while the result is not great literature, it is a heady good time and a testament to the valor, talent, and goodwill of the author. Published posthumously, as Abbey suspected it would be, the book received high praise from reviewers willing to forgo credibility and enjoy the larger-than-life escapades of the ingenious George Washington Hayduke and his gang of misfits. "Abbey's prose ranges from Whitmanesque lyricism to vulgate," says *Library Journal,* "but he has energy, passion, and an infectious comic madness."

Writing for the *New York Times Book Review,* Michael Pellecchia declares that "Abbey's rollicking style . . . can incorporate sendups of everything from industrial slide-show scripts to paperback romance novels. Every member of the gang is a perfectly realized invention, painted in broad strokes of humanity and set against the religious-industrial complex that lurks behind Goliath."

ABBEY LIVES!

"Restoring an Ecosystem Torn Asunder by a Dam" reads the headline in the June 11, 2002, edition of the *New York Times.* The dam in question is the Glen Canyon Dam, the dam Edward Abbey knew from day one was a crime against nature and a complete fiasco. Forty years after its completion, the construction, according to the *Times,* has caused "colossal loss of sand, shrinking beaches, an invasion of outside fish and plants, the extinction of native species, erosion of archaeological sites and the sudden appearance of an Asian tapeworm." All the environmental woes that the maverick and visionary Abbey predicted are coming to a head, and a dozen years after his untimely death from cancer he is cited with respect, even awe, in nearly everything written about the Southwest. And he is eloquently remembered with affection and gratitude by such fellow writers and earth advocates as Barbara Kingsolver, Terry Tempest Williams, Barry Lopez, and William Kittredge.

Abbey and his friend Jack Loeffler had made a pledge in 1974: neither would let the other die in a hospital, and each would bury whoever died first in their sleeping bag in a desert place of their choosing. When the time came, Loeffler, loving and reliable, bravely disconnected Abbey from the hospital's life-support system and brought him home. Two days later, on March 14, 1989, Abbey died in the care and company of family and friends, who then buried him in a secret site deep in the desert he loved.

In a tribute included in the 1990 reprint edition of Abbey's *Black Sun,* the author Charles Bowden, a friend of Abbey's and himself a champion of the desert, writes:

> Of course, what stopped people like myself in their tracks was not simply his style, it was his mind. He wasn't just an entertainer, he had ideas to sell, and for decades he explored his ideas, refined them, and forced us to snap awake and pay attention. . . . His words were driven by a moral energy, a biting tongue, and, thank God, by an abundant sense of humor.

An unpredictable and fruitful amalgam of Cervantes, Henry Thoreau, Mark Twain, John Steinbeck, Thomas Wolfe, Henry Miller, and Hunter S. Thompson, Abbey took writing seriously as an art and as a duty. "Why write?" he asks in "A Writer's Credo" and answers,

> Speaking for myself, I write to entertain my friends and to exasperate our enemies. I write to record the truth of our time as best as I can see it. To investigate the comedy and tragedy of human relationships. To oppose, resist, and sabotage the contemporary drift toward a global technocratic police state, whatever its ideological coloration. I write to oppose injustice, to defy power, and to speak for the voiceless.
>
> I write to make a difference. "It is always a writer's duty," said Samuel Johnson, "to make the world better." I write to give pleasure and promote aesthetic bliss. To honor life and to praise the divine beauty of the natural world. I write for the joy and exultation of writing itself. To tell my story.

Selected Bibliography

WORKS OF EDWARD ABBEY

NOVELS

Jonathan Troy. New York: Dodd, Mead, 1954.

The Brave Cowboy: An Old Tale in a New Time. New York: Dodd, Mead, 1956.

Fire on the Mountain. New York: Dial, 1962.

Black Sun. New York: Simon & Schuster, 1971. Reprint, Santa Barbara, Calif.: Capra Press, 1990. (Includes "Tribute from Charles Bowden.")

The Monkey Wrench Gang. Philadelphia: Lippincott, 1975; New York: HarperPerennial, 2000. (The HarperPerennial reprint includes an introduction by Douglas Brinkley.)

Good News. New York: Dutton, 1980.

The Fool's Progress: An Honest Novel. New York: Holt, 1988. Rev. ed., New York: Holt, 1998.

Hayduke Lives! Boston: Little, Brown, 1990.

ESSAYS, JOURNALS, POETRY

Desert Solitaire: A Season in the Wilderness. New York: McGraw-Hill, 1968.

The Journey Home: Some Words in Defense of the American West. Illustrations by Jim Stiles. New York: Dutton, 1977. (Includes "Hallelujah on the Bum" and "Telluride Blues—A Hatchet Job.")

Abbey's Road. New York: Dutton, 1979.

Down the River. Illustrated by the author. New York: Dutton, 1982.

Beyond the Wall: Essays from the Outside. New York: Holt, Rinehart and Winston, 1984.

One Life at a Time, Please. New York: Henry Holt, 1988. (Includes "A Writer's Credo.")

A Voice Crying in the Wilderness (Vox Clamantis in Deserto): *Notes from a Secret Journal.* Illustrations by Andrew Rush. New York: St. Martin's, 1990.

Confessions of a Barbarian: Selections from the Journals of Edward Abbey, 1951–1989. Illustrations by the author. Edited and with an introduction by David Petersen. Boston: Little, Brown, 1994. (All quotations from Abbey's journals are from this collection.)

Earth Apples (Pommes de Terre): *The Poetry of Edward Abbey.* Illustrations by Michael McCurdy. Collected and introduced by David Petersen. New York: St. Martin's, 1994.

READERS

Slumgullion Stew: An Edward Abbey Reader. Edited and illustrated by the author. New York: Dutton. 1984. Reprinted as *The Best of Edward Abbey.* San Francisco: Sierra Club, 1988.

The Serpents of Paradise: A Reader. Edited by John Macrae. New York: Holt, 1995.

TRAVEL AND PHOTOGRAPHY BOOKS

Appalachian Wilderness: The Great Smoky Mountains. Text by Edward Abbey. Photographs by Eliot Porter. New York: Dutton, 1970.

Slickrock: The Canyon Country of Southeast Utah. Text by Edward Abbey. Photographs and additional commentary by Philip Hyde. San Francisco: Sierra Club, 1971.

Cactus Country. New York: Time-Life, 1973.

The Hidden Canyon: A River Journey. Journal by Edward Abbey. Photographs by John Blaustein. New York: Viking, 1977.

Desert Images: An American Landscape. Text by Edward Abbey. Photographs by David Muench. New York: Harcourt, Brace, Jovanovich, 1979.

CRITICAL AND BIOGRAPHICAL STUDIES

Bishop, James, Jr. *Epitaph for a Desert Anarchist: The Life and Legacy of Edward Abbey.* Epilogue by Charles Bowden. New York: Atheneum, 1994.

Cahalan, James M. *Edward Abbey: A Life.* Tucson: University of Arizona Press, 2001.

Loeffler, Jack. *Adventures with Ed: A Portrait of Abbey.* Albuquerque: University of New Mexico Press, 2002.

McCann, Garth. *Edward Abbey.* Boise, Idaho: Boise State University, 1977.

Hepworth, James, and Gregory McNamee, eds. *Resist Much, Obey Little: Some Notes on Edward Abbey.* Salt Lake City, Utah: Dream Garden Press, 1985.

Quigley, Peter, ed. *Coyote in the Maze: Tracking Edward Abbey in a World of Words.* Salt Lake City: University of Utah Press, 1998.

Ronald, Ann. *The New West of Edward Abbey.* Albuquerque: University of New Mexico Press, 1982. (This essay cites the second edition, with an afterword by Scott Slovic, published in 2000 by the University of Nevada Press.)

BOOK REVIEWS

Cahill, Tim. "Like Huck and Jim." *New York Times Book Review,* May 30, 1982, p. 6.

Chapman, Stephen. "*Abbey's Road* by Edward Abbey." *New Republic,* August 25, 1979, pp. 37–39.

Coale, Howard. "Beer, Guns and Nietzche." *New York Times Book Review,* December 18, 1988, p. 22.

Drabelle, Dennis. "Environments and Elitists." *The Nation,* May 1, 1982, pp. 533–535.

Franks, Lucinda. Review of *Abbey's Road. New York Times Book Review,* April 5, 1979, p. 8.

Hoffman, Alice. "Land of Scorpions and Sagebrush." *New York Times Book Review,* April 15, 1984, p. 34.

Nordyke, Lewis. "Lonesome Jack Burns." *New York Times Book Review,* September 9, 1956.

Pellecchia, Michael. "Monkey Wrench Once More." *New York Times Book Review,* February 4, 1990, p. 18.

Teale, Edwin Way. Review of *Desert Solitaire. New York Times Book Review,* January 28, 1968, p. 7.

Waldhorn, Arthur. "Fiction—*Hayduke Lives!* by Edward Abbey." *Library Journal,* December 1989, p. 164.

FILM BASED ON THE WORK OF EDWARD ABBEY

Lonely Are the Brave. Screenplay by Dalton Trumbo. Directed by David Miller. Janus Films, 1962.

—DONNA SEAMAN

Margaret Atwood
1939–

MARGARET ATWOOD IS an author of novels, poetry, essays, short fiction, children's books, even radio plays. Her writings, including *The Handmaid's Tale* (1985), have been translated into more than twenty languages. While Canadian, Atwood is important to American audiences, especially since the publication of *The Handmaid's Tale,* which is recognizably set in Cambridge, Massachusetts, and draws from American rather than Canadian histories. Committed to worldwide freedom of speech, she has worked with Amnesty International and International PEN. Her writing centers on storytelling as power, dichotomies between the natural and human worlds, and the victimization of women and other marginalized groups by oppressive mythologies and societies.

Margaret Eleanor Atwood was born November 18, 1939, in Ottawa, Ontario, to Margaret Dorothy Killam Atwood and Carl Edmund Atwood, a forest entomologist. She has an older brother, Harold, and a younger sister, Ruth. During the period 1939–1945, her family spent winters in Ottawa and summers in the northern Quebec and Ontario wilderness, where her father conducted field research. Her early experience in the bush away from urban distractions helped develop both her imagination and a lifelong respect for nature. In 1946 her family settled in Toronto.

At Leaside High School, Atwood wrote for the school newspaper. At Victoria College, University of Toronto, where she studied between 1957 and 1961, she began to pursue a literary career in earnest, participating in the social and intellectual life of the college. She wrote for the literary journal, the college newsletter, and the dramatic society.

In the late 1950s the University of Toronto was a center for Canadian poetry with several important Canadian poets and critics on the faculty, including the critic Northrop Frye, author of *Anatomy of Criticism,* and the Canadian poet Jay Macpherson. The ensuing decade sparked an interest in Canadian literature, and Atwood has been an important contributor to the idea that Canadian literature, or Canlit, is a topic worthy of study.

In 1961 Atwood graduated from the University of Toronto's Victoria College and won the school's E. J. Pratt Medal for a group of poems called *Double Persephone.* She also won a Woodrow Wilson Fellowship to begin graduate study at Radcliffe College, Harvard University. She earned her M.A. in 1962 and began her doctoral studies at Harvard. Feeling exiled both from Canada and the modern poetry collection at Harvard (housed in a library that women were forbidden to enter), Atwood read a great deal of Canadian poetry. Returning to Canada in 1963, she focused her attention on Canadian literature and her own work.

Between 1963 and 1964, Atwood worked at a market research company. The following year she taught English literature at the University of British Columbia, where she wrote the first draft of *The Edible Woman* on examination booklets. In 1965 she returned to Harvard and her doctoral studies, completing all the requirements except the dissertation, which she never finished.

Writing poetry and submitting collections to editors all along, she published her first complete collection, *The Circle Game,* in 1966. In 1967 *The Circle Game* won the Governor General's Award for literature, an important Canadian honor. During the same year, Atwood married James Polk, a fellow graduate student and an American novelist. In the 1967–1968 school year Atwood taught four classes of English in Montreal, finished her next book of poems, *The Animals in That Country,* began her subsequent two books of poems, and made final cuts to *The Edible Woman,* which was published in 1969. In the next few years she taught, traveled, and published, getting involved with Anansi Press in 1971. Between 1971 and 1972, *Power Politics* (a book of poems), *Surfacing* (a novel), and *Survival* (a book of criticism) were all published, making Atwood an important if controversial Canadian writer. In 1973 she and her husband separated. She then moved to a farm in Alliston, Ontario, with the Canadian novelist Graeme Gibson, and the two became involved with the Writers' Union of Canada. Their daughter, Jess, was born in 1976. The family spent the 1978–1979 academic year in Scotland, where Gibson was writer in residence, before settling in Toronto in 1980. In the 1980s Atwood served as president of Writers' Union of Canada as well as the president of PEN Canada. All the while, she published novels, short stories, a book of essays, and poetry.

In 1985 Atwood published *The Handmaid's Tale,* the novel that made her an internationally best-selling author. The novel won her yet another Governor General's Award, the *Los Angeles Times* Award for fiction, the Arthur C. Clarke science fiction award, and was a runner-up for both the Booker Prize and the Ritz Paris Hemingway Award. The novel was made into a film that was released in 1990; the playwright Harold Pinter wrote the screenplay. Atwood continued to publish novels, short stories, and even another book of criticism, but after her *Selected Poems II: Poems Selected and New, 1976–1986* came out in 1986, she did not publish another book of poems until *Morning in the Burned House* in 1995. *Alias Grace* appeared in 1996 and won the Giller Prize. In 2000 *The Blind Assassin* won the Booker Prize. Atwood published *Negotiating with the Dead,* a book about writing, in 2002.

Because Margaret Atwood is such a prolific writer, any overview of her works is necessarily partial. Her novels garner the most popular and academic interest, and therefore it seems appropriate in a limited space to look at her ten novels in some detail while only briefly discussing her poetry and other prose.

THE EDIBLE WOMAN

Margaret Atwood's first published novel, *The Edible Woman* (1969), is the comic story of Marian McAlpin, who finds herself behaving in increasingly irrational ways. Part 1 of the novel begins with Marian trying to account for her unexpected behavior during a whirlwind weekend: "I know I was all right on Friday when I got up." But at a restaurant the following night, while listening to her boyfriend, Peter, tell an old friend of hers about hunting, she starts to cry and goes to the bathroom. When she returns, Peter gives her a smile that makes her think he was "treating me as a stage prop," and, as they are leaving, she panics and begins to run. The two men chase her. After Peter catches up to Marian, they all go to the friend's apartment, where the two men again ignore her. Despite some refusals on Marian's part, Peter drives her home; they argue in the car about whether Marian is rejecting her femininity by not behaving properly. After a short period of restored intimacy, they get engaged. Later Marian kisses a stranger with whom she has been speaking at the Laundromat. Going over her actions, Marian decides that her strange flight after dinner made sense.

Part 2 shows a shift in narration. Instead of Marian narrating her own story, the story is told in third-person past, charting the escalation of her dissociation from her own feelings. She begins a relationship with Duncan, the stranger she met at the Laundromat, but believes this has nothing to do with her engagement.

Marian's eating problems first manifest when she is out to dinner with Peter. She watches him carve his steak. When she looks down at her own half-eaten steak, she sees it as a bloody animal that has been mercilessly butchered; she cannot eat it. Over the next few weeks Marian discovers that she cannot eat an ever-increasing number of foods. Far from understanding the logic controlling her inability to eat, she tries to discover what she can still eat. Her fear "was that this thing, this refusal of her mouth to eat, was malignant."

Throughout the novel Marian conflates fertility and femininity with fat. Observing her all-female coworkers at the office Christmas party, she considers the overheard word "immature": "You were green and then you ripened: became mature. Dresses for the mature figure. In other words, fat." Critics have noted that confusing fertility and femininity with fat is common among those suffering from anorexia nervosa, a disease of body image and refusal to eat which was little understood when Atwood wrote the novel. Because of its seemingly prescient account of a woman's refusal to eat, *The Edible Woman* has been used as a case study by critics interested in eating disorders.

Marian's out-of-control behavior crescendos when at Peter's party she views Peter as a hunter trying to fix her in place with his camera. She runs away to find Duncan and has sex with him. But Duncan offers Marian no help with the problems in front of her.

Marian arranges to see the disgruntled Peter. She bakes a cake in the shape of a woman and presents it to him. "You've been trying to destroy me, haven't you," she says. "You've been trying to assimilate me. But I've made you a substitute, something you'll like much better." Without touching the cake or registering whether he understands, Peter leaves. With the engagement off Marian begins to eat the cake herself.

In part 3 Marian's first person narration resumes. She decides to clean the moldering kitchen she could not face earlier. Duncan comes over, and Marian reveals that she can eat again, having eaten a steak for lunch. He tells her that she has returned to "so-called reality, you're a consumer." He gratefully eats the cake she offers him.

Some critics argue that *The Edible Woman* is a feminist book since the female protagonist is at odds with the prevailing culture's norms. The critic John Lauber cites its indictment of consumer culture with the many barbs and comic sections surrounding Marian's work as a market research questionnaire editor. Her refusal to eat is often viewed as a reaction to a consumer culture that commodifies women as consumables, similar to the way it commodifies nature and animals.

That the story becomes alienated from Marian's voice in the second section interests many critics. Some contend that this formal device makes the novel particularly psychological, representing a disruption and alienation from the self caused by the engagement to Peter. In her article "The Dark Voyage" Catherine McLay argues that this three-part narrative enacts a classic descent into and return from the underworld with Marian's cannibal cake as a return to herself, the wedding and feast in one that ends all comedies. Robert Lecker notes that Marian's return to herself leaves her in the same position that she was in at the beginning, presenting a rather circular narrative. Lecker argues that Atwood again experiments with the circular narrative in her next two novels, *Surfacing* and *Lady Oracle,* which, he says, also chart descents to and returns from an underworld.

SURFACING

Usually considered one of Atwood's most important novels, *Surfacing* (1972) is the story of an unnamed narrator-artist who takes her boyfriend, Joe, and a crass and embattled couple, David and Anna, to the remote cabin in Quebec where she spent much of her youth. Though she has not spoken in years to her father, who is missing, she feels she must go and find out whether he is dead or alive. Finding nothing, she is reconciled to leaving: "I've finished what I came for. . . . I want to go back to where there is electricity and distraction." She wants to avoid memories of her early life on the island as well as the ex-husband and child she left.

But the travelers do not return immediately to the city. The section closes with the narrator noting, "I have to be more careful about my memories, I have to be sure they're my own . . . : if the events are wrong the feelings I remember about them will be wrong too, I'll start inventing them and there will be no way of correcting it." From this the reader knows that her "surfacing" memories will be vital throughout the rest of the novel.

The second section is in first person past, reflective of the shift in the narrator's consciousness. While she is concerned about danger on the island, she is focused more on the past. When she refuses Joe's offer of marriage, the memory of her odd wedding to her ex-husband, where the details did not fit the occasion, seems more clear to her than what is happening in the present. Later the narrator thinks, "I didn't feel awful; I realized I didn't feel much of anything, I hadn't for a long time." Her realization of her own lack of affect is key to many critics' interpretations of the novel as the narrator's recovering of her self and her emotions.

The group finds a dead heron, killed for sport. She attributes this act to the Americans, who hunt to "prove they could do it, they had the power to kill." But these needless acts of hunting and lack of compassion for nature and animals come closer to home when David fishes for bass: "I couldn't [kill] anymore, I had no right to. We didn't need it, our proper food was tin cans." When she discovers that the people she assumed were Americans are really Canadians, she is angry. "They'd killed the heron anyway," she decides. "It doesn't matter what country they're from, my head said, they're still Americans, they're what's in store for us, what we are turning into." The American imperialism of nature and Canada at large forms an important motif of the novel. Many critics compare *Surfacing* to *Survival,* Atwood's book of criticism dealing with the same national issues.

The narrator decides to find the paintings that her father had been looking for before his death. She dives off a cliff. "It was there but it wasn't a painting. . . . It was below me . . . it was dead." After she panics she is pulled into a canoe by Joe. "It was in a bottle curled up, staring out at me like a cat pickled; it had huge jelly eyes and fins instead of hands, fish gills . . . it had drowned in air. . . . It wasn't a child but it could have been one, I didn't allow it." She realizes that she had actually had an abortion recommended by her married and middle-aged lover. She was never married, never had a child, but the real memory was too painful. She recalls that this is why she withdrew from her parents. Her memory intact, she is grateful to the environment that brought back the truth for her, and she begins a shamanistic descent into the nonhuman.

The third section resumes first person present narration. She takes Joe into the woods and has sex with him to become pregnant: "I'm impatient, pleasure is redundant, the animals don't have pleasure." She believes that she can feel her lost child rising in her.

Instead of leaving the island with the others, she hides in a canoe. Listening intently to inner voices, she returns to the cabin but soon finds that everything in the cabin must be destroyed. She realizes she cannot be in any contained spaces: "I am the thing in which the trees and animals move and grow, I am a place." She sees a ghost of her mother as she used to be when she would stand so still that the jays would light on her. She sees a ghost of her father, who has taken an animal shape.

After she observes these two ghosts in their own territory, she can return to the cabin and eat canned foods again. Through this experience she has become whole, say many critics, reclaiming her past and herself. At the end she hears Joe call her name from the dock; he has come back for her. She realizes she loves and can trust him.

Often called a ghost story, *Surfacing* secured Atwood's reputation as a leading Canadian novelist, even though she had a reputation as a poet already. The Canadian literary scene found much to appreciate in this novel, from the portrayal of the Canadian wilderness to the concern about American influence. Because of *Surfacing,* feminist critics adopted Atwood as one of their own, though Atwood insists that her novels are not expressions of feminist dogma. Psychoanalytic and anthropological critics have found much to admire in the shamanistic sequence, comparing the narrator's experiences with traditional Native American practices, European notions of shamanism, and Jungian and Laingian psychology.

LADY ORACLE

A novel with five parts, *Lady Oracle* (1976) centers on Joan Foster, a woman who continually leads a double life as the rather incapable housewife turned feminist poet and secret writer of gothic romances. Part 1 reveals that Joan has faked her own death. Though she ostensibly wants to get away from her husband, her lover, and her new role as a feminist icon, she has returned to a small Italian town she visited the previous summer with her husband. Though she has been hiding both an affair and the fact that she writes escapist romances, she dreams of her husband coming romantically to rescue her from loneliness. Having returned to a town where she is known, she is forced to live a life of intrigue, going out in disguise and worrying about being recognized. Because Joan almost constantly narrates her story and appears to live her life in terms of the paranoia, roles, and conflicts of a gothic fantasy, she seems a particularly untrustworthy narrator who has internalized a great deal of the consumer culture's (and the gothic genre's) fantasies about love, romance, and life. In fact, *Lady Oracle* is studded with passages from the latest romance she is writing.

Part 2 documents Joan's relationship with her mother and her life as a fat girl. Joan recounts her embattled relationship with her mother as her mother's "product" and the justification of her unhappy life. Her mother focuses on trying to get Joan to lose weight. Joan begins to recognize her body as "disputed territory" between them—as her mother encourages Joan to "reduce," Joan defies her mother by eating gluttonously and buying outrageously conspicuous clothes to highlight her bulk and her mother's failure. Much criticism of this novel focuses on Joan and her mother's "enmeshed" relationship.

When her Aunt Lou, a fat older career woman who is the only woman in Joan's life who supports her, dies from a heart attack, Joan is left some money on the condition that she lose one hundred pounds. Despite Joan's feelings of betrayal, she begins to reduce. Joan's discipline to lose weight for Lou's money rather than her mother's appeals makes Joan's bitter mother, who has become a heavy drinker, crazy. The section closes when Joan leaves her family's house after her mother stabs her with a paring knife.

Parts 3 and 4 describe the adult life that Joan is trying to leave behind. Now a thin, vulnerable woman, Joan remakes her past. She falls into a relationship with a man from whom she learns her vocation; he writes nurse-doctor romances. She begins to write the gothic romances that will support her for her adult life. She falls in love with Arthur, whom she thinks of as "a melancholy fighter for almost-lost causes, idealistic and doomed, sort of like Lord Byron." Since he is a political activist, she remakes herself as politically astute. She leaves her lover and lies to Arthur about her past. Ultimately, Joan never tells Arthur about herself, her past as the fat lady in a picture she says is someone else, or her writing, even after they get married. She tells herself that most women ask too much of their husbands, expecting men simultaneously to understand them and fulfill their fantasies.

Finally, while conducting an experiment for one of her romances, she writes *Lady Oracle,* the book of poems that changes her life. The volume is published to immediate popular acclaim as an indictment of male-female relations. Arthur appears to feel betrayed by the book's content and is generally distant. She has an affair with an artist who calls himself the Royal Porcupine and who actually wears the long cloak of which she has dreamed, though he reveals himself eventually as an ordinary man. Since Joan is a secretive woman and a public figure, she finds herself the target of blackmail. With her worlds about to converge she lies to convince some friends to help her fake her death.

Part 5 begins with Joan's realization that she has not escaped her past. Though she has come to Italy to "start being another person," she wonders: "Where was the new life I'd intended to step into, easily as crossing a river?" The romance that she is writing also takes unexpected turns. The wife, Felicia, who is supposed to die so the heroine can marry the gothic hero, becomes the center of the story. At the heart of a maze Felicia finds the hero's other dead wives. The hero, who alternately has features of all of Joan's lovers, wants to kill Felicia so that he can replace her with a perfect gothic heroine. Clearly, the fiction must kill the real self in order for the fantasy to survive. Joan's fantasies have been denying and obscuring her own real self and feelings as well as the feelings of those she claims to care about.

The novel's ambivalent end does not suggest that Joan has learned to eschew fantasy in favor of reality and real emotions. She learns that her faked death has gotten her accomplices in trouble. A journalist finds her in her Italian flat; panicked, she hits him with a bottle. She realizes that she must get her friends out of jail and reveal her true self to Arthur. Meanwhile, she is staying in Rome, nursing the journalist, suggesting a different but equally destructive nurse-doctor fantasy.

Lady Oracle is often viewed as a gothic novel in its own right that lays bare the destructive aspects of society's mythologies about love and women's roles. Like Marian McAlpin and the unnamed narrator of *Surfacing,* Joan does not champion her own feelings or assert her own version of reality. While more comic than *Surfacing,* this circular narrative does not promise the same hope or resulting honesty that *Surfacing*'s ending would seem to imply.

LIFE BEFORE MAN

While many critics agree that Atwood's first three novels form a trilogy of concerns, Atwood's fourth novel, *Life Before Man* (1979), investigates marriage and alienation more deeply, picking up where the other novels leave off. Compared with the three earlier novels, which are plot-driven and action-packed and need a great deal of explanation even to summarize the complexities of their respective narrators' psychological realities, the plot of *Life Before Man* is simple.

Nate and Elizabeth are unhappily married people who stay together because of inertia and their children. They have affairs. But the novel so undermines the myths of romantic and marital bliss that even the affairs are not fulfilling. As the novel opens, Elizabeth grieves because her lover, Chris, has killed himself. Nate's latest affair has ended, and now he is interested in Lesje, who works with Elizabeth. Lesje is an emotionally remote young woman more compelled by the dinosaurs she studies than by her live-in boyfriend, William. The story is told alternately from the points of view of Elizabeth, Nate, and Lesje in the third person. Nate and Lesje begin an affair. Elizabeth becomes jealous and arranges to meet with William about Nate and Lesje. After William finds out about Lesje's infidelity, he rapes her, and Lesje moves out. Lesje gets her own place, but Nate vacillates about moving in with her until Elizabeth actually throws him out.

Lesje and Nate then begin the difficult process of building a life together. Nate, who had retreated from his life as a lawyer to make toys, rejoins society by practicing law again. Lesje and Nate's first fight is over his children, who are spending a weeknight at their house because Elizabeth's miserable aunt has died. Lesje, who believes her Lithuanian background prohibited former lovers from considering her for marriage and childbearing, decides to stop taking her birth control pills. She determines: "If children were the key, if having them was the only way she could stop being invisible, then she would goddamn well have some herself." The death of Elizabeth's aunt frees Elizabeth from the past and allows her to go on with her life and take care of her children. Nate and Lesje also go on, though after two months she still has not revealed her probable pregnancy to Nate.

While the plot reads like a soap opera, the narration is notable for its lack of drama and affect, with the dramatic moments mostly occurring offstage. Instead of plot events, the internal processes of the characters prove important. While a conventional narrative assumes that at least one of the characters will be likable and serve as the protagonist, reviewers and critics generally agree that each of the narrative foci in this book is distanced and unempathetic. Critics have also noted that the dated entries and present tense narration evoke the scientific observation that is Lesje's vocation. Like a scientist, the reader must synthesize a story from data.

In her article "The Canadian Mosaic" (in *Essays on Canadian Writing,* summer 1990), Carol Beran notes that there are some reasons for hope at the end. Lesje takes charge of her fertility and decides independently to have a baby, thus joining and contributing to the animal world that she has been content to observe from a safe distance. Elizabeth is able again to nurture her own children, which she had found difficult after Chris's death. In addition, Nate rejoins the society from which he had retreated. Many critics, however, find this novel to be generally depressing and hopeless.

BODILY HARM

Bodily Harm (1983) is an overtly political novel about a protagonist who wants to remain apolitical. Told in both first person and third, the narration of *Bodily Harm* serves as an explanation for a situation not revealed until the last section; the novel opens, "This is how I got here." Readers learn that Rennie Wilford is a Canadian freelance journalist specializing in light magazine pieces. In remission from breast cancer, she has just had a partial mastectomy that has left her feeling half-alive. She arrives home to find police in her apartment explaining that someone broke in and left a rope on the bed.

Upset because of the mounting pressures and dangers in her life, she hurriedly takes a travel assignment to the Caribbean island of St. Antoine. But her planned magazine story focusing on tennis courts, restaurants, hotels, and old-world charm is thwarted by political upheaval.

Her narration of St. Antoine is interspersed with other narratives. She recalls her somewhat sadomasochistic yet casual relationship with her ex-boyfriend, her narrow and repressive childhood, and her breast operation and resulting intimate but nonsexual relationship with her doctor. She offers the brutal history of Lora, a Canadian woman in St. Antoine with whom, it is revealed at the end of the narration, Rennie is sharing a prison cell. The varied narrative arcs form a complex explanation for "how I got here."

Some critics say that Rennie symbolizes Canada and the "sweet Canadians": well-meaning but politically naive. Rennie does find herself in the middle of the unrest. Dr. Minnow, a candidate for prime minister, asks her please to write about what she sees and publish it in Canada. Rennie says she will try—but later thinks better of it. Lora, a drug dealer and the sometime girlfriend of a political leader, convinces Rennie to pick up a package at the airport by telling her that it contains heart medicine. The package contains a machine gun. Paul, an attractive American, helps Rennie navigate St. Antoine, but Rennie finds out that he is actually "the connection" for guns and drugs; she has sex with him and gratefully returns to a body that she felt was already half dead.

Meanwhile, tensions are escalating. The three leaders of the island form a coalition, agreeing that Dr. Minnow will be prime minister, but Minnow is shot. Paul arranges to get Rennie out on a plane, but the airport is shut down. She is arrested and taken to a cell with Lora, which is where, the reader realizes, "here" is.

When Lora finds out that her boyfriend has been killed, she tries to kick the keepers and they beat her up. Rennie's future tense narration commences when Lora is being beaten, interrupted when a seemingly dead Lora is returned to the cell, then continues. In the future the government will apologize to Rennie and let her go, requesting that she write nothing about her experiences. Finally, Rennie realizes that she is lucky to be alive.

The ending is ambivalent. Most of the narrative is in eternal present tense, presumably until she runs out of story. Yet her escape has not happened yet, may not ever happen, as Rennie is "here," between her present-time account and the promise of her future tense narration. Maybe the future tense narration happens and the story itself is her return to serious reporting. Perhaps it is simply the story she must tell herself to keep herself alive. The critic Lorna Irvine even posits that the entire narrative is a drug-induced hallucination while Rennie is undergoing surgery.

This novel continues and escalates some of Atwood's concerns in her other work. *Bodily Harm* examines internal harm (cancer as well as the psychology of cancer and fear) and external harm (violence but also harm to the body politic). But instead of the comedy or conventional gothic, the detective thriller is the genre that some say Atwood is exploiting, undermining, and critiquing. Continuing Atwood's women-based concerns, sexual politics of misogyny, pornography, sadomasochism, rape fantasies, and women in non-Western countries all come up in *Bodily Harm*. Yet Atwood's more overt takes on violence, postcolonialism, the third world, and Canada as an inept power broaden the scope of the psychological novels she had been writing thus far. Here she begins to explore global politics and human rights violations that not only characterize the work she does for Amnesty International but which she takes on in her most famous work, *The Handmaid's Tale*.

THE HANDMAID'S TALE

Although Atwood was already lionized in Canada for her novels, poetry, and criticism, the futuristic novel *The Handmaid's Tale* (1985) made her an international best-selling author. Because *The Handmaid's Tale* is set in the United States and based on United States history, the novel remains increasingly important in the country. *The Handmaid's Tale* is the story of Offred, a woman at the center of her state's oppression.

In early twenty-first century United States, pollution and nuclear accidents have left many women infertile. A religious right group has orchestrated a coup and gained control of the government, renamed the Republic of Gilead. Women are stripped of jobs and financial independence and forced into categories. Wives of the elite stay home while fertile women are recruited to become handmaids, a position of having babies for the sterile elite. Handmaids are kept in line by threats that they will be sent to the colonies, where they could spend their last days cleaning up toxic waste. In Gilead women's roles are defined by the color of their clothing, making their status visible to all in a way that was impossible (and perhaps troubling to some) in "the time before," a society having much in common with our own. Handmaids wear red, whereas the commanders' wives wear powder blue. The young daughters born to the handmaids and brought up by the wives wear virginal white. (Men are also ranked and wear clothes befitting their station, though most of the uniforms are black, making men's roles more difficult to determine optically.)

The narrator of the novel, Offred (a patronymic: Of Fred), is a handmaid assigned to an elite family. In an antierotic ceremony meant to replicate the Biblical story in which Jacob sires a child with his wife's maidservant, the handmaid's job is to let the commander copulate with her "lower half" while she lies between the wife's legs. Likewise, when birthing a baby, the handmaid is again positioned between the wife's legs, describing spatially the handmaid's status as a mere vessel. A handmaid is allowed three unsuccessful two-year posts before she is sent to the colonies. If a handmaid does have a child, she is expected to give it up to the wife but gains the reward of never having to go to the colonies.

Offred reveals this world in "gasps," much the way she views it from under the red veil and white wings around her eyes that she must wear. Since all other distractions are forbidden, she notices everything. She remembers "the time before," focusing often on the husband and daughter taken from her. The novel begins early in her third posting at a commander's house.

The entire household listens to the Jacob and Bihlah story the night the copulation ceremony is to take place. Instead of thinking about the story, Offred remembers her college friend Moira who, at the Red Center for handmaids, tried to break out by feigning illness but was caught and tortured. Offred admires Moira's courage but knows she cannot be like her. Instead, Offred "describes." When the ceremony actually takes place, Offred states that the Commander "is fucking . . . the lower half of my body." Afterward, the Wife sends Offred away, though she is supposed to allow her to stay and rest: "There is loathing in her voice. . . . Which of us is it worse for, her or me?" Offred is clearly victimized, but she still has compassion, even for the elite.

Later that night Offred uncharacteristically breaks the rules and goes downstairs, wandering around in the dark. Virtually all the events that follow in the narrative are marked by subversion of the rules, even by those best served by them. Nick, the chauffeur, finds her and kisses her. The Commander, Nick tells Offred, wishes to see her the following night. She remembers that her courageous friend Moira finally did escape the Red Center by tying up one of the women in charge and stealing her clothes.

Since seeing a commander apart from the ceremony is not sanctioned, Offred is nervous about being called by the Commander. He wants them to be friends; she sees him regularly, playing Scrabble, reading books and magazines, using hand lotion, all normally forbidden to her. Because she has no power, she cannot refuse to see him though it is dangerous.

Offred and her assigned shopping partner, Ofglen, uneasily confess their disbelief in the regime. Ofglen notifies Offred that there is a resistance movement called May Day. She tries to convince Offred to find information that could be useful, but Offred is afraid.

Since Serena Joy, the Wife of the Commander, desperately wants a child but suspects that her husband is sterile, she asks Offred to have sex with Nick. Because the risk taken is Offred's, Serena Joy wants to give her something: a picture of Offred's daughter for her to look at. She also gives her a cigarette and a match, with which Offred considers burning the house down as she suspects Moira would do.

One night when Offred goes to see the Commander, he has a dangerous surprise for her. He dresses her up as a prostitute and takes her out to a brothel known as Jezebel's. There she finds Moira. In the washroom Moira tells her that she had indeed escaped and was able to get on the Underground Femaleroad, a resistance group that gets women out of the country. She was in Maine when she got caught and was given her choice to be a prostitute or be sent to the colonies, as she was too dangerous to be allowed back into the regimented society. Here Offred learns that while there is real hope of escape, the person most likely to make it did not. It also turns out that the Commander took Offred to Jezebel's to have sex with her in a different setting. She cannot refuse.

She does not refuse when Serena Joy arranges for her to have sex with Nick. In fact, Offred goes back to Nick again and again, an act that some critics say constitutes a defiant reclaiming of her sexuality while others argue that it reinforces her passivism.

At a public function called a Particicution, where the handmaids are encouraged to be violent, Ofglen reveals that the man accused of being a rapist is actually a member of the resistance group. Aware that the handmaids will pull him apart limb from limb, Ofglen mercifully kicks him in the head. Later, when Offred expects to meet Ofglen, she finds that a new woman, also called Ofglen, has taken her friend's place. The new Ofglen tells her that the former Ofglen hanged herself when she saw that the Eyes, an intelligence group, were coming for her. Offred is terrified.

When Serena Joy confronts Offred with the knowledge that Offred has betrayed her with the Commander, Offred waits for the Eyes to come take her away. Instead Nick comes, whispers May Day, and explains that she should leave with them under the guise of being arrested. Offred's narrative ends at that uncertain place, as she is unaware about whether she is being rescued or betrayed.

Following Offred's narrative are some "historical notes." A panel of the Gileadean Research Association, a century and a half after the tale ends, is studying Offred's story. Her narrative has been transcribed from tapes found near Maine, suggesting that she might have made it out of the country. Further, that the tapes were found far afield (clearly she could not have made them at the Commander's house) suggests that Nick did not betray her but got her onto the Underground Femaleroad. The Gileadean researchers further explain that many of Gilead's practices had historical precedents. While Offred's destiny remains uncertain, the novel ends hopefully; the academy, which had been banned in Gilead (the setting is recognizably Cambridge, Massachusetts, with Harvard having been turned into a spy center), is back in business with Gilead functioning as the subject for historical dissection.

The Handmaid's Tale is the Atwood novel most popular with academic critics. As a dystopian novel, it takes its place among, and is often compared with, dystopian classics such as Aldous Huxley's *Brave New World,* George Orwell's *1984,* Ray Bradbury's *Fahrenheit 451,* and Anthony Burgess' *A Clockwork Orange,* as well as Marge Piercy's feminist utopian novel, *Woman on the Edge of Time.* The character of Offred is also a matter of contention for many critics. Karen F. Stein argues that "Offred's narration of her tale may be the most subversive act possible for her," while Madonne Miner argues that Offred is not subversive but a passive victim. *The Handmaid's Tale* is so rich in feminist, religious, political, narrative, generic, and philosophical implications that academics of various stripes have explored this novel; perhaps the only thing they all agree on is that it is a masterwork worthy of extensive study.

CAT'S EYE

While female friendships form a theme that runs throughout Atwood's work, *Cat's Eye* (1989) pushes these concerns to the fore. *Cat's Eye* tells the life of a successful fifty-year-old artist, Elaine Risley. A retrospective of her paintings in a small feminist art gallery brings her back to Toronto, where she grew up, triggering a psychological retrospective. The present action takes place over a few days as she explores the city, expecting to see Cordelia, a childhood friend with whom she had a tense relationship, around every street corner. The novel is concerned with storytelling's link to memory and the past.

While the novel is an autobiography of Elaine's life so far, from her childhood memories to her life in art school and her first and second marriages, the story really focuses on her childhood. Elaine's family, an unconventional one that during her youth spends winters in cities and summers in the bush (her father is an entomologist like Atwood's), moves to a permanent home in Toronto when she is eight. Young Elaine expects to find friendships with girls pleasant, but because she never learned the codes that govern girls' relationships, she becomes the butt of their teasing, experiencing the cruelty accorded to an outsider. Elaine is by turns befriended, ostracized, scolded, and "improved" by the trio of Cordelia, Grace Smeath, and Carol Campbell. Grace's mother, Mrs. Smeath, who takes Elaine to church because her family does not go, still considers Elaine a heathen and condones the scapegoating. These confusing signals (Elaine calls these girls her "friends" for a long time) cause her to withdraw by shutting down emotionally. Critics note that Elaine's "cat's eye" view of the world—defensive, distanced, and distorted like looking through her favorite marble—is not only a survival strategy but also becomes her strength as an adult. When she becomes an artist, Elaine's vision and perspective are the center of her exploration and expression; they are also what make her successful.

As a child Elaine lives in tension, constantly expecting new torments. One day Cordelia tosses Elaine's hat into a frozen ravine from the bridge above. Climbing down, Elaine gets chilled and lies as if paralyzed. She has a hallucination of a magical cloaked woman who opens her heart to her and says, *"You can go home now.... It will be all right."* The event not only frees her from her paralysis at the ravine but from her paralyzing and destructive relationship with the other girls. Afterward, she finds she has grown hard and loses interest in the girls, and their power over her diminishes.

As Elaine and Cordelia grow older, their roles reverse, with Elaine gaining purpose in her life as Cordelia increasingly has trouble coping. Finally, Cordelia is in a mental hospital.

When the adult Elaine walks through her own retrospective, she comes to her paintings of Mrs. Smeath and others with more compassion. Returning to the ravine that once freed her, she sees a vision of Cordelia as a child and uses the incantation that worked before: *"It's all right. . . .You can go home now."* Looking at Cordelia with forgiveness, the hardness inside her melts.

Critics agree that *Cat's Eye* explores autobiography as a genre. At the beginning of the novel Elaine meditates on time as a dimension, that one can look through time like water. Stein argues that this meditation on time signals to the reader the instability of memory and narrative. While autobiography is purported to be fact, the autobiographer cannot help but interpret events, shaping incidents into a story.

The novel also investigates the author/artist's control of his or her creation, addressing the vexed relationship between art and interpretation. Elaine's artwork is influenced by her life—most often working out her own psychological conflicts and getting revenge on women she knew. But in the eyes of the reviewers and art critics, her work is found to be feminist, as if her focus were political rather than personal. Elaine finds these interpretations "hilarious." Because Atwood is a writer particularly subject to the "feminist" appellation, this particular concern may serve as a caution against interpreting Atwood's writing, or any work, as wholly feminist or political.

THE ROBBER BRIDE

Whereas *Cat's Eye* explores the perils of friendships among young girls *The Robber Bride* (1993) focuses on women's friendships. It is a novel about three women who bond together after being betrayed by the same femme fatale, Zenia. More important than the betrayal of these three women and how it shapes their lives, this story is about the ways the three women band together.

Like *Cat's Eye* and other Atwood novels (*Lady Oracle,* for example), *The Robber Bride* is about storytelling—each of the three women tells in third person the story of her childhood in which she rejected a part of herself and how Zenia betrayed her. Zenia, herself a storyteller (denied her own narration), tells many conflicting stories about herself, often remaking herself to exploit the women's weaknesses—not just getting their men but deeply betraying their trust.

Critics see these three victims as various triumvirates. Stein suggests that the three women are different aspects of the personality: Tony, an academic war historian, is the mind; Charis, interested in yoga, tarot, and spirituality, is the spirit; Roz, a successful executive interested in appearances, is the body. Stein also characterizes the three women as aspects of the triple goddess, and Sarah Appleton Aguiar sees them as the past (Tony), present (Roz), and future (Charis).

The novel starts when the three women, believing Zenia to be dead, see her at the restaurant where they are having lunch. The sight of her unnerves them, reminding each of her unresolved betrayal. At the book's center each woman's experience with Zenia is told from her own point of view. She manipulates the women and exploits their friendship to steal their lovers: Charis' lover, Billy; Roz's husband, Mitch; and Tony's husband, West. Since Zenia casts such a long shadow over each of the women, each sets out with her own plan to confront Zenia. Though their plans fail, each woman comes to terms with her past and finds that she can move on.

A few days after the women see Zenia in the restaurant, Zenia tempts each with a story. She tells Charis that she has AIDS, playing on

Charis' nurturing instincts. Charis almost invites her to recuperate at her island home, then thinks better of it. When Zenia's ploy does not work, she lashes out at Charis, telling her that being upset about Billy "lets you avoid your life.... Forget about him." Though disturbed by the confrontation (perhaps realizing the truth in it), Charis forgives Zenia and realizes she can move on, accepting her angry other self, called Karen, in the process. Tony, armed with a gun and a cordless drill, also goes to see Zenia. Playing on Tony's engagement with politics and war, Zenia explains that she is in danger for knowing political secrets. Tony too almost believes her, then comes to the conclusion that the story is just a ruse again to steal her husband. Roz fears that Zenia is having an affair with her son, Larry, and confronts her about it. Zenia persuades her that this is the case and that Larry is also a drug dealer. She uses this information as the grounds for blackmail. When Roz confronts her about Mitch, Zenia tells her: "You should give me a medal for getting him off your back.... You always saw him as a victim of women.... Did it ever occur to you that Mitch was responsible for his actions?" Roz leaves the confrontation not knowing what she should do about Larry, but this information instigates her first real discussion with Larry in years. It turns out he is actually gay, not having an affair with Zenia but being blackmailed by her since he did not want to his mother to know about his sexuality. He is also not a drug dealer. Though Zenia seems a compulsive and manipulative liar, she also holds a mirror up to each woman, confronting each with the truth.

The same day that each woman confronts Zenia, the women decide to have dinner together and share their experiences. They then return to Zenia's hotel to find Zenia dead. No one knows whether she killed herself or was murdered. Since no one really knows the truth of her life, it is only fitting that Zenia takes with her the truth about her death. Only her stories are left.

After the three friends scatter Zenia's ashes, they eat together and tell stories. Tony notes, "That's what they will do, increasingly in their lives: tell stories. Tonight their stories will be about Zenia."

ALIAS GRACE

Atwood's next novel focuses on storytelling so profoundly that the story a woman tells may be able to get her out of prison. Unique among Atwood's novels, *Alias Grace* (1996) is a fictionalized narrative of the real-life Grace Marks, a nineteenth-century servant accused of enticing another servant, named James McDermott, to murder their employer, Thomas Kinnear, and his housekeeper and lover, Nancy Montgomery. Grace, however, claims she cannot remember the murder of Nancy Montgomery and, therefore, cannot protest her innocence in a believable narrative. The novel also focuses on Dr. Simon Jordan, a youthful American amnesia and hysteria specialist hired to treat Grace's amnesia in hopes of finding out whether she is innocent or guilty. Simon uses an early version of the talking cure in an attempt to determine whether Grace is a liar. She reveals to him her unhappy childhood in an impoverished Irish immigrant family. Her mother died young, and Grace became a housemaid just before she turned thirteen. Except for a brief period of happiness sharing a room with her outspoken housemaid friend Mary Whitney, Grace led a sad but hardworking life until the murders when she was sixteen. She insists that McDermott forced her to be his accomplice. What Dr. Jordan does not realize is how cunning a storyteller Grace may be; he is never able to determine the truth.

What is more, the reader never knows either. It is never clear whether she lies or tells the truth, if she is very clever or rather dull but honest. The novel introduces gothic elements as well: Grace may have been possessed by her friend Mary Whitney. Grace's narrative characterizes her as observant and clever, but throughout she claims her acerbic and cynical commentary to have come originally from her friend. Dr. Jordan looks for Mary Whitney's grave but finds nothing.

As it happens, Dr. Jordan never does file a report. His young life goes topsy-turvy when he has an affair with his landlady and finds he must flee. In an odd foil to Grace's story he suffers a head injury in the Civil War and gets amnesia. Grace is eventually released from prison, and she moves to the United States, marrying an old friend who has arranged for her to have a nice home with him.

Again Atwood's work demonstrates the dangers of romantic mythologies. Grace's unlikely and convenient marriage is perhaps the happiest relationship because she has no romantic expectations. Others in the novel are not so lucky. When two flirtations result in no marriage, Lydia, the daughter of the governor of the penitentiary, is quickly married off to the head of the society group petitioning for Grace's release. Simon flees when his landlady tries to entice him to kill her returning husband. Grace's friend Mary Whitney has an affair with her employer's son and dies of a botched abortion. If one can believe Grace's narration, James McDermott's lust for Grace forms another example of the danger of romance and desire.

The novel combines Grace's story to Dr. Jordan, Grace's story to the reader, and Dr. Jordan's narration with historical artifacts such as newspaper clippings and letters. Critics note that the various versions and intertexts of the novel enhance and subvert the detective story/murder mystery of the novel. Since each chapter is named after a quilt and Grace is a skilled quilt maker, Magali Cornier Michael argues that the novel itself is a patchwork, forming a whole out of fragments even as Grace's fragments of narration form a whole though not complete story. Again Atwood writes a novel that shows the disparity between life and the stories told about it.

THE BLIND ASSASSIN

The Blind Assassin (2000), which won the Booker Prize, has multiple nested story lines. Iris, an older woman at the center of the novel, narrates her final months. She writes of the deaths of her sister, Laura, her immoral husband, and her troubled daughter, revealing the difference between the truth of and the stories told about the past; she admits that she particularly covered up the truth.

Laura's novel, called *The Blind Assassin* and published after her death, forms another layer of narrative within the larger whole. The novel, which also blends narratives, focuses on a troubled love affair between a society woman and a man who mysteriously moves from place to place, possibly wanted by the police. But the man is also a writer: during their clandestine meetings he tells his lover a science fiction/fantasy tale of virgin sacrifice, abuse of child workers, and escape. The actual person who is "the blind assassin" comes from this narrative. Interestingly, the larger story contains these themes too, including Iris' domineering husband and family, a lost daughter, sexual sacrifice, suicide, and thwarted love infused with troublesome politics.

In 2002 academic criticism had not caught up with *The Blind Assassin;* surely such a popular and critically successful novel will soon have a wealth of criticism on it.

SELECTED POEMS 1965–1975

Though most famous and revered for her novels, Margaret Atwood started her literary career as a poet. Criticism on Atwood's poetry includes David Buchbinder, Barbara Blakely, John

Wilson Foster, Frank Davey's "Atwood's Gorgon Touch," Judith McCombs' "Politics, Structure, and Poetic Development," and George Woodcock's "Metamorphosis and Survival," as well as chapters in the full-length studies on Atwood.

The poems in *The Circle Game* (1966) describe warring oppositions between the natural and human worlds. Many of the poems explore the way the human need for order becomes stultifying. "The City Planners" shows how suburbs impose an unnatural order not only on "the discouraged grass" and landscape but on the quality of life there. The city planners are characterized as insanely trying to impose "the panic of suburb / order in a bland madness of snows." In the much anthologized "This Is a Photograph of Me" the speaker lies invisibly under the water in a blurry photograph. The speaker exists and is visible only as an insistent negation.

The Animals in That Country (1968) continues the exploration of landscape, discussing the problems of country and exile. "At the Tourist Centre in Boston" investigates relations between Canada and the United States. The narrator wonders "Whose dream is this" when looking at the idealized tourist materials of her own country. In "It Is Dangerous to Read Newspapers" the speaker implicates herself and other civilians in the atrocities of war: "I reach out in love, my hands are guns, / my good intentions are completely lethal."

Atwood continues the study of exile in *The Journals of Susanna Moodie: Poems* (1970), a fictionalized poetic journal of an actual nineteenth-century English settler in Canada. "Journal I" recounts the problems of exile and being the "other." In "Death of a Young Son by Drowning" in "Journal II" Atwood's Moodie conflates private grief and the dangerous landscape with notions of land conquest: "I planted him in this country / like a flag." In "Journal III" Moodie is a genteel old lady in the growing Canadian cities. In "A Bus Along St. Clair: December," Moodie's voice is heard in the present from beyond the grave. She is now connected to the landscape she once feared, as a destroyer of the city:

there is no city;
this is the centre of a forest

your place is empty.

Atwood's book of poems charts a trajectory of exile to belonging.

In *Procedures for Underground* (1970) the animal and human worlds are again explored and compared. The shamanistic quest used in *Surfacing* turns up here. In the title poem the shaman's descent into the underworld and subsequent wisdom can be shared with the collective ("You will / tell us their names, what they want, who / has made them angry by forgetting them") but comes at a high cost: "Few will seek your help / with love, none without fear." "Dreams of the Animals" overtly contrasts the experiences of living in the wilderness with living in civilization. The animals in the wilderness dream of other animals, but the encaged animals in the human world do not. "The silver fox in the roadside zoo / dreams of digging out / and of baby foxes, their necks bitten" and the pet store iguana "dreams of sawdust." Civilization has so disturbed them that the animals are exiles even in their dreams. One cannot help but wonder by extension what civilization has done to humans.

Marking a change from Atwood's poems of landscape, *Power Politics* (1971) focuses on humans locked in the embrace and battle of a difficult romantic relationship. The poems take place in restaurants and other enclosed areas. The epigram of this collection sums up the poems:

you fit into me
like a hook into an eye

a fish hook
an open eye

The deadlock of the relationship makes both parties tormentors and victims.

You Are Happy (1974) consists of four sections: the first and last figure a relationship that is ending and beginning respectively; the two middle sections are the unspoken stories in Odysseus' relationship with the sorceress Circe. The title poem, in the first section, demonstrates that titles can be deceiving. In the middle of a landscape that is cold both emotionally and physically, the speaker says:

When you are this
cold you can think about
nothing but the cold . . .
. . . .
. . . you are happy.

Only when not thinking can the "you" or the speaker be happy. "There Is Only One of Everything" in the final section marks a change in the tone of Atwood's poetry. The poem is set in a domestic and warm scene; the speaker seems present and at peace.

. . . I can even say it,
though only once and it won't

last: I want this. I want
this.

At the end of this collection Atwood's usually cold speaker seems genuinely happy.

SELECTED POEMS II

Atwood's next collection, *Two-Headed Poems* (1978), looks at paradoxes and duplicity of language, politics, storytelling, and emotions. "Marrying the Hangman" presents the power of the storyteller to effect change. In times past a female criminal could marry a hangman to save her own life. In this poem a woman convinces the man in the next cell to become a hangman and marry her just by her voice. But always language is duplicitous. His words that had promised security and freedom become the words of order and rigidity. Her words go from the words of the flesh to words of nature and vulnerability. Has she exchanged one prison for another? Generally the poems in this collection present scenes of an ordinary household rather than the tensions displayed in *Power Politics*. "You Begin" is addressed to a young child. The poem is about language and the world and learning about the relationship between the two:

The word *hand* floats above your hand
like a small cloud over a lake.
The word *hand* anchors
your hand to this table.

An Atwood theme, the investigation of the freedom and limits of language typifies this collection.

True Stories (1981), a collection that demonstrates Atwood's overt engagement with political conscience, begins by undermining the notion that there can be a true story. In the title poem the speaker says:

The true story is vicious
and multiple and untrue

after all. Why do you
need it? . . .

The widely anthologized "Notes towards a Poem That Can Never Be Written" is about the impossibility of expressing the horrors of torture and evil in a poem: "The word *why* shrivels and empties / itself." Of those people who are suffering around the world, the speaker says:

we turn them into statistics & litanies
and into poems like this one.

Nothing works.
They remain what they are.

There are places that language does not reach.

Two sections make up Atwood's *Interlunar* (1984): "Snake Poems" and "Interlunar." In "Orpheus (1)" the poem is in the voice of Eurydice, the wife of the archetypal poet who wants to bring her back from the dead. Though Eurydice does not want to leave the underworld, his determination brings her almost to life until he looks back and she is returned to the underworld. "You could not believe I was more than your echo," the speaker accuses. "Orpheus (2)" is thematically linked to the concerns of *True Stories*. The poet has seen the horrors of the world but keeps singing though he knows he will be destroyed for it. "To sing is either praise / or defiance. Praise is defiance," the speaker affirms. Again Atwood's concerns about the political and moral values of storytelling come to the fore.

MORNING IN THE BURNED HOUSE

Atwood's first book of poems in almost ten years, *Morning in the Burned House* (1995), marks a change from her previous poems. The critic Janice Fiamengo notes that the poems demonstrate a new emotional openness in her work, that the speaker is not so wry, distant, and acerbic, but rather intimate. The collection explores, among other things, the death of the speaker's father. Unlike the accusing voice of other women poets such as Sylvia Plath, Anne Sexton, or even the speaker of Atwood's *Power Politics*, the voice here marks Atwood's foray into a new genre: the personal elegy. Continuing to explore the nature of memory, loss, and the passage of time, the speaker says: "Nothing gets finished / not dying, not mourning." *Morning in the Burned House* describes ordinary life and its frustrations and losses.

CRITICISM AND OTHER WORK

In addition to novels, poetry, and short stories Atwood has written criticism, children's books, and essays. Perhaps the most important and influential of these works is *Survival* (1972), in which Atwood argues, "every country or culture has a single unifying and informing symbol at its core." For the United States she offers the Frontier. For England, the Island. For Canada, she says, the symbol is Survival. For early Canadians it meant "bare survival in the fact of 'hostile' elements and/or natives." For contemporary Canadians the symbol refers to cultural survival, whether one is talking about the French Canadians dominated by Anglo culture or the English Canadians feeling dominated by American culture. Further, Atwood argues that Canadian literature is typified by representing victims. The end of Atwood's *Surfacing,* a book that foregrounds America's cultural domination of Canada and came out the same year as *Survival,* argues against the Canadian tendency to claim victimization: "This above all, to refuse to be a victim. Unless I can do that I can do nothing." *Survival* became a controversial bestseller, establishing Atwood as an important voice in the study of a national Canadian literature. Also notable are Atwood's *Second Words* (1982), a collection of her early essays; *Strange Things* (1995), a study of the ways in which Canadian writers imagine and write about the mysterious Canadian north; and *Negotiating with the Dead,* a collection of essays focusing on what a writer is and the particular relationship for many writers between writing and death.

The theme of victimization and the refusal or assent to being a victim comes up again and again in Atwood's many works. For some Atwood is a feminist writer, highlighting the oppression of women by society and repressive ideologies and romance mythologies. For others she is the consummate Canadian writer, concerned about the conquering of the wilderness and Canada by imperialists. But quite apart from the more narrow feminist or Canadian concerns, Atwood is a writer whose works are appreciated and studied internationally. Finally, there are many Atwoods, important to readers, writers, and scholars alike.

Selected Bibliography

WORKS OF MARGARET ATWOOD

NOVELS

The Edible Woman. Toronto: McClelland and Stewart, 1969; New York: Bantam, 1991.

Surfacing. Toronto: McClelland and Stewart, 1972; New York: Ballantine, 1987.

Lady Oracle. Toronto: McClelland and Stewart, 1976; New York: Ballantine, 1987.

Life Before Man. Toronto: McClelland and Stewart, 1979; New York: Ballantine, 1987.

Bodily Harm. Toronto: McClelland and Stewart, 1981; New York: Bantam, 1983.

The Handmaid's Tale. Toronto: McClelland and Stewart, 1985; New York: Ballantine, 1987.

Cat's Eye. Toronto: McClelland and Stewart, 1988; New York: Bantam, 1989.

The Robber Bride. New York: Nan A. Talese/Doubleday, 1993; McClelland and Stewart, 1993.

Alias Grace. New York: Nan A. Talese/Doubleday, 1996; McClelland and Stewart, 1996.

The Blind Assassin. New York: Nan A. Talese/Doubleday, 2000; McClelland and Stewart, 2000.

POETRY

Double Persephone. Toronto: Hawkshead Press, 1961. (Limited edition.)

The Circle Game. Toronto: Contact Press, 1966; Toronto: Anansi, 1967.

The Animals in That Country. Toronto: Oxford University Press, 1968.

The Journals of Susanna Moodie: Poems. Toronto: Oxford University Press, 1970.

Procedures for Underground. Toronto: Oxford University Press, 1970.

Power Politics. Toronto: Anansi, 1971.

You Are Happy. Toronto: Oxford University Press, 1974.

Selected Poems. Toronto: Oxford University Press, 1976; Boston: Houghton Mifflin, 1987. (Renamed *Selected Poems 1965–1975* for Houghton Mifflin rerelease.)

Two-Headed Poems. Toronto: Oxford University Press, 1978.

True Stories. Toronto: Oxford University Press, 1981.

Interlunar. Toronto: Oxford University Press, 1984.

Selected Poems II: Poems Selected and New 1976–1986. Toronto: Oxford University Press, 1986; Boston: Houghton Mifflin, 1987.

Morning in the Burned House. Toronto: McClelland and Stewart, 1995.

Eating Fire: Selected Poetry 1965–1995. London: Virago, 1998.

SHORT FICTION

Dancing Girls and Other Stories. Toronto: McClelland and Stewart, 1977; New York: Bantam, 1993.

Murder in the Dark: Short Fictions and Prose Poems. Toronto: Coach House, 1983.

Bluebeard's Egg and Other Stories. Toronto: McClelland and Stewart, 1983; New York: Ballantine, 1987.

Wilderness Tips. New York: Nan A. Talese/Doubleday, 1991; New York: Bantam, 1993.

Good Bones. Toronto: Couch House, 1992; Published with *Murder in the Dark* as *Good Bones and Simple Murders.* New York: Nan A. Talese/Doubleday, 1994.

A Quiet Game: And Other Early Works. Edited and annotated by Kathy Chung and Sherrill Grace. Edmonton, Alberta: Juvenilia Press, 1997.

NONFICTION

Survival: A Thematic Guide to Canadian Literature. Toronto: Anansi, 1972.

Days of the Rebels, 1815–1840. Toronto: Natural Science of Canada, 1977.

Second Words: Selected Critical Prose. Toronto: Anansi, 1982.

Strange Things: The Malevolent North in Canadian Literature. Oxford: Clarendon Press, 1995.

Negotiating with the Dead: A Writer on Writing. Cambridge: Cambridge University Press, 2002.

CHILDREN'S BOOKS

Up in the Tree. Toronto: McClelland and Stewart, 1978.

Anna's Pet. With Joyce Barkhouse. Illustrated by Ann Blades. Toronto: James Lorimer, 1980.

For the Birds. Illustrated by John Bianchi. Boxes and sidebars by Shelley Tanaka. Toronto: Douglas & McIntyre, 1990.

Princess Prunella and the Purple Peanut. Illustrated by Maryann Kovalski. New York: Workman, 1995.

RADIO AND TELEPLAYS

The Trumpets of Summer: Choral Suite for Mixed Chorus, Four Soloists, Male Speaker, and Six Instruments. Canadian Broadcasting Corporation (CBC) Radio, 1964.

The Servant Girl. CBC, 1974.

Snowbird. CBC, 1981.

WORKS EDITED BY MARGARET ATWOOD

The New Oxford Book of Canadian Verse in English. Toronto: Oxford University Press, 1982.

The Oxford Book of Canadian Short Stories in English. With Robert Weaver. Toronto: Oxford University Press, 1986.

The Canlit Foodbook: From Pen to Palate, a Collection of Tasty Literary Fare. Toronto: Totem, 1987.

The Best American Short Stories, 1989. With Shannon Ravenal. New York: Houghton Mifflin, 1989.

The Poetry of Gwendolyn MacEwen. 2 vols. With Barry Callaghan. Toronto: Exile Editions, 1993. (Contains an introduction by Atwood.)

RECORDINGS

The Poetry and Voice of Margaret Atwood. New York: Caedmon, 1977.

Margaret Atwood Reads "Unearthing Suite." Columbia, Mo.: American Audio Prose Library, 1985.

JOURNALS, CORRESPONDENCE, AND MANUSCRIPTS

The Atwood collection is at the Thomas Fisher Rare Book Library at the University of Toronto.

BIBLIOGRAPHIES

"Current Atwood Checklist." *Newsletter of the Margaret Atwood Society,* 1986–present.

McCombs, Judith, and Carole L. Palmer. *Margaret Atwood: A Reference Guide.* Boston: G. K. Hall, 1991.

CRITICAL AND BIOGRAPHICAL STUDIES

Aguiar, Sarah Appleton. "Good Girls and Evil Twins: Constructing Zenia in Margaret Atwood's *The Robber Bride.*" *Newsletter of the Margaret Atwood Society* 19:5–6, 15–16 (fall/winter 1997).

Beran, Carol L. *Living Over the Abyss: Margaret Atwood's "Life Before Man."* Toronto: ECW Press, 1993. (Introduction to the novel with an annotated bibliography.)

Blakely, Barbara. "The Pronunciation of Flesh: A Feminist Reading of Margaret Atwood's Poetry." In *Margaret Atwood: Language, Text, and System.* Edited by Sherrill E. Grace and Lorraine Weir. Vancouver: University of British Columbia Press, 1983. Pp. 33–51.

Bouson, J. Brooks. *Brutal Choreographies: Oppositional Strategies and Narrative Design in the Novels of Margaret Atwood.* Amherst: University of Massachusetts Press, 1993.

Brown, Rosellen. "Anatomy of Melancholia." *Saturday Review,* February 2, 1980, pp. 33–35. (Review of *Life Before Man.*)

Buchbinder, David. "Weaving Her Version: The Homeric Model and Gender Politics in *Selected Poems.*" In *Margaret Atwood: Visions and Forms.* Edited by Kathryn VanSpanckeren and Jan Garden Castro. Carbondale: Southern Illinois University Press, 1988. Pp.122–141.

Cameron, Elspeth. "Famininity, or Parody of Autonomy: Anorexia Nervosa and *The Edible Woman.*" *Journal of Canadian Studies* 20, no. 2:45–69 (summer 1985).

Chernin, Kim. *The Obsession: Reflections on the Tyranny of Slenderness.* New York: Harper & Row, 1981. (The analysis of the meaning of food and its rejection on pages 66–72 uses both *The Edible Woman* and *Lady Oracle* as examples to explore fasting and the fat woman, respectively.)

Cooke, Nathalie. *Margaret Atwood: A Biography.* Toronto: ECW Press, 1998.

Davey, Frank. *Margaret Atwood: A Feminist Poetics.* Vancouver: Talonbooks, 1984.

———. "Atwood's Gorgon Touch [Seven Books of Poetry from *Double Persephone* to *You Are Happy*]." In *Critical Essays on Margaret Atwood.* Edited by Judith McCombs. Boston: G. K. Hall, 1988. Pp. 134–153.

Davidson, Arnold E. *Seeing in the Dark: Margaret Atwood's "Cat's Eye."* Toronto: ECW Press, 1997. (Introduction to the novel with an annotated bibliography.)

Davidson, Cathy N., and Arnold E. Davidson. "Prospects and Retrospect in *Life Before Man.*" In *The Art of Margaret Atwood: Essays in Criticism.* Edited by Arnold E. Davidson and Cathy N. Davidson. Toronto: Anansi, 1981. Pp. 205–221.

Enos, Jennifer. "What's in a Name? Zenia and Margaret Atwood's *The Robber Bride.*" *Newsletter of the Margaret Atwood Society* 15:14 (fall/winter 1995).

Fee, Margery. *The Fat Lady Dances: Margaret Atwood's "Lady Oracle."* Toronto: ECW Press, 1993. (Introduction to the novel with an annotated bibliography.)

Fiamengo, Janice. "'A Last Time for This Also': Margaret Atwood's Texts of Mourning." *Canadian Literature* 166:145–164 (fall 2000).

Foster, John Wilson. "The Poetry of Margaret Atwood [Six Books of Poetry from *The Circle Game* to *You Are Happy*]." In *Critical Essays on Margaret Atwood.* Edited by Judith McCombs. Boston: G. K. Hall, 1988. Pp. 153–167.

Grace, Sherrill E. *Violent Duality: A Study of Margaret Atwood.* Edited by Ken Norris. Montreal: Véhicule, 1980.

———. "'Time Present and Time Past': *Life Before Man.*" *Essays on Canadian Writing* 20:165–170 (winter 1980–1981).

Greene, Gayle. *Changing the Story: Feminist Fiction and the Tradition.* Bloomington: Indiana University Press, 1991.

Hammer, Stephanie Barbé. "The World as It Will Be? Female Satire and the Technology of Power in *The Handmaid's Tale.*" *Modern Language Studies* 2, no. 2:39–49 (spring 1990).

Howells, Coral Ann. *Margaret Atwood.* Houndsmills, Eng.: Macmillan, 1996.

Irvine, Lorna. *Collecting Clues: Margaret Atwood's "Bodily Harm."* Toronto: ECW Press, 1993. (Introduction to the novel with an annotated bibliography.)

Keith, W. J. *Introducing Margaret Atwood's "The Edible Woman": A Reader's Guide.* Toronto: ECW Press, 1989. (Introduction to the novel with an annotated bibliography.)

Larkin, Joan. "Soul Survivor [*Surfacing* and *Power Politics*]." In *Critical Essays on Margaret Atwood.* Edited by Judith McCombs. Boston: G. K. Hall, 1988. Pp. 48–52.

Lauber, John. "Alice in Consumer-Land: The Self-Discovery of Marian MacAlpine [*sic*]." In *The Canadian Novel: Here and Now.* Edited by John Moss. Toronto: NC Press, 1978. Pp.19–31.

Lecker, Robert. "Janus through the Looking Glass: Atwood's First Three Novels." In *The Art of Margaret Atwood: Essays in Criticism.* Edited by Arnold E. Davidson and Cathy N. Davidson. Toronto: Anansi, 1981. Pp. 177–203.

Lovelady, Stephanie. "I Am Telling This to No One But You: Private Voice, Passing, and the Private Sphere in Margaret Atwood's *Alias Grace.*" *Studies in Canadian Literature* 24, no. 2:35–63 (1999).

Mandel, Eli. "Atwood's *Poetic Politics.*" In *Margaret Atwood: Language, Text, and System.* Edited by Sherrill E. Grace and Lorraine Weir. Vancouver: University of British Columbia Press, 1983. Pp. 53–66.

McCombs, Judith. "Politics, Structure, and Poetic Development in Atwood's Canadian-American Sequences: From an Apprentice Pair to *The Circle Game* to *Two-Headed Poems.*" In *Margaret Atwood: Visions and Forms.* Edited by Kathryn VanSpanckeren and Jan Garden Castro. Carbondale: Southern Illinois University Press, 1988. Pp. 142–162.

McLay, Catherine. "The Dark Voyage: *The Edible Woman* as Romance." In *The Art of Margaret Atwood: Essays in Criticism.* Edited by Arnold E. Davidson and Cathy N. Davidson. Toronto: Anansi, 1981. Pp. 123–138.

Michael, Magali Cornier. "Rethinking History as Patchwork: The Case of Atwood's *Alias Grace.*" *Modern Fiction Studies* 47, no. 2:421–447 (summer 2001).

Miner, Madonne. "'Trust Me': Reading the Romance Plot in Margaret Atwood's *The Handmaid's Tale.*"

Twentieth Century Literature 37, no. 2:148–168 (summer 1991).

Orbach, Susie. *Fat Is a Feminist Issue: The Anti-Diet Guide to Permanent Weight Loss.* New York: Berkley, 1978, 1994. (The exploration about what food means on pages 14–20 uses *Lady Oracle* to explore mother-daughter relationships and being fat.)

Piercy, Marge. "Margaret Atwood: Beyond Victimhood [*Survival, The Edible Woman, Surfacing,* and Five Books of Poetry]." In *Critical Essays on Margaret Atwood.* Edited by Judith McCombs. Boston: G. K. Hall, 1988. Pp. 53–66.

Rao, Eleonora. *Strategies for Identity: The Fiction of Margaret Atwood.* New York: Peter Lang, 1993.

Rigney, Barbara Hill. *Margaret Atwood.* London: Macmillan Education, 1987.

Rosowski, Susan J. "Margaret Atwood's *Lady Oracle:* Fantasy and the Modern Gothic Novel." In *Critical Essays on Margaret Atwood.* Edited by Judith McCombs. Boston: G. K. Hall, 1988. Pp. 197–208.

Solecki, Sam. "Circles of Despair." *Canadian Forum,* November 1979, pp. 28–29. (Early review finding *Life Before Man* bleak.)

Staels, Hilde. "Intertexts of Margaret Atwood's *Alias Grace.*" *Modern Fiction Studies* 46, no. 2:427–450 (summer 2000). (This analysis focuses on the psychoanalyst as detective.)

Stein, Karen F. *Margaret Atwood Revisited.* New York: Twayne Publishers, 1999. (Excellent synthesis of criticism on Atwood's oeuvre.)

Sullivan, Rosemary. *The Red Shoes: Margaret Atwood Starting Out.* Toronto: HarperFlamingo Canada, 1998.

Thompson, Lee Briscoe. *Scarlet Letters: Margaret Atwood's "The Handmaid's Tale."* Toronto: ECW Press, 1997. (Introduction to the novel with an annotated bibliography.)

VanSpanckeren, Kathryn. "Shamanism in the Works of Margaret Atwood." In *Margaret Atwood: Visions and Forms.* Edited by Kathryn VanSpanckeren and Jan Garden Castro. Carbondale: Southern Illinois University Press, 1988. Pp. 183–204.

Vogt, Kathleen. "Real and Imaginary Animals in the Poetry of Margaret Atwood." In *Margaret Atwood: Visions and Forms.* Edited by Kathryn VanSpanckeren and Jan Garden Castro. Carbondale: Southern Illinois University Press, 1988. Pp. 163–182.

Waugh, Patricia. *Feminine Fictions: Revisiting the Postmodern.* London: Routledge, 1989. Pp. 179–189.

Wilson, Sharon Rose. *Margaret Atwood's Fairy-Tale Sexual Politics.* Toronto: ECW Press, 1990.

Wilson, Sharon Rose, Thomas B. Friedman, and Shannon Hengen, eds. *Approaches to Teaching Atwood's "The Handmaid's Tale" and Other Works.* New York: Modern Language Association, 1996.

Woodcock, George. "Metamorphosis and Survival: Notes on the Recent Poetry of Margaret Atwood." In *Margaret Atwood: Language, Text, and System.* Edited by Sherrill E. Grace and Lorraine Weir. Vancouver: University of British Columbia Press, 1983. Pp. 125–142.

———. *Introducing Margaret Atwood's "Surfacing": A Reader's Guide.* Toronto: ECW Press, 1990.

York, Lorraine M., ed. *Various Atwoods: Essays on the Later Poems, Short Fiction, and Novels.* Concord, Ontario: Anansi, 1995.

INTERVIEWS

Ingersoll, Earl G., ed. *Margaret Atwood: Conversations.* Princeton, N.J.: Ontario Review Press, 1990.

Phyllis Aronoff and Howard Scott, trans. *Two Solicitudes: Conversations.* Toronto: McClelland and Stewart, 1998.

FILM AND PLAY BASED ON THE WORKS OF MARGARET ATWOOD

The Handmaid's Tale. Screenplay by Harold Pinter. Directed by Volker Schlöndorff. Cinecom, 1990.

The Edible Woman. Play by Dave Carley. First production: Ann Arbor, Michigan, 2000.

—*JOY ARBOR*

Nicholson Baker

1957–

*I*N HIS FIRST novel, *The Mezzanine* (1988), Nicholson Baker critiques the state of contemporary fiction as focusing too much on "self-love, which has been mistakenly exalted by some writers as something realer and purer and more sacredly significant than intellective memory." *The Mezzanine* illustrates this critique by trying to restore "intellective memory" to its proper sacred state. For Baker, intellective memory is the very stuff of fiction rather than a distraction. Baker's career is a consistent attempt to question what is valued, both in literature and in life. Nostalgia, acute attention to detail, formal experimentation, and wordplay are the hallmarks of his fiction and nonfiction. In his world everything matters: the minutest details of contemporary life become the point of writing rather than mere decoration. His career proves that nothing matters more than the attempt to "replenish" the "exhausted" literature of our postmodern world, to use John Barth's terms, and Baker has taken up this quest with the ardor of the romantic knight at the wellspring of fiction, Don Quixote.

Nicholson Baker was born on January 7, 1957, in New York, the son of Douglas and Ann Nicholson Baker. His love of the arts and music, evident in his fiction, began early in life and was fostered by his parents, who met when they were art students. Baker played bassoon well enough to attend the Eastman School of Music in 1974–1975. He enrolled at Haverford College, where he graduated with a degree in English in 1980. He then entered the corporate world but soon decided to commit to a writing career. After participating in a two-week writing workshop led by the experimental postmodern writer Donald Barthelme at Berkeley in 1985, Baker worked as a technical writer but moved quickly into the field of creative writing. He married Margaret Brentano in 1985, and they have two children, Alice and Elias. The daily experiences of middle-class American life yielded the raw material for Baker's early fiction: the corporate world provides the setting for his first novel, and fatherhood provides the setting for his second, *Room Temperature* (1990). Since committing himself to a career in writing he has published five novels and three books of nonfiction, and he is currently a contributing editor for *The American Scholar*.

EARLY NOVELS: UP TO THE MINUTIAE

To call Baker's first novel, *The Mezzanine*, "unconventional" is at once an understatement and a misstatement, for the novel is built upon a convention familiar to all readers: footnotes. Moreover the protagonist of the story is on a journey, one of the most conventional of all novel plots. Yet it is an unlikely and mundane journey from the ground floor of his office building to the mezzanine where he works. In the tradition of the picaresque novel, the destination of the journey is not nearly as important as the details along the way (he calls the journey "the escalator ride that is the vehicle of this memoir"). The fact that the details are composed of the narrator's observations and memories is testimony to the tedium of contemporary corporate life and evidence of the sharpness of the contemporary mind, saturated as it is with information and stimulation. The novel resists metaphor and the familiar conventions of plot in favor of a different reality, one in which the intellectual observations of the protagonist, Howie, supersede his psychological inner life. He gives us a few glimpses of his inner life, but they are overwhelmed by the details of his outer life, such as plastic drinking straws, broken shoelaces, and the design of CVS stores.

Even though his inner life is obscured, it matters to Howie, and there is a kind of cheery evasion built into the way he embraces, even loves, contemporary corporate culture. He reveals subtly that he is lonely and that he has lost L., his soul mate, without telling us what went wrong in their relationship. His uncanny observations of the world around him can nourish only the mind, not the soul. There is something almost desperate in the way he wants to "fix" the world by describing it so accurately; his life is otherwise impoverished. His final gesture in the novel is to wave to the maintenance man who is polishing the escalator's handrail one floor below him. The worker "held up his white rag for a second, then put it back down on the rubber handrail." It is a slight human connection, no different from the encounter that begins the book: Donna, a cashier at Papa Gino's, asks him if he wants a straw to go with his milk; he refuses and asks for a bag instead. These pathetic substitutions for genuine conversation are his only human contacts in a world set up to make his life as convenient as possible. The shadowy absence of L.—the woman he has loved and lost—and his desperate attempts to connect with the janitor and the cashier, lead readers to wonder about the emptiness of the life that frames this overstuffed novel, an odyssey that is a fifteen-second escalator ride during an ordinary lunch hour.

Yet the details consume and amuse the reader whose attempts to discover some revealing insight into Howie are invariably frustrated. Baker achieves this effect through his use of footnotes, which run for pages and nearly outweigh the main text. The reader of fiction is likely to lose patience with the footnotes, considered extraneous information or digressions. But Howie has a theory about them, as he does for most things, and this theory is also Baker's statement of his aesthetic. Howie admires the eighteenth-century writers James Boswell and Edward Gibbon and the nineteenth-century historian William Edward Hartpole Lecky because they "loved footnotes. They knew that the outer surface of truth is not smooth, welling and gathering from paragraph to shapely paragraph, but is encrusted with a rough protective bark of citations, quotation marks, italics, and foreign languages." He goes on to explain the digressive nature of footnotes in a way that also makes sense of the escalator-ride "plot" of the book: "Digression—a movement away from the *gradus,* or upward escalation, or the argument—is sometimes the only way to be thorough, and footnotes are the only form of graphic digression sanctioned by centuries of typesetters. And yet the MLA Style Sheet I owned in college warned against lengthy, 'essay-like' footnotes. Were they *nuts?*" As this discussion applies to the whole book, Howie's objective is to record "the outer surface of truth" and "to be thorough." He pulls our eyes away from himself to show us the hyperreality of the world around him, the world that has created him and his acute perception of it. Howie is made up of the minute details of his world, and it is clear who he is through the way he absorbs and describes those details.

Footnotes, then, are the surprising carriers of truth in the novel, a genre that for too long has been concerned with the smooth surface of reality and not concerned enough with its rough details. CVS, the homely drugstore where Howie purchases a pair of shoelaces during his lunch hour, is similarly exalted: "For now, though, the CVS pharmacy is closer to the center of life than, say, Crate & Barrel or Pier 1, or restaurants, national parks, airports, research triangles, the lobbies of office buildings, or banks. Those places are the novels of the period, while CVS is its diary." By giving this pharmacy such a prominent place in his novel, Baker is trying to restore to the novel the diary aspect that, though it has since vanished, was evident in the earliest English novels, like Daniel Defoe's *Moll Flanders* (1722). Novels have traditionally held a mirror up to the lives of common people, and Howie is extremely aware of his commonness. He remembers the exact moment when he realized this fact, regarding a man who was carefully shaven and whose shirt cuffs were expertly starched:

> I was the sort of person who said "actually" too much. I was the sort of person who stood in a subway car and thought about buttering toast—buttering raisin toast, even: when the high, crisp scrape of the butter knife is muted by occasional contact with the soft, heat-blimped forms of the raisins, and when if you cut across a raisin, it will sometimes fall right out, still intact though dented, as you lift the slice. I was the sort of person whose biggest discoveries were likely to be tricks to applying toiletries while fully dressed. I was a man, but I was not nearly the magnitude of man I had hoped I might be.

If the novel's subject is ordinary life, as James Joyce stated in his modern masterpiece *Ulysses* (1922), the narration must be extraordinary. Joyce employs a mythical scaffold; Baker employs footnotes.

These footnotes are akin to childhood memories or, as Howie calls them, the "nostalgia-driven memories . . . pulling me off course." He wonders, "Will I reach a point where there will be a good chance, I mean a more than fifty-fifty chance, that any random idea popping back into the foreground of my consciousness will be an idea that first came to me when I was an adult, rather than one I had repeatedly as a child?" One such memory of his early education partially explains his footnote fetish:

> The page I remember from first grade was a picture of Jack standing with a red wagon at the top left, and Spot waiting for him on the lower right, with a dotted line in a large Z shape connecting the two. The instructions were "Make Jack take the wagon to Spot," or something like that—and you clearly were not supposed to take the direct diagonal route, but rather were meant to travel this pointless Z with your crayon. The sideways explanation on the grown-up side of the perforation claimed that the Z path taught the child the ideal motion of the reading eyeballs—one line of type, a zag of a carriage return, another line of type.

This narrator, who has accepted his mediocrity, is dissatisfied with such conventions, and he has rebelled against them. Concerning the importance of footnotes he writes,

> The muscles of the eye . . . want vertical itineraries; the rectus externus and internus grow dazed waggling back and forth in the Zs taught in grade school: the footnote functions as a switch, offering the model-railroader's satisfaction of catching the march of thought with a superscripted "1" and routing it, sometimes at length, through abandoned stations and submerged, leaching tunnels.

The ordinary man Howie—who does not tell us his last name or his actual job or his soul mate's full name—is nearly anonymous. Upon considering popcorn he draws an analogy to the alienating reality of corporate America: "I felt somewhat like an exploding popcorn myself: a dried bicuspid of American grain dropped into a lucid gold liquid pressed from less fortunate brother kernels, subjected to heat, and suddenly allowed to flourish outward in an instantaneous detonation of weightless reversal." Yet his observations, made evident by his rebellious insistence on footnotes, make him unique and provide a thick context for his story.

Although Baker's second novel, *Room Temperature,* does not rely on the convention of footnotes, it shares some characteristics with the first. The narrator, Mike, observes life with the same acute attention to detail displayed by *The Mezzanine*'s Howie. Both characters delight in the shared minutiae of contemporary life, both are grammarians at heart, and both are obsessed with their personal pasts. Yet Mike delves into his domestic life and his private moments with little regard to his career, which he mentions only in passing. Taken together, Baker's first two novels originate from the same vantage point but look in two different directions. *Room Temperature*, as the title implies, is a more comfortable novel, free from the chilling anxiety of the corporate world.

The plots of the two novels, such as they are, can be seen as contrasts too: *The Mezzanine* is a fifteen-second journey upward, whereas *Room Temperature* is a fifteen-minute journey downward. Mike is trying to get his daughter (referred to as "the Bug") to sleep, and that mundane process provides him with an opportunity to ruminate on his life and to make connections within it. His story is as full of oddities as everyone's would be if they took the time to examine the darkest corners of them. The bulk of the narrative is composed of long treatises on the sound of a lid being twisted off a peanut butter jar or the necessity of picking one's nose or the history of the comma. What is astounding about Baker's second novel is how these disparate, incongruous elements combine and reconnect. The end result is not unlike Claude Debussy's *La Mer* (1905), the symphonic piece that Mike analyzes and returns to repeatedly. The wavelike cadence of *La Mer* as well as its mysterious resolution can be seen as a model that Baker is trying to imitate in this novel, and it is probably no coincidence that *La Mer*, like the Bug's descent into sleep, lasts about twenty minutes.

Mike quotes a line by Debussy from the composer's biography: "Listen to no one unless to the passing wind which tells us the history of the world." His attention to both *La Mer* and to this line alerts the reader not only to the structural parallels of the pieces but also to the leitmotif of the book: sound created by wind. If Marcel Proust's *Remembrance of Things Past* (1922) is a memory brought about by the taste of a madeleine cookie, *Room Temperature* is a memory brought about by the sound of a peanut butter jar opening. Baker initiates this idea in the novel's epigraph from Wallace Stevens: "I placed a jar in Tennessee." This poem, about the creation of something vast around something humble, is another model for the novel. One of Mike's projects that he never completes is to compose a symphony that begins with the conductor opening a peanut butter jar. In a hilarious sequence he imagines the effects of beginning the symphony this way, anticipating the occasional failure one encounters opening these jars.

Although humor is *Room Temperature*'s dominant note, and although the peanut butter symphony idea is ludicrous, there is a trace of seriousness attached to the way Mike sees the world. Following Debussy's advice, he is constructing a history of the world, albeit a minuscule one. Wind and sound pervade the novel; nearly all of Mike's memories have to do with one or the other or both. In the novel's opening paragraph, Mike observes "some dark birds . . . negotiating big chunks of wind," and he cannot hear them because he has removed the screens from the windows for the oncoming winter season. He is forced to sit still in his armchair in order to get his newborn daughter to sleep, and in this space he continues to observe the effects of the wind. There is nothing to listen to except the sounds his daughter makes as she breathes and sucks from a bottle. This most fundamental essence of human life—the sound of inhaling and exhaling—is nothing less than the history of the world on a tiny scale.

His daughter's suckling and breathing noises cause Mike to think about all the quirks that make him unique. The way he understands the world is linked to the way he listens to it. He pays particular attention to the spaces between sounds, which he describes as "negative spaces," a term his mother introduced to him as an art lesson in the form of an exercise to "draw the inside of a pillow." He responds to the exercise by drawing a pair of lungs "and an arrow pointing to them that said 'From a pillow'; for, as I explained to my mother, the only way to know the real nature of the inside of a pillow was to breathe in its air." He renews his appreciation for these spaces by listening to his wife, Patty, writing in a journal about their daughter's first days:

> I would find that the information-rich scribbling produced by word formation was insignificant in comparison to the very high short lisps that took place *between* words and groups of words, as Patty moved the side of her hand a short distance to the right in order to establish a new temporary base for her handwriting.

One of Mike's pet projects that he never begins is to write a short history of the comma; he argues that such a history

> would attempt to hold the library of written prose superimposedly up to a light bulb, so that one or more tiny routes would reveal themselves, as in a stack of punch cards, passing through all the stomata of individual commas directly back to the original point of momentary breath-held stillness between two phrases.

He feels as passionately about the comma as *The Mezzanine*'s Howie feels about footnotes, and he similarly criticizes critics who fail to understand its importance.

As he ruminates upon commas and music, Mike reveals a level of erudition that is stunning. His knowledge of the world and command of language are impressive. Yet they are offset by his revelation of what would almost universally be considered as disgusting habits: nose picking (as an adult) and defecating on a floor (as a young teen, in simulation of childbirth). The juxtaposition of the soaring heights of the intellect and the base depths of the body is jarring, yet it makes sense of the novel's context, for here is a startlingly intellectual man involved in the care of an infant, which always calls to mind the processes of the body. When he explains his "theory of knowledge" he comments indirectly on this particular effect and further makes sense of the epigraph from Stevens:

> I certainly believed, rocking my daughter on this Wednesday afternoon, that with a little concentration one's whole life could be reconstructed from any single twenty-minute period randomly or almost randomly selected . . . ; but you had to expect that a version of your past arrived at this way would exhibit . . . certain telltale differences of emphasis from the past you would recount if you proceeded serially, beginning with "I was born on January 5, 1957," and letting each moment give birth naturally to the next. The particular cell you started from colored your entire re-creation.

As he concludes this particular history of his life, he moves gently from recalling the past to imagining the future, his daughter's future, which will be connected to this twenty-minute space in subtle and unconscious ways.

MEMORY CRITICISM: A NEW GENRE

Baker's first two novels and a handful of uncollected short stories mark the beginning of his prolific career, and although they have strong autobiographical overtones, they are fiction. (Baker's birthday is January 7, 1957, just two days later than Mike's, and this ever-so-slight lie insists on the fictional context.) Yet Baker's nonfiction is nearly equivalent in volume to his fiction. His third book, *U and I* (1991), is nonfiction; yet to classify it more precisely is impossible. It is ostensibly an account of the author's obsession with John Updike, one of the most highly regarded, prolific American prose stylists alive. It is not a biography, an autobiography, or a work of criticism, though it has elements of all of these. It is about literary influence, literary anxiety, and literary admiration. Above all else it is a quirky look into the mind of a serious young writer.

Baker loves Updike, and most of the book serves to praise the elder writer. Baker optimistically describes his relationship with Updike as "literary friendship" even though he has met Updike only on two embarrassing occasions, both of which involve him gushing and one of which has him lying about attending Harvard. This friendship is built on professional rivalry; Baker realizes that "literary friendship is impossible . . . ; at least, it is impossible for me." It is impossible because of a kind of professional jealousy mixed with awe and respect, not unlike the feeling James Baldwin expresses in his early essays on Richard Wright. Baker admits of Updike that *"he writes better than I do and he is smarter than I am* and that's what counts. This observation will surprise no one; it came, however, as quite a shock to me." This attempt at self-deprecation surfaces repeatedly in *U and I,* but it is tempered slightly by the fact that the book is more about Baker than about Updike. Also, Baker spends a long chapter criticizing Updike, and his final gesture is to demonstrate (somewhat facetiously) that in fact he influenced Updike on one occasion, rather than the other way around. Some friendship. But part of the point of the book is to examine friendship in a literary context. The relationship between the general writer and the general reader is not exactly a friendship either. Baker begins *U and I* with an observation that demonstrates the difference between writers and readers:

> I had finished and sent off a novel, my second, and I was still full of the misleading momentum that, while it makes the completion of novels possible, also generally imparts a disappointingly thin and rushed feeling to their second halves or final thirds, as the writer's growing certainty that he is finally a pro, finally getting the hang of it, coincides exactly with that unpleasant fidgety sensation on the reader's part that he is locked into a set of characters and surroundings he knows a bit too well by now to enjoy.

Perhaps *U and I* is an attempt to understand this divide more completely as Baker scrutinizes himself as a reader as well as a writer. The pun of the title underscores the reader/writer relationship.

U and I hints that there is something wrong with both readers and writers in the contemporary literary world. Distracted by their professional jealousy of luminaries like Updike, young writers are in Baker's view like tiny insects engaged in a "dishonorable little battle up the grassblade toward some sort of eminence." He shows tremendous distaste at his own tendency to inflate his sense of his own importance; following the death of his mentor Donald Barthelme, Baker sent a brief tribute to *The New Yorker,* but he admits that he was motivated by the possibility of fame rather than by genuine grief. He then criticizes his own "self-centered, ungrieving ambition to come up with at least one sentence in it that would be in the same league as many in Updike's obituary for Nabokov, and which would as a result have the sad but not-choked-up quotability that would allow me anonymously to 'make' the Barthelme obituary, as if I were making some team." A kind of purity is lost when writers succumb to their desire for fame.

Yet readers suffer from their own maladies that contribute to the larger disease of contemporary literature. In his role as reader Baker admits *"to having read less than half the words Updike has written"* and assumes that the reader will object to this *"enraging admission."* Part of the contemporary literary crisis is the writer's awareness of the difficulty of writing when so much good literature has already been written. This is a theory that prominent critic Harold Bloom advances in *The Anxiety of Influence* (1973), and Baker jokes about his anxiety over not having read Bloom's book. Yet he claims that he understands Bloom through book reviews—book reviews, not books, being the principal engines of change in the history of thought, and contributing in that necessary role a certain class of distortions to the forward flow by allowing those works which contain plots and arguments that are easily summarized in their reviews to assume a level of cultural bulk and threat that the books themselves may or may not deserve.

Coming from a writer whose plots and arguments cannot be "easily summarized," this assessment is obviously facetious. The problem with readers is that they rely too much on such reviews, which too often substitute for the reading of longer complex works, especially novels, for "the novel is the greatest of all literary forms—the most adaptable and subspecialty-spanning and roomiest and most selfless, in the sense of not imposing artificialities on its practitioners and letting the pursuit of truth pull it forward." He gets in another jab at Bloom by admitting his "impatience with criticism as a literary form." Yet he is also swinging at Updike who has published hundreds of reviews, in contrast to Baker who has not "gotten sucked in to book reviewing." Baker implies that if literature is to regain its position of prominence in the history of thought, writers and readers should concentrate on revitalizing the forms that matter, especially the novel, by paying attention to the way language can capture experience while steering clear of the limiting tendencies of reviews and criticism.

Baker seeks to invigorate literary criticism by writing *U and I* in an unconventional way. Rather than rereading Updike's works, Baker vows to avoid opening them until he is finished composing his book-length essay. After he is done writing he checks his memory against Updike's actual words and corrects himself in brackets, usually scorning his faulty memory and praising Updike's command of language. He begins by writing down a list of phrases or scenes that he remembers from Updike and proceeds to construct an essay around this list, ranging from the depths of his personal obsession with Updike (even in dreams) to more objective assessments of him. The result is "a style of book chat that, in the unlikely event that it has not already been recognized and does not already have a name, might be called something sexy like *memory criticism,* or *phrase filtration,* or *closed book examination.*" He settles on the last of these descriptions, which is most apt because of everything he is examining, including Updike's work as well as Baker's own literary life, work, and memory, the last of which seems to deteriorate as the book progresses until he cries out, "What is wrong with me?" It may be that what is wrong with him is precisely what is right with him: he loves literature, and lovers have their shortcomings. Literature is not always as he remembers it to be, and his memory is far from perfect. As a perfectionist this fact may be tough to accept, especially as he realizes that the intelligence that produces a novel must be "more adaptable, more multiplanar, sloppier, more impatient of formal designs, roomier, and more truth-drawn than other kinds."

MIXING LITERATURE WITH DESIRE

Updike is perhaps most famous for the descriptions of sex he incorporates into his high literary style. Baker marvels at this fact and tries to remember whether he ever successfully masturbated while reading Updike. Baker's third novel, *Vox* (1992), exemplifies how desperately he wants to outdo his literary mentor. Bordering on pornography, *Vox* is sexier than virtually anything Updike has written, or, at least, Baker sustains sexual description longer than Updike ever has. *Vox* is an hours-long phone sex conversation between Jim and Abby, two lonely and unusually compatible masturbation aficionados. The novel became infamous during the exposure of the Clinton–Lewinsky affair; on March 25, 1998, independent counsel Kenneth

Starr subpoenaed a Washington bookstore for records of Lewinsky's purchases, which reportedly included *Vox* as a gift from the intern to the president. The sensational quality of this novel and its public association with the Clinton scandal indicate a new direction and focus for Baker: his name would hereafter be associated with explicitly sexual description.

Yet once one has come to terms with the almost shocking amount of graphic sexual description in the novel, it becomes easier to see it as continuous with as well as a clear departure from his earlier works. As Arthur Saltzman puts it in *Understanding Nicholson Baker* (1999), the difference between Baker's first two novels and his next two is "more or less a matter of where one trains his zoom lens." Responding to the flap over *Vox*'s involvement in the Clinton–Lewinsky affair, Baker told Laura Miller for *Salon,* "I wanted that book to be an exercise in privacy, asking what people would be willing to say given an anonymous, receptive listener and no one overhearing, except of course the reader. It's meant to be read in private. . . . That's the nice thing about books, their privacy." Regarded in this light, *Vox* has less to do with sex than it has to do with privacy, and the writer-reader relationship in *U and I* has its parallel in the speaker-listener relationship in *Vox.*

This is not to say that the sexual content of *Vox* is incidental or unimportant. The reader of hard-core pornography would not be disappointed with parts of *Vox*. It begins with the original phone sex cliché: "'What are you wearing?' he asked." Yet before long both Jim and Abby have revealed themselves as quintessential Baker narrators through their attention to detail, erudite vocabulary, and delight in digression. At the end of the novel Abby questions this final shared characteristic. She asks Jim, "Do you think we talked enough about sex?" Although it may seem like they have talked of nothing else, the reader realizes in retrospect that they have revealed a good deal of their personalities through their descriptions of their fetishes and erotic experiences.

Vox actually departs from *The Mezzanine* and *Room Temperature* not through its explicit sexual content but through Baker's creation of dual protagonists. *Vox* is based on intellective memory, just like Baker's previous three books are, but with a narrower frame. Unlike the other books, the narrator of *Vox* barely exists and utters only a handful of lines: "There was another sound of ice cubes," "There was a pause" (three times), and at the novel's conclusion, "He told her [his phone number]. She read it back to him," and "They hung up." The nearly exclusive dialogue format illustrates how Baker is yet again testing the adaptability of the novel he describes in *U and I. Vox* allows the voices of two characters to create a narrative virtually uninterrupted, and they respond to each other until they can successfully masturbate, concluding at the same time, thousands of miles apart. Not unlike a writer and reader, they must please one another without meeting. Also, the speaker must be attuned to the effects of suspense and anticipation as he or she tries to keep the other person engaged. Most importantly the two must trust one another, which means they must make themselves vulnerable and gild the truth with entertainment.

Because these would-be lovers are on an unconventional first date that allows them to hang up at any time, they can exercise certain liberties and dispense with conventions such as shyness and small talk. They are patient, cooperative, and excessively polite with one another, sensitive to each other's needs and willing to play by each other's rules. They even invent figurative language together; for instance, they decide to think of a new word for "masturbate" and work their way to the more poetic "strum." Their willingness to work together—to encourage each other's storytelling, to remember each other's desires—indicates that they are not merely using each other. When Abby admits that her own private word for a penis is "Delgado," Jim responds, "You told me the secret word you have for the adult male cock, anyway. Not for my cock, leave me out of it. For the one you think about *on your own*. See, see, this is what I need. I need to know secrets and have secrets and keep secrets. I need to be confided in." This desire, far more than Jim's sexual desire, validates Abby's teariness as she recalls a former lover. This need for secrets also establishes the trust between them: they exchange real and imagined stories—experiences and fantasies—with the knowledge that their secrets are at once safe and important to the listener. Once their inhibitions are removed they become at once more aroused and more human.

Baker's next novel, *The Fermata* (1994), is also about sexual secrets and fantasies, and it considers more intently the subject of writing and the crucial role of the reader. The narrator, Arno Strine, is able to stop time and to wander freely through the frozen world he has created through various mechanical manipulations or simply by snapping his fingers. He most frequently uses these moments (which he calls the Fermata or the Fold) to undress women, to fantasize about them, and to masturbate (a premise that earned *The Fermata* many negative reviews, one cleverly titled "Stop the World, I Want to Get Off"). Arno's imagination is overactive and perverse, and the paired, related outlets for this imagination are masturbation and writing pornography. The more Arno indulges in these activities, the more he risks offending his audience. The line between pornography and literature is deliberately fuzzy and frequently crossed in *The Fermata* as Baker further explores the life of the writer's mind and the oddities, delights, and disturbing twists of the private imagination made public.

Like Baker's other narrators, Arno is an ordinary man aware of his ordinariness; he describes himself this way: "I'm not by any means a crazy person. I don't have a flat affect. I'm friendly and likable. I go out on the occasional date. I have several male friends, even. I have had long-term relationships with three women." He announces his humble career, such as it is, parenthetically: "(I'm a temp, by the way)." Of course, his supernatural ability to manipulate time makes him extraordinary, and he sees it not only as a unique gift but as "the one thing that makes my life worth living." When he first discovers his powers in the fourth grade he is mystified by them and uncertain how he can use them to good effect. He realizes the implications of his power, what he might do with it: "Others might put it to fuller avaricious or intellectual use: government secrets, technological espionage, etc. . . . In my place, some would toggle time and cheat on their Ph.D. orals or simply take money from open cash registers. Cheating and stealing don't tempt me, though." What does tempt him from the first incident in fourth grade through his adult life is the female body. He admits, "I doubt that I would have wormed my way into the Fermata even once if I had not been motivated primarily by the desire to take women's clothes off." In this sense, and since the onset of Arno's powers coincide with puberty, the Fermata can be seen as a metaphor for deep or unconscious male sexual desire instead of just an aid for Arno's sexual fantasies. The very act of writing this book, which he calls his autobiography or "the memory thing that I've been working on," is a way of exposing this unconscious self despite the risk that his readers will judge him unfavorably.

As the book progresses and Arno takes us deeper into his fantasies, the general reader is likely to pass just such an unfavorable judgment despite the narrator's claims to normality, for Arno's erotica violates all rules of taste and decorum. Arno has readers within the book too, all of whom are women. Some of them read his erotic writings, some hear his fantasies, and some participate in his fantasies; together they represent the range of possible responses to his life and work. Toward the end of the novel one of these women, a coworker named Joyce, tells him, "You need help," which is the type of reaction he risks and does not desire; he responds, "I beg your pardon! I'm not a bad person. If you ask me to go away now, I'll go away. I'm harmless. I'm just a temp!" At another point he stops time in order to make a lengthy pornographic cassette for a woman driving next to him on the highway, and he is distraught when she tosses it out her car window. At yet another point he stops time in order to compose a pornographic story for a woman on the beach, and he is thrilled that she reads it and that it has excited her to the point that she returns home to masturbate.

Whether Arno receives a response of acceptance, tolerance, or rejection, his intent is always the same; he says, "What I want to do, and what I in fact end up doing, in the Fold is to live out my perennial wish to insert some novelty into the lives of women." His desire is not unlike that of Jim in *Vox*. Yet the fact that Arno can think of no novelty that is not graphically sexual in nature reveals a single-minded version of male desire that women can very easily dismiss; this is evident in the case of the anonymous woman who discards his cassette, or more poignantly in the case of his girlfriend Rhody, who leaves him when he hypothetically describes how he would behave if something like the Fold existed. He wants to be noticed by women, and because his Fold powers grew out of adolescent desire, his fantasies, written or acted upon, are the products of a one-track mind. (At one point he writes, "What else was there in the world beside masturbation? Nothing.") Realizing the connection between sexual desire and his writing, he describes how "the wish to create something true and valuable and even perhaps in a tiny way beautiful—combines with basic grunting cuntlapping lust, the two emotions reinforcing each other and making you, or rather me, feel almost insane with a soaringly doubled sense of mission." The Fold allows Arno to shake off as much inhibition as possible since he can remain anonymous, like someone who calls a phone sex service.

Although the Fold allows him to remain anonymous to the readers within the book as he prowls around their suspended bodies, he reveals himself fully to the reader of his autobiography. He develops over the course of the book from a mere temp, whose job is to type other people's bland data, into a writer, whose job is to delight and instruct. The writer's job is more of a strain on the soul, but it also carries greater rewards. Arno drops into the Fold not only to undress women but also to write about this experience. At one point he describes how he is developing good work habits: "I've gotten into a new and better work rhythm. I now spend every other twenty-four-hour period in Fold-furled isolation. I wake up at seven-thirty, and if it's going to be a Fold day I thick-fingeredly snap time off, shake my watch to unfreeze it, and spend the whole next twenty-four hours enclosed within the quiescent seven-thirtyness of my room, working on this book." On the one hand he is a writer of what he calls "rot" (short for erotica), and on the other he is a writer of autobiography. The Fermata allows him to develop both of these selves, one based on pure fantasy and the other on experience. The Fermata is itself a kind of writerly fantasy world where limitless time and quiet solitude are possible. It is a place where a writer can manipulate the world around him and describe it in Bakeresque detail.

The fact that this world is so filled with perverse male fantasy rather than some other content can be attributed partly to Arno's unique personality, but it can also be linked to Mike's private fantasies in *Room Temperature* when the narrator substitutes defecation for childbirth in what he feels is the male bodily equivalent for the female ability to bring life into the world. Arno's pornographic writing has an inordinate amount of anal intercourse and anal penetration. Arno notices this when he rereads what he has written: "It isn't clear to me now why Marian's adventures ended up being so unremittingly ane-oriented in content—I like to think it was just a matter of mood. After all, I had never typed the word *butthole* before in my life. It isn't a word that comes up much in business correspondence." Given the fact that nearly all of his writings and many of his Fold fantasies have the same obsession, it is clearly more than a matter of mood. The anus is not only the center of deep inhibitions, which Arno is trying to eradicate, but an erogenous zone for both men and women. At a crucial moment in his development as a writer he uses his Fold experience to drive to Cape Cod on a motorcycle and write his first piece of rot for a woman who becomes both his muse and his reader-to-be. In order to gain inspiration he undresses women as he usually does, but then he undresses himself and denies his typical desire to masturbate:

> Instead I took off my bathing suit and knelt, crouched over before the typewriter as if I were on a prayer rug, showing the ocean my open ass. . . . I didn't want anything to go *in* my asshole, no, no, I just wanted it out in the open, sunlit for once, flaunting wavewards its showered cleanness, exposed in a way that was both lewd and vulnerable. In this devotional position I worked for several intense hours, writing.

This description can be seen as a metaphor for Arno's imagination, for the writing of erotica is akin to his exposing his most private parts in a public forum. Because no one is aware of his actions in the Fold, he is able to make both his body and his imagination vulnerable without fear of judgment or ridicule. But the urge to create and to communicate more deeply with his female reader is intensified as he continues to describe the scene:

> Whenever I hesitated and needed inspiration, I simply rested my hand on the ass of the sunbathing woman beside me, sometimes sliding the fingers under her leg-hole, sometimes resting my hand on the fabric, sometimes squeezing, sometimes lightly slapping. I tried putting the typewriter on her ass but found it was too unsteady to proceed. Once, though, I pulled her bikini bottom off and sat right down on her softness, looking out past her brown legs at the tableau vivant of the waves, ass to ass with my reader-to-be. It was pleasant to wiggle and circle around, feeling our massed loose-muscled ass-flesh move as one over our deep bones: it was almost a form of communication.

Arno reveals what he claims not to understand about his own anal fixation. He regards the anus as the bodily equivalent of the unconscious, which, like masturbation, simulates and stimulates the creative imagination.

Despite his elaborate fetishes, his deepest desire is to be read. In the case of this woman on the beach he admits, "I wanted her to be holding and reading my home-grown smut so, so much! I so much wanted to have inspired a feeling of quickened curiosity in her." At another point he leaves a short, anonymous pornographic message in a book that a woman is reading and imagines her repeating the phrase to her friends at a dinner party, "and there would be whooplets of mock-shocked mirth. All because of me, all because of me." His final wish is to insert the entire autobiography into the hands of readers and to achieve the same effect: "They will read me. Word will spread. The Fermata, my Fermata, the keeper of all my secrets, will be a secret no longer." This optimistic prediction puts the final emphasis on the writer's desire for a readership rather than the desire for erotic stimulation.

Even if Arno's obsession is less about masturbation or anal penetration than it is about writing and being read, his sexual obsessions have affected his personal life: Rhody, the love of his life, leaves him because of his description of his fantasies, and especially of her fantasies. When he writes a story about her, she rejects it and regards him differently. She criticizes it as "a loveless fantasy" and dismisses Arno's description of the Fermata as "necrophilia." Arno suffers the consequences of rejection: "I felt as if my whole life were being called into question and I tried to defend myself: it's *just* an idea, *just* a fantasy, etc." Arno's feelings here are those of a writer who has received a bad review more than the feelings of a pervert who has been discovered. His desire to "insert something novel into the lives of women" is not without risks, especially when this something novel is such strong stuff. Arno is not unlike Nabokov's Humbert Humbert, another narrator who knows that his readers might consider him deviant but who attempts to insist that he is noble, worthy, and misunderstood.

NEW DIRECTIONS

If Baker's readers were surprised at the shocking sexual content of *Vox* and *The Fermata*, they were probably equally surprised by the complete absence of this content in his three most recent books, *The Size of Thoughts: Essays and Other Lumber* (1996), *The Everlasting Story of Nory* (1998), and *Double Fold: Libraries and the Assault on Paper* (2001). A gathering of writings on such subjects as fingernail clippers and model airplanes, a novel filtered through the perspective of a nine-year-old schoolgirl, and an extended work of investigative journalism about the systematic destruction of paper holdings in America's libraries, these works demonstrate Baker's versatility as well as his resistance to easy categorization. Critics who faulted *Vox* and *The Fermata* as crass (if successful) attempts to sell books were dumbstruck by these later works that are characterized by deep integrity, nostalgic tenderness, and very little best-seller potential. If the desire for fame he expresses in *U and I* was gained through *Vox* and *The Fermata,* then his next goal seems to be the establishment of critical respect, and indeed *Double Fold* won the National Book Critics Circle Award for nonfiction in 2001.

The Size of Thoughts is a miscellany of Baker's essays published from his early career in 1982 through his more ambitious recent work, including the 150-page meditation on lumber, first published in this collection. The collection demonstrates not only Baker's fiction-writing talents but also his research skills and varied interests. In *U and I* Baker criticizes Updike for wanting "to avoid clogging narratives with description" and states his preference for such Fold-like moments in fiction: "The only thing I *like* are the clogs—and when, late in most novels, there are no more in the pipeline to slow things down, I get that fidgety feeling." What many of the essays in *The Size of Thoughts* represent are the clogs that never found their way into his fiction. In his first essay, "Changes of Mind" (1982), he states a similar preference as a kind of manifesto: "I don't want the story of the feared-but-loved teacher, the book that hit like a thunderclap, the years of severe study followed by a visionary breakdown, the clench of repentance; I want each sequential change of mind in its true, knotted, clotted, viny multifariousness, with all of the colorful streamers of intelligence still taped on and flapping in the wind." Elsewhere in the collection he makes small pronouncements that might apply to his own fiction, as when he praises the novel *The Folding Star* (1994) by Alan Hollinghurst because it is "one of the few satisfying books around that treat the relationship between art and life and the secrets they keep from each other." (*The Fermata* is clearly meant to be another.)

Yet *The Size of Thoughts* is unusual and admirable as a novelist's first collection of nonfiction for its serious attention to nonliterary objects. In a section titled "Machinery" he takes us through what have to be some of the most careful considerations ever written on model airplanes, movie projectors, and (especially) fingernail clippers. (The last is supposedly a reaction to Stephen King's dismissal of *Vox* as a "meaningless little fingernail paring," but Baker does not dwell on literary criticism here: the subject is the history, manufacture, and innovation of the fingernail clipper.) In his essay "The Projector" (1994) he reveals his nostalgia for the inventions that are being obliterated in the contemporary world in the name of technological advancement. His purpose in this essay is partially to explain in meticulous detail the history and process of projecting film onto screens, but his agenda is clearly to reinforce what a curator of films tells him: "The platter is death to film." As opposed to the earlier reel projectors, platter projectors destroy the copies that they project, and in the absence of a careful program of maintenance and preservation, old films will be irreparably damaged, if not completely destroyed.

In an essay titled "Discards" (1994), Baker uses the same logic to attack the cost-driven impulse on the part of libraries to destroy card catalogs. He summarizes his complaint this way: "The unfortunate truth is that, in practice, existing frozen card catalogs, which just sit there, doing no harm to anyone, are typically being replaced by local databases that are full of new errors . . . , are much harder to browse efficiently, are less rich in cross-references and subject headings, lack local character, do not group related titles and authors together particularly well, and are in many cases stripped of whole classes of specific historical information." The crusade to save card catalogs (which have become virtually obsolete since Baker wrote the essay in 1994) may seem like a trivial pursuit, but Baker broadens the implications of his argument: if researchers are more likely to reach a "futility point" at which they abandon their online searches earlier than they would have if they had used a card catalog, "the life of the mind suffers as a result." It is clear that Baker stands for a few things at this point in his career: the reinvigoration of the novel through attention to the ordinary, the vital potential of sexual secrets to reinvigorate the novel, and the need to preserve the pursuit of intellectual perfection despite the culture's fervent acceptance of technological progress as the sine qua non of the contemporary world.

In short Baker continues to entreat his readers to slow down and pay attention to the minutiae of modern life. In his 1998 novel, *The Everlasting Story of Nory,* he accomplishes this by creating a nine-year-old protagonist whose narrative clogs are the entire point of her everlasting story. It is Baker's first novel without a first-person narrator (except *Vox,* which featured two first-person narrators and an almost nonexistent omniscient narrator). Yet the narrative is cleverly filtered through the protagonist's perspective and reproduces her language as well as her thoughts. Eleanor "Nory" Winslow is no less observant than the narrators of Baker's early novels, but because she is a child her observations are less developed than those of the adult narrators, and she does not feel the same pressure to connect that the others feel. Her everlasting story is really a series of much smaller stories, even anecdotes, and when she tires of retelling or making up a story, she writes or says "To Be Continued." She realizes how contrived this convention is: "Basically, when she wrote 'To Be Continued' at the end of a story it almost always meant 'To Never Be Continued,' that is, 'To Be Dropped Like a Hot Potato.'" At other points she abruptly writes "The End." Through telling Nory's ordinary story, which does not have the grand epiphany of a classic bildungsroman like Joyce's *A Portrait of the Artist as a Young Man* (1916), Baker is again revitalizing the very notion of storytelling.

Her story is not extraordinary, but Nory is certainly unique; in fact her oddities are what make her so appealing. She wants to be a dentist or an inventor of pop-up greeting cards and books when she grows up. She is obsessed with parasites, short people, and fans, among other things. She is an American girl living in England, and her consciousness of the cultural differences between these two countries, especially in terms of language and custom, heighten her self-consciousness. She is especially concerned with difference; reflecting on the way her younger brother learns language, she thinks, "you have to spend your whole life learning more and more about how to draw a difference between one idea and another idea and how to keep them separated out rather than totally dredged together in a sludgy mass."

The challenge to separate ideas is an internal struggle, but Nory also faces the constant heckling of her schoolmates, especially the boys. She has befriended one of the least popular girls in the class and must endure the taunts of the other children along with her. Yet her kindness is eventually rewarded: one of the teachers publicly recognizes her for her kindness to the unpopular girl. Nory has a highly advanced sense of what friendship should be at its center: "Nory believed that the core was not just to stick together and be friendly from time to time, as the case may be, and *definitely* not always to be in a competition every second, and not to just be tomboyishly friendly, but also to be able to empty your heart out to the person." In a more cynical narrative, Nory would learn that her philosophy would not work in the real world, but this novel is based upon fables as much as experience. Every story Nory enjoys has a moral. She entreats her parents to tell stories with morals, and when her little brother adds his stories without morals, "Nory added them on." The moral is the most important part of the story, even more important than a conclusion. But Nory believes that stories are meant to entertain and to reflect the world, even if they are fanciful. Hers is an almost pure Aristotelian conception of the meaning of stories, and she uses these principles to critique stories she does not like, such as *Rikki-Tikki-Tavi:* "a story should not have a small, tiny, curled-up barely alive animal be killed unless it has done a terrible thing, which it can't have done because it hasn't even uncurled itself from the egg. And the story isn't about what cobras do naturally, anyway, since it has the cobras speaking. In real life they don't speak, at least in English." Nory applies these analytical skills to life as well as to literature. Her quest for meaning is honest and forthright: she is troubled by death and cheered by small, beautiful things. The moral of her story is the cumulative moral that develops throughout the novel: nice, gentle, kind people make the world a better place. The end.

The purity of *The Everlasting Story of Nory* stands in contrast to the depraved, disturbing world of *The Fermata,* and one would be surprised to find that they were written by the same author. If one can set aside the stark differences in content, the connection between them becomes clear: they both have to do with the creation and value of stories. Nory is a budding storyteller like Arno in *The Fermata:* if his purpose is to excite female readers, Nory's purpose is to entertain and comfort the listener. She has a keen sense of how fiction works: "You really need something to fail in a story, because then when it fails it has to get better." She also realizes the potential of fiction to mediate the real and the imaginary worlds. Her fear of death prevents her from getting to sleep one night, and she calls upon her nascent powers of storytelling to remedy the situation:

Nory struggled, but finally she couldn't read for one more second—couldn't read, and couldn't go to sleep. So what she decided to herself was: "I won't read, and I won't go to sleep, I'll just think, because in reading you think and in dreaming you think, so that's exactly what I'll do—I'll think. And if the scary things come into my thoughts, fine, I'll change them."

Her imagination is a powerful thing and she feels lucky that her "thinking turned into good-dreaming." Just as Arno uses his Fold powers to write, Nory uses her storytelling imagination to comfort others. She begins by telling stories using cloth puppets in the bath and while brushing her teeth: "That was one way she would start telling stories: she would talk to the twin toothbrusher in the mirror, and then she would play a game that there were twins, asking each other questions, and then triplets." She is gradually building a sense of audience, and her games graduate to more public forums: she exchanges fables with her family and makes up storytelling games with her friends. When her unpopular friend, Pamela, tells Nory how much she has suffered because of the teasing of the other children, Nory is "suddenly reminded of something she had thought of in the mirror brushing her teeth." She proposes that the two of them write a book about their experiences of that year, and when Pamela shudders and says that she does not want to relive the experiences, Nory proposes that they write about themselves in the future, an idea that immediately comforts Pamela. This move from the past and present to the future is common to all of Baker's novels and it signals a triumph of the imagination over the constraints of the world. Nory's good-thinking mind will ultimately be stronger than any setbacks she might face.

It could be said that the climax of each of Baker's novels (pun intended, in the case of *Vox*) occurs when the protagonist's obsession with the past gives way to the future. The same is true of *U and I;* but Baker's most recent nonfiction is more of an attempt to warn about the future and to embrace the past, particularly the past as represented in our libraries. The long essay "Lumber" in *The Size of Thoughts* is born of his task to review the electronic *English Poetry Database*. He cheerfully sticks one of the CD-ROM disks on his finger and says, "I was thus able to flourish, to flaunt, around the first joint of a single finger, . . . 'all' of English poetry from 1660 to 1800." He uses the opportunity "to pick a word or a phrase, something short, and go after it, using the available equipment of intellectual retrieval, to see where we get." The word is "lumber," and Baker's etymology-based essay is even more thorough than we might expect. He exploits the many meanings of the humble word, especially one first uttered by Samuel Johnson, the phrase "lumber of the memory," which is perfect for Baker's career:

> The phrase "lumber of the memory" appealed to me because it brought to mind dim palletized piles of pressure-treated two-by-fours, their end-grain sprayed bright nonwooden colors to distinguish grades and brands, laid out in a huge, fragrant mind-hangar . . . lengths that when you bring them up to the register, intending to Make Something New with them, spring in sympathy with your steps.

Making something new out of old scraps is precisely what Baker is doing in this essay and what he has done since *The Mezzanine*. He grudgingly accepts at one point that the poetry database has helped him in this endeavor; yet he demonstrates that this database is no substitute for older-fashioned methods of library research: "While the *English Poetry Database* includes a truly astounding and thrilling number of minor poems by minor poets, it is unreliable in its coverage of minor poems, and in some cases major poems, by major prose writers." As in "The Projector" essay, Baker's argument here is that the new technology is responsible for the destruction of the old technology.

This argument informs the essay "Discards," in which Baker clearly states his objection to the space-saving practices of libraries: "Lest we become confused and forgetful, the function of a great library is to sort and store obscure books." In *Double Fold* Baker admits that the essays in *The Size of Thoughts* earned him a reputation: "I became known in the library world as a critic (and, to some, as a crank and a Luddite)." Through the publication of *Double Fold* he decides to earn this reputation and to intensify it. His cause is to encourage libraries to return to their original mission and to cease the process of destroying original documents, especially newspapers, in the misguided desire to save space, which he argues is not really the purpose or outcome of converting documents to microfilm or electronic databases.

Double Fold, like "Discards" and "Lumber," displays Baker's gifts as a researcher rather than primarily as a novelist. These works are not subtle, and Baker's message is clear: "The truth is that certain purificationally destructive transformations of old things into new things seem to excite people—otherwise polite, educated, law-abiding people—and it's up to other normally polite people to try to stop them." His research takes him well beyond the practices of libraries into the chemistry of microfilm, the composition of paper, and the economic pressures on the Library of Congress. Yet despite its thorough probing, *Double Fold* and the essays that lead into it mark the first real departure in Baker's career in terms of style. In prose that is atypically blunt, Baker concludes the book with four recommendations to cease the process of document destruction that read more like a manifesto than one of his trademark clogs.

It seems that Nicholson Baker has found a passionate cause. It is impossible to know whether it will be the lasting one in his career or just his latest fascination. Yet it is clear that Baker's intellect, his thorough love and understanding of literature, and his bold experimentation will make indelible marks on American literary history that cannot be destroyed as easily as an old newspaper.

Selected Bibliography

WORKS OF NICHOLSON BAKER

NOVELS
The Mezzanine. New York: Weidenfeld & Nicolson, 1988.
Room Temperature. New York: Grove Weidenfeld, 1990.
Vox. New York: Random House, 1992.
The Fermata. New York: Random House, 1994.
The Everlasting Story of Nory. New York: Random House, 1998.

NONFICTION
U and I: A True Story. New York: Random House, 1991.
The Size of Thoughts: Essays and Other Lumber. New York: Random House, 1996.
Double Fold: Libraries and the Assault on Paper. New York: Random House, 2001.

UNCOLLECTED WORKS
"Snorkeling." *The New Yorker,* December 7, 1981, pp. 50–55.
"K.590." In *The Best American Short Stories 1982.* Edited by John Gardner and Shannon Ravenal. Boston: Houghton Mifflin, 1982. Pp. 116–123.
"Playing Trombone." *Atlantic Monthly,* March 1982, pp. 39–58.
"Subsoil." *The New Yorker,* June 27–July 4, 1994, pp. 67–70, 72–74, 76–78.
"Infohighwaymen." *New York Times,* October 18, 1994, p. A25.
"From the Index of First Lines." *The New Yorker,* December 26, 1994–January 2, 1995, p. 83.
"My Life as Harold." *The New Yorker,* June 26–July 3, 1995, pp. 92–93.
"The Remedy." *New York Times Magazine,* August 18, 1996, pp. 38–39.
"The Author vs. the Library." *The New Yorker,* October 14, 1996, pp. 50–53, 56–62.
"China Pattern." *The New Yorker,* February 3, 1997, pp. 68–69.

"Grab Me a Gondola." *The New Yorker,* June 15, 1998, pp. 64–68.

"No Step." *The American Scholar* 70:5–7 (autumn 2001).

CRITICAL AND BIOGRAPHICAL STUDIES

Chambers, Ross. "Meditation and the Escalator Principle (On Nicholson Baker's *The Mezzanine*)." *Modern Fiction Studies* 40:765–806 (winter 1994).

Darling, Lynn. "The Highbrow Smut of Nicholson Baker." *Esquire,* February 1994, pp. 76–80.

Hall, Dennis. "Nicholson Baker's *Vox:* An Exercise in the Literature of Sensibility." *Connecticut Review* 17:35–40 (spring 1995).

Kaplan, James. "Hot *Vox.*" *Vanity Fair,* January 1992, pp. 118–121, 125–127.

Mallon, Thomas. "The Fabulous Baker Boy." *Gentleman's Quarterly,* May 1996, pp. 82–85.

Miller, Laura. "He Knows What You've Been Reading." *Salon* (http://www.salon.com/media/1998/04/03mediab.html).

Saltzman, Arthur. "To See a World in a Grain of Sand: Expanding Literary Minimalism." *Contemporary Literature* 31:423–433 (winter 1990).

———. *Understanding Nicholson Baker.* Columbia: University of South Carolina Press, 1999.

Simmons, Philip E. "Toward the Postmodern Historical Imagination: Mass Culture in Walker Percy's *The Moviegoer* and Nicholson Baker's *The Mezzanine.*" *Contemporary Literature* 33, no. 4:601–624 (1992).

—*D. QUENTIN MILLER*

Octavia Butler
1947–

Weaving together African American history and culture with the genre of science fiction has distinguished Octavia Butler as one of the most interesting writers of the twentieth century. Her novel *Kindred* (1979) is perhaps the most salient example of Butler's synthesis of these two consistently distinct areas. Using the devices of science fiction to propel the protagonist, Dana, back over a hundred years to slavery-era America, Butler poses in *Kindred* a series of important and evocative questions. Specifically, she considers the ability of contemporary African Americans to deal with the conditions of slavery and sets up difficult temporal dilemmas that oppose Dana's twentieth-century concept of slavery, particularly the question of the sexual exploitation of black women at the hands of white slave owners.

Upon returning to the past, Dana learns that her shifts in time are precipitated by the endangering of the life of a particular white boy, Rufus, who, it turns out, is Dana's great-great-grandfather. Dana also learns that Rufus must grow up to rape Alice—a slave woman—if Dana herself is to be born almost a century later. The slavery moment is complicated further by the fact that Dana's white husband, who witnesses her inexplicable vanishing into the past, holds on to Dana during one of her shifts back in time and is himself transported to the past with her. Within the slave economy, he is cast by necessity into the role designated for white people at that time—that of slaveholder. He and Dana ultimately become separated for years while she remains a slave and he travels around an America he has experienced only in history books. When Dana and her husband are reunited, Dana realizes that living in slavery-era America has rendered her once "liberal" husband more like the white people of the past, thus driving a wedge between them that is linked indelibly to a history they had thought could not, and did not, claim them.

In this way the novel brings the memory of slavery into the material present by transporting its characters to the past. By weaving the relationship between husband and wife into the politics of a slave economy, in which it was illegal and impossible for a white man to marry a black woman, *Kindred* articulates the difficulties of interracial desire that society has yet to completely solve. Using the device of time travel to encourage the investigation of a series of disconcerting ethical questions, *Butler* succeeds in making slavery—which often seems frozen in an inaccessible past—resonate for the contemporary reader. The novel also suggests, much against the grain of mainstream American thinking about race and slavery, that the ideological legacy of slavery still claims us in ways that we are not eager to acknowledge at a time when we want to see slavery as part of a primitive past from which we have evolved.

Butler sets her novel in 1976, which is significant. As not only a post-slavery moment but also a post–civil rights moment, this historical moment suggests a time in America's history when an emerging liberalism obscured the ways in which the legacy of race in the United States still claimed aspects of its citizens' consciousness. Rufus, the white forebear who keeps calling Dana back to the past, could be said to represent a damaging part of her consciousness that disables her freedom. When

Rufus' life is in danger, Dana is pulled back into the condition of slavery through a link with him that only she can (and ultimately does) sever. Rufus, who first draws Dana into the past as a young child, develops from an innocent boy, who loves the mythic and magical woman who comes to save him each time his life is in danger, into a man of his times. He rapes a slave woman (Alice, Dana's black ancestor) and sells members of families away from each other and generally behaves in the most atrocious ways allowed him, legally, under the system of chattel slavery. Dana's relationship to Rufus, which becomes complicated as her feelings about him change as he develops into a victimizing slaveholder, might be read as the presence of the racist past articulated through Dana's consciousness. As long as she is connected to that past—and needs to save it to save herself—she is bound to be dragged back into American history's worst anachronism; it is only by killing that part of her psyche that she can be free.

Ultimately, Dana kills Rufus and, in the process, loses an arm. Indeed, to "kill" this part of her past is to lose a significant and important part of herself. Losing an arm and the use of the essential hand suggests that even in rooting out the malevolent past, we also must part with a significant part of ourselves. In this way, the novel undoes the binaries between black and white set up by slavery and post-slavery discourse by suggesting that the past is not "outside" us or behind us; rather, it is alive and present within us. Furthermore, by tying a contemporary black woman's fate to a white slaveholding man, the novel makes it impossible for us to imagine that "black" and "white" people are not related, not only through biology but also through fate. The novel suggests that it is futile for us to disavow any part of American society, regardless of our racial identification, and that we are all on the same boat, so to speak. *Kindred*'s denouement indicates that while the past must be overcome and we must sever our ties with it, we also must accept that in doing so we leave a significant part of ourselves behind. The absence symbolized by Dana's missing arm is not an obliterated past, for in its very lack it implies what was once there. The void left by the destruction of the past is as much a presence as the past itself. In this way, Dana's killing of Rufus is only a gesture, but an extremely important one, as it symbolizes Dana's unwillingness to live subjected to the whims of a white slaveholding man who produced his black descendents in a violent act of perversion and power.

Often compared with Toni Morrison's novel *Beloved*, *Kindred* not only elucidates the physical brutality and reality of slavery but also coerces into coherence difficult metaphysical questions about slavery. This attention to ideology characterizes all the work of Octavia Butler, whose oeuvre is vast and varied.

CHILDHOOD AND YOUTH

Octavia Estelle Butler was born on June 22, 1947, in Pasadena, California. Her parents, Laurice and Octavia Margaret Guy Butler, endured five failed pregnancies before their daughter was born. Tragedy again struck the family when Laurice died when Butler was very young; Butler grew up with knowledge of her father gleaned only from stories told by her mother and grandmother. Growing up in a very racially diverse neighborhood, Butler came into contact with a variety of ethnic groups and cultural practices. She also experienced financial hardship as a child. Her mother was a domestic who worked in the homes of white people. This early experience, Butler has noted, in large part informed her writing of *Kindred*. She was easily able to imagine what it would be like for someone to be seen only in her role as servant. Her own childhood of ethnic diversity and class struggle is evident in her work, which focuses largely on such communities.

Butler has said that she started writing at the age of ten as a way to overcome boredom and loneliness. After graduating from John Muir High School in 1965, she went on to earn an Associate of Arts degree at Pasadena City College in 1968. She also attended California State University and the University of California, Los Angeles. She has noted, however, that her talent as a writer does not derive from her experience in higher education. She also participated in the Open Door program of the Screenwriters Guild of America and the Clarion Science Fiction and Fantasy Writers' Workshop. Her rise to success was not rapid, as she is quick to point out. She worked for years in minimum wage and hard-labor jobs—in factories, restaurants, and other such places—and she received many rejection slips before she sold her first piece of fiction. Before she was published, however, Butler took difficult jobs and wrote very early in the morning (sometimes as early as 2 A.M.), before work, on her lunch breaks, and when she got home. It was years before she could make a viable living from her writing, but through her abiding persistence she eventually made writing her profession.

Encouraged by Harlan Ellison, a master science fiction writer, Butler published her short story "Crossover" (in the 1971 collection *Clarion*) and inaugurated the themes of African American history as an integral part of her science fiction. Her first novel, *Patternmaster* (1976), was the beginning of a renowned five-volume series. She has twice won the Nebula (for "Bloodchild" in 1984 and *Parable of the Talents* in 1999) and Hugo (for "Speech Sounds" in 1984 and "Bloodchild" in 1985) awards, science fiction's highest honors. In 1995 Butler received a prestigious MacArthur Foundation genius grant.

Although Butler's work engages difficult questions of race, gender, class, and sexuality, it is not necessarily her goal when writing to expound upon these themes. She has said that she writes because she likes telling a good story and that writing for her is tied intimately to her own sense of herself. Each story forces her to grow, she has noted, and asks that she develop as a human being. For this reason, perhaps, her work has the same innovative and expanding quality that Butler says informs the writing of it.

Butler's provocative wit and sense of humor is evident in the description she has penned of herself that is included with little variation (other than her age and residence) in all of her books:

> I'm a 53-year-old writer who can remember being a 10-year-old writer and who expects someday to be an 80-year-old writer. I'm also comfortably asocial—a hermit in the middle of Seattle—a pessimist if I'm not careful, a feminist, a Black, a former Baptist, an oil-and-water combination of ambition, laziness, insecurity, certainty, and drive.

Butler's identity as a writer—as is evident from this passage (in *Parable of the Talents*)—is of central importance to her, as writing was a way that she expressed her feelings as a child. The complexity with which Butler defines herself—as oil *and* water, as lazy *and* driven, also can be said to characterize her work, which astutely captures the idea of duality and brilliantly represents the possibilities of synthesis.

Generally, Butler's work has been well received. In addition to the awards she has won for her excellence as a science fiction writer, she has garnered a wide range of academic and scholarly praise for her work, which is seen to combine issues of race and gender in ways unique to the genre of science fiction. Butler has been praised not only for her treatment of these particular issues but also for her craftily written narratives; her use of language has been described as taut and powerful and as transcendent of merely conveying a theme. Her work is understood as particularly feminist in its imaginings; as the only highly visible African American woman writing science fiction, she continues to be heralded as a trailblazer and innovator in a variety of literary genres.

THE PATTERNMASTER SERIES

Each book in the Patternmaster series stands alone and need not be read in a particular order. All of the books in this series, however, deal with the theme of difference and community, inequality and oppression, through the use of radically redefined science fiction narrative devices. In the first book of the patternmaster series, *Patternmaster,* readers are introduced to a telepathic race that is engaged in a war on two fronts—first with itself and then with the people who do not have telepathic abilities. Imposing a hierarchy that keeps them in power and the Clayarks subjected to them, the Patternists view themselves as a superior race. Within their community, however, there is much fighting for the role of Patternmaster. The "pattern" is a neurological network that binds together all of the telepaths; the Patternmaster controls them all. In a kind of Cain and Abel battle to the death, a tyrannical son of the ruling Patternmaster seeks his exiled brother so that he can destroy him and have no contestation to his ascendancy to power.

The second of the five books, *Mind of My Mind* (1977), introduces the character Doro, an ancient Nubian who discovers, almost at the moment of his own death, how to lift his spirit out of his body and enter another person's body, thereby preserving his own life. In doing so, however, he murders the soul of the person whose body he takes; thus, even while Doro is the protagonist and hero in the novel, he has the edge of a murderer about him. Eventually, Doro begins to reproduce to create a master race of telepaths.

It has been rumored that the third book in the sequence, *Survivor* (1978), is Butler's own least favorite book. She has called it her "Star Trek" novel, and it is out of print. Some dedicated Butler readers, however, herald it as one of her most intriguing novels. *Survivor* tells the story of the human Alanna, who, with other humans, flees Earth for another planet in order to escape a plague-like disease. The humans attempt to set up a colony and to resume "normal" human life, but they soon find themselves caught between two alien societies that are at war with each other, the Garkohn and the Tehkohn. Alanna is captured and then "adopted" by the Tehkohn. Later in the novel, she tries to aid the human survivors, but the humans reject her because she has been raised by aliens.

In the Patternist series Butler creates multicultural communities bound to new ways of identification. Because of the differences between them, the communities are often at war; what Butler achieves through her manipulation of human and alien identity through the tropes of telepathy, disease, and the alien is another way of demonstrating what happens when hierarchies and power intersect with difference. In the past twenty-five years, many cultural critics have sought ways to deal with and apply the dictum that race is a construction, which means that racial identity is created by society rather than biologically determined. In her Patternist series, Butler presents readers with another way to think about the negotiation of identity in a completely believable way. Furthermore, by characterizing the powerful forces of society (the "us versus them," if you will) as having to do with mental ability as opposed to physical traits, Butler demonstrates that unequal power relations are about far more than simply the color of a person's skin. Morever, inequity and hierarchies are not integral to questions of race. In other words, she shows that even in a society "without race," as we currently know it, hierarchy and unequal power relations are still at play in ways that would exploit some groups while allowing others to prosper.

This does not mean, however, that her books suggest that this is how things *should* be; rather, the Patternmaster series illustrates the complexity of power and inequality in a way that is not always possible within the oft-engaged rhetoric-laden conversations concerning race, class, gender, and sexuality. By removing the issues we are accustomed to thinking about with respect to power (i.e., race and class), Butler can draw and expose aspects of power relations from a safe distance. Because they are told from the perspective of the privileged class (the telepaths), these books also have the effect of fully investigating the psyche of the powerful, which at once exposes and humanizes them.

The book *Wild Seed* (1980) continues the story of Doro, who finally meets his match in a woman named Anyanwu. She is a shape-shifter who cannot die, and together they breed a race of people who, like the telepaths Doro "collects," will help form the "pattern" and give rise to a race of telepaths. In this book the weaving together of African forms of spirituality is clear. The name Doro means "the direction from which the sun comes," that is, east. And, the novel itself is based on the mythic figure of Atagbusi, a shape-shifting Onitsha Ado (Nigeria) woman who acted as a protector of her people and aided their commercial development by magically drawing people to the marketplace. The name Anyanwu means "the sun," and this, too, draws on African ideology. Through the clever use of these names, however, Butler articulates a feminist agenda, as the benevolent and powerful Anyanwu represents the central force of the sun, whereas Doro is merely derivative of the sun, coming only from the direction of that powerful force.

The final book in the series, *Clay's Ark* (1984), builds again on themes of the construction of a new and powerful race while introducing the idea of mutation. The civilization in *Clay's Ark* is a postindustrial one that is in the process of being destroyed. An alien life-form makes it way to Earth and merges with the humans who remain there, to create a new form of life, part human and part alien. All of the books in the Patternmaster series demonstrate a preoccupation with intermixing and its antithesis, division. The question of hierarchy, as a structure designed to keep various parts of society apart from each other, is clearly at stake in *Patternmaster, Survivor,* and *Mind of My Mind.* As the telepaths oppress and subjugate the Clayarks and mutes, the hierarchal nature of their society also turns them against one another. In opposition to this is the intermixture as represented in *Clay's Ark,* where hierarchies break down and re-form into a new synthesis. This preoccupation with intermixture is evident in Butler's later works as well, and it is especially prominent in the next series the Xenogenesis trilogy.

XENOGENESIS TRILOGY

This series, which is made up of three novels—*Dawn* (1987), *Adulthood Rites* (1988), and *Imago* (1989)—centers on issues of intermixture, colonization, and difficult questions of power. These three novels were collected into one volume, *Lilith's Brood,* and published in 2000. Colonization, a common theme in science fiction narratives, is figured through the Oankali, nomadic aliens who travel from planet to planet siphoning the resources of each, exchanging DNA with the inhabitants as a way to diversify their own gene pool, and eventually leaving. After the Oankali are finished with a planet, it is little more than a barren rock; they leave behind uninhabitable shells.

The Oankali, however, are not solely responsible for Earth's decline; the aliens arrive on the scene only after human beings wage a nuclear war that destroys most of the planet, making it an extremely hostile environment for human life. In exchange for DNA, the Oankali use their superior technology to make Earth habitable for human beings. Many critics view the Xenogenesis series as Butler's best work, owing in part to the complex and highly dynamic characterization of the Oankali, who at once "save" human beings from total extinction and yet coerce them into "gene trading," as they call it, by threatening to let them die. While the Oankali are essentially passive and nonviolent creatures who eschew murder, they are highly calculating in other, more subtle ways. They insinuate themselves into every form of human interaction, changing human relationships at the most basic level. They chemically block human beings from being able to reproduce and instead insist that humans mate through them, so that they can manipulate and meld human DNA with theirs.

Mating with the Oankali, however, is not painful or lacking in pleasure; in fact the opposite is true. The pleasure experienced when mating with the aliens is more intense than the sensations offered by human sex, which sets up a paradox for many of the characters in the novel that parallels the larger and more defining paradox of what it means to mate with the Oankali. While the Oankali save humanity from extinction, they do not allow human civilization to flourish but only to be assimilated into their own society, which many of the characters in these novels see as a kind of extinction anyway.

The first of these series of novels, *Dawn,* follows the character Lilith Iyapo who is the first human being to be impregnated by the Oankali. The Oankali who impregnates her, while she is held in a comalike state for many years, is Nikanj, who becomes something of a partner to Lilith. The Oankali are divided into three genders, the third gender being neuter and called "ooloi." It is the ooloi who serve as the intermediaries, or mediums, in procreation for all Oankali reproduction, and it is the ooloi who manipulate DNA to render a person male, female, or ooloi. The ooloi also determine how much any given child will look human or Oankali.

In *Dawn,* Lilith awakens to find herself on a strange ship. Unlike the expected metal spaceship, it is made of organic matter, and so at first it appears to her that it has no walls. She eventually learns, however, that because the ship is a living organism, it can transform into a door, a bench, a chair, a bed, a bowl, and so on, when necessary. Lilith also learns that she has been chosen as a kind of "ambassador" of all humanity; the Oankali give her the task of "awakening" the other humans, whom they have kept in stasis on their ship. Thus, Lilith becomes the hated first mother of this new group of humans, which is also the last group of humans.

Before awakening Lilith, the Oankali conduct a detailed study of humanity in all of its biological and psychological aspects. They discover that Lilith has a predisposition to cancer, and they correct this weakness in her biological makeup. Cancer is conceptualized, in the Xenogenesis series, as a strange growth, which is almost incomprehensible to the Oankali. They describe cancer as a set of cells that does not know when to stop growing and so multiplies to kill its host. This becomes a metaphor for humanity itself, because the Oankali also have found that human beings, if left to themselves, rapidly self-destruct, like a mass of cancer cells. The Oankali, who see human beings as time bombs waiting to destroy themselves, refer to this as the "human contradiction." This is one of the reasons the Oankali prohibit human procreation. As justification, they cite the current situation of the humans—which is that without the Oankali, there would be no evidence of human life anywhere in the galaxy. Yet the Oankali themselves are like a cancer; they plan to devour Earth, expanding their gene pool and resources, and then leave nothing behind but a dead shell.

In the second book of the Xenogenesis series, *Adulthood Rites,* Lilith's son, Akin, is caught up in an intense battle between the Oankali and the resisters, a group of humans that survives the nuclear holocaust and chooses to live separately from the Oankali, refusing to mate or "trade DNA" with the aliens. Seeing the very human-looking Akin, the resisters kidnap him. The Oankali, who fear that Akin's human DNA will be expressed too strongly in his character, allow him to stay with the outlaw humans so that he may learn what it means to be human. The resisters are unaware, however, that every Oankali-human child undergoes a metamorphosis that changes the child's appearance. Children who start off resembling humans often end up looking more like the Oankali, who are made up of masses of fat, wormlike tentacles. Conversely, children who look at first like Oankali often can appear more human after their metamorphosis.

Akin, whose name indicates his relationship as *kin* to both humans and Oankali, metaphorically linking the Oankali and the humans, serves as a bond between the human cause and the Oankali mission. Akin, though he ultimately concedes the Oankali point that humans have a tendency to self-destruct, also empathizes with the human resisters, who want desperately to found an "all human" society. Akin manages to persuade the Oankali to allow humans to colonize Mars and to begin to create an all-human society. This proves to be troublesome in the last book of the Xenogenesis series, *Imago.*

In *Imago* the first half-human, half-Oankali ooloi is born. In order to reproduce, however, the ooloi, named Jodahs, must find two humans with whom he can mate. That means that he must search for a mate among the resister humans who have resettled on Mars—a difficult prospect, as most of the resister humans are opposed to mating with the Oankali. The ooloi are shape-shifters and can take on the forms of their mates—thus, the title of the book, *Imago.* Like Akin in *Adulthood Rites,* Jodahs must learn to mediate between human and Oankali demands. As an ooloi, Jodahs has the power to manipulate DNA and to heal, but if this capacity is not tamed, an ooloi can mutilate or harm someone unintentionally. To be accepted by the Oankali, Jodahs is compelled to learn how to control his power. Jodahs eventually meets a group of resister humans that all still have the ability to reproduce, and so he begins a new species of half-human and half-Oankali that is able to procreate without genetic manipulation.

The Xenogenesis series has been referred to as a kind "miscegenate" fiction, indicating its concern with questions of miscegenation, or the intermixture of races. The opposition represented by the Oankali and the humans raises questions of racial mingling that characterize racist debate. During a more racist period in American history, black people were thought to belong to another species and often were seen as being the "missing link" between humankind and primates. To procreate with a black person, then, was to participate in cross-species sex—which was obviously taboo, given this flawed and oppressive characterization of black people. This series of novels elucidates many of these same concerns and issues about miscegenation. Akin and Jodahs could be seen as fulfilling the role of "tragic mulatto," as they search for a way to mediate their Oankali and human identities. In the end, there is nothing "tragic" about them, since they ultimately triumph.

The efficacy of the Xenogenesis series is that it presents a particular point of view as valid that often and aptly is maligned in contemporary discussions about interracial relationships and biracial people. The idea that people of differing races should not marry or have children now seems antiquated and anachronistic. Before 1967, when the U.S. Supreme Court, in the case *Virginia* v. *Loving,* overturned laws prohibiting miscegenation, it was a very real debate, which went to the heart of questions about humanity, identity, and group survival. The difficult questions posed in the Xenogenesis series are these: Why should the humans *not* want to "trade"

DNA with the Oankali? What is so objectionable about merging with another life-form that is superior to one's own and that can cure one of all disease and offer a more organic (and presumably better) way of life?

These questions posit the idea of a human essence—the notion that there is something indescribable that constitutes humanity, that even if it is flawed, it should thrive. This is the position of the resisters, who feel that flawed human beings are better than no human beings at all. Moreover, the notion that their DNA will exist forever through the Oankali is not enough—what the humans want is a "pure" humanity, not an intermixed one. The narrative of these novels puts readers in a position to understand both points of view. The human resisters feel a palpable violation in the prohibition to procreate, and one that is worthy of sympathy. It seems like the most basic infringement of civil rights. The analytical view offered by the Oankali however—that humanity will destroy itself and that to allow humanity to flourish is like letting a defective child grow up, only to see it die later—is compelling as well. Furthermore, readers are asked to consider whether humanity ever will become extinct, since their genes will go on, but in a metamorphosed form. In other words, why must our own likeness be reproduced exactly? The Oankali answer to this would be that human egotism, which is its downfall, motivates the desire for an unchanging humanity.

The Xenogenesis series attracted the most academic and scholarly attention of all of Butler's work. Its critical success is partly due to how it poses a set of fascinating questions about race and sexuality in a refreshing way that makes a seemingly "old" topic new and engaging. Although Butler has said that she writes to tell a story rather than to make a point, the Xenogenesis series is compelling because it manages to do both without detracting from either.

PARABLE OF THE SOWER AND *PARABLE OF THE TALENTS*

After the Patternmaster and Xenogenesis series, Butler wrote *Parable of the Sower* (1993) and its sequel, *Parable of the Talents* (1998). *Parable of the Sower* is set in 2024 in a dystopian Los Angeles. The United States, no longer the superpower that it is today, is in a state of steady decline, as lawlessness, rampant drug use, and a scarcity of such necessities as food, gasoline, and electricity change the face of life in the country. Because of unbridled crime and an impotent and inefficient police force, no one can travel unarmed or alone. College courses are taught via computer, and anyone with any kind of financial stability lives in walled and gated communities.

Lauren Olamina, the protagonist who lives in this mess of a society, looks around her and sees that her world—which has been relatively safe within the confines of her community's walls—is on the brink of collapse. As a "sharer," that is, one who can feel the pain of others, Lauren is more sensitive and intuitive than those around her. Lauren is one of many sharers in her society. She became a sharer when her mother took an experimental drug that affected Lauren's neurochemical processes. Realizing that at any moment her world could change forever, Lauren begins to prepare herself for the worst. Her father is a preacher and a leader in the community, and his example and impact have a great influence on Lauren's life.

At an early age, Lauren rejects her father's Christianity and begins to write down her own verses, which she calls Earthseed; they combine various teachings into one essential claim: God is change. Lauren realizes that she must keep her budding doctrine a secret, and so she writes the verses in her journal but shares them with no one. An unflinching pragmatism characterizes Lauren's ideology, and so, in addition to penning her verses, she studies survival guides so that when the great catastrophe comes she will be prepared to meet it. In keeping with her premonition of disaster and her practicality, Lauren keeps an emergency pack hidden away at all times, so that if she ever needs to flee immediately, she will not be without resources.

When drug addicts attack the walled-in community in which she lives, Lauren's prophesy comes true, and members of her family are killed or disappear. After spending a night hiding out, she goes back to her neighborhood for her emergency pack and begins a journey northward, looking for a new place to settle. She seeks potential members of the community that she is planning to establish, a society that will be connected by the doctrines of Earthseed. On the way, Lauren collects a variety of people by saving them from various disasters, and she teaches each of them the Earthseed philosophy. Some of them reject Earthseed but decide to stay with Lauren; among those she meets is a much older man, Bankole, who becomes her companion. Bankole, a doctor, has land in northern California that he offers to the fledgling Earthseed community. Upon arriving there, the group discovers that Bankole's sister and his family have been killed. The first act of the community is to bury and memorialize the remains of Bankole's family. In this way, the first Earthseed community, Acorn is founded.

The name "Acorn" is significant in that Lauren's community has reclaimed the edible nut that twentieth-century Americans would never have thought to eat. Acorn bread, Lauren's favorite food, represents the way her family adapted in the face of food scarcity and learned old ways to make food. The idea of adjusting to one's circumstances is central to the Earthseed philosophy, which posits not only that "God is change" but also that God exists to be shaped. For this reason, the ability or willingness to accommodate changing situations is a cornerstone of Earthseed ideology. Each chapter of *Parable of the Sower* begins with a verse from Lauren's Earthseed writings, and in this way Lauren's particular theology is foregrounded through the novel.

Parable of the Sower explores the apocalyptic possibilities of contemporary society with a twist. Instead of simply presenting the seemingly inevitable downward spiral of humanity, it also offers an alternative to mere chaos. Rather than falling back on nostalgia as a means to "restore" order to the lives of human beings, Lauren Olamina synthesizes all of the most pragmatic and logical aspects of hundreds of years of religious belief into one philosophy whose ultimate goal is to "take root among the stars." Lauren's definitive vision for her Earthseed community is that they inhabit other worlds.

This seemingly colonial imperative—this aspiration to inhabit other worlds that so mimics the desire of the people of the seventeenth and eighteenth centuries to travel to the ends of the earth—is critiqued and becomes more complicated in the sequel, *Parable of the Talents*. This second novel is in some ways a history of what happens at Acorn—what an Earthseed community would look like—but it is also an examination of Lauren and her religion. This novel picks up where its predecessor leaves off. Consisting primarily of Lauren's journals, these writings tell us that at Acorn the Earthseed community has grown to sixty-two people and that the community prospers, though without the accoutrements of modernity—such as electricity, telephones, cars, and other essential technologies. Interspersed throughout Lauren's journal entries are the words of her brother and her daughter. Her brother, Marcus, who Lauren thought was dead, reenters the narrative when Lauren finds that he is being held as a sex slave. Buying his freedom, she brings him to Acorn, where he quickly rejects Earthseed ideology and tries to preach Christianity to the community. His own ideology is questioned and rejected by the people at Acorn, who believe in

Earthseed, but Marcus nonetheless is accepted. Unable to live in what he terms a "pagan cult," however, Marcus soon flees.

Christian fundamentalism figures heavily in *Parable of the Talents,* as a new president founds an organization called Christian America, whose job is to restore peace, prosperity, and order to America by enforcing a particular kind of Christianity on all of its citizens. The new government ignores freedom of religion, as Christian America sets up "rehabilitation camps," where it enslaves "pagans and criminals" and subjects them to so-called religious training, which includes rape, violent beatings, and humiliations of every order. Christian America soon invades Acorn, Bankole is killed, and the land is stolen. All of the children, including Lauren's child, Larkin, are taken away and placed in proper Christian American homes.

The Earthseed community is enslaved for a year, until they are able—thanks to a landslide that disables their electronic collars—to kill their captors and escape. They scatter, and Lauren tries to find Larkin. She discovers that Marcus has become a leading preacher for Christian America, and when she finds him, she tells him what Acorn has suffered at their hands. Decrying the Acorn community's captors as an extreme and illegitimate subgroup of Christian America, Marcus is unable to accept that his organization has perpetrated the crimes Lauren describes. Lauren pleads with him to help her find her child. When Marcus discovers that Larkin has been adopted by Christian America parents, he decides to leave Larkin in what he considers to be a more "suitable" home rather than return her to her mother, his sister, whom he sees as a pagan and sinner. After a violent confrontation with Lauren, Marcus flees Eureka-Arcata, the area where Lauren and he find each other again, and moves to Portland, Oregon.

Much of *Parable of the Talents* is told from the perspective of Larkin, who has been renamed Asha Vere, after a Christian video game. She meets her true mother only late in life and is skeptical and resentful of her mother's ideology, because she feels that it was her mother's love for and adherence to Earthseed philosophy that made such a mess of her own life. Asha's adoptive parents, strict and unkind Christians, always compared her to their own dead daughter, Kamaria. Asha also has suffered abuse at the hands of her stepfather. Marcus, who has gained nationwide prominence as a leader of Christian America, uses his prominence in the organization to find Asha, and when she is eighteen, she moves in with her uncle. He does not intend to tell Asha who her mother is or to reintroduce the two; but Asha soon discovers who her mother is and seeks Lauren out.

When she finally meets Lauren, she sees her through a cloud of suspicion and anger. The two women are never able to recover a mother-daughter relationship. Lauren dies without being reconciled to either her brother or her daughter, but her dream, that Earthseed might take root among the stars, comes true as the first ship of Earthseed leaves Earth for the moon a few days before Lauren dies.

Asha comes to the conclusion that she could never have been her mother's daughter, because her mother favored Earthseed over everything else—including her own daughter and husband. Asha blames her father's death not on Christian America but on Earthseed and her mother. She ascribes her own abduction and horrible upbringing not to the Christians who kidnapped and raised her but to her mother's unwillingness to conform to society. Bankole several times beseeches Lauren to move into a gated (and implicitly Christian) community, where they will have a modern house and where Bankole will work as the doctor to the community. Lauren refuses to go, and it is only a few weeks later that Christian America attacks Acorn, precipitating the ensuing disastrous consequences.

Despite the extremity of the events in *The Parable of the Sower* and *The Parable of the Talents,* these texts resonate with contemporary political realities in a way that requires readers to think seriously about the possibility for catastrophe and about what one can or is willing to do after such a catastrophe. These novels convincingly sketch out a series of scenarios that are all too imaginable and terribly close to the texture and grit of the worst realities of contemporary life. Furthermore, *The Parable of the Talents* is a timely critique of religious oppression through its portrayal of a Christian America that kills and maims and seeks to eliminate any ideology besides its own. Religious freedom is one of the most important cornerstones of the American way of life. Indeed, it is what the United States was founded on—and *Parable of the Talents* is a nuanced critique of the way in which religious intolerance, in a system that legally requires the separation of church and state, still can affect the lives of people in devastating ways.

The religious oppression that is so central to the story in *Parable of the Talents* is also a metaphor for other kinds of oppression. As in all of Butler's work, oppression itself becomes the enemy, while particular identities—those of race, sex, and class—function as mere signs of the larger problem of injustice.

BLOODCHILD AND OTHER STORIES

Although she is known primarily for her novels, Butler also has written quite a few short stories. Her most famous stories are collected in *Bloodchild and Other Stories* (1995). The short story "Bloodchild" treats many of the themes that Butler later develops in the Xenogenesis series. The setting of "Bloodchild" is another planet, to which human beings fled when they were being enslaved and killed on Earth. This new planet is inhabited by strange snakelike and birdlike creatures that keep human beings confined to "reserves" and give them mood-altering "eggs," which produce a druglike euphoria in the person consuming the liquid contained within them. The creatures, called Tlic, maintain humanity for a price: human beings must serve as living incubators for their young. When he sees a man almost die as a result of this incubation, the main character of "Bloodchild," the young man Gan, experiences a crisis concerning the role he has always known he would play in the birthing of a Tlic litter.

The difficult aspect of a human-Tlic birth is that when the grubs, as the embryonic Tlic are called, begin to hatch from their eggs, they eat the eggs and then their hosts. If the grubs are not removed from a human host in time, that person will be eaten from the inside out by the larvae. After helping T'Gatoi (the Tlic who will impregnate Gan) take the grubs from the suffering man's body, Gan changes his mind about serving as incubator for the Tlic's children. When Gan realizes, however, that T'Gatoi will "take" instead his younger sister (who wants to be an incubator), he decides to go through with the process.

"Bloodchild" raises many of the same intriguing questions that are raised in the Xenogenesis series but subverts the logic of reproduction by making men the favored "incubators." While the Tlic impregnate women as well as men, they prefer men as hosts for their eggs. The cultural logic that says that only women can be reproducers of life is so strong that at first many people think the protagonist of the story is female. The undermining of this logic makes "Bloodchild" an extraordinary consideration of reproduction not only in the context of gender but also—loosely writ—in the context of "race." It poses the same set of metaphysical dilemmas that are present in Butler's *Kindred* and in her Xenogenesis trilogy. While T'Gatoi is not "forcing" her offspring on Gan, his choices are very limited. His ability to refuse does not mean that he can disrupt the systematic Tlic impregnating of human beings; it means only that he can spare *himself* this fate. Yet if a human being were to escape the reserve, that person could be used by a Tlic as an incubator, with little or no choice in the matter. The test of whether the humans are "slaves" of the Tlic comes when Gan insists on keeping a rifle, which is contraband for humans. Demanding that T'Gatoi demonstrate that Terrans are actually partners of the Tlic, as T'Gatoi claims, Gan insists that T'Gatoi leave the rifle with his family. In this way, Gan challenges T'Gatoi to prove that their relationship is not one that is defined by bondage.

This exploration of uneasily symbiotic relationships is a common theme in Butler's writing, as is the idea of an apocalyptic world where life as we know it is altered radically. In many of Butler's stories, normal human relationships are destroyed, and human beings must fight to survive. This is the situation presented in the short story "Speech Sounds." As the result of an unnamed disease, human beings find their verbal skills permanently transformed; many people can no longer talk, and others have lost their ability to read and write. The vast majority of people have endured both losses, and the result is a world characterized by a dangerous anarchy. The story follows the character Valerie Rye, who, after losing her three children and her husband, decides to travel to Pasadena to find her brothers. She is on her way there on one of the few remaining city buses when a fight breaks out and the passengers are forced to exit. Outside the bus, she meets a man named Obsidian, who is a victim of the disease of speech; the two decide to join together. Shortly after coming to this decision, all of which is conveyed through hand signals, they run into a domestic fight, which quickly escalates into violence. A man kills a woman who is presumably his wife; then he kills Obsidian. Two children run out of the nearby house, out of which the man and women previously had emerged, and quietly mourn their dead mother. Rye quickly realizes that the disease has not affected them. Despite her initial dread at adopting these children, she does so and lets them know that she, too, can talk.

The connection Butler creates between loss of language and anarchy compels us to center language, all forms of speech sounds, as important acts, without which growth and development become impossible. Many apocalyptic narratives imagine that lack of physical resources will force humanity into anarchy, but Butler subverts that logic and suggests that the things we most take for granted—like being able to talk—might actually be our Achilles' heel. The implications are intriguing when read against the afterword that Butler includes with each short story in this collection of prose. Butler writes that this story arose from a time of great pain, when one of her closest friends was dying of a rare form of cancer. In an afterward to "Speech Sounds" in the *Bloodchild* collection, Butler writes, "I began the story feeling little hope or like for the human species, but by the time I had reached the end of it, my hope had come back." In this way, her disillusionment with humanity is inverted through the very vehicle of which her characters are deprived and which leaves them violent and out of control: speech sounds. The act of writing serves the purpose of reclaiming that which is good in human beings, that which inspires us to maintain our hope in the face of life's difficulties—like illness and untimely and sometimes violent death.

Also included in this volume of short stories are two essays, both of which meditate on the writer's life. In the first, titled "Positive Obsession," Butler describes her own "obsession" with writing and her writer's life, which began when she was a child. In the second essay, "Furor Scribendi," she offers six points of advice for aspiring writers. In both essays what comes across is Butler's belief that it is not talent per se that makes the writer, but rather perseverance. She implores writers to "persist," above all other things. Her advice is insightful and remarkable because she is eagerly giving advice to aspiring writers and imparting to them the idea that it is only persistence that allows one to become a successful writer. Eschewing the idea of "talent," Butler has told interviewers that it is not that she has a particular writing talent but rather that she has a tendency to persist in her writing efforts. Butler thus extends the possibility of publication and success to every writer who works resolutely and consistently. In this way, Butler establishes herself as a Furor Scribendi with one particular positive obsession: writing. As an instructor at the Clarion Writers' Workshop, Butler instills this passion for writing in the students she teaches, and in these essays she imparts her wisdom to her readers.

Selected Bibliography

WORKS OF OCTAVIA BUTLER

NOVELS

Patternmaster. Garden City, N.Y.: Doubleday, 1976.

Mind of My Mind. Garden City, N.Y.: Doubleday, 1977.

Survivor. Garden City, N.Y.: Doubleday, 1978.

Kindred. With an introduction by Robert Crossley. Garden City, N.Y.: Doubleday, 1979.

Wild Seed. Garden City, N.Y.: Doubleday, 1980.

Clay's Ark. New York: St. Martin's Press, 1984.

Dawn. New York: Warner Books, 1987.

Adulthood Rites. New York: Warner Books, 1988.

Imago. New York: Warner Books, 1989.

Parable of the Sower. New York: Four Walls Eight Windows, 1993.

Parable of the Talents. New York: Seven Stories Press, 1998.

Lilith's Brood. New York: Aspect/Warner Books, 2000.

SHORT STORIES

Bloodchild and Other Stories. New York: Four Walls Eight Windows, 1995. (Includes all of Butler's short stories, except "The Monophobic Response.")

"The Monophobic Response." In *Dark Matter: A Century of Speculative Fiction from the African Diaspora.* Edited by Sheree R. Thomas. New York: Warner Books, 2000.

CRITICAL AND BIOGRAPHICAL STUDIES

Allison, Dorothy. "The Future of Female: Octavia Butler's Mother Lode." In *Reading Black, Reading Feminist: A Critical Anthology.* Edited by Henry Louis Gates Jr. New York: Meridian Book, 1990.

Atherton, Eric N. "Blurred Distinctions: *The Parable of the Sower* and Melville's 'One-Legged Man.'" *ANQ: A Quarterly Journal of Short Articles, Notes, and Reviews* 7, no. 3:149–153 (July 1994).

Birn, Nicholas. "Octavia Butler: Fashioning Alien Constructs." *Hollins Critic* 38, no. 3:1–14 (June 2001).

Bonner, Frances. "Difference and Desire, Slavery and Seduction: Octavia Butler's *Xenogenesis.*" *Foundation: The International Review of Science Fiction* 48:50–62 (spring 1990).

Dubey, Madhu. "Folk and Urban Communities in African-American Women's Fiction: Octavia Butler's *Parable of the Sower.*" *Studies in American Fiction* 27, no. 1:103–138 (spring 1999).

Foster, Frances S. "Octavia Butler's Black Female Future Vision." *Extrapolation* 23, no. 1:37–49 (spring 1982).

Friend, Beverly. "Time Travel as a Feminist Didactic in Works by Phyllis Eisenstein, Marlys Millhiser, and Octavia Butler." *Extrapolation* 23, no. 1:50–55 (spring 1982).

Gordon, Joan. "Two SF Diaries at the Intersection of Subjunctive Hopes and Declarative Despair." *Foundation: The International Review of Science Fiction* 72:42–38 (spring 1998).

Govan, Sandra. "Octavia E. Butler." In *Notable Black American Women*. Edited by Jessie Carney Smith. Detroit: Gale Research, Inc., 1992. Pp.144–147.

Helford, Elyce Rae. "'Would You Really Rather Die Than Bear My Young?' The Construction of Gender, Race, and Species in Octavia Butler's *Bloodchild*." *African American Review* 28, no. 2:259–271 (summer 1994).

Holden, Rebecca J. "The High Costs of Cyborg Survival: Octavia Butler's *Xenogenesis* Trilogy." *Foundation: The International Review of Science Fiction* 72:49–56 (spring 1998).

Johnson, Rebecca O. "African American Feminist Science Fiction." *Sojourner* 19, no. 6:12–14 (February 1994).

Levy, Michael M. "Ophelia Triumphant: The Survival of Adolescent Girls in Recent Fiction by Butler and Womack." *Foundation: The International Review of Science Fiction* 72:34–41 (spring 1998).

Luckhurst, Roger. "'Horror and Beauty in Rare Combination': The Miscegenate Fictions of Octavia Butler." *Women: A Cultural Review* 7, no. 1:28–38 (spring 1996).

Mellen, Philip. "Gerhart Hauptmann's *Vor Sonnenaufgang* and the *Parable of the Sower*." *Monatshefte für Deutschen Unterricht, Deutsche Sprache und Literatur* 74, no. 2:139–144 (summer 1982).

Michaels, Walter Benn. "Political Science Fictions." *New Literary History: A Journal of Theory and Interpretation* 31, no. 4:649–664 (autumn 2000).

Peppers, Cathy. "Dialogic Origins and Alien Identities in Butler's *Xenogenesis*." *Science-Fiction Studies* 22, no. 1:47–62 (March 1995).

Salvaggio, Ruth. "Octavia Butler and the Black Science Fiction Heroine." *Black American Literature Forum* 18, no. 2:78–81 (1984).

White, Eric. "The Erotics of Becoming: *Xenogenesis* and *The Thing*." *Science-Fiction Studies* 20, no. 3:394–408 (November 1993).

Zaki, Hoda. "Utopia, Dystopia, and Ideology in the Science Fiction of Octavia Butler." *Science-Fiction Studies* 17, no. 2:239–251 (1990).

INTERVIEWS

Fry, Joan. "An Interview with Octavia Butler." *Poets & Writers* 25:58–69 (March/April 1997).

"Interview with Octavia Butler." *Locus Magazine* 44:6 (June 2000).

McCaffery, Larry. *Across the Wounded Galaxies: Interviews with Contemporary American Science Fiction Writers*. Urbana: University of Illinois Press, 1990. Pp. 54–70.

—STEFANIE K. DUNNING

Stephen Dobyns

1941–

Sometimes I think communication is all we have—a voice like a silver wire extending through the dark. . . . Sometimes I don't even think that.

—Stephen Dobyns

Stephen Dobyns' literary output has been enormous. Although he commands success in multiple genres—he has produced numerous collections of poetry, as well as essays, short stories, novels, psychological thrillers, a series of mysteries, and an ongoing sequence of lengthy feature articles for the *San Diego Weekly Reader*—he considers himself first and foremost a poet. He has taught classes and workshops in many colleges and graduate writing programs and served as visiting poet at the University of Iowa, Boston University, Syracuse University, Brandeis University, College of the Holy Cross, Emerson College, and Sarah Lawrence College.

Dobyns was one of the first creative writers to put his energy into the now-ubiquitous master of fine arts writing programs. He served on the creative writing staffs of Goddard College and the prestigious Warren Wilson M.F.A. Writing Program, and he directed the M.F.A. program in creative writing at Syracuse from 1989 to 1994. His honors and awards include a Lamont Prize, a Melville Cain Award, a National Poetry Series prize, several Pushcart Prizes, and fellowships from the National Endowment for the Arts and the Guggenheim Foundation. Two of his novels were made into movies and several others are under option for future production.

EARLY INFLUENCES

Stephen Dobyns was born in Orange, New Jersey, on February 19, 1941. His mother, Barbara Johnson Dobyns, was a graduate of Columbia Teachers' College. She was an intelligent and gregarious woman, committed to liberal causes and political socialism. She taught American history at various institutions. His father, Lester Dobyns, also a graduate of Columbia, was a man of restless energy and varied passions: religion, music, and public speaking. The family home hummed with intellectual activity, and Stephen grew up surrounded by people who sought knowledge for the sake of activism. His parents' lives—their debates, their political and religious endeavors, the societal stature of some of their friends—must have made a powerful argument in the boy's consciousness, an argument stating that life has meaning, that actions have consequences, and finally that the behavior of individuals ought to serve humanity.

In dark contrast to this, Stephen Dobyns himself developed a strong tendency to conceive of the world and the human experience in existential terms. He does not believe in God, certainly not in a God that can be known. He is disturbed by the continual possibility that human life, and particularly human suffering, have no meaning. Although his parents engaged in life as a journey toward knowing, Dobyns' works consistently lament the fact that little or nothing can be known for certain. The family background of religious belief and inquiry must coexist with his sense of existential isolation. This uneasy fusion propels his poetry and his novels, charging them with intermittent strains of nostalgia, hilarity, and anguish.

Early in the 1950s Lester Dobyns studied with Paul Tillich, a renowned and controversial theologian. Tillich became known as the "apostle to the intellectuals" in his quest to incorporate existential philosophy into Christianity. Tillich's worldview ultimately may have colored Stephen Dobyns' view, since Tillich held enough influence over Stephen's father to convince him to enroll in theological seminary so he could take up a calling in the church. Tillich's biographers have pointed out that he was a man terrified of death and that he despaired of his own salvation. He suffered mental breakdowns. Dobyns' works take up the subject of death in many guises, and he frequently focuses on despair and the struggle to maintain sanity. Within Tillich's theology, "existence" is defined as the ultimate separation from God, or the "ground of being." Therefore, God, in Tillich's view, cannot be said to "exist" in the usual sense, because he is "being in itself." (This idea was later misunderstood in the "God is dead" movement.) Perhaps such philosophical tenets added shape to an underlying gloom with which Dobyns suffered from an early age.

EDUCATION

Lester Dobyns changed careers as well as locations frequently in pursuit of a calling. The Dobyns family moved to Alexandria, Virginia, in 1953, and Stephen attended seventh and eighth grade in Arlington. The next move was to State College, Pennsylvania, where Lester served as a chaplain. He was unhappy in the job, so they moved once again, this time to Michigan, and took a house on the grounds of the Cranbrook Foundation in Bloomfield Hills outside of Detroit. Cranbrook was a huge cultural complex with an art institute, a science institute, and a private girls' school, Kingswood, where Stephen's mother taught. The minister for Christ Church Cranbrook, Robert DeWitt, later became the Episcopalian bishop of Philadelphia. During the 1970s he was the first bishop to ordain women. He was a close friend of the Dobyns family and a strong personal influence on Stephen, because he took the boy seriously as a thinker and gave him books to read at a time when Stephen was floundering in his education. DeWitt guided Stephen toward the existential authors Jean-Paul Sartre, Albert Camus, Samuel Beckett, and Jean Genet. He also urged him to read Rainer Maria Rilke's *Letters to a Young Poet,* a book that eventually helped Stephen locate himself within the world of writers and begin to grasp just what sort of heart and commitment are required to develop innate talent into anything that will be of value beyond one's own ego. Dobyns' lifelong interest in Rilke resulted in one of the central essays that constitute his popular text on poets and poetry, *Best Words, Best Order* (1996).

Like many people of talent in the arts and other fields, Stephen Dobyns was badly suited to traditional educational settings, where he was expected, by his parents, teachers, and most of all by himself, to excel. Instead, he spent his time in classrooms feeling bored, restless, disorganized, and angry. He failed to hand in work. He cut school. He disobeyed rules. He refused to apologize for misdeeds. He was gruesomely shy. His schooling, from kindergarten onward, became a kind of cumulative horror story.

After being kicked out of every class he attended during the elementary years, years when other children try to please and impress their teachers, Stephen arrived at high school, where rebellion and individuation were the roles boys were expected to play. And yet, even here, his rebellion was not the garden variety of smart remarks and backtalk to authorities, nor of adolescent one-upmanship among his peers. In his shyness he abhorred the attention his bad behavior produced. Neither was he trying to insinuate himself among the overwhelming legions of females that seemed designed specifically to impose on his free will and to sweep away any equanimity he could muster.

One may ask then, what was going on inside a child who appears to have existed in a perpetual state of high alert—willing and able to go to war with his surroundings at any moment? In a remarkably candid interview for this essay, Dobyns says that he simply wanted to die. All the time? Yes. Almost every day. Did he have attention deficit disorder or some undiagnosed learning disability? Most likely. Was he clinically depressed? He supposes so, although he was not aware of it as such, and he adds with a laugh, "I don't believe in chemical Calvinism." Did his family create these problems? No. His parents loved and tried to help him. He says, wryly, that they beat their breasts and cried, "Oh how have we failed you?" His younger brother, Chris, responded to the same upbringing by becoming sociable, grounded, and successful. By comparison, Stephen's educational career was tumultuous, wide-ranging, and at times reckless.

He has characterized high school as having been utterly stultifying. He had no interest either in sports or in the classroom. He felt the school authorities treated students as the enemy, so he made sure they knew that he regarded them as such. He made it impossible for them to teach him anything, until finally they kicked him out. (Two of Dobyns' most popular novels—*The Church of Dead Girls* [1997] and *Boy in the Water* [1999]—revolve around high school educational settings and focus in part on kids who fail to fit in.)

Fortunately Stephen had the benefit of a number of individuals along the way who managed to infect him with the belief that a world of ideas and life experiences existed beyond the confines of the school hallways. He had a favorite aunt who was the superintendent of schools for New York. She brought books and read with him. Early on they read Robert Louis Stevenson's *A Child's Garden of Verses* (1885), that secure and beautiful depiction of childhood. He read the fantasies of George Macdonald: *At the Back of the North Wind* (1871) and *The Princess and the Goblins* (1872), works of profound mythic imagination and challenging vocabulary. He read adventure stories of pirates and knights and gained an underlying sense both of the necessity for human heroism and of the inevitability of human conflict, which carried over, thematically, into his writing career. Another powerful influence came by way of his love of music. His father took him to see Duke Ellington and others in concert. He collected jazz and poetry recordings, including those of the poets Kenneth Rexroth and Langston Hughes.

Following graduation from high school in 1959, Dobyns spent a year and a half at Shimer College, part of the University of Chicago at that time. Study there was based on Robert Hutchins' Great Books Theory, and students were required to tackle original works in every field rather than using textbooks. Stephen read Sigmund Freud, Jean Piaget, Karl Marx, Edward Gibbon, and Galileo. In literature, students began with the Greeks, concentrating on Aristotle's *Poetics* and expanding on world literature from there. Lectures were replaced by debate and discussion, which stimulated both Dobyns' ability and willingness to engage in the process. He felt he was getting a lot out of his readings, and yet reading remained a great challenge. Depression further complicated matters. When he went into a two-week slump, he found himself 3,000 pages behind in his studies, so he dropped out of the program.

Six months later he entered Wayne State University, where he studied off and on beginning in 1960 until 1964 when he received his bachelor of arts degree. During this time Dobyns felt emotionally unstable and at loose ends about how to proceed with his life. He applied to the Peace Corps but was turned down because he was seeing a psychiatrist. A way out appeared when he became friends with the poet Peter Cooley, whom he eventually followed to the University of Iowa Writers' Workshop.

Dobyns did not excel at Iowa in any visible way. George Starbuck, Paul Engle, and Mark Strand reigned over the program during this period. Starbuck did not like what Dobyns produced and let him know he considered not passing him at all. Strand was not visible much to his students, but he directed Dobyns toward writers that stimulated and influenced him: Philip Larkin, Alan Dugan, Robert Lowell, Sylvia Plath, Richard Wilbur, William Stafford, and James Wright. Originally the workshop had seventy students, only three of whom were women. One of these was the poet Ellen Bryan Voigt, who became a close friend and remained a professional and artistic associate throughout his career. He received his M.F.A. from Iowa in 1967.

One of the most significant phases of Dobyns' development took place when he was invited to live with a wealthy humanitarian couple on their farm outside of Lansing, Michigan. He describes them as the smartest people he ever met. He considered them his best friends as well as his benefactors. The farm was a haven of books and intellectual stimulation and offered a connection to New York City and the theater scene. Dobyns buckled down and concentrated on his writing. He gained enough confidence so that when he needed a recommendation for a grant, he decided to send his new poems to George Starbuck. Although he was terrified, the effort paid off. Starbuck loved them and wrote back in appreciative terms. In addition, he promised to recommend the manuscript to a publisher as soon as it was complete.

Starbuck first brought the poems to the attention of the poet Anne Sexton, who did not like them. However, the editor Harry Ford at Atheneum accepted them for publication. Atheneum was the premier publisher for poetry of that day—and the publisher that brought out Robert Lowell, Mark Strand, Donald Justice, James Merrill, Richard Howard, and other poets whom Dobyns most admired. Dobyns' first collection, *Concurring Beasts* (1972), took three years to come out, but it launched his career and landed him the Lamont Prize for Poetry.

Dobyns worked hard to survive financially during this period. He taught English at the State University of New York at Brockport during the 1968 academic year and then took a job as a reporter for the *Detroit News* for two years, beginning in 1969, before turning full-time to freelance writing and editing in 1971. He has maintained that he learned more about style and discipline from working as a journalist than he did from all of his schooling combined. Furthermore, as an investigative reporter he saw the dark and sordid reality of criminal behavior and observed just how frequently that behavior bleeds into elements of what is considered respectable society. He noted that the human heart is the human heart, despite its many disguises. Representing the human psyche in its entirety—at times with disgust and at times with mercy, but always faithfully—became the main focus of his many works.

By writing for news deadlines in the nonliterary, nonacademic world, Dobyns learned to get to the heart of whatever he was saying quickly and clearly. The common reader had neither the time nor the interest to wade through linguistic flourishes or intellectual constructs. Newspaper readers valued story, clarity, a democratic voice, and whenever possible, the gift of a laugh. And these became the permanent hallmarks of Dobyns' style, no matter what his genre: poetry, essay, short story, or novel.

ESSAYS

In 1996 Dobyns published *Best Words, Best Order: Essays on Poetry,* a collection of essays that discuss issues in his own writing life. Some of the essays developed from lectures given at Warren Wilson College in Asheville, North Carolina, and elsewhere. The reader receives the benefit of thirty-five years of study, as well as the practical insights Dobyns developed as he worked with young writers who attended the Syracuse Writers Program under his auspices (and other programs across the country). The first essay, "Deceptions," exposes what Dobyns sees as the basic lies that undeveloped writers tend to believe, lies that render their work obscure and uninteresting. It asserts the sometimes unpopular notion that the writer and his product are not the final goal of art. The goal is the communication possible between minds. He describes art as the clearest nonphysical way that emotion can pass from one person to another, and he insists the reader must participate in this process rather than simply witness the writers' event. To the extent that the artist is unwilling or unable to involve the audience, he fails. He points out the danger of not learning to hear one's own words as others do by recalling a line from a student poem in which the author attempted to create a poignant scene of young men sharing a cigarette the night before they must leave for war: "We passed our butts from mouth to mouth." Although this line deserves immortality, it cannot have served the poet's original intention very well. The essay is a prescription for writers who wish to avoid both solipsism and narcissism, and a scolding for those who do not.

Another essay, "Notes on Free Verse," undertakes the difficult task of defining the difference between free verse and traditional verse. Dobyns opens the essay with a paragraph that takes great pains to simplify the bewildering issues of prosody:

> Consider two systems of poetry. In the first, the reader anticipates the rhythmic direction of the poem, finds his or her anticipation verified by the reading experience and feels a sense of gratification. In the second, the reader either can't anticipate or anticipates incorrectly, while being constantly surprised with unexpected patterns and repetitions. The first system, generally speaking, is the system of traditionally metered verse. The second is the system of free verse.... Free verse employs a prosody governed by the unexpected.

Dobyns goes on to demonstrate that free verse is not somehow the antithesis of traditional verse, nor is it the absence of rhyme, meter, or indeed any other element of form. He traces the historical development of free verse in French, English, and American poetry and describes the governing impulses behind various literary movements such as symbolism, imagism, acmeism, and modernism. He highlights some of the masters whose art both inspired and articulated the political and moral values of their times, including Charles-Pierre Baudelaire, Osip Mandelstam, Walt Whitman, William Butler Yeats, T. S. Eliot, and William Carlos Williams. He leaves the reader with the analytical tools to hold free verse accountable to standards of excellence, and the willingness to do so.

Four of the essays in this collection capture the essential lives of individual writers who embody what Dobyns sees as the practical and moral attributes necessary to achieving stature as an artist: "Rilke's Growth as a Poet" tracks the almost superhuman efforts of a man who regarded the production of art as a holy calling and who had to battle his own psychological paralysis when faced with the perfection he observed in Auguste Rodin's achievements. Dobyns uses Rilke to model the process by which an artist can wrestle with the reclusive subconscious and drag its vitality kicking and screaming into the light of day, where it can serve the artist's work.

In "Chekhov's Sense of Writing as Seen Through His Letters" Dobyns provides an intimate examination of Anton Chekhov's battle to overcome what he regarded as the "slave within," by which he meant any tendency to succumb to vanity, sloth, or brutality. Dobyns highlights the underpinnings of Chekhov's philosophy, including his assertion that humility is a virtue developed by appreciating the magnitude and perfection of God and his Creation and that it must not be confused with a sense of worthlessness that comes from self-depreciation in comparison with others, or a failure to value the abilities God gives to each man. Chekhov believed that a person could perform great things in art and life only if he first mastered himself and then applied his talents with courage and vigor.

In "Mandelstam: The Poem as Event" Dobyns traces the origin of that poet's concept of how the visible and invisible worlds represent each other. He connects Mandelstam to Baudelaire, and to Emanuel Swedenborg's doctrine of "correspondences," which posits that the natural world can be read as a metaphor for the spiritual world as well as for the self. Mandelstam came to regard the process of writing not only as creative in the usual sense of that word but also as regenerative in terms of the human spirit. He insisted on the absolute reality of the spiritual realm in his claim that you should "love the existence of a thing more than the thing itself, and your own existence more than yourself."

In his essay "Ritsos and the Metaphysical Moment," Dobyns illustrates Ritsos' intense response to a metaphysical reality by highlighting a series of his poems. In each case, an inner mystery stirs the poet's soul, and he replies by bearing witness to the inner event in terms of some outer occasion—a sick man in a restaurant perceives his coming death, the colors in a sunset stir a speaker's vague anguish and longing, the leaves of a tree rustle and then fall still. Each detail is selected to indicate a vibrant, almost physical energy that flows between plains of visible and invisible realities. Dobyns describes how Ritsos fits into the long tradition of those who view the cosmos in terms of "sympathetic affinities," as the Renaissance oc-cultists termed the phenomenon, or, once again, the "correspondences" between two worlds detailed in Swedenborgian philosophy. In the poem "Maybe, Someday," Ritsos defines the poet's job as using language to force the reader to "see what he has seen," says Dobyns, and thereby reduce the intrinsic isolation of the poet as well as the reader. This can be done only when the poet strives to achieve the "true" word, the word that insists on alerting the reader to the presence of that inner event. Dobyns quotes Ritsos' poem "The Meaning of Simplicity": "Every word is a doorway / to a meeting, one often cancelled."(Dobyns points out that for Ritsos, the image a poem describes can never become an end in itself, as it did with the extremists of the symbolist movement. Neither can the poet be said to succeed if only he experiences the intensity of the inner event. He must deal in common language and trigger the reader's inner world. He does not attempt to define the mystery of that inner world, but rather his aim is to bear witness to its existence and to challenge the reader into a parallel experience of his own.

SHORT STORIES

Eating Naked, a collection of Dobyns' short stories that came out in 2000, received little media attention. The *New York Times* did not mention its publication, despite the fact that two of the stories appeared in the *Best American Short Stories* series and two others won Pushcart Prizes. However, the literary journal *Southern Review* awarded it Best First Book of Short Stories for 2001; editions of the book were published in England, Holland, and Spain; and a British company immediately bought film rights to the stories. For the most part, the central characters in each story are unexceptional in terms of talent, morality, careers, or life situations. Yet, in each case, they wind up desperately entangled in events brought about by their very mediocrity: events in the stories are driven by the compulsions, thoughtlessness, and ignorance of the all-too-familiar man in the streets. On the one hand, Dobyns presents a citizenry that fails in all sorts of intriguing ways to follow Henry David Thoreau's dictum that human beings ought to live deliberately. Or, on the other hand, his characters pursue versions of what Rilke defined as "the unlived life of which one may die." Dobyns' egalitarian treatment of a wide range of personalities does not suggest that human beings in general are necessarily capable of a great deal more than they exhibit. Dobyns' stories reflect a type of authorial sensibility adroitly described by Chekhov, who wrote that "it is not the writer's job to solve such problems as God, pessimism, etc. His job is merely to record who, under what conditions, said or thought what about God or pessimism. The artist is not meant to be the judge of his characters and what they say" (from *Chekhov's Life and Thought: Selected Letters and Commentary,* 1975).

In "Part of the Story" Dobyns has fun with one of his recurrent themes, the issue of making intentional choices in life. The protagonist is a woman who has borne five children by various men and decided (if decision making can be attributed to one who is incapable of personal reflection) to place each of them up for adoption at birth. The story features a morning when the five adults convene for the purpose of meeting their mother and one another for the first time. Naturally the fabric of their expectations is complex, and the reader is treated to almost unendurable levels of irony as Dobyns reveals each personality against the backdrop of what is already known about the mother's deficiencies. Tragic, hilarious, and preposterous as the whole setup is, Dobyns never permits the reader the right to dismiss any of these pathetic characters, especially the promiscuous and irresponsible mother. Instead one has to marvel that such stupidity, inherent as well as self-imposed, can result in ongoing lives instead of annihilation—can result in future generations and, perhaps most surprising of all, what appears to be functional careers. The crowning touch is the fact that the woman's maternal tenderness, when faced with her children's wish to learn details of their fathers, produces spontaneous and extravagant falsehoods of lineage intended to supersede the unpleasant little detail of their abandonment and provide them with an immediate wealth of self-esteem. The woman is so creative that one wonders briefly if the whole human race might not more successfully try this approach rather than pursuing the arduous and often unsuccessful efforts of responsible child rearing. In this and many of the sixteen stories that comprise this collection, Dobyns practices the art of taking a mundane idea that any reader will accept and then developing it by means of logical progression, until the reader arrives at an absurd conclusion. Readers find themselves assenting to a prosaic journey that seems almost familiar in its rightness—until they arrive at the surprise, and sometimes the scandal, of the destination.

THE NOVELS

Mystery buffs comprise perhaps the largest constituency of Dobyns' reading public. Between 1976 and 1998 he offered them a string of ten "Saratoga" mysteries that feature a likable detective, Charlie Bradshaw. He is intelligent but not good-looking. He has many everyday problems: trouble with women, trouble with cars, trouble with jobs. He is altogether unheroic—an outsider in the glamorous profession of sleuthing. The stories cover a certain period in Charlie's life, and eventually the narrative is taken over by his assistant, Victor Plotts.

Dobyns has said that he enjoyed writing the detective series and that the Saratoga stories were a blessing financially a number of times when his bank account hit the two-figure mark. One of the appeals of the mystery genre is that solving murders suggests control in the face of death—you have a murder, and you have a solution. Producing a mystery novel is the ultimate act of distancing death. One simply turns murder into an entertainment, into a rational exercise, and ultimately, in Dobyns' case, into a source of income.

Apart from the mystery series, this essay will touch on four of Dobyns' novels that share certain characteristics. Each novel presents an unusually large cast of characters. The reader has the impression that he must keep alert or he will fall too far behind to recognize the names, personalities, and relationships. This tension, in each case, is appropriate to the world Dobyns is creating, which is a world on the verge of chaos in many respects. It is in the presence of this chaos that mankind must face the reality of death. Death as a fact, as a terror, and most of all as a metaphor permeates all of Dobyns' work. A glance at his choice of subject matter, titles, and even genres (e.g., murder mysteries) might lead one to conclude that he is obsessed with death. However, his treatment of death does not emphasize the morbid. Rather he places a frantic call for life, appetite, and engagement. He returns again and again to the question "How does one live?" Much of the intrigue of these works is the exercise of observing how a host of individuals react to pressure—how they use or fail to use talent. Will they attempt to live intentionally and participate in their fate, or will they be passive and dumbfounded? One often has the impression that the characters' fates are impossibly larger than their individual wills, suggesting that the human experience, no matter how we choose to engage in it, is overwhelming. For the most part there is little serenity described in these works, for individuals, relationships, or communities as a whole. Chaos is always a factor in Dobyns' works.

AFTER SHOCKS, NEAR ESCAPES

In *After Shocks, Near Escapes* (1991), the primary source of chaos is nature itself. Dobyns sets this fiction in Chile during the earthquake of 1960. He interviewed a great many people who lived through that catastrophe, including the multigenerational family of his wife, Isabel Bize. True to his journalistic training, Dobyns presents the events of the novel in exhaustive concrete detail, faithfully recounted by the narrator Lucy Droppelman, who looks back thirty years to a time when she was eight years old and the ordered world of her Chilean village and clan exploded in a summer of earthquakes and social disintegration. The earthquake provides the ultimate metaphor for what might be called the defining moment in life: an event (whether internal or external) after which the psyche of the individual (or of the society) can never again proceed in familiar ways. The drama of such an event is that people are forced to choose to live because life no longer simply happens to them. In the case of the earthquake, every routine of employment, transportation, economy, and family life is disrupted. Nature, even the physical landscape, proceeds to devour itself as hillsides slide into fissures and rivers chew up their banks. Lakes are drained, exposing a previously hidden history of local vehicles and carcasses. Animals grow crazed, vicious, or simply unrecognizable in their behaviors, a spectacle that is particularly chilling for their human counterparts. Dobyns has a fondness for those details that alarm the senses and knock the reader off balance: cows and chickens that die of heart attacks, coffins jittering free of the chapel and bouncing along the street, a railroad track that undulates like a serpent. Such details strike the reader as utterly bizarre, and yet they are no more than minutely accurate observations of a reality we have not yet witnessed. Or, in Dobyns' view, they are a metaphor for the realms in our own psyches that we are habitually at great pains to ignore.

The defining moment, as it occurs in this novel, is not only about loss by any means. After the immediate threat of annihilation passes, the earthquake also brings about opportunity, exhilaration, and possible paradigm shifts within the society:

> Not only were we alive but there was also the sense that we had been freed from the daily world. There would be no school and our places of work had been destroyed. Despite our losses and grief and our many fears, there was also a sort of giddiness. . . . while the world which held us in bondage had received a serious blow.

The destruction caused by the earthquake is utterly democratic, affecting all classes alike. It reduces most of the population to a subsistence level where they must forage for food and clothing and where they must rely on their own resources and stamina. Under these circumstances many of the characters, old and young, rise up and take hold. One notable exception is Lucy's uncle Walterio, a man who is so indecisive and lacking in self-direction that he allows others to finish his sentences. He is self-indulgent and passive, and when the world turns to chaos around him, he simply recedes into compulsive eating and paralysis. He has no energy either to compete with others or to compel himself. He had succumbed to his mother's loving domination prior to the catastrophe, and afterward he regresses toward a kind of chubby, middle-aged babyhood. By contrast, Uncle Freddy responds to life as a moment-to-moment opportunity for entrepreneurial creativity. He lives with gusto, analyzing every situation in terms of what people need and how he can provide it for them and make a profit. Freddy generates possibilities for other people as well as for himself, offering hope of jobs, wealth, and new circumstances. He is a force for intentional change.

Dalila, Uncle Helmut's beautiful, narcissistic wife, however, represents a force for unintentional change. She idly seduces every male with enough testosterone to respond to her. She causes more disruption of the relationships in Lucy's family than the earthquake does. She does this not so much from a desire for conquest as from an inability to engage in life except through flirtation. She cannot recover from the loss of her house and her pretty things, nor can she imagine a new future. She cannot even make intentional use of her beauty to win lasting power or influence. Instead she plays men off against one another and alienates women in an effort to stave off perpetual boredom. She even finds death boring. Her creative knack is to generate a kind of unrest that disturbs the status quo and results in random and undirected change.

In direct contrast to Dalila is the matriarchal hub of the entire clan, the grandmother. She is the single strongest force for stability in the book. She dominates the lives of all her children as well as her siblings by means of food, religion, and household routines, even when the household itself no longer exists. She is enormously powerful in the face of disaster because of her monomania for family togetherness. She regards her children and grandchildren as appendages of herself and cannot imagine that any of them might hold a worldview that differs from her own, which is that human beings live a dual existence that spans the material and the metaphysical worlds. She holds an unshakeable belief that her deceased relatives scamper about in proximity to worldly activities (but occupying their own sphere), so that after the earthquake makes such a mess of the visible world, it is only a matter of practicality that she prepare to take up life in the other world just as soon as she can assemble everyone for the transition. The fact that not everyone wants to die immediately strikes her as most unimportant because God and herself generally get their way when running things.

The defining moment featured in *After Shocks* signals a contrast more wide-ranging than any of Dobyns' other works because the world of Chilean society and particularly the family unit appear to have been intact prior to the earthquake and subsequent events of the story. This is not to suggest that the particular family under scrutiny is healthy in psychological terms. But there is an underlying assumption that familial tenderness and societal integration are possible, somewhere, at some time. *After Shocks* is a book that allows for hope regarding the human condition, a level of hope that the author does not attempt to re-create in his other novels.

Ultimately the earthquake itself creates a world without façades. With the normal contexts of architecture, employment, and class expectations swept away, human nature is revealed as a series of needs and longings. But surprisingly, it is not the need for food and shelter that surfaces as the greatest motivator in the book. Rather, it is the need to be connected, to locate oneself in relation to other people, that occupies the attention of the narrator and that constitutes the vast majority of her observations regarding the rest of the characters. In *After Shocks,* Dobyns warns the reader that under normal circumstances, the routines of daily life, including the production and maintenance of wealth, distract us from reflecting upon our basic emotional needs and upon what we require in order to feel as if we are not already dead. Dobyns suggests that our obsession with façades, or with how we appear to one another (and to ourselves), dominates and deadens our deeper humanity. When our façades are wrenched from our stubborn grasp, whether by natural disaster, personal loss, or simply by life's slow process of learning to live authentically, only then can we be said to be among the living. The issue of façades and disguises dominates the next novel discussed.

THE WRESTLER'S CRUEL STUDY

In *The Wrestler's Cruel Study* (1993) Dobyns offers comedy rather than hope. Once again the book is set in chaos, but this time society, rather than nature, is the cause. The novel's dauntingly giant cast of characters includes a menagerie of so-called professional wrestlers, each with a stage name and persona as well as an everyday identity. Other characters include the so-called peacekeepers—the detectives Gapski and Brodski, who are as indistinguishable from one another as Tweedle Dum and Tweedle Dee, despite their perpetual rivalry to out perform each other; the so-called identical twins—Rose White and Violet White, who represent moral opposites but who are interchangeable in many respects; and various gangs of thugs who take their battle cries, names, and costumes from competing philosophical and religious movements—the Valentinians, the Cainites, and the Tertullian Christians all debate the finer points of divine justice and the origin of evil by means of guns and clubs.

Dobyns sets up a world where all identities, allegiances, and occupations are façades, or, as the vaudevillian wrestling coach Muldoon would say, "gimmicks." It is a world of frenetic activity, car chases, brawls, crowd scenes, and orgies on the external level, contrasted with utter stasis on the internal or psychological level. Despite the vehement identification of characters with their chosen ideologies, almost no actual thinking takes place among them. Most of the characters do not attempt to "strike through the mask," to use Herman Melville's expression. They do not analyze their own behaviors or anyone else's. They do not live deliberately.

Three characters in the novel transcend this comic-book quality and engage in self-reflection; thus, they are aware that they may not be living authentically. These characters to some extent live intentionally and make decisions by weighing consequences. One such character is Muldoon, who views all of human action as comprising layers of pretense. His occupation is to train the wrestlers and create theatrical extravaganzas for audiences. He prides himself on seeing through the layers of life in general and being able to manipulate pretense, but he is not sure there is any core within: "Years ago I believed in Gimmick in the service of truth," he says. "Now I believe only in Gimmick."

Another such character is Wally Walski, who has the wit to understand that he is an unremarkable little man with a shrewish wife, and who has the will to have a heck of a good time anyway. He chooses to accept his wife's bullying for the sake of her occasional kindness. Wally's adventures form a subplot (one among many!) that is narrated like a traditional fairy tale. He finds a magic coin. He does a good deed. He is granted wishes, and all should be well with him and his wife, but naturally it is not. The wife keeps sending him back to his benefactor with higher demands. Dobyns replaces the traditional stock elements of the fairy-tale genre with contemporary figures. The source of good fortune and high living is not a genie but a mysterious mob boss who speaks like a moral philosopher and warns repeatedly against the dangers of overstepping one's appropriate station in life.

The hero of the book is the idealist Michael Marmaduke, or Marduk the Magnificent when he is in his wrestling gear and silver elf boots. He would very much like to be a real-life hero, but he doubts his own courage and stamina. He is afraid of snakes and weapons and loud noises, and he detests violence. Unfortunately, his fiancée, Rose White, has been abducted by unsavory men in gorilla outfits, and he has to rescue her, even though he knows perfectly well that his apparent bravery and apparent prowess are simply that. During the course of the book he must encounter and embrace his dark and violent side if he wishes to be a hero, which is a serious theme underlying the comic and farce elements of the story.

In his introduction to the novel, Dobyns quotes Roland Barthes in suggesting why the activity of wrestling makes such an apt metaphor for living: "It is the euphoria of men raised for a while above . . . the ambiguity of everyday situations and placed before . . . unequivocal Nature, in which signs at last correspond to causes." Although Dobyns demonstrates throughout most of his works that the core of human life is conflict, he playfully trivializes the readers' commitment to that premise in *The Wrestler's Cruel Study* by using not legitimate wrestling but rather the pseudowrestling of the World Wrestling Federation as his overarching metaphor. Probably nowhere in modern society has such a premium been placed on façade and malarkey as in the scripted buffoonery of Saturday night wrestling. If the nature of human struggle amounts to nothing more serious than the body slams and neck wringing of the dandified wrestlers, then Muldoon is speaking for Dobyns when he says, "Peel the onion and there is always more until at last there is nothing—just a smell on the fingers and a tear in the eye." This might be read as the author's argument for nihilism, except that Muldoon also discredits himself as the ultimate spokesperson for truth and authenticity when he quotes Friedrich Nietzsche as saying, "To talk about oneself a great deal is also a way of concealing oneself."

THE CHURCH OF DEAD GIRLS

Authenticity, self-knowledge, and getting beyond appearances become the theme of Dobyns' next major novel, *The Church of Dead Girls* (1997). In this case the identity of a whole town is the novel's subject. The story is a journey from community complaisance and self-satisfaction to community awareness of its own dysfunction, in a process initiated by Franklin Moore, a newspaper editor who starts to shake things up by printing interviews of his fellow citizens in regard to social issues. These interviews often reveal more personal fragility and emotional distress than the population wants to ponder. The public issues under discussion become overshadowed by the intensity of individual responses and all the personal turmoil they inadvertently reveal. Coupled with Franklin's interviews are his aggressive editorials that hold the town council and various public officials accountable for failing to harness public funds in promoting social change. The effect of his journalism is that the population grows edgy and more self-aware. At this point, the novel's defining moment occurs, when the first of four terrifying abductions take place. A beautiful adolescent girl is kidnapped and murdered. The shock of the event changes the community's sense of its own identity and the fact of its own security forever.

At first the murder turns all eyes outward to the "real world," where horrible evil is presumed to exist, and the community asks the question "How can we protect ourselves from those others?" However, as the crimes continue it becomes increasingly clear to the townspeople that the evildoer lives among them. The question then transforms into "How can we protect ourselves from our neighbors?" As the official process of investigation churns up more and more details of rampant local perversions and misdeeds, the question evolves to the author's ultimate inquiry: "How can we protect ourselves from ourselves?" *The Church of Dead Girls* enjoyed greater popular success than anything else Dobyns had yet written. It was translated into nineteen languages, earned more than three times as much as all of Dobyns' other works combined, and bought him time to write poetry.

BOY IN THE WATER

In *Boy in the Water* (1999), Dobyns again draws on his reportorial crime background. Again he studies the psychological repercussions caused by murder, fear, and suspicion within a community—this time an educational institution. But what intrigues the reader in this book is not the central murder within the community, although this propels the plot of the story. The defining moment occurs in the life of the protagonist, Jim Hawthorne, a year prior to the events of the tale, when he could not rescue his wife and daughter from burning to death. The fact that he was having an affair at the time compounds his sense of guilt. He enters the community as one of society's walking dead, or those who sustain such severe personal and psychological trauma that they must wrest daily life by sheer force of will from the abyss of despair and the appearance that living is meaningless. He chooses to throw himself into a situation where he can be either buried alive in a lost cause or else perhaps redeemed in some sense. He does not expect to find happiness, only respite from his demons. Dobyns has facility in creating characters from this category, people who must choose to live, to put one foot in front of the other, as a daily exercise in heroism, because they do not possess whatever it is that seduces the rest of the race to keep living. It is a psychological state of isolation that lies at the core of much of Dobyns' work in the genre of poetry.

POETRY

A colleague once told Dobyns about following a cluster of young intellectuals out of a poetry reading. The poet of the evening read poems that were so dense and involuted that he communicated nothing to the audience beyond the fact that he was filled with strong emotions and that he was an intellectual giant. He wept and ranted and experienced enlightenment, but the audience did not. A few of the students admitted they had no idea what this poet was talking about, and then Stephen Dobyns' name came up. "Oh him," someone said with a dismissive gesture, "He's so accessible." Dobyns' poems are indeed "accessible" to an audience—and this is the poet's hope, his intention, and his relentless labor. Dobyns parts company with the aesthetics as well as the intentions of certain contemporary poets who he considers to be "surface poets" or poets of "apparent complexity," among whose ranks he places John Ashbery, James Merrill, and Jorie Graham. He feels their poems have too little to do with the reader or with the question "how do we live?" He has quoted Philip Larkin's criticism of such poets: "They neither help me to live nor to endure."

Despite the apparent simplicity of Dobyns' work, there is nothing "easy" in his poems: the concrete subject matter is often unsettling, the metaphors demanding, and the underlying premises consistently dark. The fact that readers can "find their way" (to use Dobyns' phrase) within his poems is because Dobyns employs those methods in his craft that will invite the reader into his world: He chooses the vocabulary of common discourse; he adopts an inclusive tone of address; he proceeds (or pretends to proceed) according to rhetorical logic; he captivates by surprises of sound, sense, and humor; and most endearingly, he tells stories. In a poem from *Cemetery Nights* (1987) called "How To Like It," one can see all these methods at work:

> These are the first days of fall. The wind
> at evening smells of roads still to be traveled,
> . . . .
> . . . like an unsettled feeling in the blood,
> the desire to get in a car and just keep driving.

The tone here is invitational as he describes a scene we all can inhabit, in a language we find familiar. We know this season, the actual and the metaphorical—the fall with its restlessness in the blood. The voice credits the reader with sensitivities equal to its own. Now the story takes off:

> A man and a dog descend their front steps.
> The dog says, Let's go downtown and get crazy
>   drunk.

> Let's tip over all the trash cans we can find.
> This is how dogs deal with the prospect of
>   change.

Now the reader clearly is being offered whimsy and entertainment. The reader may chuckle in agreement and simultaneously acknowledge that one cannot possibly accept what is being told in such matter-of-fact terms as matters of fact at all. The dog is playing a role in the poem and speaking for a charming but somehow lesser aspect of the man's psyche—of the human psyche. We immediately accept a place within a contemporary fable, knowing we are being led by the nose, and curious to be led further. Dobyns is in psychological control of the reader. Now the message darkens rapidly, although we continue to be amused because it is hard to shake off the silliness of the dog's comments:

> But in his sense of the season, the man is struck
> by the oppressiveness of his past, how his
>   memories
> which were shifting and fluid have grown more
>   solid
> until it seems he can see remembered faces
> caught up among the dark places in the trees.

Loss, regret—the man is growing morose, almost unreachable in his despondency. He is immobilized by his reflections (and will grow more so as the poem progresses). So the dog grows more urgent and, by way of contrast, more comic: "The dog says, Let's pick up some girls and just / rip off their clothes. Let's dig holes everywhere."

Cruise for girls or dig holes in the ground? The dog, or the man's primitive instincts, regards these as equal options in terms of providing distraction from the feelings of foreboding. The reader is likely to be laughing with pleasure at such juxtaposition. But despite the laugh, one is increasingly haunted by the lyrical description of the man's predicament. The reader takes in a series of ordinary things as he notices them—a wisp of cloud across the face of the moon, the man's house, the hills outside of town—all of which confirm his melancholy and his inability to exert himself:

> . . . He thinks of driving
> on that road and the dusty smell of the car
> heater which hasn't been used since last winter.

It becomes clear to the reader at this point that paralysis is the subject. Why is the man paralyzed? Is he like T. S. Eliot's Prufrock, caught up in chronic vacillation from intellectual confusion? No, his plight is a bit sadder than that. Ideas are not the problem. It is his desires that constitute the problem; not the mind but the will is hopelessly pitted against itself. His heart is confused, and he does not believe in the possibility of any of the pleasures available to him because he knows his desires will never let up. He obsesses on details, for the remainder of the poem, concerning a journey he will not undertake. Meanwhile the dog exerts heroic (for a dog) efforts to rouse him: "The dog says, Let's go down to the diner and sniff / people's legs. Let's stuff ourselves on burgers."

Eventually, the dog internalizes the man's despair and suggests they do nothing at all. After all, only the dog has been talking in this relationship. The man has neither talked nor listened. He is isolated by his pain. Suddenly the narrator takes over and cries out in a voice that speaks for the man and the audience and the poet at once:

> How is it possible to want so many things
> and still want nothing? The man wants to sleep
> and wants to hit his head again and again
> against a wall. Why is it all so difficult?

The poet's answer, in a sense, is the answer of the Stoics. Simply abide it. This is not a transformational solution, but at least it creates community, which is a high priority in Dobyns' value system. Man and dog make a sandwich together:

> . . . and that's where the man's
> wife finds him, staring into the refrigerator
> as if into the place where the answers are
>   kept . . .

But Dobyns only alludes to answers. He does not articulate them. Instead he suggests how helpful they could be in easing our discomfort, if only they existed. He confirms only that our longing is universal, that we are in good company in our unknowing.

He ends the poem by enumerating our common and urgent questions: Why get up in the morning? How is it possible to sleep at night? What comes next? But the final question is of a different order from the rest because it subtly implies a philosophical easement for the others. That question, the tough challenge that can preserve sanity in the face of our bewildering human existence, is, How to like it?

What is it in our humanity that Dobyns sees as posing the greatest threat to our peace and contentment, to our ability to lead decent lives? Time and again it is Desire that he focuses on in his poems. Not the gentle sort of pleasures that make days pass but runaway passions, desires without limits, compulsions that tear us apart and wear down our dignity. Dobyns suggests that anything can become an obsession if we allow it. In "Bowlers Anonymous" from *Cemetery Nights* he takes a comic look at a collection of miserable souls who convene from midnight to six at bowling alleys in order to resist their riotously bizarre addictions: The chicken molesters, the bicycle-seat sniffers, the lady who likes Great Danes, and the rest, are just teachers, plumbers, and grocers, apart from the lusts that torment them. In a similar vein, "Tenderly," from *Velocities* (1994), tells the story of a man who walks into an upscale restaurant, leaps onto a tabletop, grabs a butter knife, and begins trying to saw off his member. The dining public prefers to pretend nothing out of the ordinary is under way. It is only at the time of their deaths that those onlookers will recall the man as

> . . . a symbol of having had precisely
> enough, of slipping over the edge, of being whipped
>
> about the chops . . . of reacting
> with a rash mutiny against the tyranny of desire.

The tyranny of desire is treated in a more philosophical, even charming light in "The Belly," a poem from *Body Traffic* (1990): "The belly puts on a bright red wig . . . a pair of glasses . . . a hat of crushed felt . . . With its perfect disguise it is invited everywhere." This character demonstrates the vast distance between our civilized manners and our underlying appetites by revealing the duality involved in a conversation with a beautiful woman, in which the phrase "In my most considered opinion . . ." must be translated as the crudest solicitation of sex! Yet "The Body's Curse," from the same collection, offers understanding for the little shortcomings of our sensual natures:

> Greed, gluttony, sloth—but don't they all
> go back to loneliness, that sense of a barrier
>
> between oneself and others?

William Butler Yeats suggested that poets have core themes to which they return throughout their careers and that these themes spring from an inward moral battle: "Of our disagreements with others we make rhetoric. Of our disagreements with ourselves we make poetry." Dobyns' core themes relate to the question that underlies all moral philosophy, which is simply, How does one live? Or to enumerate his issues more specifically: In the face of our insatiable human appetites, in the face of persistent human depravity, in the face of inevitable death, how does one live so that our lives matter? At times the question surfaces as a hopeless lament, "How does one live?" At times it is a charge to take action, echoing Rilke's line "You must change your life!" But most often it is an injunction toward stoicism, or the process of simply hanging on in life with dignity and honor.

The critic Peter Stitt has suggested that Dobyns' use of narrative as a poetic device developed midway through his career, beginning with *The Balthus Poems* (1982). He believes that Dobyns' investigation into the nature of poetry (an investigation that produced his essays on the craft, which were collected as *Best Words Best Order*) allowed him to clarify his own path, particularly in how he chooses to manage time within his poetry. The result is a move toward narrative. He further suggests that Dobyns' three previous books of poetry failed due to excessive didacticism. Although the critical honors awarded those books would argue against classifying them as failures, it is true that Dobyns' readership expanded considerably with the next four collections: *Black Dog, Red Dog* (1984); *Cemetery Nights* (1987); *Body Traffic* (1990), and *Common Carnage* (1996).

What one critic calls didacticism in Dobyns' poems, others call guidance, wisdom, or a roadmap for living. Unquestionably, Dobyns is given to arriving at conclusions and trying to make some sort of sense, at least temporarily, of our disrupted culture. Robert Spector of *Saturday Review* says, "Dobyns looks warily at the chaotic world, dislikes what he sees, and responds to its disorder in crisply controlled verse keyed to a sardonic wit one scale above cynicism." Anthony Libby reviewed *Velocities: New and Selected Poems, 1966–1992* (1994) in the *New York Times Book Review,* saying Dobyns' "poetry of social commentary . . . is marked more by horror than by ideology." In his review of *Common Carnage* for *Poetry,* Bill Christophersen said that the poetry "blends philosophical musings with daft, deft metaphors and cheeky vernacular . . . to rib us into thought."

Dobyns gives a hint about one of his methods for composing his poems. In the afterword to *Velocities* he describes how he used static objects (in this case the paintings of Balthus) as an occasion to develop personal metaphors that would appear free from the lyrical first-person voice. One can assume that he was engaging in what Rilke called "gazing," which Dobyns later described in his essay about Rilke's life and methods. "Gazing is such a wonderful thing," wrote Rilke, when one can discipline the mind to dwell on an object with full attention. "With it we are turned completely outward but just when we are most so, things seem to be going on within us that have waited longingly to be unobserved. . . . their meaning is growing up in the object." The creation and harnessing of metaphor is one of Dobyns' strongest suits as a poet. But it is always a tool. He continues to explore the possibilities of metaphor from book to book, just as he does the possibilities of narrative, so they can be employed to bring about the lyrical moments that constitute the heart of the poems.

Some of the stories Dobyns elects to tell are horrifying indeed. In "The Gun," which opens the book *Black Dog, Red Dog,* the reader is seduced into witnessing the sexual molestation of a little boy by an older boy. The opening scene moves from innocence to perversion in a few lines, a sequence so rapid that we are dragged into it, as it were, against our wills:

Late afternoon light slices through the dormer
  window
to your place on the floor next to a stack of
  comics.
Across from you is a boy who . . .
    . . . is telling you to pull down your pants
You tell him you don't want to. His mother is out
and you are alone in the house. He has given you
  a Coke,
let you smoke . . .

The poem touches on several of Dobyns' recurrent themes: the innate depravity of human beings, the loss of innocence, and human helplessness in the face of our own desires. One of the unsettling aspects of this poem is that Dobyns does not permit the reader to marginalize the potential molester, who is after all only a pathetic eleven year old who is left unsupervised by his mother. Both boys are victims. The poem is able to pinpoint a defining moment in the life of the narrator, the boy, the audience, and the poet simultaneously because Dobyns conflates the several points of view by means of rhetorical control. As the reader exits the poem, the little boy stands out in the street with his urine-soaked pants, the symbol for his terror and his diminishment, while the narrator asks: "Where is that sense of the world you woke with / this morning? Now it is smaller. Now it has gone away."

Dobyns has commented that he attempted in this collection to free himself of the compulsion to appear thoroughly noble to the reading public. One of his goals as a poet is to embrace human totality and not simply the more civilized masks of the superego. The critic Jim Elledge assumes the book is fairly autobiographical, noting that Dobyns reveals his own secrets and hurts: "Although the nostalgic impulse asserts itself in this poem or that, it affords him no respite. Instead it serves only to underscore his pain. . . . He is left, and he leaves us with his unflinching vision, which we may not like, but whose power and honesty we cannot deny." From the same book, the poem "Bleeder" describes how kids at a camp are both intrigued and repulsed by a boy with hemophilia, in thrall to their own desire to see him bleed: "He made us want to hurt him so much we hurt / ourselves instead." In his review of *Black Dog, Red Dog* for the *New York Times,* Andy Brumer highlights lines from the title poem to show how Dobyns uses images to demonstrate "how ruthlessly we turn on ourselves and others when our animal natures aren't fully acknowledged and integrated. This is a harrowing book, not meant to please but to instruct": in the poem "Black Dog, Red Dog," the self is projected as a red sky above the darkening earth,

> . . . and they seem poised
> like two animals that have always hated each
>   other,
> each fiercely wanting to tear out the other's
>   throat:
> black dog, red dog—now more despairing, more
>   resolved.

Dobyns insists on acknowledging, even if he does not embrace, the full gamut of human emotions. He attempts also to maintain a modest hope that human beings may manage to rise above their worst natures.

In general, the two volumes that followed *Black Dog, Red Dog* incorporated more humor and more narrative distance. In the title poem from *Cemetery Nights* the vision of skeletons attempting to copulate—attempting at last to abandon themselves to the ways of the flesh when they have no flesh—speaks to the theme of human appetites. Despite the title, the collection obsesses on life, not death. In *Body Traffic* Dobyns frequently makes merry with the human body. David Kirby has pointed out Dobyns' use of humor in this book, which, he says, "functions not as a mere stylistic quality but as a mode of perception." Kirby says the poet is as fascinated with the body as St. Augustine, but unlike the church fathers he "adores the body . . . devoting individual poems to the nose, the nails, the feet. The laughter in his poetry derives . . . from a sunny awareness of the body's unflappable optimism." But even though the tone of this book is lighter than much of Dobyns' work, he does not abandon his existential premise that we feel alone in the universe, traveling our various paths to extinction. In the final poem, "The Body's Weight," he says "the body's greatest burden is itself," and he describes the process of running down, running out of steam, running out of time, until at last we are pushed through the exit door and "stand released":

> and briefly we're embraced by a joyful lightness,
> as light as smoke rising, or a phrase of music,
> or butterfly wings, and then the darkness begins.

Dobyns has said that he has an absolute horror of self-parody and that this urges him to adopt new methods in every book. His tenth book of poetry, *Pallbearers Envying the One Who Rides* (1999), was described in *Publishers Weekly* as a modern morality cycle of sixty-one poems about an Everyman-like figure named Heart "who comes to resemble Charlie Brown as seen by Charles Bukowski." The journey undertaken is for happiness rather than salvation, and Heart essentially gets nowhere on it, despite numerous brave attempts to attract the appreciation of women and solve life's other riddles. All the poems, whether funny or grim, are short except "Oh, Immobility, Death's Vast Associate," which takes a very long look at depressive inertia: what causes it, what it feels like, and why it is one of the universal states of human existence.

The Porcupine's Kisses (2002), Dobyns' eleventh book of poetry, shares many of the concerns that dominate *Pallbearers* (and his work overall) but the format and the style are entirely new. Part 1 consists of a series of prose poems that are mini-narratives of about a page each. They are interspersed with multiple one-liners or aphorisms that work as individual lyrics and offer brief insights something like a rationalist's version of the haiku experience.

The prose poems represent the lonely reveries of a central consciousness—a mind that is tempted to disassociate entirely from humanity, including the self. When he is drawn outward by gazing on the mountains, on the clouds, on the rivers, the speaker is temporarily able to forget his pain. "Wouldn't he relinquish his solitude to join that snowy company?" the voice asks ("The Clouds above the Mountains"). These meditations circle around the subject of imagination and indirectly discuss what it can and cannot do. Imagination *can* distract one from pain temporarily. It can build a city of hopes and intentions. In "Often, in Dreams, He Moved through a City" the voice describes the order and beauty of this creation. But it also admits that it can never replace the "real city," to which we all must return, and where, ultimately, we face death.

These poems explore various journeys the imagination makes when one tries to find comfort through fantasy. Each journey offers seduction but arrives nowhere that is permanent. Engaging in Art is seen as delightful but only because of the fall back into reality: "These moments that lift him far from himself, what are the rest but interruptions of envy, pride, ambition . . . that clutter the spaces between himself and what he loves? Yet without such intrusions . . . how could he know what is precious? As if only by being outside himself can he ever be within himself"("A Bach Partita"). Another journey of the imagination is nostalgia: "He Had Spent His Youth Dreaming" tells of the sort of young hopes that are often returned to obsessively. "Only in nostalgia did he roam through the rich place he had been promised, but the dream would end and again he would be left among the cold streets, full of regret and resentment." Romantic escapism is the subject of "You Take a Train through a Foreign Country," in which a man merely catches sight of a woman who is seated on another train: "What a life you invent for yourself, what a small regret to burden your contentment. These attempted escapes from your accustomed routine that take you by surprise—you can almost hear the door again bang shut."

All the aphorisms or one-liners in part 1 emanate from a disembodied voice, an unnamed character who exhibits no personality as such other than the conclusions he has gleaned. One might deem the conclusions to be folk wisdom because they resonate from a generalized voice, except that the humor and wit are so quirky.

Part 2 is a pseudodictionary of definitions in alphabetical order. They demonstrate Dobyns' propensity for metaphorical thinking and his comprehension of how the mind plays its games. Some of the definitions are psychological in nature—libido: the body's happy charioteer; juggle: your evasions looping over your defeats; fortitude: stubbornness in the face of evidence; preoccupied: two or more worries occupying the same space at the same time. Some are political—Marxist: offers your socks to others; oppressed: resentments exceed expectations; surveillance: the attention that doesn't flatter; plausible: the stupid ideas of the powerful. Some are lyric—worry: night gristle; hate: the heart's clenched fist; menial: the dog's dog; joke: air with teeth in it; twaddle: earnestness on bended knee.

Perhaps no other type of writing lends itself more to the presumption of certainties and the possibility of knowing than the dictionary format. After all, where does one go to define, delineate, and decide about the meaning of things? These "Definitions and Considerations," as he titles them, are little poems that attempt not only to employ individual metaphors but also to embody a metaphor in their very form—a metaphor that will demonstrate the concept that human beings Do know! Are certain! Have truth!—although nothing could be farther from the author's perception of the world.

CONCLUSION

Stephen Dobyns' poetry has everything to do with the pleasure principle; he thoroughly concurs with William Carlos Williams' assertion that "if it ain't a pleasure, it ain't a poem." He has frequently commented, in essays, interviews, and workshops, that pleasure is what causes him to write and that pleasure is what any reader has the right to expect from engaging in a poem. Poetry, on one level, is a game for him, as he stated in an interview for *Northeast Corridor:* "My imagination is constantly playing around. I ride my imagination as a musician uses his oboe, or my tuba, most likely." But the nature of the pleasure varies widely, from whimsy to horror. The atmosphere created at his readings is one of raucous appreciation. His followers expect a lot of entertainment but very little comfort, unless it is the comfort of hearing an unflinching admission that the human condition is wretched with pain and bloated with preposterous desire.

In every genre, in every glance, Dobyns' subject is the human heart. He observes it, meditates on it, and creates art from it. Although he has made a broad study of philosophy and religion, his tone implies no commitment to any specific ideology. He observes *desires,* particularly his own, and narrates his conclusions in terms of metaphor. What does he find out about the human heart? That if one digs around enough, one will discover universal depravity. Fortunately what keeps his conclusions from being utterly negative is the fact that he also believes people are capable of exertion, and that exertion can sometimes create community, love, or temporary respite from isolation.

An air of strenuous unease permeates everything Dobyns writes. But this unease is not on account of the coexistence of evil and good at the heart of the human race—a situation he finds inevitable but not hopeless. More likely it results from what may be Dobyns' perception, starting in his childhood, that whatever or whoever caused us to exist by definition cannot cohabit our existence—or in Paul Tillich's view, that our existence must be defined as estrangement. Dobyns' works address the chronic loneliness that he sees operating as a constant in the human equation. "At first there's the pure solipsism where we each believe we are the only outsider. Then we learn that others feel the same way. I can only address my *own* sense of being an outsider, so my writing is a way I deal with it." He admits that he has exacerbated this condition by being a poet and by being so shy. Nonetheless the process of writing also makes the world palpable to him and gives him people he can talk to, both on the page and in his audience. "The world does not exist for me until I put it into words—give significance to it."

Some critics have accused him of excessive pessimism, even nihilism, but the quantity as well as the quality of his literary output would undercut that assumption because a genuine commitment to nihilism would preclude the monstrous motivation required to bring so many works to a state of completion. It is a testimony to Dobyns' belief in the possibility of meaning that he creates narrative, humor, and poetry in the face of such evident personal discomfort. Art, he wrote in his essay "Communication," "is an antidote to madness. It allows us to define ourselves with greater or lesser accuracy in relation to our fellow human beings. Furthermore, great art, by showing us our common feeling, shows us our common responsibility. It shows us how to live."

Selected Bibliography

WORKS OF STEPHEN DOBYNS

POETRY

Concurring Beasts. New York: Atheneum, 1972.

Griffon. New York: Atheneum, 1976.

Heat Death. New York: Atheneum, 1980.

The Balthus Poems. New York: Atheneum, 1982.

Black Dog, Red Dog. New York: Holt, Rinehart and Winston, 1984.

Cemetery Nights. New York: Viking, 1987.

Body Traffic. New York: Viking, 1990.

Velocities: New and Selected Poems. New York: Viking, 1994.

Common Carnage. New York: Penguin, 1996.

Pallbearers Envying the One Who Rides. New York: Penguin, 1999.

The Porcupine's Kisses. New York: Penguin, 2002.

ESSAYS

Best Words, Best Order: Essays on Poetry. New York: St. Martins, 1996.

FICTION

A Man of Little Evils. New York: Atheneum, 1973.

Saratoga Longshot. New York: Atheneum, 1976.

Saratoga Swimmer. New York: Atheneum, 1981.

Dancer with One Leg. New York: Dutton, 1983.

Cold Dog Soup. New York: Viking, 1985.

Saratoga Headhunter. New York: Viking, 1985.

Saratoga Snapper. New York: Viking, 1986.

A Boat off the Coast. New York: Viking, 1987.

Saratoga Bestiary. New York: Viking, 1988.

The Two Deaths of Señora Puccini. New York: Viking, 1988.

The House on Alexandrine. Detroit: Wayne State University Press, 1990.

Saratoga Hexameter. New York: Viking, 1990.

After Shocks, Near Escapes. New York: Viking, 1991.

Saratoga Haunting. New York: Viking, 1993.

The Wrestler's Cruel Study. New York: Norton, 1993.

Saratoga Backtalk. New York: Norton, 1994.

Saratoga Fleshpot. New York: Norton, 1995.

The Church of Dead Girls. New York: Metropolitan Books, 1997.

Saratoga Strongbox. New York: Viking, 1998.

Boy in the Water. New York: Metropolitan Books, 1999.

Eating Naked: Stories. New York: Metropolitan Books, 2000.

CRITICAL AND BIOGRAPHICAL STUDIES

"Stephen Dobyns." In *Contemporary Authors, New Revision Series,* vol. 99. Detroit: Gale, 2002. Pp. 99–102.

Stitt, Peter. "Stephen Dobyns: The Uncertainty of Narrative." In his *Uncertainty and Plenitude: Five Contemporary Poets.* Iowa City: University of Iowa Press, 1997.

REVIEWS

Brumer, Andy. "Experience, Instinct, and Intimacy." *New York Times Book Review,* September 23, 1984, p. 14. (Review of *Black Dog, Red Dog.*)

Christophersen, Bill. Review of *Common Carnage. Poetry* 170:347 (September 1997).

Cooley, Peter. Review of *Concurring Beasts. North Atlantic Review* (spring 1973).

Elledge, Jim. "Triumphs." *Poetry* 146:297 (August 1985). (Review of *Black Dog, Red Dog.*)

Kirby, David. "Life's Goofy Splendors." *New York Times Book Review,* December 23, 1990, p. 16.

Libby, Anthony. "One Gives Us 'Happiness,' the Other, 'Gluttony.'" *New York Times Book Review,* January 15, 1995, p. 15. (Review of *Velocities.*)

Review of *Pallbearers Envying the One Who Rides. Publishers Weekly,* July 26, 1999, p. 85.

Spector, Robert D. Review of *Concurring Beasts. Saturday Review,* March 11, 1972, pp. 80–81.

INTERVIEWS

King, Janna. "Interview with S. D." *Northeast Corridor* no. 3:40–45 (1995).

———. Taped interview with Stephen Dobyns. March 3, 2002.

Ott, Bill. "Stephen Dobyns." *Booklist* 93:1798–1799 (July 1997).

FILMS BASED ON THE WORKS OF STEPHEN DOBYNS

Cold Dog Soup. Produced by Richard Abramson, William E. McEven, and Thomas Pope. Screenplay by Thomas Pope. Directed by Alan Metter. Handmade Films, 1991.

Two Deaths. Produced by Luc Roeg and Carolyn Montagu. Screen Two, BBC and Dakota Films, 1996. (Based on *The Two Deaths of Señora Puccini.*)

—JANNA KING

Leslie Fiedler

1917–2003

"Nothing if not ambivalent" was Leslie Fiedler's favorite way of summing up the strange twists and turns of his long career at the writing desk. Over a career in which he wrote some two dozen books along with hundreds of literary articles, dozens of short stories, and several novels, Fiedler's "ambivalence" was manifested as a capacity to be at once deadly serious and at the same time seriously playful. But had he written only one book—his first extended work of criticism, *Love and Death in the American Novel* (1960; a slimmed-down version was published six years later)—his lasting reputation would have been secured.

In *Love and Death,* Fiedler examines a wide range of American and European novels in detail, arguing that the principal difference between the two lies in the way that the themes of love and death are treated. As Fiedler saw it, America's most characteristic novelists are not only obsessed with death but also incapable of presenting fully imagined heterosexual relationships. American authors have shied away from permitting in their fiction the presence of any full-fledged mature women, giving readers instead "monsters of virtue or bitchery, symbols of the rejection or fear of sexuality."

The result, Fiedler famously argued, was that American fiction was largely, if not completely, of, for, and about boys. Critics were divided about how seriously they were to take such a thesis. Writing for the *Spectator,* Kingsley Amis praised the book as "witty, exasperating, energetic, penetrating," whereas Donald Davie, reviewing Fiedler's work in the *Guardian,* would have none of it: *Love and Death,* he said, is "a sustained fouling of the American nest."

One encounters little middle ground when charting how fellow critics and writers responded to Fiedler's major work. Still, *Love and Death* belongs in the company of such magisterial studies as F. O. Matthiessen's *American Renaissance* (1941) and R. W. B. Lewis' *American Adam* (1955) as a book that no serious student of American literature can ignore.

Neither can a serious student of American literature remain unacquainted with Fiedler's most influential (and infamous) essay, "Come Back to the Raft Ag'in, Huck Honey!" (1948). After one reads Fiedler's account of the homoerotic bonding between Huck and Jim and what it suggests about American literature's larger flight from domesticity, it is hard to ever again read Twain's novel as an uncomplicated example of boyhood innocence.

In a 1984 *Newsweek* profile by David Gates, Leslie Fiedler summed up the vagaries of his career this way: "The typical pattern with one of my books . . . is that when it comes out everybody abuses it. Ten years later they're still abusing it but they've begun to steal ideas from it. Twenty years go by and they decide it is a classic, . . . although nobody'd ever said anything good about it."

Fiedler was at once accurate and rueful about a literary life in which he was often seen as more provoking than provocative, and as an aging enfant terrible who desperately wanted to be a part of every radical, cutting-edge movement. As a young man who identified with the political Left, Fiedler took enormous pleasure from the fact that he was born in the same year as the Russian revolution; but by 1953 his views had changed to the extent that he wrote an essay arguing that the "atomic spies" Julius and Ethel Rosenberg, Communists who were executed after their conviction on charges of nuclear espionage in service of the Soviet Union, were not only guilty but also that those who blindly supported their cause needed to abandon political innocence for a more sophisticated grasp of realpolitik. Moreover, the same Fiedler who wrote his doctoral dissertation on the poetry of John Donne (thus placing himself firmly among the close-reading New Critics) would later insist that the distinctions that separated high art from mass culture were as artificial as they were unwarranted. What mattered, the middle-aged Fiedler now insisted, was myth, story, song, and the like—whether one found them in the works of William Shakespeare, Charles Dickens, and Mark Twain or in comic books, science fiction, popular song, and film. During the turbulent 1960s, Fiedler was a principal architect of the gradual shift in critical attention from high art to popular culture. More than any other long-established critic he expressed a growing impatience with what he regarded as a stuffy and increasingly irrelevant literary elitism. In his old age, Fiedler continued to thrive on the controversies he once generated with the happy abandon of a wet puppy shaking himself off on a living room carpet.

LIFE

Leslie Aaron Fiedler was born in Newark, New Jersey, on March 8, 1917, the son of Jacob J. (a pharmacist) and Lillian (Rosenstrauch) Fiedler. Although his father was a difficult, often sour man, his maternal grandfather, Leon Rosenstrauch, introduced the young Fiedler to the world of stories. Mark Royden Winchell's biography *"Too Good To Be True"* describes Fiedler's earliest Newark years this way:

> Before Leslie learned to read, he heard fairy tales from his grandfather. They all seemed to begin with the line: "Once there was a young man who got on a white horse and rode out into the world." Many years later, Leslie observed that his grandfather resembled the protagonist of such stories less than he did a peasant, whose youthful companions would jump on a local farmer's horse and ride into nearby orchards to steal fruit. Leon [Fiedler's maternal grandfather] had a mark on his foot, which he claimed came from a horse's hoof, although Leslie believed that the foot was probably just shaped that way. On Jewish high holy days, Leon Rosenstrauch would take his grandson to some storefront synagogue and say, "Not that I believe, but so you should remember."

What Fiedler's grandparents—on both sides—remembered was the cruelty of the Russian czars; and like many other immigrant Jews of their time and place, what they believed in was the social and economic salvation promised by Communism.

Early on, young Leslie Fiedler had a sense, however unconscious and inarticulate, that the social fabric of Newark was changing and that its Jews would soon be sharing space with blacks. Indeed, as Fiedler grew up on the south side of Newark, his experience was that there were only two groups of people in the world: Jews and blacks. (This premise seemed to be corroborated years later when Fiedler traveled to Newark to attend a conference in which the only writers on the program to have been born in Newark were Fiedler and the African American writer Amiri Baraka [Le Roi Jones]. Both of their mothers were in the audience.) His fundamental acquaintance with black people, however, was not in the context of friendship; the African Americans he knew were the maids who worked for his family and those he met on the various jobs he took on as a teenager. An aging black woman named Hattie worked for the Fiedlers during Leslie's adolescence. She enjoyed camping it up as a plantation darkie and calling Leslie's mother "Miz Lillie." While the rest of the family roared with laughter, Fiedler remembers that he stormed out of the house, "equally furious with Hattie for her play-acting and my own family for lapping it up."

This was roughly the same period during which the fifteen-year-old Fiedler campaigned to read the Newark library's "closed room" copy of James Joyce's *A Portrait of the Artist as a Young Man* and when he bought his first book with his own money—Harriet Beecher Stowe's *Uncle Tom's Cabin* (a book that played a significant role in his view of blacks, although it was years before Fiedler could reject the tyranny of the tough-minded New Critics and admit his early love for this sentimental classic). The teenage Fiedler took more advantage of the public library and the colorful down-and-outers who congregated in the city's park than he did of the colorless Newark school system. As he told Benjamin DeMott in a 1978 interview for the *New York Times Book Review,* "At 15 I had the sense of being in full possession of everything I could need for doing what I imagined I wanted to do in life.... I was growing up in a time when it wasn't possible to relish youth or play 'being young.'" Some Fiedler-watchers have speculated that his prolonged adolescence (virtually through his entire adulthood) was a way of making up for a missed childhood.

Fiedler received his B.A. degree from New York University in 1938 and his M.A. from the University of Wisconsin in 1939. That same year he married Margaret Ann Shipley, on October 6, and after he received his Ph.D. from Harvard University in 1941, the couple moved to Missoula, where Fiedler had been offered a position at Montana State University. Over the long span of time he taught at Montana State University, he and Margaret had six children: Kurt, Eric, Michael, Deborah, Jenny, and Miriam. His academic career included Fulbright lectureships at Rome and Bologna (1951–1953) and the University of Athens (1961–1962), visiting appointments at Princeton University (1956–1957), Yale University (1969), University of Sussex in England (1967–1968), and University of Vincennes in France (1971), along with assorted summer appointments at New York University, Columbia University, and the University of Letters, Indiana University. Fiedler, however, is most identified with two schools: Montana State University in Missoula, where he taught from 1941 until 1964, and the State University of New York at Buffalo, where, since 1964, he was a distinguished and highly controversial member of the English department.

The sprawling Fiedler residence at 154 Morris Avenue in Buffalo often seemed more like a hippie commune than it did the respectable domicile of a respectable professor, and this no doubt played a role in the drug raid detailed in his 1969 memoir *Being Busted.* Despite the Fiedler household's appearance of unconventionality, Fiedler's devotion to home and family was steadfast. If his critical essays on myth and mythology often focused on the ways that male protagonists avoided marriage and domesticity, his own life was a case study in home, hearth, and most important of all, fatherhood. Leslie and Margaret Fiedler remained together through an often tempestuous marriage that lasted nearly forty years. They divorced in 1973. That same year, Fiedler married the poet Sally Anderson.

Fiedler's writing has generated more than its fair share of withering criticism, but his work has also been widely honored. He was named a Rockefeller fellow at Harvard (1946–1947) and awarded a Furioso poetry prize in 1951. In 1957 he won the National Institute of Arts and Letters prize for excellence in creative writing, and in 1960, 1961, and 1970–1971 he received grants-in-aid and fellowship monies from the American Council of Learned Societies and the Guggenheim Foundation. Fiedler also received an impressive number of awards, medals, and lifetime achievement honors: in 1985 he received the Alumni Award from New York University (Heights); in 1989 he was awarded the Chancellor Charles P. Morton Medal from the State University of New York at Buffalo; and he garnered the Hubbell Medal from the Modern Language Association in 1994. In 1988 Fiedler was finally inducted into the American Academy of Letters, and in 1998 he received the Ivan Sandorf Award for Lifetime Achievement from the National Book Critics Circle. Leslie Fiedler died on January 29, 2003, following a long series of debilitating illnesses, including Parkinson's disease.

TWO EARLY CONTROVERSIAL ESSAYS

Leslie Fiedler made his debut as an American literature critic with a June 1948 essay published in the prestigious *Partisan Review*. Provocatively titled "Come Back to the Raft Ag'in, Huck Honey!" it not only changed the Twain industry but also the way that students were taught the story of a black man and a white boy playing out their respective destinies on a raft floating down the Mississippi. At the tender age of thirty-one, Fiedler announced himself as a culture critic with a penchant for pointing out patterns that more solid scholars simply missed. For Fiedler, *Huck Finn* perfectly characterizes American literature in its flight *from* the entanglements of marriage and eventual fatherhood and the ways in which this movement, often unconscious, is toward a wilderness "anti-marriage" (Fiedler's term) between a white man and a near-counterpart of color. Had Fiedler talked about this recurring phenomenon as "male bonding," it is unlikely that his revisionist view of Huck and Jim would have raised so many eyebrows. But Fiedler insisted that the proper way of describing the emotions each character brought to their sojourn on the raft was "homoeroticism," a term that many readers thought (wrongly) was interchangeable with "homosexuality." Bad enough that Fiedler was out to prove that American fiction constituted a boy's literature—with "Come Back to the Raft Ag'in, Huck Honey!" he seemed bent on smuggling X-rated themes into a boy's ripping adventures on a raft.

On the one occasion when Fiedler met Ernest Hemingway, the then-ailing novelist eyed his guest suspiciously and asked him if he still believed "that stuff about Huck Finn." What *stuff*, Fiedler might well have asked: That, as the editors of *Partisan Review* later claimed, the essay was a "put-on" and thus not to be taken seriously? That Huck and Jim were "queer as three dollar bills" (as an exasperated Fiedler declares in *Love and Death,* responding to an avalanche of misreading by professionals and general readers alike)? That, as some Queer Theorists argued beginning in the 1990s, Fiedler was, at bottom, a secret fag-basher despite his efforts to come off as an enlightened liberal? For a man who vowed he would "write his way out" of the academic gulag that was Montana State University, "Come Back to the Raft Ag'in, Huck Honey!" was surely a bold start. The essay was attacked by the left as well as the right; Fiedler's argument hit sensitive nerves across the political spectrum and, faced with the prospect of seeing Twain's novel in a new, revolutionary way, critics and academics seemed universally to fall back on the predictable and programmatic. Christopher Looby, for example, took Fiedler to task for talking as he does about "innocent homosexuality," which, Looby says, implies that, so far as Fiedler is concerned, there is "some other, 'guilty,' form of homosexuality." By contrast, writing in the conservative pages of *Commentary* magazine, Kenneth Lynn used the occasion of a review of Fiedler's 1982 collection *What Was Literature?* to revisit the article Fiedler had published more than three decades earlier and decry the objectionable foolishness that it had unleashed. Noting that Fiedler's infamous article appeared in the same year as Alfred C. Kinsey's *Sexual Behavior in the American Male,* Lynn saw connections that were alarming and patterns that were downright dangerous:

> So eager was [Fiedler] to challenge both the folk wisdom of the American people and the clinical wisdom of the psychoanalysts, so fervent was he dreaming of a Kinseyesque America of sexual pluralism and guilt-free indulgence, that he found it easy to convince himself that every important American writer from Cooper to Faulkner was on his side.

For Lynn, Fiedler's sexual reading of American literature was bad enough ("dubious statistics" did not persuade Lynn that every male was Rip Van Winkle under the skin or that the Huck-Jim relationship, however it be characterized, was a typical pattern), but far more objectionable was the way that Fiedler's essay seemed part of a hard-Left conspiracy in which Huck's refusal to return to St. Petersburg (where the process of "sivilizing" him would continue) could be viewed as symptomatic of an attack on America itself.

Fiedler's critics, including Lynn, often missed the *nuance*—both in the literature he read and the paragraphs he wrote. The complexities in "Come Back to the Raft Ag'in, Huck Honey!" proved easy enough to oversimplify and even easier to parody, but the reductions could not make Fiedler's essay go away. It shook up the Twain industry as no single essay on Huck Finn ever had, and if some Twain scholar-editors never quite forgave him for the chutzpah exhibited in the title (one does *not* add a line to a Twain novel), Twain critics—even, or perhaps most especially, those who disagreed with him—had a field day writing pieces that demonstrated precisely where Fiedler's thesis went badly wrong.

It is a safe bet that most ordinary citizens of Montana were unaware of the controversy that Fiedler's homoerotic Huck had set into motion in the literary world. But a year and a half later, in December 1949, his essay "Montana; or the End of Jean-Jacques Rousseau" appeared in the pages of *Partisan Review,* and this work by the Montana State University English professor got their attention. Once again, Fiedler drew upon a mythic understanding of his subject. For Fiedler, American literature could be best understood in terms of directional arrows: the North, the South, the East, and the West.

In "Montana; or the End of Jean-Jacques Rousseau," he identified three stages of the frontier. In the first stage, the struggle for mere survival is so intense that early settlers have no time to contemplate the gap between their romantic, utopian dreams and the barrenness of their surroundings. In the second stage, civilizing influences (e.g., the schoolmarm) cause the Dream and the Reality to confront each other, and in the process to create a kind of cultural myth: the sentimentalized image of the frontier as purveyed in pulp novels, Western movies, and fake cowboy songs. In the third stage, Western popular culture is commercialized into the dude ranch and the chamber of commerce rodeo. Montana, Fiedler argues, teeters somewhere between the second and third stages.

Nothing offended the ordinary Montana citizen more than Fiedler's description of the "Montana face":

> developed not for sociability, but for facing into the weather. It said friendly things to be sure, and meant them; but it had no adequate expressions even for friendliness, and the muscles around the mouth and eyes were obviously unprepared to cope with the demands of any more complicated emotion. . . . The poverty of experience had left the possibilities of the human face in them incompletely realized.

Fiedler's prolonged exile in Montana, with time to contemplate what the local PTA or chamber of commerce was doing to the cultural environment, was surely responsible for the sharp criticism he dishes out, singling out Missoulans as badly needing a way of self-understanding that could only come from seeing themselves as the product of myths that no longer had any justification, much less potency. The response of most Montanans to Fiedler's efforts to debunk their culture, however, was to hunker down into rock-hard denial. For many just beyond the campus, Fiedler represented the interloper extraordinaire. Not only was he an easterner who lacked a feel for the frontier West, but, worse, he was Jewish—exactly the sort who would bite the hands that fed him a monthly paycheck. No matter that Fiedler's essay had other fish to fry than his oft-quoted—and widely infuriating—portrait of the vapid Montana face; indeed, if the article had been read carefully, what these exasperated citizens would have discovered is that the essay asks them to experience nothing less than an epiphany about their lives, and then to change them.

Fiedler's Montana essay was just that, an essay, and his prescription for a state choking on its dreams was to replace outworn myths with a healthy dose of reality:

> Certainly for the bystander watching the cowboy, a comic book under his arm, lounging beneath the bright poster of the latest Roy Rogers film, there is the sense of a joke on someone—and no one to laugh. Nothing less than the total myth of the goodness of man in a state of nature is at stake every Saturday after the show at the Rialto, and, although there is scarcely anyone who sees the issue clearly or as a whole, most Montanans are driven instinctively to try to close the gap.

Fiedler's grand hypothesis is that when the average Montanan

> admits that the Noble Savage is a lie; when he has learned that his state is where the myth comes to die (it is here, one is reminded, that the original of Huck Finn ended his days, a disrespected citizen), the Montanan may find the possibilities of tragedy and poetry for which he so far has searched his life in vain.

It is hard to read such passages without reaching the conclusion that it is Fiedler and not the ordinary citizens of Montana who is filled with Romantic dreams, because, when distilled to its essence, what he is recommending is a universal Introduction to Literature class.

AN END TO INNOCENCE: WRITING ABOUT COLD WAR POLITICS

As Mark Royden Winchell observes in *"Too Good To Be True,"* Fiedler found ways of disappointing the expectations of those who worked within strictly defined disciplines. "Formalist critics think him too sociological, and sociologists think him too literary." The truth, of course, is that Fiedler was always eclectic, but even more, he had a habit of questioning people about their unquestioned beliefs. His essay about Montana and outmoded Western myths is one example; his first essay collection, *An End to Innocence: Essays on Culture and Politics* (1955), is another.

As was the case with other New York intellectuals who came of age during the Great Depression of the 1930s (one thinks of Alfred Kazin, Irving Kristol, and Irving Howe), Fiedler early identified himself as a man of the Left. Indeed, the culture of immigrant sons so embraced the Soviet Union and the worker's paradise that Marx and Lenin had brought into being that the critic Lionel Abel once remarked that certain sections of Manhattan were virtually indistinguishable from Moscow. Radical politics filled the air as America's economy teetered on the brink of collapse. Small wonder that Fiedler took so much pride in noting that he was born in the same year as the Russian revolution. But while one could argue that he remained a "revolutionary" all his life, he was hardly an ideologue of the Marxist sort. The revelations about the atrocities committed by Joseph Stalin turned Fiedler—along with others associated with the *Partisan Review*—into anti-Stalinists. What distinguished Fiedler, however, was the unflinching way he would address three of the most divisive topics of the late 1940s and early 1950s: the Hiss case, the Rosenberg trial, and McCarthyism.

In the postwar essays collected as *An End to Innocence,* Fiedler seemed less interested in strictly literary matters, particularly as they were defined by the more doctrinaire, close-reading New Critics, than he was in cultural politics. Fiedler's intention, he writes, is that essays would tell the truth "about my world and myself as a liberal, intellectual, writer, American, and Jew." And good as his word, the essays did precisely that, unpacking painful truths about a generation of Left-leaning intellectuals who simply could not bring themselves to believe that Alger Hiss had lied or that Ethel and Julius Rosenberg were traitors. After all, these were people of goodwill, people on the Left, people, in short, like them. What were the rallies they had attended (often with entertainment presented by Paul Robeson and Pete Seeger) and, indeed, the very investment of their idealistic youth if the argument of "Afterthoughts on the Rosenbergs" (first published in *Encounter,* October 1953) was correct? The same thing might be said about "Hiss, Chambers, and the Age of Innocence" (*Commentary,* August 1951), which argued, very much against the leftist cultural grain, that Hiss was, in Mark Royden Winchell's description in *"Too Good To Be True,"* "the epitome of the Popular Front Bolshevik—a Communist whose very usefulness to the party lay in appearing to be everything it theoretically hated." For the True Believers whom Fiedler's essays took to task, Hiss and the Rosenbergs could not be guilty as charged because if they were, then so too were they. Even the prospect that this just might be true was enough to cause many liberal intellectuals to close ranks and to engineer distinctions between the Larger Good (to which Hiss and the Rosenbergs were presumably devoted) and what they characterized as small legal infractions.

The sobering news Fiedler delivered was that a generation found itself on trial along with Hiss, and "not, it must be noted, for having struggled toward a better world, but for having substituted sentimentality for intelligence in that struggle, for having failed to understand the moral conditions that must determine the outcome." Thus, Fiedler early on declared himself as one who was persuaded, however reluctantly, to put away the ideological certainty shared by his generation of leftist intellectuals for a more complicated movement from a "liberalism of innocence to a liberalism of responsibility." The play of words stuck, at least during those combative times. And now Fiedler not only had the word "controversial" attached to him because of what he had to say about Huck and Jim on the raft or about the Montana sunk in its mythic despair but also because a responsible liberalism seemed a far cry from impassioned partisanship. Equally unsurprising was Fiedler's mild amusement at this turn of events, although one suspects that on certain afternoons he realized full well that he was the architect of his flamboyant, "controversial" public reputation.

MASTER OF DREAMS

The 1960 collection *Love and Death in the American Novel* expanded Fiedler's pungent thesis about the primal dream of a white male and his dark companion who flee home, hearth, and most of all, domesticity (read: fatherhood) to find freedom over the next hill, in the deepest reaches of the forest, or below the decks of oceangoing ships. Fiedler's brilliant, albeit quirky, reading of American archetypes explained why literature is, at best, one boy's book after another as well as why "the failure of the American fictionist to deal with adult heterosexual love and his consequent obsession with death, incest, and innocent homosexuality" not only defined American literature but also much that uneasily resided in America's inchoate dreams. Fiedler was drawn to those writers "in whom the consciousness of our plight is given clarity and form."

In *Love and Death,* drawing heavily from Freudian psychology, Fiedler focuses on eros and thanatos—love and death—as the drives that are most evident in American literature. Love (eros) is the drive of life, love, creativity, and sexuality. The very survival of the species depends upon it. By contrast, death (thanatos) is the drive of aggression, sadism, destruction, and violence. Fiedler sees the conflicting drives of eros and thanatos in American gothic novels that he traces from Charles Brockden Brown's *Weiland,* the work of Edgar Allan Poe, and finally to such William Faulkner novels as *Sanctuary* and *Absalom, Absalom!*

Fiedler also argues that the characters who find a home in our collective unconscious tend to be in flight from manifestations of the superego, a term that Freud defined as internalized self-criticism or what is typically called the conscience. Using this schema, Fiedler links together the likes of Natty Bumppo and Rip Van Winkle, the *Pequod*'s multicultural sailors, virtually any Poe protagonist, and Huck and Jim making their way down the Mississippi on a raft. *Love and Death in the American Novel* may have rigged the canonical deck (when writers such as Nathaniel Hawthorne or Henry James did not fit Fiedler's thesis, he sacrificed nuance for overall unity, complexity for emphasis), but its impact was enormous. Undergraduate teachers sometimes acknowledged Fiedler's influence, but most of the time they simply cribbed their lectures from *Love and Death*'s pages. And undergraduates fortunate enough to lay their hands on the book itself figured that they were highlighting paragraphs delivered from no less than the Delphic oracle. The relentless tension between eros and thanatos explained, well, *everything*—or so it seemed at a time when most literary critics were dutiful and, by comparison, tame.

Fiedler's sense of the struggles that most defined American literature—Self versus Society; Man against Nature; gothic brooding, and the coinciding but also conflicting drives of eros and thanatos—often seem unnecessarily provocative, as if he needed to be theatrically excessive if he were to get a hearing at all. Indeed, Fiedler's merging of classic American literature with the American unconscious changed not only how certain books were read but also how we saw ourselves as Americans. As Richard Gilman pointed out in the pages of *Commonweal,* "Fiedler's Freudian orientation and strong-arm tactics [are] unfailingly evocative and illuminating. You'll quarrel with him on every page, but that new light is there." Those who understood just how rare genuinely fresh insights are easily forgave Fiedler his small slips of facts and large imaginative leaps; others were not amused and figured, with some justification, that if one could not trust Fiedler's scholarship in the details, one had no basis for believing his odd analogies and the cultural consequences he drew from them.

In a reflection of how petty and backbiting academic life can be, many reviewers of *Love and Death* did not acknowledge how exciting the study was, but rather how fast and loose Fiedler had played with the facts. The truth of the matter, however, is that Fiedler had long been respected as a scholar and critic worthy of high regard. Admittedly this does not square with the "celebrity nut" image he later cultivated when invited to television talk shows or ever-larger college audiences to pontificate about popular culture.

A single example—drawn from the notebooks of Lionel Trilling—will suffice to demonstrate just how imposing a figure Fiedler already cut in the literary world of the late 1940s. Portions of an entry dated September 1948 read as follows:

Read my paper on the novel ["Art and Fortune"] to the English Institute, the response seemed very warm, hearty and prolonged applause. . . . The effort of reading 7500 words in 50 minutes enormous—to keep up the rhythm and intensity—I did it well, but ended hoarse and exhausted—wanted desperately to be praised by [Mark] Schorer and Fiedler.

Given the mantle of moral gravitas and authority that would descend on Trilling's shoulders only a few years later (his enormously influential *The Liberal Imagination* was published in 1950), it seems odd—at least in retrospect—to learn how much Trilling would have valued Fiedler's esteem. Two more different personality types could hardly be imagined—Trilling, famous (or perhaps infamous) for his Anglophilism and high-minded cultural pronouncements; Fiedler, rambunctious, free-wheeling, every inch the rebel.

Nonetheless, Trilling's self-doubt remained a considerable part of his private life (see Diana Trilling's *The Beginning of the Journey*), partly because he never developed into the novelist he had hoped to be, and partly because Trilling was a very different person away from the lectern or writing desk. Fiedler, by contrast, always wore his self-assurance easily. What you saw was what you got—and this merely increased as the years added girth to his middle and gray to his hair and beard. The young critic who often seemed to specialize in unpacking outrageous sexual myths came more and more to look like a satyr from some classical text. In one important regard, however, Fiedler and Trilling shared the frustrations of would-be creative writers: both were known more for their critical analyses than for their own poems, novels, or short stories.

For better or worse, *Love and Death* had established the terms by which nearly all Fiedler's subsequent literary criticism would be discussed, whether it be by the anonymous reviewer for *Catholic World,* who claimed of Fiedler's collection *No! In Thunder* (1960), "there is something here to offend everyone," or Willard Thorp, who more generally remarked in the *New York Herald Tribune* that "The reader who has not before encountered Mr. Fiedler at work may be in for a shock. . . . To him novels are documents from which the secret cultural history of America can be read."

If it is true that Fiedler's close textual reading of individual texts is a result of his graduate school training, it is equally true that he came to see the larger patterns that literature often makes. *Love and Death in the American Novel* is an example of seeing both forests and individual trees, of generalizations that derive from specfiic evidence. In this regard, "Archetype and Signature: The Relationship of Poet and Poem" (first published in the *Sewanee Review* in 1952 and later in *The Collected Essays of Leslie Fiedler,* 1971) is an interesting exception—not because it is laborious reading (whatever might be said of Fiedler's arguments they are always written in plain English), but because its discussion of a writer's simultaneous efforts to conceal and reveal one's "signature" is not pinned to the reading of a specific text. Interestingly enough, Fiedler came, in retrospect, to regard the essay—once one of his most famous—as a piece of self-conscious literary parody. Thus, a playful Fiedler had been taken much too solemnly by his fellow critics. Yet when some critics insisted that "Come Back to the Raft Ag'in, Huck Honey!" was too much outrageous leg-pulling, Fiedler insisted that he meant every one of its serious words.

CREATIVE WRITING

Fiedler wrote poetry throughout his long career and thought of himself, first and foremost, as a poet. Mark Royden Winchell's *"Too Good To Be True"* reproduces a number of Fiedler's poems, especially if they are revealing in terms of his biography; but reading the lines on their own, as it were, makes it clear that they are of limited aesthetic interest, and in fact, none of his poetry was ever published. His self-conscious exercises in verse lack the necessary ingredients, the "algebra and fire," that his

SUNY/Buffalo colleague John Barth felt were the indispensable ingredients of any successful piece of writing.

Fiedler had more luck as a fictionalist. His published creative work includes three novels (*The Second Stone*, 1963; *Back to China*, 1965; and *The Messengers Will Come No More*, 1974) and three collections of short fiction (*Pull Down Vanity*, 1962; *The Last Jew in America* [three novellas], 1966; and *Nude Croquet: The Stories of Leslie Fiedler*, 1969). The premise of his first novel, *The Second Stone*, is a love triangle involving Mark Stone, an ultraliberal rabbi; Clem Stone, a failed novelist and the rabbi's boyhood friend; and Mark's wife, Hilda. The action is set in Rome during an international conference devoted to love—all of which gives Fiedler ample opportunity to revisit the themes that Nathaniel Hawthorne earlier explored in his Italian novel *The Marble Faun* (1890), a book Fiedler included in his shipboard reading and that Henry James ruminated about in his international novels. As the directional arrows of Fiedler's criticism would have it, *The Second Stone* was an "Eastern," which for Fiedler often meant that there is a Jamesian drawingroom sense of how life among the leisure class is lived. At the same time, the novel offers enough instances of parody that one is never quite sure if Fiedler is appropriating the form or kicking it in the slats. For example, the novel includes so many references to Fiedler's career as a critic ("Clem" has been seen as a shortened form of Clemens, Mark Twain's real name) that the result might equally well be an Eastern in Western disguise, or perhaps a Western in Eastern disguise.

Fiedler's eminence as a critic, together with the way that, by the early 1960s, his flamboyant essays had solidified his reputation as American literature's "bad boy," meant that *The Second Stone* was widely anticipated as a literary event. Unfortunately, the event did not live up to expectations. Fiedler's characters, whatever else one might say of them "symbolically," did not seem to be fashioned from flesh and blood, nor did the twists and turns of plot ultimately convince.

Roughly the same thing was true for *Back to China*, Fiedler's "Western." Given the number of years he spent in Montana, it is understandable that he should come to think of himself as a Western writer: "It is a Montana landscape I see when I close my eyes," he wrote for *World Authors 1950–1970* (1975), "its people I imagine understanding, . . . I have to think of myself as a Western writer." This second novel is the first time Fiedler used a fictionalized Montana setting in his work; it represents a time-present against which he presents a memory of China immediately after World War II. Baro Finkelstone, a philosophy professor, is Fiedler's protagonist and mouthpiece. What protagonist and author want to explore is how a sensitive person can, perhaps *should,* respond to the atomic bomb dropped on Hiroshima. In Finkelstone's case, he undergoes sterilization as an act of atonement and then spends the next twenty years trying to preserve his youth by smoking pot with his male students and sleeping with his female ones.

Those critics who read Fiedler's novel against the popular, but often inaccurate, legends of his life, can tease out interesting parallels. They would, however, be wrong. True enough, Fiedler was no stranger to Montana bars or to the women he met there, but, as *Being Busted* makes clear, it is one thing to be a faculty adviser to a campus group seeking to legalize marijuana and quite another to be a pothead oneself. Whiskey was to Fiedler's generation what pot-smoking was to his children's.

Politics is yet another area where Fiedler and Finkelstone differ. Finkelstone's cold hedonism is balanced by his left-wing colleague, Hilber Shapiro. The Montana locals portrayed in the novel may not be familiar with the niceties of literary doubling, but, to them, the two professors are virtually interchangeable. In fact, Finkelstone gets hate mail meant for Shapiro. In truth, the two characters are a study in contrast: Shapiro is self-righteous and altogether a prig; Finkelstone is a free spirit extraordinaire.

With Finkelstone, Fiedler makes an attempt at etching the aging hippie. He is marginally successful, but the novel itself has too many loose ends, too many unbelievable twists of plot. Just as poetry lay somewhere beyond Fiedler's grasp, so too did the requirements of the novel. *The Messengers Will Come No More,* his last novel, is Fiedler's unfortunate venture into science fiction, a genre he championed but could not master himself. The novel simply sprawls, much more so than did his two previous efforts.

Fiedler writes in a more coherent, more intrinsically interesting way when he undertakes the form of the novella, represented in his collection *The Last Jew in America. The Last Jew in America* contains the title novella along with "The Last WASP in the World" and "The First Spade in the West." Set in mythical Lewis and Clark City, the series of novellas allows Fiedler the opportunity to be simultaneously playful and serious as he riffs on themes he would revisit two years later in his essay collection *The Return of the Vanishing American* (1968). Jews, blacks, and Indians dominated Fiedler's vision of the America that WASPs never fully acknowledge. But to his credit, Fiedler also knew the power of humor and the sting of satire. He did not study Mark Twain, and especially *The Adventures of Huckleberry Finn,* without having certain essential lessons rub off. The earnestness that spoiled his novels is largely absent in his freewheeling novellas, and later in his wildly funny short stories.

Lewis and Clark City exists on the "third frontier" that Fiedler first discussed in his controversial essay on Montana and the death rattle of Rousseau. The novel's setting is the fictional embodiment of what living a used-up myth means. The pop culture atmosphere that energized his Montana essay delimited his Montana novel. Fiedler was hardly the first academic novelist to have abstractions about culture get in the way of etching fully developed characters. With the novellas, however, Fiedler is able to explore a West of the mind rather than one fixed in sociological fact. That the mythopoeic Mr. Fiedler should try out his hand as a psychological tale-spinner is hardly surprising; what is surprising, however, is how much the novellas manage to resonate long after the broader landscape of their satire has gone its predictable course.

In the title story of *Nude Croquet,* the scene shifts to the Midwest and the shenanigans that occur during a gathering of writers and literary critics. The result is a thinly disguised look at the Indiana School of Letters at Bloomington that Fiedler attended for several summers during the early 1950s. Despite the title's insinuation of a lewd frolic, the stripping down that the word "nude" implies is less a matter of flesh being bared than of psyches being revealed. And since the subjects of Fiedler's dead-on satire are academics, the result is hardly a contribution to the canon of pornography; rather, the story rightly earns its place in any collection of "academic fiction." Booze is what brings the professors down.

Much the same impulse lies behind *Pull Down Vanity,* Fiedler's 1962 collection of short stories. Pretentiousness of any stripe was an anathema to everything he valued, and the stories in this collection draw on a range of easy targets. The results are often delicious but also decidedly limited. Fiedler was more effective as a cultural essayist, freed from the burden of creating believable characters and then moving them through a credible plot.

IN THE PUBLIC EYE

When the full implications of accepting an academic post, in truth the only one he was offered, in the hinterlands of Montana first hit him, Fiedler vowed that he would publish his way out. Eventually he did, but it took a much longer time—and more books—than he had imagined. In terms of confronting the West, both mythic and real, Montana State was arguably good for Fiedler's psyche and his paragraphs. But after a Western sojourn (often experienced as exile) of twenty-plus years, and after finishing his magnum opus, *Love and Death in the American Novel,* it was time for Fiedler to pull up his tent pegs and head east.

When an opening materialized at the newly created State University of New York at Buffalo, Fiedler jumped at the chance to join such interesting mavericks as the poets Charles Olson and Robert Creeley and the experimental fictionist John Barth in what was arguably the most dynamic English department in the country. The academic year was 1964–1965, the counterculture was just on the edge of explosion, and Fiedler was poised to move from influential literary critic to "celebrity nut" (Fiedler's self-descriptive term) and cultural guru. Fiedler, settled in as his department's Samuel Clemens Professor of English, seemed the very personification of the cat's meow. Fiedler thoroughly enjoyed holding court to graduate students happy to jam into a hotel room and sit at the master's feet during annual meetings of the Modern Language Association, but the background to this showmanship was Fiedler's literary workmanship: he was a professor who came to his book-lined office early every day and who stayed late, poring over novels and assorted critical tomes. Despite the seemingly relaxed style of his writing, Fiedler had the ammunition to fire off a fiercely pedantic aside when the occasion required it. And perhaps most fundamentally, what kept Fiedler looking fresh and provocative (in the best sense of these words) was his abundant intelligence, the one commodity that T. S. Eliot felt was essential to any important literary criticism.

What the larger world saw, however, was the public figure that Fiedler cut. He looked like a middle-aged hippie, he walked like a middle-aged hippie. Ergo, he *was* a hippie or at least a professor who took the side of those wearing bell-bottomed pants, tie-dyed shirts, and hair straggling down their shoulders. In 1965 he wrote an article for *Partisan Review* titled "The New Mutants" that argued on behalf of shrinking the distance between high and low culture. As the counterculture gained even more attention, Fiedler found himself eagerly embracing comic books, science fiction writers, and virtually everything that would later fly under the banner of "postmodernism," a term that he helped to popularize in literary circles. In the context of the times, Fiedler's countercultural bravado made him an accident waiting to happen; ultimately, the overly long arm of the law poked itself into his house, and he was accused of "maintaining a premise" where pot was inhaled. *Being Busted*, Fiedler's account of the brouhaha surrounding that time, that place, turned a very bad patch (financially and otherwise) into a piece of New Journalism that could hold its own with the best practitioners of nonfiction's latest wrinkle.

The book not only generated sympathy for Fiedler's embattled circumstances but it also helped advance the case for a more enlightened, less up-tight response to the youth-inspired revolution of the 1960s. For a brief, psychedelic moment, the Age of Aquarius seemed to loom just around the corner, and Fiedler took on the task of spreading the good news. In a 1972 paperback titled *Cross the Border, Close the Gap* he called for society in general to embrace whatever traveled under the wide umbrella of "the New Mutants." (At the time even Fiedler did not know—at least not consciously—that he was headed toward the moment when he would discover in "freaks" the ultimate Other he had been looking for since the salad days when he specialized in blacks and Jews, homosexuals, and Indians.)

Unfortunately, what sounded bracing, if a bit giddy, during the early 1970s began to seem dated, even dusty, just a few years later. And when Fiedler went public about his disaffections with traditional criticism and responsible teaching, his posturing seemed to undermine his relevance as a cultural and literary critic rather than enhance it. *What Was Literature?* (1982) is an extended apologia for the life Fiedler had been leading since the heyday of the mid-1960s, full of sound and fury and not a few mea culpas. If a perennial innocent such as Holden Caulfield sees life as a pitched battle between the "phonies" and the Uncorrupted Youth, Fiedler divided academe into the dryasdusts and himself. And as with Holden, the generous measures of self-congratulation take their toll. Moreover, Fiedler had more "voices" at his command (the playful, the ironic, the insightful, the learned), but he also shared with Holden, with Huck Finn, with all true-blue American outlaws the same resistance to "required" *anything* and the same wide, subversive streak.

No doubt Holden would object to reading and writing about Tarzan, *Uncle Tom's Cabin, Gone with the Wind,* or other Fiedler favorites, and one of Fiedler's unsympathetic critics has already pointed this out. Indeed, designing a curriculum that would please him is, finally, impossible, just as it was impossible to provide the education that the counterculture of the late 1960s and early 1970s presumably clamored for. Nonetheless, Fiedler, at least in his public writings, tried to be an advocate for "what's happenin' now."

But, like it or not, Fiedler was part of the literary establishment, however much he preferred to think of himself as a "barbarian *within* the gates." After all, he made out syllabi, held forth at appointed hours, set examination questions, gave grades, and not least of all, picked up a healthy paycheck. Real barbarians—within the gates or beyond them—do none of these things. More important, however, is the fact that no matter how with-it Fiedler imagined his assignments and lectures were, the bald truth of the matter is that many students are likely to plow enormous amounts of extracurricular energy into projects they insist on defining for themselves, thank you very much—everything from complicated geographies of the novelist J. R. R. Tolkien's Middle Earth or trivia about the movie *Star Trek* to (probably more commonplace) how Luke and Laura are doing on the television soap opera *General Hospital.*

The rub, alas, is that Fiedler desperately sought their approval and, worse, their adulation, as he wrote in *What Was Literature?*:

> To confess openly the passionate interest in pop which I have long shared with . . . students, but have lied about to myself as well as to them, would not just ease a classroom situation which I have come to feel intolerable, but help join together the sundered larger community, by making the university a place where we are not further separated from each other. Like all else entertained on the level of full consciousness, religion, for instance, and political ideology, what used to be "literature" divides us against ourselves; while what used to be called "trash," rooted like our dreams and nightmares in shared myth and fantasy, touches us all at a place where we have never been psychically sundered each from each.

Fiedler's vision was unashamedly utopian. It posited a university that bridges all gaps—teachers and students; fathers and sons; literatures, high and low; cultures, majority and minority—and teaches the wider world to do likewise.

Fiedler was, of course, hardly alone in exiting from the closets of popular culture (where those who had been taught better secretly binged on science fiction or comic books), but he burst forth with more pizzazz than most. Even his "shame" had a priggish smack to it, as if he knew all along that high culture was a lot of hooey. And if his mock confession upset the fuddy-duddies at staid Harvard or Structuralist Yale, so much the better. Behind their smug, starchy indignation, Fiedler argued, lies a vast reservoir of fear. They are afraid of myth, of story, of song—indeed, of anything primordial, inarticulate, unstructured, and genuinely *moving*.

Fiedler had tasted mass-cult popularity with a collection of essays in 1978 titled *Freaks*, and it seems he hankered for more. But the passage of time revealed *Freaks* to be more a curiosity than an agent of psychic change, and *What Was Literature?* comes across merely as Fiedler's attempt to keep his reserved seat on the popular-culture bandwagon, hoping against hope that the youth revolution would make a comeback and that he could be its pied piper, even as he entered his eighth decade.

CANONIZING THE JEWS

In 1959 Herzl Press published a monograph titled *The Jew in the American Novel*. It was at once a cultural history of Jewish characters in selected American novels and an effort to establish a canon of Jewish American fiction. Had the study been done by any other critic at that time it would surely have been predictable and probably destined for the dustbin. But the author was Leslie Fiedler, and the result turned out to be one of the pioneering efforts in what came to be known as the Jewish American renaissance.

A popular novelist such as Ben Hecht struck Fiedler as more hack than serious artist, and certainly as less important in the survey of Jewish American fictionists than Abraham Cahan, Daniel Fuchs, Henry Roth, and Nathanael West. Fiedler began his study of serious Jewish American fiction with Abraham Cahan's *The Rise of David Levinsky* (1917), and he went on to point out the neglected importance of the dark satires (e.g., *The Day of the Locust*) of Nathanael West. Fiedler's judgments in *The Jew in the American Novel* became the template on which subsequent courses on Jewish American fiction would be built, and several of his subjects became household names directly because of his critical attention. Indeed, few other critics have played such an important role in boosting the stock of Jewish American writers such as Henry Roth, Bernard Malamud, and Saul Bellow. What Fiedler had to say on behalf of Henry Roth was especially important because *Call It Sleep* (1934), Roth's extraordinary treatment of a young boy growing up on New York's lower East Side, was in the late 1950s nearly forgotten. A few years after Fiedler published *The Jew in the American Novel*, the journal *American Scholar* ran a feature in which selected critics were asked to nominate the most neglected novel of the twentieth century. Alfred Kazin and Leslie Fiedler both weighed in on behalf of *Call It Sleep*, and the novel was republished in 1964. The paperback edition became a huge critical and popular success.

Like the popular entertainer who gives an ongoing series of "farewell" concerts, Fiedler insisted that *The Jew in the American Novel* exhausted what he had to say on the subject of Jewish literature—but in 1991 he succumbed to the publication of *Fiedler on the Roof: Essays on Literature and Jewish Identity*, a collection that not only allowed him to put a grouping of "Jewish" essays between hard covers but also to top it off with a title that is shamelessly cheesy and characteristically audacious. Undeniably, the author's deepest subject in *Fiedler on the Roof*, his abiding concern, if you will, is *himself*. As Morris Dickstein points out in the *New York Times Book Review*, "as its show-biz title suggests, the critic himself takes the spotlight. . . . Whatever the topic at hand [be it the Holocaust or the Book of Job, Norman Mailer or the Leopold Bloom of James Joyce's *Ulysses*], the subject of this book is Leslie Fiedler." One could argue that that has always been the case with Fiedler's books, and that that is why his readers are relentlessly torn between gratitude and disgruntlement.

Still, *Fiedler on the Roof* makes it clearer than any other book that, in his self-styled mythology, Fiedler regarded himself as "the last Jew"—as Indian, as shaman, as maverick, as archetypal bad boy. In these essays, Fiedler means to shock, to provoke, to remain—in his old age—ever the iconoclast. But scrape away the Fiedler high jinks and what the collection comes to is Fiedler's realization, sometimes gleefully announced, sometimes sadly rendered, that Jewish American literature is no longer the vibrant, *living* entity it once was. Three decades after the heyday of Jewish American writing, the literature Fiedler once fought for had become part of the establishment, and the culture it reflected had been muted by assimilation. The essays in this volume reflect the views of a writer simultaneously bored with, and yet still strangely attracted to, such matters as the Holocaust or the changing faces of anti-Semitism. But they are also important, even indispensable, for anyone interested in the changing emphases that some critics of Jewish American culture have taken in the decades since the Jewish American renaissance. The Holocaust, for example, has received much more attention from Jewish American writers and critics than have novels that require readers to be Jewishly literate. Fiedler belonged to an older generation of "literary Jews" who think of themselves in largely secular terms. Small wonder then that Fiedler felt somewhat estranged from much that identifies contemporary Jewish American literature, but argue as he would that the subject no longer engaged him, as *Fiedler on the Roof* demonstrates, it clearly did.

THE NORMAL, ABNORMAL, AND DOWNRIGHT FREAKY

Tyranny of the Normal, published in 1996, is a collection of nine essays that began their life as talks delivered to a wide variety of nonliterary audiences: a World Conference of Theologians; the inaugural ceremonies for the Year of the Disabled held at the United Nations headquarters in New York City; a meeting of physicians. Fiedler was always a restless academic, someone who much preferred a lively give-and-take with nonspecialists than boring conversations about the literary niceties with English department longhairs. And given his lifelong interest in mythmaking and what has come to be known as "culture studies," it is hardly surprising that Fiedler would have been drawn to ruminating about theology and biomedical ethics—for these are the places in late-twentieth-century culture where his readings of Shakespeare and Dickens, American literature and science fiction, came to seem most applicable.

All blacks are Jews, Fiedler was always fond of declaring, and under the skin, both are Indians. But beginning in the 1970s, Fiedler appeared less and less captivated by Jewish American fiction or, indeed, by the bulk of Jewish American experience. Assimilation, he seemed to suggest, had so taken its toll that Jewish Americans had become virtually like everybody else. This being so—at least for Fiedler—his obsession with the marginalized, and the confusing syncretism he asserted among identities—racial, ethnic, sexual—reached yet another level in the late 1970s. In 1978 his book-length study of sideshow performers, titled *Freaks: Myths and Images of the Secret Self,* propelled him from academic stardom to best-sellerdom.

Throughout his long career, Fiedler tells us in the title essay of *Tyranny of the Normal,* he was

> obsessed with the image of the Stranger, the Outsider, but chiefly as it is embodied in fictional portrayals of the ethnic Other. I have concentrated, that is to say, on the myths of the Negro, the Jew, and the Indian in novel and poems written by—and primarily for—WASP Americans. More recently, however, it occurred to me that for all of

us able to think of ourselves as "normal," there is a more ultimate Other. That is, of course, the Freak, the Monster, the congenital malformation: a fellow-human born too large or too small, with too many or too few limbs, hair in the wrong places or ambiguous sexual organs.

In *Tyranny of the Normal,* Fiedler identifies a new set of cultural concepts to embrace or to vilify: the New Mutants (his term) who emerged from the cultural revolution of the late 1960s and set New Age religion into motion; politically correct euphemisms such as "physically challenged"; organ donation and how it is that most people reject the idea; and perhaps most of all, the ways in which our pervasive "tyranny of the normal" may ultimately lead to what Fiedler warns is a dangerous Cult of the Eternally Young and Fabulously Slim. Add to all this Fiedler's candor about "love and death" as he himself approached eighty, and the result is a collection packed with intriguing insights at some points, errant foolishness at others, and, always, marvelously engaged writing.

Take, for example, the essay "The Rebirth of God and the Death of Man," originally published in 1973. Fiedler writes with large measures of enthusiasm about the New Church of "actual Visionaries and Saints," premised on an ongoing revolution of the young—who stay perpetually young by abandoning bourgeois Amerika (spelt with a *k* to emphasize its links to fascism), establishing communes, and blissing out on drugs. (Granted, Fiedler worries a bit about the shivery implications of a movement that regards health itself as bourgeois; hygiene, as he rightly points out, was never a strong suit with hippies.) The rub, of course, is that none of Fiedler's giddy predictions came true. Thus, when one reads, in 1996, about the mass of disaffected young who have turned *The Whole Earth Catalogue* into a secular bible, the result seems more history lesson than an exercise in contemporary analysis. Put another way, Fiedler seemed stuck in a time warp of his own making. As a pop culture maven, he would be better off watching selected episodes of *Friends, Seinfeld,* or even *Beverly Hills 90210.*

Nonetheless, at a time when critical debates are no longer conducted in readily accessible English and when most expressions of "theory" are as tedious as they are impenetrable, Fiedler's contributions to American literature are worth revisiting. It is not just that he wrote with brio and brilliance, or even that he often failed to get full credit for pioneering aspects of feminist criticism, culture studies, or Queer theory, but, rather, that his passion for what the imagination might tell us about life stayed the course. His career needs no special pleading, much less apology. Fiedler's own words are quite enough, and, moreover, they always were.

Selected Bibliography

WORKS OF LESLIE FIEDLER

NONFICTION

An End to Innocence: Essays on Culture and Politics. Boston: Beacon, 1955.

The Jew in the American Novel. New York: Herzl Institute, 1959.

Love and Death in the American Novel. New York: Criterion, 1960. Rev. ed., New York: Stein & Day, 1966.

No! In Thunder: Essays on Myth and Literature. Boston: Beacon, 1960.

The Continuing Debate: Essays on Education. With Jacob Vincour. New York: St. Martin's, 1964.

Waiting for the End: The Crisis in American Culture and a Report on Twentieth-Century American Literature. New York: Stein & Day, 1964.

The Return of the Vanishing American. New York: Stein & Day, 1968.

Being Busted. New York: Stein & Day, 1969.

The Collected Essays of Leslie Fiedler. 2 vols. New York: Stein & Day, 1971.

Cross the Border, Close the Gap. New York: Stein & Day, 1972.

The Stranger in Shakespeare. New York: Stein & Day, 1972.

In Dreams Awake: A Historical-Critical Anthology of Science Fiction. New York: Dell, 1975.

Freaks: Myths and Images of the Secret Self. New York: Simon & Schuster, 1978.

The Inadvertent Epic: From Uncle Tom's Cabin to Roots. New York: Simon & Schuster, 1979.

Olaf Stapledon: A Man Divided. New York: Oxford University Press, 1982.

What Was Literature? Class Culture and Mass Society. New York: Simon & Schuster, 1982.

Fiedler on the Roof: Essays on Literature and Jewish Identity. Boston: Godine, 1991.

Tyranny of the Normal: Essays on Bioethics, Theology, and Myth. Boston: Godine, 1996.

A New Fiedler Reader. Amherst, N.Y.: Prometheus Books, 1999. (Includes "Come Back to the Raft Ag'in, Huck Honey!" and "Montana; or the End of Jean-Jacques Rousseau.")

NOVELS AND SHORT FICTION

Pull Down Vanity and Other Stories. Philadelphia: Lippincott, 1962. (Short stories.)

The Second Stone: A Love Story. New York: Stein & Day, 1963. (Novel.)

Back to China. New York: Stein & Day, 1965. (Novel.)

The Last Jew in America. New York: Stein & Day, 1966. (Three novellas.)

Nude Croquet: The Stories of Leslie Fiedler. New York: Stein & Day, 1969. (Short stories.)

The Messengers Will Come No More. New York: Stein & Day, 1974. (Novel.)

ESSAYS, STORIES, DRAMA

"What Can We Do About Fagin? The Jew-Villain in Western Tradition." *Commentary,* May 1949, pp. 411–418.

"Toward an American Criticism." *Kenyon Review* 2:561–574 (autumn 1950).

"The Bearded Virgin and the Blind God." *Kenyon Review* 5:540–551 (summer 1953).

"Second Thoughts on *Love and Death in the American Novel:* My First Gothic Novel." *Novel: A Forum on Fiction* 1:8–11 (fall 1967).

"The Divine Stupidity of Kurt Vonnegut." *Esquire,* September 1970, pp. 195–197, 199–200.

"The Children's Hour: or, The Return of the Vanishing Longfellow: Some Reflections of the Future of Poetry." In *Liberation: New Essays on the Humanities in Revolution.* Edited by Ihab Hassan. Middletown, Conn.: Wesleyan University Press, 1971.

"Literature as an Institution: The View from 1980." In *English Literature: Opening Up the Canon.* Edited by Leslie A. Fiedler and Houston A. Baker. Baltimore: Johns Hopkins University Press, 1981.

"New England and the Invention of the South." In *American Literature and the New England Heritage.* Edited by James Nagel and Richard Astro. New York: Garland, 1981.

"The Criticism of Science Fiction." In *Coordinates: Placing Science Fiction and Fantasy.* Edited by Georger E. Slusser, Eric S. Rabkin, and Robert Scholes. Carbondale: Southern Illinois University Press, 1983.

"Fulbright I: Italy 1952." In *The Fulbright Difference.* Edited by Richard T. Arndt and David Lee Rubin. New Brunswick, N.J.: Transaction, 1993.

"Hubbell Acceptance Speech." In *Leslie Fiedler and American Culture.* Edited by Steven G. Kellerman and Irving Malin. Newark: University of Delaware Press, 1999. (Fiedler's 1994 speech in acceptance of the Hubbell Medal for Lifetime Contribution to the Study of American Literature awarded by the Modern Language Association.)

WORKS EDITED BY FIEDLER

The Art of the Essay. 2d ed. New York: Crowell, 1969.

English Literature: Opening up the Canon. With Houston A. Baker. Baltimore: Johns Hopkins University Press, 1981.

CRITICAL AND BIOGRAPHICAL STUDIES

Barth, John. "The Accidental Mentor." In *Leslie Fiedler and American Culture.* Edited by Steven G. Kellerman and Irving Malin. Newark: University of Delaware Press, 1999.

Bauman, Bruce. "The Critic in Winter." *Salon* (http://www.salon.com/books/int/2003/01/02/fiedler/index_np.html).

Bellman, Samuel Irving. "The American Artist as European Frontiersman: Leslie Fiedler's *The Second Stone*." *Critique*, pp. 131–143 (winter 1963).

Biederman, Patricia Ward. "Leslie Fiedler: The Critics as Outlaw." *Buffalo Courier-Express,* March 7, 1982, pp. 9–11, 13–15.

Chase, Richard. "Leslie Fiedler and American Culture." *Chicago Review* 4:8–18 (autumn–winter 1960).

Cox, James M. "Celebrating Leslie Fiedler." In *Leslie Fiedler and American Culture.* Edited by Steven G. Kellerman and Irving Malin. Newark: University of Delaware Press, 1999.

Daniels, Guy. "The Sorrows of Baro Finkelstone." *New Republic,* May 22, 1965, pp. 25–27.

Dickstein, Morris. Review of *Fiedler on the Roof. New York Times Book Review,* August 4, 1991, p. 3.

Gates, David. "Fiedler's Utopian Vision." *Newsweek,* January 9, 1984, p. 11.

Kellerman, Steven G., and Irving Malin, eds. *Leslie Fiedler and American Culture.* Newark: University of Delaware Press, 1999. (See especially Kellerman's essay "The Importance of *Being Busted.*")

Kenner, Hugh. "Who Was Leslie Fiedler?" *Harper's,* November 1982, pp. 69–73.

Larson, Charles. "Leslie Fiedler: The Critic and the Myth, the Critic as Myth." *Literary Review* 4:133–143 (winter 1970–1971).

———. "The Good Bad Boy of American Letters." *Saturday Review,* December 25, 1971, pp. 27–28, 35.

Looby, Christopher. "'Innocent Homosexuality': The Fiedler Thesis in Retrospect." In *"Adventures of Huckleberry Finn": A Case Study in Critical Controversy.* Edited by Gerald Graf and James Phelan. Boston: Bedford Books of St. Martin's Press, 1995.

Lynn, Kenneth. "Back to the Raft." *Commentary,* January 1983, pp. 66, 68.

Winchell, Mark Royden. *Leslie Fiedler.* Boston: Twayne, 1985.

———. *"Too Good To Be True": The Life and Art of Leslie Fiedler.* Columbia: University of Missouri Press, 2002.

INTERVIEWS

DeMott, Benjamin. "A Talk with Leslie Fiedler." *New York Times Book Review,* March 5, 1978.

Jackson, Bruce. "Buffalo English: Literary Glory Days at UB." *Buffalo Beat,* March 4, 1999. (A series of interviews with Leslie Fiedler, taped between April 8 and August 20, 1989.)

—SANFORD PINSKER

Yusef Komunyakaa
1947–

When he received the Ruth Lilly Poetry Prize in 2001, Yusef Komunyakaa added another honor to a long list, which includes being named a chancellor of the Academy of American Poets and receiving the Bronze Star for his service as a military news correspondent in Vietnam. Komunyakaa has received most of America's major prizes for poetry, including the Pulitzer Prize, a Kingsley Tufts Award, two creative writing fellowships from the National Endowment for the Arts, and awards from the *Kenyon Review* and *Poetry*. He has been classified as a jazz poet, a southern writer, an Afro-American poet, and a "soldier poet," but it is certain that Komunyakaa, who has been described by Fran Gordon as "one of America's most receptive minds," would not care to be categorized. Komunyakaa is an original force in poetry and in his sixth decade he was continuing to produce new work at a prolific rate, always expanding his horizons, writing a poetry that is, in his own words, "constantly changing, growing. It's becoming something else in order to become itself—amorphous and cumulative until it forms a vision."

Komunyakaa was born in Bogalusa, Louisiana, to James William Brown and Mildred Washington Brown on April 29, 1947. The oldest of six children, he has four brothers and one sister. The Bogalusa of Komunyakaa's childhood was rural and bucolic, a place of hollyhocks and oak trees, as well as a paper mill that dominated the landscape with its "wheels within wheels" and "metallic syncopation." He describes the mill in a poem called "The Whistle" and generally characterized his birthplace to Susan Conley as a "typical Southern town . . . with a library that did not allow blacks" and the threat of the Ku Klux Klan always in the background. Komunyakaa, innately curious about everything and in love with the sound and look of words, found a way to get the books he needed. On his own, he read the Bible from Genesis to Revelation twice, and in school, he read Shakespeare, Edgar Allan Poe, Alfred, Lord Tennyson, and eventually the poetry of Langston Hughes, Paul Dunbar, Phyllis Wheatley, and Gwendolyn Brooks. Even though the Bogalusa Public Library was closed to him, Komunyakaa was able to borrow a copy of James Baldwin's *Nobody Knows My Name* from a small library run by the woman who had been his kindergarten teacher. He was sixteen at the time, and he maintains that Baldwin's book, which he read and reread perhaps twenty-five times, inspired him to begin writing.

Komunyakaa's father, James William Brown, was a carpenter, as was his great-grandfather, so it is not entirely surprising that at one point in his career, Komunyakaa contemplated apprenticing himself as a cabinetmaker or that he has remodeled at least one old house. The name, Komunyakaa, honors a grandfather who came to the United States from Trinidad as a stowaway and changed his name to "Brown" when he went to work on a plantation in Louisiana. According to the poet, his grandfather "never stopped whispering his name," and eventually the poet "slipped into his skin," taking the name "Komunyakaa." Not everyone in the family was happy with the change, but it was a necessary thing for Yusef, who felt his given name did not reflect what he was learning about his heritage. The name change also might have been an outward manifestation of a contest Komunyakaa had with his father. As he told Susan Conley, his father believed in a "black Calvinist illusion that menial labor could lead to great heights," but Yusef already knew that he wanted something else and spent his late teens "in far-off mental landscapes." Even though he did not seriously begin to write poetry until much later, he did write a long poem—one hundred lines in rhymed quatrains—for his high school graduating class.

After graduating from Bogalusa's Central High School in 1965, Komunyakaa traveled, stopping briefly in Puerto Rico and arriving, in 1966, in Phoenix, Arizona, where his mother had moved. He stayed in Phoenix, working on an assembly line at the McGraw Edison factory, until 1968, when he entered the U.S. Army and became an information specialist because of his natural writing ability. In early 1969 Komunyakaa was sent to Officer Candidate School but eventually transferred back into his previous field. Komunyakaa's daughter, Kimberly Ann, was born in Phoenix on April 1, 1969, and later that same month Komunyakaa began a tour of duty in Vietnam. In Vietnam, Komunyakaa was stationed at Chu Lai, where he was an editor for the military newspaper, *The Southern Cross*. As part of his job there, Komunyakaa was often sent to the front lines. "Whenever there was any engagement, I'd be ferried out on a helicopter to the action—to the middle of it—and I had to report, I had to witness," he told William Baer. Though Komunyakaa opposed the war and had even thought of going absent without leave, the idea of "bearing witness" attracted him, and once he was there, "the pressures of survival were so woven into who I was, into who we are as humans, that if placed against a war, one reacts to survive." He was awarded the Bronze Star for his journalism during the war. Komunyakaa's inner survival was helped by reading the 1970 American poetry anthology *The Voice That Is Great within Us*, edited by Hayden Carruth, and Donald Allen's 1960 anthology *New American Poetry, 1945–1960.*

After Vietnam, Komunyakaa was stationed in Fort Carson, Colorado, until he was discharged from the army in 1971. During the next couple of years, he divided his time between the mountains of Colorado, which he loved on first sight; Louisiana, where he could have long talks about his heritage with his maternal grandmother, Mary Washington; and Arizona, where his daughter lived. In 1973 he enrolled in "distributive studies" at the University of Colorado, majoring in English, sociology, and psychology; this combination allowed him to take a creative writing course with Alex Blackburn, the editor of *Writers Forum;* Komunyakaa began by writing short fiction but soon was writing poetry. Because he took on extra credit hours each semester, Komunyakaa finished his course work quickly; in December 1975 he completed his bachelor's degree magna cum laude in English and sociology. After a brief dalliance with the idea of working on a doctorate in psychology, Komunyakaa began a master's program in creative writing at Colorado State University. It was 1976, and his mentors at CSU were Bill Tremblay and Chris Howell, as well as the other poets he was able to meet and whose work he admired, including Gwendolyn Brooks, Richard Hugo, and William Matthews.

While in Colorado, Komunyakaa taught composition at CSU, began publishing work in journals such as *Chameleon, Leviathan,* and *Greensboro Review,* and, with Adam Hammer, cofounded an arts journal, *Gumbo,* which published well-known writers such as Robert Creeley during its two-year run. During this same time, Komunyakaa's first collection appeared. In 1977 his chapbook *Dedications and Other Darkhorses* was published by *Rocky Mountain Creative Arts Journal* in a poetry series edited by Paul Dilsaver.

DEDICATIONS AND OTHER DARKHORSES

The first poem in Komunyakaa's first book is, appropriately, a dedication. Dedications appear and reappear all throughout Komunyakaa's work; in his 2001 collection, *Pleasure Dome*, many of the newest poems are directly or indirectly "for" someone or something: maybe Michael Jackson, perhaps Muhammad Ali, definitely Chinua Achebe, most likely Ella Fitzgerald, and certainly Richard Johnson. In his first book, "Returning the Borrowed Road" is for Richard Hugo, one of Komunyakaa's earliest poetry teachers. The title itself is a wonder: What does it mean to return a "borrowed road"? What kind of road can be lent out and returned? This poem is about the road into writing a certain kind of poem, a way to get the stone to speak, to bring what is "a mile down in the ground" to the surface. Hugo, the "you" of the poem, is called "back across / iron months to Missoula" after he had stayed too long perhaps, "overtaken in Colorado's slow mountains." The poem is clear in its "homage" to Hugo, whose words, *"Get away / from the poem. You're too close"* teach the poet to "let each stone / seek its new mouth."

Another poem that presages later work is "Urban Renewal," in which "Everything / melts" into "the white odor of absence," while the wrecking ball, contrasted with "pigeons cooing in eaves," swings and leaves behind nothing but "parking lots." Paradise, as in the Joni Mitchell song, is paved over, and this will often be a theme in Komunyakaa's work, as the title of his 1998 book, *Thieves of Paradise,* suggests. Words related to the art of construction vie with those connected to the crudeness of destruction: the "I-beams braced for impact" are unable to withstand the jolt of "sequential sledgehammers"; the "wrecking crews" are "men unable to catch sparrows without breaking / wings into splinters." The parking lots are simultaneously an absence of what was there and the future's blueprint. This sort of coincident layering recurs throughout Komunyakaa's work, which often turns to the forms of collage, palimpsest, and medley, but even more apropos are the images in the poem, which are natural ones for a poet who knows things about buildings and tools.

In "The Tongue Is," the tongue is many things and most of them not comforting, not trustworthy. In a strange variation of the ancient metaphor of memory as a block of wax upon which images are inscribed, Komunyakaa's poem begins by saying that the tongue is "xeroxed on brainmatter," that "words spread / like dirty oil over a lake." "The tongue even lies to itself." While the poem begins like an addendum to a passage in the Bible (in the New Testament book of James, chapter 3) where "the tongue is," among other things, a "fire" and a "deadly poison," there is sympathy for that devil (and, metonymically, language and poetry) in this poem. Memory is "slow" and "erratic," and it hides itself in the poisonous oleander; no wonder then that the "tongue skips a beat" and looses a "link of truth." When a personal pronoun comes in, its purpose is to enter a

>   . . . guilty plea
> dry as the tongue of a beggar's
> unlaced shoe . . .

and the jury that is the ultimately the reader becomes even more sympathetic. The last image of the tongue laboring, "a victrola in the mad mouth-hole / of 3 A.M. sorrow," indicates that the tongue, despite its flaws, is going to make something of sorrow and is working to transform the shapeless and inexpressible into a poem.

The poems in *Dedications and Other Darkhorses* go a long way toward nullifying the second part of the book's title, because with this book Komunyakaa could never again be a complete unknown. These early poems do what Komunyakaa says the blues do: they show that life is both beautiful and painful, that the truth is difficult to say, and that letting the language carry some of the weight lightens sorrow at any hour of the day. Komunyakaa liked what he was doing in Colorado, but he wanted more time to write, more time to read. As soon as he finished his M.A. at CSU, Komunyakaa enrolled in the masters in fine arts program in creative writing at the University of California at Irvine, where the faculty included James McMichaels, Howard Moss, Robert Peters, C. K. Williams, and Charles Wright. He read voraciously, everything from Ezra Pound to Robert Hayden to Melvin Tolson; he read, in translation, poetry by Stéphane Mallarmé, Pablo Neruda, César Vallejo, and Aimé Césaire, and, in the company of other student writers—such as Garrett Hongo, Deborah Woodard, Vic Coccimiglio, Debra Thomas, and Virginia Campbell—he continued to write poetry. New poems appeared in *Black American Literature Forum, The Beloit Poetry Journal, West End,* and *Yardbird Reader.* Komunyakaa taught composition at Irvine (as he had in Colorado), but this time he was an instructor in Irvine's remedial composition program. By 1980 Komunyakaa had completed the work for his M.F.A. at UC Irvine with a thesis titled "Premonitions of the Bread Line," but even before that, in 1979, he had published another chapbook, *Lost in the Bonewheel Factory* (1979).

LOST IN THE BONEWHEEL FACTORY

From the opening poem, "Looking a Mad Dog Dead in the Eyes" and throughout the whole nightmarish trip in the Bonewheel Factory, the reader is not in for a "soft ride," as "Floor Plans" warns:

> All the cruel rooms are identical behind different-colored doors: a black cellophane window to the outside, a woman sprawled nude on a red velvet loveseat, a copy of *Premonitions of the Bread Line* on a white shag rug, as the shadow of a dagger slides along the walls. Cicadas hum fire in a valley. This is where a god gets his heart cut out. . . .

Where a woman crawls on cobblestones & a man chops off three fingers to beg bread. In a country without moon, sun, or solitary star, lies rot in the mouth.

The surrealistic qualities of Komunyakaa's second volume are obvious: influenced by reading French poets such as André Breton and (especially) Aimé Césaire, the black surrealist poet from Martinique, as well as by the Bob Dylan music of the early and mid-1970s, Komunyakaa fills the poems with bizarre juxtapositions and unrestrained images, many of them apocalyptic and disturbing. The "Tour Guide" in the poem of that name allows that

> This is where you begin
> in yourself, in the room
> alone with terror

and so it goes. In "Sitting in a Rocking Chair, Going Blind," the speaker watches as

> a black buick
>   special
>   runs down a child

while in the poem "1938" the poet Vallejo finds Death at his "boot heels" (a reference to Bob Dylan's "Mr. Tambourine Man"?), and in "S & M" the speaker temporarily becomes "a many-headed beast." The volume is filled with wild convergences: in "High on Sadness," a naked body yields its bones and becomes a "bright airplane / on an assembly line"; in "Ghost Chant, et alii," a mountain lion rides air and "a rooster struggles out of golden grass / with its head cut off"; and in "The Dog Act," the speaker claims to be the "warm-up act," which means that he is obliged to "punch [himself] in the face" and "fall through imaginary trapdoors."

> Can I have your attention now?
> I'm crawling across the stagefloor
> like a dog with four broken legs.

You're supposed to jump up
& down now, laugh & applaud.

Even though the last poem in *Lost in the Bonewheel Factory*, "Corrigenda," claims to "take it back," the images of the book reappear in the retraction: "the tumor in each of us," "death that can / hold us together like twin brothers," and the "legless beggar." Decades later, Komunyakaa told Tony Barnstone and Michael Garabedian that sometimes an artist must present "a certain reality that embraces images that are often beautiful, frightening." He continues:

> I think all of us experience all kinds of negative things, and there's a whole commodity of distractions in which we try to escape them, and we realize that's impossible, finally. So I think maybe what I'm saying is that we have the capacity to have a certain empathy for those who come into contact with that which is horrific. We have the capacity to measure out the horrors against their existence. At least I hope so.

Despite the dark mood of volume, the last lines of "Corrigenda" seem to foreshadow this statement: "If you must quote me, remember / I said that love heals from inside."

"PREMONITIONS OF THE BREAD LINE"

Komunyakaa's M.F.A. thesis, "Premonitions of the Bread Line," as already indicated, makes an intertextual appearance in *Lost in the Bonewheel Factory*, but none of its poems appear in his later selected or collected works. His thesis collection, like *Lost in the Bonewheel Factory*, is replete with juxtaposed language and imagery. Discussing "Premonitions of the Bread Line," Vince Gotera in *African American Writers* emphasizes what he calls "another of Komunyakaa's strategies," which is to couple Latinate and Anglo-Saxon words to create a "syncretic diction." One might argue that joining words of dissimilar etymology is the essence and richness of the English language, and the practice is found in poets as different from each other as Shakespeare, Walt Whitman, T. S. Eliot, Elizabeth Bishop, and Robert Hayden. One might also argue that Komunyakaa, possibly one of contemporary poetry's most voracious poetry readers, was practicing his craft in every line and phrase. Although Komunyakaa's habit of yoking together monosyllabic and multisyllabic words is perhaps a deliberate cultural strategy, used in order to demonstrate how meaningless it is to divide language into stereotypical types of diction, it seems more likely that it is his ear, informed by the jazz and blues music that poured from the radio in his mother's living room, that is at work, unconsciously. As he says in "Kit and Caboodle," which appears in *The Eye of the Poet*:

> Language is alive. For the poet, each word represents sound and meaning; the music of meaning is shaped by words that fall left or right of a single word. Each word is an increment of the whole. Perhaps we are drawn to poetry because language vibrates (is an action), and we seem to search still for a language that will keep us whole.

With his thesis completed, Komunyakaa crossed the continent to take up a fellowship at the Provincetown Fine Arts Work Center in Massachusetts, staying eight months—from October 1980 until May 1981. As he told Vince Gotera, the time in Massachusetts was a time "of semi-isolation in which I could very methodically deal with my writing . . . it was a place to develop one's voice . . . [and] to remove layers of facades and superficialities." After the gestation in Provincetown, Komunyakaa returned to the South with the book he had been working on, a book that gathers from many places, many subjects. For a while, he lived with his maternal grandmother, Mary Washington: "I went back to Bogalusa in '81, after being away for many years. It was almost like going back to a hometown inside my head, to my own psychological territory." *Copacetic* was finished in Bogalusa, but before the book appeared in 1984, Komunyakaa began teaching composition and literature at the Lakefront Campus of the University of New Orleans; at the same time, he was also working in the city's Poets-in-the-Schools program, remodeling an old house at 818 Piety Street, and running a bookstore and coffeehouse called Copacetic. It was a whirlwind time for the poet—one of many.

COPACETIC

The title of Komunyakaa's first commercially published book is a word added to the language by jazz and blues musicians; the general meaning of "copacetic" is that everything is fine and mellow, that things are cool, okay. Although jazz and blues flavor the pages of Komunyakaa's earlier books, this volume owes much more to the big wooden radio that was always playing in his childhood home, bringing him the music of Louis Armstrong, Charles Mingus, Thelonious Monk, Diane Washington, and Mahalia Jackson, to name a few. In *Copacetic* Komunyakaa uses a "gumbo" mix of voices and rhythms to describe things that surrounded him in his boyhood and early manhood. The "bloodhounds," "lynchings," "whips," "branded flesh," and "big house" combine with "piney woods" and "cottonmouth country" to let the reader know this South is seen through the eyes of an Afro-American witness and the memories are ugly and painful; the colloquial phrasings and mellow rhythms and refrains, however, do something to give the volume a sense of affirmation. For Komunyakaa, as he told Vince Gotera in an interview, the blues is a copacetic art form that has "an existential melancholy based on an acute awareness," ending up in a sort of transcendence.

"False Leads," the first poem in *Copacetic,* links interestingly with the last poem of *Lost in the Bonewheel Factory,* "Corrigenda," in which the speaker claims that he "never said there's a book inside / every tree" and claims to take back his surrealistic declarations. In "False Leads," the speaker's speech becomes the epitome of a false lead, telling "Mister Bloodhound Boss" to beware of "looking for Slick Sam / the Freight Train Hopper," giving the "Bloodhound" reasons to abandon his search: Slick Sam is "a crack shot," "a mind reader," and, besides being at home in the woods and swamps, Slick Sam "knows about bloodhounds & black pepper, / how to put a bobcat into a crocus sack." The Boss, a white man, probably from the North, obviously does not know the territory, but the speaker does, and whether or not Slick Sam "can shoot a cigarette out of a man's mouth / thirty paces of an owl's call" does not really matter. It is the "thirty paces of an owl's call" that reverberates, that conjures up the sense of mystery. How can you track someone who starts out in the air? The speaker employs other oblique threats, reporting, without comment or explanation, the fact that he had "glimpsed red / against that treeline" that very morning, followed by a line of mournful Creole, concluding with "Wise not to let night catch you out there." Everything in "False Leads," including the bravado of the speaker, who comes looking for the Man with his opening line, "Hey! Mister Bloodhound Boss," is designed to distract and worry, to create such a tangle of false and frightening leads that the search is abandoned before it begins. Ostensibly, the biggest "false lead" is the entire speech itself, which the speaker cannot help but hint at when he says "I wouldn't tell you no lie."

Many of the poems in *Copacetic* use colloquial idioms and street speech, but as always in Komunyakaa, the words show an eclectic sense of sound and meaning. "Soliloquy: Man Talking to a Mirror" opens with

> Working night shift
>   panhandling Larimer Square
> ain't been easy

and then sighs into "Lawd, this flophouse / has a hangover," telling the face in the mirror that

> you're still a born pushover,
> a tree climber
> in the devil's skull.

Besides the confrontational vernacular of the "soliloquy," there is something of a "false lead" in this poem as well: Since when is a soliloquy spoken to someone else (even if that self is one's alter-ego)? In "The Way the Cards Fall," another voice—the voice of an older woman who has "buried another / husband" since she last saw the poet "holding to the horizon"—tells him that the woman he once loved

> now lives in New Orleans
> on both sides
> of Bourbon Street.

"Reflections," another mirror poem, is another second-person talk, but in this poem, the speaker imagines himself becoming someone else—or else some other person becoming him:

> you can feel him
> grow inside you,
> straining to hoist himself,
> climbing a ladder
> of air, your feet
> in his shoes.

Like the reflections in one of Komunyakaa's most well-known poems, "Facing It," it is hard to tell what is solid and what is reflected, real or imagined.

Under the easy surface of *Copacetic* are layers of interwoven story and song, and the poems talk to each other on "both sides" of the street. In "Annabelle," "It's all to do with / a woman back in Alabama," all to do with getting "lowdown tonight," but in "Faith Healer," it is about a "laying on of hands" and leaning on Jesus. Some of the poems are tributes to personal heroes, as in "More Girl Than Boy," in which the speaker thanks a friend named "Robert Lee" for teaching him how to love jazz, but other poems summon up a remembrance of past things in New Orleans, and, as usual in Komunyakaa, the picture is double; there is always something "under a cloud of steam," as in "Untitled Blues," in which the speaker gathers a sampling of "lurid snow jobs"—that is, things that are painted to appear as what they are not. "Sure, I could say / everything's copacetic," he says, but when he goes on to mention the famous New Orleans cornet player Buddy Bolden, who ended his days in the State Mental Institution in Jackson, we know that everything is *not* copacetic. The last lines of "Untitled Blues" circle back to the beginning of the poem, where the speaker had been looking at a photo of a

>   . . . black boy
> behind a laughing white mask
> he's painted on. . . .

The conclusion is that the boy,

> locked inside your camera,
> perhaps he's lucky—
> he knows how to steal
> laughs in a place
> where your skin
> is your passport.

The blues especially inform the poems in *Copacetic*. Besides explicit titles such as "Borinken Blues," "Woman, I Got the Blues," and "Blues Chant Hoodoo Rival," hints and shades of blue show up all through in the collection; in the collection's tour de force, "Family Tree," the speaker recounts a "genealogy of blues" in which his father's childhood is a "Muddy Water's bone-song" and his grandmothers are "blues women" who

> . . . grow closer
> each year like bent oaks
> to the ground. . . .

In "Safe Subjects," the poet tells himself to "Say something," something even more true

> . . . than
> parted lips, than parted legs
> in sorrow's darkroom of potash
> & blues

and even in "Elegy for Thelonious," the night is

> . . . a lazy rhapsody of shadows,
> swaying to blue vertigo
> & metaphysical funk.

"Safe Subjects" best captures the laid-back and sometimes earnest tone of mid-book, where the speaker feels safe enough to say:

> Let truth have its way with us
> like a fishhook holds
> to life, holds dearly to nothing
> worth saying—pull it out,
> bringing with it hard facts,
> knowledge that the fine underbone
> of hope is also attached
> to inner self, underneath it all.

But toward the end of *Copacetic,* the mood has shifted to a much bleaker tone; here "The Leper's Bell" "follows" the speaker

> . . . around
> the sad blue periphery
> of other lives

and he is so low that he has not even "a dog's mercy / for company," riding the "downward wheel" of fortune, where he has "nothing / the earth wants to steal." Again, the last poem of the book is especially important. The masks and mirrors of the earlier poems come back in "Blues Chant Hoodoo Rival," which begins by saying

> my story is
> how deep the heart runs
> to hide & laugh
> with your hands
> over your blank mouth
> face behind the mask
> talking in tongues

and ends saying that

> our story is
> a rifle butt
> across our heads
> . . . .
> a post-hypnotic suggestion
> a mosaic membrane
> skin of words.

Mirrors shatter in the "gun-barrel night," and the last image in the book is a gallows.

In 1985, a year after *Copacetic* was published, Komunyakaa met Mandy Sayer, an Australian fiction writer, who came to New Orleans as a professional tap dancer. They were married around Christmas 1985, after Komunyakaa had accepted a one-year appointment as visiting professor at Indiana University. Komunyakaa spent 1986, the year after his appointment in Indiana, in Australia, where he met young performance poets at the famous Harold Park Hotel and met established Australian poets, including Gig Young, Vicki Viidikas, and Les Murray. Some of his poems appeared in the Australian journal *Blue Light Lounge.* The time in Australia, he told William Baer, was a good time to take a fresh look at his own landscape and rituals.

> For example, it seems that, as contemporary people, we're very fearful of silence. But why? Why does every moment have to be filled with some kind of external vibration coming from the radio or television or some other technological device? I don't know, but I now realize silence is not an endurance test for me, and it never was.

I APOLOGIZE FOR THE EYES IN MY HEAD

I Apologize for the Eyes in My Head was published by Wesleyan in 1986, while Komunyakaa was in Australia. In an interview with Vince Gotera, Komunyakaa said, "Actually, it's not really an apology, of course. It's the opposite of that, in an ironic satirical way," and the opening poem, "Unnatural State of the Unicorn" demonstrates his point:

> Introduce me first as a man.
> Don't mention superficial laurels
> the dead heap up on the living.

Using what is called "ostinato" in music and "anaphora" in poetry, Komunyakaa weaves a jazz-like justification of a man who will not apologize for being alive; he repeats words and phrases, replicates structures, and builds to a passionate finish:

> I have no birthright to prove,
> no insignia, no secret
> password, no fleur-de-lis.
> My initials aren't on a branding iron.
> I'm standing here in unpolished
> shoes & faded jeans, sweating
> my manly sweat. Inside my skin,
> loving you, I am this space
> my body believes in.

In many ways, this poem makes a new opening for Komunyakaa's work. He moves from *Copacetic*'s bottom of the wheel, where, to borrow a line from Kris Kristofferson, "freedom's just another word for nothing left to lose," to a place where he is able to make something out of nothing. As usual in Komunyakaa, however, the opening poem is a preview of what is *about* to happen, in stages, throughout the volume, and the poems that follow indicate how things will vacillate as the speaker works out answers. In a line that seems to invert the assured ending of "Unnatural State of the Unicorn" (and perhaps explains the word "Unnatural" in that title), the speaker in "Lightshow," who is at the window reading tarot cards, reports that "The High Priestess / says I'm wrong about losses." "Each day I badger myself with harder questions," but the "answers elude."

> I feel like a devil's decoy
> at this window, but I can't move
> till The Hanged Man says *yes*.

Before the Hanged Man says *yes* (and he does, in the last section of the last poem of the volume), the speaker takes us down an avenue that seems to intersect with Bob Dylan's "Desolation Row." In a surreal and allegorical world, "Sorrow," personified as a lethal woman, pursues the poet from Main Street to Paris and Rio de Janeiro, and

> . . . At midnight
> she climbs into bed, smiling,
> her weight no more than a clue.

In "Touch-up Man," the poet works from "Mr. Pain's notecards," and ends up "doctoring photographs, / airbrushing away the corpses." The most dominant persona in the collection is "The Thorn Merchant," who first appears in an eponymous poem, after which we meet "The Thorn Merchant's Right-Hand Man," "The Thorn Merchant's Wife," "The Thorn Merchant's Mistress," and "The Thorn Merchant's Son." ("The Thorn Merchant's Daughter" does not appear until *Thieves of Paradise*, 1998, although she is mentioned in the first poem.) The Thorn Merchant deals in pain: "There are teeth marks / on everything he loves," and the Thorn Merchant literally embodies pain:

> With his fingers around his throat
> he moans like a statue
> of straw on a hillside.
> Ready to auction off his hands
> to the highest bidder,
> he knows how death waits
> in us like a light switch.

When Alan Fox asked Komunyakaa about the last lines of this poem, Komunyakaa said that he had written the lines in California, at Irvine.

> I remembered when I wrote that line down, that image down, it was something that made me laugh and at the same time, it was something that caused a great deal of internal fear. . . . it's a realization about death, how it can come out of nowhere, it seems that it isn't something that we can rehearse for. Something we can't control.

Throughout this book, the heart and the brain struggle with each other, just as lovers come together and fall apart. In "The Heart's Graveyard Shift," the speaker concludes that

> . . . What can go wrong
> goes wrong, & between loves an empty
> space defines itself like a stone's weight

"After the Heart's Interrogation" starts out in "December's slaughterhouse," where the "wall clock picks itself apart," and

> The gun cocking outside
> my front door is another question
> I'm here to answer.

Finally, in "The Brain to the Heart," the brain says:

> . . . I know
> how hard you work
>
> in that dark place, but
> I can't be tied down
> to shadows of men
> in trenches you won't
> forget.

Many other themes and layers come into this volume: in the beautiful "Landscape for the Disappeared," Komunyakaa's "lost uncles & granddaddies / come back" from the peat bogs in Louisiana—

> . . . the ones
> we've never known, with stories
> more ours than theirs

but in "'Everybody's Reading Li Po' Silk-screened on a Purple T-Shirt," the "boy junkie, Ricardo" is "tied to night's string," and he

> . . . sways under neon
> like a black girl with red hair
> in the doorway of Lucky's.

Komunyakaa believes that the time in which one is writing affects the sound and tone of a poem, and a number of poems in this volume ("Cinderella at Big Sur," "Too Pretty for Serious Business," and "Child's Play") are discernibly of their time, 1980s America.

As Komunyakaa said, the book is not in fact an apology, even though there are two "apology" poems. The first, "When in Rome—Apologia" is an off-hand, mocking piece that apologizes to someone referred to as "sir" for

> . . . getting involved
>
> in the music—
> it's my innate weakness
>
> for the cello: so human.

Soon "cello" and "wife" become confused, just as music and sex blend. "I got carried away / by the swing of her hips" is a nice ambiguous line, but the last line, "I apologize for / the eyes in my head" is a jazzy, sarcastic way of saying "excuse me for breathing." The second apology poem is simply called "I Apologize," and again there is no actual apology. The poem, once more, is addressed to "sir" (with*out* love):

> My mind wasn't even there.
> Mirage, sir. I didn't see
> what I thought I saw.

A new kind of poem for Komunyakaa emerges in this volume: the longer, multisectioned piece, as in "Dreambook Bestiary" and "The Beast & Burden: Seven Improvisations." This sort of poem (where the sections are named and numbered) often appears in subsequent volumes and is perhaps the sort of poem where Komunyakaa takes the most risks. Improvisation, the essence of jazz, means that there is no absolute control over what is coming next, and it is fitting that it is precisely this sort of imprecise process that yields that *yes* the poet was looking for at the beginning of the volume. In "The Beast & Burden: Seven Improvisations," *"The Vicious," "The Decadent," "The Esoteric," "The Sanctimonious,"* and *"The Vindictive"* come together in *"Exorcism,"* where "beauty & ugliness conspire," and "the beast is / transmogrified into the burden."

What follows is a sort of ecstasy:

O how geranium-scented melancholia
works on the body—
smell of ether, gut string
trailing lost memories.
Detached from whatever remains,
one note of bliss still burns his tongue.

Visions of Isaiah and the burning coal occur; the tongue seems redeemed, temporarily, and in the last part of the poem, *"Epilogue: Communion,"* is able to expand on the most Joycean form of *yes:*

The beast & the burden lock-step waltz. Tiger lily & screwworm, it all adds up to this: bloodstar & molecular burning kiss.... A single sigh of glory, the two put an armlock on each other—matched for strength, leg over leg. Double bind & slow dance on ball-bearing feet. Arm in arm & slipknot. Birth, death, back to back—silent mouth against the other's ear. They sing a duet: e pluribus unum.

Yes. Amen.

TOYS IN A FIELD

Though none of the poems in *I Apologize for the Eyes in My Head* mentions Vietnam, there are indications that Komunyakaa was simultaneously working on those memories while he worked his way through stateside terrain. One poem toward the end of the book, "For the Walking Dead," describes a woman named Veronica, who dances "with boyish soldiers on their way / to the front," and who shields "amputated ghosts" "against everything they know." *I Apologize for the Eyes in My Head* won the San Francisco Poetry Center Award for the best book of poems published in 1986, but in that same year, Komunyakaa published *Toys in a Field*, a chapbook of poems about his experiences in Vietnam, and many of the poems in that book would reappear in *Dien Cai Dau* (1988), the book that brought Komunyakaa a far wider readership.

There are eighteen poems in *Toys in a Field*, twelve of which reappear in *Dien Cai Dau* and four others that are revised for *Neon Vernacular* (1993). The chapbook's opening poem, "Nothing Big," does not appear in either *Dien Cai Dau* or *Neon Vernacular* but happily reappears in *Pleasure Dome*. As is usual in Komunyakaa, the opening poem is extremely important. Memories of Vietnam come flooding back, triggered by "Nothing Big":

The hummingbird's rainbow
    lands among red
        geraniums
God's little hell-rising
helicopter flies away,

& I'm back in Danang.

Komunyakaa has often commented on the length of time between his experiences in Vietnam and writing about Vietnam. In an interview with Muna Asali, he says: "It took me fourteen years to actually excavate that whole terrain, to explore the involvement of the speaker, because perhaps beneath it all there is a cryptic guilt." When Vince Gotera asked Komunyakaa if he felt that he had been resisting memories of Vietnam, Komunyakaa agreed.

"Yes, I did at one time. Now, it's more or less a process of recall. I had pushed many of those images aside, or at least attempted to. It's amazing what the mind can do; the mind does work like a computer, storing information." The sight of the hummingbird, rising out of the geraniums, is like the "little" click that opens an entire file. Suddenly the speaker is "back in Danang . . . back at the Blue Dahlia." By the end of the poem the hummingbird turned helicopter has turned into a "flurry of wings" inside the speaker; it "stirs up trouble," and the speaker finds that he himself is "lifting off."

The poems that follow are landing points for the helicopter of memory: in "Ambush" "Stars / glint off gunbarrels," and then there is "a sound that makes you jump / in your sleep years later." In "Monsoon Season" "Dead men slip through bad weather," and in "Please" the speaker remembers how "Mistakes piled up men like clouds," and he thinks of Henry, who "went dancing on a red string / of bullets." Not surprisingly, the helicopter itself shows up in many of the poems: in "Water Buffalo" it is an "iron bird" that

> . . . rattles
> overhead again, with stars
> falling . . .

and later a "whirlwind machine / returns, hammering its gong," but in "Monsoon Season" the heavy rains makes for "grounded choppers." In "Toys in a Field" children pull themselves through the gun mounts "of abandoned helicopters / in graveyards," imitating "vultures," and by the end of the volume, in the poem "Returning (1975)," it seems the lift of the helicopter has transmogrified into a wheelchair:

> He comes toward me
>   out of white
> porcelain hallways
> in his remote control
>   contraption.

DIEN CAI DAU

In the fall of 1987, Indiana University hired Komunyakaa to teach creative writing as well as Afro-American studies, and he stayed in Bloomington for the next nine years. *Dien Cai Dau* (a Vietnamese phrase, roughly translated, meaning "crazy") was published by Wesleyan in 1988 and instantly placed Komunyakaa among the most notable soldier-poets. This full-length collection of Vietnam poems was on the American Library Association's "Best Books for Young Adults" list in 1988, and a year later it won the Dark Room Poetry Prize; many of the poems have since been translated and anthologized. In "Control Is the Mainspring," an essay that first appeared in *Hayden's Ferry Review* (1992) and later in *Blue Notes* (2000), Komunyakaa recounts how he wrote the poems in *Dien Cai Dau* in the middle of renovating an old house in the Baywater District of New Orleans. Recalling his goal to get renovations on the high hard parts of the project finished before the full blast of summer arrived, he says that he "put a pad of paper and pen on a table in the next room. This had a purpose. The images were coming so fast that, whenever I made a trek down the ladder, each line had to be worth its weight in sweat."

Apparently the ladder served its purpose well: the poems in *Dien Cai Dau* are more honed down and less surrealistic than those in the preceding collections, and a majority of them fit on the page in narrow shapes (rather like coffins); often there are no stanza breaks, and when there are, the breaks are meaningful, like a camera shifting angles. The opening poem, "Camouflaging the Chimera," is a good example of how the poems in this volume work, beginning with that very efficient word "chimera," which summons up all at once the she-monster in Greek mythology (head of lion breathing flames, goat's body, and serpent's tail) and then any imaginary monster, any illusion, any fabrication of the mind. (In what is most likely an unintentional sound coupling, "chimera" also reminds the reader of the notorious Khmer Rouge.) The poem's opening describes the "camouflaging" in the title:

> We tied branches to our helmets.
> We painted our faces & rifles
> with mud from a riverbank,
>
> blades of grass hung from the pockets
> of our tiger suits. We wove
> ourselves into the terrain,
> content to be a hummingbird's target.

The first realistic stanza flows naturally into something more metaphoric: the soldiers—that is the chimera they made as a whole—seem to become the land; they weave themselves "into the terrain" and almost disappear, leaning "against a breeze off the river." This disguising is not easy: "rock apes tried to blow our cover," and

> . . . Chameleons
>
> crawled our spines, changing from day
> to night . . .
> . . . .
> till something almost broke
> inside us. . . .

Just then the Vietcong appear on the hillside, "like black silk, / wrestling iron through grass." "We weren't there," the poet says, adding that "the river ran / through our bones," making a double-sided illusion: they were there, but they imagined they were not, and the Vietcong imagined they saw only a hillside but the camouflaged soldiers were there. By the poem's end, where "a world revolved / under each man's eyelid" we are all (soldiers and readers alike) holding our breath.

Every poem in the collection tells us something about how it was to be an American soldier in Vietnam. "Tunnels," for example, describes how the smallest man in the platoon went down,

> . . . the good soldier,
> on hands & knees, tunneling past
> death sacked into a blind corner.

The short lines of the poem, the quick narrative markers that replicate the soldier's movements, and the mixture of realistic and metaphoric imagery make this a poem that replicates, in each reading, the tunnel rat's terrible journey into the underworld. Other poems read like snapshots or film clips. "Roll Call" describes, succinctly, the ritual of remembering five dead men:

> . . . each M-16
> propped upright
> between a pair of jungle boots,
> a helmet on its barrel
> as if it were a man.

In "Fragging," five men are drawing straws to see who will "frag" a "gung ho" officer when the picture of the men "under a tree on a hillside" suddenly moves:

> They uncoil fast as a fist.
> Looking at the ground, four
> walk north, then disappear. One
> comes this way, moving through
> a bad dream. . . .

The surprising thing is how the poem ends and the questions it leaves with the reader. The grenade explodes, but it is not clear who is blown to bits, although given the title it would seem to be the lieutenant. But who is observing? Who says that the man with the grenade comes "this way" and sees how he is "married / to his devil?" And why describe the explosion, the fragmentation of a body "like a hundred red birds / released from a wooden box?" Beauty and ugliness again, the beast and its burden.

"Somewhere near Phu Bai," "Starlight Scope Myopia," and "Missing in Action" were the first three poems Komunyakaa wrote in the spring of 1984 when, as he says in "Control Is the Mainspring," poems about Vietnam "gushed out of me, and they surfaced with imagery that dredged up so much unpleasant psychic debris. . . . These poems were prompted by a need; they had fought to get out. I hadn't forgotten a single thread of evidence against myself." As it turns out, these first poems mark out various territories and tones in *Dien Cai Dau*. The scared but hapless soldier on guard duty "Somewhere near Phu Bai" reports that

> . . . In the guard shack
> I lean on the sandbags,
> taking aim at whatever.

The moon is nightmarish, "white hot," cutting through trees "like a circular saw," and the "blue-steel stars" also seem to sear the sky; "If anyone's / there, don't blame me." In "Starlight Scope Myopia," someone *is* out there; it is the Vietcong, moving again (as in "Camouflaging the Chimera") "under our eyelids": "What looks like / one step into the trees." The narrator registers the reality—"they're lifting crates of ammo / & sacks of rice"—but the reaction here is wider, more experienced than in "Somewhere near Phu Bai." Even though the "starlight scope brings / men into killing range," the narrator continues to watch, wondering what these enemies are saying, whether they are "calling the Americans / *beaucoup dien cai dau*," and longing to "place a finger" on the lips of one who is laughing or take another one, "old, bowlegged" into his arms. When the "brain closes / down" the heart opens.

"Missing in Action" appears in the last third of the book. Actually, there are no marked sections in *Dien Cai Dau*, but the poems can be loosely divided into three sections: the first describes things that happened in the combat zone; the second is about life away from the front, on the edge of the South China Sea, on Tu Do Street, and in various military installations; and the last section is set after the war and is about remembering and memorializing in various ways. In "Missing in Action," searchers are looking for the remains of men whose bodies were never found. Komunyakaa seems to have a particular incident in mind, saying

> . . . nothing can make that C-130
> over Hanoi come out of its spin,
> spiraling like a flare in green sky.

The searchers find that "there aren't / enough bones for a hash pipe" and in Washington, D.C., "they carve new names / into polished black stone." This poem makes an excellent companion poem to Komunyakaa's best-known poem, "Facing It," which begins:

> My black face fades,
> hiding inside the black granite.
> I said I wouldn't
> dammit: No tears.
> I'm stone. I'm flesh.

"Facing It," the last poem of *Dien Cai Dau*, describes the narrator looking at the Vietnam Veterans Memorial; he sees ghosts and real people, and memories collide with the present. When the narrator touches a name, he sees "the booby trap's white flash"; bird wings remind him of airplanes, and in the end it is hard to tell if the "white vet's image" is memory or reflection, if that "white vet" is inside the narrator or the stone. Years later, speaking as a member of the advisory council for the My Lai Peace Park Project in Vietnam, Komunyakaa said this about the wall in Washington D.C.: "Whoever faces the granite becomes a part of it. The reflections move into and through each other. A dance between the dead and the living." In many ways *Dien Cai Dau* is that kind of book.

FEBRUARY IN SYDNEY

In 1989 Komunyakaa published a chapbook of poems about Australia, jazz, and loneliness. The title poem, "February in Sydney," makes the jazz connection clear with opening lines where

> Dexter Gordon's tenor sax
> plays "April in Paris"
> inside my head. . .

and the poem recapitulates the mood of the entire collection in its closing:

> . . . A loneliness
> lingers like a silver needle
> under my black skin . . .

Compared with the poems in *Dien Cai Dau*, the poems *February in Sydney* lack force; they seem to wander on the pages as the poet wanders through this new but not entirely unfamiliar part of the globe. In "Short-timer's Calendar," a poem from the last section of *Dien Cai Dau*, the narrator talks about wrestling ghosts in his sleep,

> . . . with the Southern Cross
> balanced on a branch weighing a cloud
> of sparrows

so that constellation forms a sort of bridge when a reader comes to the first poem in *February in Sydney*, titled "Under the Harbour Bridge":

> America rhymes with Australia
> as I watch the Southern Cross's
> sequins fall. . . .

Many of the poems are about people and places down under. "The Man Who Carries the Desert Around Inside Himself: For Wally" describes a man who knows how to read footprints and to hear "gods / speak through blue-tongued lizards." In "Gerry's Jazz" famous Sydney dance clubs like the Trocadero as well as nearby resort towns like Tatoomba and Wollongong appear while the star of the poem, a drummer named Gerry, plays Gene Krupa on a hammered-out cymbal. There are streetwalkers and street people and a didgeridoo player named Frank, but the most moving poem of the collection is one that might have been written anywhere, though the title places it solidly in Sydney. "Blue Light Lounge Sutra for the Performance Poets at Harold Park Hotel" is a poem that begs to be read out loud; it is a continuous form poem, sans punctuation, and it is filled with repetition and syncopation:

> the need gotta be
> so deep words can't
> answer simple questions
> all night long notes
> stumble off the tongue
> & color the air indigo
> so deep fragments of gut
> & flesh cling to the song
> you gotta get into it
> so deep . . .

Jazz is always on Komunyakaa's mind, and even while its influence was showing up in his own work, he was also working (with one of his poetry students at Indiana University) on an anthology of jazz poems. In 1991 *The Jazz Poetry Anthology*, coedited with Sascha Feinstein, who has also been a jazz saxophonist, was published, and in 1996 Feinstein and Komunyakaa put together *The Second Set;* a third "set" is in the works. The same year *The Jazz Poetry Anthology* appeared, Komunyakaa was a visiting professor at the University of California at Berkeley, and in 1992 *Magic City*, Komunyakaa's book about his childhood in Louisiana, appeared. It was his eighth published collection of poems.

MAGIC CITY

At the end of "Facing It," a woman is "brushing a boy's hair," and that line from the last poem in *Dien Cai Dau* might serve as an explanation and introduction to *Magic City*. Memory, as Komunyakaa said in an early poem, is slow and erratic and can be triggered by a hummingbird hovering over a geranium or (perhaps) an image of a woman and a boy. "Life is a process of growing into oneself. An external journey that parallels that journey within, and each mirrors the other to try and make itself whole," he told Muna Asali. It took longer for Komunyakaa to write about his childhood and early manhood than it did for him to write about Vietnam, but as soon as the first poem, "Venus's-flytraps," appeared, he knew that there was a "terrain" that needed to be explored. As he told Tony Barnstone, "I had very systematically written around this, in the same way I had systematically written around the Vietnam experience. It became important to write about things I had dismissed from the territory of poetry."

"Venus's-flytraps" reminds the reader that Komunyakaa had not *entirely* dismissed his childhood and Louisiana from earlier volumes. When the narrator says, "My mama says I'm a mistake. / That I made her a bad girl," a section from *Copacetic*'s "Family Tree" comes to mind:

> my mother
> married at 15,
> with my ear pressed
> against the drum.

In fact, in "Landscape for the Disappeared," from *I Apologize for the Eyes in My Head*, Komunyakaa imagines stories "lost among Venus's-flytraps," but the language, the stories, the people, and the landscape are not lost: they come back in *Magic City* as if the time and place had been magically (but perhaps only partially) excavated. This is a land of grandfathers and grandmothers, of brothers (and sometimes the sister), of parents and neighbors, of friends and enemies. The collection shows Komunyakaa at five in "Venus's-flytraps," at eight in "Yellow Dog Café," at ten in "Blackberries," at thirteen in "Omen," at sixteen in "Nocturne," as a young man in "Butterfly-toed Shoes," and in a dozen other "human and flawed" stages in between.

Magic City is a beautiful collection, with nothing sentimental, nothing easy about it. The forty poems in this volume are (mostly) family stories, but they are also about racism and economic oppression, as the book's cover art illustrates. In "The Whistle" the paper mill that dominated Bogalusa is described as a "dragon" churning with "iron teeth" and "wheels within wheels," but

> At noon, Daddy would walk
> Across the field of goldenrod
> & mustard weed, the pollen
> Bright & sullen on his overalls.

That collision of nature's beauty and the ugly dangers of the manmade is everywhere in the collection, along with the narrator's growing awareness of what it means to be a black in the American South. In "History Lessons" a teen-aged Komunyakaa hears a driver for the local dry cleaner say that "Emmet Till had begged for it / With his damn wolf whistle," and when the young man lets a swarm of "hot words" out of his mouth, he is warned that he "*ain't gonna live long.*"

The part of the family most often discussed in *Magic City* is the parents. "The Whistle" informs readers that when the father was "kicked by the foreman, / He booted him back," and the mill whistle "burned with wrath." In "Playthings" the mother calls the boy at dusk, her voice "loud as a train whistle," and readers find out that "Once she took off her red slip / and ripped it into a kite tail." There are a number of poems that pay homage to things the father and eldest son did together: in "Banking Potatoes," as the father dropped the potatoes in the row, the boy would "march behind him / Like a peg-legged soldier"; "Immolatus," which describes a pig butchering, is naturally less bucolic, and it is the father who "did a half spin / & brought down the sledgehammer" to kill the pig. Opposition frequently arises between the father and son, as demonstrated in "Omen," when the boy pops off a snake's head and throws it at his frightened father's feet.

In its own way, *Magic City* demonstrates what Robert Hayden called the "chronic angers" of a house. In "Venus's-flytraps" we learn that "Daddy / Calls Mama honey" and on "Sunday Afternoons" the narrator and his brothers, locked out of the house,

> . . . heard cries
> Fused with gospel on the radio,
> Loud as shattered glass
> In a Saturday-night argument.

The next statement, "We were born between Oh Yeah / & Goddammit" hints at the domestic discord that becomes history in "My Father's Love Letters":

> On Fridays he'd open a can of Jax
> After coming home from the mill,
> & ask me to write a letter to my mother
> Who sent postcards of desert flowers
> Taller than men. He would beg,
> Promising to never beat her
> Again. Somehow I was happy
> She had gone . . .

NEON VERNACULAR

His collection of new and selected poems titled *Neon Vernacular* published late in 1993 earned Komunyakaa the Pulitzer, Kingsley Tufts, and William Faulkner Prizes in 1994. That same year, Komunyakaa, on leave from Indiana University, made a return visit to Australia, but most of his travels were European: in November of 1994, he toured eastern Europe, and after that he and the novelist Jane Smiley toured Russia under the U.S. government–sponsored "Corridors of Culture" program. During the same trip, he visited Prague with a group of writers including Arthur Miller and Diane Johnson. Also in 1994, a chapbook of Komunyakaa's poems, translated into French by Isabelle Cadieux, was published in France under the title *Panache de bouquets*.

Neon Vernacular is a selection of new and previously published poems, chosen to give a full range of styles and subjects, which for readers who were just then coming to Komunyakaa's work was bound to appear eclectic and wide-ranging. Vince Gotera notes in *African American Writers* that "the operative device in *Neon Vernacular* is collage, the reconstructive fine art that combines disparate fragments into a cohesive whole," and that description seems particularly apt. *Neon Vernacular* contains only a dozen new poems, but most of these poems are much longer than those in *Magic City*, which had just been published (and is the only one of Komunyakaa's previous collections not included in the selection).

Except for their length, the new poems in *Neon Vernacular* might have been part of *Magic City* because they continue the autobiographical thread of the earlier book (as well as sharing the typographical feature of capitalizing the first word in each line), but there is something different about the perspective. For example, "Fog Galleon," the first poem in *Neon Vernacular*, summons up remembrance of the second poem in *Magic City* because both focus on the paper mill in Bogalusa, but "Fog Galleon" is from a returning perspective: "I press against the taxicab / Window. I'm back." In "Moonshine" the writer says:

> That's the oak we planted
> The day before I left town,
> As if father & son
> Needed staking down to earth.

When the narrator says that he is as "lonely as those storytellers / In my father's backyard," it becomes clear that most of this new set is told in that backyard and that much of the telling has to do with loneliness and Komunyakaa's father. In fact, the last poem in the new section is "Songs for My Father," a long poem in fourteen fourteen-line sections, making a carefully constructed collage that serves as a bittersweet tribute to the carpenter-father who the poet had to "square-off and face."

"Songs for My Father" starts with early memory, when the father "had a boy's voice," and, like an austere photo album, represents a lifetime in a series of clicks. The opening section tells the reader what the writer told his brothers—that being the oldest meant being the closest and being close was not easy. Another section lets the father know that his children wanted more from him:

> . . . We always
> Walked circles around
> You, wider each year,
> Hungering for stories
> To save us from ourselves.
> Like a wife who isn't touched,
> We had to do something bad
> Before you'd look into our eyes.

In one section, where the father hides Easter eggs in "gopher holes & underneath roots," the son remembers the mother wondering "why [he] made everything so hard." In another section, after the father has hit the mother, the son says "Everyone & everything here / Is turning against you," but even after that, after the stories of the fights and frustrations, comes a section where the son remembers riding on the handlebars of a red bicycle, gliding through "the flowering / Dogwood like a thread of blood." The elegiac collage finishes with a last series of clicks: the father is old, leaning on a yard rake (still working hard) and "You smile, look into my eyes / & say you want me to write you a poem. / I stammer for words"; the son remembers breaking an old toy that had once belonged to his father and realizes that the same person can be both a font of pain and of love; the son confesses that despite everything he does not like about his father, "I never knew / We looked so much like each other."

Besides continuing the autobiographical trajectory of *Magic City*, the new poems mirror other sections of the collage that makes up *Neon Vernacular;* there are poems "recounting lost friends / As they turn into mist" ("Moonshine"); there are poems that take up the dichotomy of dark and light; there are poems about Vietnam and the ghosts that will not disappear; there are poems about living in Colorado; and there are poems infused with jazz and the blues. The poems from previous volumes are also selected for their variety and range and for the way that they come together as a whole. One gets the feeling that Komunyakaa was working by intuition as he selected, squinting his eyes the way an artist does to see how the colors work.

THIEVES OF PARADISE

In 1997, after a year as visiting professor at Washington University in St. Louis, Yusef Komunyakaa accepted an invitation to become a fellow in the Council of Humanities (the equivalent of distinguished professor) and professor of creative writing at Princeton University. *Thieves of Paradise,* published in 1998, differs from previous volumes in a number of ways: for one thing, the book is divided into sections—seven of them. Komunyakaa told Radiclani Clytus:

> I knew I wanted seven sections to the book. And I pushed for that structure. I knew I wanted those sections to stand on their own and at the same time complement the other sections. I wanted them to be in concert with each other—not in a direct way, but in more of a tonal signal between the different sections. I wanted to deal with some of the same themes even, but deal with them in a different way.

The subjects that reappear in this book include Vietnam, Australia, jazz, racial oppression, and memory and desire in all forms, but as he hoped, Komunyakaa deals with each "in a different way." Four sections of the book contain fifteen separate poems and the three other sections are made up of three very different types of single poems; once a reader notices this sort of thing, there is much more to notice, numerically and thematically. With every volume, Komunyakaa is more meticulous about structures, as if he is measuring, making rooms for the reader to inhabit.

The first section of fifteen poems is "Way Stations," which, as the title indicates, describes off-the-beaten-path places—a cave of hibernating bears, that place beyond all places on the map where "there be dragons," a cowbird's nest (stolen from a songbird), a wet nurse's breast, the head of a drum, a woman wrapped in a snake, a killing ground in colonial America, a place inside of Walt Whitman's *Leaves of Grass,* the "sweatshops of desire," the palimpsest of the modern world, a small Louisiana town in April, a Vietnamese valley that shifts into a painting by Goya, the cenotaph of a dead friend—and ends with paintings that move and images that become sound. The poems in this section (and throughout the book) are filled with erudite references, things that could be footnoted, but Komunyakaa hates footnotes, thinks adding them is not the poet's job. The more ambitious reader, the reader who takes pleasure in looking up Da Vinci's *Madonna Litta* or wondering if there was a specific incident in the *Journals* of the House of Burgesses the poet was thinking of when he wrote "Genealogy" will find much to enjoy in *Thieves of Paradise.*

The next section, "Tropic of Capricorn" is similarly shaped by its title: all fifteen poems in this section take place in the southernmost latitudes. There are poems about the early Australian settlers (prostitutes, pickpockets, forgers, and thieves), the ghosts of black Australians and the modern descendants of all of these. As in *February in Sydney,* Komunyakaa seems to love the place names: "Guichen Bay," "Bendigo & Rocky River," "Garibaldi Rock," "The Gap," and "The Great Barrier Reef." Many of the poems in this section are the closest thing to travel poems that Komunyakaa has written, but as always, the travel is undertaken for the sake of the interior voyage.

One of the long, single-poem sections of the book, "Quatrains for Ishi," is a poem that Komunyakaa wrote when he heard about a Native American who was the last member of his tribe. He told William Baer that he had meditated on the subject for eighteen months before sitting down to write the poem. "The Glass Ark," another of the single-poem sections began when Komunyakaa visited La Brea Tar Pits and imagined writing a piece that could be performed in the enclosed class space of the Tar Pits, and "Testimony," the long poem about Charlie Parker written in fourteen "double sonnet" sections, was originally commissioned by the Australian Broadcasting Company and was given a musical score by the composer Sandy Evans.

The section "Debriefing Ghosts" is a series of (of course) fifteen prose poems, and though Komunyakaa had used this form in earlier books, he had never used it to such an extent. "I wanted to have those long lines," he told Clytus, and, it would appear, he wanted to do something different with material he had covered in other volumes, or he wanted to find a way to cover more of the material, using the detail that prose more easily allows. Either or both, the poems are definitely debriefings; ghosts of men and women appear, many of them connected with Komunyakaa's time in Vietnam, and the ghosts of places and situations emerge unexpectedly and spill their stories. Following a pattern established in the fifteen-poem sections of this book, the movement is from the past to the present and the one of the last ghosts to appear is Komunyakaa's dead father.

"Blessing the Animals," the poem that opens the last section of *Thieves of Paradise,* is a semi-utopian vision of paired animals and saints, "the first scapegoats," who nevertheless "pass through / our lives, still loyal to thorns." The poems that follow pay tribute to the essential and the sensual, but the section—as its name, "The Blue Hour," indicates—has a tint of loss and pain. The signature poem is "No-Good Blues," in which autobiography is refashioned into the blues and a bit of myth:

> Working swing shift at McGraw-
> Edison, I shoot screws
> into cooler cabinets as if I was born
> to do it. But the no-good blues come
> looking for me. She's from Veracruz,
> & never wears dead colors of the factory,
> still in Frida Kahlo's world of monkeys.
> She's a bird in the caged air.

Birds are everywhere in this section, matching their wings with those of bats, ghosts, and angels. Love goes wrong, things fall apart, but the center holds and that center is simply existence, being alive, living in the body. The last poem, "Anodyne," is Komunyakaa's hymn to himself:

> I love this body, this
> solo & ragtime jubilee
> behind the left nipple,
> because I know I was born
> to wear out at least
> one hundred angels.

TALKING DIRTY TO THE GODS

A little more than a year after *Thieves of Paradise* appeared and was chosen as a finalist for the National Book Award, Komunyakaa published a very different sort of collection, *Talking Dirty to the Gods* (2000). The collection is a series of 132 poems of four quatrains each, each poem indulging a desire Komunyakaa had to talk about any subject, without restriction, compressing what he wanted to say into the sixteen-line structure. As he told David Lehman, the only thing he knew was that he wanted to begin the book with "Hearsay" and end it with "Heresy," and he would let small things and monumental things come in between, including a pantheon of gods, none of whom would keep him from talking however he pleased.

Naturally, there are poems about gods, big and little. Whatever is worshiped is questioned, while insignificant and lowly things are often elevated, as in "Infidelity."

> Zeus always introduces himself
> As one who needs stitching
> Back together with kisses

but the maggot is the "Little / Master of earth" ("Ode to the Maggot"); "Eros throws / A kiss to the teenage prostitute" ("Eros") but an old man "nuzzles the berried branches / To his mouth, like a young deer" ("September"). There are many new gods in Komunyakaa's pantheon: "The God of Broken Things," "The God of Land Mines," "The God of Variables," and "The Goddess of Quotas," and there are antigods, revisited, as in "Happenstance," in which the pain in Thomas Hardy's "Hap" modulates into "whatever":

> An airplane falls, a spaceship
> Explodes in midair over paradise,
>
> A nuclear meltdown sizzles
> In the belly of a leaden calf,
> & the Minotaur finds his way out
> Of a classic loophole. Normal
>
> Accident.

Apparently we have learned to live with "Crass Casualty" and "dicing Time." So, if there are no "real" gods to talk dirty to, what is the point? Ecstasy, for one thing—especially if another name for god is "Joy." Talking dirty—is that what John Donne did in Sonnet 14 of his *Holy*

Sonnets? Or is that just what we do now when we talk about love?

> Joy, use me like a whore.
> Turn me inside out like Donne
> Desired God to do with him.
> Show me some muscle.

The reference in "Ecstatic" is instantly clear, but as in the earlier comparison, the modern poem (perhaps intentionally) lacks force. In any case, these sorts of intertextual allusions add to the richness of the volume and allow a reader to make connections across the centuries. In "Meditations in a Swine Yard" the speaker declares that

> . . . A god isn't worth
> A drop of water in the hell of his good
>
> Imagination, if we can't curse
> Sunsets & threaten to forsake him
> In his storehouse of belladonna,
> Tiger hornets, & snakebites

and in "The Four Evangelists," he concludes that

> . . . Gods invent themselves
> So men & women see a few feet
> Into the unknown. Sympathetic
>
> Magic. . . .

The philosophical center of the volume, however, is found in "Negative Capability," where ambiguity, or as John Keats said, "being capable of being in uncertainties, Mysteries, doubts, without any irritable reaching after fact & reason" is the watermark:

> . . . I love
> What doesn't reveal every seam,
> Every droplet—when doubt owns tongue
>
> & clitoris, heart & penis. I love
> Mystery, & hope I never touch naked

> Threads of reason to answer the slimy,
> Clueless snout probing the dark.

"Probing the dark" might serve as an alternate title for *Talking Dirty to the Gods* because the book's mode is actually more exploratory than declarative, the tone more meditative than insolent. "I set out to write about mythological topics, write about folklore, the celebration of animals, insects, and human existence. I wanted to observe all those things and discover how they're connected to each other," Komunyakaa is quoted as saying in an article for *Book Magazine,* and though the connections might be difficult to find at times, the sheer audacity of the gathering, coupled with Komunyakaa's technical achievements in compression, lyric insinuation, and consistent form make this volume another major station in his career.

PLEASURE DOME

In 2001, a year after Farrar, Straus and Giroux published *Talking Dirty to the Gods,* Wesleyan published a volume of new and collected poems by Komunyakaa under the title *Pleasure Dome.* The title comes from Samuel Coleridge's "Kubla Khan": "In Xanadu did Kubla Khan / A stately pleasure-dome decree," and *Pleasure Dome,* representing more than twenty-five years of wide-ranging work, lives up to the allusion. As in *Neon Vernacular,* which was published shortly after *Magic City,* the poems of the preceding volume do not appear, which means that none of the poems from *Talking Dirty to the Gods* appear in the collected volume. Other volumes are well represented, however, and there is even a section titled "Early Uncollected" containing twenty-five short poems as well as a strong selection of "New Poems." There are more poems from the early volumes included here than there were in *Neon Vernacular,* which is why the volume subtitle describes the contents as "collected" rather than "selected," and later volumes, including *Dien Cai Dau, Magic City,* and *Thieves of Paradise* are reprinted completely intact.

In the "New Poems" section of *Pleasure Dome,* form continues to be important to Komunyakaa in a typically loose and subtle way. The first poem, "Providence," is a tour de force love song (a "pleasure dome" in itself, complete with "Abyssinian" maid), ten stanzas of seven lines each. The next poem, "Water," is a sonnet in length, and though Komunyakaa seems to have no interest in iambic pentameter or rhyme, there is a discernible turn and couplet-like closure to the ending. "Jasmine" and "The Whispering Gallery" return to Komunyakaa's familiar short-line, continuous form, each poem relaying a narrative, but the next ten poems, starting with "Tuesday Night at the Savoy Ballroom," all employ a scooped-margin tercet to describe cityscapes or recognize famous people. "Nightbird," a poem about Ella Fitzgerald, is a double sonnet without the fanfare, but "Tenebrae," a tribute to Richard Johnson written in 1990 at the request of colleague at Indiana University, has a more organic form. Johnson, the first black tenured professor at Indiana University, had been an extremely talented musician, but he found living in Bloomington so difficult that he committed suicide. Initially, Komunyakaa had a difficult time writing the poem, which was going to be combined with music. "Finally, late one Saturday night, after playing Art Blakey and the Jazz Messengers and sipping merlot, 'Tenebrae' came forth. Hundreds of lines," he says in the "Exploration" part of *Blue Notes.* "Then I spent days revising, cutting the poem down to its structure." The new poem section continues with another double sonnet, announced as such in the title, "Double Limbo" (balancing "Nightbird," numerically) and ends with "NJ Transit," a series of haiku segments that take as their subjects various commuter-train stops between New York City and Trenton, New Jersey.

The series of dedications in the "New Poems" is especially apropos because this section in *Pleasure Dome* is immediately followed by the section titled "Early Uncollected Poems," starting out with poems for Mississippi John Hurt and Langston Hughes. Many of these poems predict Komunyakaa's interests in jazz and the blues and reflect the midwestern landscape that surrounded the young poet, but though there is little to suggest the landscape of Louisiana or indicate the poet was a soldier in Vietnam, there are occasional glimpses of both. In a poem called "Legacy," the speaker talks about pinning "medals to chests" and "shadows" that "sleep in the ground, old combat boots / laced on the feet of the dead," but it is the poem's last stanza that makes sense of the fourteen years it took before this poet wrote *Dien Cai Dau:*

For as long as I can remember
men have sewn their tongues
to the roofs of their mouths.

Thankfully, Yusef Komunyakaa was willing to undo that terrible stitching and produce the poems that fill *Pleasure Dome.*

Keeping track of Komunyakaa's career is increasingly difficult. He works simultaneously on several poetry collections, and, since the 1990s, he has also been working on translations, dramatic scripts, song lyrics, and essays. After the publication of *Pleasure Dome,* he was planning a book titled "Wishbone Trilogy"—which at first centered on African American history but grew to encompass the history of blacks throughout the world—as well as a collection that would address mythologies from other cultures. In an interview with Radiclani Clytus, Komunyakaa talked about *Slip Knot,* a libretto he was composing with T. J Anderson, and said: "I'm attracted to the possibility of theater, characters getting up on stage and coming alive, saying things that surprise us, but also parallel the ideas and feelings within our own minds and bodies." Komunyakaa's interests are wide-ranging and eclectic, and in a 2002 interview with Lary Bloom, Komunyakaa revealed more projects: "Chameleon Couch," a volume of poems that came out of thinking about the Oklahoma City bombing; a series of poems from the point of view of a white Vietnam veteran; and a piece based on the life of Edmonia Lewis, a nineteenth-century African American sculptor. Komunyakaa is now married to the poet Reetika Vazirani, and together they have a son, Jehan.

"The Borrowed Road," the first poem in Komunyakaa's first collection, is dedicated to the poet Richard Hugo, who said: "So you are after those words you can own and ways of putting them in phrases and lines that are yours by right of obsessive musical deed." Few poets in America have followed this advice as well as Yusef Komunyakaa, who, with his love for jazz and the blues, has followed his obsessions to create a "neon vernacular" and who seems able to let that language "give to airy nothing / a local habitation and a name." Komunyakaa is not only a poet who has obsessions; he is also obsessive about reading and writing. "One way I read poems is that I try to read them over and over," he told Kristin Naca. "That's what really attracted me to poetry: that I could continually come to a poem and get something different from it." The same might be said for Komunyakaa's poems: we want to read them over and over, continually finding something more to admire.

Selected Bibliography

WORKS OF YUSEF KOMUNYAKAA

POETRY
Dedications and Other Darkhorses. Laramie, Wyo.: Rocky Mountain Creative Arts Journal, 1977.

Lost in the Bonewheel Factory. Amherst, Mass.: Lynx House Press, 1979.

Copacetic. Middletown, Conn.: Wesleyan University Press, 1984.

I Apologize for the Eyes in My Head. Middletown, Conn.: Wesleyan University Press, 1986.

Toys in a Field. New Orleans: Black River Press, 1986.

Dien Cai Dau. Middletown, Conn.: Wesleyan University Press, 1988.

February in Sydney. Matchbook #17. Unionville, Ind.: Matchbooks, 1989.

Magic City. Hanover, N.H.: Wesleyan University Press, published by University Press of New England, 1992.

Neon Vernacular: New and Selected Poems. Hanover, N.H.: Wesleyan University Press, published by University Press of New England, 1993.

Panache de bouquets. Translated by Isabelle Cadieux. Rennes, France: William Faulkner Foundation, Université de Haute Bretagne, 1994.

Thieves of Paradise. Hanover, N.H.: Wesleyan University Press, published by University Press of New England, 1998.

Talking Dirty to the Gods. New York: Farrar, Straus and Giroux, 2000.

Pleasure Dome. Middletown, Conn.: Wesleyan University Press, 2001.

RECORDINGS
Love Notes from the Madhouse. Poetry reading recorded at the Chopin Theatre, Chicago with the jazz ensemble 8th Harmonic Breakdown, 1998.

Yusef Komunyakaa (with Sharon Olds). Audiotape Archives. The American Academy of Poets, 1999.

Our Souls Run Deep Like the Rivers. Rhino, February 2000. Notable recordings of African American Poets. (Komunyakaa reads "Facing It" and "Venus's-flytraps.")

OTHER WORKS
The Jazz Poetry Anthology. Edited with Sascha Feinstein. Bloomington: Indiana University Press, 1991.

The Second Set: The Jazz Poetry Anthology, Volume 2. Edited with Sascha Feinstein. Bloomington: Indiana University Press, 1996.

"The Examples," by Nguyen Quang Thieu. Translated by Yusef Komunyakaa with the poet in *Mountain River: Vietnamese Poetry from the Wars, 1948–1993*. Edited by Kevin Bowen, Nguyen Ba Chung, and Bruce Weigl. Amherst, Mass.: University of Massachusetts Press, 1998. P. 225.

Blue Notes: Essays, Interviews, and Commentaries. Edited by Radiclani Clytus. Ann Arbor: University of Michigan Press, 2000.

"Kit and Caboodle." In *The Eye of the Poet: Six Views of the Art and Craft of Poetry*. Edited by David Citino. New York: Oxford University Press, 2001. Pp. 134–149.

CRITICAL AND BIOGRAPHICAL STUDIES

Aubert, Alvin. "Rare Instances of Reconciliation." *Epoch* 38, no. 1:67–72 (1989).

———. "Yusef Komunyakaa: The Unified Vision—Canonization and Humanity." *African American Review* 27, no. 1:119–123 (spring 1993). Reprinted in *Contemporary Literary Criticism*. Vol. 94. Detroit: Gale, 1997. Pp. 234–237. Also reprinted in *Black Literature Criticism Supplement*. Edited by Jeffrey W. Hunter and Jerry Moore. Detroit: Gale, 1999. Pp. 215–218.

———. "Stars and Gunbarrels. *African American Review* 28, no. 4:671–673 (1994).

Beidler, Philip D. *Re-Writing America: Vietnam Authors in Their Generation*. Athens: University of Georgia Press, 1991.

Collins, Michael. "Staying Human." *Parnassus* 18, no. 2/19, no. 1:126–149 (1993–1994). Reprinted in *Contemporary Literary Criticism*. Vol. 94. Detroit: Gale, 1997. Pp. 241–249.

Conley, Susan. "About Yusef Komunyakaa: A Profile." *Ploughshares* 23, no. 1:202–205 (spring 1997).

Derricotte, Toi. "The Tension between Memory and Forgetting in the Poetry of Yusef Komunyakaa." *The Kenyon Review* 15, no. 4:217–222 (fall 1993). Reprinted in *Contemporary Literary Criticism*. Vol. 94. Detroit: Gale, 1997. Pp. 239–241.

Engels, John. "A Cruel Happiness." *New England Review* 16, no. 1:163–169 (1994).

Fabre, Michael. "On Yusef Komunyakaa." *Southern Quarterly* 34, no. 2:5–8 (winter 1996).

Feinstein, Sascha. *Jazz Poetry from the 1920s to the Present*. Westport, Conn.: Greenwood Press, 1997.

Finklestein, Norman. "Like an Unknown Voice Rising Out of Flesh." *Ohio Review* 52:136–140 (spring 1994).

Friebert, Stuart. "The Truth of the Matter." *Field* 48:64–71 (spring 1993).

Gordon, Fran. "Blue Note in a Lyrical Landscape." *Poets and Writers* 26, no. 6:26–33 (November–December 2000).

Gotera, Vince. "'Depending on the Light': Yusef Komunyakaa's *Dien Cai Dau*." In *America Rediscovered: Critical Essays on Literature and Film of the Vietnam War*. Edited by Owen W. Gilman Jr. and Lorrie Smith. New York: Garland, 1990. Pp. 282–300. Reprinted in *Contemporary Literary Criticism*. Vol. 94. Detroit: Gale, 1997. Pp. 230–234.

———. "Killer Imagination." *Callaloo* 13, no. 2:364–371 (1990).

———. *Radical Visions: Poetry by Vietnam Veterans*. Athens: University of Georgia Press, 1994.

———. "Yusef Komunyakaa." In *African American Writers*, 2d ed. Edited by Valerie Smith. Vol. 2. New York: Scribners, 2001. Pp. 489–504.

Gwynn, R. S. "What the Center Holds." *Hudson Review* 46, no. 4:741–750 (winter 1994).

Jakubiak, Katarzyna. "Yusef Komunyakaa: Questioning Traditional Metaphors of Light and Darkness." Master's thesis, University of Northern Iowa, 1999.

Jones, Kirkland C. "Folk Idiom in the Literary Expression of Two African American Authors: Rita Dove and Yusef Komunyakaa." In *Language and Literature in the African American Imagination*. Edited by Carol Aisha Blackshire-Belay. Westport, Conn.: Greenwood Press, 1992.

Kirsch, Adam. "Verse Averse: *Talking Dirty to the Gods* by Yusef Komunyakaa; *Blue Notes: Essays, Interview, and Commentaries* by Yusef Komunyakaa." *The New Republic* 224, no. 9:38–41 (2001).

Ringnalda, Don. "Rejecting 'Sweet Geometry': Komunyakaa's *Duende*." *Journal of American Culture* 16, no. 3:21–28 (fall 1993).

———. *Fighting and Writing the Vietnam War*. Jackson: University Press of Mississippi, 1994.

Salas, Angela M. "'Flashbacks through the Heart': Yusef Komunyakaa and the Poetry of Self-Assertion." In *The Furious Flowering of African American Poetry*. Edited by Joanne V. Gabbin. Charlottesville: University Press of Virginia, 1999.

Stein, Kevin. "Vietnam and the 'Voice Within': Public and Private History in Yusef Komunyakaa's *Dien Cai Dau*." *Massachusetts Review* 36, no. 4:541–561 (1995). Reprinted as chapter 5 in his *Private Poets, Worldly Acts: Public and Private History in Contemporary American Poetry.* Athens: Ohio University Press, 1996. Pp. 90–107.

Suarez, Ernest. "Contemporary Southern Poetry and Critical Practice." *Southern Review* 30:674–688 (autumn 1994).

———. "Yusef Komunyakaa." *Five Points* 4, no. 1:15–28 (fall 1999).

Waniek, Marilyn Nelson. "The Gender of Grief." *Southern Review* 29, no. 2:405–419 (spring 1993). Reprinted in *Contemporary Literary Criticism.* Vol. 94. Detroit: Gale, 1997. Pp. 237–238.

Warren, Kenneth. "Harsh Judgment." *American Book Review* 16, no. 2:16, 19 (1994).

Whited, Stephen. "The Right Tools." *Book Magazine* (January/February 2001). Available at (http://www.bookmagazine.com/issue14/poetics.shtml).

"Yusef Komunyakaa." In *Black Literature Criticism Supplement.* Edited by Jeffrey W. Hunter and Jerry Moore. Detroit: Gale, 1999. Pp. 214–235.

"Yusef Komunyakaa." In *Contemporary American Authors.* Vol. 147. Detroit: Gale, 1995. Pp. 264–266.

"Yusef Komunyakaa: *Neon Vernacular: New and Selected Poems.*" In *Contemporary Literary Criticism.* Vol. 86. Edited by Christopher Giroux. Detroit: Gale, 1995. Pp. 190–194.

INTERVIEWS

Asali, Muna. "An Interview with Yusef Komunyakaa." *New England Review* 16, no. 1:141–147 (1994). Reprinted in Komunyakaa's *Blue Notes: Essays, Interviews and Commentaries.* Ann Arbor: University of Michigan Press, 2000. Pp. 76–84.

Baer, William. "Still Negotiating with the Images: An Interview with Yusef Komunyakaa." *The Kenyon Review* 20, nos. 3–4:5–20 (summer–fall 1998). Reprinted in *Blue Notes: Essays, Interviews and Commentaries.* Ann Arbor: University of Michigan Press, 2000. Pp. 93–106.

Barnstone, Tony, and Michael Garabedian. "The Body Is Our First Music." *Poetry Flash,* no. 227 (June–July 1998). Reprinted in *Blue Notes: Essays, Interviews and Commentaries.* Ann Arbor: University of Michigan Press, 2000. Pp. 107–125.

Bloom, Lary. "Komunyakaa's Riff: An Interview." *Hartford Courant,* "Northeast" section, June 9, 2002.

Cho, Elizabeth. "Discovering the Landscape with Yusef Komunyakaa." *The Phoenix Online: Swarthmore College's Online Student Newspaper* (http://www.sccs.swarthmore.edu/org/phoenix/1998/1998-02-27/13.html), February 27, 1998.

Clytus, Radiclani. "Notations in Blue." In *Blue Notes: Essays, Interviews and Commentaries.* Ann Arbor: University of Michigan Press, 2000. Pp. 135–143.

Carroll, Rebecca. *Swing Low: Black Men Writing.* New York: Crown, 1995.

Dawidoff, Sally. "Talking Poetry with Yusef Komunyakaa." *Africana.com* (http://www.africana.com/DailyArticles/index_20010114.htm).

Fox, Alan. "Conversation with Yusef Komunyakaa, November 28, 1997." *Rattle* 4, no. 1 (1998).

Gotera, Vince. "Lines of Tempered Steel: An Interview with Yusef Komunyakaa." *Callaloo* 13, no. 2:215–229 (1990). Interview conducted in 1986. Reprinted in *Blue Notes: Essays, Interviews and Commentaries.* Ann Arbor: University of Michigan Press, 2000. Pp. 59–75.

Johnson, Thomas C. "Yusef Komunyakaa on Etheridge Knight." *Worcester Review* 19:1–2 (1998). Reprinted in *Blue Notes: Essays, Interviews and Commentaries.* Ann Arbor: University of Michigan Press, 2000. Pp. 126–134.

Kelly, Robert. "Jazz and Poetry: A Conversation." *Georgia Review* 46, no. 4:645–661 (1992). (Komunyakaa interviewed together with William Matthews.)

Naca, Kristin. "Hotbeds and Crossing over Poetic Traditions." In *Blue Notes: Essays, Interviews, and Commentaries.* Ann Arbor: University of Michigan Press, 2000. Pp. 85–92.

Richards, David R. "Terror Aligned with Beauty: A Visit with Bloomington's Pulitzer-Prize Winning Poet." *Arts Indiana Magazine* 18, no. 1:20–21 (February 1996).

Sherman, Suzan. "Yusef Komunyakaa and Paul Muldoon." *Bomb* 65:74–80 (fall 1998).

Suarez, Ernest. In *Southbound: Interviews with Southern Poets.* Columbia: University of Missouri Press, 1999.

Washington, Dorthy A. "Seeing Surprises: An Interview with Yusef Komunyakaa." *The Black Scholar* 27, no. 1:72–73 (1997).

MUSIC BASED ON THE WORKS OF YUSEF KOMUNYAKAA

Fire Water Paper: A Vietnam Oratorio. (Includes poems from *Dien Cai Dau.*) Composed by Elliot Gondenthal. Pacific Symphony Orchestra, featuring Yo-Yo Ma. Sony, 1996.

Testimony. (Libretto by Yusef Komunyakaa.) Music by Sandy Evans. Broadcast by Australian Broadcasting Corporation, 1998.

Thirteen Kinds of Desire. (Lyrics by Yusef Komunyakaa.) Pamela Knowles, vocal composer and producer. Additional music composed by Jann Rutherford, Matt McMahon, and Alister Spence. Cornucopia Productions, 2000.

VIDEOS

Allen Ginsberg and Friends. Series Title: *Poetry Heaven.* Produced and directed by Juan Mandelbaum. Thirteen /WNET, 1998. ("You and I Are Disappearing," "Thanks," and "Facing It.")

Color: A Sampling of Contemporary African American Writing. Written by Al Young. San Francisco: The Poetry Center and American Poetry. Archives SFSU, 1994.

—JOYCE SUTPHEN

Lucy Larcom
1824–1893

"NONE OF US can think of ourselves as entirely separate beings. Even an autobiographer has to say 'we' much oftener than 'I.'" In the preface to her famous life story, *A New England Girlhood* (1889), Lucy Larcom maps out one of the assumptions that energized her writing: the interconnections between and among people. Reflecting the modesty considered appropriate for women during most of her life, Larcom suggests that important relationships include those with readers, as she tells us that "the most enjoyable thing about writing is that the relation between writer and reader may be and often does become that of mutual friendship." Contributing to many important strands of American literary tradition—including autobiography, working-class writing, regionalist writing, women's humor, and nature writing—and blending the themes of nature, religion, and human responsibilities, Larcom's work as a whole resonates with this interactive concept of reader-writer relations and makes a significant portion of her writing seem relevant and engaging for today's readers.

"ROOM AND TIME TO GROW IN": LIFE

Born on March 5, 1824, to a respectable family in Beverly, Massachusetts, Larcom included among her ancestors hard-working farmers and seamen whose hardscrabble lives had indirect benefits: "Poverty has its privileges," Larcom later reflected. "When there is very little of the seen and temporal to intercept spiritual vision, unseen and eternal realities are, or may be, more clearly beheld." Like her paternal grandfather, Jonathan Larcom, her father, Benjamin, was initially a sea captain, but he relinquished this calling sometime after the War of 1812 to assure a more stable life for his large family that eventually included ten children. Because of its involvement in sea trade, Beverly was a relatively cosmopolitan town:

> Men talked about a voyage to Calcutta, or Hong-Kong, or "up the Straits,"—meaning Gibraltar and the Mediterranean,—as if it were not much more than going to the next village. It seemed as if our nearest neighbors lived over there across the water; we breathed the air of foreign countries, curiously interblended with our own.

This interconnection was literal as well as imaginative, for "there were wanderers from foreign countries domesticated in many families, whose swarthy complexions and un-Caucasian features became familiar in our streets,—Mongolians, Africans, and waifs from the Pacific islands." After giving up his work at sea Larcom's father drew upon the wide-ranging resources of the community to establish "a store for the sale of what used to be called 'West India goods,' and various other domestic commodities." Such a community, in which many women as well as men had traveled widely, provided Larcom with a broader and more inclusive vision of human relations than many of her contemporaries and probably provided a foundation for her passionate abolitionism.

Although her father was a god-fearing and reserved man, he nevertheless managed to communicate his love for his children; his daughter also noted that "his gravity concealed a fund of rare humor," a characteristic shared by his daughter. Larcom's mother was more outgoing, "a complete contrast" in temperament to her father. "Chatty and social," Lois Barrett Larcom was naturally optimistic, although the care of her eight children—born in the space of thirteen years—meant little individual time for each. As Larcom's biographer Shirley Marchalonis observes, "the fact that her two stepchildren and her own eight children survived to adulthood suggests that she must have been a good and careful mother." The writer's only living grandparent during her childhood, Lois Barrett's father, was a Revolutionary War soldier and the sexton of Beverly's oldest church. Larcom describes him as "of French descent, piquant, merry, exceedingly polite, and very fond of us children. . . . I did not believe that there was another grandfather so delightful as ours in all the world."

In addition to her parents and grandfather, Larcom was surrounded by a lively and caring extended family and community. She recounts stories of sisters, brothers, aunts, uncles, and cousins, as well as what she calls "adopted aunts." Among the latter was "Aunt Hannah," who kept the village school in the delightful domestic surroundings of her kitchen or sitting room while she spun her flax wheel. A "kind and motherly" woman, Aunt Hannah occupied an important role in Larcom's life, teaching her the alphabet, which enabled the precocious writer to begin reading at the age of two and a half. Larcom's education advanced further with the instruction of her older sister Emeline (Emilie), who, when she discovered that little Lucy had memorized numerous hymns, challenged her to memorize a hundred and as a reward taught her to write. Although Larcom affirms that "it is always a mistake to cram a juvenile mind. . . . Children ought to be children, and nothing else," she appreciated these early educational opportunities, for such opportunities would be much abridged later.

One of the most important figures in Larcom's childhood was not a person but the sea. Larcom relates an epiphanic moment sponsored by her sister Emeline, who aroused "very little" Lucy one morning at four o'clock for a walk through the graveyard and "dewy fields." Heading east, Larcom suddenly saw "what looked to me like an immense blue wall, stretching right and left as far as I could see." In this "revelation" she tells us, "I took in at that moment for the first time something of the real grandeur of the ocean." The sea's potential for suggesting "wonders" included its inhabitants: one day, not knowing that starfish were alive, young Lucy plucked one from the beach and hung it to dry in a tree. When she returned to collect the "five-finger," as the children called them, "he had clasped with two or three of his fingers the bough where I laid him, so that he could not be removed without breaking his hardened shell." Provoking an attack of conscience, this event suggests the moral view that such proximity to nature sparked and prefigures the writer's reverence for nature.

Closely connected to nature in young Larcom's mind was religious belief. Although like most children she often chafed under the restrictions of appropriate church behavior, she loved hymns, especially those related to nature. Of one, she concluded that "there must be something like the sea in heaven" and noted that it "gave me the feeling of being rocked in a boat on a strange and beautiful ocean." "Full . . . of aspiration and hope and courage," these hymns seemed to a child "like being caught up in a strong man's arms, to gaze upon some wonderful landscape." This mood of transcendence was counterbalanced by the Calvinistic community's sense of human sin, a perspective that troubled young Larcom, who sometimes avoided sleep for fear that she would awake in "a dreadful dark Somewhere, the horror of which was that it was away from Him." In her later life, Larcom would reject this stern vision and embrace a more affirmative Christianity.

In addition to loving hymns, young Larcom also appreciated storytelling, but she devoured poetry, including work by Lord Byron and Samuel Taylor Coleridge, in part because of its rhyme and rhythm; her own poetry reveals her dedication to these formal qualities, although she would occasionally experiment, as in the blank verse of *An Idyl of Work* (1875). Significantly, her chapter on the importance of poetry to her early life juxtaposes that ostensibly masculine passion with the gendered demands of domestic labor. The reality of women's lives demanded that they learn many hateful household tasks. With unusual prescience and responsibility, her father insisted that his daughters as well as sons have "some independent means of self-support by the labor of their hands." For the girls, this meant sewing; as Larcom wryly acknowledges, "I somehow or somewhere got the idea . . . that the chief end of woman was to make clothing for mankind." One day, surveying her father, she concluded with dismay, "How tall he is! and how long his coat looks! and how many thousand stitches there must be in his coat and pantaloons! And I suppose I have got to grow up and have a husband, and put all those little stitches into *his* coats and pantaloons. Oh, I never, never can do it!" Although she retells this story with humor, readers feel the ambivalence about marriage that would figure significantly in her later decision not to marry.

The emphasis that Larcom's father placed on work was sadly fortunate for his family, for in January 1832 Benjamin Larcom died, and the carefree period of Lucy Larcom's childhood concluded. Although her mother had functioned effectively with Benjamin's guidance, and the family had lived well, though never extravagantly, Lois proved to be an ineffective money manager. After struggling for about three years in Beverly, Mrs. Larcom concluded, with the advice of family and friends, that her best option was to sell the family property and move to the burgeoning factory city of Lowell, Massachusetts, to open a boardinghouse for mill girls. Lowell had gained an international reputation, drawing as workers numerous "respectable" New England farm girls, which enabled them to save for their brothers' or their own education or marriage. In attracting these independent, largely literate women who saw themselves as temporarily employed, the owners of the mills sought to foster an environment of culture and refinement via lyceum lectures and regular church attendance. To counter charges of female immorality, they had also established a system of boardinghouses headed by respectable matrons like Mrs. Larcom.

Reflecting and challenging the nineteenth-century ideology of feminine acceptance, Larcom describes this life transformation with both pleasure and dismay. From her youthful point of view, the move meant, among other things, piles of sewing, as well as the loss of the Cape Ann landscape and the freedom to explore it. At first, however, she could attend a better school, and she was interested in the many boarders from New Hampshire and Vermont, who had "a fresh breezy sociality . . . which made them seem almost like a different race of beings." But her mother's continuing financial mismanagement soon required that the youngest children, including eleven-year-old Larcom, leave school and go to work in the mills for a dollar a week. Although Larcom wanted to help the family, she was determined to continue at some point with her education; she observes, "I had looked through an open door that I was not willing to see shut upon me." Affirming women's interdependence with others, Larcom also acknowledged her family's encouragement to cultivate her special talents. To develop these talents did not, in her view, compromise the nineteenth-century ethic of womanly service; rather, it enhanced the prospect of fulfilling this ethic.

In addition to the increased closeness with her imaginative sister Emeline, another compensation for life in Lowell was Larcom's participation in the intellectual and social life of the intelligent women workers for whom "work, study, and worship interblended." The workers developed a magazine, *The Lowell Offering,* published between 1840 and 1845, which they composed and edited and to which Larcom regularly contributed. Although Larcom gently disparages the literary contributions of the millworkers, she highlights their intelligence and passion for education, insisting that "the girls there were just such girls as are knocking on the doors of young women's colleges today." As much as any aspect of her experience in Lowell, she values the egalitarian social relations that the workers enjoyed.

It was during one of the meetings of the Lowell Improvement Society that Larcom met the great reformist poet John Greenleaf Whittier, beginning a lifelong friendship in which Whittier offered advice to Larcom, revised her work, and submitted it to prestigious periodicals and publishing houses. He also collaborated with Larcom on anthologies and when he died left her his copyrights for this work. Although his relationship with Larcom today seems to be sometimes paternalistic or selfish, he did a great deal to advance her reputation and to assist her financially.

Poetry, which was central to Larcom's early childhood, acquired another importance during her time in the mills, providing her with a creative occupation as well as a distraction from the cacophony of the machinery. This noise, combined with the confinement and pollution in the mills, finally caused a breakdown in her health that resulted, first, in a year-long visit to her married sister Louisa in Beverly, where she cared for the children and grew to enjoy certain domestic duties, and, eventually, in her move west with Emeline and her sister's new family in 1846. Emeline had married George Spaulding, an ambitious young schoolmaster headed for the ministry, and his brother, Frank, was studying medicine. All three were eager to investigate the opportunities the West offered, and Lucy, who by this time was informally engaged to Frank, decided to join them. In spite of the crude living conditions, Larcom found a measure of satisfaction in helping Emeline care for her growing family and teaching district school. Evincing the moral stance that she would continue in her poetry, she admitted a black student to one school, and, when the school committee told her it would close the school rather than permit his attendance, Larcom tutored the boy and his father privately—an action that ultimately cost her job.

Apart from its difficult and troubling aspects, however, the West provided her with the educational opportunities that she had been forced to abridge earlier. In 1848 she entered Monticello Seminary in Alton, Illinois, "a school for young women reputed to be one of the best in the country and certainly the finest in the West," wrote Marchalonis, and whose headmistress, Philena Fobes, would be a role model and friend for many years. To support herself, Larcom worked in the seminary, first as a housekeeper and then as a teacher; she reveled in the broad course of study, which included Latin, medieval and modern history, philosophy, mathematics, and botany. She continued to write, first for the *Offering* and its successor, and then, with the advice and support of the editor Harriet Farley, for other periodicals. For her first submission to the nationally known *Sartain's Magazine,* a poem titled "The Pioneer's Vision," Larcom received the generous sum of five dollars.

Around the time of Larcom's enrollment in Monticello, her fiancé caught the gold fever that infected much of the country and went to California, a decision that left Larcom conflicted and unhappy, especially when she considered the drudgery suffered by her talented sister in her marriage to George and the increasing number of dead babies that shadowed the family (by spring 1852, four of Emeline's six children would be dead). Larcom and Frank agreed that he would go West for two years while she completed her education, then he would return and they would marry. She continued her teaching and learning, though she was (and continued to be) troubled with a form of tuberculosis, and as time went on and George decided to follow Frank to California, she grew increasingly uneasy about marriage. As early as 1846, she wrote skeptically to a sister: "Talk about me getting married and settling down here in the West! I don't do that thing till I am a greater goose than I am now, for love nor money!" (quoted in *Lucy Larcom: Life, Letters, and Diary,* 1889). Under the influence of a "significant religious experience" that moved her toward a form of affirmative "Christian transcendentalism," she decided that neither continuing to teach at Monticello nor marrying Frank was the right path. When she returned to Beverly, ostensibly for a visit, in the late summer of 1852, she was on the road to becoming a professional writer.

At home Larcom called on family and friends, including the Whittiers; Elizabeth Whittier would become Larcom's lifelong friend. Renewing and extending their relationship, the famous poet encouraged her to write and helped her to publish her first book, *Similitudes, from the Ocean and Prairie* (1853), which collected short moral tales for children. She read and appreciated the work of Ralph Waldo Emerson, and, modified by her own religious beliefs, Emerson's influence would eventually be felt in her poetry. Her letters to family and friends reflected her continuing ambivalence about marriage; she wrote, "I am not 'so self-reliant and independent' that I can live and be happy without friends. But I think I can live very well without a *husband*" (cited in Marchalonis). Her straightforwardness to Frank about her feelings prompted him eventually to decide to give up their marriage; after a period of "guilt, indignation, and relief" (also in Marchalonis) followed by continued vacillation, Larcom settled into being an "old maid."

By December 1854, uneasy about finances—and dependence on her family—and uncertain about her future, Larcom began what would be a nine-year teaching career at Wheaton Seminary in Norton, Massachusetts. Her time at Wheaton proved to be both rewarding and unhappy. On the one hand, she loved the students and appreciated being able to fulfill a role of womanly service; on the other hand, her constant exhaustion, lack of time for her own studies and writing, and strong dislike for the noise and turmoil of school life caused illness and depression. As she noted in her journal, "Life in a crowd of girls has become almost a torment to me; not that the genus *girl* is disagreeable to me; I should like them all, separately, in their homes, but so much pent-up life is painful. I cannot like boarding schools" (quoted in "Lucy Larcom at Wheaton").

In December 1857 her life changed dramatically when *The Crayon,* an elite magazine, published Larcom's poem "Hannah Binding Shoes," which cast her into the national spotlight and enabled her to gain entry into all of the famous periodicals of her day, including the *Atlantic Monthly* and *The Independent.* From 1865 to 1873 she edited an important children's magazine, *Our Young Folks,* which enabled her to work with such luminaries as Henry Wadsworth Longfellow and Harriet Beecher Stowe. As she became part of the literary community, she met many celebrated writers whose work she admired, including Lydia Maria Child, Grace Greenwood, and Elizabeth Stuart Phelps. With her cheerful disposition and accommodating personality, Larcom made friends easily throughout her life.

The immediate antebellum period was a troubling time for Larcom, who was unequivocal in her support of abolition. In a letter to Whittier in 1856 later published in the *New England Quarterly* in 1930, she notes attending "Anti-slavery meetings" in Boston and declares, "We are indeed living in a revolution. It makes me ache to think I am doing nothing for the right, for *the holy cause.* What can one do? It is not very agreeable to sit still and blush to be called an American woman." One thing she could do was write poetry, including two poems still recognized today, "Weaving" and "A Loyal Woman's No."

By the time that her first book of poetry was published (*Poems*, 1868), Larcom was well into a new phase of her life as a professional writer and editor; she had also fulfilled an important dream, moving into a home of her own in Beverly Farms, close to family and friends. In the 1870s she edited three anthologies with Whittier: *Child-Life* (1871), *Child-Life in Prose* (1873), and *Songs of Three Centuries* (1876). This collaborative effort caused considerable friction, because Larcom did most of the difficult preparatory work, while Whittier, who was named as the editor, decided on final selections, wrote the prefaces, and received the royalties, while Larcom was paid a flat fee. During the same time, she edited two lucrative anthologies, *Roadside Poems for Summer Travellers* (1876) and *Hillside and Seaside in Poetry* (1877), and published her blank-verse narrative poem about several Lowell mill girls, *An Idyl of Work* (1875). Her own work was hardly idyllic, for, pressured by financial concerns, she taught school for a year, becoming very ill as a result of overwork.

Her fame, however, ultimately made possible an independent life as a writer, and she continued to publish poems and essays in magazines and newspapers. In 1879 she completed a critical assessment of major American poets, the beautifully illustrated *Landscape in American Poetry,* dovetailing with her transcendental view of nature. The most important publications of her later life were *Wild Roses of Cape Ann and Other Poems* (1880), *Larcom's Poetical Works* (1884), and *A New England Girlhood* (1889). The first of these volumes paralleled the regionalist movement in fiction and focused on her childhood surroundings, while the second formalized her importance in American literature, being published by the prestigious Houghton, Mifflin and Company, which even issued a "Household Edition." The last volume, an autobiography, provided a retrospective of the poet's early life; ostensibly written for girls, it continues to offer a window into the norms for women in the mid- to late-nineteenth-century United States. In her later years, greater financial security enabled Larcom to travel, to attend concerts and lectures, to visit family and friends, and especially to retreat to the White Mountains of New Hampshire, which Larcom found even more inspirational than the sea of her childhood.

The strong fiber of religious faith that was planted in her childhood and flowered during her travels to the West acquired even greater vitality around 1880, when she met the charismatic preacher Phillips Brooks, who became a friend and mentor. Throughout her life, Larcom was profoundly concerned with living both usefully and morally. A deeply self-reflective person who managed to negotiate for herself an independent life at a time when women were still supposed to rely on husband and family, she constructed a role that both reflected and challenged gender ideology. A learner as well as a teacher, she recognized early on that "wisdom cannot be hurried, crowded, or driven. All things worthy want room and time to grow in" (quoted in "Lucy Larcom at Wheaton).

In her last years, the deaths of family and friends influenced her profoundly. Her beloved Emeline died in July 1892, Whittier in August 1892, and Brooks in January 1893. Public announcement of Larcom's own illness in late 1892 prompted an outpouring of letters and gifts from friends, former students, and well-wishers. Secure in her faith, Larcom died on April 17, 1893.

"BOUNTEOUS FRUIT": POETRY AND EARLY WORK

Very little critical work has been done on Larcom's poetry, although a few poems are regularly anthologized, and contemporary critics emphasize the crucial role of poetry and poetry writing in Larcom's autobiography. As her career progressed, her poetry tended to be more religious and less concerned with social issues; she holds interest for today's readers for her depictions of working-class and women's experiences. Moreover, like her contemporary Celia Thaxter, who wrote many well-known poems about the Isles of Shoals off the coast of New Hampshire, and her successor Robert Frost, Larcom was primarily a nature poet. Her numerous strong poems in this vein include "Fern-Life," "November," and "Flowers of the Fallow." Having disappeared from critical view early in the twentieth century because she was widely regarded as a "sentimental" poet, Larcom's work often exceeds or complicates this mode, as Shirley Marchalonis points out. Although many of her poems tend to be metrically regular and to draw conventional connections between a transcendent nature and God, a significant number deserve close attention.

Larcom describes poetry as "the one unattainable something which I must reach out after, because I could not live without it. The thought of it was to me like the thought of God and of truth. To leave out poetry would be to lose the real meaning of life." Her most famous early poem, "Hannah Binding Shoes," demonstrates how easily Larcom is misinterpreted today. Marrying her young lover, Hannah remains at home when he leaves for a fishing voyage from Marblehead, Massachusetts. Even after twenty years, she seeks news of her lost husband, as she sits overlooking the harbor at her work. The poem initially seems cloyingly sentimental, highlighting the domestic values of love and home. From a more critical perspective, however, the poem encodes the suffering of a women who, lacking her husband's economic support, must labor endlessly at a poorly paid occupation to support herself: "Twenty winters / Bleach and tear the ragged shore she views." Given the poet's understanding of the realities of domestic life, we could easily read Larcom's poem as political, critiquing domestic ideology for its unreality and for the powerlessness and implied poverty that it imposes on the waiting wife—a role that Larcom herself declined to take in her early relationship with Frank. Early reviewers acknowledged Larcom's realism—one praised her "perfect simplicity and self-control" and the "life-like" quality of "Hannah Binding Shoes"—and her originality, referring to her as a "genius." Harriet Prescott Spofford, herself a celebrated and well-paid writer, reviewed Larcom's early work in terms that unequivocally distinguished her from her peers and emphasized her originality: "In conclusion, it may be said of these verses that there is not one syllable to be found in them of that maudlin sentimentality which sickens on the pages of so many poets, nor is there any trace of imitation of another." Larcom herself advises aspiring young women poets in *A New England Girlhood,* "Don't sentimentalize! Write more of what you see than of what you feel."

Other poems that addressed the situation of women, both directly and indirectly, include the Civil War poem "A Loyal Woman's No," in which a woman who rejects slavery also rejects her fiancé, who has Southern sympathies and refuses to fight for the Union. Appearing in the *Atlantic Monthly* in 1863, the poem was widely approved for its "strong statement of true womanly nobility and patriotic feeling," according to Marchalonis. As Marchalonis notes, the poem also reflected Larcom's personal situation, in particular, her disdain for Frank and those like him who avoided conflict: "I am not yours, because you love yourself: / Your heart has scarcely room for me beside." If men could not take the moral view, it was women's responsibility to do so: "If such as you, when Freedom's ways are rough, / Cannot walk in them, learn that women can!"

The passion and pain haunting this poem emerge differently in a "children's" poem, "A Little Old Girl," which, again reflecting her view of Emeline's difficult life, dissents strongly from domestic cultural norms. The protagonist Prudence imitates her adult female counterparts, "knitting stockings, / Sweeping floors, and baking pies." Prudence occupies "a world that women work in . . . a world where men grow rich." Each season has its work, from sewing to gardening to tending animals. Reflecting her own interrupted girlhood, in which she was removed from the idyll of Beverly and forced to work in the factory beginning at age eleven, Larcom suggests that her girl intuits another life:

> Something more has haunted Prudence
>   In the song of bird and bee,
> In the low wind's dreamy whisper
>   Through the light-leaved poplar tree.
>
> Something lingers, bends above her,
>   Leaning at the mossy well;
> Some sweet murmur from the meadows,
>   On the air some gentle spell.

Prudence ignores the call of nature and its mysteries, blaming it on "witches," but Larcom inserts her own views directly in the penultimate stanza, intimating that Prudence merely follows her mother's perspective that "work is good for child or woman" and commenting, "Childhood's jailer,—'tis a shame!" "A Little Old Girl" not only critiques the patriarchal status quo, but also offers a biting commentary on women's collusion with this state of affairs, for at the end of the poem, it is the *female* "gossips," the older women themselves, who smilingly approve of Prudence's work: "What a good wife she will make!" In her autobiography Larcom avers, "it was . . . a pity that we were set to hard work while so young." Although she repeatedly insists on the value of work throughout *A New England Girlhood,* she underlines the need for children to play, addressing mothers at least as much as their children. Like many nineteenth-century American women writers, Larcom found in children's literature (including *A New England Girlhood*) an amenably indirect method of social analysis and criticism. As Marchalonis observes, Larcom was never directly involved in the woman's rights movement, but she contributed obliquely to the affirmation of women's perspectives in much of her writing, including such poems as "Getting Along," "Unwedded," "Her Choice," "Sylvia," and "A Gambrel Roof."

Larcom's most familiar poem to modern readers, "Weaving," continues the theme of women's social and moral responsibility and adds the concept of interracial connections. As is often the case in Larcom's work, nature provides a framework for her insights. "Weaving" demonstrates an understanding of cultural ecology—specifically, the matrix of exploitation involving Southern slave women, Northern white women factory workers, and cotton production. The poem opens with a blurring of the border between inside and outside as well as between imagination and "reality":

> All day she stands before her loom;
>   The flying shuttles come and go;
> By grassy fields, and trees in bloom,
>   She sees the winding river flow:
> And fancy's shuttle flieth wide,
> And faster than the waters glide.

Musing in a voice that speaks to herself and to readers, the weaver affirms the connection between culture and nature, as the river becomes a metaphor for life itself:

> The river glides along, one thread
>   In nature's mesh, so beautiful!
> The stars are woven in; the red
>   Of sunrise; and the rain-cloud dull.
> Each seems a separate wonder wrought;
> Each blends with some more wondrous thought.

"Each" of the natural elements here is both "a separate wonder" and "blends" with others; Larcom insists that only God can perceive the "full pattern" that the "separate shreds" finally compose.

Nevertheless, she ventriloquizes through the voice of the weaver—in a clear reference to the poet's vocation—to underscore her own comprehensive vision, a vision that perceives "nature's mesh" paralleling the connections between and among women. The river fosters this imaginative link:

> Wind on, by willow and by pine,
>   Thou blue, untroubled Merrimack!
> Afar, by sunnier streams than thine,
>   My sisters toil, with foreheads black;
> And water with their blood this root,
> Whereof we gather bounteous fruit.

Nature mediates conscience for Larcom, as she notes the connection between the livelihood of Northern factory women and the lives of Southern slave women. By the light of sunset, she imagines the Merrimack's "calm flood / Were changed into a stream of blood," as if, seen in another light, nature reflects and remarks on human—and here, specifically female—sins—and even more significantly, female responsibilities. She insists: "Thy sister's keeper know thou art!" Larcom deploys nature to critique the exploitative class system of manual labor that undermines the ideology and reality of "America."

Nature forms the subject or metaphoric frame for the large majority of Larcom's poem, and she admired William Cullen Bryant as much as she did Whittier, Emerson, and other contemporaries. "Flowers of the Fallow" investigates the conventional affiliation between women and nature. Resisting the Romantic ideal of nature as pure, and purely beautiful, the poem opens:

> I like these plants that you call weeds,—
>   Sedge, hardhack, mullein, yarrow,—
> That knit their seeds
> Where any grassy wheel-track leads
>   Through country by-ways narrow.

Larcom emphasizes the consonants in these plant names to reinforce the perspective of a nature both "wild" and "cultivated." These powerfully invasive "weeds" are paradoxically linked to the presence of culture via the metaphor of "seeds" and the observation of the literal inroads made by the technology of wheels. Although the "wild" weeds occupy the position of social outcasts, the next stanza revalues these plants, asserting their chronological (and metaphoric) priority, before the emergence of hill farms themselves "grown old with cultivation."

The second stanza also introduces the image of female nature—described as a "matron"—who in the third stanza emerges as "Mother Earth." But this mother resists the human urge to transform the natural world and fills the spaces created by plows with "humbler blossoms" that speak from "flowery lips." Larcom acknowledges the historical role of men in the literal and conceptual creation of the American landscape, for stanza five articulates another perspective on the relationship between humans and nature, which "yielded to your axe, with pain, / Her free, primeval glory." Yet the poet goes beyond this depiction and links postlapsarian nature with the image of the aging woman, reenvisioned in "Flowers of the Fallow" as powerful:

> You say, "How dull she grows! how plain!"
>   The old, mean, selfish story!

> Her wildwood sod you may subdue,
>   Tortured by hoe and harrow;
> But leave her for a year or two,
> And see! she stands and laughs at you
>   With hardhack, mullein, yarrow!

Larcom creates an old, tired Mother Nature with whom she identifies, as the poem's final stanza envisions the weeds as tangible evidence of "heaven's breath" and herself as deeply connected to them: "And I lie down at blessèd ease / Among thy weeds and grasses." Exposing the objectification of Mother Nature and of women, especially old women, in American culture, Larcom offers a reappraisal of the affiliations between women and nature that reinforce cultural gender norms and hierarchies.

Another important poem for today's readers also investigates gender roles—frequently with nature as a central metaphor—and also revisits the role of class structures in U.S. society. *An Idyl of Work* revisits Larcom's experience as a Lowell mill girl and questions how social class is often constructed through language. Also contributing to ongoing discussions about regionalism and regional life, Larcom modestly articulates her goal: "A truthful sketch of factory-life . . . and a sketch only, for this 'Idyl' does not claim completeness either as poem or as narrative,—is all that she has sought to produce. The routine of such a life is essentially prosaic." Set in a brief New England summer, *An Idyl* presents the story of several mill girls. Anticipating Robert Frost's New England women in his 1915 volume *North of Boston* (though without their psychological sophistication), Larcom's "girls" nevertheless reveal distinctive characters: motherly Esther cares for the group members and ministers to the community; Eleanor is the delicate consumptive; Minta is the educated New Hampshire country girl, a worker and teacher who aspires to something better than marriage to a dull and narrow local farmer; and Isabel is the ladylike but reckless worker who endangers her reputation by falling in love with a rogue. With its focus on social class and on women as important characters beyond their role as romantic partners for men, *An Idyl of Work* reinvents and indirectly critiques Alfred, Lord Tennyson's popular *Idylls of the King* (1859–1885), a series of poems about the King Arthur myth. In her poem, Larcom points to another kind of heroism—the heroism of work and of everyday life—while she underlines the healing powers of nature.

Preceding the midcentury wave of Irish immigrants, the mill girls had a fluid understanding of class identity. In *An Idyl of Work* Larcom records the discomfort of many nonworking women about this fluidity. In the first section one of Larcom's protagonists muses on the definition of "lady": "'Lady.' Who defines / That word correctly?" We discover that "There's something more in it than feeding folks / With bread or with ideas." In contrast to the views of the genteel mill girl protagonists, a "town-dame" laments

> that now even factory-girls
> Shine with gold watches, and you cannot tell,
> Therefore, who are the ladies.

Such questioning about social roles—especially by a famous poet—would not go unnoticed. *An Idyl of Work* received a notice in the powerful *Atlantic,* which referred to *The Lowell Offering* in slighting terms but compared American working-class "girls" favorably to their British counterparts ("the vicious and stupid operative class of the Old World"). The reviewer praised Larcom's work for its realism ("faithfulness to the life it depicts"), as well as its "sincerity," "boldness," and ability to "move one to a compassionate sympathy with girlhood struggling to keep life pretty and nice and even noble in circumstances so adverse." Although the reviewer lamented what he saw as Larcom's timidity, wishing for "something more decided and dramatic than she has done," he praised the "Wordsworthian courage" of her realism. Few well-known poets at this time—a period of turbulent class relations in the United States—attempted the direct exploration of social differences, especially as such differences related to gender. During her earlier experience teaching at Wheaton Seminary, she reflected in her journal on the educational disparities between men and women and their respective teachers: "girls will be ill-educated, till their teachers are allowed the time and thought which teachers of *men* are expected to take." Larcom's denunciation of superficial markers of class indicates her lifelong emphasis on education and freedom from external sources of valuation.

In addition to forecasting Frost's dramatic verse, Larcom's poetry also anticipates Frost' nature lyrics, as we see in "Swinging on a Birch-Tree," a children's poem affiliated with Frost's "Birches" in title, shape, and mood. As her life drew to a close Larcom returned to poems about nature and the region she loved. Invoking places specific to Cape Ann, such as "Agawam," "Wenham Lake," "Chebacco woods," and "Jeffrey's Creek"—just as Frost would cite Lancaster, New Hampshire, in "A Hundred Collars" and Bow, New Hampshire, in "The Generations of Men"—"My Mariner" begins with a jaunty and romanticized ballad-form vision of a seafaring husband. But after four stanzas the poem changes in tone and form, providing in blank verse a more domesticated and realistic—though sometimes nostalgic—portrait of what is left behind. Larcom invites her readers to journey with her along the shore as it was twenty years earlier as, admiring hidden byways, she depicts the landscape's complex beauties:

> Even now,
> You slip into those rose-roads unaware,
> Just out of reach of landscape gardeners,
> And farmers beauty-blind, whose synonym
> For poison-oak and rose is—underbrush!

Humorously reinventing the concept of beauty to include "poison-oak" along with "rose," Larcom criticizes both "landscape gardeners" who have altered the wild landscape for the worse ("everything / That hints of Nature closely taken in hand / By patronizing Wealth, and stroked and smoothed / Into suburban elegance") and purely utilitarian farmers.

The poem concludes with another passage that is simultaneously romantic and critical of the romantic vision of its initial ballad form:

> The fisher's child scarce knows if sea or shore
> Is most his home; and yet must Georges' name—
> The dragon-shoal that counts his wrecks by scores—
> Bring dreams of nightmare-terror to the babe
> Who hears it only through a mother's moan.

Although Larcom's poem ends with a generalized invocation to "the fisher child" and invokes the myth of St. George slaying the dragon, it specifies the locale of Cape Ann with the reference to the Georges' Bank fishing ground. "My Mariner" and similar poems in Larcom's *Cape Ann* underline for readers, as many of Frost's North of Boston poems would do, the quiet heroism of many New Englanders in the face of daunting weather, cultural transformation, and personal disaster.

"THIS GREEN, ROCKY STRIP OF SHORE": A NEW ENGLAND GIRLHOOD REVISITED

Larcom's most interesting prose work for today's readers is *A New England Girlhood* (1889), the volume on which most contemporary criticism is focused. Critics have remarked on its embeddedness in poetry and poetic vision, on its emphasis on useful work and on women's education, its philosophy of a "balance between autonomy and relationship" and on its careful handling of details to provide a simultaneously intimate and veiled, stylistically impressionistic portrait of the author's childhood. Marchalonis underscores the volume's "controlled nostalgia—not a simplistic urging to return to the past, but a looking back with love on parallel childhoods, her own and that of the country." Among her contemporaries the book was an enormous popular success with male as well as female readers and with people of all ages, even though it was ostensibly written for an audience of girls. Reviewers in all the powerful magazines praised the volume, with the *Atlantic* noting that "it will not be the young who will draw the greatest pleasure from the performance" and *The Dial* concluding that "Nothing better of its kind has come under our notice" (quoted in Marchalonis).

To many modern readers, the book may seem occasionally marred by excess religiosity, but for others Larcom's depiction of a transcendental worldview framed by belief in a loving deity may be more appealing. Virtually all will acknowledge the book's lyrical attention to landscape and place, its appealing descriptions of an older way of life and family connections, and its often unexpected, self-subversive humor that counterbalances its emphatic effort toward cheeriness in difficult circumstances. With stark personal experience, she also provides a window into the fragile class system in the United States and the reality that underlay the American Dream. Larcom's preface acknowledges the significance of a writer's life to all of her work: "It is hardly possible for an author to write anything sincerely without making it something of an autobiography." Larcom conceptualizes herself as a child and, later, girl character in her life story. Although she appreciates her child self, who "seems to me like my little sister, at play in a garden where I can at any time return and find her," she is more critical of "the older girl," whose "faults" include "her habit of lapsing into listless reveries, her cowardly shrinking from responsibility and vigorous endeavor."

Nevertheless, she sounds a note of self-acceptance—"Still, she is myself, and I could not be quite happy without her companionship"—and invokes, characteristically, a natural image: "The moon does not, except in appearance, lose her first thin, luminous curve, nor her silvery crescent, in rounding to her full. The woman is still the child and the girl, in the completeness of womanly character." Assuming a conventionally feminine stance of self-deprecation, Larcom nevertheless affirms the value of her character (in both senses). Her autobiography as a whole emerges from a dual narrative perspective combining masculine self-assertiveness—to tell one's story at all represents an act of pride and reflects one's importance—with feminine self-erasure. This strategic self-erasure frames the book, as she depicts her book in the preface as shared "gossip" with "friends" and states, "I should like far better to listen to my girl-readers' thoughts about life and themselves to be writing out my own experiences." As Amy Kort acknowledges, Larcom's self-diminishing and reader-responsive style undercuts the norms for the speaker's authority in standard autobiographical writing.

In her portraits of herself—as a precocious child who valued reading and writing over traditionally female employments such as sewing—and of supportive female family members and friends, Larcom dissents from standard, limiting portraits of women and encourages female achievement. For example, despite Aunt Hannah's conventionally female context and domestic employments—keeping school in her home, and teaching even as she sits at the spinning wheel—in her role as schoolteacher she expects girls to attend to their education as diligently as boys, and, indeed, although she castigates any student who exhibits inattentiveness and stupidity, she reserves a conspicuously "feminine" punishment for the girls: they receive a "rap on the head with the teacher's thimble; accompanied with a half-whispered, impatient ejaculation, which sounded very much like 'Numskull!'" Another important model is her father's sister, for whom Larcom is named. She writes, "I learned that 'Lucy' means 'with light'" and describes how "my aunt, like my father, was always studying something. Some map or book always lay open before her, when I went to visit her." Later in the narrative, Larcom admires both her sister Emilie (Emeline), who announces her desire to be an "old maid" and defends the usefulness of such women, and the mill girls with whom she works: "the girls who toiled together at Lowell were clearing away a few weeds from the overgrown track of independent labor for other women." These strong women served as complements and counterpoints to her more conventional and impractical mother.

As she grew older and began to read novels, Lucy compared herself unfavorably with the heroines, which reflected her increasing dissatisfaction with her appearance, a concern that, she humorously suggests, occupied too many young women of her time. She also anticipates her youthful awkwardness as she grew to be much taller than many women of her era; by the time the family moved to Lowell, Larcom, at eleven, had reached her adult height, and her family insisted that she dress like a woman even though she did not feel like one. In Beverly, however, although she was not allowed to play with boys other than her brothers, she enjoyed the freedom often given to children of both sexes in rural communities. Reflecting a dual narrative perspective that both celebrated her accomplishments and criticized her failings, her story conveys ambivalence about self-presentation and complicates our understanding about the tradition of American autobiography, with its emphasis on the public lives of famous and successful men.

This dual perspective appears in one episode when she goes for a walk with her little sister, and the latter jumps into "a bog by the roadside, where sweet-flag and cat-tails grew. Out in the middle of the bog, where no venturesome boy had ever attempted their seizure, there were many tall, fine-looking brown cat-tails growing." Her sister plunges forward while Lucy watches, "petrified with horror" because she "knew all about that dangerous place." When her sister begins to sink, Larcom "felt the power of a giant suddenly taking possession of my small frame," and, giving "one tremendous pull," she "dragged her back to the road." In a self-deprecatingly feminine fashion, Larcom attributes her strength to "some unseen Power [that] had taken possession of me for a moment, and made me do it," but alert readers can see in this narrative a story of small heroism that serves as a counterpoint to the previous chapter, "Naughty Children and Fairy Tales," in which most of the heroines occupy entirely conventional romantic roles. Here Larcom represents herself as more daring than any "venturesome boy" and as salvifically powerful. Ignoring her heroic actions, her family members scold her "for not taking better care of [her] little sister"; significantly, a part of the damage done is to her sister's fashionable "brand-new pair of red morocco boots" which "were never again *red*."

Later in the book Larcom addresses the question of women's roles—and eventually, her own professional authorship—directly. She notes that although in earlier times girls were expected to "to become good wives and mothers" and describes these roles as "natural and laudable," in her childhood girls were encouraged "to cultivate and make use of their individual powers." Although such encouragement emerged within a moral framework in which women were to be of use, "to develop any talent we might possess, or at least to learn how to do some one thing which the world needed, or which would make it a pleasanter world," it enabled Larcom early on to dream, first of teaching, and eventually of writing. After describing the independent, hard-working, intelligent young women of Lowell, she avows,

> A girl's place in the world is a very strong one: it is a pity that she does not always see it so.... She often lets her life get broken into fragments among the flimsy trellises of fashion and conventionality, when it might be a perfect thing in the upright beauty of its own consecrated freedom.

She goes on to describe women as helpers, for men or for the poor or for children, but again emphasizes "courage and self-reliance" as appropriate female virtues. Underneath the sometimes flowery rhetoric is a belief in female self-empowerment and independence, themes that reappear throughout *A New England Girlhood*.

Another important concern in the autobiography is class difference, a subject on which she diverges from the normative perspective of Benjamin Franklin's autobiography. Like Franklin, Larcom values hard work, but she values it less for its power to bring financial success and more for its ability to build character, for its own sake. Paradoxically, Larcom indicates that her earliest awareness of this difference was only through reading: "a ragged, half-clothed child, or one that could really be called poor, in the extreme sense of the world, was the rarest of all sights in a thrifty New England town fifty years ago." Even less obvious were beggars: "I believe I had more curiosity about a beggar, and more ignorance, than about a king." Differences in rank were obscured, and to be a "servant" in the Old World sense was entirely confusing to her. She observes, "I settled down upon the conclusion that 'rich' and 'poor' were book-words only, describing something far off, and having nothing to do with our every-day experience." It was only later, after the death of her father, and "poverty was a possible visitation to our own household," that she would learn what it meant to "earn my own living." Such experience would prompt her years later to ask her publisher James T. Fields to make one book as inexpensive as possible so that more people could afford it.

After she had worked in the mills, Larcom revisted the idea of a "servant," coming to affirm the old-fashioned idea of interdependent "help" so prevalent in New England households earlier in the nineteenth century:

> A girl came into a family as one of the home-group, to share its burdens, to feel that they were her own. The woman who employed her, if her nature was at all generous, could not feel that money alone was an equivalent for a heart's service; she added to it her friendship, her gratitude and esteem.

Referring to the late-century difficulty of middle-class and wealthy women in finding reliable and loyal servants, Larcom concludes, "The domestic problem can never be rightly settled until the old idea of mutual help is in some way restored." Fostered by her early childhood experience, her egalitarian views grew even stronger after her experience in the Lowell mills.

Coupled with her religious faith this experience led her to protest against false social distinctions and to echo the sentiments in "Weaving": "it is the first duty of every woman to recognize the mutual bond of universal womanhood." Rejecting Franklin's individualism, Larcom imagines a community vision that is necessary in an economic environment in which "changes of fortune come so abruptly that the millionaire's daughter of to-day may be glad to earn her living by sewing or sweeping to-morrow." Expanding on her earlier investigation of the subject in *An Idyl of Work,* she asserts that "perhaps it is the fault of ladies themselves that the word 'lady' has nearly lost its original meaning (a noble one) indicating sympathy and service;—bread-giver to those who are in need." In spite of her recognition of false distinctions, however, she argues that the term should be earned through behavior and attitude, rather than referring to "something external in dress and attitude." Here again she highlights the New World attitudes of the mill girls as she constructs a proud model of independent American womanhood. Larcom's account of working in the mills and her lifelong struggle for financial security places her account within a tradition of working-class writing that critics have only recently begun to explore.

As "Weaving" indicates, Larcom was not only concerned with class differences but also with race and ethnic differences. In *A New England Girlhood* this theme forms a subtle undercurrent to the narration. She recalls as a child seeing "families of black people [who] were scattered about the place, relics of a time when even New England had not freed her slaves," and in spite of their participation in the community describes them in sad terms: "they seemed pathetically out of place, although they lived among us on equal terms, respectable and respected." In contrast, her journal records with pleasure meeting at the Whittiers' home "an educated mulatto girl, refined, lady-like in every respect, and a standing reply to those who talk of the 'inferiority of the colored race.'" Larcom's attitude toward slavery emerges later in an account of Whittier's visit to Lowell: "It is strange now to think that a cause like that should not have always been our country's cause,—our country,—our own free nation! But antislavery sentiments were then regarded by many as traitorous heresies." She notes, "If the vote of the mill-girls had been taken, it would doubtless have been unanimous on the antislavery side. But those were also the days when a woman was not expected to give, or even to have, an opinion on subjects of public interest." Larcom's optimism and praise for the mill girls in this retrospective account constitutes another strand in her construction of both progressive American womanhood and American identity more generally; she constructs an indelible and self-aware image of American girlhood: "They were making their own traditions, to hand down to their Republican descendants."

Native Americans in *An American Girlhood* emerge either as potential religious converts or as attractive, orientalized objects for pleasant observation; as she looks out the window at the mills in the summer and sees a group of Penobscot Indians "glide noiselessly up the river" in their canoes and land on a "green point almost always in sight from our windows," she observes:

> Their strange endeavors to combine civilization with savagery were a great source of amusement to us; men and women clad alike in loose gowns, stove-pipe hats, and moccasons; grotesque relics of aboriginal forest-life. The sight of these uncouth-looking red men made the romance fade entirely out of the Indian stories we had heard. Still their wigwam camp was a show we would not willingly have missed.

In spite of Larcom's relatively egalitarian and realistic vision elsewhere, she and her friends seek a romantic vision of Native Americans, whom they view with amused condescension. Her narrative unwittingly tells us a great deal, however, about the Indians' ability to synthesize, to take from white society what they found most useful and to adapt it to their own culture.

Irish immigrants also retain some of their romantic appeal, as Larcom describes a mud cabin with a thatched roof

> that looked as if it had emigrated bodily from the bogs of Ireland. It had settled itself down in a green hollow by the roadside, and it looked as much at home with the lilac-tinted crane's-bill [geraniums] and yellow buttercups as if it had never lost sight of the shamrocks of Erin.

Preceding the description of the Penobscots, this account of the Irish immigrants' housing is noteworthy because of the absence of the inhabitants. Larcom follows this passage, however, with a stereotypical account of a "real beggar," one of the many who sought food from the New England residents. Although in the

1830s the Lowell mills still employed predominantly native New England workers and it was only in the late 1840s, following a series of famines, that Irish workers would immigrate en masse, a few Irish families came to the United States earlier. In spite of a lack of her characteristic sensitivity in these descriptions of Indians and Irish people, Larcom provides an important, lively portrait of a multiethnic, multicultural United States. At its best, this America, her "affiliative autobiography" suggests more broadly, emphasizes appreciation of difference, of community and connection over disparity and individual achievement.

Given many twentieth-century readers' misleading understanding of her as a sentimental writer, a surprising component of Larcom's autobiography is her unremitting humor, often aimed at herself, even emerging in a religious context. She tells us that when she was a small child,

> When the minister read, "Cut it down: why cumbereth it the ground?" I thought he meant to say "cu-cumbereth." These vegetables grew on the ground, and I had heard that they were not very good for people to eat. I honestly supposed that the New Testament forbade the cultivation of cucumbers.

Her literalness causes additional difficulties when she hears an aunt pray, "Oh Lord, Thou knowest that we are all groveling worms of the dust" and returns home to repeat the sentence to her family, "begging to know whether everybody did sometimes have to crawl about in the dust" like worms. Another glimpse of her naïveté comes when she begins to read and write in earnest; in the process of collecting a "library" at the age of four, she finds in the attic a copy of *The Life of John Calvin*. Although it is missing half its cover, Larcom treasures the volume, which she juxtaposes on the shelf next to the only other book that she could find, Byron's *Vision of Judgment,* which was similarly disfigured. Acknowledging as an adult the humorous incompatibility of placing the sternly religious John Calvin beside the worldly Byron, she concludes, "to me they were two brother-books, like each other in their refusal to wear limp covers." She also admits that "John Calvin was left to a lonely fate, and I am afraid that at last the mice devoured him," intimating wittily that the Byron volume did not suffer a similar conclusion. Larcom's humor adds to the tradition of American women's humor that begins with Anne Bradstreet and continues in the nineteenth century with writers such as Frances Miriam Berry Whitcher, Rose Terry Cooke, Marietta Holley, and Kate Sanborn.

Larcom's principal appeal for today's readers is as a regionalist and nature writer. The opening of *A New England Girlhood* affirms her fundamental connection to place: "It is strange that the spot of earth where we were born should make such a difference to us. People can live and grow anywhere, but people as well as plants have their *habitat,*—the place where they belong, and where they find their happiest, because their most natural life." For Larcom, this place is in northeastern Massachusetts, on "this green, rocky strip of shore," where "these gray ledges hold me by the roots, as they do the bayberry bushes, the sweet-fern, and the rock-saxifrage." As her description makes clear, people flourish or fail because of their roots, and many of Larcom's descriptions connect people to natural phenomena or describe them in metaphors based in nature.

Following in the tradition of such regionalist and nature writing as Susan Fenimore Cooper's *Rural Hours* (1850), Henry David Thoreau's *Walden* (1854), and Celia Thaxter's *Among the Isles of Shoals* (1873), and anticipating Thaxter's *An Island Garden* (1894) and Sarah Orne Jewett's *The Country of the Pointed Firs* (1896), Larcom's regionalist voice describes the Beverley of her childhood in idyllic terms. The herbs and flowers, the terrain, the cultivated land all figure largely, expanding the young writer's vision: "Those dandelion fields were like another heaven dropped down upon the earth, where our feet wandered at will among the stars." The water, however, holds a special place in the writer's imagination: "An 'arm of the sea' I was told that our river was, and it did seem to reach around the town and hold it in a liquid embrace. Twice a day the tide came in and filled its muddy bed with a sparkling flood." More maternal than menacing, the river and sea signify possibility. And indeed, they are full of wonderful creatures:

> One [of the snails] we called a "butter-boat"; it had something shaped like a seat across the end of it on the inside. And the curious sea-urchin, that looked as if he was made only for ornament, when he had once got rid of his spines,—and the transparent jelly-fish, that seemed to have no more right to be alive than a ladleful of mucilage,—and the razor-shells, and the barnacles, and the knotted kelp, and the flabby green sea-aprons,—there was no end to the interesting things I found when I was trusted to go down to the edge of the tide alone.

In much of *A New England Girlhood,* as in Thaxter and Jewett's work, nature attains the presence and status of a character. As in Emily Dickinson's poetry, nature's wonders offer opportunities for human imagination and spiritual transcendence.

Part of the allure of Larcom's home territory derives from its heterogeneity, from the things global as well as local. Describing the mixing of people and things from abroad, she recalls how "mantel-pieces were adorned with nautilus and conch-shells, and with branches and fans of coral"; how the community was "accustomed to seeing barrels full of cocoa-nuts rolled about; and there were jars of preserved tropical fruits, tamarinds, ginger-root, and other spicy appetizers, almost as common as barberries and cranberries, in the cupboards of most housekeepers." Among the common wonders were "many living reminders of strange lands across the sea":

> Green parrots went scolding and laughing down the thimbleberry hedges that bordered the cornfields, as much at home out of doors as within. Java sparrows and canaries and other tropical song-birds poured their music out of sunny windows into the street, delighting the ears of passing school children long before the robins came.

Larcom makes clear that her local environment is a diverse world environment as well, painting a picture of "a rural Paradise." The importance of nature to Larcom's life and aesthetic vision continues even when her rural idyll is dislodged by the realities of impending poverty and hard work. In the mills, she has another view of a river, the mighty Merrimack, as an omnipresent feature of the landscape. Reminding readers that "we were children still," she observes, "Nature still held us close to her motherly heart." Close to the mill gates is green grass; "violets and geraniums grew by the canals."

Larcom repeatedly underscores the transcendental nature of her vision, which she felt from earliest childhood. In describing how she learned to read the Bible and acquired her sense of God's familiarity—meaning both accustomed and familial—she evokes an ecstatic moment:

> Sitting on the floor in a square of sunshine made by an open window, the leaf-shadows from the great boughs outside dancing and wavering around me, I seemed to be talking to them and they to me in unknown tongues, that left within me an ecstasy yet unforgotten. The shadows brought a message from an unseen Somewhere. . . . The wonder of that moment often returns. Shadow-traceries of bough and leaf still seem to me like the hieroglyphics of a lost language.

Echoing Walt Whitman's resonant visions of nature and anticipating today's ecocritics' concerns with the language of nature, Larcom evokes an intense presence that opens toward divine revelation and forecasts the work of such modern and contemporary women nature writers as Mary Hunter Austin, Annie Dillard, and Diane Ackerman.

Throughout her autobiography Larcom negotiates between the cultural ideology of female self-sacrifice and the self-assertive requirements of the genre of autobiography, but this tension intensifies near the end. In her depictions of her literary precocity and passion for reading and writing, Larcom presents as an almost accidental author, and she indicates that she (modestly) did not consider writing as a career until well into adulthood. She also observes that "certainly the world needs deeds more than it needs words. I should never have been willing to be *only* a writer, without using my hands to some good purpose besides." It is her siblings, friends, and family who acknowledge her gift and pressure her to develop her skills. The *Lowell Offering* provided a hospitable venue for publication and, although (or perhaps because) it drew attention to the young author, she felt compelled to insist that "fame . . . never had much attraction for me." She comments sadly on the financial exigencies of her life when she acknowledges that poetry was possible to her only "as an aside from other employments. Whether I should have written better verses had circumstances left me free to do what I chose, it is impossible to know now." The concluding pages are full of conventional apology and self-retraction. In acknowledging her successes, Larcom avows diminishingly, "I have always regarded it as a better ambition to be a true woman than to be a successful writer"; she insists that "my little story is not a remarkable one"; and, astonishingly—given the evidence of her increasing professionalism over the years—concludes by quoting a writer who asserted "I never had a career." However much she might demur, *A New England Girlhood* testifies not only to a remarkable life but also to Larcom's skill and authority as a prose writer and poet.

Finally, Larcom's poetics of community regards poets—and perhaps, by extension, poetic prose writers—as "the voices of common humanity" (quoted in *Lucy Larcom: Life, Letters, and Diary*). At the center of one of her most important poems, the metaphor of weaving represents the best figure for Larcom's vision of literature and life. Enabling her to maintain the importance of individuality while insisting upon social connection, the writer draws upon her life in Lowell to conclude:

> Every little thread must take its place as warp or woof, and keep in it steadily. Left to itself, it would only be a loose, useless filament. Trying to wander in an independent or disconnected way among the other threads, it would make of the whole web an inextricable snarl. Yet each little thread must be as firmly spun as if it were the only one, or the result would be a worthless fabric. That we are entirely separate, while yet we entirely belong to the Whole, is a truth that we learn to rejoice in.

Selected Bibliography

WORKS OF LUCY LARCOM

NONFICTION AND COLLECTED ESSAYS

"Recollections of L. L." *Lowell Offering* 5:211–216, 220–223 (September and October 1845).

Landscape in American Poetry. New York: Appleton, 1879.

"Among Lowell Mill-Girls." *Atlantic Monthly* 48:593–612 (1881).

"American Factory Life—Past, Present, and Future." *Journal of Social Science* 16:141–146 (1882).

Semi-Centennial Sketch of Wheaton Seminary. Cambridge, Mass.: Riverside Press, 1885.

A New England Girlhood, Outlined from Memory. Boston: Houghton, Mifflin and Co., 1889.

"In the Ossipee Glens." *New England Magazine* 13, no. 2:192–207 (October 1892).

POETRY

Poems. Boston: Fields, Osgood, 1868.

Childhood Songs. Boston: Osgood, 1875. (Children's book.)

An Idyl of Work. Boston: Osgood, 1875.

Wild Roses of Cape Ann and Other Poems. Boston: Houghton Osgood, 1880.

Larcom's Poetical Works [also titled *Lucy Larcom's Poems*]. Boston: Houghton, Mifflin and Co., 1884.

The Crystal Hills. With John Greenleaf Whittier. Illustrated by F. Schuyler Mathews. Boston: Prang, 1889.

EDITED COLLECTIONS AND PERIODICALS

Our Young Folks. Boston: Ticknor & Fields. Edited with J. T. Trowbridge and Gail Hamilton, 1865–1867; with J. T. Trowbridge, 1867–1873. (Serial.)

Child-Life. With John Greenleaf Whittier. Boston: Osgood, 1871.

Child-Life in Prose. With John Greenleaf Whittier. Boston: Osgood, 1873.

Roadside Poems for Summer Travellers. Boston: Osgood, 1876.

Songs of Three Centuries. With John Greenleaf Whittier. Boston: Osgood, 1876.

Hillside and Seaside in Poetry: A Companion to "Roadside Poems." Boston: Osgood, 1877.

DEVOTIONAL WORKS

Similitudes, from the Ocean and Prairie. Boston: Jewett, 1853. (Children's book.)

Lottie's Thought-Book. Philadelphia: American Sunday-School Union, 1858. (Children's book.)

Ships in the Mist, and Other Stories. Boston: Hoyt, 1860. (Children's book.)

Leila among the Mountains. Boston: Hoyt, 1861. (Children's book.)

Breathings of a Better Life. Boston: Fields, Osgood, 1866. (Poetry anthology edited by Larcom.)

Beckonings for Every Day: A Calendar of Thought. Boston: Houghton, Mifflin and Co., 1886. (Edited by Larcom.)

Easter Messengers: A New Poem of the Flowers. New York: White, Stokes, and Allen, 1886.

Easter Gleams. Boston: Houghton, Mifflin and Co., 1890. (Poetry.)

As It Is in Heaven. Boston: Houghton, Mifflin and Co., 1891.

At the Beautiful Gate, and Other Songs of Faith. Boston: Houghton, Mifflin and Co., 1892.

The Unseen Friend. Boston: Houghton, Mifflin and Co., 1892.

PAPERS

Major collections of Lucy Larcom's papers are in the Beverly Historical Society and the Beverly Public Library, Beverly, Massachusetts; the Essex Institute, Salem, Massachusetts; the Houghton Library, Harvard University; the Boston Public Library and the Massachusetts Historical Society, Boston; Wheaton College Library, Norton, Massachusetts; the Huntington Library, San Marino, California; and the University of Virginia Library.

The Lucy Larcom Collection in the Marion B. Gebbie Archives and Special Collections at the Madeleine Clark Wallace Library of Wheaton College includes letters, manuscripts for poems and lectures, copybooks, diaries, and artwork by Larcom. There are also letters at the Boston Athenaeum and the Essex Institute.

CRITICAL AND BIOGRAPHICAL STUDIES

Abbott, William F. "The Genealogy of the Larcom Family." *Essex Institute Historical Collections* 58:41–48, 129–150 (January and April 1922).

Addison, Daniel Dulany. *Lucy Larcom: Life, Letters, and Diary.* Boston: Houghton, Mifflin and Co., 1894.

Alves, Susan. "A Thousand Times I'd Rather Be a Factory Girl: The Politics of Reading American and British Female Factory Workers' Poetry, 1840–1914." Ph.D. dissertation, Northeastern University, 1996.

———. "Lucy Larcom." *Nineteenth-Century American Women Writers: A Bio-Bibliographical Sourcebook.* Edited by Denise D. Knight. Westport, Conn.: Greenwood Press, 1997. Pp. 292–297.

Bennett, Paula Bernat. "Lucy Larcom." In her *Nineteenth-Century American Women Poets: An Anthology.* Malden, Mass.: Blackwell, 1998. Pp. 111–113.

Brooks, Van Wyck. *The Flowering of New England: 1815–1865.* New York: Dutton, 1936.

———. *New England: Indian Summer, 1865–1915.* New York: Dutton, 1940.

Cott, Nancy. Foreword to *A New England Girlhood.* Boston: Northeastern University Press, 1986. Pp. xi–xvii.

Dow, Mary Larcom. *Old Days at Beverly Farms.* Beverly: North Shore, 1921.

Dublin, Thomas. *Women at Work: The Transformation of Work and Community in Lowell, Massachusetts, 1826–1860.* New York: Columbia University Press, 1979.

———. "Women, Work, and Protest in the Early Lowell Mills: 'The Oppressing Hand of Avarice Would Enslave Us.'" In *The Working Class and Its Culture.* Edited by Neil Larry Shumsky. New York: Garland, 1996. Pp. 127–144.

Eisler, Benita, ed. *The Lowell Offering: Writings by New England Mill Women (1840–1845).* New York: Norton, 1998.

Foner, Philip S., ed. *The Factory Girls: A Collection of Writings on Life and Struggles in the New England Factories of the 1840s.* Urbana: University of Illinois Press, 1977.

Geissler, Kathleen Mary. "The Social Meaning of Women's Literacy in Nineteenth-Century America." Ph.D. dissertation, University of Southern California, 1986.

Gray, Janet, ed. *She Wields a Pen: American Women Poets of the Nineteenth Century.* Iowa City: University of Iowa Press, 1997.

Harris, Sharon M., ed. *American Women Prose Writers, 1870–1920.* Detroit: Gale, 2000.

Helmreich, Paul C. "Lucy Larcom at Wheaton." *The New England Quarterly: A Historical Review of New England Life and Letters* 63, no. 1:109–120 (March 1990).

Holly, Carol. "Nineteenth-Century Autobiographies of Affiliation: The Case of Catharine Maria Sedgwick and Lucy Larcom." *American Autobiography: Retrospect and Prospect.* Edited by Paul John Eakin. Madison: University of Wisconsin Press, 1991. Pp. 216–234.

Kilcup, Karen. *Robert Frost and Feminine Literary Tradition.* Ann Arbor: University of Michigan Press, 1998.

———. "'Something of a Sentimental Sweet Singer': Robert Frost, Lucy Larcom, and 'Swinging Birches.'" In *Roads Not Taken; Rereading Robert Frost.* Edited by Earl J. Wilcox and Jonathan Barron. Columbia: University of Missouri Press, 2000. Pp. 11–31.

Kort, Amy. "Lucy Larcom's Double Exposure: Strategic Obscurity in *A New England Girlhood.*" *American Literary Realism* 13, no. 1:25–40 (fall 1998).

Lewis, Jessica. "'Poetry Experienced': Lucy Larcom's Poetic Dwelling in *A New England Girlhood.*" *Legacy: A Journal of American Women Writers* 18, no. 2:182–192 (2001).

Marchalonis, Shirley. "*Legacy* Profile: Lucy Larcom." *Legacy: A Journal of American Women Writers* 5, no. 1:45–52 (1988).

———. "A Model for Mentors? Lucy Larcom and John Greenleaf Whittier." In her *Patrons and Protégées: Gender, Friendship, and Writing in Nineteenth-Century America.* New Brunswick, N.J.: Rutgers University Press, 1988. Pp. 94–121.

———. *The Worlds of Lucy Larcom, 1824–1893.* Athens: University of Georgia Press, 1989.

Norman, Rose. "New England Girlhoods in Nineteenth-Century Autobiography." *Legacy: A Journal of American Women Writers* 8, no. 2:104–107 (fall 1992).

Pickett, La Salle Corbell. *Across My Path: Memories of People I Have Known.* New York: Brentano's, 1916.

"Recent Literature." *Atlantic Monthly* 36:242 (August 1875). (Review of Larcom's *An Idyl of Work.*)

Review of *Poems* by Lucy Larcom. *Atlantic Monthly* 23:136 (January 1869).

Robinson, Harriet. *Loom and Spindle: or, Life among the Early Mill Girls.* New York: Crowell, 1898.

Savage, Elizabeth. "Innovation as Interrogation in American Poetics." Ph.D. dissertation, Duquesne University, 1998.

Shaw, Justin Henry. "Centenary of a New England Poet: Lucy Larcom." *Boston Evening Transcript,* March 8, 1924.

Shepard, Grace Florence, ed. "Letters of Lucy Larcom to the Whittiers." *New England Quarterly* 3:501–518 (1930).

S[pofford], H[arriet] P[rescott]. "Lucy Larcom's Poems." *Galaxy* 7:299 (1869).

———. *A Little Book of Friends*. Boston: Little, Brown, 1916.

Walker, Cheryl. *The Nightingale's Burden: Women Poets and American Culture before 1900*. Bloomington: Indiana University Press, 1982.

———. "Lucy Larcom." In her *American Women Poets of the Nineteenth Century: An Anthology*. New Brunswick, N.J.: Rutgers University Press, 1992. P. 216.

Watson, Mrs. Robert A. *Poet-Toilers in Many Fields*. London: T. Woolmer, 1884.

Ward, Susan Hayes, ed. *The Rushlight: Special Number in Memory of Lucy Larcom*. Boston: Ellis, 1894.

Watts, Emily Stipes. *The Poetry of American Women from 1632 to 1945*. Austin: University of Texas Press, 1977. P. 191.

Whitney, Adeline Dutton Train. "Lucy Larcom." In *Our Famous Women*. Hartford, Conn.: A. D. Worthington, 1885. Pp. 415–436.

———. *White Memories*. Boston: Houghton, Mifflin and Co., 1893.

—KAREN L. KILCUP

Horace McCoy

1897–1955

AMONG THE GREAT practitioners of the American roman noir, Horace McCoy remains the most neglected. While Dashiell Hammett, James M. Cain, and Raymond Chandler reign as recognized giants of the "hard-boiled" school, McCoy—easily their artistic equal—began his descent into near total obscurity early in his career, after achieving brief notoriety with his first novel, *They Shoot Horses, Don't They?* (1935). To a large extent, Horace McCoy was the architect of his own anonymity. His greatest sin as a literary artist was to virtually abandon fiction for Hollywood screenwriting early on. Consequently, his output was small: only five short novels over a twenty-year period. Furthermore, McCoy, unlike most of his tough guy compatriots, did not work in the safe confines of the mystery/detective genre. Much of his fiction, not surprisingly, deals with Hollywood: usually a one-shot topic for a writer, not an established popular genre. Third, as part of a literary generation famous for its somber outlook on life, McCoy, as novelist, often exceeded his contemporaries in sheer nihilism: a trait not endearing to a reading public that prefers titillation, adventure, and escapist fare. Even after the 1969 release of Sydney Pollack's excellent film version of *They Shoot Horses,* there was no discernible McCoy revival. Nor is there likely to be one any time soon, which is a pity, because Horace McCoy is the most intriguing of the "tough guy" writers.

EARLY YEARS

The eldest of five children, Horace Stanley McCoy was born on April 14, 1897, near Pegram Station, Tennessee, a whistle-stop hamlet twenty miles west of Nashville. His father, James Harris McCoy, was a country schoolteacher turned railroad conductor for the Nashville, Chattanooga, and St. Louis Railroad. His mother, Nannie (later Nancye) Holt McCoy, was descended from John Peter Pegram, after whom the town was named. An impoverished but cultured and well-educated descendant of Southern aristocracy, Nancye McCoy instilled a love of reading in her oldest son. James McCoy took a freight-house job in 1899 and moved his family to Nashville. To supplement the family income, young Horace began working as a newsboy at the age of six. In the fall of 1912 McCoy enrolled at the newly established Hume-Fogg High School on Broad Street in Nashville. Only a mediocre student, McCoy quit school at the end of the 1912–1913 academic year. At first he worked as an auto mechanic. He later joined his father as a traveling coffee and tea salesman for the Jewel Tea Company. In 1915 the McCoy family moved to Dallas, Texas. McCoy, then eighteen years old, took a job as a taxi driver in Dallas.

DOUGHBOY

After the United States declared war on Germany (on April 6, 1917), McCoy was caught up in the patriotic fervor that swept the nation. On May 30, 1917, he enlisted as a private in Troop G, First Cavalry, Texas Guard, which was—along with all other state guard units—immediately federalized. National Guard units from Texas and Oklahoma soon were combined to form the Thirty-sixth Infantry Division, which trained at Camp Bowie, a 1,400-acre facility hastily built near Fort Worth, Texas. Because of his experience as a driver and a mechanic, McCoy was transferred from Camp Bowie to Fifth Company, Third Motor Mechanics Regiment, at Camp Hancock, Georgia, in January 1918. From March until June, McCoy received further training at Camp Greene, North Carolina, before shipping overseas on the French transport ship *Patria*. After a relatively uneventful Atlantic crossing that took twenty-seven days, McCoy's outfit disembarked at Brest on July 5, 1918, and was assigned to "Romo," Production Center No. 2, a huge airplane assembly and repair facility located near the village of Romorantin, 150 kilometers south of Paris. After spending a couple of weeks outfitting combat airplanes with wireless sets, McCoy was assigned to the Air Service (a branch of the Signal Corps). He saw action in the Verdun–Saint-Mihiel sector along the Meuse River before being moved up to the front near Château-Thierry in late July to participate in the first major Allied offensive in more than a year.

In what became the Second Battle of the Marne, McCoy saw regular air combat as an "observer" (bombardier and reconnaissance photographer) in a big de Havilland Airco D.H.4 biplane bomber, sometimes called the "flaming coffin." On August 5, on a reconnaissance mission near Barricourt, McCoy's plane was attacked by four Fokker D.VII fighters. McCoy's pilot was killed, and McCoy was hit by two machine gun bullets that passed clean through his body. Despite his wounds, he was able to shoot down one of his pursuers, land the riddled bomber, and deliver valuable negatives: a feat of skill and courage that earned him the Croix de Guerre. After a three-week hiatus recovering from his wounds, McCoy returned to combat duty in September, flying twenty-four reconnaissance missions over the Saint-Mihiel salient, a German-occupied wedge of territory between Verdun and Nancy. During the great Meuse-Argonne offensive, which began on September 26, McCoy logged fifty-four combat sorties in October, thirty of which included bombing. Wounded again, and gassed, he added a palm to his Croix de Guerre. By the time hostilities ceased on November 11, McCoy had logged more than four hundred hours over enemy lines.

During his time overseas McCoy had begun to write short fiction. In the eight-month period between the Armistice and his being shipped back to America (November 1918 to July 1919), McCoy made the transition from combat flyer to writer and publicist. On April 14, 1919 (his twenty-second birthday), McCoy was thrilled to be appointed one of the editors of the *Romo Exhaust,* the official weekly newspaper for the Romorantin facility. Ambitious, energetic, and popular with his fellow soldiers, McCoy also served as a columnist and sports editor. Just ten days later he was tapped for a more conspicuous honor: publicity man for "The Romo Follies of 1919," a fifty-person touring variety show that included a thirteen-piece band and, in McCoy's breathless prose, "15 real, honest-to-goodness American girls" from the Overseas Theatrical Unit. (A Follies musician later recalled there being only "two former young ladies from the Y" on the tour.) McCoy spent a busy and exhilarating May and June traveling with the Follies troupe as it entertained Allied Expeditionary Force troops at sites all over Europe.

DALLAS

Having acquired public relations experience during his final weeks in Europe, McCoy began to believe that journalism was his calling. Upon discharge from the service on August 19, 1919, McCoy returned to Dallas and applied for a job at the *Dallas Morning News* under false pretenses, claiming that he had been a reporter with the *New York Tribune*. Fired almost immediately, McCoy toiled at menial labor for two months before landing a job as a columnist and news reporter at the *Dallas Dispatch* in October 1919. During his six-month stint at the *Dispatch*, McCoy wrote signed sports and entertainment columns and covered the police beat as well. On May 23, 1920, McCoy left the job at the *Dispatch* to join the *Dallas Journal,* the first newspaperman in the history of the city to be hired away from one paper by another. Harry Clay Withers, managing editor of the *Journal,* was impressed with McCoy's seeming ability to scoop rival papers, until he discovered that McCoy mostly fabricated his sensational news stories. Instead of firing McCoy, Withers assigned him to the sports desk, where he could do little real damage. McCoy flourished there; he was soon promoted to sports editor, a job he held until 1929. Though chronically profligate and an inveterate teller of tall tales, the affable, large-hearted McCoy was well liked by his colleagues.

In 1921 McCoy married a fellow journalist, Loline Scherer (who later became Texas's first woman radio announcer). A son, Stanley, was born in 1924. Not one to settle easily into fatherhood and domesticity, the ever restless McCoy took up acting with Dallas's celebrated Little Theatre, then in its fifth season in 1925, under the capable direction of Oliver ("Skipper") Hindsell. Six feet tall, athletic, and handsome, McCoy was not afraid to strut his stuff. Over the next six years he would act in ten Little Theatre productions and in at least two plays put on by an amateur group in the suburb of Oak Cliff. His Little Theatre roles were diverse and challenging for a fledgling actor: a part in Philip Barry's comedy *The Youngest;* the stalwart farmer Andy Mayo in Eugene O'Neill's *Beyond the Horizon;* the good-natured rube Merton in the George S. Kaufman–Marc Connelly play *Merton of the Movies* (a popular comedy brought to the screen three times, in 1923, 1932, and 1947); a hapless Dutch sailor, Geert, in Herman Heijermans' *Good Hope;* the villainous Deputy Sheriff Weeks in Lula Vollmer's *Sun-Up;* the "glamour-boy roughneck" title character in Ferenc Molnár's *Liliom* (the basis for the musical *Carousel*); a rakish hired man, Joe, in Sidney Howard's *They Knew What They Wanted;* the debonair Anthony Cavendish in George S. Kaufman and Edna Ferber's *Royal Family;* the menacing Ned Galloway in Martin Flavin's *Criminal Code* (a play brought to the screen by Howard Hawks in 1931); and Pratt, a newspaperman, in Bartlett Cormack's *Racket.*

McCoy's creative energies found another outlet in fiction. In March of 1927 his first published short story, "Brass Buttons," appeared in Dallas's *Holland's Magazine*. A second story, "The Man Who Wanted to Win," appeared in the July issue of *Holland's*. By the end of the year McCoy had graduated to *Black Mask,* the famous pulp fiction magazine founded by H. L. Mencken and George Jean Nathan in 1920 to support their money-losing but prestigious literary publication, *Smart Set*. By the time McCoy began submitting to *Black Mask* it had changed ownership, was edited by Joseph T. ("Cap") Shaw, and had become exclusively devoted to hard-boiled detective stories. Between December 1927 and October 1934, McCoy published seventeen stories in *Black Mask,* all but two featuring the exploits of an airborne Texas Ranger named Jerry Frost. Drawing on his air combat experiences in World War I, McCoy had no trouble concocting credible aviation tales, which he combined with the stock elements of the Western fiction genre to create a hybrid form that garnered a loyal following.

In the waning years of the 1920s the personal and professional life that McCoy had built in Dallas began to unravel. In 1928, after seven years of marriage, McCoy and his wife, Loline, divorced. The exact reasons for the split are unknown but not difficult to surmise: McCoy's chronic insolvency, frenetic social and professional life, and intense personal ambition must have made him a less than an ideal husband and father. After the separation, McCoy seems to have shared lodgings at the Dallas Athletic Club with Eddie Barr, an ex-colleague from the *Dallas Dispatch*. He then lived with his parents until September 1929.

After that, McCoy shared, with five other young men—all aspiring artists—a large three-story stucco house at 2411 North Pearl Street, in the "Old Mexico" section of Dallas. (Sardonically dubbed the "Pearl Dive" by its tenants, the communal house on North Pearl became Dallas's prime bohemian enclave in the 1930s.) McCoy's housemates were a talented and cultured lot: James Buchanan ("Buck") Winn Jr., a muralist; the brothers Emil and Marcel Robin, artists from France; and O'Neil Ford and David Reichard Williams, architects. Dave Williams already was gaining notoriety as a leading proponent of "indigenous architecture," a regionalist style that borrowed heavily from Texas pioneer-era buildings. At forty years of age, Williams was the oldest and most accomplished member of the household, a status that made him unofficial leader. Of a less impressive pedigree than his cohorts, McCoy overcompensated by assuming the affect of a jazz age dandy in his brown-and-white coonskin coat and brown-and-white spectator shoes. Miss Violet Short, a frequent social guest at the Pearl Dive, told McCoy's biographer, John Thomas Sturak, that McCoy came off as a "superficially phony" but "desperately lonely man . . . ashamed of his background and frantic because so much of his life had gone by before he discovered his flair for writing. He was stepping to the beat of a distant drummer—which we never heard."

Just before moving to Pearl Street in September 1929, McCoy either quit or was fired—accounts vary—from the *Dallas Journal* after nine years and four months of employment there. He immediately joined the staff of the *Dallasite,* a short-lived imitation of *The New Yorker* founded by R. C. Dyer, a prominent Dallas printer, and his socialite daughter, recently married into millions, who was anxious to bring cosmopolitan sophistication to central Texas. The *Dallasite* began publishing on September 28, 1929, under the editorship of Wilbur Shaw Jr., a former city editor of the *Dallas Times Herald.* Closely modeled on *The New Yorker* format, the *Dallasite* featured a "Rambling about Town" column, humor and cartoons, poetry, "slice of life" sketches, sports, fashions, personals, and "What's Doing in Town" listings. Part of a staff of eight writers and three artists, McCoy contributed the lion's share of copy, writing weekly signed theater and sports columns, supplying much of the data for the entertainment listings, and regularly contributing to the "Rambling about Town" department. The ill-fated magazine had been publishing for only a month when the stock market crashed in late October of 1929: an event that sealed the *Dallasite*'s eventual demise. In February of 1930 Wilbur Shaw died suddenly, and McCoy replaced him as editor. Circulation and advertising revenue, never strong, fell precipitously as the Great Depression began to take hold. In a futile attempt to breathe life into the Dyer family's fading venture, McCoy discarded the faux *New Yorker* format and turned the *Dallasite* into something of a muckraking magazine that purported to investigate crime and city corruption and to berate rival publications for laziness, timidity, or censorship. But McCoy was just bluffing; he had no real dirt to dish on local politicos, and his attacks on other journalists came off as unsubstantiated bluster. Steadily sinking into the red, the *Dallasite* ceased publication with its April 5, 1930, issue. It had lasted just five months.

After the demise of the magazine, McCoy remained in Dallas for another year, acting in his last three Little Theatre productions and scraping up rent money by publishing a story every month or two in *Black Mask* and other pulps, such as *Battle Aces, Detective Action Stories,* and *Detective-Dragnet Magazine.* In May 1931 McCoy's stage mentor, Oliver Hindsell, was hired as a director at Metro-Goldwyn-Mayer. Hindsell, who could not drive, promised McCoy that he would do his best to get him a screen test at MGM if McCoy would chauffeur him out to California. Harboring his own dream of success as a Hollywood actor, McCoy readily agreed.

HOLLYWOOD

Through Hindsell's influence, McCoy got his screen test with MGM. Although it was not spectacular, the test went well enough. Unfortunately, McCoy clashed with Ben Piazza, an irascible studio executive who wielded the power to make or break aspiring actors. Cast adrift by MGM, McCoy, nearly destitute, soon ended up in the skid row district of downtown Los Angeles, reduced, in Sturak's words, to "sleeping in parks or in automobiles in used car lots; jerking sodas for $1.50 a day; cadging room and board where he could." Indeed, McCoy's timing could not have been worse. By the spring of 1931 America was in the firm grip of the depression, and despite the lingering excitement over the advent of "talkies," the motion picture industry likewise had fallen on hard times, owing to sagging attendance and the enormous costs involved in retooling for sound. (In the early 1930s there were reputed to be 20,000 Hollywood extras out of work.) Despite his rebuff by MGM and the enormous odds against him, McCoy wrote screen treatments, kept on penning for the pulps, and continued to try to break into pictures. He did manage to land uncredited bit parts in a number of B movies: *Heartbreak* (1931), a Charles Merrill war romance, directed by Alfred L. Werker for Fox; *Surrender* (1931), another war romance, starring Warner Baxter and directed by William K. Howard for Fox; *Is My Face Red?* (1932), a newspaper picture directed by William A. Seiter and based on a play by Ben Markson and Allen Rivkin, for which McCoy also wrote dialogue.

McCoy was luckier in love than in his search for employment. In the fall of 1931 he met—and fell in love with—Helen Vinmont. The daughter of a wealthy oilman with powerful Hollywood connections, Vinmont probably helped McCoy stay afloat financially during his leanest moments. Then, near the end of 1932, McCoy's employment situation suddenly changed. After peddling original screen stories (with such titles as "Death in Hollywood" and "Murder Is Murder") to the studios for more than a year, McCoy finally sold one entitled *The Luxury Girl.* Shortly thereafter, Columbia Studios hired him to write dialogue for fifty dollars a week and promptly filmed one of his original scenarios, *Dangerous Crossroads* (1933), an action picture directed by Lambert Hillyer. His first screenplay for Columbia, co-written with Charles R. Condon, was an adaptation of a story by a fellow pulp writer and combat aviator, Thomson Burtis, entitled *Soldiers of the Storm* (released April 4, 1933). McCoy chalked up his first solo screenwriting credit with a mystery-thriller called *Hold the Press* (1933). The next year Columbia Pictures released *Fury of the Jungle,* a Donald Cook–Peggy Shannon vehicle, co-written by McCoy, Ethel Hill, and Dore Schary. After 1933 McCoy found steady work in Hollywood for the rest of his life. Finally on firm ground, he was ready to marry Helen Vinmont. Though the Vinmont family bitterly objected to one of their own marrying beneath her social class, the couple wed on November 4, 1933.

With a wealthy wife and his steady, albeit rather modest, salary as a studio writer, McCoy had enough financial independence to prioritize the writing of fiction. He began to rework and extend a short story he had started in late 1931 entitled "Marathon Dance," later retitled *They*

Shoot Horses, Don't They? After a year spent revising the manuscript, McCoy showed the book to his friend, the writer Michael Fessier, who sent it to Harold Matson, then vice president of Ann Watkins, Inc., a literary agency. Impressed, Matson became McCoy's agent (and later his literary executor). Matson, in turn, sold the novel to Simon & Schuster, which published it in July 1935. The publishing firm of Arthur Barker brought out a British edition at the same time.

THEY SHOOT HORSES, DON'T THEY?

While *They Shoot Horses* is permeated by a dark pessimism that undoubtedly reflected the hard times McCoy experienced during his first year in Hollywood, the specific phenomenon that inspired the novel was a bizarre American fad known as the dance marathon. Frank Calabria, author of *Dance of the Sleepwalkers,* describes the dance marathon as "a Poor Man's Nightclub . . . the dog-end of American show business, a bastard form of entertainment which borrowed from vaudeville, burlesque, nightclub acts and sports." An ebullient product of the jazz age craze for setting endurance records of all sorts, the dance marathon devolved into a gruesome, sadomasochistic spectacle during the depression years. As Calabria notes, "Two-person teams, a female and a male, were virtually incarcerated for weeks or months at a time; they were segregated in living quarters, deprived of normal sleep, and required to compete daily in arduous walking and running contests. Spontaneity and freedom were sacrificed for routine and regulation." The last couple to remain upright on the dance floor split a prize of $1,000 to $5,000, an enormous sum in the cash-strapped 1930s. Show business hoopla aside, dance marathons essentially were protracted torture exhibitions with audience members paying a fee to watch hobbled, suffering contestants slowly succumb to exhaustion.

Having attended a dance marathon on the Santa Monica pier, McCoy was struck by its ritualized brutality. He also intuited that these sad and pointless contests constituted a perfect metaphor for the Darwinian absurdities of capitalist society in its dotage, where the masses were regimented, humiliated, and run ragged by venal hucksters promising elusive rewards. In the unpublished short story that formed the basis of the novel, McCoy used the sentencing hearing of a convicted murderer as the framing device for the story of how the killing came about. In classic noir fashion, there is no whodunit murder mystery; instead the narrative's intrigue revolves around the question of the killer's motivation. As he revised and expanded his original story idea, McCoy hit on another device: he prefaced each of the novel's thirteen chapters with another small installment of the judge's death sentence as it was being read. The book's designer, Philip Van Doren Stern, suggested that these successive fragments of the sentence progressively increase one point in size of type, until the final phrase, "MAY GOD HAVE MERCY ON YOUR SOUL," visually shouts at the reader. This gradual crescendo effect, though somewhat gimmicky and contrived, does not detract appreciably from the impact of the narrative proper, which remains exceptionally compelling.

The first-person narrator-protagonist, Robert Syverten, is a down-and-out drifter in his twenties who meets Gloria Beatty, also young and destitute, on the streets of Los Angeles. From Arkansas and Texas, respectively, Robert and Gloria have been lured to Hollywood by the glamorous hokum of movie magazines but have found only unemployment and hunger. After getting acquainted, Gloria persuades Robert to join her in entering a dance marathon; though they are unlikely to win the big prize, they at least will have free bed and board and public exposure that might lead to the proverbial "big break." Cheerful, naive, and obsessively ambitious, Robert stands in stark contrast to Gloria, who is tough, supremely cynical, foul-mouthed, and desperately unhappy. Indeed, the uneasy partnership of Robert and Gloria can be seen as epitomizing the conflicted and inherently unstable relationship between the polar opposites that reside in every human psyche: Eros, the hopeful impulse to affirm life, and Thanatos, the nihilistic impulse to negate it. Most likely, Robert and Gloria also reflect their author's own ambivalence and self-division, whereby Robert embodies McCoy's bonhomie and zeal for commercial and popular success, and Gloria represents darker and more closely guarded facets—his inner despair, self-contempt, and alienation from a society that he found unutterably corrupt.

Though recovering from intestinal flu, Robert proves to be the stronger of the two—at least physically. He supports Gloria during the grueling running derbies meant to winnow down the field of contestants (the last couple to finish is eliminated) and smoothes feathers ruffled by Gloria's caustic wit and sarcasm. But Gloria, by the sheer force of her withering negativism, easily dominates Robert. As Sturak puts it in an article on McCoy's "objective lyricism," among female characters in American fiction, Gloria Beatty is "unique in her unremitting, evil-tempered, nihilistic despair and total estrangement." Though such relentless gloom is debilitating to her and extremely unpleasant for those around her, it does afford Gloria a degree of ideological clarity almost unheard of among her contemporaries. Predisposed to see things in the worst light, Gloria is not susceptible to the wish-fulfillment fantasies of eventual success and happiness that keep her more gullible peers enthralled. Possessing no illusions, Gloria has nothing to insulate her from the ultimate and universal existential dilemma: Why go on living in an absurd, godless world without any hope of redemption? As Albert Camus argued in *The Myth of Sisyphus* (1942), "There is but one truly serious philosophical problem and that is suicide."

In the emotionally climactic tenth chapter, Gloria finally loses her struggle to remain even marginally enthusiastic about a life that is anathema to her. Boiling with frustrated rage at the self-congratulatory moral hypocrisy of a couple of representatives of the Mothers' League for Good Morals, she blasts the old ladies with a string of expletives. Having spent all her anger, Gloria collapses in sobbing despair. When the dance marathon is shut down after an audience member is shot, thirty-seven days of agony end in utter futility, and Gloria realizes that her last, tenuous connection to life has been broken. She asks Robert to "pinch hit for God" by shooting her and putting her out of her misery. Robert quite deliberately obliges, recognizing the justice of her claim and reasoning that "they shoot [crippled] horses, don't they?" In the end, Gloria's ferocious nihilism not only destroys her but also engulfs and destroys Robert, thus suggesting that it is a much more potent and real force than Robert's placid conformism. A naturalistic novel in the sense that it clearly depicts the destructive, demoralizing influences of an impoverished and brutal environment, *They Shoot Horses* transcends naturalism by showing that Gloria and Robert react differently to the same situation and freely choose their own fates. Though certainly not an example of 1930s proletarian fiction, McCoy's grim novella is as radical as more explicitly political work in its scathing condemnation of an amoral, culturally vapid society.

Publishing a deeply depressing novel at the nadir of the Great Depression would not seem to bode well for sales. *They Shoot Horses* also was ill timed in a more specific way. Coming out in the shadow of James M. Cain's *Postman Always Rings Twice* (1934), *They Shoot Horses* was unjustly deemed derivative by some critics—even though McCoy had conceived and outlined his novel well before the appearance of *Postman.* Although it was no best-seller, McCoy's book did reasonably well, selling nearly four thousand copies in the United States and a similar number in Great Britain. Reviews ran from hostile to adulatory, but quite a few were ambivalent, indicating that reviewers did not know what to make of so original and singular a work. In an appraisal for the *New York Times* (July 25, 1935), Robert Van Gelder predicted the McCoy's book would "be seen as both the best and worst of the hard-boiled novels." Van Gelder went on to call the book "a remarkably accurate—though at the same time artfully sketchy—study of moronia, and of a girl who was just a little bit too smart to be anything but miserable in the environment into which she was born and from which she had no avenue of escape." Ted Robinson, reviewing the book for the *Cleveland Plain Dealer* (July 28, 1935), called it a "sordid tragedy" but also "a little masterpiece." James Hilton, writing for the London *Daily Telegraph,* termed McCoy's novel "as near a masterpiece as its school has yet produced." Likewise, a reviewer for the *Providence Journal* called it "a raw, bitter book that startles one by its vigor and consummate tragedy."

NO POCKETS IN A SHROUD

By the time McCoy placed *They Shoot Horses,* he had a second novel already well under way, based on a 1935 short story he had written about Hollywood extras, entitled "Looks Like They'll Never Learn." He originally titled the new book "The Madman Beats a Drum" but later changed the title to "Death Cannot Spoil the Spring" and then changed it a third time, to "No Angels in Heaven," before adopting the final title, *No Pockets in a Shroud* (derived from an old proverb, "Our last garment is made without pockets"). McCoy promised Simon & Schuster a completed manuscript by the fall of 1935. Busy with screenwriting assignments and short fiction, he was not able to deliver a first draft that year. Instead, he brought out "The Grandstand Complex," his only published short story between 1935 and 1943, which appeared in the December 1935 issue of *Esquire.* When McCoy finally submitted a draft of *No Pockets* in late March 1936, the editors at Simon & Schuster found it intriguing but unfocused and asked for revisions. The ever-hasty McCoy turned the manuscript around in less than a month. Still unsatisfied, Simon & Schuster passed, as in subsequent months did Knopf, Covici-Friede, Viking, Morrow, Macaulay, and Dutton.

While Matson shopped around McCoy's fiction, his client had a busy year as a screenwriter. Besides writing numerous treatments and concocting story ideas that were later or never produced, McCoy helped churn out four features in 1936. Collaborating with Grover Jones and Harvey Thew for Paramount, McCoy toiled on a fourth screen adaptation of John Fox's 1908 popular novel about feuding moonshiners, *The Trail of the Lonesome Pine* (silent film versions appeared in 1914, 1916, and 1923). McCoy's next assignment was for Universal: a crime drama entitled *Postal Inspector,* for which he co-wrote the original story with Robert Presnell Sr. and then penned the screenplay himself. McCoy worked with Presnell again on *Parole,* another B crime film, co-written with Kubec Glasmon and Joel Sayre. McCoy returned to Paramount for *Fatal Lady,* a forgettable mystery co-written with Harry Seagall and Samuel Ornitz. Though Knopf rejected *No Pockets in a Shroud,* they nonetheless admired *They Shoot Horses* and wanted to publish McCoy. On December 11, 1936, McCoy's agent, Harold Matson, wired with good news: "SOLD YOU TO KNOPF FIVE HUNDRED ADVANCE FIVE HUNDRED ON ACCEPTANCE." The novel, in progress, that Knopf optioned would turn out to be another bitter and sordid Hollywood saga with a typically downbeat McCoy title: *I Should Have Stayed Home*. Not long after being picked up by Knopf, McCoy got more good news. Early in 1937 Matson sent *No Pockets in a Shroud* to Arthur Barker, the British firm that had published *They Shoot Horses, Don't They?* Unlike their American counterparts, the editors at Barker immediately liked the book, bought it, and published it on August 23, 1937. McCoy's burgeoning reputation in Europe was enhanced further by Portuguese, Norwegian, and Dutch translations of *They Shoot Horses* that same year.

McCoy's most autobiographical novel, *No Pockets in a Shroud*, fictionalizes—and greatly embellishes—his last two years in Dallas, when he juggled paradoxical careers as a muckraking magazine editor, amateur stage actor, debonair man-about-town and shameless social climber. His protagonist and alter ego is the handsome Michael Dolan, a crusading sports reporter for *The [Colton] Daily Times-Gazette* (a mythical version of the *Dallas Journal*). Dolan is called on the carpet by his managing editor about a potentially explosive story he wrote on local baseball corruption *and* for owing money to local merchants who happen to be the paper's biggest advertisers. Threatened with termination, Dolan quits the paper. Immediately thereafter, he borrows $1,500 from Johnny London, a wealthy Little Theatre colleague, to start his own magazine, a fictitious version of the *Dallasite*, called the *Cosmopolite*. (The masthead motto reads, "The Truth, the Whole Truth, and Nothing But the Truth.")

Supposedly a glitzy society magazine in *The New Yorker* format, the *Cosmopolite* seems to have closer affinities to a magazine like *Confidential*, the notorious scandal sheet that specialized in sensational exposés in the 1950s. Soon immersed in dangerous intrigues connected with the magazine's investigations, Dolan is equally hard pressed to keep up with a complicated love life that revolves around Colton's debutantes.

At one point Dolan impulsively elopes with a senator's daughter but subsequently accepts $35,000 as a payoff from the woman's family to agree to an annulment, a sum that enables him to clear his debts and keep the magazine going. Although Dolan prefers to date society ladies, he becomes involved unwittingly in a sexually charged love-hate relationship with an attractive employee named Myra Barnovsky. An ardent Communist, Myra is puzzled and dismayed by her boss's eagerness to break into high society, a penchant that Dolan attributes to a vague sense of inferiority rooted in his humble origins. Rather predictably, Dolan and Barnovsky wed—an event that signals a salutary readjustment of Dolan's value system. Unfortunately, there is no "happily ever after," as Dolan's muckraking crusades prove to be his eventual undoing.

After publishing the baseball exposé originally suppressed by the *Daily Times-Gazette*, Dolan goes on to investigate Harry Carlisle, a society doctor who has performed illegal abortions that resulted in three fatalities. When minions of the doctor's powerful and ruthless brother hijack an issue of the *Cosmopolite* that contains an exposé of Carlisle, Dolan hires his own "gorillas" to ensure that another printing reaches the newsstands. His reputation ruined, Dr. Carlisle commits suicide. The doctor's brother, Jack Carlisle, exacts vengeance by having thugs armed with lead pipes attack and very nearly kill Dolan. Undaunted, Dolan launches another investigation into the Crusaders, a clandestine white racist organization that resembles groups like the Ku Klux Klan or the United Brotherhood of Americans (i.e., the Black Legion, a 1930s Midwest fascist alliance). He manages to infiltrate a Crusaders secret rally, during which one black man is tarred and feathered and another is castrated. Sickened and "in a frenzy of hatred," Dolan publishes an exposé in the *Cosmopolite* that names Colton's "leading citizens" as Crusaders, among them his bitter nemesis, Jack Carlisle. Upon leaving his office that day, Dolan proceeds down a back alley to his car, when he is approached from behind. A shot rings in his ears and then "the top of his head [flies] off, and he [falls] face downward across [a] garbage can, trying to get his fingers up to hold his nose."

As Sturak suggests in his biography of McCoy, the figure of Michael Dolan was probably a composite of McCoy himself and a crusading newspaperman named Walter W. Liggett, Minnesota publisher of a muckraking newspaper, the *Midwest American*. Liggett was a radical activist who aggressively investigated organized crime in Minneapolis despite intimidation, sabotage, bribery offers, death threats, and beatings. A mob leader named Kid Cann finally shot Liggett to death in the alley behind his home in full view of his wife and ten-year-old daughter in December 1935. Another model for Dolan was almost certainly Wilford Bascom "Pitchfork" Smith (1884–1939), a lawyer turned radical newspaperman who published *Plaintalk* (later renamed *The Pitchfork*), a muckraking monthly journal for Kansas City. Driven out of Kansas City in 1909 for his fiery rhetoric and radical views on race relations, Smith moved to Dallas and continued to publish *The Pitchfork* until his death in 1939. It is highly likely that McCoy knew Smith personally. While McCoy obviously thought of himself as an idealistic, crusading journalist during and after his *Dallasite* days, his identification with the likes of Walter Liggett and Wilford Smith suggest a Walter Mitty–like romanticism that borders on the fatuous. Likewise, Mike Dolan's incongruous duality as a muckraking journalist and a social climber strains the novel's credibility, as does the unlikely notion that the *Cosmopolite* would resemble *The New Yorker* in style and format—even though, for a time, the *Dallasite*, actually did.

While critical notices of *No Pockets in a Shroud* were mixed, every critic found something to praise. A reviewer for the *Times Literary Supplement* (August 28, 1937) thought that the novel was "done in the best 'tough' manner, alert and sure and economical, dramatic to the last degree, extremely readable" but also "profoundly unsatisfying," because its purportedly shallow characterization of Dolan made it difficult to identify with him. Writing for the *New Statesman and Nation* (August 28, 1937), V. S. Pritchett did not think that the novel would win any literary prizes but nonetheless applauded the book's "speed and skill of talk and narrative" and its power to make the reader feel "important indignation." Another critic, for the *London Daily Mail* (August 26, 1937), decried the book's "hysterical and despairing fury" but tempered his assessment by noting that "the best and most characteristic American writers are social reformers first and novelists afterwards." A reviewer for the London *Evening Standard* (September 10, 1937) felt that the book's depiction of widespread corruption was rendered "with great brilliance" and had "the unmistakable impress of truth." Writing for the London *Sunday Times* (August 22, 1937), the critic Ralph Straus thought *No Pockets in a Shroud* a much better book, in every way, than *They Shoot Horses, Don't They?* because of its "author's passionate cry for that much much-vaunted freedom and equality which, in his view, it is so difficult to find in the America of today." Generally favorable reviews, coupled with a British hankering for American tough guy fiction, made *No Pockets* a modest hit in England, selling more than eight thousand copies in the first four years following its publication.

I SHOULD HAVE STAYED HOME

In mid-August 1937, just as the British edition of *No Pockets in a Shroud* was coming out, McCoy delivered the completed manuscript of his third novel, *I Should Have Stayed Home,* to Alfred Knopf's wife, Blanche, who was "delighted" with it. She wrote McCoy, "God knows it is a bitter book that you have written but it is good." Nonetheless, Mrs. Knopf requested "slight changes" that she thought "would definitely improve the book." Perhaps inspired by the novelist William Faulkner's stylistic flourishes, McCoy began and ended the manuscript with long, parenthetical passages set in italic. Knopf's editors felt that these passages did not integrate well with the narrative proper and should be eliminated. They also objected to the lurid, melodramatic ending, in which the protagonist committed suicide. McCoy readily agreed to drop the italicized passages and rewrite the ending. He hastily made the specified changes but did not bother to alter numerous harbingers of Ralph Carston's suicide scattered throughout the narrative: an omission that would prove somewhat damaging to the novel in its published form. At any rate, McCoy returned the altered manuscript to Knopf, via his agent, Matson, within a week's time. In a letter dated August 23, 1937, Blanche Knopf wrote back to McCoy, telling him that the novel was "in fine shape now" and that the publication process could begin.

Published six months later, in February 1938, *I Should Have Stayed Home* tells the story of Ralph Carston and Mona Matthews, two unemployed Hollywood extras in their early twenties who share a bungalow, a platonic relationship, and hopeless dreams of stardom. When their friend, another unemployed extra, named Dorothy Trotter, is sentenced to the California women's prison in Tehachapi for three years on a shoplifting conviction, an outraged Mona stands up in court and calls the presiding judge "a fine son of a bitch." The judge threatens Mona with a thirty-day contempt sentence if she does not apologize. When she refuses with another shouted obscenity, he doubles her sentence to sixty days. Fortunately, municipal politics comes to Mona's rescue. Up for reelection, the judge releases her in a matter of hours, so that he can garner favorable publicity as a "Great Humanitarian."

After Mona's outburst makes headlines, she and Ralph are invited to a fundraising party for the Scottsboro Boys hosted by Mrs. Smithers, a rich, aging Beverly Hills nymphomaniac with a penchant for young men. Mrs. Smithers seduces Ralph while Mona fends off the sexual advances of Laura Eubanks, a lesbian starlet. Hoping that Mrs. Smithers can help him get a screen test with a prominent director, Ralph becomes her "protégé" (a wry euphemism for gigolo) but tries to back out when he is overcome with fear and disgust by her sexual advances. Insulted but undaunted, Mrs. Smithers continues to pursue Ralph. In the meantime Mona lands a job for $35 a week as Laura Eubanks' stand-in, and Dorothy suddenly shows up at the bungalow, having escaped from Tehachapi and stolen a car to return to Los Angeles. When Ralph and Dorothy are arrested in the stolen car, Dorothy is returned to prison, and Ralph is charged with abetting her escape attempt; he gets out of trouble, thanks to Mrs. Smithers' money and influence. Unable to face the prospect of a return to prison and an even longer sentence, Dorothy hangs herself in her downtown holding cell. (Responding to a request for the "Instrument of Death" by news photographers at the morgue, a bitter Mona places movie magazines in Dorothy's hands.)

After Dorothy's death, Ralph summons the courage to end his degrading affair with Mrs. Smithers, and his place is quickly taken by Johnny Hill, a young, alcoholic, would-be actor only too eager to sell out any integrity he might have had. Fired for organizing a successful actor's strike to improve working conditions for extras, Mona comes to the realization that "there's no escape." Irrevocably estranged from Hollywood and its dreams, she answers a lonely-hearts ad, marries a farmer, and retreats to the country: a move that causes Ralph to think that he should have stayed home—hence the book's title. In the end, despite the decadence, corruption, and tragedy he has witnessed, Ralph Carston retains his simpleminded optimism: "I hadn't stayed home, I was here, on the famous boulevard, in Hollywood, where miracles happen, and maybe today, maybe the next minute some director would pick me out passing by."

Reviews of the novel were generally favorable, although Hollywood itself seemed rankled by McCoy's bitter portrayal. Writing for the *Hollywood Citizen-News* (March 19, 1938), Morton Thompson denounced the book as "nauseating" in its "striving for effect in an inverted gutter, both arms to the elbows in scum." Other reviews were considerably less vitriolic. An anonymous notice that appeared in the *Dallas News* (April 1937) characterized the book as "an indictment against Hollywood for the glittering promises it holds out but rarely fulfills to American youth." Iris Barry, writing for the *New York Herald-Tribune* (February 20, 1938) recognized that McCoy was "dealing not with frustration so much as with folly, for by the symptoms which he reveals Ralph Carston had only the slightest chance of being anything but a small-town nobody." A critic writing for the *Saturday Review* (February 19, 1938) sardonically noted "Horace McCoy hates Hollywood, not enough to stay away from it but enough to get all the bile out of his system in a short, bitter, name-calling novel." A more sympathetic review appeared in the *New York Times* (February 20, 1938): "The background, the talk and the vague ending are all realistic, and tough-minded readers seeking the truth about Hollywood's lower depths will not object to the violent language used to express it."

Hollywood novels were nothing new in the late 1930s, but McCoy was the first writer to subvert the cliché show biz success story and characterize Hollywood as a squalid nightmare landscape of hypocrisy and broken dreams. In the ensuing years, other writers would follow McCoy's lead and turn his vision into a still thriving subgenre. In 1939 Nathanael West's apocalyptic novel, *The Day of the Locust,* was published. Though he died of a heart attack before he could complete it, F. Scott Fitzgerald's *Last Tycoon* was edited and polished by Edmund Wilson and published in 1941. That same year also saw the publication of Budd Schulberg's *What Makes Sammy Run?,* his scathing portrait of a maniacally driven Hollywood powerbroker.

INTERREGNUM

A decade would pass between the publication of *I Should Have Stayed Home* and McCoy's next novel, *Kiss Tomorrow Good-bye* (1948). During these years McCoy and his wife had two children: Amanda (born 1940) and Peter (born 1945). McCoy continued to write dialogue, film treatments, and screenplays for a wide array of B movies during the war years. In 1939 he and William R. Lipman began to adapt stories for Paramount from *Persons in Hiding,* a 1938 book by the director of the Federal Bureau of Investigation, J. Edgar Hoover, that told the story of the "G-men" (special agents of the FBI) in pursuit of notorious 1930s criminals. No fewer than four movies resulted: *Persons in Hiding* (1939), *Undercover Doctor* (1939), *Queen of the Mob* (1940), and *Parole Fixer* (1940). Busy with his work for the studios, McCoy had little time for his own fiction. He published only three stories during this period: "Flight for Freedom," a story adapted from a screen treatment that appeared in the *Women's Home Companion* in January 1943 (and for which McCoy received the astonishing sum of $2,000—the most he ever earned for a short story); "The Girl in the Grave," a short story based on a "movie idea" told by a character in *I Should Have Stayed Home,* which appeared in an anthology edited by Charles Grayson entitled *Half-a-Hundred: Tales by Great American Writers* (1945); and "Destiny and the Lieutenant," which appeared in the July 25, 1948, edition of *This Week Magazine*.

After a few years' experience as a studio hack, McCoy's weekly paycheck soared to the then enormous sum of $1,000 a week. Though still profligate and always in debt, McCoy managed, in 1943, to buy a sizable house at 608 North Alpine Drive, a "nice and quiet" Beverly Hills street off Sunset Boulevard. He wrote in his off time in what he described in an *Esquire* piece as "a little cubicle over a little garage." Always artistically and intellectually restless, McCoy took up a number of sidelines in the late 1930s. A jazz record collector and aficionado for many years, McCoy ably reviewed jazz records for the *Los Angeles Daily News* in the 1940s. He also took up photography and soon produced work of professional quality. A third passion was oil painting. Besides producing original work, McCoy specialized in making exact copies of works by Maurice Utrillo.

Throughout this period, unbeknownst to McCoy, his literary reputation in Europe was growing steadily as his first three novels were translated into other languages on a regular basis. A Swedish edition of *They Shoot Horses* appeared in 1938, followed by a French edition in 1946 and a Brazilian edition in 1947. Norwegian, Danish, and French translations of *No Pockets in a Shroud* appeared in 1938, followed in 1940 and 1946, respectively, by Swedish and French editions. In 1939 a Danish translation of *I Should Have Stayed Home* came out, followed in 1944 and 1948, respectively, by Finnish and French editions. In sum, fourteen separate foreign-language editions of McCoy's first three novels were published in Europe between 1936 and 1948—clear evidence of extraordinary interest in McCoy—while his work was barely noticed in the United States.

Part of the European attraction to McCoy undoubtedly was his fascinating depiction of the dark underbelly of American society, rendered in concise tough-guy prose that made for haunting, emotionally powerful narratives. Ravaged by economic depression, fascism, and war, Europeans likely took some comfort in the realization that the Arsenal of Democracy harbored nihilism and anomie every bit as desperate and deranged as the European variety. Furthermore, McCoy's tragic sense of life and the stark existentialist aura that hangs over his books were all of a piece with European sensibilities before, during, and immediately after World War II. McCoy's deracinated protagonists shift for themselves in an absurd, godless world that foregrounds the radical contingency of life and the constant proximity of death. Some McCoy characters, like Robert Syverten and Ralph Carston, live in what the French writer Jean-Paul Sartre refers to as "bad faith," that is, they avoid angst-inducing existential responsibility for their own being by basing their lives on received values, rote custom, and moral convention, which allows them to dwell in comforting dream worlds. Likewise, Mona Matthews, who knows better, *acts* in bad faith when she settles for a loveless marriage in exchange for a modicum of financial security. Other McCoy characters, like Gloria Beatty and Dorothy Trotter, are too alienated to adhere to status quo ideology; they harbor no illusions about the beneficence of society or possible escape from the underclass. True existentialist heroines, Gloria and Dorothy freely choose self-murder rather than live in an utterly oppressive and sterile world. The case of Michael Dolan is more complicated. Much like his creator, Dolan recognizes societal injustice and commits himself to fighting it through his writing but, at the same time, succumbs to the blandishments of the capitalist consumption and status-seeking ethos. Inwardly divided between rebellion and conformity, Dolan is not able to resolve his conflicted character before he dies. Indeed, he evinces no real awareness of the contradiction at the center of his being.

Shortly after the war, word finally reached America that McCoy was a venerated writer in Europe, especially in France. Returning from a trip abroad in the winter of 1946, Allene Talmey, an editor for *Vogue* (January 15, 1947), reported: "Everyone in the knowledgeable world talks about American writers, about a curious trinity: Hemingway, Faulkner, and McCoy. . . . Horace McCoy . . . has a wide public of French literary fans who know his two works, *They Shoot Horses, Don't They?* and *No Pockets in a Shroud.*" (The French edition of *I Should Have Stayed Home* was not yet published.) Four months later Albert Guerard Jr., another returning expatriate, echoed Talmey's assessment in a letter to the *New Republic* (May 19, 1947): "Horace McCoy and the late Nathanael West, still virtually unknown in this country, occupy a very high place in the smoky pantheon of the Boulevard St. Germaine."

KISS TOMORROW GOOD-BYE

The European rediscovery of Horace McCoy could not have come at a better time for him. By the beginning of 1947 McCoy was nearly fifty years old, unemployed after fifteen years as a Hollywood scrivener, dead broke, and described by his fellow screenwriter and friend P. J. Wolfson in *The Life and Writings of Horace McCoy* as "extremely depressed and full of fear . . . of losing his only means of income, his ability to write." After a ten-year hiatus from longer fiction, McCoy struggled to start a fourth novel about a criminal psychopath that he had been mulling over for at least seven years. Aware that his initial efforts were "very bad," a discouraged McCoy was ready to quit and return to MGM when a friend alerted him to the notice that had appeared in *Vogue*. In a letter quoted in *The Life and Writings of Horace McCoy* (dated April 16, 1948) to Victor Weybright, editor of New American Library, McCoy recalled in that "shortly thereafter the storm broke: pictures, interviews, even the *New Republic* took notice of the spectacle of a dead man rising." Caught up in the excitement, Bennett Cerf, founder of Random House, begged to see McCoy's novel in progress. McCoy went behind the back of his agent and obliged Cerf, a move that annoyed Matson and angered Alfred Knopf, whose firm already had a first refusal option on the new book. (Knopf eventually passed, and Random House published the book after all.) His confidence restored, McCoy attacked his new novel, tentatively titled *You Can Kiss Tomorrow Goodbye,* energized by the conviction that this was his last chance to secure fame and an honorable literary reputation. In his letter to Weybright, which is quoted from *The Life and Writings of Horace McCoy,* he recalled, "I began to train like a prize fighter, I dieted strictly, I took off weight, I even began to squeeze a handball to strengthen my fingers, because I write in longhand and they tired too quickly. Such dramatics you have never seen!" After numerous false starts, dead ends, and detours, McCoy finally started to accumulate pages, and the novel took shape.

Kiss Tomorrow Good-bye is the first-person story of a highly intelligent but deranged career criminal whose real name and life history are concealed by two aliases: Ralph Cotter and Paul Murphy, which signify the protagonist's divided self. At the outset of his narrative, Cotter shoots and kills Toko, another inmate, while the two are escaping from a prison farm. On the run, Cotter joins up with Toko's sister, a nymphomaniac named Holiday Tokowanda, who abetted the escape but is unaware that he has murdered her brother. After robbing a supermarket and brutally murdering an employee, Cotter is interrogated by a corrupt police inspector, whom he then blackmails by surreptitiously recording an incriminating interview. Looking for a place to safeguard the tapes, Cotter meets the daughter of the multimillionaire Ezra Dobson, Margaret Dobson, who triggers vague, disquieting memories of his dead grandmother. The two have a brief affair and impulsively marry, but separate the same day. In a gratuitous replay of an incident described in *No Pockets in a Shroud,* Margaret's father offers Cotter $35,000 to agree to annul the marriage. Cotter refuses the money and changes his alias to Paul Murphy. He then organizes a daring daylight robbery that nets $50,000 of protection money from local gangsters. In the course of the robbery, Cotter-Murphy, Holiday, and other accomplices murder the gangsters and roll their corpse-filled car into a nearby lake. Oblivious to Cotter-Murphy's criminality and impressed that he refused his buyout offer, Ezra Dobson offers him "a million dollars in cash" if he will take care of the none-too-stable Margaret for life.

Pondering the lucrative offer, Cotter-Murphy accompanies Margaret to a party at a country club. Bored with the festivities and wanting to make love, Margaret leads Cotter-Murphy across the golf course to an oak tree by a lake. Intoxicated by alcohol and Benzedrine, Cotter-Murphy smells the hallucinatory odor of Huele de Noche (Oil of Night), the perfume his grandmother used to wear—a sense memory that triggers access to a horrifying incident he has repressed for more than twenty-five years. It seems that Cotter-Murphy often hid under his grandmother's skirts when he was a young child. He suddenly remembers that when he was six or seven years old, he had become sexually aroused under her skirts one day and began to grope his grandmother's legs. Angered by his behavior, she told him that his grandfather would "do to him what he did to the ram," that is, castrate him. To silence her, the terrified boy killed his grandmother with a rock and then claimed that she had fallen from a horse. Realizing that Margaret Dobson will always conjure his grandmother, he leaves her—and the million dollars—only to be shot and killed by Holiday, who has discovered that Cotter-Murphy murdered her brother. It is a desolate ending that is trademark McCoy.

Steeped in lurid Freudianism, grotesque violence, and a bleak aura of corruption and nihilism, *Kiss Tomorrow Good-bye* proved to be too heady a mixture for critics who reviewed the book upon its release in May 1948. In a review for the *New York Times* (June 13, 1948), Wilson Follett was somewhat less than enthusiastic: "If you discount the psychological fiddle-faddle what you have left is a straight crime thriller of the fast, tough school in the first person singular with all the brutal cynicism of the graduate jailbird." Guardian of middlebrow taste, *Time* magazine (May 10, 1948) responded with vitriol, calling McCoy's novel a "gutter-minded, gutter-tongued shocker of alley cat sex, sadism, and unmourned murders . . . one of the nastiest novels ever published in this country." Likewise, the novelist Nelson Algren, in a scathing review for the *Philadelphia Inquirer* (May 2, 1948), called *Kiss Tomorrow Good-bye* "just one more loud and badly written novel [which] adds up to a world of cardboard psychopaths, papier mache gargoyles and pulp-fiction Frankensteins." A review appearing in the *San Francisco Chronicle* (May 6, 1948) dismissed the book as a "murky ditch of hyperpituitary desire and unalloyed profanity."

SCALPEL

Having poured his heart and soul into *Kiss Tomorrow Good-bye,* McCoy regarded it not only as his most profound and accomplished novel but also as a last ditch attempt to be taken seriously as a writer so that he could quit his labors as a "Hollywood hand." Consequently, he was stung by the vicious criticism it garnered and deeply disappointed that his masterwork was so badly misconstrued. It is likely that the emotional stress McCoy experienced following the book's release was a factor in his first heart attack, which occurred in the summer of 1948. He was bedridden for seven weeks and lost twenty-two pounds. Still, he soldiered on, attempting to start another novel called "The Alligator Horse," which did not get much beyond the synopsis stage. Despite the harsh reviews, *Kiss Tomorrow Good-bye* sold moderately well (7,500 hardbound copies at three dollars per copy). Soon after publication, the film producer William Cagney bought the screen rights and made McCoy's novel into a Warner Brothers film (1950) starring his famous brother, James Cagney. Cagney's previous role as the psychopathic, mother-fixated Cody Jarrett in Raoul Walsh's *White Heat* (1949) bore a strong resemblance to his role as Ralph Cotter. Overshadowed by *White Heat* and John Huston's *Asphalt Jungle* (1950), the film version of *Kiss Tomorrow Good-bye* was considered derivative and quickly forgotten.

Frustrated on one literary front, McCoy had advanced on another by contracting with New American Library to publish a paperback edition of *They Shoot Horses, Don't They?* (1948) in a "near record first printing of 300,000 copies," as quoted from *The Life and Writings of Horace McCoy*. That same year New American Library published a 200,000-copy printing of a revised edition of *No Pockets in a Shroud*. What amounted to the first U.S. edition deleted all the references to Communism or political radicalism that had appeared in the original edition, published in England eleven years earlier. This was a telling barometer of the American political climate less than a year after the House Un-American Activities Committee hearings to investigate subversive activities concluded with the conviction and imprisonment of the "Hollywood Ten," writers who refused to testify before the committee and name possible Communist sympathizers. They were prosecuted as "unfriendly" witnesses.

Early in 1951 McCoy sold *Scalpel,* an original screen treatment about a surgeon's life, to Hal Wallis Productions for a reputed $100,000, a sum the company probably recouped when Columbia Pictures brought *Scalpel* to the screen in 1954 as *Bad for Each Other,* a mediocre movie starring Charlton Heston and Lizabeth Scott. Suddenly wealthy, McCoy immediately took his family to Europe, his first visit since he had shipped back home after World War I in 1919. McCoy did attend various dinners and receptions in his honor, but he was hampered by an inability to speak French. To his disappointment, anticipated meetings with Sartre and other literary luminaries never happened, but there were other positive developments stemming from the *Scalpel* script. John Mock, Wallis' Hollywood story editor, mentioned his new acquisition to the Appleton-Century-Crofts editor Archie Ogden and opined in *The Life and Writings of Horace McCoy* that it "had the markings of a superior novel." Ogden read the manuscript, agreed with Mock, and subsequently offered McCoy an advance of $3,000 to turn the treatment into a full-fledged book. In less than ten months—from March 1951 to January 1952—McCoy took his 282-page film script and turned it into a 512-page novel. Used to working against deadlines, McCoy wrote with demonic speed and intensity; most of those 512 pages were written in the month of December 1951. The novel, McCoy's fifth, was published on June 23, 1952, to positive reviews and sales strong enough to put it on the *New York Times* best-seller list for several weeks.

The success of *Scalpel* owed to its upbeat story of the American Dream fulfilled—a radical departure for McCoy, whose other novels plotted opposite trajectories. Dr. Tom Owen, son of a Pennsylvania coal miner, returns home from his Army Medical Corps post in Berlin to investigate the death of his brother in a mining accident. He meets Helen Curtis, the divorced daughter of the mine owner, who persuades him to leave the military and start a private practice in Pittsburgh. Lacking confidence in his own skills, Owen comes to rely heavily on his superb surgical nurse, Joan Lasher. Owen soon falls in love with her and seduces her, despite his affair with Helen and Joan's engagement to another doctor on his staff. Cognizant of Owen's superior abilities, Nurse Lasher arranges things so that Owen will overcome his dependency on her. In the end, she returns to her fiancé, and Owen reunites with Helen and looks forward to a new career as Professor of Medicine at Harvard University—an authorial wish-fulfillment fantasy for McCoy, who always dreamed of great success, social prominence, and intellectual prestige.

FINAL YEARS

In September 1952 McCoy received a $2,500 advance from Appleton-Century-Crofts for a sixth novel, entitled "The Hard Rock Man." Unfortunately, he suffered a second heart attack in 1953 and was never able to complete the book. That same year Serie Noire published *Pertes et Fracas* (Loss and Uproar), the French translation of a 1950 McCoy screen treatment for *The Turning Point,* a 1952 noir film about Special Prosecutor John Conroy (Edmond O'Brien), who sets out to fight organized crime in his city by appointing his cop father, Matt (Tom Tully) as chief investigator—unaware that Matt has ties to the mob. In the end, despite terrible losses, the incorruptible Conroy prevails, wins the girl he loves, and gets the opportunity to run for governor. Some years later Dell published *Corruption City,* a paperback edition of *The Turning Point.* Horace McCoy died of a third heart attack on December 15, 1955, at the age of fifty-eight, never having attained the literary stature he sought.

Selected Bibliography

WORKS OF HORACE McCOY

NOVELS

They Shoot Horses, Don't They? New York: Simon & Schuster, 1935.

No Pockets in a Shroud. London: Barker, 1937; rev. ed., New York: New American Library, 1948.

I Should Have Stayed Home. New York: Knopf, 1938.

Kiss Tomorrow Good-bye. New York: Random House, 1948.

Scalpel. New York: Appleton-Century-Crofts, 1952.

Corruption City. New York: Dell, 1959.

UNCOLLECTED SHORT STORIES

"Brass Buttons." *Holland's Magazine* (March 1927).

"The Man Who Wanted to Win." *Holland's Magazine* (July 1927).

"The Devil Man." *Black Mask* (December 1927).

"Rustling Syndicate." *Brief Stories* (March 1928).

"Dirty Work." *Black Mask* (September 1929).

"Hell's Stepsons." *Black Mask* (October 1929).

"Renegades of the Rio." *Black Mask* (December 1929).

"Kid's Christmas." *Dallasite* (December 21, 1929).

"The Little Black Book." *Black Mask* (January 1930).

"Frost Rides Alone." *Black Mask* (March 1930).

"The Sky-Horse." *Southwest Review* (April 1930).

"Somewhere in Mexico." *Black Mask* (July 1930).

"The Gun-Runners." *Black Mask* (August 1930).

"The Mailed Fist." *Black Mask* (December 1930).

"Killer's Killer." *Detective-Dragnet Magazine* (December 1930).

"Orders to Die." *Battle Aces* (December 1930).

"Night Club." *Detective Action Stories* (February 1931).

"Death Alley." *Detective-Dragnet Magazine* (March 1931).

"Headfirst into Hell." *Black Mask* (May 1931).

"The Sky Hellion." *Battle Aces* (May 1931).

"A Matter of Honor." *Man Stories* (July 1931).

"Juggernaut of Justice." *Detective-Dragnet Magazine* (August 1931).

"A Pair of Sixes." *Western Trails* (August 1931).

"The Passing of Nowata." *Western Trails* (August 1931).

"The Mopper Up." *Black Mask* (November 1931).

"The Trail to the Tropics." *Black Mask* (March 1932).

"The Golden Rule." *Black Mask* (June 1932).

"Murder in Error." *Black Mask* (August 1932).

"Wings over Texas." *Black Mask* (October 1932).

"Flight at Sunrise." *Black Mask* (May 1934).

"Somebody Must Die." *Black Mask* (October 1934).

"The Grandstand Complex." *Esquire* (December 1935).

"Flight for Freedom." *Women's Home Companion* (January 1943).

"The Girl in the Grave." In *Half-a-Hundred: Tales by Great American Writers*. Edited by Charles Grayson. Philadelphia: Blakiston, 1945.

"Destiny and the Lieutenant." *This Week Magazine* (July 25, 1948).

SCREENPLAYS AND ORIGINAL STORIES
ADAPTED TO FILM

Dangerous Crossroads. Story. Columbia, 1933.

Hold the Press. Columbia, 1933.

Soldiers of the Storm. Screenplay, with Charles R. Condon. Columbia, 1933.

Fury of the Jungle. With Ethel Hill and Dore Schary. Columbia, 1934.

Speed Wings. Screenplay and story. Columbia, 1934.

Fatal Lady. With Harry Seagall and Samuel Ornitz. Paramount, 1936.

Parole. With Kubec Glasmon and Joel Sayre. Universal, 1936.

Postal Inspector. Screenplay and story, with Robert Presnell Sr. Universal, 1936.

The Trail of the Lonesome Pine. Adaptation, with Grover Jones and Harvey F. Thew. Paramount, 1936.

Dangerous to Know. With William R. Lipman. Paramount, 1938.

Hunted Men. With William R. Lipman. Paramount, 1938.

King of the Newsboys. Story, with Samuel Ornitz. Republic, 1938.

Prison Farm. Uncredited. Paramount, 1938.

Island of Lost Men. With William R. Lipman. Paramount, 1939.

Persons in Hiding. With William R. Lipman. Paramount, 1939.

Television Spy. With William R. Lipman and Lillie Hayward. Paramount, 1939.

Undercover Doctor. With William R. Lipman. Paramount, 1939.

Parole Fixer. With William R. Lipman. Paramount, 1940.

Queen of the Mob. With William R. Lipman. Paramount, 1940.

The Texas Rangers Ride Again. With William R. Lipman. Paramount, 1940.

Women without Names. With William R. Lipman. Paramount, 1940.

Texas. With Michael Blankfort and Lewis Meltzer. Columbia, 1941.

Gentleman Jim. With Vincent Lawrence. Warner Brothers/First National, 1942.

Valley of the Sun. RKO, 1942.

Appointment in Berlin. With Michael Hogan. Columbia, 1943.

Flight for Freedom. Story. RKO, 1943.

There's Something About a Soldier. With Barry Trivers. Columbia, 1943.

The Fabulous Texan. With Lawrence Hazard. Republic, 1947. Reissued as *The Texas Uprising.*

The Fireball. With Tay Garnett. Twentieth Century-Fox, 1950. Also known as *The Challenge.*

Bronco Buster. With Lillie Hayward. Universal, 1952.

The Lusty Men. With David Dortort. RKO, 1952.

Montana Belle. With Norman S. Hall. RKO, 1952.

The Turning Point. Story. Paramount, 1952.

The World in His Arms. Additional dialogue. Universal, 1952.

Bad for Each Other. Screenplay and Story, with Irving Wallace. Columbia, 1953.

Destinées. 1953. Also released as *Daughters of Destiny.*

El Alaméin. Columbia, 1953. Released in the United Kingdom as *Desert Patrol.*

Dangerous Mission. Also story, with W. R. Burnett and Charles Bennett. RKO, 1954. Also known as *Rangers of the North.*

Rage at Dawn. RKO, 1955. Also known as *Seven Bad Men.*

The Road to Denver. With Allen Rivkin. Republic, 1955.

Texas Lady. Screenplay and story. RKO, 1955.

PAPERS

Horace McCoy's papers are held in the Special Collections Department, University of California, Los Angeles Library.

CRITICAL AND BIOGRAPHICAL STUDIES

Brennan, Carol. "Horace (Stanley) McCoy, 1897–1955." *Contemporary Authors Online.* Detroit: Gale Group, 2000.

Calabria, Frank. *Dance of the Sleepwalkers: The Dance Marathon Fad.* Bowling Green, Ohio: Bowling Green State University, Popular Press, 1993.

Kutt, Inge. "Horace McCoy, April 14, 1897–December 15, 1955." In *Dictionary of Literary Biography.* Vol. 9, *American Novelists, 1910–1945.* Edited by James J. Martine. Detroit: Gale, 1981. Pp. 200–208.

Sturak, John Thomas. *The Life and Writings of Horace McCoy 1897–1955.* Ann Arbor, Mich.: University Microfilms, 1967.

———. "Horace McCoy's Objective Lyricism." In *Tough Guy Writers of the Thirties.* Edited by David Madden. Carbondale: Southern Illinois University Press/Arcturus, 1979. Pp. 137–162.

Winchell, Mark Royden. *Horace McCoy.* Boise, Idaho: Boise State University, 1982.

—ROBERT NIEMI

Terry McMillan
1951–

Any critical discussion of Terry McMillan and her works seems to begin with a discussion of McMillan's own anxieties about her place in the literary canon. McMillan believes that successful writers, especially black writers, have an obligation to support other black writers, but she feels slighted by the women that she most admires and respects, especially Alice Walker. The debate, if one could call it that, has been well publicized and the consensus seems to be that McMillan's success speaks for itself and the opinion of other women writers is not germane to appreciating her work.

Indeed, Terry McMillan's contributions to African American literature are of note for several reasons. Although she is often criticized for not being "literary," she is also acknowledged as the writer who has opened the door for a particular kind of black fiction and as the writer who has forced the publishing companies to reevaluate their markets. Although some critics have denounced her work as being popular "fluff" with little to contribute to African American literature, insisting that she is not at all on the scale of some other notable African American women writers, other critics have pointed out that she has uncovered a voice that has hitherto been unheard in black literature, a voice that resonates with many readers and results in a phenomenal commercial success. This voice is that of the educated contemporary black woman. Writing stories of young (or middle-aged) black women, women who live in suburban areas with suburban problems, women who are educated, women who have trouble with their children and with their men and with their careers, McMillan has hit a nerve with a market that was previously ignored. Black women (and men) do read, and like to read, about themselves. White women (and men) will actually read stories about black women and will not feel that the stories are necessarily about someone foreign to them. Seemingly able to bridge a gap that not even Spike Lee's movies are always able to do, McMillan's movies attract audiences of all socioeconomic backgrounds. McMillan's profound and largely unanticipated commercial success bears some examination.

Another contribution that McMillan has made to the literary world was not of her own intention. Many of her works are admittedly thinly fictionalized versions of her own autobiography, and she has been accused by some who know her of being too honest, of revealing too many personal secrets. The accusations reached their peak when Leonard Welch, the father of her son, sued her for defamation of character because one of her fictional characters was so closely based on him, and the fictional love affair about which she wrote portrayed so accurately some of the actual events in their relationship. The case had wide implications for the entire publishing industry, setting a legal precedent in the favor of fiction writers everywhere when the case was thrown out.

Finally, McMillan has provided an example for all writers who aspire to being published. Although the publishing market is notably difficult to break into, and despite the fact that myriad books are published that never make it to the best-seller lists or become well known, McMillan almost single-handedly created her own market. She sent out letters to booksellers, black studies programs, colleges, newspapers, and radio and television stations across the country, promoting her first novel. She generated such an interest, staging a promotion that the publishing company itself simply could not afford to stage, that her first novel was released to much interest. Rather than relying upon events to unfold as they may, hoping to get some ads, some favorable book reviews, and some readings, she made these things happen for herself, an approach that had been hitherto virtually unheard of in the publishing industry. She created her own success from a relatively inauspicious beginning.

These facts alone establish a significant place for McMillan in any discussion of twentieth-century literature, and her works warrant greater critical attention than they have been hitherto given.

LIFE

Terry Lynn McMillan's mother, Madeline Katherine Washington, became pregnant with her first child when she was seventeen years old and in the eleventh grade. She married the baby's father, twenty-one-year-old Edward Lewis McMillan, in June 1951 in Port Huron, Michigan, and Terry was born six months later, on October 18, 1951. Within the next five years, four more children—Edwin, Rosalyn, Crystal, and Vicki—were born to Madeline and Edward.

Life was difficult for the McMillans. Edward, a sanitation worker, was a diabetic and an alcoholic, and he became abusive when he was drunk. In interviews, Terry McMillan has said that in fights between her parents, her mother could give as well as she could get, and at times the children would have to intervene to prevent serious injury. Terry, as the eldest, ended up having to care for her younger siblings a good deal of the time, and she felt responsible for maintaining the peace in the family. Madeline and Edward finally divorced acrimoniously in May 1963, and Madeline was awarded custody of the children: Terry was eleven, Edwin ten, Rosalyn nine, Crystal seven, and Vicki six.

Despite (or perhaps because of) being a single mother with five young children and no real career skills, never having finished high school, Madeline was a strong woman. She worked at various jobs to support the family, at one time as an auto worker and at another in a pickle factory. Madeline made sure that the children were clean and educated and tried to keep them out of trouble as best she could. She was determined that her children should not make the same mistakes that she had made, but she was equally determined that she would enjoy her own life as much as was possible, without fear or complaint. She refused to wallow in her situation, believing that she was the only person who could affect her own destiny. Madeline had an affair with a man who was thirteen years younger than she, Alvin Tillman, for which she was criticized by her family and by her own children, but she scorned such criticism, insisting on her own happiness and sexual fulfillment. She married Alvin on October 9, 1967, when Terry was fifteen years old. Alvin was twenty, Madeline was almost thirty-four, and the discrepancy in their ages and the difficulties they encountered in their relationship had a deep impact on Terry McMillan later in her life. In a short time, the marriage between Madeline and Alvin became strained, at best. Terry McMillan has spoken of the night when Alvin attacked Madeline with a knife; Terry, enraged, wrested the knife from Alvin and held it to his neck, threatening him with death if he should ever hurt her mother again. Thirteen months after their marriage, Madeline divorced Alvin, citing "acts of extreme and repeated cruelties" as well as fear for her life and for the welfare of her children. That same year, Edward, Terry McMillan's father, died of diabetes complicated by his alcoholism.

Although much of the United States was experiencing racial turmoil throughout the 1960s, Port Huron was insulated from most of it, and Terry McMillan did not grow up with any particular sense of black pride or interest in social justice. McMillan's first real sense of black pride came when she was sixteen and working in the public library shelving books; there she discovered that not all authors were white when she shelved a book with an author photograph of a black man. James Baldwin was thus her first encounter with a voice that she felt was closer to her own than any other she had heard. Still, she was not politically motivated by the black pride movement of the 1960s, and she knew virtually nothing about figures such as Malcolm X. When she finally left Port Huron in the fall of 1969, she was relieved to be getting away from what she perceived as its stifling atmosphere. She headed for California (soon to be followed by her mother and several siblings), where she found a job as a typist and attended courses at the Los Angeles Community College. Enrolled in a class in African American literature, she was intrigued to find that there were many blacks writing about issues that she found relevant to her own life. The move to California had opened up a very different awareness of her race for McMillan, and she began to develop a sense of self that she had not discovered at home.

McMillan never had any plan to become a writer, despite her interest in black writers. She recalls that her first experience with writing poetry was almost accidental, growing out of the pain she felt after the breakup with her first serious boyfriend. A friend who worked at the campus black literary magazine came across the poem accidentally and offered to publish it, to McMillan's surprise. Thereafter, she published quite a few poems in the campus magazine, but recognizing that most writers made little money from their work, she discarded the idea of making a living at writing. With the intention of pursuing a career in social work, she transferred to the University of California at Berkeley, but she quickly lost interest in social work and became a journalism major, writing short stories and editorials for the college newspaper. Although she graduated with a bachelor's degree in journalism, she still had not decided on any particular career, finding herself dissatisfied with the rigid mandates of news writing. Meanwhile, she became more and more involved in the Bay Area literary scene, working with Ishmael Reed, whom she had met at Berkeley and who was to be her teacher and mentor.

Living in San Anselmo, California, just north of San Francisco, after graduation, McMillan—an extraorinarily adept typist—made a living working at word processing and data entry. In 1979, still longing to put her creative skills to work, she entered the master's degree program at the Columbia University Film School in New York City, where she planned to study screenwriting. Without completing the program, McMillan quit the school at the end of two years, reportedly because she felt she was being racially discriminated against. She returned to work as a typist, now for a law firm in New York, so that she could support herself while working on her short stories. In 1982, while she was living in Brooklyn, she met Leonard Welch, a construction worker; the attraction was immediate. She and Welch moved in together, and she became increasingly successful as a typist, making a considerable amount of money and in high demand. During the early 1980s she also began to drink heavily and to use cocaine; although her substance abuse apparently had no detrimental effect on her work, she recognized that she was repeating her father's patterns, and quit drugs and alcohol for good.

In spite of long hours at work, she continued to write, joining the Harlem Writers Guild, a group that met weekly to discuss one another's writing and prospects. She also spent time at two different artists' colonies in 1982 and 1983—Yaddo (in Saratoga Springs, New York) and MacDowell (in Peterborough, New Hampshire)—and returned feeling rejuvenated and inspired. Shortly after her return from MacDowell in 1983, while she was becoming more and more successful as a word processor, and as Welch began to have trouble finding consistent work in construction, McMillan found that she was pregnant. On April 24, 1984, she gave birth to a son, Solomon Welch. Less than a year later, she left Leonard, disappointed by their relationship.

Feeling that her life was stagnating at this time, she sent out a collection of her short stories for publication. Her writing attracted the interest of the publisher Houghton Mifflin, but the editors there felt that short stories from an unknown writer would be difficult to market, and they were more interested in the manuscript of McMillan's novel in progress, a gritty story with a strong narrative voice, based closely on her own life. When Houghton Mifflin made her an offer on the book, McMillan accepted eagerly but was disappointed to find that the publishers would not spend much effort to distribute and publicize a first novel, so she took it upon herself to market the book personally. Writing letters to booksellers and to black studies programs across the country, she forced the publisher to support a self-generated tour of readings and interviews. When *Mama* was released in January 1987, there was already a considerable amount of interest in it, and the initial run of five thousand copies had sold out the day before the original publication date. The book was in its third printing six weeks after its release date owing to continued demand. Critical response was mixed, but popular response was supportive and enthusiastic.

Shortly afterward, McMillan was offered a position at the University of Wyoming in Laramie as a teacher of creative writing, thanks to Ishmael Reed's recommendation. She accepted, despite having had no teaching experience, and she and Solomon moved to Laramie in June 1987. After a year in Wyoming that included an unfamiliarly harsh winter, in May 1988 she moved to the University of Arizona in Tucson to take a position as associate professor of creative writing.

McMillan's next novel was a love story told in chapters that alternated between a man's voice and a woman's voice, and she sent the partial manuscript to Houghton Mifflin, who expressed interest but refused to pay the amount of advance on royalties that she had requested. They also advised that she drop the alternate voices, suggesting that it would be a stronger story told from one perspective, but McMillan insisted that that was not the story she wanted to tell. She took the manuscript to Viking Penguin and got the amount she wanted. *Disappearing Acts* came out in August 1989, and like *Mama* it received mixed critical reviews, but it generated much public excitement.

McMillan continued to teach in Arizona. Her mother joined her in Tucson in 1990; the Arizona air seemed to help toward alleviating her mother's asthma. By August of that year, however, McMillan had tired of Arizona—as a single black woman, she felt socially bereft in Tucson. She was hoping to return to northern California, although she was too busy to do much about it except write to Ishmael Reed. That fall, she was a member of the panel to choose the winner of the 1990 National Book Award for fiction, a panel that eventually chose Charles Johnson for his novel *Middle Passage*. She was also editing an anthology of black writers' short fiction, a project generated by her experience as a teacher: frustrated by the relative absence of black fiction in more mainstream anthologies, she was hoping to make examples of "black" writing more readily available. In the introduction to the anthology, *Breaking Ice* (1990), she demonstrates again the self-consciousness about her critical reception that seems to plague her. She posits what amounts to a defense of her own work as well as a defense of the choices she made for inclusion in the collection. These works, she explains pointedly, are not trying to "represent" all black people, or to be the definitive voice for a particular group, or to re-create a stereotype. They are only trying to tell stories, and therefore they ought not to be criticized for failing at that which they are not trying to do in the first place.

Many of her critics accuse McMillan of not being political enough in her own writing, of not responsibly rising to the role of "black writer" by dealing with the more activist issues of racism and oppression, of "copping out" by writing about subjects such as romance and friendship and family, as if black literature must only reflect either rural or urban situations, showing crime and poverty and tragedy in order to demonstrate the plight of black people everywhere. But, McMillan argues, her stories are not meant to be political; she is trying to reach people who can recognize themselves in her tales, and she knows that everyone has experience with romance and friendship and family. Far from "copping out," she believes that she is giving a voice to a large group of people who are sometimes treated as if they themselves have "copped out." Contemporary successful black people must contend with a culture that sometimes accuses them of having assimilated into white culture so well that they have lost their sense of "blackness." Believing this to be untrue, McMillan writes about what it means to be black and successful, and includes stories in the anthology that reflect a wide range of contemporary black experience. Ultimately, however, as she says in the introduction to the anthology, "good fiction is not preaching." She is only trying to present the stories, not trying to espouse a political point.

Meanwhile, *Disappearing Acts* was selling quite well. The novel is a love story that revolves around Zora (named for Zora Neale Hurston, another black woman writer admired by McMillan), a young woman who is struggling to launch a singing career, and Franklin Swift, a young construction worker who is struggling in his career, and the story is again closely tied to McMillan's own life. Leonard Welch, the father of McMillan's son, furiously objected to the portrayal of a character whom he felt was clearly based on him. Despite McMillan's assurances that she meant the story lovingly, and her warnings that she took liberties with their story to make it more novelistic, Welch resented the implications that he was a drunk, drugged-out, lazy, homophobic, abusive rapist, implications that he felt personally defamed him because the rest of the portrayal was so thinly disguised. The stories about their fights, the issues behind their breakup, his physical description, the way that they met, the fact that he was still married but separated, that he had a child who lived with his wife, and that he had a sister who had spent some time in a mental hospital were all based firmly in the reality of their relationship; what McMillan perceived as a love story, Welch perceived as slander that warranted $4,750,000 in damages. The case was watched closely by publishing houses and fiction writers everywhere, as most fiction is based at least somewhat on reality: the maxim to "write what you know" has always been good advice. To tell writers that they may no longer use the truth to tell a story would be a tremendous stricture, and many people were alarmed at the possibilities for future lawsuits. In 1991 a judge dismissed the case, noting that although there were certainly similarities to real life, the character of Franklin Swift was also obviously a fiction, and the characterization could not slander Welch because Welch was not an abusive, racist, homophobic, alcoholic rapist. The relief felt throughout the publishing industry was great, and the legal precedent has in effect allowed "truth in fiction" to continue.

McMillan and her son again uprooted in late 1992, moving from Arizona to Danville, California, an affluent suburb east of San Francisco. She continued to work on a novel that she had begun before *Mama* but that she had found difficult to finish (*A Day Late and a Dollar Short*, ultimately published in 2001). Before finishing that, however, she wrote *Waiting to Exhale,* a story about four black women living in Arizona who are good friends but who are having trouble finding men who are not deeply flawed, if not entirely worthless. Published in 1992, the story was immensely popular, again not only with black women, despite its man-bashing (or perhaps because of it). The amount paid to McMillan for the book broke records for the amount paid to an African American author, and in fact it was on the high end of payments to any author for a single novel. Negotiations had already begun for the movie rights, and McMillan became involved in writing the screenplay. Still, the overwhelming commercial success of the book was a surprise to most people.

Critically, the book did less well. Accusations that there was too much profanity in the book, accusations that had also been proffered against the previous books, abounded. McMillan argued that she only represented the way that black women really talked, and that she was simply being true to the voice that told the story.

Another criticism against the book related to McMillan's use of brand names to tell the story, referring to particular products in order to demonstrate status. The argument suggested that McMillan was "selling out" by naming specific brands, in the same way that companies pay to have their products shown in movies, and that these brand names detract from the sense of timelessness that critics believe make up "literariness" in texts. Brand names, suggest these critics, make a text little more than a cultural artifact and foster artificial nostalgia. McMillan has argued that many suburban women identify status among themselves by their use of particular products, and that referring to clothing and furniture and vehicles by their name works more as a code for characterization, such a code being consistent with both McMillan's fictional style and with the way she characterized her people. In failing to appreciate the way that McMillan uses the brand names in the novel, for instance, to demonstrate the shallowness of one character's failed life, the critics seemed to have missed a key point that McMillan makes regarding contemporary women of all races: the expensive gadgets and name-brand products do not equate with a happy home. The use of brand names to illustrate such a point is far more clever than a simple recitation of the adage that has become a cliché.

Finally, many people argued that the book was too one-sided, that there was entirely too much man-bashing, and that men were not nearly as bad as McMillan represented. There are several responses to such criticism. First, the astonishing popularity of both the book and the movie might seem to suggest that perhaps these bad-relationship stories are not quite the anomalies some would prefer to believe. After all, revenge stories were seeing a great spurt in popularity; *The First Wives' Club* did well as both a book (1992) and a movie (1996), and *Butterfly* (1995) by Kathryn Harvey had a particular and devoted audience. The common thread here was women who were treated badly by their men, but who refused to tolerate such treatment and who plotted outrageous revenge. A second defense is one posed by McMillan: history is full of stories about misogynists whose authors have never had to defend themselves. Finally, critics again seem to have missed the overall message behind the novel: although each of the characters encounters some dreadful men, none of the women gives up hope of finding a man who will be good for her, and half of them succeed in doing so. McMillan had done what had worked for her before, touching a nerve, and not only with black women. Her ability to do so was bringing in a healthy living for McMillan and her son.

Although McMillan always did what she could for her family, in early September 1993 she decided more deliberately to spread around some of her new wealth, buying her mother a new car, a house, and dentures. She wanted to see her mother finally comfortable after her years of sacrifice and struggle. On September 30, only a couple of weeks later, fifty-nine-year-old Madeline was staying with Solomon while Terry McMillan was on tour in Europe to promote *Waiting to Exhale,* and she died unexpectedly during an asthma attack. Terry McMillan was inconsolable. Shortly after her mother's death, McMillan's best friend, Doris Jean Austin, was diagnosed with inoperable liver cancer; she died less than a year later.

McMillan, distraught, went alone to Jamaica on vacation to try to rejuvenate her spirit. There she met Jonathan Plummer, a Jamaican man who was nearly half her age, and they fell in love. McMillan fictionalized this story in *How Stella Got Her Groove Back,* a book that was written in three weeks and released in May 1995. After she submitted the manuscript, she sent for Jonathan to join her, and they moved in together. She was very anxious about their age difference, especially after having seen what had happened between her mother and Alvin, and she was insecure about Plummer's reasons for being with her. Furthermore, as a literary celebrity, McMillan's personal life was on public view. Conscious of being accused of choosing a "boy toy," McMillan made it clear that Plummer was from a wealthy Jamaican family and was choosing a career in the hotel industry. However, she enjoyed the fact that he was not aware of (and not overly impressed by) the fact that she was a famous novelist; he loved her for herself, and she reveled in the relationship. They had a house custom built in Danville, and they married in September 1998, after the film rights to *Stella* had been sold.

Her next book, *A Day Late and a Dollar Short,* which had been in drafts since the mid-1980s, appeared in 2001. Here, she follows an entire family: a mother and father, three sisters, and one brother. She tells the story of a family whose children are grown, and the struggles that each individual has with trying to make it in a world that is less than friendly to him or her, with a mother who will not let them use that as an excuse to fail. Once again, McMillan draws heavily from her own experiences.

THE NOVELS

In some ways, Terry McMillan's works follow the tradition of other well-known African American writers. Writers such as Toni Morrison, Alice Walker, Zora Neale Hurston, Maya Angelou, and others have written about the struggles that blacks have faced, about the tensions between assimilation and heterogeneity. They have celebrated black culture by focusing on, among other things, the insular nature of family and community, the strength that is called upon in adversity, the triumph over tremendous pain. They focus on issues that are endemic to a people who must struggle to stay ahead and to stay together. Frequently situated in the South or in rural areas, the works of these writers reflect on the experience of slavery and its aftermath, not in order to dwell on it but in order to come to terms with it and to understand its impact on the formation of a culture. These works often reflect what W. E. B. Du Bois, in *The Souls of Black Folk,* calls a "double-consciousness" that is familiar to readers (and writers) of African American literature: attempts to reconcile participation in the dominant culture of America as well as the marginalized black culture create an essential duality, and a conflict in self.

Toni Morrison, in *Playing in the Dark* (1992), discusses the literary images of black and white, dark and light, and makes a compelling argument that the use of these dichotomies in literature reinforces a chronic judgment about race. She is, of course, discussing texts that were written primarily by white authors, particularly men (the texts that make up the literary canon). The subconsciousness of this reinforcement has been perpetuated easily because of the void between white voices and black voices: when black voices have been silent for so long, the white voices are heard so much more powerfully. However, she and other black authors (not the least of whom are those authors who have had a powerful impact on McMillan, such as James Baldwin, Ralph Ellison, Countee Cullen, and the women already mentioned, to name just a few) have attempted to deconstruct the hierarchy inherent in the dichotomies, and do so by writing literature from an ethnocentric perspective.

Although McMillan's works are based in this same tradition—hoping to give a voice to blacks who have not had one in the past, hoping to add her voice to the tumultuous voices she only encountered later in her life—her works also operate from within a different tradition. As she has said on numerous occasions, it took her some time to realize that when she read, she was not hearing the voices of people that she encountered or knew, or even of her own voice, even when she read the works of some African American authors. She was experiencing her own kind of double consciousness, and as Du Bois knew, "It is a peculiar sensation . . . this sense of always looking at one's self through the eyes of others, of measuring one's soul by the tape of a world that looks on in amused contempt and pity." Her consciousness is that she is both black and an American, and that the demarcations for her as a contemporary woman are not as divergent as they were for blacks in the past. She wants to show the way that African Americans today struggle in society, in a society that is not only black or white but is often mixed, in a society where black people are not always relegated to the "wrong side of the rural tracks" or to the urban ghetto, but in a society where blacks can be found in the suburbs, in law firms, in television producing, in universities, in banks.

The issues affecting the women McMillan writes of are the same issues that affect women of any age and race, but they are complicated by race. She knows that within contemporary black culture there are stories of despair and poverty, of pain and heartbreak, of crime and violence, of drug and alcohol abuse; but there are also stories of triumph and wealth, of joy and love, of reform and recovery. The world McMillan speaks of is a world with hope, hope that is accessible to anyone, rather than the bleak vision of a potential, "maybe one day" future that so many African American authors seem to posit. She recognizes that although there is far to go, blacks had made progress at the end of the twentieth century, and that progress ought to be celebrated, or at least discussed. McMillan refuses to allow her characters to stagnate at a particular painful time in the past (either the individual or the collective past), preferring instead to modernize her characters. Perhaps the people of whom McMillan speaks are not as downtrodden as those of whom other authors choose to speak, and perhaps they are not as vitally in need of being given a voice as those who are more downtrodden, or so her critics imply. The point, however, is that McMillan speaks about people who have largely been ignored, for one reason or another (as suggested above), and now McMillan is writing about their experience, an experience that is still very much racialized even if it is more suburban and successful. The issues that middle-class blacks have to face still impact black culture, in some ways even more than the kinds of stories that people such as Spike Lee might present: there is much conflict within black culture about what might be perceived as assimilation.

MAMA

McMillan's first novel, *Mama*, is a testimony to her own mother's experiences raising five children. The book's family of mother and siblings is nearly identical to McMillan's own family, and the story takes place in Point Haven, Michigan, a place that resembles Port Huron, McMillan's hometown, in many transparent ways: the town is described as being in the same geographic location as Port Huron, and even the name of the only bar that serves blacks in Port Huron, the Red Shingle, is left as The Shingle in the book. The father (whose nickname is "Crook" both in the book and in real life) is abusive and alcoholic, leaving the family after much violence. The breakup between Madeline and Edward was virtually identical to the version told in the story about Mildred and Crook. Later in the story, the diabetic Crook, like Edward, dies because he is unable to stop drinking and eating sweets. "Money" is the nickname of the only son in the book, as it is the nickname of Madeline's only son in real life. The mother in the novel, Mildred, has an affair with a much younger man, Billy, finally marrying him. There is a scene where Freda, the eldest daughter, intervenes when Billy pulls a knife on Mildred, a scene more than reminiscent of the event Terry McMillan recounts as having happened between herself and Madeline and Alvin. Freda leaves Point Haven to go to California, and her mother and sisters follow soon after. The sister to remain, Bootsey, does so to marry, having several children at an early age; McMillan's sister Rosalyn (affectionately known as "Booge") remained in Michigan to marry, and she also had several children; both Bootsey and Rosalyn work in the auto factories until deciding to go into different careers. (Rosalyn followed McMillan's example and became a writer as well.) McMillan's disclaimers—"This book is a work of fiction. Names, characters, places and incidents are either products of the author's imagination or are used fictitiously. Any resemblance to actual events or locales or persons, living or dead, is entirely coincidental"—gives her some literary license but has fooled few people, if any.

Perhaps it is this proximity to McMillan's own life that allows her to maintain such consistency with the voices of her characters. Although *Mama* is told by a third-person narrator, the sense throughout is that the narrative voice is that of whomever is the center of the action. The story, although the perspective changes now and then, is most definitely that of Mildred, and it begins compellingly:

> Mildred hid the ax beneath the mattress of the cot in the dining room. She poured lye in a brown paper bag and pushed it behind the pots and pans under the kitchen sink. Then she checked all three butcher knives to make sure they were razor sharp. She knew where she could get her hands on a gun in fifteen minutes, but ever since she'd seen her brother shot for stealing a beer from the pool hall, she'd been afraid of guns. Besides, Mildred didn't want to kill Crook, she just wanted to hurt him.

The smooth introduction of an old antagonism, as well as the establishment of a history of frightening violence, hints at what Mildred has had to face in her life, as well as confirming Mama as an indomitable type: she would clearly not tolerate victimization. This, perhaps above all else, is what McMillan espouses in all her novels. Being black does not necessitate victimization. Her own mother could have been a victim, and certainly faced her share of demons throughout her life, but never did she allow a sense of defeat to conquer her or her children, and never did she allow victimization to become an excuse for failure. Far from using oppression as a justification for violence and crime, effectually continuing black exploitation, McMillan wants to point out that other blacks have managed to rise above the same obstacles in hopeful and meaningful ways. Much of this is conveyed in McMillan's opening paragraph, when Mama's voice is heard through that of the narrator.

The narrative technique that McMillan deploys through this novel, and indeed throughout many of her novels, might be considered consistent with a feminist voice. A transgressive narration might be any voice other than that of the educated, self-centric voice of an omniscient (or even partially omniscient) narrator, and part of the feminist argument is that women need to use a different kind of voice and a different kind of narrative technique than that which has been handed down through the canon. Although this is a terribly simplistic way to think of feminist writing, McMillan is clearly experimenting with different styles of narration, styles that are consciously not self-centric; in fact, there are some who have suggested that the smooth transition from one point of view to another reflects more of a blues aesthetic than a feminist one. A true omniscient narrator would be far more objective and less malleable than McMillan's narrator is; her narrator adapts his or her voice to suit the subject under discussion, so that in the end, the sense is that readers have seen varying points of view that are all valid and sympathetic, even the perspectives of those with whom readers might not ordinarily sympathize. Rather than establishing any moralistic rhetoric, McMillan promotes tolerance of many perspectives and situations, since tolerance comes with understanding.

DISAPPEARING ACTS

With *Disappearing Acts*, McMillan takes this narrative approach a step further. By alternating the chapters so that both Zora and Franklin are heard, in each of their own first-person voices, McMillan has taken great pains to establish sympathy for both sides of this story about failed love. As the saying goes, there are two sides to every story: yours, mine, and truth. (After going to such extremes to treat the subject "fairly" and to give the male perspective of the relationship, McMillan must have been dumbfounded to learn of Welch's lawsuit against her.) McMillan hopes to demonstrate that the truth lies somewhere between the two versions of events, in a way that truly undermines the dichotomies that are so often portrayed in black literature. Here, the relationship itself, between the man and the woman, represents that dichotomy and in fact the Du Boisian double consciousness: although both individuals love each other and long for union, they also remain individuals. The tension lies in the efforts to have both individualism and union, a tension that mimics racial double consciousness. By allowing readers to hear both voices, McMillan illustrates that tension admirably, as well as illustrating the sense that someone else is watching and judging: not only does each character feel that the other is judging him or her, weighing the relationship based on events, but the very fact of each narration implies an audience that expects some kind of justification and reconciliation.

Zora is a young woman who is struggling to make a name for herself as a singer, supporting herself by teaching but finding little creative satisfaction in that. Franklin is a construction worker who has a hard time finding work because of his race and because he is not unionized. As her career takes off, his career becomes increasingly difficult, and in his despair at the situation, he begins to drink and use drugs. He grows less inclined to seek work and finally stops looking entirely. He picks fights, cheats on Zora, and loses any sense of self-worth, spiraling into self-destruction. Zora, meanwhile, becomes pregnant. With little hope in their situation, Zora has an abortion, without telling Franklin that she was pregnant. Upset when he learns what she has done, he assures her that he wants a child, another chance to raise a family; he already has a child by a woman he is still legally married to (albeit separated from). He swears that he will support Zora and any baby that they may have, that he will finally get a divorce from his first wife. When Zora gets pregnant again, she decides to have this baby, and she names her son Jeremiah. After she brings the baby home, she throws Franklin out, unable to sustain sympathy for his excuses any longer, and she and Jeremiah are on their own. Perhaps the greatest weakness of the story is its ending: in a few short pages (which is supposed to span three months), Franklin returns to school and finds work, motivated by his love for Zora to get his life together at last, and he returns to her in the end with a new resolve. The ending is a bit too pat, and it is the primary place where McMillan deviates widely from her own experience, since she and Welch did not reunite. Perhaps the ending is the part that she hoped Welch would read as a loving tribute to their relationship, a hint of hope in their otherwise failed relationship. Either way, after a strong buildup of the rest of the story, the ending seems to tie up all the loose ends implausibly. Nonetheless, McMillan's success at maintaining the two voices throughout the novel, consistently representing the give and take within the relationship and within the narrative itself, makes the novel one of McMillan's best.

WAITING TO EXHALE

Waiting to Exhale, her next novel, uses a narrative style similar to that in *Mama*. Following the stories of four black women, friends who learn that they can rely only on one another, the narrator alternates the voice according to whose story is being told. Again, the narration is not first-person, but it may as well be. One of the women, Bernadine, a bookkeeper who aspires to be a caterer, is going through an ugly and painful divorce after her husband announces that he is leaving her for his younger, blond, white secretary. Another of the foursome, Robin, who works for an insurance agency, is unable to break off her connection with a man who will not remain faithful to her and who causes her nothing but heartache. The third, Gloria, a divorced hairstylist who owns her own beauty salon, is seemingly using her weight to avoid the pain of relationships while she raises her son alone; her pain comes from having her husband leave her for a gay man. The fourth woman is Savannah, a publicist for a television station, who is hoping to break into producing, and hoping above all to find a man with whom she can have a successful relationship. Savannah is the one who articulates the problem for all four of the women, and indeed the problem that many people have with the book itself: "From the outside, everything looks good: I've got a decent job, money in the bank, live in a nice condo, and drive a respectable car. I've got everything I need except a man." The idea that a successful woman can never be fulfilled without a man is distasteful for many, and McMillan's own reputation as a new feminist voice suffered from the implication. Through all their tribulations, the four women in the book work their way toward a resolution of their problems, although with varying degrees of success. In the end, Bernadine has a new man and revenge on the old one. Robin finally dumps her man, but only after she becomes pregnant with his child, a child she determines to raise herself with the help of her girlfriends. Gloria has a heart attack, and the close call leads her to a new resolve about her health and about a potential for love with a new neighbor; her son is on his way to being successful and responsible. Savannah gets rid of the married man that she was hung up on and embraces her new life. Apparently, each of the women is able to exhale at last.

Although the story is entertaining and was certainly embraced by many of McMillan's fans, it lacked the depth of her earlier two books. It made good Hollywood material, but seemed to steer away from the innovative narration that McMillan had been striving for. The voices of her characters were distinct, but not so divergent as those in, for example, *Disappearing Acts,* and although the women each had separate problems, their voices seemed to vary mostly in their level of anger or desperation. If McMillan were truly trying to appeal to a literary crowd, *Waiting to Exhale* was not the book to do so, a fact that she seemed to recognize in her complaint that too many people seemed to identify her only by that book rather than by some of her others.

HOW STELLA GOT HER GROOVE BACK

Another hint that McMillan is not in total disagreement with her critics regarding *Exhale*—and perhaps a glimpse at McMillan's insecurity about her literary status and her own concerns about being pigeonholed as the writer of *Exhale*—comes in the amusingly self-referential passage that she included in her next book, *How Stella Got Her Groove Back.* McMillan's first-person narrator, Stella Payne, is in Jamaica, trying to figure out what her beach reading ought to be, and she comments upon the choices available to her:

> I pick up the hardcover version of *Waiting to Exhale* by that Terry McMillan which I bought when it first came out and I've been meaning to read for a couple of years now and after reading like the first fifty or sixty pages I don't know what all the hoopla is about and why everybody thinks she's such a hot writer because her shit is kind of weak when you get right down to it and this book here has absolutely no literary merit whatsoever at least none that I can see and she uses entirely too much profanity. Hell, I could write the same stuff she writes cause she doesn't exactly have what you'd call a style but anyway I can sort of relate to some of her characters even though the main reason I didn't read this book was because from what I heard a couple of these women sounded too much like me although I'm not as stupid as a few of them.

Allowing Stella this little aside also enabled McMillan to take a jab at the critics who pan her for things such as obscenity or shallow women characters.

How Stella Got Her Groove Back is about a forty-two-year-old woman who is divorced, working as a successful investment analyst, and raising her son by herself. She is close to her problematic family, but she feels unfulfilled and wants some time away from her life, so she takes off by herself for a vacation to Jamaica, to the horror of many of her friends and family who believe that taking a vacation alone is a sign of instability. When she gets there, she meets Winston Shakespeare, a tall, extraordinarily good-looking Jamaican man who is half her age. They have an affair that is filled with excitement but also with the misunderstandings that result from Stella's insecurity about their age difference. When Stella returns home, she finds that she has lost her job, a fact that does not distress her as much as she thought it might, and she decides to return to Jamaica to see if her feelings for Winston have any foundation or whether the infatuation was just an anomaly. The affair resumes with passion, but also with wariness, and Stella invites Winston to return to California with her. The story traces their affair in Jamaica as well as their attempts to fit that relationship into a life. Her anxieties about their age discrepancy wreak havoc on their time together, and almost prevent her from agreeing when Winston proposes marriage to her at the end of the novel; although she does accept his proposal, this character seems to be unaware of the advice that Mama had given in the first novel, advice that Madeline McMillan had also given to her children: "Feel the fear but do it anyway." Mildred (and Madeline) did not care what others thought of her relationship with

Billy (and Alvin), but clearly Stella (and McMillan) had grave concerns about her relationship with Winston (Jonathan).

How Stella Got Her Groove Back received much more negative critical attention than her previous novels had. Many people felt that the story was implausible, that there was little to recommend the book except for a somewhat fantastic romantic romp. Many complained that McMillan's powers of description failed her in the novel, noting that her greatest strength lies in dialogue and character development rather than description. Others objected to the lack of punctuation in the novel, as it was written in what McMillan considers to be stream of consciousness. By using this style, she hoped to convey a sense of the narrator's enthusiasm and euphoria about her new relationship. McMillan says that she wrote as she thought and, more importantly, as Stella thought. Although there is clearly a huge difference between the Joycean stream of consciousness of *Ulysses* or, obviously, *Finnegans Wake,* and McMillan's nearly run-on sentences, McMillan does manage to convey the urgency of Stella's thoughts, and she is experimenting with alternative styles of narration. The effect, many argue, is unsuccessful, and the style may be more distracting than literary. Nonetheless, the voice in this novel remains consistent throughout, and McMillan's following does not seem to mind the narrative technique. The book, either in spite of or because of the fantastic nature of the story, sold well. Again, the appeal of the book extended beyond the target market of black women, and the movie did the same. The challenge of a beautiful young couple trying to extend their relationship beyond the infatuation of a vacation tryst was dynamic. And yet, the book did seem to lose McMillan still more of the critical acclaim that she had been seeking, even if the "fantastic" story was not far from the truth of McMillan's real experiences in Jamaica.

A DAY LATE AND A DOLLAR SHORT

A Day Late and a Dollar Short (2001)—the manuscript on which McMillan had been working for years but which she found difficult to complete (especially after the death of her mother)—is a novel about a family of grown children who are living their separate, complicated lives but who still struggle with their familial bonds. The book, like her others, is heavily autobiographical, and the parallels with McMillan's life make it easy to see why this novel should have been so difficult to complete.

The mother is Viola Price, a woman who has worked hard all her life to keep her family together and who is tired now, still strong but very tired. The father, Cecil, has left the family once again—this time apparently for good, despite the skepticism of the rest of the family—and has moved in with a sometime girlfriend. When the girlfriend ends up pregnant, Cecil takes responsibility, although it is uncertain that he is the father; he is both puzzled at the way he ended up in this situation and excited by the prospect of getting to start over again with another family. Viola is in poor health with asthma and is barely holding it together, worried about each of her children and grandchildren. Paris, the eldest daughter, is divorced, raising her seventeen-year-old son by herself in California and working as a successful party planner. Much like Savannah in *Waiting to Exhale,* however, Paris is battling her own demons of depression and prescription drugs. Lewis, the brother, is in and out of trouble with the law, hung up on his former wife and unable to hold down the job that would allow him to see his son. (Every brother—in the sibling sense—that McMillan creates seems to have trouble with his temper, with drugs, with the law; it is in fact easy to see why some critics have accused her of always putting black men in stereotypically bad situations, even when she does let readers empathize with them.) Lewis seems to remain at the level of his family's expectations, which are not high, and he cannot seem to control his violent frustration with the course of his life. Janelle, the baby of the family, has just found out that her second husband has been molesting her teenaged daughter, his step-daughter, and she throws him out of the house just as she is realizing that she is pregnant with his child. Charlotte, who appears to be another character modeled on Rosalyn McMillan, has her own husband and children in Chicago and prefers to try to stay out of the trouble that everyone else seems continually to get into, apparently feeling that her own life allows her a certain superiority over the others.

In this book, McMillan returns to a more interesting and challenging narrative technique. As in *Disappearing Acts,* she gives us the first-person narrative of each individual, rather than a centralized perspective. But where *Disappearing Acts* offers two perspectives, *A Day Late and a Dollar Short* offers six: all four children and both parents. McMillan is proficient at juggling her characters and their stories and at maintaining consistency in their voices. Able to create a believable father who is somewhat bumbling but loving, a strong and domineering but lonely mother, a well-intentioned but problem-plagued brother, and three sisters who are each controlling in varying degrees, McMillan presents a microcosm of family life in all its joys and sorrows.

Beyond situational coincidences with McMillan's life, the obvious parallel is the death of the mother, Viola Price. While Paris is in Europe, her niece, Shanice (Janelle's daughter), is staying with Viola to get away from her stepfather. Viola, in the midst of one of her frequent asthma attacks, dies. Each family member's reaction to the news is shown; even though they were often at odds with one another and with their mother, they are all distraught. Viola's dying request, well-organized beforehand, is that the family—all the children and their father—should spend Thanksgiving in one house that year. Having written each of them a letter, she wants the letters read to one another out loud on Thanksgiving, hoping that they will effect a reconciliation of her family. The novel ends with the letters being read and with plans being made to spend the next Thanksgiving together as well.

Once again, the novel ends a bit too neatly, with all the ends tied up and everyone on his or her way to happiness and accord. Satisfying and hopeful though this may be, McMillan seems to lose the thread of the characterizations when she deploys this kind of ending. Although this sense of hope may be what McMillan is trying to convey in her work as a body, it seems improbable as a way of ending the story, even if the device of a mother's death might indeed require a reevaluation of priorities.

Perhaps a critical discussion on McMillan's works should center on a consideration of what McMillan is trying to accomplish with her invariably happy endings. The implication seems to be that everyone, regardless of condition, can rise above obstacles. The tensions of racial double consciousness can be overcome, according to her novels, although that is not the same as saying that racial tension itself is avoidable. By presenting scenarios for American blacks that have been considered too mundane for literature, McMillan is not exactly preaching, but she is making it clear that contemporary black America is not simply about assimilation. The argument about conformity or success as being assimilation remains a hot topic within black studies and black culture, in discussions about everything from education and language to jobs and crime. McMillan, however, avoids being just another black writer who is espousing assimilation: her novels focus far more on self-autonomy, of rising above all kinds of adversity, but most important, of refusing to play the role of victim. Ultimately, McMillan would argue, the role of victim has been overplayed (indeed, she feels that victims are boring and present no new challenges for a fiction writer), and although there is much victimization still occurring in the world, the appeal that her novels have for people of all races should suggest that adversity is a universal issue, not a black issue. A refusal to accept the role of victim is the only way to attain any level of happiness in the world, whether that happiness is financial, emotional, spiritual, or sexual. Fulfillment, McMillan has clearly shown, can be achieved in a number of ways, and no two individuals, even within the same race, are alike in that respect. The variety of solutions for her characters' happiness should suggest to a discerning reader that McMillan recognizes the impossibility of becoming the "definitive" voice for any group of people. Perhaps the new tension that should be examined in contemporary black literature is that between what we think we want and what would be good for us, regardless of our socioeconomic backgrounds.

Selected Bibliography

WORKS OF TERRY McMILLAN

NOVELS

Mama. New York and Boston: Houghton Mifflin, 1987.

Disappearing Acts. New York: Viking, 1989.

Waiting to Exhale. New York: Viking, 1992.

How Stella Got Her Groove Back. New York: Viking, 1996.

A Day Late and a Dollar Short. New York: Viking, 2001.

WORKS EDITED BY TERRY McMILLAN

Breaking Ice: An Anthology of Contemporary African-American Fiction. New York: Penguin, 1990.

CRITICAL AND BIOGRAPHICAL STUDIES

"McMillan, Terry." In *Modern Black Writers Supplement.* Edited by Steven R. Serafin. New York: Continuum, 1995.

Patrick, Diane. *The Unauthorized Biography: Terry McMillan.* New York: St. Martin's, 1999. (The primary source of information about Terry McMillan's life, but not very well written. Patrick devotes much space to complaining about McMillan's lack of cooperation with the project. Much material seems to have been gleaned from published interviews.)

Richards, Paulette. *Terry McMillan: A Critical Companion.* Westport, Conn.: Greenwood Press, 1999. (An overview of McMillan's life as well as readings of her work; this is the only real critical source for McMillan's works.)

Sellers, Frances Stead. "Terry McMillan." *Times Literary Supplement,* November 6, 1992, p. 20.

Thompson, Kathleen. "McMillan, Terry." In *Black Women in America: A Historical Encyclopedia.* 2 vols. Edited by Darlene Clark Hine. Brooklyn, N.Y.: Carlson, 1993.

INTERVIEWS

Hubbard, Ken. "On Top of Her Game." *People Weekly,* April 29, 1996, pp. 111–112.

Randolph, Laura B. "Sisters Speak: Me As I Wanna Be." *Ebony,* July 1996, p. 20.

—KATHY HEININGE

Terrence McNally

1939–

TERRENCE MCNALLY'S FIRST Broadway production opened to scathing reviews and closed two weeks later. It was quite lucky for theater that the playwright's brother reminded him that he had "no place to go but up." Forty years later McNally is one of America's finest and most successful playwrights. He has won, among other things, numerous Tonys, an Emmy, two Guggenheim Fellowships, and a Rockefeller grant. A member of the Dramatists Guild Council since 1970, he served as vice president from 1981 to 1999. He is also often labeled as America's premier gay playwright. Yet he resists such a limiting classification. This reluctance to be burdened with designations extends throughout his career in comedies, dramas, tragedies, musicals, operas, and characters of every kind. Despite his eclectic body of work, there are threads that tie his corpus together. The most striking is the theme of alienation and human beings' desire for connection: "I think that that issue, the barriers between people, and why they stay there, will always interest me" (quoted in Steven Drukman, "Terrence McNally"). McNally now has the rare distinction of being a playwright whose new plays will always be produced. But this is not because he writes conventionally appealing plays; rather, he is continually innovating theater with controversial ideas and experimental deliveries. As McNally writes in his article "What I Know about Being a Playwright," every play is important: "If a play isn't worth dying for—not to mention months, perhaps years of rewrites and frustration—maybe it isn't worth writing."

BIOGRAPHY

Terrence McNally was born on November 3, 1939, in St. Petersburg, Florida, to Hubert and Dorothy Rapp McNally. His family soon moved to Corpus Christi, Texas, where he and his younger brother, Peter, spent their childhoods. Although the small southern town lacked a regional theater, McNally was introduced to different theatrical forms. He saw *Annie Get Your Gun* with Ethel Merman in New York in his early years and was enchanted. Although he remembers seeing only two New York shows in his youth, his parents went to the city regularly. Their playbills from the shows would be on the coffee table for months afterward. A nun at McNally's school first introduced him to opera, to which he would then listen every Saturday on the radio. McNally's love for opera would influence his plays from the very beginning of his career.

In hindsight McNally can recognize these early theatrical leanings, yet when he went to New York to attend college at Columbia, theater was not in the forefront of his mind. Journalism was more appealing, and McNally obtained the appropriate degree. Before he left college, however, he wrote his first show upon discovering that no one had yet penned the annual Columbia varsity show.

After his graduation in 1960, McNally headed off to Mexico to write the great American novel. He ended up writing a play instead, which he sent to the Actors Studio. When they accepted it, he moved back to New York. The studio nurtured the young playwright, who learned by working as a stage manager. His *And Things*

That Go Bump in the Night was first produced in 1962 (under the title *There Is Something Out There*). After revisions it was produced again and transferred to Broadway in 1965. He was twenty-five. John Guare remembers hearing that "at one performance an audience member jumped on stage and slapped its star Eileen Heckart for appearing in such an immoral play." Guare decided that anything so upsetting to its audience must have potential. When he saw the production, he determined, "It was filled with the future." Guare was right. McNally has matured into one of the most versatile and consistently powerful voices in the theater. Terrence McNally's later plays, however varied, are always identifiable in their use of music, their delicately crafted dialogue, and their appeal to what is best in the human spirit.

EARLY PLAYS

And Things That Go Bump in the Night was McNally's first Broadway show. The play is a surreal family drama about dysfunction and was among many premiering in the 1960s that attacked the myth of the perfect American family. In it, one can see the author working out the ideas and influences of the likes of Edward Albee and Harold Pinter.

McNally says of the set that there should be "no shadows or semitones." The play is stark and disturbing. Although the play is set in the "present," this present is a time when there is a nightly curfew. Something is "out there," prompting the family to erect a large electric fence around their house. The characters—Fa and his wife, Ruby; their children, Sigfrid and Lakme; and Grandfa—live in fear of the threat outside but also of each other. Grandfa wheels around the house despondently. The audience gradually learns that the family has a nightly guest to distract them from their painful interactions. It becomes clear that their days are much the same; they are caught in a cruel routine.

Indeed, the play feels very much like a dynamic *Endgame*. And as in Samuel Beckett's *Endgame,* there is the possibility for change in each day. Grandfa will be leaving the house in the morning to go to an old folks home, but this particular change is never seen. Instead, Fa dies quietly in his chair while Ruby and her children mentally torture their guest for the evening, Clarence. Sigfrid has rediscovered his old classmate and brought him home to seduce him. The family taunts Clarence as they play the tape they made of the seduction. This cruel replay of his first sexual experience is too much for the sweet, socially minded Clarence. He runs from the house and is electrified on the fence. The play ends with the surviving characters trying in vain to make sense of the events of the evening and the repetitive events of their lives. Throughout the second act the lights go on and off, and in the third act thunderous "thumps" or bumps are heard. The play ends in darkness with a tumultuous bump.

The play is very self-conscious about its critique of the potential destructiveness of the American family. Sigfrid points out the consequences of such a critique: "You *acknowledged* it . . . the way we live. You can't do that, Ruby. You'll wreck it . . . the set-up . . . *everything*. It all falls apart then." Clarence represents not only the victimized homosexual but also the ultimately defeated protestor, thwarted in his attempts to get rid of the play's great menace. Grandfa becomes the voice of the 1960s playwright, writing the truth in times of denial. He spends much of the play writing his chronicle, his description of what goes on in the family. He is continually mocked; Ruby insists that he is writing a fictional novel, as he cannot possibly be recording the truth. He is the only character who pities Clarence and even tries to warn him of the danger the family poses. Yet his dire caveats go unheeded, and he is caught in the end, like everyone else, listening to the bumps. He writes "No" as his last act of defiance, just before the darkness.

When they were not writing negative reviews of *Bump,* critics were crafting press about McNally's sexuality. That is, the new playwright was not much discussed in terms of his work but in terms of his past relationship with Edward Albee. Despite all the bad press, McNally's play struck a chord with many theatergoers. Some even campaigned outside the theater, encouraging passersby to see the show. It is probable they recognized McNally's first experimentation with themes that would carry through all his work—the inability of people to connect coupled with their dire need to do so. Yet it would be a few years before audiences saw a mature expression of the reason why McNally's characters have such a difficult time connecting: "I do believe there is a divinity in all of us, and we are all perfect in a way.... I think it's out of terror of one another and of intimacy that we become racist and homophobic and sexist and all these things" (quoted in Drukman).

McNally took a short sabbatical from playwriting after *Bump*'s disastrous reviews. He soon began experimenting with short plays. McNally's plays from this period are usually classified as comedies, although they are mostly satires: comedy is used in the plays to critique serious problems in society. Although the characters are underdeveloped, the author's wit is evident. Like many playwrights of his generation, his satire in the late 1960s and early 1970s often involved a critique of the conflict in Vietnam. For example, *Next* (1967) is set in an examination room. Marion Cheever tries desperately to get out of the draft. The female examiner is impassive to his protests. The play starts out as comical, but the audience quickly discovers the seriousness of the situation as Cheever's excuses rise in absurdity.

Tour, which also premiered in 1967, makes fun of American tourists. The play is a series of snapshots of their travels abroad. The minimalist set allows the audience to concentrate on the American couple's ability to ignore the misery they see around them as they write notes to their son, stationed in Vietnam. *Next* and *Tour* were both produced for television by Channel 13, the Public Broadcasting Station, in New York.

After the success of *Next* and *Tour*'s television productions, McNally wrote his first teleplay, *Botticelli,* in 1968. The play is set in the jungles of Vietnam. The two protagonists engage in a guessing game: Wayne is "a dead European male in the arts beginning with P." Stu must ask questions until he guesses the identity. They continue to play even when they come under fire and a man is shot to death in front of them. Stu never wins the game.

Witness (1968) is named for what the main character needs. Young Man, the protagonist, is about to attempt a presidential assassination. He has tied and gagged Man to witness the event. Man is temporarily forgotten, however, when a window washer enters. The window washer and a young woman become additional witnesses. The play effectively brings together concerns over both Vietnam and the Kennedy assassination. The young man reads from a letter to the president: "You will undoubtedly be curious why I have 'assassinated' you. Actually I am sick and tired of all the assassinations and I don't want another one to happen again.... People have got to learn that killing people doesn't change anything." Rifle shots come from the other buildings before Young Man has the chance to shoot. The audience learns that the Young Man's gun is full of blanks.

The theme of homophobia is drawn into the Vietnam commentary in 1969's *Bringing It All Back Home.* The play opens with a brother and sister teasing each other over their teenage experimentation with their peers. They are interrupted by their brother, Jimmy, who comes home in a box from Vietnam. A reporter, Miss Horne, then arrives to interview the family about their loss. It becomes clear that Jimmy's death has saved him from accusations of homosexuality. As his father explains, "Dying, you see, my son, is the real test of a man's masculinity. And Jimmy passed it." After Miss Horne is kicked out for asking "communist" questions, the audience is left with Jimmy's mother mourning him.

The Ritz (1975) was McNally's first big commercial success. The clever farce's action revolves around a straight man's calamities as he hides from the mob in a gay bathhouse. The play was extremely subversive when it premiered. For the play to work, the audience would have to set aside their homophobia; they would have to recognize that the heterosexuals in the play were the bad guys. These were huge barriers to overcome, but the play succeeded. McNally notes that the play has become dated because the specter of AIDS prevents it from being performed. Nevertheless, the play was produced successfully in San Francisco in 2002.

LATER PLAYS

It's Only a Play (1985) marks a turning point in McNally's career. Until this point he was best known for comedies (mostly satire). While some critics and scholars believe *The Lisbon Traviata* was McNally's first play that moved away from comedy, McNally maintains that *It's Only* was never meant to be performed as pure farce. As he says in "A Few Words of Introduction": "*It's Only a Play* is a comedy, but it's one of the most serious plays I have ever written. It's my attempt to describe exactly what it was like to work in the Broadway theater in the 1980s. It is probably the closest thing I will ever write to a documentary." The original title when it premiered in Philadelphia was *Broadway, Broadway*. The title changed when it went to the Manhattan Theatre Club (MTC) and Lynne Meadow, the club's artistic director.

The play has many conventions that may lead a director to interpret it as farcical. The whole of the action takes place in a bedroom of a townhouse while an opening night party for *The Golden Egg* rages downstairs. Various characters enter and feed quick jokes to the audience about what is happening downstairs. The driving force in the action is that they are all waiting for the reviews. Act 1 ends with a major review arriving; act 2 opens with the group of characters preparing to read it. The review is contemptuous of every aspect of the production. After various insults and comforts, the group comes together again—they have an idea for a new play. The desperation is both funny and tragic. Most telling is a moment in act 1 when the playwright gets down on his knees to pray: "You who have given me the greatest gift of all, the gift to realize that no matter what happens tonight, it's only a play . . . give us just one more thing . . . surely you can give us a hit tonight."

This may be the play that is McNally's most self-referential in terms of playwriting. His shadow can been seen in the following conversation between Ira (the critic) and Peter (the playwright) after Peter prays:

> IRA: You know, Mr. Austin, there was a genuine sincerity when you spoke.
> PETER: That surprises you?
> IRA: From the author of this evening's play, quite frankly, yes.

Perhaps McNally accurately anticipated that critics would be reluctant to see a comic writer tackling serious material. (These critics had obviously forgotten McNally's biting satires of Vietnam.)

However one might view *It's Only a Play*, its importance can never be underestimated if only because it is the play that forged McNally's relationship with Lynne Meadow and the Manhattan Theatre Club. McNally explains in "A Few Words of Introduction": "It was during one of the previews of *It's Only a Play* that Lynne Meadow said she would produce my next play sight unseen. It was the best Christmas present any playwright ever got." The relationship between McNally and the MTC has lasted over fifteen years.

Although opera music featured heavily in many of McNally's plays (starting with *And Things That Go Bump in the Night*'s Ruby, who considers herself an opera diva), *The Lisbon Traviata* is the first play to be centered around this particular obsession. *Traviata* was also the most difficult play for McNally in all respects. Critical response prompted him to rewrite the ending, only to meet with more critical response. For all its difficulty, however, it is the play for which McNally says he holds the most affection. This is perhaps because McNally was able to explore the opera-fan part of his personality. The first act consists of two friends, Stephen and Mendy, discussing opera. Though many people in the audience will not get all the opera jokes, the first act is quite funny. It is not without serious moments, however, as the audience comes to understand that Stephen's relationship with his partner, Mike, has problems. A tense moment between the lovers is witnessed as Mike hurries away for a date with another man. Stephen's attempt to date outside their relationship fails, as he is stood up.

The second act takes place in Stephen and Mike's apartment when Stephen returns early to find Mike still asleep with his new lover, Paul. The tension in the second act is heavy. After Paul leaves, Stephen and Mike have their last fight—Mike is to live with Paul. Something has gone wrong in their relationship, but neither of them quite knows what it is. Stephen is desperate. In the first version of the play (1985), he stabs Mike with scissors to keep him from leaving—scissors Mike had used to cut up the last pictures of them when they were happy. Critics denounced the operatic ending. When the play appeared again in 1989, Stephen brandished the scissors, but Mike left unharmed.

Sam Abel's article on the play addresses the rewrites and the variety of reactions to the play from both gay and straight audiences. Many members of the gay audience felt that McNally was exploiting gay stereotypes. Abel reminds us that the play does not give its audience a monolithic view of gay men. Rather, McNally is seen as investigating an idea that he will revisit in *Love! Valour! Compassion!*—that of the generation gap in the homosexual community. More specifically, men raised in eras past have a greater tendency toward self-loathing, whereas the younger generation benefits from being raised in a society that is more accepting. They are the inheritors of hard-won hope.

Critics across the board were displeased by the dissimilarity in tone between the two acts. The rewrite did not solve this problem. McNally addresses these concerns in his introduction: "It is clearly not a well-made play in which the first act prepares us for everything that happens in the second. Yesterday did not prepare me for what happened today. Life is a lousy playwright that way. I was merely trying to reflect that in *The Lisbon Traviata*." While often not prepared for what happens, we can often recognize things in hindsight. Stephen's stabbing of Mike is foreshadowed when Mendy playfully stabs Stephen while acting out the end of *Carmen*. *Carmen* becomes an allegory for Stephen and Mike's relationship in the first act. Mendy notes, "If he's with someone else, it sounds like the first act of *Carmen* is turning into the last." In retrospect he is perfectly right.

Stephen's melodramatic act seems unsurprising when one considers that the main theme of this play is obsession. Stephen and Mendy are both obsessed with opera, and more specifically, with Maria Callas. Mendy is uncompromising in his affection for Callas. Stephen, however, is able to see Callas' flaws. What he cannot see are the flaws in his relationship; Mike is his

Callas. As McNally says, "I don't think we live in a very romantic age, but Stephen is a romantic character, and it is romantic characters who are driven to acts of violence" (quoted in John L. DiGaetani, "Terrence McNally"). Ultimately, Stephen lives in an opera world and Mike does not belong there.

Whereas *The Lisbon Traviata* is about the end of a relationship, *Frankie and Johnny in the Clair de Lune* is about the beginning of one. The character Johnny best sums up the plot of this 1987 play: "There's a man and a woman. Not young, not old. No great beauties, either one. . . . They meet but they don't connect." This is not, however, a typical boy-meets-girl story. McNally explores the difficulty that working-class, middle-aged people have in making a start. Unlike young lovers, they have histories, memories, and scars. Throughout most of the play Frankie keeps bringing up "the million reasons not to love." Johnny is persistent: "I said I was passionate. I don't let go of old things easy and I grab new things hard." As McNally says of the play in his introduction to the Plume edition: "The unattainable is pursued at great length and at great risk."

The play opens with a dark stage and a couple of minutes of the sound of lovemaking. We have entered at a time of connection. Almost immediately afterward, Frankie starts to push Johnny away. Somehow he manages to stay, although his passion and intensity put her off. We learn about their childhoods, their adult misfortunes, and their dreams. We learn about the failings of their bodies—Johnny's allergies, Frankie's inverted nipples. We also learn about the self-inflicted scars on Johnny's hands and the scar on Frankie's face that an ex-lover put there. Johnny experiences momentary impotence. Frankie confesses that she cannot have children because of the scars her ex-lover left.

The play takes place in the hours before dawn. The couple fights, makes love, eats, and dances. Claude Debussy's "Clair de Lune" becomes a major player. When Johnny calls the radio station to check the title of the music Frankie had admired ("The Goldberg Variations"), he asks the disc jockey to play "the most beautiful music ever written." Thus "Clair de Lune" is played at the close of act 1 as they are about to attempt to make love a second time. The disc jockey gives an encore, dedicated to Frankie and Johnny, at the close of act 2 as they watch the sunrise and brush their teeth together.

When *Frankie and Johnny* opened in 1987, some critics tried to label it as "gay," arguing that the characters must be allegorical for a gay couple because both the names are male. Frankie might well be speaking to them when she says, "You put too much stock in this name business, John." McNally responds, "No, *Frankie and Johnny* examines intimacy and what people who are over forty do about having a relationship" (quoted in Jackson R. Bryer, "Terrence McNally"). This play is the first play that is centered on the idea of connecting, which will become McNally's dominating theme. Johnny is as overt in his desire to connect as Frankie is in her attempts to refuse:

> JOHNNY: I want you to notice how we're connecting. My hand is flowing into yours. My eyes are trying to see inside yours.
> FRANKIE: That's not connecting. That's holding and staring. Connecting is when the other person isn't even around and you could die from just thinking of them.
> JOHNNY: That's missing. This is connecting.

Frankie is understandably cautious. The apartments around her are filled with frightening relationships—the neighbors who do not talk to each other, the other neighbors who engage in domestic abuse. When she finally seems to let go, to let the "wall of disparity" break down, the audience understands that this night has required great courage from them both.

Prelude and Liebestod (1989) was McNally's first attempt to dramatize the world of the opera rather than the world of its fans. The play opens as an opera is about to begin. After the music starts, we are given insight into the mind of the conductor, happy with the reception from the audience, save his wife, who is reading. We are then treated to the internal monologues of all of the various characters who share their fears and desires as the music plays. The conductor confesses: "The only satisfying sexual experience I ever had was with a man. . . . The kind of sexual experience this music is about." As in *The Lisbon Traviata*, the audience is reminded that plays about opera have operatic endings. The conductor, who feels he has not connected with another human since a sexual experience he had when he was twenty-two, stabs himself with a seppuku blade.

Terrence McNally has said that *Lips Together, Teeth Apart* is his most operatic play. It is also the one he considers his best. The play, which opened at the Manhattan Theatre Club on May 28, 1991, is indeed masterful. The action takes place on the Fourth of July at a beach house on Fire Island, complete with an onstage pool. The three acts are set in the morning, afternoon, and night. Sally Truman has inherited the beach house from her brother, who recently died of AIDS. She and her husband, Sam, have come to the island to decide what they should do with the house. Sam's sister, Chloe Haddock, and her husband, John, accompany them. In *Frankie and Johnny* one couple was struggling to connect; in *Lips* two couples struggle to connect; accordingly, the problem of alienation is magnified. The characters' frequent soliloquies not only give voice to inner thoughts but also demonstrate the fundamental problem the characters have—they do not hear each other.

Sally and John have had an affair. Their spouses know it, and the tension is high. Several other factors complicate the scene: In the beginning of the play, Sally sees a young man go into the ocean. She worries over him until he is washed up, drowned, at the end of act 2. Sally feels that she should give the house to her brother's widower; aside from her mourning, she is living with the secret that she aided her brother in his death. Additionally, she is pregnant yet reluctant to tell her husband because of her previous miscarriages. John wants to continue his relationship with Sally, despite her rebukes. He has been diagnosed with cancer and attempts to keep it from Sally and Sam throughout most of the play. Chloe and Sam must contend with their knowledge of the affair. Sam does so through hostility. He and John eventually get into a "deadly serious" physical altercation that ends only after John almost breaks Sam's arm. Chloe, also coping with her husband's illness, constantly attempts to distract herself from the situations at hand: "I talk too much, probably because it's too horrible to think about what's really going on."

The day is also fraught with more subtle conflicts. Sally is representative of feminism when Chloe apologizes for using exclusionary language in front of her. Sally explains to John why she married Sam: "I don't want to be married to a man who thinks he can control his wife. Or wants to. Or needs to." Sam sees himself as a victim of John's classism although Sam and John are linked together in their racist remarks. The greatest source of anxiety, however, is heterosexism. The critic John M. Clum calls this play "the American theater's most probing satire on homophobia." Sam and John are clearly uncomfortable in gay paradise. While Chloe and Sally do not use pejoratives when discussing the neighbors, they nevertheless reveal their own prejudices. Much of the characters' discomfort centers around the swimming pool. Although the characters constantly talk about getting into the water, they do not. Sally verbalizes the reason why: "We all think it's infected. We all think it's polluted. We all think we'll get AIDS and die if we go in. . . .

One drop of water in your mouth or on an open sore and we'll be infected with my brother and his black lover and God knows who else was in here."

Despite all the problems, the third act allows for some cathartic moments as the characters confront their fears and each other. Sally splashes the pool water on John and, after drinking it, kisses Sam. John then spits the water into Chloe's face: "Now we're all infected." Later, John's cancer is revealed. Sam and Sally discuss the possibility of having a gay child.

Some critics have questioned McNally's decision to have the gay neighbors as offstage presences. McNally responds: "I thought it was very *theatrical* of me not to have the gay men onstage—I could've put them on so easily—and then to read that the play is homophobic, when the gays are reduced to offstage characters, it *completely* misses the point of what I was trying to do" (quoted in Drukman). The neighbors are a dynamic part of the play. There is steady interaction between them and the couples as they yell to each other across the decks. The characters see them dancing, swimming, and loving. Sam describes in a soliloquy an act of lovemaking he observes. This momentary visage allows him to universalize lovemaking beyond his heterosexual experience. The neighbors donate American flags for the couples to wave as the patriotic fireworks go off. The play is heavily infused with music (McNally chose specific pieces); the music comes from the decks of the neighbors. The notable exception is Chloe's tape of bad piano accompaniment to her dance routine. This is one of many ways in which McNally shows the lives of the gay neighbors as more amenable than those of the distracted, distanced couples. As the scholar Benilde Montgomery says, "We know, among other things, and significantly in contrast to what we observe of the others, that the gay community is open and welcoming; that they dance; that they make love; that they are attractive and wealthy; that they are comfortable with their bodies."

Light and darkness are also strong themes in the play. The pool so recently belonging to a dying man is the main source of light in the last act. The other light source is a bug lamp. The last act is punctuated by the zapping of insects. The fireworks go off near the end of the play as the couples make their last confessions and a sort of peace with each other. The characters are then frozen as they observe a shooting star—the light reflected from a burning, dying meteor. The last image is of people who are trying to celebrate, to live, although surrounded by reminders of death—a drowned swimmer, a dead brother, miscarried children, a dying man. Perhaps the star is a sign that Sally's earlier prayer has been heard: "God, every single day for the rest of my life, with your help, I want to renew my membership in the human race. Amen. Thank you."

A Perfect Ganesh was first produced at the Manhattan Theatre Club on June 4, 1993. It is McNally's least realistic and most metaphysical play. In many ways *Ganesh* may be seen as harking back to the experimental expressionism that filled the theater decades earlier. Rather than being a mere throwback, *Ganesh* is expressionistic, as it is mythological in both scope and theme. That is, McNally shows us a journey through India and a journey through two souls. The play follows Margaret Civil and Katharine Brynne as they travel in India. The work has dream sequences, but they are waking dreams; they are the fulfillment of the characters' desires. The audience is guided by the god Ganesha, who is aided by Man. They both play many parts.

Katharine is a warm, if brash, woman. She has two goals in India—to kiss a leper and to find the perfect Ganesh (also called Ganesha) figurine. Both of these goals represent finding the part of herself that can love unconditionally.

She feels the need to do this because she failed her son in this respect; she was unable to love him until he died. Notably, he was a victim of homophobic violence. Margaret is more concerned with appearances and more closed than Katharine. She also needs to heal but only confides her fears about a breast lump to Katharine near the end of the play. She never tells Katharine that she, too, has lost a son.

The play confronts many modern -isms—racism, sexism, heterosexism, and classism. The heroines are not immune to any of these -isms. Their journey does not magically free them from the trappings of their prejudices, yet they do become more aware of these feelings and of the consequences of failing to love others. Katharine's homophobia, for example, makes her complicit in her son's death. Katharine is trying to correct this as she strives to be better: "I choose to be happy. I choose to be loving. I choose to be good." Katharine is not able to kiss a leper, but she and Margaret are able to find solace in the perfect Ganesh they receive from two AIDS-stricken men at the end.

Like most of McNally's plays, this piece is ultimately about connecting. Katharine wants to connect to her lost son (as does Margaret). Indeed, their sons are mirrored in that they both died from a crushed skull. Margaret feels disconnected from her husband, who is engaged in a long-term affair. But this play centers on the women's ability to connect to each other. They spend a lot of dialogue questioning their own relationship. McNally also illustrates their disconnect in staging: "*A bolt of blue fabric is rolled across the white floor of the stage. It is a river. KATHARINE and MARGARET will find themselves on different sides of it.*"

Ganesha embodies the McNally theme that humans are all divine, that divinity is everywhere: "I am in your kiss. I am in your cancer." The audience and the characters are implored to recognize "these two little, insignificant, magnificent lives." Only by accepting the transcendental ideal of divinity will characters be able to come together. In the penultimate scene of the play Katharine gives Margaret a Ganesh. Margaret compliments Katharine for the first time in the play: "You're a kind woman." And then, they connect: "*They just look at each other a moment. It would be hard to say who opens her arms to the other first. They embrace. They kiss.*"

Following closely on the heels of *Ganesh*, the acclaimed *Love! Valour! Compassion!* premiered at the MTC on November 1, 1994. It was quickly transferred to Broadway, where it opened on January 20, 1995, and it won the Tony award for best play in the same year. The action takes place at Gregory's country house over three summer holiday weekends (one for each act). The other characters are Gregory's friends—his partner, Bobby; the married couple, Perry and Arthur; Buzz, the musical theater fan; John Jeckyll and his young lover, Ramon; and later in the play, James, John's twin brother. The play chronicles how these men love, live, get along, and do not get along. Even in the idyllic setting, there are problems. Gregory is a dancer/choreographer whose body no longer allows him to dance his own creations. Additionally, he has a stutter. Bobby is blind and therefore unable to see his lover's dances. Perry and Arthur celebrate their fourteenth anniversary over one of the weekends—they struggle, as all couples do, with getting older, with subtle changes in their relationship. Buzz and James both have AIDS. Various conflicts arise throughout the summer: Ramon seduces Bobby for a tryst. Bobby's sister dies in a freak accident. Yet the most difficult task for the men seems to be putting up with John. It is made clear early in the play that no one particularly likes him, but when compared with his brother, his callous nature is glaringly obvious.

Much of what is learned about the characters' histories is given to us through asides. McNally updates the convention by making the asides more interactive between characters: sometimes other characters hear the speeches and comment on them so that the asides become a group effort. The most striking direct audience addresses come very near the end of the play. The men gather together, arms intertwined, to rehearse "Dance of the Swans" for an AIDS benefit, complete with white tutus. One by one, the men step out to tell us how they will die. But Bobby cannot see his death. Gregory offers to tell him, but Bobby does not want to know. The motif of blindness, so powerful throughout the play, is physically extended to the other characters after the death monologues when the power goes out. Candlelight illuminates the rest of the play.

This piece is, of course, mainly about connection. One of the complicating factors is a theme McNally explores earlier in *The Lisbon Traviata*—generational conflict and difference. Ramon and Bobby are both in their early twenties, while the rest of the men are in their thirties and forties. Ramon and Bobby's bodies are continual reminders of the aging bodies of the other characters. Gregory is aware in his end monologue that Bobby will leave him eventually because of age. Although Gregory resents Ramon for interfering in his relationship with Bobby, he asks Ramon to dance his new project. He fulfills Ramon's dream and passes the torch at the same time. McNally also shows what the next generation will have to offer. Ramon becomes the voice of self-love, the antithesis of the self-hating gay man. He reminds the others, "We don't love one another because we don't love ourselves."

As the title indicates, love is the most dominant theme in the play. The characters, and therefore the audience members, are encouraged to love each other and themselves. The theme of the negative consequences for failing to do so carries over from *A Perfect Ganesh*. Arthur seems to channel Ganesha when he notes about pejoratives: "We hurt ourselves when we use them. We're all diminished." The absence of love is embodied in the aptly named John Jeckyll. Although James is quickly wasting away, he is still able to find love with Buzz. John knows he will die alone and will not be mourned. The audience is to understand that he is by far the sickest person in the play. As he tells his dying brother, "I resent everything about you. You had Mum and Dad's unconditional love and now you have the world's. . . . You got the good soul. I got the bad one. Think about leaving me yours."

While most critics praised the play, some said the play was just an excuse to show nude male bodies. This surely says more about the critics than about the plays. There is indeed nudity in the production—the men are fond of skinny-dipping in the lake outside the house. And the audience gets to see all the bodies celebrated—not just the pretty ones. We are encouraged to love Buzz's love handles so that we may better love Buzz, especially as we know that Buzz will not be around for long. Death hangs over the play. Glimpses of it hinder the men's joy, just as the rain that comes every holiday weekend hinders their outdoor fun. The play makes clear that the rain will eventually fall on everyone. The young Ramon will die in a plane crash. Bobby's sister's death is a startling reminder about the universality of the human condition. Although the characters are all gay men, McNally wants his audience to see beyond that: "The most common comment I get is that by the end of act 1 the person has forgotten that the play is about gay men, and just thinks about them as human beings they can identify with—and I take that as a compliment" (quoted in Toby Silverman Zinman, "The Muses of Terrence McNally").

The play *Master Class* (1996) was McNally's chance to write about his beloved opera diva, Maria Callas, the absent costar of *The Lisbon Traviata*. The play is a fictionalized rendering of the famous master classes Callas taught at Juilliard at the end of her career. Callas demonstrates that she is every bit the diva as she berates her three "victims" who have come for instruction. Through her lapses into memory, however, we see the woman who has suffered so much to come so far. Callas' voice is broken. The effect of this tragedy is evident when recordings of her work fill the stage. Although certainly about Callas, the play is also an exploration of teaching and art. *Master Class* won the Tony for best play in 1996.

In remembering the horrendous reviews he received for *And Things That Go Bump in the Night,* McNally once quipped to Jackson R. Bryer, "They haven't called for my actual death since the first play." This statement remained true until *Corpus Christi,* McNally's 1998 play. The plan to produce the play resulted in numerous threats from Christian groups. Additionally, the National Security Movement of America threatened McNally's life and warned the Manhattan Theatre Club that if the play were to go on, the theater would be burned and all staff executed. For the first time the Manhattan Theatre Club backed away from the playwright who made them what they are, postponing the play because of potential violence. Other playwrights immediately came to McNally's defense. Some, such as Athol Fugard, withdrew their plays from the MTC until *Corpus* was put back on the schedule. The opposing groups' victory was therefore short-lived and *Corpus Christi* premiered on September 22, 1998 (it opened for its full run on October 13), only a few months behind schedule. Upon the opening of the play in London in 1999, a British Muslim group issued a fatwa against McNally. Should he venture to a Muslim state, he may be arrested and summarily executed.

Corpus Christi is a modern passion play. It is, according to McNally's preface to the Grove edition of the play, "The life of Joshua, a young man from south Texas . . . told in the theatrical tradition of medieval morality plays." McNally grew up in Corpus Christi, Texas. His childhood and Joshua's took place at roughly the same time, the 1950s. Some critics have pointed out that this play may be McNally revisiting his youth—the picture of a young gay man in the Bible Belt of America. While this is one way to read the play, it is incomplete, for Joshua is obviously not McNally. It is in fact his resemblance to Christ, whose story is the one most often told in the "theatrical tradition of medieval morality plays," that caused controversy. There is just enough resemblance to Christ to make Joshua's sexuality offensive to many Christians and Muslims.

The play begins with the actors changing into costume and being christened by John as their characters. Through direct addresses the audience is introduced to the characters and to the few props that will be used on the blank stage. These addresses also serve to set the tone for the play—this is a serious subject, but McNally's comic voice has not been excised. When these preliminaries are taken care of, Joshua is born in a motel room. Joseph vetoes the name Jesus because it "sounds like a Mexican," and this would be dangerous in the climate of south Texas. Joshua learns from God that he will teach the world a secret: "All men are divine." Major moments of the Christ story are mirrored one by one. For example, Joshua presiding over the marriage of two of his disciples replaces Christ's blasphemy of healing on the Sabbath day. The story, as the actors have promised, unfolds predictably. Joshua heals, is betrayed, and is killed for being "queer." In this version of the passion story, Joshua is mocked as being "King of the Queers." One of the last lines, directed to the audience, is "If we have offended, so be it."

That this passion play was not meant to represent the life of the historical Christ is, to many observers, self-evident considering the setting. Yet the mirroring cannot but make the audience think of Christ throughout the production. This play, more than any other, has a very clear social message—McNally's overriding theme that we are all divine and deserving of love. Yet overtly didactic social theater usually calls for something other than traditional realism. Hence, the play is McNally's most Brechtian. According to the stage directions, all of the actors are continually on the stage, on benches in the back when not performing: "While seated, the actors observe the scene in progress and may even comment on it, either to the actors in the scene, among themselves, or to the audience." The spectators observe the actors change from street clothes in to the "*'uniform' of the play: white shirt, khaki trousers, and bare feet.*" When the actors address the audience about their characters, they do so in third person. The actor playing Thomas encourages the members of the audience to suspend their disbelief. Yet this address undermines their ability to do so. Instead, it invites the audience to consider the consequences of suspending their disbelief. Bertolt Brecht's goal was to make the theatricality of theater more visible. That is, he drew the audience's attention to the techniques of creating the spectacle in order to distance it from the action on the stage. This, Brecht hoped, would encourage the audience members to think critically about what they were seeing. Additionally, he wanted them to be able to see connections from the histories he presented to their own time so that they might be able to keep history from repeating itself.

Although he says in the preface, "I'm a playwright, not a theologian," McNally, who was educated by nuns and exposed to Catholicism, knows what purpose a morality play serves. A morality play is to be repeated throughout time so humans do not forget why Jesus died. This play warns that people should not crucify one another for their differences, sexual differences in particular. McNally was, as usual, a step ahead of the world around him. Before McNally's message could be heeded, a young gay man was literally crucified. In his preface McNally says, "At the same time [the play] asks you to look at what they did to Joshua, it asks that we look at what they did one cold October night to a young man in Wyoming as well. Jesus Christ died again when Matthew Shepard did." *Corpus Christi* may be read as a play similar to *The Crucible*. Both works tell a familiar story about historical figures who were wrongly executed. Both serve as a warning to the contemporary society.

OTHER WRITINGS

Andre's Mother (1988) is a short play set at a funeral. The four characters each release a balloon after they have said their good-byes to Andre. The play is the first of McNally's to deal specifically with an AIDS-related death. When Cal and Andre's mother are left at the graveside, Cal tells Andre's mother about his relationship with Andre and about Andre's death. He explains why Andre hid both his sexuality and his illness from her: "The only thing that frightened him was you." *Andre's Mother* was converted for television in 1990 and won an Emmy for best writing.

McNally's theatrical successes prompted Hollywood interest. McNally wrote all the screenplays for the films based on his works. *The Ritz* was made into a movie in 1976, *Frankie and Johnny* in 1991, and *Love! Valour! Compassion!* in 1997. Critics complain that his films are not as edgy as his plays. They blame this on Hollywood's desire for mainstream appeal. While the script for *Love!* does not differ very much from its play version, *Frankie and Johnny* is quite different from *Frankie and Johnny in the Clair de Lune*. McNally says that he approaches his screenplays as if he is writing something new, not just reworking play scripts. In the case of *Frankie and Johnny* he rightly surmised that the cramped setting of the play would not work on screen. The movie version takes place over months rather than one night, and many more characters appear. McNally's goal in writing the screenplay versions of his plays is to capture the essence of the pieces, not to stay true to his original scripts. McNally is rare in that he has not been wooed away from the theater by the glamour of Hollywood. The actress Zoe Caldwell, in Toby Silverman Zinman's interview, praises McNally: "Terrence has never abandoned the theatre as so many playwrights have."

In 1984 McNally began experimenting with musicals. His first attempt was the book for *The Rink,* which was followed by the highly acclaimed book for *Kiss of the Spider Woman* in 1992. His book for *Ragtime* (1997) was also well received. *Kiss* and *Ragtime* both won Tonys for best book. He wrote the book for the musical *The Full Monty* in 2000 and for *The Visit in 2001.* He also went back on his longtime refusal to try his hand at writing an opera of his own with his libretto for the opera version of *Dead Man Walking,* produced by the San Francisco Opera. In 2002 McNally was said to be working on a biography of Tennessee Williams and the screenplay for *A Perfect Ganesh.*

THE WRITING PROCESS

McNally is unique in his writing process. He notes that other playwrights start with ideas while he begins with characters. Once he has his characters, McNally plays with them by putting them in situations to see what they will do. His frequent trips to the theater enable him to scope out actors, designers, and directors with whom he hopes to work as well as those gifted people who have the capacity to be "McNally actors." McNally actors are those who have faith in McNally's words (they should not add a breath) but also a spirit of open collaboration. He often has a specific actor in mind for his characters and hears their delivery as he is writing. Many of the theater minds with whom he has collaborated have gone on to great success, most notably Kathy Bates and Nathan Lane.

As the former vice president of Dramatists Guild Council, McNally is passionately dedicated to nurturing young playwrights and working to get the youth of America into the theaters. He frequently teaches playwriting at Juilliard with John Guare. The theater is, for him, a community: he says in his article "What I Know about Being a Playwright," "We are all in this together—young and old, man and woman—and the more we help and support each other, the stronger we all are, and so is the theatre." McNally believes that the theater is worth fighting for and argues with those who say the theater is dying. In "Some Thoughts," a preface to *Love! Valour! Compassion!* he notes: "The American theater has never been healthier. It's Broadway that's sick. The American theater is no longer Broadway. It is Los Angeles, it is Seattle, it is Louisville, it is everywhere but the west side of midtown Manhattan."

McNally's devotion to the arts is not limited to the theater, however. He is adamant in his commitment to his beloved opera:

> There are too many young people too ready to listen only to contemporary pop music which makes no demands on their minds or hearts other than the quickest kind of gratification. . . . We have to give our best all the time. Every single night. A production of *Carmen* should be a matter of life and death. Every *Butterfly* may be our last one. . . . The stakes are that high. We have to prove over and over again that opera is relevant to the way we live (quoted in Marc A. Scorca, "The Three Balances").

MAJOR THEMES

In "The Muses of Terrence McNally" Zinman notes that McNally's late plays have a strong commonality: "The most recent plays . . . are celebrations of love between people in the face of emotional danger—damaged, neurotic people whose capacity to love is almost always increased in the course of the drama." Zinman explains that we arrive at the theme of connection through his use of two other motifs: "If music is for McNally a redemptive, life-giving force, death is always the fact, the point of a play's departure—that which makes not only the action of the play but the writing of the play necessary." Music's importance is most evident in his musicals and librettos, but music becomes a character even in his plays. The most obvious examples are in *The Lisbon Traviata* and *Master Class* as opera features so prominently in them. Yet almost every play is dependent on music. Even in his first, *And Things That Go Bump in the Night*, McNally chose specific pieces of music to achieve his purpose. What would Frankie and Johnny have done without the "Clair de Lune"? Critics most often cite the opening stage directions to *Lips Together, Teeth Apart* when discussing McNally's use of music—as if he is conducting his characters rather than writing them:

Music begins: the farewell trio from Mozart's Così fan tutte. *As the trio progresses, the stage and the actors will slowly come to "life."*

The first movement will be the gentle stirrings of an ornamental flag in the early-morning breeze.

Then SALLY will begin to paint, CHLOE to drink coffee in the kitchen, JOHN to turn the pages of his New York Times, *SAM to retrieve the chlorine indicator—but all in time to the music, not reaching naturalistic behavior until the end of the piece. By the time the trio ends, we will be in "real" time.*

Although his critics often speak of his use of music, they seem less concerned with his use of dance. Yet dancing also features heavily in his plays. In fact, various characters quote the line "Shut up and dance" from *Gypsy* in three of his plays: *Lips Together, Teeth Apart; A Perfect Ganesh;* and *Love! Valour! Compassion!* After all, McNally is not just an opera fan. He is found often at the ballet. McNally says of dance, "Sometimes dance and music make me feel inarticulate. Dance is the most beautiful expression of sensual love; in theatre, that's the hardest thing to convey" (quoted in Zinman, "Muses"). Not only does dance allow McNally to represent love between characters, sometimes it represents love itself. Dance allows the characters to connect, however briefly, in *Lips Together, Teeth Apart*. Katharine gets to dance with her dead son in a dream sequence in *A Perfect Ganesh*. Margaret also dances with him, expressing her desires for her own lost boy. When the men in *Love!* dance, they are expressing the joy found in the human form and therefore the joy that can be found in all of us.

If music and dance express the life force, they do so in the strong shadow of death. AIDS lingers in the background of all the later works, just as the vision of Vietnam was present in his early plays. Many critics of McNally's plays are concerned solely with the gay male body and the issues for which it is specifically coded, such as the assumption that it is vulnerable to HIV. For example, when David Román argues that *Kiss of the Spider Woman, the Musical* is an AIDS allegory, a main part of his evidence is simply that McNally is the author. Román further postulates, "It is no longer possible to stage a gay representation without invoking the experience of AIDS. . . . And the context of AIDS now informs all productions of gay male representation regardless of the actual content of the representation."

Yet AIDS is not the only agent of sickness or death. Most of McNally's characters have some sort of physical ailment. One recurring theme in the plays is the characters' acceptance of the failings of their own bodies and the bodies of others. McNally's audience learns that the former is necessary for the latter and that both are as necessary as they are difficult. McNally's obsession with the body on the road to death is ultimately about finding the beauty in life—something which is, of course, only possible through the fallible body. In speaking of death,

McNally says, "I think I was once more frightened of it than I am now. I don't see death now as punitive. In the early plays it's more terrible, the worst thing that can happen to you; now it's part of the process of being alive" (quoted in Zinman, *Terrence McNally: A Casebook*).

McNally shows his audience failing bodies that demand compassion to encourage reconciliation between the body and its owner. Though this aim could be accomplished by showing only one kind of body (a gay one) with one kind of illness (HIV/AIDS), McNally confronts us with a variety of bodies with a striking variety of ailments. As John says in *Lips*: "Not everyone is dying from AIDS, Sally. There are other malevolent forces at work on God's miraculous planet." Additionally, death comes in accidents. *Love! Valour! Compassion!*'s Bobby loses his sister to an ill-fated carnival ride. *A Perfect Ganesh*'s Katharine loses her husband in a car crash while she is away. Death also comes from deliberate acts of violence. Katharine confesses that she spent years dreading the phone call in which her son would tell her he had AIDS. Instead, she received a phone call because homophobic men beat him to death.

These varied representations of death can be explained by considering McNally's desire to make his plays inclusive—to write not as a "gay playwright," despite criticism from the gay press: "I don't think there's gay theatre anymore. . . . A gay play has to be not as good as a 'straight play' but as good as a play should be" (quoted in Savran, *The Playwright's Voice*). McNally explains the nudity in *Love! Valour! Compassion!* to the audience: "I'm saying these people have dicks—just like you—some of them have flabby asses and some don't—just like you." John M. Clum comments on how McNally can critique homophobia and still have universal appeal: "McNally's alternation of plays about homosexuals and heterosexuals shows that poverty of the spirit, lack of compassion, are human traits, which in heterosexuals are most dramatically seen in their hatred or fear of homosexuals."

When looking over his corpus, one is struck with the idea of inclusiveness. Surely that is what McNally wants to teach—to love one another. In play after play he shows the consequences of refusing to connect with one another. Katharine's son complains, "She should have loved me not just for falling down and scraping my knee when I was a little boy but for standing tall when I was a young man and telling her I loved other men." Love is the great healer. Gregory's stutter disappears whenever he is alone and at peace with his lover. Katharine discovers love's potential as she seeks to rectify her life:

> KATHARINE: Why are you diseased and hideous? What can I do to change that?
> MAN: Love me.

The potential power of love is made manifest in *Corpus Christi* when Joshua heals his fellow man through love, through the acceptance of others despite their various "sins." Just as McNally seeks to reconcile the mind with the body through whatever form of unconditional love as can be humanly achieved, he seeks to bring together gay and mainstream theater, rejecting Cartesian models of a binary system of thought which would seek to rip apart the body and mind, the power of theater, and the community of people that inhabit his audience.

Terrence McNally goes to the theater at least three nights a week (the other nights are for opera and the ballet). He believes in the vitality and life of the theater in an age when the majority of the American public ignores theater. His works are part of the reason why the rest of us can keep believing. Perhaps people do not picket anymore when a play should be seen, like they did for McNally's first play. If America were populated with people who were willing to demonstrate for great theater, McNally's plays would give them something to picket for.

Selected Bibliography

WORKS OF TERRENCE McNALLY

PLAYS

Apple Pie: Three One Act Plays. New York: Dramatists Play Service, 1968. (Contains *Tour; Next; Botticelli.*)

Three Plays by Terrence McNally. New York: Plume, 1990. (Contains *The Lisbon Traviata, Frankie and Johnny in the Clair de Lune, It's Only a Play,* and "A Few Words of Introduction.")

Lips Together, Teeth Apart. New York: Plume, 1992.

Terrence McNally: 15 Short Plays. Lyme, N.H.: Smith and Kraus, 1994. (Contains *Bringing It All Back Home; Noon; Botticelli; Next; ¡Cuba Si!; Sweet Eros; Witness; Whiskey; Bad Habits; The Ritz; Prelude & Liebestod; Andre's Mother; The Wibbly, Wobbly, Wiggly Dance That Cleopatterer Did; Street Talk; Hidden Agendas,* and a preface by McNally.)

Love! Valour! Compassion! and A Perfect Ganesh: Two Plays. New York: Plume, 1995. (Includes "Some Notes" by McNally.)

Master Class. New York: Plume, 1995.

Terrence McNally: Collected Plays. Lyme, N.H.: Smith and Kraus, 1996. (Contains *And Things That Go Bump in the Night* and *Where Has Tommy Flowers Gone?*)

Corpus Christi: A Play. New York: Grove, 1998. (Includes a preface by McNally.)

SCREENPLAYS

The Ritz. Directed by Richard Lester. Warner, 1976.

Frankie and Johnny. Directed by Garry Marshall. Paramount, 1991.

Love! Valour! Compassion! Directed by Joe Mantello. Krost/Chapin, 1997.

OTHER WORKS

The Rink (book for the musical). Music by John Kander; lyrics by Fred Ebb. New York: French's Musical Library, 1985.

Kiss of the Spider Woman (book for the musical). Music by John Kander, lyrics by Fred Ebb. New York: Fiddleback Music Publishing Co./Kander & Ebb, Inc., 1993.

"What I Know about Being a Playwright." *American Theatre* 15, no. 9:25–26 (November 1998).

CRITICAL AND BIOGRAPHICAL STUDIES

Abel, Sam. "Uneasy Transitions: Reassessing *The Lisbon Traviata* and Its Critics." In *Terrence McNally: A Casebook.* Edited by Toby Silverman Zinman. Pp. 37–54.

Clum, John M. "Where We Are Now: *Love! Valour! Compassion!* and Contemporary Gay Drama. *Terrence McNally: A Casebook.* Edited by Toby Silverman Zinman. Pp. 95–116.

Guare, John. Introduction to *15 Short Plays.* Lyme, N.H.: Smith and Kraus, 1994. P. ix.

Montgomery, Benilde. "*Lips Together, Teeth Apart:* Another Version of Pastoral." *Modern Drama* 36, no. 4:547–555 (December 1993).

Román, David, and Alberto Sandoval. "Caught in the Web: Latinidad, AIDS, and Allegory in *Kiss of the Spider Woman, the Musical.*" *American Literature* 67, no. 3:553–585 (September 1995).

Scorca, Marc A. "The Three Balances." *Opera America* (http://www.operaam.org/3balla.htm), 1999.

Straub, Deborah A. "McNally, Terrence." In *Contemporary Authors, New Revision Series.* Vol. 2. Detroit: Gale, 1962–1981. Pp. 457–458.

Zinman, Toby Silverman. "The Muses of Terrence McNally." *American Theatre* 12, no. 3:12–17 (March 1995).

———, ed. *Terrence McNally: A Casebook.* New York: Garland, 1997. (See, especially, her "Interview with Zoe Caldwell," pp. 151–156.)

INTERVIEWS

Bryer, Jackson R. "Terrence McNally." In his *The Playwright's Art: Conversations with Contemporary American Dramatists.* New Brunswick, N.J.: Rutgers University Press, 1995. Pp. 182–204.

DiGaetani, John L. "Terrence McNally." In his *A Search for a Postmodern Theater: Interviews with Contemporary Playwrights.* New York: Greenwood, 1991. Pp. 219–228.

Drukman, Steven. "Terrence McNally." In *Speaking on Stage: Interviews with Contemporary American Playwrights.* Edited by Philip C. Kolin and Colby H. Kullman. Tuscaloosa: University of Alabama Press, 1996. Pp. 332–345.

Savran, David. *The Playwright's Voice: American Dramatists on Memory, Writing, and the Politics of Culture.* New York: Theatre Communications Group, 1990.

—KARMA WALTONEN

Pat Mora

1942–

Patricia Estella Mora is a highly anthologized Mexican American writer whose prizes include the Premio Aztlán (1997), founded by Chicano writer Rudolfo Anaya and his wife, Patricia, and four Southwest Book Awards given by the Border Regional Library Association. Mora's birthplace and ancestry are keys to understanding her prolific work as a poet, memoirist, children's writer, and essayist. She was born on July 19, 1942, in El Paso, Texas, to Raúl Antonio Mora and Estela (Delgado) Mora. More than half of the population of El Paso is Spanish-speaking, and Mora is a strong activist on behalf of bilingualism and literacy for non-English speaking children, through her own work and through the annual Día de los niños/Día de los libros (Day of Children/Day of Books) festival she founded in 1997. The Chihuahuan desert surrounds El Paso and forms the setting for many of her poems as well as for her memoir, *House of Houses* (1997). Place and her Mexican ancestry are at the heart of Mora's work, but Nicolás Kanellos, whose Arte Público Press publishes many of Mora's books, rightly points out that the uniting metaphor in her writing is the concept of borders. Her second poetry collection was called *Borders,* and her 1993 essay collection, *Nepantla: Essays from the Land in the Middle,* uses the term *nepantla,* an indigenous Mexican term (from the Nahuatl) for "place in the middle," to indicate that she grew up in "the land corridor bordered by the two countries which have most influenced my perception of reality." As she told interviewer Darwin L. Henderson, she had the special experience of being able to see the ancestral land of her family just by looking across the river into Mexico.

Mora's father was an optician, her mother a housewife. The story of their lives is told comprehensively in the autobiography, *House of Houses,* whose title refers both to her actual childhood home, a stone house at 704 Mesita, and to a mental construction in which all of her family, living members and dead ancestors, dwell. Mora was educated in El Paso, attending St. Patrick's School in the lower grades, then Loretto Academy, a Catholic high school for girls. She completed a Bachelor of Arts degree at what was then called Texas Western College in 1963. She married William H. Burnside in 1963 and had three children with him, William, Elizabeth, and Cecilia. The marriage ended in divorce in 1981. In 1967 she completed a master's degree in English at the same institution, now renamed the University of Texas at El Paso. Mora held jobs in the local schools during the years 1963 to 1966 and then taught English and communications at El Paso Community College from 1971 to 1978. She taught English at the University of Texas at El Paso during 1979–1981, then was employed as assistant to the vice president of academic affairs in the years 1981–1988. In 1988–1989 she served as director of the university museum and as assistant to the president. In *House of Houses* she notes the irony of her having served as an administrator at a university that her uncle, Lalo Delgado, could not afford to attend. Since 1989 she has been an independent writer and highly successful reader and lecturer. She married again, in 1984, to Vernon Lee Scarborough, an archaeologist, and she now divides her time between Cincinnati, Ohio, and Santa Fe, New Mexico.

EARLY POEMS

Mora's first book publication was a collection of poetry, *Chants,* published by Arte Público in 1984. The poems are brief, written in free verse, and dominated stylistically by parallel forms. Her early work has some problems with line breaks: they often seem arbitrary. The first six poems are about the desert, which is treated as a beneficent mother (an attitude echoed in her award-winning children's book *The Desert Is My Mother/El desierto es mi madre,* published in 1994). In the essay "Tradition and Mythology: Signatures of Landscape in Chicana Poetry," Tey Diana Rebolledo observes that for Mora the desert is always personified as a mother and teacher, and the poet presents herself as a mediator. For Southwestern writers like Mora, Rebolledo says, the desert is not a desolate wasteland but a setting that, for all its heat and aridity, is full of life. Mora's idyllic view of the nurturing role of the desert has affinities with the sensibility of William Wordsworth, a similarity that will be apparent to any reader who concedes that nature poetry need not be set in the English Lake Country or the lush Wye River Valley above Tintern Abbey.

Human society, by contrast, is not idyllic in *Chants.* Many of the poems deal with harsh facts of life in villages where women are victims of machismo, the social code that allows and even expects men to act in ways that are dominant and oppressive. Mora creates characters who are anxious about losing their virginity before marriage or being thought impure on their wedding nights. In the article "Conserving Natural and Cultural Diversity: The Prose and Poetry of Pat Mora," Patrick Murphy comments on the way that Mora's writing demonstrates her desire to conserve Mexican culture while at the same time she presents a critique of sexual attitudes within that culture. These poems are not set in a contemporary urban world: they could take place on either side of the border but seem as a group to take place in Mexico, for among them are poems drawing on the mythology and folklore of the indigenous peoples of that country.

Mayan and Aztec myths are re-created, like the legend of Ixtabai (a kind of evil enchantress) in "Mayan Warning," and Mora nostalgically describes the beauties of the Toltec center at Tula in "Leyenda" (legend). Among the cultural practices that Mora would conserve is the healing practice of *curanderismo,* the Mexican herbalist tradition that shades off into magic. In an essay in *Nepantla,* "Poet as *Curandera,*" Mora has suggested that such a healer can serve as a symbol of the poet's vocation. She distinguishes the figure of the witch, or *bruja,* who seeks power through sinister magical practices, from the *curandera,* who relies on an intimate knowledge of nature and traditional white magic to effect healing. In a poem in *Chants* titled "Curandera," she describes a healer who lives in a two-room house in the desert and gathers herbs, which she incorporates with dried snake or ground wild bees into her cures. The curandera listens to the stories of the townspeople who come to her, but she also "listens / to the desert, always to the desert." Rebolledo says that for writers like Mora "the curandera represents both intuition and natural knowledge. She can harness nature's secrets and is in harmony with both order and disorder." The contrasting figure, the *bruja,* uses power for evil purposes. Mora's poem, "Bruja: Witch," shows a woman casting a spell by taking a shamanistic journey through a magical union with her familiar spirit, an owl. In this form the witch terrifies an unfaithful husband by catching him in the act with his lover and laughing at him from a nearby tree. He runs back to his wife, who will pay the *bruja* three dollars. In the meantime, the witch enjoys flying till dawn, dancing among the white stars. Mora's story, "Hands," published in 1982, presents a woman who pays a *bruja* for a spell to shrink the breasts of her husband's mistress. The spell works, but the husband's loyalty remains with the mistress. The contrasting figure, the *bruja,* is often suspected of using magical powers for evil purposes, though Mora's witches seem mischievous rather than malignant.

A Mexican folk practice, the Day of the Dead, furnishes the imagery for "Love Ritual," one of the best poems in *Chants.* On November 1, All Souls Day, Mexican families build altars heaped with marigolds at home or at the cemetery. Pictures of deceased relatives are usually placed on the altar. The marigolds, which were the flowers of the dead in the ancient Mexican mythology, guide the spirits to the altar, which is ablaze with candles. The altar has an *ofrenda,* or offering, a kind of symbolic feast, which may include *pan dulce* (sweet bread) in the form of bones and skulls, along with candies, fruits, tequila, cigarettes, and other items that gave the ancestor pleasure in life. The speaker in Mora's highly sensuous poem imagines covering her doorway with marigold blossoms, placing an erotic picture of herself and her desired lover on the door, and lighting a green votive candle, all of these measures to draw the living spirit to her. A similar love poem uses the image of *mielvirgen* (literally "virgin honey"), a clarified syrup used in Mexico for sugar making, to evoke memories of the sweetness of love.

Mora's first volume has some anticipations of her later explorations of family. In a particularly touching work, "Pushing 100," she writes about the pains of old age as experienced by a spinster aunt of ninety-four, and "Family Ties" looks wryly at a grandmother who gives the narrator gifts of chalk-white uniforms, when the granddaughter herself prefers designer jeans. In "1910" she makes her first exploration of the family sagas that are so important in the memoir *House of Houses.* The poem tells the story of a woman who immigrated to El Paso to escape Pancho Villa and then is humiliated by a store owner, Upton, who insists that all Mexican customers leave their bags, shawls, and even gloves outside his store—all Mexicans being, in his mind, thieves. The woman wears her gloves and shawl the day that she walks over the ashes of his store after it burns down for unknown reasons. The same incident appears in *House of Houses.*

A pair of poems, "Illegal Alien" and "Legal Alien," look toward future work by Mora on the border theme. In "Illegal Alien," the speaker addresses her maid, who comes from across the Rio Grande. The maids—the usual term along the border—are an important element in the economy of the region, freeing the women who hire them to pursue careers. The maid is symbolically named "Socorro," meaning aid or salvation, which is appropriate because she frees the narrator from housework. But her story is a painful one: she has a husband who beats her. The speaker wants to comfort the woman, take her in her arms, as they both have Mexican blood and are both married women. But she feels inhibited and can only offer words, which the poem calls "band-aid helps." The speaker is left feeling like the alien. The companion poem explores the discomfort of someone who is American but believes herself doubly excluded. Bilingual and bicultural, this dual status leaves her feeling merely "hyphenated" rather than empowered: both Anglos and Mexicans (of Mexico) find her exotic or alien, "an American to Mexican / a Mexican to Americans." The paradoxical title, "Legal Alien," expresses the ambiguous situation of someone who is "legal" but still alien—and alienated.

Mora won the Southwest Books Award for *Chants* and won it a second time for her second volume of poetry, *Borders* (1986), published by Arte Público in 1986. Her second collection explores several kinds of borders, including boundaries between men and women. The title poem opens with a quotation from Carol Gilligan suggesting that men and women speak different languages, and then poses a question raised by the poet: "if we're so bright, / then why didn't we notice?" Mora uses the image of side-by-side translations in books (e.g., *luna* opposite "moon") to convey the gulf between the speaker and a long-time spouse or partner in their understanding of the words they speak to each other. The speaker realizes that she has been wrong to assume that words like "success" and "happiness" had the same meaning to both her and her partner. What the couple needs, she says, is a listener who can hear their words "side by side" and translate "us to us."

The opening section of *Borders* considers other borders, primarily social, ethnic, and political ones. In one poem she celebrates the life of Tomás Rivera, a Chicano novelist and university administrator who was the son of migrant workers and had struggled to obtain an education. Rivera was chief executive officer at the University of Texas at El Paso in 1978 just before Mora began working there. He eventually became chancellor of the University of California at Riverside, the first Chicano to hold such a position in an American university, and he wrote a classic of Chicano literature, *Y no se lo trago la tierra* (*And the Earth Did Not Cover Him*), a work about the misfortunes of migrant workers. (In 1997 Mora published a prize-winning children's book about Rivera, *Tomás and the Library Lady,* that tells the tale of his discovery of books.) Mora's poem is perhaps too reverential in tone, but it celebrates a genuine culture-hero,

> the boy from Crystal City, Texas
> not a legend to be shelved
> but a man whose *abrazos* [embraces] still warm
> us yet say, "Now you."

Social mobility and education are related themes in the opening section of *Borders.* Traditionally immigrants and members of minority groups in America seek to advance themselves through education. Mora writes in "Immigrants" about those who "wrap their baby in the American flag" and hope the child will be taken for "our fine American / boy, our fine American girl." In "University Avenue" she evokes those who walk to classes knowing that "their people" have prepared this path for them: therefore they "do not travel alone." In perhaps the bitterest poem in the book, "Withdrawal Symptoms," she speaks for those like her who excelled in school, craving the gold stars from their "pale teachers." After graduation, she says, such students experiencing the "push and pound" of board rooms and committee rooms realize that "I am the only Mexican American here." The teachers, she suggests, created an addiction to a sweet sticky poison, praise.

A pair of poems, "Sonrisas" (smiles) and "Bilingual Christmas," explore the ambiguities of being bilingual and Mexican on the border. In "Sonrisas," the narrator says she lives in "a doorway / between two rooms." In one room, she listens to discussions of tenure and curriculum from women in crisp beige suits who have "quick beige smiles / that seldom sneak into their eyes." In the other room, she can hear señoras who drink "sweet milk coffee" (*café con leche*) in a room full of the steam of fresh tamales. Tamale-making is a traditional women's activity on Christmas Eve. These women have smiles "in their dark, Mexican eyes."

The next poem, "Bilingual Christmas," has an epigraph from a Christmas song, *"Do you hear what I hear?"* The poem is addressed to bilingual professionals (like herself at the time of *Borders*) who may add "a dash of color / to conferences and corporate parties," but in fact are likely to be conscious of a very different social reality from their non-Mexican colleagues. The question "do you hear what I hear" might summon up images not of twinkling lights, but of "search lights / seeking illegal aliens /outside our thick windows." The University of Texas at El Paso, where Mora worked at the time she was writing *Borders,* is a short distance from the Rio Grande, and it is not uncommon for anyone working on the campus to see the searchlights of the Border Patrol from its windows at night.

The final poem in the opening section, "Now and Then, America," affirms Mexican American identity in the midst of a society of boardrooms and pinstripe suits. The speaker craves a chance to bring a little color into such a world and wants to be buried with the flowers of the dead, marigolds (*zempasúchitl*), which she envisions being planted on the grave along with organ cactus: wild creatures can live in the orange blooms and wrens can nest in the cactus. Clearly Mora was impatient with her successful career as a university administrator, and she left it three years after *Borders.*

The second and third sections of the book are more personal than the poetry in her first volume. Part 2 has poems about family, a number of them about children. The third part deals with marriage breakup and its aftermath. As Linda C. Fox says in her essay "From *Chants* to *Borders* to *Communion,*" the borders explored in Mora's second book are multiple: some are political and ethnic, but she also looks at borders "between mother and children and the border between men and women." The prophetic family poem is "Family History," in which Mora describes taping interviews with her favorite aunt, Ygnacia Delgado, known to Mora and her siblings as "Lobo," meaning wolf, because she used to call them her *lobitos,* "little wolves." One of the best of her poems about the effects of marriage breakup is "Out of Business," a declaration by the speaker that she is not running a first-aid station for newly divorced men: she will not tend their wounds.

The fourth and final section of *Borders* is composed of poems that are personal, but personal in various ways. Some of the poems are realistic in an autobiographical sense: the section includes a poem about a cancer scare, two poems about the experiences of a traveling writer, and another poem, "To Big Mary from an Ex-Catholic," that is addressed to the Virgin Mary, the traditional role model for women in Mexican culture. The speaker has turned away from Mary, and although she can speak contemptuously of her in the title of the poem, she still fears retribution, imagining Mary kicking her in the teeth.

A more interesting kind of personal poem appropriates the shamanistic experience attributed to the *bruja* in *Chants,* creating a kind of imaginative alter ego. In "Home," an ecstatic woman spinning in the moonlit desert is surrounded by owls (the familiar spirit of the earlier "Bruja"), rabbits, and mice, and then, eyes shut, she rises to the moon in a trance. Later the moon leaves her on the desert floor. Whether the home of the title is the moon (a common destination in shamanism) or the desert is not explained. In a similar poem, "Luna, Luna," the speaker, who listens to "the wise wind" and the owls, is hypnotized by the moon and in her trance is able to draw it down to her lap and slice off pieces to give to women "sad with their bodies." In the numbered sections of "Spring," each beginning with "Somehow to," a woman wishes to enter into natural experience, to dive into a sparrow's song or the perfume of a wild rose. The final poem, "Success," has a humbler aspiration, to identify with the wild mint, *yerbabuena,* a renowned remedy, a tea that Mora says can soothe a weary woman.

The culmination of Mora's early period is the volume *Communion* (1991). In this collection her world has widened: there are poems about travels to India, Pakistan, Cuba, and the Dominican Republic. In 1986 she had received a Kellogg National Fellowship that underwrote her travels. Linda Fox proposes in "From *Chants* to *Borders* to *Communion*" that one effect of Mora's foreign travel was to supplant her awareness of borders with an aspiration toward community, as suggested by the title. Certainly travel enabled Mora to put the situation of Mexican Americans in a world perspective. She is acutely sensitive to the situation of women throughout the work, and a number of the poems are narrated by women of the developing world: "Señora X No More" is a monologue by a woman learning to read as an adult, whereas "Abuelita's Ache" is a vegetable seller's lament over her granddaughter's love affair, which will end in village gossip. Mora is aware that the sensitive observer is nevertheless an outsider, a point she dramatizes in "Peruvian Child." The child's poverty is so great that the narrator prefers to see her in a white-bordered picture than to confront her mud-encrusted feet in real life. In a Mexican poem, "Picturesque: San Cristóbal de las Casas," the narrator says that no one prepared her for the poverty she witnesses in a Mexican town: the scene is horrifying, not picturesque. The recurring image of that poverty in the poem is one of bare feet.

Two of the most powerful poems tell stories of domestic violence. In "Perfume" a woman becomes the victim of her murderously jealous husband, whose machismo is offended when she has to work outside the house. The woman in the following poem, "Emergency Room," is not a murder victim, but she lies in a hospital bed for a similar reason: she put on her green dress to go out seeking work. Her jealous husband gave her a new "dress," blue bruises from head to toe. Mora has always been a feminist—the poems of village life in her first book are good examples of her attitude—but the sense of outrage is stronger than ever before in *Communion*.

Her most sustained story of a third-world woman comes in "Mini-novela: *Rosa y sus espinas*," a six-episode poem that tells the story of a woman who has eleven children by the son of the *patrón* on an estate. The woman is disturbed throughout her life by the whine of horseflies. She loses the lover to witchcraft by another woman, takes up with a second man, and eventually sees most of her children take the bus to the border. The story is melodramatic and modeled on Mexican soap operas, *telenovelas*. The bewitching of the lover is brilliantly written: his skin breaks open and pours out insects, then he grows progressively lighter and dryer and smaller till he becomes child-sized and dies. At the end the woman spends her time listening to soap operas (a self conscious and postmodern touch) and turns the volume up loud to drown out the sound of the horseflies.

Communion, like its predecessors, is divided into thematically linked sections, three in this case. The opening section, "Old Bones" concentrates on elderly people, though the "old bone" image comes from a nature poem, "Bosque del Apache Wildlife Refuge," in which each stanza begins, "if the earth's old bones smile." The book's second part, "Espinas" (thorns), focuses on painful events and sights encountered while traveling, and the concluding section, "A Voice," deals with a number of voices, some negative like the egocentric tone of "The Conference Male." But the best poem in the final section, "The Young Sor Juana," tells the story of Mexico's great woman poet and scholar, a prodigy of the seventeenth century. (In 2002 Mora published a children's book, titled *A Library for Juana*, about this important historical figure.) The poem in *Communion* ends with Juana's achievement of her goal of becoming a scholar, but also makes clear the price she paid: she had to become a nun, and Mora shows her obsessively clipping her hair short.

Two poems look ahead to the memoir *House of Houses*. The first poem in the book, "Gentle Communion" tells the story of Mora's relationship with Mamande, an affectionate name for her maternal grandmother, Sotero Amelia Landavazo. The grandmother is dead, but her spirit wanders through the poet's rooms making beds and folding socks. In *House of Houses*, likewise, the dead wander through an imaginary house, carrying out domestic activities and telling stories. Mora ends "Gentle Communion" with a vivid memory of sitting in her grandmother's lap as Mamande peels grapes for her. When the "luminous coolness" of a grape is placed on her tongue, she says:

> I know not to bite or chew. I wait
> for the thick melt,
> our private green honey.

A poem near the end of the collection, "My Word-house," is the germ of her memoir, *House of Houses*. The "word-house" grows in the desert as if it were a natural being: it is an image of the reconciliation of human beings and nature. It has an inner courtyard where domesticated birds—parrots and canaries—teach wild sparrows to sing, as if, in Shakespeare's phrase from *The Winter's Tale,* the art itself were nature. The courtyard of a traditional southwestern house is modeled on Moorish houses, and a fountain and fish pool are essential. The harmony of the house leads the personified moon to come down to the household and dance with white-haired women. Some of Mora's key images are the moon, the desert, and dancing: "Home" in her first book brought all three together. At the end of "My Word-house," the dancing is succeeded by blissful sleep of the old and the young, human and nonhuman:

> Bodies and butterflies rest in the slow breaths
> of water. *La luna* hums with the earth's dark
> rhythms, hums lullabies of yellowed lace.

The final image of yellowed lace captures one color state of the moon exactly. Mora's poem expresses a utopian dream of harmony, a complete communion on all levels of being. Passages from this poem open the first essay in Mora's *Nepantla,* published in 1993.

NEPANTLA

Pat Mora's collection of essays deals with many topics. The volume offers sketches of family members, including her mother and her beloved Aunt Lobo, essays on travel, discussions of writing, and strong statements on Chicano and Latino issues, especially bilingual education. The meaning of *Nepantla,* "land in the middle," is variable: Mora was born in the middle of the border area between countries, she occupies a middle place in the generations between her mother and her daughters, she finds herself in the middle of disputes about language—the list could be extended. Her own image in "Sonrisas" (from *Borders*) comes to mind: she has lived in the middle between a traditional culture of women cooking together and a culture of academic discussions. Her middle position is not one of compromise but opportunity: she takes strong stands in debate over racism and bilingual education, and three years after the publication of *Nepantla* she took action on bilingualism by founding the Día de los niños/ Día de los libros.

The longest essay in *Nepantla,* "Universities: A Mirage?" is perhaps the weakest. It lacks the focus of her other efforts, covering too many issues. It starts by examining the frustrations faced by writers, shifts to a discussion of the frustrations in university life, and ends with a reasonable plea for a larger role for minorities in university education. Perhaps more of her experiences as a university administrator might have been brought to bear on the topic. She does conclude with a vivid image: the campus where she worked in El Paso had a view of houses in Mexico that had no running water. She turns the situation around and explains that from Juarez the American city looks like a dream.

Far more effective is "Endangered Species," a plea for what she calls cultural conservation. Folk cultures are being lost or damaged all over the world. She praises a small minority in the United States that seeks to preserve the languages, customs, and traditions of various cultural heritages, and she gives examples of individuals, organizations (like Cultural Survival), and programs dedicated to this work. Her Kellogg Foundation Fellowship enabled her to travel in search of cultural organizations and indigenous groups. Naturally she has a special interest in the preservation of Latino cultures and she calls for more minority teachers in schools.

Mora is a Mexican American, but in her essays she most often uses the more inclusive terms for American speakers of Spanish: Latinos and Latinas. As she says in "Bienvenidos," the introduction to *Nepantla,* the reader of her essays may at times be confused by the use of the pronoun "we," wondering about the referent. She has "purposely let the meaning shift and slide as it does in my life." She asks, "Who are the we of me," and answers, "my family, writers, Chicanas, Southwesterners, mothers, women of color, daughters, Latinas, college graduates, Hispanas, wives, Mexicans, U.S. citizens, readers, advocates, Mexican Americans, women, educators, learners?" Mora knows that a diverse culture is made up of overlapping identities, and even terms for race have various uses.

By using "Latino" and "Latina" so often in *Nepantla,* she affirms the Spanish speakers in the United States, who share some (but by no means all) cultural qualities with each other: Chicanos, Puerto Ricans, Dominicans, Cubans.

Not all of the essays are on public issues. The book includes accounts of her trips to Mexico, Guatemala, Pakistan, and the Dominican Republic. Other essays look at family life: there are personal essays on her mother and on her three children. An important essay, "Remembering Lobo," uses the Mexican Day of the Dead as a focus for her memories of a beloved aunt. (The Day of the Dead ritual is also an important element in *House of Houses.*)

Mora's essays on writing have much to say about her attitudes toward her own practice. Most valuable is "Poet as *Curandera.*" As mentioned earlier, the essay formulates her view of the poet as a kind of healer. Although *curanderismo* continues to be practiced in Mexico and the rural American Southwest, Mora reports that she first encountered it through reading Rudolfo Anaya's classic Chicano novel, *Bless Me, Ultima* (1972), which portrays a *curandera* with extraordinary powers, closer in some ways to shamanism than to ordinary healing through herbs. Not long after reading Anaya, Mora says, she heard of a *bruja* practicing near El Paso, and that information inspired the poem "Bruja: Witch" that appears in *Chants.*

The *curandera* has the support of a culture that values her practices, and she offers a holistic medicine based on tradition rather than formal education. Mora sees a model for the poet here: "Like the *curandera,* then, the writer creates an informal atmosphere conducive to holistic healing—the healing of affirmation, of identification, of confirmation, of wholeness," and ideally can practice in a supportive community. Mora observes that her own culture tends to value collectivity over individuality, and the role of the poet can be a communal one from this point of view. "Writers of Color, Chicana writers, feel a moral responsibility to serve their own," she maintains, and she says that "the Chicana writer seeks to heal cultural wounds of historical neglect."

Mora's other essays on writing also speak to minority issues. In "To Gabriela, a Young Writer," she gives familiar advice about willingness to fail, the place of curiosity, and the need to revise. She also highlights the notion that a young Chicana writer should be proud of her cultural roots. In the essay on "Emerging Voices: The Teaching of Writing," she emphasizes that her writing is a way of working for her group, of writing about "the stories of men and women still invisible in our cultural landscape." In the final essay of *Nepantla,* wryly titled "A Poet for President," she suggests that a society that does not take poets seriously is defective. The poet is too often seen as someone removed from ordinary life. Like Walt Whitman, whose preface to the 1855 edition of *Leaves of Grass* imagines of the United States, "Their presidents shall not be their common referee so much as their poets shall," Mora conceives of the poet as a reconciler and arbiter in a multicultural society. She suggests that the ethnic legacy of Americans is their sixth sense, and the poet helps preserve and communicate that inheritance. In 1994, the year after the publication of *Nepantla,* Mora won a National Endowment for the Arts Fellowship in Creative Writing.

WORKS FOR CHILDREN AND YOUNG ADULTS

Pat Mora's books for children are a means of preserving an ethnic legacy. She has published most of them in Spanish as well as English. One of her deepest concerns is the scarcity of reading materials for Latino children. She often addresses teachers and librarians on the subject. One of her best essays, on the need for books for Hispanic children, "Confessions of a Latina Author," began as a presentation to a Booklist Forum at the Modern Languages Association Convention in 1997.

Her first children's book, *A Birthday Basket for Tía* (1992) appeared a year before *Nepantla.* It tells the story of a little girl named Cecilia, who discovers that the right present for her ninety-year-old *tía* (aunt) is a basket of homemade cookies. This title won a Southwest Books Award. It was followed by two bilingual books, *Listen to the Desert/Oye al desierto* (1994) and in the same year, *The Desert Is My Mother/El desierto es mi madre,* both of which express Mora's love for the Southwestern desert. The second book won the Honor Award in Nature and Ecology from *Stepping Stones* magazine in 1995. She has written numerous books in Spanish and books issued in Spanish translations. Her first collection of poems for children, published as *Confetti* (1996), explores family life and nature in the Southwest. It was followed by another original collection centered on the Southwest, *This Big Sky* (1998), which won the Book Publishers Prize of the Texas Institute of Letters in the children's literature category. She is also the editor of a poetry anthology, *Love to Mamá: A Tribute to Mothers* (2001), a collection by thirteen Latino poets.

Perhaps her finest work for the young is *Tomás and the Library Lady,* the story of Tomás Rivera's initiation into reading. As the son of migrant workers from Texas at work in Iowa, the young Rivera was not eligible for a library card. A generous librarian provided him with books on her own card, and when his family was on the verge of returning to Texas, she gave him a book. As Mora tells the story, the librarian asks the child to teach her some Spanish words. And before the family leaves town, they bring her a gift of *pan dulce,* Mexican sweet bread. The didactic aim is clear but not overstated: individuals can sometimes transcend racial barriers and the results may be incalculable. Appropriately enough, the book won the Tomas Rivera Mexican American Children's Book Award in 1998. In 1999 Mora published *The Rainbow Tulip,* another book about a Chicano child entering the American educational system. The work is based on the experiences of "Estelita," Pat Mora's mother, in the first grade. Estelita participates in the school's May Day celebrations. All the girls were to wear "tulip" skirts, and only Estelita chose to wear a skirt with all the tulip colors, which makes a subtle point about the need for diversity in American life.

In 1996 Mora conceived of the literary festival she founded and still advocates for, El día de los niños/El día de los libros (The Day of Children/The Day of Books). In an interview with Darwin L. Henderson ("Listening to the Desert") she described how the idea for the festival came to her when she was being interviewed on public radio at the University of Arizona. The interviewer asked her to read from her children's work in Spanish for a program on April 30, explaining that April 30 is a children's day in Mexico. Mora then imagined connecting the idea of a children's day with literacy, and she especially wanted to reach children whose first language is not English. Ultimately the festival she envisioned came to be celebrated in a number of libraries in the United States, and her family established the annual Raúl and Estela Mora Award for a library which makes special efforts to celebrate the day. The statement of purpose on Mora's website reads: "The purpose of the celebration includes creating an occasion for all language groups to celebrate the power of being bilingual, for involving non-English-speaking families in literacy activities, and for featuring books in other languages and about bilingual children written by authors from those various cultures."

In 2000 the publisher of Mora's first three books, Arte Público, issued work from them as *My Own True Name: New and Selected Poems for Young Adults, 1984–1999*. The volume is divided into three parts, "Blossoms," "Thorns," and "Roots." The choices are good, the only serious omissions being "Bruja: Witch" and "Curandera." The preface to the book dispenses advice for young writers without pomposity. Mora encourages reading, persistent practice in writing, collecting "facts and phrases and stories," being nosy and given to eavesdropping, and respecting one's own work.

LATER POEMS

Pat Mora's fourth book, *Agua Santa/Holy Water*, published in 1995, reveals a deepening art. The stanza forms are more complex, and she experiments with refrains. A number of the poems are long narratives or meditations. The volume is unified by images of water—holy water, rivers, the sea—and sometimes the water has miraculous creative powers. In a long review, Alison Townsend describes the work as "a mythical journey into the abundant waters of the imagination," and she suggests that "storytelling is what this book is about." Some of the narratives are about real human beings; others are about mythical figures.

The core of the work comes in the section titled "Where We Were Born," which has a prologue, "Litany to the Dark Goddess," evoking the mythical figure of Coatlicue (a mother-destroyer deity in Aztec mythology). The prologue is followed by a "Cuareto Mexicano," a set of astonishing poems presented as "talk show interviews" with the four most important female symbols in Mexican culture: Coatlicue herself; Malinche, the symbolic mother of the Mexican people and traitor of Mexican history; the revered Virgin of Guadalupe; and La Llorona, the murderous mother and ghost out of folklore. The section title refers to the cultural matrix from which Mexican and Mexican American women have drawn their identity.

Coatlicue is a rich symbolic figure, and Mora's litany provides a list of epithets for her, beginning with "Mother of All Gods," then itemizes various other mythological images associated with her, such as her skirt of snakes. The poem finally modulates into epithets for the Virgin Mary, such as "House of Gold" and "Morning Star." The litany ends by asking the mother figure to speak through the babble of epithets: "we're straining to hear," the narrator says. The ensuing poems imply that one archetype is behind all the female beings in Mexican thought. The great precedent for this syncretism is the Virgin of Guadalupe, whose appearance to the Indian Juan Diego (canonized in July 2002) on a hill sacred to the goddess Tonantzin (another ambiguous mother and destroyer) made it possible for Mexican Indians to join the new Catholic faith: the image of the Virgin of Guadalupe is Indian, not European.

The talk-show interviews, an amusing take-off on a form of entertainment that is extremely popular in Mexico, put very contemporary views in the mouth of the ancient beings. The first poem is "Coatlicue's Rules: Advice from an Aztec Goddess." Her rules are gained from her experience as a divine housewife and mother of 401 children plus one extraordinary baby, the sun god Huitzilopochtli, who was conceived after she swallowed a mysterious ball of feathers. The first of her nine rules is "Beware of offers to make you famous." After all, that might lead to talk shows. Rule 4, "Avoid housework," is followed by Rule 5: "Avoid housework. It bears repeating." Coatlicue is presented as superhuman not through divine powers so much as through her extraordinary motherhood. Mora makes rich comedy out of Coatlicue's attempt to advise ordinary mortals. The goddess manages to sound like a contemporary spin doctor: one of her rules is "Retain control of your own publicity," advice extended in Rule 8, "Insist on personal interviews." The eighth rule is explained in clear feminist terms:

> Past is present, remember. Men carved me,
> wrote my story, and Eve's, Malinche's,
>   Gaudalupe's,
> Llorona's, snakes everywhere, even in our
>   mouths.

The final rule, "Be selective about what you swallow," refers both to the ball of feathers and to acceptance of male stereotyping.

The second poem in "Cuarteto Mexicano," titled "Malinche's Tips: Pique from Mexico's Mother," rehabilitates a hated figure from Mexican history, the woman who served as interpreter and mistress for Hernán Cortés. She is often considered a traitor to the indigenous peoples of Mexico, though she herself had been sold by her Aztec mother to another Indian tribe, which might explain her lack of loyalty. In his study of the Mexican psyche, *The Labyrinth of Solitude* (1950), Octavio Paz identifies Malinche as a key to the Mexican character, her children by Cortés being the first mestizos—that is, children of mixed Spanish and American Indian ancestry—who now constitute the majority population of Mexico. Malinche has become a symbol of the violation of Mexico by the Spanish conquerors. She is a constant presence in Mexican cultural memory: goddesses like Coatlicue are much more remote. Mora's Malinche is as aware of the dangers of bad publicity as Coatlicue. Her second tip is: "Write / your own rumors / or hire your own historians." She demands fair treatment, pointing out that she is called "whore, traidora [traitor], slut. / What happened to mother?" Later she says,

> I hear
> prostitute, puta, hooker, bitch.
> Try saying mamá.

Mora celebrates the fact that Malinche was a gifted translator; in emphasizing the power of knowing more than one language, Mora may be influenced by the notion of bilingual "code-switching" that is praised as a strength in Gloria Anzaldúa's 1999 book *Borderlands/La Frontera: The New Mestiza*. The last two tips speak to the whole question of mestizos as being a "bastard" race because the descendants of the unions of conquering Spanish males and Indian women could rarely trace their fathers. Mora's Tip 9 says,

> . . . Children are
> not bastards;
> children are children.

And the last tip says,

> Face it:
> Hating your mother
> ruins your skin.

This idea is explored further in *House of Houses*, where Mora notes the tendency in Mexican and Mexican American society to admire light skin and look down on dark.

The third poem, "Consejos de Nuestra Señora de Guadalupe: Counsel from the Brown Virgin," lets the most important Mexican icon give some surprising advice to women. The Virgin of Guadalupe is depicted everywhere in Mexican society: the first flag in the revolution against Spain had her image on it, and Mora suggests that she is a "muse amused" by the use of her image in "auto-shops, / buses, bars." In stanzas that have a chorus of Spanish-language epithets for the Virgin Mary, she gives shrewd advice, belying her exalted and unspeaking image. She tells her *hijas* (daughters) to beware of altars and legends, she herself having been transformed by men from an Aztec goddess to a queen of the Americas, with her cult moved from pyramid to cathedral. She is thoroughly contemporary:

> Hijas, value contemplation. Alone, I write
> my own legends. . . . Play the symbols.
> I loan my cape to women in tennis shoes who fly
> back and forth across the Río Grande.

Mary's blue mantle becomes a version of a superheroine's cape. This introspective and benevolent Mary is very different from the fearsome figure in the poem from *Borders*, "To Big Mary from an Ex-Catholic."

The final poem in the set, "Llantos de La Llorona: Warnings from the Wailer," is spoken by the ghostly mother who is said to haunt bodies of water weeping for her children, children she drowned or stabbed. The origins of the legend are unclear, but one account sees her as Malinche herself, who supposedly drowned her son when she realized that Cortés would desert her and take the child to Spain. Mora's ghostly figure suggests that the killings are not literal reasons for her tears, a woman already has sufficient reason to weep in a male-dominated world. "Oye [listen]," she says. "Sometimes raising the voice does get attention." Weeping can be a healing and sanctifying act, like holy water in folk medicine: "Oye: Agua santa can come from our eyes." She ends by saying: "Oye: Never underestimate the power of the voice."

The presentation of superhuman figures in the anachronistic framework of talk shows is effective satire. Mora goes further in the last section of the book, "Wondrous Wetness," creating her own myths, whereas in previous work she relied on Mayan and Aztec legends. She rewrites male-centered creation stories in "Un cuento de agua santa" (A story of holy water). The male creator is a rather listless king whose world has no light, no water, no wind. Three times a female liberator persuades the servants of the god to open the clay jars in which he hides his secrets. The first time, light enters the world; the second time, water; the third time, wind. The next poem, titled in Greek, "Agio Neró" (which, like *agua santa,* means "holy water"), celebrates the sight and sound of water in a variety of places in Greece. More interesting is the final poem, "Cuentista" (storyteller), which portrays the teller of stories as a water spirit who carries the green river in her arms. Mora—a poet who loves the desert and, indeed, grew up in the arid Southwest, views water as sacred, perhaps because she knows so well its preciousness. In "El Río Grande," she envisions La Llorona as the river, turning her from a malign ghost to a water goddess. Earlier poems in the book deal with water through the lens of natural history, ranging from a celebration of the grand baleen whale in "Ballena" to writing accurately about a lowly species of stingless jellyfish in "Aurelia: Moon Jellies."

Some of the poems in *Agua Santa* foreshadow elements of her memoir, *House of Houses.* "Ofrenda for Lobo" is a verbal equivalent of the offering put out for a dead ancestor on the Mexican Day of the Dead: her aunt Lobo returns to the page as an important source of family history in *House of Houses*. In "Depression

Days," she describes the racial predicament faced by her uncle Lalo (Eduardo Delgado), and Lalo's experience is discussed in more detail in the autobiography: her uncle had a difficult time not because he was dark but because he was so fair that he created confusion and hostility in racists who could not understand the conjunction of a Mexican name and a Caucasian exterior.

Agua Santa includes some poetry in Spanish: Mora's longest effort in this respect comes in "Corazón del Corrido," a poem dedicated to her father that draws on the *corrido* tradition. The *corrido* is a ballad form that has been practiced along the Mexican-American border since at least the early nineteenth century. Many *corridos* dealt with heroic figures like Gregorio Cortez, who one day in 1902 was falsely accused of stealing a horse. Because of an error in translation, Cortez got into a gun battle with a sheriff and killed him. Shortly after, he killed another sheriff and eluded capture by the vaunted Texas Rangers for some time. Cortez was the subject of an immensely popular ballad, and that song became the subject of an extremely influential book titled *With His Pistol in His Hand,* by the Mexican American folklorist Américo Paredes. Paredes saw the *corrido* as resistance literature, and he excoriated the celebrated Texas Rangers and the scholars who helped to sustain their image of nobility and courage. Paredes, like Tomás Rivera, was an inspirational figure for Chicano writers.

The "Corrido de Gregorio Cortez" describes the man as defending himself "con su pistola en la mano" (with his pistol in his hand). By contrast, as Mora tells the story of her hardworking father, who was not a rancher like Cortez but an optician, she emphasizes that his accomplishments were achieved "sin pistola en la mano" ("without a pistol in his hand")—thus revising the notion of heroism to honor those who do their duty in a normal calling.

HOUSE OF HOUSES

Such heroes are plentiful in Mora's intricate memoir, *House of Houses,* which won the Premio Aztlán Award in 1997 as well as a Southwest Books Award. In this "relational memoir," to use a phrase coined by Paul John Eakin, Mora tells the story of her own life, but she devotes more space to her relatives than to herself. Her father came to the United States as a child in 1916, brought by his parents from the city of Chihuahua. They were fleeing Pancho Villa's reign of terror during the Mexican Revolution. Her maternal grandfather, Eduardo Luis Delgado, had made a similar flight in 1913 with his daughters, fording the Rio Grande in a carriage.

The book is set in an imaginary house somewhere along the Rio Grande between the cities of El Paso (the pass of the north) and Santa Fe (holy faith). Mora has been influenced by Gaston Bachelard's *The Poetics of Space* (1964) and quotes his phrase, "protected intimacy." Bachelard's discussion of domestic spaces encouraged her to create an imaginary domicile where her relatives and ancestors could be brought together in a kind of refuge from time and change. Her imaginary house is a "Wordhouse," as in her poem from *Communion,* and a place where she can gather her relatives, alive and dead—even those who never met, even those who lived in different centuries—into intimate connection with one another. They share stories with the narrator, who gathers the generations and their intertwined history into a work of art, a rich prose correlative of the family tree and set of portraits that she provides at the outset. In a perceptive review of the book, Héctor A. Torres says that Mora's representative account of the Mexican diaspora and its aftermath in the lives of the immigrants and their children is more than a family history and memoir because it speaks about much more than a single self or a single family." He calls it an "epic spiritual narrative."

The dead who dwell in the house (her father, for example) are presented as translucent spirits, capable of shape-shifting—although Mora is adamant that she is not a magic realist, a label that is often affixed to works with a Latino origin as if all writers in Spanish are Gabriel García Márquez. The farthest she goes in that direction is to present a visit of the Virgin of Guadalupe to the house on the feast of the Archangel Rafael. The angel comes too and leaves a feather behind. But magic realism treats extraordinary events as if they were true, whereas Mora frequently reminds the reader that the house and its tenants are really constructions of her imagination, a utopian ideal of family gathered in one place and harmonized with each other and with nature.

The characteristic perception of harmony in nature, and in particular the abundance of flower imagery, that infuses Mora's writing from her earliest collections of poetry reaches a high point in the idealized landscape of *House of Houses*. The gardens around the imaginary house are carefully tended, and the memoir abounds with blossoming plants: flowers are described with loving detail, to the point that the book is in part a herbal. At one point, a deceased ancestor says good night to the trees. Also characteristically, Mora's passion for the desert is balanced in her work with a preoccupation with water imagery, and the inner garden of the house has a fountain. Since Moorish times, Spanish architecture has included a fountain as an essential feature, a nurturing source as important in the American southwest as it was on the arid plains of Castile. The inner fountain is often alluded to in the memoir. The walls of the house are adobe, the brown clay that not only comes from the desert but suggests the human body, which in the Biblical tradition is often referred to as being made of clay. Mora's "house of clay" is in a way Mora herself: her own being is the shelter for her family's stories. The spirits of her family are souls dwelling in the house through her imaginative reanimation of them. The intense blue of the desert sky overarches the house and becomes a spiritual presence in the memoir's cosmography. The family spirits are the souls dwelling in the house. The intense blue of the desert sky overarches it all and becomes a spiritual presence in the memoir's cosmography.

Mora purposefully fills her imaginary house with Mexican culture. She frequently quotes *dichos*, the proverbs so important in that culture, and she provides a list of them at the back of the book. Various folk practices and folktales are imparted in the course of the book. For example, she has her aunt Chole talk about the need to cover windows in a storm so that lightning will not strike the house. Traditional remedies and recipes are described. Mora uses a calendar year scheme, naming the chapters of her book for months, and she is careful to name the religious festivals and saints associated with each month. Although she did not arrange the book by the liturgical year, which begins at Advent, she mentions that she has drawn on her Aunt Lobo's missal for much of the liturgical information provided in the book. The use of the missal affirms her interest in her family's religious traditions.

Traditional Catholic piety is represented by the memoir's most remote ancestor, Anacleta Manquera, a great great grandmother, known in the book as Mamá Cleta. She seeks harmony without quite understanding her modern descendants, and she tries to involve them in pious activities. Her wholeness of vision is represented by her habit of synesthesia, experiencing one sense in terms of another; other characters cannot share in this vision, but Mora as narrator manifests an acute sensory awareness of her own, reveling in the senses without blurring them together. Cleta is presented as a compulsive housekeeper, always making teas and tending flowers, the archetype of the obsessive nurturer of children and houses. Through this archaic figure, Mora manages to come to terms with the traditional role of Mexican women while keeping some distance from it. She can also present the Virgin of Guadalupe in a favorable light through the mediation of Mamá Cleta, who invites the Virgin and Rafael to have *café con leche* on his feast day, September 29. At the other extreme from Mamá Cleta, Mora's adult children are present in the book as a younger generation who often fail to understand the Mexican cultural background.

The narrative tells the story of the Delgado family first, through Lobo, who skillfully narrates reminiscences of life in Mexico and the early days in El Paso that make the realities of life for Mexican immigrants clear. The story of the Mora family is constructed through the memories of Aunt Chole and Mora's father. The Mexican diaspora began to receive much attention as the twentieth century came to a close, but Mora's version is not based on statistics but on rich family memories. She used taped interviews and a notebook kept by her mother in youth as sources.

Mora describes the discrimination that Mexican immigrants and their children faced in America. The Anglo appearance of Mora's mother and Uncle Lalo makes their situation even more complicated, creating misunderstandings, especially for Lalo, whose skin did not match his surname, which caused suspicion at border crossings. And discrimination against dark skin extends to the Mexican community, Mora tells us: her father would never have been accepted by his light-skinned father-in-law, the judge from Chihuahua, but the old man was incapacitated by a stroke and did not realize that a courtship was going on. Mora's father found that his dark skin color was a problem in his business dealings. He said once to his daughter, "I have a map of Mexico in my face."

Mora's commitment to speaking against racism is strong, but the tone of the book is generally tender rather than angry, and much of it commemorates her aunts, her uncle, and her parents. Her father's quiet heroism in struggling for his family, "sin pistola en la mano," gets much of her space. The descriptions of his illness and death are among the most powerful in the book.

The celebration of the Day of the Dead (a festival that has also become important in the United States as a means for Mexican Americans to conserve their cultural heritage) provides Mora with a framework for summoning her ancestors to the work in a Yeatsian phantasmagoria, as the inhabitants of her imaginary house create altars and *ofrendas* for all family members who have died. For her maternal grandfather, Lázaro Delgado, who was a tailor, the *ofrenda* is "a photograph of him with his sons in his tailor shop, good cloth for making men's jackets, needles, measuring tape, a radio playing classical music, beer, a plate of *mole*." Then in a ceremony of her own invention, she and her children place votive candles in little boats and launch them on the Rio Grande. The candles represent the souls of the entire extended family. The ceremony is a moving conclusion to her Day of the Dead narrative.

An essay in *Nepantla*, "Remembering Lobo," suggests that one way to understand the Latino population in the United States is to realize that for them "family ties are so strong that not even death can sever them." Mora's affectionate memoir documents the power of such ties. She has found a literary form to perpetuate them.

AUNT CARMEN'S BOOK OF PRACTICAL SAINTS

In 1997, the same year that *House of Houses* appeared, Pat Mora published a poetry collection that drew from the same well of Chicano folklore used in the memoir. Perhaps taking her cue from folklorists like the Texas writer J. Frank Dobie, who appropriated the legends and songs of Mexican Americans into his own tale-telling, Mora makes her own delightful and audacious appropriation of the Anglo-American literary tradition in *Aunt Carmen's Book of Practical Saints*. Although the title of Mora's work will make readers think of T. S. Eliot's *Old Possum's Book of Practical Cats,* and Eliot is one of the most prestigious poets in the English and American tradition, the two works have little in common, except that Aunt Carmen sometimes treats her saints with the familiarity given to pets. They are indeed practical saints: she talks to them, exhorts them, addresses litanies to them, complains to them about her husband, and looks to them for inspiration in her life. Along with poems addressed to saints, the book includes poems about members of the Holy Family: the Virgin Mary is addressed in five poems. The titles of the poems give the names of the beings addressed in English and Spanish. One subtle touch is the italicizing of the English part of the title, making English the foreign language.

The magnificent illustrations of Mora's book are with one exception images from the Museum of International Folk Art (a branch of the Museum of New Mexico) in Santa Fe. Some of the images are by twentieth-century artists, but they all come out of the *santo*-making tradition of northern New Mexico. In this isolated region, a folk-art tradition began in the eighteenth century that featured wood carvings and paintings on wood of *santos* (saints) and other religious figures. The works depicted in Mora's book are charming (or in the case of "*Death*/La Muerte," terrifying) folk art. The poet provides an appendix giving the stories of each saint or member of the Holy Family.

Mora's Aunt Carmen is an eighty-year-old woman who works as the sacristan in a New Mexico church. The priest is intimidated by her. She is in some ways conservative, disliking the loss of Latin in the liturgy, but she is socially aware, and especially concerned about the mistreatment of women. Mora's brilliant characterization of an elderly feminist folk Catholic will leave most readers surprised and amused: Aunt Carmen suggests that "*Saint Michael the Archangel*/San Miguel Arcángel" should use his skills and his spears against oppressive landlords and religious hypocrites, giving her a touch of the social revolutionary. The intimate tone adopted by Aunt Carmen resembles Mora's Aunt Chole in *House of Houses:* Chole talks to God in a very familiar way, referring to him with a diminutive form, *Mi diosito,* which means "my little God." Mora knows that folk religion can take a very personal attitude toward the saints, and in one captivating poem "*Saint Anthony of Padua*/San Antonio de Padua," Aunt Carmen uses a mild form of magic with the saint's image. Saint Anthony is prayed to by those who wish to find lost objects or to conceive a child. It is a common Mexican folk practice to turn a little statue of the saint upside down to pressure him to grant petitions. When one of Carmen's daughters went missing, she took extreme measures, suspending his image upside down in the well for two weeks until the girl was found.

The poems addressed to the Virgin Mary have a positive tone, quite different from Mora's "To Big Mary from an Ex-Catholic." Aunt Carmen's attitude in "*Our Lady of the Annunciation*/ Nuestra Señora de la Anunciación" is reverential, but she also makes a feminist point, observing that painters depict the Mary of the Annunciation as a passive individual because they fear her fire: "This old world is still scared of women." The Virgin of Guadalupe gets her own poem, one that sees her as a source of light and consolation. In "*The Visitation*/La Visitación" Aunt Carmen imagines the meeting of the Virgin Mary and her cousin Elizabeth when they were both pregnant, one with Jesus, the other with St. John the Baptist. Mora provides a realistic detail: they laugh when they hug and their stomachs bump. The curved shape of the poem suggests a pregnant abdomen. The most touching and unusual poem is the last one, "*The*

Good Shepherdess/La Buena Pastora." In the painting reproduced in the book, Mary appears without a halo, in a casual pose, very different from the traditional splendor of depictions of the Virgin. The poem is a way of pointing to the feminine in the sacred, for Christ is traditionally the Good Shepherd. It also celebrates natural beauty, and "cranky Carmen" asks Mary to teach her the "practicality of beauty."

The poems show Mora experimenting with form. Her earlier work was in free verse. These poems often use the four-line rhymed stanza (abcb) of the *corrido*. She also includes a sestina, a villanelle, and a poem in terza rima. "*Christ on the Cross*/Nuestro Señor Crucificado" is in the shape of a cross. The diction of the poems sometimes includes Latin—Aunt Carmen adapts litanies and invocations from the Catholic liturgy—and Spanish. One of the most delightful poems is "*St Anne*/Santa Ana." It makes use of a lullaby in Spanish that contains some amusing nonsense syllables: "ru-rru-que-rru-rru." The double "rr" in Spanish is a heavily trilled form of the "r" sound and is a favorite sound in Hispanic nursery rhymes.

The collection represents Mora's most sustained use of Mexican folk culture. Readers without a Catholic background will find it exotic, and the northern New Mexico setting will be unfamiliar to most readers. The poet still manages to speak across cultures. Pat Mora's writing is a sustained dialogue with Mexican American culture—its machismo is critiqued, for example, and figures like the Virgin of Guadalupe are scrutinized, but her writing carries on a dialogue with the rest of American society as well. A daughter of the borderlands, she has created a body of work that uses the tensions and the opportunities of her special position in American life to warn, reconcile, and celebrate. The "*Febrero loco*/Crazy February" chapter of *House of Houses* gives a genealogy beginning, "I am Patricia Mora, born in El Paso, Texas, daughter of the desert, of the border, of the Río Grande." Mora has clearly made good use of her heritage.

Selected Bibliography

WORKS OF PAT MORA

POETRY

Chants. Houston: Arte Público, 1984.

Borders. Houston: Arte Público, 1986.

Communion. Houston: Arte Público, 1991.

Agua Santa/Holy Water. Boston: Beacon Press, 1995.

Aunt Carmen's Book of Practical Saints. Boston: Beacon Press, 1997.

AUTOBIOGRAPHY AND COLLECTED ESSAYS

House of Houses. Boston: Beacon Press, 1997.

Nepantla: Essays from the Land in the Middle. Albuquerque: University of New Mexico Press, 1993.

BOOKS FOR CHILDREN AND YOUNG ADULTS

A Birthday Basket for Tía. Illustrated by Cecily Lang. New York: Macmillan, 1992.

Agua, Agua, Agua. Illustrated by José Ortega. Glenville, Ill.: GoodYear, 1994.

Listen to the Desert/Oye al desierto. Illustrated by Francisco X. Mora. New York: Clarion, 1994.

The Desert Is My Mother/El desierto es mi madre. With art by Daniel Lechón. Houston: Piñata Books, 1994.

Pablo's Tree. Illustrated by Cecily Lang. New York: Macmillan, 1994.

The Gift of the Poinsettia/El regalo de la flor de nochebuena. With Charles Ramírez Berg. Houston: Piñata, 1995.

The Race of Toad and Deer. Illustrated by May Itzna Brooks. New York: Orchard Books, 1995.

Confetti: Poems for Children. Illustrated by Enrique O. Sanchez. New York: Lee and Low, 1996.

Uno, dos, tres/One, Two, Three. Illustrated by Barbara Lavallee. New York: Clarion Books, 1996.

Tomás and the Library Lady. Illustrated by Raúl Colón. New York: Knopf, 1997.

Delicious Hullabaloo/Pachanga deliciosa. Illustrated by Francisco X. Mora. Spanish translation by Alba Nora Martínez and Pat Mora. Houston: Piñata, 1998.

This Big Sky. Illustrated by Steve Jenkins. New York: Scholastic, 1998.

The Rainbow Tulip. Illustrated by Elizabeth Sayles. New York: Viking, 1999.

My Own True Name: New and Selected Poems for Young Adults, 1984–1999. Houston: Piñata, 2000.

The Night the Moon Fell: A Maya Myth Retold. Illustrated by Domi. Toronto: Groundwood/Douglas & McIntyre, 2000.

The Bakery Lady / La señora de la panadería. Illustrated by Pablo Torrecilla. Houston: Piñata, 2001.

Love to Mamá: A Tribute to Mothers. New York: Lee and Low Books, 2001. (Anthology of thirteen selections by Latino poets, edited by Mora.)

A Library for Juana: The World of Sor Juana Inés. Illustrated by Beatriz Vidal. New York: Knopf, 2002.

Maria Paints the Hills. With paintings by Maria Hesch. Santa Fe: Museum of New Mexico Press, 2002.

SHORT FICTION

"Hands." *Revista chicana-riqueña* 10, no. 3:32–37 (summer 1982). Collected in *Infinite Divisions: An Anthology of Chicana Literature.* Edited by Tey Diana Rebolledo and Eliana S. Rivero. Tucson: University of Arizona Press, 1993. Pp. 222–226.

ESSAYS

"A Latina in Kentucky." *The Horn Book,* May–June 1994, pp. 298–300.

"The Leader in the Mirror." *Teaching Tolerance* (publication of the Southern Poverty Law Center, Montgomery, Ala.), fall 1994, pp. 62–63.

"The Lure of Languages." *Southwest Conference on Language Teaching Newsletter,* September 1997, pp. 12ff.

"April 30: Día de los niños/Día de los libros: Bilingual Literacy Day." *United States Board on Books for Young People, Inc., Newsletter,* spring 1998, pp. 15–18.

"Confessions of a Latina Author." *The New Advocate* 11, no. 4:279–290 (fall 1998).

"Let's Lift Our Spirits by Reaffirming Our Shared Humanity." *Dallas Morning News,* December 31, 1999, pp. 1C and 6C.

"The Seeds of Stories." *The Dragon Lode* (journal of the International Reading Association Children's Literature and Reading Special Interest Group) 18, no. 2:55–59 (spring 2000).

OTHER

Pat Mora's website (http://www.patmora.com) contains information about her writings and Día de los niños/Día de los libros.

CRITICAL AND BIOGRAPHICAL STUDIES

Almon, Bert. *This Stubborn Self: Texas Autobiographies.* Fort Worth: Texas Christian University Press, 2002. Pp. 271–306. (Discusses *House of Houses* at length.)

Anzaldúa, Gloria. *Borderlands/La Frontera: The New Mestiza.* 2d ed. San Francisco: Aunt Lute, 1999.

Barrera, Rosalinda. "Pat Mora: Fiction/Nonfiction, Writer and Poet." *Language Arts* 75, no. 3:221–227 (March 1998).

Day, Frances Ann. "Pat Mora." In *Latina and Latino Voices in Literature for Children and Teenagers.* Portsmouth, N.H.: Heinemann, 1997. Pp. 122–131.

Fast, Robin Riley. "Nature and Creative Power: Pat Mora and Patricia Hampl." *San Jose Studies* 15, no. 2:29–40 (1989).

Fox, Linda C. "From *Chants* to *Borders* to *Communion*: Pat Mora's Poetic Journey to Nepantla." *Bilingual Review* 21, no. 3:259–270 (September–December 1996).

———. "Four *Imaginarios Femeninos* in Pat Mora's 'Cuarteto Mexicano.'" *Americas Review* 25:166–178 (1999).

Kanellos, Nicolás. "Pat Mora." In *Dictionary of Literary Biography.* Vol. 209. *Chicano Writers, Third Series.* Detroit: Gale, 1999. Pp. 160–163.

McCracken, Ellen. *New Latina Narrative: The Feminine Space of Postmodern Ethnicity.* Tucson: University of Arizona Press, 1999.

McKenna, Teresa. *Migrant Song: Politics and Process in Contemporary Chicano Literature.* Austin: University of Texas Press, 1997.

Milligan, Bryce. "Ever Radical: A Survey of Tejana Writers." In *Texas Women Writers: A Tradition of Their Own.* Edited by Sylvia Ann Grider and Lou Halsell Rodenberger. College Station: Texas A&M Press, 1997. Pp. 223–228.

Munson, Sammye. "Pat Mora." In *Today's Tejano Heroes.* Austin, Tex.: Eakin Press, 2000. Pp. 40–45.

Murphy, Patrick D. "Grandmother Borderland: Placing Identity and Ethnicity." *Interdisciplinary Studies in Literature and Enviroment* 1, no. 1:35–41 (spring 1993).

———. "Conserving Natural and Cultural Diversity: The Prose and Poetry of Pat Mora." In his *Farther Afield in the Study of Nature-Oriented Literature.* Charlottesville: University Press of Virginia, 2000. Pp. 132–145.

Nigro, Kirsten. "Mujeres fuertes: La poesía de Pat Mora." *Cuadernos Americanos: Nueva Epoca* 1, no. 55:118–130 (1996).

Passman, Kristina. "Demeter, Kore, and the Birth of the Self: The Quest for Identity in the Poetry of Alma Villanueva, Pat Mora, and Cherríe Moraga." *Monographic Review* 6:35–41 (1990).

Rebolledo, Tey Diane. "Tradition and Mythology: Signatures of Landscape in Chicana Literature." In *The Desert Is No Lady: Southwestern Landscapes in Women's Writing and Art.* Edited by Vera Norwood and Janice Monk. New Haven, Conn.: Yale University Press, 1987. Pp. 96–124.

———. *Women Singing in the Snow: A Cultural Analysis of Chicana Literature.* Tucson: University of Arizona Press, 1995.

Saldívar-Hull, Sonia. "Feminism on the Border: From Gender Politics to Geopolitics." In *Criticism in the Borderlands: Studies in Chicano Literature, Culture, and Ideology.* Edited by Héctor Calderón and José David Saldívar. Durham, N.C.: Duke University Press, 1991.

Spencer, Laura Gutierrez. "The Desert Blooms: Flowered Songs by Pat Mora." *Bilingual Review* 20:28–37 (January–April 1995).

Wadham, Tim. "Spotlight on Pat Mora." In *Programming with Latino Children's Materials: A How-To-Do-It Manual for Librarians.* New York: Neal-Schuman Publishers, Inc., 1999. Pp. 48–50.

BOOK REVIEWS

Jarolim, Edie. "Books in Brief: Nonfiction." *New York Times,* June 29, 1997, Section 7, p. 20. (Review of *House of Houses.*)

Peery, Janet. "Daughter of Memory." *Washington Post,* June 26, 1997, p. E2. (Review of *House of Houses.*)

Torres, Héctor A. Review of *House of Houses. Aztlán* 23:233–238 (fall 1998).

Townsend, Alison. "Women in the Middle." *Women's Review of Books* 13:40–41 (July 1996). (Review of *Agua Santa/Holy Water.*)

INTERVIEWS

Ada, Alma Flor. "Ventana a un rostro: Pat Mora." In *Cuentaquetecuento: Revista latinoamericana de literatura para niños y jovenes.* San José, Costa Rica: Fundación Educativa San Judas Tadeo, 1998. Pp. 109–113.

Alarcón, Norma. "Interview with Pat Mora." *Third Woman: Texas and More* 3, nos. 1–2:121–126 (1986).

Conlan, Maureen. "Writing from Two Worlds: Pat Mora Draws on Her Mexican Heritage." *Cincinnati Post,* May 18, 1996, pp. 1B, 3B.

Corsaro, Julie. "Talking with Pat Mora." *Book Links,* September 1997, pp. 25–29.

Gersh, Rachel. "Voz de la cultura escritora hispana comenta sobre la conexión entre el lenguaje y la cultura." *Santa Fe New Mexican,* October 11, 1999, p. A10.

Henderson, Darwin L. "Listening to the Desert: A Conversation with Pat Mora." *Ohio Journal of English Language Arts* 41:12–16 (fall 2000).

Ikas, Karin Rosa. "Pat Mora: Poet, Writer, and Educator." In her *Chicana Ways: Conversations with Ten Chicana Writers.* Reno: University of Nevada Press, 2001. Pp. 126–149.

Jácquez-Ortiz, Michele. "Land of Enchantment Inspires New Book for Author Pat Mora." *La Herencia del Norte,* fall 1997, pp. 32–33.

Milligan, Bryce. "A Conversation with Sandra Cisneros and Pat Mora." *Texas Journal of Ideas, History, and Culture* 17, no. 1:12–17 (fall–winter 1994).

Racine, Marty. "Border Voice." *Houston Chronicle,* May 30, 1999, pp. 1F, 4F.

Rebolledo, Tey Diana. "Pat Mora." In *This Is About Vision: Interviews with Southwestern Writers.* Edited by John F. Crawford, William Balassi, and Annie O. Eysturoy. Albuquerque: University of New Mexico Press, 1990. Pp. 129–139.

Rentería, Ramón. "A Passion for Writing." *El Paso Times,* June 11, 2000, pp. 1F, 8F.

Versace, Candelora. "Pat Mora: Bringing the Latino Experience to Children's Literature." *The Santa Fe New Mexican,* October 6, 1996, pp. D5.

—BERT ALMON

Walter Mosley

1952–

THE STORY OF Walter Mosley's career thus far has two parts: doing and undoing. First, questing his way past the nervous gatekeepers of American publishing, Mosley disguised the newness of his work by wrapping his themes in a genre everyone recognized—the detective novel. Once inside the gates, he has struggled to escape categories. Thus, the self-evident truth about Mosley is not that he is a mystery novelist—or that he is an African American mystery novelist. Nor is it that he is an African American mystery novelist who is also Jewish and a mystery novelist who has now written almost as many books in other genres. It does not even work to say that he is *not* a mystery novelist.

An impatience with modifiers—Walter Mosley is a novelist, full stop—is the salient feature of Mosley's career. Readers have identified literary influences as divergent as Ralph Ellison, Ralph Waldo Emerson, and (as critic after critic has insisted, even after Mosley himself disputed the idea) Chester Himes. Why have critics fixed on Chester Himes? The answer seems to be that Himes was a black man, like Mosley, who wrote hard-boiled mysteries, like Mosley. In a 1993 interview with Thulani Davis, Mosley characteristically implied that such commonalities of category are no basis from which to infer influence: "People say Chester Himes about me. . . . I don't feel like I came out of Himes. . . . I don't live under the kind of racism he lived under. . . . I learned more from Chandler." Indeed, Mosley's novels do echo and rework aspects of Raymond Chandler's detective novels, from the tough lyricism to the Los Angeles setting to the emphasis on the connection between gritty street violence and corruption in high places.

Nevertheless, it is natural and correct to locate Mosley in an African American literary tradition. Reviewer Greg Tate sees affinities between Mosley's work and that of Richard Wright, and Mosley himself has cited Langston Hughes and Zora Neale Hurston as influences. Critics Helen Lock and Alice Mills have perceptively added W. E. B. Du Bois to the list. At the same time, Mosley claims to belong in the broadest way (as one could say of all the African American writers listed here) to the discourse of writers across centuries and continents; he has at various times also named Graham Greene, Albert Camus, Ross Macdonald, Shakespeare, Dickens, and Thucydides as literary models.

Mosley refuses to merely entertain. He is equally reluctant to consign himself to obscurity by writing exclusively serious books about serious issues, which he believes many African American writers feel obliged to do. His agenda, though, is a serious one: to tell "his people's stories," as he said in a conversation with writer Colson Whitehead (transcribed in the May 2001 issue of *Book* under the title "Eavesdropping"), and to establish those stories in the mainstream as windows into the human condition. Shakespeare and Dickens, he points out, were popular writers. A theme that runs through his work, growing more pronounced in recent years, is the argument that poverty and oppression increase the pressure of ethical dilemmas on daily life, and that African Americans are therefore particularly well situated to participate in broad philosophical debates about ethics and morality. Novelists, Mosley told Whitehead, are the closest thing America has to philosophers.

CHILDHOOD INFLUENCES

Mosley's resistance to being categorized began early, with his birth on January 12, 1952, to an interracial couple. His father, LeRoy Mosley, was African American, a veteran of World War II who had moved to Los Angeles from the repressive pre–civil rights era South. That emigration, as one might call it, was not unlike the one made by the forebears of Walter Mosley's mother, Ella, who were Jews from Poland and Russia. In both cases, large sections of the original communities transferred themselves, sending word to those left behind that in the new place one could, as Mosley puts it in an essay titled "The World of Easy Rawlins," eat "off the trees" and sleep "right outside under the moon." Both of Mosley's parents, who met while working for the Los Angeles School District, were storytellers: "If you go to either of them," Mosley said in an interview with the *Observer*, "they'd be telling stories of living in ghettos, of being hanged and burnt and prejudice against us." Mosley's use of the first-person plural—*us*—to describe groups of people with roots in different parts of the world encapsulates his impatience with the conventional categories through which people understand "us and them." According to Mosley, "we" are not members of a single race, creed, or nationality; "we" are simply ghetto dwellers whose friends and relatives have been hanged or burned.

As a child in South Central Los Angeles, Mosley did not encounter racism because he had little contact with white people other than his mother and her relatives. The two sides of his family got along, and according to the journalist David Streitfeld, Mosley describes the cultural and political tolerance of his relatives in terms of food:

I couldn't have a bar mitzvah because I wasn't practicing so we just had a big party. Everybody got along and everybody joked and everybody had a good time and we had a lot of food. My Jewish family were almost all communists or socialists or intellectuals . . . so they all ate everything.

Until his early teens, Mosley and his parents lived in a small house on 76th Place, near Central Avenue. In that house, Mosley heard his father exchange tales with friends and relatives about a shared past in Texas and Louisiana. In interviews and articles, Mosley has emphasized his father's skill as a storyteller. Perhaps that childhood intimacy with places and times not within his personal experience is behind the streak of nostalgia that runs through Mosley's fiction—a sense, especially strong in *RL's Dream* (1995), that the most vital passages in the lives of the characters have happened before the narrative action and in some other setting. Storytelling also seems to have been at the root of a rare phenomenon Mosley experienced, a Los Angeles neighborhood with a sense of community. Although his family was poor, Mosley told Thulani Davis, he had a sense of security as a child: "My father gave me the feeling, when I was a kid, that nothing bad would ever happen to me. I knew that if the police came to get me that he would protect me. I knew that if somebody was trying to kill me, he would be out there with a gun." His mother, too, was protective, letting him walk to the store by himself at the age of six, but following him on the other side of the street. She kept out of sight, however, allowing him a sense of independence. In other words, Mosley was not so much sheltered from the world as helped into it. The Mosleys insisted on their right to imagine a successful professional career for their child, despite the racism that had prevented LeRoy Mosley from progressing past the position of maintenance supervisor at his job in the school district. As Mosley told Lynell George, "It wasn't: 'Walter can get a job at the garage, maybe, if he's lucky.' [My father] was saying,

'My son is going to make it, 'cause I'm going to make something out of my son.'"

Mosley's adolescence was not so comfortable. LeRoy Mosley owned a number of residential properties (as the character Easy Rawlins would do after him), and the family moved into one of them, a fourplex in another neighborhood. Mosley's sense of community was severed. As a teenager, George reports, Mosley experienced the Los Angeles of legend, "the flat, hot vastness." LeRoy Mosley made the house itself into a kind of refuge, though, surrounding it with an "exotic array of vegetables, fruits, and flowers." The theme of the garden oasis appears repeatedly in Mosley's fiction.

When he left home at the age of eighteen to attend Goddard College in Vermont, Mosley seems to have entered a period of wandering. He soon dropped out of Goddard. Over the following years, he moved from one Vermont school to another, eventually earning a bachelor's degree in political science from Johnson State College in 1977. While working toward a Ph.D. at the University of Massachusetts–Amherst, Mosley met his future wife, the choreographer Joy Kellman. He took up computer programming and moved to New York City in 1982, where he started a consulting business. With a restlessness that may have had something to do with the ambitions his parents had for him or with a sense of having something important to offer—perhaps because of the family stories fermenting inside him?—Mosley tried one creative endeavor after another: painting, pottery, music. Finally, language seemed to break out of him: "I was . . . working for Mobil Oil," he told the *Observer*. "It was a Saturday. Nobody was there. I got tired of writing computer code and I wrote a sentence."

GONE FISHIN'

Mosley completed his first novel in 1988, although it was not published until 1997. *Gone Fishin'* introduces Raymond "Mouse" Alexander and Ezekiel "Easy" Rawlins, whose partnership will become the foundation of Mosley's famous mystery series. They travel to Mouse's hometown of Pariah, Texas, carrying readers into the Southern past that Mosley knows so well from his father's stories. The lyricism of the prose conveys Easy's, if not Mosley's own, feelings for the landscape: "If [people] could see Texas in the early dawn like I saw it that day they would know a Texas that is full of potential from the smallest rock to the oldest woman on the farm." "Potential" implies magic—the power to transform the impossible into the conceivable—and magic is beauty, an ominous kind of beauty: "magic hides in the early morning. If you get up early enough you might find something so beautiful that it would be all right if you just died right then because nothing else in life could ever be better."

Easy's experiences in Mouse's hometown are as transformative as these passages promise, but the transformation takes place through terror as well as beauty. The friends wander through a swampy landscape. Whereas Mouse knows his way around this treacherous place, Easy does not. Easy contracts a fever and suffers from delirium. He makes love against his will with a giant witch who keeps her husband's skull on her mantelpiece; he learns a brutal fishing technique (hence the novel's title); and he meets the witch's son, a hunchback named Domaque, who lives in a molasses shack surrounded by a wild garden that is "like an inside room or greenhouse only with the sky for a roof." (Domaque's garden is described as a garden "right out of the Bible," but in this Eden there is a pile of mutilated "hard-rubber baby dolls" that looks like "a pile of infant corpses." These dolls, on which Domaque takes out his rage, signal the extent of the mistreatment he receives from the world.) Easy also witnesses his best friend shoot dogs "like ducks in an arcade." He watches Mouse kill an abusive stepfather and pin the blame on another man. Easy thus becomes the only witness to crimes he can never report because he knows that Mouse inevitably turns his killing instincts on anyone perceived as a traitor. The nightmare events bind Easy to Mouse and set up an entanglement that continues into the subsequent mystery series; Mouse's reflexive, remorseless violence runs through the novels as an effective survival strategy that Easy both relies on and dreads.

Also important in *Gone Fishin'* is Easy's encounter with Miss Dixon, a tight-fisted, small-minded, hard-willed old white woman who urges him to learn to read. If he could read the Bible, she suggests, he would know about the prophet he is named after. This allusion to the biblical Ezekiel, the most explicit one that occurs in any of the Easy Rawlins novels, invites not just the narrator but also his readers to reflect on the significance of the name.

The biblical Ezekiel has a special relation to the written word. "Eat what is offered you," the voice of God tells him, "eat this scroll, and go, speak to the House of Israel." The scroll tastes "sweet as honey" (Ezekiel 3:1–3). Ezekiel is an anxious personality, embodying the nervousness and uncertainty he is to bring to his people; he is doomed to "eat [his] bread with quaking and drink [his] water in trembling and fearfulness" (Ezekiel 12:17). Similarly, the prose in which Easy tells his story is sweetly lyrical, but, like the divine scrolls, full of "lamentation and mourning and woe" (Ezekiel 2:10). Moreover, Ezekiel Rawlins, like his namesake, is in a state of moral anxiety about the world he inhabits, even as he learns to make his "face hard against their faces, and [his] forehead hard against their foreheads" (Ezekiel 3:8).

Despite these parallels, the biblical allusions in *Gone Fishin'* must ultimately be seen as ironic. Ezekiel Rawlins shortens his name to Easy, after all, and he practices an easier, more pragmatic version of morality than does his namesake. He tells his story from the point of view of an outsider, as prophets generally do, but he remains bound to the underworld despite a basic decency. Repeatedly, he is compelled to choose between ethical principles and his own survival—and chooses survival. As Mosley puts it in "The World of Easy Rawlins," Easy is "a man who, finding himself with a dark skin, has decided that he's going to live his life and do what's right, in that order." Easy diverges from the biblical Ezekiel in another way: any written words he consumes he intends to "make [his] own." *Gone Fishin'* makes it clear that this habit of reworking stories has cultural roots. Domaque, who has learned to read under the tutelage of Miss Dixon, does the same thing, changing biblical stories to suit his purposes. Moreover, in the secular setting of Pariah's general store and bar, people who gather to socialize "trade lies," ornamenting and improvising upon the truth. As Mary Young has noted, Easy is participating in an African American oral culture that is also prominent in the work of Zora Neale Hurston; characters in *Gone Fishin'* demonstrate their social fluency and their willingness to be a part of the community by "telling lies." In this way, Mosley has made the biblical Ezekiel "his own." He has made him African American.

Gone Fishin' is an important novel, not just because it is beautifully written, not just because it introduces themes that Mosley develops in later novels, but also because it went unpublished for nine years. The experience of rejection of what was, after all, a very good first novel shaped Mosley's relationship with the publishing industry and his artistic direction in many ways, the most obvious of which was his resort to the mystery form as a way of getting heard.

When Mosley finished *Gone Fishin'*, he sent it to a number of agents, none of whom saw any prospect of selling it. "They told me, 'White people don't read about black people,'" Mosley said in an interview with Peter Werbe, "black women don't like black men, and black men don't read." Mosley responded with *Devil in a Blue Dress* (1990), which put Easy and Mouse into a fictional category that publishers could recognize as commercially viable. Frederic Tuten, with whom Mosley was studying at City College of New York, took the manuscript to his own agent; the agent sold it in six weeks. The success of the Easy Rawlins mystery series has helped prove that there are many readers for work about black men, so it is easy to forget how few such novels were being published in the United States before the first Easy Rawlins mystery appeared in 1990.

Throughout his career, Mosley has continued to react to the closed doors he initially experienced. Once he had the clout to do so, he began to diagnose the problem in public forums. In "A Closed Book," published in 1994 in the *Los Angeles Times Book Review*, he charges publishers with "a passive kind of liberal racism . . . the kind of racism where you stick to your own kind without hating those who are different." He points to the word-of-mouth hiring practices of the industry and argues that the people getting hired onto editorial staffs tend to be from the same social circles. He initiated a remedy to this practice in 1997, when he proposed the creation of a publishing institute at City College to train and provide internships for urban students. The Publishing Certificate Program resulted from this effort, supported by money Mosley provided out of his own pocket, as well as by donations from major publishing houses. When, in the mid-1990s, Mosley was in a position to choose any publisher he wanted for *Gone Fishin'*, he gave the book to a small independent house, Black Classic Press.

THE EASY RAWLINS MYSTERIES

The six Easy Rawlins books that have appeared so far—*Devil in a Blue Dress*, *A Red Death* (1991), *White Butterfly* (1992), *Black Betty* (1994), *A Little Yellow Dog* (1996), and *Bad Boy Brawly Brown* (2002)—originated in a strategic career move. Nevertheless, Mosley has claimed that the mystery form suits his material artistically; the "structure of revelation," he told Lynell George, is paradigmatic of the way he understands plotting. Although he dislikes being labeled a mystery novelist, Mosley does not cast aspersions on the "low" form that has made his career possible.

Some of Mosley's critics are suspicious of the genre. Robert Crooks and Roger Berger have suggested that the structure and conventions of the hard-boiled detective tradition carry with them a reactionary ideology. In every novel, Berger notes, Easy undergoes physical ordeals that prove his strength and stamina. Mosley's protagonist, in other words, participates in the masculinist warrior code defined by his hard-boiled precursors. That code insists on individualist solutions to social problems; Berger also worries, as does Patricia Turner, that Mosley has absorbed the traditional sexism of the genre. Crooks constructs a genealogy for the hard-boiled loner, locating the roots of the figure in the individualism of a frontier ideology that rationalized European American assaults on Native Americans. Both Berger and Crooks point to Easy's intense pursuit of private property as evidence that the narrator-protagonist of the series (and possibly the author as well) has been co-opted by the ideology of getting ahead.

The sense that the trappings of the detective novel are a liability is not universally shared among Mosley's critics. Greg Tate, for instance, perceives the mystery elements in Mosley's writing as inactive ingredients—the binders holding together a potent mix of psychological and philosophical explorations into the anxieties and vulnerabilities of black men. Others believe that the genre elements actually sharpen Mosley's discussion of racial issues. Helen Lock argues that the hard-boiled formulas have a special resonance when the protagonist is African American. One might add, by way of example, that if a private investigator is harassed or beaten by representatives of the established order—an almost obligatory scene in a hard-boiled detective novel—the episode has a special air of plausibility when the victim of police brutality is black.

Lock is particularly interested in the contrast between Easy's hard-boiled narrative voice, which reports the action in standard, or "white," English, and the black vernacular he speaks in dialogue passages. Lock, John Lowe, and Mary Young all have spotted the shape shifting of the folkloric African American trickster in Easy's linguistic slipperiness. Perhaps Easy also exemplifies W. E. B. Du Bois's famous concept of double consciousness as defined in *The Souls of Black Folk* (1903):

> It is a peculiar sensation, this double-consciousness, this sense of always looking at one's self through the eyes of others, of measuring one's soul by the tape of a world that looks on in amused contempt and pity. One ever feels his two-ness—an American, a Negro; two souls, two thoughts, two unreconciled strivings; two warring ideals in one dark body, whose dogged strength alone keeps it from being torn asunder.

As a traditional hard-boiled, first person narrator, Easy talks about himself in the language of the majority culture. He ratchets up the "tension," as Lowe calls it, by emphasizing his preference for the "vernacular-warmed" speech patterns of his childhood. Elsewhere, still in mainstream English, he complains about a black policeman who speaks "white" English and describes his (mistaken) assumption that a black woman who speaks standard English must be a snob.

One consequence of all this is the destabilization of the marketing philosophy behind the claim that "white people don't read about black people, black women don't like black men, and black men don't read." Implicit in that philosophy is the notion that readers look for protagonists with whom they can identify—white with white, black with black, women with women, men with men. Mosley turns that notion on itself, using the mechanics by which writers solicit identification to lever readers out of their demographic niches. Readers of different ethnic backgrounds are encouraged to identify with the narrative "I" and to share in Easy's fears and triumphs, only to be reminded, when Easy speaks between quotation marks, that if they are not African American, he is "other," or, more precisely, that *they* are "other" in his world. For black readers, the same narrative tension provides an opportunity to see the classic African American experience of double consciousness taken out of the margins of cultural life and made normative.

As critics on all sides of the debate acknowledge, the moral universe of the Easy Rawlins series is more ambiguous than the worlds described by earlier practitioners of the hard-boiled–detective genre. Part of that complexity derives from the fact that Mosley draws on other traditions as well. Kristina Knotts has pointed to the existentialism of the series, which is full of ethical conundrums pitting the narrator's personal survival against his loyalty and generosity.

Ethics are a luxury. Nevertheless, Easy does have some absolute values that take precedence over survival. These signifiers of decency help, perhaps, to make him sympathetic to readers. The most unyielding of his values is love of children. That trait separates him from traditional private investigators. In the course of the series, he rescues and adopts two children: Jesus, a Mexican boy who has been sexually abused, and Feather, a mixed-race baby girl who is orphaned by events in *White Butterfly*. "When I first saw her," Easy says of Feather, "she was sucking her toe. I looked down and she smiled at me and said something in baby talk that I thought meant 'Tickle my stomach and push my nose.'" Easy, in other words, has a soft spot; it compromises both the toughness and the lonesomeness that characterize the traditional private eye. When he adopts Jesus and Feather, he knits himself into a web of responsibilities and community ties.

Mosley's characterization of the community has occasioned some nervousness. William Frieburger complains that the prevalence of crime, vice, and violence in the novels borders on stereotype. He also worries that in *A Red Death* the only "genuinely admirable" character is a white one, the communist Chaim Wenzler, whom Easy spies on for the FBI. In his interview with the writer Thulani Davis, Mosley suggested a possible response to the charge by indicating that the flawed characters who populate the world of Easy Rawlins are drawn with love. The autodidact Jackson Blue, for instance, is intensely interesting to write about because he is both a brilliant intellect and a "small-minded," irresponsible coward. Mosley's colorful characters are not perfect, but his affection for them shines through his prose, humanizing the community he is introducing to the world in a way that would not be possible if his affection required perfection from its objects.

One might add that "good" and "bad" are ambiguous terms in the Easy Rawlins series. Wenzler, for example, is considered a good man (a label other characters often attach to Easy throughout the series), but perhaps, after all, he is not genuinely admirable. His idealism is shown to depend on a kind of willed naiveté. Wenzler's goodness turns out to be as much a flaw as a virtue because it is incompatible with survival. "Chaim was a good man," Easy says in *A Red Death*, "better than a lot of people in Washington, and a lot of black people I knew. But he was dead. He was history, as they say, and I was holding a gun in the dark; being real." Easy has already said that he does not believe in history; it does not seem "real" to him. If Chaim is "history" and history is "not real," then Mosley seems to be saying that Chaim is, on some level, not real. Easy, as an imperfect, not genuinely admirable black-everyman figure, is, however, real.

Just as "good" is not an absolute good in Easy's world, so "bad" is not wholly bad. Mouse, for instance, is as bad as Wenzler is good. He is so bad that critic Mary Young sees another figure from African American folklore in him—the "bad Black man," also called the "badman." The almost mythical stature Mouse has in the novels supports this appeal to folklore. The descriptions of his exploits read like tall tales, or oral lies put into print.

Despite—perhaps because of—his badness, Mouse is an attractive character. He makes himself indispensable to Easy in the treacherous world of mid-century Los Angeles. "Easy, you gotta have somebody at yo' back," he says in *Devil in a Blue Dress*. "That's just a lie them white men give 'bout makin' it on they own. They always got they backs covered." Mosley also locates Mouse's appeal to readers in the character's self-love. Mouse does not feel inferior to white people, and, as Mosley has told Davis, he has "a rock solid certainty" about his ability to prevail "that most black people don't have." In *Bad Boy Brawly Brown*, Mosley sums up Mouse's abilities—a set of superficially disparate talents that together suggest a single word: potency.

> Raymond Alexander was the most perfect human being a black man could imagine. He was a lover and a killer and one of the best storytellers you ever heard. He wasn't afraid of white people in general or the police in particular. Women who went to church every week would skip out on Sunday school to take off their clean white panties for him.

Mouse's successes as a lover are explicitly contrasted with Easy's more troubled encounters. Despite a violent streak that makes even his best friend quake at his every mood change, women anticipate pleasure from Mouse and do not fear him at all. Mouse is a towering figure among men, but next to women he looks small enough to justify his name. In *White Butterfly* his lover Minnie leaps up and yells "Oh boy!" when he enters her apartment. She is "a head taller and fifty pounds heavier than Mouse." When she picks him up and swings him from side to side, Mouse has to plead to be set down. "Stop it, Minnie. Stop it fo' you send me to the hospital."

Is Mouse's relative meekness with women organic to his character? Or is it a domestication on Mosley's part, a concession like Easy's love of children? Perhaps readers need some signs of underlying softness if they are going to find a badman (or a trickster) likable. If Mouse were to exercise his trademark hair-trigger violence on women—just imagine—he might lose his appeal, regardless of his mythic dimensions. "Bad" may not be all bad in the world of Easy Rawlins, but neither is it all good.

At any rate, the strategies of both trickster and badman carry a price. Easy's habits of dissembling make him incapable of intimacy, a theme explored extensively in *White Butterfly*. Also, as Young notes, Mouse is more sadistic than a traditional badman. The pleasure he takes in killing is a source of anxiety for Easy and an expression of ambivalence on the part of the author about a survival strategy that relies on having violent backup. Throughout the series, Easy struggles to keep his personality from merging with Mouse's, alternately running from his friend and summoning his help. Mouse is a dangerous weapon; more than once he threatens to turn on Easy, and in this respect he is like the destructive side of a split personality, developed as a defense against abuse from outside. Mouse is a shadow self; in *Black Betty*, Easy calls him "the darkness on the other side of the moon."

Much has been written about Easy's materialism, his bourgeois values, and his eagerness to join the middle class. What Easy yearns for most poignantly, though, is the middle-class luxury of being a good man without also having to be a bad man. This theme perhaps accounts for the lyrical energy Easy invests in making his home a world apart. In every book of the series he has a private Eden, usually a harbor inside the shade of plants. *A Red Death* gives a characteristic description of such a place: "I had daylilies and wild roses . . . strawberries and potatoes. . . . There was a trellis that enclosed my porch, and I always had flowering vines growing there." The resonance with Domaque's fantastical garden bower in *Gone Fishin'* is evident and suggests a layer of significance beyond social climbing. Easy calls Domaque's molasses shack a kind of Eden in *Gone Fishin'*, and in *Black Betty* he describes the untraditional home he has created with two adopted children as "our own paradise." In both cases, embattled characters have built fragile oases against all odds.

The meaning Mosley has invested in these eccentric garden settings is further illuminated by a comparison with a passage from *Black Betty* that describes the vast, park-like grounds of a powerful white family: "The Cain mansion, first seen through bars of wrought iron painted pink, looked like heaven. It was on top of a hill of sloping grass, dotted now and then with various fruit trees. The structure rose high in the center with giant pillars." Immense wealth looks like heaven, which has some things in common with Eden—greenery and fruit trees—but is uncomfortably more distant and unwelcoming. In *White Butterfly*, Mosley adds the distancing effect of irony to a similar description, giving the scene a touch of kitsch: swans preening and "a large white rabbit" that "held one ear aloft as he nibbled in the grass."

Heaven may not be attainable, Mosley seems to say—who wants it, anyway?—but the oppressive silliness of utopian visions does not mean that all idealistic yearning is fruitless. In *Bad Boy Brawly Brown,* the space Easy creates at home with Jesus, Feather, and Bonnie, his new girlfriend, is safe enough that he can begin to imagine alternatives to the dissembling of the trickster, the fearlessness of the badman, and the fear of intimacy intrinsic to both of those survival strategies. Bonnie offers Easy one such alternative when she explains to him that she loves him not because he saved her from an attacker, but because he cared that she was okay. Easy almost accepts this unfamiliar value system, looking into her eyes and concluding that her heart is "too vast for me to comprehend." There is a sense here of an impossibly large space opening up within the small confines of Easy's "own paradise."

Is the mystery form ultimately a liability for Mosley? One must not forget that technical problems as well as ideological ones are inherent in any series with an ongoing cast of characters. In each succeeding book, characters must be reintroduced. Plot points from previous books must be rehashed. Incidents from early in the series, reappearing as backstory in the later Easy Rawlins novels, sometimes do not sparkle as they did at the first telling. *A Little Yellow Dog* and *Bad Boy Brawly Brown* in particular show signs of weariness. Nevertheless, the form has on the whole served well. Mosley's detective novels have put him on the best-seller list, have amplified his voice across several other genres, and have given him a framework for the language, the world, and the characters whose story he began to tell in *Gone Fishin'*.

FEARLESS JONES

In his conversation with Colson Whitehead, Mosley said that he wrote four Easy Rawlins novels before he realized that "one of the subjects of my books is black male heroes." That realization gave new direction to his work, and after the publication in 1994 of *Black Betty,* Mosley began a period of heightened productivity. He tried out new genres and new protagonists, at least in part as vehicles for his theme.

Exploration of black male heroism seems to be the point of Fearless Jones, who first appeared in a short story, "Fearless," in 1995. That agenda may explain an authorial choice that has bewildered at least one reviewer; Jesse Berrett has questioned why Mosley bothered to launch a new series set in the same time and place as the Easy Rawlins series, but with different characters. Fearless is a more "perfect human being" even than Mouse, effortlessly Herculean, endlessly attractive to women, and as generous as Easy with waifs. He also subscribes to a personal code of chivalry. When attacked by two racist cops wielding pistols, Fearless disarms them; then, instead of shooting them as Mouse would do instantly, he tosses the pistols away and offers to fight both men with his bare hands.

It is as if Mosley, having decided to explore the theme of black male heroes, has reshuffled the personality traits he previously divided between Easy and Mouse. The hero still is split in two: like Mouse, Fearless has an ambivalent best friend, Paris Minton, who serves as a narrator. The novel *Fearless Jones* (2001), which followed the short story, makes the comparison with Mouse's potent bravado explicit: "Fearless considered himself and maybe three other people he'd ever met to be *full bad*"—as opposed to half or three-quarters bad. Mouse's given name, Raymond Alexander, is on the list of those considered full bad.

Paris Minton, like Easy Rawlins, is a reader of books (he owns a used-bookstore) who relies on ratiocination to unravel the plots that threaten his survival. Unlike Easy, he is also a coward whose instinct for self-preservation always trumps his sense of honor. Paris does not join in Fearless' battles against injustice; when Fearless takes on the police, two against one, Paris watches from the sidelines. He does call out to warn Fearless of a knife attack coming from behind, but he cringes at having committed himself even that far, clapping his hand over his mouth as soon as the words are out.

A slapstick, cartoon quality, apparent in this scene from the short story, may be part of what made Berrett uncomfortable with the novel. In an essay written for the Internet, "The Writing of *Fearless Jones*" (2002), Mosley acknowledges that the Fearless episodes are not as substantial as his other work, calling the novel "comic noire" with "fringe of social realism" and hoping that readers will find it "an entertaining interlude."

THE SOCRATES FORTLOW STORIES

The mood is different in *Always Outnumbered, Always Outgunned* (1998) and in *Walkin' the Dog* (1999), two short story collections whose protagonist is the meaningfully named ex-convict Socrates Fortlow. *Fearless Jones* extracts and condenses the comic-heroic elements of the Easy Rawlins series; the Socrates stories are to the same degree earnest and melancholy. The heroism Mosley illustrates here is psychological, encompassing courage, persistence, and a refusal to despair. Nevertheless, Mosley also marks Socrates as a hero, as he does Fearless, Mouse, and Easy, by giving him larger-than-life physical prowess. The stories refer repeatedly to Socrates' "rock-breaking hands," his "great hands."

Socrates fears his own strength, which, together with hair-trigger reactions and a deep-seated reflexive anger, has enabled him, thirty-five years before the action of the stories, to kill his best friend and to rape and kill his best friend's girlfriend, a crime Mosley explains in *Always Outnumbered, Always Outgunned*:

Three young people, blind drunk.

Back at Shep's, Muriel gave Socrates the eye. He danced with her until Shep broke it up. But then Shep fell asleep. When he awoke to find them rolling on the floor the fight broke out in earnest.

Socrates knocked Shep back to the floor and then he finished his business with Muriel. . . . when she started to scream and she hit Socrates with that chair he hit her back.

The strength and reflexes that get Socrates in so much trouble constitute, precisely, the survival strategy that makes Mouse "full bad." Mouse is not a moral being, but Socrates, despite his terrible crimes, is. Hence the latter, fearing his own power, embodies the dilemma also embodied in the alter-ego relationship of Mouse and Easy.

Socrates suffers from a pervasive sense of guilt, an oppressive sense of being in the wrong, even when he has done nothing wrong. In *Walkin' the Dog*, Mosley writes that Socrates "was guilty, guilty, all the way around. He was big and he was black, he was an ex-convict and he was poor. . . . you could see by looking at him that he wasn't afraid of any consequences no matter how harsh."

Mosley is describing a state of mind, not objective reality, when he calls Socrates guilty, and he emphasizes this distinction in *Always Outnumbered, Always Outgunned*: "he was evil. That's what Socrates thought. That's what he believed." But in using an unqualified indicative form of the verb "to be"—Socrates "was" guilty—Mosley perhaps is getting at a cultural metaphysics of guilt as well. Socrates has no voice in the reality constructed by the dominant culture. That reality defines him—"guilty"—without reference to survival needs, and so, in trying to survive, he *is* guilty, absolutely, always. Socrates inhabits a universe whose God does not cherish him. In fact, God is so distant that he is blue, as Socrates remembers his aunt telling him in *Always Outnumbered, Always Outgunned*: "Blue like the ocean. . . . Sad and cold and far away like the sky is far and blue. You got to go a long long way to get to God. And even if you get there he might not say a thing." In his distance and coldness, God is reminiscent of the vast, park-like properties of powerful white people. God—culturally defined righteousness, one might say—is, like heaven, unattainable to Socrates.

Socrates does not despair, however. He harnesses his anger and the knowledge he has acquired from his bleak experiences in prison, engaging people in Socratic dialogues on ethical issues and struggling against untenable living conditions. When a drug addict named Petis commits a series of murders, Socrates holds a meeting with residents of the terrorized neighborhood. The participants give testimony and make arguments for and against informing the police or imposing the death penalty on their own. Socrates presides, questioning witnesses, applying rules of evidence, and leading the group to a decision. They decide not to turn Petis in to the police because the effectiveness and fair-mindedness of the police are in question and not to execute him because "killin' ain't no answer for civilized men," but to exile him from the neighborhood. In this homegrown justice system, Socrates is the hero, not only working out a solution but also serving as an enforcer. The strength and anger that have gotten him into trouble in the past enable him to frighten Petis into compliance. His opposition to the "death penalty," it becomes clear, has more to do with his intimate understanding of what it means to have blood on his hands than with any softheartedness about Petis's fate. When he confronts Petis, Socrates is pragmatic and far from gentle:

> "We know what you been doin', Petis," Socrates said.
> "What?"
> Socrates slapped the young man so hard that he fell.
> "Get back up in the chair, boy."

This interaction resembles a police interrogation Easy Rawlins undergoes at the hands of a corrupt policeman in *Black Betty*. It differs from that scene, however, in that Socrates lacks the sadism Mosley attributes to the many powerful men who populate his novels—racist white policemen, crooked white politicians, thuggish white real estate developers, and flamboyant black killers like Mouse. Socrates is not a congenial hero, but he exercises his power soberly.

Another component of his heroism is his mentoring of Darryl, a twelve-year-old boy. In Darryl's "hard convict stare," Socrates sees a resemblance to his own younger self that initially enrages him. When they meet, Socrates senses murder on Darryl's conscience, but the remedy he prescribes in this case contrasts sharply with the justice he metes out to Petis. Instead of punishing Darryl or turning him in, Socrates acts as confessor, wringing from him an admission of a crime whose memory Darryl would prefer to repress. Darryl learns to acknowledge that he has done wrong without being consumed with self-hatred, hatred of the world, and bitterness at the world's distant, blue God.

The interest these stories have in the sensation of futility and the psychology of frustration suggests that Mosley may have written them in dialogue with W. E. B. Du Bois's *Souls of Black Folk*. They share not only themes with Du Bois's work but also the still-resonant imagery with which Du Bois described the experience of racially based dispossession nearly a hundred years earlier:

> their youth shrunk into tasteless sycophancy, or into silent hatred . . . or wasted itself in a bitter cry. . . . The shades of the prison-house closed round us all: walls strait and stubborn to the whitest, but relentlessly narrow, tall, and unscalable to sons of night who must plod darkly on in resignation, or beat unavailing palms against the stone, or steadily, half hopelessly, watch the streak of blue above.

RL'S DREAM

The theme of a distant God—"the streak of blue above"—might account for an aspect of *RL's Dream,* its take on blues music, that has distressed at least one critic. Arguably Mosley's most ambitious and complex novel, *RL's Dream* follows the final months in the life of a Delta Blues guitarist named Soupspoon Wise, who once played with the legendary Robert Johnson; now Soupspoon is dying of lung cancer in the unenchanted New York of the 1990s. The book has a striking emotional energy, manifest in the intensity of all its characters, from Robert "RL" Johnson himself to Soupspoon, who is obsessed with Johnson, to Kiki, a wounded, young white woman who grants Soupspoon a reprieve from death by scooping him off the street, bathing and feeding him, and forging him a health insurance policy so that he can get cancer treatments.

RL's Dream is Mosley's first published novel that is not a mystery. Its atmospheric effects have received praise, as have its musical prose, vibrant characterizations, and psychological insights. The novel also has provoked expressions of uneasiness. David Ulin, for instance, believes that the protagonist lacks the complexity of Easy Rawlins and characterizes Mosley's take on the blues as "out of date," "wrong-headed," and "stereotypical." This critical distress is occasioned by Soupspoon's description of the blues as "devil's music" and of Robert Johnson as "Satan's favorite son." Ulin finds this treatment of the blues something of an enigma, given that Mosley "clearly reveres the genre."

One solution to the enigma might be that most of the pronouncements about the blues in *RL's Dream* are filtered through Soupspoon's point of view, and that protagonist and author are not necessarily univocal. Soupspoon is a dying man in a heightened state of mind—a state of feeling, one might say. Nevertheless, what is at stake in *RL's Dream,* as in the Socrates Fortlow stories, is more than a picture of one man's psychological complexities. The additional layer of significance becomes clearer when one reads Soupspoon's descriptions of the blues in light of Du Bois's "blue streak above" or Socrates' notion of a God as distant as the sky. In the one world Soupspoon really knows, the world of the Mississippi Delta, where the blues originated, God may be good—by definition—but the white deity that presides over that world is not kind to black people. Almost anything Soupspoon does in his own interest—earning money by playing music at the side of the road, for instance—could get him in trouble with a white sheriff. To be good, in other words, is to abdicate life. Soupspoon remembers black men and women carrying hundred-pound sacks of cotton on their backs, "Sacks bigger than they were. Like God's big white toe about to crush out what little misery they had to let them know that they were alive." In this context, the opposite of godliness is freedom, and "freedom had a name. It was called the blues." If one no longer had the heart for pleasures like "whiskey, women, and the blues," Soupspoon says, "it was time to die." Thus, behind the dichotomy between godly hard work and evil revelry lurk familiar existential specters: the futility of life, the endpoint of death.

Robert Johnson, whom Soupspoon considers a far more authentic blues artist than he, is the only man he has ever met who could face those specters "and still be a man. . . . he never let himself know that he was scared." The so-called evilness of the undaunted R. L., like the badness of Mouse, is not all bad. Robert Johnson embodies the will to live and retains a spooky vibrancy fifty years after his death. He appears at Soupspoon's deathbed as a young man lighting a cigarette, revealing his "evil, handsome face in the flame." When the match goes out, his face stays "alight."

By contrast, the musician whose dying consciousness hosts this vision feels like a "weak shadow." Soupspoon knows that his musical performances have made people happy. Still, he thinks of his music as "just . . . some echo of somethin' that happened a long time ago." His life of fifty years ago has telescoped into the present, as if the intervening years are irrelevant: "It's like everything I did seems to be happenin' all the time," he says. He sees himself as a vessel of memories—important only because of his encounters with Robert Johnson and his knowledge of a past that is almost lost to history.

The narrative structure of the novel allows us to accept this self-assessment, showing by the very interiority of Soupspoon's current experiences that a world of riches will die with him if he does not manage to hand them off. When the novel opens, he is dying, alone in an apartment from which he will soon be evicted. A throat infection renders him literally mute. Part of the narrative tension of the novel rests in the question of whether his experiences will vanish when his body shuts down. Soupspoon, like Mosley's other protagonists, can be characterized as a "black male hero," but his heroism has a different flavor; his triumph consists of recovering long enough to transfer his memories onto a cassette tape, which he sends to a historian.

In the end, Soupspoon's throat infection returns, along with the cancer. He falls mute again and dies anonymously. Mosley does not insist that the triumph over existential despair is complete. Regret and nostalgia pervade the very premise of the book—the past, for all its horrors, seems somehow more authentic than the present, and it is the past, rather than the future, that characters look to for an alternative to the present. Indeed, Mosley leaves readers with the question of whether Soupspoon can be said ever to have existed at all. As he dies, Soupspoon suspects that "I'ma wake up and all this I been goin' through is just a dream. The kinda dream that somebody like RL would have. A evil long-lastin' dream about all the bad things could happen here." It is a view of Soupspoon's life both melancholy and plausible that his experiences of the past fifty years might be a figment of Robert Johnson's imagination.

It may be worth noting that Robert Johnson was born Robert Leroy (hence the intials R. L.) Johnson. Mosley's father, whose first name was LeRoy, died of lung cancer in 1993, and the book is dedicated to him. The confluence of names and events suggests an emotional source for the almost uninterrupted lyricism of *RL's Dream,* the force of its nostalgia, and the existential question it asks: Who is more real—the man who lives legends, or the man who survives to tell the stories?

The earnest tone of the book has made some readers cringe. Gary Giddins, for instance, objects to the allegorical implications of Soupspoon's last name and complains about "moments of unreality." To this criticism, one might add that Mosley's ideas sometimes show—with passion—through the fabric of the story. On occasion, his characters sound more like vehicles for those ideas than real people. The ideas themselves are generally interesting. Whether such moments are seen as weaknesses in the writing or as different-colored threads that increase the strength and density of the weave depends, ultimately, on what readers think novels are for.

BLUE LIGHT

In a clean break from "gritty realism," Mosley imagines an event defined as impossible in his preceding works: blue streaks of heaven descend on the world. The divine is brought to earth in *Blue Light* (1998). Variously described as "a din of radiance," "God's tears," "the word," and a kind of cosmic sperm, the blue rays have a quickening effect. Everything they fall on either perishes from the intensity of the experience or awakens to its fullest potential. Thus, "wide-eyed mackerel and barracuda" discover a desire "to swim up onto shore." A philosophy-school dropout becomes a prophet with a cult following, a "smart black girl" who has been living a vicarious life through books becomes a multilingual world traveler with encyclopedic knowledge, and a man who has just died of cancer becomes a zombie. This last character, called Gray Man, is potently, implacably murderous—in some ways like Mouse. Gray Man, however, has none of Mouse's vibrancy. He is not interested in sex or money or flashy clothes; he dislikes what he sees as the contamination of blue light by the admixture of flesh and blood. Gray Man is, in fact, pure death. In his determination to send the blue light back to the heavens, he drives the plot of the novel, stalking and killing the other beings who have been exposed to the blue light, the "blues." While *Blue Light* is generally classed as science fiction, the novel also reads like horror fiction because divine power in this work, as in Mosley's other books, is not necessarily benevolent.

Given his predilection for large ideas, it is not surprising that Mosley would turn to writing what he calls speculative fiction—fiction that takes an imaginative or counterfactual premise as its starting point. More remarkable, because by the mid-1990s he had the authority of five best-sellers behind him, is that his usual publishers refused the book. When Little, Brown finally published *Blue Light,* Mosley was accused of "new age posturing" by *Guardian* reviewer Hettie Judah. Reviewers also complained that the book dabbled in too many styles and ideas. Most of all, they worried, like Mel Watkins, that *Blue Light* had replaced the "gut-real encounters" of the Easy Rawlins series with allegory and archetype.

The novel has its defenders too. David Smith has suggested that *Blue Light*'s philosophical underpinnings are Emersonian. Smith demonstrates that the everyday state from which Mosley's blue light awakens its recipients resembles the numb half-oblivion described by Emerson as limiting most human lives. Likewise, the powers that the blue light intensifies in its recipients—prophecy in the case of Ordé, sexuality in the case of Claudia Heart, dreaming in the case of Wanita, evasion and escape in the case of Reggie, and warrior strength in the case of Alacrity—can be read as examples of what Emerson called genius. Emerson defined genius as the combination of qualities that differentiates one being from another; one's genius gives one purpose. It is interesting to note that in another context Mosley uses the term with similar precision. In his introduction to *Black Genius* (1999), a book of essays he edited, Mosley distances himself from the common usage that associates genius with extraordinary intelligence. For him, the term refers to "that quality which crystallizes the hopes and talents and character of a people. . . . It is the possibility for a people to look into their hearts and see a life worth living." Mosley is talking about a collective rather than an individual genius—the genius of a people. Otherwise, his use of the term is closely allied to Emerson's.

One thing that separates this philosophy from watered-down, New Age notions of finding oneself is the stress Emerson placed on intensity of experience, application, and discipline. *Blue Light* shares that emphasis, describing the single-mindedness, even ruthlessness, with which "the blues" follow their callings. Ordé, who makes it his mission to save others from the sleepwalking state he has transcended, sometimes kills his disciples in the process. The intensity of Claudia Heart's sexuality is similarly dangerous to her lovers. These and other blues exhibit a coldness, a misanthropy, and an intolerance that call intensity as a value per se into question.

Mosley does not blithely imagine that Emersonian intensity is a path to utopia. Instead of advocating for such a world, Mosley simply posits its existence and then explores the implications. As Smith points out, Emerson recognized that a society full of people relentlessly following their own geniuses is likely to devolve into conflict and violence. The solution Emerson proposed is something called "double consciousness," a concept that resonates in more than homonymic ways with the better-known phenomenon of double consciousness described by Du Bois. To have double consciousness in Emerson's sense is to occupy an individual perspective and a collective, or community, perspective simultaneously, one always checking the other.

Mosley does seem to believe that there is too little of the "blue" way of life in today's world. Part of his task as a writer, he has intimated, is to give readers a taste of heightened experience, to elate them. He expresses his admiration for other writers in similar terms: a piece by Albert Camus is "like that one-tenth of one percent of life that is truly ecstatic," he says in "Writing About the Universe" (1998); John Edgar Wideman's prose, he says in "Love Among the Ruins," a 1998 review of Wideman's *Two Cities*, "is crafted to please as it elates."

This articulation of Mosley's goals in writing—along with the leap *Blue Light* makes across the boundaries of genre—raises another question about the book: How do racial issues, so central in Mosley's other works, figure into *Blue Light*? Mosley does not believe African Americans should be confined to writing about their "chains," he has told Sarah Lyall, but he includes the theme of racial oppression in his books because it is a part of life. In *Blue Light* one of the blues articulates a similar take on what the light means for racial identification: "This body is like a uniform, Chance. I'm like a soldier. I'm proud of the colors and buttons, but they are only vestiges of the spirit that wears them." The need to love one's roots without getting trapped in a ghetto is a theme that gains prominence in much of Mosley's later work.

WORKIN' ON THE CHAIN GANG AND *FUTURELAND*

Mosley's first book-length work of nonfiction, written on the occasion of the millennium, characterizes contemporary racism and its progenitor, slavery, as manifestations of "a much larger malignancy" that affects people of all races. *Workin' on the Chain Gang: Shaking Off the Dead Hand of History* (2000) also sees the experiences of African Americans as a key to solving the problems facing humanity in the new century. The resistance African Americans have "put up to a system that has kept us down" could serve as a model for others, he writes.

As its title suggests, *Workin' on the Chain Gang* takes the plantations of the South as paradigmatic metaphors for the contemporary corporate economy. For this reason, it makes sense to read it in tandem with *Futureland: Nine Stories of an Imminent World* (2001). *Futureland* is a collection of cyber-punk stories in which technological marvels initially seem to promise that humanity will eventually slip its chains—both social chains and natural ones like those Mosley identifies in *Workin' on the Chain Gang:* "the aging process, vulnerability to disease, failing eyesight," and death, "the final link . . . the eyebolt that holds fast all our other chains." That promise is betrayed in *Futureland,* and the stories grow darker as the collection progresses. They culminate in the collapse of the technologically advanced, hyper-controlled Futureland into chaos and ethnic warfare.

The theme of escape runs countercurrent to the darker themes in *Futureland*. In episode after episode, Mosley's protagonists make elaborate, artistic escapes. A prisoner in a for-profit prison (a type of institution Mosley characterizes as "dangerously close to . . . slavery" in *Workin' on the Chain Gang*) uses a computer virus to outwit an electronic shackle that conditions behavior through an interface with the central nervous system. Likewise, a man accused of murder ties an electronic judge-and-jury machine in logical knots; although he is ultimately executed, his consciousness is accepted into the jury pool, whose members he promptly liberates. The most influential escape artist, perhaps, is Chill, a heroic ex-convict who

> had been obsessed with escape ever since the day he was convicted of armed robbery. The only way he could fall asleep in his cell at night was by imagining himself a slave who had slipped his chains, pried open the bars, and outrun the dogs. Even after his release Chill needed this fantasy to drop off most nights.

As a result of Chill's efforts, his nephew, Ptolemy, escapes indoctrination in Futureland's schools and grows up outside the influence of the hegemonic media. Ptolemy reappears later in the collection as a revolutionary who frees another protagonist from workplace misery.

In *Workin' on the Chain Gang,* Mosley argues that two traits, apparent in Chill, are crucial elements in African American resistance to oppression. The first trait is self-love despite a deluge of negative messages about oneself. How does this work? "Simple," Mosley says. "You accept the images given and love them anyway. . . . We love our features, our foibles, and the unique way in which we hold off oblivion. This love is ecstatic and ambivalent." The second trait is the conscious knowledge of dispossession from another world. "We might not remember Africa," Mosley writes, "but . . . at least we know it wasn't always like this." Mosley offers this willingness to imagine other realities as a crucial remedy for the totalitarian notion that the economic laws by which the contemporary world is governed are immutable. In *Futureland,* however, Mosley clearly sets out to describe not some other world that could be, but what is. The collection conforms to science fiction conventions in a way that *Blue Light* does not, following the science fiction principle that futuristic stories are generally about the present.

"Productivity" is a key word in *Futureland.* Neil, the protagonist of "En Masse," works at "the data production house of General Specifix," where he is not an employee, but a "prod." In crowded rooms, the prods work seven to a table inserting "logic currents." They are monitored and given "D-marks" for lapses in concentration, illness, symptoms of a stress-related disorder called *labor nervosa,* and, in Neil's case, fainting. Seventeen D-marks result in unemployment. The unemployed are confined to a giant underground facility called Common Ground, in which people whom the market cannot accommodate are warehoused, eat cheap food in twenty-two-minute shifts, and spend their days in waiting rooms looking at washed-out video images of the upper world. Common Ground, in other words, is the opposite of an Emersonian world.

Neil tends to faint because he suffers from claustrophobia. If discovered, the condition could get him assigned to permanent unemployment. Instead, he is suddenly transferred to a special project with more humane working conditions, where he enjoys freedoms he had never imagined: he can turn his chair to face the window, he has a whole table to work at, he can take breaks whenever he needs them, and, he discovers, he and a coworker can put up a do-not-disturb sign and make love on company time. The "unit controller" of this project is called M Un Fitt, a tip-off, perhaps, that the project is illicit. The project turns out to be Ptolemy's creation, and its goal is to enhance human potential. Neil has been chosen precisely because his inability to tolerate the harsh work environment of General Specifix enables him to "dream of something other than [his] mind locked into this world." Un Fitt, in other words, is the expression of a defiant anti–social Darwinism.

Archetypes and allegory prevail in *Futureland* to a greater extent than in *RL's Dream* or even *Blue Light*. Mosley is more interested here in ideas than in characterization or well-crafted prose. Indeed, the quality of the writing does not match that of his other books. The narrative voices that tell the stories are weak; the point of view is at best ad hoc and colorless and at worst inconsistent. Nevertheless, the critical reception, although muted, has not been hostile. Perhaps the rubric of science fiction, more unambiguously applicable than in the case of *Blue Light*, has sheltered the book. Perhaps, also, Mosley has trained the literary world to expect surprises from him and to allow him a freer range in which to experiment.

CONCLUSION

Frederic Tuten, the City College instructor who mentored Mosley, is quoted by Lynell George as saying, "There is a lyricism there that you don't find in much American writing today." The passion for ideas and the thematic sweep of Mosley's work also are rare. Those qualities have sometimes discomfited a literary establishment that tends to expect a becoming modesty of scope from fiction writers. Mosley's agenda—the novelist as philosopher—could have put him on a collision course with the twin taboos of contemporary American letters: intellectualism and naïveté. For the most part, Mosley steers a nuanced course between these dangers. If there are flaws in his later works, they perhaps loom larger in the current climate than they might in a place or time governed by other fears. Given the context, Mosley's persistence—finding a way to move Easy Rawlins from the margins of cultural discourse toward the center, finding (and funding) a way to diversify the staffs of publishing houses, and finding a way to open the emotional and intellectual range of contemporary American fiction—could be seen as heroism on par with that of his protagonists.

Selected Bibliography

WORKS OF WALTER MOSLEY

NOVELS
Devil in a Blue Dress. New York: Norton, 1990.
A Red Death. New York: Norton, 1991.
White Butterfly. New York: Norton, 1992.
Black Betty. New York: Norton, 1994.
RL's Dream. New York: Norton, 1995.
A Little Yellow Dog. New York: Norton, 1996.
Gone Fishin': An Easy Rawlins Novel. Baltimore: Black Classic Press, 1997.
Blue Light: A Novel. Boston: Little, Brown, 1998.
Fearless Jones: A Novel. Boston: Little, Brown, 2001.
Bad Boy Brawly Brown. Boston: Little, Brown, 2002.

SHORT STORIES
"Voodoo." *Callaloo* 38:153–155 (winter 1989).
"Fearless." In *Spooks, Spies, and Private Eyes: Black Mystery, Crime, and Suspense Fiction.* Edited by Paula L. Woods. New York: Doubleday, 1995. Pp. 135–157.
Always Outnumbered, Always Outgunned. New York: Norton, 1998.
"Pet Fly." *The New Yorker,* December 13, 1999, pp. 90–97.
Walkin' the Dog. Boston: Little, Brown, 1999.
"The Black Woman in the Chinese Hat." *Gentleman's Quarterly,* August 2000, pp. 94–100.
"Life and Death." *Savoy,* February 2001, pp. 82–85, 112. (This is the first of the "Tempest Tales," a series of ten short stories that appeared over the course of a year. Best described as fantasy or speculative fiction, the Tempest Tales narrate the after-death experiences of Tempest Landry, who is refused entry to heaven by St. Peter but challenges the decision.)
"Charity." *Savoy,* March 2001, pp. 76–79. (Tempest Tale II.)
"The Kingdom of Heaven." *Savoy,* April 2001, pp. 68–71. (Tempest Tale III.)
"Desire." *Savoy,* May 2001, pp. 74–77. (Tempest Tale IV.)
"Trinity." *Savoy,* June/July 2001, pp. 67–69. (Tempest Tale V.)

"The Fight." *Savoy,* August 2001, pp. 70–72. (Tempest Tale VI.)

"Lady." *Savoy,* September 2001, pp. 72–74. (Tempest Tale VII.)

"The Wake." *Savoy,* October 2001, pp. 74–76. (Tempest Tale VIII.)

"A New Morning." *Savoy,* November 2001, pp. 76–78. (Tempest Tale IX.)

"Gone Fishin'." *Savoy,* December 2001/January 2002, pp. 84–86. (Tempest Tale X.)

Futureland: Nine Stories of an Imminent World. New York: Warner, 2001. (The stories in this collection first appeared as e-books.)

NONFICTION

"The Black Dick." In *Critical Fictions: The Politics of Imaginative Writing.* Edited by Philomena Mariani. Seattle, Wash.: Bay Press, 1991. Pp. 131–133. (Mosley talks about the history of his attempt to sell his first novel and his decision to gain entry to the publishing world through the mystery genre.)

"The World of Easy Rawlins." *Los Angeles Times Book Review,* July 14, 1991, p. 1.

"A Closed Book." *Los Angeles Times Book Review,* May 29, 1994, p. 2. (Mosley discusses the publishing industry.)

"Love Among the Ruins." *New York Times Book Review,* October 4, 1998, section 7, p. 12. (Review of John Edgar Wideman's novel *Two Cities.*)

"Black to the Future." *New York Times Magazine,* November 1, 1998, pp. 6, 32.

"Writing About the Universe." *Whole Earth,* winter 1998, p. 1.

"Giving Back." In *Black Genius: African American Solutions to African American Problems.* Edited by Walter Mosley, Manthia Diawara, Clyde Taylor, and Regina Austin. Introduction by Walter Mosley. New York: Norton, 1999. Pp. 36–49.

"No Renaissance without Our Editors and Publishers." In *Defining Ourselves: Black Writers in the 90s.* Edited by Elizabeth Nunez and Brenda M. Greene. New York: Peter Lang, 1999. Pp. 9–14.

Workin' on the Chain Gang: Shaking Off the Dead Hand of History. New York: Ballantine Publishing Group, 2000.

"The Writing of *Fearless Jones.*" Available at ⟨http://www.twbookmark.com/features/waltermosley/article.html⟩, 2002.

CRITICAL AND BIOGRAPHICAL STUDIES

Berger, Roger A. "'The Black Dick': Race, Sexuality, and Discourse in the L.A. Novels of Walter Mosley." *African American Review* 31, no. 2:281–294 (summer 1997).

Berrett, Jesse. "Same Time, Same Place: Walter Mosley's Mystery Is in Familiar Territory but with a New Hero." *New York Times Book Review,* June 10, 2001, p. 24.

Bruckner, D. J. R. "Mystery Stories Are Novelist's Route to Moral Questions." *New York Times,* September 4, 1990, p. C13.

Christian, Barbara T. "Walter Mosley." In *The Norton Anthology of African American Literature.* Edited by Nellie Y. McKay and Henry Louis Gates Jr. New York: Norton, 1996. Pp. 2594–2595.

Crooks, Robert. "From the Far Side of the Urban Frontier: The Detective Fiction of Chester Himes and Walter Mosley." *College Literature* 22, no. 3:68–90 (October 1995).

Frieburger, William. "James Ellroy, Walter Mosley, and the Politics of the Los Angeles Crime Novel." *Clues: A Journal of Detection* 17, no. 2:87–104 (fall–winter 1996).

George, Lynell. "Walter Mosley's Secret Stories: A Ride with a Mystery Writer Who Evokes the Uncliched." *Los Angeles Times Magazine,* May 22, 1994, p. 14.

Giddins, Gary. "Soupspoon's Blues." *New York Times Book Review,* August 13, 1994, p. 11.

Hitchens, Christopher. "The Tribes of Walter Mosley." *Vanity Fair* 56, no. 2:46–48 (February 1993).

Judah, Hettie. "Portrait: I Intend to Destroy the World." *The Guardian,* April 6, 1999, p. 4.

Knotts, Kristina L. "Walter Mosley." In *Contemporary African American Novelists: A Bio-Bibliographical Critical Sourcebook.* Edited by Emmanuel S. Nelson. Westport, Conn.: Greenwood Press, 1999. Pp. 350–354.

Lock, Helen. "Invisible Detection: The Case of Walter Mosley." *MELUS* 26, no. 1:77–89 (spring 2001).

Lomax, Sara M. "Double Agent Easy Rawlins." *American Visions* 7, no. 2:32–34 (April–May 1992).

Lowe, John. "Wake-up Call from Watts." *World and I* 13, no. 5:250–260 (May 1998).

Lyall, Sarah. "Los Angeles Memories and an Unlikely Hero." *New York Times,* June 15, 1994, p. C1.

Mason, Theodore O., Jr. "Walter Mosley's Easy Rawlins: The Detective and Afro-American Fiction." *The Kenyon Review* 14, no. 4:173–183 (fall 1992).

Mills, Alice. "Warring Ideals in Dark Bodies: Cultural Allegiances in the Work of Walter Mosley." *PALARA: Publication of the Afro-Latin/American Research Association* 4:23–39 (fall 2000).

Mullen, Bill V. "Breaking the Signifying Chain: A New Blueprint for African American Literary Studies." *Modern Fiction Studies* 47, no. 1:145–163 (spring 2001). (Mullen discusses *Workin' on the Chain Gang* as an example of the class-conscious approach he advocates for African American literary studies.)

Muller, Gilbert H. "Double Agent: The Los Angeles Crime Cycle of Walter Mosley." In *Los Angeles in Fiction: A Collection of Essays,* rev. ed. Edited by David Fine. Albuquerque: University of New Mexico Press, 1995. Pp. 287–301.

Pinckley, Diana. "Mystery Writer and Novelist Walter Mosley Wraps His Tales Around Issues." *Times Picayune,* August 20, 1995, p. D1.

Smith, David L. "Walter Mosley's *Blue Light:* (Double Consciousness) Squared." *Extrapolation* 42, no. 1:7–26 (spring 2001).

Streitfeld, David. "The Clues to the City of L.A.: Walter Mosley's Gumshoe Tracks Decades of Despair." *Washington Post,* November 10, 1992, p. C1.

Tate, Greg. "Ain't That a Shamus." *Voice Literary Supplement,* October 1992, p. 22.

Turner, Patricia A. "From Talma Gordon to Theresa Galloway: Images of African American Women in Mysteries." *Black Scholar* 28, no. 1:23–26 (spring 1998).

Ulin, David L. "Where Memory and Reality Intersect: Soupspoon Wise Faces the Winter of His Life." *Los Angeles Times Book Review,* August 6, 1995, pp. 3, 8.

———. "A Grand Contrivance." *Atlantic Monthly,* July/August 2002, p. 186.

Watkins, Mel. "Primary Color." *New York Times Book Review,* November 15, 1998, p. 20. (Review of *Blue Light.*)

Wesley, Marilyn C. "Power and Knowledge in Walter Mosley's Devil in a Blue Dress." *African American Review* 35, no. 1:103–116 (spring 2001). (Using the terminology of Michel Foucault, Wesley discusses dominance and power as themes in the first Easy Rawlins novel. She argues that Mosley ultimately shows knowledge to be more powerful than violence.)

Whetstone, Muriel L. "Walter Mosley: Hollywood Discovers Best-selling Author." *Ebony* 51:106–112 (December 1995).

Young, Mary. "Walter Mosley, Detective Fiction, and Black Culture." *Journal of Popular Culture* 32, no. 1:141–150 (summer 1998).

INTERVIEWS

Cuza, Bobby. "Q&A with Walter Mosley: Practical Words to Live By." *Los Angeles Times,* March 19, 2000, p. B2.

Davis, Thulani. "Walter Mosley." *Bomb* 44:52–57 (summer 1993).

"Eavesdropping." *Book,* May 2001, pp. 44–47. (An unnamed journalist "eavesdrops" as Mosley converses with fellow writer Colson Whitehead.)

Frumkes, Lewis Burke. "A Conversation with . . . Walter Mosley." *The Writer* 112, no. 12:20–22 (December 1999).

Gregg, Sandra. "Writing Out of the Box." *Black Issues Book Review* 2, no. 5:50–52 (September 2000).

Hahn, Robert C. "*PW* Talks with Walter Mosley." *Publishers Weekly,* May 28, 2001, p. 54.

McCormick, Kathryn. "Tackling Racism in the Mystery Novel." *New York Newsday,* February 1, 1993, p. 35.

Perez, Hugo. "Walter Mosley Talks Technology, Race and His Return Trip into *Futureland.*" *Science Fiction Weekly* 7, no. 45 (http://www.scifi.com/sfw/issue237/index.html), November 5, 2001.

"Walter Mosley: The Books Interview." *The Observer,* April 11, 1999, p. 13. (An unnamed interviewer discusses *Blue Light* with Mosley.)

Werbe, Peter. "Hard-boiled: A Profile of Walter Mosley." *The Progressive* 64, no. 4:32–34 (April 2000).

*PLAYS, FILMS, AND TELEVISION
SHOWS BASED ON THE WORKS
OF WALTER MOSLEY*

Always Outnumbered, Always Outgunned. Adapted by Mosley; directed by Michael Apted. HBO, 1998.

Devil in a Blue Dress. Screenplay and direction by Carl Franklin. TriStar Pictures, 1995.

A Red Death. Stage adaptation by playwright David Barr; directed by Delia Jolly Gray. First production: Chicago Theatre Company, 1997.

—REBECCA BERG

John Nichols

1940–

THERE ARE TWO books that a visitor to any part of New Mexico will have no trouble finding. Whether browsing thriving bookstores in Albuquerque, Santa Fe, or Taos, or seeking curiosities in struggling gift shops in Pojoaque, Shakespeare, or Chimayo, one will always come across copies of *Death Comes for the Archbishop* by Willa Cather and *The Milagro Beanfield War* by John Nichols. Indeed, these two novels are considered required reading for all newcomers who are fortunate enough to settle in the Land of Enchantment, as well as those who have experienced the haunting beauty of that land but must be content to daydream about its splendors from far away.

Cather's Pulitzer Prize–winning story chronicles the struggles and triumphs of Bishop Jean Baptist L'Amy, who was sent from his native France in 1850 to build churches, schools, and hospitals in the New Mexico territory. It is an honest portrayal of the problems that arise when an outside force, in this case the Catholic Church, seeks to exert its will on an indigenous population. Nichols' book, set in modern New Mexico, tells the story of another outside force (a greedy land developer) and a local bean farmer who rallies his neighbors to fight the planned destruction of their way of life. The book established Nichols as the somewhat reluctant literary spokesman for those New Mexicans who stand firm against capitalism's continuing attempts to rape their beloved state. Although it was not well received by most critics, the novel quickly became a cult classic as many New Mexicans recognized the sometimes unflattering but always honest presentation of themselves and their uniqueness. Today John Nichols is as inextricably a part of the New Mexico consciousness as the luscious sunsets and the piñon-scented air. But it is often overlooked that there were two Nichols novels published before *The Milagro Beanfield War*. They and the story of Nichols' journey to New Mexico are worthy of consideration.

EARLY YEARS AND EDUCATION

The genealogical roots of John Nichols' penchant for storytelling can be traced back to his maternal great-grandfather, Anatole Le Braz, who lived between 1859 and 1926. Le Braz, known as the Bard of Brittany, was a prolific storyteller and poet whose most famous work, *La Légende de la mort,* is a vast collection of folktales that celebrates the customs, superstitions, and lifestyle of the far western territory of his native France. Additionally, Nichols' paternal forebears were whalers and merchant sea captains, natural tellers of tall tales, who hailed from Salem, Massachusetts, and Mastic, Long Island.

Nichols' paternal grandfather, and the source for his name, was the renowned naturalist and ichthyologist John Treadwell Nichols. Grandfather Nichols, a curator at the Museum of Natural History in New York, founded the American Society of Ichthyologists and Herpetologists in 1913 and was instrumental in the investigation of four mysterious deaths in the waters off the New Jersey shore in the summer of 1916. It was determined that the deaths were the result of the first recorded shoreline shark attack in America, a determination that was verified by the capture of a seven-and-a-half-foot-long, three-hundred-pound great white whose stomach was found to contain fifteen pounds of human flesh and bones. *Close to Shore: A True Story of Terror in an Age of Innocence* (2001) by Michael Capuzzo recalls that summer and Nichols' role in the events.

Nichols' father, David Gelston Nichols, followed his own father's interests and was employed in his late teens as a field collector in the museum's department of mammalogy. The work allowed him to venture far west of the family home: he traveled on horseback through Nevada, and along with the specimens he collected for the museum, he brought back legendary tales of his adventures—sitting down to play cards with the notorious bank robber Pretty Boy Floyd in Reno, getting bitten by a rattlesnake and having to slash open the wound and suck out the poison—the sort of tales that were just true enough to fascinate his young son many years later. In his 1982 book *The Last Beautiful Days of Autumn* Nichols describes his father as having a passion for "making the physical universe seem knowable and important to others." "Today he is a scientist, a linguist, a zoologist, an ornithologist, an ethologist, a psychologist—in short, an intellectual with a deep curiosity about the world."

Nichols' mother, Monique Robert Le Braz, enjoyed a childhood of wealth and privilege due in part to her grandfather Le Braz's third wife, an American with family connections to the multimillionaire J. P. Morgan. Monique journeyed to America with her stepgrandmother in 1932. After a few months of dinner parties and dances in Manhattan and at the family estate at Peacock Point on Long Island, Monique indulged her fascination with the American Southwest by boarding the Twentieth Century Chief for Santa Fe, New Mexico. On January 4, 1933, she wrote in her diary that from her window in Santa Fe's La Fonda hotel she could see all the stars of heaven. Two days after that she wrote of a visit to San Ildefonso Pueblo, a few miles northwest of Santa Fe. On the surface it is not a very unusual story; she attends two ceremonial dances, looks in on one of the dancers, and exchanges gifts with him—all told in a rather breathless young girl fashion. What is remarkable, and what impressed Nichols, is the fact that she felt a strong, almost sacred affinity for the native people, an affinity she somehow passed on to her son in the brief time she had with him. She returned to New York and was given a position in the Museum of Natural History's anthropology department. She met and fell in love with David Nichols, and the two were married in Paris in 1938.

When they returned to the United States, they moved to Berkeley, California, where the twenty-two-year-old David began his undergraduate studies. It was a happy marriage of two strong individuals who shared a passionate interest in the mysteries of nature. Monique often accompanied David on his specimen collecting trips throughout California and the neighboring states, and their cramped student apartment was filled with unusual flora and fauna and ongoing experiments. They were not, however, merely dilettantes dabbling in arcane knowledge; indeed, they were pre-environmental movement activists. An example of the Nicholses' fervent determination to fight for the rights of man and endangered beast occurred in 1939, when David fought to prevent the California state legislature from declaring open season on the sea lions that fishermen claimed were depleting their fishing areas.

In 1940 their only child was born, and the dedicated naturalists chose to send announcements that read:

NAME John Treadwell Nichols 2nd
DATE July 23rd
LOCALITY 1713 Dwight Way, Berkeley, Cal.
SEX Male
TOTAL LENGTH 20 in.
WEIGHT 7 lbs. 5 oz.
LOCAL HABITAT Alta Bates Hospital

COLLECTORS Monique & David Nichols
FIELD NO. 1

In an autobiographical essay he wrote for *Contemporary Authors*, Nichols recalls:

> Apparently, I was a delightful tyke—blond, blue-eyed, always cheerful. According to Pop, I took after my mother, whom he usually refers to as a kind of saint: always upbeat, gentle, very loving. I have some of her letters and early diaries, and I must admit, she comes across quite even-keeled and sweet. In photographs, she is a lovely blond Bretonne woman, whose beautiful youthfulness is eternal because she died so young.

Monique was only twenty-seven when a general staph infection stopped her weak heart in Miami in 1942.

In his grief David deposited his young son with an aunt and uncle in Smithtown, Long Island, joined the marines, and spent the war years in the South Pacific. Though thousands of miles apart, David kept close to his boy by sending him letters. "I was born in 1940," Nichols says in *The Last Beautiful Days of Autumn*, "But my first real rememberable contact with Dad occurred late in World War II. I received letters from him, full of crayon drawings not of the war, but featuring the jungle trees and beautifully colored exotic birds of the Solomon Islands."

When David returned after the war, he married Esther Gleason of Montpelier, Vermont. Montpelier was one of the first of many cities that were to be the temporary home of Nichols. "We moved often during my childhood, touching down in eight states and twice that many towns," he writes in *If Mountains Die: A New Mexico Memoir* (1979). As disrupting as this must have been, Nichols recalls that there was one constant in his life, his father's family mansion, Mastic, on Long Island. There he was free to roam its six hundred acres of forest and burrow through the attic, a treasure trove for a young boy filled with Civil War uniforms and Revolutionary War weaponry. Stays at his late mother's family home at Peacock Point provided a different but equally enjoyable experience. There he lived a life of Gatsbyian luxury; breakfast was served to him in bed by a maid carrying a tray of silver-domed plates.

Growing up, Nichols exhibited a vivid imagination and wide-ranging curiosity. He often traipsed behind his father on specimen collecting forays in the early morning; He writes in *The Last Beautiful Days of Autumn:* "He gave me a passion to experience the natural world up close, touch it if I could, marveling over a butterfly's habits, or over an intricate spiderweb, an oriole nest, a feather." Nichols learned how to identify animals by their tracks and birds by their songs, and he learned the common and Latin names of plants. He enjoyed a communion with his father and nature that is similar to the relationship the young Ernest Hemingway had with Dr. Hemingway and northern Michigan. Indeed, Nichols' remembrance of himself as a young boy going out alone one summer morning in a canoe to catch perch for breakfast brings to mind Hemingway's Nick Adams.

Despite his ability quickly to learn the wonders of the natural world, when it came time for him to enter formal education, he proved to be at best an indifferent student. As early as kindergarten he stood his ground against the system by resolutely refusing to learn how to tell time. This stubbornness continued throughout grade school in Vermont and New York. In 1949 Nichols' father moved the family, which now included two more sons, David and Tim, to Berkeley so that he might finish his interrupted college work. It was here that Nichols escalated his rebellious behavior by resorting to petty theft. He was arrested for shoplifting a Hopalong Cassidy pistol and holster set. The police later discovered a cache of five hundred dollars worth of previously stolen merchandise hidden under the Nichols' front porch. Nichols was put on probation. Upon receiving his degree from Berkeley, Nichols' father left for Alaska to collect mammals for the Museum of Natural History. Nichols moved with his stepmother and half brothers to Wilton, Connecticut, where, although his grades improved, his rebellious spirit got him into trouble with his classmates and teachers. The family was reunited in Colvin Run, Virginia, and Nichols experienced his first all-white school. The academic standards in this rural town were so low that Nichols easily made straight A's in all his courses. He writes in *Dancing on the Stones* (2000), "I was always the teacher's pet because I could write poetry and wasn't missing three fingers from trying to pull weeds free of a jammed sickle bar. I earned A's in math because I *knew* I had ten toes and thirty-two teeth." Eventually Nichols' father decided it was time for his son to receive a better education, and perhaps some discipline and direction, at a boarding school. With the promise of financial help from his aunt, Nichols took the entrance exam for admission to the Loomis Chaffee School in Windsor, Connecticut. "The math and social studies and history were difficult," he says in *Dancing on the Stones*. "But finally I reached a question right up my alley: *Imagine that your great-grandfather was a settler traveling west in a covered wagon in the 1870s. Give a description of his journey.*" Nichols launched into a now lost masterpiece of teenage hyperbole. "Commenting on my entrance exam, the admissions director said, 'Well, your math scores stink, but you sure can sling the bull.'" He was accepted at Loomis but was required to take two years of remedial English.

> Though English was supposed to be my strong suit, I found it flabbergastingly difficult. I never understood the difference between a dangling participle and a gerund, and I split every infinitive that meandered down the pike. In a trunk somewhere I still have stashed many long essays so marred by red marks they look like surgical operating aprons in the emergency room of a big city hospital on a turbulent Saturday night in July.

At Loomis, Nichols was a curious combination of teenage rebel and crew-cut jock, an avid instigator of pranks, and a star player on the football, hockey, and track teams. He was an indifferent student yet contributed stories to the school's newspaper and its literary magazine, *The Loom,* and he was a voracious reader who could easily absorb literature but could not critically analyze it. The school's teachers and administrators had ample cause to expel Nichols on several occasions, but the fact that he was a favorite among the students, a member of the student council, and a dorm advisor weighed heavily in his favor, and he was allowed to remain.

Sometime during his junior year Nichols won an essay contest sponsored by the National Association of Student Councils. The prize was a trip to the national conference in Roswell, New Mexico. At the last minute, however, it was discovered that Nichols' school had not sent its membership fee, and Nichols was disqualified. It was a crushing blow to the sixteen-year-old boy who was anxious to get away from the pressures of school and the upheaval caused by his father's decision to divorce Esther. He explains in his autobiographical book *An American Child Supreme* (2001) that the divorce shook the comfortable and predictable foundation of his life.

> It became clear to me in about thirty seconds that there is no stability on earth, particularly if you depend on dysfunctional relatives to provide it for you. Fearful of being set adrift, I made a conscious decision to tow the line at Loomis, a simple survival tactic and a fairly cynical act, given my budding rebellious worldview. When I returned to school for my junior year I sucked in my gut, began modestly brownnosing the status quo, and my life became immeasurably easier. Fawning isn't pretty, but occasionally it promotes longevity.

His understanding and generous father did not fail him. He gave him one hundred dollars and a letter of introduction to the director of the

American Museum of Natural History's Southwest Research Station in Portal, Arizona. The summer between his junior and senior years at Loomis, Nichols boarded a Greyhound bus and began a journey into adulthood. He states often in his memoirs, essays, and other nonfiction work that the two months he spent in the Southwest during the summer of 1957 changed his life.

He arrived in Albuquerque, New Mexico, and made his way north to Santa Fe and on to Taos. Like his mother who made her first trip to the region at the same age twenty-four years earlier, Nichols kept a diary. His entries, however, some of which are remembered in *If Mountains Die,* describe little more than what he bought (a cowboy hat and a switchblade knife) what he ate (steak, French fries, and a salad for eighty-seven cents in Santa Fe) and the fact that he saw a Jayne Mansfield movie. He does record visits to Taos Pueblo, the Ranchos de Taos church, and an exhibit of paintings by D. H. Lawrence's friend Dorothy Brett. For the week he stayed in Taos he worked for Justin Locke, who provided him with room and board in exchange for backbreaking work on Locke's house and land. Twenty-two years later he writes, "I still believe that house and its view to be among the most beautiful I have ever known."

Nichols' experiences in Portal were just as physically demanding. He worked for room and board at the research station, collecting lizards, rattlesnakes, and gloriosa beetles. A United States Forest Service ranger offered him a job tracking down and extinguishing fires that had been spotted from lookout towers. The job paid one dollar and fifty cents an hour for twenty-four hour shifts, but it benefited Nichols in ways other than monetary; he was thrown in with a culture of people he would not have met in New England. These were Chicanos and Mexican nationals who worked for low wages in miserable conditions, enduring the abuse of racist foremen. Nichols found himself gravitating toward class betrayal. He enjoyed working hard and drinking hard with his new companions and resented being associated, because of the color of his skin, with the prejudiced and scornful bosses. In his autobiographical book *An American Child Supreme* Nichols writes, "I must have desired liberation from the repressed sand traps of my own family and culture, though I had no concept of poverty's damnation." He celebrated the end of his summer of adventure and insight by going into town with his comrades for a night of Rabelaisian debauchery. The memories he took back East with him sustained him through the next eleven, sometimes difficult years.

Although he stuck to his resolve to do better at Loomis, his final average at the end of his senior year was so low that he was allowed to graduate only after a faculty committee voted in his favor. His academic record would ordinarily have made admission to college very difficult if not impossible. It was his achievements as captain of the Loomis hockey team that enabled Nichols to continue his formal education. He applied to four "hockey" schools: Middlebury, Clarkson, Hamilton, and St. Lawrence. To his surprise he was immediately accepted by all four. "The moral?" he says in *Dancing on the Stones.* "The shortest distance between two points on the line between academic standards and student admissions is a good slap shot."

He chose Hamilton, a small liberal arts college in upstate New York. After the rigors of Loomis, Nichols found life at Hamilton to be relatively easy. He joined a fraternity—Theta Delta Chi—played hockey and football, was elected to his class's honor society, and, during his junior and senior years, served as a member of the honor court, a judicial body that enforced the school's honor code. Beneath this "all-American boy" facade, however, the first stirrings of a social consciousness were making themselves felt. Nichols had, of course, come face-to-face with the ugly fact of segregation when he lived in Virginia, but like the majority of his generation, the so-called "silent generation," he saw it as an insurmountable reality. In college he became enamored of American folk music, the music of the Deep South that told poignantly and angrily the stories of inequality, injustice, despair, and violence. He learned to play the guitar and performed for his college friends such songs as "Strange Fruit," a song about lynching that was made famous by Billie Holiday. In his sophomore year he contracted blood poisoning. During his two-week convalescence in the college's infirmary, he wrote *Don't Be Forlorn,* a novel based on the 1955 lynching of Emmett Till. Reflecting on this effort in *An American Child Supreme* several years later, Nichols writes, "The plot of *Don't Be Forlorn* is seriously warped by the weight of catastrophically maudlin writing. Mawkish stereotypes and an absolute lack of subtlety abound on both sides of the race question; my writing is outlandishly melodramatic." He adds, "But my story does indicate a desire for social justice. One page touches on the brutality of 'free' enterprise; another angrily explains why, in a county 63 percent black, not a single registered black voter is able to qualify for a jury." Unfortunately, the novel was never published; the manuscript is tucked away in Nichols' storage locker in Taos.

In the summer of 1960 Nichols and a friend from college vacationed in Europe. His maternal grandmother, Mamita, had a home in Barcelona, Spain, and the young men used it as their base of operations. Their experiences are straight out of Hemingway: attending bullfights, running before the bulls in Pamplona, visiting the grave of the famous matador Manolete, and touring Paris, Cannes, and Rome. When he returned for his junior year, Nichols began submitting stories to the college's magazine, *The Continental,* and newspaper *The Hamilton Spectator.* In his essay for *Contemporary Authors,* he says:

> Immediately upon our return to Hamilton in September, I got drunk and regaled everybody with my cape and muleta on the fraternity house lawn. Then I cranked out a bundle of stories for our literary magazine, all of them enthusiastic Hemingway imitations full of Spanish swearwords, bullfighters, and prostitutes with hearts of gold.

At this time in his life Nichols considered his writing to be merely a pleasant way to pass time. His hope of a lucrative career after college was pinned on his ever-increasing prowess at hockey. But that hope came to an abrupt and painful end when in the middle of his junior year he sustained an injury during the annual alumni hockey game. The cartilage in his left knee was torn, and the anterior cruciate ligament in each knee was severed. He spent the summer of 1961 in New York City living in rather sumptuous luxury thanks to a generous aunt who gave him the use of a penthouse apartment. He divided his time between writing— "For six weeks, like a little pasha ensconced in a fringed litter atop a decorated elephant, I scribbled industriously in a pair of thick green notebooks"—and absorbing the unusual people and places in Greenwich Village and the Bronx.

In his senior year Nichols received a letter from the United States Selective Service ordering him to appear for a physical. The war in Vietnam was escalating, and it was a certainty that if a young man were found fit for service he would be sent along with hundreds of thousands of others to fight. Nichols passed his first physical but was granted another when he demanded that an orthopedic specialist be allowed to examine his injured knees. Subsequently he was classified 4-F, unfit for combat.

Nichols spent the year after graduation at Mamita's home in Barcelona. He taught English at the Instituto Americano and worked on a manuscript that would become his first published novel, *The Sterile Cuckoo* (1965). The poverty and injustice he had observed in New Mexico, Arizona, and New York City made living with Mamita difficult for Nichols. He was embarrassed by the presence of a cook, a maid, and a chauffeur and tried to avoid their ever-available help. Often he was able to escape to Paris, where he fell in love with a girl named Claude Mégérlin, whose family welcomed the young American into their household. There is no evidence that Nichols saw Claude again after he left Europe; there is, however, reason to believe that Nichols did not leave willingly. In *Dancing on the Stones* Nichols tells the story of how he, a budding revolutionist, made an obscene gesture at Francisco Franco as the dictator's motorcade drove past Mamita's residence in the spring of 1963. The Guardia Civil quickly arrested Nichols and deported him back to New York.

Although wealthy relatives made generous offers to help the unemployed twenty-three-year-old, Nichols cherished his independence above all things and declined. He rented a small apartment on the corner of West Broadway and Prince Street for forty-two dollars and fifty cents a month and began making the rounds of publishing houses trying to sell his novel. As rejection slips from Knopf, Random House, and Viking arrived, Nichols returned to his desk, an odd piece of furniture constructed from boxes and a door found in the streets, and rewrote and resubmitted the work many times. Part-time jobs kept him from starvation. He found work as a short-order cook and dishwasher in Greenwich Village cafés, sold pen-and-ink drawings of nudes for five dollars each on the sidewalk, and played guitar for spare change in coffeehouses.

The early 1960s was a time of transition in the music world. The jazz of the beatnik era of the 1950s was giving way to a new type of American folk music, a folk music that pleaded the cause of social, economic, and political reform. Singers and songwriters such as Joan Baez, Bob Dylan, Joni Mitchell, and Phil Ochs were emerging as the poetic voices of a revolutionary new generation that demanded nothing less than an end to war, a ban on nuclear weapons, and a society that lived by the tenets of peace and love. For a moment Nichols thought that music would be his means of artistic expression. Indeed, he rotated sets with Phil Ochs at Bruce Clayman's launching ground for new talent, the World Café. Clayman invited Nichols to join him and several others on a trip around the world, but Nichols declined, returning to his apartment to work on yet another rewrite of *The Sterile Cuckoo* and to begin a novella that would become his second published work, *The Wizard of Loneliness* (1966). Sixteen years later in his essay for *Contemporary Authors* Nichols says: "Oh Lord, for such fertile and freewheeling days again! I produced bad literature with reckless abandon. I had so much energy! I rewrote draft after draft of *The Sterile Cuckoo*. Simultaneously, I worked on *The Wizard of Loneliness*." After seven months of rejections, rewrites, and recommendations that he get a real job, Nichols was contacted by the David McKay publishing house. They expressed interest in *The Sterile Cuckoo*, a one-hundred-ten-page novella at the time, and asked Nichols to double its length. It took Nichols only three weeks to satisfy McKay, and his novel of love and loss between two college students was accepted for publication.

THE STERILE CUCKOO

The Sterile Cuckoo is a first-person narrative told by Jerry Payne. On the opening page Jerry tells his readers that in the second half of his junior year in college, unable to decide whether to marry or desert a girl, he had signed a suicide pact with her. Now, several years after the potentially fatal agreement, he relates what led the couple to consider such a drastic act. The account begins when he meets the girl, Pookie Adams, at an Oklahoma bus depot where he and the other passengers are having a meal stop. As he is sitting outside waiting to board the bus and continue his journey, Pookie saunters out of the restaurant and sits by him. She is "a skinny, scrubby-haired, dark-eyed, pale girl, with a thin-lipped sarcastic, almost-smiling mouth, balancing a toothpick on her tongue. . . . Before I could catch my breath, she managed to say more mixed-up things than, up until that time, I had heard collectively in my life." Pookie is exasperatingly direct, yet so unlike anyone Jerry has ever known that he sits in stunned silence as she greets him:

> You're a kind of shaggy, scruffy-looking, bag of bones—the real cowboy role—aren't you? . . . And judging from the intense expression on your incredibly boyish face, you are thinking of either punching a gorgeous naked broad in her big white belly, or else catching a flock of tame canaries in a huge net just before they fall into the Mississippi River.

This is hardly a promising beginning for a romantic involvement that three years later will find Jerry and Pookie in the situation described in the novel's first sentence. Jerry does his best to extricate himself from the attentions of this screwball chatterbox, but Pookie is not easily put off. Although he does not exhibit any interest in her whatsoever, she proceeds to tell him the story of her life in her maddening, rapid-fire, stream of consciousness style.

Seventeen-year-old Pookie is on her way home to Merritt, Indiana, after spending the summer with her aunt and uncle in Los Angeles. She dreads returning to her lackluster and somewhat dysfunctional parents and the coming senior year of high school. Jerry is overwhelmed by the onslaught of personal information this strange girl seems compelled to share with him. He begrudgingly gives her tidbits of his own life: he is eighteen, lives with his parents in Riverdale, New York, and will soon be entering an all-male New England college as a freshman. He, like Nichols once did, has spent the summer working at a research center in Arizona, where he collected specimens and chopped down trees that had been struck by lightning and posed a fire hazard. When they board the bus, Pookie convinces Jerry to sit beside her. She takes his hand, and the virginal Jerry is shocked into a fit of stuttering. His reluctance makes Pookie angry. "Talk about furious!" Jerry says,

> I suppose she had a right to be, but she overdid it a lot, asking me if my testicles hadn't dropped or *what* was the matter? Hearing a girl say "testicles" electrocuted me into numbness, and all I did was sit and listen with amazement while she lashed out at me.

Pookie manages to overcome Jerry's shyness, and the two awkwardly kiss. The next morning at the St. Louis depot, they have a quick breakfast together and Pookie says she must change buses. After Jerry reboards his bus Pookie realizes that she does not know Jerry's name or how to get in touch with him. He shouts the information to her as his bus pulls away.

Jerry is deluged with long, rambling letters from Pookie that tell of her senior year in high school. Although he does not write back, her letters keep coming at the rate of a least one every two weeks. As a Christmas card she sends Jerry a piece she wrote entitled "A Parable or Something." It is a "once upon a time" type of schoolgirl fantasy of true love finally arriving beneath her bedroom window. When the love-struck young girl steps out onto the window ledge, however, she falls on her lover's head and smashes his guitar. The letters keep coming, and feeling some vague obligation to respond, Jerry sends Pookie a short note of thanks. Nichols uses an interesting device here; Pookie receives Jerry's note as she is writing to him about a horrific automobile accident that involved herself and several friends. All died save Pookie, who was thrown from the car. She writes that she lay in a state of semiparalysis all night, listening to her friends die, before she was found and transported to a hospital. The letter breaks off abruptly in midsentence, and Jerry realizes that that is when she must have received his pitiful attempt at communication. When she resumes her letter a few days later, she explodes in anger and biting sarcasm. "How devastatingly wonderful it was to receive your letter the other day; however did you find the time to write such an informative and captivating piece of shit?" The letter continues in this vein for several more sentences before Pookie concludes with the declaration that she would commit suicide if she had the proper means.

For the next several months Jerry hears nothing more from Pookie, and he exhibits no interest in discovering what ever became of her. Indeed, he has filled his life at school with a determined pursuit of drunkenness and other self-destructive behaviors. One morning in October of his sophomore year, in one of his few moments of lucidity, Jerry sees a photograph of Pookie in a publication called *The Freshman Scoop*. The magazine is from a girl's college that is about four hours away by car from Jerry's school, and he convinces his friends Roe Billins and Harry Schoonover to make the journey. The drunken trio arrive at Pookie's dormitory at half past seven in the morning and awaken the campus with the sounds of falling beer cans and amplified guitar music. Pookie is by turns humiliated, angry, and delighted by Jerry's arrival. They spend an idle afternoon wandering the campus, catching up on all that has happened to them since Pookie sent her last letter. At the end of the day Jerry realizes that he is in love with this mysterious and maddening girl.

Jerry travels to Pookie's campus by bus nearly every weekend and stays in a boardinghouse that is within easy walking distance to Pookie's dorm. "Saturday afternoons were spent viewing art shows, or sniffing flowers in the campus greenhouses, or talking in some popular café over mugs of chocolate and coffee, or simply going for long walks. I suppose we walked millions of miles in those days." Back at his own school, Jerry daydreams about Pookie and skips classes so that he will be at his door the minute the mailman arrives with Pookie's weekly letter. The couple's early physical relationship consists of kissing and feverish groping but not intercourse. Shyly, Jerry puts the question to Pookie, asking her if she is willing to take the next step. She sends a telegram that shouts with agreement—"YOU BET I AM!" Nichols' genius for comic writing propels the story of their long-delayed consummation—a series of slapstick mishaps and awkward fumbling punctuated by Pookie's constant flow of words. Their coupling, however, is lovingly and tenderly told. They awake the next morning and see the sun shining on snowcapped mountains.

Jerry's problems at school become serious when his growing infatuation with Pookie causes him to skip not only an occasional class but entire days. He manages to avoid expulsion by promising to stay at school and work on his assignments during the spring holiday. This promise means that he will have to withdraw his invitation to Pookie to stay with him at his parents' house during that period. Pookie, however, will not stand for it. She invites herself to stay with Jerry at school, and despite his strong objections and pleas that he must have time to study, she wears him down and he feebly agrees to her plan. They spend the holiday week in Jerry's deserted fraternity house, Jerry working on papers and Pookie exploring. In the evenings they cook hamburgers, make love, and sleep peacefully. One morning Pookie is awakened from a fascinating dream by two raucous crows; she vows she will shoot at least one of them. She rummages through the frat house and finds a rifle, goes into town to buy several boxes of ammunition, and spends the afternoon perfecting her aim by shattering Coke bottles she has lined up on a distant fence. After several failed attempts she finally hits one of the crows and rushes out barefoot to claim its carcass. The glass from the Coke bottles tears a dangerous wound in her foot. After a quick trip to the doctor's office where her injury is sutured, she returns with Jerry to the frat house, gathers up the rifle and the dead crow, and insists that her picture be taken even though it means standing in a torrential downpour. Near the end of their campus idyll, Pookie recites a poem to Jerry that she has been working on all week. It is a curious bit of nonsense in the style of Edmund Lear and Dr. Seuss entitled "The Lavendar Grella." His less than enthusiastic response to the work hints that Jerry may have had about all the "Pookieness" he can stand.

It is interesting that throughout their spring holiday together there is a noticeable absence of alcohol. Even the bottles Pookie shatters with the rifle are specifically identified as Coke bottles. Jerry, who fills his time away from Pookie with drinking bouts that are bacchanalian in their excess, seems content to forgo the dubious pleasures of drunkenness when in Pookie's dizzying presence. Nichols does not glamorize excessive alcohol consumption among college students. His honest depictions in this novel of the severely debilitating effects of chronic inebriation and the painful aftermath of binging are as horrifying as scenes from Charles Jackson's novel *The Lost Weekend* or J. P. Miller's play *Days of Wine and Roses*. Throughout their first months together Pookie's involvement with alcohol amounts to little more than sharing a single bottle of wine with Jerry on the night of their first lovemaking; her abstemious behavior changes drastically in the novel's final chapters.

Jerry finds in the intervening weeks that his fascination with Pookie has begun to cool. He is able to concentrate enough on his studies to restore his shaky academic standing to an acceptable level. Pookie arrives for spring house parties at Jerry's school. He leaves off drinking heavily at one of the parties long enough to pick her up at the train station. Pookie's enthusiastic embrace on the platform knocks Jerry down, and the resulting crack to his head requires seven stitches. The weekend dissolves into one long drunken orgy culminating in a visit to the campus cemetery on Sunday. Fortified with a potent potable called Purple Jesus, Jerry, Pookie, and another couple cavort among the graves and sing raucously upon a tomb. An old English professor who stands at the gate with flowers in his hands silently interrupts them. The foursome realize with some shock and self-loathing that they are standing on the tomb of the grieving man's wife. Pookie has had enough and returns to her school.

Jerry and Pookie do not see each other during the summer months; she has gone home to work for her father's real estate business in Indiana. When they meet again in the fall of Jerry's junior year, they take up where they left off, crawling from one party to another. Pookie boasts of the fact that she has been training hard all summer to become a "speed drinker." "My record's five seconds. And you should have seen my old man's face. Instead of smashing the beer bottle on the floor, I chucked it out the window. The window happened to be closed." There is a hardness to Pookie now, a desperate need for alcohol and mindless sex. They decide to get away from the campus party crowd and spend a weekend together in New York. The adventure begins well enough: Pookie is filled with her usual overabundance of joy, and they talk of marriage and having children, but their happiness and hopes are again washed away by alcohol. Arguments and despair escalate; it becomes clear that although they love each other, they are not capable of becoming a mutually supportive couple. Pookie says, "Agony in a Nutshell, that's us," and recites a poem she has written on hotel stationery:

Oh, Hi-ho in the Lavender Woods
A Sterile Cuckoo is crying;

Oh, Hi-ho in the Lavender Snow
A Sterile Cuckoo is dying.

Cuckoo! Cuckoo!
Cuckoo! Cuckoo!

In the real dark night of her soul it's always three
   o'clock in the morning.
(F. S. Fitz—P. Adams)

The reference to F. Scott Fitzgerald is appropriate. The master of doomed young love surely experienced the drunken despair with his wife, Zelda, that Pookie and Jerry are suffering. Hungover and depressed they sign a suicide pact and agree that overdosing on aspirin would be their method. However, yet another argument ensues, and they retreat from their decision. The next morning Pookie declares that she is not returning to school; she is instead going home for good. Their taxi ride to the train station is reminiscent of another ill-fated couple's taxi ride, that of Jake Barnes and Brett Ashley in *The Sun Also Rises* who "could have had such a damned good time together." A year passes before Jerry hears from Pookie again. She sends him a letter that is also a suicide note. Jerry smothers his first instinct to investigate whether or not she is still alive, preferring instead always to wonder about the fate of the strange young woman who was his first love.

The appeal of *The Sterile Cuckoo* lies in the portrayal of a completely new type of young American woman, Pookie Adams. Pookie has a desperate zaniness that is Salingeresque in its heights of happiness and depths of despair. Like Franny Glass in J. D. Salinger's *Franny and Zooey,* Pookie's intellect and offbeat view of the world separate her from her peers. She is hopelessly trapped by her own uniqueness, a uniqueness that attracts Jerry but also defines the insurmountable differences between them. Contemporary critics were divided on the novel's merits. Granville Hicks declared it to be "the best of many novels I have read about sex and the younger generation." Eliot Fremont-Smith, however, dismissed it as "adolescent jabbering." High school and college students responded to the novel's honest portrayal of their angst, and it remains a cult classic.

Nichols' next published work, *The Wizard of Loneliness* (1966) is a fictional account of his years spent in the care of relatives while his father was fighting in the Pacific during World War II. Ten-year-old Wendall Oler is sent from New York to live with his father's family in rural Stebbinsville, Vermont. His anger over the death of his mother and the absence of his father causes him to become a holy terror intent on disrupting the lives of those around him. The unconditional love of his caring new family, however, has a mellowing effect on the rebellious boy. The novel was well received, and Nichols could have continued to write successfully about the trials and tribulations of strange girls and Tom Sawyer-ish boys were it not for a trip he took in 1964.

GUATEMALA

With the five-hundred-dollar advance he received for *The Sterile Cuckoo,* Nichols took a trip to visit his college friend Alan Howard, who was working on a Fulbright Fellowship in Guatemala City. In his letters to Nichols about life in Central America, Howard admonished Nichols that it was time for the young writer to develop a social conscience. Nichols rejected the idea, claiming that art and politics should not mix. His experiences in Guatemala changed that belief forever—but not immediately.

Initially, he enjoyed his stay in Guatemala; he spent his time working on the copyedited manuscript of *The Sterile Cuckoo,* drinking with Howard and a new friend, Michael Kimmel, and sight-seeing. When he returned to New York, however, he was haunted by images of poverty, brutality, and injustice. It had been only ten years since the CIA's first covert operation in Latin America had ousted the democratically elected president of Guatemala, Jacobo Arbenz Guzmán, and installed a series of military dictators to rule the country in a manner that the United States and the United Fruit Company thought best. As he relates in *An American Child Supreme,* Nichols was ashamed of the fact that his own country would be the creator of such misery, he was ashamed of his own privileged life, and he was ashamed of his expensive education that had left him so politically naive.

> That miserable country was like a ghostly homeless person that I had to step over every time I started off in another direction with cash jingling in my pockets. Guatemala made it impossible for me to feel comfortable or free. Like it or not, Guatemala insisted that everything is interconnected and that the price of wealth for some is an ache of want for many.

Nichols began to reeducate himself, reading such classics of radical politics as *The Autobiography of Malcolm X,* Piri Thomas' *Down These Mean Streets,* Seymour Melman's *Our Depleted Society,* and later Barry Commoner's *The Closing Circle.*

Ironically, as Nichols became more sensitive to the plight of the world's poor and downtrodden, he found himself showered with fame and fortune. Avon purchased the paperback rights to *The Sterile Cuckoo,* the producer Alan Pakula bought the movie rights, and *The Wizard of Loneliness* was published by Putnam. Suddenly the budding Marxist was in demand by the rich and famous. Literary cocktail parties and first-class flights to California, where he worked on the screenplay of *The Sterile Cuckoo* and mingled with the likes of Robert Redford, Roddy McDowall, Natalie Wood, and the newcomer Liza Minnelli, who was nominated for an Academy Award for her portrayal of Pookie Adams, began to confuse his growing belief in the evils of capitalism. Add to this his decision in April 1965 to enter into what would quickly become a difficult marriage with Ruth "Ruby" Harding, and a picture of Nichols emerges that shows a young man trying to find a new direction in one of the most complicated decades in American cultural history.

He became involved with various antiwar groups, participated in protest rallies, marched on the Pentagon, and suffered the indignity of being pelted with eggs by onlookers and clubbed by the police. As his frustration and anger increased, Nichols turned to a writer he admired greatly, Bernard Malamud, for advice. In his 1966 letter to the novelist, as recorded in *An American Child Supreme,* Nichols "confessed to being torn between art and activism and asked Malamud if he felt that writing was a valid act against atrocities like Vietnam." To Nichols' surprise, Malamud quickly replied, telling Nichols that "it was possible to write, teach, and engage in politics simultaneously." Malamud added, "What a writer must say changes as he rids himself of provincialism, fear; yet he must always struggle to make it art." Nichols struggled through several attempts to create political fiction, but his anger rendered his efforts shrill and unpublishable. By 1969 Nichols was nearly broke; he had not published a book in three years, and it was becoming impossible to live in New York. The day after Neil Armstrong put his foot on the surface of the moon, Nichols moved his family to a place almost as remote and peaceful: Taos, New Mexico.

NEW MEXICO

Eight thousand dollars from the Literary Guild enabled Nichols to make a down payment on an adobe house that was situated about a mile north of the Taos plaza. He and Ruby and their son Luke, who was born in 1966, settled into a life that was unlike anything they had known in New York. Their one-and-a-half-acre property was soon thriving with vegetables and fruit and became home to chickens, turkeys, goats, two Shetland ponies, and numerous dogs and cats. After spending his days tending to the garden and the animals, gathering firewood, cleaning the irrigation ditches, and catching trout for dinner, Nichols spent his nights writing. He wrote articles for the *New Mexico Review,* a political journal published in Santa Fe, and through that work became closely involved with the concerns and struggles of the people of the Taos valley. He became intimate with the historical, cultural, sociological, and economic structures of the area. His research skills proved invaluable to the indigenous poor who struggled to fight the government's attempts to violate long-standing land and water rights. Here in northern New Mexico, Nichols found Malamud's words to be true; he could "write, teach, and engage in politics simultaneously." Now his challenge was to "make it art."

The political/agrarian lifestyle did not suit Nichols' wife, however. After the birth of their second child, Tania, in 1970, Ruby began to spend more time in Albuquerque, over one hundred miles south of Taos. The commuter marriage began to fall apart, and eventually Ruby was raising Tania in Albuquerque while attending nursing school, and Nichols was left in Taos with Luke. Despite the hardships of these times, Nichols discovered a new joy in life. The warm and welcoming people of the Taos valley and the serenity of the valley itself displaced a lot of Nichols' unfocused anger, and he became an organizer and activist in communal grassroots endeavors. Nichols found that happiness was possible and even permissible in an unjust world. A major liberating force at this time in Nichols' life was the revolutionary activist and artist Rini Templeton. Her voluptuous and bawdy love of life released Nichols from some joy-smothering inhibitions. In *An American Child Supreme* he says that for the first time in his life he felt fully alive and hopeful. "It's, like, all of a sudden the sun came out."

Nichols' work for the *New Mexico Review* came to an end in 1972 when the journal ceased publication. In an attempt to revive his long-dormant literary career, Nichols poured everything he had learned in his three years in New Mexico into a new novel, *The Milagro Beanfield War* (1974). He finished the manuscript in eleven weeks, and much to Nichols' surprise and delight, Holt, Rinehart and Winston quickly bought it and provided him with a much-needed ten-thousand-dollar advance.

The Milagro Beanfield War is like a good southwestern-style stew, hearty, robust, and satisfying, a blend of many ingredients, not one of which overpowers the others to stand out as the central flavor. Although the novel does not have one central character or protagonist, there is a primary instigator of the "war," a thirty-six-year-old unemployed general handyman and perpetual troublemaker named Joe Mondragón. Joe has no greater purpose in mind when he irrigates an arid patch of land that has belonged to his family for generations; all he wants to do is raise a few beans. But when he diverts water from an irrigation canal to his bean field, he unwittingly and unwillingly becomes something of a folk hero. Although not an act of open defiance, Joe's action inspires a determination in the people of Milagro to battle an unscrupulous developer and the governmental powers that back him.

Ladd Devine III is the grandson of a man who developed a large sheep ranching enterprise in Milagro in the late 1800s. In 1935 the Interstate Water Compact split Milagro in two and made it impossible for small sheep farmers on the west side to survive. The barren, abandoned, and apparently worthless west side land was bought cheaply by the Devine Company, which began to make elaborate plans to create the Miracle Valley Recreation Area. The plans call for the construction of a dam at the mouth of Milagro Canyon that would create a mile-and-a-half-long lake. The cost of this project would be paid for by the creation of a water conservancy district that would incorporate the destitute village of Milagro. To sweeten the deal Devine offers to return water rights to the west side, but the citizens slowly come to the realization that taxes and conservancy assessments would bankrupt the village and drive its inhabitants from their land.

Joe's attempt to bring life to a small patch of the west side is an inspiration for some but a source of concern for others. Those who depend on Devine for their livelihood ask, "What's that little half-pint son of a bitch want to cause so much trouble for?" Older members of the community, such as ninety-three-year-old Amarante Córdova, are excited by the possibility of resistance to the corporate takeover of their village. Amarante chides those who exhibit reluctance or a "wait and see" attitude: "'That's the trouble with this younger generation,' Amarante whined petulantly. 'They don't give a damn about anything important anymore.'"

News of Joe's act soon reaches Devine at his Dancing Trout Dude Ranch and the state governor in Santa Fe. Both men are keenly aware of the delicate balance that exists between the Anglo and Hispanic cultures and are reluctant to do anything that might upset it. An undercover agent, Kyril Montana, is sent to Milagro to investigate the situation and perhaps to find a way to undermine Joe's influence among his people.

Two things happen that make Montana's job much harder than expected. First, Amarante Córdova, who has dusted off his old revolver, has a vision in his dreams. He sees a rainbow in bright sunlight arching over Milagro and an angel limping along the road.

> No shining angel with a golden halo straight from Tiffany's, a French horn, and wings fabricated out of pristine Chinese swansdown arrived to bless Amarante's fertile imagination; rather, a half-toothless, one-eyed bum sort of coyote dressed in tattered blue jeans and sandals, and sporting a pair of drab moth-eaten wings that looked as if they had come off the remainder shelves of a disreputable cut-rate discount store during a fire-damage sale, appeared.

Amarante asks the coyote angel why there would be a rainbow in broad daylight over the arid town. The coyote angel answers, "Maybe it's because for once in your lives you people are trying to do something right." Meanwhile, Joe Mondragón watches the early morning departure of his friends and neighbors as they travel to menial jobs for Devine or the mines in Doña Luz or the hotels and restaurants in Chamisaville.

> And abruptly the strangest feeling he had ever known came over him; as suddenly as a summer hailstorm in the mountains, it caught him by surprise, and it damn near made him fall over backward. . . . No getting around it, though: suddenly he held a profound tenderness for his people, that's what it was. His people.

Joe's sudden concern for something bigger than himself combines with Amarante's conviction that theirs is a holy quest and helps to stop those who seek to undermine their way of life.

The novel's more than four hundred pages give the reader an almost palpable experience of life in a northern New Mexico village. The sights, smells, tastes, sounds, and feel of daily life are presented honestly with no attempt to prettify or make quaint the often harsh realities that near-poverty imposes. Even the novel's ending avoids the temptation to portray the downtrodden as victorious over the oppressors; Milagro wins only a temporary reprieve from Devine's machinations.

Nichols completed what was to become known as his New Mexico trilogy with *The Magic Journey* (1978) and *The Nirvana Blues* (1981). Both novels continue the central theme of the first, the loss of an indigenous culture to Anglo ignorance, arrogance, and greed. Nichols says in *An American Child Supreme* that *The Magic Journey* (1978) is his favorite book: "The novel I care about most, *The Magic Journey,* contains everything in my macroscopic overview that I feel defines life as well as seeks to destroy it." He hopes that this, "a real kitchen sink" as he calls it in the preface to the 2000 edition, will be the work for which he is remembered.

The time span that Nichols covers in *The Magic Journey* is more ambitious than its predecessor in the trilogy. Nichols traces the destruction of the native culture of northern New Mexico from the 1930s through the 1970s. A school bus explodes in the small town of Chamisaville, dislodging hot springs. Tourists flock to the scene, which becomes a shrine to the Dynamite Virgin, and spas, hotels, and restaurants are built to accommodate them. Dozens of characters grapple with the influx of tourism, strip-mining, and casino gambling that inexorably robs them of their communal, rural economy. *The Nirvana Blues* again takes up the story of Chamisaville and the Anglos' success in ridding the area of its last Chicano inhabitant. Nichols manages to blend a profound sense of loss with a surprisingly uncynical sense of humor. His anguish and anger over capitalism's rape of his adopted state are real, but he is no longer the shrill, ineffectual writer he was in the late 1960s. He sugarcoats the bitter pill of revolution with laughter; as he says in an *American Child Supreme,* "You can't overthrow the jerks without an ironclad indestructible sense of humor."

In *A Ghost in the Music* (1979), a novel that was published before *The Nirvana Blues,* Nichols' focus shifts from communal tribulations to the troubles encountered in family relationships. The book tells the story of a forty-seven-year-old "writer, theater and film director, actor, real-estate mogul, stunt man and poet, songwriter, perverse womanizer, masochist, health faddist, worrywart, child in a grown man's jeans," Bart Darling. Bart lives in New Mexico and is having some serious trouble with his pregnant girlfriend, Lorraine, over a dangerous movie stunt he wants to perform. Lorraine feels that the stunt is too risky and declares that if Bart goes ahead with his plan, she will leave him. Bart calls upon his twenty-nine-year-old son, Marcel, who lives in New York, to come and calm things down. There has been a long-established pattern of Bart's calls for help, and Marcel has learned to accept the histrionics for what they are, a guilt-ridden father's attempt to keep in touch with his illegitimate son. All of Nichols' trademark humor is present here, but there is a tenderness and compassion in this story of a father and son struggling to love and be loved that hark back to his first two published novels.

At the end of the 1970s, with five novels published, Nichols decided to branch out into other means of expression. The year 1979 saw the publication of his first book of essays on northern New Mexico, *If Mountains Die: A New Mexico Memoir.* Nichols wrote the text that accompanies the beautiful color photographs by his friend Bill Davis. A similar volume, *The Last Beautiful Days of Autumn,* was published in 1982, with Nichols' own photographs. In the early 1980s Nichols turned again to script writing. Undaunted by his brush with Hollywood fame and fortune some fifteen years earlier, Nichols was hired, fired, and rehired in 1986 by Robert Redford to write the screenplay for *The Milagro Beanfield War* (1988). He recounts the delights and demands of writing the screenplay and participating in the filming of his book in an essay published in *Dancing on the Stones* entitled "Night of the Living Beanfield: How an Unsuccessful Cult Novel Became an Unsuccessful Cult Film in Only Fourteen Years, Eleven Nervous Breakdowns, and $20 Million."

DIVORCES AND ILL HEALTH

Nichols' rocky marriage to Ruby ended in divorce sometime in the late 1970s. In 1985 he married Juanita Wolf. Two more volumes of Nichols' tributes to New Mexico were published, *On the Mesa* (1986) and *A Fragile Beauty: John Nichols' Milagro Country: Text and Photographs from His Life and Work* (1987). Any notions that Nichols had been lulled into a state of contentment by the peaceful beauty of his surroundings were sent fleeing by the publication of his first novel in six years, *American Blood* (1987).

American Blood is a harsh, violent, humorless novel that explores the personal consequences of America's involvement in the Vietnam War. Michael P. Smith and his fellow platoon member Tom Carp are products of the horrors in which they participated overseas. Smith accepts Carp's invitation to come to New Mexico, where he meets Janine Tarr and her teenaged daughter, Cathie. Smith is on the verge of finding a fragile peace with the two women when Cathie, a symbol of an innocent America that will never exist again, is savagely murdered.

Nichols and Juanita traveled to Europe to celebrate the publication of *American Blood*, but visiting her relatives in the Netherlands and his in Brittany and Spain did nothing to improve what had become a tempestuous marriage. They were divorced in 1989. Nichols lost his house in the divorce settlement, and it would appear that he lost more than that. His next book, *The Sky's the Limit: A Defense of the Earth* (1990), another photo essay on northern New Mexico, displays a rather hopeless pessimism regarding even our best efforts to preserve the environment. He expresses that it is no longer possible for him to behold an unspoiled landscape without fearing its pending destruction; he can no longer line up a perfect vista in his viewfinder without imagining a bulldozer just outside the frame waiting to reduce pristine beauty to rubble.

Concern not only for the planet's health but also for his own pervade his next two books, *Keep It Simple: A Defense of the Earth* (1992) and *An Elegy for September* (1992). *Keep It Simple* is a slim volume of fourteen pages of text and seventy-two of Nichols' photographs. In it he recounts his efforts to simplify his life after experiencing some early warning signs of heart problems. There is nothing simple about the life revealed in Nichols' novella *An Elegy for September*. It is a poignant story of middle-aged writer living in New Mexico, struggling through his second divorce and facing the fact of his own mortality. He begins receiving fan letters from a nineteen-year-old college junior who makes it clear that it is her intention to seduce him. The pathetic chaos she brings to his life is almost more than his diseased heart can bear.

Nichols abandoned his determination to lead a more serene life when he accepted visiting professorships for the spring semester of 1992 and the fall semester of 1993 at the University of New Mexico in Albuquerque. There he taught two graduate-level courses on creative writing. In 1994 he complicated his life further by marrying a young dancer, Miel Castanga; they were divorced within a few years. Also in 1994 he returned to film work. In *An American Child Supreme* he explains why:

Why movies? Because on the whole Hollywood's product is reactionary, yet it wields enormous power around the globe. This behooves us to create antidote works of a more progressive nature. So projects that I wrote dealt with Haitian refugees, nuclear holocaust, science and human values in the twentieth century, Kayapo Indian rights in Amazonia, Pancho Villa and the Mexican Revolution, the life of Che Guevara. It's important for me to point out that while I live in a small New Mexico town, much of my work has been international in scope.

It was while working with Ridley Scott on the Kayapo Indian movie in 1994 that Nichols contracted endocarditis, a bacterial infection of the heart that had claimed his mother fifty-two years earlier. After a brief recovery period

Nichols embarked on a three-week book tour to promote his biting satire on the institution of marriage, *Conjugal Bliss: A Comedy of Marital Arts* (1994). The stress was too much, and congestive heart failure was the result. It was determined that he must have open-heart surgery to repair a prolapsed mitral valve. Nichols gruesomely describes the pain and fear he experienced when he came out of anesthesia in "The Longest Night of My Life," an essay in *Dancing on the Stones.* Recovery was slow, and it would be six years before his next book was published.

A LIBERATION ECOLOGIST IN THE NEW MILLENNIUM

The year 2000 saw a revival of interest in Nichols' work. Henry Holt published new editions of his New Mexico trilogy, and Ancient City Press in Santa Fe published a paperback edition of *The Last Beautiful Days of Autumn* with a new introduction by Nichols. A selection of essays that span thirty years, *Dancing on the Stones,* was also published that year, and on May 13, 2000, he received an honorary degree from the University of New Mexico. His speech to the graduates is recorded in *An American Child Supreme:* "When I graduated from college thirty-eight years ago," he begins,

> I had to start over, as you most certainly will, learning everything from scratch. My formal education had prepared me to succeed in our culture, but not to really understand the planet or to sympathize with it in a compassionate manner. I knew very little about love or work or the tragedy of environment and people under attack by material development.

He goes on to describe his awakening to the evils of capitalism that he had observed in Guatemala and his disillusionment with the United States during the Vietnam War. He ends his talk by expressing how New Mexico has restored his hope:

> Being the poorest state in our nation allies us intimately with most of the rest of the people on earth. Folks I love and have been inspired by in this place are the salt of the earth. Rarely do they receive accolades or even modest recognition. Many kill themselves for minimum wages, and they do not have the safety nets of retirement pensions or health care insurance plans. They defend the acequias, pick the vegetables that go on our tables, and build the houses we live in. Their jobs can be deadening or dangerous, and higher education for them is often out of reach.
>
> But they make the world work, and they labor so hard on behalf of everyone.

Nichols does more than pay lip service to the plight of the poor; indeed, he steadfastly refuses to become a part of the economic system that relies on the poverty of many for the enrichment of few. He spends very little of the money he makes on himself and is often seen in Taos wearing thrift shop shirts and pants with shoes held together by duct tape. What money he has in excess of that which is necessary to meet his few needs, he gives away.

In 2001 he published his credo, *An American Child Supreme: The Education of a Liberation Ecologist.* In it he calls for a new philosophy.

> We need environmentalists—liberation ecologists!—able to speak like George Jackson or Malcolm X and urban activists willing to incorporate John Muir and Rachel Carson. . . . Our task is to reinvent our economic philosophy and principles to meet the commandments of our *democratic* institutions. That means an end to officially sanctioned selfishness.

Today Nichols lives alone in a small adobe home in the Taos region he loves so well. He is a disciplined writer who works most often at night after a day of fly fishing in the mountain streams or running errands in town. He keeps a storage unit in Taos that is jammed with a lifetime of manuscripts, the majority of them unpublished.

Nichols' 2001 novel, *The Voice of the Butterfly*, gives clear evidence that the sixty-one-year-old author has neither mellowed nor backed off from his uncompromising battle against capitalism's destruction of the environment and its economic enslavement of the majority of the world's population. The novel's narrator is an aging 1960s radical, Charley McFarland, who jumps at the chance to battle once again the powers that be. The politicians of Suicide City have proposed that a highway bypass be built through their city. Apart from the destruction and displacement that Proposition X would cause Charley and his neighbors on Willow Road, the stretch of highway would run through a piece of land that is the last breeding ground of the rare Rocky Mountain phistic copper butterfly. Charley rallies a ragtag group of sympathizers, the Butterfly Coalition, and in a series of sometimes comic and sometimes tragic misadventures manages to defeat the proposition. Despite achieving the desired outcome, Charley is troubled that it took so much of his energy to win a relatively small victory, that it was so difficult to convince others to join him, and that his son has apparently evolved into a "berserk ideologue who'd spend the rest of his born days mired down in anarchical demagogic zealotry." Charley wonders, *"How could we ever feed and clothe the hungry, and end racism, and save the environment, and build suitable economies, and redistribute the wealth if it took so much effort just to stop one . . . idiotic . . . highway . . . bypass?"*

It is remarkable given the escalating destruction of the environment, oppression of the poor, and the fragile state of his health that Nichols has not lapsed into morose cynicism. But he is a tenacious fighter, a living example of Hemingway's belief that "a man can be destroyed but not defeated." Indeed, on his sixtieth birthday Nichols, accompanied by his daughter, overcame the harsh physical demands of climbing to the top of Lake Fork Peak and was rewarded with a spectacular view of the Taos valley. In spite of everything, Nichols' indomitable high spirits and riotous sense of humor prevail and sustain him. One strongly suspects, however, that he is laughing to keep from crying.

Selected Bibliography

WORKS OF JOHN NICHOLS

FICTION

The Sterile Cuckoo. New York: McKay, 1965; New York: Norton, 1997.

The Wizard of Loneliness. New York: Putnam, 1966; New York: Norton, 1987.

The Milagro Beanfield War. Illustrations by Rini Templeton. New York: Holt, Rinehart and Winston, 1974; New York: Henry Holt, 2000.

The Magic Journey: A Novel. Illustrations by the author. New York: Holt, Rinehart and Winston, 1978; New York: Henry Holt, 2000.

A Ghost in the Music. New York: Holt, Rinehart and Winston, 1979; New York: Norton, 1996.

The Nirvana Blues. New York: Holt, Rinehart and Winston, 1981; New York: Henry Holt, 2000.

American Blood. New York: Henry Holt, 1987; New York: Ballantine, 1988.

An Elegy for September: A Novel. New York: Henry Holt, 1992; New York: Ballantine, 1993.

Conjugal Bliss: A Comedy of Marital Arts. New York: Henry Holt, 1994; New York: Ballantine, 1995.

The Voice of the Butterfly. San Francisco: Chronicle Books, 2001.

NONFICTION

If Mountains Die: A New Mexico Memoir. Photographs by William Davis. New York: Knopf, 1979; New York: Norton, 1994.

The Last Beautiful Days of Autumn. Photographs by the author. New York: Holt, Rinehart and Winston, 1982; Santa Fe, N.Mex.: Ancient City Press, 2000.

On the Mesa. Photographs by the author. Salt Lake City, Utah: Peregrine Smith, 1986.

A Fragile Beauty: John Nichols' Milagro Country: Text and Photographs from His Life and Work. Salt Lake City, Utah: Peregrine Smith, 1987.

The Sky's the Limit: A Defense of the Earth. Photographs by the author. New York: Norton, 1990.

Keep It Simple: A Defense of the Earth. Photographs by the author. New York: Norton, 1992.

Dancing on the Stones: Selected Essays. Albuquerque: University of New Mexico Press, 2000.

An American Child Supreme: The Education of a Liberation Ecologist. Minneapolis: Milkweed, 2001. (Includes a bibliography of Nichols' books, book reviews, book introductions, sound recordings, uncollected essays and stories, video recordings, anthology appearances, interviews, and film credits.)

CRITICAL AND BIOGRAPHICAL STUDIES

Colby, Vineta. "Nichols, John (Treadwell)." In *World Authors, 1980–1985.* Edited by Vineta Colby. New York: H. W. Wilson, 1991.

Contemporary Authors Online. Gale Group (www.infotrac.galenet.com), 2001. (Includes an autobiographical essay by Nichols written in 1984 with a postscript dated 2000.)

Shirley, Carl R. "John Nichols." In *Dictionary of Literary Biography: Yearbook, 1982.* Edited by Richard Ziegfeld. Detroit: Gale Research, 1983.

Wild, Peter. *John Nichols.* Boise, Idaho: Boise State University, 1986.

BOOK REVIEWS

Becker, Alida. "Assault and Battery by Way of Vietnam." *Newsday,* May 6, 1987, p. 14. (Review of *American Blood.*)

Bowden, Charles. "Not Just Another Pastel Coyote." *Los Angeles Times Book Review,* June 28, 1992, p. 1. (Review of *An Elegy for September.*)

Busch, Frederick. Review of *The Milagro Beanfield War. New York Times Book Review,* October 27, 1974, p. 53–54.

Cook, Bruce. "A Half-Baked Miracle Awakens a Sleepy Town." *Washington Post,* June 17, 1978, p. B4. (Review of *The Magic Journey.*)

Eder, Richard. "Vietnam: Uncured Plague of Violence in America." *Los Angeles Times Book Review,* April 29, 1987, p. 1. (Review of *American Blood.*)

Fisher, Barbara. Review of *An Elegy for September. New York Times Book Review,* June 21, 1992, p. 16.

Fleming, Thomas J. "The Sorrows of Wendall." *New York Times Book Review,* March 6, 1966, p. 52. (Review of *The Wizard of Loneliness.*)

Fremont-Smith, Eliot. "Life with Pookie, Life Without." *New York Times,* January 15, 1965, p. 41. (Review of *The Sterile Cuckoo.*)

Grumbach, Doris. Review of *If Mountains Die: A New Mexico Memoir. New York Times Book Review,* June 10, 1979, p. 18.

Hepworth, James R. Review of *Dancing on the Stones. Bloomsbury Review* 20, no. 3 (May/June 2000).

Hicks, Granville. "Labor Leader's Lost Love." *Saturday Review,* February 26, 1966, p. 29–30. (Review of *The Wizard of Loneliness.*)

Milligan, Bryce. "Welcome to a 'Marriage from Hell.'" *Chicago Tribune,* February 27, 1994, p. 146. (Review of *Conjugal Bliss.*)

INTERVIEWS

Allen, Steven Robert. "Keeping It Simple: An Interview with John Nichols." *Alibi* 9, no. 25, June 22–28, 2000. Available at (http://www.alibi.com/alibi/2000-06-22/feat4.html).

Blei, Norbert. "Being in Love with Words and Uncomfortable with Money." *Washington Post,* March 31, 1985, p. K3.

SCREENPLAY

Missing. Screenplay by John Nichols (uncredited). Directed by Constantin Costa-Gavras. Polygram/Universal, 1982.

FILMS BASED ON THE WORKS OF JOHN NICHOLS

The Milagro Beanfield War. Screenplay by John Nichols and David S. Ward. Directed by Robert Redford. Universal Pictures, 1988.

The Sterile Cuckoo. Screenplay by John Nichols (uncredited). Directed by Alan J. Pakula. Paramount, 1969.

The Wizard of Loneliness. Screenplay by John Nichols (uncredited). Directed by Jenny Bowen. Skouras Pictures, 1988.

—CHARLES R. BAKER

Naomi Shihab Nye

1952–

Naomi Shihab Nye, a poet, essayist, children's writer, and distinguished anthologist, was born in St. Louis, Missouri, on March 12, 1952, to Aziz and Miriam (Allwardt) Shihab. Her father is a Palestinian, and her Arab American background has become increasingly important: she is not a propagandist by any means, and she is neither a Muslim nor fluent in Arabic; however, her close ties to relatives in Palestine have given her an anguished concern over the violence in the Middle East. Her work has consistently shown a love of human diversity, whether she is writing about a broom maker in Jerusalem or her Mexican American neighbors in San Antonio, Texas.

Nye received her early education in St. Louis. Upon moving to the United States her father set out to be a minister in the Unity School of Christianity, a sect that was influenced by Emersonian transcendentalism and has much in common with Christian Science. Her mother, who was raised as a Lutheran, brought up Naomi and her younger brother in the Vedanta Society of St. Louis, complete with a swami and sandalwood incense, according to Nye's essay collection *Never in a Hurry: Essays on People and Places* (1996). Nye also attended Unity Sunday school. Her highly affirmative point of view may owe something to Unity, and the kind of toleration she encourages in her poetry and multicultural anthologies may have been influenced by Vedantic teachings. In "Thank You in Arabic," an essay in *Never in a Hurry,* she says she was raised to be ecumenical, although she did not learn the word until college. She observes that the stories about Jesus had less influence on her than the way "our Hindu swami said a single word three times, 'Shanti, shanti, shanti'—peace, peace, peace," the formula that concludes T. S. Eliot's *The Waste Land.* Peace has been one of her preoccupations. It is fitting that since 1999 she has served on the National Council on the Humanities, the advisory body to the National Endowment for the Humanities.

When she was fourteen, Nye's family moved to Palestine for a year, where she attended an Armenian school, St. Tarkmanchatz, in East Jerusalem, which was then under the jurisdiction of Jordan. Her father wanted the family to become familiar with his homeland. (His 1993 book, *A Taste of Palestine: Menus and Memories,* is an interesting combination of cookbook, memoir, and ethnography.) His daughter's experiences in the Jerusalem area were the basis of her semi-autobiographical novel for young readers, *Habibi* (1997). After a year, the outbreak of war between Israel and its Arab neighbors forced the Shihab family to return to the United States. In "Thank You in Arabic" she observes that "*Home* had grown different forever. . . . Back *home* again in my own country, it seemed impossible to forget the place we had just left: the piercing call of the *muezzin* from the mosque at prayer time, the dusky green tint of the olive groves, the sharp, cold air that smelled as deep and old as my grandmother's white sheets flapping from the line on her roof."

The family moved to San Antonio, Texas, where Nye still lives. She attended Trinity University in that city and received her B.A. in 1974. Not until she was on the verge of graduating did she realize that there were programs in creative writing, though she had pursued poetry on her own for years. Her first poem was written at the age of six as a response to a visit to Chicago, and her first publication as a poet came at the age of seven, in a children's magazine, *Wee Wisdom*. Later she published in *Seventeen* magazine. In an interview with Rachel Barenblat in *The Best of Pif Magazine Off-line* she says that her interest in poetry was fostered by seeing Carl Sandburg on black-and-white television; his accessible and populist poetry must have influenced her, and she eventually performed with the guitar, just as he did.

She published her first chapbook, *Tattooed Feet*, with a small press, Texas Portfolio, in 1977. A second chapbook, *Eye-to-Eye*, appeared the following year. It was dedicated to her friend John Phillip Santos, the author of the distinguished memoir *Places Left Unfinished at the Time of Creation* (1999). In 1978 she married Michael Nye, a San Antonio lawyer and photographer. Their son, Madison Cloudfeather Nye, was born in 1986, and the family lives in the King William neighborhood of San Antonio, near the river and the downtown district. Nye has supported herself without the full-time academic employment common among American writers. She spent fifteen years as a visiting writer in the public schools for the Texas Commission on the Arts and has held a number of visiting appointments with colleges and universities. As of 2003, she was serving as the poetry editor of *The Texas Observer*. A well-known poetry reader, she won the Charity Randall Citation for Spoken Poetry in 1988 and made a recording, *The Spoken Page*, for the International Poetry Forum in Pittsburgh. She has become a familiar public figure, with appearances on two PBS series, *The Language of Life* with Bill Moyers (1995) and *The United States of Poetry* (1996), and on Garrison Keillor's radio programs *A Prairie Home Companion* and *The Writer's Almanac*. The United States Information Agency has sent her on three tours abroad.

EARLY POEMS

In addition to her work as a poet Nye enjoyed writing and performing folk and children's songs from her teens to her mid-thirties. She used the musical numbers to warm up or relax audiences at schools and other group settings and recorded two albums of her original songs with the San Antonio Flying Cat label, *Rutabaga-Roo: I've Got a Song and It's for You* (1979) and *Lullaby Raft* (1981). Her first full-length collection of poems, *Different Ways to Pray*, appeared in 1980. She included only a few of the poems from the two chapbooks.

Nye has been forthcoming about her early influences. Her writing is not reducible to a set of precedents, but she has a definite lineage, which is made clear in her interview with Bryce Milligan, "Writing to Save Our Lives." She read W. S. Merwin when she was sixteen and made "exuberant notes" on his work. She admires his sense of "mystery" and "the whole exquisitely insightful consciousness of language and imagery." Merwin offered her an example of a poet who can create subtle effects without a loss of clarity. Her greatest influence has surely been William Stafford, whose work she began reading at age fifteen. His sense of the value of the situations of daily life has its counterpart in Nye's work. She wrote the introduction for *The Way It Is*, a posthumous selection of Stafford's work, and she often praises him in interviews. Her second chapbook, *Eye-to-Eye*, contains a poem, "In a Dark Room, Furniture," dedicated to Stafford. She told Milligan that she had "always felt attracted to the Stafford notion of images leading you where you need to go, to something you may need to discover." Like Stafford she often discovers a striking final image in the process of recounting an apparently ordinary situation or event. A poem in *Different Ways to Pray*, "You Know Who You Are," has often been taken to be about Stafford, but she has said that the subject is actually David Ignatow.

In Stafford-like fashion Nye dedicated *Different Ways to Pray* both to her husband and to "the woman with the lamb on the train in Peru." The woman appears not inside the book but on its cover in a striking photograph wearing a straw hat and cradling a lamb. Nye's Middle Eastern collection, *19 Varieties of Gazelle* (2002), has a front cover photograph of a Palestinian girl holding up a poem that she wrote for her mother. Such pictures are meant to affirm a compassionate view of humanity, and the otherness of the subjects—a Peruvian woman, a member of a Palestinian family—serves to remind her American readership of the diversity in the world. She also values diversity within cultures: in the title poem of *Different Ways to Pray* she describes Palestinian relatives who pray in conventional ways and postures but ends with an eccentric:

And occasionally there would be one
who did none of this,
the old man Fowzi, for example, Fowzi the fool,
who beat everyone at dominoes,
insisted he spoke with God as he spoke with
   goats,
and was famous for his laugh.

Another influence on Nye that may surprise some of her readers is Jack Kerouac. In her interview with Bryce Milligan she mentions that she has the same birthday as Kerouac and that on her twentieth birthday she telephoned Kerouac's widow and then went to Florida to visit her. Lawrence Ferlinghetti read at Trinity University in 1974 when Nye was a student, and she told him that she was "The World's Greatest Kerouac Fan." Kerouac's love of American places, his generous attitudes toward people, and his spontaneous style seem to have influenced her work, and like him she values travel as a theme. One of the best poems in her third book, *Yellow Glove* (1986), is "Where the Soft Air Lives," a set of San Antonio nocturnes that starts with a quotation from Kerouac's *On the Road* praising her city's nighttime atmosphere.

A number of the poems in *Different Ways to Pray* grow out of travel in the Latin American countries of Colombia, Guatemala, and Peru. She describes the people encountered more than the scenery and historical sites. One of the best poems in the book, "Biography of an Armenian Schoolgirl," is set in Jerusalem. It deals with an actual classmate of Nye's at St. Tarkmanchatz who was sent to Syria at age fifteen to marry a man of fifty whom she had never met. Other poems evoke members of Nye's family: her parents, her maternal grandfather, her reclusive Palestinian uncle Mohammed, and her younger brother.

Another subject addressed in her first book (and in her later work) is the nature of the self. The poem "White Silk" opens with a saying by a Zen master who advises seeing oneself as a length of white silk. The speaker explores the image through dreams, but a Zen-like gesture ends the poem with a moment shopping for silk in a store. In "The Whole Self" the narrator describes the struggle to create wholeness of being. She is willing to settle for less, the wholeness of one toe. Finding a state of wholeness elusive, the speaker accepts a provisional process: the self is "a current, a fragile cargo, / a raft someone was paddling through the jungle." And the acceptance of the journey metaphor makes some kind of continuity possible: "I would be there at the other end." Nye won the Voertman Poetry Prize of the Texas Institute of Letters in 1980 for her debut volume. She won it a second time in 1982 for her next book, *Hugging the Jukebox*, which was selected by the poet Josephine Miles for the National Poetry Series, a major competition.

In *Hugging the Jukebox* Nye takes a strong interest in the people and neighborhoods of San Antonio: the trashpickers; a boy named Carlos who is supposed to write a dream-poem for her but can only think of his lost parrot; and the label-snobs of the north side who encourage their children to buy designer clothes. The most sustained poem in the book is the dramatic monologue "The Mother Writes to the Murderer: A Letter." Nye's desire to understand all human beings takes an unusual form in this poem as the mother seeks to explain her love for her daughter to the man who has killed her. The title poem, set in a dance hall in the Caribbean, is quite different in tone, with its wry portrait of a child named Alfred who spends his time hugging a jukebox and singing along with the selections. The child, sent to his grandparents by his parents, seems content to sing for everyone and everything, and his grandmother finds some hope in his singing, which will continue even when a hurricane "brewing near Barbados" cuts off the electricity. He will continue to hug the darkened jukebox, and he will command his grandmother to put a coin in his mouth. The affirmations of life and song in the poem are typical of Nye.

The poems in *Yellow Glove,* published in 1986 and dedicated to Nye's infant son, Madison Cloudfeather, represent a noticeable step forward. The images are sharper in this volume, and she makes fine use of objects, as some of the titles indicate: "Old Iron," "Yellow Glove," "The Brick," "Arabic Coffee," "The Traveling Onion," "Wood," "Ropes." The poems are likely to grow out of an image rather than being projected from a lyrical speaker. She discusses her love of objects in an interview with Bill Moyers for his *Language of Life* television series, an exchange transcribed for Moyers' book of the same name that was published in 1995. Moyers asks her how "daily and mundane objects" find their way into so many of her poems, and she replies that she lives her life among such objects and believes that they have a wisdom to impart, "if I would only pay the right kind of attention to them." She cites the precedent of William Stafford and says that many poems deal with "the things which often go unnoticed—these poems all say: 'Pause. Take Note. A story is being told through this thing.'" Typical of her stance is the suggestion that poets need not wait for splendid experiences because "the tiniest moments are the most splendid."

One advantage of such focus on small and mundane objects is that the poet manages to convey insights without being didactic: even moral judgments can be implied through poems about such ordinary images as an onion, which, she says in "The Traveling Onion," has "an honorable career": "For the sake of others, / disappear." In "Yellow Glove" an article of clothing lost one winter and found months later implies the "difference between floating and going down" through the miracle of its survival.

The timbre of the collection grows deeper in *Yellow Glove,* manifesting a fuller and richer awareness of loss through the images, particularly in the poems set in India, such as "At Mother Teresa's." The Middle East is another concern, as it is so often in Nye's books. She writes about Jerusalem and Nablus, reminding her American readers that these cities are inhabited by people with complex and often tragic lives. One of her best-known poems, "The Man Who Makes Brooms," set in Jerusalem, uses a homely household object and an ordinary man in a Wordsworthian "spot of time": she describes a man who sits on a short stool working "thumb over thumb, / straw over straw." The poem was written as a reply both to those who have "maps in your heads," preconceptions about the Middle East, and those who want doctrinaire statements ("voices chiding me to / 'speak for my people'"). The poem "speaks for her people" by affirming the dignity of a simple workman.

Reviewing *Yellow Glove* in 1989, the poet Philip Booth emphasized what he saw as Nye's strengths, like an attentive eye and compassion for her subjects, and what he considered her weakness, a deficiency of music: her prosody and syntax, he said, are not notable. He thought that her "extraordinary consciousness should become extraordinary actuality on the page." A plain style writer like Nye, or like her mentors Stafford and Sandburg, is open to such criticisms, especially when the work is written in free verse. In her interview with Bryce Milligan she says that Booth's review is the most perceptive she has received, and she is willing, she says, to think about "what he wished were different." So far Nye has received many awards, and most reviews of her work are respectful, though there are few critiques of any length.

In 1988 Nye received a Peter I. B. Lavan Younger Poets Award from the Academy of American Poets, a choice made by W. S. Merwin. Her three early collections, *Different Ways to Pray, Hugging the Jukebox,* and *Yellow Glove,* were published in 1995 as *Words under the Words: Selected Poems.* She dedicated the book to the memory of William Stafford: "The day I found his poems was a lucky day. And every day thereafter." The very term "day" is from Stafford's characteristic vocabulary. In the preface to the book she describes her poems as snapshots from an album. "What was said that made us all look that way at just that moment? The gleam of particulars." Nye's poems strive to capture that "gleam of particulars." In the poet Robert Pinsky's terms she is a nominalist, a writer who finds meaning in the particular more than in the universal. She sums up her conception of the poem in a 1998 interview with Teri Lesesne: "Poetry invites us to be intimate, descriptive, metaphorical and odd. Essential elements for a human life, I think."

By the appearance of the *Words under the Words* compilation, Nye had published a selection of new poems in a four-poet volume titled *Texas Poets in Concert: A Quartet* (1990), several chapbooks—*Invisible: Poems* (1987), *Mint* (1991), and *Travel Alarm* (1993)—and a major volume, *Red Suitcase* (1994). A selection of nineteen of her poems appeared in *Texas Poets in Concert* under the heading "Twenty Other Worlds." Only five of them were gathered in *Red Suitcase,* while one more, "The Turtle Shrine near Chittagong," was included in her book *Fuel* in 1998. Some of the reprint omissions are surprising, for they are significant works. "The Sail Made of Rags" meditates on the third world and its poverty but escapes glib sermonizing by approaching the subject through a concrete situation, a glimpse of a ship on a river in Bangladesh, a good example of her use of gleaming particulars. "Through the Kitchen Window, Chiapas," set in a region of Mexico that would later become well-known for the Zapatista insurrection, also eschews didacticism for vivid images that show the reader life in another society.

The works in *Mint,* the best of her chapbooks, are best classified as prose poems, though she indicates in the preface that she prefers the less lofty term "paragraph." "The paragraph, standing by itself, has a lovely pocket-sized quality. It garnishes the page, as mint garnishes a plate." She points out that many people say they do not like poetry, but "I've never heard anyone say they don't like paragraphs. It would be like disliking 5 minute increments on the clock." All but four of the paragraphs in the chapbook were reprinted in *Mint Snowball* in 2001. One of the poems that was not reprinted, "Trouble with the Stars and Stripes," deals with what might be called her lover's quarrel with her country. The speaker says that she will not make her usual flag cake on the Fourth of July: the war (referring to the Gulf War with Iraq, which began in January 1991) having made the holiday painful: "Let's talk about the difference between victory and public relations." She observes that "all forms of righteousness begin to terrify."

Most of the paragraphs deal with small moments, the sorts of experiences she often treats in her essays. The image of mint (a favorite herb in Middle Eastern cookery) turns up frequently in her poetry. The title poem of the chapbook celebrates the plant and its uses. With skill she modulates from talking about its use in lemonade and as a decoration to describing two uncles fighting with their fists near a mint bed. At the end—a typical moment of reconciliation in Nye's work—the two uncles are "laughing, drinking tea with mint." Nye's poetry shows a deep longing for harmony. She, like her contemporary readers, lives in a time when harmony is constantly threatened and disrupted by conflict.

In her next full volume, *Red Suitcase,* she arranges the poems in thematically related sections. The first part, "In Every Language," has poems that deal with Palestine, Mexico City, and other places distant from San Antonio. The second part, "Living Where We Do," stays close to home, though poems about letters and a trip to Niagara keep the section from being too narrow. In the final section, "Brushing Lives," the poet emphasizes individuals, including some of her Palestinian relatives and a thirteen-year-old girl, a victim of violence ("For the 500th Dead Palestinian, Ibtisam Bozieh"). Although some of the poems about people stress sorrow, she says in "First Hawaiian Bank," "*Lives unlike mine,* you save me. I would grow so tired were it not for you." Some of the poems in the collection deal with the writer's vocation and the teaching of poetry in schools and community centers. The responsibility of the writer is suggested by the epigraph to the collection, a saying from a Moroccan folktale: "A person was carrying a very heavy red leather suitcase. / When opened, it contained nothing but a blank sheet of paper." Paper represents an opportunity, the image implies, as well as a burden.

Nye has made contributions to two translations of the works of Arabic writers. She helped with the translation of poems contained in the autobiography of the Palestinian poet Fadwa Tuqan, *A Mountainous Journey* (1990), and she edited English translations of the poetry of the Syrian author Muhammad al-Maghut for the book *The Fan of Swords* (1991). In 1991 Gregory Orfalea wrote an article on Nye, "Doomed by Our Blood to Care," which emphasized her growing political awareness as a person of Palestinian descent. That consciousness would manifest itself in some of her children's books and anthologies.

ANTHOLOGIES AND BOOKS FOR
YOUNGER READERS

Nye's first original children's book, *Sitti's Secrets* (1994), was dedicated to her grandmother, Sitti Khadra Shihab Idais Al-Zer of Palestine, "still alive at 105." It tells a simple story of a girl named Mona who visits her *sitti* (grandmother) on the other side of the world and develops a strong relationship with her, although they do not share a language. They communicate nonverbally, sharing sights and smells and daily activities like cooking. After Mona, who is called *habibi* (darling) by her grandmother, returns home, she writes a letter to the president of the United States expressing concern about the news she has seen on television. She assures the president that "I vote for peace. My grandmother votes with me." The child's feeling is established in concrete terms before the message for peace is presented, a gentle and effective kind of didacticism. The story won a Jane Addams Children's Book Award from the Cooperative Children's Book Center.

The following year Nye published *Benito's Dream Bottle,* a story about a boy who learns that his grandmother has stopped dreaming. He attempts to help her by finding images for the magic bottle from which he believes dreams are replenished. In 1997 a picture book called *Lullaby Raft* appeared, based on the title song of Nye's 1981 album.

Nye's 1997 novel *Habibi,* written for young adults, is a strong narrative and is heavily autobiographical. She bases the story on her own experiences as a fourteen year old in Jerusalem, and she dedicates it to her parents and other relatives and "all the Arabs and Jews who would rather be cousins than enemies." When Nye lived in Palestine, the area was under the control of Jordan, but the Six Day War, which cut short her stay in the region, left East Jerusalem and the West Bank under the control of Israel. The novel reflects that change and the tensions that followed. Her protagonist, Liyana Abboud, moves from St. Louis to Palestine. She and her family—an Arab father, an American mother, and a younger brother, Rafik—take a house between Jerusalem and the West Bank town of Ramallah. She meets her Palestinian relatives, who live in a village near Ramallah, and becomes deeply attached to her grandmother. The way of life in the grandmother's village is described in sensuous detail. Liyana, like the young Naomi Shihab, attends an Armenian school called St. Tarkmanchatz. She persuades the priest in charge to admit her by mentioning her love for the great Armenian American writer William Saroyan.

Some elements of the novel are almost inevitable in a book for adolescents, like agitation over a first kiss, the relationship with her younger brother, and a clandestine romance. The romance is with a young man whom Liyana meets in a ceramics shop. She thinks he is called by the Arabic name Omar, but it turns out that he is Jewish and his name is actually Omer. Their relationship requires considerable diplomacy to survive the hostile atmosphere of the country. Omer actually visits the grandmother's village, and though the situation is tense, he achieves a rapport with her.

This hopeful element in the novel is set against deepening political troubles: a bomb going off in a marketplace and the shooting and hospitalization of Liyana's friend Khaled, a Palestinian boy who lives in a West Bank refugee camp. Nye tries to balance realism and the unpleasant facts of history with the kind of utopian aspiration that permeates much of her work. The novel ends with a happy scene, a trip to Galilee with Liyana's family (including her grandmother) and Omer. They share a meal, and her father comments that his fish is not "*quite*—delicious," a way of implying that not all is right with the world even when a momentary rapprochement of Arab and Israeli has been achieved. The reader of *Habibi* may wonder if Nye will use her fictional skills to write a novel that transcends the young adult category.

One of the strong points of the book is Nye's treatment of the imaginative powers of her protagonist. Unobtrusively, the story presents a young woman who writes, sketches, and perceives poetry in daily life. Liyana's intelligence is so intense that the symbolic dreams she has throughout the book (an old narrative device) seem plausible. The book has an array of good qualities: it presents a highly gifted protagonist, makes the Middle East tangible, and looks at political upheaval without falling into despair. It won the Judy Lopez Memorial Award for Children's Literature and the Middle East Book Award. It also won her a second Jane Addams award and the Book Publishers of Texas Award from the Texas Institute of Letters. The book appeared on a number of prestigious lists, including the American Library Association (ALA) Best Books for Young Adults, ALA Notable Children's Books, and New York Public Library Books for the Teen Age. In 2000 Nye published a collection of original poems for children, *Come with Me: Poems for a Journey.* She made good use of the page, sometimes centering the poems, sometimes using right justification. The poems could be more verbally charged. She has a good knowledge of the world of the child, stating, "First grade takes twenty years to get through. / But second grade only takes ten."

Nye's anthologies for children and young adults are particularly fine, with good choices of poetry supplemented with outstanding illustrations. The first one, *This Same Sky: A Collection of Poems from around the World*, published in 1992, contains 162 poems from sixty-eight countries and includes a map. The germ of the collection was a group of Iraqi poems she assembled during the Gulf War as a counterpoise to hostility toward Arabs: she read them to schoolchildren to show that people the world over have experiences and feelings in common. The choices in the anthology include many poems from non-Western nations. In "Lights in the Windows," an article about the book published in the *ALAN Review,* an on-line journal, she suggests that poetry can create empathy: "Other countries stop seeming quite so 'foreign,' or inanimate, or strange, when we listen to the intimate voices of their citizens." One sign of the unsettled times is the note on the copyright page indicating that because of political conflicts, the origins of some poems are given by region rather than by country.

Perhaps her best anthology overall is *The Tree Is Older Than You Are* (1995), which brings together poems and paintings from Mexico. It received the Paterson Poetry Prize. *The Space between Our Footsteps: Poems and Paintings from the Middle East* (1998) collects works primarily by poets from Palestine, Iraq, Israel, and Egypt. An abridged version of this book, *The Flag of Childhood: Poems from the Middle East,* was issued in 2002 with the goal of encouraging understanding of the Middle East. The didactic aim is well-supported by the good choice of poems. Childhood is not just the theme of another anthology, *Salting the Ocean* (2000): it comprises poems written by children themselves.

Two of Nye's anthologies classified as books for younger readers have a wider reach. An outstanding collection, *I Feel a Little Jumpy around You,* coedited in 1996 with Paul Janeczko, deals with the ambiguities of male-female relations. The work juxtaposes poems by men and women, and the relationships of the poems (unintended by the poets) are interesting to explore. In *What Have You Lost?* (1999), which is illustrated by her husband's photographs, she gathers works by 140 poets on the theme of loss. The possible varieties of loss are almost infinite, and the responses here range from deep grief to mild regret. The book grew out of her experience teaching writing in schools. She would begin a class by asking, "What have you lost?" as a way to start young people writing. Many of the poets included are not well-known, but the standard is good. The reviewer Mary Kay Rummel praised the book for inviting student readers into dialogue about their own losses. She also commended the global perspective offered by the many works in translation. The anthology won the 2000 Lee Bennett Hopkins Poetry Award for children's literature.

ART OF THE ESSAY: *NEVER IN A HURRY*

Nye frequently publishes personal essays in forums ranging from *The Iowa Review* to the magazine *Organica.* In 1996 she gathered many of her essays into *Never in a Hurry: Essays on People and Places.* The volume is richly autobiographical, and readers of her poems can recognize many of the verses' sources, like the encounter with a broom maker in the old city of Jerusalem, or the story of her classmate at St. Tarkmanchatz that went into "Biography of an Armenian Schoolgirl." While the book is not a continuous memoir, it reaches from Nye's childhood in St. Louis to her year in Jerusalem to her adult life in San Antonio.

Nye has mentioned William Saroyan and Phillip Lopate as influences on her essays. She shares Saroyan's zestfulness, love of ordinary people, and enthusiasm for the texture of American life. She would undoubtedly endorse Lopate's claim in *The Art of the Personal Essay* that "the hallmark of the personal essay is its intimacy. The writer seems to be speaking directly into your ear, confiding everything from gossip to wisdom." Nye's tone is friendly, and her emotions are made clear whether she expresses sorrow or joy. She has that casual organization that distinguishes many good personal essays: the work may appear to ramble, but it can suddenly lead to an epiphany or an emotional response. All these qualities—intimacy, a tone of familiarity with the reader, a rambling organization—have been marks of the essay since Michel de Montaigne in the sixteenth century. The very title of Nye's collection conveys a pervasive attitude, an acceptance of life on its own terms by a writer who is eager for experience. However, as she told Pamela Colloff in *Texas Monthly,* she knows the saying (apparently Thai in origin), "Life is so short, we must move very slowly." Nye, like John Keats, believes that indolence can be an element in creative life.

The opening section of *Never in a Hurry,* "Gateway to the West," deals primarily with her early life, though in the second chapter she meditates on her married name, Nye, as a way of talking about identity. Amusingly, she was so curious about the name that she and her husband once called all the Nyes in the San Antonio phone directory and invited them to a potluck dinner. The third essay, "The Cookies," describes selling Girl Scout cookies in St. Louis, the city known as "the Gateway to the West." She was immensely successful, for she was accompanied by her maternal grandmother, who knew every elderly lady in her building. With one of those implied transitions that the essayist relies upon, Nye turns in the next essay, "Commerce," to her parents' less than successful import shops. She gives a few scenes from her childhood in "Three Pokes of a Thistle," an essay that ends with the struggle to persuade her parents to buy her a training bra. More interesting by far is "Thank You in Arabic," which describes her family's move to Palestine when she was fourteen. The essay overlaps with similar events in *Habibi.*

The parental gift shops in St. Louis were called World Gifts, and Nye gives that name to the next section of her collection, which is devoted to travel experiences, as if to say that encounters in the world are boons. Two of the essays are rich evocations of her family's village in Palestine, but she also writes about looking for moose in Maine and taking a camel safari in the Indian region of Rajasthan. One brief essay, "Roses for Lubbock," stays at home in Texas, in the most rootless kind of setting, an airport departure lounge where fog has stranded the fliers. The steadily drooping roses carried by a mother and son in the San Antonio lounge become a symbol of the longing for human contact. Nye writes that at the time of this incident she was carrying a book called *Someday, Maybe,* a reference that serves as a quiet tribute to its unnamed author, William Stafford.

Nye stays mostly at home in the twenty essays of the third and fourth sections of the book, "Lucky People" and "Troubled Land." After "Tulips," a prelude about her family's flowers in St. Louis, the essays discuss her life in her colorful San Antonio neighborhood, King William. The essays in part four, "Troubled Land," emphasize the poverty and social problems of the area. Many of the neighbors described are eccentric, and most of the eccentrics are Mexican Americans, but Nye delicately manages to give them their stubborn individuality without patronizing them or turning them into folk exhibits. She perceives their eccentricity as a mark of individuality. Her South Main Avenue has something of Tortilla Flat but nothing of Tobacco Road, not even when she describes a homeless pop can gatherer in "Keys." Two of the finest essays deal with Pablo Tamayo, a baker with a profound understanding of pie crust for whom "poetry is the fluted edge of dough."

The most capacious essay in the book is "David Crockett's Other Life," which begins by describing a bored driver of a purple tourist trolley who makes up elaborate stories about the sights of the city. Nye spins an elaborate story herself about an automobile accident and a mysterious drive-in, and she ends by celebrating Davey Crockett, the notorious tall tale spinner who died in San Antonio's famous battle at the Alamo.

Not as complex but delightfully circumstantial in its own way is "My Life with Medicine," which covers a variety of extraordinary ailments and remarkable cures, suggesting an authorial personality that is balanced between skepticism and curiosity. Having been cured of bronchitis and hyperventilation by a Filipina psychic without charge (at the David Crockett Hotel-Motel behind the Alamo), Nye is inclined to give miracles the benefit of the doubt: "I always think people with closed minds must never have had any ineffable experiences in their lives. Otherwise how could they be that way?" Exposure to the Unity faith, with its affinity to Christian Science, must have had some effect. She does not demand that the reader accept the occult: she says that the faith healer merely explained that Nye was breathing too deeply and should cure her hyperventilation by panting like a dog.

In "The World and All Its Teeth" she confronts the painful side of her neighborhood through several strands of narrative. She tells a story of elder abuse: Pablo Tamayo's son beats him up. She also describes the lives of the students in a community creative writing class she taught at the West Side Food Bank. She notes that one member of the class, a student who was merely working off detentions by taking the course, ends a touching poem about his grandfather by saying, "He got shot." She says all of the students want to write about "someone being shot. And the worst thing is, they all know somebody." She ends the essay on a bleak note, telling of Erica, a student who wrote a story about having to sleep in the car every night because there were no more beds in her house.

The final section of *Never in a Hurry*, "Still the Sky," is a miscellany. The longest essay, "Used Cars on Oahu," deals with a comic struggle to find a good used car during Nye's one-semester teaching stint at the University of Hawaii. A very brief essay, "Poetry," talks about her vocation as a poet, which was confirmed for her in the first grade when she wrote her poem about Chicago and had it posted on a bulletin board by the teacher. A fellow student noticed it and later said, "I read it—and I know what you *mean*." Nye very effectively follows this affirmative piece with "Banned Poem," about an incident in 1992 when Israeli censors banned the Arabic translation of her elegy for Ibtisam Bozieh, the young girl shot dead at thirteen. Nye was in Palestine at the time of the banning and felt that the text, marked with red slashes throughout and then stamped "REJECTED ENTIRELY" in Hebrew and Arabic, was an honorable linkage with her father's people.

Her final essay, "One Moment on Top of the Earth," strives for optimism and reconciliation: the dedication reads, "For Palestine and for Israel." She uses a family crisis, the near-fatal illness of her 105-year-old grandmother, who lived on "the lip of a beautiful mountain" in what the television called "*the ravaged West Bank,*" for symbolic weight. The grandmother recovers, so perhaps, Nye suggests, "an old country with many names could be that lucky too."

FUEL AND *MINT SNOWBALL*

Naomi Shihab Nye received a Guggenheim Fellowship in 1997. She published *Fuel* in 1998, her first full-length collection of new adult poems since *Red Suitcase* four years earlier. The book seeks out sources that foster people: The opening poem, "Muchas Gracias Por Todo," uses the ordinary idiom "thanks to" as a litany of actual gratitude, with some qualifications: the river has not disappeared "thanks to that one big storm," but "the springs dried up." The poem suggests that we may be nourished in some way by the smallest things: "Thanks to the fan, we are still breathing. / Thanks to the small toad that lives in cool mud at the base of the zinnias." The following poem, "Bill's Beans," expresses more complex gratitude. It is dedicated to Nye's late mentor, William Stafford, and honors him by celebrating his simple gift, beans, now growing in the garden, where the poet delights in pulling up "a perfect question mark and two lean twins." "We'll thank him forever for our breath, / and the brevity of bean," the poem concludes.

She celebrates other gifts of life in the book: a chance to hold a stranger's baby on a plane trip ("Wedding Cake"); her relationship with her young son, who appears in a number of poems; the life-giving qualities of books ("Because of Libraries We Can Say These Things"). The image of fuel appears in two poems. The more powerful is "Hidden," which suggests that a loved one can become a force that sustains you.

> If you place a fern
> under a stone
> the next day it will be
> nearly invisible
> as if the stone
> has swallowed it.
>
> If you tuck the name of a loved one
> under your tongue too long
> without speaking it
> it becomes blood
> sigh
> the little sucked-in breath of air
> hiding everywhere
> beneath your words.
>
> No one sees
> the fuel that feeds you.

The title poem of *Fuel* juxtaposes beans (they seem to be Stafford's beans), a symbol of what is given to us by life, with a scene from the speaker's school days when she was put on a "high stool / for laughing." The classmates admired her in this exalted position instead of belittling her. And she was aware of a world beyond the schoolroom:

> I pinned my gaze out the window
> on a ripe line of sky.
>
> That's where I was going.

This is not quite the poet with flashing eyes and floating hair in Samuel Taylor Coleridge's "Kubla Khan," but it seems a presage of a vocation.

Although the volume has many affirmative moments and some fine flashes of wit, there is a ground bass of sorrow, an awareness of mortality ("Estate Sale") and of the kind of urban renewal that demolishes more than it renews ("Last Song for the Mend-It Shop"). She laments the passing of old people in her neighborhood ("Alphabet"): their rusted chairs stand in the same places but their memories of how things were ninety years ago vanish with them.

The deepest sorrow in *Fuel* arises from events in the Middle East. In "My Uncle's Favorite Coffee Shop" she laments an uncle who went back to Palestine to live out his life but died only a week after he arrived. One of Nye's best poems to date is "The Small Vases from Hebron," which moves from fragile objects—the delicate glass vases and the intricate flowers placed in them—to human loss, the destruction of human bodies:

> the child of Hebron sleeps
> with the thud of her brothers falling
> and the long sorrow of the color red.

Nye's volumes are carefully arranged, and "Darling," the poem that follows "The Small Vases from Hebron," presents a different kind of vase: on a visit to a refugee camp near the

Golan Heights the speaker observes a tin can with a vine "springing pinkly" from it. She ends the poem by celebrating words that console us, like "darling" and "together."

The book ends with a half dozen poems that praise the consolations discovered in the course of a life. One of them, "Quiet of the Mind," describes a "creamy cloud / ignited" by the sunset: glimpsing "that lit stillness" on the road between Presidio and Marfa provided months of consolation "whenever the cities pressed us, / rubbed us down." This is a poem in the tradition of William Wordsworth's "Daffodils." In "Vocabulary of Dearness," as in "Darling," she says that a single word (like "tempestuous" or "suffer") can prevent the days from becoming "thin sticks / thrown down in a clutter of leaves" for which there is no rake. "Pollen" is less consolatory than cautionary, a nudge toward valuing small things like the pollen of foxglove and cedars. Even conflict can be transcended by the gifts of life, Nye suggests in "The Last Days of August," a subtle poem about a man sitting under a pear tree reading. He becomes aware that the pears are falling off the tree, and this sign of ripening and change has a symbolic heft, as he has written a letter to his father about the fear and anxiety that the father created in him. The tone of the poem transforms such conflicts: life bestows gifts as well as conflicts, which she represents through the pears. Action is required as well as contemplation: the pears have to be gathered, processed: "It is hard not to love the pile of peelings / growing on the counter next to the knife."

In *Mint Snowball* (2001) Nye stands by her earlier statement in *Mint* about preferring to call her prose poems "paragraphs," which avoids the difficult question of how a prose work can be a poem. The nineteenth-century French poets Charles Baudelaire and Arthur Rimbaud are usually acknowledged as the first important practitioners of this paradoxical literary form, which uses rhythms, images, and figurative speech that we usually identify with poetry, but without meter or line breaks. Nye's hero, Jack Kerouac, wrote paragraphs and sentences of similar stylistic weight in his novels.

Nye says rather modestly in the preface to *Mint Snowball* that she has trouble growing mint in her drought-stricken Texas soil, with the implication that good paragraphs are also hard to cultivate. The "Mint Snowball" of her title (a piece reprinted from *Never in a Hurry*) has no Middle Eastern connection. Nye writes about a maternal great-grandfather of hers who kept a soda fountain in his drugstore. He invented a dessert concocted of shaved ice flavored with mint syrup. He sold the secret recipe to a man who seems never to have used it, leaving Nye's grandfather feeling hurt, disinherited. Nye uses this vanished recipe as a key to her own character, suggesting that she has a feeling of discontent that proceeds from this lost secret. Her utopian longing for the mint snowball gains symbolic significance, as if growing her "pathetic sprigs from my sunbaked Texas earth" represents a quest for Eden. In *Fuel* she suggests that words like "darling," "together," "tempestuous," and "suffer" can offer emotional redemption. In "Mint Snowball" the mantra is "refreshment": "Can we follow the long river of the word 'refreshment' back to its spring?" She concludes her book with "Mint Snowball II," a little story in which she travels through Shelbyville, Illinois, and actually finds an old man who had tasted one of the desserts.

Prose poems come in various kinds, including narratives and parables. The most common approach to the prose poem in recent American poetry is the "object poem" of the sort written by Robert Bly, who sees the genre as a way of getting in touch with the physical world. Some of Nye's paragraphs are indeed object centered ("The Mind of Squash," "Mint," and "The Urge for Epasote"—a Mexican herb) but most often they encapsulate narratives, like "Heirs," the story of a battered child, or work like brief essays, drawing conclusions from an experience. Generally, the shorter the works are, the more they seem like poems rather than essays or stories.

Mint Snowball is grouped into four sections: "Deep Time," works considering the past and family history; "Piecemeal Lives," compositions dealing mostly with other people; "Sunday Papers," reflections on public issues; and "Appetite," more personal observations united by a pervasive awareness that forces of desire or even greed keep the world going. The epilogue, "Mint Snowball II," acts as a coda, bringing together the past—as family history—and the themes of travel and desire that run through many of the individual pieces.

19 VARIETIES OF GAZELLE

In 2000 Naomi Shihab Nye was named a Witter Bynner Fellow, a distinction given by the Library of Congress at the suggestion of the poet laureate Robert Pinsky. On September 11 of the following year she, like other Americans, was shocked by the terror attacks on the United States. She was also appalled by the hostility shown by some people toward Arab Americans. Her responses to the situation were meant to counter tendencies to demonize Muslims.

She wrote an open letter, "To Any Would-Be Terrorists," which reached a remarkably wide audience via the Internet. She initially sent it to a few friends, who sent it on to their own friends. It gained momentum: the letter showed up in various unlikely places, including an Arabic translation in a Beirut newspaper and a copy tacked on the wall of a Buddhist temple in San Francisco. The essay was published in William Heyen's 2002 anthology *September 11, 2001: American Writers Respond.*

Nye's letter patiently explains the suffering caused to Arab Americans by the September 11 attacks. She begins by discussing how much she hates the word "terrorist" and explains that her father, a refugee from Palestine since 1948, "has written columns and stories saying the Arabs are not terrorists; he has worked all his life to defy that word." "Arabs have always been famous for their generosity," she points out. As for tolerance, she observes that "there is no way everyone on earth could travel on the same road, or believe in exactly the same religion." Adhering to the personal, she gives the example of her Palestinian grandmother as a person who saw Islam as "a welcoming religion." She also observes that the Palestinian cause cannot be helped by such abhorrent means, that well-disposed people in America have spoken in favor of the Palestinians. She advises would-be terrorists to read the poetry of their own tradition and American poetry for its humanizing influence. She advises them to plant mint, which might seem odd advice for anyone not aware of its symbolic weight for her.

Nye's faith in poetry comes through in "A Backlash of Kindness," an article she published in *Hope* in January/February 2002. She noted that people "of every hue and history are trading clues, snippets of uplift," including poems. The poet Mary Karr reported the same phenomenon in an article published in the *New York Times* the same month, "Negotiating the Darkness, Fortified by Poets' Strength." Nye received many letters from friends and strangers who realized that as an Arab American she would be doubly pained by recent events. Her poem "Kindness," from *Different Ways to Pray,* was posted constantly on the Internet. Her most widely distributed comment on the effects of the terror attacks on Arab Americans, "This Is Not Who We Are," was published in the April 2002 issue of *O: The Oprah Magazine,* with its circulation of almost three million. She, like Karr, suggests that poetry is a source of strength: "As a direct line to human feeling, empathic experience, genuine language and detail, poetry is everything that headline news is not." Once again she turns to her grandmother's tolerant and generous attitude as an example of wisdom. Nye says that her grandmother appeared in her dreams with the injunction to "say this is not who we are." In a brief follow-up in the November 2002 issue Nye says, "Moderate voices have to speak more loudly. We have to shout as moderates even if it is not our style." She then advocates the activities of groups that promote dialogue. She has also admonished her fellow citizens to keep in mind the historical roots of the terror attack, speaking out in the *Houston Chronicle* on matters of foreign policy in a piece titled "Naomi Shihab Nye: U.S. Mideast-History a Harbinger of 9-11?" She opens the article with a quotation from Bertolt Brecht about singing "in the dark times." In her follow-up article in the same newspaper on September 11, 2002, "In Such Times, Ties Must Bind," she discusses the influence of the terror attacks on her Arab cousins in San Antonio and declares that "tribalism is obsolete." She says that her heroes are those who make efforts to create dialogue. Nye has also given a lengthy interview about poetry and the Middle East for the PBS program *NOW with Bill Moyers*. In her conversation with Moyers she discusses her faith in the power of words during a time of crisis, making it clear that words are a means of discovery rather than a means of proclaiming things. She emphasizes poetry as a means of conversation with oneself and with the world. Once again she mentions the inspiration she has derived from her grandmother's tolerance and wisdom.

The poet responded to the dreams in which her grandmother implored her to speak by publishing *19 Varieties of Gazelle,* a collection of her previously published poems about the Middle East augmented by a considerable number of new works. A portion of the proceeds of the sales is designated for Seeds of Peace, an organization that attempts to foster dialogue and understanding between Arabs and Jews. The book was a National Book Awards finalist in Young People's Literature for 2002. The introduction to the collection begins with a poem about a young man named Flinn, released that day from prison, riding a bus three hours after the fall of the World Trade Center. Ignorant of the news, he was full of optimism, touchingly resolved to give up "assault with deadly weapons." The speaker does not have the heart to tell him about the new violence loose in the United States. From this poem Nye moves to the issues she dealt with through prose in "To Any Would-Be Terrorists," "A Backlash of Kindness," and "This Is Not Who We Are." She keeps to her faith in poetry as a consolation and as a means of understanding experience more effectively than through television. Once more she invokes her grandmother's tolerance. The preface ends with a plea for peace, and the reader of *Never in a Hurry* may recall the strong impression that the swami made on her when he invoked the traditional formula, "shanti, shanti, shanti."

As mentioned earlier, the front cover of *19 Varieties of Gazelle* has a photograph of a Palestinian girl holding a poem she wrote for her mother. The back cover speaks by implication to the violence of life in the region. It has a picture of a man in Arab headdress standing next to a young boy and holding a photograph of a young adult male. The reader must guess at the family relationships: perhaps a grandfather and grandson, with the grandfather holding a memorial picture of the missing generation.

The title poem, one of the book's new works, uses a visit to a wildlife sanctuary in Bahrain to suggest that the beauty of natural beings offers consolation to human beings distressed by history, headlines, and human voices, a kind of comfort common in poetry since the Romantics. But history and human voices inevitably dominate much of the poetry, as in "Mr. Dajani, Calling from Jericho," an account of phone conversations with a weatherman in Jericho who calls the speaker to talk about books and remains cheerful even as bombs are falling. Dajani is a voice calling for reconciliation and mutual respect between Israelis and Palestinians. Although many of Nye's poems are angry, her basic stance is conciliatory. She says at the beginning of "Jerusalem," a poem reprinted from *Red Suitcase:*

> I'm not interested in
> who suffered the most.
> I'm interested in
> people getting over it.

And at the end of the poem she declares, "It's late but everything comes next."

One of the most complex of the new poems, "Things Don't Stop," contrasts nature imagery with human suffering. It is notable among her works for the sheer number of its unexpected turns, and it may represent a new enrichment of her art. The poem begins with a description of Palestinian girls waiting in line for hours to receive pieces of bread, then moves to the harder case of a boy who has to sleep under the wall of a shattered house. He no longer fears dead people because he has seen so many. From those scenes of desolation the speaker turns to a newly learned fact of natural history, asking if the reader has a seen a "bee's little bucket," the basket some bees form from pollen and nectar in order to scoop up pollen. "Why are bees so lucky?" the speaker wonders, obviously thinking of the girls standing in line for food. From that question she turns to the image of "the boy in my house," which by implication is not a broken house, who has grown very tall. He, also by implication, has been adequately fed. Yet another turn in the poem introduces a neighbor, Mr. Laguna, who still thinks of the boy as "The Baby," not realizing that he has grown as tall—figuratively—as the Pioneer flour mill. The reference to the mill makes the speaker think of workers who go home with "flour in their cuffs," a sign of American abundance and an implied contrast with the lineup of girls waiting for a bit of food. Next year in Hawaii, the narrator says, the boy will learn to say "I am not sorry" in Hawaiian. The poem ends:

> We are not sorry.
> We are not sorry.
> We can't be sorry enough.

The "we" in the final lines is perhaps the human race, which is not as lucky or harmonious as a colony of bees. Human beings have much to be sorry for but cannot be sorry enough even if they wish to be. Nye's longer poems have generally been written in sections; this one is riskier.

A poet who worries if we can ever be sorry enough naturally deplores the reduction of complex issues to headlines, but here and there she herself writes poems that seem too close to journalism, as in "Top Israeli Official Hints at 'Shared' Jerusalem." Her final poem, "Postscript," regrets her carelessness in letting a journalist who interviewed her on the phone come away with a sound bite that distorted her views. She resolves to be more careful with words. This is the writer whose poem in *Different Ways to Pray,* "The Art of Disappearing," advocated a thoroughly private life: reject invitations to parties, reject public recognition; she advises her reader and herself to pay attention to the subject matter of lyric poetry, like trees and monastery bells at sunset. But the pressure of painful public events has prevented Nye from practicing the art of disappearing. The results for her poetry have not been bad: her work has deepened in response to the crises she cannot ignore.

Not every poem in *19 Varieties of Gazelle* is about the Arab-Israeli conflict. One of the most powerful is "Rock," which looks compassionately at the effects of an earthquake in Iran, contrasting that suffering with her own society where there is time for growing bean sprouts and discussing the virtues of vegetarianism. In

Iran the people themselves were eaten by the earthquake. Other poems celebrate the joy of living or look closely at the daily lives of people in the Middle East. Without mentioning terrorism she honors traditional Arab hospitality in "Red Brocade": the old saying was that a stranger appearing at one's door should be fed for three days before being asked any questions about his identity and purposes. The poem is an implicit reply to murderous hatred: meet the Other with a red brocade pillow, snip mint for his tea, she suggests.

Daily life in the United States is the subject of a quietly utopian poem, "Steps," in which an Arab American grocer letters a sign in both his languages. The Arabic takes longer to dry because of its "thick swoops and curls," an image that simultaneously points to the richness of the Arab heritage and to the slowness with which it has been accepted into mainstream American culture. The grocer sells candy to immigrant children, who have learned to use American dimes. The poem says,

> One of these children will tell a story that keeps her people
> alive. We don't know yet which one she is.

Nye is one of those poets who wants to keep a people alive. Like the grocer and the children she has overlapping but not contradictory identities as an American conscious of her Arabic heritage. A book on Texas memoirists titled *This Stubborn Self: Texas Autobiographies* discusses her briefly as a member of the Arab diaspora but also observes that she is "thoroughly multicultural by birth, origins, and commitment."

Nye affirmed her commitments in an important essay, "This Crutch That I Love," which was published in 2002 by the U.S. Department of State in *Writers on America,* an ethnically diverse anthology by fifteen distinguished American authors. In this essay, she talks about her own mixed ethnic origins and her interest in writing about details of the varied life in America, stressing ethnic diversity. Living in a Latino city like San Antonio, she speculates, has made her aware of what it is to be an Arab American. Near the end of the essay she says "How various we are in our eccentric, multicolored land, our trails dotting so many landscapes, cultures and histories up till now." At the same time, the practice of writing is "a daily declaration of independence," a reminder that the individual transcends his or her background. Naomi Shihab Nye's vision is, to use her own word, "ecumenical," a term that, after all, is not distant from the American motto e pluribus unum—"Out of many, one."

Selected Bibliography

WORKS OF NAOMI SHIHAB NYE

POETRY

Tattooed Feet (as Naomi Shihab). Texas City: Texas Portfolio Press, 1977. (Chapbook.)

Eye-to-Eye (as Naomi Shihab). Texas City: Texas Portfolio Press, 1978. (Chapbook.)

Different Ways to Pray: Poems. Portland, Ore.: Breitenbush, 1980.

On the Edge of the Sky. Madison, Wis.: Iguana, 1981. (Chapbook.)

Hugging the Jukebox. New York: Dutton, 1982; Portland, Ore.: Breitenbush, 1984.

Yellow Glove. Portland, Ore.: Breitenbush, 1986.

Invisible: Poems. Denton, Tex.: Trilobite, 1987. (Chapbook.)

"Twenty Other Worlds." In *Texas Poets in Concert: A Quartet.* Denton: University of North Texas Press, 1990. Pp. 76–105.

Mint. Brockport, N.Y.: State Street, 1991. (Chapbook.)

Travel Alarm. Houston: Wings, 1993. (Chapbook.)

Red Suitcase: Poems. Brockport, N.Y.: BOA Editions, 1994.

Words under the Words: Selected Poems. Portland, Ore.: Eighth Mountain, 1995.

Fuel: Poems. Rochester, N.Y.: BOA Editions, 1998.

Mint Snowball. Tallahassee, Fla.: Anhinga, 2001.

19 Varieties of Gazelle: Poems of the Middle East. New York: Greenwillow, 2002.

BOOKS FOR CHILDREN AND YOUNG ADULTS

Sitti's Secrets. Illustrated by Nancy Carpenter. New York: Four Winds, 1994.

Benito's Dream Bottle. Illustrated by Yu Cha Pak. New York: Simon & Schuster Books for Young Readers, 1995.

Habibi. New York: Simon & Schuster Books for Young Readers, 1997.

Lullaby Raft. Illustrated by Vivienne Flesher. New York: Simon & Schuster Books for Young Readers, 1997.

Come with Me: Poems for a Journey. Illustrated by Dan Yaccarino. New York: Greenwillow, 2000.

Baby Radar. Illustrated by Nancy Carpenter. New York: Greenwillow, 2003.

ESSAYS

"On the Front Steps of the Hall Where W. S. Merwin Is Reading." *Paintbrush* 18, no. 35:53–55 (spring 1991).

"Music of the Deep Well." *Mid-American Review* 13, no. 1:159–160 (fall 1992).

"Lights in the Windows." *The ALAN Review* (http://scholar.lib.vt.edu/ejournals/ALAN/spring95/Nye.html), spring 1995.

Never in a Hurry: Essays on People and Places. Columbia: University of South Carolina Press, 1996.

Tribute to Allen Ginsberg. *The Massachusetts Review* 39, no. 2:207–208 (summer 1998).

"Your Poem Is Happening All Over." *Texas Observer,* August 3, 2001, pp. 36–39.

"Naomi Shihab Nye: U.S.-Mideast History a Harbinger of 9-11?" *Houston Chronicle,* December 29, 2001, Lifestyle section, p. 1.

"This Crutch That I Love: A Writer's Life, Past and Present." In *Writers on America.* Washington, D.C.: Office of International Information Programs, U.S. Department of State, 2002. Pp. 54–57. Available online at (http://usinfo.state.gov/products/pubs/writers/nye.htm).

"To Any Would-Be Terrorists." In *September 11, 2001: American Writers Respond.* Edited by William Heyen. Silver Spring, Md.: Etruscan, 2002. Pp. 287–291.

"A Backlash of Kindness." *Hope,* January/February 2002, pp. 30–32.

"This Is Not Who We Are." *O: The Oprah Magazine,* April 2002, pp. 83–86.

"Children's Books." *New York Times Book Review,* August 11, 2002, p. 18.

"In Such Times, Ties Must Bind." *Houston Chronicle,* September 11, 2002, special section, p. 5.

"What Can We Do?" *O: The Oprah Magazine,* November 2002, p. 235.

ANTHOLOGIES EDITED BY NAOMI SHIHAB NYE

This Same Sky: A Collection of Poems from around the World. New York: Four Winds, 1992; New York: Aladdin, 1996.

The Tree Is Older Than You Are: A Bilingual Gathering of Poems and Stories from Mexico with Paintings by Mexican Artists. New York: Simon & Schuster Books for Young Readers, 1995.

I Feel a Little Jumpy around You: A Book of Her Poems and His Poems Collected in Pairs. Coedited by Paul B. Janeczko. New York: Simon & Schuster Books for Young Readers, 1996.

The Space between Our Footsteps: Poems and Paintings from the Middle East. New York: Simon & Schuster Books for Young Readers, 1998.

What Have You Lost? Photographs by Michael Nye. New York: Greenwillow, 1999.

Salting the Ocean: 100 Poems by Young Poets. Illustrated by Ashley Bryan. New York: Greenwillow, 2000.

The Flag of Childhood: Poems from the Middle East. New York: Aladdin, 2002. (Abridged version of *The Space between Our Footsteps.*)

TRANSLATIONS

Tuqan, Fadwa. *A Mountainous Journey: An Autobiography.* Translated by Olive Kenny; poetry translated by Naomi Shihab Nye with the help of the editor, Salma Khadra Jayyusi. St. Paul, Minn.: Graywolf, 1990.

al-Maghut, Muhammad. *The Fan of Swords: Poems.* Translated by May Jayyusi and Naomi Shihab Nye and edited by Salma Khadra Jayyusi. Washington, D.C.: Three Continents, 1991.

RECORDINGS

Rutabaga-Roo: I've Got a Song and It's for You. San Antonio: Flying Cat, 1979. (Songs.)

Lullaby Raft. San Antonio: Flying Cat, 1981. (Songs.)

The Spoken Page. Pittsburgh: International Poetry Forum, 1988. (Poetry reading.)

CRITICAL AND BIOGRAPHICAL STUDIES

Almon, Bert. Review of *Words under the Words* and *Never in a Hurry*. Western American Literature 31, no. 3:265–266 (fall 1996).

———. "Conclusion: Are Texans Still Texans?" In *This Stubborn Self: Texas Autobiographies.* Fort Worth: Texas Christian University Press, 2002. Pp. 355–357.

Booth, Philip. "Loners Whose Voices Move." *Georgia Review* 43, no. 1:161–178 (spring 1989). (Review of *Yellow Glove*.)

Clausi, Victoria. Review of *Fuel*. *Ploughshares* 24, no. 4:224–227 (winter 1998/1999).

Colloff, Pamela. "The Literature of an Examined Life: Naomi Shihab Nye." *Texas Monthly,* September 1998, pp. 111–113.

Gómez-Vega, Ibis. "The Art of Telling Stories in the Poetry of Naomi Shihab Nye." *MELUS* 26, no. 4:245–252 (2002).

McKee, Louis. "Ranting and Raving about Naomi Shihab Nye." *Swamp Root* (spring 1989). Pp. 83–89.

Orfalea, Gregory. "Doomed by Our Blood to Care: The Poetry of Naomi Shihab Nye." *Paintbrush* 18, no. 35:56–66 (spring 1991).

Rummel, Mary Kay. "Books for Adolescents." *Journal of Adolescent & Adult Literacy* 43, no. 5:496–497 (February 2000). (Review of *What Have You Lost?*)

Seale, Jan Epton. "Three Contemporary Poets: Naomi Shihab Nye, Pattiann Rogers, and Betsy Feagan Colquitt." In *Texas Women Writers: A Tradition of Their Own.* Edited by Sylvia Ann Grider and Lou Halsell Rodenberger. College Station: Texas A&M University Press, 1997. Pp. 310–320.

Shihab, Aziz. *A Taste of Palestine: Menus and Memories.* San Antonio: Corona, 1993.

Tanner, Jane L. "Naomi Shihab Nye." In *Dictionary of Literary Biography.* Volume 120, *American Poets Since World War II,* Third Series, edited by R. S. Gwynn. Detroit: Gale, 1992. Pp. 223–226.

INTERVIEWS

Barenblat, Rachel. "One on One: Email Interview with Naomi Shihab Nye." In *The Best of Pif Magazine Off-line.* Edited by Camille Renshaw. Irving, Tex.: Fusion, 2000. Pp. 83–88.

Lesesne, Teri. "Honoring the Mystery of Experience." *Teacher Librarian* 26, no. 2:59–61 (November/December1998).

Milligan, Bryce. "Writing to Save Our Lives: An Interview with Naomi Shihab Nye." *Paintbrush* 18, no. 35:31–49 (spring 1991).

Moyers, Bill. "Naomi Shihab Nye." In *The Language of Life: A Festival of Poets.* New York: Doubleday, 1995. Pp. 319–334.

———. "Naomi Shihab Nye." *NOW with Bill Moyers* (http://www.pbs.org/now/transcript/transcript_nye.html), October 11, 2002. (Transcript of television program.)

—BERT ALMON

Tillie Olsen

1912/13–

*T*ILLIE OLSEN IS not a prolific writer. Her entire literary reputation rests on five short stories, a book of essays, and an unfinished novel. Yet few figures have contributed so much to revolutionizing the short story form, and few are as beloved or have been as influential in bringing to light the lost works of women and working-class people. As Margaret Atwood argued in the *New York Times Book Review,* "Among women writers in the United States, 'respect' is too pale a word: 'reverence' is more like it. This is presumably because women writers, even more than their male counterparts, recognize what a heroic feat it is to have held down a job, raised four children and still somehow managed to become and remain a writer." And Atwood is not alone in her admiration of Olsen's contribution and presence. Alice Walker, for instance, has described Olsen as "a writer of such generosity and honesty she literally saves our lives" (quoted from *Protest and Possibility in the Writing of Tillie Olsen.*).

BIOGRAPHY

Tillie Olsen's parents, Ida Beber and Samuel Lerner, were Russian Jews who met in the Minsk Bund and emigrated from Russia to the United States after the failed 1905 revolution to overthrow the czars. After arriving in New York, they moved to Nebraska, where Samuel held various jobs to support his young family, working variously as a miner, farmworker, and packinghouse worker, among other occupations.

In 1912 or 1913, their second child, Tillie, was born on January 14 on a tenant farm in Mead, Nebraska. Around 1917, the family moved to Omaha, where Samuel joined the Socialist Party of America and worked to organize workers. The Lerner household became a center for secular Jewish socialists and other activists, and Samuel later was elected state secretary of the Nebraska Socialist Party. Young Tillie suffered often from childhood illnesses during her elementary school years, but staying at home because of sickness created time for her to read even amid the responsibility of helping to care for her five siblings. Although she was shy because of a stutter, Tillie absorbed a great deal from the political tenor of the activists who frequented her home. Samuel was blacklisted during the early 1920s because of his involvement in a failed packinghouse strike. Yet within the ranks, Samuel Lerner was so admired that he served as the party's candidate for lieutenant governor in 1928. Also during the 1920s, Samuel organized men to travel to Tulsa to help blacks rebuild their homes after they were burned down in a race riot. Her parents' everyday heroism and integrity impacted the young Tillie Olsen profoundly, serving to fuel her commitment to social justice.

In 1925 Olsen attended Central High School, Omaha's only public academic high school, crossing the tracks from her home and, for the first time, directly experiencing class-based discrimination. She wrote a column for the school paper and read passionately, intending to read all the fiction in the Omaha public library (she reached M), all the while having to earn money at jobs that included shelling almonds, serving as a nanny, or working as a grocery clerk. When she was just fifteen, Olsen stumbled across a couple of old copies of the *Atlantic*

Monthly in a used bookstore in Omaha, bought them for a dime, and encountered the unsigned story "Life in the Iron Mills." It would be years later (1958) before she would learn that the story's author was Rebecca Harding Davis, and Olsen would use her influence to get an edition of *Life in the Iron Mills* into print. But the encounter galvanized the young Olsen into believing she, too, could write of the plight of the working class, gleaning from Davis' example that "literature can be made out of the lives of despised people" (quoted from *Silences*).

After her junior year, Olsen dropped out of high school, and, as the Great Depression began, she was forced to work a series of low-skill, low paying jobs, at one point serving as a pork trimmer in a packinghouse. In 1931 Olsen joined the Young Communist League (YCL) against her parents' wishes. She attended the party school in the Kansas-Missouri area, and she was jailed in Kansas City for distributing flyers to workers in area packinghouses. The case was never brought to trial, but Olsen spent seven weeks in jail, where she came down with pleurisy that later developed into incipient tuberculosis. In 1932, after moving to Faribault, Minnesota, to recover from tuberculosis, she began writing her novel *Yonnondio* (which remained unpublished until 1974), and she gave birth to her first daughter, Karla (named after Karl Marx), in Minneapolis.

After Karla's birth, Olsen moved to California and experienced the deprivation of single motherhood during the Great Depression that she later chronicled in "I Stand Here Ironing," the most straightforwardly autobiographical of her stories. Despite her hardships, her early days in the socialist movement were exciting, fueled by a sincere optimism that it was possible to create a more egalitarian society. In interviews between 1988–1990, Olsen discussed how she internalized her parents' political drive, recalling her father's words: "We could not wait for a messiah to bring a beautiful future. We realized that we ourselves, acting together, must be the Messiah," as recorded in Joanne Frye's *Tillie Olsen: A Study of the Short Fiction*. And when asked how coming from a working-class background had shaped her work, Olsen replied, "it has shaped what I am as well as all I've written."

Once in California, Olsen worked in Venice and Stockton at various menial jobs before settling in San Francisco, where she met the young labor organizer Jack Olsen. Through the Young Communist League, Olsen became active in the San Francisco maritime strike that began in May 1934, and after the deadly fighting between police and strikers of July 5, 1934—known as Bloody Thursday—she got involved in the general strike of West Coast dockworkers, writing leaflets and providing clerical support for the cause. She was arrested at the home of communist friends and jailed for "vagrancy" along with hundreds of other activists and strikers. From this period of fervid activism came her first published work, appearing in the leftist periodicals *Partisan Review* and *New Republic*: two published poems—"I Want You Women Up North To Know" and "There Is a Lesson"—as well as her short story "The Iron Throat" and two essays, "The Thousand Dollar Vagrant" and "The Strike." "The Iron Throat" (which later became part of the first chapter of *Yonnondio*) gained the most attention. Reviewing the story in the *New Republic*, Robert Cantwell called it a work of "early genius," and declared "the imagery, the metaphors distilled out of common speech, are startling in their brilliance" (quoted in *The Critical Response to Tillie Olsen*). Publishers interested in finding this promising young writer tried to contact Olsen through the *New Republic*, which was no small feat, given that Olsen was in jail under a false name (Teresa Landale) to protect her parents. Because of the interest her story garnered, through the advocacy of literary editors and agents who took up her cause, she was eventually released. She was even offered a book contract for the novel she was working on, including a regular stipend if she submitted a chapter a month.

In 1935 Olsen was one of a handful of women writers (thirty-six women out of four thousand delegates) invited to attend the American Writers Congress in New York, where she presented an address to that prestigious group and rubbed elbows with writers such as Richard Wright, Nathanael West, and Theodore Dreiser. Despite such auspicious beginnings, Olsen's novel was later abandoned, for as Olsen states in *Silences,* "the simplest circumstances for creation did not exist."

In 1936 Tillie began living with Jack Olsen and in 1937 began writing occasional pieces for the communist newspaper *People's World.* In 1946 she began writing a column for *People's World* which argued, among other issues, that motherhood was political work and should be considered as such, campaigning for such radical ends as equal pay, an increase in the minimum wage, and publicly subsidized childcare. (Indeed, in *Silences,* Olsen points out that "the atomic bomb was in manufacture before the first automatic washing machine.") In 1938 Olsen gave birth to a second daughter, Julie, named for Julius "Jack" Eggan, to whom the short story "Hey Sailor, What Ship?" would later be dedicated. In the next few years, Olsen continued to organize warehouse unions, became director of the California Congress of Industrial Organizations (CIO), served as president of the CIO Women's Auxiliary directing the northern California war relief after World War II began, and served on the CIO Serviceman's Committee.

In 1943, still living in San Francisco, Olsen gave birth to a third daughter, Katherin Jo, and married Jack Olsen before he was drafted. While he was away, she raised three daughters alone while working for canteen and family services as part of the war effort. She also became president of the parent-teacher organization at her daughters' school and was instrumental in establishing San Francisco's first public day care center. Olsen continued to work for better schools and libraries, and she was responsible for the addition of a playground and library to her daughters' school. In addition to advocating for better public schools, Olsen helped found an independent women's division of the International Longshoremen's and Warehousemen's Union. In 1948 her last daughter, Laurie, was born.

In the early 1950s the House Un-American Activities Committee targeted both Olsen and her husband as subversives. During a 1990 interview (quoted in the biography by Mickey Pearlman and Abby Werlock), Olsen recalled how a neighbor phoned and told her to turn on the radio, where a disembodied voice droned, "Tillie Olsen, alias Tillie Lerner, alias Teresa Landale," accusing her of being, "an agent of Stalin working in San Francisco Public Schools to take over the public schools." Tillie Olsen was never subpoenaed, but Jack Olsen was called before the committee in December 1953. As a result, Jack Olsen lost his union job and was blacklisted from working in the sensitive waterfront areas. Forced to start over, at the age of forty he began a six-year apprenticeship to a printer. Meanwhile, Tillie Olsen could not stay longer than a month at any given job before the FBI would appear and she would be fired. In response to the mounting tensions of the cold war and the devastating effect of the detonation of the atomic bomb over Hiroshima and Nagasaki, Olsen became involved in the disarmament movement.

When her youngest child began grade school in 1954, Olsen enrolled in a creative writing course at San Francisco State University and her renaissance as a writer began. She did not complete the course, but the instructor was so encouraging he gave Olsen the confidence to apply for the prestigious Stegner Creative Writing Fellowship at Stanford University; she received the fellowship and attended Stanford in 1955–1956. Olsen, an older, unknown reentry student, shared the workshop table with such writers as James Baldwin, Bernard Malamud, Flannery O'Connor, and Katherine Ann Porter during those auspicious eight months. The time to devote to writing that the Stegner fellowship afforded Olsen led to her most prolific period. She published "Help Her to Believe" (the story that would later become "I Stand Here Ironing") in 1956, and "Hey Sailor, What Ship?" and "Baptism" (which she later retitled "O Yes") followed the next year. Moreover, "I Stand Here Ironing" appeared in *Best American Short Stories* in 1957.

Olsen began work on the novella "Tell Me a Riddle" while still in the program at Stanford. In 1959, amid scribbling on notecards while snatching writing time on the bus to and from work, or using the ironing board as a writing desk after putting the children to sleep, Olsen received a Ford Foundation Grant in Literature. The grant came almost too late, she later wrote in *Silences:* her work had virtually "died." "What demanded to be written, did not. It seethed, bubbled, clamored, peopled me.... Time granted does not necessarily coincide with time that can be most fully used, as the congested time of fullness would have been." The grant did in fact allow her to finish "Tell Me a Riddle," which was anthologized in 1960 and went on to win the O. Henry Award for Best Story of the Year in 1961. *Tell Me a Riddle*, which collected the title novella along with the earlier stories "I Stand Here Ironing," "Hey Sailor, What Ship?" and "O Yes," was published in 1961; *Time* magazine named it one of the ten best books of the year.

Invited on Anne Sexton's recommendation, from 1962 through 1964 Olsen joined the poets Sexton and Maxine Kumin as fellows at Radcliffe Institute, and there she began collecting material for what would later become the nonfiction volume *Silences,* published in 1978. In 1963 Olsen delivered a speech as part of her Radcliffe fellowship, an edited version of which was later published in *Harpers* magazine as "Silences: When Writers Don't Write." The talk and the article concerned Olsen's increasing interest in the "unnatural silences" that prevent or obstruct literary creation, and for examples she chronicled the silences of such writers as Herman Melville, Thomas Hardy, and Gerard Manley Hopkins.

In 1967 Olsen received a National Endowment for the Arts grant that allowed her time to work on her next short story. In 1969 she accepted a position at Amherst College as a professor and writer in residence; at Amherst she first started teaching a course concerned with the issues of the working class: "The Literature of Poverty, Work, and the Struggle for Human Freedom." Here Olsen introduced into the classroom a text central to her worldview: the United Nations Declaration of Universal Human Rights. This course was also the genesis for Olsen's creation of a reading list of lost women writers. These reading lists became an underground phenomenon as mimeographed copies circulated by hand and later were distributed at the 1971 Modern Language Association panel on which Olsen presented with Adrienne Rich.

In 1970 the beginning of what was to be a larger piece appeared in the *Iowa Review* as "Requa." It was reprinted as "Requa I" in *The Best American Short Stories of 1971* in an issue dedicated to Olsen. The next year, Olsen returned to Stanford as a visiting instructor and continued her research into the unnatural thwarting of creative potential, presenting "One Out of Twelve: Writers Who Are Women in Our Century" at the Modern Language Association, a talk that eventually became the second chapter of *Silences.* In that same year, 1972, Jack Olsen stumbled across some old papers among which he discovered the manuscript of Olsen's long lost, unfinished novel *Yonnondio,* which had been abandoned in 1937 amid the demands of raising four children and holding down survival-wage jobs. Olsen spent five months reconstructing and reworking the manuscript of *Yonnondio* at the MacDowell Writers Colony. At the time, she was also writing an afterword to Rebecca Harding Davis' *Life in the Iron Mills,* which she had convinced Florence Howe at the Feminist Press to reissue. Olsen also convinced Howe to make it a central mission of the press to reprint lost texts by important women writers. Around the same time, the *Women Studies Newsletter* began publishing "Tillie Olsen's Reading Lists," recovering and rediscovering unjustly forgotten women writers like Zora Neale Hurston, Agnes Smedly, and Sarah Wright, all of whose work was then obscure and out of print. In 1973 the Feminist Press published *Life in the Iron Mills* accompanied by the lengthy "A Biographical Interpretation" by Olsen. The press published Smedly's *Daughter of Earth* (a book even more central to Olsen than *Life in The Iron Mills*) the next year, and it went on to reprint works by Charlotte Perkins Gilman, Paule Marshall, Dorothy West, Josephine Herbst, Sarah Wright, and Zora Neale Hurston, among many others, in the years following.

In 1973 Olsen took a position as writer in residence at the Massachusetts Institute of Technology, and in 1974 she served as distinguished visiting professor at the University of Massachusetts in Boston. Olsen's novel *Yonnondio: From the Thirties,* was finally published in 1974, forty years after it was originally abandoned. In 1975 Olsen received an award for her distinguished contribution to American literature from the American Academy and National Institute of Arts and Letters, followed by a Guggenheim Fellowship. She became a Copeland Fellow at Amherst in 1977, all of which provided much-needed time to realize her manuscript for *Silences,* which was published in 1978.

The following year, Olsen was awarded an honorary doctorate from the University of Nebraska; she received five other honorary degrees in the years that followed. In 1980 she received the Ministry to Women Award granted by the Unitarian Universalist Federation, traveled as an international visiting scholar to Norway, and was named Radcliffe's centennial lecturer. She was also honored for her work by the British Post Office, with a special award for "the American woman writer best exemplifying in our time their ideals and literary excellence" (quoted from *The Critical Response to Tillie Olsen*). In tandem with that award, stamps were issued internationally to commemorate women writers such the Brontë sisters, Elizabeth Gaskell, and George Eliot. The same year, 1980, also saw the release of a film version of "Tell Me a Riddle," directed by Lee Grant. On May 18, 1981, the city of San Francisco celebrated Tillie Olsen Day by order of the mayor and the board of supervisors (eight years later, a month after his death, Jack Olsen was honored in San Francisco with an official remembrance day, on March 25, 1989). In 1983 five colleges in the Quad City area of Iowa and Illinois jointly hosted Tillie Olsen Week and Symposium, and Olsen was awarded a Senior Fellowship from the National Endowment for the Humanities.

In 1984 Olsen realized a lifelong dream to visit to the home of her Russian immigrant parents when she traveled with her husband to the USSR as a guest of the Soviet Writers' Union. This trip was followed by a visit to China with a coalition of women writers including Alice Walker and Paule Marshall, and both journeys were important cultural moments for a writer who still considers herself a committed socialist. *Mother to Daughter, Daughter to Mother* appeared in 1984; this daybook and reader with selections by Olsen featured writers as diverse as Harriet Beecher Stowe and Audre Lorde. It also included Olsen's own essay "Dream Vision," a moving account of Olsen's mother's deathbed hallucination later reprinted in *Ms. Magazine*. She was named Bunting Fellow at Radcliffe College in 1985, Gund Professor at Kenyon College in 1986, and Regents Lecturer at the University of California at Los Angeles in 1987.

Tillie Olsen's long partnership with Jack Olsen came to an end with his death in 1989, but along with sadness, 1989 brought still more honors. Olsen was feted with a special session at the Modern Language Association called "*Silences:* Ten Years Later." In the company of the writers Gwendolyn Brooks and May Sarton, Olsen was honored at Clark University in Worcester, Massachusetts, that year as well. Despite her grief at the loss of her husband, Olsen returned to work, spending September and October of 1990 at the Leighton Arts Colony in Banff, Canada. In 1994 Olsen received the prestigious Rea Award for advancing the art of the short story. In a Dungannon Foundation announcement, the selection committee characterized her work as combining the "lyric intensity of an Emily Dickinson poem and the scope of a Balzac novel" (as quoted in *Tillie Olsen: A Study of the Short Fiction*). The year 1994 also saw the publication of new editions of *Tell Me a Riddle* and *Yonnondio* (containing previously unreleased material). In her early nineties, Olsen continued to be generous with her time and energy, traveling the country giving readings and interviews, inspiring all who had the good fortune to hear her speak in person or who read her words on the page.

THE LITERATURE

Despite her significant contributions as an activist and humanist, Tillie Olsen's relatively small literary output is what has secured her place as an important American writer. Marked by a stream-of-consciousness style, a dense lyrical poeticism, and stylistic use of fragments, Olsen's prose style is experimental and innovative, and has done much to elevate the artistry of the short story genre. Her prose makes demands on the reader, eschewing linear plot development in favor of shifts in time and associative links in her characters' psyches. The language is rich, textured, imagistic; dialogue captures the cadences of spoken language. The stories are compressed and complex, impressionistic; yet they are embedded in historical context, and "novelistic" in scope despite their economy.

Olsen told Joanne Frye that when she writes, "The form comes primarily out of what it is I am trying to get said in the best way I can say it." Yet Olsen's stylistic innovations reveal a greater truth. As Olsen says in a 1983 interview with Frye included in *Tillie Olsen: A Study of the Short Fiction,* "how can you say what is generally not accepted with unmistakable force and clarity, when the context has not been established? That can happen only after a movement has articulated different perceptions, truths." Her fiction is rooted in an experiential, bodily means of experiencing the world, and it concretizes the metaphor of mental and spiritual maiming. The images of constriction are bodily: one notes, for instance, her use of the word "festering" in *Silences,* while "clogged" and "clotted" are her metaphors of choice in "I Stand Here Ironing." In interviews, Olsen has discussed the phenomenon of how years of physical labor come to be encoded in one's flesh; indeed Olsen attributes instances of her own physical illness as having been caused by the obligation to prematurely cease writing and return to paid work: "I was sometimes hospitalized," she told Frye, because "the harm had entered my body." As Olsen says in Deborah Rosenfelt's "From the Thirties: Tillie Olsen and the Radical Tradition," she has come by her knowledge in "an earned way, a bone way." Indeed, Olsen ends a section of *Silences* with the assertion, "We are the injured body."

Olsen's form demands participation from the reader, making the reading experience a collaborative one. She relies heavily on ellipses in punctuating her sentences, building into her sentence structure places to pause and speculate. In this manner, her very sentences resist closure. Olsen's use of fragments implies, on the syntactical level, the elliptical nature of the associative consciousness of her characters, creating an intimacy between character and reader, as she has dispensed with formal modes of description in favor of a shorthand. Elizabeth Meese connects this impulse with the ecriture feminine espoused by the philosopher Hélène Cixous, arguing that "'feminine' texts are 'without ending,' with the "pages' blank spaces" providing "open invitations to the reader to participate in the text's creation." Joanne Trautmann Banks concurs, saying, "Olsen works with empty space as if it were as important an element as language. Many of her sentences are fragments, italicized, parenthetical." Both Constance Coiner and Linda Park-Fuller have written compellingly on Olsen's intent to bring to voice those silenced and marginalized. Coiner notes how in "Tell Me a Riddle," Olsen "disrupts our passivity, demanding that we as readers share responsibility for completing Eva's story." This strategy is nothing less than radical. Olsen destabilizes the implied hierarchies of author and reader in her prose. In forcing the reader out of complacency, Olsen is modeling—on the sentence level of her fiction—the very democratizing she has enacted on the social and political levels with her resurrection of forgotten working-class and women writers and with her lifelong labor activism.

EARLY WORK

Olsen's early work published in the 1930s is the stuff of polemic. Yet in poems such as "I Want You Women Up North To Know," the seeds of Olsen's later style are apparent in her use of the female body as the site of metaphor. The poem catalogs the suffering of Latinas working in sweatshops in San Antonio to produce the fine hand-sewn children's clothing sold in exclusive department stores up North. The power of the poem is not just in the move to implicate the potential reader in an economy predicated on exploitation, but also lies in Olsen's intertwining of the producer and the product, the very bodies of the exploited women becoming the fabric they sew, their blood the dye. Olsen's other published poem from the period, "There Is a Lesson," is similar in the way it takes what is usually abstract and concretizes the suffering into the bodies of children, again utilizing the trope of body and blood.

Olsen's other pieces from the period, the essays "The Thousand Dollar Vagrant" and "The Strike," are more reportorial in execution, but just as political in intent. "The Strike" is particularly revealing, as it highlights a central dilemma for Olsen: the primacy of the pull between political activism and the detached role of the artist. Olsen writes, "Do not ask me to write of the strike and the terror; I am on a battlefield." This dramatic statement is later contradicted by her admittance that she is, in fact, "sitting up in headquarters, typing accounts of the events . . . this is all I can do, because this is what I am supposed to do." Yet in times of such political turmoil, Olsen often made the difficult decision to engage in political action, perhaps at the expense of greater literary output. Yet, for a single mother of her political convictions and class background, such engagement was mandatory. Despite the early attention her work generated—the heady exhilaration of participating in the American Writers Congress with the literary luminaries of the day and the offer of a book contract (and stipend) when Olsen published her short story "The Iron Throat"—Olsen's passion for language ultimately had to take a back seat to the demands of subsistence wage earning, raising four children alone during the war, and continued work for meaningful social change.

THE SHORT STORIES

Olsen's literary reputation was forged mainly as a result of the four short stories collected in *Tell Me a Riddle*. This slim volume, only 116 pages long, contains the stories "I Stand Here Ironing," "Hey Sailor, What Ship?" "O Yes," and the title novella, "Tell Me a Riddle." The stories were all written during Olsen's midlife writing renaissance, facilitated by her youngest daughter starting school in the mid-1950s. Olsen has said that much of the first story, "I Stand Here Ironing," was in fact written and rewritten on the ironing table late at night. The story is the moving interior monologue of a mother trying to make sense of the set of circumstances that have made up the life of her eldest daughter, Emily. The meditation is occasioned by a call from a well-meaning school official, and the story opens, "I stand here ironing, and what you asked me moves back and forth tormented with the iron." The story is an indictment of the ways in which those in positions of authority repeatedly fail the young, single mother, and it captures the anguish the mother feels about witnessing the scarring effects of such deprivation manifest in her daughter.

In a deft economy of words (the story is only twelve pages long), readers get an agonizing portrait of a childhood in which Emily's mother is forced to work menial jobs for their survival, leave her in poor care, send her away to relatives. The mother contemplates, "I will become engulfed in all I did or did not do, with what should have been and what cannot be helped"— yet Olsen argues it is a mistake for readers to interpret the mother's anguish as guilt. After all, guilt is predicated on responsibility, which implies circumstances within the mother's control, an opportunity to choose differently. Lamenting the "lacerations of group life in nurseries," the narrator tells us that "it would have made no difference if I had known. It was the only place there was. It was the only way we could be together." Responding to the label of maternal guilt some readers are so quick to assign to the narrator, Olsen has said, "One is guilty only for what one oneself is responsible for." She argues against "the use of the word 'guilt' to define the actual anguish, the justifiable anguish, the legitimate anguish which has never been legitimized . . . having to raise children in a society not concerned with, even hostile to, human flowering" (quoted in Frye's *Tillie Olsen: A Study of the Short Fiction*). "Mother blaming" is what Olsen calls in *Silences* the tendency to see guilt "where it is not guilt at all but the workings of an intolerable situation."

The sense of powerlessness is tangible in the story, highlighted by the narrator's repeated use of the pronoun "they," which lacks a clear referent, suggesting the impersonal dismissal of social workers and others in positions of authority. And lest readers be inclined to read the narrator's daughter as resilient and well-adjusted because she has sublimated her alienation into a talent for comedy, when they actually encounter nineteen-year-old Emily near the end of the story, she blithely reveals her sense of hopelessness. She tells her mother not to wake her for midterm exams the following morning because "in a couple of years when we'll all be atom-dead they won't matter a bit." The story ends with the mother's plea: "Let her be. So all that is in her will not bloom—but in how many does it? There is still enough left to live by. Only help her to know—help make it so there is cause for her to know—that she is more than this dress on the ironing board, helpless before the iron." The mother begs only for Emily's survival, that she be spared from the overwhelming mechanizing forces that threaten to annihilate her. The image simultaneously evokes the dehumanizing conditions of working-class toil and powerfully indicts the confining gender roles of domesticity—ideas that recall Olsen's own early short story "The Iron Throat," and Davis' *Life in the Iron Mills* as well.

"Hey Sailor, What Ship?" is the next story in the collection, and the first of the remaining three that treat individual members of an extended family. Olsen originally intended that the individual pieces concerning the family be part of a larger whole, but the larger work was never realized. Whitey, an aging alcoholic seaman, is the protagonist of "Hey Sailor." The story chronicles his ongoing relationship with Lennie and Helen and their three daughters, Jeannie, Carol, and Allie. Despite Whitey's decline, Helen and Lennie are attached to him and view him as a member of the family, remembering better days when Whitey saved Lennie's life back in the 1934 strike. They remember Whitey's compassion for Helen in helping with housework when she was exhausted, and the fact that he gave them money when they were struggling financially. There are touching moments in the present as well—one scene makes clear the affection the young Allie holds for Whitey, as she passes out in his arms feeling safe after a bad dream. The story offers a powerful parable of unconditional love and a prototype of the modern notion of blended families. It also offers a lesson in tolerance, as Helen takes the teenaged Jeannie to task for her embarrassment over Whitey's cursing and drunken behavior. Helen beseeches her to move beyond judgment to compassion, to see the intention behind the behavior, and to remember that their family is Whitey's only home, his only family. Jeannie's appearance in "Hey Sailor" allows for the evolution of her character in the following stories; she is the character who changes most dramatically over the course of the different narratives.

Olsen has said she based the character of Whitey on many seamen she knew, and that among those the most poignant were the Filipino seamen, because Filipino women were not allowed into the country, so her family was the only family they had. She is also adamant that what is central to Whitey's descent into alcoholism is "how he came to be so—what losses, betrayals, separations were *not* because he was drinking" (quoted from *Tillie Olsen: A Study of the Short Fiction*). Rather than judging Whitey's alcoholism, Olsen invokes compassion in readers, subtly creating the context of everyday humiliations to which Whitey is subject as his brand of heroism and way of life slowly fade.

The next story in the collection, "O Yes," primarily concerns Jeannie's younger sister Carol (the middle child) and Helen. The two attend a black church service for the baptism of Carol's childhood friend Parialee (Parry). The scene in the church is almost hypnotic in its power. Carol is overwhelmed by the intensity of the parishioners' emotions during the call-and-response part of the sermon and nearly faints as the cacophony imprints upon her. Alva, Parry's mother and Helen's friend, attempts to explain the fervor of the congregation's release, calling the church a place where they are free to let go of the burdens they must carry: "And they're home, Carol, church is home. Maybe the only place they can feel how they feel and maybe let it come out. So they can go on. And it's all right."

The story is decidedly about race, but it is also about the circumstances that separate friends of different races as they mature, tracked in a school system that places white students in academic classes and sends black students into vocational training. In a particularly poignant moment, readers are privy to Parry's humiliation when Carol is home sick with the mumps and Parry attempts to bring Carol's assignments home to her when a racist teacher assumes that Parry's mother must work for Carol's family as a maid. Jeannie appears in the story as a world-weary teenager surprised by her own parents' naïveté, unpersuaded when Helen insists on the injustice of tracking junior high students, protesting, "Now wait, Jeannie. Parry's just as bright, just as capable." Through most of the story, Helen is left feeling inadequate in the face of explaining the injustices of the world to her middle daughter, who is unable to articulate her painful incomprehension at the societal forces conspiring to keep her and her childhood friend apart. Yet despite the little hope that exists for the two girls to remain friends as they mature in a world hostile to such friendship, Helen and Alva's alliance as adults holds some hope for eventual friendship and coalition-building against the societal forces that keep races separate.

The story ends when Helen turns on the radio, and Carol, ill with the mumps, runs downstairs in a feverish state, hysterical at the gospel music emanating from the radio. Helen tries to soothe her daughter, as Carol admits she has betrayed her friendship with Parry in the face of the teacher's prejudice. Crying, Carol implores her mother, "Why is it like it is and why do I have to care?" Helen's unspoken response is a microcosm of Olsen's world view, "*caring asks doing.*" Helen goes on to wonder, "*It is a long baptism into the seas of humankind, my daughter. Better immersion than to live untouched.... Yet how will you sustain?*"

While "I Stand Here Ironing" is probably Olsen's most anthologized piece of fiction, critics tend to read her novella "Tell Me a Riddle" as her masterpiece, her most profound and fully realized literary work. In "Tell Me a Riddle" Olsen has woven an imagistic, masterfully crafted fable of transformation. On the surface it may appear a depressing story of a bitter old woman dying a miserable death; however, the metamorphoses are manifold. Two of the most resonant are the main character's movement from life into death and from silence into voice. In "Tell Me a Riddle" the granddaughter Jeannie serves as a midwife in the grandmother's transition into death, and in this way she also becomes an agent of the grandmother's struggle to move from embittered silence into voice as Jeannie helps Eva heal into death. It is only the granddaughter Jeannie (curiously not one of Eva's many children) who is able to facilitate this passage. The space of a generation is significant, for it is only the adult grandchild, who lives some distance away from the grandmother, who can serve this function so selflessly by being fully present with Eva. Eva's husband and children are too close, too invested in their own reactions to the years of Eva's bitterness and emotional withholding, too acute in their personal feelings of deprivation to function out of anything other than their own all-encompassing need—of who they need Eva to be.

Eva's feelings about mothering are complex. She notices a familiar paradox when visiting her daughter Vivi, a new mother: the attraction of motherhood ("the maze of the long lovely drunkenness") as well as the impending loss of control. To Olsen, the mother's own subjectivity is at risk of being devoured, her own needs silenced, and Eva's withdrawal is self-protective. Here the "torrent" of the maternal instinct is so strong Eva describes it as a powerful, living entity; the violent struggle against this leviathan that drowns or immolates all in its path is almost Mephistophelean in proportion, for in the act of becoming a mother Eva in many ways has lost her self. And this powerful creature of mother instinct does not subside into the underworld from which it emerged; it fights to live long after it is needed.

The question of silence is one that permeates much of Olsen's work. Eva is described as a "mute old woman"; the novella is a chronicle of Eva's metaphorical journey to voice after her existential acknowledgement of the profound, sad irony of the human condition precipitates her realization that she is dying. Olsen employs the technique of stream of consciousness to invoke the grandmother's unmitigated immediacy of insight. Much like Carol's reaction to the music in "O Yes," Eva experiences a singing choir as oppressive, spurring a painful epiphany in which the old woman struggles with the juxtaposition between the hope she hears in the voices and the way that hope is set in relief against life's suffering and disappointment:

> Yet they sang like like Wondrous! Humankind one has to believe So strong for what? To rot not grow? . . . Singing. Unused the life in them . . . Everywhere unused the life And who has meaning? Century after century still all in us not to grow? . . . And when will it end. Oh, *the end* . . . Man . . . will destroy ourselves?

To Eva, the naive, touching optimism of the singers' voices rings hollow against the species' impulse to self-destruct: to "destroy ourselves." For Eva, the tragedy is one of thwarted potential, and the scene becomes an impetus for the bitter, silent, constricted woman she has become to move inward, back in time to recover her lost idealist self, which has been forced underground by the demands of poverty and motherhood.

Olsen uses a water motif throughout the story's description of Eva's experience of mothering; in particular, she connects drowning imagery to the complex nature of Eva's feelings about motherhood. An image of "the painful damming back of what still surged," the "thin pulsing," recalls the discomfort of the nursing mother as her milk comes in. Water becomes a powerful metaphor for strong instinctual drives as well as a primal liberating force for healing, for, like air, it is what we are all most dependent upon for our survival. Water is also a powerful elemental force: streams will eventually carve through stone; a tidal wave or hurricane will swallow all in its path. Olsen employs words such as "torrent," "riverbed," "desert," and "springs"—all words we associate with water or drought—when speaking of Eva as a mother, as a way of emphasizing Eva's powerlessness against the pull.

When Vivi's newborn baby is thrust in her lap, Eva launches into a reverie in which she remembers the "long drunkenness; the drowning into needing and being needed." The connection with inebriation is an apt one, for what may be lovely and intoxicating when first experienced often has longer-lasting negative effects. A loss of control, mounting addiction, or a yearning to recover the drunken state are all inherent in the pleasure of that drunken state and are analogous to Eva's experience of mothering. Eva's lament over motherhood is complex, however, for the image of drowning indicates the loss of identity or self that is the residual effect of such intense, primal connection with another, which has precipitated her closed-down affect and movement toward solitude.

The dilemma for the mother is that there is no one to feed once the children are grown, a withering of purpose that Olsen represents in metaphors that shift to the barrenness of the desert in contrast to the sense of fecundity that infused the beginning of the passage. The "springs . . . the older power that beat for life" is Eva's muffled, buried voice forced underground. Eva finds herself unwilling to hold her new grandbaby; instead she must reclaim a small part of her own identity from the primal tidal wave that is all-consuming. Olsen repeats allusions to being devoured, eaten alive, suggesting a kind of cannibalism: "warm flesh like this that had claims and nuzzled away all else and with lovely mouths devoured; hot-living like an animal—intensely and now; the turning maze; the long drunkenness; the drowning into needing and being needed . . . the shudder seized her again, and the sweat." One may wonder if this is the scene of a birth or a death. The scene is primal, and may literally refer to the act of breast-feeding, but the implication is that something greater is being consumed than merely mother's milk. It is as though Eva's lifeblood (and voice, and selfhood) is draining from her in a kind of vampirism. The mouths are "lovely," and the mothering instinct is pleasurable, a "long drunkenness," yet Eva, facing the end of her life, now yearns only to withdraw: "It was not that she had not loved her babies, her children . . . but [she] could no longer hold nor help. . . . Somewhere an older power that beat for life . . . If they would but leave her in the air now stilled of clamor, in the reconciled solitude, to journey on."

This theme of motherhood is a central one for Olsen, who has consciously campaigned to bring the long-silenced experience of motherhood into the literary canon. As Constance Coiner notes, Olsen has explored the paradox of motherhood as both the "last explored and tormentingly complex *core* of women's oppression," while arguing that it can also potentially be a source of "transport." The specter of the mother's importance leaves its seal even in a narrative where she is tellingly absent, as in the short story "Requa."

"Requa" is Olsen's only uncollected short story, and thus it is also her least read and one that has had scant critical attention afforded it. The occasion for the story is the death of a mother, and the attempt of Stevie, the mother's teenage son, to move through grief, to come to terms with the loss of his mother as he forges a new relationship with his ill-equipped guardian, his bachelor uncle, Wes. Olsen envisioned "Requa" as the beginning of a greater whole, as a novella or novel, hence it was designated "Requa I" (as in part 1) in the *Best American Short Stories of 1971.*

The title literally refers to the name of the logging town in the Klamath Valley of northern California where Wes brings Stevie after the boy's mother's death. The town is named after the Native American "Rekwoi," but the title is particularly evocative in the way it simultaneously recalls the words "reckoning" and "requiem," which both resonate with the story given that Stevie is undergoing a reckoning during his initial cocooning into the paralysis of grief. The story also serves as a requiem for the lost mother, as the boy moves into the imperfect nurturing of his uncle and a greater immigrant community in her absence.

As the story opens, Wes and Stevie are in the cab of Wes's pickup truck as Wes drives them to Requa after the mother's funeral. Stevie is so exhausted from the physical stress of standing vigil at the dying woman's bedside as her only caretaker that he can barely hold up his head. But as the days unfold, and Stevie remains in an almost catatonic state, barely speaking, it becomes clear that his exhaustion is not merely physical. It is only through the embrace of the extended immigrant community, and that community's patience in letting Stevie experience his grief, that readers encounter the seeds of Stevie's resurrection.

The story is set during the Great Depression, and Wes (and later Stevie) works in a junkyard where nomadic families sell off their last belongings for a few gallons of gas to get farther down the road. Olsen's writing is particularly poetic in the descriptions of the litany of "junk" that moves though the place, and the heroic ability Wes has to transform it into something usable, an image mirrored in Stevie's own eventual resurrection. Even Olsen herself admits to the lyrical qualities of the junk passages in Frye's *Tillie Olsen: A Study of the Short Fiction,* "It is immodest to say, but the sections of 'Requa' describing these tasks, these tools, have the precision of, the rhythm, the sound, of true poetry. If I read it aloud to you, you'd hear— but words in the service of everyday work, or tools, are not accorded such recognition." But in the world of Olsen's prose they are:

Disorder twining with order. The discarded, the broken, the torn from the whole: weathereaten weatherbeaten: mouldering or waiting for use-need. *Broken existences that yet continue.*

> Hasps switches screws plugs tubings drills
> Valves pistons shears planes punchers sheaves
> Clamps sprockets coils bits braces dies
>
> How many shapes and sizes; how various, how cunning in application. Human mastery, human skill. Hard, defined, enduring, they pass through his hands.

The delight in the sounds of the words, detached from any sense of their meanings, is reminiscent of language poetry, and the cadences of the text are percussive, as Olsen takes good advantage of the words' onomatopoeic possibilities and rhythms, capturing the beauty normally ignored in consideration of such utilitarian objects. Olsen approaches the language with an almost childlike sense of wonder and play—and she knows the terminology of which she speaks, because at one point in her life she worked in the office of a junkyard. (Notably, *Yonnondio* also has a junkyard scene, in which the Holbrook children scavenge amid the junk heap.) While despairing of the necessity born of desperation, Olsen celebrates the human ingenuity that enables a man like Wes, a man lacking formal education, to work with his hands: "Requa" demonstrates that both invention and innovation can be found in a junk heap, and the story is a moving tribute to the incredible human capacity for resilience. The story is certainly in keeping with Olsen's central theme, that of the tragedy of those circumstances (sex, race, class) that thwart human potential, and the amazing courage, hope, and beauty of those men and women who struggle against those circumstances in an effort to transform them, making meaning of their lives against damning odds.

YONNONDIO

Although Olsen wrote much of the novel *Yonnondio* in the 1930s, she had abandoned the manuscript and later considered it lost, until it resurfaced among her papers in 1972. As Olsen says in her preface, by the time it was published in 1974, "the book ceased to be solely the work of the long ago, young writer and, in arduous partnership, became this older one's as well. But it is all the old manuscripts—no rewriting, no new writing," except, of course, the new subtitle, *From the Thirties,* which summons the spirit of the time in which the nineteen-year-old Olsen began to compose it. While certainly thematically linked to the political propaganda of Olsen's early period, *Yonnondio* is a work of fiction, and as such, contains the seeds of the artistry that makes such an impact in *Tell Me a Riddle* and "Requa." The novel is unfinished, but it hardly reads as such to a contemporary reader. What is there is all of a piece, and does not come across as a fragment of a larger work.

The novel follows the lives of the Holbrook family—Anna and Jim and their children Mazie, Will, Ben, Jimmie, and baby Bess—as they struggle to eke out a living in the American heartland. When the novel begins, Jim is working in the coal mines of Wyoming, "da bowels of earth." Dreaming of a bucolic life living off the land, the family moves on to an ill-fated attempt at tenant farming in South Dakota, where the family nearly starves and freezes to death during the harsh winter. The Holbrooks finally settle in the squalor of the slaughterhouse ghettos in an unnamed midwestern city. The novel is decidedly proletarian in intent, and the young Olsen does a masterful job of depicting the cycle of domestic and sexual violence exacerbated by the desperation and hopelessness of poverty. In his despair, Jim beats Anna. Out of frustration and exhaustion, Anna beats the children. Yet amid the violence, Olsen evokes a compassion for her characters. While Jim's rape of Anna while she is in the early stages of another exhausted pregnancy is brutal, causing her to miscarry and fall dangerously ill, he is not simply demonized as a character. There are times when Jim shows true tenderness, holding Mazie in his lap and calling her "Bigeyes." Olsen is sensitive to his dilemma:

He lifted her and carried her toward home, her father.... "Were you scared? Momma's sick, awful sick . . . and the doctor says she needs everything she cant get, tells me everything she needs, but not how to get it...."

"And Bess's pretty sick, ... And medicine, he says. Everything, but not how to get it...."

No, he could speak no more.... Covering up Anna and the baby. No, he could speak no more. And as he sat there in the kitchen with Mazie against his heart, and dawn beat up like a drum, the things in his mind so vast and formless, so terrible and bitter cannot be spoken, will never be spoken—till the day that hands will find a way to speak this; hands.

Although the family's economic situation is certainly bleak, the characters exhibit moments of transcendence and lyricism, demonstrated particularly in Anna's strength and Mazie's prescience, and to a lesser extent in the talent of young Ben, who is musical—breaking into spontaneous descant before he can speak. Anna is bound and determined her children are going to get an "edjication," believing it to be their only means of escape. In one lovely scene, Anna takes the children to an empty lot outside of town to pick greens and falls into a kind of revelry before remembering the mantle of her responsibilities and the desperation of the family's circumstances.

The novel ends hopefully with the powerful metaphor of baby Bess asserting herself and the human capacity to endure, as she bangs on kitchen pots:

She releases, grabs, releases, grabs. I can do. Bang! I can do. I! A Neanderthal look of concentration is on her face. That noise! In triumphant, astounded joy she clashes the lid down. Bang, slam, whack . . . Centuries of human drive work in her; human ecstasy of achievement, satisfaction deep and fundamental as sex. *I achieve, I use my powers; I! I!*

Furthermore, the last lines of the novel symbolize a more tempered optimism, as Anna says to Jim, "The air's changin, Jim. I see for it [the heat wave] to end tomorrow, at least get tolerable."

Something is known of how Olsen originally intended to end the story, which she outlined according to Rosenfelt's "From the Thirties: Tillie Olsen and the Radical Tradition." Jim was to finally get so discouraged he would eventually abandon the family. Anna would die trying to end a pregnancy. Mazie and Will would go out west and become labor organizers; the future would lie in the hands of Mazie and Ben, the nascent artists in the family.

Like "Requa," the title of *Yonnondio* is an indigenous word. The novel is bookended by an epigraph and a closing note from the author that both borrow words from the poem "Yonnondio" by Walt Whitman (a great favorite of Olsen's). The novel opens:

Lament for the aborigines . . . the word itself a dirge . . .

No picture, poem, statement, passing them to the future:
Yonnondio! Yonnondio!—unlimn'd they disappear;
To-day gives place, and fades—the cities, farms, factories fade;
A muffled, sonorous sound, a wailing word is borne through the air for a moment,
Then blank and gone and still, and utterly lost.

The book's powerful epigraph is especially apropos to Olsen's aim, which was to capture the lives of the dispossessed, those whose lives were not deemed the stuff of which great literature is made. Moreover, it is exceptionally poignant given that the lives of the characters in Olsen's *Yonnondio* were lost for forty years, and very nearly remained so.

SILENCES

Silences was a groundbreaking book and has become a seminal text of the women's movement, much like Virginia Woolf's *A Room of One's Own*, from which it draws inspiration and with which it often reads as though it is in dialogue. The book's structure is pastiche, drawing heavily on quotations from other writers, as well as Olsen's own autobiography, and it is a powerful indictment of the circumstances that disallow creative flowering. The book includes a discussion of Olsen's recovery work on Rebecca Harding Davis, even going so far as to excerpt *Life in the Iron Mills* at the end, making Davis' work available to a new audience.

Olsen is not concerned with the fallow periods of creative ebb and flow, which she terms "natural silences." Rather, the book focuses on those circumstances of race, gender, and class, as well as censorship, compulsory motherhood, illiteracy, and lack of education, that serve to thwart human potential. Olsen considers the literary silences of writers such as Jean Toomer and Ralph Ellison, who produced one masterpiece and then never published again during their lifetimes; of writers like Franz Kafka and Herman Melville, who were silenced though the drudgery of bureaucratic work; as well as the silences of countless of those "Shakespeare's sisters" (to use Woolf's term), who were never taught to read at all.

The book opens with the following dedication:

> For our silenced people, century after century their beings consumed in the hard, everyday essential work of maintaining human life. Their art, which still they made—as their other contributions—anonymous, refused respect, recognition; lost.
>
> For those of us (few yet in number, for the way is punishing), their kin and descendants, who begin to emerge into more flowered and rewarded use of our selves in ways denied to them;—and by our achievement bearing witness to what was (and still is) being lost, silenced.

The book is a powerful testament to bearing witness to such silences, such thwarted potentials, for as Olsen writes: "we who write are survivors."

Like Virginia Woolf's *A Room of One's Own* before it, *Silences* is concerned with the question of what conditions creation demands for full flowering. Olsen builds on the notion of the Angel in the House delineated in Virginia Woolf's essay "Professions for Women," by complicating the gender-role issues of the original incarnation of the Angel with the additional burden of class. Olsen expands on Woolf's pernicious phantom, introducing the idea of what Olsen calls "essential angels," those women on whom the material existence of the family depends. For unlike Woolf, and others of the privileged classes who could afford servants, the "essential angel must assume the physical responsibilities for daily living, for the maintenance of life." The mother in "I Stand Here Ironing" is an essential angel, as was Eva in "Tell Me a Riddle," and Anna in *Yonnondio*. The lot of such characters is not chosen, nor is it merely socialized. Lives hang in the balance, dependent upon their toil. As Olsen makes clear, "it is no accident that the first work I considered publishable began: 'I stand here ironing, and what you asked me moves tormented back and forth with the iron.'" Such words are fitting testament to a life spent as an essential angel.

By far Olsen's most controversial book, and perhaps ultimately her most influential, *Silences* created a sensation when it was published in 1978. Some critics bemoaned its writing, believing Olsen's time and energy would have been better served creating more beautiful, haunting short stories like those that first brought her acclaim in *Tell Me a Riddle*. Yet others heralded its arrival on the literary scene, gathering in one place those speeches and essays that had created such a stir in earlier incarnations, making accessible to a much larger audience Olsen's ideas about the silences in literature and the conditions that obstruct and preclude literary creation.

One cannot begin to consider the revolution in canon formation that occurred during the 1970s and 1980s without acknowledging the monumental influence of *Silences*. Olsen's influence is palpable when considering that the now-classic works of Charlotte Perkins Gilman or Zora Neale Hurston, featured almost ubiquitously today on high school and college syllabi, were out of print and forgotten before Olsen and others took up the cause of the literary recovery of important works by women writers. Olsen can rightly be considered the mother of the literary recovery movement, beginning with her reading lists brought out by the *Women's Studies Newsletter* and her advocacy with Florence Howe and the Feminist Press on behalf of getting these works back into print, and culminating in the powerful argument she puts forward in *Silences*.

Those who champion *Silences* emphasize the importance of its content, while those who find fault with it object to its form. These poles were established early on in two reviews by prominent women writers. Margaret Atwood calls the form "a scrapbook, a patchwork quilt: bits and pieces joined to form a powerful whole. And, despite the condensed and fragmentary quality of this book, the whole is powerful. Even the stylistic breathlessness—the elliptical prose . . . is reminiscent of a biblical messenger, sole survivor of a relentless and obliterating catastrophe." Joyce Carol Oates is less forgiving, allowing that "*Silences* is necessarily uneven, and it is certainly not an academic or scholarly study." Oates finds fault with what she interprets as the book's "numerous inconsistencies and questionable statements offered as facts," noting how "unexamined, unverified, and indeed unverifiable statements are offered as facts again and again." Oates attributes these textual offenses to shoddy editing, or "lack thereof," calling it editorial "indifference." So while Oates laments such problematic textual elements, Atwood argues that "what Tillie Olsen has to say . . . is of primary importance to those who want to understand how art is generated or subverted and to those trying to create it themselves."

Critics are not wrong to note the urgency and desperation that imbue *Silences*. At least one writer, Rose Kamel, has called *Silences* an "apologia, a lamentation for her own sparse literary output." (Olsen's biographer Mickey Pearlman has exposed Kamel's own misreadings and sloppy scholarship in Kamel's essay on *Yonnondio*.) Perhaps Valerie Trueblood sums it up best, noting the paradox of how, on the one hand, *Silences* at times "reads like a lawsuit" in that "it amasses, marshals evidence," while, on the other hand, "in its distressed rhythm and integrity of emotion it is more a poem than an argument." She points out, furthermore, that regardless of whether a reader approves or disapproves of the book's form, the documentation Olsen has amassed is itself a "gold mine."

OLSEN'S LEGACY

Olsen may be best remembered for her role as a literary foremother, a generous mentor who gave of her energies perhaps at the expense of her own literary output. Mickey Pearlman writes that, magnificent short stories notwithstanding, "Olsen is known and admired much more for what she represents than because of what she's written"—damning praise indeed. On the one hand, it is a tribute that acknowledges the way Tillie Olsen has spent so much of her life giving tirelessly of her self for the greater good, and it is a testament to how she has meaningfully intervened in the politics of canon formation. As Pearlman notes, "without doubt, a significant number of novels, short stories, essays and anthologies—as well as the criticism and canon reforms spurred on by sweeping changes in academia and the culture at large—exist partly because of the vision, talent, and determination Olsen has released and encouraged in her contemporaries." But such praise belies the stunning innovations Olsen has introduced into the literary genre of the short story. Tillie Olsen has changed the literary landscape not only through her untiring advocacy on behalf of the important writers she has rescued from literary obscurity, but through her own significant literary achievement as well, having produced some of the most exquisitely crafted, hauntingly evocative stories in the English language.

Selected Bibliography

WORKS OF TILLIE OLSEN

POETRY
"I Want You Women Up North To Know." *Partisan* 1:4 (March 1934).

"There Is a Lesson." *Partisan* 1:4 (April 1934).

SHORT STORIES
"The Iron Throat." *Partisan Review* 1, no. 2:3–9 (April–May 1934). ("The Iron Throat" later became the first chapter of *Yonnondio*.)

"Help Her to Believe." *Pacific Spectator* 10:55–63 (1956). (Reprinted as "I Stand Here Ironing" and collected in *Tell Me a Riddle*.)

"Baptism." *Prairie Schooner* 31:70–80 (1957). (Reprinted as "O Yes" and collected in *Tell Me a Riddle*.)

"Hey Sailor, What Ship?" *New Campus Writing 2*. Edited by Nolan Miller. New York: Putnam, 1957. Pp. 199–213. (Collected in *Tell Me a Riddle*.)

"Tell Me a Riddle." *New World Writing 16*. Edited by Stewart Richardson and Corlies M. Smith. Philadelphia: Lippincott, 1960. Pp. 11–67. (Collected as the title story in *Tell Me a Riddle*.)

"Requa." *Iowa Review* 1, no. 3:54–74 (1970). (Reprinted as "Requa I" in *Best American Short Stories*, edited by Martha Foley and David Burnett [Boston: Houghton Mifflin, 1971], an issue dedicated to Olsen.)

SHORT STORY COLLECTIONS AND NOVELS
Tell Me a Riddle. Philadelphia: Lippincott, 1961. (Quotes taken from Delta 1971 paperback edition.)

Yonnondio: From the Thirties. New York: Delacorte Press/Seymour Lawrence, 1974. (Quotes taken from Delta 1975 paperback edition.)

NONFICTION
"The Thousand Dollar Vagrant." *New Republic*, August 29, 1934, pp. 67–69. (Reprinted in *Years of Protest: A Collection of American Writings of the 1930s*, edited by Jack Salzman [New York: Pegasus, 1967].)

"The Strike." *Partisan Review* 1:3–9 (September/October 1934). (Reprinted in *Years of Protest: A Collection of American Writings of the 1930s*, edited by Jack Salzman [New York: Pegasus, 1967] and in *Writing Red: An Anthology of American Women Writers, 1930–1940*, edited by Charlotte Nekola and Paula Rabinowitz [New York: Feminist Press, 1987].)

"Silences: When Writers Don't Write." *Harpers*, October 1965, pp. 153–161. (Reprinted in *Silences*.)

"A Biographical Interpretation." In *Life in the Iron Mills; or, The Korl Woman*, by Rebecca Harding Davis. New York: Feminist Press, 1972. (Reprinted in revised form in *Silences*.)

"Women Who Are Writers in Our Century: One out of Twelve." *College English* 34:6–17 (1972). (From a talk presented at the Modern Language Association, December 28, 1971, and reprinted in *Silences*.)

Silences. New York: Delacorte Press/Seymour Lawrence, 1978. (Quotes taken from the Delta/Seymour Lawrence paperback edition.)

"Foreword." In *Black Women Writers at Work*. Edited by Claudia Tate. New York: Continuum, 1983.

"Dream Vision." In *Mother to Daughter, Daughter to Mother: Mothers on Mothering: A Daybook and Reader*. Edited by Tillie Olsen. Old Westbury, N.Y.: Feminist Press, 1984. (Reprinted in *Ms.*, December 1984.)

Mothers and Daughters: That Special Quality: An Exploration in Photographs. Essays by Tillie Olsen with Julie Olsen Edwards and Estelle Jussim. Edited by Dianne Lyon and Nan Richardson. New York: Aperture, 1987.

MANUSCRIPT COLLECTIONS
Part of the manuscript of *Yonnondio* is housed in the Berg Collection of English and American Literature at the New York Public Library.

BIBLIOGRAPHIES

Wilds Craft, Brigette. "Tillie Olsen: A Bibiography of Review and Criticism, 1934–1991." *Bulletin of Bibliography* 50, no. 3:189–206 (September 1993).

CRITICAL AND BIOGRAPHICAL STUDIES

Atwood, Margaret. "Obstacle Course." *New York Times Book Review,* July 30, 1978, pp. 1, 17. (Reprinted in Nelson and Huse, eds., *The Critical Response to Tillie Olsen,* pp. 250–251.)

Banks, Joanne Trautmann. "Death Labors." *Literature and Medicine* 9:162–171 (1990). (Reprinted in Nelson and Huse, eds., *The Critical Response to Tillie Olsen,* pp. 158–168).

Burkom, Selma, and Margaret Williams. "De-Riddling Tillie Olsen's Writings." *San Jose Studies* 2, no. 1:65–83 (February 1976). (Reprinted in Nelson and Huse, eds., *The Critical Response to Tillie Olsen,* pp. 33–53.)

Cantwell, Robert. "The Literary Life in California." *New Republic,* August 22, 1934, p. 49. (Reprinted in Nelson and Huse, eds., *The Critical Response to Tillie Olsen,* pp. 21–22.)

Coiner, Constance. "'No One's Private Ground': A Bakhtinian Reading of Tillie Olsen's *Tell Me A Riddle.*" *Feminist Studies* 18, no. 2:257–281 (summer 1992). (Reprinted with revisions in Nelson and Huse, eds., *The Critical Response to Tillie Olsen,* pp. 169–195.)

Duncan, Erika. "The Hungry Jewish Mother." In *The Lost Tradition: Mothers and Daughter in Literature.* Edited by Cathy N. Davidson and E. M. Broner. New York: Frederick Ungar, 1980. Pp. 231–241.

Elman, Richard M. "The Many Forms Which Loss Can Take." *Commonweal* 8:295–296 (December 1961). (Reprinted in Nelson and Huse, eds., *The Critical Response to Tillie Olsen,* pp. 113–114.)

Faulkner, Mara. *Protest and Possibility in the Writing of Tillie Olsen.* Charlottesville: University Press of Virginia, 1993.

Fisher, Elizabeth. "The Passion of Tillie Olsen." *The Nation,* April 10, 1972, pp. 472, 474. (Reprinted in Nelson and Huse, eds., *The Critical Response to Tillie Olsen,* pp. 115–117.)

Frye, Joanne S. "'I Stand Here Ironing': Motherhood as Experience and Metaphor." *Studies in Short Fiction* 18, no. 3:287–292 (summer 1981). (Reprinted in Nelson and Huse, eds., *The Critical Response to Tillie Olsen,* pp. 128–133.)

———. *Tillie Olsen: A Study of the Short Fiction.* New York: Twayne, 1995.

Gelfant, Blanche H. "After Long Silence: Tillie Olsen's 'Requa.'" *Studies in American Fiction* 12, no. 1:61–69 (spring 1984). (Reprinted in Nelson and Huse, eds., *The Critical Response to Tillie Olsen,* pp. 206–215.)

Hedges, Elaine, and Shelley Fisher Fishkin. *Listening to Silences: New Essays in Feminist Criticism.* New York: Oxford University Press, 1994.

Howe, Irving. "Stories: New, Old, and Sometimes Good." *New Republic,* November 13, 1961, p. 22. (Reprinted in Nelson and Huse, eds., *The Critical Response to Tillie Olsen,* pp. 111–112.)

Jacobs, Naomi M. "Olsen's 'O Yes': Alva's Vision as Childbirth Account." *Notes on Contemporary Literature* 16, no. 1:7–8 (January 1986). (Reprinted in Nelson and Huse, eds., *The Critical Response to Tillie Olsen,* pp. 134–135.)

Kamel, Rose. "Literary Foremothers and Writers' Silences: Tillie Olsen's Autobiographical Fiction." In *Melus* 12, no. 3:55–71 (fall 1985).

Lyons, Bonnie. "Tillie Olsen: The Writer as a Jewish Woman." *Studies in American Jewish Literature* 5:89–102 (1986). (Reprinted in Nelson and Huse, eds., *The Critical Response to Tillie Olsen,* pp. 144–157.)

Meese, Elizabeth. "Deconstructing the Sexual Politic: Virginia Woolf and Tillie Olsen." In *Crossing the Double Cross: The Practice of Feminist Criticism.* Edited by Elizabeth Meese. Chapel Hill: University of North Carolina Press, 1986. Pp. 89–113.

Nelson, Kay Hoyle, and Nancy Huse. *The Critical Response to Tillie Olsen.* Westport, Conn.: Greenwood Press, 1994.

Oates, Joyce Carol. "*Silences* by Tillie Olsen." *New Republic,* July 29, 1978, pp. 32–34. (Reprinted in Nelson and Huse, eds., *The Critical Response to Tillie Olsen,* pp. 245–249.)

O'Connor, William Van. "The Short Stories of Tillie Olsen." *Studies in Short Fiction* 1, no. 1:12–25 (fall 1963).

Orr, Elaine Neil. *Tillie Olsen and a Feminist Spiritual Vision.* Jackson: University Press of Mississippi, 1987.

Park-Fuller, Linda M. "Voices: Bakhtin's Heteroglossia and Polyphany, and the Performance of Narrative Literature." *Literature in Performance* 7, no. 1:1–12 (November 1986). (Reprinted in Nelson and Huse, eds., *The Critical Response to Tillie Olsen,* pp. 90–103.)

Pearlman, Mickey, and Abby H. P. Werlock. *Tillie Olsen.* Boston: Twayne, 1991.

Pratt, Linda Ray. "The Circumstances of Silence: Literary Representation and Tillie Olsen's Omaha Past." In *The Critical Response to Tillie Olsen.* Edited by Kay Hoyle Nelson and Nancy Huse. Westport, Conn.: Greenwood Press, 1994. Pp. 229–243.

Roberts, Nora Ruth. *Three Radical Women Writers: Class and Gender in Meridel Le Sueur, Tillie Olsen, and Josephine Herbst.* New York: Garland, 1996.

Rosenfelt, Deborah. "From the Thirties: Tillie Olsen and the Radical Tradition." *Feminist Studies* 7, no. 3:371–406 (fall 1981). (Reprinted in Nelson and Huse, eds., *The Critical Response to Tillie Olsen,* pp. 54–89.)

Staub, Michael E. "Labor Activism and the Post-War Politics of Motherhood: Tillie Olsen in the *People's World.*" In *The Critical Response to Tillie Olsen.* Edited by Kay Hoyle Nelson and Nancy Huse. Westport, Conn.: Greenwood Press, 1994. Pp. 104–109.

Trueblood, Valerie. "Books: Tillie Olsen, *Silences.*" *American Poetry Review,* May–June 1979, pp. 18–19. (Reprinted in Nelson and Huse, eds., *The Critical Response to Tillie Olsen,* pp. 253–254.)

Yalom, Marilyn. "Tillie Olsen." In her *Women Writers of the West Coast: Speaking of Their Lives and Careers.* Santa Barbara, Calif.: Capra Press, 1983. Pp. 57–68.

INTERVIEWS

"Breaking Silence." With Kenneth Turan. *New West,* August 28, 1978, pp. 56–59.

Reading: Selected Passages from the Novel Yonnondio: From the Thirties, *"I Stand Here Ironing," "Tell Me A Riddle"; and Interview with Tillie Olsen.* Audiotape. Clinton, N.Y.: Hamilton College, 1979.

"Tillie Olsen: From a Public Dialogue between Olsen and Marilyn Yalom." Stanford Center for Research on Women, November 5, 1980. (See also Yalom's entry under criticism.)

Tillie Olsen: A Profile. With Susan Stamberg. *All Things Considered.* Audiotape. National Public Radio. AT800303.01/01-C. 1980. 29 minutes.

"'Surviving Is Not Enough': A Conversation with Tillie Olsen." With Kay Mills. *Los Angeles Times,* August 26, 1981, p. 3.

Tillie Olsen Interview with Kay Bonetti. Audiotape. American Audio Prose Library. AAPL 1132. 1981. 51 minutes.

"An Interview with Tillie Olsen." With Linda Park-Fuller. *Literature in Performance* 4, no. 1:75–77 (November 1983).

"A Riddle of History for the Future." With Naomi Rubin. *Sojourner,* July 1983, pp. 4, 18.

"Tillie Olsen." With Lisa See. Interview on *Mother to Daughter, Daughter to Mother. Publishers Weekly,* November 23, 1984, pp. 76, 79.

FILMS AND PLAYS BASED ON THE WORKS OF TILLIE OLSEN

Tell Me A Riddle. Screenplay by Joyce Eliason. Produced by Susan O'Connell, Rachel Lyon, and Mindy Affrime. Directed by Lee Grant. Berkeley, Calif.: Godmother Productions, 1980.

Throughout the 1970s and 1980s, there were attempts to dramatize Olsen's stories on stage with varying degrees of success. For a good breakdown of the varying productions, see Kay Hoyle Nelson's introduction to *The Critical Response to Tillie Olsen.*

—JENNIFER M. HOOFARD

Luis Omar Salinas

1937–

Luis Omar Salinas has been a leading Chicano poet as well as an important voice in contemporary American poetry since the publication of his first book, *Crazy Gypsy,* in 1970. Considered a classic of Chicano literature, *Crazy Gypsy* reflects the struggle for political empowerment and ethnic identity of Mexican Americans in the mid-twentieth century. In the late 1960s and early 1970s Salinas was a prominent member of the literary community at California State College at Fresno (now California State University at Fresno, or familiarly Fresno State). The poems in *Crazy Gypsy* are noted for their immediacy, their raw emotional sensibility, and their unusual imagery. They showed Salinas to be a poet willing to engage alienation, despair, anger, and psychological turmoil, both his own and that of others similarly disfranchised.

Salinas' second full-length book of poetry, *Afternoon of the Unreal,* was published in 1980. In the ten years after writing *Crazy Gypsy,* Salinas had developed and refined his craft. In *Afternoon of the Unreal* he combined a deeper exploration of imagery and the surreal with a targeting of specific emotional states, revealing to the reader his mature voice. A sense of melancholy, a romantic longing and wildness balanced by wit and irony, would be evident in Salinas' subsequent books—*Prelude to Darkness* (1981), *Darkness under the Trees / Walking behind the Spanish* (1982), and *The Sadness of Days: Selected and New Poems* (1987).

By the time *Sometimes Mysteriously* was published in 1997, Salinas had entered his sixth decade, and his poems and his vision had developed and changed. In these late poems a reader can detect an element of hope, of wistful resignation. Despite Salinas' acknowledgment of hardships, his disposition in these poems is one of acceptance and praise as opposed to anger and complaint. A chapbook published in 2002, *Greatest Hits 1969–1996,* part of a series by Pudding House Publications in Ohio that showcases twelve poems from a poet's oeuvre, is remarkable not only for its selection of poems written over twenty-seven years, but also for Salinas' narrative reflections on the poems and their histories, in keeping with the series' format. In this book, Salinas talks about the title poem of *Sometimes Mysteriously,* articulating a new direction in his creative life:

> This poem was a turning point in my life. . . . I was beginning to attain more authority in my life and in my work. Having survived, almost miraculously, so much of my life, having found my poetry, I began more often to take a positive outlook on the days I have left.

LIFE AND CAREER

Salinas was born seventeen miles from the Gulf of Mexico, in Robstown, Texas, on June 27, 1937, to Rosendo and Olivia Treviño Salinas. His father was a merchant and owner of a small grocery in Robstown. During the winter of 1939 he moved the family south to Monterrey, Mexico, and opened a general store. In 1941 after Olivia Salinas died from tuberculosis, four-year-old Luis was adopted by his aunt and uncle Oralia and Alfredo Salinas; his younger sister, Irma, also went to live with relatives. Another aunt, Bessie, began to tutor Salinas in languages, literature, math, and some geography and history. By age five he was living again in Robstown with his aunt and uncle and was admitted to St. Anthony's, an all-Mexican elementary school. Fluent in English and Spanish, he was proficient at reading, and in his first years of school he won prizes for reading aloud to the class. Salinas grew up watching Mexican movies, mainly melodramas dealing with machismo and featuring Mexican songs. His heroes included the singing movie stars of the 1930s and 1940s Pedro Infante and Jorge Negrete, and as a youngster he wanted to be an actor or singer. He had musical training on trumpet and violin and wrote his own songs.

Because of racial discrimination against Mexican Americans in Nueces County, Texas, Salinas' adoptive parents moved the family to Daly City, California, where Salinas' uncle Alfredo found work in a clothing store in San Francisco. After five months, the family moved to Fresno, where Salinas attended Webster Elementary School, Longfellow Junior High, and Roosevelt High School. He was active in several sports, played in the school orchestra at Longfellow, and read all of Jack London's novels. In the summer of 1954 Alfredo moved the family to Bakersfield, following the promise of a better job. Salinas finished high school in Bakersfield and eventually took classes at Bakersfield City College, receiving an Associate of Arts degree in history. Just out of high school, Salinas had joined the U.S. Marine Reserves, and while attending Bakersfield City College he formed a band called the Momboleros, a six-piece combo in which he played trumpet. Salinas was also drawn to drama and once had a minor part in Shakespeare's *Twelfth Night*.

In 1958 Salinas moved to Los Angeles and enrolled at California State College. In Los Angeles, he rejoined his natural father. Salinas alternated several jobs with various attempts at success in college until he suffered a mental breakdown and was hospitalized for eleven months. He discovered the Spanish poet Gustavo Adolfo Bécquer and re-enrolled at Cal State in 1963; he studied with the poet Henri Coulette, who encouraged Salinas' reading of Sylvia Plath, Anne Sexton, W. D. Snodgrass, and Donald Justice, poets whose willingness to engage the personal in poetry had an influence on the direction of his work. Omar, as his friends knew him, published his first poem in the college magazine *Statement*. When Salinas' uncle moved to Sanger, a small town near Fresno, to start a business, Salinas decided to move with him. Coulette recommended that Omar attend Fresno State College and study with the poet Philip Levine, whose work they had read and discussed in class.

Salinas began attending classes at Fresno State in 1966 and enrolled in Levine's Intermediate Poetry Workshop, where his work was well received. He met fellow poets Larry Levis, B. H. Boston, DeWayne Rail, Greg Pape, David St. John, and other poets who achieved renown as members of the Fresno literary community in the 1960s and 1970s. Salinas took other Levine workshops and subsequently participated in workshops taught by Peter Everwine and later Robert Mezey. The late 1960s was a turbulent time on the campus of Fresno State as it was on college campuses throughout the United States. There were protests against the Vietnam War, for equal rights, for social and academic status for groups historically not recognized or enfranchised in the academic community. Those years saw the emergence of courses in black studies, women's studies, and Chicano studies, or La Raza studies as the subject was first called on some campuses. The young and the educated were questioning authority—political and academic—at every turn, and they were asserting their rights as students and citizens, as individuals.

It was in Mezey's class that Salinas began to write his first political poems, including "Guevara . . . Guevara" (about the South American revolutionary Che Guevara), which was included in his first book, as well as poems of social and political protest, poems in support of the Chicano political movement, poems against racial prejudice, and assertive poems of personal awareness. "Crazy Gypsy," which became the title poem of his first book, was a poem of personal and political revolution, and it was the first poem of Salinas' mature work to be published, appearing in the anthology *Speaking for Ourselves: American Ethnic Writing* (1969), edited by Lillian Faderman and Barbara Bradshaw. Salinas spent three years at Fresno State, and toward the end of his time there he befriended the Fresno poets Gary Soto, Ernesto Trejo, and Jon Veinberg, who became important supporters of his literary efforts. After publishing *Crazy Gypsy* in 1970, in 1973 Salinas and Faderman coedited the poetry collection *From the Barrio: A Chicano Anthology.*

In the 1970s Salinas' work was well known in California and among readers of Chicano literature and scholars in Chicano studies throughout the United States. By the end of the 1980s Salinas' poetry had been recognized as an original and significant contribution to contemporary American poetry. In 1980 Salinas was awarded the Earl Lyon Award for poetry writing from Fresno State University, and in 1982 he won the Stanley Kunitz award from *Columbia* magazine at Columbia University for his poem "Letter Too Late to Vallejo." In 1984 he received a prestigious General Electric Foundation Award to support his writing. In 1985 he was invited to read at the Library of Congress with the author Sandra Cisneros.

Since the 1970s Salinas has lived in or near Fresno. He has worked at many part-time jobs—as a field-worker and a shoe salesman, in a packinghouse and in home construction, as a court interpreter, and in the clothing business run by his uncle and godfather. Salinas' father died in 1996; his uncle Alfredo died in 1998. In 2002 Salinas lived with his aunt in Sanger, California, where he read and wrote daily, remaining active at his craft. Selections of Salinas' poetry, along with his prose commentary on his subjects and writing life, have appeared in several notable poetry anthologies, including *What Will Suffice: Contemporary American Poets on the Art of Poetry* (1995); *The Geography of Home: California's Poetry of Place* (1999); and *How Much Earth: The Fresno Poets* (2001).

CRAZY GYPSY

In 1969 a group of Chicanos occupied Baker Hall on the campus of Fresno State College, and a main boulevard by the school was blocked as they demanded equal rights and academic considerations from the administration. Given Salinas' willingness to engage social and political subjects in his poetry, a number of faculty and staff members at Fresno State collaborated to publish his work the following year. *Crazy Gypsy* was published in 1970 by Origines Publications—a press spearheaded by two faculty members from the La Raza studies department, Guillermo Martínez and Eliezar Risco-Lozado, who also wrote the book's introduction. The evening of the publication, Salinas read to a large audience, which was predominantly Chicano, and was given an enthusiastic reception; his career as a poet was born. About four thousand copies of *Crazy Gypsy,* in two editions, sold in eight months, a significant sales record for a book of poetry even by mainstream standards.

Crazy Gypsy collected poems written between 1964 and 1969. It was an unpolished but promising book, which resonated with the times in the anarchy of spirit it embraced—many poems were dark, angry, and unhopeful. Readers responded to the poems' emotional honesty and jarring imagery.

The title poem appears first in the volume, set off from the other five sections of the book as a proem. It announces the tone, style, and voice of the book. In this poem we encounter many of the hallmarks of Salinas' early style as well as recurring themes and subjects. In the first stanza of section 2 we meet the lyrical Salinas, who mourns the death of his mother when he was a child, and we meet the political Salinas, the angry rebel, throwing stones at policemen. Whereas these first lines are forthright, the stanza ends with Salinas introducing an image from the subconscious, which alerts us to the range of his voice and imagination, expanding the emotional center of the poem.

> I am Omar
> > the crazy gypsy
> > > I write songs
> > > > to my dead mother
> > > > > hurl stones
> > > > > > at fat policemen
> > > > > > > and walk on seaweed
> > > > > > > > in my dreams.

Salinas' ability to combine these disparate elements into a sharp poetic movement marks his original style—the lyrical or narrative woven with the political and what many critics have labeled the surreal in his work—the arresting seaweed/dream image at the end. Also in this premier poem the reader first sees Salinas' conceit of using an alter ego as the poem's speaker, a device he will employ in books to come. Here, Salinas gives notice that he is a gypsy, a character who is unpredictable, self-made and self-determined, a desperate character with many undisclosed powers, a clever and to some extent menacing psyche who has his eye on everything around him. In the last section of the poem we first hear the lyric voice, then encounter the terror of the speaker's subconscious vision, and finally confront an image with surreal texture—the social/political fact of racism/hate cast in an image of physical reality.

> I am Omar
> > the Mexican gypsy
> . . . .
> > I speak of Love
> > > as something
> > > > whimsical and aloof
> > > as something
> > > > naked and cruel
> I speak of death
> > as something inhabiting
> > > the sea
> > > > awkward and removed
> I speak of hate
> > as something
> > > nibbling my ear

"Aztec Angel" is a poem similar to "Crazy Gypsy," but it even more strongly emphasizes the speaker's alienation from society. Of all of Salinas' early work, this poem is the most anthologized, and in the early years of the 1970s it alone brought in $1,500 in royalties to Salinas. It combines political and cultural assertiveness along with sociopolitical complaint, and as always, the personal lyric touches are interwoven with Salinas' trademark inventive imagery. The poem is in five sections; here are some representative passages:

> I am an Aztec angel
> > criminal
> > > of a scholarly
> > > > society
> . . . .
> I am the Aztec angel
> > fraternal partner
> > > of an orthodox
> > > > society
> > > > > where pachuco children
> > > > > > hurl stones
> > > > > > > through poetry rooms
> and end up in a cop car
> . . . .
> Drunk
> > lonely
> > > bespectacled
> > the sky
> > > > opens my veins
> > > > > like rain
> > > > clouds go berserk
> > > > > around me
> > > > > > my Mexican ancestors
> > > > > > > chew my fingernails . . .

Many of the poems in *Crazy Gypsy* embrace political subjects: there are appraisals of the war ("Death in Viet Nam"), an elegy for the Latin American revolutionary leader Che Guevara ("Guevara . . . Guevara"), and a rather camp college fight-song or revolution piece ("Stand Up"). The political stance is left of center, and Salinas is keen in his observations and loyal to the Chicano movement of the times, especially in "Death in Viet Nam." In the middle of this poem he takes the theme beyond the predictable details of war and its atrocities to focus on the social and racial ramifications of the war, which in his view was preceded by hundreds of years of injustice:

>   and now choir boys are ringing
> bells
> another sacrifice for America
> a Mexican
> comes home
> his beloved country
> gives homage
> and mothers sleep
> in cardboard houses.

Poems in this collection are also noteworthy for their ability to concisely and poignantly narrate. "Through the Hills of Spain" is an intense lyric elegy, an imagistic narrative about the great Spanish poet Miguel Hernández, which demonstrates Salinas' affinity for the surreal image-making practiced by Hernández and other Spanish poets of the 1920s and 1930s, including Federico García Lorca, Juan Ramón Jiménez, and Antonio Machado y Ruiz, as well as the South American poets Pablo Neruda and César Vallejo. Salinas had first been introduced to these poets while in Levine's workshop at Fresno State, and in an interview published in *Quarterly West,* he commented on this early influence and affinity: "I read and admired them all. . . . They spoke my language. That is Spanish."

"Mexico, Age Four" and "Robstown" are remarkable for the economy of their lyric narration and for the way in which they are resolved through sensory and thematic imagery. A melodic narrative quality is also found in one of the last poems in the book, "Saturday." The poem moves beyond the lyric to conclude with surrealistic imagery and announces the complex voice and emotional strategies of Salinas' most representative poetry.

> It is Saturday . . . day of apples and turnips
> on heavy trucks that pass my aunt's house
> sleeping. My cousin is awake quibbling with
> his painful back, this corner of the earth
> surrenders to the anarchy of crows.
>
> We are off to see the movies and the flesh
> of night is torn into small, little children
> as angels eat breaded clouds and spiders
> tell stories to the rabbits of the neighborhood.

In a 1982 essay, Gary Soto writes candidly about Salinas' early achievement:

> *Crazy Gypsy* is an uneven book of 39 poems, some of which are ungrammatical, scattered in thought, and poorly crafted. . . . The book was so rushed into production that no one person—Levine, Everwine, or Mezey—had the opportunity to pencil in corrections and revised lines. . . . But these problems aside, what we find are many deeply felt, highly imaginative and psychologically true and vulnerable poems . . . remarkable poems written with an apparent ease. They are direct, evocative, and succinct—qualities that are characteristic of mature writing. Moreover, they are remarkable for their integrity and their propensity to deal directly with facts.

Soto was one of the first to write at length about Salinas and to point out the candor with which Salinas explored his own psyche, the honesty and objectivity that characterize these early poems.

AFTERNOON OF THE UNREAL

Between 1970 and 1979 Salinas published two small groups of poems. Five poems appeared in a small anthology, *Entrance: Four Chicano Poets,* in 1975, alongside the work of Soto, Ernesto Trejo, and Leonard Adamé. In 1979 a group of ten poems, *I Go Dreaming Serenades,* was published as a chapbook. All of these poems and thirty others comprised the manuscript of *Afternoon of the Unreal,* which was published in Fresno in 1980.

The craft of *Afternoon of the Unreal* is superior to *Crazy Gypsy;* the extended period between book publications provided for the poems' development, and editing produced a strong and consistent collection. The original imagery in the poetry was familiar to readers of *Crazy Gypsy,* yet with this second volume one could sense a darkening of emotional skies as Salinas attempted to understand the hardships and unjust turns of fate in his life during intensified bouts of manic depression. However, two of the earliest poems in the book are more lyrical and narrative by comparison with the rest of the book; they are elegies for his mother ("Olivia") and for his grandfather ("Going North"). The latter is the most direct and linear of these poems.

> Those streets in my youth,
> hilarious and angry,
> cobblestoned by Meztizos,
> fresh fruit
> and dancing beggars.
> Gone are the soldiers
> and the nuns. . . .
> I hum Spanish tunes
> waiting for the bus
> in Fresno.
> These avenues
> I watch
> carefree
> young, open collared
> like my grandfather
> who died in a dream
> going North.

There is an understated pathos here as Salinas tries to resolve past and present in his life as well as his dreams in the face of family and cultural history and reality. "Olivia" is an equally poignant poem, and although it is also an elegy, Salinas' trademark style comes through as he translates the emotional pain of experience through more associative and surreal imagery, especially as seen in the last third of the poem.

> I didn't come to this world
> to be frightened
> yet your death sticks
> in my stomach
> and I must clean the kitchen
> with my hands
> and I must wander on
> into the night of leavened bread
> and pursue truth
> like a tube needing air.

In a 1982 review of *Afternoon of the Unreal,* Donald Wolff offered valuable insights into Salinas' techniques, subjects, and motivations. Speaking of an "unlooked for joy" that counters or balances much of the melancholy and despair in Salinas' work, Wolff wrote,

> Salinas is a thoroughly Spanish, thoroughly Mexican, proudly Chicano, assuredly American, deeply human, yet quintessentially personal poet. It may be the way all these strains are effortlessly evoked that accounts for what joy the poet can discover—he is never alone. While the joy is never pure or unmixed, the confluence, even when bitter, is at once sharp and expansive.

"Ode to the Mexican Experience" is a poem in which are all of the elements that Wolff describes; at the end of the poem, the poet's personal past, his ancestry, and the joy he discovers in poetry, in "singing" about his perceptions and experience, are resolved amid flourishes of associative imagery.

> The happy poet talks in his sleep,
> the eyes of his loved one
> pressing against him—
> her lips have the softness
> of olives crushed by rain

> . . . .
> The soft aggressive spiders
> came out to play in the sunlight,
> and suffering violins in pawn shops,
> hell and heaven and murdered angels
> and all the incense of the living
> in poisoned rivers
> wandering aimlessly among dead fish,
> dead dreams, dead songs.
> I was an altar boy,
> a shoeshine boy,
> an interventionist in family affairs,
> a ruthless connoisseur of vegetables,
> a football player.
> To all living things I sing
> The most terrible and magnificent
> Ode to my ancestry.

Salinas is writing from Monterrey, from Mazatlán; he is recalling his Aztec heritage, and all of the suffering and dreams and songs. Yet this is an ode, and he sings to all that he remembers, invoking supporting images of suffering violins and murdered angels, out of the creative visions of Salvador Dali and Giorgio De Chirico, to expand the creative vision. In the *Quarterly West* interview, Salinas commented on observations Wolff made in his review of *Afternoon of the Unreal*, specifically with regard to Salinas' surreal style and its connection to a "dark side of the soul," as Wolff put it. Salinas responded:

> I wanted to somehow come to terms with the tragic and through the tragic, gain a vision which transcends the world. I tapped freely into my unconscious, and thus, living in a fantastic world, I conjured many visions and idiosyncrasies into a poem. . . . certainly the surreal events of those years left an imprint, and I would later use it in my poetry, that is, my impressions, thoughts, etc. would fuse, and fantastic imagery could, for me, convey reality.

In *Afternoon of the Unreal,* Salinas loosens the reins on his imagination as witnessed in the poems' rapid turns of subconscious and surreal imagery and also in poems in which he creates an alter ego to speak and act. This other "Salinas" suffers as well, but at the same time is capable of grand gestures toward the world, of extensive absorbing and resolving. In "Salinas Is on His Way" he announces that

> After dreams get through with me
> I shall devour books, sing arias,
> walk on snow,
> have arguments with darkness
> and crawl into the corner of the sea.

Yet in the end of the poem Salinas is "making a mad dash through the night / making certain everything is secure." Here the poet is capable of moving beyond tragedy and psychic difficulties. The little poem "Salinas Sends Messengers to the Stars" gives a more humble, yet finally grand and romantic Salinas, again capable of overcoming physical and emotional poverty.

> Sir. You understand. I am poor.
> I work from sunup to sundown.
> Never mind what I do . . .
> yet, I'll tell:
> I send messengers to the stars.
>
> With all the trouble and madness
> on this earth
> I feel the stars to be
> more human.
> I think I'll weave
> blankets
> and tell them
> I love them so dearly.

With its short lines and uncomplicated diction, this poem conveys humility and pathos without self-pity. The leaps of imagination are supported by a simple assertiveness, a plainspoken voice making a fantastic claim to employment, a job fit only for a poet of supreme imagination and dedication.

In the main, the method of *Afternoon of the Unreal* is one of counterpoint, of juxtaposing brilliant and unexpected imagery with emotional darkness, and yet ultimately the poems reflect an imagination that finds joy in the craft of poetry, which makes it possible to look upon circumstance with irony and humor, and offer praise for mere survival. Here are the fifth and last stanzas of "Magnificent Little Gift."

> I have a dog that follows me
> from room to room
> like a doctor.
> The wives of the moon
> sit silent.
> A berserk seagull dances
> on the shore
> . . . .
> As I said, life is fighting me.
> I shall aim a blow at its ears
> breathing poetry
> counting stars in the evening
> floating with the universe
> thanking God for this gift,
> this life.

PRELUDE TO DARKNESS

Completed not long after publication of *Afternoon of the Unreal*, *Prelude to Darkness* is a book of struggle—personal, emotional, and psychological. The poems embody the experience of an expansive soul, an individual who desires to be generous, righteous, and accepting, yet who at almost every turn is confronted by the many unmanageable and unkind particulars of the world—financial constraints, professional concerns, romantic unfulfillment.

Some poems plunge Salinas and the reader into darkness, into a desperation that the poems convince readers is all too justified. Section 3 of "I Sigh in the Afternoon" is representative.

> And I've been smiling too long
> to be overworked
>   and underpaid.
> I've got to find someone
>   to talk to.
> I have a ruthless rendezvous
>   with humanity,
> and I will not rest half-ignorant
>   in the cubicle of thought,
> alienated from the happy condition
>   which plagues man.
> I'm learning to question
> *psychiatry psychology*
> the label given to genius.
> I am questioning the modern term
> *man.*
> We have to take a scrutinizing
>   look, a deep haunting courageous
>   blissful look into the mirror
>   of our ways, or
> our crazy souls will not rest.

The poetic method here is direct statement; only about half of the poems in the book rely on Salinas' keen and unusual image making. Yet to be sure, in this book Salinas continues to transform a dark emotional state by means of imagery, as seen in the last half of a short poem about blossoms, titled "Visitors":

> Gaunt-legged
> bosoms of snow,
> timid little voyeurs
> of dusk
> in terrible
> conversation with my
> brain.
>
> I take them in my hand
> and walk in my malice,
> wildly eating the air.

Salinas' ability to distill an emotional and psychological state into objective and wild images is what marks his work; the blossoms, falling here in "terrible / conversation" with his brain, his consciousness, effectively translate to the reader the tension experienced by the speaker.

In other poems in this book the poet wins out over his circumstances, if only marginally. In "Last Tango in Fresno" the speaker is accepting fate, doing his best with humor, a little wit, to arrive at an apparently hopeful resignation despite being down on his romantic luck.

> Midnoon and I'm between
> a pastrami and a dream.
> In love with bad love
> I put out my cigarette
> and count my blessings.
> Bad kharma and no lover.
> I want to seduce
> the nearest woman
> and run off to the
> nearest motel.
> But the nearest woman
> is thinking of vegetables
> and buying a gift
> for her lover.
> So I waltz down
> the avenue,
> feeling great
> and important
> and bump into
> a lesbian friend
> who is out of
> work and needs a job.
> I give her five bucks
> and feel
> that in the next life
> I'll get it all back.

Few poets can manage such a distilled narrative, one that jumps from one event and mood to the next while remaining emotionally coherent. The speaker may take comfort in the adage that there is always someone worse off than oneself, but there is of course no "tango" here, no dance or romance. We have only one soul pinned down by fate helping another, and a reader comes away—given the wit and ironic texture—doubting that the speaker truly believes in an afterlife or reincarnation, and hence in his reward.

The subject of this book is not darkness, but rather the day-to-day battle, those manic clips of experience that could very well lead to darkness. It is then the strength of these poems that they can present a balance between affirmation and denial of a cosmic order. The title poem offers this tension, the bruised places of the heart in conflict with the hope of the spiritual. Here we have the poet alone, in the night of his imagination, outside a dancehall in Fresno, listening to Mexican music and watching lovers who seem to find each other effortlessly. The second half of the poem offers the example of romance and desire in the world that countervails the spiritual order, or lack of that order.

> Pedro Infante's singing
> "Tu Solo Tu" and
> the country girls who dance
> once a week and go to church
> are leaving the Rainbow Ballroom
> on the strong arm of Jorge Negrete
> . . . .
> Who could have dreamed this
> agony up? The nuns
> with their sorrowful mysteries
> and dark beads? Jesus
> with a bad memory?

A more concentrated reflective mode surfaces in the fourth section of the book. While poems here are not optimistic, they are calmer, almost hopeful. They show Salinas rising past eloquent or forceful complaint. He has approached darkness but not succumbed to hopelessness. The last poem, "As Evening Lays Dying," has Salinas winning the struggle and gives a soul that for all its suffering, survives and goes expansively and compassionately into the world. Once more, Salinas is buoyed by his vocation, his craft, and his commitment to poetry.

> And feel each passing
> day, like gypsies,
> while I feel orphanages
> in the sky and
> in my thumbs singing.
> As the evening lays dying,
> I announce this heart
> for all its irony,
> and venture forward
> into the world,
> poetic and unassuming.

DARKNESS UNDER THE TREES / WALKING BEHIND THE SPANISH

In 1979–1980 Salinas lived on his own in Fresno. When he was not working at a part-time job, he would often stay up most of the night writing or talking about poetry with friends. Given Salinas' history of manic depression, his associates feared he might suffer another breakdown. Nevertheless, this was a tremendously productive period for Salinas, who was sometimes writing two or three poems a day. The manuscript of *Prelude to Darkness* had been ready for publication by 1979, and by the time Gary Soto and his wife, Carolyn, had helped Salinas secure a publisher for his next book, Salinas had in fact completed two books of poetry. Since both works issued from the period 1979 through 1981, the Chicano Studies Library Publications at the University of California, Berkeley, decided to publish the two books under one cover. *Darkness under the Trees / Walking behind the Spanish* was released in 1982.

In an essay in *Recovering the U.S. Hispanic Literary Heritage* (1993), Raymund A. Paredes makes instructive observations about Chicano writers in general and Salinas in particular. "In the last decade or so, much of the most satisfying work by Chicano writers has tended toward introspection within carefully-bounded environments rather than toward broad representational characterization and sweeping cultural perspectives. . . . Much of Salinas' power derives from the courage and honesty with which he confronts his frail and flawed psyche." So while many of the thirty-six poems making up "Darkness under the Trees" reflect a dark mood in the wake of a disastrous love affair, an equal number of poems direct the book away from pessimism through the use of irony and a philosophic mode, in the examination of such notions as God and fate. One of the first poems in the collection is "I'm on My Way," and Salinas is seen as a caricature, taking an almost humorous look at himself, yet sending a warning to God.

> Evening becomes evening,
> and I'm not letting up, God.
> I'm still sleeping
> with my neighbor's wife
> on Sundays—
> and sometimes drive nails
> into flowers out of boredom
> and bump into beggars
> when morning goes dead
> . . . .
> I'll make it
> to heaven on a motorbike yet—
> beardless Leo Da Vinci
> singing Spanish folk songs.

Salinas is confronting God, the human condition, and attempting to come to some conclusions that will serve him emotionally and intellectually, that will help him resolve some of his more immediate emotional quandaries. Other poems in a highly introspective and speculative mode are "Salinas Summering at the Caspian and Thinking of Hamlet" and "Salinas Wakes Early and Goes to the Park to Lecture Sparrows." Again to his advantage, he establishes a distance between himself and the character of "Salinas" and is thus able to reason both more objectively and imaginatively.

"Fragments for Fall"—a longer poem in eight sections—should not be overlooked. Not long after reading Saul Bellow's *Humboldt's Gift* and rereading the poetry of Delmore Schwartz, Salinas wrote this poem, assuming the character of Schwartz. The poem is remarkable for its sustained imagery and lyric vision. Salinas surely must have found a kindred spirit in Schwartz, and in this highly evocative poem is able to step into Schwartz's skin and elicit the paranoia and pathos of a great yet tragic poetic soul. Here are the main portions of the last two sections of this tour-de-force persona poem:

> I accuse the world
> of having stolen
> the pigeons from
> my window,
> and beneath the benches
> feed them cocktail sandwiches
> from the night before.
> I am Schwartz

the magnanimous,
smooth of wit,
facile, glib, and true
as a meteor
in my castigations.

I am the best
of my age,
its hands and eyes,
and say so
while the clock ticks,
forlorn
as the frosted grass.

This poem is important in Salinas' work as it demonstrates his considerable range and skills. Here he demonstrates not only that he is a poet of great empathy, but that he is a poet capable of intricate strategies—a sustained longer poem developed by imagistic progression and theme and variation.

While the atmosphere in this collection may be bleak, Salinas manages to endure with grit and determination. The last portion of "Soto Thinking of the Ocean" concludes with the directness and honesty of which Paredes wrote:

The incoming waves
catch us
in our
amazement,
that we are mortal,
that we could drown
near shore
and be remembered,
be recognized
like strong
tobacco,
and like pelicans
considered
in a strange way
romantics.

We are all being
beaten by the waves
under this
August sky.

"[Caught] / in our / amazement" refers to the denial of mortality, the tendency of humans to daydream their way through life, neglecting to focus on essential matters. Salinas serves up an understated indictment of a society that is too comfortable, too complaisant.

The ending of the title poem shows Salinas as wrestling with the idea of God, challenging God's purported effects in the world. I wish I could explain to God,

ask forgiveness, but I'm awkward
with the sentimental.
Don Quixote and I have lost
our minds—this is
another involuntary jump
into the darkness under the trees . . .

Leonardo da Vinci, Miguel de Cervantes' great character Don Quixote—despite his desperation Salinas nonetheless finds kin and companions to help him bear the burden of loneliness and disappointment. Like Quixote—who is a frequent touchstone for Salinas—the poet manages the fortitude, the grit, to continue on in life despite the odds, and often, as in the case in the poem "The Odds," he can do so with the great irony and resoluteness found in the last stanza.

Let the dead-mad divide and
anger the moon, but I prefer
to simply go unadorned
among kings and hold my head
high among the common towns
I come from, unnoticed in my
open coat and summer hat.
I've known dogs in my life
who have died gallantly
with feet straight up in the air.

Salinas sees it as unlikely that he will prevail against the odds, but no matter what the outcome, says the poem, he will meet his fate gallantly, like the dog in this unexpected but appropriate concluding image. Finding a code, a way to survive while interpreting experience, is Salinas' primary project in this book. At the same time, he has not abandoned his affinity for lyric themes and dazzling imagery. One of the last poems in the book, "This Is What I Said" shows all of these elements.

> "I'm a very metaphysical cat,
> someday I'll be slicing apples
> in heaven." . . .
> . . . .
> Deep inside me, I think
> difficult thoughts and wonder
> whether my intellect is sharp
> enough for this, or if I can
> translate the feeling that
> overcame me when my grandfather died,
> or the time I had a high fever
> and saw ghosts in the garden
> and my mother consoled me
> . . . .
> I realize I'm nothing;
> yet, if something kind were
> to come from nowhere,
> I'd start believing all over
> again, and smile at a girl's
> fancifulness, gather myself,
> and make a life.

Certainly, these are personal poems under the desolate trees of Salinas' world, yet he presents his difficulties with candor and approaches them with an idiosyncratic reason. From that frank approach and the brilliance of his imagery, he is able to see the irony in life and identify possible ways to survive.

Although written only a few months after the manuscript of "Darkness under the Trees," "Walking behind the Spanish," a collection of forty-one poems, marks a large step forward in Salinas' poetic accomplishment. Here Salinas is at the height of his imagistic powers, displaying concentrated and inventive imagery rarely matched in contemporary poetry. As well, Salinas takes this opportunity to praise and eulogize the great Spanish poets who were writing in the 1920s and 1930s, to show compassion and empathy for their dedication to poetry and humanity, which in many instances brought the poets their early deaths at the hands of the Spanish dictator Francisco Franco and the fascists. Salinas embraces the example of their lives and the example of their poetry and enlarges his own vision.

To be sure, Salinas is still trying to decipher his fate and the complex emotions in which he finds himself tangled, and these subjects take up the first section of this book. The last poem in section 1 shows Salinas' mastery of the short line as it serves his unexpected turns of imagery and tight narration. Here is all of "When We Have To."

> An evening stroll
> has declared me sane
> for the world.
> The hurried days
> walk beside
> me like stray dogs;
> I've invented
> no one today,
> no ghost to walk beside
> me and act as a shepherd
> in the night.
> Left this way
> to the motion of flowers
> and lovers who
> have shunned me,
> I discover the air—
> air is air
> yet the arithmetic
> of birds
> with their songs
> becomes my waltz,
> unheroic . . .
> With the cry of the mudlark
> all bitterness
> leaves
> as if starbound
> knowing
> we shine in the paleness
> when we have to.

While the catalyst for the poem may have been "lovers who/ have shunned me," the ambition finally is much larger than that required for a worn romantic complaint. The speaker here is aware of his mental and emotional condition, and by extension, of the human condition. He realizes, with the help of practical discovery—"air is air"—coupled with poetic discovery—"the arithmetic / of birds"—that the personal can be overcome when one looks beyond oneself, both practically and inventively, to human beings collectively.

The project for the central section of the book is to transform emotion and experience into original imagery. "A Clever Magician Carrying My Heart" announces a more distilled surrealist method than seen before in Salinas:

> . . . In the garden
> the woman is breathing roses
> and the sky is on horseback
> opening like a huge bone.

These images do not exist for their own sake but to magnify and make accessible the poem's emotional center—the perplexed heart and mind of the poet walking through the world.

The height of Salinas' achievement, however, comes in the third section of the book in the poems dedicated to the Spanish and South American poets and writers who have inspired him, "The Generation of Spanish Civil War Poets," in Salinas' words. Here, Salinas reaches beyond anything he had written to this point to a deeper sense of his poetic being, for the kinship he feels with these poets stems not merely from poetic influence but from a spiritual and humanistic bond. Lorca, Jiménez, Machado, Hernández, Neruda, and Vallejo—clearly Salinas was attracted to these poets' music, the freshness and flair of their imagery, their explorations of the surreal, and that gave him a license to pursue his own brand of imagistic bravado. Perhaps Salinas' most significant connection to these poets, however, is philosophical or political. Soto, in his 1982 essay on Salinas, wrote incisively to this point:

> This influence is not strictly one of style but also of spirit. He saw them as touchstones against an unjust world—poets who lived to some purpose. They were blessed with a profound sense of community, and this is what attracted Luis to them. What they gave to the world, Luis returned by writing poems that affirmed that their lives had been significant.

Indeed, the first poem in this last section, "I'm Walking behind the Spanish," announces the subject and style at the heart of this book; fully in Salinas' own voice the poems combine the details of the poets' lives and deaths with Salinas' original imagery. The specificity of his imaginative musings reveal the extent to which these ghosts haunt Salinas' poetic landscape. Here is most of the first section.

> Neruda sound asleep
> Juan Ramon placing yellow flowers
> in his kitchen.
> Miguel in jail.
> Lorca playing flamenco
> to a house full of romanceros.
> Cesar Vallejo walking through
> the streets of Paris.
> I walk behind you
> carrying this heart
> of white rain which has
> come out of the barrio
> with the turbulence of
> the Guadalquivir
> . . . .
> And this petty inquisitive
> brain has watched you
> enter my life.
> Miguel weeping.
> Lorca clean shaven and alert
> murdered standing.
> Neruda calm like dropping fruit.
> Juan Ramon Jimenez
> in a portrait of yellow flowers.
> And Vallejo drunk with the ghost
> of compassion, sipping cold coffee.
> Behind time I'm
> like a lost finger
> in the sea.
> Thrashing about
> looking for a lost heaven
> . . . .

> I'm taking everything
> to the sea, toss bird bones
> there, eat bread and hold on.

Salinas has seemingly internalized every detail of these lives, and though the time of their experience is lost to him, he takes inspiration from and finds courage in the example of their poetry and struggle.

"Someone Is Buried" is an elegy to Lorca, and Salinas demonstrates his understanding of Lorca's sensibilities, his emotional concision, fashioning this poem in only fifteen lines. "Black ribbons under an anonymous moon" is certainly Salinas' poetic nod to Lorca, but otherwise a reader encounters the more romantic and sometimes off-beat or unexpected imagery particular to Salinas—"The children are going to the clouds / to hear flamenco . . ." and "In heaven an angel fixes his trousers." Yet, to anchor this flourish of imagery, Salinas concludes with pathos and the actual, and with a slowed rhythm for emphasis:

> Someone is being buried.
> There is no marker on your grave
> In Granada, Federico Garcia Lorca.

A moving poem of homage to Vallejo, "Letter Too Late to Vallejo," derives from Vallejo's poem "Black Stone Lying on a White Stone." While the poem ends with an echo of Vallejo's phrasing, the narration and imagery are Salinas'. Additionally, this last section contains an "Ode to Cervantes," a figure who has inspired many of Salinas' poems, a figure with whom he finds great kinship:

> I of sound mind
> and wind in my logic
> want to go against the State,
> be imprisoned there,
> and give compassion
> to the luminous underdogs.

This book, and especially this final section, offers poems that pay homage to many heroes, not only the heroes of literature but also political heroes such as the Mexican revolutionist Emiliano Zapata. One of the most moving poems, however, concerns an unlikely hero, the poet's adopted father. "My Father Is a Simple Man" is direct and simply spoken, as befits its subject. Salinas imagines himself as walking behind this great man, using simple facts, observed in his mature style and voice, which need little embellishment. This is the last third of the poem:

> I'd gladly give my life
> for this man with a sixth
> grade education, whose kindness
> and patience are true . . .
> The truth of it is, he's the scholar
> and when the bitter-hard reality
> comes at me like a punishing
> evil stranger, I can always
> remember that here was a man
> who was a worker and provider,
> who learned the simple facts
> in life and lived by them,
> who held no pretense.
> And when he leaves without
> benefit of fanfare or applause
> I shall have learned what little
> there is about greatness.

In all cases, Salinas is out to learn through his poetry. Often flamboyant in his style, he is also capable of great lyricism and directness as befits his subject. Over the years, the instinct to praise in his poetry has been more and more evident. In this book he seeks to convey what he has learned about himself and what he values from other lives, simple, political, and poetic. We hear an honest voice, one that takes the risks of involvement, of wrestling with the world, emotionally, poetically, and aesthetically.

THE SADNESS OF DAYS

There are fourteen new poems in *The Sadness of Days: Selected and New Poems* (1987), written between 1982 and 1986. This was a transitional period and not a particularly productive time for Salinas. Nevertheless, this is a fully realized group of poems with characteristic flashes of surreal brilliance supporting an essentially lyric subject. Even though Salinas revisits situations of psychological distress and loneliness, we find him looking outside himself, with compassion for the poor and institutionally committed, and closing the book with a very straightforward poem of commiseration, "How Much Are You Worth."

In the title poem, "The Sadness of Days," the poet is hoping for relief from emotional distress; he wants to be able to offer compassion to others, to understand himself and thereby believe in the future:

> Honestly I want to find myself,
> to sit under a tree with its dusty fruit
> of salvation. I will take my place,
> Listen up, and have faith in all things.

Yet Salinas is weary battling for sanity, companionship, and the small salvations of poetry, as we see at the end of "Letter to Soto."

> And a woman somewhere, whispering
> To the lilacs, "Omar is crazy."
> Yes, ladies, yes, yes, yes to anything.
> And the big theater of loneliness,
> Like a huge hand dropping out of the sky.
> Yet, I can hear my friends in the distance,
> Like doves saying, "Omar
> It's alright, it's alright."
> And the mind adds zeros. The flesh talks of
>   youth
> And its heart. The heart is silent,
> Like the dangling string on the package
> Of cigarettes in the asylum.
> And they find me on bad elbows by the meadow
> With a copy of Omar Khayyam, whiskey,
> And my poems that can't find an ear.

Salinas' particular talent is found in lines such as "the dangling string on the package / of cigarettes in the asylum." This is of course an unlikely image to convey the silence of a lonely heart, and yet it is fresh, original, comes directly from experience, and is apt given what readers imagine must be endured in an asylum, given the tenuous connection to stability.

The next poem in the volume, "Beyond the Sea (at the sanatorium)," has a similar context. The poem, which resolves in the second half, presents images at once realistic and far removed from the scene, in keeping with Salinas' long-established style of using surprising imagistic and contextual combinations.

> And this ship of the lost won't move.
> Only John and Gertrude move
> And it's like a long dip
> In the ocean.
> Their bodies are pressed together
> Like something from the sea—
> Making the small noises
> Of whales that have no end.

The last three poems in this group have the poet overcoming his circumstances. "In the Thick of Darkness" concludes with Salinas rising, clean shaven, "wearing the hard crust / of silence" and walking away from darkness. "On a Visit to a Halfway House after a Long Absence" gives us a firsthand, unflinching assessment of places that serve shattered lives; here are the most telling lines of the poem.

> The damned and the defeated
> share coffee here
> like lost apostles, but
> no saint or prayer can
> change the hunger or the cold
> . . . .
> I leave this place and its
> aroma of suicides, for the lost
> have gathered here
> like wounded sparrows;
> and the inhuman
> and the human
> suffocate in this air,
> in this terrible refuge.

Finally, a very direct poem concludes the book; "How Much Are You Worth" is a poem with only one arresting image; the tone is that of admonition. Having been too long a witness to suffering, Salinas has lost patience and wishes to exhort his readers to do something practical and positive. Here, the voice of a modern-day scourge best serves his purposes, yet his ability to juxtapose even common items and objects draws a reader's attention sharply to the subject and ideas at hand.

> Come sit with poverty for an hour.
> Capitalism is a large room with idiotic stares.
> And seagulls might as well recite the rosary.
> Money that runs its hand over your face.
> Anger that does not approach justice.
> Come sit by the Martyrs of the highway.
> Tie the shoelace of the beggar.
> Come make yourself useful.
> Boil an egg. Fry some cheese.
> Run after Senators—stop their cars.
> Wash the feet of the poor.

On those occasions when Salinas is political in theme, he manages to keep his poetry from becoming rhetorical by means of his inventiveness and use of concrete detail. Here, despite the abstractions of "capitalism," "anger," and "justice," the unexpected seagulls and the highway martyrs join with shoelaces, an egg, and fried cheese to render his vision and his theme original, specific, personal, and engaging. The image of capitalism, its implied precepts, is here conjunct with the nonsense of seagulls reciting the rosary. A New Testament image ends the poem, in what might be an effort by Salinas to place poverty into a larger, more redemptive perspective.

SOMETIMES MYSTERIOUSLY

In 1991 a selection of twenty-two new poems by Salinas won the annual chapbook contest from Flume Press, in Chico, California, which published the collection as *Follower of Dusk*. The poems in this chapbook formed the core of a full-length poetry manuscript, published in 1997 as *Sometimes Mysteriously* by Salmon Run Press after winning the Alaska publisher's annual book contest. Following *The Sadness of Days*, there was a period of inactivity for Salinas and then through the early 1990s he began to write anew. The vision in these more recent poems is tempered; while not openly optimistic, they are less strident than the poems of previous works. The sense of anxiety that marks much of Salinas' early poems is mitigated somewhat here, although Salinas continues to employ his distinctive image making to translate his difficulties. In a 1999 review of *Sometimes Mysteriously*, Donald Wolff again offered keen insight into the development and achievement of Salinas' poetry: "This book of forty-five poems represents the maturation of Salinas' vision while recording the losses that accumulate over the years. Salinas' staccato succession of images are always arresting, but in this book they are more modulated and the reader is included in the vision before he or she knows it."

"Love Rushes By" gives the reader a good indication of this evolution in temperament. It begins with a familiar lyric subject:

> I'm thinking of those
> evenings of love
> rushing by me
> as thrushes rustle through
> the leaves of autumn.
> And I want to wrestle
> with fate and toss it about.

This poem continues in Salinas' characteristic manner with fanciful and original imagery; however, it resolves in a positive mood, as do many in this collection.

> I take leave of the patio
> where birds dance about
> like unconcerned acrobats—
> for like them
> I want to learn
> the lesson of unforgetfulness.

I put on my jacket
and drive through
the fields . . . a full moon
is rising—I light a cigarette
and sing to all the madonnas
of faith.

This is an autumnal book; the voice of the poet is wiser, calmer, more reflective. "Prayer to the Child of Prague" uses the compelling rhythms of formal prayer while at the same time transforming Salinas' uneasy speculation by means of original imagery.

And the Child of Prague in his
sweet sleep cannot imagine
bitterness like I can,
though even in the worst saint
one can find comfort.
Being full of fear in a sanitarium,
I too need your solace
Child, in my bitter castle,
in my rootless abode.
Shelter me from the cynical,
the faithless and arrogant,
all the weeds grown up
around the weak heart.
Give me courage and strength
to bear up and let me believe
for much strife comes
bundled up like an old man
who holds his shoes
in his hands for sale.

Salinas makes excellent use of the melody and rhetoric of supplication in this poem, and yet the examples and details are internalized. The poem offers no formulated affirmation but rather a mature, and to one with Salinas' history, accurate, image, one that portrays—in the old man with his shoes for sale—realistic and specific loss on an everyday scale.

This tone of sober resignation is also found in "My Fifty-Plus Years Celebrate Spring." The occasion for the poet is the arrival of spring in the San Joaquin Valley, a cause for personal—and ultimately political—observation and reflection.

Forty years
in this valley,
the wind, the sun
building its altars
of salt, the rain that
holds nothing back,
and with the crop
at its peak
packing houses burn
into morning,
their many diligent
Mexican workers stacking up
the trays and hard hours
that equal their living.

I've heard it said
hard work ennobles
the spirit—
If that is the case,
the road to heaven
must be crowded
beyond belief.

Salinas alludes here to the idea of a valley of plenty, but in this valley the poor never have enough. In the last line of the poem, the idiomatic expression "beyond belief," meaning outside common understanding, becomes truly meaningful only in its literal sense. Salinas would like to believe in reward and redemption, but his experience and that of those he observes fills him with doubt and makes belief in the transcendent difficult if not impossible.

Yet there is also an element of joy to be found among these poems. "After a Party" has Salinas responding to the past, and thus to fate:

I've been invited to forget
all this,
to go on being friendly,
to disappear
on country roads
with a wave and a laugh.

"The Beginning of Enthusiasm" offers a speaker exuberant and hopeful:

It's as if a new road
opened up in my life

and I, sitting on a train,
waved goodbye.
It's as if the world rolled
me inside a batch of prayers
and hope put on its coat
among feminine whispers.
I am the merchant
on the edge of a marquee
arranging letters that say,
"Poetry For Sale"
as I live
in the soft embrace
of handkerchiefs,
in the swollen rivers,
in the market,
in the barrio's swift slap.
Yes, I live away from the insane,
the suicides, sharpening my tongue,
waiting for my key to a room,
for my imaginary wife,
and my chauffeur, an angel
who'll get me there on time!

Here Salinas turns a litany of the everyday into an affirmation.

In the interview published in *Quarterly West*, Salinas comments on this book and its title poem:

> *Sometimes Mysteriously* is a more tempered book, a sort of acceptance of life and reality. I try to handle it all with irony, humor, and of course with truth. In the title poem, the theme of loneliness appears again. However here it takes a different turn. It finds a solution. Before it was madness or the edge of madness that seemed to rule over most everything I wrote. Now, I am more seriously looking for answers and being quiet; I am more concerned with an affirmation of life rather than just a negative irresponsibility. I am moving in the direction of a responsible self rather than a self betrayed, so to speak, by life.

"Sometimes Mysteriously" is a short, candid poem with subtle emotional turns and a lyric center that demonstrates the maturity of Salinas' vision. This poem, as well as most of the poems making up this book, does not utilize the surreal tour de force images to the extent that previous Salinas poems do. Rather, here is a poem of eloquence, discovery, and honesty.

Sometimes in the evening when love
tunes its harp and the crickets
celebrate life, I am like a troubadour
in search of friends, loved ones,
anyone who will share with me
a bit of conversation. My loneliness
arrives ghostlike and pretentious,
it seeks my soul, it is ravenous
and hurting. I admire my father
who always has advice in these matters,
but a game of chess won't do, or
the frivolity of religion.
I want to find a solution, so I
write letters, poems, and sometimes
I touch solitude on the shoulder
and surrender to a great tranquility.
I understand I need courage
and sometimes, mysteriously,
I feel whole.

Salinas, who turned sixty-five in 2002, had begun rereading the English Romantic poets. Throughout his work, he has always had a "romantic" proclivity, a desire for the grand gesture, to embrace the world and move through it magnanimously. He would happily be the troubadour in "Sometimes Mysteriously." Certainly he is a poet who has found contentment in survival and in his writing, and this last book admits the possibility of hope, of life ultimately turning out for the better.

Selected Bibliography

WORKS OF LUIS OMAR SALINAS

POETRY

Crazy Gypsy. Fresno, Calif.: Origines, 1970.
I Go Dreaming Serenades. San Jose, Calif.: Mango, 1979.

Afternoon of the Unreal. Fresno, Calif.: Abramás, 1980.

Prelude to Darkness. San Jose, Calif.: Mango, 1981.

Darkness under the Trees / Walking behind the Spanish. Berkeley: Chicano Studies Library Publications, University of California, 1982.

The Sadness of Days: Selected and New Poems. Houston, Tex.: Arte Publico, 1987.

Follower of Dusk. Chico, Calif.: Flume, 1991.

Sometimes Mysteriously. Anchorage, Alaska: Salmon Run, 1997.

Greatest Hits 1969–1996. Johnstown, Ohio: Pudding House, 2002.

PROSE

"Sometimes Mysteriously." Commentary. In *What Will Suffice: Contemporary American Poets on the Art of Poetry.* Edited by Christopher Buckley and Christopher Merrill. Salt Lake City, Utah: Gibbs-Smith, 1995. P. 130.

"Luis Omar Salinas." Autobiography and commentary. In *The Geography of Home: California's Poetry of Place.* Edited by Christopher Buckley and Gary Young. Berkeley, Calif.: Heyday, 1999. P. 314.

"Luis Omar Salinas." Autobiography and commentary. In *How Much Earth: The Fresno Poets.* Edited by Christopher Buckley, David Oliveira, and M. L. Williams. Berkeley, Calif.: Roundhouse, 2001. P. 195.

"A Steady Stream." Commentary. In his *Greatest Hits 1969–1996.* Johnstown, Ohio: Pudding House, 2002. Pp. 7–11.

OTHER WORKS

From the Barrio: A Chicano Anthology. Editor, with Lillian Faderman. San Francisco: Canfield, 1973.

CRITICAL AND BIOGRAPHICAL STUDIES

Alarcón McKesson, Norma. Review of *From the Barrio: A Chicano Anthology. Revista Chicano-Riqueña* 2, no. 2:53–54 (spring 1974).

Alves Pereira, Teresinka. Review of *Darkness under the Trees / Walking behind the Spanish. Imagine* 1, no. 1:132–133 (summer 1984).

Buckley, Christopher. Review of *Prelude to Darkness.* In *Appreciations: Selected Reviews, Views, and Interviews, 1975–2000.* Santa Barbara, Calif.: Millie Grazie, 2000. Pp. 30–34.

Library Journal. Review of *From the Barrio: A Chicano Anthology.* Vol. 98, July 1973, p. 2072.

Lomelí, Francisco A., and Carl R. Shirley, eds. *Chicano Writers, First Series.* Detroit: Gale Research, 1989. Pp. 234–238.

Lomelí, Francisco A., and Donaldo W. Urioste. *Chicano Perspectives in Literature: A Critical and Annotated Bibliography.* Albuquerque, N.Mex.: Pajarito, 1976. Pp. 32, 68, 103, 106.

Magill, Frank N., ed. "The Poetry of Luis Omar Salinas." In *Masterpieces of Latino Literature.* New York: Harper Collins, 1994. Pp. 475–478.

Ortego y Gasca, Filipe. "An Introduction to Chicano Poetry." In *Modern Chicano Writers: A Collection of Critical Essays.* Edited by Joseph Sommers and Tomás Ybarra-Fausto. Englewood Cliffs, N.J.: Prentice Hall, 1979. Pp. 108–116.

Paredes, Raymund A. "Mexican-American Literature: An Overview." In *Recovering the U.S. Hispanic Literary Heritage.* Vol. 1. Edited by Ramón Gutiérrez and Genaro Padilla. Houston, Tex.: Arte Público, 1993. P. 48.

Peña, Manuel H. "Salinas, Luis Omar (1937–)." In *Chicano Literature: A Reference Guide.* Edited by Julio A. Martínez and Francisco A. Lomelí. Westport, Conn.: Greenwood Press, 1985. Pp. 353–365.

Revelle, Keith. "El Librero/The Crazy Gypsy: A Life Worth Preserving." *La Voz del Pueblo* 3, no. 8:3 (1970).

Rios, Alberto. "Chicano Borderlands Literature and Poetry." In his *Contemporary Latin American Culture: Unity and Diversity.* Tempe, Ariz.: Center for Latin American Studies, 1984. Pp. 79–93.

Risco-Lozada, Eliezar, and Guillermo Martínez. Introduction to *Crazy Gypsy.* Fresno, Calif.: Origines, 1970. Pp. 7–11.

Soto, Gary. "Luis Omar Salinas: Chicano Poet." *MELUS* 9, no 2:47–82 (summer 1982).

———. "Voices of Sadness and Silence." *Bloomsbury Review,* July 1988, p. 21.

———. Introduction to *Sometimes Mysteriously.* Anchorage, Alaska: Salmon Run, 1997. Pp. 5–7.

Shirley, Carl R., and Paula W. Shirley, *Understanding Chicano Literature.* Columbia: University of South Carolina Press, 1988. P. 25.

Tatum, Charles M. *A Selected and Annotated Bibliography of Chicano Studies.* Manhattan, Kans.: Society of Spanish and Spanish-American Studies, 1976. Pp. 59–60, 67–68, 77–78, 85.

———. "Other Social Poets." *Chicano Literature.* Boston: Twayne, 1982. P. 149.

Villanueva, Tino. "Más allá del grito: Poesía engagée chicana." *De Colores* 2, no. 2:27–42 (1975).

Wolff, Donald. "Strange Hours of the Day." Review of *Afternoon of the Unreal. Berkeley Poetry Review* 14, no 1:55–58 (1982).

———. "A Life Charmed and Haunted." Review of *Sometimes Mysteriously. SOLO* 3:156–159 (1999).

Wright, Charlotte M. Review of *The Sadness of Days: Selected and New Poems. Western American Literature* 23:91 (spring 1988).

INTERVIEWS

Binder, Wolfgang, ed. *Partial Autobiographies: Interviews with Twenty Chicano Poets.* Erlangen, Germany: Palm & Enke, 1985. (See pages 147–149.)

Buckley, Christopher. "Any Good Fortune." *Quarterly West* vol. 55 (fall/winter 2002/2003).

Veach, Cindy. *Northwest Review* 20, nos. 2–3:238–241 (1982).

—CHRISTOPHER BUCKLEY

William Jay Smith

1918–

WILLIAM JAY SMITH was born in Winnfield, Louisiana, on April 22, 1918, the child of Georgia Ella Campster Smith and Jay Smith, who was a soldier and for most of his career a clarinet player in the Sixth Infantry Band of the U.S. Army. In his memoir *Army Brat* (1980) the poet offers vivid recollections of his first twenty years at Jefferson Barracks on the edge of the Mississippi in the years between the wars. The peacetime "brown boot" army was an oddly pacific setting in which a child could grow up. Indeed, as Smith remarks:

> The woods on the reservation were a child's paradise; we knew every inch of these acres: here we followed the fern-lined muddy streams to our swimming holes, fished for crawfish with strips of bacon fat, and on the banks built our tree houses and lean-tos of sassafras in air blue with bluebells and heavy with the perfume of sweet william.

He was educated in St. Louis at the Blow School between 1924 and 1931 and then at Cleveland High School, from which he graduated in 1935. He won a scholarship to Washington University in St. Louis, where his literary abilities were recognized and where as a sophomore he became friends with Tennessee Williams, who was a senior. At the end of his junior year Smith studied for three months at the Institut de Touraine in Tours, France. He earned a B.A. in French in 1939 and an M.A. in that subject in 1941. During World War II he served as a lieutenant in the United States Naval Reserve in the Atlantic, and in the Pacific as a liaison officer aboard a French war vessel. After the war he studied at Columbia University (1946–1947); at Wadham College, Oxford, where he was a Rhodes Scholar (1947–1948); and at the University of Florence (1948–1950).

Smith began teaching before the war—as an assistant in French at Washington University—and he continued his academic connections with appointments at Columbia University, Williams College, and later at Hollins College (now Hollins University) in Virginia, where he was writer in residence and then a professor of English. Not wholly or solely an academic, however, he served for a couple of years as a Democratic member of the Vermont House of Representatives. He has been the Consultant in Poetry to the Library of Congress (the position is now called Poet Laureate) and poet in residence at the Cathedral of St. John the Divine in New York City. Smith has been a lecturer at the Salzburg Seminar in American Studies and a Fulbright Lecturer at Moscow State University, and he has been the recipient of numerous awards, including an award from the Henry Bellamann Memorial Foundation, the Loines Award, and the New England Poetry Club's Golden Rose. For his translations he has been honored by the French Academy, the Swedish Academy, and the Hungarian government. He is a member of the American Academy and Institute of Arts and Letters and was its vice president for literature during the period 1986–1989. In 1973 he received an honorary D. Litt from New England College in Henniker, New Hampshire. In 1947 he married the poet Barbara Howes, from whom he was divorced in 1965; in 1966 he married Sonja Haussmann, with whom he lives in Paris in an apartment near Montparnasse and on a wooded hillside in Cummington, Massachusetts, in a house that once belonged to the poet William Cullen Bryant.

What is initially striking about Smith's life and work—and turns out to be central to an understanding of his sensibility—is his enormous range, the way in which he comprehends what appear to be not only inconsistencies but also polarities. He is an international figure, living in both urbane Paris and rural western Massachusetts. He is cosmopolitan in his interests and translates from a great number of languages and cultures and is proud of his Native American heritage—he is part Choctaw and a descendant of Chief Moshulatubbee, one of the heads of the Choctaw nation. He is also an erudite, sophisticated poet who is at least as well known for his light verse and his work for children as he is for his "serious" poetry intended for adults. (Any attempt to draw a clear line between the different kinds of poetry is bound to fail, but the failure can actually be instructive: Smith's *Typewriter Town* of 1960, a children's book of verses accompanied by typewriter drawings of the sort that he had begun to make as early as 1947, anticipated by some years the avant-garde vogue for concrete poetry.)

EARLY POETRY

The pattern of Smith's publication has been atypical. Rather than issuing a series of slender volumes that led toward and contributed to a larger and more comprehensive collection, he has responded to the vagaries of publishing—in which editors leave or die and books are allowed to go out of print—by repeatedly revising and expanding his canon. *New and Selected Poems* appeared from Delacorte Press in 1970; *The Traveler's Tree: New and Selected Poems* came out in 1980 from Persea and Carcanet; *Collected Poems: 1939–1989* was published in 1990 by Scribners; and *The World Below the Window: Poems 1937–1997* was issued by the Johns Hopkins University Press in 1998.

In a general way one can look at the early work of poets to see what they were reading and, more particularly, what was exciting to them, inviting imitation and experiment, for a poet does not begin by addressing the world directly. Instead, he or she looks to the models of what other artists have been doing for instruction, inspiration, or at the very least suggestions about ways to proceed. A student of French literature and to some extent a product of his times, Smith looked at Eliot and at Jules Laforgue, who was the source of many of Eliot's own ideas about prosody, and he looked at the often dreamlike Valery Larbaud. A young poet also tries various voices and timbres to see what is comfortable in his own head and larynx. From his earliest work it is clear that Smith had an acute eye and a delicate and supple ear. From the constraints of tight forms—with which he would later sometimes dispense but which he would never abandon—he took strength, producing memorably pithy formulations that resonate far beyond their immediate occasions.

One particularly instructive example of a poem following a tight form is "The Closing of the Rodeo," which Smith says began with a simple announcement in the *New York Times* that the rodeo that had been at Madison Square Garden was about to close down. From this donnée Smith made an elegant miniature that he printed in his first book, *Poems* (1947), and then, in a slightly different version, reprinted in *Celebration at Dark* (1950) and in subsequent volumes.

> The lariat snaps, the cowboy rolls
>   His pack, and mounts and rides away.
> Back to the land the cowboy goes.
>
> Plumes of smoke from the factory sway
>   In the setting sun. The curtain falls,
> A train in the darkness pulls away.
>
> Goodbye, says the rain on the iron roofs.
>   Goodbye, say the barber poles.
> Dark drum the vanishing horses' hooves.

The critic Henry Taylor observes:

> The quiet, declarative tone of these lines, and the precision of words like "snaps," enable the poem to remain completely "factual" in tone, even through lines that might have appeared in one of Smith's poems for children. Aside from articles, conjunctions, and prepositions, only three words—*cowboy, away,* and *Good-bye*—occur more than once, in a pattern that underscores the permanence of this closing, and suggests extinction.

And extinction, of one kind or another, is what the poem is clearly "about."

One of Smith's best-known poems, "American Primitive," first appeared in *Poems: 1947–1957*. The poem, a short, elegant, dark piece, is only twelve lines long, but it has been widely anthologized and taught in schools and colleges.

> Look at him there in his stovepipe hat,
> His high-top shoes, and his handsome collar;
> Only my Daddy could look like that,
> And I love my Daddy like he loves his Dollar.
>
> The screen door bangs, and it sounds so funny—
> There he is in a shower of gold;
> His pockets are stuffed with folding money,
> His lips are blue, and his hands feel cold.
>
> He hangs in the hall by his black cravat,
> The ladies faint, and the children holler:
> Only my Daddy could look like that,
> And I love my Daddy like he loves his Dollar.

Clear enough, one might think, but as Smith reports in "A Frame for Poetry," one of the essays in his book *The Streaks of the Tulip: Selected Criticism* (1972), the reactions have been curious and paradoxical:

> I have frequently been asked to discuss this poem with grade-school children and, although it may appear a macabre choice on the part of the teacher, I have discovered that children respond to it without hesitation. They understand that a child is speaking and that the father has hanged himself for some reason involving money. College students, on the other hand, have often found this piece bewildering; they have lost the down-to-earth metaphorical approach of childhood and cannot follow the simple words to their unexpected conclusion. I think that I scarcely need add that although "American Primitive" is a bitter poem in the tradition of Edwin Arlington Robinson's "Richard Cory," it is certainly not intended as my sole view of the American scene.

He also offers some insight into his method of composition, letting us know that even though the piece may look as if it were dashed off in one quick, inspired take, it took rather longer. "It was indeed a delight," he says,

> to write it right off—as it now stands—after working on it at odd moments for a period of five years. I cannot recall how many versions I put down during this period, most of them discarded. I knew exactly where I wanted to get to; the problem was getting there, and getting there with directness and *élan*—and without fuss. I had in mind a Mississippi River guitar tune—absolutely mechanical in its rhythm—an out-and-out child's innocent unadorned view of horror—horror with the resonant twang of strings to it.

In an odd way, then, the ease with which grade-schoolers read it and the difficulty that college students seem to find with it are both hallmarks of Smith's success.

In the same essay he prints one of the rejected "little ballad bits" that was in the original version of the poem:

> I fear the feel of frozen steel,
>   I fear the scarlet dagger;
> But more than these I fear the eel,
>   I fear the carpetbagger.

He realized, as many craftsmanly poets come often to realize, that "less is more," and he adduces these lines to demonstrate his method of refining and winnowing.

> I had indeed the vision of the carpetbagger who had made his money in some suspect manner; and

with the sunlight and the screen door I wish to suggest the large, open, airy southern house that I remembered from childhood. The most difficult line for me to get in the poem was the one that now seems the simplest, and it is the turning point: "He hangs in the hall by his black cravat." Poetry is all in verbs, in verbs and nouns, and it seems to me it is all here in the verb "hangs."

"Death of a Jazz Musician," another poem from Smith's 1957 volume that he has reprinted in later collections, offers insights into the subtleties and contradictions of his poetic practice. It is another simple—almost deceptively simple—piece:

> I dreamed that when I died a jukebox played,
> And in the metal slots bright coins were laid;
> Coins on both my eyes lay cold and bright
> As the boatman ferried my thin shade into the night.
>
> I dreamed a jukebox played. I saw the flame
> Leap from a whirling disk which bore my name,
> Felt fire like music sweep the icy ground—
> And forward still the boatman moved, and made no sound.

There are two *aabb* quatrains, and their regularity is relieved only by the length of the fourth line of each stanza—which is actually an alexandrine, a line that does not fall naturally on an American ear. The childlike, or rather the folklike quality of the first three lines is converted into something sophisticated and, in emotional terms, attenuated, etiolated. The coins on the eyes are both classical and southern. (Readers may think of the lines from "Waynesboro Cotton Mill Blues": "He'd take the nickels off a dead man's eyes / to buy a Coca-Cola and an Eskimo Pie.") What Smith does is to take the nickels from the jukebox—that is what they used to require—and convert them into the traditional funerary offering, which makes the jukebox itself spooky and supernatural. The flame, of an old Wurlitzer maybe, leaps "from a whirling disk which bore my name," which is the record. And then the speaker's death itself is dramatized by the eerie silence in which the boatman progresses, a stark contrast to the playing jukebox.

Another early poem with which Smith fiddled over the years, first printed in *The Tin Can* (1966) and consistently reprinted in later volumes, is the powerful "Quail in Autumn." In this poem he seems to be borrowing from some of Robert Frost's practice, writing about a walk in the woods that is, of course, much more than that. In an essay in *The Streaks of the Tulip*, the downwardness of the imagery is clear but subtle in a manner at least as close to Robert Herrick as to Frost:

> The woods in Missouri on the banks of the Mississippi through which I used to tramp endlessly as a boy had their terrifying aspects. All around in them were sinkholes left by an earthquake; at the bottom of each was an overgrown black hole that I was convinced was a bottomless pit that would surely swallow me up if I allowed myself to slip into it. As I went along skirting the sinkholes, I would come at times on a snake and at other times on a covey of quail. In the absolute stillness of the autumn woods both were terrifying, but in the vision of the quail there was not only terror but a haunting beauty as well.
>
> Autumn has turned the dark trees toward the hill;
> The wind has ceased; the air is white and chill.
> Red leaves no longer dance against your foot,
> The branch reverts to tree, the tree to root.

The main action of the stanza, the important verb, is oddly abstract—"reverts." In the middle stanza the walker in this all but metaphysical woodland—Smith uses the second person for its intimacy and immediacy—flushes that covey of quail:

> And now in this bare place your step will find
> A twig that snaps flintlike against the mind;
> Then thundering above your giddy head,
> Small quail dart up, through shafting sunlight fled.

Not surprisingly, the walker is—and the reader is—startled, as Smith had been years before. Indeed, the experience turns out to be a kind of shock treatment, which is why the head is quite properly described as "giddy."

> Like brightness buried by one's sullen mood
> The quail rise startled from the threadbare wood;
> A voice, a step, a swift sun-thrust of feather
> And earth and air come properly together.

The shift to the third person in the final stanza is a clinical distancing: "one's sullen mood" is a depression, and the shock that the subject of the poem receives from the noise and flash of the ascending birds causes the depression to be, as it is said, lifted. It is a moment of grace, a blessed relenting, but its machinery is reported with telegraphic rapidity in the penultimate line. The heaviness of earth and the lightness of air are restored to their proper proportion, the walker is healed and, therefore, for him at least, the world is healed.

Smith wrote "Quail in Autumn" as a college student but did not publish it, sensing that there was something wrong with it. And he says in his essay that the only real difference between the early and the published versions is in the first two lines of the last stanza, which read, originally, "The quail rise startled from the autumn wood, / Love makes its brief appearance as it should." Candidly he says:

> I realized, of course, that to a young man of twenty love is what always appears, or should appear, at any time of the day or night, but in middle age, I could see that what I had really experienced so long ago—and was still experiencing—was the chilling beauty, the terror, of poetry itself.

This remark seems to slight love poetry, but then we remember that Smith is particularly successful in that realm. His 2002 book *The Girl in Glass: Love Poems* is a compilation of his love poetry, and on the Internet there is a website that offers young men and women possibilities of what might be read at their weddings. One of the suggested offerings is Smith's "A Pavane for the Nursery," which is as witty and playful as a children's poem (it has appeared in many anthologies for children) but is intimate and tender with its peculiarly Smith-like conclusion:

> So touch the air softly,
> And swing the broom high.
> We will dust the gray mountains,
> And sweep the blue sky;
> And I'll love you as long
> As the furrow the plow,
> As However is Ever,
> And Ever is Now.

TRANSITIONAL POETRY

In the 1960s a good number of poets who had been writing tight, formal poems began, perhaps in response to the cultural moment and the winds of fashion, to loosen up. For most American poets, the models for this prosodic relaxation were William Carlos Williams and Walt Whitman. For Smith, a student of French literature, there was a more comfortable and congenial point of access. As he says in his interview with Robert Phillips in *New Letters,* his model was not Whitman then but Laforgue:

> What he did I did. He first wrote very tight lyrics, then broke them all up. . . . And in the 1950s I translated Valery Larbaud. In his *Poems of a Multimillionaire* he had been influenced by Whitman but was a very witty and sophisticated writer in a way not at all Whitmanesque. . . .
>
> Some critics said at the time that I had been influenced by the Beats, Ginsberg, Corso, and the others. That's not true. I had my own interest in free verse quite independently of theirs. . . . I objected to the carelessness, the sloppiness of much of their work. I thought then—and I think now—that free verse ought to be just as carefully written as formal metrical verse.

While Smith's longer lines allowed him a new freedom, he did not abandon the constraints of form. Indeed, it could be said—not only of Smith's but of all poets' work—that there is nothing free about "free verse" if there are not available alternatives. Smith never gave up the competence and grace that formal poetry requires, and these craftsmanly qualities show to excellent advantage in the longer lines of such poems as "Morels," with which he opened his 1966 collection, *The Tin Can*. It begins:

> A wet gray day—rain falling slowly, mist over the
> > valley, mountains dark circumflex
> smudges in the distance—
>
> Apple blossoms just gone by, the branches feathery still
> > as if fluttering with half-visible antennae—
>
> A day in May like so many in these green mountains, and
> > I went out just as I had last year
>
> At the same time, and found them there under the big maples—
> > by the bend in the road—right where they had stood
>
> Last year and the year before that, risen from the dark duff
> > of the woods, emerging at odd angles
>
> From spores hidden by curled and matted leaves, a fringe of
> > rain on the grass around them,
>
> Beads of rain on the mounded leaves and mosses round them,
>
> Not in a ring themselves but ringed by jack-in-the-pulpits
> > with deep eggplant-colored stripes.

One notices the line breaks on such words as "the," "and," and "of," and the grammar, a heaping up of clauses for five lines until we arrive at the subject of the sentence, the "I" in the sixth line. The entire poem, all thirty-eight lines of it, is actually a single hurtling sentence, an almost breathless account of what turns out to be breath itself, for as the speaker says:

> These mushrooms of the gods, resembling human organs
> > uprooted, rooted only on the air,
>
> Looking like lungs wrenched from the human body, lungs
> > reversed, not breathing internally
>
> But being the externalization of breath itself, these
> > spicy, twisted cones,
>
> These perforated brown-white asparagus tips—these morels,
> > smelling of wet graham crackers mixed with maple leaves.

One delights in the meticulous specificity of the description and yields to its authority. There is also a playfulness in the occurrence of the word "duff," which came up once at a Cummington dinner party where Smith and his friend and neighbor Richard Wilbur were both at the table. Everyone agreed that it was a miraculously accurate low-frequency word, not something one could use often, but a word that would have its inevitable occasion. Among other things, then, this poem turns out to be Smith's entry in the sweepstakes of which of the poets could use the word first.

Smith's speaker puts the morels in a damp brown paper bag and carries them home.

> . . . you held them
>
> Under cold bubbling water and sliced them with a surgeon's
> > stroke clean through,
>
> And sautéed them over a low flame, butter-brown; and we ate
> > them then and there—

Tasting of the sweet damp woods and of the rain
one inch
above the meadow:

It was like feasting upon air.

The staccato of "stroke clean through" is worth noticing as a mimesis of the act of cutting, as is the rhyme of "there" and "air," with which the poem achieves its music of closure. It is altogether a deft, technical display, and a delicious exhibition of a moment of joy. Inspiration—the drawing in of breath—is what poetry comes from and what, in the end, it is about.

The oddly named title poem of the collection is a reference to the Japanese expression "kanzume," or the "tin can," which is, as the headnote explains, the kind of retreat into which one goes if one has a lot of work to do, especially writing. As Smith's source, Herbert Passin, says in "The Mountain Hermitage: Pages from a Japanese Notebook," "When someone gets off by himself to concentrate, they say, 'He has gone into the tin can.'" The poem is in very long lines with hanging indents, almost biblical in their cadence. It begins:

I have gone into the tin can; not in late spring,
fleeing a stewing,
meat-and-fish smelling city of paper
houses,

Not when wisteria hangs, a purple cloud, robbing
the pines of
their color, have I sought out the gray
plain, the indeterminate
outer edge of a determined world,

Not to an inn nestling astride a waterfall where
two mountains
meet and the misty indecisiveness of
Japanese ink-drawn pines
frames the afternoon, providing from a
sheer bluff an adequate
view of infinity,

But here to the tin can in midwinter: to a sagging
New England
farmhouse in the rock-rooted mountains,
where wind rifles the
cracks,

Here surrounded by crosshatched, tumbling stone
walls, where
the snow plow with its broad orange side-
thrust has outlined
a rutted road,

Where the dimly cracked gray bowl of the sky
rests firmly on the
valley and gum-thick clouds pour out at
the edges,

Where in the hooded afternoon a pock-marked,
porcupine-
quilled landscape fills with snow-swirls,
and the tin can settles
in the snow.

I have gone into the tin can, head high, resolute,
ready to confront
the horrible, black underside of the world.

In an essay on Smith, Dana Gioia remarks that the unit here is what Smith himself calls the "verset," a French term for a long line that is roughly equivalent "to the capacity of breath from full lungs." Gioia also observes, quite rightly, that the poems in *The Tin Can* mark not only the beginning of Smith's free verse but also a new and more direct use of his own life experience. Smith introduces himself as a character. "This new direction," Gioia says, "raises a new set of challenges for the poet. One recalls Louis Simpson's observation on giving up formal poetry and trying to write more personal poems: 'I must work not at techniques, but at improving my character.'" It is, as Simpson and Gioia and Smith know perfectly well, more complicated than that. An improvement in Marcel Proust's character might have meant for a disimprovement in the novel. Gioia says, "Smith's personal work now succeeds or fails on the quality and depth of the experience he describes."

This particular poem describes and enacts the speaker's ordeal during a dark night of the soul and the restoration of health and equipoise that he achieves not by fighting off the depression but by contriving a way of embracing it ever more closely. When wrestling with an angel, one does not let go. The poetics of the transaction are characteristically witty and Smith-like in that the Japanese "tin can" becomes, in one way or another, a nonmetaphorical tin can, first of the kind that children play with.

> In the tin can I hear a murmur of voices speaking of the life in other
> tin cans, of death sifting through them.
>
> A vision of bodies blasted on the black earth; and I think of those
> photographs my father kept from the Nicaraguan Insurrection,
> was it?—that we played with as children on a sun-spotted
> floor—
>
> Brown bodies spread out over the jungle floor, the figures beside
> them wide-eyed and bewildered, toy soldiers in ridiculous
> stances in a meaningless world;
>
> I think of the photographs rubbed vinegar-brown in the sunlight;
> and of how we placed them around us, lined our toy fortress
> with them,
>
> And talked to one another through tin-can telephones, while
> from out the photographs the jungle's green arm tapped our
> small brown shoulders.

The speaker struggles to come to terms with the small details of life that can betray with a perverse tendency to turn nightmarish, and the equipment he brings into the engagement seems unreliable:

> When am I to emerge? Dirt falls; eyes blur; memory confounds;
> multiple voices move furred and batlike round my ears; and
> then no sound—
>
> Only the grating of a pencil over a page—an army of ant words
> swarming up to consciousness.
>
> When will they break through to a bright remembered world, up
> through the top of the tin?
>
> Snow-swirl—hemlocks hunching toward the window—gray-
> black shadow cutting over black, fan shaken over fan . . .
>
> From here the windows open their white mouths to swallow the
> wind-driven snow.
>
> And I remember salmon sky, fine-boned sunsets sweeping the
> spiny mountains; and I have seen the snow
>
> In banks driven back from the road, the black edges scraggly and
> bearded, the snowbanks under the birches like milk from
> buckets overturned and frozen . . .
>
> Will the words rise? Will the poem radiate with morning? Here
> where I see nothing, I have seen the Cyclops-eye ballooning
> over a frozen world. . . .

And just as the reader is on the verge of despair, Smith finds a memory of a sexual encounter in his youth, an incident of which he is at the same time proud and ashamed, exultant and remorseful, and it is strong enough, vivid enough to be, in its odd way, sufficiently life-affirming as to be redemptive:

> O bodies my body has known! Bodies my body has touched and

remembered—in beds, in baths, in
streams, on fields and streets
—will you remember?

Sweet vision of flesh known and loved, lusted
after, cherished,
repulsed, forgotten and remembered, will
you remember my
body buried now and forgotten? . . .

In childhood we played for hours in the sun on a
dump near a
cannery; and the long thin ribbons of tin
rippled round us,
and we ran by the railroad track and into
the backyard behind
the asparagus and through the feathers of
green our bodies
touched and the strips of tin radiated their
rainbows of light—

And our bodies were spiralled with tin and
wondrous with light—

Now out of darkness here from the tin can,
through snow-swirl
and wind-dazzle, let the tin ribbons ride
again and range in
new-found freedom;

Let the tin rip and rustle in the wind; let the
green leaves rise and
rift the wondrous windows, leaving behind
the raging women,
and the sickening mould of money, rust,
and rubble . . .

And the words clean-spun and spiraling orbit that
swift-seeing,
unseen immensity that will never be
contained!

What Smith does, of course, is to take an image and mine it until it yields something surprising, something quite different from what it was at the beginning. This re-vision is the action of the poem, a way of "making good" from his—and the reader's—dismal beginnings. The foray takes him to the boundary between verse and prose, where readers are lulled by the rhetorical waves, so that it is only by an effort of technical scrutiny that one realizes how unusual it is, in the concluding section, to find "rift" as a verb, one of the units in the barrage of "r" sounds ("rip," "rustle," "rise," "rift," "raging," "rust," and "rubble") that gather momentum for the liftoff of the last lines.

Smith's relaxation into these longer lines was not so much a matter of principle, it seems, as of temperament, or of his response to the particular artistic occasion of a particular poetic problem. He has been able at any moment to return to his earlier practice of the small, intricately wrought bijou. Such a poem is "Journey to the Interior" (first appearing in *Collected Poems*), another description of a walk, later and much darker than that of "Quail in Autumn." It is an open-ended metaphor that makes its suggestion in the second line, where the speaker talks explicitly about "the wooded mind in wrath," but the rest is all vehicle to which one can assume a tenor. This short poem, as poised as the best of Emily Dickinson's, is as close to a representation of utter despair as any in contemporary poetry:

He has gone into the forest,
to the wooded mind in wrath;
he will follow out the nettles
and the bindweed path.

He is torn by tangled roots,
he is trapped by mildewed air;
he will feed on alder shoots
and on fungi: in despair

he will pursue each dry creek-bed,
each hot white gully's rough raw stone
till heaven opens overhead
a vast jawbone

and trees around grow toothpick-thin
and a deepening dustcloud swirls about
and every road leads on within
and none leads out.

LATE POETRY

Beginning in *Collected Poems: 1939–1989,* Smith opens a new vein with "The Players," a bizarre but historically accurate account of how, as Smith says in the headnote, in May 1840, during the Second Seminole War, a traveling Shakespearean troupe left their baggage unattended in St. Augustine, Florida, and it was stolen by the Seminoles. The following March, when Chief Coacoochee and his followers appeared at Fort Cummings to discuss a treaty with the commander of the United States forces, Coacoochee (whose name means "The Wild Cat") and his entourage were wearing the feathers and spangled vests that are the basis of the present-day costume of the Seminoles—and that came out of the luggage of the actors. As Smith explains in his headnote, "Hamlet's headgear became the badge of the Seminole Medicine man."

It is an extraordinary occasion and an extraordinary poem, but it is important in other ways—as a harbinger of significant new work, when it appears as part of a seven-poem suite in *The World Below the Window: Poems 1937–1997.* And then, to those seven, Smith added another eleven to make *The Cherokee Lottery: A Sequence of Poems,* which was published in 2000.

One has the sense—and it seems the poet has it as well—that Smith's whole life has been a preparation for *The Cherokee Lottery.* He says in the acknowledgments and notes at the end of the volume:

> The removal of the Southern Indian Tribes—the great American tragedy of the "Trail of Tears"—has been something of an obsession with me since I first discovered seventy years ago that members of my mother's family in Mississippi, Oklahoma, and Arkansas, by reason of their Choctaw blood, claimed to have played a part in it. I have given the details of that discovery in *Army Brat* . . . my memoir about the twenty years (1921–1941) spent growing up in and around Jefferson Barracks, Missouri, just south of St. Louis, the United States Army's first permanent base west of the Mississippi. As the son of an enlisted man, a corporal in the Sixth Infantry Band, I concluded then: "While I was brought up on an Army garrison founded as an outpost in the Indian Wars, I knew that I had forebears on the outside and in the enemy's camp, and that knowledge gave me a new strength to face the limited—and limiting—aspects of military life."

That sense Smith had of being an outsider is important not only for his poetry but more generally for much of contemporary literature. The strategic advantages of being southern (for William Faulkner, Eudora Welty, or Flannery O'Connor) or Jewish (for Saul Bellow, Norman Mailer, or Philip Roth) or black (for Ralph Ellison or James Baldwin) consisted largely of twentieth-century writers' ability to see and feel beyond the limitations of the dominant culture.

The small poem of despair he had written earlier, "Journey to the Interior," Smith puts at the beginning of the volume as a frontispiece, a warning to readers of the mood of what will follow and an invitation to join in the grieving. The next poem is what would be, in a classical epic, the invocation to the muse, but Smith's muse is an Aztec eagle warrior, a

> . . . life-size ceramic man costumed as an eagle,
> . . . .
> preserved because the conquistadors,
> on their arrival in the city
> of the Aztecs, had thrown it into the lake.

Smith describes the figure, which is also represented on the opposite page in a black-and-white photograph, and the rhetorical effect is that one can check to see that his description is absolutely accurate. Readers thus have acquired a certain confidence, or he has achieved a certain authority, and are likelier to believe what Smith says as he goes on with the poem. Then comes the invocation, direct, old-fashioned, and as serious as Homer's or Virgil's:

O Eagle-warrior, surrogate of the sun,
        fly off in my mind now
to circle the sun, that "ascending eagle,"
and with your penetrating eye
and your calligraphic wing-span
            printed high upon the air,
follow the westward movement
           of every vanquished tribe.
O Eagle-warrior, quick-eyed, fierce-beaked,
        tense-taloned,
be their emblem, be their witness, be their scribe.

Smith, however, is not an epic poet, though it may be said that he is stretching the limits of the lyric to their furthest extent. His method is to provide the reader with a series of glimpses and leave those images and cadences to grow into a context in which the artistic whole is larger than the sum of its parts. He has cited Stanley Kunitz's remark about how lyric poets respond "to the changing weathers of a landscape, to the motions of the mind, to the complications and surprises of the human comedy." Smith goes beyond Kunitz in that his weather observations become, finally, a judgment about climate.

The eponymous section of the sequence begins with an account of the outrageous behavior of the citizens of Georgia in 1838 as the Cherokee lands were given out to the whites in the Cherokee lottery:

            When the Cherokees refused to
  leave,
the state set up a lottery
        to rid them of their land:
a clumsy wooden wheel
          sat poised above the great black
numbers painted on bright squares—
         woodpecker red and watermelon
  green,
wild azalea orange
        and morningglory blue—
to designate the farms
         that now were up for grabs:
and while the wheel creaked
        slowly round, the Georgians
danced and sang:
         "All we want in this creation
        is a pretty little girl
        and a big plantation
        way down yonder
        in the Cherokee Nation!"
and laughed until they cried.

In eleven brisk lines General Winfield Scott arrives to declare to the Cherokees that they must leave before the next full moon, and then his troops sweep in with bayonets fixed. The Cherokees, Smith states,

              . . . stripped
of everything they owned,
        at last lined up to go.

Their going is understated, Smith's restraint a combination of artistic good taste and civilized good manners, which turn out to belong more to the Indians than to the white man:

White-haired Going Snake,
        the eighty-year-old chief,
on his pony led the way,
        followed by young men on
  horseback.
Then the women and children,
        with the rustling sound
wind makes in tall dry grass,
        came on, and no one spoke,
no one cried: only the dogs
        howled as if they alone
could voice the nation's grief
        while the procession slowly wound
  its way
off through the tall pines
        over the red clay.

At the moment they began to move,
        a low rumble of distant thunder
broke directly westward
        and a dark spiral cloud rose
above the horizon,
        but the sun was unclouded,
the thunder rolled away,
        and no rain fell.

It is painful to read, and one tries to be literary about it, looking perhaps to those lines of another poet who also came from St. Louis. In *The Waste Land* T. S. Eliot wrote:

> There is not even silence in the mountains
> But dry sterile thunder without rain
> There is not even solitude in the mountains
> But red sullen faces sneer and snarl
> From doors of mudcracked houses.

But Eliot's lines, more general in application, more mannered and decorative, are a refuge from Smith's sterner passage.

Not that Smith disdains the decorative, but he does put literary embellishment to odd and novel uses, and readers have to readjust their expectations. There are gestures that seem almost mannerist and hyperaesthetic, as in the following lines in "The Trail":

> Past corn
>   brown-tasseled
> shredded
>   against gray sky
> yellow hickory
>   bronze oak
> hairy spiraled
>   moss falling
> wind-driven
>   black boughs
> bending over
>   black water
> twisted vines
>   circling
> red clay
>   burrows
> wrinkled
>   leaves blowing
> dark clouds
>   massing
> thunder
>   splitting
> lightning
>   forking
> torsades
>   of rain
> falling

The very short lines are like details in a painting, and if they are almost fussily observed, they seem to reveal that Smith is inviting—or daring?—the reader to look as closely as he has, to see how it was, to take in its fullest horror and dimension. A torsade is a twisted ribbon, usually used as a decoration on a hat, and while he could have said "ribbons of rain," that would not have included the spin and torque he has imagined and that readers are obliged to imagine also. From the rain he then turns to the other downpour:

> tears
> constant flowing
> salt scene
> never-ending
> tear
> trail

The poem continues through another fifteen sections in various moods and timbres, some celebratory, some angry, some contemptuous, and some heartbreakingly sad. In one Smith chooses the point of view of an army lieutenant who guards the Cherokees on their way west, and who tells a story about the act of kindness of a farmer who invites the starving Indians to take what is in his pumpkin field, and the Indians fall upon the pumpkins and gorge themselves. What this scene turns into in the lieutenant's mind—and in Smith's account, of course—is quite vivid, moving, and also surrealistic:

> "What have we done to these people?"
> I cried out . . . And then a silence fell;
> across the dark I saw
> row after row of pumpkins carved and slit,
> their crooked eyes
> and pointed teeth all candle-lit within,
> not pumpkins but death's-heads they were
> with features of the vacant
> hungry faces I had seen,
> stretching to infinity
> and glowing in the dark—
> and glowing still when I awoke—
>
> as they do now, and as they always will.

The grief and the rage are not unexpected. What is truly magisterial—in the root sense, in which

Smith demonstrates his mastery over the material and shows the spiritual poise that is necessary to contemplate this sorry history—is that the poem is, in places, very funny. It is dark humor, like that of Richard Pryor, which turns pain into laughter without ever taming it, and it is all the more persuasive for its acknowledgment of how bizarre life can be.

"The Players," which first appeared in *Collected Poems: 1939–1989,* tells of the encounter of Chief Coacoochee, in Shakespearean costume, with General Walker Keith Armistead, Commander of the United States forces in the swamps of the Everglades that are the Seminoles' allies. As the speaker of the poem says to Armistead:

> You hear the constant sloshing of your troops through ever-present water . . .
>
> . . . and lifted to your steady gaze, the swamp's black mirror,
> cut by alligator-blade and skeletal palmetto,
> swathe of egret feathers, the heron's bony legs,
> dainty stag hoof, dank panther paw, the seething saw grass,
> the fangs of water moccasins, the smear of glutinous eggs,
> a swarm of black flies circling the even blacker water
> like a convocation of Jesuits,
> croaking frog-chorale that kept you company at midnight.

And into this scene comes the preposterous but nonetheless menacing figure:

> Tap . . . tap . . . tap . . .
>   Hamlet advances,
> holding in one hand a skull—
> or is that only a piece of coral from the reef
> with all the perforations of the human brain? . . .
> . . . .
> —A wild wind rakes your fort, a hurricane
> across the tense peninsula . . .
>   and in the silent eye
> a voice that cleaves the quiet water:

> "There will be no surrender, General. There will be no peace;
> only the murderer who waits, only the poetry that kills."

The final section of the poem is unsettling, a fierce satire called "Full Circle: The Connecticut Casino," which is about Foxwoods Resort Casino, the Mashantucket Pequot extravagance north of New London:

> It was with this Casino that the Mashantucket Pequot Nation
> finally tricked the Great White Father Trickster
> or outfoxed the Great White Fox.
> It is no accident that the tribe's logo
> displays a *small* white fox poised against a tree
> perched on a rocky knoll representing Mashantucket,
> this "much wooded land" where the natives once hunted and prospered.

What has come full circle is the gambling wheel, the slot machines and the roulette wheels that are not unlike the "faint ghostly creaking of the clumsy wooden wheel" in the Cherokee lottery. The tables are turned:

> A night of bitter memory but also one of celebration
> for with the Trickster tricked
> and all the gold stolen from the Cherokees in Georgia
> seeming to return now to the Pequots in Connecticut,
> the moonlight releases those legendary Indian mischief makers,
> Rabbit and Coyote, who hop, prance, slink and weave
> through the house with their endless bags of tricks:
> to create greater and greater excitement
> they explode canisters of laughter in every corner
> and in their various guises, in dungarees and dinner jackets,
> in cowboy hats and Reeboks,
> they hover over the gambling tables,
> egging the players on to ever-increasing extravagance

in their betting, helping the Fox People
with the lure of moonlit gold,
to continue to outfox the Great White Fox.

It is an extraordinary achievement, comparable to that of William Heyen's fine *Crazy Horse in Stillness,* which is a longer work but also more diffuse, and which deserves to be much better known than it has been. Smith's poem has its own character, its own strength and delicacy and—what is rare in this extremely civilized poet's work—its own personal rage. Both collections are accomplishments of a high order and are, moreover, crucially important documents in our nation's culture.

CHILDREN'S POETRY

In his interview with Robert Phillips, Smith remarks, "There are some readers who know me *only* as a writer for children while others know nothing of my children's books. But I don't know why those worlds should be so separate." One can speculate about the possible reasons for this disjunction. One plausible explanation has to do with the fact that poems are now so much used as teaching material in English courses—which is not what poets have in mind when they are writing. Teachers of English tend to be serious about what they are doing, and the earnestness of their approach and their enterprise puts light verse and children's verse at a severe disadvantage. The idea that people might read poetry for pleasure or, even more subversively, for fun is a threat to the decorum of the classroom.

Still, the work of so august a figure as T. S. Eliot—whose *Old Possum's Book of Practical Cats* has not only been the most profitable holding of his literary estate but which, at least according to the poet Elizabeth Sewell, is a central part of his oeuvre—is essential to an understanding of his poetics as *The Waste Land* or *Four Quartets.*

Smith has both children and grandchildren, and he can remember something of his own childhood. He has confirmed this knowledge through a careful reading of St.-John Perse, whose *Eloges* are, as Smith points out in his essay on that poet's work, "poems of praise." Recognizing Perse's peculiar vividness, Smith says,

> He recreates from memory the living world of childhood through a reiteration of sensuous images: bright everyday household things are evoked alongside old and indistinct ones like the disparate objects heaped up by a hurricane, grown over with old roots and green vines. The long, winding *versets* themselves—and in this the form is superbly fitted to the subject—suggest the gnarled and twisted lianas reaching out to claim everything in their path.

What poets do is at the same time serious and playful. And the delight young children take in the rhythms and rhyme patterns of English is a quality that may be bruised and battered but, for poets and readers of poetry, has never quite died. Or more accurately, it has never been altogether subjugated by terrible teachers in the primary grades. Smith finds this painful to contemplate. "How natural and harmonious it all is at the beginning," he says in *The Streaks of the Tulip* of children's delight in language,

> and yet what happens along the way later to make poetry to many children the dullest and least enjoyable of literary expressions? It is usually along about the fifth grade in our schools that children decide poetry is not for them. It is then that they are exposed to—and often made to memorize—some insipid lines from which they never recover.

He is perfectly cheerful about relating how he started writing children's poetry. His interest, he says,

> began with a particular child on a special day. When my son David was four years old, I was sitting in the living room of our Greenwich Village

apartment. . . . I was working with a pad on my lap, when David, as four-year-olds will, came parading up and down the room reciting to the rhythm of his step:

A Jack-in-the-Box
Fell in the coffee
And hurt himself.

At first I paid no attention and went on with my work, but he also went on, coming down hard on every syllable again and again. I can't remember whether or not I actually wrote the phrase down, but it certainly stayed with me. It stayed until that night when I lay awake—in a huge, dark, brocaded four-poster bed that made me feel a child again myself. I made up the poem:

A Jack-in-the-Box
On the pantry shelf
Fell in the coffee
And hurt himself.
Nobody looked
To see what had happened:
There by the steaming
Hot urn he lay;
So they picked him up
With the silverware,
And carried him off
On the breakfast tray.

It seems not at all incidental that Smith, as he describes the experience, reveals that he had been made himself to feel a child again. The careful diminution of the poem's rhetoric of the experience of death—which is clearly what it is about—is a kind of pastoral. But while he would have been perfectly capable both before and after the fact of making such an analysis, he was, at the time of composition, almost entirely within the experience. His conscious attention would have been to the prosody, the insertion of that crucial second line with its the pre-rhyme for "himself." The enjambment of the "steaming / Hot urn" keeps the poem from being too predictable and jog-trot in its structure. And the "silverware" and the "breakfast tray" are evocative enough of the trappings of exequies and funerary rites to be suggestive without overwhelming either the poem or the audience for which it is intended.

Another of Smith's well-known children's poems that demonstrates his abilities in the pastoral mode is "The Floor and the Ceiling," which he has included in several collections for children and alongside his adult work in *Collected Poems 1939–1989* and *The World Below the Window: Poems 1937–1997*.

Winter and summer, whatever the weather,
The Floor and the Ceiling were happy together
In a quaint little house on the outskirts of town
With the Floor looking up and the Ceiling
  looking down.

The Floor bought the Ceiling an ostrich-plumed
  hat,
And they dined upon drippings of bacon fat,
Diced artichoke hearts and cottage cheese
And hundreds of other such delicacies.

It starts out as pure whimsy, all charming silliness of the kind that children like, but then:

The years went by as the years they will,
And each little thing was fine until
One evening, enjoying their bacon fat,
The Floor and the Ceiling had a terrible spat.

They argue, insult each other, and while the Floor "settled down, / The Ceiling packed up her gay wallflower gown," and she departs:

Took a coat from the hook and a hat from the
  rack,
And flew out the door—farewell to the Floor!—
And flew out the door, and was seen no more,
And flew out the door, and *never* came back!

In a quaint little house on the outskirts of town,
Now the shutters go bang, and the walls tumble
  down;
And the roses in summer run wild through the
  room,
But blooming for no one—then why should they
  bloom?

> For what is a Floor now that brambles have grown
> Over window and woodwork and chimney of stone?
> For what is a Floor when the Floor stands alone?
> And what is a Ceiling when the Ceiling has flown?

The image of the derelict house is not at all fantastic, and even children can make the connection between houses and households, physical and social structures, a home and the life of a home.

Not all his children's poetry is this dark, of course. *Ho for a Hat* (1964) is cheerful, almost boisterous fun, like Dr. Seuss but with a little more class and panache. *Birds and Beasts* (1990) has a wry Edward Lear–like charm (and includes the striking woodcuts of Jacques Hnizdovsky, whose fine work graces several of Smith's volumes). The important thing is that nowhere in his poetry for children does Smith ever condescend or even relax; he demands of himself work worthy of the kind of elegant child he imagines and, as he suggests in his essay on children's poetry, all but becomes himself.

TRANSLATIONS

Smith is one of the preeminent translators of his time, and readers look at his renditions into English from the French, Italian, Spanish, Russian, Romanian, Swedish, Hungarian, Danish, and Portuguese not only to read the work of those poets he is translating but also to find out about Smith's own tastes and proclivities. As he says in the *New Letters* interview, "No poet should undertake the translation of the work of a foreign poet for whom he feels no affinity. This affinity may be difficult to gauge because one is perhaps drawn to a writer who represents something one lacks, or wishes to fortify, in one's own work."

With some diffidence then, one looks to see what poets have drawn Smith's attention and how their work in his versions seems to be exemplary of his own virtues. As Josephine Jacobsen points out in her *Hollins Critic* essay, Smith

> writes excellent prose, a thing surprisingly rare among poets; and reading his translations of Laforgue's poems, for example, one sees how he is able to reproduce that painter's eye of Laforgue's, that passionately accurate seeing of detail, color, shape, the true *look* of things. When he writes of babies, ". . . their nostrils wide, their eyes glazed by the future . . . ," two sorts of observation mesh. Laforgue said of Corbière that he had "an incurably indelicate ear." Smith and Laforgue share the delicate ear and eye.

What Smith and Laforgue also share is a tendency toward the epigrammatic that they play on and with. Smith's version of Laforgue's poem "Moon Solo" reads in part:

> How cool it is now, how cool,
> And what if now at this very hour
> She also strolls at the edge of some wood
> Drowning her sorrow
> In a wedding of light! . . .
> (And how she loves to stroll at night!)
> Having forgotten the scarf for her throat tonight,
> She is sure to take cold in such cold, clear light!
> Oh, my darling, I beg of you, do take care;
> That cough is more than one can bear.

Dudley Fitts remarks of Smith's translating abilities, "There is such a clear contour to the writing that one rarely feels that one is reading the poet in anything but the original." One can hear even in the English what it was in Laforgue that attracted T. S. Eliot and that enabled him, so that the echoes are apparent in those nervous lines in "The Love Song of J. Alfred Prufrock," and in *The Waste Land*. One can also pick up resonances of Laforgue's style in Smith's precise, almost fussy diction in "The Floor and the Ceiling," in which part of the fun is that he is performing in this stylized manner.

Smith's book *The Traveler's Tree: New and Selected Poems,* which his wife, Sonja Haussmann, translated from English into French under the title *L'Arbre du voyageur,* presumably with his collaboration and certainly with his approval, shows something of that rigorous fidelity that is his goal in translating, and the kinds of liberties he approves of taking in order to maintain that faithfulness. Thus, in the translation, for example, of "Quail in Autumn" into French, the rhyme scheme (hill/chill; foot/root) changes but the tightness of the stanzas remains the same:

> L'automne courbe les arbres noirs vers la colline,
> L'air est d'une froide blancheur, le vent apaisé,
> Les feuilles écarlates ne dansent plus à tes pieds,
> La branche est devenue arbre, l'arbre racine.

The piece is easy and assured and yet has the epigrammatic stylishness and inevitability of a polished performance; but then one realizes that there was the preexisting English poem, and one's admiration, unstinting to begin with, only intensifies. This is the kind of miraculous transformation that only the best—and luckiest—translators are able to manage.

CRITICISM

Aside from his memoir *Army Brat,* some of Smith's intellectual autobiography is available in his one collection of literary criticism, *The Streaks of the Tulip,* now, sadly, out of print. The odd title is from a phrase by Samuel Johnson about how "the business of the poet . . . is to examine, not the individual, but the species; to remark general properties and large appearances; he does not number the streaks of the tulip, or describe the different shades in the verdure of the forest." Smith uses that remark as one of his epigraphs, the other being from Louis MacNeice: "Dr. Johnson has said that the poet is not concerned with the minute particulars, with 'the streaks of the tulip.' This, I thought, was just where he was wrong. . . ."

Smith, as a critic, is useful, interesting, and entertaining—criticism, after all, is a kind of literature and ought to offer its own peculiar pleasures—but it is especially enlightening for readers of his poetry to look at *The Streaks of the Tulip* to see how the sensibility reacts to those works that are congenial or admirable or, sometimes, not. There are essays on poets Smith enjoys and wants to share with others, such as A. D. Hope, who was probably Australia's best poet and who is little known in America. There is the moving tribute to and appreciation of the work of Louise Bogan, with whom Smith collaborated on the fine anthology of poetry for young people, *The Golden Journey* (1965), and who was not much talked of in the late twentieth century but was a marvelous modern metaphysical poet. There is the long essay, first published as a book and recently reprinted, on the Spectra hoax, the prank of Witter Bynner and Arthur Davison Ficke, who invented the school of Spectra writers founded by the fictitious Emanuel Morgan and Anne Knish, whose poetry Bynner and Ficke wrote and got published fairly widely—and reviewed, too—even though it was deliberate nonsense. There are occasional essays such as the one about Smith's service in the Vermont state legislature. And there is the down-in-the-trenches criticism he wrote for *Harper's* annual "Poetry Chronicle" between 1963 and 1966. One can see his likes and dislikes. Just as important, one can see his fairness and generosity, so that when a poet writes something Smith does not like and of which he does not approve, thinking it wrongheaded or even offensive, he is likely to find aspects of the work or of the talent that produced it that are somehow appealing. One explanation for this geniality is that for a reviewer to pick something from the pile of books of poetry to mention in the constrained space of a magazine column, there has to be something important about it, something worth talking about. Still, Smith's generosity of spirit is not manufactured. His preferences and his abilities as a practicing poet seem not to have limited him as a reader and a critic, and this is a measure of his self-confidence. Poets who are unlike him, and poetry that is not like his own, are not threatening.

Paradoxically, his geniality allows him to be, on occasion, deftly sharp in his observation of defects without putting readers off or causing them to suspect him of mean-spiritedness. Elizabeth Bishop's reputation has grown since the 1980s, and although she wrote many fine poems, it is bracing to read Smith's observation in 1966 that

> Miss Bishop overworks the adjective "little": there is something little on almost every page—little pearls, little bottles, little people, little moons, a little filling station. The effect of all this is sometimes to put things in proper perspective, but by its very insistence it often becomes merely peculiar and tiresome.

He reminds us that she "is so fine a poet, so individual an artist, that she can only momentarily disappoint us," but he also prompts his readers to maintain high standards of taste and judgment, which is what criticism ought to do.

In "The Making of Poems," another of the essays in *The Streaks of the Tulip,* Smith alludes to the odd Catalan custom of a poets' competition in Barcelona:

> After the poems have been read aloud, the judges award the prizes in a most unusual fashion. The author of the third best poem receives a rose made of silver, the author of the second best, a rose made of gold, and the author of the best—the most enduring and most original—a real rose.

There are only a few poets who deserve that real rose. William Jay Smith surely is one of them.

Selected Bibliography

WORKS OF WILLIAM JAY SMITH

POETRY

Poems. New York: Banyan Press, 1947.

Celebration at Dark: Poems. London: Hamish Hamilton; New York: Farrar, Straus, 1950.

Poems 1947–1957. Boston: Seymour Lawrence/Little, Brown, 1957.

The Tin Can, and Other Poems. New York: Seymour Lawrence/Delacorte Press, 1966.

New and Selected Poems. New York: Seymour Lawrence/Delacorte Press, 1970.

Venice in the Fog. Greensboro, N.C.: Unicorn Press, 1975.

Journey to the Dead Sea. Omaha, Nebr.: Abattoir, 1979.

The Traveler's Tree: New and Selected Poems. Woodcuts by Jacques Hnizdovsky. New York: Persea, 1980; Manchester, Eng.: Carcanet, 1980.

Collected Translations: Italian, French, Spanish, Portuguese. Woodcuts by Jacques Hnizdovsky. St. Paul, Minn.: New Rivers Press, 1985.

Plain Talk: Epigrams, Epitaphs, Satires, Nonsense, Occasional, Concrete, and Quotidian Poems. New York: Center for Book Arts, 1988.

Collected Poems 1939–1989. New York: Scribners, 1990.

L'Arbre du voyageur. Translated by Sonja Haussmann. Woodcuts by Jacques Hnizdovsky. Marseille: Sud, 1990. (A translation into French of selections from *The Traveler's Tree.*)

Primitif américain: poèmes. Translated by Alain Bosquet. Paris: Belfond, 1993. (A translation into French of selections from *Collected Poems 1939–1989* and *The Traveler's Tree: New and Selected Poems.*)

The World Below the Window: Poems 1937–1997. Baltimore: The Johns Hopkins University Press, 1998.

The Cherokee Lottery: A Sequence of Poems. Willimantic, Conn.: Curbstone Press, 2000.

The Girl in Glass: Love Poems. Woodcuts by Jacques Hnizdovsky. New York: Books & Co., 2002.

POETRY FOR CHILDREN

Laughing Time. Illustrated by Juliet Kepes. Boston: Seymour Lawrence/Little, Brown, 1955; London: Faber and Faber, 1956.

Boy Blue's Book of Beasts. Illustrated by Juliet Kepes. Boston: Seymour Lawrence/Little, Brown, 1957.

Puptents and Pebbles: A Nonsense ABC. Illustrated by Juliet Kepes. Boston: Seymour Lawrence/Little, Brown, 1959; London: Faber and Faber, 1960.

Typewriter Town. New York: Dutton, 1960.

What Did I See? Illustrated by Don Almquist. New York: Crowell-Collier, 1962.

My Little Book of Big and Little. 3 vols. Illustrated by Don Bolognese. Riverside, N.J.: Rutledge, 1963. (Includes *Little Dimity, Big Gumbo,* and *Big and Little.*)

Ho for a Hat. Illustrated by Ivan Chermayeff. Boston: Little, Brown, 1964; rev. ed., illustrated by Lynn Munsinger, 1989.

The Golden Journey: Poems for Young People. Compiled with Louise Bogan. Woodcuts by Fritz Kredel. Chicago: Reilly and Lee, 1965; Chicago: Contemporary Books, 1990.

If I Had a Boat. Illustrated by Don Bolognese. New York: Macmillan, 1966.

Mr. Smith and Other Nonsense. Illustrated by Don Bolognese. New York: Seymour Lawrence/Delacorte Press, 1968.

Around My Room, and Other Poems. Illustrated by Don Madden. New York: Lancelot Press, 1969.

Grandmother Ostrich, and Other Poems. Illustrated by Don Madden. New York: Lancelot Press, 1969.

Laughing Time, and Other Poems. Illustrated by Don Madden. New York: Lancelot Press, 1969.

Laughing Time: Nonsense Poems. Illustrated by Fernando Krahn. New York: Seymour Lawrence/Delacorte Press, 1980.

Laughing Time: Collected Nonsense. Illustrated by Fernando Krahn. New York: Farrar, Straus and Giroux, 1990.

Birds and Beasts. Woodcuts by Jacques Hnizdovsky. Boston: David Godine, 1990.

Behind the King's Kitchen: A Roster of Rhyming Riddles. Compiled with Carol Ra. Woodcuts by Jacques Hnizdovsky. Honesdale, Pa.: Wordsong/Boyds Mills Press, 1992.

TRANSLATIONS

Poems of a Multimillionaire, by Valery Larbaud. New York: Bonacio and Saul with Grove Press, 1955.

Selected Writings of Jules Laforgue. New York: Grove Press, 1956.

Children of the Forest, by Elsa Beskow. New York: Seymour Lawrence/Delacorte Press, 1969.

Two Plays by Charles Bertin: Christopher Columbus and Don Juan. Minneapolis: University of Minnesota Press, 1970.

The Pirate Book, by Lennart Hellsing. Illustrated by Poul Ströyer. New York: Seymour Lawrence/Delacorte Press; London: Benn, 1972.

The Telephone, by Kornei Chukovsky. Translated with Max Hayward. New York: Seymour Lawrence/Delacorte Press, 1977.

Agadir, by Artur Lundkvist. Translated with Leif Sjöberg. Pittsburgh: International Poetry Forum, 1979.

The Pact: My Friendship with Isak Dinesen, by Thorkild Bjørnvig. Translated with Ingvar Schousboe. Baton Rouge: Louisiana State University Press, 1983; London: Souvenir Press, 1984.

Moral Tales, by Jules Laforgue. New York: New Directions, 1985; London: Picador, 1987.

Wild Bouquet: Nature Poems, by Harry Martinson. Translated with Leif Sjöberg. With drawings by the author. Kansas City, Mo.: Bookmark Press, College of Arts and Sciences, University of Missouri–Kansas City, 1985.

An Arrow in the Wall: Selected Poetry and Prose of Andrei Voznesenskii. Edited with F. D. Reeve. Introduction by William Jay Smith. New York: Holt; London: Secker and Warburg, 1986.

Eternal Moment: Selected Poems, by Sándor Weöres. Translated with Alan Dixon et al. Minneapolis: New Rivers; London: Anvil Press, 1988.

The Madman and the Medusa, by Tchicaya U Tam'si. Translated with Sonja Haussmann Smith. Charlottesville: University Press of Virginia, 1989.

Epitaph for Vysotsky, by Andrei Voznesenskii. Roslyn, N.Y.: The Stone House Press, 1990.

Songs of Childhood, by Federico García Lorca. Wood engravings by John De Pol. Roslyn, N.Y.: The Stone House Press, 1994.

Berlin: The City and the Court, by Jules Laforgue. Photographs by Simone Sassen. New York: Turtle Point Press, 1996.

What You Have Almost Forgotten: Selected Poems, by Gyula Illyés. Budapest: Kortárs Kiadó; Willimantic, Conn.: Curbstone Press, 1999. (Edited with an introduction by William Jay Smith.)

OTHER WORKS

The Spectra Hoax. Middletown, Conn.: Wesleyan University Press, 1961; Ashland, Ore.: Story Line Press, 2000. (Criticism.)

Children and Poetry: A Selective, Annotated Bibliography. Compiled with Virginia Haviland. Washington, D.C.: Library of Congress, 1969; rev. ed., 1979.

The Streaks of the Tulip: Selected Criticism. New York: Seymour Lawrence/Delacorte Press, 1972.

Army Brat: A Memoir. New York: Persea, 1980; New York: Penguin, 1981; Ashland, Ore.: Story Line Press, 1990.

CRITICAL AND BIOGRAPHICAL STUDIES

Frank, Elizabeth. "The Pleasures of Formal Poetry." *Atlantic Monthly,* September 1998, pp. 134–137. (Review of *The World Below the Window: Poems 1937–1997.*)

Gioia, Dana. "The Journey of William Jay Smith." *Cumberland Poetry Review* 2, no. 2:35–49 (spring 1983).

Hall, Dorothy Judd. "The Lightness of William Jay Smith." *Southern Humanities Review* (summer 1968).

Jacobsen, Josephine. "The Dark Train and the Green Place: The Poetry of William Jay Smith." *The Hollins Critic* 12, no. 1:1–14 (February 1975). (Includes a bibliography.)

Phillips, Robert. "William Jay Smith at Eighty: An Interview." *New Letters* 65, no. 3:90–119 (1999).

Taylor, Henry. "William Jay Smith: Enter the Dark House." In his *Compulsory Figures: Essays on Recent American Poets.* Baton Rouge: Louisiana State University Press, 1992. Pp. 267–282.

—DAVID R. SLAVITT

Index

Arabic numbers printed in bold-face type refer to extended treatment of a subject.

"A" (Zukofsky), **Supp. III Part 2:** 611, 612, 614, 617, 619, 620, 621, 622, 623, 624, 626, 627, 628, 629, 630, 631; **Supp. IV Part 1:** 154
Aal, Katharyn, **Supp. IV Part 1:** 332
Aaron, Daniel, **IV:** 429; **Supp. I Part 2:** 647, 650
Aaron's Rod (Lawrence), **Supp. I Part 1:** 255
Abacus (Karr), **Supp. XI: 240–242,** 248, 254
Abádi-Nagy, Zoltán, **Supp. IV Part 1:** 280, 289, 291
"Abandoned Newborn, The" (Olds), **Supp. X:** 207
Abbey, Edward, **Supp. VIII:** 42; **Supp. X:** 24, 29, 30, 31, 36; **Supp. XIII: 1–18**
Abbey's Road (Abbey), **Supp. XIII:** 12
Abbott, Edith, **Supp. I Part 1:** 5
Abbott, George, **Supp. IV Part 2:** 585
Abbott, Grace, **Supp. I Part 1:** 5
Abbott, Jack Henry, **Retro. Supp. II:** 210
Abbott, Jacob, **Supp. I Part 1:** 38, 39
Abbott, Lyman, **III:** 293
Abbott, Sean, **Retro. Supp. II:** 213
ABC of Color, An: Selections from Over a Half Century of Writings (Du Bois), **Supp. II Part 1:** 186
ABC of Reading (Pound), **III:** 468, 474–475
"Abdication, An" (Merrill), **Supp. III Part 1:** 326
Abel, Lionel, **Supp. XIII:** 98
Abel, Sam, **Supp. XIII:** 199
Abelard, Peter, **I:** 14, 22
Abeles, Sigmund, **Supp. VIII:** 272
Abercrombie, Lascelles, **III:** 471; **Retro. Supp. I:** 127, 128
Abernathy, Milton, **Supp. III Part 2:** 616
Abhau, Anna. *See* Mencken, Mrs. August (Anna Abhau)
"Ability" (Emerson), **II:** 6
Abish, Walter, **Supp. V:** 44
"Abishag" (Glück), **Supp. V:** 82

"Abortion, The" (Sexton), **Supp. II Part 2:** 682
"Abortions" (Dixon), **Supp. XII:** 153
"About Hospitality" (Jewett), **Retro. Supp. II:** 131
"About Kathryn" (Dubus), **Supp. VII:** 91
About the House (Auden), **Supp. II Part 1:** 24
About Town: "The New Yorker" and the World It Made (Yagoda), **Supp. VIII:** 151
"Above Pate Valley" (Snyder), **Supp. VIII:** 293
Above the River (Wright), **Supp. III Part 2:** 589, 606
"Abraham" (Schwartz), **Supp. II Part 2:** 663
Abraham, Nelson Algren. *See* Algren, Nelson
"Abraham Davenport" (Whittier), **Supp. I Part 2:** 699
"Abraham Lincoln" (Emerson), **II:** 13
Abraham Lincoln: The Prairie Years (Sandburg), **III:** 580, 587–589, 590
Abraham Lincoln: The Prairie Years and the War Years (Sandburg), **III:** 588, 590
Abraham Lincoln: The War Years (Sandburg), **III:** 588, 589–590
"Abraham Lincoln Walks at Midnight" (Lindsay), **Supp. I Part 2:** 390–391
"Abram Morrison" (Whittier), **Supp. I Part 2:** 699
Abramovich, Alex, **Supp. X:** 302, 309
"Absalom" (Rukeyser), **Supp. VI:** 278–279
Absalom, Absalom! (Faulkner), **II:** 64, 65–67, 72, 223; **IV:** 207; **Retro. Supp. I:** 75, 81, 82, 84, 85, 86, 87, 88, 89, 90, 92, 382; **Supp. V:** 261; **Supp. X:** 51
"Absence of Mercy" (Stone), **Supp. V:** 295
"Absentee, The" (Levertov), **Supp. III Part 1:** 284
Absentee Ownership (Veblen), **Supp. I Part 2:** 642
"Absent Thee from Felicity Awhile" (Wylie), **Supp. I Part 2:** 727, 729
"Absolution" (Fitzgerald), **Retro. Supp. I:** 108
"Abuelita's Ache" (Mora), **Supp. XIII:** 218
Abysmal Brute, The (London), **II:** 467
"Academic Story, An" (Simpson), **Supp. IX:** 279–280
"Accident" (Minot), **Supp. VI: 208–209**
"Accident, The" (Southern), **Supp. XI:** 295
"Accident, The" (Strand), **Supp. IV Part 2:** 624
Accident/A Day's News (Wolf), **Supp. IV Part 1:** 310
Accidental Tourist, The (Tyler), **Supp. IV Part 2:** 657, 668–669; **Supp. V:** 227
Accordion Crimes (Proulx), **Supp. VII:** 259–261
"Accountability" (Dunbar), **Supp. II Part 1:** 197, 204
"Accusation, The" (Wright), **Supp. III Part 2:** 595
"Accusation of the Inward Man, The" (Taylor), **IV:** 156
"Accusing Message from Dead Father" (Karr), **Supp. XI:** 244
Ace, Goodman, **Supp. IV Part 2:** 574
Achievement in American Poetry (Bogan), **Supp. III Part 1:** 63–64
Acker, Kathy, **Supp. XII: 1–20**
Ackerman, Diane, **Supp. XIII:** 154
"Acknowledgment" (Lanier), **Supp. I Part 1:** 364
Ackroyd, Peter, **Supp. V:** 233
"Acquaintance in the Heavens, An" (Dillard), **Supp. VI:** 34
"Acquainted with the Night" (Frost), **II:** 155; **Retro. Supp. I:** 137
Across Spoon River (Masters), **Supp. I Part 2:** 455, 457, 459, 460, 466, 474–475, 476
Across the Layers: Poems Old and New

(Goldbarth), **Supp. XII:** 181, **187–189**
Across the River and into the Trees (Hemingway), **I:** 491; **II:** 255–256, 261; **Retro. Supp. I:** 172, **184–185**
"Actfive" (MacLeish), **III:** 18–19, 22
Actfive and Other Poems (MacLeish), **III:** 3, 17–19, 21
Action (Shepard), **Supp. III Part 2:** 446
Active Anthology (Pound), **Supp. III Part 2:** 617
Active Service (Crane), **I:** 409
Acton, Patricia Nassif, **Supp. X:** 233
Actual, The (Bellow), **Retro. Supp. II:** 33
"Actual Experience, Preferred Narratives" (Julier), **Supp. IV Part 1:** 211
Acuff, Roy, **Supp. V:** 335
Ada (Nabokov), **Retro. Supp. I:** 265, 266, 270, 276–277, 278, 279
"Ada" (Stein), **IV:** 43
Ada; or Ardor (Nabokov), **III:** 247
"Adagia" (Stevens), **IV:** 78, 80, 88, 92
"Adam" (Hecht), **Supp. X:** 62
"Adam" (W. C. Williams), **Retro. Supp. I:** 422, 423
"Adam and Eve" (Eugene), **Supp. X:** 204
Adam and Eve" (Shapiro), **Supp. II Part 2:** 712
"Adam and Eve" (Shapiro), **Supp. II Part 2:** 708
Adam Bede (Eliot), **II:** 181
Adamé, Leonard, **Supp. XIII:** 316
Adam & Eve & the City (W. C. Williams), **Retro. Supp. I:** 423
"Adamic Purity as Double Agent" (Whalen-Bridge), **Retro. Supp. II:** 211–212
Adams, Althea. *See* Thurber, Mrs. James (Althea Adams)
Adams, Annie. *See* Fields, Annie Adams
Adams, Brooks, **Supp. I Part 2:** 484
Adams, Charles, **Supp. I Part 2:** 644
Adams, Charles Francis, **I:** 1, 4; **Supp. I Part 2:** 484
Adams, Franklin P., **Supp. I Part 2:** 653; **Supp. IX:** 190
Adams, Henry, **I:** **1–24**, 111, 243, 258; **II:** 278, 542; **III:** 396, 504; **IV:** 191, 349; **Retro. Supp. I:** 53, 59; **Retro. Supp. II:** 207; **Supp. I Part 1:** 299–300, 301, 314; **Supp. I Part 2:** 417, 492, 543, 644; **Supp. II Part 1:** 93–94, 105; **Supp. III Part 2:** 613; **Supp. IV Part 1:** 31, 208
Adams, Henry B., **Supp. I Part 1:** 369
Adams, J. Donald, **IV:** 438

Adams, James Truslow, **Supp. I Part 2:** 481, 484, 486
Adams, John, **I:** 1; **II:** 103, 301; **III:** 17, 473; **Supp. I Part 2:** 483, 506, 507, 509, 510, 511, 517, 518, 520, 524
Adams, John Luther, **Supp. XII:** 209
Adams, John Quincy, **I:** 1, 3, 16–17; **Supp. I Part 2:** 685, 686
Adams, Léonie, **Supp. I Part 2:** 707; **Supp. V:** 79; **Supp. IX:** 229
Adams, Luella, **Supp. I Part 2:** 652
Adams, Mrs. Henry (Marian Hooper), **I:** 1, 5, 10, 17–18
Adams, Phoebe, **Supp. IV Part 1:** 203; **Supp. VIII:** 124
Adams, Samuel, **Supp. I Part 2:** 516, 525
"Ad Castitatem" (Bogan), **Supp. III Part 1:** 50
Addams, Jane, **Supp. I Part 1:** **1–26;** **Supp. XI:** 200, 202
Addams, John Huy, **Supp. I Part 1:** 2
"Addendum" (Wright), **Supp. V:** 339
Addiego, John, **Supp. XII:** 182
Adding Machine, The (Rice), **I:** 479
Adding Machine, The: Selected Essays (Burroughs), **Supp. III Part 1:** 93, 97
Addison, Joseph, **I:** 8, 105, 106–107, 108, 114, 131, 300, 304; **III:** 430
"Addressed to a Political Shrimp, or, Fly upon the Wheel" (Freneau), **Supp. II Part 1:** 267
"Address to My Soul" (Wylie), **Supp. I Part 2:** 729
Address to the Government of the United States on the Cession of Louisiana to the French, An (Brown), **Supp. I Part 1:** 146
"Address to the Scholars of New England" (Ransom), **III:** 491
"Address with Exclamation Points, A" (Simic), **Supp. VIII:** 283
"Adjutant Bird, The" (Banks), **Supp. V:** 5
Adkins, Nelson F., **II:** 20
Adler, Alfred, **II:** 248
Adler, Betty, **III:** 103
Adler, George J., **III:** 81
Adler, Renata, **Supp. X:** 171
Admiral of the Ocean Sea: A Life of Christopher Columbus (Morison), **Supp. I Part 2:** 486–488
"Admirals" (Chabon), **Supp. XI:** 72
"Admonition, An" (Brodsky), **Supp. VIII:** 33
"Adolescence" (Dove), **Supp. IV Part 1:** 245
"Adolescence" (Olds), **Supp. X:** 211

"Adolescence II" (Dove), **Supp. IV Part 1:** 242, 244–245
"Adonais" (Shelley), **II:** 516, 540; **Retro. Supp. II:** 291
Adorno, Theodor, **Supp. I Part 2:** 645, 650; **Supp. IV Part 1:** 301
"Adrienne Rich: The Poetics of Change" (Gelpi), **Supp. I Part 2:** 554
"Adultery" (Banks), **Supp. V:** 15
"Adultery" (Dubus), **Supp. VII:** 85
Adultery and Other Choices (Dubus), **Supp. VII:** 83–85
Adulthood Rites (O. Butler), **Supp. XIII:** 63, **64–65**
Adult Life of Toulouse Lautrec by Henri Toulouse Lautrec, The (Acker), **Supp. XII:** 5, 6, **8–9**
Adventure (London), **II:** 466
Adventures in Ancient Egypt (Goldbarth), **Supp. XII:** 191
Adventures in Value (Cummings), **I:** 430
"Adventures of a Book Reviewer" (Cowley), **Supp. II Part 1:** 137, 142
Adventures of Augie March, The (Bellow), **I:** 144, 147, 149, 150, 151, 152–153, 154, 155, 157, 158–159, 164; **Retro. Supp. II:** 19, 20, **22–23,** 24, 30; **Supp. VIII:** 234, 236–237
Adventures of a Young Man (Dos Passos), **I:** 488, 489, 492
Adventures of Captain Bonneville (Irving), **II:** 312
Adventures of Huckleberry Finn, The (Twain), **I:** 307, 506; **II:** 26, 72, 262, 266–268, 290, 418, 430; **III:** 101, 112–113, 357, 554, 558, 577; **IV:** 198, 201–204, 207; **Retro. Supp. I:** 188; **Retro. Supp. II:** 121; **Supp. I Part 1:** 247; **Supp. IV Part 1:** 247, 257; **Supp. IV Part 2:** 502; **Supp. V:** 131; **Supp. VIII:** 198; **Supp. X:** 230; **Supp. XII:** 16
Adventures of Roderick Random, The (Smollett), **I:** 134
Adventures of the Letter I (Simpson), **Supp. IX:** 266, **273–274**
Adventures of Tom Sawyer, The (Twain), **II:** 26; **III:** 223, 572, 577; **IV:** 199–200, 203, 204; **Supp. I Part 2:** 456, 470
Adventures While Preaching the Gospel of Beauty (Lindsay), **Supp. I Part 2:** 374, 376, 381, 382–384, 389, 399
Adventures with Ed (Loeffler), **Supp. XIII:** 1
Advertisements for Myself (Mailer), **III:** 27, 35–38, 41–42, 45, 46;

Retro. Supp. II: 196, 199, 200, 202, 203, 212; **Supp. IV Part 1:** 90, 284
"Advertisements for Myself on the Way Out" (Mailer), **III:** 37
"Advice to a Prophet" (Wilbur), **Supp. III Part 2:** 555–557
Advice to a Prophet and Other Poems (Wilbur), **Supp. III Part 2:** 554–558
"Advice to a Raven in Russia" (Barlow), **Supp. II Part 1:** 65, 74, 80, 83
Advice to the Lovelorn (film), **Retro. Supp. II:** 346
Advice to the Privileged Orders, Part I (Barlow), **Supp. II Part 1:** 80
"Aeneas and Dido" (Brodsky), **Supp. VIII:** 24–25
"Aeneas at Washington" (Tate), **IV:** 129
Aeneid (Virgil), **I:** 396; **II:** 542; **III:** 124
Aeneus Tacticus, **I:** 136
Aerial View (Barabtarlo), **Retro. Supp. I:** 278
Aeschylus, **I:** 274, 433; **III:** 398; **IV:** 358, 368, 370; **Retro. Supp. I:** 65; **Supp. I Part 2:** 458, 494
Aesop, **I:** 387; **II:** 154, 169, 302; **III:** 587
Aesthetic (Croce), **III:** 610
"Aesthetics" (Mumford), **Supp. II Part 2:** 476
"Aesthetics of Silence, The" (Sontag), **Supp. III Part 2:** 459
"Aesthetics of the Shah" (Olds), **Supp. X:** 205
"Affair at Coulter's Notch, The" (Bierce), **I:** 202
"Affair of Outposts, An" (Bierce), **I:** 202
Affliction (Banks), **Supp. V:** 15, 16
Affluent Society, The (Galbraith), **Supp. I Part 2:** 648
"Aficionados, The" (Carver), **Supp. III Part 1:** 137
"Afloat" (Beattie), **Supp. V:** 29
Afloat and Ashore (Cooper), **I:** 351, 355
Africa, Its Geography, People, and Products (Du Bois), **Supp. II Part 1:** 179
Africa, Its Place in Modern History (Du Bois), **Supp. II Part 1:** 179
"Africa, to My Mother" (D. Diop), **Supp. IV Part 1:** 16
African American Writers (Smith, ed.), **Supp. XIII:** 115, 127
"African Book" (Hemingway), **II:** 259
"African Chief, The" (Bryant), **Supp. I Part 1:** 168
"African Fragment" (Brooks), **Supp. III Part 1:** 85
African Queen, The (film), **Supp. XI:** 17
"African Roots of War, The" (Du Bois), **Supp. II Part 1:** 174
African Silences (Matthiessen), **Supp. V:** 203
African Treasury, An (Hughes, ed.), **Supp. I Part 1:** 344
"Afrika Revolution" (Baraka), **Supp. II Part 1:** 53
"AFRO-AMERICAN LYRIC" (Baraka), **Supp. II Part 1:** 59
After All: Last Poems (Matthews), **Supp. IX:** 155, **167–169**
After and Before the Lightning (Ortiz), **Supp. IV Part 2:** 513
"After a Party" (Salinas), **Supp. XIII:** 327
"After Apple-Picking" (Frost), **Retro. Supp. I:** 126, 128
"After Arguing against the Contention That Art Must Come from Discontent" (Stafford), **Supp. XI:** 327
"After Dark" (Rich), **Retro. Supp. II:** 283–284
After Experience (Snodgrass), **Supp. VI:** 314–316, 317
"After great pain, a formal feeling comes" (Dickinson), **Retro. Supp. I:** 37
"After Hearing a Waltz by Bartók" (Lowell), **II:** 522
After Henry (Didion), **Supp. IV Part 1:** 195, 196, 199, 207, 208, 211
"After Henry" (Didion), **Supp. IV Part 1:** 211
"After Holbein" (Wharton), **IV:** 325; **Retro. Supp. I:** 382
After Ikkyu and Other Poems (Harrison), **Supp. VIII:** 42
"After-Image" (Caldwell), **I:** 309
After-Images: Autobiographical Sketches (Snodgrass), **Supp. VI:** 314, **319–323**, 324, 326–327
After I's (Zukofsky), **Supp. III Part 2:** 628, 629
Afterlife (Monette), **Supp. X:** 153
Afterlife (Updike), **Retro. Supp. I:** 322
Afterlife, The (Levis), **Supp. XI:** 259, **260–264**
"After Magritte" (McClatchy), **Supp. XII:** 264
"After Making Love" (Dunn), **Supp. XI:** 153
Aftermath (Longfellow), **II:** 490
"Aftermath" (Longfellow), **II:** 498
"Afternoon" (Ellison), **Supp. II Part 1:** 238
"Afternoon at MacDowell" (Kenyon), **Supp. VII:** 159
"Afternoon Miracle, An" (O. Henry), **Supp. II Part 1:** 390
Afternoon of a Faun (Hearon), **Supp. VIII: 63–64**
Afternoon of an Author: A Selection of Uncollected Stories and Essays (Fitzgerald), **II:** 94
"Afternoon of a Playwright" (Thurber), **Supp. I Part 2:** 620
Afternoon of the Unreal (Salinas), **Supp. XIII:** 311, **316–318**
"Afternoon with the Old Man, An" (Dubus), **Supp. VII:** 84
"After Punishment Was Done with Me" (Olds), **Supp. X:** 213
"After Reading *Barely and Widely,*" (Zukofsky), **Supp. III Part 2:** 625, 631
"After Reading 'In the Clearing' for the Author, Robert Frost" (Corso), **Supp. XII:** 130
"After Reading *Mickey in the Night Kitchen* for the Third Time before Bed" (Dove), **Supp. IV Part 1:** 249
"After Reading Tu Fu, I Go Outside to the Dwarf Orchard" (Wright), **Supp. V:** 343
"After Reading Wang Wei, I Go Outside to the Full Moon" (Wright), **Supp. V:** 343
After Shocks, Near Escapes (Dobyns), **Supp. XIII: 80–82**
"After Song, An" (W. C. Williams), **Retro. Supp. I:** 413
After Strange Gods (Eliot), **I:** 588
"After the Alphabets" (Merwin), **Supp. III Part 1:** 356
"After the Argument" (Dunn), **Supp. XI:** 149
"After the Burial" (Lowell), **Supp. I Part 2:** 409
"After the Curfew" (Holmes), **Supp. I Part 1:** 308
"After the Death of John Brown" (Thoreau), **IV:** 185
"After the Denim" (Carver), **Supp. III Part 1:** 144
"After the Dentist" (Swenson), **Supp. IV Part 2:** 645
After the Fall (A. Miller), **III:** 148, 149, 156, 161, 162, 163–165, 166
"After the Fire" (Merrill), **Supp. III Part 1:** 328
After the Fox (film), **Supp. IV Part 2:** 575
After the Genteel Tradition (Cowley),

Supp. II Part 1: 143
"After the Heart's Interrogation" (Komunyakaa), Supp. XIII: 120
After the Lost Generation: A Critical Study of the Writers of Two Wars (Aldridge), Supp. IV Part 2: 680
"After the Night Office—Gethsemani Abbey" (Merton), Supp. VIII: 195–196
"After the Persian" (Bogan), Supp. III Part 1: 64
"After the Pleasure Party" (Melville), III: 93
"After the Resolution" (Dunn), Supp. XI: 151
After the Stroke (Sarton), Supp. VIII: 264
"After the Surprising Conversions" (Lowell), I: 544, 545; II: 550; Retro. Supp. II: 187
"After 37 Years My Mother Apologizes for My Childhood" (Olds), Supp. X: 208
"Afterthoughts on the Rosenbergs" (Fiedler), Supp. XIII: 99
"After Twenty Years" (Rich), Supp. I Part 2: 559–560
"Afterwake, The" (Rich), Supp. I Part 2: 553
"Afterward" (Wharton), Retro. Supp. I: 372
"After Working Long" (Kenyon), Supp. VII: 170
"After Yitzl" (Goldbarth), Supp. XII: 186
"After You, My Dear Alphonse" (Jackson), Supp. IX: 119
"Again" (Dixon), Supp. XII: 157
"Again, Kapowsin" (Hugo), Supp. VI: 141
"Against" (Goldbarth), Supp. XII: 193
"Against Decoration" (Karr), Supp. XI: 248
Against Interpretation (Sontag), Supp. III Part 2: 451, 455
"Against Interpretation" (Sontag), Supp. III Part 2: 456–458, 463
"Against Modernity" (Ozick), Supp. V: 272
"Against Nature" (Karr), Supp. XI: 243
Against Nature (Updike), Retro. Supp. I: 323
"Against the Crusades" (Stern), Supp. IX: 300
Against the Current: As I Remember F. Scott Fitzgerald (Kroll Ring), Supp. IX: 63
Agapida, Fray Antonio (pseudonym). *See* Irving, Washington

"Agassiz" (Lowell), Supp. I Part 2: 414, 416
Agassiz, Louis, II: 343; Supp. I Part 1: 312; Supp. IX: 180
Agee, Emma, I: 26
Agee, James, I: **25–47**, 293; IV: 215; Supp. IX: 109
"Agent, The" (Wilbur), Supp. III Part 2: 557–561
Age of Anxiety, The (Auden), Supp. II Part 1: 2, 19, 21
"Age of Conformity, The" (Howe), Supp. VI: 117
Age of Grief, The: A Novella and Stories (Smiley), Supp. VI: 292, **299–301**
Age of Innocence, The (Wharton), IV: 320–322, 327–328; Retro. Supp. I: 372, 374, **380–381**; Supp. IV Part 1: 23
Age of Longing, The (Koestler), I: 258
Age of Reason, The (Paine), Supp. I Part 2: 503, 515–517, 520
"Age of Strolling, The" (Stern), Supp. IX: 297
"Ages, The" (Bryant), Supp. I Part 1: 152, 155, 166, 167
"Aging" (Jarrell), II: 388
Aging and Gender in Literature (George), Supp. IV Part 2: 450
"Agio Neró" (Mora), Supp. XIII: 224
"Agitato ma non Troppo" (Ransom), III: 493
"Agnes of Iowa" (Moore), Supp. X: 165, 178
Agnes of Sorrento (Stowe), Supp. I Part 2: 592, 595–596
Agnon, S. Y., Supp. V: 266
"Agosta the Winged Man and Rasha the Black Dove" (Dove), Supp. IV Part 1: 246–247
Agrarian Justice (Paine), Supp. I Part 2: 517–518
"Agricultural Show, The" (McKay), Supp. X: 139
Agua Fresca: An Anthology of Raza Poetry (Rodríguez, ed.), Supp. IV Part 2: 540
Agua Santa/Holy Water (Mora), Supp. XIII: **222–225**
Agüero Sisters, The (García), Supp. XI: **185–190**
Aguiar, Sarah Appleton, Supp. XIII: 30
Ah, Wilderness! (O'Neill), III: 400–401; Supp. IV Part 2: 587
Ah, Wilderness!: The Frontier in American Literature (Humphrey), Supp. IX: 104
Ahearn, Barry, Retro. Supp. I: 415

Ahearn, Frederick L., Jr., Supp. XI: 184
Ahearn, Kerry, Supp. IV Part 2: 604
Ahmed Arabi Pasha, I: 453
Ahnebrink, Lars, III: 328
Ah Sin (Harte), Supp. II Part 1: 354–355
"Ah! Sun-flower" (Blake), III: 19
AIDS and Its Metaphors (Sontag), Supp. III Part 2: 452, 466–468
Aids to Reflection (Coleridge), II: 10
Aiieeeee! An Anthology of Asian-American Writers (The Combined Asian Resources Project), Supp. X: 292
Aiken, Conrad, I: **48–70**, 190, 211, 243; II: 55, 530, 542; III: 458, 460; Retro. Supp. I: 55, 56, 57, 58, 60, 62; Supp. X: 50, 115
"Aim Was Song, The" (Frost), Retro. Supp. I: 133
Ainsworth, Linda, Supp. IV Part 1: 274
Ainsworth, William, III: 423
Air-Conditioned Nightmare, The (H. Miller), III: 186
Airing Dirty Laundry (Reed), Supp. X: 241
"Air Plant, The" (Crane), I: 401
Air Raid: A Verse Play for Radio (MacLeish), III: 21
"Airs above the Ground" (Sarton), Supp. VIII: 261
Air Tight: A Novel of Red Russia. See We the Living (Rand)
"Airwaves" (Mason), Supp. VIII: 146
Airways, Inc. (Dos Passos), I: 482
Aitken, Robert, Supp. I Part 2: 504
Akhmadulina, Bella, Supp. III Part 1: 268
Akhmatova, Anna, Supp. III Part 1: 268, 269; Supp. VIII: 20, 21, 25, 27, 30
Akhmatova Translations, The (Kenyon), Supp. VII: 160
"Akhnilo" (Salter), Supp. IX: 260
Aksenev, Vasily P., Retro. Supp. I: 278
"Al Aaraaf" (Poe), III: 426–427
Al Aaraaf, Tamerlane, and Minor Poems (Poe), III: 410
Alarcón, Justo, Supp. IV Part 2: 538, 539, 540
À la Recherche du Temps Perdu (Proust), IV: 428
"Alastor" (Shelley), Supp. I Part 2: 728
"Alatus" (Wilbur), Supp. III Part 2: 563

"Alba" (Creeley), **Supp. IV Part 1:** 150
Albee, Edward, **I: 71–96,** 113; **II:** 558, 591; **III:** 281, 387; **IV:** 4, 230; **Retro. Supp. II:** 104; **Supp. VIII:** 331; **Supp. XIII:** 196, 197
Albers, Joseph, **Supp. IV Part 2:** 621
Albright, Margery, **Supp. I Part 2:** 613
"Album, The" (Morris), **III:** 220
Alcestiad, The (Wilder), **IV:** 357, 374
"Alchemist, The" (Bogan), **Supp. III Part 1:** 50
"Alchemist in the City, The" (Hopkins), **Supp. IV Part 2:** 639
"Alcmena" (Winters), **Supp. II Part 2:** 801
Alcott, Abba. *See* Alcott, Mrs. Amos Bronson (Abigail May)
Alcott, Amos Bronson, **II:** 7, 225; **IV:** 172, 173, 184; **Retro. Supp. I:** 217; **Supp. I Part 1:** 28, 29–32, 35, 39, 41, 45; **Supp. II Part 1:** 290
Alcott, Anna. *See* Pratt, Anna
Alcott, Louisa May, **IV:** 172; **Supp. I Part 1: 28–46; Supp. IX:** 128
Alcott, May, **Supp. I Part 1:** 41
Alcott, Mrs. Amos Bronson (Abigail May), **IV:** 184; **Supp. I Part 1:** 29, 30, 31, 32, 35
Alcuin: A Dialogue (Brown), **Supp. I Part 1:** 126–127, 133
Alden, Hortense. *See* Farrell, Mrs. James T. (Hortense Alden)
Alden, John, **I:** 471; **II:** 502–503
Aldington, Mrs. Richard. *See* Doolittle, Hilda
Aldington, Perdita, **Supp. I Part 1:** 258
Aldington, Richard, **II:** 517; **III:** 458, 459, 465, 472; **Retro. Supp. I:** 63, 127; **Supp. I Part 1:** 257–262, 270
Aldrich, Thomas Bailey, **II:** 400; **Supp. II Part 1:** 192
Aldrich, Tom, **Supp. I Part 2:** 415
Aldridge, John W., **Supp. I Part 1:** 196; **Supp. IV Part 1:** 286; **Supp. IV Part 2:** 680, 681; **Supp. VIII:** 189; **Supp. XI:** 228
Aleck Maury Sportsman (Gordon), **II:** 197, 200, 203–204
Alegría, Claribel, **Supp. IV Part 1:** 208
Aleichem, Sholom, **IV:** 3, 10; **Supp. IV Part 2:** 585
"Alert Lovers, Hidden Sides, and Ice Travelers: Notes on Poetic Form and Energy" (Dunn), **Supp. XI:** 153
"Ale[009a] Debeljak" (Simic), **Supp. VIII:** 279
"Alex" (Oliver), **Supp. VII:** 232

Alexander, George, **II:** 331
Alexander, Michael, **Retro. Supp. I:** 293
"Alexander Crummell Dead" (Dunbar), **Supp. II Part 1:** 207, 208–209
Alexander's Bridge (Cather), **I:** 313, 314, 316–317, 326; **Retro. Supp. I:** 1, 6, 7, 8
Alexander the Great, **IV:** 322
"Alexandra" (Cather), **Retro. Supp. I:** 7, 9, 17
Alexandrov, V. E., **Retro. Supp. I:** 270
Algonquin Round Table, **Supp. IX:** 190, 191, 197
Algren, Nelson, **I:** 211; **Supp. V:** 4; **Supp. IX: 1–18; Supp. XII:** 126; **Supp. XIII:** 173
Alhambra, The (Irving), **II:** 310–311
Alias Grace (Atwood), **Supp. XIII:** 20, **31–32**
"Alice Doane's Appeal" (Hawthorne), **II:** 227
Alice in Wonderland (Carroll), **Supp. I Part 2:** 622
"Alicia and I Talking on Edna's Steps" (Cisneros), **Supp. VII:** 64
"Alicia Who Sees Mice" (Cisneros), **Supp. VII:** 60
Alison, Archibald, **Supp. I Part 1:** 151, 159
Alison's House (Glaspell), **Supp. III Part 1:** 182, 188, 189
Alive and Writing: Interviews with American Authors of the 1980s (McCaffery and Gregory), **Supp. X:** 260
"Alki Beach" (Hugo), **Supp. VI:** 135
ALL: The Collected Poems, 1956–1964 (Zukofsky), **Supp. III Part 2:** 630
ALL: The Collected Short Poems, 1923–1958 (Zukofsky), **Supp. III Part 2:** 629
"All Around the Town" (Benét), **Supp. XI:** 48, 58
All at Sea (Lardner), **II:** 427
"All Boy" (Rawlings), **Supp. X:** 222
Allegiances (Stafford), **Supp. XI: 322–323,** 329
"Allegory of the Cave" (Dunn), **Supp. XI:** 150
Allen, Brooke, **Supp. VIII:** 153
Allen, Dick, **Supp. IX:** 279
Allen, Donald, **Supp. VIII:** 291; **Supp. XIII:** 112
Allen, Frank, **Supp. XI:** 126; **Supp. XII:** 186
Allen, Frederick Lewis, **Supp. I Part 2:** 655
Allen, Gay Wilson, **IV:** 352; **Supp. I Part 2:** 418

Allen, Paula Gunn. *See* Gunn Allen, Paula
Allen, Walter, **I:** 505; **III:** 352; **Supp. IV Part 2:** 685; **Supp. IX:** 231
Allen, Woody, **Supp. I Part 2:** 607, 623; **Supp. IV Part 1:** 205; **Supp. X:** 164; **Supp. XI:** 307
"Aller et Retour" (Barnes), **Supp. III Part 1:** 36
Aller Retour New York (H. Miller), **III:** 178, 182, 183
Allessandrini, Goffredo, **Supp. IV Part 2:** 520
Alleys of Eden, The (R. O. Butler), **Supp. XII:** 62, **62–64,** 68
All God's Children Need Traveling Shoes (Angelou), **Supp. IV Part 1:** 2, 9–10, 12–13, 17
All God's Chillun Got Wings (O'Neill), **III:** 387, 391, 393–394
All Gone (Dixon), **Supp. XII:** 148, 149
"All Hallows" (Glück), **Supp. V:** 82
"All I Can Remember" (Jackson), **Supp. IX:** 115
"Alligators, The" (Updike), **IV:** 219
"ALL IN THE STREET" (Baraka), **Supp. II Part 1:** 53
"All I Want" (Tapahonso), **Supp. IV Part 2:** 508
"All Little Colored Children Should Play the Harmonica" (Patchett), **Supp. XII:** 309
"All Mountains" (Doolittle), **Supp. I Part 1:** 271
All My Friends Are Going to Be Strangers (McMurtry), **Supp. V:** 224, 228, 229
All My Pretty Ones (Sexton), **Supp. II Part 2:** 678, 679–683
"All My Pretty Ones" (Sexton), **Supp. II Part 2:** 681–682
"All My Sad Captains" (Jewett), **Retro. Supp. II:** 134
All My Sons (A. Miller), **III:** 148, 149, 150, 151–153, 154, 155, 156, 158, 159, 160, 164, 166
"All Night, All Night" (Schwartz), **Supp. II Part 2:** 665
All Night Long (Caldwell), **I:** 297
"All Our Lost Children: Trauma and Testimony in the Performance of Childhood" (Pace), **Supp. XI:** 245
"All Out" (Hecht), **Supp. X:** 72
All Over (Albee), **I:** 91–94
"Allowance" (Minot), **Supp. VI:** 206, 207–208
"Alloy" (Rukeyser), **Supp. VI:** 279
"All Parrots Speak" (Bowles), **Supp. IV Part 1:** 89
Allport, Gordon, **II:** 363–364

All Quiet on the Western Front (Remarque), **Supp. IV Part 1:** 380, 381
"ALL REACTION IS DOOMED-!-!-!" (Baraka), **Supp. II Part 1:** 59
"All Revelation" (Frost), **II:** 160–162
"All Souls" (Wharton), **IV:** 315–316; **Retro. Supp. I:** 382
"All Souls' Night" (Yeats), **Supp. X:** 69
All Souls' Rising (Bell), **Supp. X:** 12, **13–16,** 17
"All-Star Literary Vaudeville" (Wilson), **IV:** 434–435
Allston, Washington, **II:** 298
All Stories Are True (Wideman), **Supp. X:** 320
"All That Is" (Wilbur), **Supp. III Part 2:** 563
"All the Bearded Irises of Life: Confessions of a Homospiritual" (Walker), **Supp. III Part 2:** 527
"All the Beautiful Are Blameless" (Wright), **Supp. III Part 2:** 597
All the Dark and Beautiful Warriors (Hansberry), **Supp. IV Part 1:** 360, 374
All the Days and Nights: The Collected Stories (Maxwell), **Supp. VIII:** 151, 158, 169
"All the Dead Dears" (Plath), **Retro. Supp. II:** 246; **Supp. I Part 2:** 537
All the Good People I've Left Behind (Oates), **Supp. II Part 2:** 510, 522, 523
"All the Hippos Were Boiled in Their Tanks" (Burroughs and Kerouac), **Supp. III Part 1:** 94
All the King's Men (Warren), **I:** 489; **IV:** 243, 248–249, 252; **Supp. V:** 261; **Supp. VIII:** 126; **Supp. X:** 1
All the Little Live Things (Stegner), **Supp. IV Part 2:** 599, 604, 605, 606, 609–610, 611, 613
All the Pretty Horses (film), **Supp. VIII:** 175
All the Pretty Horses (McCarthy), **Supp. VIII:** 175, **182–183,** 188
All the Sad Young Men (Fitzgerald), **II:** 94; **Retro. Supp. I:** 108
"All the Time in the World" (Dubus), **Supp. VII:** 91
"All the Way to Flagstaff, Arizona" (Bausch), **Supp. VII:** 47, 49
"All This and More" (Karr), **Supp. XI:** 243
"All Too Real" (Vendler), **Supp. V:** 189
All-True Travels and Adventures of Lidie Newton (Smiley), **Supp. VI:** 292, **305–307**
All We Need of Hell (Crews), **Supp. XI:** 114
Almack, Edward, **Supp. IV Part 2:** 435
al-Maghut, Muhammad, **Supp. XIII:** 278
"Almanac" (Swenson), **Supp. IV Part 2:** 641
Almanac of the Dead (Silko), **Supp. IV Part 2:** 558–559, 560, 561, 570–571
Almon, Bert, **Supp. IX:** 93
Almost Revolution, The (Priaulx and Ungar), **Supp. XI:** 228
Alnilam (Dickey), **Supp. IV Part 1:** 176, 186, 188–189
"Alone" (Levine), **Supp. V:** 184, 185, 186
"Alone" (Poe), **Retro. Supp. II:** 266
"Alone" (Singer), **IV:** 15
"Alone" (Winters), **Supp. II Part 2:** 786, 811
Aloneness (Brooks), **Supp. III Part 1:** 85, 86
Alone with America (Corso), **Supp. XII:** 131
Alone with America (Howard), **Supp. IX:** 326
"Along the Color Line" (Du Bois), **Supp. II Part 1:** 173
Along the Illinois (Masters), **Supp. I Part 2:** 472
"Alphabet" (Nye), **Supp. XIII:** 283
Alphabet, An (Doty), **Supp. XI:** 120
Alphabet of Grace, The (Buechner), **Supp. XII:** 52
"Alphabet of My Dead, An" (Pinsky), **Supp. VI:** 235, 250
"Alphabet of Subjects, An" (Zukofsky), **Supp. III Part 2:** 624
"Alpine Christ, The" (Jeffers), **Supp. II Part 2:** 415, 419
Alpine Christ and Other Poems, The (Jeffers), **Supp. II Part 2:** 419
"Alpine Idyll, An" (Hemingway), **II:** 249; **Retro. Supp. I:** 176
Al Que Quiere! (W. C. Williams), **Retro. Supp. I:** 414, 416, **417,** 428
Alsop, Joseph, **II:** 579
"Altar, The" (Herbert), **Supp. IV Part 2:** 646
"Altar, The" (MacLeish), **III:** 4
"Altar Boy" (Fante), **Supp. XI:** 160, 164
"Altar of the Dead, The" (James), **Retro. Supp. I:** 229
"Altars in the Street, The" (Levertov), **Supp. III Part 1:** 280
Alter, Robert, **Supp. XII:** 167

Altgeld, John Peter, **Supp. I Part 2:** 382, 455
Althea (Masters), **Supp. I Part 2:** 455, 459
Altick, Richard, **Supp. I Part 2:** 423
Altieri, Charles, **Supp. VIII:** 297, 303
Altman, Robert, **Supp. IX:** 143
"Altra Ego" (Brodsky), **Supp. VIII:** 31–32
A Lume Spento (Pound), **Retro. Supp. I:** 283, 285
"Aluminum House" (F. Barthelme), **Supp. XI:** 26
Alvares, Mosseh, **Supp. V:** 11
Alvarez, A., **Supp. I Part 2:** 526, 527; **Supp. II Part 1:** 99; **Supp. IX:** 248
Alvarez, Julia, **Supp. VII:** 1–21; **Supp. XI:** 177
Always Outnumbered, Always Outgunned (Mosley), **Supp. XIII:** 242
"Always the Stories" (Ortiz), **Supp. IV Part 2:** 499, 500, 502, 504, 512
Always the Young Strangers (Sandburg), **III:** 577–578, 579
"Amahl and the Night Visitors: A Guide to the Tenor of Love" (Moore), **Supp. X:** 167
"Am and Am Not" (Olds), **Supp. X:** 212
"Amanita, The" (Francis), **Supp. IX:** 81
Amaranth (Robinson), **III:** 509, 510, 512, 513, 522, 523
Amazing Adventures of Kavalier and Clay, The (Chabon), **Supp. XI:** 68, 76, **77–80**
Amazons: An Intimate Memoir by the First Woman to Play in the National Hockey League (DeLillo), **Supp. VI:** 2
Ambassadors, The (H. James), **II:** 320, 333–334, 600; **III:** 517; **IV:** 322; **Retro. Supp. I:** 215, 218, 219, 220, 221, **232–233**
Ambelain, Robert, **Supp. I Part 1:** 260, 273, 274
"Ambition Bird, The" (Sexton), **Supp. II Part 2:** 693
Ambler, Eric, **III:** 57
Ambrose Holt and Family (Glaspell), **Supp. III Part 1:** 175, 181, 184, 187, 188
"Ambrose Seyffert" (Masters), **Supp. I Part 2:** 464
"Ambush" (Komunyakaa), **Supp. XIII:** 122
Amen Corner, The (Baldwin), **Retro. Supp. II:** 5, 7; **Supp. I Part 1:** 48, 51, 54, 55, 56
America (Benét), **Supp. XI:** 46, 47, 51

"America" (Ginsberg), **Supp. II Part 1:** 58–59, 317
"America" (song), **IV:** 410
"America, America!" (poem) (Schwartz), **Supp. II Part 2:** 665
"America, Seen Through Photographs, Darkly" (Sontag), **Supp. III Part 2:** 464
America: The Story of a Free People (Commager and Nevins), **I:** 253
"America! America!" (story) (Schwartz), **Supp. II Part 2:** 640, 658–659, 660
America and Americans (Steinbeck), **IV:** 52
"America and the Vidal Chronicles" (Pease), **Supp. IV Part 2:** 687
America as a Civilization (Lerner), **III:** 60
"America Independent" (Freneau), **Supp. II Part 1:** 261
America Is Worth Saving (Dreiser), **Retro. Supp. II:** 96
American, The (James), **I:** 226; **II:** 326–327, 328, 331, 334; **IV:** 318; **Retro. Supp. I:** 220, **221**, 228, 376, 381
Americana (DeLillo), **Supp. VI:** 2, 3, 5, 6, 8, 13, 14
American Adam, The (R. W. B. Lewis), **II:** 457–458; **Supp. XIII:** 93
American Almanac (Leeds), **II:** 110
American Anthem (Doctorow and Suares), **Supp. IV Part 1:** 234
"American Apocalypse" (Gunn Allen), **Supp. IV Part 1:** 325
American Blood, (Nichols), **Supp. XIII:** 268
American Blues (T. Williams), **IV:** 381, 383
American Caravan: A Yearbook of American Literature (Mumford, ed.), **Supp. II Part 2:** 482
American Cause, The (MacLeish), **III:** 3
American Childhood, An (Dillard), **Supp. VI:** **19–21**, 23, 24, 25, 26, 30, 31
"American Childhood in the Dominican Republic, An" (Alvarez), **Supp. VII:** 2, 5
American Child Supreme, An: The Education of a Liberation Ecologist (Nichols), **Supp. XIII:** 256, 257, 258, 264, 265, 266, 267, 268, 269
American Claimant, The (Twain), **IV:** 194, 198–199
American Crisis I (Paine), **Supp. I Part 2:** 508
American Crisis II (Paine), **Supp. I Part 2:** 508
American Crisis XIII (Paine), **Supp. I Part 2:** 509
"American Critic, The" (J. Spingarn), **I:** 266
American Democrat, The (Cooper), **I:** 343, 346, 347, 353
American Diary (Webb), **Supp. I Part 1:** 5
American Drama since World War II (Weales), **IV:** 385
American Dream, An (Mailer), **III:** 27, 33–34, 35, 39, 41, 43, 44; **Retro. Supp. II:** 203, **204–205**
American Dream, The (Albee), **I:** 74–76, 77, 89, 94
"American Dreams" (Simpson), **Supp. IX:** 274
American Earth (Caldwell), **I:** 290, 308
"American Emperors" (Poirier), **Supp. IV Part 2:** 690
American Exodus, An (Lange and Taylor), **I:** 293
American Experience, The (Parkes), **Supp. I Part 2:** 617–618
American Express (Corso), **Supp. XII:** 129
"American Express" (Salter), **Supp. IX:** 260–261
"American Fear of Literature, The" (Lewis), **II:** 451
American Fictions (Hardwick), **Supp. X:** 171
American Fictions, 1940–1980 (Karl), **Supp. IV Part 1:** 384
"American Financier, The" (Dreiser), **II:** 428
American Folkways (book series), **I:** 290
American Heroine: The Life and Legend of Jane Addams (Davis), **Supp. I Part 1:** 1
American Historical Novel, The (Leisy), **Supp. II Part 1:** 125
"American Horse" (Erdrich), **Supp. IV Part 1:** 333
American Humor (Rourke), **IV:** 339, 352
American Hunger (Wright), **Supp. IV Part 1:** 11
American Indian Anthology, An (Tvedten, ed.), **Supp. IV Part 2:** 505
"American Indian Women: At the Center of Indigenous Resistance in Contemporary North America" (Jaimes and Halsey), **Supp. IV Part 1:** 331
"American in England, An" (Wylie), **Supp. I Part 2:** 707

American Jitters, The: A Year of the Slump (Wilson), **IV:** 427, 428
American Journal (Hayden), **Supp. II Part 1:** 367
"American Land Ethic, An" (Momaday), **Supp. IV Part 2:** 488
American Landscape, The, **Supp. I Part 1:** 157
American Language, The (Mencken), **II:** 289, 430; **III:** 100, 104, 105, 108, 111, 119–120
American Language, The: Supplement One (Mencken), **III:** 111
American Language, The: Supplement Two (Mencken), **III:** 111
"American Letter" (MacLeish), **III:** 13
"American Liberty" (Freneau), **Supp. II Part 1:** 257
American Literary History (Harrison), **Supp. VIII:** 37
American Mercury, **Supp. XI:** 163, 164
American Mind, The (Commager), **Supp. I Part 2:** 650
American Moderns: From Rebellion to Conformity (Geismar), **Supp. IX:** 15; **Supp. XI:** 223
"American Names" (Benét), **Supp. XI:** 47
American Nature Writers (Elder, ed.), **Supp. IX:** 25
American Nature Writers (Winter), **Supp. X:** 104
American Negro, The (W. H. Thomas), **Supp. II Part 1:** 168
American Notebooks, The (Hawthorne), **II:** 226
American Novel Since World War II, The (Klein, ed.), **Supp. XI:** 233
"American Original, An: Learning from a Literary Master" (Wilkinson), **Supp. VIII:** 164, 165, 168
American Pastoral (P. Roth), **Retro. Supp. II:** 297, 307, **310–311**; **Supp. XI:** 68
American Places (Porter, Stegner and Stegner), **Supp. IV Part 2:** 599
"American Poet" (Shapiro), **Supp. II Part 2:** 701
"American Poetry" (Simpson), **Supp. IX:** 272
"American Poetry and American Life" (Pinsky), **Supp. VI:** 239–240
American Poetry since 1945: A Critical Survey (Stepanchev), **Supp. XI:** 312
American Poetry since 1960 (Mesic), **Supp. IV Part 1:** 175
American Primer, An (Boorstin), **I:** 253
American Primer, An (Whitman), **IV:** 348

"American Primitive" (W. J. Smith), **Supp. XIII:** 333
American Primitive: Poems (Oliver), **Supp. VII:** 234–237, 238
American Procession, An: The Major American Writers from 1830–1930—the Crucial Century (Kazin), **Supp. VIII: 105–106,** 108
"American Realist Playwrights, The" (McCarthy), **II:** 562
American Register, or General Repository of History, Politics, and Science, The (Brown, ed.), **Supp. I Part 1:** 146
American Renaissance (Matthiessen), **I:** 259–260; **III:** 310; **Supp. XIII:** 93
"American Rendezvous, An" (Beauvoir), **Supp. IX:** 4
American Scene, The (James), **II:** 336; **III:** 460; **Retro. Supp. I:** 232, 235
American Scenes (Kozlenko, ed.), **IV:** 378
"American Scholar, The" (Emerson), **I:** 239; **II:** 8, 12–13; **Retro. Supp. I:** 62, 74–75, 149, 298; **Retro. Supp. II:** 155; **Supp. I Part 2:** 420; **Supp. IX:** 227, 271
"American Soldier, The" (Freneau), **Supp. II Part 1:** 269
American Songbag, The (Sandburg), **III:** 583
"American Student in Paris, An" (Farrell), **II:** 45
"American Sublime, The" (Stevens), **IV:** 74
American Tragedy, An (Dreiser), **I:** 497, 498, 499, 501, 502, 503, 511–515, 517, 518, 519; **III:** 251; **IV:** 35, 484; **Retro. Supp. II:** 93, 95, **104–108**
"American Triptych" (Kenyon), **Supp. VII:** 165
"American Use for German Ideals" (Bourne), **I:** 228
American Village, The (Freneau), **Supp. II Part 1:** 256, 257
"American Village, The" (Freneau), **Supp. II Part 1:** 256
America's Coming-of-Age (Brooks), **I:** 228, 230, 240, 245, 258; **IV:** 427
America's Humor: From Poor Richard to Doonesbury (Blair and Hill), **Retro. Supp. II:** 304
America's Rome (Vance), **Supp. IV Part 2:** 684
America Was Promises (MacLeish), **III:** 16, 17
"Amerika" (Snyder), **Supp. VIII:** 301
Ames, Fisher, **Supp. I Part 2:** 486

Ames, Lois, **Supp. I Part 2:** 541, 547
Ames, William, **IV:** 158
Ames Stewart, Beatrice, **Supp. IX:** 200
Amichai, Yehuda, **Supp. XI:** 267
Amidon, Stephen, **Supp. XI:** 333
Amiel, Henri F., **I:** 241, 243, 250
Amis, Kingsley, **IV:** 430; **Supp. IV Part 2:** 688; **Supp. VIII:** 167; **Supp. XIII:** 93
Amis, Martin, **Retro. Supp. I:** 278
Ammons, A. R., **Supp. III Part 2:** 541; **Supp. VII: 23–38; Supp. IX:** 41, 42, 46; **Supp. XII:** 121
Ammons, Elizabeth, **Retro. Supp. I:** 364, 369; **Retro. Supp. II:** 140
"Among Children" (Levine), **Supp. V:** 192
Among My Books (Lowell), **Supp. I Part 2:** 407
"Among School Children" (Yeats), **III:** 249; **Supp. IX:** 52
"Among the Hills" (Whittier), **Supp. I Part 2:** 703
Among the Isles of Shoals (Thaxter), **Supp. XIII:** 152
"Among Those Present" (Benét), **Supp. XI:** 53
"Amoral Moralist" (White), **Supp. I Part 2:** 648
Amory, Cleveland, **Supp. I Part 1:** 316
Amory, Fred, **Supp. III Part 1:** 2
Amos (biblical book), **II:** 166
"Am Strand von Tanger" (Salter), **Supp. IX:** 257
"AMTRAK" (Baraka), **Supp. II Part 1:** 60
Amy and Isabelle (Strout), **Supp. X:** 86
Amy Lowell: Portrait of the Poet in Her Time (Gregory), **II:** 512
"Amy Lowell of Brookline, Mass." (Scott), **II:** 512
"Amy Wentworth" (Whittier), **Supp. I Part 2:** 694, 696
Anabase (Perse), **III:** 12
"Anabasis (I)" (Merwin), **Supp. III Part 1:** 342, 346
"Anabasis (II)" (Merwin), **Supp. III Part 1:** 342, 346
Anagrams: A Novel (Moore), **Supp. X:** 163, 164, 167, **169–171,** 172
Analects (Confucius), **Supp. IV Part 1:** 14
Analects, The (Pound, trans.), **III:** 472
Analogy (J. Butler), **II:** 8
"Analysis of a Theme" (Stevens), **IV:** 81
Anarchiad, The, A Poem on the Restoration of Chaos and Substantial Night, in Twenty Four Books (Barlow), **Supp. II Part 1:** 70
Anatomy Lesson, The (P. Roth), **Retro. Supp. II:** 304, 308; **Supp. III Part 2:** 422–423, 425
Anatomy of Criticism (Frye), **Supp. XIII:** 19
Anatomy of Melancholy (Burton), **III:** 78
Anatomy of Nonsense, The (Winters), **Supp. II Part 2:** 811, 812
Anaya, Rudolfo A., **Supp. IV Part 2:** 502; **Supp. XIII:** 213, 220
Ancestors (Maxwell), **Supp. VIII:** 152, 168
"Ancestors, The" (Tate), **IV:** 128
Ancestral Voice: Conversations with N. Scott Momaday (Woodard), **Supp. IV Part 2:** 484, 485, 486, 489, 493
"Anchorage" (Harjo), **Supp. XII:** 220–221
Ancient Child, The: A Novel (Momaday), **Supp. IV Part 2:** 488, 489–491, 492, 493
"Ancient Egypt/Fannie Goldbarth" (Goldbarth), **Supp. XII:** 191–192
Ancient Evenings (Mailer), **Retro. Supp. II:** 206, 210, 213
Ancient Law, The (Glasgow), **II:** 179–180, 192
Ancient Musics (Goldbarth), **Supp. XII:** 191–192
"Ancient Semitic Rituals for the Dead" (Goldbarth), **Supp. XII:** 191–192
"Ancient World, The" (Doty), **Supp. XI:** 122
& (And) (Cummings), **I:** 429, 431, 432, 437, 445, 446, 448
Andersen, Hans Christian, **I:** 441; **Supp. I Part 2:** 622
Anderson, Charles R., **Supp. I Part 1:** 356, 360, 368, 371, 372
Anderson, Frances, **I:** 231
Anderson, Guy, **Supp. X:** 264, 265
Anderson, Henry J., **Supp. I Part 1:** 156
Anderson, Irwin M., **I:** 98–99
Anderson, Jon, **Supp. V:** 338
Anderson, Judith, **III:** 399
Anderson, Karl, **I:** 99, 103
Anderson, Margaret, **I:** 103; **III:** 471
Anderson, Margaret Bartlett, **III:** 171
Anderson, Mary Jane. *See* Lanier, Mrs. Robert Sampson (Mary Jane Anderson)
Anderson, Maxwell, **III:** 159
Anderson, Mrs. Irwin M., **I:** 98–99
Anderson, Mrs. Sherwood (Tennessee Mitchell), **I:** 100; **Supp. I Part 2:** 459, 460

Anderson, Quentin, **Retro. Supp. I:** 392
Anderson, Robert, **Supp. I Part 1:** 277; **Supp. V:** 108
Anderson, Sally, **Supp. XIII:** 95
Anderson, Sherwood, **I: 97–120,** 211, 374, 375, 384, 405, 423, 445, 480, 487, 495, 506, 518; **II:** 27, 38, 44, 55, 56, 68, 250–251, 263, 271, 289, 451, 456–457; **III:** 220, 224, 382–383, 453, 483, 545, 576, 579; **IV:** 27, 40, 46, 190, 207, 433, 451, 482; **Retro. Supp. I:** 79, 80, 177; **Supp. I Part 2:** 378, 430, 459, 472, 613; **Supp. IV Part 2:** 502; **Supp. V:** 12, 250; **Supp. VIII:** 39, 152; **Supp. IX:** 14, 309; **Supp. XI:** 159, 164; **Supp. XII:** 343
Anderson, T. J., **Supp. XIII:** 132
Anderssen, A., **III:** 252
"And Hickman Arrives" (Ellison), **Retro. Supp. II:** 118, 126; **Supp. II Part 1:** 248
And in the Hanging Gardens (Aiken), **I:** 63
And I Worked at the Writer's Trade (Cowley), **Supp. II Part 1:** 137, 139, 141, 143, 147, 148
Andorra (Cameron), **Supp. XII:** 79, 81, **88–91**
Andral, Gabriel, **Supp. I Part 1:** 302
Andre, Michael, **Supp. XII:** 117–118, 129, 132, 133–134
Andre's Mother (McNally), **Supp. XIII:** 206
Andress, Ursula, **Supp. XI:** 307
"Andrew Jackson" (Masters), **Supp. I Part 2:** 472
Andrews, Bruce, **Supp. IV Part 2:** 426
Andrews, Roy Chapman, **Supp. X:** 172
Andrews, Tom, **Supp. XI:** 317
Andrews, Wayne, **IV:** 310
Andrews, William L., **Supp. IV Part 1:** 13
Andreyev, Leonid Nikolaevich, **I:** 53; **II:** 425
Andria (Terence), **IV:** 363
"Andromache" (Dubus), **Supp. VII:** 84
"And Summer Will Not Come Again" (Plath), **Retro. Supp. II:** 242
"And That Night Clifford Died" (Levine), **Supp. V:** 195
And the Band Played On (Shilts), **Supp. X:** 145
"And the Moon Be Still as Bright" (Bradbury), **Supp. IV Part 1:** 106
"And the Sea Shall Give up Its Dead" (Wilder), **IV:** 358
And Things That Go Bump in the Night (McNally), **Supp. XIII: 196–197,** 205, 208
"And *Ut Pictura Poesis* Is Her Name" (Ashbery), **Supp. III Part 1:** 19
"Anecdote and Storyteller" (Howe), **Supp. VI:** 127
"Anecdote of the Jar" (Stevens), **IV:** 83–84
"Anemone" (Rukeyser), **Supp. VI:** 281, 285
"Angel, The" (Buck), **Supp. II Part 1:** 127
Angela's Ashes (McCourt), **Supp. XII: 271–279,** 283, 285
"Angel at the Grave, The" (Wharton), **IV:** 310; **Retro. Supp. I:** 365
"Angel Butcher" (Levine), **Supp. V:** 181
Angel City (Shepard), **Supp. III Part 2:** 432, 445
"Angel Is My Watermark!, The" (H. Miller), **III:** 180
Angell, Carol, **Supp. I Part 2:** 655
Angell, Katharine Sergeant. *See* White, Katharine
Angell, Roger, **Supp. I Part 2:** 655; **Supp. V:** 22; **Supp. VIII:** 139
Angel Landing (Hoffman), **Supp. X: 82–83**
"Angel Levine" (Malamud), **Supp. I Part 2:** 431, 432, 433–434, 437
Angel of Bethesda, The (Mather), **Supp. II Part 2:** 464
"Angel of the Bridge, The" (Cheever), **Supp. I Part 1:** 186–187
"Angel of the Odd, The" (Poe), **III:** 425
Angelo Herndon Jones (Hughes), **Retro. Supp. I:** 203
"Angel on the Porch, An" (Wolfe), **IV:** 451
Angelou, Maya, **Supp. IV Part 1: 1–19; Supp. XI:** 20, 245; **Supp. XIII:** 185
"Angel Poem, The" (Stern), **Supp. IX:** 292
Angels and Earthly Creatures (Wylie), **Supp. I Part 2:** 709, 713, **724–730**
Angels in America: A Gay Fantasia on National Themes (Kushner), **Supp. IX:** 131, 134, **141–146**
"Angels of the Love Affair" (Sexton), **Supp. II Part 2:** 692
"Angel Surrounded by Paysans" (Stevens), **IV:** 93
Angel That Troubled the Waters, The (Wilder), **IV:** 356, 357–358
"Anger" (Creeley), **Supp. IV Part 1:** 150–152
Anger (Sarton), **Supp. VIII:** 256
"Anger against Children" (Bly), **Supp. IV Part 1:** 73
Angle of Ascent (Hayden), **Supp. II Part 1:** 363, 367, 370
"Angle of Geese" (Momaday), **Supp. IV Part 2:** 485
Angle of Geese and Other Poems (Momaday), **Supp. IV Part 2:** 487, 491
Angle of Repose (Stegner), **Supp. IV Part 2:** 599, 605, 606, 610–611
"*Angle of Repose* and the Writings of Mary Hallock Foote: A Source Study" (Williams-Walsh), **Supp. IV Part 2:** 611
Anglo-Saxon Century, The (Dos Passos), **I:** 474–475, 483
Angoff, Charles, **III:** 107
"Angola Question Mark" (Hughes), **Supp. I Part 1:** 344
Angry Wife, The (Sedges), **Supp. II Part 1:** 125
"Angry Women Are Building: Issues and Struggles Facing American Indian Women Today" (Gunn Allen), **Supp. IV Part 1:** 324
"Animal, Vegetable, and Mineral" (Bogan), **Supp. III Part 1:** 66
"Animal Acts" (Simic), **Supp. VIII:** 278
Animal and Vegetable Physiology Considered with Reference to Natural Theology (Roget), **Supp. I Part 1:** 312
Animal Dreams (Kingsolver), **Supp. VII:** 199, 204–207
"Animals, The" (Merwin), **Supp. III Part 1:** 348
"Animals Are Passing from Our Lives" (Levine), **Supp. V:** 181, 182
Animals in That Country, The (Atwood), **Supp. XIII:** 20, 33
Animals of the Soul: Sacred Animals of the Oglala Sioux (Brown), **Supp. IV Part 2:** 487
"Animula" (Eliot), **Retro. Supp. I:** 64
Ankor Wat (Ginsberg), **Supp. II Part 1:** 323
"Annabelle" (Komunyakaa), **Supp. XIII:** 117
"Annabel Lee" (Poe), **Retro. Supp. I:** 273; **Retro. Supp. II:** 266
Anna Christie (O'Neill), **III:** 386, 389, 390
Anna Karenina (Tolstoy), **I:** 10; **II:** 290; **Retro. Supp. I:** 225; **Supp. V:** 323
"*Anna Karenina*" (Trilling), **Supp. III Part 2:** 508
"Anna Who Was Mad" (Sexton), **Supp.**

II Part 2: 692
"Ann Burlak" (Rukeyser), **Supp. VI:** 280
"Anne" (Oliver), **Supp. VII:** 232
"Anne at the Symphony" (Shields), **Supp. VII:** 310
"Anne Bradstreet's Poetic Voices" (Requa), **Supp. I Part 1:** 107
Anne Sexton: The Artist and Her Critics (McClatchy), **Supp. XII:** 253
"Ann from the Street" (Dixon), **Supp. XII:** 146–147
"Ann Garner" (Agee), **I:** 27
"Anniad, The" (Brooks), **Supp. III Part 1:** 77, 78
Annie (musical), **Supp. IV Part 2:** 577
Annie Allen (Brooks), **Supp. III Part 1:** 76–79
Annie Dillard Reader, The (Dillard), **Supp. VI:** 23
Annie Hall (film), **Supp. IV Part 1:** 205
Annie John (Kincaid), **Supp. VII:** 184–186, 193
Annie Kilburn, a Novel (Howells), **II:** 275, 286, 287
Anniversary (Shields), **Supp. VII:** 320, 322, 323, 324
"Annunciation, The" (Le Sueur), **Supp. V:** 130
Ann Vickers (Lewis), **II:** 453
"A No-Account Creole, A" (Chopin), **Retro. Supp. II:** 64
"Anodyne" (Komunyakaa), **Supp. XIII:** 130
Another America/Otra America (Kingsolver), **Supp. VII:** 207–209
"Another Animal" (Swenson), **Supp. IV Part 2:** 639
Another Animal: Poems (Swenson), **Supp. IV Part 2:** 639–641, 649
Another Antigone (Gurney), **Supp. V:** 97, 98, 100, 101, 102, 105
"Another August" (Merrill), **Supp. III Part 1:** 326
"Another Beer" (Matthews), **Supp. IX:** 158
Another Country (Baldwin), **Retro. Supp. II:** 9–11, 14; **Supp. I Part 1:** 51, 52, 56–58, 63, 67, 337; **Supp. II Part 1:** 40; **Supp. VIII:** 349
"Another Language" (Jong), **Supp. V:** 131
Another Mother Tongue: Gay Words, Gay Worlds (Grahn), **Supp. IV Part 1:** 330
"Another Night in the Ruins" (Kinnell), **Supp. III Part 1:** 239, 251
"Another Old Woman" (W. C. Williams), **Retro. Supp. I:** 423

Another Part of the Forest (Hellman), **Supp. I Part 1:** 282–283, 297
Another Republic: 17 European and South American Writers (Strand, trans.), **Supp. IV Part 2:** 630
Another Roadside Attraction (Robbins), **Supp. X:** 259, 261, 262, 263, 264, 265–266, **267–269**, 274, 275, 277, 284
"Another Spring Uncovered" (Swenson), **Supp. IV Part 2:** 644
Another Thin Man (film), **Supp. IV Part 1:** 355
Another Time (Auden), **Supp. II Part 1:** 15
Another Turn of the Crank (Berry), **Supp. X:** 25, 35
"Another upon the Same" (Taylor), **IV:** 161
"Another Voice" (Wilbur), **Supp. III Part 2:** 557
"Another Wife" (Anderson), **I:** 114
Another You (Beattie), **Supp. V:** 29, 31, 33–34
Anouilh, Jean, **Supp. I Part 1:** 286–288, 297
Ansky, S., **IV:** 6
Ansky, Shloime, **Supp. IX:** 131, 138
"Answer, The" (Jeffers), **Supp. III Part 2:** 423
Answered Prayers: The Unfinished Novel (Capote), **Supp. III Part 1:** 113, 125, 131–132
"Answering the Deer: Genocide and Continuance in the Poetry of American Indian Women" (Gunn Allen), **Supp. IV Part 1:** 322, 325
"Answer of Minerva, The: Pacifism and Resistance in Simone Weil" (Merton), **Supp. VIII:** 204
Antaeus (Wolfe), **IV:** 461
"Ante-Bellum Sermon, An" (Dunbar), **Supp. II Part 1:** 203–204
Antheil, George, **III:** 471, 472; **IV:** 404
Anthem (Rand), **Supp. IV Part 2:** 523
Anthology of Holocaust Literature (Glatstein, Knox, and Margoshes, eds.), **Supp. X:** 70
Anthology of Twentieth-Century Brazilian Poetry, An (Bishop and Brasil, eds.), **Retro. Supp. II:** 50; **Supp. I Part 1:** 94
Anthon, Kate, **I:** 452
Anthony, Saint, **III:** 395
Anthony, Susan B., **Supp. XI:** 200
"Anthropologist as Hero, The" (Sontag), **Supp. III Part 2:** 451
"Anthropology of Water, The" (Carson), **Supp. XII:** 102–103
Anthropos: The Future of Art (Cummings), **I:** 430
Antichrist (Nietzsche), **III:** 176
"Anti-Father" (Dove), **Supp. IV Part 1:** 246
"Anti-Feminist Woman, The" (Rich), **Supp. I Part 2:** 550
Antigone (Sophocles), **Supp. I Part 1:** 284; **Supp. X:** 249
Antin, David, **Supp. VIII:** 292; **Supp. XII:** 2, 8
Antin, Mary, **Supp. IX:** 227
Anti-Oedipus: Capitalism and Schizophrenia (Deleuze and Guattari), **Supp. XII:** 4
Antiphon, The (Barnes), **Supp. III Part 1:** 43–44
"Antiquities" (Mather), **Supp. II Part 2:** 452
"Antiquity of Freedom, The" (Bryant), **Supp. I Part 1:** 168
"Antislavery Tocsin, An" (Douglass), **Supp. III Part 1:** 171
Antoine, Andre, **III:** 387
Antonioni, Michelangelo, **Supp. IV Part 1:** 46, 47, 48
Antony and Cleopatra (Shakespeare), **I:** 285
"Antony on Behalf of the Play" (Burke), **I:** 284
"An trentiesme de mon Eage, L'" (MacLeish), **III:** 9
"Ants" (Bly), **Supp. IV Part 1:** 71
Anxiety of Influence, The (Bloom), **Supp. XIII:** 46
"Any Object" (Swenson), **Supp. IV Part 2:** 640
"Any Porch" (Parker), **Supp. IX:** 194
"Anywhere Out of This World" (Baudelaire), **II:** 552
Any Woman's Blues (Jong), **Supp. V:** 115, 123, 126
Anzaldúa, Gloria, **Retro. Supp. II:** 292; **Supp. IV Part 1:** 330; **Supp. XIII:** 223
"Aphorisms on Society" (Stevens), **Retro. Supp. I:** 303
Apollinaire, Guillaume, **I:** 432; **II:** 529; **III:** 196; **IV:** 80; **Retro. Supp. II:** 344
Apologies to the Iroquois (Wilson), **IV:** 429
"Apology, An" (Malamud), **Supp. I Part 2:** 435, 437
"Apology for Bad Dreams" (Jeffers), **Supp. II Part 2:** 427, 438
"Apology for Crudity, An" (Anderson), **I:** 109
Apology for Poetry (Sidney), **Supp. II Part 1:** 105
"Apostle of the Tules, An" (Harte),

Supp. II Part 1: 356
"Apostrophe to a Dead Friend" (Kumin), **Supp. IV Part 2:** 442, 451, 452
"Apostrophe to a Pram Rider" (White), **Supp. I Part 2:** 678
"Apostrophe to Man (on reflecting that the world is ready to go to war again)" (Millay), **III:** 127
"Apostrophe to Vincentine, The" (Stevens), **IV:** 90
"Apotheosis" (Kingsolver), **Supp. VII:** 208
"Apotheosis of Martin Luther King, The" (Hardwick), **Supp. III Part 1:** 203–204
Appalachia (Wright), **Supp. V:** 333, 345
"Appalachian Book of the Dead III" (Wright), **Supp. V:** 345
"Appeal to Progressives, An" (Wilson), **IV:** 429
Appeal to Reason (Paine), **I:** 490
Appeal to the World, An (Du Bois), **Supp. II Part 1:** 184
Appearance and Reality (Bradley), **I:** 572
"Appendix to 'The Anniad'" (Brooks), **Supp. III Part 1:** 77
Apple, Max, **Supp. VIII:** 14
"Apple, The" (Kinnell), **Supp. III Part 1:** 250
Applegarth, Mabel, **II:** 465, 478
"Apple of Discord, The" (Humphrey), **Supp. IX:** 109
"Apple Peeler" (Francis), **Supp. IX:** 82
Appleseed, Johnny (pseudonym). See Chapman, John (Johnny Appleseed)
Appleton, Nathan, **II:** 488
Appleton, Thomas Gold, **Supp. I Part 1:** 306; **Supp. I Part 2:** 415
"Applicant, The" (Plath), **Retro. Supp. II:** 252; **Supp. I Part 2:** 535, 544, 545
"Applications of the Doctrine" (Hass), **Supp. VI:** 100–101
Appointment, The (film), **Supp. IX:** 253
Appointment in Samarra (O'Hara), **III:** 361, 363–364, 365–367, 371, 374, 375, 383
Appreciation of Sarah Orne Jewett (Cary), **Retro. Supp. II:** 132
"Approaches, The" (Merwin), **Supp. III Part 1:** 350
"Approaching Artaud" (Sontag), **Supp. III Part 2:** 470–471
"Approaching Prayer" (Dickey), **Supp. IV Part 1:** 175

"Approach to Thebes, The" (Kunitz), **Supp. III Part 1:** 265–267
"Après-midi d'un faune, L'" (Mallarmé), **III:** 8
"April" (Winters), **Supp. II Part 2:** 788
"April" (W. C. Williams), **Retro. Supp. I:** 422
April Galleons (Ashbery), **Supp. III Part 1:** 26
"April Galleons" (Ashbery), **Supp. III Part 1:** 26
April Hopes (Howells), **II:** 285, 289
"April Lovers" (Ransom), **III:** 489–490
"April Showers" (Wharton), **Retro. Supp. I:** 361
"April Today Main Street" (Olson), **Supp. II Part 2:** 581
April Twilights (Cather), **I:** 313; **Retro. Supp. I:** 5
"Apt Pupil" (King), **Supp. V:** 152
Arabian Nights, **I:** 204; **II:** 8; **Supp. I Part 2:** 584, 599; **Supp. IV Part 1:** 1
"Arabic Coffee" (Nye), **Supp. XIII:** 276
"Araby" (Joyce), **I:** 174; **Supp. VIII:** 15
Aragon, Louis, **I:** 429; **III:** 471; **Retro. Supp. II:** 85, 339
Arana-Ward, Marie, **Supp. VIII:** 84
Ararat (Glück), **Supp. V:** 79, 86–87
Arbre du voyageur, L' (W. J. Smith; Haussmann, trans.), **Supp. XIII:** 347
Arbus, Diane, **Supp. XII:** 188
Arbuthnott, John (pseudonym). See Henry, O.
Archaeologist of Morning (Olson), **Supp. II Part 2:** 557
"Archaic Maker, The" (Merwin), **Supp. III Part 1:** 357
Archer (television show), **Supp. IV Part 2:** 474
Archer, William, **IV:** 131; **Retro. Supp. I:** 228
Archer at Large (Macdonald), **Supp. IV Part 2:** 473
Archer in Hollywood (Macdonald), **Supp. IV Part 2:** 474
"Archetype and Signature: The Relationship of Poet and Poem" (Fiedler), **Supp. XIII:** 101
"Archibald Higbie" (Masters), **Supp. I Part 2:** 461
"Architect, The" (Bourne), **I:** 223
Arctic Dreams (Lopez), **Supp. V:** 211
Arctic Refuge: A Circle of Testimony (Haines), **Supp. XII:** 205

Arendt, Hannah, **II:** 544; **Retro. Supp. I:** 87; **Retro. Supp. II:** 28, 117; **Supp. I Part 2:** 570; **Supp. IV Part 1:** 386; **Supp. VIII:** 98, 99, 100, 243; **Supp. XII:** 166–167
Arensberg, Walter, **IV:** 408; **Retro. Supp. I:** 416
Aren't You Happy for Me? (Bausch), **Supp. VII:** 42, 51, 54
Areopagitica (Milton), **Supp. I Part 2:** 422
"Are You a Doctor?" (Carver), **Supp. III Part 1:** 139–141
"Are You Mr. William Stafford? (Stafford), **Supp. XI:** 317
"Argonauts of 49, California's Golden Age" (Harte), **Supp. II Part 1:** 353, 355
Aria da Capo (Millay), **III:** 137–138
Ariel (Plath), **Retro. Supp. II:** 250–255; **Supp. I Part 2:** 526, 539, 541; **Supp. V:** 79
"Ariel" (Plath), **Supp. I Part 2:** 542, 546
"Ariel Poems" (Eliot), **I:** 579
Arise, Arise (Zukofsky), **Supp. III Part 2:** 619, 629
"Aristocracy" (Emerson), **II:** 6
Aristocracy and Justice (More), **I:** 223
Aristophanes, **I:** 436; **II:** 577; **Supp. I Part 2:** 406
Aristotle, **I:** 58, 265, 280, 527; **II:** 9, 12, 198, 536; **III:** 20, 115, 145, 157, 362, 422, 423; **IV:** 10, 18, 74–75, 89; **Supp. I Part 1:** 104, 296; **Supp. I Part 2:** 423; **Supp. IV Part 1:** 391; **Supp. IV Part 2:** 526, 530; **Supp. X:** 78; **Supp. XI:** 249; **Supp. XII:** 106
Aristotle Contemplating the Bust of Homer (Rembrandt), **Supp. IV Part 1:** 390, 391
"Arkansas Traveller" (Wright), **Supp. V:** 334
"Armadillo, The" (Bishop), **Supp. I Part 1:** 93
Armadillo in the Grass (Hearon), **Supp. VIII:** 58–59
"Armageddon" (Ransom), **III:** 489, 492
Armah, Aiy Kwei, **Supp. IV Part 1:** 373
Armies of the Night, The (Mailer), **III:** 39–40, 41, 42, 44, 45, 46; **Retro. Supp. II:** 205, 206–207, 208; **Supp. IV Part 1:** 207
"Arm in Arm" (Simpson), **Supp. IX:** 267–268
Arminius, Jacobus, **I:** 557

Armitage, Shelley, **Supp. IV Part 2:** 439
Arm of Flesh, The (Salter), **Supp. IX:** 251
"Armor" (Dickey), **Supp. IV Part 1:** 179
Armored Attack (film), **Supp. I Part 1:** 281
Arms, George W., **Supp. I Part 2:** 416–417
Armstrong, George, **Supp. I Part 2:** 386
Armstrong, Louis, **Retro. Supp. II:** 114
"Army" (Corso), **Supp. XII:** 117, 127
Army Brat (W. J. Smith), **Supp. XIII:** 331, 347
Arna Bontemps Langston Hughes: Letters 1925–1967 (Nichols), **Retro. Supp. I:** 194
Arner, Robert D., **Retro. Supp. II:** 62
Arnold, Edwin T., **Supp. VIII:** 189
Arnold, George W., **Supp. I Part 2:** 411
Arnold, Marilyn, **Supp. IV Part 1:** 220
Arnold, Matthew, **I:** 222, 228, 275; **II:** 20, 110, 338, 541; **III:** 604; **IV:** 349; **Retro. Supp. I:** 56, 325; **Supp. I Part 2:** 416, 417, 419, 529, 552, 602; **Supp. IX:** 298
Arnold, Thurman, **Supp. I Part 2:** 645
Aronson, Steven M. L., **Supp. V:** 4
Around about America (Caldwell), **I:** 290
"Arrangement in Black and White" (Parker), **Supp. IX:** 198
"Arrival at Santos" (Bishop), **Retro. Supp. II:** 46; **Supp. IX:** 45–46
"Arrival of the Bee Box, The" (Plath), **Retro. Supp. II:** 255
Arrivistes, The: Poem 1940–1949 (Simpson), **Supp. IX:** 265, 267–268
"Arrow" (Dove), **Supp. IV Part 1:** 250
Arrowsmith (Lewis), **I:** 362; **II:** 445–446, 449
"Arsenal at Springfield, The" (Longfellow), **Retro. Supp. II:** 168
"Arson Plus" (Hammett), **Supp. IV Part 1:** 343
"Ars Poetica" (Dove), **Supp. IV Part 1:** 250
"Ars Poetica" (Dunn), **Supp. XI:** 154
"Ars Poetica" (MacLeish), **III:** 9–10
"*Ars Poetica*: A Found Poem" (Kumin), **Supp. IV Part 2:** 455
"Ars Poetica; or, Who Lives in the Ivory Tower" (McGrath), **Supp. X:** 117
"Ars Poetica: Some Recent Criticism" (Wright), **Supp. III Part 2:** 603

"Art" (Emerson), **II:** 13
"Art and Neurosis" (Trilling), **Supp. III Part 2:** 502
Art and Technics (Mumford), **Supp. II Part 2:** 483
Art & Ardor: Essays (Ozick), **Supp. V:** 258, 272
Art as Experience (Dewey), **I:** 266
Art by Subtraction (Reid), **IV:** 41
Art de toucher le clavecin, L' (Couperin), **III:** 464
Artemis to Actaeon and Other Verse (Wharton), **Retro. Supp. I:** 372
Arte of English Poesie (Puttenham), **Supp. I Part 1:** 113
Arthur, Anthony, **Supp. IV Part 2:** 606
Arthur Mervyn; or, Memoirs of the Year 1793 (Brown), **Supp. I Part 1:** 137–140, 144
Articulation of Sound Forms in Time (Howe), **Supp. IV Part 2:** 419, 431–433
"Artificial Nigger, The" (O'Connor), **III:** 343, 351, 356, 358; **Retro. Supp. II:** 229, 232
Artist, The: A Drama without Words (Mencken), **III:** 104
"Artist of the Beautiful, The" (Hawthorne), **Retro. Supp. I:** 149
Artistry of Grief (Torsney), **Retro. Supp. I:** 224
"Artists' and Models' Ball, The" (Brooks), **Supp. III Part 1:** 72
"Art of Disappearing, The" (Nye), **Supp. XIII:** 287
Art of Fiction, The (Gardner), **Supp. VI:** 73
"Art of Fiction, The" (H. James), **Retro. Supp. I:** 226; **Retro. Supp. II:** 223
Art of Hunger, The (Auster), **Supp. XII:** 22
"Art of Keeping Your Mouth Shut, The" (Heller), **Supp. IV Part 1:** 383
"Art of Literature and Commonsense, The" (Nabokov), **Retro. Supp. I:** 271
Art of Living and Other Stories, The (Gardner), **Supp. VI:** 72
"Art of Poetry, The" (McClatchy), **Supp. XII:** 262
"Art of Romare Bearden, The" (Ellison), **Retro. Supp. II:** 123
"Art of Storytelling, The" (Simpson), **Supp. IX:** 277
Art of Sylvia Plath, The (Newman), **Supp. I Part 2:** 527
Art of the Moving Picture, The (Lindsay), **Supp. I Part 2:** 376, 391–392, 394

Art of the Novel (H. James), **Retro. Supp. I:** 227
"Art of Theodore Dreiser, The" (Bourne), **I:** 235
Art of the Personal Essay, The (Lopate), **Supp. XIII:** 280–281
Art of the Self, The: Essays a Propos "Steps" (Kosinski), **Supp. VII:** 222
Arts and Sciences (Goldbarth), **Supp. XII:** 184–186
"Art's Bread and Butter" (Benét), **Retro. Supp. I:** 108
Arts of the Possible: Essays and Conversations (Rich), **Retro. Supp. II:** 292
Arvin, Newton, **I:** 259; **II:** 508; **Retro. Supp. I:** 19, 137
Asali, Muna, **Supp. XIII:** 121, 126
Asbury, Herbert, **Supp. IV Part 1:** 353
Ascent of F6, The (Auden), **Supp. II Part 1:** 11, 13
Ascent to Truth, The (Merton), **Supp. VIII:** 208
Asch, Sholem, **IV:** 1, 9, 11, 14; **Retro. Supp. II:** 317
Ascherson, Neal, **Supp. XII:** 167
As Does New Hampshire and Other Poems (Sarton), **Supp. VIII:** 259
"As Evening Lays Dying" (Salinas), **Supp. XIII:** 319
"As Flowers Are" (Kunitz), **Supp. III Part 1:** 265
Ashbery, John, **Retro. Supp. I:** 313; **Supp. I Part 1:** 96; **Supp. III Part 1:** 1–29; **Supp. III Part 2:** 541; **Supp. IV Part 2:** 620; **Supp. VIII:** 272; **Supp. IX:** 52; **Supp. XI:** 139; **Supp. XIII:** 85
"Ashes" (Levine), **Supp. V:** 188
Ashes: Poems Old and New (Levine), **Supp. V:** 178, 188–189
"Ashes of the Beacon" (Bierce), **I:** 209
Ashford, Margaret Mary (Daisy), **II:** 426
Ash Wednesday (Eliot), **I:** 570, 574–575, 578–579, 580, 582, 584, 585; **Retro. Supp. I:** 64
"Ash Wednesday" (Eliot), **Supp. IV Part 2:** 436
"Ash Wednesday" (Garrett), **Supp. VII:** 109–110
"Ash Wednesday" (Merton), **Supp. VIII:** 199
Asian American Authors (Hsu and Palubinskas, eds.), **Supp. X:** 292
Asian American Heritage: An Anthology of Prose and Poetry (Wand), **Supp. X:** 292
Asian Figures (Mervin), **Supp. III Part 1:** 341

Asian Journal of Thomas Merton, The (Merton), **Supp. VIII:** 196, 206, 208
"Asian Peace Offers Rejected without Publication" (Bly), **Supp. IV Part 1:** 61
"Asides on the Oboe" (Stevens), **Retro. Supp. I:** 305
"As I Ebb'd with the Ocean of Life" (Whitman), **IV:** 342, 345–346; **Retro. Supp. I:** 404, 405
As I Lay Dying (Faulkner), **II:** 60–61, 69, 73, 74; **IV:** 100; **Retro. Supp. I:** 75, 82, 84, 85, 86, 88, 89, 91, 92; **Supp. IV Part 1:** 47; **Supp. VIII:** 37, 178; **Supp. IX:** 99, 103, 251
"As I Lay with My Head in Your Lap, Camerado" (Whitman), **IV:** 347
Asimov, Isaac, **Supp. IV Part 1:** 116
Asinof, Eliot, **II:** 424
"As Is the Daughter, So Is Her Mother" (Patchett), **Supp. XII:** 310
"As It Was in the Beginning" (Benét), **Supp. XI:** 56
"As I Walked Out One Evening" (Auden), **Supp. II Part 1:** 13
"As I Went Down by Havre de Grace" (Wylie), **Supp. I Part 2:** 723
"Ask Me" (Stafford), **Supp. XI:** 326–327
Ask Me Tomorrow (Cozzens), **I:** 365–367, 379
Ask the Dust (Fante), **Supp. XI:** 159, 160, 166, **167–169,** 172, 173, 174
Ask Your Mama (Hughes), **Supp. I Part 1:** 339, 341–342
Ask Your Mama: 12 Moods for Jazz (Hughes), **Retro. Supp. I:** 210, 211
"As One Put Drunk into the Packet Boat" (Ashbery), **Supp. III Part 1:** 18
Aspects of the Novel (Forster), **Retro. Supp. I:** 232; **Supp. VIII:** 155
"Aspen and the Stream, The" (Wilbur), **Supp. III Part 2:** 555, 556
Aspern Papers, The (James), **Supp. V:** 101, 102
"Aspern Papers, The" (James), **Retro. Supp. I:** 219, 227, 228
Asphalt Jungle (film, Huston), **Supp. XIII:** 174
"Asphodel" (Welty), **IV:** 265, 271
"Asphodel, That Greeny Flower" (W. C. Williams), **Retro. Supp. I:** 429
"Aspic and Buttermilk" (Olds), **Supp. X:** 213
Asquith, Herbert Henry, **Retro. Supp. I:** 59
"Ass" (Cisneros), **Supp. VII:** 67
Assante, Armand, **Supp. VIII:** 74
Assassins, The (Oates), **Supp. II Part 2:** 512, 517–519
"Assault" (Millay), **III:** 130–131
"Assemblage of Husbands and Wives, An" (Lewis), **II:** 455–456
Assembly (O'Hara), **III:** 361
Assignment, Wildlife (LaBastille), **Supp. X:** 99, 104
Assistant, The (Malamud), **Supp. I Part 2:** 427, 428, 429, 431, 435, 441–445, 451
Assommoir, L' (Zola), **II:** 291; **III:** 318
Assorted Prose (Updike), **IV:** 215–216, 218; **Retro. Supp. I:** 317, 319, 327
Astor, Mary, **Supp. IV Part 1:** 356; **Supp. XII:** 173
Astoria, or, Anecdotes of an Enterprise beyond the Rocky Mountains (Irving), **II:** 312
"Astounding News by Electric Express via Norfolk! The Atlantic Crossed in Three Days Signal Triumph of Mr. Monck's Flying-Machine . . ." (Poe), **III:** 413, 420
Astraea (Holmes), **III:** 82
Astro, Richard, **Supp. I Part 2:** 429, 445
"Astrological Fricassee" (H. Miller), **III:** 187
"As Weary Pilgrim" (Bradstreet), **Supp. I Part 1:** 103, 109, 122
As We Know (Ashbery), **Supp. III Part 1:** 9, 21–25
"As We Know" (Ashbery), **Supp. III Part 1:** 21–22
Aswell, Edward C., **IV:** 458, 459, 461
"As You Like It" (Chopin), **Supp. I Part 1:** 217
As You Like It (Shakespeare), **Supp. I Part 1:** 308
"At a Bar in Charlotte Amalie" (Updike), **IV:** 214
"At a Lecture" (Brodsky), **Supp. VIII:** 33
"At a March against the Vietnam War" (Bly), **Supp. IV Part 1:** 61
"At a Reading" (McClatchy), **Supp. XII:** 256–257
"Atavism of John Tom Little Bear, The" (O. Henry), **Supp. II Part 1:** 410
"At Chênière Caminada" (Chopin), **Supp. I Part 1:** 220
"At Chinese Checkers" (Berryman), **I:** 182
Atchity, Kenneth John, **Supp. XI:** 227
At Eighty-Two (Sarton), **Supp. VIII:** 264
"At Every Gas Station There Are Mechanics" (Dunn), **Supp. XI:** 144
At Fault (Chopin), **Retro. Supp. II:** 57, 60, **62–63; Supp. I Part 1:** 207, 209–211, 220
At Heaven's Gate (Warren), **IV:** 243, 247–248, 251
Atheism Refuted: in a Discourse to Prove the Existence of God (Paine), **Supp. I Part 2:** 517
"Athénaïse" (Chopin), **Retro. Supp. II:** 66, 67; **Supp. I Part 1:** 219–220
Atherton, Gertrude, **I:** 199, 207–208
Athey, Jean L., **Supp. XI:** 184
At Home: Essays, 1982–1988 (Vidal), **Supp. IV Part 2:** 682, 687, 688
"At Kino Viejo, Mexico" (Ríos), **Supp. IV Part 2:** 541
Atkinson, Brooks, **IV:** 288; **Supp. IV Part 2:** 683
Atlantis (Doty), **Supp. XI:** 121, **126–129**
"Atlantis" (Doty), **Supp. XI:** 127–128
Atlas, James, **Supp. V:** 233
Atlas of the Difficult World, An: Poems, 1988–1991 (Rich), **Retro. Supp. II:** 292–293
Atlas Shrugged (Rand), **Supp. IV Part 2:** 517, 521, 523, 524–526, 528, 531
At Liberty (T. Williams), **IV:** 378
"At Majority" (Rich), **Retro. Supp. II:** 283
"At Melville's Tomb" (H. Crane), **I:** 393; **Retro. Supp. II:** 76, 78, 80, 82
"At Mother Teresa's" (Nye), **Supp. XIII:** 276
At Night the Salmon Move (Carver), **Supp. III Part 1:** 142
"At North Farm" (Ashbery), **Supp. III Part 1:** 1–2
At Paradise Gate (Smiley), **Supp. VI:** 292, **293–294**
"At Paso Rojo" (Bowles), **Supp. IV Part 1:** 87
At Play in the Fields of the Lord (Matthiessen), **Supp. V:** 199, 202, 204–206, 212
"At Pleasure By" (Pinsky), **Supp. VI:** 245
At Risk (Hoffman), **Supp. X:** 87
"At Sea" (Hemingway), **II:** 258
"At Shaft 11" (Dunbar), **Supp. II Part 1:** 212
"At Slim's River" (Haines), **Supp. XII:** 208–209
"At St. Croix" (Dubus), **Supp. VII:** 83, 87
At Sundown (Whittier), **Supp. I Part 2:** 704
"At Sunset" (Simic), **Supp. VIII:** 282
Attebery, Brian, **Supp. IV Part 1:** 101
"At That Time, or The History of a Joke" (Paley), **Supp. VI:** 229–230

At the Back of the North Wind (Macdonald), **Supp. XIII:** 75
"At the Birth of an Age" (Jeffers), **Supp. II Part 2:** 432
"At the Bomb Testing Site" (Stafford), **Supp. XI:** 317–318, 321, 323
At the Bottom of the River (Kincaid), **Supp. VII:** 182–184, 185
"At the 'Cadian Ball" (Chopin), **Retro. Supp. II:** 64, 65, 68
"At the Chelton-Pulver Game" (Auchincloss), **Supp. IV Part 1:** 27
"At the Drugstore" (Taylor), **Supp. V:** 323
At the Edge of the Body (Jong), **Supp. V:** 115, 130
At the End of the Open Road (Simpson), **Supp. IX:** 265, 269, **271–273,** 277
At the End of This Summer: Poems 1948–1954, **Supp. XII:** 211
"At the End of War" (Eberhart), **I:** 522–523
"At the Executed Murderer's Grave" (Wright), **Supp. III Part 2:** 595, 597
"At the Fishhouses" (Bishop), **Retro. Supp. II:** 45; **Supp. I Part 1:** 90, 92
"At the Grave of My Guardian Angel: St. Louis Cemetery, New Orleans" (Levis), **Supp. XI:** 268–269
"At the Gym" (Doty), **Supp. XI:** 135
"At the Lake" (Oliver), **Supp. VII:** 244
"At the Landing" (Welty), **IV:** 265–266; **Retro. Supp. I:** 348
At the Root of Stars (Barnes), **Supp. III Part 1:** 34
"At the Slackening of the Tide" (Wright), **Supp. III Part 2:** 597
"At the Tomb of Walt Whitman" (Kunitz), **Supp. III Part 1:** 262
"At the Tourist Centre in Boston" (Atwood), **Supp. XIII:** 33
"At the Town Dump" (Kenyon), **Supp. VII:** 167
"At the Worcester Museum" (Pinsky), **Supp. VI:** 251
"Atticus Finch and the Mad Dog: Harper Lee's *To Kill a Mockingbird*" (Jones), **Supp. VIII:** 128
"Atticus Finch—Right and Wrong" (Freedman), **Supp. VIII:** 127–128
"Attic Which Is Desire, The" (W. C. Williams), **Retro. Supp. I:** 422
"At Times in Flight: A Parable" (H. Roth), **Supp. IX:** 234
Attitudes toward History (Burke), **I:** 274

"At White River" (Haines), **Supp. XII:** 208–209
Atwood, Margaret, **Supp. IV Part 1:** 252; **Supp. V:** 119; **Supp. XI:** 317; **Supp. XIII: 19–39,** 291, 306
"Atwood's Gorgon Touch" (Davey), **Supp. XIII:** 33
"Aubade: Opal and Silver" (Doty), **Supp. XI:** 129
"Au Bal Musette" (Van Vechten), **Supp. II Part 2:** 735
Auchincloss, Hugh D., **Supp. IV Part 2:** 679
Auchincloss, Louis, **I:** 375; **III:** 66; **Retro. Supp. I:** 370, 373; **Supp. IV Part 1: 21–38**
"Auction" (Simic), **Supp. VIII:** 278
"Auction, The" (Crane), **I:** 411
"Auction Model 1934" (Z. Fitzgerald), **Supp. IX:** 61
Auden, W. H., **I:** 71, 381, 539; **II:** 367, 368, 371, 376, 586; **III:** 17, 134, 269, 271, 292, 476–477, 504, 527, 530, 542, 615; **IV:** 136, 138, 240, 430; **Retro. Supp. I:** 430; **Retro. Supp. II:** 183, 242, 244, 279, 341; **Supp. I Part 1:** 270; **Supp. I Part 2:** 552, 610; **Supp. II Part 1: 1–28;** **Supp. III Part 1:** 2, 3, 14, 26, 60, 61, 64, 341; **Supp. III Part 2:** 591, 595; **Supp. IV Part 1:** 79, 84, 136, 225, 302, 313; **Supp. IV Part 2:** 440, 465; **Supp. V:** 337; **Supp. VIII:** 19, 21, 22, 23, 30, 32, 155, 190; **Supp. IX:** 94, 287, 288; **Supp. X:** 35, 57, 59, 115–116, 117, 118–119; **Supp. XI:** 243, 244; **Supp. XII:** 253, 264–265, 266, 269–270
"Auden's OED" (McClatchy), **Supp. XII:** 264–265
"Audition" (Alvarez), **Supp. VII:** 10
Audubon, John James, **III:** 210; **IV:** 265; **Supp. IX:** 171
Auer, Jane. *See* Bowles, Jane
Auerbach, Eric, **III:** 453
Auerbach, Nina, **Supp. I Part 1:** 40
"August" (Oliver), **Supp. VII:** 235
"August" (Rich), **Supp. I Part 2:** 564
"August 1968" (Auden), **Supp. II Part 1:** 25
"August Darks, The" (Clampitt), **Supp. IX:** 43, **50–51,** 52
Augustine, Saint, **I:** 279, 290; **II:** 537; **III:** 259, 270, 292, 300; **IV:** 69, 126; **Retro. Supp. I:** 247; **Supp. VIII:** 203; **Supp. XI:** 245; **Supp. XIII:** 89
August Snow (Price), **Supp. VI:** 264
"Au Jardin" (Pound), **III:** 465–466
"Au lecteur" (Baudelaire), **Retro.**

Supp. II: 282
Aunt Carmen's Book of Practical Saints (Mora), **Supp. XIII: 227–229**
"Aunt Cynthy Dallett" (Jewett), **II:** 393
"Aunt Gladys" (Karr), **Supp. XI:** 241
"Aunt Imogen" (Robinson), **III:** 521
"Aunt Jemima of the Ocean Waves" (Hayden), **Supp. II Part 1:** 368, 379
"Aunt Jennifer's Tigers" (Rich), **Retro. Supp. II:** 279
Aunt Jo's Scrapbooks (Alcott), **Supp. I Part 1:** 43
"Aunt Mary" (Oliver), **Supp. VII:** 232
"Aunt Mary" (Stowe), **Supp. I Part 2:** 587
"Aunt Moon's Young Man" (Hogan), **Supp. IV Part 1:** 400
"Aunt Sarah" (Lowell), **II:** 554
"Aunt Sue's Stories" (Hughes), **Retro. Supp. I:** 197, 199
"Aunt Violet's Canadian Honeymoon/ 1932" (Shields), **Supp. VII:** 311
"Aunt Violet's Things" (Shields), **Supp. VII:** 311–312
"Aurelia: Moon Jellies" (Mora), **Supp. XIII:** 224
Aurora Leigh (E. Browning), **Retro. Supp. I:** 33; **Supp. XI:** 197
Auroras of Autumn, The (Stevens), **Retro. Supp. I:** 297, 300, **309–312**
"Auroras of Autumn, The" (Stevens), **Retro. Supp. I:** 311, 312; **Supp. III Part 1:** 12
"Auspex" (Frost), **Retro. Supp. I:** 122
"Auspex" (Lowell), **Supp. I Part 2:** 424
Austen, Jane, **I:** 130, 339, 375, 378; **II:** 272, 278, 287, 568–569, 577; **IV:** 8; **Retro. Supp. I:** 354; **Supp. I Part 1:** 267; **Supp. I Part 2:** 656, 715; **Supp. IV Part 1:** 300; **Supp. VIII:** 125, 167; **Supp. IX:** 128; **Supp. XII:** 310
Auster, Paul, **Supp. XII: 21–39**
Austerities (Simic), **Supp. VIII: 276–278,** 283
"Austerities" (Simic), **Supp. VIII:** 277
Austin, Mary Hunter, **Retro. Supp. I:** 7; **Supp. IV Part 2:** 503; **Supp. X:** 29; **Supp. XIII:** 154
"Authentic Unconscious, The" (Trilling), **Supp. III Part 2:** 512
Author and Agent: Eudora Welty and Diarmuid Russell (Kreyling), **Retro. Supp. I:** 342, 345, 347, 349–350
"Author at Sixty, The" (Wilson), **IV:** 426
"Author of 'Beltraffio,' The" (James), **Retro. Supp. I:** 227
"Author's House" (Fitzgerald), **Retro.**

Supp. I: 98
"Author's Reflections, An: Willie Loman, Walter Younger, and He Who Must Live" (Hansberry), **Supp. IV Part 1:** 370
"Author to Her Book, The" (Bradstreet), **Supp. I Part 1:** 119; **Supp. V:** 117–118
"Autobiographical Note" (H. Miller), **III:** 174–175
"Autobiographical Notes" (Baldwin), **Supp. I Part 1:** 54
"Autobiographical Notes" (Holmes), **Supp. I Part 1:** 301
"Autobiographic Chapter, An" (Bourne), **I:** 236
Autobiography (Franklin), **II:** 102, 103, 108, 121–122, 302
Autobiography (James), **I:** 462
"Autobiography" (MacLeish), **III:** 20
Autobiography (Van Buren), **III:** 473
Autobiography (W. C. Williams), **Supp. I Part 1:** 254
Autobiography (Zukofsky), **Supp. III Part 2:** 627
"Autobiography of a Confluence, The" (Gunn Allen), **Supp. IV Part 1:** 321
Autobiography of Alice B. Toklas, The (Stein), **IV:** 26, 30, 35, 43; **Supp. IV Part 1:** 11, 81
Autobiography of an Ex-Colored Man, The (Johnson), **Supp. II Part 1:** 33, 194
Autobiography of Benjamin Franklin (Franklin), **Supp. IV Part 1:** 5
Autobiography of LeRoi Jones, The (Baraka), **Retro. Supp. I:** 411
Autobiography of Malcolm X (Little), **Supp. I Part 1:** 66; **Supp. X:** 27; **Supp. XIII:** 264
Autobiography of Mark Twain, The (Twain), **IV:** 209
Autobiography of My Mother, The (Kincaid), **Supp. VII:** 182, 188–190, 191, 192, 193
Autobiography of Red: A Novel in Verse (Carson), **Supp. XII:** 97, **106–110**
Autobiography of Upton Sinclair, The (Sinclair), **Supp. V:** 276, 282
Autobiography of W. E. B. Du Bois, The (Du Bois), **Supp. II Part 1:** 159, 186
Autobiography of William Carlos Williams, The (W. C. Williams), **Retro. Supp. I:** 51, 428
Autocrat of the Breakfast-Table, The (Holmes), **Supp. I Part 1:** 306–307
"Automatic Gate, The" (Southern), **Supp. XI:** 294

"Automotive Passacaglia" (H. Miller), **III:** 186
"Autopsy Room, The" (Carver), **Supp. III Part 1:** 137
"Auto Wreck" (Shapiro), **Supp. II Part 2:** 706
"Autre Temps" (Wharton), **IV:** 320, 324
"Autumn Afternoon" (Farrell), **II:** 45
"Autumnal" (Eberhart), **I:** 540–541
"Autumn Begins in Martins Ferry, Ohio" (Wright), **Supp. III Part 2:** 599
"Autumn Courtship, An" (Caldwell), **I:** 309
"Autumn Equinox" (Rich), **Retro. Supp. II:** 280
Autumn Garden, The (Hellman), **Supp. I Part 1:** 285–286, 290
"Autumn Garden, The: Mechanics and Dialectics" (Felheim), **Supp. I Part 1:** 297
"Autumn Holiday, An" (Jewett), **II:** 391; **Retro. Supp. II:** 140–141
"Autumn Musings" (Harte), **Supp. II Part 1:** 336
"Autumn Within" (Longfellow), **II:** 499
"Autumn Woods" (Bryant), **Supp. I Part 1:** 164
"Au Vieux Jardin" (Aldington), **Supp. I Part 1:** 257
"Aux Imagistes" (W. C. Williams), **Supp. I Part 1:** 266
Avakian, Aram, **Supp. XI:** 294, 295, 309
Avedon, Richard, **Supp. I Part 1:** 58; **Supp. V:** 194; **Supp. X:** 15
"Avenue" (Pinsky), **Supp. VI:** 248
Avenue Bearing the Initial of Christ into the New World: Poems 1946–1964 (Kinnell), **Supp. III Part 1:** 235, 239–241
"Avenue of the Americas" (Simic), **Supp. VIII:** 278
"Average Torture" (Karr), **Supp. XI:** 243
Avery, John, **Supp. I Part 1:** 153
"Avey" (Toomer), **Supp. IX:** 317
Avon's Harvest (Robinson), **III:** 510
Awake and Sing! (Odets), **Supp. II Part 2:** 530, 531, 536–538, 550; **Supp. IV Part 2:** 587
Awakening, The (Chopin), **Retro. Supp. I:** 10; **Retro. Supp. II:** 57, 59, 60, 67, **68–71**, 73; **Supp. I Part 1:** 200, 201, 202, 211, 220–225; **Supp. V:** 304; **Supp. VIII:** 198; **Supp. XII:** 170
Awful Rowing Toward God, The (Sexton), **Supp. II Part 2:** 694–696
Awiakta, Marilou, **Supp. IV Part 1:** 319, 335
Awkward Age, The (James), **II:** 332; **Retro. Supp. I:** 229, **230–231**
Axe Handles (Snyder), **Supp. VIII:** **303–305**
Axel's Castle: A Study in the Imaginative Literature of 1870 to 1930 (Wilson), **I:** 185; **II:** 577; **IV:** 428, 431, 438, 439, 443; **Supp. VIII:** 101
"Ax-Helve, The" (Frost), **Retro. Supp. I:** 133
Azikewe, Nnamdi, **Supp. IV Part 1:** 361
"Aztec Angel" (Salinas), **Supp. XIII:** 314
B. F.'s Daughter (Marquand), **III:** 59, 65, 68, 69
Babbitt (Lewis), **II:** 442, 443–445, 446, 447, 449; **III:** 63–64, 394; **IV:** 326
Babbitt, Irving, **I:** 247; **II:** 456; **III:** 315, 461, 613; **IV:** 439; **Retro. Supp. I:** 55; **Supp. I Part 2:** 423
Babcock, Elisha, **Supp. II Part 1:** 69
Babel, Isaac, **IV:** 1; **Supp. IX:** 260; **Supp. XII:** 308–309
Babel to Byzantium (Dickey), **Supp. IV Part 1:** 177, 185
Babeuf, François, **Supp. I Part 2:** 518
"Babies, The" (Strand), **Supp. IV Part 2:** 625
Baby, Come on Inside (Wagoner), **Supp. IX:** 335
"Baby, The" (Barthelme), **Supp. IV Part 1:** 49
Baby Doll (T. Williams), **IV:** 383, 386, 387, 389, 395
"Baby Face" (Sandburg), **III:** 584
"Babylon Revisited" (Fitzgerald), **II:** 95; **Retro. Supp. I:** 109
"Baby or the Botticelli, The" (Gass), **Supp. VI:** 92
"Baby Pictures of Famous Dictators" (Simic), **Supp. VIII:** 276
"Baby's Breath" (Bambara), **Supp. XI:** 15, 16
"Babysitter, The" (Coover), **Supp. V:** 43–44
"Baby Villon" (Levine), **Supp. V:** 182
Bacall, Lauren, **Supp. IV Part 1:** 130
"Baccalaureate" (MacLeish), **III:** 4
Bacchae, The (Euripides), **Supp. VIII:** 182
Bach, Johann Sebastian, **Supp. I Part 1:** 363; **Supp. III Part 2:** 611, 612, 619
Bache, Richard, **Supp. I Part 2:** 504
Bachelard, Gaston, **Supp. XIII:** 225
Bachmann, Ingeborg, **Supp. IV Part**

1: 310; **Supp. VIII:** 272
Bachofen, J. J., **Supp. I Part 2:** 560, 567
Back Bog Beast Bait (Shepard), **Supp. III Part 2:** 437, 438
Back Country, The (Snyder), **Supp. VIII: 296–299**
"Background with Revolutionaries" (MacLeish), **III:** 14–15
Back in The World (Wolff), **Supp. VII:** 345
Back in the World (Wolff), **Supp. VII:** 344
"Backlash Blues, The" (Hughes), **Supp. I Part 1:** 343
"Backlash of Kindness, A" (Nye), **Supp. XIII:** 285, 286
Back to China (Fiedler), **Supp. XIII: 102–103**
Back to Methuselah (Shaw), **IV:** 64
"Backwacking: A Plea to the Senator" (Ellison), **Retro. Supp. II:** 126; **Supp. II Part 1:** 248
Backward Glance, A (Wharton), **Retro. Supp. I:** 360, 363, 366, 378, 380, 382
"Backward Glance o'er Travel'd Roads, A" (Whitman), **IV:** 348
Bacon, Francis, **II:** 1, 8, 11, 15–16, 111; **III:** 284; **Retro. Supp. I:** 247; **Supp. I Part 1:** 310; **Supp. I Part 2:** 388; **Supp. IX:** 104
Bacon, Helen, **Supp. X:** 57
Bacon, Leonard, **II:** 530
Bacon, Roger, **IV:** 69
"Bacterial War, The" (Nemerov), **III:** 272
Bad Boy Brawly Brown (Mosley), **Supp. XIII:** 237, 239, 240–241
Bad Boys (Cisneros), **Supp. VII:** 58
"Bad Dream" (Taylor), **Supp. V:** 320
Badè, William Frederic, **Supp. IX:** 178
"Bad Fisherman, The" (Wagoner), **Supp. IX:** 328
Bad for Each Other (film), **Supp. XIII:** 174
"Badger" (Clare), **II:** 387
Badger, A. G., **Supp. I Part 1:** 356
Badley, Linda, **Supp. V:** 148
Bad Man, A (Elkin), **Supp. VI: 47**
Bad Man Blues: A Portable George Garrett (Garrett), **Supp. VII:** 111
"Bad Music, The" (Jarrell), **II:** 369
"Bad Woman, A" (Fante), **Supp. XI:** 165
Baeck, Leo, **Supp. V:** 260
Baecker, Diann L., **Supp. VIII:** 128
Baer, William, **Supp. XIII:** 112, 118, 129
Baez, Joan, **Supp. IV Part 1:** 200; **Supp. VIII:** 200, 202
Bag of Bones (King), **Supp. V:** 139, 148, 151
"Bagpipe Music" (MacNeice), **Supp. X:** 117
"Bahá'u'lláh in the Garden of Ridwan" (Hayden), **Supp. II Part 1:** 370, 378
"Bailbondsman, The" (Elkin), **Supp. VI:** 49, **50,** 58
Bailey, Gamaliel, **Supp. I Part 2:** 587, 590
Bailey, William, **Supp. IV Part 2:** 631, 634
Bailey's Café (Naylor), **Supp. VIII: 226–228**
Bailyn, Bernard, **Supp. I Part 2:** 484, 506
Bair, Deirdre, **Supp. X:** 181, 186, 187, 188, 192, 194, 195, 196, 197
Baird, Linnett, **Supp. XII:** 299
Baird, Peggy, **I:** 385, 401
Bakan, David, **I:** 59
Baker, Carlos, **II:** 259
Baker, David, **Supp. IX:** 298; **Supp. XI:** 121, 142, 153; **Supp. XII:** 175, 191–192
Baker, George Pierce, **III:** 387; **IV:** 453, 455
Baker, Houston A., Jr., **Retro. Supp. II:** 121; **Supp. IV Part 1:** 365; **Supp. X:** 324
Baker, Nicholson, **Supp. XIII: 41–57**
Bakerman, Jane S., **Supp. IV Part 2:** 468
Bakhtin, Mikhail, **Retro. Supp. II:** 273; **Supp. IV Part 1:** 301; **Supp. X:** 120, 239
Bakst, Léon, **Supp. IX:** 66
Bakunin, Mikhail Aleksandrovich, **IV:** 429
Balbuena, Bernado de, **Supp. V:** 11
Balch, Emily Greene, **Supp. I Part 1:** 25
Balcony, The (Genet), **I:** 84
Bald Soprano, The (Ionesco), **I:** 74
Baldwin, David, **Supp. I Part 1:** 47, 48, 49, 50, 51, 54, 65, 66
Baldwin, James, **Retro. Supp. II: 1–17; Supp. I Part 1: 47–71,** 337, 341; **Supp. II Part 1:** 40; **Supp. III Part 1:** 125; **Supp. IV Part 1:** 1, 10, 11, 163, 369; **Supp. V:** 201; **Supp. VIII:** 88, 198, 235, 349; **Supp. X:** 136, 324; **Supp. XI:** 288, 294; **Supp. XIII:** 46, 111, 181, 186, 294
Baldwin, Samuel, **Supp. I Part 1:** 48
Balkian, Nona, **Supp. XI:** 230
"Ballad: Between the Box Cars" (Warren), **IV:** 245
"Ballade" (MacLeish), **III:** 4
"Ballade at Thirty-Five" (Parker), **Supp. IX:** 192
"Ballade for the Duke of Orléans" (Wilbur), **Supp. III Part 2:** 556
"Ballade of Broken Flutes, The" (Robinson), **III:** 505
"Ballade of Meaty Inversions" (White), **Supp. I Part 2:** 676
"Ballad of Billie Potts, The" (Warren), **IV:** 241–242, 243, 253
"Ballad of Carmilhan, The" (Longfellow), **II:** 505
"ballad of chocolate Mabbie, the" (Brooks), **Supp. IV Part 1:** 15
"Ballad of Dead Ladies, The" (Villon), **Retro. Supp. I:** 286
"Ballad of East and West" (Kipling), **Supp. IX:** 246
"Ballad of Jesse Neighbours, The" (Humphrey), **Supp. IX:** 100
"Ballad of Jesus of Nazareth, A" (Masters), **Supp. I Part 2:** 459
"Ballad of John Cable and Three Gentlemen" (Merwin), **Supp. III Part 1:** 342
"Ballad of Nat Turner, The" (Hayden), **Supp. II Part 1:** 378
"Ballad of Pearl May Lee, The" (Brooks), **Supp. III Part 1:** 74, 75
Ballad of Remembrance, A (Hayden), **Supp. II Part 1:** 367
"Ballad of Remembrance, A" (Hayden), **Supp. II Part 1:** 368, 372, 373
"Ballad of Ruby, The" (Sarton), **Supp. VIII: 259–260**
"Ballad of Sue Ellen Westerfield, The" (Hayden), **Supp. II Part 1:** 364
Ballad of the Brown Girl, The (Cullen), **Supp. IV Part 1:** 167, 168, 169–170, 173
"Ballad of the Brown Girl, The" (Cullen), **Supp. IV Part 1:** 168
"Ballad of the Children of the Czar, The" (Schwartz), **Supp. II Part 2:** 649
"Ballad of the Girl Whose Name Is Mud" (Hughes), **Retro. Supp. I:** 205
"Ballad of the Goodly Fere," **III:** 458
"Ballad of the Harp-Weaver" (Millay), **III:** 135
"Ballad of the Sad Cafe, The" (McCullers), **II:** 586, 587, 588, 592, 595, 596–600, 604, 605, 606
"Ballad of the Sixties" (Sarton), **Supp. VIII:** 259
"Ballad of Trees and the Master, A" (Lanier), **Supp. I Part 1:** 370

"Ballad of William Sycamore, The" (Benét), **Supp. XI:** 44, 47
Ballads and Other Poems (Longfellow), **II:** 489; **III:** 412, 422; **Retro. Supp. II:** 157, 168
Ballads for Sale (Lowell), **II:** 527
"Ballads of Lenin" (Hughes), **Supp. I Part 1:** 331
Ballantyne, Sheila, **Supp. V:** 70
Ballard, Josephine. *See* McMurtry, Josephine
"Ballena" (Mora), **Supp. XIII:** 224
"Ballet in Numbers for Mary Ellen, A" (Karr), **Supp. XI:** 241
"Ballet of a Buffoon, The" (Sexton), **Supp. II Part 2:** 693
"Ballet of the Fifth Year, The" (Schwartz), **Supp. II Part 2:** 650
"Ball Game, The" (Creeley), **Supp. IV Part 1:** 140
"Balloon Hoax, The" (Poe), **III:** 413, 420
Balo (Toomer), **Supp. III Part 2:** 484
Balsan, Consuelo, **IV:** 313–314
Balthus, **Supp. IV Part 2:** 623
Balthus Poems, The (Dobyns), **Supp. XIII:** 87
Baltimore, Lord, **I:** 132
Balzac, Honoré de, **I:** 103, 123, 339, 376, 474, 485, 499, 509, 518; **II:** 307, 322, 324, 328, 336, 337; **III:** 61, 174, 184, 320, 382; **IV:** 192; **Retro. Supp. I:** 91, 217, 218, 235; **Retro. Supp. II:** 93; **Supp. I Part 2:** 647
Bambara, Toni Cade, **Supp. XI:** 1–23
Banana Bottom (McKay), **Supp. X:** 132, **139–140**
Bancal, Jean, **Supp. I Part 2:** 514
Bancroft, George, **I:** 544; **Supp. I Part 2:** 479
Band of Angels (Warren), **IV:** 245, 254–255
Bang the Drum Slowly (Harris), **II:** 424–425
Banjo: A Story without a Plot (McKay), **Supp. X:** 132, **138–139**
"Banjo Song, A" (Dunbar), **Supp. II Part 1:** 197
Bankhead, Tallulah, **IV:** 357; **Supp. IV Part 2:** 574
"Banking Potatoes" (Komunyakaa), **Supp. XIII:** 126
"Bank of England Restriction, The" (Adams), **I:** 4
Banks, Joanne Trautmann, **Supp. XIII:** 297
Banks, Russell, **Supp. V:** 1–19, 227; **Supp. IX:** 153; **Supp. X:** 85; **Supp. XI:** 178; **Supp. XII:** 295, 309, 343

"Banned Poem" (Nye), **Supp. XIII:** 282
Bannon, Barbara, **Supp. XI:** 228
"Banyan" (Swenson), **Supp. IV Part 2:** 651, 652
"Baptism" (Olsen).*See* "O Yes" (Olsen)
Baptism, The (Baraka), **Supp. II Part 1:** 40, 41–42, 43
Baptism of Desire (Erdrich), **Supp. IV Part 1:** 259
"B.A.R. Man, The" (Yates), **Supp. XI:** 341
Barabtarlo, Gennady, **Retro. Supp. I:** 278
Baraka, Imamu Amiri (LeRoi Jones), **Retro. Supp. I:** 411; **Retro. Supp. II:** 298; **Supp. I Part 1:** 63; **Supp. II Part 1: 29–63,** 247, 250; **Supp. III Part 1:** 83; **Supp. IV Part 1:** 169, 244, 369; **Supp. VIII:** 295, 329, 330, 332; **Supp. X:** 324, 328; **Supp. XIII:** 94
"Bar at the Andover Inn, The" (Matthews), **Supp. IX:** 168
"Barbados" (Marshall), **Supp. XI:** 281
"Barbara Frietchie" (Whittier), **Supp. I Part 2:** 695–696
Barbarella (film), **Supp. XI:** 293, **307–308**
"Barbarian Status of Women, The" (Veblen), **Supp. I Part 2:** 636–637
Barbarous Coast, The (Macdonald), **Supp. IV Part 2:** 472, 474
Barbary Shore (Mailer), **III:** 27, 28, 30–31, 33, 35, 36, 40, 44; **Retro. Supp. II: 199–200,** 207
Barber, David, **Supp. IV Part 2:** 550; **Supp. XII:** 188–189
Barber, Rowland, **Supp. IV Part 2:** 581
Barber, Samuel, **Supp. IV Part 1:** 84
"Barclay of Ury" (Whittier), **Supp. I Part 2:** 693
Bard of Savagery, The: Thorstein Veblen and Modern Social Theory (Diggins), **Supp. I Part 2:** 650
"Barefoot Boy, The" (Whittier), **Supp. I Part 2:** 691, 699–700
Barefoot in the Park (Simon), **Supp. IV Part 2:** 575, 578–579, 586, 590
Bare Hills, The (Winters), **Supp. II Part 2:** 786, 788
"Bare Hills, The" (Winters), **Supp. II Part 2:** 790
Barely and Widely (Zukofsky), **Supp. III Part 2:** 627, 628, 635
Barenblat, Rachel, **Supp. XIII:** 274
Barfield, Owen, **III:** 274, 279
"Bargain Lost, The" (Poe), **III:** 411
Barker, Arthur, **Supp. XIII:** 167

Barker, Clive, **Supp. V:** 142
"Barking Man" (Bell), **Supp. X:** 9
Barking Man and Other Stories (Bell), **Supp. X:** 9
Barksdale, Richard, **Retro. Supp. I:** 202, 205; **Supp. I Part 1:** 341, 346
Barlow, Joel, **Supp. I Part 1:** 124; **Supp. I Part 2:** 511, 515, 521; **Supp. II Part 1: 65–86,** 268
Barlow, Ruth Baldwin (Mrs. Joel Barlow), **Supp. II Part 1:** 69
Barnaby Rudge (Dickens), **III:** 421
Barnard, Frederick, **Supp. I Part 2:** 684
Barnard, Rita, **Retro. Supp. II:** 342
Barn Blind (Smiley), **Supp. VI: 292–293**
"Barn Burning" (Faulkner), **II:** 72, 73; **Supp. IV Part 2:** 682
Barnes, Djuna, **Supp. III Part 1: 31–46; Supp. IV Part 1:** 79, 80
Barnett, Samuel, **Supp. I Part 1:** 2
Barnstone, Tony, **Supp. XIII:** 115, 126
Barnstone, Willis, **Supp. I Part 2:** 458
Barnum, P. T., **Supp. I Part 2:** 703
Baroja, Pío, **I:** 478
"Baroque Comment" (Bogan), **Supp. III Part 1:** 56, 58
"Baroque Sunburst, A" (Clampitt), **Supp. IX:** 49
"Baroque Wall-Fountain in the Villa Sciarra, A" (Wilbur), **Supp. III Part 2:** 553
Barr, Robert, **I:** 409, 424
Barracks Thief, The (Wolff), **Supp. VII:** 344–345
Barren Ground (Glasgow), **II:** 174, 175, 178, 179, 184–185, 186, 187, 188, 189, 191, 192, 193, 194; **Supp. X:** 228
Barrés, Auguste M., **I:** 228
Barrett, Elizabeth, **Supp. IV Part 2:** 430
Barrett, George, **Supp. IX:** 250
Barrett, Ralph, **Supp. I Part 2:** 462
Barron, Jonathan, **Supp. IX:** 299
Barrow, John, **II:** 18
Barrus, Clara, **I:** 220
Barry, Iris, **Supp. XIII:** 170
Barry, Philip, **Retro. Supp. I:** 104; **Supp. IV Part 1:** 83; **Supp. V:** 95
Bartas, Seigneur du, **IV:** 157
Barth, John, **I: 121–143; Supp. I Part 1:** 100; **Supp. III Part 1:** 217; **Supp. IV Part 1:** 48, 379; **Supp. V:** 39, 40; **Supp. IX:** 208; **Supp. X:** 263, 301, 302, 307; **Supp. XI:** 309; **Supp. XII:** 29, 289, 316; **Supp. XIII:** 41, 101, 104
Barth, Karl, **III:** 40, 258, 291, 303,

309; **IV:** 225; **Retro. Supp. I:** 325, 326, 327
Barthé, Richmond, **Retro. Supp. II:** 115
Barthelme, Donald, **Supp. IV Part 1: 39–58,** 227; **Supp. V:** 2, 39, 44; **Supp. VIII:** 75, 138; **Supp. X:** 263; **Supp. XI:** 25; **Supp. XII:** 29; **Supp. XIII:** 41, 46
Barthelme, Frederick, **Supp. XI: 25–41**
Barthelme, Peter, **Supp. XI:** 25
Barthelme, Steven, **Supp. XI:** 25, 27, 37
Barthes, Roland, **Supp. IV Part 1:** 39, 119, 126; **Supp. XIII:** 83
"Bartleby, the Scrivener; A Story of Wall-Street" (Melville), **III:** 88–89; **Retro. Supp. I:** 255
Bartleby in Manhattan and Other Essays (Hardwick), **Supp. III Part 1:** 204, 210
Bartlet, Phebe, **I:** 562
Bartlett, Lee, **Supp. VIII:** 291
Bartlett, Mary Dougherty, **Supp. IV Part 1:** 335
Barton, Bruce, **III:** 14; **Retro. Supp. I:** 179
Barton, Priscilla. *See* Morison, Mrs. Samuel Eliot (Priscilla Barton)
Barton, Rev. William E., **Retro. Supp. I:** 179
Bartram, John, **Supp. I Part 1:** 244
Bartram, William, **II:** 313; **Supp. IX:** 171; **Supp. X:** 223
"Basement" (Bambara), **Supp. XI:** 5
"Base of All Metaphysics, The" (Whitman), **IV:** 348
"Base Stealer, The" (Francis), **Supp. IX:** 82
Bashevis, Isaac. *See* Singer, Isaac Bashevis
Basil Stories, The (Fitzgerald), **Retro. Supp. I:** 109
Basin and Range (McPhee), **Supp. III Part 1:** 309
"Basin of Eggs, A" (Swenson), **Supp. IV Part 2:** 645
"Basket, The" (Lowell), **II:** 522
"Basketball and Beefeaters" (McPhee), **Supp. III Part 1:** 296
"Basketball and Poetry: The Two Richies" (Dunn), **Supp. XI:** 140
Baskin, Leonard, **Supp. X:** 58, 71
Basso, Hamilton, **Retro. Supp. I:** 80
Bastard, The (Caldwell), **I:** 291, 292, 308
"Bat, The" (Kenyon), **Supp. VII:** 168
Bataille, Georges, **Supp. VIII:** 4; **Supp. XII:** 1
"Batard" (London), **II:** 468–469

Bate, W. J., **II:** 531
Bates, Arlo, **Retro. Supp. I:** 35
Bates, Kathy, **Supp. XIII:** 207
Bates, Lee, **Retro. Supp. II:** 46
Bates, Milton J., **Supp. XII:** 62
Bates, Sylvia Chatfield, **II:** 586
"Bath, The" (Carver), **Supp. III Part 1:** 144, 145
"Bath, The" (Snyder), **Supp. VIII:** 302
Bathwater Wine (Coleman), **Supp. XI:** 83, 90, **91**
"Batter my heart, three person'd God" (Donne), **Supp. I Part 2:** 726
"Battle, The" (Simpson), **Supp. IX:** 268–269
Battle-Ground, The (Glasgow), **II:** 175, 176, 177, 178, 193
"Battle Hymn of the Republic" (Sandburg), **III:** 585
"Battle Hymn of the Republic, The" (Howe), **III:** 505
"Battle Hymn of the Republic, The" (Updike), **Retro. Supp. I:** 324
Battle of Angels (T. Williams), **IV:** 380, 381, 383, 385, 386, 387
"Battle of Lovell's Pond, The" (Longfellow), **II:** 493
Battle of the Atlantic, The (Morison), **Supp. I Part 2:** 490
"Battle of the Baltic, The" (Campbell), **Supp. I Part 1:** 309
"Battle of the Bunker, The" (Snodgrass), **Supp. VI:** 319–320
"***Battle of the Century!!!, The***" (Goldbarth), **Supp. XII:** 193
Battle-Pieces and Aspects of the War (Melville), **II:** 538–539; **III:** 92; **IV:** 350; **Retro. Supp. I:** 257
"Battler, The" (Hemingway), **II:** 248; **Retro. Supp. I:** 175
"Baudelaire" (Schwartz), **Supp. II Part 2:** 663
Baudelaire, Charles, **I:** 58, 63, 384, 389, 420, 569; **II:** 543, 544–545, 552; **III:** 137, 141–142, 143, 409, 417, 418, 421, 428, 448, 466, 474; **IV:** 74, 79, 80, 87, 211, 286; **Retro. Supp. I:** 56, 90; **Retro. Supp. II:** 261, 262, 340, 344; **Supp. I Part 1:** 271; **Supp. III Part 1:** 4, 6, 105; **Supp. XIII:** 77, 284
Baudrillard, Jean, **Supp. IV Part 1:** 45
Bauer, Dale, **Retro. Supp. I:** 381
Bauer, Douglas, **Supp. XII:** 290
Baum, L. Frank, **Supp. I Part 2:** 621; **Supp. IV Part 1:** 101, 113; **Supp. XII:** 42
Baumann, Walter, **III:** 478
Bausch, Richard, **Supp. VII: 39–56**
Bawer, Bruce, **Supp. VIII:** 153; **Supp.**

IX: 135; **Supp. X:** 187
Baxter, Charles, **Supp. XII:** 22
Baxter, John, **Supp. XI:** 302
Baxter, Richard, **III:** 199; **IV:** 151, 153; **Supp. I Part 2:** 683
"Bay City Blues" (Chandler), **Supp. IV Part 1:** 129
Baylies, William, **Supp. I Part 1:** 153
Baym, Nina, **Supp. IV Part 2:** 463; **Supp. X:** 229
Bayou Folk (Chopin), **Retro. Supp. II: 64–65,** 73; **Supp. I Part 1:** 200, 216, 218
Beach, Joseph Warren, **I:** 309, 500; **II:** 27; **III:** 319
Beach, Sylvia, **IV:** 404; **Retro. Supp. I:** 109, 422
"Beach Women, The" (Pinsky), **Supp. VI:** 241
"Beaded Pear, The" (Simpson), **Supp. IX:** 276
Beagle, Peter, **Supp. X:** 24
Beam, Jeffrey, **Supp. XII:** 98
Beaman, E. O., **Supp. IV Part 2:** 604
Bean, Michael, **Supp. V:** 203
Bean, Robert Bennett, **Supp. II Part 1:** 170
Bean Eaters, The (Brooks), **Supp. III Part 1:** 79–81
Be Angry at the Sun (Jeffers), **Supp. II Part 2:** 434
"Beanstalk Country, The" (T. Williams), **IV:** 383
Bean Trees, The (Kingsolver), **Supp. VII:** 197, 199–201, 202, 207, 209
"Bear" (Hogan), **Supp. IV Part 1:** 412
Bear, The (Faulkner), **Supp. VIII:** 184
"Bear, The" (Faulkner), **II:** 71–72, 73, 228; **IV:** 203; **Supp. IV Part 2:** 434; **Supp. IX:** 95; **Supp. X:** 30
"Bear, The" (Kinnell), **Supp. III Part 1:** 244
"Bear, The" (Momaday), **Supp. IV Part 2:** 480, 487
Bear and His Daughter: Stories (Stone), **Supp. V:** 295, 308
Beard, Charles, **I:** 214; **IV:** 429; **Supp. I Part 2:** 481, 490, 492, 632, 640, 643, 647
Beard, James, **I:** 341
Beard, Mary, **Supp. I Part 2:** 481
"Bearded Oaks" (Warren), **IV:** 240
Bearden, Romare, **Retro. Supp. I:** 209; **Supp. VIII:** 337, 342
Beardsley, Aubrey, **II:** 56; **IV:** 77
"Bears" (Rich), **Retro. Supp. II:** 280
"Beast" (Swenson), **Supp. IV Part 2:** 639
"Beast & Burden, The: Seven Improvisations" (Komunyakaa), **Supp.**

XIII: 120, 121
Beast God Forgot to Invent, The (Harrison), **Supp. VIII:** 37, 46, **51–52**
Beast in Me, The (Thurber), **Supp. I Part 2:** 615
"Beast in the Jungle, The" (James), **I:** 570; **II:** 335; **Retro. Supp. I:** 235; **Supp. V:** 103–104
Beast in View (Rukeyser), **Supp. VI:** 272, 273, 279, 280
"Beat! Beat! Drums!" (Whitman), **III:** 585
"Beatrice Palmato" (Wharton), **Retro. Supp. I:** 379
Beattie, Ann, **Supp. V: 21–37; Supp. XI:** 26; **Supp. XII:** 80, 139, 294
Beatty, General Sam, **I:** 193
Beaty, Jerome, **Supp. IV Part 1:** 331
Beaumont, Francis, **Supp. I Part 2:** 422
"Beauties of Santa Cruz, The" (Freneau), **Supp. II Part 1:** 260
Beautiful and Damned, The (Fitzgerald), **II:** 88, 89–91, 93, 263; **Retro. Supp. I: 103–105**, 105, 106, 110; **Supp. IX:** 56, 57
Beautiful Changes, The (Wilbur), **Supp. III Part 2:** 544–550
"Beautiful Changes, The" (Wilbur), **Supp. III Part 2:** 549, 550
"Beautiful Child, A" (Capote), **Supp. III Part 1:** 113, 125
"Beautiful & Cruel" (Cisneros), **Supp. VII:** 63, 67
"Beautiful Woman Who Sings, The" (Gunn Allen), **Supp. IV Part 1:** 326
"Beauty" (Emerson), **II:** 2, 5
"Beauty" (Wylie), **Supp. I Part 2:** 710
"Beauty and the Beast" (Dove), **Supp. IV Part 1:** 245
"Beauty and the Beast" (fairy tale), **IV:** 266; **Supp. X:** 88
"Beauty and the Shoe Sluts" (Karr), **Supp. XI:** 250
Beauty of the Husband, The: A Fictional Essay in Twenty-Nine Tangos (Carson), **Supp. XII: 113–114**
Beauty's Punishment (Rice), **Supp. VII:** 301
Beauty's Release: The Continued Erotic Adventures of Sleeping Beauty (Rice), **Supp. VII:** 301
Beauvoir, Simone de, **IV:** 477; **Retro. Supp. II:** 281; **Supp. I Part 1:** 51; **Supp. III Part 1:** 200–201, 208; **Supp. IV Part 1:** 360; **Supp. IX:** 4
"Because I could not stop for Death—" (Dickinson), **Retro. Supp. I: 38–40**, 41, 43, 44

"Because It Happened" (Goldbarth), **Supp. XII:** 192
"Because of Libraries We Can Say These Things" (Nye), **Supp. XIII:** 283
"Because You Mentioned the Spiritual Life" (Dunn), **Supp. XI:** 154
Bech: A Book (Updike), **IV:** 214; **Retro. Supp. I:** 329, 335
Beck, Dave, **I:** 493
Beck, Jack, **Supp. IV Part 2:** 560
Becker, Carl, **Supp. I Part 2:** 492, 493
Becker, Paula. *See* Modersohn, Mrs. Otto (Paula Becker)
Beckett, Samuel, **I:** 71, 91, 142, 298, 461; **III:** 387; **IV:** 95; **Retro. Supp. I:** 206; **Supp. IV Part 1:** 297, 368–369; **Supp. IV Part 2:** 424; **Supp. V:** 23, 53; **Supp. XI:** 104; **Supp. XII:** 21, 150–151; **Supp. XIII:** 74
Beckett, Tom, **Supp. IV Part 2:** 419
Beckford, William, **I:** 204
Beckonings (Brooks), **Supp. III Part 1:** 85
"Becky" (Toomer), **Supp. III Part 2:** 481, 483; **Supp. IX:** 312
Becoming a Man: Half a Life Story (Monette), **Supp. X:** 146, 147, 149, 151, 152, **155–157**
"Becoming a Meadow" (Doty), **Supp. XI:** 124–125
"Becoming and Breaking: Poet and Poem" (Ríos), **Supp. IV Part 2:** 539
Becoming Canonical in American Poetry (Morris), **Retro. Supp. I:** 40
Becoming Light: New and Selected Poems (Jong), **Supp. V:** 115
Bécquer, Gustavo Adolfo, **Supp. XIII:** 312
"Bed, The" (Dixon), **Supp. XII:** 154
Beddoes, Thomas Lovell, **III:** 469; **Retro. Supp. I:** 285
Bedichek, Roy, **Supp. V:** 225
Bedient, Calvin, **Supp. IX:** 298; **Supp. XII:** 98
"Bed in the Sky, The" (Snyder), **Supp. VIII:** 300
Bednarik, Joseph, **Supp. VIII:** 39
"Bedrock" (Proulx), **Supp. VII:** 253
"Bee, The" (Lanier), **Supp. I Part 1:** 364
Beecher, Catharine, **Supp. I Part 2:** 581, 582–583, 584, 586, 588, 589, 591, 599; **Supp. X:** 103; **Supp. XI:** 193
Beecher, Charles, **Supp. I Part 2:** 588, 589
Beecher, Edward, **Supp. I Part 2:** 581, 582, 583, 584, 588, 591

Beecher, Harriet. *See* Stowe, Harriet Beecher
Beecher, Henry Ward, **II:** 275; **Supp. I Part 2:** 581; **Supp. XI:** 193
Beecher, Lyman, **Supp. I Part 2:** 580–581, 582, 583, 587, 588, 599; **Supp. XI:** 193
Beecher, Mrs. Lyman (Roxanna Foote), **Supp. I Part 2:** 580–581, 582, 588, 599
Beeching, Jack, **Supp. X:** 114, 117, 118, 123, 125, 126
"Beehive" (Toomer), **Supp. IX:** 317
"Bee Hunt, The" (Irving), **II:** 313
"Beekeeper's Daughter, The" (Plath), **Retro. Supp. II:** 246–247
"Bee Meeting, The" (Plath), **Retro. Supp. II:** 254–255
Bee Poems (Plath), **Retro. Supp. II:** 254–255
Beer, Thomas, **I:** 405
Beerbohm, Max, **III:** 472; **IV:** 436; **Supp. I Part 2:** 714
"Beer in the Sergeant Major's Hat, or The Sun Also Sneezes" (Chandler), **Supp. IV Part 1:** 121
Beethoven, Ludwig van, **II:** 536; **III:** 118; **IV:** 274, 358; **Supp. I Part 1:** 363; **Supp. VIII:** 103
Beet Queen, The (Erdrich), **Supp. IV Part 1:** 259, 260, 264–265, 266, 273, 274, 275
Befo' de War: Echoes in Negro Dialect (Gordon), **Supp. II Part 1:** 201
"Before" (Goldbarth), **Supp. XII:** 175
"Before" (Snyder), **Supp. VIII:** 301
Before Adam (London), **II:** 466
Before Disaster (Winters), **Supp. II Part 2:** 786, 800
"Before Disaster" (Winters), **Supp. II Part 2:** 801, 815
"Before I Knocked" (D. Thomas), **III:** 534
"Before March" (MacLeish), **III:** 15
"Before the Altar" (Lowell), **II:** 516
"Before the Birth of one of her children" (Bradstreet), **Supp. I Part 1:** 118
"Before the Sky Darkens" (Dunn), **Supp. XI:** 155
"Begat" (Sexton), **Supp. II Part 2:** 693
Beggar on Horseback (Kaufman and Connelly), **III:** 394
"Beggar Said So, The" (Singer), **IV:** 12
Beggar's Opera, The (Gay), **Supp. I Part 2:** 523
Begiebing, Robert, **Retro. Supp. II:** 210
Begin Again (Paley), **Supp. VI:** 221

"Beginning and the End, The" (Jeffers), **Supp. II Part 2:** 420–421, 424
"Beginning of Decadence, The" (Jeffers), **Supp. II Part 2:** 420
"Beginning of Enthusiasm, The" (Salinas), **Supp. XIII:** 327–328
Beginning of Wisdom, The (Benét), **I:** 358; **Supp. XI:** 44
Be Glad You're Neurotic (Bisch), **Supp. I Part 2:** 608
"Begotten of the Spleen" (Simic), **Supp. VIII:** 277
"Behaving Like a Jew" (Stern), **Supp. IX: 290–291,** 294
"Behavior" (Emerson), **II:** 2, 4
Behavior of Titans, The (Merton), **Supp. VIII:** 201
Behind a Mask (Alcott), **Supp. I Part 1:** 36–37, 43–44
"Behind a Wall" (Lowell), **II:** 516
"Behold the Key" (Malamud), **Supp. I Part 2:** 437
Behrendt, Stephen, **Supp. X:** 204
Behrman, S. N., **Supp. V:** 95
Beidler, Peter G., **Supp. IV Part 2:** 557
Beidler, Philip D., **Supp. XII:** 69
Beige Dolorosa (Harrison), **Supp. VIII:** 40, 51
Beiles, Sinclair, **Supp. XII:** 129
Beiliss, Mendel, **Supp. I Part 2:** 427, 446, 447, 448
"Being a Lutheran Boy-God in Minnesota" (Bly), **Supp. IV Part 1:** 59, 67
Being and Race (Johnson), **Supp. VI:** 193, 199
Being and Time (Heidegger), **Supp. VIII:** 9
Being Busted (Fiedler), **Supp. XIII:** 95, 102, 104
Being There (Kosinski), **Supp. VII:** 215, 216, 222–223
Beiswanger, George, **Retro. Supp. II:** 220
Bel Canto (Patchett), **Supp. XII:** 307, 310, **320–322**
"Beleaguered City, The" (Longfellow), **II:** 498
Belfry of Bruges, The, and Other Poems (Longfellow), **II:** 489; **Retro. Supp. II:** 157, 168
"Belief" (Levine), **Supp. V:** 186, 190
"Beliefs of Writers, The" (Doctorow), **Supp. IV Part 1:** 235–236
"Believers, The/Los Creyentes" (Kingsolver), **Supp. VII:** 208
Belinda (Rice), **Supp. VII:** 301–302
"Belinda's Petition" (Dove), **Supp. IV Part 1:** 245

"Belita" (Ríos), **Supp. IV Part 2:** 541
Belitt, Ben, **Supp. XII:** 260
Bell, Clive, **IV:** 87
Bell, Daniel, **Supp. I Part 2:** 648
Bell, George Kennedy Allen, **Retro. Supp. I:** 65
Bell, Madison Smartt, **Supp. X: 1–20**
Bell, Marvin, **Supp. V:** 337, 339; **Supp. IX:** 152; **Supp. XI:** 316
Bell, Michael, **Retro. Supp. II:** 139
Bell, Pearl, **Supp. XI:** 233
Bell, Quentin, **Supp. I Part 2:** 636
Bell, Whitfield J., Jr., **II:** 123
Bellafante, Gina, **Supp. VIII:** 85
Bellamy, Edward, **II:** 276; **Supp. I Part 2:** 641; **Supp. XI:** 200, 203
Bellarosa Connection, The (Bellow), **Retro. Supp. II:** 31, 32
"Belle Dollinger" (Masters), **Supp. I Part 2:** 463
Belleforest, François de, **IV:** 370
"Belle Zoraïde, La" (Chopin), **Supp. I Part 1:** 215–216
Bell Jar, The (Plath), **Retro. Supp. II:** 242, **249–250; Supp. I Part 2:** 526, 527, 529, 531–536, 539, 540, 541, 542, 544
Belloc, Hilary, **III:** 176; **IV:** 432
Bellow, Saul, **I:** 113, 138–139, **144–166,** 375, 517; **II:** 579; **III:** 40; **IV:** 3, 19, 217, 340; **Retro. Supp. II: 19–36,** 118, 297, 325, 342; **Supp. I Part 2:** 428, 451; **Supp. II Part 1:** 109; **Supp. IV Part 1:** 30; **Supp. V:** 258; **Supp. VIII:** 98, 176, 234, 236–237, 245; **Supp. IX:** 212, 227; **Supp. XI:** 64, 233; **Supp. XII:** 159, 165, 170, 310; **Supp. XIII:** 106
"Bells, The" (Poe), **III:** 593; **Retro. Supp. II:** 266; **Supp. I Part 2:** 388
"Bells, The" (Sexton), **Supp. II Part 2:** 673
"Bells for John Whiteside's Daughter" (Ransom), **III:** 490
"Bells of Lynn, The" (Longfellow), **II:** 498
"Bells of San Blas, The" (Longfellow), **II:** 490–491, 493, 498
"Bell Tower, The" (Melville), **III:** 91
"Belly, The" (Dobyns), **Supp. XIII:** 87
Beloved (Morrison), **Supp. III Part 1:** 364, 372–379; **Supp. IV Part 1:** 13–14; **Supp. V:** 259; **Supp. VIII:** 343; **Supp. XIII:** 60
Beloved Lady: A History of Jane Addams' Ideas on Reform and Peace (Farrell), **Supp. I Part 1:** 24
Benchley, Robert, **I:** 48, 482; **II:** 435; **III:** 53; **Supp. IX:** 190, 195, 204
Benda, W. T., **Retro. Supp. I:** 13

Bend Sinister (Nabokov), **III:** 253–254; **Retro. Supp. I:** 265, 266, 270
"Beneath the Sidewalk" (Dunn), **Supp. XI:** 145
Benedict, Ruth, **Supp. IX:** 229
Benefactor, The (Sontag), **Supp. III Part 2:** 451, 455, 468, 469
"Benefit Performance" (Malamud), **Supp. I Part 2:** 431
Benét, Laura, **Supp. XI:** 44
Benét, Rosemary, **Supp. XI:** 44, 51
Benét, Stephen Vincent, **I:** 358; **II:** 177; **III:** 22; **IV:** 129; **Supp. XI: 43–61**
Benét, William Rose, **II:** 530; **Retro. Supp. I:** 108; **Supp. I Part 2:** 709; **Supp. XI:** 43, 44
Ben Franklin's Wit and Wisdom (Franklin), **II:** 111
Ben-Hur (film), **Supp. IV Part 2:** 683
Benigna Machiavelli (Gilman), **Supp. XI:** 201, 208
Benitez, R. Michael, **Retro. Supp. II:** 264
Benito Cereno (Lowell), **II:** 546; **Retro. Supp. II:** 181
"Benito Cereno" (Melville), **III:** 91; **Retro. Supp. I:** 255; **Retro. Supp. II:** 188
Benito's Dream Bottle (Nye), **Supp. XIII:** 278
"Bênitou's Slave, The" (Chopin), **Retro. Supp. II:** 64
Benjamin, Walter, **Supp. IX:** 133
Benjamin Franklin (Van Doren), **Supp. I Part 2:** 486
"Benjamin Pantier" (Masters), **Supp. I Part 2:** 461
Bennett, Anne Virginia, **II:** 184
Bennett, Arnold, **I:** 103; **II:** 337
Bennett, Elizabeth, **Supp. VIII:** 58
Bennett, Patrick, **Supp. V:** 225
Bennett, Paula, **Retro. Supp. I:** 29, 33, 42
Bennett, William, **Supp. VIII:** 245
Benson, Jackson J., **Supp. IV Part 2:** 613
Benstock, Shari, **Retro. Supp. I:** 361, 368, 371, 382
Bentham, Jeremy, **I:** 279; **Supp. I Part 2:** 635
Bentley, Eric R., **IV:** 396
Bentley, Nelson, **Supp. IX:** 324
Bentley, Richard, **III:** 79, 86
Benton, Robert, **Supp. IV Part 1:** 236
Beowulf, **Supp. II Part 1:** 6
Beran, Carol, **Supp. XIII:** 25
"Berck-Plage" (Plath), **Retro. Supp. II:** 253–254
Bercovitch, Sacvan, **Retro. Supp. I:**

408; **Retro. Supp. II:** 343, 348; **Supp. I Part 1:** 99; **Supp. I Part 2:** 659
Berdyaev, Nikolai, **I:** 494; **III:** 292
"Bereaved Apartments" (Kingsolver), **Supp. VII:** 203
"Bereavement in their death to feel" (Dickinson), **Retro. Supp. I:** 43, 44
"Berenice" (Poe), **III:** 415, 416, 425; **Retro. Supp. II:** 270
Bérénice (Racine), **II:** 573
Berenson, Bernard, **Retro. Supp. I:** 381; **Supp. IV Part 1:** 314
Berg, Stephen, **Supp. IV Part 1:** 60
Berger, Charles, **Retro. Supp. I:** 311
Berger, Roger, **Supp. XIII:** 237
Berger, Thomas, **III:** 258; **Supp. XII:** 171
Bergman, Ingmar, **I:** 291
Bergson, Henri, **I:** 224; **II:** 163, 165, 166, 359; **III:** 8, 9, 488, 619; **IV:** 86, 122, 466, 467; **Retro. Supp. I:** 55, 57, 80; **Supp. IV Part 1:** 42
Berkeley, Anthony, **Supp. IV Part 1:** 341
Berkeley, George, **II:** 10, 349, 357, 480, 554
Berkowitz, Gerald, **Supp. IV Part 2:** 590
Berlin Stories (Isherwood), **Supp. IV Part 1:** 82
Berlyne, Daniel E., **Supp. I Part 2:** 672
Bernard Clare (Farrell), **II:** 38, 39
Bernard of Clairvaux, Saint, **I:** 22; **II:** 538
Bernays, Thekla, **Retro. Supp. II:** 65
Berne, Suzanne, **Supp. XII:** 320
Berneis, Peter, **IV:** 383
Bernhardt, Sarah, **I:** 484; **Retro. Supp. I:** 377
Bernice (Glaspell), **Supp. III Part 1:** 179
"Bernice Bobs Her Hair" (Fitzgerald), **II:** 88; **Retro. Supp. I:** 103
Bernstein, Aline, **IV:** 455, 456
Bernstein, Andrea, **Supp. IX:** 146
Bernstein, Charles, **Supp. IV Part 2:** 421, 426
Bernstein, Elizabeth, **Supp. XII:** 318
Bernstein, Leonard, **I:** 28; **Supp. I Part 1:** 288, 289; **Supp. IV Part 1:** 83, 84
Bernstein, Michael André, **Retro. Supp. I:** 427
Bernstein, Richard, **Supp. IX:** 253, 262; **Supp. XII:** 113
Berrett, Jesse, **Supp. XIII:** 241, 242
"Berry" (Hughes), **Supp. I Part 1:** 329, 330

Berry, Faith, **Retro. Supp. I:** 194, 201
Berry, Walter, **IV:** 313–314, 326
Berry, Wendell, **Supp. VIII:** 304; **Supp. X: 21–39; Supp. XII:** 202; **Supp. XIII:** 1–2
"Berry Feast, A" (Snyder), **Supp. VIII:** 289, 297
Berryman, John, **I: 167–189,** 405, 441–442, 521; **II:** 554; **III:** 273; **IV:** 138, 430; **Retro. Supp. I:** 430; **Retro. Supp. II:** 175, 178; **Supp. I Part 2:** 546; **Supp. II Part 1:** 109; **Supp. III Part 2:** 541, 561, 595, 596, 603; **Supp. IV Part 2:** 620, 639; **Supp. V:** 179–180, 337; **Supp. IX:** 152; **Supp. XI:** 240
Berryman, Mrs. John, **I:** 168–169
Berryman's Sonnets (Berryman), **I:** 168, 175–178
"Berry Territory" (Snyder), **Supp. VIII:** 304
Berthoff, Warner, **Supp. I Part 1:** 133
Bertolucci, Bernardo, **Supp. IV Part 1:** 94
"Bertrand Hume" (Masters), **Supp. I Part 2:** 463–464
Best American Essays 1988, The (Dillard, ed.), **Supp. VIII:** 272
Best American Essays 1997, The (Frazier, ed.), **Supp. VIII:** 272
Best American Poetry, The: 1988 (Ashbery, ed.), **Supp. III Part 1:** 26
Best American Short Stories, **I:** 174; **II:** 587; **III:** 443; **Supp. IV Part 1:** 102, 315; **Supp. IX:** 114; **Supp. X:** 301
Best American Short Stories, 1915–1950, The, **Supp. IX:** 4
Best American Short Stories of 1942, The, **Supp. V:** 316
Best American Short Stories of 1944, The, **Supp. IX:** 119
Best American Short Stories of the Century (Updike, ed.), **Supp. X:** 163
Best American Short Stories of the Eighties, The (Ravenal, ed.), **Supp. IV Part 1:** 93
"Best China Saucer, The" (Jewett), **Retro. Supp. II:** 145–146
Best Hour of the Night, The (Simpson), **Supp. IX: 277–279**
Bestiaire, Le (Apollinaire), **IV:** 80
Bestiary, A (Wilbur), **Supp. III Part 2:** 552
"Bestiary for the Fingers of My Right Hand" (Simic), **Supp. VIII:** 274, 275
Best Man, The: A Play About Politics (Vidal), **Supp. IV Part 2:** 683
"Best of Everything, The" (Yates),

Supp. XI: 341
Best Short Plays, The (Mayorga), **IV:** 381
Best Short Stories, The (O'Brien, ed.), **I:** 289
Best Short Stories by Negro Writers, The (Hughes, ed.), **Supp. I Part 1:** 345
Best Times, The: An Informal Memoir (Dos Passos), **I:** 475, 482
Best Words, Best Order: Essays on Poetry (Dobyns), **Supp. XIII:** 74, **76–78,** 87
"BETANCOURT" (Baraka), **Supp. II Part 1:** 33, 34
Bête humaine, La (Zola), **III:** 316, 318
"Bethe" (Hellman), **Supp. I Part 1:** 293
Bethea, David, **Supp. VIII:** 27
Bethel Merriday (Lewis), **II:** 455
Bethlehem in Broad Daylight (Doty), **Supp. XI:** 121, **122–123**
Bethune, Mary McLeod, **Retro. Supp. I:** 197; **Supp. I Part 1:** 333
Bethurum, Dorothy, **IV:** 121
"Betrayal" (Lanier), **Supp. I Part 1:** 364
"Betrothed" (Bogan), **Supp. III Part 1:** 49–51
Bettelheim, Bruno, **Supp. I Part 2:** 622; **Supp. X:** 77, 84
Better Days (Price), **Supp. VI:** 264
Better Sort, The (James), **II:** 335
Betty Leicester (Jewett), **II:** 406
Betty Leicester's Christmas (Jewett), **II:** 406; **Retro. Supp. II:** 145
Between Angels (Dunn), **Supp. XI: 149–159**
"Between Angels" (Dunn), **Supp. XI:** 150
Between Fantoine and Agapa (Pinget), **Supp. V:** 39
"Between the Porch and the Altar" (Lowell), **II:** 540–541
"Between the World and Me" (Wright), **Supp. II Part 1:** 228
Between Time and Timbuktu (Vonnegut), **Supp. II Part 2:** 753, 759
Bevis, Howard L., **Supp. I Part 2:** 611
Bevis, John, **Supp. I Part 2:** 503
"Bewitched" (Wharton), **IV:** 316
Bewley, Marius, **I:** 336
Beyle, Marie Henri. *See* Stendhal
Beyond (Goldbarth), **Supp. XII:** 192
Beyond Black Bear Lake (LaBastille), **Supp. X:** 95, **99–102,** 108
"Beyond Charles River to the Acheron" (Lowell), **II:** 541
Beyond Criticism (Shapiro), **Supp. II**

Part 2: 703, 711
Beyond Culture (Trilling), **Supp. III Part 2:** 508–512
Beyond Desire (Anderson), **I:** 111
Beyond Document: The Art of Nonfiction Film (Warren, ed.), **Supp. IV Part 2:** 434
Beyond Good and Evil (Nietzsche), **Supp. IV Part 2:** 519
"Beyond Harm" (Olds), **Supp. X:** 210
"Beyond the Alps" (Lowell), **II:** 547, 550
"Beyond the Bayou" (Chopin), **Supp. I Part 1:** 215
Beyond the Horizon (O'Neill), **III:** 389
Beyond the Hundredth Meridian: John Wesley Powell and the Second Opening of the West (Stegner), **Supp. IV Part 2:** 599, 603–604, 611
"Beyond the Kittery Bridge" (Hatlen), **Supp. V:** 138
Beyond the Law (film) (Mailer), **Retro. Supp. II:** 205
"Beyond the Sea (at the sanatorium)" (Salinas), **Supp. XIII:** 325
Beyond the Wall: Essays from the Outside (Abbey), **Supp. XIII:** 13
Beyond Tragedy (Niebuhr), **III:** 300–303
Bezner, Kevin, **Supp. XII:** 202
Bhagavad Gita, **III:** 566; **IV:** 183
"Biafra: A People Betrayed" (Vonnegut), **Supp. II Part 2:** 760
Bianchi, Martha Dickinson, **I:** 470; **Retro. Supp. I:** 35, 37, 38
Bible, **I:** 191, 280, 414, 421, 490, 506; **II:** 6, 12, 15, 17, 108, 231, 237, 238, 252, 267, 302; **III:** 28, 199, 308–309, 341, 343, 350, 356, 402, 492, 519, 565, 577; **IV:** 11, 13, 42, 57, 60, 67, 152, 153, 154, 155, 164, 165, 296, 337, 341, 367, 369, 370, 371, 438; **Retro. Supp. I:** 91; **Supp. I Part 1:** 4, 6, 63, 101, 104, 105, 113, 193, 369; **Supp. I Part 2:** 388, 433, 494, 515, 516, 517, 583, 584, 587, 589, 653, 689, 690, 691; **Supp. IV Part 1:** 284; **Supp. VIII:** 20; **Supp. IX:** 246. *See also* names of biblical books; New Testament; Old Testament
Biblia Americana (Mather), **Supp. II Part 2:** 442
Bibliography of the King's Book, A; or, Eikon Basilike (Almack), **Supp. IV Part 2:** 435
"Bibliography of the King's Book, A, or, Eikon Basilike" (Howe), **Supp. IV Part 2:** 435
Bickel, Freddy. *See* March, Fredric

Bidart, Frank, **Retro. Supp. II:** 48, 50, 52, 182, 183, 184
Bid Me to Live (Doolittle), **Supp. I Part 1:** 258, 260, 268, 269, 270
"*Bien* Pretty" (Cisneros), **Supp. VII:** 70
"Bienvenidos" (Mora), **Supp. XIII:** 220
Bierce, Albert, **I:** 191, 209
Bierce, Ambrose, **I: 190–213**, 419; **II:** 74, 264, 271; **IV:** 350; **Retro. Supp. II:** 72
Bierce, Day, **I:** 195, 199
Bierce, General Lucius Verus, **I:** 191
Bierce, Helen, **I:** 210
Bierce, Leigh, **I:** 195, 198, 208
Bierce, Marcus, **I:** 190, 191
Bierce, Mrs. Ambrose, **I:** 194–195, 199
Bierce, Mrs. Marcus, **I:** 190, 191
Biffle, Kent, **Supp. V:** 225
"Bi-Focal" (Stafford), **Supp. XI:** 318, 321
Big as Life (Doctorow), **Supp. IV Part 1:** 231, 234
"Big Bite" (Mailer), **Retro. Supp. II:** 204
"Big Blonde" (Parker), **Supp. IX:** 189, 192, 193, 195, 196, 203
Big Bozo, The (Glaspell), **Supp. III Part 1:** 182
Bigelow, Gordon, **Supp. X:** 222, 227, 229
Bigelow, Jacob, **Supp. I Part 1:** 302
Bigelow Papers, Second Series, The (Lowell), **Supp. I Part 2:** 406, 415–416
Bigelow Papers, The (Lowell), **Supp. I Part 2:** 406, 407, 408, 410, 411–412, 415, 417, 424
"Bight, The" (Bishop), **Retro. Supp. II:** 38, 45
Big Hunger: Stories 1932–1959 (Fante), **Supp. XI:** 160
Big Knife, The (Odets), **Supp. II Part 2:** 546, 547, 548
Big Knockover, The (Hammett), **Supp. I Part 1:** 292; **Supp. IV Part 1:** 344, 345, 356
Big Laugh, The (O'Hara), **III:** 362, 373–375
Big Money, The (Dos Passos), **I:** 482, 483, 486–487, 489; **Supp. I Part 2:** 646, 647
"Big Rock Candy Figgy Pudding Pitfall, The" (Didion), **Supp. IV Part 1:** 195
Big Rock Candy Mountain, The (Stegner), **Supp. IV Part 2:** 596, 597, 598, 599, 600, 603, 604, 605, 606–607, 608, 610–611

Bigsby, C. W. E. (Christopher), **Supp. IX:** 137, 140
Big Sea, The (Hughes), **Retro. Supp. I:** 195, 197, 199, 201, 204; **Supp. I Part 1:** 322, 332, 333; **Supp. II Part 1:** 233–234
Big Sky, The (Mora), **Supp. XIII:** 221
Big Sleep, The (Chandler), **Supp. IV Part 1:** 122–125, 127, 128, 134
Big Sleep, The (film), **Supp. IV Part 1:** 130
Big Sur (Kerouac), **Supp. III Part 1:** 230
Big Sur and the Oranges of Hieronymous Bosch (H. Miller), **III:** 189–190
Big Town, The (Lardner), **II:** 426, 429
"Big Two-Hearted River" (Hemingway), **II:** 249; **Retro. Supp. I:** 170–171; **Supp. IX:** 106
"Big Wind" (Roethke), **III:** 531
"Big Winner Rises Late, The" (Dunn), **Supp. XI:** 146
"Bilingual Christmas" (Mora), **Supp. XIII:** 216–217
"Bilingual Sestina" (Alvarez), **Supp. VII:** 10
"Bill" (Winters), **Supp. II Part 2:** 792
"Bill, The" (Malamud), **Supp. I Part 2:** 427, 430, 434
Billings, Gladys. *See* Brooks, Mrs. Van Wyck
Bill of Rites, a Bill of Wrongs, a Bill of Goods, A (Morris), **III:** 237
"Bill's Beans" (Nye), **Supp. XIII:** 283
"Billy" (Gordon), **Supp. IV Part 1:** 306
Billy Bathgate (Doctorow), **Supp. IV Part 1:** 217, 219, 222, 224, 227, 229–231, 231, 232, 233, 238
Billy Bathgate (film), **Supp. IV Part 1:** 236
Billy Budd, Sailor (Melville), **III:** 40, 93–95; **IV:** 105; **Retro. Supp. I:** 249, **258–260**
Billy Phelan's Greatest Game (Kennedy), **Supp. VII:** 131, 132, 134, 135, 142–147, 149, 151, 153, 155
Billy the Kid, **Supp. IV Part 2:** 489, 490, 492
Biloxi Blues (Simon), **Supp. IV Part 2:** 576, 577, 584, 586–587, 590
"Bimini" (Hemingway), **II:** 258
Bingham, Millicent Todd, **I:** 470; **Retro. Supp. I:** 36
Bingo Palace, The (Erdrich), **Supp. IV Part 1:** 259, 260, 261, 263–264, 265, 266–267, 268–269, 270, 271–273, 274, 275

"Binsey Poplars" (Hopkins), **Supp. I Part 1:** 94; **Supp. IV Part 2:** 639
Biographia Literaria (Coleridge), **II:** 10; **Retro. Supp. I:** 308
"Biography" (Francis), **Supp. IX:** 77
"Biography" (Pinsky), **Supp. VI:** 235, 236, 239, 241, **243,** 249, 250
Biography and Poetical Remains of the Late Margaret Miller Davidson (Irving), **II:** 314
"Biography in the First Person" (Dunn), **Supp. XI:** 144
"Biography of an Armenian Schoolgirl" (Nye), **Supp. XIII:** 275, 280
"Biography of a Story" (Jackson), **Supp. IX:** 113
Biondi, Joann, **Supp. XI:** 103
"Biopoetics Sketch for *Greenfield Review*" (Harjo), **Supp. XII:** 216
"Birchbrook Mill" (Whittier), **Supp. I Part 2:** 699
"Birches" (Frost), **II:** 154; **Retro. Supp. I:** 132; **Supp. XIII:** 147
Bird, Alan, **Supp. I Part 1:** 260
Bird, Gloria, **Supp. XII:** 216
Bird, Isabella, **Supp. X:** 103
Bird, Robert M., **III:** 423
"Bird, The" (Simpson), **Supp. IX:** 269–270
"Bird, the Bird, the Bird, The" (Creeley), **Supp. IV Part 1:** 149
"Bird came down the Walk, A" (Dickinson), **Retro. Supp. I:** 37
"Bird Frau, The" (Dove), **Supp. IV Part 1:** 245
"Bird in Hand" (screen story) (West and Ingster), **Retro. Supp. II:** 348
Bird Kingdom of the Mayas (LaBastille), **Supp. X:** 96
Birds and Beasts (W. J. Smith), **Supp. XIII:** 346
Bird's Nest, The (Jackson), **Supp. IX: 124–125**
Birds of America (McCarthy), **II:** 579–583; **Supp. X:** 177
Birds of America (Moore), **Supp. X:** 163, 165, 167, 168, 171, **177–179**
"Birds of Killingsworth, The" (Longfellow), **Retro. Supp. II:** 164
Birds of North America (Audubon Society), **Supp. X:** 177
"Bird-Witted" (Moore), **III:** 214
Birkerts, Sven, **Supp. IV Part 2:** 650; **Supp. V:** 212; **Supp. VIII:** 85; **Supp. X:** 311
Birkhead, L. M., **III:** 116
"Birmingham Sunday" (Hughes), **Supp. I Part 1:** 343
Birnbaum, Henry, **Supp. XII:** 128
Birnbaum, Robert, **Supp. X:** 13

Birney, James G., **Supp. I Part 2:** 587, 588
Birstein, Ann, **Supp. VIII:** 100
Birthday Basket for Tía, A (Mora), **Supp. XIII:** 221
"Birthday Cake for Lionel, A" (Wylie), **Supp. I Part 2:** 721
"Birthday of Mrs. Pineda, The" (Ríos), **Supp. IV Part 2:** 542, 546
"Birthday Poem, A" (Hecht), **Supp. X:** 64
"Birthday Present, A" (Plath), **Supp. I Part 2:** 531
"Birthmark, The" (Ellison), **Retro. Supp. II:** 116; **Supp. II Part 1:** 237–238
"Birth-mark, The" (Hawthorne), **Retro. Supp. I:** 152
Birth-mark, The: Unsettling the Wilderness in American Literary History (Howe), **Supp. IV Part 2:** 422, 431, 434
Birth of a Nation, The (film), **Supp. I Part 1:** 66
Birth of the Poet, The (Gordon), **Supp. XII:** 7
Birth of Tragedy, The (Nietzsche), **Supp. IV Part 1:** 105, 110; **Supp. IV Part 2:** 519; **Supp. VIII:** 182
"Birth of Venus, The" (Botticelli), **IV:** 410
"Birth of Venus, The" (Rukeyser), **Supp. VI:** 281
"Birthplace Revisited" (Corso), **Supp. XII:** 123
"Birthright" (McKay), **Supp. X:** 136
Bisch, Louis E., **Supp. I Part 2:** 608
Bishop, Elizabeth, **Retro. Supp. I:** 140, 296, 303; **Retro. Supp. II: 37–56,** 175, 178, 189, 233, 234, 235; **Supp. I Part 1: 72–97,** 239, 320, 326; **Supp. III Part 1:** 6, 7, 10, 18, 64, 239, 320, 326; **Supp. III Part 2:** 541, 561; **Supp. IV Part 1:** 249, 257; **Supp. IV Part 2:** 439, 626, 639, 641, 644, 647, 651, 653; **Supp. V:** 337; **Supp. IX:** 40, 41, 45, 47, 48; **Supp. X:** 58; **Supp. XI:** 123, 136; **Supp. XIII:** 115, 348
Bishop, James, Jr., **Supp. XIII:** 1, 5, 6, 7, 9, 11, 15
Bishop, John Peale, **I:** 432, 440; **II:** 81, 85, 86–87, 91, 209; **IV:** 35, 140, 427; **Retro. Supp. I:** 109; **Supp. I Part 2:** 709
Bishop, John W., **Supp. I Part 1:** 83
Bishop, Morris, **Supp. I Part 2:** 676
Bishop, William Thomas, **Supp. I Part 1:** 83

"Bishop's Beggar, The" (Benét), **Supp. XI:** 56
Bismark, Otto von, **Supp. I Part 2:** 643
"Bistro Styx, The" (Dove), **Supp. IV Part 1:** 250–251
Bitov, Andrei, **Retro. Supp. I:** 278
"Bitter Drink, The" (Dos Passos), **Supp. I Part 2:** 647
"Bitter Farce, A" (Schwartz), **Supp. II Part 2:** 640, 657–658
"Bitter Pills for the Dark Ladies" (Jong), **Supp. V:** 118
Bitter Victory (Hardy; Kinnell, trans.), **Supp. III Part 1:** 235
Bixby, Horace, **IV:** 194
Bjorkman, Frances Maule, **Supp. V:** 285
Björnson, Björnstjerne, **II:** 275
Blackamerican Literature, 1760–Present (R. Miller), **Supp. X:** 324
Black American Literature Forum, **Supp. XI:** 86, 92, 93
"Black and Tan" (Bell), **Supp. X:** 9
Black Armour (Wylie), **Supp. I Part 2:** 708, 709, 712–714, 729
"Black Art" (Baraka), **Supp. II Part 1:** 49, 50–51, 59, 60
"Black Art, The" (Sexton), **Supp. II Part 2:** 682
"Black Ball, The" (Ellison), **Retro. Supp. II:** 124
Black Bart and the Sacred Hills (Wilson), **Supp. VIII:** 330, 331
Black Beetles in Amber (Bierce), **I:** 204, 209
"Blackberries" (Komunyakaa), **Supp. XIII:** 126
"Blackberry Eating" (Kinnell), **Supp. III Part 1:** 250
Blackberry Winter (Warren), **IV:** 243, 251, 252
Black Betty (Mosley), **Supp. XIII:** 237, **Supp. XIII:** 240, 243
"Black Birch in Winter, A" (Wilbur), **Supp. III Part 2:** 561
Black Boy (Wright), **IV:** 477, 478, 479, 480–482, 488, 489, 494; **Retro. Supp. II:** 117; **Supp. II Part 1:** 235–236; **Supp. IV Part 1:** 11
"Black Boys and Native Sons" (Howe), **Retro. Supp. II:** 112
Blackburn, Alex, **Supp. XIII:** 112
Blackburn, William, **IV:** 100
"Black Buttercups" (Clampitt), **Supp. IX:** 42
Black Cargo, The (Marquand), **III:** 55, 60
Black Cargoes: A History of the Atlantic Slave Trade (Cowley), **Supp. II**

Part 1: 140
"Black Cat, The" (Poe), III: 413, 414, 415; Retro. Supp. II: 264, 267, 269, 270
"Black Christ, The" (Cullen), Supp. IV Part 1: 170, 171–172
Black Christ and Other Poems, The (Cullen), Supp. IV Part 1: 166, 170
"Black Cottage, The" (Frost), Retro. Supp. I: 128
"BLACK DADA NIHILISMUS" (Baraka), Supp. II Part 1: 39, 41
"Black Death" (Hurston), Supp. VI: 153
Black Dog, Red Dog (Dobyns), Supp. XIII: 87, 88–89
"Black Dog, Red Dog" (Dobyns), Supp. XIII: 89
"Black Earth" (Moore), III: 197, 212
Black Fire (Jones and Neal, eds.), Supp. X: 324, 328
Black Fire: An Anthology of Afro American Writing (Baraka, ed.), Supp. II Part 1: 53
Black Flame, The (Du Bois), Supp. II Part 1: 159, 185–186
Black Folk, Then and Now: An Essay in the History and Sociology of the Negro Race (Du Bois), Supp. II Part 1: 159, 178, 183, 185
"Black Fox, The" (Whittier), Supp. I Part 2: 692
Black Freckles (Levis), Supp. XI: 257, 271
"Black Gang," IV: 406, 407
Black Genius (Mosley, ed.), Supp. XIII: 246
"Black Hood, The" (Francis), Supp. IX: 83, 91
Black House, The (Theroux), Supp. VIII: 319
Black Humor (Johnson), Supp. VI: 187, 199
Black Image in the White Mind, The (Fredrickson), Supp. I Part 2: 589
"Black Is My Favorite Color" (Malamud), Supp. I Part 2: 437
"Black Jewel, The" (Merwin), Supp. III Part 1: 355
Black Light (Kinnell), Supp. III Part 1: 235, 243
"Blacklist and the Cold War, The" (Kramer), Supp. I Part 1: 295
Black Literature in America (Baker), Supp. X: 324
Black Magic, A Pictorial History of the Negro in American Entertainment (Hughes), Supp. I Part 1: 345
Black Magic: Collected Poetry 1961–1967 (Baraka), Supp. II Part 1: 45, 49–50
"Blackmailers Don't Shoot" (Chandler), Supp. IV Part 1: 121–122
Black Manhattan (Johnson), Supp. IV Part 1: 169
Black Mass, A (Baraka), Supp. II Part 1: 46, 48–49, 56, 57
"Black Mesa, The" (Merrill), Supp. III Part 1: 328
Black Metropolis (Cayton and Drake), IV: 475, 486, 488
Black Misery (Hughes), Supp. I Part 1: 336
Blackmur, Helen Dickson (Mrs. R. P. Blackmur), Supp. II Part 1: 90
Blackmur, Richard P., I: 50, 63, 67, 280, 282, 386, 455, 472; II: 320, 537; III: 194, 208, 462, 478, 497; Supp. II Part 1: 87–112, 136; Supp. II Part 2: 543, 643; Supp. XII: 45
Black Music (Baraka), Supp. II Part 1: 47, 51
Black Nativity (Hughes), Retro. Supp. I: 196
"Black Panther" (Hughes), Retro. Supp. I: 211
Black Power (Wright), IV: 478, 488, 494
"Black Rainbow, A: Modern Afro-American Poetry" (Dove and Waniek), Supp. IV Part 1: 244
Black Reconstruction (Du Bois), Supp. II Part 1: 159, 162, 171, 182
Black Riders and Other Lines, The (Crane), I: 406, 419
"Black Rook in Rainy Weather" (Plath), Supp. I Part 2: 543, 544
Blacks (Brooks), Supp. III Part 1: 69, 72, 86, 87
Blacks, The (Genet), Supp. IV Part 1: 8
Black Skin, White Masks (Fanon), Retro. Supp. II: 118
Black Spear, The (Hayden), Supp. II Part 1: 375
Black Spring (H. Miller), III: 170, 175, 178, 180–182, 183, 184; Supp. X: 187
"Black Stone Lying on a White Stone" (Vallejo), Supp. XIII: 324
Black Sun (Abbey), Supp. XIII: 4, 8–9, 17
"Black Swan, The" (Jarrell), II: 382
Black Swan, The (Merrill), Supp. III Part 1: 319, 320
"Black Tambourine" (Crane), I: 387–388; II: 371
"Black Tuesday" (Swenson), Supp. IV Part 2: 646
Black Voices (Chapman), IV: 485
"Blackwater Mountain" (Wright), Supp. V: 335, 340
"Black Wedding, The" (Singer), IV: 12–13
Blackwell, Alice Stone, Supp. XI: 195, 197
Blackwell, Elizabeth, Retro. Supp. II: 146
Black Woman, The (Bambara, ed.), Supp. XI: 1
"Black Workers" (Hughes), Retro. Supp. I: 202
"Black Writer and the Southern Experience, The" (Walker), Supp. III Part 2: 521
Black Zodiac (Wright), Supp. V: 333, 344, 345
Blade Runner (film), Supp. XI: 84
Blaine, Anita McCormick, Supp. I Part 1: 5
Blair, Hugh, II: 8, 17; Supp. I Part 2: 422
Blair, Robert, Supp. I Part 1: 150
Blair, Walter, II: 20; Retro. Supp. II: 304
Blake, William, I: 381, 383, 389, 390, 398, 447, 476, 525, 526, 533; II: 321; III: 5, 19, 22, 195, 196, 197, 205, 485, 528, 540, 544–545, 567, 572; IV: 129; Retro. Supp. II: 76, 318; Supp. I Part 1: 80; Supp. I Part 2: 385, 514, 517, 539, 552, 708; Supp. V: 208, 257, 258; Supp. VIII: 26, 99, 103; Supp. X: 120; Supp. XII: 45
Blakely, Barbara, Supp. XIII: 32
Blanc, Marie Thérèse, Retro. Supp. II: 135
Blanc-Bentzon, Mme. Thérèse, II: 405
Blanchard, Paula, Retro. Supp. II: 131, 133–134, 135
Blancs, Les (Hansberry), Supp. IV Part 1: 359, 364, 365, 369, 372–374
Blancs, Les: The Collected Last Plays of Lorraine Hansberry (Nemiroff, ed.), Supp. IV Part 1: 365, 368, 374
"'Blandula, Tenulla, Vagula'" (Pound), III: 463; Supp. V: 336, 337, 345
Blankenship, Tom, IV: 193
Blanshard, Rufus A., I: 67
Blauvelt, William Satake, Supp. V: 171, 173
Blavatsky, Elena Petrovna, III: 176
"Blazing in Gold and Quenching in

Purple" (Dickinson), **Retro. Supp. I:** 30
Bleak House (Dickens), **II:** 291; **Supp. IV Part 1:** 293
Blechman, Burt, **Supp. I Part 1:** 290
"Bleeder" (Dobyns), **Supp. XIII:** 88
"Bleeding" (Swenson), **Supp. IV Part 2:** 646–647
"Blessed Is the Man" (Moore), **III:** 215
"Blessed Man of Boston, My Grandmother's Thimble, and Fanning Island, The" (Updike), **IV:** 219
"Blessing, A" (Wright), **Supp. III Part 2:** 600, 606
"Blessing the Animals" (Komunyakaa), **Supp. XIII:** 129–130
"Blessing the Children" (Hogan), **Supp. IV Part 1:** 401
Bless Me, Ultima (Anya), **Supp. XIII:** 220
Bligh, S. M., **I:** 226
Blind Assassin, The (Atwood), **Supp. XIII:** 20, **32**
Blind Bow-Boy, The (Van Vechten), **Supp. II Part 2:** 737, 740–742
Blind Date (Kosinski), **Supp. VII:** 215, 224–225
Blind Lion, The (Gunn Allen), **Supp. IV Part 1:** 324
"Blind Man's Holiday" (O. Henry), **Supp. II Part 1:** 401
Blindness and Insight (de Man), **Retro. Supp. I:** 67
"Blind Poet, The: Sidney Lanier" (Warren), **Supp. I Part 1:** 371, 373
Blithedale Romance, The (Hawthorne), **II:** 225, 231, 239, 241–242, 271, 282, 290; **IV:** 194; **Retro. Supp. I:** 63, 149, 152, 156–157, **162–163**; **Supp. I Part 2:** 579; **Supp. II Part 1:** 280; **Supp. VIII:** 153, 201
Blitzstein, Marc, **Supp. I Part 1:** 277
Blix (Norris), **III:** 314, 322, 327, 328, 333
Blixen, Karen Denisen Baroness. *See* Dinesen, Isak
"Blizzard in Cambridge" (Lowell), **II:** 554
Blok, Aleksandr Aleksandrovich, **IV:** 443
"Blood" (Singer), **IV:** 15, 19
Blood, Bread, and Poetry: Selected prose, 1979–1985 (Rich), **Retro. Supp. II:** 283, 292
Blood, Tin, Straw (Olds), **Supp. X: 212–215**
Blood and Guts in High School (Acker), **Supp. XII:** 5, 6, **11–12**
"Blood Bay, The" (Proulx), **Supp. VII:** 262–263

"Blood-Burning Moon" (Toomer), **Supp. III Part 2:** 483; **Supp. IX:** 314–315
"Bloodchild" (O. Butler), **Supp. XIII:** 61, **69–70**
Bloodchild and Other Stories (O. Butler), **Supp. XIII:** 69
Blood for a Stranger (Jarrell), **II:** 367, 368–369, 370–371, 375, 377
Blood Issue (Crews), **Supp. XI:** 103
Bloodlines (Wright), **Supp. V:** 332, 335, 340
Blood Meridian; or, The Evening Redness in the West (McCarthy), **Supp. VIII:** 175, 177, **180–182**, 188, 190
"Blood of the Conquistadores, The" (Alvarez), **Supp. VII:** 7
"Blood of the Lamb, The" (hymn), **Supp. I Part 2:** 385
Blood of the Martyr (Crane), **I:** 422
"Blood of the Martyrs, The" (Benét), **Supp. XI:** 56, 58
Blood of the Prophets, The (Masters), **Supp. I Part 2:** 458, 459, 461
Blood on the Forge (Attaway), **Supp. II Part 1:** 234–235
"Blood Returns, The" (Kingsolver), **Supp. VII:** 209
Bloodshed and Three Novellas (Ozick), **Supp. V:** 259–260, 261, 266–268
"Blood Stains" (Francis), **Supp. IX:** 86
Bloody Crossroads, The: Where Literature and Politics Meet (Podhoretz), **Supp. VIII: 241–242**
Bloom, Alice, **Supp. IV Part 1:** 308
Bloom, Allan, **Retro. Supp. II:** 19, 30, 31, 33–34
Bloom, Claire, **Retro. Supp. II:** 299; **Supp. IX:** 125
Bloom, Harold, **Retro. Supp. I:** 67, 193, 299; **Retro. Supp. II:** 81, 210, 262; **Supp. IV Part 2:** 620, 689; **Supp. V:** 178, 272; **Supp. VIII:** 180; **Supp. IX:** 146, 259; **Supp. XII:** 261; **Supp. XIII:** 46, 47
Bloom, Larry, **Supp. XIII:** 133
Bloom, Leopold, **I:** 27, 150; **III:** 10
Bloom, Lynn Z., **Supp. IV Part 1:** 6
Bloomfield, Leonard, **I:** 64
"Blossom and Fruit" (Benét), **Supp. XI:** 52–53
Blotner, Joseph, **Retro. Supp. I:** 88
Blouin, Lenora, **Supp. VIII:** 266
"Blue Battalions, The" (Crane), **I:** 419–420
"Bluebeard" (Barthelme), **Supp. IV Part 1:** 47
"Bluebeard" (Millay), **III:** 130

"Blueberries" (Frost), **Retro. Supp. I:** 121, 128
Blue Calhoun (Price), **Supp. VI:** 265–266
Blue City (Macdonald, under Millar), **Supp. IV Part 2:** 466–467
Blue Dahlia, The (Chandler), **Supp. IV Part 1:** 130
Blue Estuaries, The: Poems, 1923–1968 (Bogan), **Supp. III Part 1:** 48, 57, 66
Blue Hammer, The (Macdonald), **Supp. IV Part 2:** 462
"Blue Hotel, The" (Crane), **I:** 34, 415–416, 423
"Blue Hour, The" (Komunyakaa), **Supp. XIII:** 130
Blue in the Face (Auster), **Supp. XII:** 21
Blue Jay's Dance, The: A Birth Year (Erdrich), **Supp. IV Part 1:** 259–260, 265, 270, 272
"Blue Juniata" (Cowley), **Supp. II Part 1:** 144
Blue Juniata: Collected Poems (Cowley), **Supp. II Part 1:** 140
Blue Light (Mosley), **Supp. XIII: 245–247**, 248, 249
"Blue Light Lounge Sutra for the Performance Poets at Harold Park Hotel" (Komunyakaa), **Supp. XIII:** 125
"Blue Meridian" (Toomer), **Supp. III Part 2:** 476, 487; **Supp. IX:** 320
"Blue Moles" (Plath), **Supp. I Part 2:** 539
Blue Mountain Ballads (music) (Bowles), **Supp. IV Part 1:** 84
Blue Movie (Southern), **Supp. XI:** 309
"Blue Notes" (Matthews), **Supp. IX:** 169
Blue Pastures (Oliver), **Supp. VII:** 229–230, 245
"Blueprints" (Kingsolver), **Supp. VII:** 203
"Blue Ribbon at Amesbury, A" (Frost), **Retro. Supp. I:** 138
"Blues Ain't No Mockin Bird" (Bambara), **Supp. XI:** 3
"Blues Chant Hoodoo Rival" (Komunyakaa), **Supp. XIII:** 117, 118
"Blues for Another Time" (Dunn), **Supp. XI:** 148
"Blues for Jimmy" (McGrath), **Supp. X:** 116
"Blues for John Coltraine, Dead at 41" (Matthews), **Supp. IX:** 157
Blues for Mister Charlie (Baldwin), **Retro. Supp. II:** 8; **Supp. I Part 1:**

48, 61–62, 63
"Blues for Warren" (McGrath), **Supp. X:** 116
Blues If You Want (Matthews), **Supp. IX:** 155, **163–165**
"Blues I'm Playing, The" (Hughes), **Retro. Supp. I:** 204
"Blue Sky, The" (Snyder), **Supp. VIII:** 306
"Blues on a Box" (Hughes), **Retro. Supp. I:** 208
"Blues People" (Ellison), **Retro. Supp. II:** 124
Blues People: Negro Music in White America (Baraka), **Retro. Supp. II:** 124; **Supp. II Part 1:** 30, 31, 33–35, 37, 41, 42, 53
Bluest Eye, The (Morrison), **Supp. III Part 1:** 362, 363–367, 379; **Supp. IV Part 1:** 2, 253; **Supp. VIII:** 213, 214, 227; **Supp. XI:** 4, 91
Bluestone, George, **Supp. IX:** 7, 15
Blue Swallows, The (Nemerov), **III:** 269, 270, 271, 274–275, 278, 284, 286–288
Blue Voyage (Aiken), **I:** 53, 56
Blum, Morgan, **I:** 169
Blum, W. C (pseudonym). *See* Watson, James Sibley, Jr.
Blumenthal, Nathaniel. *See* Branden, Nathaniel
Blumenthal, Sidney, **Supp. VIII:** 241
Blunt, Wilfrid Scawen, **III:** 459
Bly, Robert, **I:** 291; **Supp. III Part 2:** 599; **Supp. IV Part 1: 59–77,** 177; **Supp. IV Part 2:** 623; **Supp. V:** 332; **Supp. VIII:** 279; **Supp. IX:** 152, 155, 265, 271, 290; **Supp. X:** 127; **Supp. XI:** 142; **Supp. XIII:** 284
"Boarder, The" (Simpson), **Supp. IX:** 269
Boarding House Blues (Farrell), **II:** 30, 43, 45
Boas, Franz, **I:** 214; **Supp. I Part 2:** 641; **Supp. VIII:** 295; **Supp. IX:** 329
"Boat, The" (Oliver), **Supp. VII:** 247
"Boat, The" (Sexton), **Supp. II Part 2:** 692
Boating Party, The (Renoir), **Supp. XII:** 188
Boat of Quiet Hours, The (Kenyon), **Supp. VII:** 167–169, 171
"Boat of Quiet Hours, The" (Kenyon), **Supp. VII:** 168
"Bob and Spike" (Wolfe), **Supp. III Part 2:** 580
Bob the Gambler (F. Barthelme), **Supp. XI:** 30, 31, 32, 34–35, 36–37

Boccaccio, Giovanni, **III:** 283, 411; **IV:** 230
Bocock, Maclin, **Supp. X:** 79
Bodenheim, Maxwell, **II:** 42, 530; **Retro. Supp. I:** 417; **Supp. I Part 1:** 257
"Bodies" (Oates), **Supp. II Part 2:** 520
"Bodies and Souls: The Haitian Revolution and Madison Smartt Bell's *All Souls' Rising*" (Trouillot), **Supp. X:** 14
Bodies of Work: Essays (Acker), **Supp. XII:** 7
Bodily Harm (Atwood), **Supp. XIII:** 25–27
Bodley Head Jack London (London), **II:** 483
Body (Crews), **Supp. XI:** 108–109
"Body, The" (Heldreth), **Supp. V:** 151
"Body and Soul: A Meditation" (Kumin), **Supp. IV Part 2:** 442, 452
Body and the Song, The (Bishop), **Retro. Supp. II:** 40
Body of This Death: Poems (Bogan), **Supp. III Part 1:** 47, 49–52, 58
Body of Waking (Rukeyser), **Supp. VI:** 274, 281
"Body of Waking" (Rukeyser), **Supp. VI:** 279
Body Rags (Kinnell), **Supp. III Part 1:** 235, 236, 243–245, 250, 253, 254
"Body's Curse, The" (Dobyns), **Supp. XIII:** 87
"Body's Weight, The" (Dobyns), **Supp. XIII:** 89
Body Traffic (Dobyns), **Supp. XIII:** 87, 89
"'Body with the Lamp Lit Inside, The'" (Mills), **Supp. IV Part 1:** 64
Boehme, Jakob, **I:** 10
Bogan, Louise, **I:** 169, 185; **Retro. Supp. I:** 36; **Supp. I Part 2:** 707, 726; **Supp. III Part 1: 47–68;** **Supp. VIII:** 171, 265; **Supp. IX:** 229; **Supp. X:** 58, 102; **Supp. XIII:** 347
Bogan, Major Benjamin Lewis, **IV:** 120
Bogart, Humphrey, **Supp. I Part 2:** 623; **Supp. IV Part 1:** 130, 356
Bogdanovich, Peter, **Supp. V:** 226
"Bohemian, The" (Harte), **Supp. II Part 1:** 339
"Bohemian Girl, The" (Cather), **Retro. Supp. I:** 7
"Bohemian Hymn, The" (Emerson), **II:** 19
Boissevain, Eugen, **III:** 124
Boit, Edward, **Retro. Supp. I:** 366
Bojorquez, Jennifer, **Supp. XII:** 318

"Bold Words at the Bridge" (Jewett), **II:** 394
Boleyn, Anne, **Supp. I Part 2:** 461
Bolivar, Simon, **Supp. I Part 1:** 283, 284, 285
Bolton, Guy, **Supp. I Part 1:** 281
Bolts of Melody: New Poems of Emily Dickinson (Todd and Bingham, eds.), **I:** 470; **Retro. Supp. I:** 36
"Bomb" (Corso), **Supp. XII:** 117, 124, 125–126, 127
Bombs Away (Steinbeck), **IV:** 51–52
"Bona and Paul" (Toomer), **Supp. IX:** 307, 318–319
Bonaparte, Marie, **III:** 418; **Retro. Supp. II:** 264, 266
"Bon-Bon" (Poe), **III:** 425
Bone, Robert, **Supp. IX:** 318–319; **Supp. XI:** 283
Bone by Bone (Matthiessen), **Supp. V:** 199, 212, 213, 214
"Bones" (Goldbarth), **Supp. XII:** 173–174
"Bones and Jewels" (Monette), **Supp. X:** 159
"Bones of a House" (Cowley). *See* "Blue Juniata"
Bonetti, Kay, **Supp. VIII:** 47, 152, 159, 160, 165, 168, 170, 223; **Supp. XII:** 61
Bonfire of the Vanities, The (Wolfe), **Supp. III Part 2:** 584–586
Bonhoeffer, Dietrich, **Supp. VIII:** 198
Boni and Liveright, **Retro. Supp. I:** 59, 80, 178
Bonicelli, Vittorio, **Supp. XI:** 307
Bonifacius (Mather), **Supp. II Part 2:** 461, 464
Bonnefoy, Yves, **Supp. III Part 1:** 235, 243
Bonner, Robert, **Retro. Supp. I:** 246
Bonneville, Mme. Marguerite, **Supp. I Part 2:** 520, 521
Bonneville, Nicolas de, **Supp. I Part 2:** 511, 518, 519
Bonney, William. *See* Billy the Kid
Bontemps, Arna, **Retro. Supp. I:** 194, 196, 203; **Supp. I Part 1:** 325; **Supp. IV Part 1:** 170; **Supp. IX:** 306, 309
Book, A (Barnes), **Supp. III Part 1:** 36, 39, 44
Book about Myself, A (Dreiser), **I:** 515; **Retro. Supp. II:** 104
"Book as a Container of Consciousness, The" (Gass), **Supp. VI:** 92
"Bookies, Beware!" (Heller), **Supp. IV Part 1:** 383
Book of American Negro Poetry, The

(Johnson), **Supp. IV Part 1:** 165, 166
Book of Americans, A (Benét), **Supp. XI:** 46, 47, 51
Book of Beb, The (Buechner), **Supp. XII:** 53
Book of Breeething, The (Burroughs), **Supp. III Part 1:** 97, 103
Book of Burlesques, A (Mencken), **III:** 104
Book of Common Prayer, A (Didion), **Supp. IV Part 1:** 196, 198, 203–205, 207, 208
Book of Daniel, The (Doctorow), **Supp. IV Part 1:** 218, 219, 220–222, 227, 231, 237–238, 238; **Supp. V:** 45
Book of Dreams (Kerouac), **Supp. III Part 1:** 225
"Book of Ephraim, The" (Merrill), **Supp. III Part 1:** 330–334
Book of Folly, The (Sexton), **Supp. II Part 2:** 691, 692–694
Book of Gods and Devils, The (Simic), **Supp. VIII:** 281
"Book of Hours of Sister Clotilde, The" (Lowell), **II:** 522
Book of Jamaica, The (Banks), **Supp. V:** 11, 12, 16
Book of Medicines, The (Hogan), **Supp. IV Part 1:** 397, 410, 411–414
"Book of Medicines, The" (Hogan), **Supp. IV Part 1:** 412, 413
"Book of Memory, The" (Auster), **Supp. XII:** 21–22
Book of Negro Folklore, The (Hughes, ed.), **Supp. I Part 1:** 345
Book of Nightmares, The (Kinnell), **Supp. III Part 1:** 235, 236, 243, 244, 246–254
Book of Prefaces, A (Mencken), **III:** 99–100, 105
Book of Repulsive Women, The (Barnes), **Supp. III Part 1:** 33
Book of Roses, The (Parkman), **Supp. II Part 2:** 597, 598
"Book of the Dead, The" (Rukeyser), **Supp. VI:** 272, 278, 279
"Book of the Grotesque, The" (Anderson), **I:** 106
Book of the Homeless, The (Wharton), **Retro. Supp. I:** 377
Book of the Hopi (Waters), **Supp. X:** 124
Book of Tobit (Bible), **Supp. XII:** 54
Book of Verses, A (Masters), **Supp. I Part 2:** 458
"Book of Yolek, The" (Hecht), **Supp. X:** 69, 70–71
"Books Considered" (Bloom), **Supp. I Part 1:** 96

Books in My Life, The (H. Miller), **II:** 176, 189
"Books/P,L,E, The" (Goldbarth), **Supp. XII:** 190
Bookviews, **Supp. XI:** 216
"Boom" (Nemerov), **III:** 278
Boom! (T. Williams), **IV:** 383
Boom Town (Wolfe), **IV:** 456
"Boom Town" (Wolfe), **IV:** 469
Boone, Daniel, **II:** 207; **III:** 444; **IV:** 192, 193
Boorstin, Daniel, **I:** 253
Booth, Charles, **Supp. I Part 1:** 13
Booth, General William, **Supp. I Part 2:** 384, 386
Booth, John Wilkes, **III:** 588
Booth, Philip, **I:** 522; **Supp. IX:** 269; **Supp. XI:** 141; **Supp. XIII:** 277
Borah, William, **III:** 475
Borden, Lizzie, **II:** 5
Borderlands/La Frontera: The New Mestiza (Anzaldúa), **Supp. XIII:** 223
Borders (Mora), **Supp. XIII:** 213, 215–217
Border Trilogy (McCarthy), **Supp. VIII:** 175, 182
Borel, Pétrus, **III:** 320
Borges, Jorge Luis, **I:** 123, 135, 138, 140, 142; **Supp. III Part 2:** 560; **Supp. IV Part 2:** 623, 626, 630; **Supp. V:** 238; **Supp. VIII:** 15, 348, 349; **Supp. XII:** 21, 147
"Borinken Blues" (Komunyakaa), **Supp. XIII:** 117
"Born a Square: The Westerner's Dilemma" (Stegner), **Supp. IV Part 2:** 595; **Supp. V:** 224
"Born Bad" (Cisneros), **Supp. VII:** 62
Borrowed Time: An AIDS Memoir (Monette), **Supp. X:** 145, 146, 147, 152, 154, 155
"Bosque del Apache Wildlife Refuge" (Mora), **Supp. XIII:** 218
"Boston" (Hardwick), **Supp. III Part 1:** 201
Boston (Sinclair), **Supp. V:** 282, 288–289
Boston, B. H., **Supp. XIII:** 312
Boston Adventure (Stafford), **Retro. Supp. II:** 177, 178
"Boston Common" (Berryman), **I:** 172
"Boston Hymn" (Emerson), **II:** 13, 19
Bostonians, The (James), **I:** 9; **II:** 282; **IV:** 202; **Retro. Supp. I:** 216, 225
"Boston Nativity, The" (Lowell), **II:** 538
Boswell: A Modern Comedy (Elkin), **Supp. VI:** 42, 44–45, 57

Boswell, James, **IV:** 431; **Supp. I Part 2:** 656
Bosworth, Patricia, **Supp. IV Part 2:** 573, 591
Botticelli (McNally), **Supp. XIII:** 197
Botticelli, Sandro, **IV:** 410; **Retro. Supp. I:** 422
"Botticellian Trees, The" (W. C. Williams), **Retro. Supp. I:** 422
"Bottle of Milk for Mother, A" (Algren), **Supp. IX:** 3
"Bottle of Perrier, A" (Wharton), **IV:** 316
"Bottles" (Kenyon), **Supp. VII:** 171
Bottom: On Shakespeare (Zukofsky), **Supp. III Part 2:** 622, 624, 625, 626, 627, 629
"Bottom Line, The" (Elkin), **Supp. VI:** 52, **53**
Boucher, Anthony, **Supp. IV Part 2:** 473
Boulanger, Nadia, **Supp. IV Part 1:** 81
"Boulot and Boulette" (Chopin), **Supp. I Part 1:** 211
Boulton, Agnes, **III:** 403
Bound East for Cardiff (O'Neill), **III:** 388
"Bouquet, The" (Stevens), **IV:** 90
"Bouquet of Roses in Sunlight" (Stevens), **IV:** 93
Bourdin, Henri L., **Supp. I Part 1:** 251
Bourgeois Poet, The (Shapiro), **Supp. II Part 2:** 701, 703, 704, 713, 714–716
Bourget, James, **IV:** 319
Bourget, Paul, **II:** 325, 338; **IV:** 311, 315; **Retro. Supp. I:** 224, 359, 373
Bourjaily, Vance, **III:** 43; **Supp. IX:** 260
Bourke-White, Margaret, **I:** 290, 293, 295, 297
Bourne, Charles Rogers, **I:** 215
Bourne, Mrs. Charles Rogers, **I:** 215
Bourne, Randolph, **I:** **214–238**, 243, 245, 246–247, 251, 259; **Supp. I Part 2:** 524
Bowden, Charles, **Supp. XIII:** 17
Bowditch, Nathaniel, **Supp. I Part 2:** 482
Bowen, Barbara, **Supp. IX:** 311
Bowen, Elizabeth, **Retro. Supp. I:** 351; **Supp. IV Part 1:** 299; **Supp. VIII:** 65, 165, 251, 265; **Supp. IX:** 128
Bowen, Francis, **Supp. I Part 2:** 413
Bowen, Louise de Koven, **Supp. I Part 1:** 5
Bowen, Michael, **Supp. VIII:** 73
Bowers, John, **Supp. XI:** 217–218

"Bowlers Anonymous" (Dobyns), **Supp. XIII:** 86
Bowles, Jane (Jane Auer), **II:** 586; **Supp. IV Part 1:** 89, 92
Bowles, Paul, **I:** 211; **II:** 586; **Supp. II Part 1:** 17; **Supp. IV Part 1: 79–99**
Bowles, Samuel, **I:** 454, 457; **Retro. Supp. I:** 30, 32, 33
"Bowl of Blood, The" (Jeffers), **Supp. II Part 2:** 434
"Bowls" (Moore), **III:** 196
Bowman, James, **I:** 193
"Bows to Drouth" (Snyder), **Supp. VIII:** 303
Box, Edgar (pseudonym). *See* Vidal, Gore
Box and Quotations from Chairman Mao Tse-tung (Albee), **I:** 89–91, 94
Box Garden, The (Shields), **Supp. VII:** 314–315, 320
"Box Seat" (Toomer), **Supp. III Part 2:** 484; **Supp. IX:** 316, 318
Boy, A (Ashbery), **Supp. III Part 1:** 5
Boyce, Horace, **II:** 136
Boyd, Brian, **Retro. Supp. I:** 270, 275
Boyd, Janet L., **Supp. X:** 229
Boyd, Nancy (pseudonym). *See* Millay, Edna St. Vincent
Boyd, Thomas, **I:** 99; **IV:** 427
Boyesen, H. H., **II:** 289
"Boyhood" (Farrell), **II:** 28
"Boy in France, A" (Salinger), **III:** 552–553
Boy in the Water (Dobyns), **Supp. XIII:** 75, **84**
Boyle, Kay, **IV:** 404
Boyle, T. C. (Thomas Coraghessan), **Supp. VIII: 1–17**
Boyle, Thomas John. *See* Boyle, T. C.
Boynton, H. W., **Supp. IX:** 7
Boynton, Percy Holmes, **Supp. I Part 2:** 415
"Boy on a Train" (Ellison), **Retro. Supp. II:** 124
"Boy Riding Forward Backward" (Francis), **Supp. IX:** 82
"Boys and Girls" (Cisneros), **Supp. VII:** 59–60
Boy's Froissart, The (Lanier), **Supp. I Part 1:** 361
Boy's King Arthur, The (Lanier), **Supp. I Part 1:** 361
Boy's Mabinogion, The (Lanier), **Supp. I Part 1:** 361
"Boys of '29, The" (Holmes), **Supp. I Part 1:** 308
Boys of '76, The (Coffin), **III:** 577
Boy's Percy, The (Lanier), **Supp. I Part 1:** 361
Boy's Town (Howells), **I:** 418

Boy's Will, A (Frost), **II:** 152, 153, 155–156, 159, 164, 166; **Retro. Supp. I:** 124, 127, 128, 131; **Retro. Supp. II:** 168
"Boy Who Wrestled with Angels, The" (Hoffman), **Supp. X:** 90
"Boy with One Shoe, The" (Jewett), **Retro. Supp. II:** 132
"Brace, The" (Bausch), **Supp. VII:** 48
Bracebridge Hall, or, The Humorists (Irving), **I:** 339, 341; **II:** 308–309, 313
Bracher, Frederick, **I:** 378, 380; **Supp. I Part 1:** 185
Brackenridge, Hugh Henry, **Supp. I Part 1:** 124, 127, 145; **Supp. II Part 1:** 65
Brackett, Leigh, **Supp. IV Part 1:** 130
Bradbury, John M., **I:** 288–289; **IV:** 130, 135
Bradbury, Malcolm, **Supp. VIII:** 124
Bradbury, Ray, **Supp. I Part 2:** 621–622; **Supp. IV Part 1: 101–118**
Braddon, Mary E., **Supp. I Part 1:** 35, 36
Bradfield, Scott, **Supp. VIII:** 88
Bradford, Gamaliel, **I:** 248, 250
Bradford, Roark, **Retro. Supp. I:** 80
Bradford, William, **Retro. Supp. II:** 161, 162; **Supp. I Part 1:** 110, 112; **Supp. I Part 2:** 486, 494
Bradlee, Ben, **Supp. V:** 201
Bradley, Bill, **Supp. VIII:** 47
Bradley, F. H., **Retro. Supp. I:** 57, 58
Bradley, Francis Herbert, **I:** 59, 567–568, 572, 573
Bradshaw, Barbara, **Supp. XIII:** 313
Bradstreet, Anne, **I:** 178–179, 180, 181, 182, 184; **III:** 505; **Retro. Supp. I:** 40; **Retro. Supp. II:** 286; **Supp. I Part 1: 98–123,** 300; **Supp. I Part 2:** 484, 485, 496, 546, 705; **Supp. V:** 113, 117–118; **Supp. XIII:** 152
Bradstreet, Elizabeth, **Supp. I Part 1:** 108, 122
Bradstreet, Mrs. Simon. *See* Bradstreet, Anne
Bradstreet, Simon, **I:** 178; **Supp. I Part 1:** 103, 110, 116
Brady, Alice, **III:** 399
"Bragdowdy and the Busybody, The" (Thurber), **Supp. I Part 2:** 617
"Brahma" (Emerson), **II:** 19, 20
Brahms, Johannes, **III:** 118, 448
"Brain and the Mind, The" (James), **II:** 346
"Brain Damage" (Barthelme), **Supp. IV Part 1:** 44
"Brain to the Heart, The"

(Komunyakaa), **Supp. XIII:** 120
Braithewaite, W. S., **Retro. Supp. I:** 131
Braithwaite, William Stanley, **Supp. IX:** 309
Brakhage, Stan, **Supp. XII:** 2
Bramer, Monte, **Supp. X:** 152
Branch Will Not Break, The (Wright), **Supp. III Part 2:** 596, 598–601; **Supp. IV Part 1:** 60; **Supp. IX:** 159
Brancusi, Constantin, **III:** 201; **Retro. Supp. I:** 292
Brande, Dorothea, **Supp. I Part 2:** 608
Branden, Nathaniel, **Supp. IV Part 2:** 526, 528
"Brand-Name Blues" (Kaufmann), **Supp. XI:** 39
Brand New Life, A (Farrell), **II:** 46, 48
Brando, Marlon, **II:** 588; **Supp. IV Part 2:** 560
Brandon, Henry, **Supp. I Part 2:** 604, 612, 618
Brandt, Alice, **Supp. I Part 1:** 92
Brandt, Carl, **Supp. XI:** 45
Brant, Sebastian, **III:** 447, 448
Braque, Georges, **III:** 197; **Supp. IX:** 66
Brashford, Jake, **Supp. X:** 252
Brasil, Emanuel, **Supp. I Part 1:** 94
"Brasília" (Plath), **Supp. I Part 2:** 544, 545
"Brass Buttons" (McCoy), **Supp. XIII:** 161
"Brass Candlestick, The" (Francis), **Supp. IX:** 89
Brass Check, The (Sinclair), **Supp. V:** 276, 281, 282, 284–285
"Brass Ring, The" (Carver), **Supp. III Part 1:** 137
"Brass Spittoons" (Hughes), **Supp. I Part 1:** 326–327
Brautigan, Richard, **III:** 174; **Supp. VIII:** 42, 43; **Supp. XII:** 139
Brave Cowboy, The (Abbey), **Supp. XIII:** 4–5
Brave New World (Huxley), **II:** 454; **Supp. XIII:** 29
"Brave New World" (MacLeish), **III:** 18
Bravery of Earth, A (Eberhart), **I:** 522, 524, 525, 526, 530
"Brave Words for a Startling Occasion" (Ellison), **Retro. Supp. II:** 118
Braving the Elements (Merrill), **Supp. III Part 1:** 320, 323, 325–327, 329
Bravo, The (Cooper), **I:** 345–346, 348
"Bravura" (Francis), **Supp. IX:** 90
Brawley, Benjamin, **Supp. I Part 1:** 327, 332
Brawne, Fanny, **I:** 284; **II:** 531

Braxton, Joanne, **Supp. IV Part 1:** 12, 15
Brazil (Bishop), **Retro. Supp. II:** 45; **Supp. I Part 1:** 92
"Brazil" (Marshall), **Supp. XI:** 281
Brazil (Updike), **Retro. Supp. I:** 329, 330, 334
"Brazil, January 1, 1502" (Bishop), **Retro. Supp. II:** 47
Braziller, George, **Supp. X:** 24
Brazzi, Rossano, **Supp. IV Part 2:** 520
"Bread" (Dickey), **Supp. IV Part 1:** 182
"Bread" (Olds), **Supp. X:** 206
"Bread Alone" (Wylie), **Supp. I Part 2:** 727
Bread in the Wilderness (Merton), **Supp. VIII:** 197, 208
Bread of Idleness, The (Masters), **Supp. I Part 2:** 460
"Bread of This World, The" (McGrath), **Supp. X:** 119, 127
Bread of Time, The (Levine), **Supp. V:** 180
Bread without Sugar (Stern), **Supp. IX: 297–298**
"Break, The" (Sexton), **Supp. II Part 2:** 689
Breakfast at Tiffany's (Capote), **Supp. III Part 1:** 113, 117, 119–121, 124, 126
Breakfast of Champions (Vonnegut), **Supp. II Part 2:** 755, 759, 769, 770, 777–778
Breaking Ice (McMillan, ed.), **Supp. XIII:** 182–183
Breaking Open (Rukeyser), **Supp. VI:** 274, 281
"Breaking Open" (Rukeyser), **Supp. VI:** 286
Breaking Ranks: A Political Memoir (Podhoretz), **Supp. VIII: 239–241,** 245
"Breaking Up of the Winships, The" (Thurber), **Supp. I Part 2:** 616
Breast, The (Roth), **Retro. Supp. II:** 305–306; **Supp. III Part 2:** 416, 418
"Breast, The" (Sexton), **Supp. II Part 2:** 687
"Breasts" (Simic), **Supp. VIII:** 275
"Breath" (Levine), **Supp. V:** 185
Breathing Lessons (Tyler), **Supp. IV Part 2:** 669–670
Breathing the Water (Levertov), **Supp. III Part 1:** 274, 283, 284
Breaux, Zelia, **Retro. Supp. II:** 114
Brecht, Bertolt, **I:** 60, 301; **III:** 161, 162; **IV:** 394; **Supp. I Part 1:** 292; **Supp. II Part 1:** 10, 26, 56; **Supp. IV Part 1:** 359; **Supp. IX:** 131, 133, 140; **Supp. X:** 112; **Supp. XIII:** 206, 286
Breen, Joseph I., **IV:** 390
Breit, Harvey, **I:** 433; **III:** 575; **Retro. Supp. II:** 230
Bremer, Fredrika, **Supp. I Part 1:** 407
Brendan: A Novel (Buechner), **Supp. XII:** 53
Brent, Linda, **Supp. IV Part 1:** 12, 13
Brentano, Franz, **II:** 350
Brer Rabbit (tales), **Supp. IV Part 1:** 11, 13
Breslin, James E. B., **Retro. Supp. I:** 430
Breslin, John B., **Supp. IV Part 1:** 308
Breslin, Paul, **Supp. VIII:** 283
Bresson, Robert, **Supp. IV Part 1:** 156
"Bresson's Movies" (Creeley), **Supp. IV Part 1:** 156–157
Breton, André, **III:** 425; **Supp. XIII:** 114
Brett, George, **II:** 466; **Supp. V:** 286
Brevoort, Henry, **II:** 298
Brew, Kwesi, **Supp. IV Part 1:** 10, 16
"Brewing of Soma, The" (Whittier), **Supp. I Part 2:** 704
Brewsie and Willie (Stein), **IV:** 27
Brewster, Martha, **Supp. I Part 1:** 114
"Brian Age 7" (Doty), **Supp. XI:** 136
"Briar Patch, The" (Warren), **IV:** 237
Briar Rose (Coover), **Supp. V:** 52
"Briar Rose (Sleeping Beauty)" (Sexton), **Supp. II Part 2:** 690
Brice, Fanny, **II:** 427
"Brick, The" (Nye), **Supp. XIII:** 276
"Bricklayer in the Snow" (Fante), **Supp. XI:** 164–165
"Brick Layer's Lunch Hour, The" (Ginsberg), **Supp. II Part 1:** 318
"Bricks, The" (Hogan), **Supp. IV Part 1:** 413
"Bridal Ballad, The" (Poe), **III:** 428
Bridal Dinner, The (Gurney), **Supp. V:** 109, 110
"Bride Comes to Yellow Sky, The" (Crane), **I:** 34, 415, 416, 423
"Bride in the 30's, A" (Auden), **Supp. II Part 1:** 9
Bride of Lammermoor (Scott), **II:** 291
Bride of Samoa (film), **Supp. IV Part 1:** 82
Bride of the Innisfallen, The (Welty), **IV:** 261, 275–279
"Bride of the Innisfallen, The" (Welty), **IV:** 278–279; **Retro. Supp. I:** 353
Bride of the Innisfallen, The, and Other Stories (Welty), **Retro. Supp. I:** 352–353, 355
Brides of the South Wind: Poems 1917–1922 (Jeffers), **Supp. II Part 2:** 419
Bridge, Horatio, **II:** 226
"BRIDGE, THE" (Baraka), **Supp. II Part 1:** 32, 36
Bridge, The (H. Crane), **I:** 62, 109, 266, 385, 386, 387, 395–399, 400, 402; **IV:** 123, 341, 418, 419, 420; **Retro. Supp. I:** 427; **Retro. Supp. II:** 76, 77, 81, 83, **84–87; Supp. V:** 342; **Supp. IX:** 306
Bridge at Remagen, The (film), **Supp. XI:** 343
"Bridge Burners, The" (Van Vechten), **Supp. II Part 2:** 733
Bridge of San Luis Rey, The (Wilder), **I:** 360; **IV:** 356, 357, 360–363, 365, 366
Bridge of Years, The (Sarton), **Supp. VIII:** 253
"Bridges" (Kingsolver), **Supp. VII:** 208
Bridges, Harry, **I:** 493
Bridges, Robert, **II:** 537; **III:** 527; **Supp. I Part 2:** 721; **Supp. II Part 1:** 21
Bridgman, P. W., **I:** 278
"Bridle, The" (Carver), **Supp. III Part 1:** 138
"Brief Début of Tildy, The" (O. Henry), **Supp. II Part 1:** 408
"Brief Encounters on the Inland Waterway" (Vonnegut), **Supp. II Part 2:** 760
Briefings (Ammons), **Supp. VII:** 29
Brief Interviews with Hideous Men (Wallace), **Supp. X: 308–310**
"Brief Interviews with Hideous Men" (Wallace), **Supp. X:** 309
"Briefly It Enters, and Briefly Speaks" (Kenyon), **Supp. VII:** 174
Briffault, Robert, **Supp. I Part 2:** 560, 567
"Brigade de Cuisine" (McPhee), **Supp. III Part 1:** 307–308
Brigadier and the Golf Widow, The (Cheever), **Supp. I Part 1:** 184–185, 192
Briggs, Charles F., **Supp. I Part 2:** 411
"Bright and Morning Star" (Wright), **IV:** 488
Bright Book of Life: American Novelists and Storytellers from Hemingway to Mailer (Kazin), **Supp. VIII:** 102, 104
Bright Center of Heaven (Maxwell), **Supp. VIII: 153–155,** 164
Brighton Beach Memoirs (Simon), **Supp. IV Part 2:** 576, 577, 584, 586–587, 590
Bright Procession (Sedges), **Supp. II**

Part 1: 125
Bright Room Called Day, A (Kushner), **Supp. IX:** 133, **138–141,** 142
"Brilliance" (Doty), **Supp. XI:** 124, 128
"Brilliant Leaves" (Gordon), **II:** 199
"Brilliant Sad Sun" (W. C. Williams), **Retro. Supp. I:** 422
"Bringing Back the Trumpeter Swan" (Kumin), **Supp. IV Part 2:** 454
Bringing It All Back Home (McNally), **Supp. XIII:** 197–198
"Bringing the Strange Home" (Dunn), **Supp. XI:** 141
"Bring the Day!" (Roethke), **III:** 536
Brinkley, Douglas, **Supp. XIII:** 9
Brinkmeyer, Robert H., Jr., **Supp. XI:** 38
Brinnin, John Malcolm, **IV:** 26, 27, 28, 42, 46
Brissot, Jacques Pierre, **Supp. I Part 2:** 511
"Britain's Negro Problem in Sierra Leone" (Du Bois), **Supp. I Part 1:** 176
"British Guiana" (Marshall), **Supp. XI:** 281–282
"British Poets, The" (Holmes), **Supp. I Part 1:** 306
"British Prison Ship, The" (Freneau), **Supp. II Part 1:** 261
Britten, Benjamin, **II:** 586; **Supp. II Part 1:** 17; **Supp. IV Part 1:** 84
Broadwater, Bowden, **II:** 562
Broadway, Broadway (McNally). *See It's Only a Play* (McNally)
Broadway, J. William, **Supp. V:** 316
Broadway Bound (Simon), **Supp. IV Part 2:** 576, 577, 584, 586–587, 590
"Broadway Sights" (Whitman), **IV:** 350
Broccoli, Albert R. "Cubby," **Supp. XI:** 307
Bröck, Sabine, **Supp. XI:** 275, 277, 278
Brodhead, Richard, **Retro. Supp. II:** 139
Brodkey, Harold, **Supp. VIII:** 151; **Supp. X:** 160
Brodskii, Iosif Alexsandrovich. *See* Brodsky, Joseph
Brodsky, Joseph, **Supp. VIII:** 19–35; **Supp. X:** 65, 73
"Brokeback Mountain" (Proulx), **Supp. VII:** 264–265
"Broken Balance, The" (Jeffers), **Supp. II Part 2:** 426
"Broken Field Running" (Bambara), **Supp. XI:** 10, 11
Broken Ground, The (Berry), **Supp. X:** 30

"Broken Home, The" (Merrill), **Supp. III Part 1:** 319, 325
"Broken Oar, The" (Longfellow), **Retro. Supp. II:** 169
"Broken Promise" (MacLeish), **III:** 15
Broken Span, The (W. C. Williams), **IV:** 419; **Retro. Supp. I:** 424
"Broken Tower, The" (H. Crane), **I:** 385, 386, 400, 401–402; **Retro. Supp. II:** 89, 90
Broken Vessels (Dubus), **Supp. VII:** 90–91; **Supp. XI:** 347
"Broken Vessels" (Dubus), **Supp. VII:** 90
"Broker" (H. Roth), **Supp. IX:** 234
Bromfield, Louis, **IV:** 380
Bromwich, David, **Retro. Supp. I:** 305; **Supp. XII:** 162
"Broncho That Would Not Be Broken, The" (Lindsay), **Supp. I Part 2:** 383
Bronner, Stephen Eric, **Retro. Supp. II:** 293
Brontë, Anne, **Supp. IV Part 2:** 430
Brontë, Branwell, **I:** 462
Brontë, Charlotte, **I:** 458; **II:** 175; **Retro. Supp. II:** 286; **Supp. IV Part 2:** 430; **Supp. IX:** 128; **Supp. XII:** 104, 303
Brontë, Emily, **I:** 458; **Retro. Supp. I:** 43; **Supp. IV Part 2:** 430; **Supp. IX:** 128; **Supp. X:** 78, 89
"Bronze" (Francis), **Supp. IX:** 76
"Bronze" (Merrill), **Supp. III Part 1:** 336
"Bronze Buckaroo, The" (Baraka), **Supp. II Part 1:** 49
"Bronze Horses, The" (Lowell), **II:** 524
"Bronze Tablets" (Lowell), **II:** 523
Bronzeville Boys and Girls (Brooks), **Supp. III Part 1:** 79
"Bronzeville Mother Loiters in Mississippi, A. Meanwhile, a Mississippi Mother Burns Bacon" (Brooks), **Supp. III Part 1:** 80
"Brooch, The" (Singer), **IV:** 20
Brook, Peter, **Retro. Supp. II:** 182
Brooke, Rupert, **II:** 82; **III:** 3
Brook Evans (Glaspell), **Supp. III Part 1:** 182–185
"Brooking Likeness" (Glück), **Supp. V:** 85
"Brooklyn" (Marshall), **Supp. XI:** 281, 282
Brooks, Cleanth, **I:** 280, 282; **III:** 517; **IV:** 236, 279; **Retro. Supp. I:** 40, 41, 90; **Retro. Supp. II:** 235; **Supp. I Part 2:** 423; **Supp. III Part 2:** 542; **Supp. V:** 316; **Supp. IX:** 153, 155; **Supp. X:** 115, 123

Brooks, David, **Supp. IV Part 2:** 623, 626, 630; **Supp. VIII:** 232
Brooks, Gwendolyn, **Retro. Supp. I:** 208; **Supp. III Part 1: 69–90;** **Supp. IV Part 1:** 2, 15, 244, 251, 257; **Supp. XI:** 1, 278; **Supp. XIII:** 111, 112, 296
Brooks, Mel, **Supp. IV Part 1:** 390; **Supp. IV Part 2:** 591
Brooks, Mrs. Van Wyck (Eleanor Kenyon Stimson), **I:** 240, 245, 250, 252
Brooks, Mrs. Van Wyck (Gladys Billings), **I:** 258
Brooks, Paul, **Supp. IX:** 26, 31, 32
Brooks, Phillips, **II:** 542; **Retro. Supp. II:** 134; **Supp. XIII:** 142
Brooks, Van Wyck, **I:** 106, 117, 215, 222, 228, 230, 231, 233, 236, **239–263,** 266, 480; **II:** 30, 271, 285, 309, 337, 482; **III:** 394, 606; **IV:** 171, 312, 427, 433; **Retro. Supp. II:** 46, 137; **Supp. I Part 2:** 423, 424, 650; **Supp. II Part 1:** 137; **Supp. VIII:** 98, 101
Broom of the System, The (Wallace), **Supp. X:** 301, **302–305,** 310
"Brooms" (Simic), **Supp. VIII:** 275
Brosnan, Jim, **II:** 424–425
Brother Carl (Sontag), **Supp. III Part 2:** 452
"Brother Death" (Anderson), **I:** 114
Brotherhood of the Grape, The (Fante), **Supp. XI:** 160, **171–172**
"Brothers" (Anderson), **I:** 114
Brothers, The (F. Barthelme), **Supp. XI:** 25, 28, 29, 30, 32–33
Brothers and Keepers (Wideman), **Supp. X:** 320, 321–322, 323, **325–327,** 328, 329–330, 331, 332
Brothers Ashkenazi, The (Singer), **IV:** 2
Brothers Karamazov, The (Dostoyevsky), **II:** 60; **III:** 146, 150, 283; **Supp. IX:** 102, 106; **Supp. XI:** 172; **Supp. XII:** 322
Brother to Dragons: A Tale in Verse and Voices (Warren), **IV:** 243–244, 245, 246, 251, 252, 254, 257
Broughton, Rhoda, **II:** 174; **IV:** 309, 310
Broun, Heywood, **I:** 478; **II:** 417; **IV:** 432; **Supp. IX:** 190
Broussais, François, **Supp. I Part 1:** 302
Browder, Earl, **I:** 515
Brower, David, **Supp. X:** 29
Brown, Alice, **II:** 523; **Retro. Supp. II:** 136
Brown, Ashley, **Retro. Supp. II:** 48;

Supp. I Part 1: 79, 80, 82, 84, 92
Brown, Charles Brockden, **I:** 54, 211, 335; **II:** 74, 267, 298; **III:** 415; **Supp. I Part 1:** 124–149; **Supp. II Part 1:** 65, 292
Brown, Clifford, **Supp. V:** 195
Brown, Dee, **Supp. IV Part 2:** 504
Brown, Elijah, **Supp. I Part 1:** 125
Brown, George Douglas, **III:** 473
Brown, Harry, **Supp. IV Part 2:** 560
Brown, John, **II:** 13; **IV:** 125, 126, 172, 237, 249, 254; **Supp. I Part 1:** 345; **Supp. VIII:** 204
Brown, Joseph Epes, **Supp. IV Part 2:** 487
Brown, Leonard, **Supp. IX:** 117
Brown, Mary Armitt, **Supp. I Part 1:** 125
Brown, Mrs. Charles Brockden (Elizabeth Linn), **Supp. I Part 1:** 145, 146
Brown, Percy, **II:** 20
Brown, Robert E., **Supp. X:** 12
Brown, Scott, **Supp. XI:** 178
Brown, Slater, **IV:** 123; **Retro. Supp. II:** 79
Brown, Solyman, **Supp. I Part 1:** 156
Brown, Sterling, **Retro. Supp. I:** 198; **Supp. IV Part 1:** 169
Brown, Wesley, **Supp. V:** 6
Brown Decades, The (Mumford), **Supp. II Part 2:** 475, 478, 491–492
Brown Dog (Harrison), **Supp. VIII:** 51
"Brown Dwarf of Rügen, The" (Whittier), **Supp. I Part 2:** 696
Browne, Charles Farrar, **II:** 289; **IV:** 193, 196
Browne, Roscoe Lee, **Supp. VIII:** 345
Browne, Thomas, **II:** 15–16, 304; **III:** 77, 78, 198, 487; **IV:** 147; **Supp. IX:** 136; **Supp. XII:** 45
Browne, William, **Supp. I Part 1:** 98
Brownell, W. C., **II:** 14
Brownell, William Crary, **Retro. Supp. I:** 365, 366
Brown Girl, Brownstones (Marshall), **Supp. XI:** 275, 276, 278–280, 282
Brownies' Book, The (Hughes), **Supp. I Part 1:** 321
Browning, Elizabeth Barrett, **I:** 458, 459; **Retro. Supp. I:** 33, 43
Browning, Robert, **I:** 50, 66, 103, 458, 460, 468; **II:** 338, 478, 522; **III:** 5, 8, 467, 469, 484, 511, 521, 524, 606, 609; **IV:** 135, 245, 366, 416; **Retro. Supp. I:** 43, 55, 217; **Retro. Supp. II:** 188, 190; **Supp. I Part 1:** 2, 6, 79, 311; **Supp. I Part 2:** 416, 468, 622; **Supp. III Part 1:** 5, 6; **Supp. IV Part 2:** 430; **Supp. X:** 65

Brownmiller, Susan, **Supp. X:** 252
"Brown River, Smile" (Toomer), **Supp. IV Part 1:** 16
Brownstone Eclogues and Other Poems (Aiken), **I:** 65, 67
Broyard, Anatole, **Supp. IV Part 1:** 39; **Supp. VIII:** 140; **Supp. X:** 186; **Supp. XI:** 348
Bruccoli, Matthew, **Retro. Supp. I:** 98, 102, 105, 114, 115, 359; **Supp. IV Part 2:** 468, 470
Bruce, Lenny, **Supp. VIII:** 198
Bruce, Virginia, **Supp. XII:** 173
Bruce-Novoa, Juan, **Supp. VIII:** 73, 74
Bruchac, Joseph, **Supp. IV Part 1:** 261, 319, 320, 321, 322, 323, 325, 328, 398, 399, 403, 408, 414; **Supp. IV Part 2:** 502, 506
Brueghel, Pieter, **I:** 174; **Supp. I Part 2:** 475
Brueghel, Pieter, the Elder, **Retro. Supp. I:** 430
Bruell, Edwin, **Supp. VIII:** 126
"Bruja: Witch" (Mora), **Supp. XIII:** 214, 220, 221, **Supp. XIII:** 222
Brulé, Claude, **Supp. XI:** 307
Brumer, Andy, **Supp. XIII:** 88
Brunner, Emil, **III:** 291, 303
Brustein, Robert, **Supp. VIII:** 331
Brutus, **IV:** 373, 374; **Supp. I Part 2:** 471
"Brutus and Antony" (Masters), **Supp. I Part 2:** 472
"Bryan, Bryan, Bryan, Bryan" (Lindsay), **Supp. I Part 2:** 394, 395, 398
Bryan, George, **Retro. Supp. II:** 76
Bryan, Sharon, **Supp. IX:** 154
Bryan, William Jennings, **I:** 483; **IV:** 124; **Supp. I Part 2:** 385, 395–396, 455, 456
Bryant, Austin, **Supp. I Part 1:** 152, 153
Bryant, Frances, **Supp. I Part 1:** 153
Bryant, Louise, **Supp. X:** 136
Bryant, Mrs. William Cullen (Frances Fairchild), **Supp. I Part 1:** 153, 169
Bryant, Peter, **Supp. I Part 1:** 150, 151, 152, 153. *See also* George, Peter
Bryant, William Cullen, **I:** 335, 458; **II:** 311; **III:** 81; **IV:** 309; **Retro. Supp. I:** 217; **Retro. Supp. II:** 155; **Supp. I Part 1:** 150–173, 312, 362; **Supp. I Part 2:** 413, 416, 420; **Supp. IV Part 1:** 165; **Supp. XIII:** 145
Bryer, Jackson R., **Supp. IV Part 2:** 575, 583, 585, 586, 589, 591; **Supp.**

XIII: 200, 205
Bryher, Jackson R. (pseudonym). *See* Ellerman, Winifred
"Bubbs Creek Haircut" (Snyder), **Supp. VIII:** 306
Buber, Martin, **II:** 228; **III:** 45, 308, 528; **IV:** 11; **Supp. I Part 1:** 83, 88
Buccaneers, The (Wharton), **IV:** 327; **Retro. Supp. I:** 382
Buchanan Dying (Updike), **Retro. Supp. I:** 331, 335
Buchbinder, David, **Supp. XIII:** 32
Buchwald, Art, **Supp. XII:** 124–125
Buck, Dudley, **Supp. I Part 1:** 362
Buck, Gene, **II:** 427
Buck, Pearl S., **Supp. II Part 1:** 113–134
"Buckdancer's Choice" (Dickey), **Supp. IV Part 1:** 191
Buckdancer's Choice (Dickey), **Supp. IV Part 1:** 176, 177, 178, 180
Bucke, Richard Maurice, **Retro. Supp. I:** 407
"Buck Fever" (Humphrey), **Supp. IX:** 109
"Buck in the Snow, The" (Millay), **III:** 135
Buckley, Christopher, **Supp. IX:** 169; **Supp. XI:** 257, 329
Buckminster, Joseph, **Supp. II Part 1:** 66–67, 69
Bucolics (Auden), **Supp. II Part 1:** 21, 24
Budd, Louis J., **IV:** 210
Buddha, **I:** 136; **II:** 1; **III:** 173, 179, 239, 567; **Supp. I Part 1:** 363; **Supp. I Part 2:** 397
"Buddha's Last Instruction, The" (Oliver), **Supp. VII:** 239
Budding Prospects: A Pastoral (Boyle), **Supp. VIII:** 8–9
Buechner, Frederick, **III:** 310; **Supp. XII:** 41–59
Buell, Lawrence, **Supp. V:** 209; **Supp. IX:** 29
"Buffalo, The" (Moore), **III:** 215
"Buffalo Bill." *See* Cody, William
Buffalo Girls (McMurtry), **Supp. V:** 229
Buffalo Girls (screenplay) (McMurtry), **Supp. V:** 232
Buffett, Jimmy, **Supp. VIII:** 42
Buffon, Comte de, **II:** 101
Buford, Fanny McConnell, **Retro. Supp. II:** 117
Bugeja, Michael, **Supp. X:** 201
"Buglesong" (Stegner), **Supp. IV Part 2:** 606
"Buick" (Shapiro), **Supp. II Part 2:** 705

"Builders" (Yates), **Supp. XI:** 342–343
Builders, The (Glasgow), **II:** 183–184, 193
Builders of the Bay Colony (Morison), **Supp. I Part 2:** 484–485
"Builders of the Bridge, The" (Mumford), **Supp. II Part 2:** 475
"Building" (Snyder), **Supp. VIII:** 305
"Building, Dwelling, Thinking" (Heidegger), **Retro. Supp. II:** 87
"Building of the Ship, The" (Longfellow), **II:** 498; **Retro. Supp. II:** 159, 167, 168
"Build Soil" (Frost), **Retro. Supp. I:** 138, 139
"Build Soil" (Snyder), **Supp. VIII:** 304
Build-Up, The (W. C. Williams), **Retro. Supp. I:** 423
Bukowski, Charles, **Supp. III Part 1:** 147; **Supp. XI:** 159, 161, 172, 173
"Bulgarian Poetess, The" (Updike), **IV:** 215, 227; **Retro. Supp. I:** 329
Bull, Ole, **II:** 504
"Bulldozer, The" (Francis), **Supp. IX:** 87
"Bullet in the Brain" (Wolff), **Supp. VII:** 342–343
Bullet Park (Cheever), **Supp. I Part 1:** 185, 187–193, 194, 195
Bullfight, The (Mailer), **Retro. Supp. II:** 205
Bullins, Ed, **Supp. II Part 1:** 34, 42
Bullock, Sandra, **Supp. X:** 80
"Bull-Roarer, The" (Stern), **Supp. IX:** 297
"Bully, The" (Dubus), **Supp. VII:** 84
Bultmann, Rudolf, **III:** 309
Bulwark, The (Dreiser), **I:** 497, 506, 516–517; **Retro. Supp. II:** 95, 96, 105, 108
Bulwer-Lytton, Edward George, **IV:** 350
"Bums in the Attic" (Cisneros), **Supp. VII:** 62
Bunche, Ralph, **Supp. I Part 1:** 343
"Bunchgrass Edge of the World, The" (Proulx), **Supp. VII:** 263
"Bunner Sisters, The" (Wharton), **IV:** 317
Bunting, Basil, **Retro. Supp. I:** 422; **Supp. III Part 2:** 616, 620, 624
Buñuel, Luis, **III:** 184; **Retro. Supp. II:** 355
Bunyan, John, **I:** 445; **II:** 15, 104, 228; **IV:** 80, 84, 156, 437; **Supp. I Part 1:** 32
Burana, Lily, **Supp. XI:** 253
Burbank, Luther, **I:** 483
Burbank, Rex, **IV:** 363

Burchfield, Alice, **Supp. I Part 2:** 652, 660
Burden of Southern History, The (Woodward), **Retro. Supp. I:** 75
Burdens of Formality, The (Lea, ed.), **Supp. X:** 58
Burger, Gottfried August, **II:** 306
Burgess, Anthony, **Supp. IV Part 1:** 227; **Supp. IV Part 2:** 685; **Supp. V:** 128
Burgh, James, **Supp. I Part 2:** 522
"Burglar of Babylon, The" (Bishop), **Retro. Supp. II:** 47; **Supp. I Part 1:** 93
Burgum, E. B., **IV:** 469, 470
Buried Child (Shepard), **Supp. III Part 2:** 433, 447, 448
"Buried Lake, The" (Tate), **IV:** 136
Burke, Edmund, **I:** 9; **III:** 310; **Supp. I Part 2:** 496, 511, 512, 513, 523; **Supp. II Part 1:** 80
Burke, Kenneth, **I:** 264–287, 291; **III:** 497, 499, 546; **IV:** 123, 408; **Retro. Supp. I:** 297; **Retro. Supp. II:** 117, 120; **Supp. I Part 2:** 630; **Supp. II Part 1:** 136; **Supp. VIII:** 105; **Supp. IX:** 229
"Burly Fading One, The" (Hayden), **Supp. II Part 1:** 366
"Burned" (Levine), **Supp. V:** 186, 192
"Burned Diary, The" (Olds), **Supp. X:** 215
Burnett, David, **Supp. XI:** 299
Burnett, Frances Hodgson, **Supp. I Part 1:** 44
Burnett, Whit, **III:** 551; **Supp. XI:** 294
Burnham, James, **Supp. I Part 2:** 648
Burnham, John Chynoweth, **I:** 59
"Burning, The" (Welty), **IV:** 277–278; **Retro. Supp. I:** 353
Burning Bright (Steinbeck), **IV:** 51, 61–62
Burning City (Benét), **Supp. XI:** 46, 58
Burning Daylight (London), **II:** 474, 481
Burning House, The (Beattie), **Supp. V:** 29
"Burning of Paper Instead of Children, The" (Rich), **Supp. I Part 2:** 558
Burning the Days: Recollections (Salter), **Supp. IX:** 245, 246, 248, 260, **261–262**
"Burning the Small Dead" (Snyder), **Supp. VIII:** 298
Burns, David, **III:** 165–166
Burns, Robert, **II:** 150, 306; **III:** 592; **IV:** 453; **Supp. I Part 1:** 158; **Supp. I Part 2:** 410, 455, 683, 685, 691, 692; **Supp. IX:** 173; **Supp. XII:** 171; **Supp. XIII:** 3

Burnshaw, Stanley, **Retro. Supp. I:** 298, 303; **Supp. III Part 2:** 615
"Burn the Cities" (West), **Retro. Supp. II:** 356
Burnt Norton (Eliot), **I:** 575, 580–581, 582, 584, 585; **III:** 10
"Burnt Norton" (Eliot), **Retro. Supp. I:** 66
Burnt-Out Case, A (Greene), **Supp. VIII:** 4
"Burnt-out Spa, The" (Plath), **Retro. Supp. II:** 246
Burr, Aaron, **I:** 7, 549, 550; **II:** 300; **IV:** 264; **Supp. I Part 2:** 461, 483
Burr: A Novel (Vidal), **Supp. IV Part 2:** 677, 682, 684, 685, 687, 688, 689, 691
Burr Oaks (Eberhart), **I:** 533, 535
Burroughs, Edgar Rice, **Supp. IV Part 1:** 101
Burroughs, John, **I:** 220, 236, 506; **IV:** 346; **Supp. IX:** 171
Burroughs, William S., **III:** 45, 174, 258; **Supp. II Part 1:** 320, 328; **Supp. III Part 1:** 91–110, 217, 226; **Supp. IV Part 1:** 79, 87, 90; **Supp. XI:** 297, 308; **Supp. XII:** 1, 3, 118, 121, 124, 129, 131, 136
Burrow, Trigant, **Supp. II Part 1:** 6
Burrows, Ken, **Supp. V:** 115
Burt, Steve, **Supp. V:** 83
Burtis, Thomson, **Supp. XIII:** 163
Burton, Robert, **II:** 535; **III:** 77, 78; **Supp. I Part 1:** 349
Burton, William Evans, **III:** 412
"Burying Ground by the Ties" (MacLeish), **III:** 14
Bury My Heart at Wounded Knee (Brown), **Supp. IV Part 2:** 504
Bury the Dead (Shaw), **IV:** 381
"Bus Along St. Clair: December, A" (Atwood), **Supp. XIII:** 33
Busch, Frederick, **Supp. X:** 78; **Supp. XII:** 343
Bush, Barney, **Supp. XII:** 218, 222
Bush, Douglas, **Supp. I Part 1:** 268
"Busher Comes Back, The" (Lardner), **II:** 422
"Busher's Letters Home, A" (Lardner), **II:** 418–419, 421
"Business Deal" (West), **IV:** 287
"Business Man, A" (Jewett), **Retro. Supp. II:** 132
Buss, Helen M., **Supp. IV Part 1:** 12
"Butcher, The" (Southern), **Supp. XI:** 294
"Butcher Shop" (Simic), **Supp. VIII:** 273
Butler, Benjamin, **I:** 457

Butler, Dorothy. *See* Farrell, Mrs. James T. (Dorothy Butler)
Butler, Elizabeth, **Supp. I Part 1:** 260
Butler, James D., **Supp. IX:** 175
Butler, Joseph, **II:** 8, 9
Butler, Judith, **Supp. XII:** 6
Butler, Maud. *See* Falkner, Mrs. Murray C. (Maud Butler)
Butler, Nicholas Murray, **I:** 223; **Supp. I Part 1:** 23; **Supp. III Part 2:** 499
Butler, Octavia, **Supp. XIII:** 59–72
Butler, Robert Olen, **Supp. XII:** 61–78, 319
Butler, Samuel, **II:** 82, 86; **IV:** 121, 440; **Supp. VIII:** 171
Butler-Evans, Elliot, **Retro. Supp. II:** 121
"But Only Mine" (Wright), **Supp. III Part 2:** 595
Butscher, Edward, **Supp. I Part 2:** 526
"Buttercups" (Lowell), **Retro. Supp. II:** 187
Butterfield 8 (O'Hara), **III:** 361
Butterfield, R. W., **I:** 386
Butterfield, Stephen, **Supp. IV Part 1:** 3, 11
Butterfly (Harvey), **Supp. XIII:** 184
"Butterfly, The" (Brodksy), **Supp. VIII:** 26
"Butterfly and the Traffic Light, The" (Ozick), **Supp. V:** 263, 265
"Butterfly-toed Shoes" (Komunyakaa), **Supp. XIII:** 126
Butter Hill and Other Poems (Francis), **Supp. IX:** 88, 89
Buttons, Red, **Supp. IV Part 2:** 574
Buttrick, George, **III:** 301; **Supp. XII:** 47–48
"But What Is the Reader to Make of This?" (Ashbery), **Supp. III Part 1:** 25
Butz, Earl, **Supp. X:** 35
"Buz" (Alcott), **Supp. I Part 1:** 43
By Avon River (Doolittle), **Supp. I Part 1:** 272
"By Blue Ontario's Shore" (Whitman), **Retro. Supp. I:** 399, 400
"By Disposition of Angels" (Moore), **III:** 214
"By Earth" (Olds), **Supp. X:** 214
"By Fire" (Olds), **Supp. X:** 214
By Land and by Sea (Morison), **Supp. I Part 2:** 492
By-Line: Ernest Hemingway (Hemingway), **II:** 257–258
By Love Possessed (Cozens), **I:** 358, 365, 372–374, 375, 376, 377, 378, 379
"By Morning" (Swenson), **Supp. IV Part 2:** 642

"By Night" (Francis), **Supp. IX:** 76
Bynner, Witter, **II:** 513, 527; **Supp. XIII:** 347
Byrd, William, **Supp. IV Part 2:** 425
Byrne, Donn, **IV:** 67
Byron, George Gordon, Lord, **I:** 343, 568, 577; **II:** 135, 193, 296, 301, 303, 310, 315, 331, 566; **III:** 82, 137, 170, 409, 410, 412, 469; **IV:** 245, 435; **Supp. I Part 1:** 150, 312, 349; **Supp. I Part 2:** 580, 591, 683, 685, 719; **Supp. XIII:** 139
"Bystanders" (Matthews), **Supp. IX:** 160
By the North Gate (Oates), **Supp. II Part 2:** 504
"By the Waters of Babylon" (Benét), **Supp. XI:** 56, 58
By Way of Orbit (O'Neill), **III:** 405
"C 33" (H. Crane), **I:** 384; **Retro. Supp. II:** 76
Cabala, The (Wilder), **IV:** 356, 358–360, 369, 374
Cabbages and Kings (O. Henry), **Supp. II Part 1:** 394, 409
Cabell, James Branch, **II:** 42; **III:** 394; **IV:** 67, 359, 360; **Retro. Supp. I:** 80; **Supp. I Part 2:** 613, 714, 718, 721; **Supp. X:** 223
"Cabin, The" (Carver), **Supp. III Part 1:** 137, 146
Cabinet of Dr. Caligari, The (film), **Retro. Supp. I:** 268
Cable, George Washington, **II:** 289; **Retro. Supp. II:** 65; **Supp. I Part 1:** 200; **Supp. II Part 1:** 198
Cables to the Ace; or, Familiar Liturgies of Misunderstanding (Merton), **Supp. VIII:** 208
Cabot, James, **II:** 14; **IV:** 173
Cabot, John, **Supp. I Part 2:** 496, 497
"Caddy's Diary, A" (Lardner), **II:** 421–422
"Cadence" (Dubus), **Supp. VII:** 84–85
Cadieux, Isabelle, **Supp. XIII:** 127
"Cadillac Flambé" (Ellison), **Retro. Supp. II:** 119, 126; **Supp. II Part 1:** 248
Cadillac Jack (McMurtry), **Supp. V:** 225
Cadle, Dean, **Supp. I Part 2:** 429
Cady, Edwin H., **II:** 272
"Caedmon" (Garrett), **Supp. VII:** 96–97
Caesar, Julius, **II:** 12, 502, 561–562; **IV:** 372, 373
Caesar, Sid, **Supp. IV Part 2:** 574, 591
"Cafeteria, The" (Singer), **Retro. Supp. II:** 334
Cage, John, **Supp. IV Part 1:** 84;

Supp. V: 337, 341
"Cage and the Prairie: Two Notes on Symbolism, The" (Bewley), **Supp. I Part 1:** 251
Cage of Spines, A (Swenson), **Supp. IV Part 2:** 641–642, 647
Cagney, James, **Supp. IV Part 1:** 236; **Supp. XIII:** 174
Cagney, William, **Supp. XIII:** 174
Cahalan, James, **Supp. XIII:** 1, 2, 3, 4, 12
Cahan, Abraham, **Supp. IX:** 227; **Supp. XIII:** 106
Cahill, Tim, **Supp. XIII:** 13
Cain, James M., **III:** 99; **Supp. IV Part 1:** 130; **Supp. XI:** 160; **Supp. XIII:** 159, 165
Cairns, Huntington, **III:** 103, 108, 114, 119
Cairo! Shanghai! Bombay! (Williams and Shapiro), **IV:** 380
Cakes and Ale (Maugham), **III:** 64
Calabria, Frank, **Supp. XIII:** 164
Calamity Jane (Martha Jane Canary), **Supp. V:** 229–230; **Supp. X:** 103
"Calamus" (Whitman), **IV:** 342–343; **Retro. Supp. I:** 52, 403, 404, 407
Calasso, Roberto, **Supp. IV Part 1:** 301
Calderón, Hector, **Supp. IV Part 2:** 544
Caldwell, Christopher, **Supp. IV Part 1:** 211
Caldwell, Erskine, **I:** 97, 211, **288–311**; **IV:** 286; **Supp. IV Part 2:** 601
Caldwell, Mrs. Erskine (Helen Lannegan), **I:** 289
Caldwell, Mrs. Erskine (Margaret Bourke-White), **I:** 290, 293–295, 297
Caldwell, Mrs. Erskine (Virginia Fletcher), **I:** 290
Caldwell, Reverend Ira Sylvester, **I:** 289, 305
Caldwell, Zoe, **Supp. XIII:** 207
Caleb Williams (Godwin), **III:** 415
"Calendar" (Creeley), **Supp. IV Part 1:** 158
Calhoun, John C., **I:** 8; **III:** 309
"California" (Didion), **Supp. IV Part 1:** 195
"California, This Is Minnesota Speaking" (Dunn), **Supp. XI:** 146
California and Oregon Trail, The (Parkman), **Supp. I Part 2:** 486
Californians (Jeffers), **Supp. II Part 2:** 415, 418, 420
"California Oaks, The" (Winters), **Supp. II Part 2:** 798
"California Republic" (Didion), **Supp.**

IV Part 1: 205
California Suite (film), **Supp. IV Part 2:** 589
California Suite (Simon), **Supp. IV Part 2:** 581, 582
"Caligula" (Lowell), **II:** 554
Callahan, John F., **Retro. Supp. II:** 119, 126, 127
"Call at Corazón" (Bowles), **Supp. IV Part 1:** 82, 87
Calle, Sophia, **Supp. XII:** 22
"Called Back" (Kazin), **Supp. VIII:** 104
Calley, Captain William, **II:** 579
Calley, John, **Supp. XI:** 305
Calligrammes (Apollinaire), **I:** 432
"Calling Jesus" (Toomer), **Supp. III Part 2:** 484
Calling Myself Home (Hogan), **Supp. IV Part 1:** 397, 399, 400, 401, 413
Call It Experience (Caldwell), **I:** 290–291, 297
"Call It Fear" (Harjo), **Supp. XII:** 220
Call It Sleep (H. Roth), **Supp. VIII:** 233; **Supp. IX:** 227, 228, **229–231**; **Supp. XIII:** 106
"Call Letters: Mrs. V. B." (Angelou), **Supp. IV Part 1:** 15
Call Me Ishmael (Olson), **Supp. II Part 2:** 556
Call of the Gospel, The (Mather), **Supp. II Part 2:** 448
Call of the Wild, The (London), **II:** 466, 470–471, 472, 481
"Call of the Wild, The" (Snyder), **Supp. VIII:** 301
"Calloway's Code" (O. Henry), **Supp. II Part 1:** 404
"Call to Arms" (Mumford), **Supp. II Part 2:** 479
Call to Arms, The (film), **Retro. Supp. I:** 325
Calmer, Ned, **Supp. XI:** 219
Calvert, George H., **Supp. I Part 1:** 361
Calverton, V. F., **Supp. VIII:** 96
Calvin, John, **II:** 342; **IV:** 160, 490
Calvino, Italo, **Supp. IV Part 2:** 623, 678
Cambridge Edition of the Works of F. Scott Fitzgerald, The (Bruccoli, ed.), **Retro. Supp. I:** 115
"Cambridge Thirty Years Ago" (Lowell), **Supp. I Part 2:** 419
Cambridge University Press, **Retro. Supp. I:** 115
"Camellia Sabina" (Moore), **III:** 208, 215
"Cameo Appearance" (Simic), **Supp. VIII:** 283

Camera Obscura (Nabokov), **III:** 255
Cameron, Elizabeth, **I:** 10, 17
Cameron, Kenneth W., **II:** 16
Cameron, Peter, **Supp. XII: 79–95**
Cameron, Sharon, **Retro. Supp. I:** 43; **Retro. Supp. II:** 40
Camerson, Don, **I:** 10, 17
Camino, Léon Felipe, **Retro. Supp. II:** 89
Camino Real (T. Williams), **IV:** 382, 385, 386, 387, 388, 391, 392, 395, 398
Camões, Luiz Vaz de, **II:** 133; **Supp. I Part 1:** 94
"Camouflaging the Chimera" (Komunyakaa), **Supp. XIII: 122–123**
Camp, Walter, **II:** 423
Campana, Dino, **Supp. V:** 337
Campbell, Alan, **Supp. IV Part 1:** 353; **Supp. IX:** 196, 198, 201
Campbell, Alexander, **Supp. I Part 2:** 381, 395
Campbell, Donna, **Retro. Supp. II:** 139
Campbell, Helen, **Supp. XI:** 200, 206
Campbell, James, **Supp. XII:** 127
Campbell, James Edwin, **Supp. II Part 1:** 202
Campbell, Joseph, **I:** 135; **IV:** 369, 370; **Supp. IX:** 245
Campbell, Lewis, **III:** 476
Campbell, Thomas, **II:** 8, 303, 314; **III:** 410; **Supp. I Part 1:** 309, 310
Campbell, Virginia, **Supp. XIII:** 114
Campbell (Hale), Janet, **Supp. IV Part 2:** 503
"Campers Leaving: Summer 1981" (Kenyon), **Supp. VII:** 169
"Camp Evergreen" (Kenyon), **Supp. VII:** 168
"Camping in Madera Canyon" (Swenson), **Supp. IV Part 2:** 649
Campion, Thomas, **I:** 439; **Supp. VIII:** 272
Camus, Albert, **I:** 53, 61, 292, 294, 494; **II:** 57, 244; **III:** 292, 306, 453; **IV:** 6, 211, 236, 442, 487; **Retro. Supp. I:** 73; **Retro. Supp. II:** 20; **Supp. I Part 2:** 621; **Supp. VIII:** 11, 195, 241; **Supp. XI:** 96; **Supp. XIII:** 74, 165, 233, 247
Camuto, Christopher, **Supp. V:** 212–213
"Canadian Mosaic, The" (Beran), **Supp. XIII:** 25
"Canadians and Pottawatomies" (Sandburg), **III:** 592–593
"Can a Good Wife Be a Good Sport?" (T. Williams), **IV:** 380

"Canal, The: A Poem on the Application of Physical Science to Political Economy" (Barlow), **Supp. II Part 1:** 73
Canary, Martha Jane. *See* Calamity Jane (Martha Jane Canary)
"Canary for One, A" (Hemingway), **Retro. Supp. I:** 170, 189
Canary in a Cat House (Vonnegut), **Supp. II Part 2:** 758
"Canary in Bloom" (Dove), **Supp. IV Part 1:** 248
Canby, Henry Seidel, **IV:** 65, 363
"Cancer" (McClatchy), **Supp. XII:** 266
"Cancer Match, The" (Dickey), **Supp. IV Part 1:** 182
"Canción y Glosa" (Merwin), **Supp. III Part 1:** 342
Candide (Hellman), **I:** 28; **Supp. I Part 1:** 288–289, 292
Candide (Voltaire), **Supp. I Part 1:** 288–289; **Supp. XI:** 297
Candide (Voltaire; Wilbur, trans.), **Supp. III Part 2:** 560
Candle in the Cabin, The (Lindsay), **Supp. I Part 2:** 398, 400
"Candles" (Plath), **Retro. Supp. II:** 248, 257
Candles in Babylon (Levertov), **Supp. III Part 1:** 283
Candles in the Sun (T. Williams), **IV:** 381
Candles of Your Eyes, The (Purdy), **Supp. VII:** 278
Candy (Southern), **Supp. XI:** 297, **298–299,** 305
"Candy-Man Beechum" (Caldwell), **I:** 309
Cane (Toomer), **Supp. III Part 2:** 475, 481–486, 488; **Supp. IV Part 1:** 164, 168; **Supp. IX:** 305, 306, 307, **308–320**
"Cane in the Corridor, The" (Thurber), **Supp. I Part 2:** 616
Canfield, Cass, **Supp. I Part 2:** 668
Canfield, Dorothy, **Retro. Supp. I:** 4, 11, 14, 18. *See also* Fisher, Dorothy Canfield
Can Grande's Castle (Lowell), **II:** 518, 524
"Canicula di Anna" (Carson), **Supp. XII: 101–102**
"Canis Major" (Frost), **Retro. Supp. I:** 137
Cannery Row (Steinbeck), **IV:** 50, 51, 64–65, 66, 68
Cannibal Galaxy, The (Ozick), **Supp. V:** 270
Cannibals and Christians (Mailer), **III:**

38–39, 40, 42; **Retro. Supp. II:** 203, 204, 205
Canning, George, **I:** 7, 8
Canning, Richard, **Supp. X:** 147
Cannon, Jimmy, **II:** 424
Cannon, Steve, **Retro. Supp. II:** 111
Cannon between My Knees, A (Gunn Allen), **Supp. IV Part 1:** 324
"Canso" (Merwin), **Supp. III Part 1:** 344
Can Such Things Be? (Bierce), **I:** 203, 204, 205, 209
Canterbury Tales (Chaucer), **II:** 504; **III:** 411; **IV:** 65
"Canto Amor" (Berryman), **I:** 173
Canto I (Pound), **III:** 469, 470; **Retro. Supp. I:** 286
Canto II (Pound), **III:** 470
Canto III (Pound), **III:** 470
Canto IV (Pound), **III:** 470
Canto VIII (Pound), **III:** 472
Canto IX (Pound), **III:** 472
Canto X (Pound), **III:** 472
Canto XIII (Pound), **III:** 472
Canto XXXIX (Pound), **III:** 468
Canto LXV (Pound), **Retro. Supp. I:** 292
Canto LXXXI (Pound), **III:** 459; **Retro. Supp. I:** 293
Cantor, Lois, **Supp. IV Part 1:** 285
Cantos (Pound), **I:** 482; **III:** 13–14, 17, 457, 462, 463, 466, 467, 469–470, 472–473, 474, 475, 476, 492; **Retro. Supp. I:** 284, 292, 292–293, 293, 427; **Supp. I Part 1:** 272; **Supp. II Part 1:** 5; **Supp. II Part 2:** 420, 557, 564, 644; **Supp. IV Part 1:** 153; **Supp. V:** 343, 345; **Supp. VIII:** 305
"Cantus Planis" (Pound), **III:** 466
Cantwell, Robert, **Retro. Supp. I:** 85; **Supp. VIII:** 96; **Supp. XIII:** 292
"Can You Carry Me" (O'Hara), **III:** 369
Canzoneri, Robert, **IV:** 114, 116
Canzoni (Pound), **Retro. Supp. I:** 286, 288, 413
"Cap" (Shaw), **Supp. IV Part 1:** 345
"Cape Breton" (Bishop), **Supp. I Part 1:** 92; **Supp. IX:** 45
Cape Cod (Thoreau), **II:** 540
Capitalism: The Unknown Ideal (Rand), **Supp. IV Part 2:** 518, 527, 531, 532
Caponi, Gena Dagel, **Supp. IV Part 1:** 95
Capote, Truman, **Supp. I Part 1:** 291, 292; **Supp. III Part 1:** 111–133; **Supp. III Part 2:** 574; **Supp. IV Part 1:** 198, 220; **Supp. VIII:** 105; **Supp. XII:** 43, 249

Capouya, Emile, **Supp. I Part 1:** 50
Cappetti, Carla, **Supp. IX:** 4, 8
Capra, Fritjof, **Supp. X:** 261
Capron, Marion, **Supp. IX:** 193
"Capsule History of Conservation, A" (Stegner), **Supp. IV Part 2:** 600
"Captain Carpenter" (Ransom), **III:** 491
Captain Craig (Robinson), **III:** 508, 523; **Supp. II Part 1:** 192
"Captain Jim's Friend" (Harte), **Supp. II Part 1:** 337
"Captain Jones's Invitation" (Freneau), **Supp. II Part 1:** 261
"Captain's Son, The" (Taylor), **Supp. V:** 314, 325, 327
"Captain's Wife, The" (Salter), **Supp. IX:** 261
"Capt Christopher Levett (of York)" (Olson), **Supp. II Part 2:** 576, 577
"Captivity and Restoration of Mrs. Mary Rowlandson, The" (Howe), **Supp. IV Part 2:** 419, 431, 434
"Captivity of the Fly" (MacLeish), **III:** 19
"Captured Goddess, The" (Lowell), **II:** 520
Caputi, Jane, **Supp. IV Part 1:** 334, 335
Caputo, Philip, **Supp. XI:** 234
Capuzzo, Michael, **Supp. XIII:** 254
Car (Crews), **Supp. XI:** 110–111
Carabi, Angels, **Supp. VIII:** 223; **Supp. XII:** 215
"Caravaggio: Swirl & Vortex" (Levis), **Supp. XI:** 258, 269
Carby, Hazel B., **Supp. IV Part 1:** 13
"Carcassonne" (Faulkner), **Retro. Supp. I:** 81
Card, Antha E., **Supp. I Part 2:** 496
Cárdenas, Lupe, **Supp. IV Part 2:** 538, 539, 540
Cardinale, Ernesto, **Supp. XII:** 225
"Cardinal Ideograms" (Swenson), **Supp. IV Part 2:** 645
"Cards" (Beattie), **Supp. V:** 31
"Careful" (Carver), **Supp. III Part 1:** 138
Careful and Strict Enquiry into the Modern Prevailing Notions of That Freedom of Will, Which Is Supposed to be Essential to Moral Agency, Vertue and Vice, Reward and Punishment, Praise and Blame, A (Edwards), **I:** 549, 557, 558, 562
Carel: A Poem and Pilgrimage in the Holy Land (Melville), **III:** 92–93
"Carentan O Carentan" (Simpson), **Supp. IX:** 267

Carew, Thomas, **IV:** 453
Cargill, Oscar, **Supp. II Part 1:** 117
Caribbean as Columbus Saw It (Morison and Obregon), **Supp. I Part 2:** 488
Carl, K. A., **III:** 475
"Carlos Who Died, and Left Only This, The" (Ríos), **Supp. IV Part 2:** 547
Carlotta (empress of Mexico), **Supp. I Part 2:** 457
Carl Sandburg (Golden), **III:** 579
Carlyle, Thomas, **I:** 103, 279; **II:** 5, 7, 11, 15–16, 17, 20, 145, 315; **III:** 82, 84, 85, 87; **IV:** 169, 182, 338, 350; **Retro. Supp. I:** 360, 408; **Supp. I Part 1:** 2, 349; **Supp. I Part 2:** 410, 422, 482, 485, 552
"Carma" (Toomer), **Supp. III Part 2:** 481–483; **Supp. IX:** 312–313
"Carmen de Boheme" (Crane), **I:** 384
Carmen Jones (film), **Supp. I Part 1:** 66
Carmina Burana, **Supp. X:** 63
Carnegie, Andrew, **I:** 483; **IV:** 192; **Supp. I Part 2:** 639, 644; **Supp. V:** 285
Carnegie, Dale, **Supp. I Part 2:** 608
"Carnegie Hall: Rescued" (Moore), **III:** 215
Carne-Ross, D. S., **Supp. I Part 1:** 268, 269
Carnes, Mark C., **Supp. X:** 14
Carnovsky, Morris, **III:** 154
Caroling Dusk: An Anthology of Verse by Negro Poets (Cullen), **Supp. IV Part 1:** 166, 169
"Carol of Occupations" (Whitman), **I:** 486
"Carpe Diem" (Frost), **Supp. XII:** 303
"Carpe Noctem, if You Can" (Thurber), **Supp. I Part 2:** 620
Carpenter, Dan, **Supp. V:** 250
Carpenter, David, **Supp. VIII:** 297
Carpenter, Frederic I., **II:** 20
Carpentered Hen and Other Tame Creatures, The (Updike), **IV:** 214; **Retro. Supp. I:** 320
Carpenter's Gothic (Gaddis), **Supp. IV Part 1:** 288, 289–291, 293, 294
Carr, Dennis W., **Supp. IV Part 2:** 560
Carr, Rosemary. *See* Benét, Rosemary
Carrall, Aaron, **Supp. IV Part 2:** 499
Carrel, Alexis, **IV:** 240
"Carrell/Klcc/and Cosmos's Groom" (Goldbarth), **Supp. XII:** 183
"Carriage from Sweden, A" (Moore), **III:** 212
Carrie (King), **Supp. V:** 137
Carried Away (Harrison), **Supp. VIII:** 39

Carrier of Ladders (Merwin), **Supp. III Part 1:** 339, 346, 350–352, 356, 357
"Carriers of the Dream Wheel" (Momaday), **Supp. IV Part 2:** 481
Carriers of the Dream Wheel: Contemporary Native American Poetry (Niatum, ed.), **Supp. IV Part 2:** 484, 505
Carrington, Carroll, **I:** 199
"Carrion Spring" (Stegner), **Supp. IV Part 2:** 604
Carroll, Charles, **Supp. I Part 2:** 525
Carroll, Lewis, **I:** 432; **II:** 431; **III:** 181; **Supp. I Part 1:** 44; **Supp. I Part 2:** 622, 656
"Carrots, Noses, Snow, Rose, Roses" (Gass), **Supp. VI:** 87
Carrouges, Michel, **Supp. IV Part 1:** 104
"Carrousel, The" (Rilke), **III:** 558
Carruth, Hayden, **Retro. Supp. II:** 281; **Supp. IV Part 1:** 66; **Supp. VIII:** 39; **Supp. IX:** 291; **Supp. XIII:** 112
"Carry" (Hogan), **Supp. IV Part 1:** 412
"Carrying On" (Dunn), **Supp. XI:** 145
Cars of Cuba (García), **Supp. XI:** 190
Carson, Anne, **Supp. XII: 97–116**
Carson, Johnny, **Supp. IV Part 2:** 526
Carson, Rachel, **Supp. V:** 202; **Supp. IX: 19–36; Supp. X:** 99
Carson, Tom, **Supp. XI:** 227
Cart, Michael, **Supp. X:** 12
Carter, Elliott, **Supp. III Part 1:** 21
Carter, Jimmy, **Supp. I Part 2:** 638
Carter, Marcia, **Supp. V:** 223
Carter, Mary, **Supp. IV Part 2:** 444
Carter, Stephen, **Supp. XI:** 220
Cartesian Sonata and Other Novellas (Gass), **Supp. VI: 92–93**
Cartier, Jacques, **Supp. I Part 2:** 496, 497
Cartier-Bresson, Henri, **Supp. VIII:** 98
"Cartographies of Silence" (Rich), **Supp. I Part 2:** 571–572
Carver, Raymond, **Supp. III Part 1: 135–151; Supp. IV Part 1:** 342; **Supp. V:** 22, 23, 220, 326; **Supp. VIII:** 15; **Supp. X:** 85, 167; **Supp. XI:** 26, 65, 116, 153; **Supp. XII:** 79, 139, 289, 294
Cary, Alice, **Retro. Supp. II:** 145
Cary, Richard, **Retro. Supp. II:** 132, 137
"Casabianca" (Bishop), **Retro. Supp. II:** 42; **Supp. I Part 1:** 86
Casablanca (film), **Supp. VIII:** 61
Case of the Crushed Petunias, The (T. Williams), **IV:** 381
Case of the Officers of Excise (Paine), **Supp. I Part 2:** 503–504
Casey, John, **Supp. X:** 164
Cash, Arthur, **Supp. IV Part 1:** 299
Cashman, Nellie, **Supp. X:** 103
Casino Royale (film), **Supp. XI: 306–307**
"Cask of Amontillado, The" (Poe), **II:** 475; **III:** 413; **Retro. Supp. II:** 268, 269, 270, 273
Cassada (Salter), **Supp. IX: 251–252**
Cassady, Neal, **Supp. II Part 1:** 309, 311
"Cassandra Southwick" (Whittier), **Supp. I Part 2:** 693
Cassell, Verlin, **Supp. XI:** 315
Cassill, R. V., **Supp. V:** 323
Cassirer, Ernst, **I:** 265; **IV:** 87, 89
Cass Timberlane (Lewis), **II:** 455–456
Cast a Cold Eye (McCarthy), **II:** 566
Castaway (Cozzens), **I:** 363, 370, 374, 375, 379
"Caste in America" (Du Bois), **Supp. II Part 1:** 169
Castiglione, Baldassare, **I:** 279; **III:** 282
"Castilian" (Wylie), **Supp. I Part 2:** 714
Castillo, Ana, **Supp. XI:** 177
"Castles and Distances" (Wilbur), **Supp. III Part 2:** 550
Castle Sinister (Marquand), **III:** 58
Castro, Fidel, **II:** 261, 434
"Casual Incident, A" (Hemingway), **II:** 44
"Cat, The" (Matthews), **Supp. IX: 157–158**
"Catbird Seat, The" (Thurber), **Supp. I Part 2:** 623
"Catch" (Francis), **Supp. IX:** 82
Catch-22 (Heller), **III:** 558; **Supp. IV Part 1:** 379, 380, 381–382, 383, 384–386, 387, 390, 391, 392, 393, 394; **Supp. V:** 244, 248; **Supp. XII:** 167–168
Catcher in the Rye, The (Salinger), **I:** 493; **III:** 551, 552, 553–558, 567, 571; **Retro. Supp. I:** 102; **Retro. Supp. II:** 222, 249; **Supp. I Part 2:** 535; **Supp. V:** 119; **Supp. VIII:** 242; **Supp. XI:** 65
"Catching Frogs" (Kenyon), **Supp. VII:** 170
catechism of d neoamerican hoodoo church (Reed), **Supp. X:** 240, 241
Catered Affair, The (film), **Supp. IV Part 2:** 683
"Cathay" (Goldbarth), **Supp. XII:** 185, 186
Cathay (Pound), **II:** 527; **Retro. Supp. I:** 289
Cathedral (Carver), **Supp. III Part 1:** 144–146; **Supp. XII:** 139
"Cathedral" (Carver), **Supp. III Part 1:** 144–145
Cathedral, The (Lowell), **Supp. I Part 2:** 407, 416–417
Cather, Willa, **I: 312–334**, 405; **II:** 51, 96, 177, 404, 412; **III:** 453; **IV:** 190; **Retro. Supp. I: 1–23**, 355, 382; **Retro. Supp. II:** 71, 136; **Supp. I Part 2:** 609, 719; **Supp. IV Part 1:** 31; **Supp. VIII:** 101, 102, 263; **Supp. X:** 103; **Supp. XIII:** 253
Catherine, Saint, **II:** 211
Catherine II, **Supp. I Part 2:** 433
Catholic Art and Culture (Watkin), **Retro. Supp. II:** 187
"Catholic Novelist in the Protestant South, The" (O'Connor), **Retro. Supp. II:** 223, 224
"Cathy Queen of Cats" (Cisneros), **Supp. VII:** 59
Cat Inside, The (Burroughs), **Supp. III Part 1:** 105
"Cat in the Hat for President, The" (Coover), **Supp. V:** 44, 46–47
Cato, **II:** 114, 117
Cat on a Hot Tin Roof (T. Williams), **II:** 190; **IV:** 380, 382, 383, 386, 387, 389, 390, 391, 394, 395, 397–398
Cat's Cradle (Vonnegut), **Supp. II Part 2:** 758, 759, 767–768, 770, 771, 772; **Supp. V:** 1
Cat's Eye (Atwood), **Supp. XIII:** 29–30
"Cat's Meow, A" (Brodsky), **Supp. VIII:** 31
"Catterskill Falls" (Bryant), **Supp. I Part 1:** 160
Catullus, **Supp. XII:** 2, 13, **112**
Catullus (Gai Catulli Veronensis Liber) (Zukofsky), **Supp. III Part 2:** 625, 627, 628, 629
"Catullus: *Carmina*" (Carson), **Supp. XII: 112**
Catullus, Gaius Valerius, **I:** 381; **Supp. I Part 1:** 261; **Supp. I Part 2:** 728
Caudwell, Christopher, **Supp. X:** 112
"Caul, The" (Banks), **Supp. V:** 10–11
Cause for Wonder (Morris), **III:** 232–233
"Causerie" (Tate), **IV:** 129
"Causes of American Discontents before 1768, The" (Franklin), **II:** 120
Cavafy, Constantine P., **Supp. IX:** 275; **Supp. XI:** 119, 123
Cavalcade of America, The (radio program), **III:** 146

Cavalcanti (Pound, opera), **Retro. Supp. I:** 287
Cavalcanti, Guido, **I:** 579; **III:** 467; **Supp. III Part 2:** 620, 621, 622, 623
Cavalieri, Grace, **Supp. IV Part 2:** 630, 631
"Cavalry Crossing the Ford" (Whitman), **IV:** 347
Cave, The (Warren), **IV:** 255–256
Cavell, Stanley, **Retro. Supp. I:** 306–307, 309
Cavender's House (Robinson), **III:** 510
Caviare at the Funeral (Simpson), **Supp. IX:** 266, **276–277**
"Cawdor" (Jeffers), **Supp. II Part 2:** 431
Caxton, William, **III:** 486
Cayton, Horace, **IV:** 475, 488
Cazamian, Louis, **II:** 529
Celan, Paul, **Supp. X:** 149; **Supp. XII:** 21, 110–111
"Celebrated Jumping Frog of Calaveras County, The" (Twain), **IV:** 196
Celebrated Jumping Frog of Calaveras County, The, and Other Sketches (Twain), **IV:** 197
Celebration (Crews), **Supp. XI:** 103, **108**
Celebration at Dark (W. J. Smith), **Supp. XIII:** 332
"Celebration for June 24th" (McGrath), **Supp. X:** 116
"Celery" (Stein), **IV:** 43
"Celestial Globe" (Nemerov), **III:** 288
Celestial Navigation (Tyler), **Supp. IV Part 2:** 662–663, 671
"Celestial Railroad, The" (Hawthorne), **Retro. Supp. I:** 152; **Supp. I Part 1:** 188
Celibate Season, A (Shields), **Supp. VII:** 323, 324
"Cemetery at Academy, California" (Levine), **Supp. V:** 182
Cemetery Nights (Dobyns), **Supp. XIII:** 85, 87, 89
"Censors As Critics: *To Kill a Mockingbird* As a Case Study" (May), **Supp. VIII:** 126
"Census-Taker, The" (Frost), **Retro. Supp. I:** 129
"Centaur, The" (Swenson), **Supp. IV Part 2:** 641
Centaur, The (Updike), **IV:** 214, 216, 217, 218, 219–221, 222; **Retro. Supp. I:** 318, 322, 324, 331, 336
"Centennial Meditation of Columbia, The" (Lanier), **Supp. I Part 1:** 362
Centeno, Agusto, **IV:** 375

"Centipede" (Dove), **Supp. IV Part 1:** 246
"Central Man, The" (Bloom), **Supp. IV Part 2:** 689
"Central Park" (Lowell), **II:** 552
Century of Dishonor, A (Jackson), **Retro. Supp. I:** 31
"Cerebral Snapshot, The" (Theroux), **Supp. VIII:** 313
"Ceremonies" (Rukeyser), **Supp. VI:** 279
Ceremony (Silko), **Supp. IV Part 1:** 274, 333; **Supp. IV Part 2:** 557–558, 558–559, 559, 561–566, 570
Ceremony (Wilbur), **Supp. III Part 2:** 550–551
"Ceremony, The" (Harjo), **Supp. XII:** 230
Ceremony in Lone Tree (Morris), **III:** 229–230, 232, 238, 558
Ceremony of Brotherhood, A (Anaya and Ortiz, eds.), **Supp. IV Part 2:** 502
Cerf, Bennett, **III:** 405; **IV:** 288; **Retro. Supp. II:** 348; **Supp. XIII:** 172
"Certain Attention to the World, A" (Haines), **Supp. XII:** 201
Certain Distance, A (Francis), **Supp. IX:** 85
"Certain Music, A" (Rukeyser), **Supp. VI:** 273
Certain Noble Plays of Japan (Pound), **III:** 458
Certain People (Wharton), **Retro. Supp. I:** 382
"Certain Poets" (MacLeish), **III:** 4
"Certain Testimony" (Bausch), **Supp. VII:** 48
Certificate, The (Singer), **IV:** 1; **Retro. Supp. II:** **332–333**
Cervantes, Lorna Dee, **Supp. IV Part 2:** 545
Cervantes, Miguel de, **I:** 130, 134; **II:** 8, 272, 273, 276, 289, 302, 310, 315; **III:** 113, 614; **IV:** 367; **Retro. Supp. I:** 91; **Supp. I Part 2:** 406; **Supp. V:** 277; **Supp. XIII:** 17
Césaire, Aimé, **Supp. X:** 132, 139; **Supp. XIII:** 114
"Cesarean" (Kenyon), **Supp. VII:** 173
Cézanne, Paul, **II:** 576; **III:** 210; **IV:** 26, 31, 407; **Supp. V:** 333, 341–342
Chabon, Michael, **Supp. XI:** **63–81**
Chaboseau, Jean, **Supp. I Part 1:** 260
Chaikin, Joseph, **Supp. III Part 2:** 433, 436–437
"Chain, The" (Kumin), **Supp. IV Part 2:** 452
Chainbearer, The (Cooper), **I:** 351, 352–353

"Chain of Love, A" (Price), **Supp. VI:** **258–259**, 260
Chains of Dew (Glaspell), **Supp. III Part 1:** 181
Challacombe, Robert Hamilton, **III:** 176
Chalmers, George, **Supp. I Part 2:** 514, 521
"Chambered Nautilus, The" (Holmes), **Supp. I Part 1:** 254, 307, 312–313, 314
Chamberlain, John, **Supp. I Part 2:** 647; **Supp. IV Part 2:** 525
Chamberlain, Neville, **II:** 589; **Supp. I Part 2:** 664
Chamber Music (Joyce), **III:** 16
Chambers, Richard, **Supp. III Part 2:** 610, 611, 612
Chambers, Whittaker, **Supp. III Part 2:** 610; **Supp. IV Part 2:** 526
"Champagne Regions" (Ríos), **Supp. IV Part 2:** 553
"Champion" (Lardner), **II:** 420–421, 428, 430
Champion, Laurie, **Supp. VIII:** 128
Champollion-Figeac, Jean Jacques, **IV:** 426
"Chance" (Doolittle), **Supp. I Part 1:** 271
Chance, Frank, **II:** 418
Chance Acquaintance, A (Howells), **II:** 278
"Chanclas" (Cisneros), **Supp. VII:** 61
Chandler, Raymond, **Supp. III Part 1:** 91; **Supp. IV Part 1: 119–138**, 341, 344, 345; **Supp. IV Part 2:** 461, 464, 469, 470, 471, 472, 473; **Supp. XI:** 160, 228; **Supp. XII:** 307; **Supp. XIII:** 159, 233
Chaney, "Professor" W. H., **II:** 463–464
Chang, Leslie C., **Supp. IV Part 1:** 72
"Change, The: Kyoto-Tokyo Express" (Ginsberg), **Supp. II Part 1:** 313, 329
Changeling (Middleton), **Retro. Supp. I:** 62
"Changeling, The" (Lowell), **Supp. I Part 2:** 409
"Changeling, The" (Whittier), **Supp. I Part 2:** 697
Change of World, A (Rich), **Retro. Supp. II:** 279; **Supp. I Part 2:** 551, 552
"Changes of Mind" (Baker), **Supp. XIII:** 52
"Change the Joke and Slip the Yoke" (Ellison), **Retro. Supp. II:** 118
Changing Light at Sandover, The (Merrill), **Supp. III Part 1:** 318,

319, 323, 327, 332, 335–336; **Supp. XII:** 269–270
"Changing Same, The" (Baraka), **Supp. II Part 1:** 47, 51, 53
Chanler, Mrs. Winthrop, **I:** 22; **IV:** 325
Channing, Carol, **IV:** 357
Channing, Edward, **Supp. I Part 2:** 479–480
Channing, Edward Tyrrel, **Supp. I Part 1:** 155; **Supp. I Part 2:** 422
Channing, William Ellery, **I:** 336; **II:** 224, 495; **IV:** 172, 173, 176, 177; **Retro. Supp. I:** 54; **Supp. I Part 1:** 103; **Supp. I Part 2:** 589
Channing, William Henry, **IV:** 178; **Supp. II Part 1:** 280, 285
Chanson de Roland, La, **I:** 13
"Chanson un Peu Naïve" (Bogan), **Supp. III Part 1:** 50–51
"Chanteuse" (Doty), **Supp. XI:** 119
"Chant for May Day" (Hughes), **Supp. I Part 1:** 331
Chants (Mora), **Supp. XIII: 214–215**
Chaos (Dove), **Supp. IV Part 1:** 243
"Chaperone, The" (Van Vechten), **Supp. II Part 2:** 728
Chaplin, Charles Spencer, **I:** 27, 32, 43, 386, 447; **III:** 403; **Supp. I Part 2:** 607; **Supp. IV Part 1:** 146; **Supp. IV Part 2:** 574
"Chaplinesque" (H. Crane), **Retro. Supp. II:** 79
"Chapman" (Rukeyser), **Supp. VI:** 273
Chapman, Abraham, **IV:** 485
Chapman, George, **Supp. I Part 2:** 422
Chapman, John (Johnny Appleseed), **Supp. I Part 2:** 397
Chapman, John Jay, **IV:** 436
Chapman, Stephen, **Supp. XIII:** 12
Chappell, Fred, **Supp. IV Part 1:** 69; **Supp. XI:** 317
Chapters in a Mythology: The Poetry of Sylvia Plath (Kroll), **Supp. I Part 2:** 541–543
Chapters on Erie (Adams and Adams), **Supp. I Part 2:** 644
Chapter Two (Simon), **Supp. IV Part 2:** 575, 586
"Chapter VI" (Hemingway), **II:** 252
"Character" (Emerson), **II:** 6
"Character of Presidents, The" (Doctorow), **Supp. IV Part 1:** 224
"Character of Socrates, The" (Emerson), **II:** 8–9
Character of the Poet, The (Simpson), **Supp. IX:** 273, 275, 278
"Characters in Fiction" (McCarthy), **II:** 562
"Charades" (Moore), **Supp. X:** 178

"Charge It" (Fante), **Supp. XI:** 164–165
Charlatan, The (Singer), **IV:** 1
"Charles" (Jackson), **Supp. IX:** 125
Charles Goodnight: Cowman and Plainsman (Haley), **Supp. V:** 226
Charles Simic: Essays on the Poetry (Weigl), **Supp. VIII:** 269
Charles the Bold, Duke of Burgundy, **III:** 487
Charleville, Victoria Verdon, **Supp. I Part 1:** 200–201, 205, 206, 210
Charley's Aunt (B. Thomas), **II:** 138
Charlie Chan Is Dead: An Anthology of Contemporary Asian American Fiction (Hagedorn), **Supp. X:** 292
"Charlie Christian Story, The" (Ellison), **Retro. Supp. II:** 121
"Charlie Howard's Descent" (Doty), **Supp. XI:** 122
Charlotte: A Tale of Truth (Rowson), **Supp. I Part 1:** 128
Charlotte's Web (White), **Supp. I Part 2:** 655, 656, 658, 667, 670
Charm, The (Creeley), **Supp. IV Part 1:** 139, 141, 144, 149–150
Charmed Life, A (McCarthy), **II:** 571–574
Charms for the Easy Life (Gibbons), **Supp. X:** 45, **47–48**
Charnel Rose, The (Aiken), **I:** 50, 57, 62
Charon's Cosmology (Simic), **Supp. VIII: 276–278**
Charterhouse, The (Percy), **Supp. III Part 1:** 388
Charvat, William, **II:** 244
Chase, Mary Ellen, **Retro. Supp. II:** 243, 245
Chase, Richard, **IV:** 202, 443; **Retro. Supp. I:** 40, 395
Chase, Salmon P., **Supp. I Part 2:** 584
Chase, Stuart, **Supp. I Part 2:** 609
Chase, The (Foote), **Supp. I Part 1:** 281
"Chaste Land, The" (Tate), **IV:** 122
Château, The (Maxwell), **Supp. VIII:** 152, 160, **165–167**, 168, 169
Chatham, Russell, **Supp. VIII:** 40
Chatterton, Thomas, **Supp. I Part 1:** 349; **Supp. I Part 2:** 410, 716
Chatterton, Wayne, **Supp. IX:** 2, 4, 11–12
Chatwin, Bruce, **Supp. VIII:** 322
Chaucer, Geoffrey, **I:** 131; **II:** 11, 504, 516, 542, 543; **III:** 283, 411, 473, 492, 521; **Retro. Supp. I:** 135, 426; **Supp. I Part 1:** 356, 363; **Supp. I Part 2:** 422, 617; **Supp. V:** 259; **Supp. XII:** 197

Chauncy, Charles, **I:** 546–547; **IV:** 147
Chavez, César, **Supp. V:** 199
Chávez, Denise, **Supp. IV Part 2:** 544; **Supp. XI:** 316
Chavez, Lydia, **Supp. VIII:** 75
Chavkin, Allan, **Supp. IV Part 1:** 259
Chavkin, Nancy Feyl, **Supp. IV Part 1:** 259
Chayefsky, Paddy, **Supp. XI:** 306
Cheang, Shu Lea, **Supp. XI:** 20
"Cheers" (Carver), **Supp. III Part 1:** 138
Cheetham, James, **Supp. I Part 2:** 521
Cheever, Benjamin Hale, **Supp. I Part 1:** 175
Cheever, David W., **Supp. I Part 1:** 304
Cheever, Ezekiel, **Supp. I Part 1:** 174, 193
Cheever, Federico, **Supp. I Part 1:** 175
Cheever, Fred, **Supp. I Part 1:** 174
Cheever, Frederick L., **Supp. I Part 1:** 174
Cheever, John, **Retro. Supp. I:** 116, 333, 335; **Supp. I Part 1: 174–199;** **Supp. V:** 23, 95; **Supp. VIII:** 151; **Supp. IX:** 114, 208; **Supp. XI:** 65, 66, 99; **Supp. XII:** 140
Cheever, Mary Liley, **Supp. I Part 1:** 174
Cheever, Mrs. John (Mary Winternitz), **Supp. I Part 1:** 175
Cheever, Susan. *See* Cowley, Susan Cheever (Susan Cheever)
Cheever Evening, A (Gurney), **Supp. V:** 95
Chekhov, Anton, **I:** 52, 90; **II:** 27, 38, 44, 49, 198, 542; **III:** 362, 467; **IV:** 17, 53, 359, 446; **Retro. Supp. I:** 5, 355; **Retro. Supp. II:** 317; **Supp. I Part 1:** 196; **Supp. II Part 1:** 6; **Supp. IV Part 2:** 585; **Supp. V:** 265; **Supp. VIII:** 153, 332; **Supp. IX:** 260, 265, 274; **Supp. XI:** 66; **Supp. XII:** 94, 307; **Supp. XIII:** 79
"Chekhov's Sense of Writing as Seen Through His Letters" (Dobyns), **Supp. XIII:** 77–78
"Chemin de Fer" (Bishop), **Retro. Supp. II:** 41; **Supp. I Part 1:** 80, 85, 86
Cheney, Brainard, **Retro. Supp. II:** 229
Chenzira, Ayoka, **Supp. XI:** 19
Cherkovski, Neeli, **Supp. XII:** 118, 132, 134
Chernyshevski, Nikolai, **III:** 261, 262, 263; **Retro. Supp. I:** 269
Cherokee Lottery, The: A Sequence of

Poems (W. J. Smith), **Supp. XIII:** 340–344
Cherry (Karr), **Supp. XI:** 239, 251–254
Cherry Orchard, The (Chekhov), **IV:** 359, 426; **Supp. VIII:** 153
Cheslock, Louis, **III:** 99, 118, 119
Chesnutt, Charles Waddell, **Supp. II Part 1:** 174, 193, 211; **Supp. IV Part 1:** 257
"Chess House, The" (Dixon), **Supp. XII:** 139
Chessman, Caryl, **Supp. I Part 2:** 446
Chester, Alfred, **Retro. Supp. II:** 111, 112; **Supp. X:** 192
Chesterfield, Lord, **II:** 36
Chesterton, Gilbert Keith, **I:** 226; **IV:** 432
Cheuse, Alan, **Supp. IV Part 2:** 570
Chevigny, Bell Gale, **Supp. XI:** 283
"Chicago" (Sandburg), **III:** 581, 592, 596; **Supp. III Part 1:** 71
Chicago (Shepard), **Supp. III Part 2:** 439
Chicago: City on the Make (Algren), **Supp. IX:** 1, 3
"*Chicago Defender* Sends a Man to Little Rock, The" (Brooks), **Supp. III Part 1:** 80–81
"Chicago Hamlet, A" (Anderson), **I:** 112
Chicago Loop (Theroux), **Supp. VIII:** 324
"Chicago Picasso, The" (Brooks), **Supp. III Part 1:** 70–71, 84
Chicago Poems (Sandburg), **III:** 579, 581–583, 586
"Chicano/Borderlands Literature and Poetry" (Ríos), **Supp. IV Part 2:** 537, 538, 542, 545
Chick, Nancy, **Supp. IV Part 1:** 1
"Chickamauga" (Bierce), **I:** 201
"Chickamauga" (Wolfe), **IV:** 460
Chickamauga (Wright), **Supp. V:** 333, 343–344
"Chickamauga" (Wright), **Supp. V:** 334
"Chiefly about War Matters" (Hawthorne), **II:** 227; **Retro. Supp. I:** 165
"Child" (Plath), **Supp. I Part 2:** 544
Child, Lydia Maria, **Supp. XIII:** 141
"Child, The" (Ríos), **Supp. IV Part 2:** 543
"Child by Tiger, The" (Wolfe), **IV:** 451
"Childhood" (Wright), **Supp. V:** 341
Childhood, A: The Biography of a Place (Crews), **Supp. XI:** 102–103, 245
"Childhood, When You Are in It . . ." (Kenyon), **Supp. VII:** 160, 170
"Childhood Sketch" (Wright), **Supp. III Part 2:** 589
"Child Is Born, A" (Benét), **Supp. XI:** 46
"Child Is the Meaning of This Life, The" (Schwartz), **Supp. II Part 2:** 659–660
"Childlessness" (Merrill), **Supp. III Part 1:** 323
"Childless Woman" (Plath), **Supp. I Part 2:** 544
Child-Life (Whittier and Larcom, eds.), **Supp. XIII:** 142
Child-Life in Prose (Whittier and Larcom, eds.), **Supp. XIII:** 142
Childlike Life of the Black Tarantula, The (Acker), **Supp. XII:** 4, 6, 7–8
"Child Margaret" (Sandburg), **III:** 584
"Child of Courts, The" (Jarrell), **II:** 378, 379, 381
Child of God (McCarthy), **Supp. VIII:** 177–178
"CHILD OF THE THIRTIES" (Baraka), **Supp. II Part 1:** 60
"Child on Top of a Greenhouse" (Roethke), **III:** 531
Children (Gurney), **Supp. V:** 95, 96
"Children" (Stowe), **Supp. I Part 2:** 587
Children, The (Wharton), **IV:** 321, 326; **Retro. Supp. I:** 381
"Children, the Sandbar, That Summer" (Rukeyser), **Supp. VI:** 274
Children and Others (Cozzens), **I:** 374
Children Is All (Purdy), **Supp. VII:** 277, 278, 282
"Children of Adam" (Whitman), **IV:** 342; **Retro. Supp. I:** 403, 405
Children of Light (Stone), **Supp. V:** 304–306
Children of Light and the Children of Darkness, The (Niebuhr), **III:** 292, 306, 310
Children of the Frost (London), **II:** 469, 483
"Children of the Lord's Supper, The" (Tegnér), **Retro. Supp. II:** 155, 157
Children of the Market Place (Masters), **Supp. I Part 2:** 471
"Children on Their Birthdays" (Capote), **Supp. III Part 1:** 114, 115
"Children Selecting Books in a Library" (Jarrell), **II:** 371
Children's Hour, The (Hellman), **Supp. I Part 1:** 276–277, 281, 286, 297
"Children's Rhymes" (Hughes), **Supp. I Part 1:** 340
Childress, Mark, **Supp. X:** 89
Child's Garden of Verses, A (Stevenson), **Supp. IV Part 1:** 298, 314; **Supp. XIII:** 75
"Child's Reminiscence, A" (Whitman), **IV:** 344
Childwold (Oates), **Supp. II Part 2:** 519–520
Chill, The (Macdonald), **Supp. IV Part 2:** 473
Chills and Fever (Ransom), **III:** 490, 491–492, 493
Chilly Scenes of Winter (Beattie), **Supp. V:** 21, 22, 23, 24, 26, 27
"Chimes for Yahya" (Merrill), **Supp. III Part 1:** 329
Chin, Frank, **Supp. V:** 164, 172
"China" (Johnson), **Supp. VI:** 193–194
"Chinaman's Hat" (Kingston), **Supp. V:** 169
China Men (Kingston), **Supp. V:** 157, 158, 159, 160, 161, 164–169; **Supp. X:** 292
China Trace (Wright), **Supp. V:** 332, 340, 341, 342
Chinese Classics (Legge), **III:** 472
Chinese Materia Medica (P. Smith), **III:** 572
"Chinese Nightingale, The" (Lindsay), **Supp. I Part 2:** 392–393, 394
Chinese Nightingale and Other Poems, The (Lindsay), **Supp. I Part 2:** 392
Chinese Siamese Cat, The (Tan), **Supp. X:** 289
"Chinoiseries" (Lowell), **II:** 524–525
Chirico, Giorgio de, **Supp. III Part 1:** 14
"Chiron" (Winters), **Supp. II Part 2:** 801
Chodorov, Jerome, **IV:** 274
"Choice, The" (Karr), **Supp. XI:** 251
"Choice of Profession, A" (Malamud), **Supp. I Part 2:** 437
Chomei, Kamo No, **IV:** 170, 171, 184
Chomsky, Noam, **Supp. IV Part 2:** 679
Choosing not Choosing (Cameron), **Retro. Supp. I:** 43
Chopin, Felix, **Supp. I Part 1:** 202
Chopin, Frédéric, **Supp. I Part 1:** 363
Chopin, Jean, **Supp. I Part 1:** 206
Chopin, Kate, **II:** 276; **Retro. Supp. I:** 10, 215; **Retro. Supp. II:** 57–74; **Supp. I Part 1:** 200–226; **Supp. V:** 304; **Supp. X:** 227
"Choral: The Pink Church" (W. C. Williams), **Retro. Supp. I:** 428
"Chord" (Merwin), **Supp. III Part 1:** 356
Choruses from Iphigenia in Aulis (Doolittle, trans.), **Supp. I Part 1:** 257, 268, 269

"Chosen Blindness" (Karr), **Supp. XI:** 251

Chosen Country (Dos Passos), **I:** 475, 490–491

Chosen Place, The Timeless People, The (Marshall), **Supp. XI:** 275, 276, **282–284**

Chosön (Lowell), **II:** 513

Choukri, Mohamed, **Supp. IV Part 1:** 92

Chovteau, Mane Thérèse, **Supp. I Part 1:** 205

Chrisman, Robert, **Supp. IV Part 1:** 1

Christabel (Coleridge), **Supp. IV Part 2:** 465

"Christ for Sale" (Lowell), **II:** 538

Christian, Graham, **Supp. XII:** 193

Christian Dictionary, A (Wilson), **IV:** 153

"Christian in World Crisis, The" (Merton), **Supp. VIII:** 203

Christianity and Power Politics (Niebuhr), **III:** 292, 303

"Christianity and the Survival of Creation" (Berry), **Supp. X:** 30

"Christian Minister, The" (Emerson), **II:** 10

Christian Philosopher, The (Mather), **Supp. II Part 2:** 463–464

Christian Realism and Practical Problems (Niebuhr), **III:** 292, 308

"Christian Roommates, The" (Updike), **IV:** 226–227; **Retro. Supp. I:** 319, 323

Christiansen, Carrie, **I:** 210

Christie, Agatha, **Supp. IV Part 1:** 341; **Supp. IV Part 2:** 469

Christine (King), **Supp. V:** 139, 148

"Christ Light, The" (Chopin), **Retro. Supp. II:** 61

"Christmas 1944" (Levertov), **Supp. III Part 1:** 274

"Christmas, or the Good Fairy" (Stowe), **Supp. I Part 2:** 586

"Christmas Banquet, The" (Hawthorne), **II:** 227

Christmas Card, A (Theroux), **Supp. VIII:** 322

Christmas Carol, A (Dickens), **Retro. Supp. I:** 196; **Supp. I Part 2:** 409–410; **Supp. X:** 252, 253

"Christmas Eve at Johnson's Drugs N Goods" (Bambara), **Supp. XI:** 11–12

"Christmas Eve in the Time of War: A Capitalist Meditates by a Civil War Monument" (Lowell), **II:** 538

"Christmas Eve under Hooker's Statue" (Lowell), **II:** 539–540

"Christmas Gift" (Warren), **IV:** 252–253

"Christmas Greeting, A" (Wright), **Supp. III Part 2:** 601

"Christmas Hymn, A" (Wilbur), **Supp. III Part 2:** 557

Christmas Memory, A (Capote), **Supp. III Part 1:** 118, 119, 129

"Christmass Poem" (West), **Retro. Supp. II:** 356

Christmas Story (Mencken), **III:** 111

"Christmas to Me" (Lee), **Supp. VIII:** 113

Christographia (Taylor), **IV:** 164–165

"Christ on the Cross/Nuestro Señor Crucificado" (Mora), **Supp. XIII:** 229

"Christopher Cat" (Cullen), **Supp. IV Part 1:** 173

Christopher Columbus, Mariner (Morison), **Supp. I Part 2:** 488

Christophersen, Bill, **Supp. IX:** 159, 167; **Supp. XI:** 155; **Supp. XIII:** 87

"Christ's Passion" (Karr), **Supp. XI:** 251

Christus: A Mystery (Longfellow), **II:** 490, 493, 495, 505–507; **Retro. Supp. II:** 161, 165, 166

Chroma (F. Barthelme), **Supp. XI:** 30, 33, 34

"Chroma" (F. Barthelme), **Supp. XI:** 31

"Chronicle of Race Relations, A" (Du Bois), **Supp. II Part 1:** 182

Chronicle of the Conquest of Granada (Irving), **II:** 310

"Chronologues" (Goldbarth), **Supp. XII:** 183, 184

"Chrysanthemums, The" (Steinbeck), **IV:** 53

"Chrysaor" (Longfellow), **II:** 498

Chu, Louis, **Supp. X:** 291

Chuang, Hua, **Supp. X:** 291

Chuang-Tzu, **Supp. VIII:** 206

"Chunk of Amethyst, A" (Bly), **Supp. IV Part 1:** 72

Church, Margaret, **IV:** 466

"Church and the Fiction Writer, The" (O'Connor), **Retro. Supp. II:** 223, 233

Churchill, Winston, **I:** 9, 490; **Supp. I Part 2:** 491

Church of Dead Girls, The (Dobyns), **Supp. XIII:** 75, **83–84**

"Church Porch, The" (Herbert), **IV:** 153

Church Psalmody, Selected from Dr. Watts and Other Authors (Mason and Greene, ed.), **I:** 458

Ciannic, Saint, **II:** 215

Ciano, Edda, **IV:** 249

Ciardi, John, **I:** 169, 179, 535; **III:** 268; **Supp. IV Part 1:** 243; **Supp. IV Part 2:** 639; **Supp. IX:** 269, 324; **Supp. XII:** 119

Cicada (Haines), **Supp. XII: 206–207**

"Cicadas" (Wilbur), **Supp. III Part 2:** 549

Cicero, **I:** 279; **II:** 8, 14–15; **III:** 23; **Supp. I Part 2:** 405

Cider House Rules, The (Irving), **Supp. VI:** 164, **173–175**

"Cigales" (Wilbur), **Supp. III Part 2:** 549

"Cimetière Marin, Le" (Valéry), **IV:** 91–92

Cimino, Michael, **Supp. X:** 126

Cincinnati Kid, The (film), **Supp. XI:** **306**

"Cinderella" (Jarrell), **II:** 386

"Cinderella" (Perrault), **IV:** 266, 267

"Cinderella" (Sexton), **Supp. II Part 2:** 691

"Cinema, The" (Salter), **Supp. IX:** 257

Cinema of Tony Richardson, The: Essays and Interviews (Phillips), **Supp. XI:** 306

Cinthio, **IV:** 370

CIOPW (Cummings), **I:** 429

"Circe" (Welty), **Retro. Supp. I:** 353

Circle Game, The (Atwood), **Supp. XIII:** 20, 33

"Circle in the Fire, A" (O'Connor), **III:** 344–345, 349–350, 351, 353, 354; **Retro. Supp. II:** 229, 232

"Circle of Breath" (Stafford), **Supp. XI:** 318, 322

"Circles" (Emerson), **I:** 455, 460

"Circles" (Lowell), **II:** 554

"Circus, The" (Porter), **III:** 443, 445

"Circus Animals' Desertion" (Yeats), **I:** 389

"Circus in the Attic" (Warren), **IV:** 253

Circus in the Attic, The (Warren), **IV:** 243, 251–253

"Circus in Three Rings" (Plath), **Retro. Supp. II:** 243; **Supp. I Part 2:** 536

Circus of Needs, A (Dunn), **Supp. XI:** **147–148**

"Cirque d'Hiver" (Bishop), **Supp. I Part 1:** 85

Cisneros, Sandra, **Supp. IV Part 2:** 544; **Supp. VII: 57–73**; **Supp. XI:** 177

Cities of the Interior (Nin), **Supp. X:** 182

Cities of the Plain (McCarthy), **Supp. VIII:** 175, **186–187**

Cities of the Red Night (Burroughs),

Supp. III Part 1: 106
"Citizen Cain" (Baraka), **Supp. II Part 1:** 49
Citizen Kane (film), **Retro. Supp. I:** 115; **Supp. V:** 251; **Supp. XI:** 169
"Citizen of the World" (Goldsmith), **II:** 299
"City" (Francis), **Supp. IX:** 87
City and the Pillar, The (Vidal), **Supp. IV Part 2:** 677, 680–681
"*City and the Pillar, The,* as Gay Fiction" (Summers), **Supp. IV Part 2:** 680–681
City in History, The (Mumford), **Supp. II Part 2:** 495
"City in the Sea, The" (Poe), **III:** 411; **Retro. Supp. II:** 274
City Life (Barthelme), **Supp. IV Part 1:** 44, 47
City of Glass (Auster), **Supp. XII:** 22, **24–26**
City of God, The (St. Augustine), **IV:** 126
City of the Living and Other Stories, The (Stegner), **Supp. IV Part 2:** 599, 609, 613
City of Your Final Destination, The (Cameron), **Supp. XII:** 79, 82, **91–94**
"City on a Hill" (Lowell), **II: 552**
"City Person Encountering Nature, A" (Kingston), **Supp. V:** 170
"City Planners, The" (Atwood), **Supp. XIII:** 33
City Without Walls (Auden), **Supp. II Part 1:** 24
Civil Disobedience (Thoreau), **IV:** 185; **Supp. I Part 2:** 507
Civilization in the United States (Stearns), **I:** 245
"Civil Rights" (Lanier), **Supp. I Part 1:** 357
Cixous, Hélène, **Supp. X:** 102; **Supp. XIII:** 297
Claiborne, William, **I:** 132
Claiming of Sleeping Beauty, The (Rice), **Supp. VII:** 301
Clampitt, Amy, **Supp. IX: 37–54;** **Supp. X:** 120; **Supp. XI:** 249
Clancy's Wake, At (Crane), **I:** 422
Clara Howard; or, The Enthusiasm of Love (Brown), **Supp. I Part 1:** 145
Clara's Ole Man (Bullins), **Supp. II Part 1:** 42
Clare, John, **II:** 387; **III:** 528
Clarel: A Poem and Pilgrimage in the Holy Land (Melville), **Retro. Supp. I:** 257
Clarissa (Richardson), **II:** 111; **Supp. I Part 2:** 714; **Supp. V:** 127

Clark, Alex, **Supp. XII:** 307
Clark, Charles, **I:** 470
Clark, Eleanor. *See* Warren, Mrs. Robert Penn (Eleanor Clark)
Clark, Francis Edward, **II:** 9
Clark, Geoffrey, **Supp. XI:** 342
Clark, Harry Hayden, **Supp. I Part 2:** 423
Clark, John Bates, **Supp. I Part 2:** 633
Clark, Thomas, **Supp. III Part 2:** 629; **Supp. IV Part 1:** 140, 145, 147
Clark, Walter, **Supp. XI:** 315
Clark, William, **III:** 14; **IV:** 179, 283
Clark, Willis Gaylord, **Supp. I Part 2:** 684
Clarke, James Freeman, **Supp. II Part 1:** 280
Clarke, John, **Supp. IV Part 1:** 8
Clarke, John J., **III:** 356
Clarke, Samuel, **II:** 108
Clark Lectures, **Retro. Supp. I:** 65
Clash by Night (Odets), **Supp. II Part 2:** 531, 538, 544–546, 550, 551
Classical Tradition, The (Highet), **Supp. I Part 1:** 268
Classic Ballroom Dances (Simic), **Supp. VIII:** 271, **276–278,** 283
Classics and Commercials: A Literary Chronicle of the Forties (Wilson), **IV:** 433
"CLASS STRUGGLE" (Baraka), **Supp. III Part 1:** 55
Claudel, Paul, **I:** 60
Claudelle Inglish (Caldwell), **I:** 304
Clausen, Jan, **Retro. Supp. II:** 292
Clavel, Marcel, **I:** 343
"CLAY" (Baraka), **Supp. II Part 1:** 54
Clay, Henry, **I:** 8; **Supp. I Part 2:** 684, 686
Clay's Ark (O. Butler), **Supp. XIII:** 63
Clayton, John J., **Supp. IV Part 1:** 238
"Clean, Well Lighted Place, A" (Hemingway), **Retro. Supp. I:** 181
"Clear, with Light Variable Winds" (Lowell), **II:** 522
"Clear Days" (White), **Supp. I Part 2:** 664, 665
Clearing (Berry), **Supp. X:** 22
"Clearing, A" (Simpson), **Supp. IX:** 280
"Clearing, The" (Kenyon), **Supp. VII:** 174
"Clearing the Title" (Merrill), **Supp. III Part 1:** 336
"Clearing Up the Question of Stesichoros' Blinding by Helen" (Carson), **Supp. XII:** 107–108
"Clear Morning" (Glück), **Supp. V:** 88
"Clearness" (Wilbur), **Supp. III Part**

2: 544, 550
"Clear Night" (Wright), **Supp. V:** 341
Clear Pictures: First Loves, First Guides (Price), **Supp. VI:** 253, 254, 255, 256, 265
Clear Springs (Mason), **Supp. VIII:** 134–136, 137–138, 139, 147
Cleaver, Eldridge, **Retro. Supp. II:** 12; **Supp. IV Part 1:** 206; **Supp. X:** 249
Cleland, John, **Supp. V:** 48, 127
Clemenceau, Georges, **I:** 490
Clemens, Jane, **I:** 247
Clemens, Mrs. Samuel Langhorne (Olivia Langdon), **I:** 197, 208, 247; **Supp. I Part 2:** 457
Clemens, Orion, **IV:** 193, 195
Clemens, Samuel Langhorne. *See* Twain, Mark
Clemens, Susie, **IV:** 208
Clementine Recognitions (novel), **Supp. IV Part 1:** 280
Clemons, Walter, **Supp. IV Part 1:** 305, 307
Cleopatra, **III:** 44; **IV:** 373; **Supp. I Part 1:** 114
"Clepsydra" (Ashbery), **Supp. III Part 1:** 10–15
"Clerks, The" (Robinson), **III:** 517–518
Cleveland, Carol, **Supp. IX:** 120, 125
Cleveland, Ceil, **Supp. V:** 222
Cleveland, Grover, **II:** 126, 128, 129, 130, 137, 138; **Supp. I Part 2:** 486
"Clever Magician Carrying My Heart, A" (Salinas), **Supp. XIII:** 323
Cliff, Michelle, **Retro. Supp. II:** 293–294
Clifford, Craig, **Supp. IX:** 99
Clift, Montgomery, **III:** 161
Climate of Monastic Prayer, The (Merton), **Supp. VIII:** 205, 207
"Climber, The" (Mason), **Supp. VIII:** 140–141
"Climbing the Tower" (Crews), **Supp. XI:** 102
Clinton, De Witt, **I:** 338
"Clipped Wings" (H. Miller), **III:** 176–177
Clive, Robert, **Supp. I Part 2:** 505
"Clock in the Square, A" (Rich), **Retro. Supp. II:** 279
Clock Winder, The (Tyler), **Supp. IV Part 2:** 661–662, 670
Clock Without Hands (McCullers), **II:** 587–588, 604–606
Clockwork Orange, A (Burgess), **Supp. XIII:** 29
Clorindy (Cook), **Supp. II Part 1:** 199

"Close Calls" (Wolff), **Supp. VII:** 332–333

"Closed Book, A" (Mosley), **Supp. XIII:** 237

Close Range: Wyoming Stories (Proulx), **Supp. VII:** 261–265

Close the Book (Glaspell), **Supp. III Part 1:** 179

"Close the Book" (Lowell), **II:** 554

Close to Shore: A True Story of Terror in an Age of Innocence (Capuzzo), **Supp. XIII:** 254

Closet Writing & Gay Reading: The Case of Melville's Pierre (Creech), **Retro. Supp. I:** 254

Closing Circle, The (Commoner), **Supp. XIII:** 264

Closing of the American Mind, The (Bloom), **Retro. Supp. II:** 19, 30, 31

"Closing of the Rodeo, The" (W. J. Smith), **Supp. XIII:** 332

Closing Time (Heller), **Supp. IV Part 1:** 382, 386, 391–394

Closset, Marie, **Supp. VIII:** 251, 265

"Cloud, The" (Shelley), **Supp. I Part 2:** 720

"Cloud and Fame" (Berryman), **I:** 173

Cloud Forest, The: A Chronicle of the South American Wilderness (Matthiessen), **Supp. V:** 202, 204

"Cloud on the Way, The" (Bryant), **Supp. I Part 1:** 171

"Cloud River" (Wright), **Supp. V:** 341

"Clouds" (Levine), **Supp. V:** 184

Cloudsplitter (Banks), **Supp. V:** 16

"Clover" (Lanier), **Supp. I Part 1:** 362–364

Clover and Other Poems (Lanier), **Supp. I Part 1:** 362

"Clown" (Corso), **Supp. XII:** 127

Clown in the Belfry, The: Writings on Faith and Fiction (Buechner), **Supp. XII:** 53

Cluck, Julia, **Supp. I Part 2:** 728

Clum, John M., **Supp. XIII: 200,** 201, 209

Cluny, Hugo, **IV:** 290

Clurman, Harold, **I:** 93; **IV:** 381, 385

Clytus, Radiclani, **Supp. XIII:** 128, **Supp. XIII:** 129, 132

"Coal: Beginning and End" (Winters), **Supp. II Part 2:** 791

Coale, Howard, **Supp. XIII:** 15

"Coast, The" (column), **Supp. IV Part 1:** 198

"Coast Guard's Cottage, The" (Wylie), **Supp. I Part 2:** 723

Coast of Trees, A (Ammons), **Supp. VII:** 24, 34

"Coast-Range Christ, The" (Jeffers), **Supp. II Part 2:** 414, 419

"Coast-Road, The" (Jeffers), **Supp. II Part 2:** 425

Coates, Joseph, **Supp. VIII:** 80

Coates, Robert, **I:** 54; **IV:** 298

"Coatlicue's Rules: Advice from an Aztec Goddess" (Mora), **Supp. XIII:** 223

"Coats" (Kenyon), **Supp. VII:** 172

Cobb, Lee J., **III:** 153

Cobb, Ty, **III:** 227, 229

Cobbett, William, **Supp. I Part 2:** 517

"Cobbler Keezar's Vision" (Whittier), **Supp. I Part 2:** 699

"Cobweb, The" (Carver), **Supp. III Part 1:** 148

Cobwebs From an Empty Skull (Bierce), **I:** 195

Coccimiglio, Vic, **Supp. XIII:** 114

"Cock-a-Doodle-Doo!" (Melville), **III:** 89

"Cockayne" (Emerson), **II:** 6

"Cock-Crow" (Gordon), **II:** 219

Cock Pit (Cozzens), **I:** 359, 378, 379

Cockpit (Kosinski), **Supp. XII:** 21

Cockpit: A Novel (Kosinski), **Supp. VII:** 215, 223–224, 225

"Cock Robin Takes Refuge in the Storm House" (Snodgrass), **Supp. VI:** 319

Cocktail Hour, The (Gurney), **Supp. V:** 95, 96, 100, 101, 103, 105, 108

Cocktail Hour and Two Other Plays: Another Antigone and *The Perfect Party* (Gurney), **Supp. V:** 100

Cocktail Party, The (Eliot), **I:** 571, 582–583; **III:** 21; **Retro. Supp. I:** 65; **Supp. V:** 101, 103

Cocteau, Jean, **III:** 471; **Retro. Supp. I:** 82, 378; **Supp. IV Part 1:** 82

"Coda: Wilderness Letter" (Stegner), **Supp. IV Part 2:** 595

"Code, The" (Frost), **Retro. Supp. I:** 121, 128

Codman, Florence, **Supp. II Part 1:** 92, 93

Codman, Ogden, Jr., **Retro. Supp. I:** 362, 363

Cody, William ("Buffalo Bill"), **I:** 440; **III:** 584; **Supp. V:** 230

Coffey, Michael, **Supp. V:** 243

Coffey, Warren, **III:** 358

Coffin, Charles, **III:** 577

Cogan, David J., **Supp. IV Part 1:** 362

Coghill, Nevill, **Supp. II Part 1:** 4

Cohan, George M., **II:** 427; **III:** 401

Cohen, Hettie, **Supp. II Part 1:** 30

Cohen, Marty, **Supp. X:** 112

Cohen, Norman J., **Supp. IX:** 132, 143

Cohen, Sarah Blacher, **Supp. V:** 273

"Coin" (Goldbarth), **Supp. XII:** 187

Coindreau, Maurice, **III:** 339

Coiner, Constance, **Supp. XIII:** 297, 302

Coit, Lille Hitchcock, **Supp. X:** 103

"Coitus" (Pound), **III:** 466

"Cold, The" (Kenyon), **Supp. VII:** 164

"Cold, The" (Winters), **Supp. II Part 2:** 790–791, 809, 811

"Cold-blooded Creatures" (Wylie), **Supp. I Part 2:** 729

Colden, Cadwallader, **Supp. I Part 1:** 250

"Colder the Air, The" (Bishop), **Supp. I Part 1:** 86

Cold Feet (Harrison), **Supp. VIII:** 39

Cold Ground Was My Bed Last Night (Garrett), **Supp. VII:** 98

"Cold Ground Was My Bed Last Night" (Garrett), **Supp. VII:** 100

"Cold Night, The" (W. C. Williams), **Retro. Supp. I:** 418

"Cold Plunge into Skin Diving, A" (Knowles), **Supp. XII:** 241

Cold Spring, A (Bishop), **Retro. Supp. II:** 45

Cold Springs Harbor (Yates), **Supp. XI:** 348

Cold War American Poetry, **Supp. V:** 182

Cold War and the Income Tax, The (Wilson), **IV:** 430

Cole, Goody, **Supp. I Part 2:** 696–697

Cole, Lester, **Retro. Supp. II:** 347

Cole, Nat King, **Retro. Supp. I:** 334; **Supp. X:** 255

Cole, Thomas, **Supp. I Part 1:** 156, 158, 171

"Coleman" (Karr), **Supp. XI:** 244

Coleman, Wanda, **Supp. XI: 83–98**

Coleridge, Samuel Taylor, **I:** 283, 284, 447, 522; **II:** 7, 10, 11, 19, 71, 169, 273, 301, 502, 516, 549; **III:** 77, 83–84, 424, 461, 488, 523; **IV:** 74, 173, 250, 349, 453; **Retro. Supp. I:** 65, 308; **Retro. Supp. II:** 292; **Supp. I Part 1:** 31, 311, 349; **Supp. I Part 2:** 376, 393, 422; **Supp. IV Part 2:** 422, 465; **Supp. V:** 258; **Supp. IX:** 38, 50; **Supp. XIII:** 139

Coles, Katharine, **Supp. IV Part 2:** 630

Colette, **Supp. VIII:** 40, 171

"Coliseum, The" (Poe), **III:** 411

Collage of Dreams (Spencer), **Supp. X:** 196

"Collapse of Tomorrow, The" (Mumford), **Supp. II Part 2:** 482

"Collar, The" (Herbert), **Retro. Supp. II:** 282
Collected Earlier Poems (Hecht), **Supp. X:** 58, 59
Collected Earlier Poems (W. C. Williams), **Retro. Supp. I:** 414, 428
Collected Earlier Poems 1940–1960 (Levertov), **Supp. III Part 1:** 273, 275
Collected Early Poems, 1950–1970 (Rich), **Retro. Supp. II:** 280
Collected Essays (Tate), **IV:** 133–134
Collected Essays of Ralph Ellison, The (Ellison), **Retro. Supp. II:** 119
Collected Essays of Robert Creeley, The (Creeley), **Supp. IV Part 1:** 153, 154
Collected Later Poems (W. C. Williams), **Retro. Supp. I:** 428
Collected Plays (A. Miller), **III:** 158
Collected Plays, 1974–1983 (Gurney), **Supp. V:** 99
Collected Poems (Aiken), **I:** 50
Collected Poems (Burke), **I:** 269
Collected Poems (Cummings), **I:** 430, 439, 441
Collected Poems (Doolittle), **Supp. I Part 1:** 264–267, 269
Collected Poems (Frost), **Retro. Supp. I:** 136
Collected Poems (Lindsay), **Supp. I Part 2:** 380, 387, 392, 396–397, 400
Collected Poems (Moore), **III:** 194, 215
Collected Poems (Price), **Supp. VI:** 267
Collected Poems (Simpson), **Supp. IX:** 279
Collected Poems (Winters), **Supp. II Part 2:** 791, 810
Collected Poems (Wright), **Supp. III Part 2:** 602
Collected Poems (W. C. Williams), **IV:** 415; **Retro. Supp. I:** 430
Collected Poems 1909–1935 (Eliot), **I:** 580; **Retro. Supp. I:** 66
Collected Poems 1909–1962 (Eliot), **I:** 583
Collected Poems 1917–1952 (MacLeish), **III:** 3, 4, 19
Collected Poems 1921–1931 (W. C. Williams), **Retro. Supp. I:** 422
Collected Poems 1930–1960 (Eberhart), **I:** 522, 525–526, 540, 541
Collected Poems, 1923–1953 (Bogan), **Supp. III Part 1:** 64
Collected Poems, 1936–1976 (Francis), **Supp. IX:** 77, 80, **87**
Collected Poems: 1939–1989 (W. J. Smith), **Supp. XIII:** 332, 340, 343, 345
Collected Poems: 1940–1978 (Shapiro), **Supp. II Part 2:** 703, 717
Collected Poems: 1951–1971 (Ammons), **Supp. VII:** 24, 26–29, 32, 33
Collected Poems: 1956–1976 (Wagoner), **Supp. IX:** 323, **328–329**
Collected Poems, The (Stevens), **III:** 273; **IV:** 75, 76, 87, 93; **Retro. Supp. I:** 296, 309
Collected Poems of Amy Clampitt, The (Clampitt), **Supp. IX:** 37, 44, 53
Collected Poems of George Garrett (Garrett), **Supp. VII:** 109
Collected Poems of Hart Crane, The (Crane), **I:** 399–402
Collected Poems of James Agee, The (Fitzgerald, ed.), **I:** 27–28
Collected Poems of James T. Farrell, The (Farrell), **II:** 45
Collected Poems of Langston Hughes, The (Rampersad and Roessel, ed.), **Retro. Supp. I:** 194, 196, 212
Collected Poems of Muriel Rukeyser, The (Rukeyser), **Supp. VI:** 274
Collected Poems of Thomas Merton, The, **Supp. VIII:** 207, 208
Collected Poetry (Auden), **Supp. II Part 1:** 18
Collected Prose (Wright), **Supp. III Part 2:** 596
Collected Prose, The (Bishop), **Retro. Supp. II:** 51
Collected Recordings (W. C. Williams), **Retro. Supp. I:** 431
Collected Short Stories, The (Wharton), **Retro. Supp. I:** 362, 363, 366
Collected Sonnets (Millay), **III:** 136–137
Collected Stories, 1939–1976 (Bowles), **Supp. IV Part 1:** 92
Collected Stories, The (Paley), **Supp. VI:** 218
Collected Stories, The (Price), **Supp. VI:** 266
Collected Stories, The (Theroux), **Supp. VIII:** 318
Collected Stories, The (Wharton), **Retro. Supp. I:** 361
Collected Stories of Eudora Welty, The (Welty), **Retro. Supp. I:** 355
Collected Stories of Isaac Bashevis Singer (Singer), **Retro. Supp. II: 325–326**
Collected Stories of Katherine Anne Porter (Porter), **III:** 454
Collected Stories of Peter Taylor (Taylor), **Supp. V:** 314, 320, 323–324, 325, 326
Collected Stories of Richard Yates, The, **Supp. XI:** 349
Collected Stories of Wallace Stegner (Stegner), **Supp. IV Part 2:** 599, 605
Collected Stories of William Faulkner (Faulkner), **II:** 72; **Retro. Supp. I:** 75
Collected Stories of William Humphrey, The (Humphrey), **Supp. IX:** 106
Collected Works (Bierce), **I:** 204, 208–210
Collected Works of Buck Rogers in the 25th Century, The (Bradbury), **Supp. IV Part 1:** 101
Collected Writings, The (Z. Fitzgerald; Bruccoli, ed.), **Supp. IX:** 65, 68
Collection of Epigrams, **II:** 111
Collection of Poems, on American Affairs, and a Variety of Other Subjects . . . (Freneau), **Supp. II Part 1:** 274
Collection of Select Aphorisms and Maxims (Palmer), **II:** 111
"Collectors" (Carver), **Supp. III Part 1:** 141–142
Collingwood, R. G., **I:** 278
Collins, Billy, **Supp. XI:** 143
Collins, Doug, **Supp. V:** 5
Collins, Eddie, **II:** 416
Collins, Richard, **Supp. XI:** 171
Collins, Wilkie, **Supp. I Part 1:** 35, 36; **Supp. IV Part 1:** 341
Collins, William, **Supp. I Part 2:** 714
Collinson, Peter, **II:** 114
Collinson, Peter (pseudonym). *See* Hammett, Dashiell
Colloff, Pamela, **Supp. XIII:** 281
Colloque Sentimental (ballet), **Supp. IV Part 1:** 83
"Colloquy in Black Rock" (Lowell), **II:** 535; **Retro. Supp. II:** 178
"Colloquy of Monos and Una, The" (Poe), **III:** 412
Colônia, Regina, **Retro. Supp. II:** 53
Color (Cullen), **Supp. IV Part 1:** 164, 166, 167, 168
"Colorado" (Beattie), **Supp. V:** 27
Color and Democracy: Colonies and Peace (Du Bois), **Supp. II Part 1:** 184, 185
Color Curtain, The (Wright), **IV:** 478, 488
"Colored Americans" (Dunbar), **Supp. II Part 1:** 197
"Color Line, The" (Douglass), **Supp. III Part 1:** 163–165
Color Line, The (W. B. Smith), **Supp. II Part 1:** 168
Color of a Great City, The (Dreiser),

Retro. Supp. II: 104
Color of Darkness (Purdy), **Supp. VII:** 271
Color Purple, The (Walker), **Supp. III Part 2:** 517, 518, 520, 525–529, 532–537; **Supp. VIII:** 141; **Supp. X:** 252, 330
Color Schemes (Cheang; film), **Supp. XI:** 20
"Colors of Night, The" (Momaday), **Supp. IV Part 2:** 490
"Colors without Objects" (Swenson), **Supp. IV Part 2:** 645
Colossus, The (Plath), **Retro. Supp. II:** 245–247; **Supp. I Part 2:** 529, 531, 536, 538, 540; **Supp. V:** 79; **Supp. XI:** 317
"Colossus, The" (Plath), **Retro. Supp. II:** 250
Colossus of Maroussi, The (H. Miller), **III:** 178, 185–186
"Colt, The" (Stegner), **Supp. IV Part 2:** 600
Coltelli, Laura, **Supp. IV Part 1:** 323, 330, 335, 409; **Supp. IV Part 2:** 493, 497, 559
Coltrane, John, **Supp. VIII:** 197
Colum, Mary, **I:** 246, 252, 256; **Supp. I Part 2:** 708, 709
Columbiad, The (Barlow), **Supp. II Part 1:** 67, 72, 73, 74, 75–77, 79
"Columbian Ode" (Dunbar), **Supp. II Part 1:** 199
"Columbia U Poesy Reading—1975" (Corso), **Supp. XII:** 134
Columbus, Christopher, **I:** 253; **II:** 6, 310; **III:** 8; **Supp. I Part 2:** 397, 479, 480, 483, 486–488, 491, 495, 497, 498
"Columbus to Ferdinand" (Freneau), **Supp. II Part 1:** 255
Comanche Moon (McMurtry), **Supp. V:** 232
"Come, Break With Time" (Bogan), **Supp. III Part 1:** 52
Come Along with Me (Jackson), **Supp. IX:** 117, 118, 122
Comeback, The (Gurney), **Supp. V:** 97
"Come Back to the Raft Ag'in, Huck Honey!" (Fiedler), **Supp. XIII:** 93, 96–97, 101
Come Blow Your Horn (Simon), **Supp. IV Part 2:** 574, 575, 577, 578, 586, 587, 591
"Come Dance with Me in Ireland" (Jackson), **Supp. IX:** 119
"Comedian as the Letter C, The" (Stevens), **IV:** 84–85, 88; **Retro. Supp. I:** 297, 301, 302
"Comedy Cop" (Farrell), **II:** 45

"Comedy's Greatest Era" (Agee), **I:** 31
"Come In" (Frost), **Retro. Supp. I:** 139
"Come on Back" (Gardner), **Supp. VI:** 73
"Come Out into the Sun" (Francis), **Supp. IX:** 82
Come Out into the Sun: Poems New and Selected (Francis), **Supp. IX:** 82–83
"Come out the Wilderness" (Baldwin), **Supp. I Part 1:** 63
Comer, Anjanette, **Supp. XI:** 305
Comer, Cornelia, **I:** 214
Come with Me: Poems for a Journey (Nye), **Supp. XIII:** 279
"Comforts of Home, The" (O'Connor), **III:** 349, 351, 355; **Retro. Supp. II:** 237
Comic Artist, The (Glaspell and Matson), **Supp. III Part 1:** 182
"Comic Imagination of the Young Dickens, The" (Wright), **Supp. III Part 2:** 591
Comic Tragedies (Alcott), **Supp. I Part 1:** 33
"Coming Close" (Levine), **Supp. V:** 192
Coming Forth by Day of Osiris Jones, The (Aiken), **I:** 59
"Coming Home" (Gordon), **Supp. IV Part 1:** 309
"Coming in From the Cold" (Walker), **Supp. III Part 2:** 526
Coming into Eighty (Sarton), **Supp. VIII:** 262
"Coming into Eighty" (Sarton), **Supp. VIII:** 262
Coming into the Country (McPhee), **Supp. III Part 1:** 298, 301–306, 309, 310
Coming Into Writing (Cixous), **Supp. X:** 102
Coming of Age in Mississippi (Moody), **Supp. IV Part 1:** 11
Comings Back (Goldbarth), **Supp. XII:** 180
Coming to Canada: Poems (Shields), **Supp. VII:** 311–312
"Coming to Canada—Age Twenty Two" (Shields), **Supp. VII:** 311
"Coming to the Morning" (Merwin), **Supp. III Part 1:** 356
"Coming to This" (Strand), **Supp. IV Part 2:** 627
Comiskey, Charles, **II:** 422
Commager, Henry Steele, **I:** 253; **Supp. I Part 1:** 372; **Supp. I Part 2:** 484, 647, 650
Command the Morning (Buck), **Supp. II Part 1:** 125

"Commencement Address, A" (Brodsky), **Supp. VIII:** 31
"Commencement Day Address, The" (Schwartz), **Supp. II Part 2:** 660
Commentaries (Caesar), **II:** 502, 561
"Commentary" (Auden), **Supp. II Part 1:** 13
"Comment on Curb" (Hughes), **Supp. I Part 1:** 340
"Commerce" (Nye), **Supp. XIII:** 281
Commins, Saxe, **Retro. Supp. I:** 73; **Retro. Supp. II:** 355
Commodity of Dreams & Other Stories, A (Nemerov), **III:** 268–269, 285
Common Carnage (Dobyns), **Supp. XIII:** 87
"Common Ground, A" (Levertov), **Supp. III Part 1:** 277
"Common Life, The" (Auden), **Supp. IV Part 1:** 302, 313
Common Room, A: Essays 1954–1987 (Price), **Supp. VI:** 264–265, 267
Commons, John, **Supp. I Part 2:** 645
Common Sense (Paine), **II:** 117; **Supp. I Part 1:** 231; **Supp. I Part 2:** 505, 506–508, 509, 513, 516, 517, 521
"Communication" (Dobyns), **Supp. XIII:** 91
"Communion" (Dubus), **Supp. VII:** 91
Communion (Mora), **Supp. XIII:** 217–219
Communist Manifesto, The (Marx), **II:** 463
"Community Life" (Moore), **Supp. X:** 178
Comnes, Gregory, **Supp. IV Part 1:** 283, 284, 291
"Companions, The" (Nemerov), **III:** 269, 278, 287
Company of Poets, A (Simpson), **Supp. IX:** 265, 275
Company of Women, The (Gordon), **Supp. IV Part 1:** 302–304, 304, 306, 313
Company She Keeps, The (McCarthy), **II:** 562, 563–566
Compass Flower, The (Merwin), **Supp. III Part 1:** 353, 357
"Compassionate Friendship" (Doolittle), **Supp. I Part 1:** 257, 258, 259, 260, 271
"Compendium" (Dove), **Supp. IV Part 1:** 248
"Complaint" (W. C. Williams), **Retro. Supp. I:** 418
Complete Collected Poems of William Carlos Williams, 1906–1938, The (W. C. Williams), **Retro. Supp. I:** 424

"Complete Destruction" (W. C. Williams), **IV:** 413
"Complete Life of John Hopkins, The" (O. Henry), **Supp. II Part 1:** 405
Complete Poems (Frost), **II:** 155, 164
Complete Poems (Sandburg), **III:** 590–592, 594, 596
Complete Poems, The (Bishop), **Retro. Supp. II:** 49; **Supp. I Part 1:** 72, 82, 94
Complete Poems, The (Bradbury), **Supp. IV Part 1:** 105
Complete Poems, The: 1927–1979 (Bishop), **Retro. Supp. II:** 51
Complete Poems of Emily Dickinson, The (Bianchi and Hampson, eds.), **Retro. Supp. I:** 35
Complete Poems of Emily Dickinson, The (Johnson, ed.), **I:** 470
Complete Poems of Frederick Goddard Tuckerman, The (Momaday), **Supp. IV Part 2:** 480
Complete Poems of Hart Crane, **Retro. Supp. II:** 81
Complete Poems to Solve, The (Swenson), **Supp. IV Part 2:** 652
Complete Poetical Works (Hulme), **III:** 464
Complete Poetical Works (Longfellow), **Retro. Supp. II:** 154
Complete Poetical Works (Lowell), **II:** 512, 516–517
Complete Stories (O'Connor), **Supp. X:** 1
"Complete with Starry Night and Bourbon Shots" (Goldbarth), **Supp. XII:** 192–193
Complete Works of Kate Chopin, The (Seyersted, ed.), **Supp. I Part 1:** 212, 225
Complete Works of the Gawain-Poet (Gardner), **Supp. VI:** 64, 65
"Complicated Thoughts About a Small Son" (White), **Supp. I Part 2:** 678
"Compliments of the Season" (O. Henry), **Supp. II Part 1:** 392, 399
"Compline" (Auden), **Supp. II Part 1:** 23
Composition as Explanation (Stein), **IV:** 32, 33, 38
"Composition as Explanation" (Stein), **IV:** 27, 28
"Compounding of Consciousness" (James), **II:** 358–359
Comprehensive Bibliography (Hanneman), **II:** 259
Compton-Burnett, Ivy, **I:** 93; **II:** 580
"Comrade Laski, C.P.U.S.A. [M.L.]" (Didion), **Supp. IV Part 1:** 200

Comstock, Anthony, **Retro. Supp. II:** 95
Comus (Milton), **II:** 12; **Supp. I Part 2:** 622
Conan Doyle, Arthur. *See* Doyle, Arthur Conan
Conceptions of Reality in Modern American Poetry (Dembo), **Supp. I Part 1:** 272
"Concept of Character in Fiction, The" (Gass), **Supp. VI:** 85, **86**
Concept of Dread, The (Kierkegaard), **III:** 305
Concerning Children (Gilman), **Supp. XI:** 206
"Concerning Some Recent Criticism of His Work" (Doty), **Supp. XI:** 131
Concerning the End for Which God Created the World (Edwards), **I:** 549, 557, 559
Concerto for Two Pianos, Winds, and Percussion (Bowles), **Supp. IV Part 1:** 83
Conchologist's First Book, The (Poe), **III:** 412
Conclusive Evidence (Nabokov), **III:** 247–250, 252
"Concord Hymn" (Emerson), **II:** 19
"Concrete Universal, The: Observations on the Understanding of Poetry" (Ransom), **III:** 480
Concurring Beasts (Dobyns), **Supp. XIII:** 76
Condensed Novels and Other Papers (Harte), **Supp. II Part 1:** 342
Condition of Man, The (Mumford), **Supp. II Part 2:** 483, 484, 486, 495–496, 498
"Condolence" (Parker), **Supp. IX:** 191
"Condominium, The" (Elkin), **Supp. VI:** 49, **50–51,** 55, 56
Condon, Charles R., **Supp. XIII:** 163
Condorcet, Marquis de, **Supp. I Part 2:** 511
Conduct of Life, The (Emerson), **II:** 1–5, 8
Conduct of Life, The (Mumford), **Supp. II Part 2:** 485, 496–497
"Conductor of Nothing, The" (Levine), **Supp. V:** 189
"Conference Male, The" (Mora), **Supp. XIII:** 218
Confession de Claude, La (Zola), **I:** 411
"Confession of a House-Breaker, The" (Jewett), **Retro. Supp. II:** 146–147
Confession of Jereboam O. Beauchamp, The (pamphlet), **IV:** 253
Confessions (Augustine), **I:** 279
Confessions (Rousseau), **I:** 226

Confessions of a Barbarian: Selections from the Journals of Edward Abbey, 1951–1989 (Petersen, ed.), **Supp. XIII:** 2, 4
"Confessions of a Latina Author" (Mora), **Supp. XIII:** 221
Confessions of Nat Turner, The (Styron), **IV:** 98, 99, 105, 113–117; **Supp. X:** 16, 250
Confetti (Mora), **Supp. XIII:** 221
Confidence (James), **II:** 327, 328
Confidence-Man, The (Melville), **III:** 91; **Retro. Supp. I:** 255–256, 257; **Retro. Supp. II:** 121
Confidence Man, The (Van Vechten), **Supp. II Part 2:** 737
Confidential Clerk, The (Eliot), **I:** 570, 571–572, 583, 584; **Retro. Supp. I:** 65
Confident Years, 1885–1915, The (Brooks), **I:** 257, 259; **Supp. I Part 2:** 650
"Configurations" (Ammons), **Supp. VII:** 28
Confronting the Horror: The Novels of Nelson Algren (Giles), **Supp. IX:** 11, 15
Confucius, **II:** 1; **III:** 456, 475; **Supp. IV Part 1:** 14
Confusion (Cozzens), **I:** 358, 359, 377, 378
Congo (film), **Supp. IV Part 1:** 83
"Congo, The" (Lindsay), **Supp. I Part 2:** 388–389, 392, 395
Congo and Other Poems, The (Lindsay), **Supp. I Part 2:** 379, 382, 389, 390, 391
"Congress of the Insomniacs, The" (Simic), **Supp. VIII:** 281–282
Congreve, William, **III:** 195; **Supp. V:** 101
Coningsby (Disraeli), **II:** 127
Conjectures of a Guilty Bystander (Merton), **Supp. VIII:** 197, 206, 207
Conjugal Bliss: A Comedy of Marital Arts (Nichols), **Supp. XIII:** 269
"Conjugation of the Paramecium, The" (Rukeyser), **Supp. VI:** 271
"Conjuration" (Wilbur), **Supp. III Part 2:** 551
Conjure (Reed), **Supp. X:** 240, 242
Conjure (recording), **Supp. X:** 241
Conjure Woman, The (Chesnutt), **Supp. II Part 1:** 193
Conklin, Grof, **Supp. I Part 2:** 672
Conkling, Hilda, **II:** 530
Conkling, Roscoe, **III:** 506
Conley, Robert J., **Supp. V:** 232
Conley, Susan, **Supp. XIII:** 111, 112
Connaroe, Joel, **Supp. IV Part 2:** 690

"Connecticut Lad, A" (White), **Supp. I Part 2:** 677

"Connecticut Valley" (Cowley), **Supp. II Part 1:** 141–142

Connecticut Yankee in King Arthur's Court, A (Twain), **I:** 209; **II:** 276; **IV:** 205

Connell, Norreys (pseudonym). *See* O'Riordan, Conal Holmes O'Connell

Connelly, Marc, **III:** 394; **Supp. I Part 2:** 679; **Supp. IX:** 190

"Connoisseur of Chaos" (Stevens), **IV:** 89; **Retro. Supp. I:** 306

Connors, Elizabeth. *See* Lindsay, Mrs. Vachel (Elizabeth Connors)

Conover, Roger, **Supp. I Part 1:** 95

Conquering Horse (Manfred), **Supp. X:** 126

"Conqueror Worm, The" (Poe), **Retro. Supp. II:** 261

Conquest of Canaan (Dwight), **Supp. I Part 1:** 124

Conquistador (MacLeish), **III:** 2, 3, 13–14, 15

Conrad, Alfred, **Retro. Supp. II:** 245, 280, 286

Conrad, Alfred H., **Supp. I Part 2:** 552

Conrad, David, **Supp. I Part 2:** 552

Conrad, Jacob, **Supp. I Part 2:** 552

Conrad, Joseph, **I:** 123, 343, 394, 405, 409, 415, 421, 485, 506, 575–576, 578; **II:** 58, 73, 74, 91, 92, 144, 263, 320, 338, 595; **III:** 28, 102, 106, 328, 464, 467, 491, 512; **IV:** 476; **Retro. Supp. I:** 80, 91, 106, 108, 231, 274, 377; **Retro. Supp. II:** 222; **Supp. I Part 1:** 292; **Supp. I Part 2:** 621, 622; **Supp. IV Part 1:** 197, 341; **Supp. IV Part 2:** 680; **Supp. V:** 249, 251, 262, 298, 307, 311; **Supp. VIII:** 4, 310

Conrad, Paul, **Supp. I Part 2:** 552

Conrad, Peter, **Supp. IV Part 2:** 688

"Conrad Aiken: From Savannah to Emerson" (Cowley), **Supp. II Part 1:** 43

Conroy, Frank, **Supp. VIII:** 145; **Supp. XI:** 245

Conscience with the Power and Cases thereof (Ames), **IV:** 158

"Conscientious Objector, The" (Shapiro), **Supp. II Part 2:** 710

"Consciousness and Dining" (Harrison), **Supp. VIII:** 46

"Conscription Camp" (Shapiro), **Supp. II Part 2:** 705

"Consejos de Nuestra Señora de Guadalupe: Counsel from the Brown Virgin" (Mora), **Supp. XIII:** 224

"Conserving Natural and Cultural Diversity: The Prose and Poetry of Pat Mora" (Murphy), **Supp. XIII:** 214

"Considerations by the Way" (Emerson), **II:** 2, 5

Considine, Bob, **II:** 424

"Consolation" (Bausch), **Supp. VII:** 48

"Consolations" (Stafford), **Supp. XI:** 329

"Conspiracy of History, The: E. L. Doctorow's *The Book of Daniel*" (Levine), **Supp. IV Part 1:** 221

Conspiracy of Kings, The (Barlow), **Supp. II Part 1:** 80

Conspiracy of Pontiac, The (Parkman), **Supp. II Part 2:** 590, 595, 596, 599–600

Constab Ballads (McKay), **Supp. X:** 131, 133

Constance (Kenyon), **Supp. VII:** 170–172

"Constructive Work" (Du Bois), **Supp. II Part 1:** 172

"Consumption" (Bryant), **Supp. I Part 1:** 169–170

"Contagiousness of Puerperal Fever, The" (Holmes), **Supp. I Part 1:** 303–304

"Contemplation in a World of Action" (Merton), **Supp. VIII:** 204

"Contemplation of Poussin" (Sarton), **Supp. VIII:** 261

"Contemplations" (Bradstreet), **Supp. I Part 1:** 112, 113, 119–122

Contemporaries (Kazin), **Supp. VIII:** 102, **103–104**

Contemporary American Poetry (Poulin, ed.), **Supp. IX:** 272; **Supp. XI:** 259

"Contentment" (Holmes), **Supp. I Part 1:** 307

"Contest, The" (Paley), **Supp. VI:** 223, 230, 231

"Contest for Aaron Gold, The" (Roth), **Supp. III Part 2:** 403

Continental Drift (Banks), **Supp. V:** 13–14, 16, 227

Continental Op, The (Hammett), **Supp. IV Part 1:** 344

Continuity of American Poetry, The (Pearce), **Supp. I Part 1:** 111; **Supp. I Part 2:** 475

Continuous Harmony, A: Essays Cultural and Agricultural (Berry), **Supp. X:** 33

Continuous Life, The (Strand), **Supp. IV Part 2:** 630, 631–633

Contoski, Victor, **Supp. XII:** 181

"Contract" (Lardner), **II:** 432

"Contraption, The" (Swenson), **Supp. IV Part 2:** 643

"Contrariness of the Mad Farmer, The" (Berry), **Supp. X:** 35

"Contrition" (Dubus), **Supp. VII:** 84

"Control Burn" (Snyder), **Supp. VIII:** 301

"Control Is the Mainspring" (Komunyakaa), **Supp. XIII:** 122, 124

Control of Nature, The (McPhee), **Supp. III Part 1:** 310–313

"Conventional Wisdom, The" (Elkin), **Supp. VI:** 52–53

"Convergence" (Ammons), **Supp. VII:** 28

"Convergence of the Twain, The" (Hardy), **Supp. VIII:** 31, 32

Conversation (Aiken), **I:** 54

Conversation at Midnight (Millay), **III:** 138

"Conversation of Eiros and Charmion, The" (Poe), **III:** 412

"Conversation on Conversation" (Stowe), **Supp. I Part 2:** 587

"Conversations in Moscow" (Levertov), **Supp. III Part 1:** 282

Conversations on Some of the Old Poets (Lowell), **Supp. I Part 2:** 405

Conversations with Byron (Blessington), **Retro. Supp. II:** 58

Conversations with Eudora Welty (Prenshaw, ed.), **Retro. Supp. I:** 339, 340, 341, 342, 343, 352, 354

Conversations with Ishmael Reed (Dick and Singh, eds.), **Supp. X:** 244

Conversations with James Baldwin (Standley and Pratt, eds.), **Retro. Supp. II:** 6

Conversations with Richard Wilbur (Wilbur), **Supp. III Part 2:** 542–543

"Conversation with My Father, A" (Paley), **Supp. VI:** 220

"Conversion of the Jews, The" (Roth), **Retro. Supp. II:** 299; **Supp. III Part 2:** 404, 406

Conway, Jill, **Supp. I Part 1:** 19

Coode, John, **I:** 132

Cook, Bruce, **Supp. XII:** 130, 131, 133–134

Cook, Captain James, **I:** 2

Cook, Eleanor, **Retro. Supp. I:** 311

Cook, Elisha, **Supp. IV Part 1:** 356

Cook, Elizabeth Christine, **II:** 106

Cook, Mercer, **Supp. IV Part 1:** 368

Cooke, Alistair, **III:** 113, 119, 120

Cooke, Delmar G., **II:** 271

Cooke, Grace MacGowan, **Supp. V:** 285
Cooke, Philip Pendleton, **III:** 420
Cooke, Rose Terry, **II:** 401; **Retro. Supp. II:** 51, 136, 138; **Supp. XIII:** 152
"Cookie" (Taylor), **Supp. V:** 320
"Cookies, The" (Nye), **Supp. XIII:** 281
Cook-Lynn, Elizabeth, **Supp. IV Part 1:** 325
Coolbrith, Ina, **I:** 193, 196
"Coole Park" (Yeats), **Supp. VIII:** 155, 159
"Coole Park and Ballylee" (Yeats), **Supp. VIII:** 156
Cooley, John, **Supp. V:** 214
Cooley, Peter, **Supp. XIII:** 76
Coolidge, Calvin, **I:** 498; **II:** 95; **Supp. I Part 2:** 647
"Cool Million, A" (screen story) (West and Ingster), **Retro. Supp. II:** 348
Cool Million, A (West), **III:** 425; **IV:** 287, 288, 297–299, 300; **Retro. Supp. II:** 339, 340–341, 346, **353–355**
"Cool Tombs" (Sandburg), **III:** 554
Coon, Ross, **IV:** 196
"Coon Hunt" (White), **Supp. I Part 2:** 669
Co-op (Sinclair), **Supp. V:** 290
Cooper, Bernard, **Supp. XI:** 129
Cooper, Gary, **Supp. IV Part 2:** 524
Cooper, James Fenimore, **I:** 211, 257, **335–357**; **II:** 74, 277, 295–296, 302, 306, 309, 313, 314; **III:** 51; **IV:** 205, 333; **Retro. Supp. I:** 246; **Retro. Supp. II:** 160; **Supp. I Part 1:** 141, 155, 156, 158, 171, 372; **Supp. I Part 2:** 413, 495, 579, 585, 652, 660; **Supp. IV Part 1:** 80; **Supp. IV Part 2:** 463, 469; **Supp. V:** 209–210; **Supp. VIII:** 189
Cooper, Mrs. James Fenimore (Susan A. De Lancey), **I:** 338, 351, 354
Cooper, Mrs. William, **I:** 337
Cooper, Susan Fenimore, **I:** 337, 354
Cooper, William, **I:** 337–338, 351
Coover, Robert, **Supp. IV Part 1:** 388; **Supp. V: 39–55**; **Supp. XII:** 152
Copacetic (Komunyakaa), **Supp. XIII:** **116–118,** 126
Copland, Aaron, **II:** 586; **Supp. I Part 1:** 281; **Supp. III Part 2:** 619; **Supp. IV Part 1:** 79, 80–81, 84
Coplas de Don Jorge Manrique (Longfellow, trans.), **II:** 488, 492
Coppée, François Edouard Joachim, **II:** 325

Copperhead, The (Frederic), **II:** 134–135
Copper Sun (Cullen), **Supp. IV Part 1:** 167, 168
Coppola, Francis Ford, **Supp. XI:** 171, 172; **Supp. XII:** 75
Coprolites (Goldbarth), **Supp. XII:** **177–178,** 180, 183
"Coral Ring, The" (Stowe), **Supp. I Part 2:** 586
"Cora Unashamed" (Hughes), **Supp. I Part 1:** 329, 330
"Corazón del Corrido" (Mora), **Supp. XIII:** 225
Corbett, Gentlemen Jim, **II:** 416
Corbett, William, **Supp. XI:** 248
Corbière, Jean Antoine, **II:** 354–355, 528
Cording, Robert, **Supp. IX:** 328; **Supp. XII:** 184
Corelli, Marie, **III:** 579
Corey, Lewis, **Supp. I Part 2:** 645
"Coriolan" (Eliot), **I:** 580
"Coriolanus and His Mother" (Schwartz), **Supp. II Part 2:** 643, 644–645
"Corkscrew" (Hammett), **Supp. IV Part 1:** 345, 347
Corkum, Gerald, **I:** 37
Corliss, Richard, **Supp. VIII:** 73
Corman, Cid, **Supp. III Part 2:** 624, 625, 626, 627, 628; **Supp. IV Part 1:** 144; **Supp. VIII:** 292
"Corn" (Lanier), **Supp. I Part 1:** 352, 353, 354, 356–361, 364, 366
Corn, Alfred, **Supp. IX:** 156
Corneille, Pierre, **Supp. I Part 2:** 716; **Supp. IX:** 131
Cornell, Esther, **I:** 231
Cornell, Katherine, **IV:** 356
"Corners" (Dunn), **Supp. XI:** 148
Cornhuskers (Sandburg), **III:** 583–585
"Corn-Planting, The" (Anderson), **I:** 114
"Corporal of Artillery" (Dubus), **Supp. VII:** 84, 85
"Corpse Plant, The" (Rich), **Supp. I Part 2:** 555
Corpus Christi (McNally), **Supp. XIII:** **205–206,** 209
Corradi, Juan, **Supp. IV Part 1:** 208
"Correspondences" (Baudelaire), **I:** 63
"Corrido de Gregorio Cortez" (Mora), **Supp. XIII:** 225
"Corrigenda" (Komunyakaa), **Supp. XIII:** 115, 116
Corruption City (McCoy), **Supp. XIII:** 175
Corso, Gregory, **Supp. II Part 1:** 30; **Supp. IV Part 1:** 90; **Supp. XII:** **117–138**
Corsons Inlet (Ammons), **Supp. VII:** 25–26, 28–29, 36
"Corsons Inlet" (Ammons), **Supp. VII:** 25–26
Cortázar, Julio, **Retro. Supp. I:** 278
"Cortège for Rosenbloom" (Stevens), **IV:** 81
Cortez, Hernando, **III:** 2
Coser, Lewis, **Supp. I Part 2:** 650
Cosgrave, Patrick, **Retro. Supp. II:** 185
Cosmic Optimism: A Study of the Interpretation of Evolution by American Poets from Emerson to Robinson (Conner), **Supp. I Part 1:** 73
Cosmological Eye, The (H. Miller), **III:** 174, 184
"Cosmological Eye, The" (H. Miller), **III:** 183
"Cosmos" (Beattie), **Supp. V:** 35
"Cost, The" (Hecht), **Supp. X:** 62–63
Costello, Bonnie, **Retro. Supp. II:** 40
Costner, Kevin, **Supp. VIII:** 45
"Cost of Living, The" (Malamud), **Supp. I Part 2:** 429, 437
"Cottage Street, 1953" (Wilbur), **Supp. III Part 2:** 543, 561
"Cottagette, The" (Gilman), **Supp. XI:** 207
Cotten, Joseph, **Supp. IV Part 2:** 524
Cotter, James Finn, **Supp. X:** 202
Cotton, John, **Supp. I Part 1:** 98, 101, 110, 111, 116
Cotton, Joseph, **Supp. XII:** 160
Cotton, Seaborn, **Supp. I Part 1:** 101
"Cotton Song" (Toomer), **Supp. IX:** 312
Couch, W. T., **Supp. X:** 46
Coughlin, Ruth Pollack, **Supp. VIII:** 45
Coulette, Henri, **Supp. V:** 180; **Supp. XIII:** 312
"Council of State, A" (Dunbar), **Supp. II Part 1:** 211, 213
"Countee Cullen at 'The Heights'" (Tuttleton), **Supp. IV Part 1:** 166
Counterfeiters, The (Gide), **Supp. IV Part 1:** 80; **Supp. IV Part 2:** 681
"Countering" (Ammons), **Supp. VII:** 28
Counterlife, The (Roth), **Retro. Supp. II:** 297, 298, 309; **Supp. III Part 2:** 424–426
Counter-Statement (Burke), **I:** 270–272; **IV:** 431
"Countess, The" (Whittier), **Supp. I Part 2:** 691, 694

Count Frontenac and New France Under Louis XIV (Parkman), **Supp. II Part 2:** 607, 609–610
"Counting Small-Boned Bodies" (Bly), **Supp. IV Part 1:** 62
"Counting the Mad" (Justice), **Supp. VII:** 117
Count of Monte Cristo, The (Dumas), **III:** 386, 396
"Country Boy in Boston, The" (Howells), **II:** 255
Country By-Ways (Jewett), **II:** 402
Country Doctor, A (Jewett), **II:** 391, 392, 396, 404–405; **Retro. Supp. II:** 131, 141, 146
"Country Full of Swedes" (Caldwell), **I:** 297, 309
Country Girl, The (Odets), **Supp. II Part 2:** 546, 547, 548–549
"Country House" (Kumin), **Supp. IV Part 2:** 446
"Country Husband, The" (Cheever), **Supp. I Part 1:** 184, 189
Countrymen of Bones (R. O. Butler), **Supp. XII:** 62, 65–66
"Country Mouse, The" (Bishop), **Retro. Supp. II:** 37, 38, 51
Country Music: Selected Early Poems (Wright), **Supp. V:** 332, 335, 338, 342
Country of a Thousand Years of Peace, The (Merrill), **Supp. III Part 1:** 321, 322, 331
"Country of Elusion, The" (O. Henry), **Supp. II Part 1:** 407
Country of Marriage, The (Berry), **Supp. X:** 33
Country of the Pointed Firs, The (Jewett), **II:** 392, 399, 405, 409–411; **Retro. Supp. I:** 6; **Retro. Supp. II:** 134, 136, 139, 140, 141, 145, 146, 147; **Supp. VIII:** 126; **Supp. XIII:** 152
"Country Printer, The" (Freneau), **Supp. II Part 1:** 269
Coup, The (Updike), **Retro. Supp. I:** 331, 334, 335
"Coup de Grâce, The" (Bierce), **I:** 202
Couperin, François, **III:** 464
"Couple, The" (Olds), **Supp. X:** 206
"Couple of Hamburgers, A" (Thurber), **Supp. I Part 2:** 616
"Couple of Nuts, A" (Z. Fitzgerald), **Supp. IX:** 58, 71, 72
Couples (Updike), **IV:** 214, 215, 216, 217, 227, 229–230; **Retro. Supp. I:** 320, 327, 330; **Supp. XII:** 296
Cournos, John, **III:** 465; **Supp. I Part 1:** 258
"Course in Creative Writing, A" (Stafford), **Supp. XI:** 327
"Course of a Particular, The" (Stevens), **Retro. Supp. I:** 312
Courtier, The (Castiglione), **III:** 282
"'Courtin,' The" (Lowell), **Supp. I Part 2:** 415
"Courting of Sister Wisby, The" (Jewett), **Retro. Supp. II:** 134, 135, 146
"Courtship" (Dove), **Supp. IV Part 1:** 248
"Courtship, Diligence" (Dove), **Supp. IV Part 1:** 248
Courtship of Miles Standish, The (Longfellow), **II:** 489, 502–503; **Retro. Supp. II:** 155, **161–162**, 163, 166, 168
"Cousin Aubrey" (Taylor), **Supp. V:** 328
Cousine Bette (Balzac), **Retro. Supp. II:** 98
Couturier, Maurice, **Supp. IV Part 1:** 44
"Covered Bridges" (Kingsolver), **Supp. VII:** 203
Cowan, Lester, **III:** 148
Cowan, Louise, **IV:** 120, 125
Coward, Noel, **Retro. Supp. I:** 65; **Supp. I Part 1:** 332; **Supp. V:** 101
"Cowardice" (Theroux), **Supp. VIII:** 313
Cowboy Mouth (Shepard), **Supp. III Part 2:** 441–442
"Cowboys" (Salter). *See* "Dirt" (Salter)
Cowboys (Shepard), **Supp. III Part 2:** 432
Cowboys #2 (Shepard), **Supp. III Part 2:** 437, 438
Cowell, Henry, **Supp. IV Part 1:** 80, 82
Cowen, Wilson Walker, **Supp. IV Part 2:** 435
Cowie, Alexander, **IV:** 70
"Cow in Apple Time, The" (Frost), **II:** 154; **Retro. Supp. I:** 131
Cowl, Jane, **IV:** 357
Cowley, Abraham, **III:** 508; **IV:** 158; **Supp. I Part 1:** 357
Cowley, Malcolm, **I:** 246, 253, 254, 255, 256, 257, 283, 385; **II:** 26, 57, 94, 456; **III:** 606; **IV:** 123; **Retro. Supp. I:** 73, 91, 97; **Retro. Supp. II:** 77, 83, 89, 221, 348; **Supp. I Part 1:** 174; **Supp. I Part 2:** 609, 610, 620, 647, 654, 678; **Supp. II Part 1:** 103, **135–156**; **Supp. VIII:** 96
Cowley, Marguerite Frances Baird (Mrs. Malcolm Cowley), **Supp. I Part 2:** 615; **Supp. II Part 1:** 138, 139
Cowley, Muriel Maurer (Mrs. Malcolm Cowley), **Supp. II Part 1:** 139
Cowley, Susan Cheever (Susan Cheever), **Supp. I Part 1:** 175; **Supp. IX:** 133
Cowper, William, **II:** 17, 304; **III:** 508, 511; **Supp. I Part 1:** 150, 151, 152; **Supp. I Part 2:** 539
"Cow Wandering in the Bare Field, The" (Jarrell), **II:** 371, 388
Cox, Martha Heasley, **Supp. IX:** 2, 4, 11–12
Cox, Sidney, **Retro. Supp. I:** 131
Cox, Stephen, **Supp. IV Part 2:** 523, 524
Coxey, Jacob, **II:** 464
"Coxon Fund, The" (James), **Retro. Supp. I:** 228
Coyne, Patricia, **Supp. V:** 123
"Coyote Ortiz: *Canis latrans latrans* in the Poetry of Simon Ortiz" (P. C. Smith), **Supp. IV Part 2:** 509
Coyote's Daylight Trip (Gunn Allen), **Supp. IV Part 1:** 320, 324
Coyote Was Here (Ortiz), **Supp. IV Part 2:** 499
Cozzens, James Gould, **I: 358–380; II:** 459
Crabbe, George, **II:** 304; **III:** 469, 508, 511, 521
"Crab-Boil" (Dove), **Supp. IV Part 1:** 249
"Cracked Looking-Glass, The" (Porter), **III:** 434, 435, 446
"Cracker Chidlings" (Rawlings), **Supp. X:** 224, 228
Cracks (Purdy), **Supp. VII:** 277–278
"Crack-Up, The" (Fitzgerald), **I:** 509; **Retro. Supp. I:** 113, 114
Crack-Up, The (Fitzgerald), **II:** 80; **III:** 35, 45; **Retro. Supp. I:** 113, 115; **Supp. V:** 276; **Supp. IX:** 61
"Crack-up of American Optimism, The: Vachel Lindsay, the Dante of the Fundamentalists" (Viereck), **Supp. I Part 2:** 403
Cradle Will Rock, The (Blitzstein), **Supp. I Part 1:** 277, 278
Craft of Fiction, The (Lubbock), **I:** 504; **Supp. VIII:** 165
Craft of Peter Taylor, The (McAlexander, ed.), **Supp. V:** 314
Craig, Gordon, **III:** 394
Crain, Jane Larkin, **Supp. V:** 123; **Supp. XII:** 167, 168
Cram, Ralph Adams, **I:** 19
Cramer, Stephen, **Supp. XI:** 139
Crandall, Reuben, **Supp. I Part 2:** 686

Crane, Agnes, **I:** 406
Crane, Edmund, **I:** 407
Crane, Hart, **I:** 61, 62, 97, 109, 116, 266, **381–404; II:** 133, 215, 306, 368, 371, 536, 542; **III:** 260, 276, 453, 485, 521; **IV:** 122, 123–124, 127, 128, 129, 135, 139, 140, 141, 341, 380, 418, 419; **Retro. Supp. I:** 427; **Retro. Supp. II: 75–91; Supp. I Part 1:** 86; **Supp. II Part 1:** 89, 152; **Supp. III Part 1:** 20, 63, 350; **Supp. V:** 342; **Supp. VIII:** 39; **Supp. IX:** 38, 229, 320; **Supp. X:** 115, 116, 120; **Supp. XI:** 123, 131; **Supp. XII:** 198
Crane, Jonathan, Jr., **I:** 407
Crane, Jonathan Townley, **I:** 406
Crane, Luther, **I:** 406
Crane, Mrs. Jonathan Townley, **I:** 406
Crane, Nellie, **I:** 407
Crane, R. S., **Supp. I Part 2:** 423
Crane, Stephen, **I:** 34, 169–170, 201, 207, 211, **405–427,** 477, 506, 519; **II:** 58, 144, 198, 262, 263, 264, 276, 289, 290, 291; **III:** 314, 317, 334, 335, 454, 505, 585; **IV:** 207, 208, 256, 350, 475; **Retro. Supp. I:** 231, 325; **Retro. Supp. II:** 97, 123; **Supp. I Part 1:** 314; **Supp. III Part 2:** 412; **Supp. IV Part 1:** 350, 380; **Supp. IV Part 2:** 680, 689, 692; **Supp. VIII:** 98, 105; **Supp. IX:** 1, 14; **Supp. X:** 223; **Supp. XI:** 95; **Supp. XII:** 50
Crane, William, **I:** 407
Cranford (Gaskell), **Supp. IX:** 79
Crashaw, William, **IV:** 145, 150, 151, 165
"Crash Report" (McGrath), **Supp. X:** 116
Crater, The (Cooper), **I:** 354, 355
Cratylus (Plato), **II:** 10
"Craven Street Gazette" (Franklin), **II:** 119
Crawford, Brad, **Supp. XI:** 133
Crawford, Eva, **I:** 199
Crawford, F. Marion, **III:** 320
Crawford, Joan, **Supp. I Part 1:** 67
Crawford, Kathleen, **I:** 289
"Crayon House" (Rukeyser), **Supp. VI:** 273
Crayon Miscellany, The (Irving), **II:** 312–313
"Crazy about her Shrimp" (Simic), **Supp. VIII:** 282
"Crazy Cock" (H. Miller), **III:** 177
Crazy Gypsy (Salinas), **Supp. XIII:** 311, **313–315,** 316
"Crazy Gypsy" (Salinas), **Supp. XIII:** 313–314

Crazy Horse, **Supp. IV Part 2:** 488, 489
Crazy Horse (McMurtry), **Supp. V:** 233
Crazy Horse in Stillness (Heyen), **Supp. XIII:** 344
"Creation, According to Coyote, The" (Ortiz), **Supp. IV Part 2:** 505
Creation: A Novel (Vidal), **Supp. IV Part 2:** 677, 685, 688
"Creation of Anguish" (Nemerov), **III:** 269
"Creation Story" (Gunn Allen), **Supp. IV Part 1:** 325
"Creative and Cultural Lag" (Ellison), **Retro. Supp. II:** 116; **Supp. II Part 1:** 229
Creative Criticism (Spingarn), **I:** 266
Creative Present, The (Balkian and Simmons, eds.), **Supp. XI:** 230
Creatures in an Alphabet (illus. Barnes), **Supp. III Part 1:** 43
"Credences of Summer" (Stevens), **IV:** 93–94
"Credo" (Du Bois), **Supp. II Part 1:** 169
"Credo" (Jeffers), **Supp. II Part 2:** 424
"Credos and Curios" (Thurber), **Supp. I Part 2:** 606, 613
Creech, James, **Retro. Supp. I:** 254
"Creed for Americans, A" (Benét), **Supp. XI:** 52
"Creed of a Beggar, The" (Lindsay), **Supp. I Part 2:** 379
Creekmore, Hubert, **II:** 586
Creeley, Robert, **Retro. Supp. I:** 411; **Supp. II Part 1:** 30; **Supp. III Part 1:** 2; **Supp. III Part 2:** 622, 626, 629; **Supp. IV Part 1: 139–161,** 322, 325; **Supp. XI:** 317; **Supp. XIII:** 104, 112
"Cremona Violin, The" (Lowell), **II:** 523
"Crêpe de Chine" (Doty), **Supp. XI:** 128
"Cressy" (Harte), **Supp. II Part 1:** 354, 356
"Cretan Woman, The" (Jeffers), **Supp. II Part 2:** 435
Crèvecoeur, Michel-Guillaume Jean de, **I:** 229; **Supp. I Part 1: 227–252**
Crèvecoeur's Eighteenth-Century Travels in Pennsylvania and New York (Adams), **Supp. I Part 1:** 251
Crewe Train (Macaulay), **Supp. XII:** 88
Crews, Harry, **Supp. X:** 11, 12; **Supp. XI: 99–117,** 245
"Crickets" (R. O. Butler), **Supp. XII:** 71

Criers and Kibitzers, Kibitzers and Criers (Elkin), **Supp. VI: 45–46,** 57
Crime and Punishment (Dostoyevsky), **II:** 60, 130; **IV:** 484; **Supp. IV Part 2:** 525; **Supp. VIII:** 282; **Supp. XII:** 281
Crisis papers (Paine), **Supp. I Part 2:** 508–509, 510
"Criteria of Negro Arts" (Du Bois), **Supp. II Part 1:** 181
"Critiad, The" (Winters), **Supp. II Part 2:** 794, 799
Critical Essays on Charlotte Perkins Gilman (Karpinski, ed.), **Supp. XI:** 201
Critical Essays on Peter Taylor (McAlexander), **Supp. V:** 319, 320, 323–324
Critical Essays on Robert Bly (Davis), **Supp. IV Part 1:** 64, 69
Critical Essays on Wallace Stegner (Arthur), **Supp. IV Part 2:** 606
Critical Fable, A (Lowell), **II:** 511–512, 527, 529–530
Critical Guide to Leaves of Grass, A (J. Miller), **IV:** 352
Critical Response to Joan Didion, The (Felton), **Supp. IV Part 1:** 210
"Critic as Artist, The" (Wilde), **Supp. X:** 189
Criticism and Fiction (Howells), **II:** 288
Criticism and Ideology (Eagleton), **Retro. Supp. I:** 67
Criticism in the Borderlands (Calderón and Saldívar, eds.), **Supp. IV Part 2:** 544
"Critics, The" (Jong), **Supp. V:** 119
"Critics and Connoisseurs" (Moore), **III:** 209
Critic's Notebook, A (Howe), **Supp. VI: 126–128**
"Critic's Task, The" (Kazin), **Supp. VIII:** 103
"Critic Who Does Not Exist, The" (Wilson), **IV:** 431
"Critique de la Vie Quotidienne" (Barthelme), **Supp. IV Part 1:** 50
Croce, Benedetto, **I:** 58, 255, 265, 273, 281; **III:** 610
Crockett, Davy, **II:** 307; **III:** 227; **IV:** 266; **Supp. I Part 2:** 411
Crofter and the Laird, The (McPhee), **Supp. III Part 1:** 301–302, 307
Croly, Herbert, **I:** 229, 231, 235; **IV:** 436
Cromwell, Oliver, **IV:** 145, 146, 156; **Supp. I Part 1:** 111
Cronin, Dr. Archibald, **III:** 578
Cronin, Justin, **Supp. X:** 10

Crooke, Dr. Helkiah, **Supp. I Part 1:** 98, 104
Crooks, Alan, **Supp. V:** 226
Crooks, Robert, **Supp. XIII:** 237
"Crop, The" (O'Connor), **Retro. Supp. II:** 223–225
Crosby, Caresse, **I:** 385; **III:** 473; **Retro. Supp. II:** 85; **Supp. XII:** 198
Crosby, Harry, **I:** 385; **Retro. Supp. II:** 85
"Cross" (Hughes), **Supp. I Part 1:** 325
Crossan, John Dominic, **Supp. V:** 251
"Cross Country Snow" (Hemingway), **II:** 249
Cross Creek (Rawlings), **Supp. X:** 223, 226, 228, **231–232**, 233, 234, 235
Cross Creek Cookery (Rawlings), **Supp. X:** 233
Crossing, The (McCarthy), **Supp. VIII:** 175, **184–186**
"Crossing, The" (Swenson), **Supp. IV Part 2:** 644
"Crossing Brooklyn Ferry" (Whitman), **IV:** 333, 340, 341; **Retro. Supp. I:** 389, 396, 397, 400–401
Crossings (Chuang), **Supp. X:** 291
"Crossings" (Hogan), **Supp. IV Part 1:** 412
Crossing the Water (Plath), **Retro. Supp. II:** 248; **Supp. I Part 2:** 526, 538
Crossing to Safety (Stegner), **Supp. IV Part 2:** 599, 606, 612, 613–614
"Cross of Snow, The" (Longfellow), **II:** 490; **Retro. Supp. II:** 169–170
"Crossover" (O. Butler), **Supp. XIII:** 61
"Cross-Roads, The" (Lowell), **II:** 523
"Crossroads of the World Etc." (Merwin), **Supp. III Part 1:** 347, 348
Cross-Section (Seaver), **IV:** 485
Cross the Border, Close the Gap (Fiedler), **Supp. XIII:** 104
"Croup" (Karr), **Supp. XI:** 243
Crouse, Russel, **III:** 284
"Crow" (Hogan), **Supp. IV Part 1:** 405
"Crow, The" (Creeley), **Supp. IV Part 1:** 148–149
"Crowded Street, The" (Bryant), **Supp. I Part 1:** 168
Crowder, A. B., **Supp. XI:** 107
"Crow Jane" (Baraka), **Supp. II Part 1:** 38
Crowninshield, Frank, **III:** 123; **Supp. IX:** 201
Crown of Columbus (Erdrich and Dorris), **Supp. IV Part 1:** 260

"Crows, The" (Bogan), **Supp. III Part 1:** 50, 51
Crucial Instances (Wharton), **Retro. Supp. I:** 365, 367
Crucible, The (A. Miller), **III:** 147, 148, 155, 156–158, 159, 166; **Supp. XIII:** 206
"Crucifix in the Filing Cabinet" (Shapiro), **Supp. II Part 2:** 712
"Crude Foyer" (Stevens), **Retro. Supp. I:** 310
"Cruel and Barbarous Treatment" (McCarthy), **II:** 562, 563
Cruise of the Dazzler, The (London), **II:** 465
Cruise of the Snark, The (London), **II:** 476–477
"'Crumbling Idols' by Hamlin Garland" (Chopin), **Supp. I Part 1:** 217
"Crusade of the Excelsior, The" (Harte), **Supp. II Part 1:** 336, 354
"Crusoe in England" (Bishop), **Retro. Supp. II:** 50; **Supp. I Part 1:** 93, 95, 96; **Supp. III Part 1:** 10, 18
Cry, the Beloved Country (Paton), **Supp. VIII:** 126
Cryer, Dan, **Supp. VIII:** 86, 88; **Supp. XII:** 164
Crying of Lot 49, The (Pynchon), **Supp. II Part 2:** 618, 619, 621, 630–633
"Crying Sisters, The" (Rand), **Supp. IV Part 2:** 524
"Crystal, The" (Aiken), **I:** 60
"Crystal, The" (Lanier), **Supp. I Part 1:** 364, 370
"Crystal Cage, The" (Kunitz), **Supp. III Part 1:** 258
Cry to Heaven (Rice), **Supp. VII:** 300–301
"Cuba" (Hemingway), **II:** 258
"Cuba Libre" (Baraka), **Supp. II Part 1:** 33
Cudjoe, Selwyn, **Supp. IV Part 1:** 6
"Cudjo's Own Story of the Last American Slaver" (Hurston), **Supp. VI:** 153
Cudlipp, Thelma, **I:** 501
Cudworth, Ralph, **II:** 9, 10
"Cuentista" (Mora), **Supp. XIII:** 224
"Cuento de agua santa, Un" (Mora), **Supp. XIII:** 224
Cujo (King), **Supp. V:** 138–139, 143, 149, 152
Cullen, Countee, **Retro. Supp. I:** 207; **Retro. Supp. II:** 114; **Supp. I Part 1:** 49, 325; **Supp. III Part 1:** 73, 75, 76; **Supp. IV Part 1: 163–174;** **Supp. IX:** 306, 309; **Supp. X:** 136, 140; **Supp. XIII:** 186

"Cultivation of Christmas Trees, The" (Eliot), **I:** 579
"Cult of the Best, The" (Arnold), **I:** 223
"Cultural Exchange" (Hughes), **Supp. I Part 1:** 341
"Culture" (Emerson), **III:** 2, 4
"Culture, Self, and Style" (Gass), **Supp. VI:** 88
"Culture and Anarchy" (Rich), **Retro. Supp. II:** 291
"Culture and Religion" (Olds), **Supp. X:** 214
Culture of Cities, The (Mumford), **Supp. II Part 2:** 492, 494–495
Cummings, E. E., **I:** 44, 48, 64, 105, 176, **428–450,** 475, 477, 482, 526; **III:** 20, 196, 476; **IV:** 384, 402, 415, 427, 433; **Retro. Supp. II:** 178, 346; **Supp. I Part 2:** 622, 678; **Supp. III Part 1:** 73; **Supp. IV Part 2:** 637, 641; **Supp. IX:** 20
Cummings, Robert, **Supp. IV Part 2:** 524
Cunard, Lady, **III:** 459
Cunningham, Merce, **Supp. IV Part 1:** 83
Cunningham, Michael, **Supp. XII:** 80
Cup of Gold (Steinbeck), **IV:** 51, 53, 61–64, 67
"Cupola, The" (Bogan), **Supp. III Part 1:** 53
"Curandera" (Mora), **Supp. XIII:** 214, 222
Curé de Tours, Le (Balzac), **I:** 509
Cure for Dreams, A: A Novel (Gibbons), **Supp. X: 45–47,** 48, 50
Curie, Marie, **IV:** 420, 421; **Supp. I Part 2:** 569
Curie, Pierre, **IV:** 420
Curiosa Americana (Mather), **Supp. II Part 2:** 463
Curiosities (Matthews), **Supp. IX:** 151, 152
"Curious Shifts of the Poor" (Dreiser), **Retro. Supp. II:** 97
"Currents and Counter-Currents in Medical Science" (Holmes), **Supp. I Part 1:** 305
"Curried Cow" (Bierce), **I:** 200
Curry, Professor W. C., **IV:** 122
Curse of the Starving Class (Shepard), **Supp. III Part 2:** 433, 447–448
"Curtain, The" (Chandler), **Supp. IV Part 1:** 122
Curtain of Green, A (Welty), **IV:** 261–264, 268, 283
"Curtain of Green, A" (Welty), **IV:** 263–264
Curtain of Green and Other Stories, A

(Welty), **Retro. Supp. I**: 343, 344, 345, 346, 347, 355
Curtain of Trees (opera), **Supp. IV Part 2**: 552
"Curtain Raiser, A" (Stein), **IV**: 43, 44
"Curtains" (Cisneros), **Supp. VII**: 66
Curtin, John, **Supp. IX**: 184
Curtis, George William, **Supp. I Part 1**: 307
Curve (Goldbarth), **Supp. XII**: 181
Curve of Binding Energy, The (McPhee), **Supp. III Part 1**: 301
Curzon, Mary, **III**: 52
Cushing, Caleb, **Supp. I Part 2**: 684, 686
Cushman, Howard, **Supp. I Part 2**: 652
Cushman, Stephen, **Retro. Supp. I**: 430
"Custard Heart, The" (Parker), **Supp. IX**: 201
Custer, General George, **I**: 489, 491
Custer Died for Your Sins (Deloria), **Supp. IV Part 1**: 323; **Supp. IV Part 2**: 504
"Custom House, The" (Hawthorne), **II**: 223; **Retro. Supp. I**: 147–148, 157
Custom of the Country, The (Wharton), **IV**: 318; **Retro. Supp. I**: 374, 375–376
"Cut" (Plath), **Retro. Supp. II**: 253
"Cut-Glass Bowl, The" (Fitzgerald), **II**: 88
Cutting, Bronson, **III**: 600
"Cuttings, *later*" (Roethke), **III**: 532
"Cycles, The" (Pinsky), **Supp. VI**: 250–252
Cynic's Word Book, The (Bierce), **I**: 197, 205, 208, 209, 210
Cynthia Ozick (Lowin), **Supp. V**: 273
Cynthia Ozick's Comic Art (Cohen), **Supp. V**: 273
Cynthia Ozick's Fiction (Kauvar), **Supp. V**: 273
D. H. Lawrence: An Unprofessional Study (Nin), **Supp. X**: 182–183
Dacey, Philip, **Supp. IV Part 1**: 70
Dacier, André, **II**: 10
"Dad" (Cullen), **Supp. IV Part 1**: 167
"Daddy" (Plath), **Retro. Supp. II**: 250–251; **Supp. I Part 2**: 529, 542, 545, 546; **Supp. II Part 2**: 688
"Daemon, The" (Bogan), **Supp. III Part 1**: 58, 61
"Daemon Lover, The" (Jackson), **Supp. IX**: 116–117
"Daffodils" (Wordsworth), **Supp. XIII**: 284
"Daffy Duck in Hollywood" (Ashbery), **Supp. III Part 1**: 18

D'Agata, John, **Supp. XII**: 97, 98
Dago Red (Fante), **Supp. XI**: 160, 169
Dahl, Roald, **Supp. IX**: 114
Dahlberg, Edward, **I**: 231; **Retro. Supp. I**: 426; **Supp. III Part 2**: 624
Daiches, David, **Retro. Supp. II**: 243; **Supp. I Part 2**: 536
Daily Modernism (Podnieks), **Supp. X**: 189
Dain Curse, The (Hammett), **Supp. IV Part 1**: 348
"Daisies" (Glück), **Supp. V**: 88
"Daisy" (Oates), **Supp. II Part 2**: 523
Daisy Miller (James), **Retro. Supp. I**: 216, 220, 222, 223, 228, 231
"Daisy Miller" (James), **II**: 325, 326, 327, 329; **IV**: 316
Dale, Charlie, **Supp. IV Part 2**: 584
Dali, Salvador, **II**: 586; **Supp. IV Part 1**: 83; **Supp. XIII**: 317
Dalibard, Thomas-François, **II**: 117
"Dallas-Fort Worth: Redband and Mistletoe" (Clampitt), **Supp. IX**: 45
"Dalliance of Eagles, The" (Whitman), **IV**: 348
Dalva (Harrison), **Supp. VIII**: 37, 45, 46, **48–49**
Daly, Carroll John, **Supp. IV Part 1**: 343, 345
Daly, John, **II**: 25, 26
Daly, Julia Brown, **II**: 25, 26
"Dalyrimple Goes Wrong" (Fitzgerald), **II**: 88
"Dam, The" (Rukeyser), **Supp. VI**: 283
Damas, Leon, **Supp. X**: 139
Damascus Gate (Stone), **Supp. V**: 308–311
Damballah (Wideman), **Supp. X**: 319, 320, 321, 322, 323, 326, 327, 331, 333–334
Damnation of Theron Ware, The (Frederic), **II**: 140–143, 144, 146, 147; **Retro. Supp. I**: 325
"Damned Thing, The" (Bierce), **I**: 206
Damon, Matt, **Supp. VIII**: 175
Damon, S. Foster, **I**: 26; **II**: 512, 514, 515
"Damon and Vandalia" (Dove), **Supp. IV Part 1**: 252
Dana, H. W. L., **I**: 225
Dana, Richard Henry, **I**: 339, 351; **Supp. I Part 1**: 103, 154, 155; **Supp. I Part 2**: 414, 420
Dana, Richard Henry, Jr., **III**: 81
Dana, Robert, **Supp. V**: 178, 180
"Dance, The" (Crane), **I**: 109
"Dance, The" (Roethke), **III**: 541
Dance of Death, The (Auden), **Supp. II Part 1**: 10

Dance of Death, The (Bierce and Harcourt), **I**: 196
Dance of the Sleepwalkers (Calabria), **Supp. XIII**: 164
"Dance of the Solids, The" (Updike), **Retro. Supp. I**: 323
Dances with Wolves (film), **Supp. X**: 124
Dancing After Hours (Dubus), **Supp. VII**: 91
Dancing Bears, The (Merwin), **Supp. III Part 1**: 343–344
Dancing on the Stones (Nichols), **Supp. XIII**: 256, 257, 259, 267, 269
"Dancing the Jig" (Sexton), **Supp. II Part 2**: 692
Dandelion Wine (Bradbury), **Supp. IV Part 1**: 101, 109–110
Dandurand, Karen, **Retro. Supp. I**: 30
"Dandy Frightening the Squatters, The" (Twain), **IV**: 193–194
Dangerous Crossroads (film), **Supp. XIII**: 163
Dangerous Moonlight (Purdy), **Supp. VII**: 278
"Dangerous Road Before Martin Luther King" (Baldwin), **Supp. I Part 1**: 52
"Dangerous Summer, The" (Hemingway), **II**: 261
"Dangers of Authorship, The" (Blackmur), **Supp. II Part 1**: 147
Dangling Man (Bellow), **I**: 144, 145, 147, 148, 150–151, 153–154, 158, 160, 161, 162, 163; **Retro. Supp. II**: 19, 20–21, 22, 23; **Supp. VIII**: 234
Daniel (biblical book), **Supp. I Part 1**: 105
Daniel (film), **Supp. IV Part 1**: 236
Daniel, Arnaut, **III**: 467
Daniel, Robert W., **III**: 76
Daniel, Samuel, **Supp. I Part 1**: 369
Daniel Deronda (Eliot), **I**: 458
Danielson, Linda, **Supp. IV Part 2**: 569
D'Annunzio, Gabriele, **II**: 515
Danny O'Neill pentalogy (Farrell), **II**: 35–41
Danse Macabre (King), **Supp. IV Part 1**: 102; **Supp. V**: 144
"Danse Russe" (W. C. Williams), **IV**: 412–413
"Dans le Restaurant" (Eliot), **I**: 554, 578
Dans l'ombre des cathédrales (Ambelain), **Supp. I Part 1**: 273
Dante Alighieri, **I**: 103, 136, 138, 250, 384, 433, 445; **II**: 8, 274, 278, 289, 490, 492, 493, 494, 495, 504, 508,

524, 552; **III:** 13, 77, 124, 182, 259, 278, 448, 453, 467, 533, 607, 609, 610–612, 613; **IV:** 50, 134, 137, 138, 139, 247, 437, 438; **Retro. Supp. I:** 62, 63, 64, 66, 360; **Retro. Supp. II:** 348; **Supp. I Part 1:** 256, 363; **Supp. I Part 2:** 422, 454; **Supp. III Part 2:** 611, 618, 621; **Supp. IV Part 2:** 634; **Supp. V:** 277, 283, 331, 338, 345; **Supp. VIII:** 27, 219–221; **Supp. X:** 120, 121, 125; **Supp. XII:** 98
Danziger, Adolphe, **I:** 199–200
Dar (Nabokov), **III:** 246, 255
"Dare's Gift" (Glasgow), **II:** 190
Dark Angel, The (Bolton), **Supp. I Part 1:** 281
"Dark Angel Travels With Us to Canada and Blesses Our Vacation, The" (Dunn), **Supp. XI:** 146
Dark Carnival (Bradbury), **Supp. IV Part 1:** 102
Darker (Strand), **Supp. IV Part 2:** 619, 626–628
Darker Face of the Earth, The (Dove), **Supp. IV Part 1:** 255–257
Dark Fields of the Republic: Poems, 1991–1995 (Rich), **Retro. Supp. II:** 293
Dark Green, Bright Red (Vidal), **Supp. IV Part 2:** 677
Dark Half, The (King), **Supp. V:** 141
Dark Harbor: A Poem (Strand), **Supp. IV Part 2:** 633–634
"Dark Hills, The" (Robinson), **III:** 523
Dark Laughter (Anderson), **I:** 111, 116; **II:** 250–251
"Darkling Alphabet, A" (Snodgrass), **Supp. VI:** 323
Darkling Child (Merwin and Milroy), **Supp. III Part 1:** 346
"Darkling Summer, Ominous Dusk, Rumorous Rain" (Schwartz), **Supp. II Part 2:** 661
"Darkling Thrush" (Hardy), **Supp. IX:** 40
"Dark Men, The" (Dubus), **Supp. VII:** 86
Darkness and the Light, The (Hecht), **Supp. X:** 58
"Darkness on the Edge of Town" (O'Brien), **Supp. V:** 246
Darkness under the Trees/Walking behind the Spanish (Salinas), **Supp. XIII:** 311, **319–324**
Dark Night of the Soul, The (St. John of the Cross), **I:** 1, 585
"Dark Ones" (Dickey), **Supp. IV Part 1:** 182
Dark Princess: A Romance (Du Bois),
Supp. II Part 1: 179, 181–182
Dark Room, The (T. Williams), **IV:** 381
"Dark Summer" (Bogan), **Supp. III Part 1:** 51, 53
Dark Summer: Poems (Bogan), **Supp. III Part 1:** 52–53, 57
"Dark Tower, The" (column), **Supp. IV Part 1:** 168, 170
Dark Tower, The: The Gunslinger (King), **Supp. V:** 152
Dark Tower IV, The: Wizard and Glass (King), **Supp. V:** 139
Dark Tunnel, The (Macdonald, under Millar), **Supp. IV Part 2:** 465, 466
"Dark TV Screen" (Simic), **Supp. VIII:** 282
"Dark Voyage, The" (McLay), **Supp. XIII:** 21
"Dark Walk, The" (Taylor), **Supp. V:** 320–321, 322, 326
Darkwater: Voices from Within the Veil (Du Bois), **Supp. II Part 1:** 178, 180, 183
Dark Waves and Light Matter (Goldbarth), **Supp. XII:** 176, 193
"Darling" (Nye), **Supp. XIII:** 283–284
"Darling, The" (Chekhov), **Supp. IX:** 202
Darnell, Linda, **Supp. XII:** 173
Darragh, Tina, **Supp. IV Part 2:** 427
Darreu, Robert Donaldson, **Supp. II Part 1:** 89, 98, 102
Darrow, Clarence, **Supp. I Part 1:** 5; **Supp. I Part 2:** 455
Darwin, Charles, **I:** 457; **II:** 323, 462, 481; **III:** 226, 231; **IV:** 69, 304; **Retro. Supp. I:** 254; **Retro. Supp. II:** 60, 65; **Supp. I Part 1:** 368; **Supp. IX:** 180; **Supp. XI:** 203
Daryush, Elizabeth, **Supp. V:** 180
Dash, Julie, **Supp. XI:** 17, 18, 20
Dashell, Alfred, **Supp. X:** 224
"DAS KAPITAL" (Baraka), **Supp. II Part 1:** 55
"Datum Centurio" (Wallace), **Supp. X:** 309
Daudet, Alphonse, **II:** 325, 338
"Daughter" (Caldwell), **I:** 309
Daughter of Earth (Smedly), **Supp. XIII:** 295
Daughter of the Snows, A (London), **II:** 465, 469–470
"Daughters" (Anderson), **I:** 114
Daughters (Marshall), **Supp. XI:** 275, 276, 277, **286–288,** 289, 290
Daughters, I Love You (Hogan), **Supp. IV Part 1:** 397, 399, 401
"Daughters of Invention" (Alvarez), **Supp. VII:** 9
Daughters of the Dust (Dash; film),
Supp. XI: 17, 18
Daumier, Honoré, **IV:** 412
Dave, R. A., **Supp. VIII:** 126
Davenport, Abraham, **Supp. I Part 2:** 699
Davenport, Gary, **Supp. IX:** 98
Davenport, Herbert J., **Supp. I Part 2:** 642
Davenport, James, **I:** 546
Daves, E. G., **Supp. I Part 1:** 369
Davey, Frank, **Supp. XIII:** 33
"David" (Garrett), **Supp. VII:** 109–110
"David" (Gordon), **Supp. IV Part 1:** 298–299
David Copperfield (Dickens), **I:** 458; **II:** 290; **Retro. Supp. I:** 33
"David Crockett's Other Life" (Nye), **Supp. XIII:** 282
Davideis (Cowley), **IV:** 158
David Harum (Westcott), **I:** 216
"David Lynch Keeps His Head" (Wallace), **Supp. X:** 314
David Show, The (Gurney), **Supp. V:** 97
Davidson, Donald, **I:** 294; **III:** 495, 496; **IV:** 121, 122, 124, 125, 236; **Supp. II Part 1:** 139
Davidson, John, **Retro. Supp. I:** 55
Davidson, Michael, **Supp. VIII:** 290, 293, 294, 302–303
Davidson, Sara, **Supp. IV Part 1:** 196, 198, 203
Davidsz de Heem, Jan, **Supp. XI:** 133
Davie, Donald, **III:** 478; **Supp. IV Part 2:** 474; **Supp. V:** 331; **Supp. X:** 55, 59
Davies, Arthur, **III:** 273
Davies, Sir John, **III:** 541
Da Vinci, Leonardo, **I:** 274; **II:** 536; **III:** 210
Davis, Allen F., **Supp. I Part 1:** 1, 7
Davis, Allison, **Supp. I Part 1:** 327
Davis, Angela, **Supp. I Part 1:** 66; **Supp. X:** 249
Davis, Bette, **I:** 78; **Supp. I Part 1:** 67
Davis, Bill, **Supp. XIII:** 267
Davis, Donald, **Supp. XIII:** 93
Davis, Elizabeth Gould, **Supp. I Part 2:** 567
Davis, George, **II:** 586
Davis, Glover, **Supp. V:** 180, 182, 186
Davis, Jefferson, **II:** 206; **IV:** 122, 125, 126
Davis, Katie, **Supp. VIII:** 83
Davis, L. J., **Supp. XI:** 234
Davis, Lydia, **Supp. XII:** 24
Davis, Ossie, Jr., **Supp. IV Part 1:** 362
Davis, Rebecca Harding, **Supp. I Part 1:** 45; **Supp. XIII:** 292, 295, 305
Davis, Richard Harding, **III:** 328;

Supp. II Part 1: 393
Davis, Robert Gorham, **II:** 51; **IV:** 108
Davis, Stuart, **IV:** 409
Davis, Thulani, **Supp. XI:** 179; **Supp. XIII:** 233, 234, 239
Davis, William V., **Supp. IV Part 1:** 63, 64, 68, 69, 70
Dawn (Dreiser), **I:** 498, 499, 503, 509, 515, 519
Dawn (O. Butler), **Supp. XIII:** 63, **64**
"Dawnbreaker" (Hayden), **Supp. II Part 1:** 370
Dawson, Edward, **IV:** 151
Dawson, Emma, **I:** 199
Dawson, Ruth, **Supp. XI:** 120
Day, Dorothy, **II:** 215; **Supp. I Part 2:** 524; **Supp. X:** 142
Day, Georgiana, **Supp. I Part 2:** 585
Dayan, Joan, **Retro. Supp. II:** 270
Day Book, A (Creeley), **Supp. IV Part 1:** 155
"Daybreak" (Kinnell), **Supp. III Part 1:** 250
"Daybreak in Alabama" (Hughes), **Retro. Supp. I:** 211; **Supp. I Part 1:** 344
Day by Day (Lowell), **Retro. Supp. II:** 184, 186, 191
"Day-Care Field Trip: Aquarium" (Karr), **Supp. XI:** 243
"Day-Dream, A" (Bryant), **Supp. I Part 1:** 160
"Day for Poetry and Song, A" (Douglass), **Supp. III Part 1:** 172
Day Late and a Dollar Short, A (McMillan), **Supp. XIII:** 184, **Supp. XIII:** 185, **191–192**
"Day longs for the evening, The" (Levertov), **Supp. III Part 1:** 274
Day of a Stranger (Merton), **Supp. VIII:** 203
"Day of Days, A" (James), **II:** 322
Day of Doom (Wigglesworth), **IV:** 147, 155, 156
Day of the Locust, The (West), **I:** 298; **IV:** 288, 299–306; **Retro. Supp. II:** 339, 341, 342, 347, **355–356**; **Supp. II Part 2:** 626; **Supp. XI:** 296; **Supp. XII:** 173; **Supp. XIII:** 170
"Day on the Big Branch, A" (Nemerov), **III:** 275–276
"Day on the Connecticut River, A" (Merrill), **Supp. III Part 1:** 336
Day Room, The (DeLillo), **Supp. VI:** 4
"Days" (Emerson), **II:** 19, 20
Days: Tangier Journal, 1987–1989 (Bowles), **Supp. IV Part 1:** 94
"Days and Nights: A Journal" (Price), **Supp. VI:** 265

Days Before, The (Porter), **III:** 433, 453
"Days of 1935" (Merrill), **Supp. III Part 1:** 325, 328
"Days of 1964" (Merrill), **Supp. III Part 1:** 328, 352
"Days of 1971" (Merrill), **Supp. III Part 1:** 328
"Days of 1981" (Doty), **Supp. XI:** 123
"Days of 1941 and '44" (Merrill), **Supp. III Part 1:** 336
"Days of Edward Hopper" (Haines), **Supp. XII:** 210
Days of Our Lives (soap opera), **Supp. XI:** 83
Days of Our Lives Lie in Fragments: New and Old Poems (Garrett), **Supp. VII:** 109–110, 111
Days of the Phoenix (Brooks), **I:** 266
Days of Wine and Roses (J. P. Miller), **Supp. XIII:** 262
Days to Come (Hellman), **Supp. I Part 1:** 276, 277–278
Days without End (O'Neill), **III:** 385, 391, 397
"Day's Work, A" (Capote), **Supp. III Part 1:** 120
"Day's Work, A" (Porter), **III:** 443, 446
"Day the Presidential Candidate Came to Ciudad Tamaulipas, The" (Caldwell), **I:** 309
Day the World ended, The (Coover), **Supp. V:** 1
"Day with Conrad Green, A" (Lardner), **II:** 428–429, 430
"Deacon's Masterpiece, The" (Holmes), **Supp. I Part 1:** 302, 307
"Dead, The" (Joyce), **I:** 285; **III:** 343
Dead and the Living, The (Olds), **Supp. X:** 201, **204–206**, 207
"Dead Body, The" (Olds), **Supp. X:** 210
"Dead by the Side of the Road, The" (Snyder), **Supp. VIII:** 301
Dead End (Kingsley), **Supp. I Part 1:** 277, 281
Dead Father, The (Barthelme), **Supp. IV Part 1:** 43, 47, 50–51
"Dead Fiddler, The" (Singer), **IV:** 20
Dead Fingers Talk (Burroughs), **Supp. III Part 1:** 103
"Dead Hand" series (Sinclair), **Supp. V:** 276, 277, 281
"Dead Languages, The" (Humphrey), **Supp. IX:** 109
Dead Lecturer, The (Baraka), **Supp. II Part 1:** 31, 33, 35–37, 49
Deadline at Dawn (Odets), **Supp. II Part 2:** 546

Dead Man's Walk (McMurtry), **Supp. V:** 231, 232
Dead Man's Walk (screenplay) (McMurtry and Ossana), **Supp. V:** 231
Dead Man Walking (opera libretto, McNally), **Supp. XIII:** 207
Dead Souls (Gogol), **I:** 296
"Dead Souls on Campus" (Kosinski), **Supp. VII:** 222
"Dead Wingman, The" (Jarrell), **II:** 374
"Dead Yellow Women" (Hammett), **Supp. IV Part 1:** 345
Dead Zone, The (King), **Supp. V:** 139, 143, 144, 148, 152
Dean, James, **I:** 493
Dean, Man Mountain, **II:** 589
Deane, Silas, **Supp. I Part 2:** 509, 524
"Dean of Men" (Taylor), **Supp. V:** 314, 323
Dean's December, The (Bellow), **Retro. Supp. II:** 30–31
"Dear Adolph" (Benét), **Supp. XI:** 46
"Dear America" (Ortiz), **Supp. IV Part 2:** 503
"Dear Judas" (Jeffers), **Supp. II Part 2:** 431–432, 433
Dear Juliette (Sarton), **Supp. VIII:** 265
Dear Lovely Death (Hughes), **Retro. Supp. I:** 203; **Supp. I Part 1:** 328
"Dear Villon" (Corso), **Supp. XII:** 135
"Dear World" (Gunn Allen), **Supp. IV Part 1:** 321
"Death" (Corso), **Supp. XII:** 127
"Death" (Lowell), **II:** 536
"Death" (Mailer), **III:** 38
"Death" (West), **IV:** 286
"Death" (W. C. Williams), **Retro. Supp. I:** 422
"Death and Absence" (Glück), **Supp. V:** 82
Death and Taxes (Parker), **Supp. IX:** 192
"Death and the Child" (Crane), **I:** 414
"Death as a Society Lady" (Hecht), **Supp. X:** 71–72
Death before Bedtime (Vidal, under pseudonym Box), **Supp. IV Part 2:** 682
"Death by Water" (Eliot), **I:** 395, 578
Death Comes for the Archbishop (Cather), **I:** 314, 327, 328–330; **Retro. Supp. I:** 16–18, 21; **Supp. XIII:** 253
Death in the Afternoon (Hemingway), **II:** 253; **IV:** 35; **Retro. Supp. I:** 182; **Supp. VIII:** 182
"Death in the Country, A" (Benét),

Supp. XI: 53–54
Death in the Family, A (Agee), **I:** 25, 29, 42, 45
Death in the Fifth Position (Vidal, under pseudonym Box), **Supp. IV Part 2:** 682
"Death in the Woods" (Anderson), **I:** 114, 115
Death in the Woods and Other Stories (Anderson), **I:** 112, 114, 115
Death in Venice (Mann), **III:** 231; **Supp. IV Part 1:** 392; **Supp. V:** 51
"Death in Viet Nam" (Salinas), **Supp. XIII:** 315
Death Is a Lonely Business (Bradbury), **Supp. IV Part 1:** 102, 103, 111–112, 115
"Death Is Not the End" (Wallace), **Supp. X:** 309
Death Kit (Sontag), **Supp. III Part 2:** 451, 468–469
Death Likes It Hot (Vidal, under pseudonym Box), **Supp. IV Part 2:** 682
"*Death*/La Muerta" (Mora), **Supp. XIII:** 228
Death Notebooks, The (Sexton), **Supp. II Part 2:** 691, 694, 695
"Death of a Jazz Musician" (W. J. Smith), **Supp. XIII:** 334
Death of a Kinsman, The (Taylor), **Supp. V:** 324, 326
"Death of an Old Seaman" (Hughes), **Retro. Supp. I:** 199
"Death of a Pig" (White), **Supp. I Part 2:** 665–668
Death of a Salesman (A. Miller), **I:** 81; **III:** 148, 149, 150, 153–154, 156, 157, 158, 159, 160, 163, 164, 166; **IV:** 389; **Supp. IV Part 1:** 359
"Death of a Soldier, The" (Stevens), **Retro. Supp. I:** 299, 312. *See also* "Lettres d'un Soldat" (Stevens)
"Death of a Soldier, The" (Wilson), **IV:** 427, 445
"Death of a Toad" (Wilbur), **Supp. III Part 2:** 550
"Death of a Traveling Salesman" (Welty), **IV:** 261; **Retro. Supp. I:** 344
"Death of a Young Son by Drowning" (Atwood), **Supp. XIII:** 33
Death of Bessie Smith, The (Albee), **I:** 76–77, 92
Death of Billy the Kid, The (Vidal), **Supp. IV Part 2:** 683
Death of Cock Robin, The (Snodgrass), **Supp. VI:** 315, **317–319,** 324
"Death of General Wolfe, The" (Paine), **Supp. I Part 2:** 504
"Death of Halpin Frayser, The" (Bierce), **I:** 205
"Death of Justina, The" (Cheever), **Supp. I Part 1:** 184–185
Death of Life, The (Barnes), **Supp. III Part 1:** 34
Death of Malcolm X, The (Baraka), **Supp. II Part 1:** 47
"Death of Marilyn Monroe, The" (Olds), **Supp. X:** 205
"Death of Me, The" (Malamud), **Supp. I Part 2:** 437
"Death of Slavery, The" (Bryant), **Supp. I Part 1:** 168–169
"Death of St. Narcissus, The" (Eliot), **Retro. Supp. I:** 291
"Death of the Ball Turret Gunner, The" (Jarrell), **II:** 369–370, 372, 374, 375, 376, 378
"Death of the Fathers, The" (Sexton), **Supp. II Part 2:** 692
"Death of the Flowers, The" (Bryant), **Supp. I Part 1:** 170
Death of the Fox (Garrett), **Supp. VII:** 99, 101–104, 108
"Death of the Hired Man, The" (Frost), **III:** 523; **Retro. Supp. I:** 121, 128; **Supp. IX:** 261
Death of the Kapowsin Tavern (Hugo), **Supp. VI:** 133–135
"Death of the Kapowsin Tavern" (Hugo), **Supp. VI:** 137, 141
"Death of the Lyric, The: The Achievement of Louis Simpson" (Jarman and McDowell), **Supp. IX:** 266, 270, 276
"Death of Venus, The" (Creeley), **Supp. IV Part 1:** 143, 144–145
"Death on All Fronts" (Ginsberg), **Supp. II Part 1:** 326
"Deaths" (Dunn), **Supp. XI:** 147
"Death Sauntering About" (Hecht), **Supp. X:** 72
Deaths for the Ladies (and Other Disasters) (Mailer), **Retro. Supp. II:** 203
Death's Jest-Book (Beddoes), **Retro. Supp. I:** 285
Death Song (McGrath), **Supp. X:** 127
"Death the Carnival Barker" (Hecht), **Supp. X:** 72
"Death the Film Director" (Hecht), **Supp. X:** 72
"Death the Judge" (Hecht), **Supp. X:** 72
"Death the Mexican Revolutionary" (Hecht), **Supp. X:** 72
"Death the Oxford Don" (Hecht), **Supp. X:** 72
"Death the Painter" (Hecht), **Supp. X:** 72
Death the Proud Brother (Wolfe), **IV:** 456
"Death to Van Gogh's Ear!" (Ginsberg), **Supp. II Part 1:** 320, 322, 323
"Death Warmed Over!" (Bradbury), **Supp. IV Part 1:** 104–105, 112
Débâcle, La (Zola), **III:** 316
"Debate with the Rabbi" (Nemerov), **III:** 272
Debeljak, Ale[009a], **Supp. VIII:** 272
De Bellis, Jack, **Supp. I Part 1:** 366, 368, 372
De Bosis, Lauro, **IV:** 372
"Debriefing" (Sontag), **Supp. III Part 2:** 468–470
Debs, Eugene, **I:** 483, 493; **III:** 580, 581; **Supp. I Part 2:** 524; **Supp. IX:** 1, 15
Debt to Pleasure, The (Lanchester), **Retro. Supp. I:** 278
Debussy, Claude, **Retro. Supp. II:** 266; **Supp. XIII:** 44
Decameron (Boccaccio), **III:** 283, 411; **Supp. IX:** 215
"Deceased" (Hughes), **Retro. Supp. I:** 208
"December" (Oliver), **Supp. VII:** 245
"December 1, 1994" (Stern), **Supp. IX:** 299
"December Eclogue" (Winters), **Supp. II Part 2:** 794
Deception (Roth), **Retro. Supp. II:** 309; **Supp. III Part 2:** 426–427
"Deceptions" (Dobyns), **Supp. XIII:** 77
De Chiara, Ann. *See* Malamud, Mrs. Bernard (Ann de Chiara)
De Chirico, Giorgio, **Supp. XIII:** 317
"Decided Loss, A" (Poe), **II:** 411
"Decisions to Disappear" (Dunn), **Supp. XI:** 144
Decker, James A., **Supp. III Part 2:** 621
Declaration of Gentlemen and Merchants and Inhabitants of Boston, and the Country Adjacent, A (Mather), **Supp. II Part 2:** 450
"Declaration of Paris, The" (Adams), **I:** 4
Declaration of the Rights of Man and the Citizen, **Supp. I Part 2:** 513, 519
Declaration of Universal Peace and Liberty (Paine), **Supp. I Part 2:** 512
Decline and Fall (Waugh), **Supp. I Part 2:** 607
Decline and Fall of the English System of Finance, The (Paine), **Supp. I**

Part 2: 518
Decline and Fall of the Roman Empire, The (Gibbons), **Supp. III Part 2:** 629
"Decline of Book Reviewing, The" (Hardwick), **Supp. III Part 1:** 201–202
Decline of the West, The (Spengler), **I:** 270; **IV:** 125
"Decoration Day" (Jewett), **II:** 412; **Retro. Supp. II:** 138
Decoration of Houses, The (Wharton and Codman), **IV:** 308; **Retro. Supp. I:** 362, 363–364, 366
"Decoy" (Ashbery), **Supp. III Part 1:** 13–14
"De Daumier-Smith's Blue Period" (Salinger), **III:** 560–561
"Dedication and Household Map" (Erdrich), **Supp. IV Part 1:** 272
"Dedication Day" (Agee), **I:** 34
"Dedication for a Book of Criticism" (Winters), **Supp. II Part 2:** 801
"Dedication in Postscript, A" (Winters), **Supp. II Part 2:** 801
Dedications and Other Darkhorses (Komunyakaa), **Supp. XIII:** 112, **113–114**
"Dedication to Hunger" (Glück), **Supp. V:** 83
"Dedication to My Wife, A" (Eliot), **I:** 583
Dee, Ruby, **Supp. IV Part 1:** 362
"Deep Breath at Dawn, A" (Hecht), **Supp. X:** 58
Deeper into Movies: The Essential Kael Collection from '69 to '72 (Kael), **Supp. IX:** 253
Deep Green Sea (R. O. Butler), **Supp. XII:** 62, **74**
Deephaven (Jewett), **II:** 398–399, 400, 401, 410, 411; **Retro. Supp. II:** 133, 134, 135, 136, 137, 138, 140, 141, 143, 144
"Deep Sight and Rescue Missions" (Bambara), **Supp. XI:** 18–19
Deep Sightings and Rescue Missions: Fiction, Essays, and Conversations (Bambara), **Supp. XI:** 1, 3, **14–20**
Deep Sleep, The (Morris), **III:** 224–225
Deep South (Caldwell), **I:** 305, 309, 310
"Deep Water" (Marquand), **III:** 56
"Deep Woods" (Nemerov), **III:** 272–273, 275
"Deer at Providencia, The" (Dillard), **Supp. VI:** 28, 32
"Deer Dancer" (Harjo), **Supp. XII:** 224–225

"Deer Ghost" (Harjo), **Supp. XII:** 225
Deer Park, The (Mailer), **I:** 292; **III:** 27, 31–33, 35–36, 37, 39, 40, 42, 43, 44; **Retro. Supp. II: 200–202**, 205, 207, 211
Deer Park, The: A Play (Mailer), **Retro. Supp. II:** 205
Deerslayer, The (Cooper), **I:** 341, 349, 350, 355; **Supp. I Part 1:** 251
"Defence of Poesy, The" (Sidney), **Supp. V:** 250
"Defence of Poetry" (Longfellow), **II:** 493–494
"Defender of the Faith" (Roth), **Retro. Supp. II:** 299; **Supp. III Part 2:** 404, 407, 420
"Defenestration in Prague" (Matthews), **Supp. IX:** 168
Defenestration of Prague (Howe), **Supp. IV Part 2:** 419, 426, 429–430
Defense, The (Nabokov), **III:** 251–252; **Retro. Supp. I:** 266, 268, **270–272**
"Defense of Poetry" (Francis), **Supp. IX:** 83–84
Defiant Ones, The (film), **Supp. I Part 1:** 67
"Defining the Age" (Davis), **Supp. IV Part 1:** 64
"Defining the Space That Separates" (Rich), **Retro. Supp. II:** 292
"Definition" (Ammons), **Supp. VII:** 28
Defoe, Daniel, **I:** 204; **II:** 104, 105, 159, 304–305; **III:** 113, 423; **IV:** 180; **Supp. I Part 2:** 523; **Supp. V:** 127
De Forest, John William, **II:** 275, 280, 288, 289; **IV:** 350
Degas, Brian, **Supp. XI:** 307
Degler, Carl, **Supp. I Part 2:** 496
"Degrees of Fidelity" (Dunn), **Supp. XI:** 148, 156
De Haven, Tom, **Supp. XI:** 39; **Supp. XII:** 338–339
Deitch, Joseph, **Supp. VIII:** 125
"Dejection" (Coleridge), **II:** 97
DeJong, Constance, **Supp. XII:** 4
DeJong, David Cornel, **I:** 35
de Kooning, Willem, **Supp. XII:** 198
Delacroix, Henri, **I:** 227
De La Mare, Walter, **III:** 429; **Supp. II Part 1:** 4
Delamotte, Eugenia C., **Supp. XI:** 279
De Lancey, James, **I:** 338
De Lancey, Mrs. James (Anne Heathcote), **I:** 338
De Lancey, Susan A. *See* Cooper, Mrs. James Fenimore
De Lancey, William Heathcote, **I:** 338, 353

Delano, Amasa, **III:** 90
Delattre, Roland A., **I:** 558
De Laurentiis, Dino, **Supp. XI:** 170, 307
De la Valdéne, Guy, **Supp. VIII:** 40, 42
De l'éducation d'un homme sauvage (Itard), **Supp. I Part 2:** 564
"Delft" (Goldbarth), **Supp. XII:** 189
Delft: An Essay-Poem (Goldbarth), **Supp. XII:** 187
Délie (Scève), **Supp. III Part 1:** 11
DeLillo, Don, **Retro. Supp. I:** 278; **Retro. Supp. II:** 297; **Supp. VI: 1–18; Supp. IX:** 212; **Supp. XI:** 68; **Supp. XII:** 21, 152
DeLisle, Anne, **Supp. VIII:** 175
Deliverance (Dickey), **Supp. IV Part 1:** 176, 186–188, 190; **Supp. X:** 30
Deliverance, The (Glasgow), **II:** 175, 176, 177–178, 181
"Delivering" (Dubus), **Supp. VII:** 87
Dell, Floyd, **I:** 103, 105; **Supp. I Part 2:** 379
"Della Primavera Trasportata al Morale" (W. C. Williams), **Retro. Supp. I:** 419, 422
Deloria, Vine, Jr., **Supp. IV Part 1:** 323; **Supp. IV Part 2:** 504
"Delta Autumn" (Faulkner), **II:** 71
"Delta Factor, The" (Percy), **Supp. III Part 1:** 386
Delta of Venus: Erotica (Nin), **Supp. X:** 192, 195
Delta Wedding (Welty), **IV:** 261, 268–271, 273, 281; **Retro. Supp. I:** 349–350, 351
Delusions (Berryman), **I:** 170
de Man, Paul, **Retro. Supp. I:** 67
DeMars, James, **Supp. IV Part 2:** 552
Dembo, L. S., **I:** 386, 391, 396, 397, 398, 402; **III:** 478; **Supp. I Part 1:** 272
Demeter, Anna, **Retro. Supp. II:** 285
Demetrakopoulous, Stephanie A., **Supp. IV Part 1:** 12
DeMille, Cecil B., **Supp. IV Part 2:** 520
Demme, Jonathan, **Supp. V:** 14
Democracy (Adams), **I:** 9–10, 20; **Supp. IV Part 1:** 208
Democracy (Didion), **Supp. IV Part 1:** 198, 208–210

"Democracy" (Lowell), **Supp. I Part 2:** 419
Democracy and Education (Dewey), **I:** 232
Democracy and Other Addresses (Lowell), **Supp. I Part 2:** 407
Democracy and Social Ethics (Addams), **Supp. I Part 1:** 8–11
Democracy in America (Tocqueville), **Retro. Supp. I:** 235
Democratic Vistas (Whitman), **IV:** 333, 336, 348–349, 351, 469; **Retro. Supp. I:** 408; **Supp. I Part 2:** 456
Democritus, **I:** 480–481; **II:** 157; **III:** 606; **Retro. Supp. I:** 247
"Demon Lover, The" (Rich), **Supp. I Part 2:** 556
"Demonstrators, The" (Welty), **IV:** 280; **Retro. Supp. I:** 355
DeMott, Benjamin, **Supp. IV Part 1:** 35; **Supp. V:** 123; **Supp. XIII:** 95
DeMott, Robert, **Supp. VIII:** 40, 41
Demuth, Charles, **IV:** 404; **Retro. Supp. I:** 412, 430
"Demystified Zone" (Paley), **Supp. VI:** 227
Denmark Vesey (opera) (Bowles), **Supp. IV Part 1:** 83
Denney, Joseph Villiers, **Supp. I Part 2:** 605
Denney, Reuel, **Supp. XII:** 121
Dennie, Joseph, **II:** 298; **Supp. I Part 1:** 125
Denniston, Dorothy Hamer, **Supp. XI:** 276, 277
"Den of Lions" (Plath), **Retro. Supp. II:** 242
"Dental Assistant, The" (Simpson), **Supp. IX:** 280
Den Uyl, Douglas, **Supp. IV Part 2:** 528, 530
"Deodand, The" (Hecht), **Supp. X:** 65
"Departing" (Cameron), **Supp. XII:** 81
"Departure" (Glück), **Supp. V:** 89
"Departure" (Plath), **Supp. I Part 2:** 537
"Departure, The" (Freneau), **Supp. II Part 1:** 264
Departures (Justice), **Supp. VII:** 124–127
Departures and Arrivals (Shields), **Supp. VII:** 320, 322
"Depressed by a Book of Bad Poetry, I Walk Toward an Unused Pasture and Invite the Insects to Join Me" (Wright), **Supp. III Part 2:** 600
"Depressed Person, The" (Wallace), **Supp. X:** 309
"Depression Days" (Mora), **Supp. XIII:** 224–225

De Puy, John, **Supp. XIII:** 12
D'Erasmo, Stacey, **Supp. IX:** 121
De Reilhe, Catherine, **Supp. I Part 1:** 202
De Rerum Natura (Lucretius), **II:** 162
"De Rerum Virtute" (Jeffers), **Supp. II Part 2:** 424
De Rioja, Francisco, **Supp. I Part 1:** 166
"Derivative Sport in Tornado Alley" (Wallace), **Supp. X:** 314
Derleth, August, **Supp. I Part 2:** 465, 472
Deronda, Daniel, **II:** 179
Derrida, Jacques, **Supp. IV Part 1:** 45
Deruddere, Dominique, **Supp. XI:** 173
Der Wilde Jäger (Bürger), **II:** 306
Derzhavin, Gavrila Romanovich, **Supp. VIII:** 27
De Santis, Christopher, **Retro. Supp. I:** 194
Descartes, René, **I:** 255; **III:** 618–619; **IV:** 133
Descendents, The (Glasgow), **II:** 173, 174–175, 176
Descending Figure (Glück), **Supp. V:** 83–84
"Descending Theology: Christ Human" (Karr), **Supp. XI:** 251
"Descending Theology: The Garden" (Karr), **Supp. XI:** 251
"Descent, The" (W. C. Williams), **Retro. Supp. I:** 428, 429
"Descent from the Cross" (Eliot), **Retro. Supp. I:** 57, 58
"Descent in the Maelström, A" (Poe), **Retro. Supp. II:** 274
"Descent into Proselito" (Knowles), **Supp. XII:** 237
"Descent into the Maelström, A" (Poe), **III:** 411, 414, 416, 424
Descent of Man (Boyle), **Supp. VIII:** 1, 12–13
"Descent of Man" (Boyle), **Supp. VIII:** 14
Descent of Man, The (Wharton), **IV:** 311; **Retro. Supp. I:** 367
Descent of Man and Other Stories, The (Wharton), **Retro. Supp. I:** 367
Descent of Winter, The (W. C. Williams), **Retro. Supp. I:** 419, 428
De Schloezer, Doris, **III:** 474
"Description" (Doty), **Supp. XI:** 126
"Description of the great Bones dug up at Clavarack on the Banks of Hudsons River A.D. 1705, The" (Taylor), **IV:** 163, 164
"Description without Place" (Stevens), **Retro. Supp. I:** 422

"Desert" (Hughes), **Retro. Supp. I:** 207
"Deserted Cabin" (Haines), **Supp. XII:** 203
Deserted Village, The (Goldsmith), **II:** 304
Desert Is My Mother, The/El desierto es mi madre (Mora), **Supp. XIII:** 214, 221
Desert Music, The (W. C. Williams), **IV:** 422; **Retro. Supp. I:** 428, 429
"Desert Music, The" (W. C. Williams), **Retro. Supp. I:** 428, 429
"Desert Places" (Frost), **II:** 159; **Retro. Supp. I:** 121, 123, 129, 138, 299
Desert Rose, The (McMurtry), **Supp. V:** 225, 231
Desert Solitaire (Abbey), **Supp. X:** 30; **Supp. XIII:** 7–8, 12
"Design" (Frost), **II:** 158, 163; **Retro. Supp. I:** 121, 126, 138, 139; **Supp. IX:** 81
"Designated National Park, A" (Ortiz), **Supp. IV Part 2:** 509
Des Imagistes (Pound), **II:** 513; **Supp. I Part 1:** 257, 261, 262
"Desire" (Beattie), **Supp. V:** 29
"Désirée's Baby" (Chopin), **Retro. Supp. II:** 64, 65; **Supp. I Part 1:** 213–215
Desire under the Elms (O'Neill), **III:** 387, 390
"Desolate Field, The" (W. C. Williams), **Retro. Supp. I:** 418
"Desolation, A" (Ginsberg), **Supp. II Part 1:** 313
Desolation Angels (Kerouac), **Supp. III Part 1:** 218, 225, 230
"Desolation Is a Delicate Thing" (Wylie), **Supp. I Part 2:** 729
Despair (Nabokov), **Retro. Supp. I:** 270, 274
"Despisals" (Rukeyser), **Supp. VI:** 282
Des Pres, Terrence, **Supp. X:** 113, 120, 124
"Destiny and the Lieutenant" (McCoy), **Supp. XIII:** 171
"Destruction of Kreshev, The" (Singer), **IV:** 13; **Retro. Supp. II:** 325
Destruction of the European Jews, The (Hilberg), **Supp. V:** 267
"Destruction of the Goetheanum, The" (Salter), **Supp. IX:** 257
"Destruction of the Long Branch, The" (Pinsky), **Supp. VI:** 239, 240, 243–244, 245, 247, 250
Destructive Element, The (Spender), **Retro. Supp. I:** 216
"Detail & Parody for the poem 'Paterson'" (W. C. Williams), **Retro.**

Supp. I: 424
Detmold, John, **Supp. I Part 2:** 670
Deuce, The (R. O. Butler), **Supp. XII:** 62, **69–70,** 72
Deuteronomy (biblical book), **II:** 166
Deutsch, Andre, **Supp. XI:** 297, 301
Deutsch, Babette, **Supp. I Part 1:** 328, 341
Deutsch, Michel, **Supp. IV Part 1:** 104
"Devaluation Blues: Ruminations on Black Families in Crisis" (Coleman), **Supp. XI:** 87
Devane, William, **Supp. XI:** 234
"Development of the Literary West" (Chopin), **Retro. Supp. II:** 72
"Development of the Modern English Novel, The" (Lanier), **Supp. I Part 1:** 370–371
DeVeriante (Herbert of Cherbury), **II:** 108
"Devil and Daniel Webster, The" (Benét), **III:** 22; **Supp. XI:** 45–46, 47, 50–51, 52
Devil and Daniel Webster and Other Writings, The (Benét), **Supp. XI:** 48
"Devil and Tom Walker, The" (Irving), **II:** 309–310
Devil At Large, The: Erica Jong on Henry Miller (Jong), **Supp. V:** 115, 131
Devil Finds Work, The (Baldwin), **Retro. Supp. II:** 14; **Supp. I Part 1:** 48, 52, 66–67
Devil in a Blue Dress (Mosley), **Supp. XIII:** 237, 239
"Devil in Manuscript, The" (Hawthorne), **II:** 226; **Retro. Supp. I:** 150–151
Devil in Paradise, A (H. Miller), **III:** 190
"Devil in the Belfry, The" (Poe), **III:** 425; **Retro. Supp. II:** 273
"Devil Is a Busy Man, The" (Wallace), **Supp. X:** 309
Devil's Dictionary, The (Bierce), **I:** 196, 197, 205, 208, 209, 210
Devil's Stocking, The (Algren), **Supp. IX:** 5, 16
Devil's Tour, The (Karr), **Supp. XI:** 240, **242–244**
Devil Tree, The (Kosinski), **Supp. VII:** 215, 222, 223
"Devising" (Ammons), **Supp. VII:** 28
De Voto, Bernard, **I:** 247, 248; **II:** 446; **Supp. IV Part 2:** 599, 601
"Devout Meditation in Memory of Adolph Eichmann, A" (Merton), **Supp. VIII:** 198, 203
De Vries, Peter, **Supp. I Part 2:** 604

Dewberry, Elizabeth, **Supp. XII:** 62, 72
Dewey, John, **I:** 214, 224, 228, 232, 233, 266, 267; **II:** 20, 27, 34, 229, 361; **III:** 112, 294–295, 296, 303, 309–310, 599, 605; **IV:** 27, 429; **Supp. I Part 1:** 3, 5, 7, 10, 11, 12, 24; **Supp. I Part 2:** 493, 641, 647, 677; **Supp. V:** 290; **Supp. IX:** 179
Dewey, Joseph, **Supp. IX:** 210
Dewey, Thomas, **IV:** 161
De Young, Charles, **I:** 194
Dhairyam, Sagari, **Supp. IV Part 1:** 329, 330
Dharma Bums, The (Kerouac), **Supp. III Part 1:** 230, 231; **Supp. VIII:** 289, 305
D'Houdetot, Madame, **Supp. I Part 1:** 250
"Diabetes" (Dickey), **Supp. IV Part 1:** 182
Diaghilev, Sergei, **Supp. I Part 1:** 257
Dial (publication), **I:** 58, 109, 115, 116, 215, 231, 233, 245, 261, 384, 429; **II:** 8, 430; **III:** 194, 470, 471, 485; **IV:** 122, 171, 427; **Retro. Supp. I:** 58; **Retro. Supp. II:** 78; **Supp. I Part 2:** 642, 643, 647; **Supp. II Part 1:** 168, 279, 291; **Supp. II Part 2:** 474; **Supp. III Part 2:** 611
"Dialectics of Love, The" (McGrath), **Supp. X:** 116
"Dialogue" (Rich), **Supp. I Part 2:** 560
Dialogue, A (Baldwin and Giovanni), **Supp. I Part 1:** 66
"Dialogue: William Harvey; Joan of Arc" (Goldbarth), **Supp. XII:** 178
"Dialogue Between Franklin and the Gout" (Franklin), **II:** 121
"Dialogue Between General Wolfe and General Gage in a Wood near Boston, A" (Paine), **Supp. I Part 2:** 504
"Dialogue between Old England and New" (Bradstreet), **Supp. I Part 1:** 105–106, 110–111, 116
"Dialogue between the Writer and a Maypole Dresser, A" (Taylor), **IV:** 155
Dialogues (Bush, ed.), **III:** 4
Dialogues in Limbo (Santayana), **III:** 606
"Diamond as Big as the Ritz, The" (Fitzgerald), **II:** 88–89
Diamond Cutters and Other Poems, The (Rich), **Retro. Supp. II:** 280; **Supp. I Part 2:** 551, 552, 553
"Diamond Guitar, A" (Capote), **Supp. III Part 1:** 124
"Diana and Persis" (Alcott), **Supp. I**

Part 1: 32, 41
Diaries of Charlotte Perkins Gilman (Knight, ed.), **Supp. XI:** 201
Diary of Anaïs Nin, The (1931–1974), **Supp. X:** 181, 185–189, 191, 192, 193, 195
Diary of a Yuppie (Auchincloss), **Supp. IV Part 1:** 31, 32–33
Diary of "Helena Morley," The (Bishop, trans.), **Retro. Supp. II:** 45, 51; **Supp. I Part 1:** 92
Díaz del Castillo, Bernál, **III:** 13, 14
Dickens, Charles, **I:** 152, 198, 505; **II:** 98, 179, 186, 192, 271, 273–274, 288, 290, 297, 301, 307, 316, 322, 559, 561, 563, 577, 582; **III:** 146, 247, 325, 368, 411, 421, 426, 572, 577, 613–614, 616; **IV:** 21, 192, 194, 211, 429; **Retro. Supp. I:** 33, 91, 218; **Retro. Supp. II:** 204; **Supp. I Part 1:** 13, 34, 35, 36, 41, 49; **Supp. I Part 2:** 409, 523, 579, 590, 622, 675; **Supp. IV Part 1:** 293, 300, 341; **Supp. IV Part 2:** 464; **Supp. VIII:** 180; **Supp. IX:** 246; **Supp. XI:** 277; **Supp. XII:** 335, 337; **Supp. XIII:** 233
Dickey, James, **I:** 29, 535; **III:** 268; **Retro. Supp. II:** 233; **Supp. III Part 1:** 354; **Supp. III Part 2:** 541, 597; **Supp. IV Part 1:** **175–194;** **Supp. V:** 333; **Supp. X:** 30; **Supp. XI:** 312, 317
Dick Gibson Show, The (Elkin), **Supp. VI:** 42, **48–49**
Dickie, Margaret, **Retro. Supp. II:** 53, 84
Dickinson, Donald, **Retro. Supp. I:** 206, 212
Dickinson, Edward, **I:** 451–452, 453
Dickinson, Emily, **I:** 384, 419, 433, **451–473;** **II:** 272, 276, 277, 530; **III:** 19, 194, 196, 214, 493, 505, 508, 556, 572, 576; **IV:** 134, 135, 331, 444; **Retro. Supp. I: 25–50;** **Retro. Supp. II:** 39, 40, 43, 45, 50, 76, 134, 155, 170, 281, 286; **Supp. I Part 1:** 29, 79, 188, 372; **Supp. I Part 2:** 375, 546, 609, 682, 691; **Supp. II Part 1:** 4; **Supp. III Part 1:** 63; **Supp. III Part 2:** 600, 622; **Supp. IV Part 1:** 31, 257; **Supp. IV Part 2:** 434, 637, 641, 643; **Supp. V:** 79, 140, 332, 335; **Supp. VIII:** 95, 104, 106, 108, 198, 205, 272; **Supp. IX:** 37, 38, 53, 87, 90; **Supp. XII:** 226; **Supp. XIII:** 153, 339
Dickinson, Gilbert, **I:** 469
Dickinson, Lavinia Norcross, **I:** 451,

453, 462, 470
Dickinson, Mrs. Edward, **I:** 451, 453
Dickinson, Mrs. William A. (Susan Gilbert), **I:** 452, 453, 456, 469, 470
Dickinson, William Austin, **I:** 451, 453, 469
Dickinson and the Strategies of Reticence (Dobson), **Retro. Supp. I:** 29, 42
Dickson, Helen. *See* Blackmur, Helen Dickson
Dickstein, Morris, **Supp. XIII:** 106
"Dick Whittington and His Cat," **Supp. I Part 2:** 656
"DICTATORSHIP OF THE PROLETARIAT, THE" (Baraka), **Supp. II Part 1:** 54
Dictionary of Literary Biography (Kibler, ed.), **Supp. IX:** 94, 109; **Supp. XI:** 297
Dictionary of Modern English Usage, A (Fowler), **Supp. I Part 2:** 660
"Dictum: For a Masque of Deluge" (Merwin), **Supp. III Part 1:** 342–343
"Didactic Poem" (Levertov), **Supp. III Part 1:** 280
Diderot, Denis, **II:** 535; **IV:** 440
Didion, Joan, **Retro. Supp. I:** 116; **Retro. Supp. II:** 209; **Supp. I Part 1:** 196, 197; **Supp. III Part 1:** 302; **Supp. IV Part 1:** 195–216; **Supp. XI:** 221; **Supp. XII:** 307
Dido, **I:** 81
"Did You Ever Dream Lucky?" (Ellison), **Supp. II Part 1:** 246
"Die-Hard, The" (Benét), **Supp. XI:** 54–55, 56
Diehl, Digby, **Supp. IV Part 1:** 204
Dien Cai Dau (Komunyakaa), **Supp. XIII:** 121, **122–124,** 125, 131, 132
"Dies Irae" (Lowell), **II:** 553
Die Zeit Ohne Beispiel, (Goebbels), **III:** 560
Different Drummer, A (Larkin; film), **Supp. XI:** 20
Different Fleshes (Goldbarth), **Supp. XII:** 181–182, 188
Different Hours (Dunn), **Supp. XI:** 139, 142, 143, 155
Different Seasons (King), **Supp. V:** 148, 152
Different Ways to Pray (Nye), **Supp. XIII:** 274, 275, 277, 285, 287
"Different Ways to Pray" (Nye), **Supp. XIII:** 275
"Difficulties of a Statesman" (Eliot), **I:** 580
"Difficulties of Modernism and the Modernism of Difficulty" (Poirier),

Supp. II Part 1: 136
Diff'rent (O'Neill), **III:** 389
DiGaetani, John L., **Supp. XIII:** 200
"Digging in the Garden of Age I Uncover a Live Root" (Swenson), **Supp. IV Part 2:** 649
Diggins, John P., **Supp. I Part 2:** 650
Digregorio, Charles, **Supp. XI:** 326
"Dilemma of Determinism, The" (James), **II:** 347–348, 352
"Dilettante, The" (Wharton), **IV:** 311, 313
"Dilettante, The: A Modern Type" (Dunbar), **Supp. II Part 1:** 199
Dillard, Annie, **Supp. VI:** 19–39; **Supp. VIII:** 272; **Supp. X:** 31; **Supp. XIII:** 154
Dillard, R. H. W., **Supp. XII:** 16
Dillman, Bradford, **III:** 403; **Supp. XII:** 241
Dillon, Brian, **Supp. X:** 209
Dillon, George, **III:** 141; **Supp. III Part 2:** 621
Dillon, Millicent, **Supp. IV Part 1:** 95
Dilsaver, Paul, **Supp. XIII:** 112
Dilthey, Wilhelm, **I:** 58
Dime-Store Alchemy: The Art of Joseph Cornell, **Supp. VIII:** 272
"Diminuendo" (Dunn), **Supp. XI:** 152–153
"Dimout in Harlem" (Hughes), **Supp. I Part 1:** 333
Dinesen, Isak, **IV:** 279; **Supp. VIII:** 171
Dining Room, The (Gurney), **Supp. V:** 105–106
"Dinner at ———, A" (O. Henry), **Supp. II Part 1:** 402
"Dinner at Sir Nigel's" (Bowles), **Supp. IV Part 1:** 94
Dinner at the Homesick Restaurant (Tyler), **Supp. IV Part 2:** 657, 667–668
"Dinner at Uncle Borris's" (Simic), **Supp. VIII:** 272
Dinner Bridge (Lardner), **II:** 435
Dinosaur Tales (Bradbury), **Supp. IV Part 1:** 103
"Diogenes Invents a Game" (Karr), **Supp. XI:** 240–241
"Diogenes Tries to Forget" (Karr), **Supp. XI:** 241
Dionysis in Doubt (Robinson), **III:** 510
Diop, Birago, **Supp. IV Part 1:** 16
Diop, David, **Supp. IV Part 1:** 16
DiPrima, Diane, **Supp. III Part 1:** 30
Direction of Poetry, The: Rhymed and Metered Verse Written in the English Language since 1975 (Richman), **Supp. XI:** 249

"Directive" (Bishop), **Retro. Supp. II:** 42
"Directive" (Frost), **III:** 287; **Retro. Supp. I:** 140; **Supp. VIII:** 32, 33
"Dire Cure" (Matthews), **Supp. IX:** 168
"Dirge" (Dunbar), **Supp. II Part 1:** 199
"Dirge without Music" (Millay), **III:** 126
"Dirt" (Salter), **Supp. IX:** 257, 260, 261
"Dirt and Desire: Essay on the Phenomenology of Female Pollution in Antiquity" (Carson), **Supp. XII:** 111
"Dirty Memories" (Olds), **Supp. X:** 211
"Dirty Word, The" (Shapiro), **Supp. II Part 2:** 710
Disappearances (Auster), **Supp. XII:** 23
"Disappearances" (Hogan), **Supp. IV Part 1:** 401
Disappearing Acts (McMillan), **Supp. XIII:** 182, 183, **188–189,** 192
"Disappointment, The" (Creeley), **Supp. IV Part 1:** 143
"Disappointment and Desire" (Bly), **Supp. IV Part 1:** 71
"Discards" (Baker), **Supp. XIII:** 53, 55–56
Discerning the Signs of the Times (Niebuhr), **III:** 300–301, 307–308
"Disciple of Bacon, The" (Epstein), **Supp. XII:** 163–164
"Discordants" (Aiken), **I:** 65
Discourse on Method (Descartes), **I:** 255
"Discovering Theme and Structure in the Novel" (Schuster), **Supp. VIII:** 126
"Discovery" (Freneau), **Supp. II Part 1:** 258
"Discovery of the Madeiras, The" (Frost), **Retro. Supp. I:** 139
"Discovery of What It Means to Be an American, The" (Baldwin), **Supp. I Part 1:** 54–55
Discovery! The Search for Arabian Oil (Stegner), **Supp. IV Part 2:** 599
"Discrete Series" (Zukofsky), **Supp. III Part 2:** 616
"Discretions of Alcibiades" (Pinsky), **Supp. VI:** 241
"Disease, The" (Rukeyser), **Supp. VI:** 279
Disenchanted, The (Schulberg), **II:** 98; **Retro. Supp. I:** 113
"Dish of Green Pears, A" (Ríos), **Supp. IV Part 2:** 552

Dismantling the Silence (Simic), **Supp. VIII: 273–274,** 275, 276
Disney, Walt, **III:** 275, 426
"Disney of My Mind" (Chabon), **Supp. XI:** 63
Dispatches (Herr), **Supp. XI:** 245
"Displaced Person, The" (O'Connor), **III:** 343–344, 350, 352, 356; **Retro. Supp. II:** 229, 232, 236
"Disposal" (Snodgrass), **Supp. VI:** 314
Dispossessed, The (Berryman), **I:** 170, 172, 173, 174, 175, 176, 178
"Disquieting Muses, The" (Plath), **Supp. I Part 2:** 538
Disraeli, Benjamin, **II:** 127
Dissent (Didion), **Supp. IV Part 1:** 208
"Dissenting Opinion on Kafka, A" (Wilson), **IV:** 437–438
Dissent in Three American Wars (Morison, Merk, and Freidel), **Supp. I Part 2:** 495
Dissertation on Liberty and Necessity, Pleasure and Pain, A (Franklin), **II:** 108
Dissertations on Government; the Affairs of the Bank: and Paper Money (Paine), **Supp. I Part 2:** 510
"Distance" (Carver), **Supp. III Part 1:** 146
"Distance" (Paley), **Supp. VI:** 222
"Distance, The" (Karr), **Supp. XI:** 241
"Distance Nowhere" (Hughes), **Retro. Supp. I:** 207
"Distant Episode, A" (Bowles), **Supp. IV Part 1:** 84–85, 86, 90
Distant Episode, A: The Selected Stories (Bowles), **Supp. IV Part 1:** 79
Distinguished Guest, The (S. Miller), **Supp. XII: 299–301**
Distortions (Beattie), **Supp. V:** 21, 23, 24, 25, 27
"Distrest Shepherdess, The" (Freneau), **Supp. II Part 1:** 258
District of Columbia (Dos Passos), **I:** 478, 489–490, 492
Disturber of the Peace (Manchester), **III:** 103
Disturbing the Peace (Yates), **Supp. XI:** 345, 346
"Diver, The" (Hayden), **Supp. II Part 1:** 368, 372, 373
"Divided Life of Jean Toomer, The" (Toomer), **Supp. III Part 2:** 488
Divina Commedia (Longfellow, trans.), **II:** 490, 492, 493
"Divine Collaborator" (Simic), **Supp. VIII:** 282
Divine Comedies (Merrill), **Supp. III Part 1:** 324, 329–332

Divine Comedy (Dante), **I:** 137, 265, 400, 446; **II:** 215, 335, 490, 492, 493; **III:** 13, 448, 453; **Supp. V:** 283, 331, 338, 345; **Supp. X:** 253
"Divine Image, The" (Blake), **Supp. V:** 257
Divine Pilgrim, The (Aiken), **I:** 50, 55
Divine Tragedy, The (Longfellow), **II:** 490, 500, 505, 506, 507; **Retro. Supp. II:** 165, 166
Divine Weekes and Workes (Sylvester, trans.), **Supp. I Part 1:** 104
Divine Weeks (Du Bartas), **IV:** 157–158
"Diving into the Wreck: Poems 1971–1972" (Rich), **Supp. I Part 2:** 550, 559–565, 569
Diving into the Wreck: Poems, 1971–1972 (Rich), **Retro. Supp. II:** 284
Diving Rock on the Hudson, A (H. Roth), **Supp. IX:** 236, **237–238**
"Divinity in Its Fraying Fact, A" (Levis), **Supp. XI:** 271
"Divinity School Address" (Emerson), **II:** 12–13
"Divisions upon a Ground" (Hecht), **Supp. X:** 58
"Divorce" (Karr), **Supp. XI:** 244
Dix, Douglas Shields, **Supp. XII:** 14
Dixon, Ivan, **Supp. IV Part 1:** 362
Dixon, Stephen, **Supp. XII: 139–158**
Dixon, Thomas, Jr., **Supp. II Part 1:** 169, 171, 177
Djinn (Robbe-Grillet), **Supp. V:** 48
D'Lugoff, Burt, **Supp. IV Part 1:** 362, 370
Do, Lord, Remember Me (Garrett), **Supp. VII:** 98–100, 110
"Doaksology, The" (Wolfe), **IV:** 459
Dobie, J. Frank, **Supp. V:** 225; **Supp. XIII:** 227
Dobriansky, Lev, **Supp. I Part 2:** 648, 650
Dobson, Joanne, **Retro. Supp. I:** 29, 31, 42
Dobyns, Stephen, **Supp. XIII: 73–92**
"Docking at Palermo" (Hugo), **Supp. VI:** 137–138
"Dock Rats" (Moore), **III:** 213
"Dock-Witch, The" (Ozick), **Supp. V:** 262, 264
"Doc Mellhorn and the Pearly Gates" (Benét), **Supp. XI:** 55
"Doctor, The" (Dubus), **Supp. VII:** 80–81
"Doctor and the Doctor's Wife, The" (Hemingway), **II:** 248; **Retro. Supp. I:** 174, 175
Doctor Breen's Practice, a Novel (Howells), **I:** 282

Doctor Faustus (Mann), **III:** 283
"Doctor Jekyll" (Sontag), **Supp. III Part 2:** 469
"Doctor Leavis and the Moral Tradition" (Trilling), **Supp. III Part 2:** 512–513
Doctor Martino and Other Stories (Faulkner), **II:** 72; **Retro. Supp. I:** 84
"Doctor of the Heart, The" (Sexton), **Supp. II Part 2:** 692
Doctorow, E. L., **Retro. Supp. I:** 97; **Supp. III Part 2:** 590, 591; **Supp. IV Part 1: 217–240; Supp. V:** 45
Doctor Sax (Kerouac), **Supp. III Part 1:** 220–222, 224–227
Doctor Sleep (Bell), **Supp. X: 9–11**
"Doctors' Row" (Aiken), **I:** 67
Doctor's Son and Other Stories, The (O'Hara), **III:** 361
Doctor Stories, The (W. C. Williams), **Retro. Supp. I:** 424
"Doctor's Wife, The" (Ozick), **Supp. V:** 262, 265
Doctor Zhivago (Pasternak), **IV:** 434, 438, 443
"Documentary" (Simic), **Supp. VIII:** 282
Dodd, Elizabeth, **Supp. V:** 77
Dodd, Wayne, **Supp. IV Part 2:** 625
Dodson, Owen, **Supp. I Part 1:** 54
Dodsworth (Lewis), **II:** 442, 449–450, 453, 456
Doenitz, Karl, **Supp. I Part 2:** 491
Does Civilization Need Religion? (Niebuhr), **III:** 293–294
"Does 'Consciousness' Exist?" (James), **II:** 356
"Does Education Pay?" (Du Bois), **Supp. II Part 1:** 159
Dog (Shepard), **Supp. III Part 2:** 434
"Dog Act, The" (Komunyakaa), **Supp. XIII:** 114–115
"Dog and the Playlet, The" (O. Henry), **Supp. II Part 1:** 399
Dog Beneath the Skin, The (Auden), **Supp. II Part 1:** 10
"Dog Creek Mainline" (Wright), **Supp. V:** 340
Dog in the Manger, The (Vega; Merwin, trans.), **Supp. III Part 1:** 341, 347
Dogs Bark, The: Public People and Private Places (Capote), **Supp. III Part 1:** 120, 132
Dog Soldiers (Stone), **Supp. V:** 298, 299–301
Dog & the Fever, The (Quevedo), **Retro. Supp. I:** 423
"Dogwood, The" (Levertov), **Supp. III**

Part 1: 276
"Dogwood Tree, The: A Boyhood" (Updike), IV: 218; **Retro. Supp. I:** 318, 319
"Doing Battle with the Wolf" (Coleman), **Supp. XI:** 87–88
Doings and Undoings (Podhoretz), **Supp. VIII: 236–237**
"Dolce Far' Niente" (Humphrey), **Supp. IX:** 106
Dolci, Carlo, **III:** 474–475
"Dollhouse, The" (Haines), **Supp. XII:** 204
Dollmaker's Ghost, The (Levis), **Supp. XI:** 259, 260, **264–268**
Doll's House, A (Ibsen), **III:** 523; **IV:** 357
Dolmetsch, Arnold, **III:** 464
Dolores Claiborne (King), **Supp. V:** 138, 141, 147, 148, 149–150, 152
"Dolph Heyliger" (Irving), **II:** 309
Dolphin, The (Lowell), **Retro. Supp. II:** 183, 186, 188, **190–191; Supp. XII:** 253–254
"Dolphins" (Francis), **Supp. IX:** 83
Dome of Many-Coloured Class, A (Lowell), **II:** 515, 516–517
Domesday Book (Masters), **Supp. I Part 2:** 465, 466–469, 471, 473, 476
"Domestic Economy" (Gilman), **Supp. XI:** 206
"Domestic Manners" (Hardwick), **Supp. III Part 1:** 211
"Dominant White, The" (McKay), **Supp. X:** 134
Dominguez, Robert, **Supp. VIII:** 83
Dominique, Jean. *See* Closset, Marie
Donahue, Phil, **Supp. IV Part 2:** 526; **Supp. X:** 311
Doña Perfecta (Galdós), **II:** 290
"DON JUAN IN HELL" (Baraka), **Supp. II Part 1:** 33
"Donna mi Prega" (Cavalcanti), **Supp. III Part 2:** 620, 621, 622
Donn-Byrne, Brian Oswald. *See* Byrne, Donn
Donne, John, **I:** 358–359, 384, 389, 522, 586; **II:** 254; **III:** 493; **IV:** 83, 88, 135, 141, 144, 145, 151, 156, 165, 331, 333; **Retro. Supp. II:** 76; **Supp. I Part 1:** 80, 364, 367; **Supp. I Part 2:** 421, 424, 467, 725, 726; **Supp. III Part 2:** 614, 619; **Supp. VIII:** 26, 33, 164; **Supp. IX:** 44; **Supp. XII:** 45, 159; **Supp. XIII:** 94, 130
Donoghue, Denis, **I:** 537; **Supp. IV Part 1:** 39; **Supp. VIII:** 105, 189
Donohue, H. E. F., **Supp. IX:** 2, 3, 15, 16

Donovan, Josephine, **Retro. Supp. II:** 138, 139, 147
Don Quixote (Cervantes), **I:** 134; **II:** 291, 434; **III:** 113, 614; **Supp. I Part 2:** 422; **Supp. IX:** 94
Don Quixote: Which Was a Dream (Acker), **Supp. XII:** 5, **12–14**
Don't Ask (Levine), **Supp. V:** 178
Don't Ask Questions (Marquand), **III:** 58
"Don't Shoot the Warthog" (Corso), **Supp. XII:** 123
Don't You Want to Be Free? (Hughes), **Retro. Supp. I:** 203; **Supp. I Part 1:** 339
"Doodler, The" (Merrill), **Supp. III Part 1:** 321
Doolan, Moira, **Retro. Supp. II:** 247
Doolittle, Hilda (H. D.), **II:** 517, 520–521; **III:** 194, 195–196, 457, 465; **IV:** 404, 406; **Retro. Supp. I:** 288, 412, 413, 414, 415, 417; **Supp. I Part 1: 253–275; Supp. I Part 2:** 707; **Supp. III Part 1:** 48; **Supp. III Part 2:** 610; **Supp. IV Part 1:** 257; **Supp. V:** 79
Doolittle, Thomas, **IV:** 150
"Doomed by Our Blood to Care" (Orfalea), **Supp. XIII:** 278
"Doomsday" (Plath), **Retro. Supp. II:** 242
Doomsters, The (Macdonald), **Supp. IV Part 2:** 462, 463, 472, 473
"Door, The" (Creeley), **Supp. IV Part 1:** 145, 146, 156–157
"Door, The" (White), **Supp. I Part 2:** 651, 675–676
"Door in the Dark, The" (Frost), **II:** 156
Door in the Hive, A (Levertov), **Supp. III Part 1:** 283, 284
"Door of the Trap, The" (Anderson), **I:** 112
"Doors, Doors, Doors" (Sexton), **Supp. II Part 2:** 681
Doors, The, **Supp. X:** 186
Doreski, William, **Retro. Supp. II:** 185
Dorfman, Ariel, **Supp. IX:** 131, 138
Dorfman, Joseph, **Supp. I Part 2:** 631, 647, 650
Dorman, Jen, **Supp. XI:** 240
Dorn, Edward, **Supp. IV Part 1:** 154
Dorris, Michael, **Supp. IV Part 1:** 260, 272
Dos Passos, John, **I:** 99, 288, 374, 379, **474–496,** 517, 519; **II:** 74, 77, 89, 98; **III:** 2, 28, 29, 70, 172, 382–383; **IV:** 340, 427, 433; **Retro. Supp. I:** 105, 113, 187; **Retro. Supp. II:** 95, 196, 285; **Supp. I Part 2:** 646;

Supp. III Part 1: 104, 105; **Supp. V:** 277; **Supp. VIII:** 101, 105
"Dos Passos: Poet Against the World" (Cowley), **Supp. II Part 1:** 143, 145
Dostoyevsky, Fyodor, **I:** 53, 103, 211, 468; **II:** 60, 130, 275, 320, 587; **III:** 37, 61, 155, 174, 176, 188, 189, 267, 272, 283, 286, 354, 357, 358, 359, 467, 571, 572; **IV:** 1, 7, 8, 17, 21, 50, 59, 106, 110, 128, 134, 285, 289, 476, 485, 491; **Retro. Supp. II:** 20, 204, 317; **Supp. I Part 1:** 49; **Supp. I Part 2:** 445, 466; **Supp. IV Part 2:** 519, 525; **Supp. VIII:** 175; **Supp. X:** 4–5; **Supp. XI:** 161; **Supp. XII:** 322
Doty, M. R. *See* Dawson, Ruth; Doty, Mark
Doty, Mark, **Supp. IX:** 42, 300; **Supp. XI: 119–138**
Double, The (Dostoyevsky), **Supp. IX:** 105
"Double, The" (Levis), **Supp. XI:** 260, **261–263**
Double, The (Rank), **Supp. IX:** 105
Double Agent, The (Blackmur), **Supp. II Part 1:** 90, 108, 146
Double Axe, The (Jeffers), **Supp. II Part 2:** 416, 434
Doubleday, Frank, **I:** 500, 502, 515, 517; **III:** 327
Doubleday, Mrs. Frank, **I:** 500
Double Down (F. and S. Barthelme), **Supp. XI:** 27, 34, 35, 36–38
Double Dream of Spring, The (Ashbery), **Supp. III Part 1:** 11–13
Double Fold: Libraries and the Assault on Paper (Baker), **Supp. XIII:** 52, 56
Double Game (Calle), **Supp. XII:** 22
"Double Gap, The" (Auchincloss), **Supp. IV Part 1:** 33
"Double-Headed Snake of Newbury, The" (Whittier), **Supp. I Part 2:** 698
Double Image, The (Levertov), **Supp. III Part 1:** 274, 276
"Double Image, The" (Sexton), **Supp. II Part 2:** 671, 677–678
Double Indemnity (film), **Supp. IV Part 1:** 130
"Double Limbo" (Komunyakaa), **Supp. XIII:** 132
Double Man, The (Auden), **Supp. III Part 1:** 16; **Supp. X:** 118
"Double Ode" (Rukeyser), **Supp. VI:** 282–283, 286
Double Persephone (Atwood), **Supp. XIII:** 19
Doubles in Literary Psychology

(Tymms), **Supp. IX:** 105
Double Vision: American Thoughts Abroad (Knowles), **Supp. XII:** 249
"Doubt on the Great Divide" (Stafford), **Supp. XI:** 322
Dougherty, Steve, **Supp. X:** 262
Douglas, Aaron, **Supp. I Part 1:** 326
Douglas, Alfred, **Supp. X:** 151
Douglas, Ann, **Supp. XII:** 136
Douglas, Claire, **III:** 552
Douglas, George (pseudonym). *See* Brown, George Douglas
Douglas, Kirk, **Supp. XIII:** 5–6
Douglas, Lloyd, **IV:** 434
Douglas, Melvyn, **Supp. V:** 223
Douglas, Michael, **Supp. XI:** 67
Douglas, Paul, **III:** 294
Douglas, Stephen A., **III:** 577, 588–589; **Supp. I Part 2:** 456, 471
Douglas, William O., **III:** 581
Douglass, Frederick, **Supp. I Part 1:** 51, 345; **Supp. I Part 2:** 591; **Supp. II Part 1:** 157, 195, 196, 292, 378; **Supp. III Part 1: 153–174; Supp. IV Part 1:** 1, 2, 13, 15, 256; **Supp. VIII:** 202
Douglass Pilot, The (Baldwin, ed.), **Supp. I Part 1:** 49
Dove, Belle, **I:** 451
Dove, Rita, **Supp. IV Part 1: 241–258**
"Dover Beach" (Arnold), **Retro. Supp. I:** 325
Dow, Lorenzo, **IV:** 265
Dowd, Douglas, **Supp. I Part 2:** 645, 650
"Do We Understand Each Other?" (Ginsberg), **Supp. II Part 1:** 311
Dowie, William, **Supp. V:** 199
Do with Me What You Will (Oates), **Supp. II Part 2:** 506, 515–517
Dowling, Eddie, **IV:** 394
"Down at City Hall" (Didion), **Supp. IV Part 1:** 211
"Down at the Cross" (Baldwin), **Retro. Supp. II:** 1, 2, 7, 12, 13, 15; **Supp. I Part 1:** 60, 61
"Down at the Dinghy" (Salinger), **III:** 559, 563
"Down by the Station, Early in the Morning" (Ashbery), **Supp. III Part 1:** 25
Downhill Racer (film), **Supp. IX:** 253
"Down in Alabam" (Bierce), **I:** 193
Downing, Ben, **Supp. XII:** 175, 189, 190–191
Downing, Major Jack (pseudonym). *See* Smith, Seba
Down in My Heart (Stafford), **Supp. XI:** 313, 315
Down Mailer's Way (Solotaroff), **Retro. Supp. II:** 203
Down the River (Abbey), **Supp. XIII:** 12–13
"Down the River with Henry Thoreau" (Abbey), **Supp. XIII:** 12–13
Down These Mean Streets (P. Thomas), **Supp. XIII:** 264
Down the Starry River (Purdy), **Supp. VII:** 278
"Downward Path to Wisdom, The" (Porter), **III:** 442, 443, 446
"Down Where I Am" (Hughes), **Supp. I Part 1:** 344
Dowson, Ernest C., **I:** 384
Doyle, Arthur Conan, **Retro. Supp. I:** 270; **Supp. IV Part 1:** 128, 341; **Supp. IV Part 2:** 464, 469; **Supp. XI:** 63
Doyle, C. W., **I:** 199
"Dr. Bergen's Belief" (Schwartz), **Supp. II Part 2:** 650
"Dr. Jack-o'-Lantern" (Yates), **Supp. XI:** 340–341
Dr. Strangelove; or, How I Learned to Stop Worrying and Love the Bomb (film), **Supp. XI:** 293, **301–305**
Drabble, Margaret, **Supp. IV Part 1:** 297, 299, 305
Drabelle, Dennis, **Supp. XIII:** 13
Drach, Ivan, **Supp. III Part 1:** 268
Dracula (film), **Supp. IV Part 1:** 104
"Draft Horse, The" (Frost), **Retro. Supp. I:** 141
"Draft Lyrics for *Candide*" (Agee), **I:** 28
Draft of XVI Cantos, A (Pound), **III:** 472; **Retro. Supp. I:** 292
Draft of XXX Cantos, A (Pound), **III:** 196; **Retro. Supp. I:** 292
Drafts &Fragments (Pound), **Retro. Supp. I:** 293
Dragon Country (T. Williams), **IV:** 383
Dragon Seed (Buck), **Supp. II Part 1:** 124
Dragon's Teeth (Sinclair), **Supp. V:** 290
Drake, Benjamin, **Supp. I Part 2:** 584
Drake, Daniel, **Supp. I Part 2:** 584
Drake, Sir Francis, **Supp. I Part 2:** 497
Drake, St. Clair, **IV:** 475
Dramatic Duologues (Masters), **Supp. I Part 2:** 461
"Draught" (Cowley), **Supp. II Part 1:** 141, 142
Drayton, Michael, **IV:** 135; **Retro. Supp. II:** 76
"Dreadful Has Already Happened, The" (Strand), **Supp. IV Part 2:** 627
"Dream, A" (Ginsberg), **Supp. II Part 1:** 312
"Dream, A" (Tate), **IV:** 129
"Dream, The" (Hayden), **Supp. II Part 1:** 368, 377
Dream at the End of the World, The: Paul Bowles and the Literary Renegades in Tangier (Green), **Supp. IV Part 1:** 95
"Dream Avenue" (Simic), **Supp. VIII:** 282
"Dream Boogie" (Hughes), **Retro. Supp. I:** 208; **Supp. I Part 1:** 339–340
"Dreambook Bestiary" (Komunyakaa), **Supp. XIII:** 120
Dreamer (Johnson), **Supp. VI:** 186, **196–199**
"Dreamer in a Dead Language" (Paley), **Supp. VI:** 217
Dreaming in Cuban (García), **Supp. XI:** 178, **179–185,** 190
"Dreaming the Breasts" (Sexton), **Supp. II Part 2:** 692
"Dream Interpreted, The" (Paine), **Supp. I Part 2:** 505
Dream Keeper, The (Hughes), **Supp. I Part 1:** 328, 332, 333, 334
Dream Keeper and Other Poems, The (Hughes), **Retro. Supp. I:** 201, 202
"Dream-Land" (Poe), **Retro. Supp. II:** 274
Dream Life of Balso Snell, The (West), **IV:** 286, 287, 288–290, 291, 297; **Retro. Supp. II:** 339, 340, 345, 346, **348–350**
Dream of a Common Language, The: Poems, 1974–1977 (Rich), **Retro. Supp. II: 287–290; Supp. I Part 2:** 551, 554, 569–576
Dream of Arcadia: American Writers and Artists in Italy (Brooks), **I:** 254
Dream of Governors, A (Simpson), **Supp. IX:** 265, **269–270**
"Dream of Italy, A" (Masters), **Supp. I Part 2:** 458
"Dream of Mourning, The" (Glück), **Supp. V:** 84
"Dream of the Blacksmith's Room, A" (Bly), **Supp. IV Part 1:** 73
"Dream of the Cardboard Lover" (Haines), **Supp. XII:** 204
Dream of the Golden Mountains, The (Cowley), **Supp. II Part 1:** 139, 141, 142, 144
"Dream Pang, A" (Frost), **II:** 153
"Dreams About Clothes" (Merrill), **Supp. III Part 1:** 328–329
Dreams from Bunker Hill (Fante), **Supp. XI:** 160, 166, **172–173**

"Dreams of Adulthood" (Ashbery), **Supp. III Part 1:** 26
"Dreams of Math" (Kenyon), **Supp. VII:** 160–161
"Dreams of the Animals" (Atwood), **Supp. XIII:** 33
"Dream Variations" (Hughes), **Retro. Supp. I:** 198; **Supp. I Part 1:** 323
"Dream Vision" (Olsen), **Supp. XIII:** 295–296
Dream Work (Oliver), **Supp. VII:** 234–235, 236–238, 240
Dred: A Tale of the Great Dismal Swamp (Stowe), **Supp. I Part 2:** 592
Dreiser, Theodore, **I:** 59, 97, 109, 116, 355, 374, 375, 475, 482, **497–520;** **II:** 26, 27, 29, 34, 38, 44, 74, 89, 93, 180, 276, 283, 428, 444, 451, 456–457, 467–468; **III:** 40, 103, 106, 251, 314, 319, 327, 335, 453, 576, 582; **IV:** 29, 35, 40, 135, 236, 237, 475, 482, 484; **Retro. Supp. I:** 325, 376; **Retro. Supp. II: 93–110,** 114, 340; **Supp. I Part 1:** 320; **Supp. I Part 2:** 461, 468; **Supp. III Part 2:** 412; **Supp. IV Part 1:** 31, 236, 350; **Supp. IV Part 2:** 689; **Supp. V:** 113, 120; **Supp. VIII:** 98, 101, 102; **Supp. IX:** 1, 14, 15, 308; **Supp. XI:** 207
"Drenched in Light" (Hurston), **Supp. VI:** 150–151
Dresser, Paul, **Retro. Supp. II:** 94, 103
Dress Gray (Truscott), **Supp. IV Part 2:** 683
Dress Gray (teleplay), **Supp. IV Part 2:** 683
"Dressing for Dinner" (Ríos), **Supp. IV Part 2:** 548
Dressing Up for the Carnival (Shields), **Supp. VII:** 328
Drew, Bettina, **Supp. IX:** 2, 4
Drew, Elizabeth, **Retro. Supp. II:** 242, 243
Dreyfus, Alfred, **Supp. I Part 2:** 446
Drift and Mastery (Lippmann), **I:** 222–223
"Drinker, The" (Lowell), **II:** 535, 550
"Drinking from a Helmet" (Dickey), **Supp. IV Part 1:** 180
Drinking Gourd, The (Hansberry), **Supp. IV Part 1:** 359, 365–367, 374
Drinks before Dinner (Doctorow), **Supp. IV Part 1:** 231, 234–235
"Drive Home, The" (Banks), **Supp. V:** 7
"Driver" (Merrill), **Supp. III Part 1:** 331
"Driving through Minnesota during the Hanoi Bombings" (Bly), **Supp. IV Part 1:** 61
"Driving through Oregon" (Haines), **Supp. XII:** 207
"Driving toward the Lac Qui Parle River" (Bly), **Supp. IV Part 1:** 61
"Drone" (Coleman), **Supp. XI:** 85–86
"Drowned Man, The: Death between Two Rivers" (McGrath), **Supp. X:** 116
Drowning Pool, The (film), **Supp. IV Part 2:** 474
Drowning Pool, The (Macdonald), **Supp. IV Part 2:** 470, 471
Drowning Season, The (Hoffman), **Supp. X:** 82
Drowning with Others (Dickey), **Supp. IV Part 1:** 176, 178, 179
"Drowsy Day, A" (Dunbar), **Supp. II Part 1:** 198
Drugiye Berega (Nabokov), **III:** 247–250, 252
"Drug Shop, The, or Endymion in Edmonstoun" (Benét), **Supp. XI:** 43
"Drug Store" (Shapiro), **Supp. II Part 2:** 705
"Drugstore in Winter, A" (Ozick), **Supp. V:** 272
Drukman, Steven, **Supp. XIII:** 195, 197, 202
"Drum" (Hogan), **Supp. IV Part 1:** 413
"Drum, The" (Alvarez), **Supp. VII:** 7
"Drumlin Woodchuck, A" (Frost), **II:** 159–160; **Retro. Supp. I:** 138
Drummond, William, **Supp. I Part 1:** 369
Drummond de Andrade, Carlos, **Supp. IV Part 2:** 626, 629, 630
Drum-Taps (Whitman), **IV:** 346, 347, 444; **Retro. Supp. I:** 406
"Drunken Fisherman, The" (Lowell), **II:** 534, 550
"Drunken Sisters, The" (Wilder), **IV:** 374
Drunk in the Furnace, The (Merwin), **Supp. III Part 1:** 345–346
"Drunk in the Furnace, The" (Merwin), **Supp. III Part 1:** 346
Dryden, John, **II:** 111, 542, 556; **III:** 15; **IV:** 145; **Retro. Supp. I:** 56; **Supp. I Part 1:** 150; **Supp. I Part 2:** 422; **Supp. IX:** 68
Drye, Captain Frank, **Retro. Supp. II:** 115
Dry Salvages, The (Eliot), **I:** 581
"Dry Salvages, The" (Eliot), **Retro. Supp. I:** 66
"Dry September" (Faulkner), **II:** 72, 73
Dry Sun, Dry Wind (Wagoner), **Supp. IX:** 323, 324
D'Souza, Dinesh, **Supp. X:** 255
"Dual" (Goldbarth), **Supp. XII:** 188
"Dual Curriculum" (Ozick), **Supp. V:** 270
"Dualism" (Reed), **Supp. X:** 242
Duane's Depressed (McMurtry), **Supp. V:** 233
Du Bartas, Guillaume, **Supp. I Part 1:** 98, 104, 111, 118, 119
Duberman, Martin, **Supp. I Part 2:** 408, 409
"Dubin's Lives" (Malamud), **Supp. I Part 2:** 451
Dubliners (Joyce), **I:** 130, 480; **III:** 471; **Supp. VIII:** 146
Du Bois, Nina Gomer (Mrs. W. E. B. Du Bois), **Supp. II Part 1:** 158
Du Bois, Shirley Graham (Mrs. W. E. B. Du Bois), **Supp. II Part 1:** 186
Du Bois, W. E. B., **I:** 260; **Supp. I Part 1:** 5, 345; **Supp. II Part 1:** 33, 56, 61, **157–189,** 195; **Supp. IV Part 1:** 9, 164, 170, 362; **Supp. X:** 133, 134, 137, 139, 242; **Supp. XIII:** 185, 186, 233, 238, 243, 244, 247
Dubreuil, Jean, **Supp. IV Part 2:** 425
Dubus, Andre, **Supp. VII: 75–93;** **Supp. XI:** 347,**Supp. XI:** 349
Duchamp, Marcel, **IV:** 408; **Retro. Supp. I:** 416, 417, 418, 430; **Supp. IV Part 2:** 423, 424; **Supp. XII:** 124
"Duchess at Prayer, The" (Wharton), **Retro. Supp. I:** 365
Duchess of Malfi, The (Webster), **IV:** 131
Duck Soup (film), **Supp. IV Part 1:** 384
Dudley, Anne. *See* Bradstreet, Anne
Dudley, Joseph, **III:** 52
Dudley, Thomas, **III:** 52; **Supp. I Part 1:** 98, 99, 110, 116
"Duet, With Muffled Brake Drums" (Updike), **Retro. Supp. I:** 319
Duet for Cannibals (Sontag), **Supp. III Part 2:** 452, 456
Duffey, Bernard, **Supp. I Part 2:** 458, 471
Duffus, R. L., **Supp. I Part 2:** 650
Duffy, Martha, **Supp. IV Part 1:** 207
Dufy, Raoul, **I:** 115; **IV:** 80
Dugan, Alan, **Supp. XIII:** 76
Dujardin, Edouard, **I:** 53
"Duke de l'Omelette, The" (Poe), **III:** 411, 425
"Duke in His Domain, The" (Capote), **Supp. III Part 1:** 113, 126

Duke of Deception, The (G. Wolff), **Supp. II Part 1:** 97; **Supp. XI:** 246
"Duke's Child, The" (Maxwell), **Supp. VIII:** 172
"Dulham Ladies, The" (Jewett), **II:** 407, 408; **Retro. Supp. II:** 143
Duluth (Vidal), **Supp. IV Part 2:** 677, 685, 689, 691–692
Dumas, Alexandre, **III:** 386
"Dumb Oax, The" (Lewis), **Retro. Supp. I:** 170
"Dummy, The" (Sontag), **Supp. III Part 2:** 469
"Dump Ground, The" (Stegner), **Supp. IV Part 2:** 601
Dunbar, Alice Moore (Mrs. Paul Laurence Dunbar), **Supp. II Part 1:** 195, 200, 217
Dunbar, Paul Laurence, **Supp. I Part 1:** 320; **Supp. II Part 1:** 174, 191–219; **Supp. III Part 1:** 73; **Supp. IV Part 1:** 15, 165, 170; **Supp. X:** 136; **Supp. XI:** 277; **Supp. XIII:** 111
Duncan, Isadora, **I:** 483
Duncan, Robert, **Retro. Supp. II:** 49; **Supp. III Part 2:** 625, 626, 630, 631; **Supp. VIII:** 304
Dunciad, The (Pope), **I:** 204
Dunford, Judith, **Supp. VIII:** 107
Dunlap, William, **Supp. I Part 1:** 126, 130, 137, 141, 145
Dunn, Stephen, **Supp. XI: 139–158**
Dunne, Finley Peter, **II:** 432
Dunne, John Gregory, **Supp. IV Part 1:** 197, 198, 201, 203, 207
"Dunnet Shepherdess, A" (Jewett), **II:** 392–393; **Retro. Supp. II:** 139
Dunning, William Archibald, **Supp. II Part 1:** 170
Dunnock, Mildred, **III:** 153
Dunster, Henry, **Supp. I Part 2:** 485
"Duo Tried Killing Man with Bacon" (Goldbarth), **Supp. XII:** 176
Dupee, F. W., **I:** 254; **II:** 548; **Supp. VIII:** 231; **Supp. IX:** 93, 96
DuPlessis, Rachel Blau, **Supp. IV Part 2:** 421, 426, 432
Duplicate Keys (Smiley), **Supp. VI:** 292, **294–296**
Durable Fire, A (Sarton), **Supp. VIII:** 260
Durand, Asher, B., **Supp. I Part 1:** 156, 157
Durand, Régis, **Supp. IV Part 1:** 44
"Durango Suite" (Gunn Allen), **Supp. IV Part 1:** 326
"Durations" (Matthews), **Supp. IX:** 152–153, 154

Dürer, Albrecht, **III:** 212; **Supp. XII:** 44
"During Fever" (Lowell), **II:** 547
Durkheim, Émile, **I:** 227; **Retro. Supp. I:** 55, 57; **Supp. I Part 2:** 637, 638
Durrell, Lawrence, **III:** 184, 190; **IV:** 430; **Supp. X:** 108, 187
Dürrenmatt, Friedrich, **Supp. IV Part 2:** 683
Duse, Eleonora, **II:** 515, 528
Dusk and Other Stories (Salter), **Supp. IX: 260–261**
Dusk of Dawn: An Essay Toward an Autobiography of a Race Concept (Du Bois), **Supp. II Part 1:** 159, 183, 186
"Dusting" (Alvarez), **Supp. VII:** 4
"Dusting" (Dove), **Supp. IV Part 1:** 247, 248
"Dust of Snow" (Frost), **II:** 154
Dust Tracks on a Road (Hurston), **Supp. IV Part 1:** 5, 11; **Supp. VI:** 149, 151, 158–159
"Dusty Braces" (Snyder), **Supp. VIII:** 302
Dutchman (Baraka), **Supp. II Part 1:** 38, 40, 42–44, 54, 55
"Dutch Nick Massacre, The" (Twain), **IV:** 195
"Dutch Picture, A" (Longfellow), **Retro. Supp. II:** 171
Dutton, Charles S., **Supp. VIII:** 332, 342
Dutton, Clarence Earl, **Supp. IV Part 2:** 598
Duvall, Robert, **Supp. V:** 227
"Duwamish" (Hugo), **Supp. VI:** 136
"Duwamish, Skagit, Hoh" (Hugo), **Supp. VI:** 136–137
"Duwamish No. 2" (Hugo), **Supp. VI:** 137
Duyckinck, Evert, **III:** 77, 81, 83, 85; **Retro. Supp. I:** 155, 247, 248; **Supp. I Part 1:** 122, 317
Duyckinck, George, **Supp. I Part 1:** 122
"Dvonya" (Simpson), **Supp. IX:** 274
Dwellings: A Spiritual History of the Living World (Hogan), **Supp. IV Part 1:** 397, 410, 415–416, 417
Dwight, Sereno E., **I:** 547
Dwight, Timothy, **Supp. I Part 1:** 124; **Supp. I Part 2:** 516, 580; **Supp. II Part 1:** 65, 69
Dworkin, Andrea, **Supp. XII:** 6
Dybbuk, A, or Between Two Worlds: Dramatic Legend in Four Acts (Kushner), **Supp. IX:** 138
Dybbuk, The (Ansky), **IV:** 6
Dyer, Geoff, **Supp. X:** 169

Dyer, R. C., **Supp. XIII:** 162
Dying Animal, The (Roth), **Retro. Supp. II:** 306
"Dying Elm, The" (Freneau), **Supp. II Part 1:** 258
"Dying Indian, The" (Freneau), **Supp. II Part 1:** 262
"Dying Man, The" (Roethke), **III:** 540, 542, 543–545
Dylan, Bob, **Supp. VIII:** 202; **Supp. XIII:** 114, 119
Dynamo (O'Neill), **III:** 396
"Dysfunctional Nation" (Karr), **Supp. XI:** 245
Dyson, A. E., **Retro. Supp. II:** 247
E. E. Cummings (Marks), **I:** 438
E. E. Cummings: A Miscellany (Cummings), **I:** 429, 441
E. E. Cummings: A Miscellany, Revised (Cummings), **I:** 429
E. L. Doctorow (Harter and Thompson), **Supp. IV Part 1:** 217
E. M. Forster (Trilling), **Supp. III Part 2:** 496, 501, 504
"Each and All" (Emerson), **II:** 19
Each in His Season (Snodgrass), **Supp. VI:** 324, 327
"Each Like a Leaf" (Swenson), **Supp. IV Part 2:** 644
Eager, Allen, **Supp. XI:** 294
"Eagle, The" (Tate), **IV:** 128
"Eagle and the Mole, The" (Wylie), **Supp. I Part 2:** 710, 711, 713, 714, 729
"Eagle Poem" (Harjo), **Supp. XII:** 224, 226
"Eagles" (Dickey), **Supp. IV Part 1:** 186
Eagle's Mile, The (Dickey), **Supp. IV Part 1:** 178, 185–186
"Eagle That Is Forgotten, The" (Lindsay), **Supp. I Part 2:** 382, 387
Eagleton, Terry, **Retro. Supp. I:** 67
Eakin, Paul John, **Supp. VIII:** 167, 168; **Supp. XIII:** 225
Eames, Roscoe, **II:** 476
"Earl Painter" (Banks), **Supp. V:** 14–15
"Early Adventures of Ralph Ringwood, The" (Irving), **II:** 314
Early Ayn Rand, The: A Selection of Her Unpublished Fiction (Rand), **Supp. IV Part 2:** 520
Early Dark (Price), **Supp. VI:** 262
Early Diary of Anaïs Nin, The, **Supp. X:** 184, 192
Early Elkin (Elkin), **Supp. VI: 42–43,** 45
"Early Evenin' Blues" (Hughes), **Retro. Supp. I:** 205
Early Lectures of Ralph Waldo Emer-

son, The (Emerson), **II:** 11
Early Lives of Melville, The (Sealts), **Retro. Supp. I:** 257
Early Martyr and Other Poems, An (W. C. Williams), **Retro. Supp. I:** 423
"Early Morning: Cape Cod" (Swenson), **Supp. IV Part 2:** 641
"Early Spring between Madison and Bellingham" (Bly), **Supp. IV Part 1:** 71
Earnhardt, Dale, **Supp. XII:** 310
Earnshaw, Doris, **Supp. IV Part 1:** 310
"Earth" (Bryant), **Supp. I Part 1:** 157, 164, 167
"Earth, The" (Sexton), **Supp. II Part 2:** 696
"Earth and Fire" (Berry), **Supp. X:** 27
"Earth Being" (Toomer), **Supp. IX:** 320
"Earthly Care a Heavenly Discipline" (Stowe), **Supp. I Part 2:** 586
"Earthly City of the Jews, The" (Kazin), **Retro. Supp. II:** 304
Earthly Possessions (Tyler), **Supp. IV Part 2:** 665–666, 671
Earth Power Coming (Ortiz, ed.), **Supp. IV Part 2:** 502
"Earth's Holocaust" (Hawthorne), **II:** 226, 231, 232, 242; **III:** 82; **Retro. Supp. I:** 152
East Coker (Eliot), **I:** 580, 581, 582, 585, 587
"East Coker" (Eliot), **Retro. Supp. I:** 66; **Supp. VIII:** 195, 196
"Easter" (Toomer), **Supp. III Part 2:** 486
"Easter, an Ode" (Lowell), **II:** 536
"Easter Morning" (Ammons), **Supp. VII:** 34
"Easter Morning" (Clampitt), **Supp. IX:** 45
"Easter Ode, An" (Dunbar), **Supp. II Part 1:** 196
Easter Parade, The (Yates), **Supp. XI:** 346, 349
"Easter Sunday: Recollection" (Gunn Allen), **Supp. IV Part 1:** 322
"Easter Wings" (Herbert), **Supp. IV Part 2:** 646
"East European Cooking" (Simic), **Supp. VIII:** 277
East Is East (Boyle), **Supp. VIII:** 1–3
Eastlake, William, **Supp. XIII:** 12
East Lynne (Wood), **Supp. I Part 1:** 35, 36; **Supp. I Part 2:** 459, 462
Eastman, Elaine Goodale, **Supp. X:** 103
Eastman, Max, **Supp. III Part 2:** 620; **Supp. X:** 131, 134, 135, 137

East of Eden (Steinbeck), **IV:** 51, 56–57, 59
"East of the Sun and West of the Moon" (Merwin), **Supp. III Part 1:** 344
Easton, Alison, **Retro. Supp. II:** 143, 144, 145
Easton, Bret Ellis, **Supp. XI:** 65
Easton, Robert, **Supp. IV Part 2:** 461, 474
East Wind (Lowell), **II:** 527
East Wind: West Wind (Buck), **Supp. II Part 1:** 114–115
Easy Rawlins mysteries, **Supp. XIII:** 236, **237–241,** 242
Easy Rider (film), **Supp. XI:** 293, **308,** 309
Eat a Bowl of Tea (Chu), **Supp. X:** 291
Eating Naked (Dobyns), **Supp. XIII: 78–79**
"Eating Poetry" (Strand), **Supp. IV Part 2:** 626
Eaton, Edith, **Supp. X:** 291
Eaton, Peggy, **Supp. I Part 2:** 461
Eaton, Winnifred, **Supp. X:** 291
"Eatonville Anthology, The" (Hurston), **Supp. VI:** 152
"Ebb and Flow, The" (Taylor), **IV:** 161
Eben Holden (Bacheller), **I:** 216
Eberhardt, Isabelle, **Supp. IV Part 1:** 92
Eberhart, Mrs., **I:** 521–522, 530
Eberhart, Richard, **I: 521–543; II:** 535–536; **III:** 527; **IV:** 416; **Retro. Supp. II:** 176, 178; **Supp. I Part 1:** 83; **Supp. XII:** 119
Eble, Kenneth E., **Supp. I Part 1:** 201
Eccentricities of a Nightingale (T. Williams), **IV:** 382, 385, 397, 398
Ecclesiastica Historia Integram Ecclesiae (Taylor), **IV:** 163
"Echo, The" (Bowles), **Supp. IV Part 1:** 84, 86, 87
Echoes inside the Labyrinth (McGrath), **Supp. X:** 127
Eckhart, Maria, **Supp. V:** 212
Eclipse (Hogan), **Supp. IV Part 1:** 397, 400, 402
Eclogues (Virgil), **Supp. VIII:** 31
"Ecologue" (Ginsberg), **Supp. II Part 1:** 326
"Ecologues of These States 1969–1971" (Ginsberg), **Supp. II Part 1:** 325
"Economics of Negro Emancipation in the United States, The" (Du Bois), **Supp. II Part 1:** 174
"Economic Theory of Women's Dress, The" (Veblen), **Supp. I Part 2:** 636
Economy of the Unlost: Reading Simo-

nides of Keos with Paul Celan (Carson), **Supp. XII:** 110–111
Ecotactics: The Sierra Club Handbook for Environmental Activists (Mitchell and Stallings, eds.), **Supp. IV Part 2:** 488
"Ecstasy" (Olds), **Supp. X:** 206
"Ecstatic" (Komunyakaa), **Supp. XIII:** 131
Edda, **Supp. X:** 114
Eddy, Mary Baker, **I:** 583; **III:** 506
Edel, Leon, **I:** 20; **II:** 338–339; **Retro. Supp. I:** 218, 224, 231
Edelberg, Cynthia, **Supp. IV Part 1:** 155
"Eden and My Generation" (Levis), **Supp. XI:** 270
Edenbaum, Robert, **Supp. IV Part 1:** 352
Eder, Richard, **Supp. XII:** 189
Edgar Huntly; or, Memoirs of a Sleep-Walker (Brown), **Supp. I Part 1:** 140–144, 145
"Edge" (Plath), **Retro. Supp. II:** 256; **Supp. I Part 2:** 527, 547
Edge, Mary E., **II:** 316
"Edge of the Great Rift, The" (Theroux), **Supp. VIII:** 325
Edge of the Sea, The (Carson), **Supp. IX:** 19, **25–31,** 32
Edgeworth, Maria, **II:** 8
Edible Woman, The (Atwood), **Supp. XIII:** 19, 20, **20–21**
"Edict by the King of Prussia, An" (Franklin), **II:** 120
Edison, Thomas A., **I:** 483; **Supp. I Part 2:** 392
Edith Wharton (Joslin), **Retro. Supp. I:** 376
Edith Wharton: A Biography (Lewis), **Retro. Supp. I:** 362
Edith Wharton: A Woman in Her Time (Auchincloss), **Retro. Supp. I:** 370
Edith Wharton: Matters of Mind and Spirit (Singley), **Retro. Supp. I:** 373
Edith Wharton: Traveller in the Land of Letters (Goodwyn), **Retro. Supp. I:** 370
Edith Wharton's Argument with America (Ammons), **Retro. Supp. I:** 364
Edith Wharton's Brave New Politics (Bauer), **Retro. Supp. I:** 381
Edith Wharton's Letters from the Underworld (Waid), **Retro. Supp. I:** 360
Editing of Emily Dickinson, The (Franklin), **Retro. Supp. I:** 41
"Editor and the Schoolma'am, The"

(Frederic), **II:** 130
"Editor's Easy Chair" (Howells), **II:** 276
"Editor's Study, The" (Howells), **II:** 275, 276, 285
"Editor Whedon" (Masters), **Supp. I Part 2:** 463
Edlin, Mari, **Supp. X:** 266
Edman, Irwin, **III:** 605
Edmundson, Mark, **Retro. Supp. II:** 262
Edsel (Shapiro), **Supp. II Part 2:** 703, 704, 717–719
Edson, Russell, **Supp. VIII:** 279
"Educated American Woman, An" (Cheever), **Supp. I Part 1:** 194
"Education, An" (Ozick), **Supp. V:** 267
Education and Living (Bourne), **I:** 252
"Education of a Storyteller, The" (Bambara), **Supp. XI:** 20
Education of Black People, The (Du Bois), **Supp. II Part 1:** 186
Education of Harriet Hatfield, The (Sarton), **Supp. VIII:** 257–258
Education of Henry Adams, The (Adams), **I:** 1, 5, 6, 11, 14, 15–18, 19, 20–21, 111; **II:** 276; **III:** 504; **Retro. Supp. I:** 53, 59; **Supp. IX:** 19
"Education of Mingo, The" (Johnson), **Supp. VI:** 193, 194
"Education of Norman Podhoretz, The" (Goldberg), **Supp. VIII:** 238
Education of Oscar Fairfax, The (Auchincloss), **Supp. IV Part 1:** 25, 36
"Education of the Poet" (Glück), **Supp. V:** 78, 80
Education sentimentale (Flaubert), **III:** 315
Edwards, Eli. *See* McKay, Claude
Edwards, Esther, **I:** 545
Edwards, John, **I:** 478
Edwards, Jonathan, **I:** 544–566; **II:** 432; **Retro. Supp. II:** 187; **Supp. I Part 1:** 301, 302; **Supp. I Part 2:** 552, 594, 700; **Supp. IV Part 2:** 430; **Supp. VIII:** 205
Edwards, Sarah, **I:** 545
Edwards, Timothy, **I:** 545
Edwards-Yearwood, Grace, **Supp. VIII:** 81
"Edwin Arlington Robinson" (Cowley), **Supp. II Part 1:** 144
Edwin Arlington Robinson (Winters), **Supp. II Part 2:** 812
Edwin Booth (play), **Supp. IV Part 1:** 89
"Effects of Analogy" (Stevens), **Retro. Supp. I:** 297

"Effort at Speech between Two People" (Rukeyser), **Supp. VI:** 276, 284
"Efforts of Affection" (Moore), **III:** 214
"Efforts of Affection: A Memoir of Marianne Moore" (Bishop), **Retro. Supp. II:** 52
"Egg, The" (Anderson), **I:** 113, 114
"Egg, The" (Snyder), **Supp. VIII:** 302
"Eggplant Epithalamion, The" (Jong), **Supp. V:** 119
"Eggs" (Olds), **Supp. X:** 206
"Eggshell" (Stern), **Supp. IX:** 299
Egoist, The (Meredith), **II:** 186
Egorova, Lubov, **Supp. IX:** 58
"Egotism, or the Bosom Sergent" (Hawthorne), **II:** 227, 239
"Egyptian Pulled Glass Bottle in the Shape of a Fish, An" (Moore), **III:** 195, 213
Ehrenpreis, Irvin, **Supp. XII:** 128
Eichmann, Adolf, **Supp. XII:** 166
Eichmann in Jerusalem (Arendt), **Retro. Supp. II:** 28; **Supp. VIII:** 243; **Supp. XII:** 166
"Eichmann in New York: The New York Intellectuals and the Hannah Arendt Controversy" (Rabinbach), **Supp. XII:** 166
"Eidolon" (Warren), **IV:** 239
Eight Cousins (Alcott), **Supp. I Part 1:** 29, 38, 42, 43
18 Poems from the Quechua (Strand, trans.), **Supp. IV Part 2:** 630
1876: A Novel (Vidal), **Supp. IV Part 2:** 677, 684, 688, 689, 691, 692
"18 West 11th Street" (Merrill), **Supp. III Part 1:** 323, 328
"Eighth Air Force" (Jarrell), **II:** 373–374, 377
Eight Harvard Poets, **I:** 429, 475
"Eighth Ditch, The" (Baraka), **Supp. II Part 1:** 40
"'80s Pastoral: Frederick Barthelme's *Moon Deluxe* Ten Years On" (Peters), **Supp. XI:** 39
Eight Men (Wright), **IV:** 478, 488, 494
80 Flowers (Zukofsky), **Supp. III Part 2:** 631
Eikon Basilike, The, **Supp. IV Part 2:** 435
Eileen (Masters), **Supp. I Part 2:** 460
Eimi (Cummings), **I:** 429, 433, 434, 439–440
"Einstein" (MacLeish), **III:** 5, 8, 10–11, 18–19
Einstein, Albert, **I:** 493; **III:** 8, 10, 21, 161; **IV:** 69, 375, 410, 411, 421; **Retro. Supp. I:** 63; **Supp. I Part 2:** 609, 643; **Supp. III Part 2:** 621;

Supp. V: 290; **Supp. XII:** 45
Eiseley, Loren, **III:** 227–228
Eisenhower, Dwight D., **I:** 136, 376; **II:** 548; **III:** 215; **IV:** 75; **Supp. I Part 1:** 291; **Supp. III Part 2:** 624; **Supp. V:** 45
Eisenstein, Sergei, **I:** 481
Eisinger, Chester E., **I:** 302; **II:** 604; **Supp. IX:** 15
Eisner, Douglas, **Supp. X:** 155
Elam, Angela, **Supp. XI:** 290
El Bernardo (Balbuena), **Supp. V:** 11
Elbert, Sarah, **Supp. I Part 1:** 34, 41
Elder, Donald, **II:** 417, 426, 435, 437
Elder, John, **Supp. IX:** 25
Elder, Lonne, III, **Supp. IV Part 1:** 362
Elder, Richard, **Supp. XII:** 172
"Elder Sister, The" (Olds), **Supp. X:** 205–206
Elder Statesman, The (Eliot), **I:** 572, 573, 583; **Retro. Supp. I:** 53, 65
Eldredge, Kay, **Supp. IX:** 254, 259
Eldridge, Florence, **III:** 154, 403; **IV:** 357
Eleanor of Aquitaine, **III:** 470
Eleanor of Guienne, **I:** 14
"Elect, The" (Taylor), **Supp. V:** 323
"Elections, Nicaragua, 1984" (Kingsolver), **Supp. VII:** 208
Elective Affinities (Goethe; Bogan and Mayer, trans.), **Supp. III Part 1:** 63
Electra (Euripides), **III:** 398
Electra (Sophocles), **III:** 398; **IV:** 370; **Supp. IX:** 102
"Electra on Azalea Path" (Plath), **Supp. I Part 2:** 538
"Electrical Storm" (Bishop), **Supp. I Part 1:** 93
"Electrical Storm" (Hayden), **Supp. II Part 1:** 370
"Electric Arrows" (Proulx), **Supp. VII:** 256
"Electricity Saviour" (Olds), **Supp. X:** 215
Electric Kool-Aid Acid Test, The (Wolfe), **Supp. III Part 2:** 575–577, 582–584; **Supp. XI:** 239
Electric Lady, The (film), **Supp. XI:** 309
Elegant Extracts (Knox), **II:** 8
Elegiac Feelings American (Corso), **Supp. XII:** 131–134
Elegies (Rukeyser), **Supp. VI:** 273
"Elegies" (Rukeyser), **Supp. VI:** 272
"Elegies for Paradise Valley" (Hayden), **Supp. II Part 1:** 363
Elegy (Levis), **Supp. XI:** 257, 259, 261, **271–272**

"Elegy" (Merwin), **Supp. III Part 1:** 351
"Elegy" (Stafford), **Supp. XI:** 322
"Elegy" (Tate), **IV:** 128
"Elegy, for the U.S.N. Dirigible, Macon, An" (Winters), **Supp. II Part 2:** 810
"Elegy Ending in the Sound of a Skipping Rope" (Levis), **Supp. XI:** 271–272
"Elegy for D. H. Lawrence, An" (W. C. Williams), **Retro. Supp. I:** 421
"Elegy for My Father" (Strand), **Supp. IV Part 2:** 628
"Elegy for My Mother" (Wagoner), **Supp. IX:** 330
Elegy for September, An (Nichols), **Supp. XIII:** 268
"Elegy for Thelonious" (Komunyakaa), **Supp. XIII:** 118
"Elegy for the U.S.N. Dirigible, Macon, A" (Winters), **Supp. II Part 2:** 810
"Elegy of Last Resort" (Nemerov), **III:** 271
"Elegy with a Thimbleful of Water in the Cage" (Levis), **Supp. XI:** 272
Elegy Written in a Country Churchyard (Gray), **I:** 68
"Elementary Scene, The" (Jarrell), **II:** 387, 388, 389
"Elements" (Frank), **Supp. X:** 213
Elements of Style, The (Strunk), **Supp. I Part 2:** 670
"Elenita, Cards, Palm, Water" (Cisneros), **Supp. VII:** 64
"Eleonora" (Poe), **III:** 412
Eleothriambos (Lee), **IV:** 158
"Elephants" (Moore), **III:** 203
"Elevator, The" (Dixon), **Supp. XII:** 154
"Elevator Boy" (Hughes), **Retro. Supp. I:** 200; **Supp. I Part 1:** 326
"Eleven" (Cisneros), **Supp. VII:** 69
Eleven Essays in the European Novel (Blackmur), **Supp. II Part 1:** 91, 111
Eleven Kinds of Loneliness (Yates), **Supp. XI: 340–343,** 349
Eleven Poems on the Same Theme (Warren), **IV:** 239–241
"Eleven Times a Poem" (Corso), **Supp. XII:** 132, 133
El Greco (Doménikos Theotokópoulos), **I:** 387; **III:** 212
"El-Hajj Malik El-Shabazz" (Hayden), **Supp. II Part 1:** 379
"Eli, the Fanatic" (Roth), **Supp. III Part 2:** 407–408
Eliot, Charles W., **I:** 5; **II:** 345; **Supp. I Part 2:** 479; **Supp. IX:** 94
Eliot, Charles William, **Retro. Supp. I:** 55
Eliot, George, **I:** 375, 458, 459, 461, 467; **II:** 179, 181, 191–192, 275, 319, 324, 338, 577; **IV:** 311, 322; **Retro. Supp. I:** 218, 220, 225; **Supp. I Part 1:** 370; **Supp. I Part 2:** 559, 579; **Supp. IV Part 1:** 31, 297; **Supp. IV Part 2:** 677; **Supp. V:** 258; **Supp. IX:** 38, 43, 51; **Supp. XI:** 68; **Supp. XII:** 335
Eliot, T. S., **I:** 48, 49, 52, 59, 60, 64, 66, 68, 105, 107, 215–216, 236, 243, 256, 259, 261, 266, 384, 386, 395, 396, 399, 403, 430, 433, 441, 446, 475, 478, 479, 482, 521, 522, 527, **567–591; II:** 65, 96, 158, 168, 316, 371, 376, 386, 529, 530, 532, 537, 542, 545; **III:** 1, 4, 5, 6, 7–8, 9, 10, 11, 14, 17, 20, 21, 23, 26, 34, 174, 194, 195–196, 205–206, 220, 236, 239, 269, 270–271, 277–278, 301, 409, 428, 435, 436, 453, 456–457, 459–460, 461–462, 464, 466, 471, 476, 478, 485, 488, 492, 493, 498, 504, 509, 511, 517, 524, 527, 539, 572, 575, 586, 591, 594, 600, 613; **IV:** 27, 74, 82, 83, 95, 122, 123, 127, 129, 134, 138, 140, 141, 191, 201, 237, 331, 379, 402, 403, 418, 419, 420, 430, 431, 439, 442, 491; **Retro. Supp. I: 51–71,** 74, 80, 89, 91, 171, 198, 210, 283, 289, 290, 292, 296, 298, 299, 311, 324, 359, 411, 413, 414, 416, 417, 420, 428; **Retro. Supp. II:** 79, 178, 189, 262, 292, 344; **Supp. I Part 1:** 257, 264, 268, 270, 274, 299; **Supp. I Part 2:** 387, 423, 455, 536, 554, 624, 659, 721; **Supp. II Part 1:** 1, 4, 8, 20, 30, 91, 98, 103, 136, 314; **Supp. III Part 1:** 9, 10, 26, 31, 37, 41, 43, 44, 48, 62–64, 73, 91, 99–100, 105–106, 273; **Supp. III Part 2:** 541, 611, 612, 617, 624; **Supp. IV Part 1:** 40, 47, 284, 380, 404; **Supp. IV Part 2:** 436; **Supp. V:** 79, 97, 101, 338, 343, 344; **Supp. VIII:** 19, 21, 93, 102, 105, 182, 195, 205, 290, 292; **Supp. IX:** 158–159, 229; **Supp. X:** 59, 115, 119, 124, 187, 324; **Supp. XI:** 242; **Supp. XII:** 45, 159, 198, 308; **Supp. XIII:** 77, 104, 115, 332, 341–342, 344, 346
Eliot's Early Years (Gordon), **Retro. Supp. I:** 55
"Elizabeth" (Longfellow), **I:** 502
Elizabeth Appleton (O'Hara), **III:** 362, 364, 375–377

"Elizabeth Bishop (1911–1979)" (Merrill), **Retro. Supp. II:** 53
"Elizabeth Bishop in Brazil" (Brown), **Supp. I Part 1:** 96
"Elizabeth Bishop's *North & South*" (Lowell), **Retro. Supp. II:** 40–41
"Elizabeth Gone" (Sexton), **Supp. II Part 2:** 674, 681
Elk Heads on the Wall (Ríos), **Supp. IV Part 2:** 540
Elkin, Stanley, **Supp. VI: 41–59**
"Elk Song" (Hogan), **Supp. IV Part 1:** 406
Ella in Bloom (Hearon), **Supp. VIII: 70–71**
Elledge, Jim, **Supp. XIII:** 88
Ellen Foster: A Novel (Gibbons), **Supp. X:** 41, **42–44,** 46, 47, 49, 50
Ellen Rogers (Farrell), **II:** 42–43
Eller, Ernest, **Supp. I Part 2:** 497
Ellerman, Winifred, **Supp. I Part 1:** 258–259. *See also* McAlmon, Mrs. Robert (Winifred Ellerman)
"*El libro de la sexualidad*" (Simic), **Supp. VIII:** 283
Ellington, Duke, **Retro. Supp. II:** 115; **Supp. IV Part 1:** 360; **Supp. IX:** 164
Elliot, Charles, **Supp. V:** 161
Elliott, George B., **III:** 478
Ellis, Albert, **Supp. IV Part 2:** 527
Ellis, Bret Easton, **Supp. XII:** 81
Ellis, Brett Easton, **Supp. X:** 7
Ellis, Charles, **Supp. I Part 1:** 99
Ellis, Havelock, **II:** 276
Ellis, John Harvard, **Supp. I Part 1:** 103
Ellis, Katherine, **IV:** 114
Ellison, Harlan, **Supp. XIII:** 61
Ellison, Ralph, **IV:** 250, 493; **Retro. Supp. II:** 3, **111–130; Supp. II Part 1:** 33, **221–252; Supp. IV, Part 1:** 374; **Supp. VIII:** 105, 245; **Supp. IX:** 114, 316; **Supp. X:** 324; **Supp. XI:** 18, 92, 275; **Supp. XIII:** 186, 233, 305
Ellmann, Maud, **Supp. IV Part 1:** 302
Ellmann, Richard, **Supp. VIII:** 105
Elman, Richard, **Supp. V:** 40
"Elmer" (Faulkner), **Retro. Supp. I:** 79, 80
Elmer Gantry (Lewis), **I:** 26, 364; **II:** 447–449, 450, 455
Elmer the Great (Lardner), **II:** 427
"Elms" (Glück), **Supp. V:** 85
Eloges (Perse), **Supp. XIII:** 344
"Eloquence of Grief, An" (Crane), **I:** 411
"El Río Grande" (Mora), **Supp. XIII:** 224

"*El* Round up" (Alvarez), **Supp. VII:** 11

"El Salvador: Requiem and Invocation" (Levertov), **Supp. III Part 1:** 284

Elsasser, Henry, **I:** 226

"Elsa Wertman" (Masters), **Supp. I Part 2:** 462–463

Elsie Venner (Holmes), **Supp. I Part 1:** 243, 315–316

Éluard, Paul, **III:** 528; **Supp. IV Part 1:** 80

Elvins, Kells, **Supp. III Part 1:** 93, 101

Ely, Richard T., **Supp. I Part 1:** 5; **Supp. I Part 2:** 640, 645

"Emancipation. A Life Fable" (Chopin), **Retro. Supp. II:** 59; **Supp. I Part 1:** 207–208

"Emancipation in the British West Indies" (Emerson), **II:** 13

"Emancipation Proclamation, The" (Emerson), **II:** 13

Emanuel, James, **Supp. I Part 1:** 346

Embargo, The (Bryant), **Supp. I Part 1:** 152–153

Embarrassments (James), **Retro. Supp. I:** 229

Embezzler, The (Auchincloss), **Supp. IV Part 1:** 24, 30–31

"Emerald" (Doty), **Supp. XI:** 131

"Emerald, The" (Merrill), **Supp. III Part 1:** 328

"Emergence of Flight from Aristotle's Mud, The" (Goldbarth), **Supp. XII:** 190

"Emergency Room" (Mora), **Supp. XIII:** 218

"Emerging Voices: The Teaching of Writing" (Mora), **Supp. XIII:** 220

Emerson, Ellen, **Supp. I Part 1:** 33

Emerson, Ralph Waldo, **I:** 98, 217, 220, 222, 224, 228, 239, 246, 251, 252, 253, 257, 260, 261, 283, 386, 397, 402, 424, 433, 444, 447, 455, 458, 460–461, 463, 464, 485, 561; **II: 1–24,** 49, 92, 127–128, 169, 170, 226, 233, 237, 273–274, 275, 278, 289, 295, 301, 313, 315, 336, 338, 344, 402, 491, 503; **III:** 53, 82, 171, 174, 260, 277, 409, 424, 428, 453, 454, 507, 576–577, 606, 614; **IV:** 60, 167, 169, 170, 171, 172, 173–174, 176, 178, 183, 186, 187, 192, 201, 202, 211, 335, 338, 340, 342, 350; **Retro. Supp. I:** 34, 53, 54, 57, 62, 74–75, 76, 125, 148–149, 152–153, 159, 217, 250, 298, 392, 400, 403; **Retro. Supp. II:** 96, 113, 135, 142, 155, 207, 262; **Supp. I Part 1:** 2, 28–29, 31, 33, 188, 299, 308–309, 317, 358, 365, 366, 368; **Supp. I Part 2:** 374, 383, 393, 407, 413, 416, 420, 422, 474, 482, 580, 582, 602, 659, 679; **Supp. II Part 1:** 280, 288; **Supp. III Part 1:** 387; **Supp. IV Part 2:** 439, 597, 619; **Supp. V:** 118; **Supp. VIII:** 42, 105, 106, 108, 198, 201, 204, 205, 292; **Supp. IX:** 38, 90, 175, 176, 181; **Supp. X:** 42, 45, 121, 223; **Supp. XI:** 203; **Supp. XIII:** 141, 145, 233, 246, **Supp. XIII:** 247

"Emerson and the Essay" (Gass), **Supp. VI:** 88

"Emerson the Lecturer" (Lowell), **Supp. I Part 2:** 420, 422

Emerson-Thoreau Award, **Retro. Supp. I:** 67

Emery, Clark, **III:** 478

Emily Dickinson: Woman Poet (Bennett), **Retro. Supp. I:** 42

"Emily Dickinson and Class" (Erkkila), **Retro. Supp. I:** 42–43

Emily Dickinson Editorial Collective, **Retro. Supp. I:** 47

Eminent Victorians (Strachey), **Supp. I Part 2:** 485

"Emma and Eginhard" (Longfellow), **III:** 505

"Emma Enters a Sentence of Elizabeth Bishop's" (Gass), **Supp. VI:** 93

Emperor Jones, The (O'Neill), **II:** 278; **III:** 391, 392

Emperor of Haiti (Hughes), **Supp. I Part 1:** 339

"Emperor of Ice Cream, The" (Stevens), **IV:** 76, 80–81

"Emperors" (Dunn), **Supp. XI:** 155

"Emperor's New Clothes, The" (Anderson), **I:** 441

"Empire" (Ford), **Supp. V:** 69

Empire: A Novel (Vidal), **Supp. IV Part 2:** 677, 684, 686, 690

"Empire Builders" (MacLeish), **III:** 14

Empire Falls (Russo), **Supp. XII: 339–343**

Empire of Summer, The (Doty), **Supp. XI:** 120

Empire of the Senseless (Acker), **Supp. XII: 5, 6, 14–16**

"Empires" (Simic), **Supp. VIII:** 282

"Emporium" (Shapiro), **Supp. II Part 2:** 705

Empress of the Splendid Season (Hijuelos), **Supp. VIII: 86–89**

Empson, William, **I:** 522, 533; **II:** 536; **III:** 286, 497, 498, 499; **IV:** 136, 431; **Retro. Supp. I:** 263; **Retro. Supp. II:** 253, 292

"Empty Hills, The" (Winters), **Supp. II Part 2:** 792, 793, 796

Empty Mirror, Early Poems (Ginsberg), **Supp. II Part 1:** 308, 311, 313–314, 319, 329

"Empty Room" (Hughes), **Supp. I Part 1:** 337

"Empty Threat, An" (Frost), **II:** 159

"Encantadas, The" (Melville), **III:** 89

Enchanter, The (Nabokov), **Retro. Supp. I:** 266

"Encomium Twenty Years Later" (Tate), **I:** 381

"Encounter, The" (Pound), **III:** 466

Encounter in April (Sarton), **Supp. VIII:** 259

"Encounter in April" (Sarton), **Supp. VIII:** 259

"Encountering the Sublime" (McClatchy), **Supp. XII:** 261

"Encounter on the Seine: Black Meets Brown" (Baldwin), **Retro. Supp. II:** 2

Encounters with Chinese Writers (Dillard), **Supp. VI:** 19, 23, 31

Encounters with the Archdruid (McPhee), **Supp. III Part 1:** 292–294, 301; **Supp. X:** 30

"End, The" (Olds), **Supp. X:** 205

"Endangered Species" (Mora), **Supp. XIII:** 219–220

Endecott and the Red Cross (Lowell), **II:** 545

Endgame (Beckett), **Supp. XIII:** 196

"Endgame" (Tan), **Supp. X:** 290

"Endicott and the Red Cross" (Hawthorne), **Retro. Supp. II:** 181, 187–188

"End of Books, The" (Coover), **Supp. V:** 53

End of Education, The (Postman), **Supp. XI:** 275

"End of Season" (Warren), **IV:** 239–240

"End of Something, The" (Hemingway), **II:** 248

End of the Affair, The (Greene), **Supp. XI:** 99

End of the Age of Innocence, The (Price), **Retro. Supp. I:** 377

"End of the Line, The" (Jarrell), **III:** 527

"End of the Rainbow, The" (Jarrell), **II:** 386

End of the Road (film), **Supp. XI:** 309

End of the Road, The (Barth), **I:** 121, 122, 126–131; **Supp. XI:** 309

"End of the World, The" (MacLeish), **III:** 8

Endor (Nemerov), **III:** 269, 270, 279

"Ends" (Dixon), **Supp. XII:** 153

End to Innocence, An: Essays on Culture and Politics (Fiedler), **Supp. XIII: 98–99**

Endure: The Diaries of Charles Walter Stetson (Stetson), **Supp. XI:** 196

"Enduring Chill, The" (O'Connor), **III:** 349, 351, 357; **Retro. Supp. II:** 236

Enduring Vision of Norman Mailer, The (Leeds), **Retro. Supp. II:** 204

Endymion (Keats), **IV:** 405; **Retro. Supp. I:** 412

End Zone (DeLillo), **Supp. VI:** 2, 3, 4, 10, 11, 12

Enemies: A Love Story (Singer), **IV:** 1; **Retro. Supp. II: 328–329**

Enemy, The: Time (T. Williams), **IV:** 391

Enemy of the People, An (adapt. Miller), **III:** 154–156

"Energy Vampire" (Ginsberg), **Supp. II Part 1:** 326

"Enforcement of the Slave Trade Laws, The" (Du Bois), **Supp. II Part 1:** 161

"Engaging the Past" (Bell), **Supp. X:** 17

Engel, Bernard F., **I:** 532

Engels, Friedrich, **IV:** 429, 443–444; **Supp. I Part 1:** 13

Engineer of Moonlight (DeLillo), **Supp. VI:** 4

Engineers and the Price System, The (Veblen), **I:** 475–476; **Supp. I Part 2:** 638, 642, 648

"England" (Moore), **III:** 203, 207, 214

Engle, Paul, **III:** 542; **Retro. Supp. II:** 220, 221; **Supp. V:** 337; **Supp. XI:** 315; **Supp. XIII:** 76

English Elegy, The: Studies in the Genre from Spenser to Yeats (Sacks), **Supp. IV Part 2:** 450

English Hours (James), **II:** 337; **Retro. Supp. I:** 235

Englishmen of Letters (James), **II:** 327

English Notebooks, The (Hawthorne), **II:** 226, 227–228

English Novel, The (Lanier), **Supp. I Part 1:** 371

English Poets, The: Lessing, Rousseau (Lowell), **Supp. I Part 2:** 407

English Prosody and Modern Poetry (Shapiro), **Supp. II Part 2:** 710

English Traits (Emerson), **II:** 1, 5, 6–7, 8

"English Writers on America" (Irving), **II:** 308

Engstrand, Stuart, **Supp. I Part 1:** 51

"Enoch and the Gorilla" (O'Connor), **Retro. Supp. II:** 225

Enormous Changes at the Last Minute (Paley), **Supp. VI:** 218

"Enormous Changes at the Last Minute" (Paley), **Supp. VI:** 226, 232

"Enormous Radio, The" (Cheever), **Supp. I Part 1:** 175–177, 195

Enormous Radio and Other Stories, The (Cheever), **Supp. I Part 1:** 175–177

Enormous Room, The (Cummings), **I:** 429, 434, 440, 445, 477

"Enough for a Lifetime" (Buck), **Supp. II Part 1:** 127

Enough Rope (Parker), **Supp. IX:** 189, 192

Enquiry Concerning Political Justice (Godwin), **Supp. I Part 1:** 126, 146

Entered From the Sun (Garrett), **Supp. VII:** 105–106, 107–109

"Entering the Kingdom" (Oliver), **Supp. VII:** 234

Entertaining Strangers (Gurney), **Supp. V:** 98, 99

Entrance: Four Chicano Poets, **Supp. XIII:** 316

Entrance to Porlock, The (Buechner), **Supp. XII:** 52

Entries (Berry), **Supp. X:** 23

"Entropy" (Pynchon), **Supp. II Part 2:** 619, 621

Environmental Imagination, The (Buell), **Supp. V:** 209; **Supp. IX:** 29

"Envoys, The" (Merrill), **Supp. III Part 1:** 326

"Envy; or, Yiddish in America" (Ozick), **Supp. V:** 263, 265–266

"Eolian Harp, The" (Coleridge), **I:** 284

"Ephemera, The" (Franklin), **II:** 121

Ephesians (biblical book), **Supp. I Part 1:** 117

Epictetus, **III:** 566

"Epicurean, The" (Auchincloss), **Supp. IV Part 1:** 25

Epicurus, **I:** 59

"Epigram" (Lowell), **II:** 550

"Epilogue" (Lowell), **Retro. Supp. II:** 191

"Epimanes" (Poe), **III:** 411

"Epimetheus" (Longfellow), **II:** 494

"Epipsychidion" (Shelley), **Supp. I Part 2:** 718

Episode in Palmetto (Caldwell), **I:** 297, 307

Epistle to a Godson (Auden), **Supp. II Part 1:** 24

"Epistle to Be Left in the Earth" (MacLeish), **III:** 13

"Epistle to George William Curtis" (Lowell), **Supp. I Part 2:** 416

"Epistle to Léon-Paul Fargue" (MacLeish), **III:** 15

"Epitaph Ending in And, The" (Stafford), **Supp. XI:** 321–322

Epitaph for a Desert Anarchist (Bishop), **Supp. XIII:** 1

"Epitaph for Fire and Flower" (Plath), **Supp. I Part 2:** 537

"Epitaph for the Race of Man" (Millay), **III:** 127–128

"Epithalamium" (Auden), **Supp. II Part 1:** 15

"Epstein" (Roth), **Retro. Supp. II:** 299; **Supp. III Part 2:** 404, 406–407, 412, 422

Epstein, Jason, **Supp. VIII:** 233

Epstein, Joseph, **Supp. IV Part 2:** 692; **Supp. VIII:** 236, 238

Epstein, Leslie, **Supp. XII: 159–174**

Epstein, Philip, **Supp. XII:** 159

"Equal in Paris" (Baldwin), **Retro. Supp. II:** 3; **Supp. I Part 1:** 52

"Equilibrists, The" (Ransom), **III:** 490, 494

"Equipment for Pennies" (H. Roth), **Supp. IX:** 233

"Erat Hora" (Pound), **III:** 463; **Retro. Supp. I:** 413

Erdrich, Louise, **Supp. IV Part 1: 259–278,** 333, 404; **Supp. X:** 290

"Erectus" (Karr), **Supp. XI:** 243

"Ere Sleep Comes Down to Soothe the Weary Eyes" (Dunbar), **Supp. II Part 1:** 199, 207–208

Erikson, Erik, **I:** 58, 214, 218

Erisman, Fred, **Supp. VIII:** 126

Erkkila, Betsy, **Retro. Supp. I:** 42

"Ernest: or Parent for a Day" (Bourne), **I:** 232

Ernst, Max, **Retro. Supp. II:** 339

"Eros" (Komunyakaa), **Supp. XIII:** 130

Eros and Civilization (Marcuse), **Supp. XII:** 2

"Eros at Temple Stream" (Levertov), **Supp. III Part 1:** 278–279

Eros the Bittersweet (Carson), **Supp. XII:** 97, **98–99**

"Eros Turannos" (Robinson), **III:** 510, 512, 513–516, 517, 518

"Eroticism in Women" (Nin), **Supp. X:** 195

"Errand" (Carver), **Supp. III Part 1:** 149

Erskine, Albert, **IV:** 261; **Retro. Supp. II:** 117

Erskine, John, **I:** 223; **Supp. X:** 183

Erstein, Hap, **Supp. IV Part 2:** 589, 590

"Escape" (MacLeish), **III:** 4
Escape Artist, The (Wagoner), **Supp. IX:** 324, **334–335**
Escher, M. C., **Supp. XII:** 26
Espen, Hal, **Supp. X:** 15
Espey, John, **III:** 463, 468, 478
Essais (Renouvier), **II:** 344–345
"Essay: The Love of Old Houses" (Doty), **Supp. XI:** 136
Essay Concerning Human Understanding, An (Locke), **I:** 554; **II:** 8, 348–349
Essay on American Poetry (Brown), **Supp. I Part 1:** 156
"Essay on Aristocracy" (Paine), **Supp. I Part 2:** 515
"Essay on Friendship, An" (McClatchy), **Supp. XII:** 258–259
Essay on Man (Pope), **II:** 111; **Supp. I Part 2:** 516
Essay on Our Changing Order (Veblen), **Supp. I Part 2:** 629, 642
"Essay on Poetics" (Ammons), **Supp. VII:** 29–31
Essay on Projects (Defoe), **II:** 104
"Essay on Psychiatrists" (Pinsky), **Supp. VI:** 237, 238, 241, 242, 249, 250
Essay on Rime (Shapiro), **I:** 430; **Supp. II Part 2:** 702, 703, 708–711
"Essay on Sanity" (Dunn), **Supp. XI:** 147
"Essay on the Character of Robespierre" (Paine), **Supp. I Part 2:** 515
Essay on the Chinese Written Character (Fenollosa), **III:** 474
"Essay on What I Think About Most" (Carson), **Supp. XII: 111–112**
Essays (Emerson), **II:** 1, 7, 8, 12–13, 15, 21
Essays, Speeches, and Public Letters by William Faulkner (Meriweather, ed.), **Retro. Supp. I:** 77
Essays in Anglo-Saxon Law (Adams), **I:** 5
Essays in London (James), **II:** 336
Essays in Radical Empiricism (James), **II:** 355, 356–357
Essays on Norman Mailer (Lucid), **Retro. Supp. II:** 195
Essays on the Nature and Principles of Taste (Alison), **Supp. I Part 1:** 151
Essays to Do Good (Mather), **II:** 104; **Supp. II Part 2:** 461, 467
"Essay Toward a Point of View, An" (Brooks), **I:** 244
Essential Haiku, The (Hass), **Supp. VI:** 102
Essential Keats (Levine, ed.), **Supp. V:** 179

"Essential Oils—are wrung" (Dickinson), **I:** 471; **Retro. Supp. I:** 43, 46
"Essentials" (Toomer), **Supp. III Part 2:** 486
Essentials: A Philosophy of Life in Three Hundred Definitions and Aphorisms (Toomer), **Supp. III Part 2:** 486
Essentials: Definitions and Aphorisms (Toomer), **Supp. IX:** 320
"Essentials of Spontaneous Prose" (Kerouac), **Supp. III Part 1:** 227–228
"Estate Sale" (Nye), **Supp. XIII:** 283
Estess, Sybil, **Supp. IV Part 2:** 449, 452
Esther (Adams), **I:** 9–10, 20
"Esther" (Toomer), **Supp. IX:** 313–314
"Esthétique du Mal" (Stevens), **IV:** 79; **Retro. Supp. I:** 300, 311, 312
"Estoy-eh-muut and the Kunideeyahs (Arrowboy and the Destroyers)" (film), **Supp. IV Part 2:** 560
Estrada, Genaro, **Retro. Supp. II:** 89
Estray, The (Longfellow, ed.), **Retro. Supp. II:** 155
Esty, William, **III:** 358
"Etching, An" (Masters), **Supp. I Part 2:** 458
"Eternal Goodness, The" (Whittier), **Supp. I Part 2:** 704
"Eternity, An" (W. C. Williams), **Retro. Supp. I:** 423
"Eternity Is Now" (Roethke), **III:** 544–545
"Ethan Brand" (Hawthorne), **II:** 227
Ethan Frome (Wharton), **IV:** 316–317, 327; **Retro. Supp. I:** 372–373; **Supp. IX:** 108
Ethics (Spinoza), **IV:** 12; **Retro. Supp. II:** 318
Etulain, Richard, **Supp. IV Part 2:** 597, 601, 604, 606, 607, 608, 610, 611
Euclid, **III:** 6, 620
"Euclid Alone Has Looked on Beauty Bare" (Millay), **III:** 133
Eugene, Frank, **Supp. X:** 204
Eugene Onegin (Pushkin), **III:** 246, 263
Eugene Onegin (Pushkin; Nabokov, trans.), **Retro. Supp. I:** 266, 267, 272
Eugénie, Empress, **IV:** 309
Eugénie Grandet (Balzac), **II:** 328
"Eugénie Grandet" (Barthelme), **Supp. IV Part 1:** 47
"Eulogy for Richard Hugo (1923–

1982)" (Wagoner), **Supp. IX:** 330–331
"Eulogy on the Flapper" (Z. Fitzgerald), **Supp. IX:** 71
Eumenides (Aeschylus), **Retro. Supp. I:** 65
"E Unibus Pluram: Television and U.S. Fiction" (Wallace), **Supp. X:** 315–316
"Euphemisms" (Matthews), **Supp. IX: 167–168**
Eureka (Poe), **III:** 409, 424, 428–429
Eurekas (Goldbarth), **Supp. XII:** 181
Euripides, **I:** 325; **II:** 8, 282, 543; **III:** 22, 145, 398; **IV:** 370; **Supp. I Part 1:** 268, 269, 270; **Supp. I Part 2:** 482; **Supp. V:** 277
"Euripides and Professor Murray" (Eliot), **Supp. I Part 1:** 268
"Euripides—A Playwright" (West), **IV:** 286; **Retro. Supp. II:** 344
"Europe" (Ashbery), **Supp. III Part 1:** 7–10, 13, 18
European Discovery of America, The: The Northern Voyages (Morison), **Supp. I Part 2:** 496–497
European Discovery of America, The: The Southern Voyages (Morison), **Supp. I Part 2:** 497
Europeans, The (James), **I:** 452; **II:** 327, 328; **Retro. Supp. I:** 216, 220
"Europe! Europe!" (Ginsberg), **Supp. II Part 1:** 320, 322
Europe of Trusts, The: Selected Poems (Howe), **Supp. IV Part 2:** 420, 422, 426
Europe without Baedeker (Wilson), **IV:** 429
Eurydice in the Underworld (Acker), **Supp. XII:** 7
Eustace, Saint, **II:** 215
Eustace Chisholm and the Works (Purdy), **Supp. VII:** 273–274, 279–280
"Euthanasia" (Tate), **IV:** 122
"Evangeline" (Dixon), **Supp. XII:** 153
Evangeline (Longfellow), **II:** 489, 501–502; **Retro. Supp. II:** 155, **156–159,** 162, 164; **Supp. I Part 2:** 586
Evans, Mary Ann. *See* Eliot, George
Evans, Oliver, **Supp. IV Part 1:** 85, 91
Evans, Sandy, **Supp. XIII:** 129
Evans, Walker, **I:** 36, 38, 293; **Retro. Supp. II:** 85
"Eve" (W. C. Williams), **Retro. Supp. I:** 423
Even Cowgirls Get the Blues (Robbins), **Supp. X:** 259, 260, 261,

262–263, 264, 266, **269–271**, 272, 274, 277, 284; **Supp. XIII:** 11
"Evening" (Carver), **Supp. III Part 1:** 148
Evening (Minot), **Supp. VI:** 204–205, 208, **213–215**
"Evening at a Country Inn" (Kenyon), **Supp. VII:** 167
"Evening in a Sugar Orchard" (Frost), **Retro. Supp. I:** 133
"Evening in Nuevo Leon, An" (Caldwell), **I:** 309
"Evening in the Sanitarium" (Bogan), **Supp. III Part 1:** 61
"Evening on the Cote d'Azur" (Yates), **Supp. XI:** 349
Evening Performance, An: New and Selected Short Stories (Garrett), **Supp. VII:** 109
"Evenings at Home" (Hardwick), **Supp. III Part 1:** 195–196
"Evening's at Seven, The" (Thurber), **Supp. I Part 2:** 616
"Evening Star" (Bogan), **Supp. III Part 1:** 56
Evening Star, The (McMurtry), **Supp. V:** 230
Evening Star, The (screenplay) (McMurtry), **Supp. V:** 232
"Evening Sun" (Kenyon), **Supp. VII:** 168
"Evening Wind, The" (Bryant), **Supp. I Part 1:** 164
"Evening without Angels" (Stevens), **Retro. Supp. I:** 302
Evening with Richard Nixon, An (Vidal), **Supp. IV Part 2:** 683
"Even Sea, The" (Swenson), **Supp. IV Part 2:** 641
Even Stephen (Perelman and West), **Retro. Supp. II:** 346
"Event, An" (Wilbur), **Supp. III Part 2:** 547, 554
"Event, The" (Dove), **Supp. IV Part 1:** 242, 247–248
"Eventide" (Brooks), **Supp. III Part 1:** 73
"Eventide" (Purdy), **Supp. VII:** 270
Eve of Saint Agnes, The (Keats), **II:** 82, 531
"Eve of St. Agnes, The" (Clampitt), **Supp. IX:** 40
"Ever a Bridegroom: Reflections on the Failure of Texas Literature" (McMurtry), **Supp. V:** 225
Everett, Alexander Hill, **Supp. I Part 1:** 152
Everlasting Story of Nory, The (Baker), **Supp. XIII:** 52, **Supp. XIII: 53–55**
Evers, Medgar, **IV:** 280; **Retro. Supp. II:** 13; **Supp. I Part 1:** 52, 65

Everwine, Peter, **Supp. V:** 180; **Supp. XIII:** 312
"Everybody's Protest Novel" (Baldwin), **Retro. Supp. II:** 4; **Supp. I Part 1:** 50, 51
"Everybody's Reading Li Po' Silkscreened on a Purple T-Shirt" (Komunyakaa), **Supp. XIII:** 120
"Everybody Was Very Nice" (Benét), **Supp. XI:** 53
"Every-Day Girl, A" (Jewett), **Retro. Supp. II:** 132
"Everyday Use" (Walker), **Supp. III Part 2:** 534
"Every-Day Work" (Jewett), **Retro. Supp. II:** 132
Every Pleasure (Goldbarth), **Supp. XII:** 181
Every Soul Is a Circus (Lindsay), **Supp. I Part 2:** 384, 394, 399
"Everything Is a Human Being" (Walker), **Supp. III Part 2:** 527
Everything Is Illuminated (Foer), **Supp. XII:** 169
"Everything Stuck to Him" (Carver), **Supp. III Part 1:** 143
Everything That Rises Must Converge (O'Connor), **III:** 339, 348–349, 350–351; **Retro. Supp. II:** 235, **236–237**
"Everything That Rises Must Converge" (O'Connor), **III:** 349, 352, 357; **Retro. Supp. II:** 236
Eve's Diary (Twain), **IV:** 208–209
"Eve the Fox" (Gunn Allen), **Supp. IV Part 1:** 331
"Evidence" (Harjo), **Supp. XII:** 219
Evidence of the Senses, The (Kelley), **Supp. IV Part 2:** 529
Evidence of Things Not Seen, The (Baldwin), **Retro. Supp. II:** 15
"Evil Seekers, The" (Sexton), **Supp. II Part 2:** 696
"Evolution" (Swenson), **Supp. IV Part 2:** 639
Ewing, Jon, **Supp. X:** 253
Ewings, The (O'Hara), **III:** 383
"Examination of the Hero in a Time of War" (Stevens), **Retro. Supp. I:** 305–306, 308
"Excavation of Troy" (MacLeish), **III:** 18
Excellent Becomes the Permanent, The (Addams), **Supp. I Part 1:** 25
"Excelsior" (Longfellow), **Retro. Supp. II:** 169
"Excerpts from Swan Lake" (Cameron), **Supp. XII:** 80, **84**
"Excerpts from the Epistemology Workshops" (Rand), **Supp. IV Part 2:** 529
"Excess of Charity" (Wylie), **Supp. I Part 2:** 720
"Exchange, The" (Swenson), **Supp. IV Part 2:** 644
"Exclusive" (Olds), **Supp. X:** 206
"Excrement Poem, The" (Kumin), **Supp. IV Part 2:** 448
"Excursion" (Garrett), **Supp. VII:** 100
Excursions (Thoreau), **IV:** 188
Executioner's Song, The (Mailer), **Retro. Supp. II:** 108, 209
Ex-Friends: Falling Out with Allen Ginsberg, Lionel and Diana Trilling, Lillian Hellman, Hannah Arendt, and Norman Mailer (Podhoretz), **Supp. VIII:** 239, **242–244**
"Exhausted Bug, The" (Bly), **Supp. IV Part 1:** 73
"Exhortation" (Bogan), **Supp. III Part 1:** 58
"Exhortation" (McKay), **Supp. X:** 135
"Exile" (Gass), **Supp. VI:** 92
"Exile" (Oates), **Supp. II Part 2:** 523
Exile, The (Buck), **Supp. II Part 1:** 119, 131
"Exiles, The" (Bradbury), **Supp. IV Part 1:** 113
"Exiles, The" (Whittier), **Supp. I Part 2:** 692–693
Exiles and Fabrications (Scott), **II:** 512
Exile's Daughter, The (Spencer), **Supp. II Part 1:** 121
"Exile's Departure, The" (Whittier), **Supp. I Part 2:** 683
Exiles from Paradise: Zelda and Scott Fitzgerald (Mayfield), **Supp. IX:** 65
"Exile's Letter" (Karr), **Supp. XI:** 241
Exile's Return (Cowley), **Supp. III Part 1:** 136, 138, 140, 141, 144, 147, 148
"Exile's Return, The" (Lowell), **II:** 539; **Retro. Supp. II:** 187
"Existences" (Stafford), **Supp. XI:** 324
Exit to Eden (Rampling), **Supp. VII:** 301–302
Exodus (biblical book), **IV:** 300
Exodus (Uris), **Supp. IV Part 1:** 379
"Exorcism" (Snodgrass), **Supp. VI:** 314
"Exorcism, An" (Malamud), **Supp. I Part 2:** 435
Exorcist, The (film), **Supp. I Part 1:** 66
"Expanses" (Dickey), **Supp. IV Part 1:** 186
"Ex Parte" (Lardner), **II:** 432

"Expectant Father Compares His Wife to a Rabbit, An" (White), **Supp. I Part 2:** 678
"Expedition to the Pole, An" (Dillard), **Supp. VI:** 32, 34
"Expelled" (Cheever), **Supp. I Part 1:** 174, 186
Expense of Greatness, The (Blackmur), **Supp. II Part 1:** 90, 107
Expense of Vision, The (Holland), **Retro. Supp. I:** 216
"Expensive Gifts" (S. Miller), **Supp. XII:** 294
"Expensive Moment, The" (Paley), **Supp. VI:** 222, **227–228**, 230
Expensive People (Oates), **Supp. II Part 2:** 509, 510–511
"Experience and Fiction" (Jackson), **Supp. IX:** 121
"Experience and the Objects of Knowledge in the Philosophy of F. H. Bradley" (Eliot), **I:** 572; **Retro. Supp. I:** 59
Experience of Literature, The (Trilling), **Supp. III Part 2:** 493
"Experiences and Principles of an Historian" (Morison), **Supp. I Part 2:** 492
Experimental Death Unit # 1 (Baraka), **Supp. II Part 1:** 46
"Experimental Life, The" (Bourne), **I:** 217, 220
"Experiment in Misery, An" (S. Crane), **I:** 411; **Retro. Supp. II:** 97
Experiments and Observations on Electricity (Franklin), **II:** 102, 114–115
"Expiation" (Wharton), **Retro. Supp. I:** 367
"Explaining Evil" (Gordon), **Supp. IV Part 1:** 310
"Explanation" (Stevens), **IV:** 79
Explanation of America, An (Pinsky), **Supp. VI:** 237, **241–243**
"Exploit" (Wharton), **IV:** 324
"Exploration in the Great Tuolumne Cañon" (Muir), **Supp. IX:** 181
"Explorer, The" (Brooks), **Supp. III Part 1:** 79–80
"Exploring the Magalloway" (Parkman), **Supp. II Part 2:** 591
Expositor's Bible, The (G. A. Smith), **III:** 199
Expressions of Sea Level (Ammons), **Supp. VII:** 24, 28, 36
Extract from Captain Stormfeld's Visit to Heaven (Twain), **IV:** 209–210
Extracts from Adam's Diary (Twain), **IV:** 208–209
"Exulting, The" (Roethke), **III:** 544

"Eye, The" (Bowles), **Supp. IV Part 1:** 93
Eye, The (Nabokov), **III:** 251
Eye-Beaters, Blood, Victory, Madness, Buckhead and Mercy, The (Dickey), **Supp. IV Part 1:** 178, 182–183
"Eye for an Eye, An" (Humphrey), **Supp. IX:** 108
"Eye in the Rock, The" (Haines), **Supp. XII:** 208, 209
"Eye-Mote, The" (Plath), **Retro. Supp. II:** 246, 247
"Eye of Paris, The" (H. Miller), **III:** 183–184
Eye of the Poet, The: Six Views of the Art and Craft of Poetry (Citino, ed.), **Supp. XIII:** 115
"Eye of the Rock, The" (Haines), **Supp. XII:** 208
"Eye of the Story, The" (Porter), **IV:** 279
Eye of the Story, The: Selected Essays and Reviews (Welty), **Retro. Supp. I:** 339, 342, 344, 345, 346, 351, 354, 355, 356
"Eyes, The" (Wharton), **IV:** 315
"Eyes like They Say the Devil Has" (Ríos), **Supp. IV Part 2:** 543, 544
Eyes of the Dragon, The (King), **Supp. V:** 139, 152
Eyes of the Heart: A Memoir of the Lost and Found (Buechner), **Supp. XII:** 53
"Eyes of Zapata" (Cisneros), **Supp. VII:** 70
"Eyes to See" (Cozzens), **I:** 374
Eye-to-Eye (Nye), **Supp. XIII:** 274
Eysturoy, Annie O., **Supp. IV Part 1:** 321, 322, 323, 328
Ezekiel (biblical book), **II:** 541
Ezekiel, Mordecai, **Supp. I Part 2:** 645
"Ezra Pound: His Cantos" (Zukofsky), **Supp. III Part 2:** 612, 619, 622
Ezra Pound's Mauberley (Espey), **III:** 463
"Ezra Pound's Very Useful Labors" (Schwartz), **Supp. II Part 2:** 644
"F. S. F., 1896–1996, R.I.P." (Doctorow), **Retro. Supp. I:** 97
F. Scott Fitzgerald: A Critical Portrait (Piper), **Supp. IX:** 65
Faas, Ekbert, **Supp. VIII:** 292
"Fabbri Tape, The" (Auchincloss), **Supp. IV Part 1:** 21–22
Faber, Geoffrey, **Retro. Supp. I:** 63
"Fable" (Merwin), **Supp. III Part 1:** 343
"Fable" (Wylie), **Supp. I Part 2:** 714
Fable, A (Faulkner), **II:** 55, 73; **Retro. Supp. I:** 74
"Fable, A" (Glück), **Supp. V:** 86
"Fable, The" (Winters), **Supp. II Part 2:** 792, 793, 796
Fable for Critics, A (Lowell), **Supp. I Part 2:** 406, 407–408, 409, 412–413, 416, 420, 422
"Fable of the War, A" (Nemerov), **III:** 272
Fables (Gay), **II:** 111
Fables and Distances: New and Selected Essays (Haines), **Supp. XII:** 197, 199, 207–208, 211
Fables for Our Time (Thurber), **Supp. I Part 2:** 610
Fables of Identity: Studies in Poetic Mythology (Frye), **Supp. X:** 80
Fables of La Fontaine, The (Moore), **III:** 194, 215
"Fables of the Fallen Guy" (Rosaldo), **Supp. IV Part 2:** 544
"Fables of the Moscow Subway" (Nemerov), **III:** 271
Fabulators, The (Scholes), **Supp. V:** 40
Face against the Glass, The (Francis), **Supp. IX:** 80–81
Face of Time, The (Farrell), **II:** 28, 34, 35, 39
Faces of Jesus, The (Buechner), **Supp. XII:** 53
"Facing It" (Komunyakaa), **Supp. XIII:** 117, 124, 125
"Facing West from California's Shores" (Jeffers), **Supp. II Part 2:** 437–438
"Fact in Fiction, The" (McCarthy), **II:** 562
"Facts" (Levine), **Supp. V:** 193
"Facts" (Oliver), **Supp. VII:** 231–232
"Facts" (Snyder), **Supp. VIII:** 301
"Facts, The" (Lardner), **II:** 431
Facts, The: A Novelist's Autobiography (Roth), **Retro. Supp. II:** 298, 309; **Supp. III Part 2:** 401, 405, 417, 426
"Facts and Traditions Respecting the Existence of Indigenous Intermittent Fever in New England" (Holmes), **Supp. I Part 1:** 303
"Facts in the Case of M. Valdemar, The" (Poe), **III:** 416
Faderman, Lillian, **Retro. Supp. II:** 135; **Supp. XIII:** 313
Fadiman, Clifton, **II:** 430, 431, 443, 591–592; **Supp. IX:** 8
"Fado" (McClatchy), **Supp. XII:** 265–266
Faerie Queen, The (Spencer), **III:** 487; **IV:** 253

Faery, Rebecca Blevins, **Retro. Supp. I:** 374
Fagan, Kathy, **Supp. V:** 180
Fahrenheit 451 (Bradbury), **Supp. IV Part 1:** 101, 102, 104, 107–109, 110, 113; **Supp. XIII:** 29
"Failure of David Barry, The" (Jewett), **Retro. Supp. II:** 132
Faint Perfume (Gale), **Supp. I Part 2:** 613
Fair, Bryan K., **Supp. VIII:** 128
Fairchild, Frances. *See* Bryant, Mrs. William Cullen (Frances Fairchild)
Fairfield, Flora (pseudonym). *See* Alcott, Louisa May
Fairly Conventional Woman, A (Shields), **Supp. VII:** 312, 316, 318
"Fairly Sad Tale, A" (Parker), **Supp. IX:** 192
Fair Warning (R. O. Butler), **Supp. XII:** 62, **75–76**
Faith (Goldbarth), **Supp. XII:** 181, **182–183**
Faith and History (Niebuhr), **III:** 308
Faith and the Good Thing (Johnson), **Supp. VI:** 187, **188–190**, 191, 193, 194, 196
Faith for Living (Mumford), **Supp. II Part 2:** 479–480
Faithful Narrative of the Surprising Works of God in the Conversion of Many Hundred Souls in Northampton, and the Neighboring Towns and Villages of New-Hampshire in New-England, A (Edwards), **I:** 545, 562
"Faith Healer" (Komunyakaa), **Supp. XIII:** 117
"Faith in a Tree" (Paley), **Supp. VI:** 217–218, 224, 230
"Faith in Search of Understanding" (Updike), **Retro. Supp. I:** 327
"Faith of an Historian" (Morison), **Supp. I Part 2:** 492
Falcoff, Mark, **Supp. VIII:** 88
Falcon (Hammett), **Supp. IV Part 1:** 351
Falconer (Cheever), **Supp. I Part 1:** 176, 193–195, 196
"Falcon of Ser Federigo, The" (Longfellow), **II:** 505
Falk, Peter, **Supp. XI:** 174
Falkner, Dean, **II:** 55
Falkner, John, **II:** 55
Falkner, Mrs. Murray C. (Maud Butler), **II:** 55
Falkner, Murray, **II:** 55
Falkner, Murray C., **II:** 55
Falkner, William C., **II:** 55
"Fall" (Francis), **Supp. IX:** 76
"Fall 1961" (Lowell), **II:** 550

"Fall in Corrales" (Wilbur), **Supp. III Part 2:** 556
Falling (Dickey), **Supp. IV Part 1:** 178, 181–182
"Falling" (Dickey), **Supp. IV Part 1:** 182
"Falling Asleep over the Aeneid" (Lowell), **II:** 542; **Retro. Supp. II:** 188
Falling in Place (Beattie), **Supp. V:** 28–29
"Falling into Holes in Our Sentences" (Bly), **Supp. IV Part 1:** 71
"Fall Journey" (Stafford), **Supp. XI:** 322
Fall of America, The: 1965–1971 (Ginsberg), **Supp. II Part 1:** 323, 325, 327
Fall of the City, The: A Verse Play for Radio (MacLeish), **III:** 20
"Fall of the House of Usher, The" (Poe), **III:** 412, 414, 415, 419; **Retro. Supp. II:** 270
Fallows, James, **Supp. VIII:** 241
Fall & Rise (Dixon), **Supp. XII:** 147–148, 148, 153, 157
"Falls, The" (Olds), **Supp. X:** 215
"Falls Fight, The" (Howe), **Supp. IV Part 2:** 431–432
Falon, Janet Ruth, **Supp. IV Part 2:** 422
"False Dawn" (Wharton), **Retro. Supp. I:** 381
"False Documents" (Doctorow), **Supp. IV Part 1:** 220, 236
"False Leads" (Komunyakaa), **Supp. XIII:** 116
Fame & Folly: Essays (Ozick), **Supp. V:** 272
"Familiar Epistle to a Friend, A" (Lowell), **Supp. I Part 2:** 416
"Family" (Wilson), **IV:** 426
"Family Affair, A" (Chopin), **Retro. Supp. II:** 71
Family Arsenal, The (Theroux), **Supp. VIII:** 322
"Family History" (Mora), **Supp. XIII:** 217
Family Life (Banks), **Supp. V:** 7
"Family Matters" (Alvarez), **Supp. VII:** 10
Family Moskat, The (Singer), **IV:** 1, 17, 20, 46; **Retro. Supp. II:** 322
"Family of Little Feet, The" (Cisneros), **Supp. VII:** 61
Family Party, A (O'Hara), **III:** 362
Family Pictures (Brooks), **Supp. III Part 1:** 69, 85, 86
Family Pictures (S. Miller), **Supp. XII:** 291, **295–297**, 299

Family Reunion, The (Eliot), **I:** 570–571, 572, 581, 584, 588; **Retro. Supp. I:** 62, 65
"Family Secrets" (Kingsolver), **Supp. VII:** 208
"Family Sideshow, The" (Karr), **Supp. XI:** 245
"Family Ties" (Mora), **Supp. XIII:** 215
"Family Tree" (Komunyakaa), **Supp. XIII:** 117–118, 126
Famous American Negroes (Hughes), **Supp. I Part 1:** 345
"Famous Gilson Bequest, The" (Bierce), **I:** 204
Famous Negro Music Makers (Hughes), **Supp. I Part 1:** 345
"Famous New York Trials" (Ellison), **Supp. II Part 1:** 230
Fanatics, The (Dunbar), **Supp. II Part 1:** 213–214
Fancher, Edwin, **Retro. Supp. II:** 202
"Fancy and Imagination" (Poe), **III:** 421
"Fancy Flights" (Beattie), **Supp. V:** 25
"Fancy's Show Box" (Hawthorne), **II:** 238
"Fancy Woman, The" (Taylor), **Supp. V:** 316–317, 319, 323
"Fang" (Goldbarth), **Supp. XII:** 190
Fanny: Being the True History of the Adventures of Fanny Hackabout-Jones (Jong), **Supp. V:** 115, 127
Fanny Hill (Cleland), **Supp. V:** 48, 127
Fan of Swords, The (al-Maghut), **Supp. XIII:** 278
Fanon, Frantz, **Retro. Supp. II:** 118; **Supp. X:** 131, 141
Fanshawe (Hawthorne), **II:** 223–224; **Retro. Supp. I:** 149, 151
"Fantasia on 'The Nut-Brown Maid'" (Ashbery), **Supp. III Part 1:** 19
"Fantasia on the Relations between Poetry and Photography" (Strand), **Supp. IV Part 2:** 631
"Fantastic Fables" (Bierce), **I:** 209
Fante, John, **Supp. XI:** **159–176**
Faraday, Michael, **I:** 480–481
"Farewell" (Emerson), **II:** 13
Farewell, My Lovely (Chandler), **Supp. IV Part 1:** 122, 125–126, 127, 128, 130
"Farewell, My Lovely!" (White), **Supp. I Part 2:** 661–663, 665
"Farewell Performance" (Merrill), **Supp. III Part 1:** 336–337
Farewell-Sermon Preached at the First Precinct in Northampton, after the People's Publick Rejection of their Minister, A (Edwards), **I:** 548, 562
"Farewell Sweet Dust" (Wylie), **Supp.**

INDEX / 423

I Part 2: 727–728
Farewell to Arms, A (Hemingway), **I:** 212, 421, 476, 477; **II:** 68–69, 248–249, 252–253, 254, 255, 262, 265; **Retro. Supp. I:** 171, 178, **180–182**, 187, 189; **Retro. Supp. II:** 108; **Supp. IV Part 1:** 380–381, 381; **Supp. VIII:** 179; **Supp. XII:** 241–242
"Farewell to Miles" (Berryman), **I:** 173
Farewell to Reform (Chamberlain), **Supp. I Part 2:** 647
"Farewell to the Middle Class" (Updike), **Retro. Supp. I:** 321
Far Field, The (Roethke), **III:** 528, 529, 539, 545, 547–548
"Far Field, The" (Roethke), **III:** 537, 540
Far-Flung (Cameron), **Supp. XII:** 81
Far from the Madding Crowd (Hardy), **II:** 291
Faris, Athénaïse Charleville, **Supp. I Part 1:** 204
Farley, Abbie, **I:** 458
Farley, Harriet, **Supp. XIII:** 140
"Farm, The" (Creeley), **Supp. IV Part 1:** 155
Farmer (Harrison), **Supp. VIII:** 39, **44–45**
"Farmers' Daughters, The" (W. C. Williams), **Retro. Supp. I:** 423
Farmers Hotel, The (O'Hara), **III:** 361
"Farmer's Sorrow, A" (Jewett), **Retro. Supp. II:** 132
"Farmer's Wife, The" (Sexton), **Supp. II Part 2:** 676
"Farm Implements and Rutabagas in a Landscape" (Ashbery), **Supp. III Part 1:** 13
Farming: A Hand Book (Berry), **Supp. X:** 31, 35
"Farm on the Great Plains, The" (Stafford), **Supp. XI:** 322
Farnol, Jeffrey, **Supp. I Part 2:** 653
Far North (Shepard), **Supp. III Part 2:** 433, 435
"Far Northern Birch, The" (Francis), **Supp. IX:** 90
Farnsworth, Elizabeth, **Supp. XI:** 139
Farrand, Max, **II:** 122
Farrar, Geraldine, **Retro. Supp. I:** 10
Farrar, John, **II:** 191; **Supp. XI:** 47
Farrell, James Francis, **II:** 25, 26
Farrell, James T., **I:** 97, 288, 475, 508, 517, 519; **II:** **25–53**, 416, 424; **III:** 28, 114, 116, 118, 119, 317, 382; **IV:** 211, 286; **Retro. Supp. II:** 196, 345; **Supp. I Part 2:** 679; **Supp. VIII:** 96, 97
Farrell, John, **II:** 26

Farrell, John C., **Supp. I Part 1:** 24
Farrell, Kevin, **II:** 26
Farrell, Mary, **II:** 25
Farrell, Mrs. James T. (Dorothy Butler), **II:** 26
Farrell, Mrs. James T. (Hortense Alden), **II:** 26, 27, 45, 48
"Far Rockaway" (Schwartz), **Supp. II Part 2:** 649
Far Side of the Dollar, The (Macdonald), **Supp. IV Part 2:** 473
Farther Off from Heaven (Humphrey), **Supp. IX:** 93, 96, 101, **103–104**, 105, 109
Far Tortuga (Matthiessen), **Supp. V:** 201, 206–207
"Fascinating Fascism" (Sontag), **Supp. III Part 2:** 465
"Fascination of Cities, The" (Hughes), **Supp. I Part 1:** 325
Fashion, Power, Guilt and the Charity of Families (Shields), **Supp. VII:** 323
Fasman, Jonathan, **Supp. V:** 253
Fast, Howard, **Supp. I Part 1:** 295
Fast, Jonathan, **Supp. V:** 115
Fast and Loose (Wharton), **Retro. Supp. I:** 361
"Fastest Runner on Sixty-first Street, The" (Farrell), **II:** 45
"Fat" (Carver), **Supp. III Part 1:** 141
Fatal Interview (Millay), **III:** 128–129, 130
"Fatality" (Bausch), **Supp. VII:** 54
Fatal Lady (film), **Supp. XIII:** 166
"Fate" (Emerson), **II:** 2–3, 4, 16
"Fate" (Mailer), **Retro. Supp. II:** 207
"Fate of Pleasure, The" (Trilling), **Supp. III Part 2:** 510
Fate of the Jury, The (Masters), **Supp. I Part 2:** 466, 468, 469
"Fat Girl, The" (Dubus), **Supp. VII:** 84, 85
"Father" (Levine), **Supp. V:** 188
"Father" (Walker), **Supp. III Part 2:** 522
"Father, The" (Carver), **Supp. III Part 1:** 137, 140
Father, The (Olds), **Supp. X:** **209–211**
"Father Abraham" (Faulkner), **Retro. Supp. I:** 81, 82
Fatheralong: A Meditation on Fathers and Sons, Race and Society (Wideman), **Supp. X:** 320, 332–333, 334, 335
"Father and Daughter" (Eberhart), **I:** 539
Father and Glorious Descendant (Lowe), **Supp. X:** 291
"Father and Son" (Eberhart), **I:** 539

Father and Son (Farrell), **II:** 34, 35, 290, 291
Father and Son (Gosse), **Supp. VIII:** 157
"Father and Son" (Hughes), **Retro. Supp. I:** 204; **Supp. I Part 1:** 329, 339
"Father and Son" (Kunitz), **Supp. III Part 1:** 262
"Father and Son" (Schwartz), **Supp. II Part 2:** 650
Father Bombo's Pilgrimage to Mecca (Freneau), **Supp. II Part 1:** 254
"Father Guzman" (Stern), **Supp. IX:** **293,** 296
"Father out Walking on the Lawn, A" (Dove), **Supp. IV Part 1:** 246
"Fathers" (Creeley), **Supp. IV Part 1:** 157–158
Fathers, The (Tate), **IV:** 120, 127, 130, 131–133, 134, 141; **Supp. X:** 52
"Fathers and Sons" (Hemingway), **II:** 249, 265–266; **Retro. Supp. I:** 175
"Father's Body, The" (Dickey), **Supp. IV Part 1:** 176
"Father's Story, A" (Dubus), **Supp. VII:** 88
"Father's Voice" (Stafford), **Supp. XI:** 322
"Fat Man, Floating" (Dunn), **Supp. XI:** 144
Faulkner: A Collection of Critical Essays (Warren), **Retro. Supp. I:** 73
Faulkner, William, **I:** 54, 97, 99, 105, 106, 115, 117, 118, 123, 190, 204–205, 211, 288, 289, 291, 292, 297, 305, 324, 374, 378, 423, 480, 517; **II:** 28, 51, **54–76**, 131, 174, 194, 217, 223, 228, 230, 259, 301, 306, 431, 458–459, 542, 594, 606; **III:** 45, 70, 108, 164, 218, 220, 222, 236–237, 244, 292, 334, 350, 382, 418, 453, 454, 482, 483; **IV:** 2, 4, 33, 49, 97, 98, 100, 101, 120, 131, 203, 207, 211, 217, 237, 257, 260, 261, 279, 280, 352, 461, 463; **Retro. Supp. I: 73–95**, 215, 339, 347, 356, 379, 382; **Retro. Supp. II:** 19, 221, 344; **Supp. I Part 1:** 196, 197, 242, 372; **Supp. I Part 2:** 450, 621; **Supp. III Part 1:** 384–385, 396; **Supp. IV Part 1:** 47, 130, 257, 342; **Supp. IV Part 2:** 434, 463, 468, 502, 677, 682; **Supp. V:** 58, 59, 138, 210, 226, 237, 261, 262, 334–336; **Supp. VIII:** 37, 39, 40, 104, 105, 108, 175, 176, 180, 181, 183, 184, 188, 189, 215; **Supp. IX:** 20, 95; **Supp. X:** 44, 228; **Supp. XI:** 92, 247; **Supp. XII:** 16, 289, 310, 313;

Supp. XIII: 100, 169
Faulkner at Nagano (Jelliffe, ed.), I: 289; II: 63, 65
Faulkner-Cowley File, The: Letters and Memories 1944–1962 (Cowley, ed.), **Retro. Supp. I:** 73, 92; **Supp. II Part 1:** 140, 141
"Faun" (Plath), **Supp. I Part 2:** 537
"Fauna" (Jeffers), **Supp. II Part 2:** 415
Fauset, Jessie, **Supp. I Part 1:** 321, 325; **Supp. IV Part 1:** 164
Faust (Goethe), **I:** 396; **II:** 489; **III:** 395; **Supp. II Part 1:** 16; **Supp. IX:** 141
Faust, Clarence H., **II:** 20
Faute de l'Abbé Mouret, La (Zola), **III:** 322
Favor Island (Merwin), **Supp. III Part 1:** 346, 347
"Favrile" (Doty), **Supp. XI:** 131
Fay, Bernard, **IV:** 41
"Fear, The" (Frost), **Retro. Supp. I:** 128
"Fear & Fame" (Levine), **Supp. V:** 192
"Fearless" (Mosley), **Supp. XIII:** 241
Fearless Jones (Mosley), **Supp. XIII: 241–242**
Fear of Fifty: A Midlife Memoir (Jong), **Supp. V:** 114, 115, 116, 131
Fear of Flying (Jong), **Supp. V:** 113, 115, 116, 119–123, 124, 129
"Feast, The" (Kinnell), **Supp. III Part 1:** 239, 250
Feast of All Saints, The (Rice), **Supp. VII:** 299–301
Feast of Snakes, A (Crews), **Supp. XI:** 102, **107–108**
"Feast of Stephen, The" (Hecht), **Supp. X:** 63–64
"Featherbed for Critics, A" (Blackmur), **Supp. II Part 1:** 93, 151
Feather Crowns (Mason), **Supp. VIII: 146–147**
"Feathers" (Carver), **Supp. III Part 1:** 145
Feathers (Van Vechten), **Supp. II Part 2:** 736, 749
"Feathers, The" (Hogan), **Supp. IV Part 1:** 416
"February" (Ellison), **Supp. II Part 1:** 229
"February: Thinking of Flowers" (Kenyon), **Supp. VII:** 171
February in Sydney (Komunyakaa), **Supp. XIII: 124–125**, 129
"February in Sydney" (Komunyakaa), **Supp. XIII:** 125
"February 14th" (Levine), **Supp. V:** 194

"Feces" (McClatchy), **Supp. XII:** 266, 267–268
Fechner, Gustav, **II:** 344, 355, 358, 359, 363
Feder, Lillian, **IV:** 136
Federal Arts Project, **Supp. III Part 2:** 618
Federigo, or, The Power of Love (Nemerov), **III:** 268, 276, 282, 283–284, 285
"Fedora" (Chopin), **Supp. I Part 1:** 220
Fedorko, Kathy A., **Retro. Supp. I:** 361, 374
"Feeling and Precision" (Moore), **III:** 206
"Feeling of Effort, The" (James), **II:** 349
"Feel Like a Bird" (Swenson), **Supp. IV Part 2:** 639
"Feel Me" (Swenson), **Supp. IV Part 2:** 647
Feeney, Mary, **Supp. IX:** 152, 154
Feinstein, Sascha, **Supp. XIII:** 125
Feldman, Charles K., **Supp. XI:** 307
Fellini, Federico, **Supp. XII:** 172
"Fellow Citizens" (Sandburg), **III:** 553
Fellows, John, **Supp. I Part 2:** 520
"Felo de Se" (Wylie), **Supp. I Part 2:** 727, 729
Felton, Sharon, **Supp. IV Part 1:** 210
"Female Author" (Plath), **Retro. Supp. II:** 243
"Female Frailty" (Freneau), **Supp. II Part 1:** 258
"Female Voice in *To Kill a Mockingbird*, The: Narrative Strategies in Film and Novel" (Shakelford), **Supp. VIII:** 129
"Feminine Landscape of Leslie Marmon Silko's *Ceremony*, The" (Gunn Allen), **Supp. IV Part 1:** 324
Feminism and the Politics of Literary Reputation: The Example of Erica Jong (Templin), **Supp. V:** 116
"Feminismo" (Robbins), **Supp. X:** 272
"Feminist Criticism in the Wilderness" (Showalter), **Supp. X:** 97
"Fence, The" (Oliver), **Supp. VII:** 232
"Fence Posts" (Snyder), **Supp. VIII:** 304
Fences (Wilson), **Supp. VIII:** 329, 330, 331, **334–337**, 350
Fenick, Elizabeth, **Retro. Supp. II:** 221
"Fenimore Cooper's Literary Offenses" (Twain), **IV:** 204–205
Fenollosa, Ernest, **III:** 458, 465, 466, 474, 475, 477; **Retro. Supp. I:** 289; **Supp. IV Part 1:** 154

Fenollosa, Mrs. Ernest, **III:** 458
Fenton, Charles, **Supp. XI:** 43
Ferdinand: Including "It Was" (Zukofsky), **Supp. III Part 2:** 630
"Fergus" (Bourne), **I:** 229
Ferguson, James, **Supp. I Part 2:** 503
Ferguson, Otis, **Supp. IX:** 7
Ferguson, William, **Supp. XII:** 189
Ferguson Affair, The (Macdonald), **Supp. IV Part 2:** 473
Fergusson, Francis, **I:** 265, 440
Ferlinghetti, Lawrence, **Supp. IV Part 1:** 90; **Supp. VIII:** 290, 292; **Supp. XII:** 121, 125; **Supp. XIII:** 275
Fermata, The (Baker), **Supp. XIII: 49–52**, 54
"Fern" (Toomer), **Supp. III Part 2:** 481; **Supp. IX:** 313
Fern, Fanny, **Retro. Supp. I:** 246; **Supp. V:** 122
Fernández, Enrique, **Supp. VIII:** 73
Fernandez, Ramon, **Retro. Supp. I:** 302, 303
"Fern-Beds in Hampshire Country" (Wilbur), **Supp. III Part 2:** 558
"Fern Hill" (D. Thomas), **IV:** 93
"Fern-Life" (Larcom), **Supp. XIII:** 143
Ferreo, Guglielmo, **Supp. I Part 2:** 481
Fessenden, Thomas Green, **II:** 300
Fessier, Michael, **Supp. XIII:** 164
"Festival Aspect, The" (Olson), **Supp. II Part 2:** 585
Fêtes galantes (Verlaine), **IV:** 79
"Fetish" (McClatchy), **Supp. XII:** 256
Fetterley, Judith, **Retro. Supp. II:** 139
"Fever" (Carver), **Supp. III Part 1:** 145
"Fever 103[00b0]" (Plath), **Supp. I Part 2:** 541
Fever: Twelve Stories (Wideman), **Supp. X:** 320
Fever Pitch (Hornby), **Supp. XII:** 286
"Few Don'ts by an Imagiste, A" (Pound), **III:** 465; **Retro. Supp. I:** 288; **Supp. I Part 1:** 261–262
"Few Words of Introduction, A" (McNally), **Supp. XIII:** 198–199
Fiamengo, Janice, **Supp. XIII:** 35
Ficke, Arthur Davison, **Supp. XIII:** 347
"Fiction" (Stafford), **Supp. XI:** 327
"Fiction: A Lens on Life" (Stegner), **Supp. IV Part 2:** 595, 596, 600
Fiction and the Figures of Life (Gass), **Supp. VI:** 85
Fiction of Joseph Heller, The (Seed), **Supp. IV Part 1:** 391
Fiction of Paule Marshall, The

(Denniston), **Supp. XI:** 276
Fiction of the Forties (Eisinger), **I:** 302; **II:** 604
"Fiction Writer and His Country, The" (O'Connor), **III:** 342; **Retro. Supp. II:** 223, 225; **Supp. II Part 1:** 148
Fidelity (Glaspell), **Supp. III Part 1:** 177
Fiedler, Leslie A., **II:** 27; **III:** 218; **Retro. Supp. II:** 298, 342; **Supp. II Part 1:** 87; **Supp. IV Part 1:** 42, 86; **Supp. IX:** 3, 227; **Supp. X:** 80; **Supp. XIII: 93–110**
Fiedler on the Roof: Essays on Literature and Jewish Identity (Fiedler), **Supp. XIII:** 106–107
"Fie! Fie! Fi-Fi!" (Fitzgerald), **Retro. Supp. I:** 100
Field, Eugene, **Supp. II Part 1:** 197
Field, John, **IV:** 179
Field Guide, (Hass), **Supp. VI:** 97–98, **99–101,** 102, 103, 106
Field Guide to Contemporary Poetry and Poetics (Friebert and Young, eds.), **Supp. XI:** 270
"Field Guide to the Western Birds" (Stegner), **Supp. IV Part 2:** 609
Fielding, Henry, **I:** 134; **II:** 302, 304–305; **III:** 61; **Supp. I Part 2:** 421, 422, 656; **Supp. IV Part 2:** 688; **Supp. V:** 127; **Supp. IX:** 128; **Supp. XI:** 277
"Field-larks and Blackbirds" (Lanier), **Supp. I Part 1:** 355
Field of Vision, The (Morris), **III:** 226–228, 229, 232, 233, 238
"Field Report" (Corso), **Supp. XII:** 124, **136**
Fields, Annie Adams, **II:** 401, 402, 403–404, 406, 412; **IV:** 177; **Retro. Supp. II:** 134, 135, 142; **Supp. I Part 1:** 317
Fields, James T., **II:** 274, 279, 402–403; **Retro. Supp. II:** 135; **Supp. I Part 1:** 317; **Supp. XIII:** 150
Fields, Joseph, **IV:** 274
Fields, Mrs. James T. *See* Fields, Annie Adams
Fields, W. C., **II:** 427; **IV:** 335
"Fields at Dusk, The" (Salter), **Supp. IX:** 260
Fields of Wonder (Hughes), **Retro. Supp. I:** 206, 207; **Supp. I Part 1:** 333–334
Fierce Invalids Home from Hot Climates (Robbins), **Supp. X:** 267, 276–277, **282–285**
Fiery Chariot, The (Hurston), **Supp. VI:** 155–156
15 Poems (Banks), **Supp. V:** 5

"Fifteenth Farewell" (Bogan), **Supp. III Part 1:** 51, 58
"Fifth Avenue, Uptown" (Baldwin), **Supp. I Part 1:** 52
Fifth Book of Peace, The (Kingston), **Supp. V:** 173
Fifth Chinese Daughter (Wong), **Supp. X:** 291
Fifth Column, The (Hemingway), **II:** 254, 258; **Retro. Supp. I:** 184
Fifth Decad of Cantos, The (Pound), **Retro. Supp. I:** 292
"Fifth Movement: *Autobiography*" (Zukofsky), **Supp. III Part 2:** 611
Fifth Sunday (Dove), **Supp. IV Part 1:** 251, 252–253
"Fifth Sunday" (Dove), **Supp. IV Part 1:** 252
Fifty Best American Short Stories (O'Brien), **III:** 56
"Fifty Dollars" (Elkin), **Supp. VI: 43–44**
"55 Miles to the Gas Pump" (Proulx), **Supp. VII:** 264
55 Poems (Zukofsky), **Supp. III Part 2:** 611, 621
"Fifty Grand" (Hemingway), **II:** 250, 424; **Retro. Supp. I:** 177
50 Poems (Cummings), **I:** 430, 440, 442–443, 444–445, 446
"Fifty Suggestions" (Poe), **Retro. Supp. II:** 266
"52 Oswald Street" (Kinnell), **Supp. III Part 1:** 251
"Fifty Years Among the Black Folk" (Du Bois), **Supp. II Part 1:** 169
"Fifty Years of American Poetry" (Jarrell), **Retro. Supp. I:** 52
Fight, The (Mailer), **Retro. Supp. II:** 207, 208
Fight Back: For the Sake of the People, For the Sake of the Land (Ortiz), **Supp. IV Part 2:** 497, 498, 499, 503, 510–512, 514
Fight for Freedom (Hughes), **Supp. I Part 1:** 345
Fightin': New and Collected Stories (Ortiz), **Supp. IV Part 2:** 513
Fighting Angel (Buck), **Supp. II Part 1:** 119, 131
Fighting France; From Dunkerque to Belfort (Wharton), **Retro. Supp. I:** 377, 378
"Figlia che Piange, La" (Eliot), **I:** 570, 584; **III:** 9
Figliola, Samantha, **Supp. V:** 143
"Figure a Poem Makes, The" (Frost), **Retro. Supp. I:** 139
"Figured Wheel, The" (Pinsky), **Supp. VI:** 243, 244, 245, 246

Figured Wheel, The: New and Collected Poems (Pinsky), **Supp. VI:** 247–248
"Figure in the Carpet, The" (James), **Retro. Supp. I:** 228, 229
"Figure in the Doorway, The" (Frost), **Retro. Supp. I:** 138
Figures from the Double World (McGrath), **Supp. X: 118–119**
"Figures in the Clock, The" (McCarthy), **II:** 561–562
Figures of Time (Hayden), **Supp. II Part 1:** 367
"Filling Out a Blank" (Wagoner), **Supp. IX:** 324
Fillmore, Millard, **III:** 101
Film Flam: Essays on Hollywood (McMurtry), **Supp. V:** 228
Films of Ayn Rand, The (Cox), **Supp. IV Part 2:** 524
Filo, John, **Supp. XII:** 211
Filson, John, **Retro. Supp. I:** 421
Final Beast, The (Buechner), **Supp. XII: 49–51**
"Finale" (Longfellow), **II:** 505, 506–507
"Final Fear" (Hughes), **Supp. I Part 1:** 338
Final Harvest: Emily Dickinson's Poems (Johnson, ed.), **I:** 470, 471
Final Payments (Gordon), **Supp. IV Part 1:** 297, 299, 300–302, 304, 306, 314
"Final Report, A" (Maxwell), **Supp. VIII:** 169
"Final Soliloquy of the Interior Paramour" (Stevens), **Retro. Supp. I:** 312
Final Solution, The (Reitlinger), **Supp. XII:** 161
Financier, The (Dreiser), **I:** 497, 501, 507, 509; **Retro. Supp. II:** 94, 101–102, 105
Find a Victim (Macdonald), **Supp. IV Part 2:** 467, 472, 473
"Fin de Saison Palm Beach" (White), **Supp. I Part 2:** 673
Finding a Form (Gass), **Supp. VI:** 91–92, 93
Finding a Girl in America (Dubus), **Supp. VII:** 85–88
"Finding a Girl in America" (Dubus), **Supp. VII:** 87
"Finding Beads" (Hogan), **Supp. IV Part 1:** 400
"Finding of Zach, The" (Dunbar), **Supp. II Part 1:** 212
Findings and Keepings: Analects for an Autobiography (Mumford), **Supp. II Part 2:** 483

Finding the Center: Narrative Poetry of the Zuni Indians (Tedlock), **Supp. IV Part 2:** 509
Finding the Islands (Merwin), **Supp. III Part 1:** 353, 357
"Finding the Place: A Migrant Childhood" (Stegner), **Supp. IV Part 2:** 597
"Find the Woman" (Macdonald, under Millar), **Supp. IV Part 2:** 466
Fine, David, **Supp. XI:** 160
Fine Clothes to the Jew (Hughes), **Retro. Supp. I:** 200, 201, 203, 205; **Supp. I Part 1:** 326–328
"Fine Old Firm, A" (Jackson), **Supp. IX:** 120
Finer Grain, The (James), **II:** 335
Finished Man, The (Garrett), **Supp. VII:** 96, 97–98
Fink, Mike, **IV:** 266
Finley, John H., **II:** 418
Finn, David, **Supp. VIII:** 106–107
Finnegans Wake (Joyce), **III:** 7, 12, 14, 261; **IV:** 182, 369–370, 418, 421; **Supp. I Part 2:** 620; **Supp. II Part 1:** 2; **Supp. XIII:** 191
"Finnish Rhapsody" (Ashbery), **Supp. III Part 1:** 26
Firbank, Ronald, **IV:** 77, 436
"Fire" (Hughes), **Supp. I Part 1:** 327
Fire: From "A Journal of Love," the Unexpurgated Diary of Anaïs Nin, 1934–1937, **Supp. X:** 184, 185, 189, 194, 195
"Fire and Cloud" (Wright), **IV:** 488
"Fire and Ice" (Frost), **II:** 154; **Retro. Supp. I:** 133
Fire and Ice (Stegner), **Supp. IV Part 2:** 598, 607–608
"Fire and the Cloud, The" (Hurston), **Supp. VI:** 158
"Fire and the Hearth, The" (Faulkner), **II:** 71
Firebird (Doty), **Supp. XI:** 119–120, 121, **132–133**, 134
"Firebombing, The" (Dickey), **Supp. IV Part 1:** 180–181, 187, 189–190
"Fireborn Are at Home in Fire, The" (Sandburg), **III:** 591
"Fire Chaconne" (Francis), **Supp. IX:** 87
Firecrackers (Van Vechten), **Supp. II Part 2:** 740, 742–744, 749
Fireman's Wife and Other Stories, The (Bausch), **Supp. VII:** 48, 54
Fire Next Time, The (Baldwin), **Retro. Supp. II:** 5, 8, 9; **Supp. I Part 1:** 48, 49, 52, 60–61
"Fire Next Time, The" (Baldwin). *See* "Down at the Cross" (Baldwin)

"Fire of Driftwood, The" (Longfellow), **II:** 499; **Retro. Supp. II:** 159, 168
"Fire of Life" (McCullers), **II:** 585
Fire on the Mountain (Abbey), **Supp. XIII:** 6
"Fire Poem" (Merrill), **Supp. III Part 1:** 321
"Fires" (Carver), **Supp. III Part 1:** 136–139, 147
Fires: Essays, Poems, Stories (Carver), **Supp. III Part 1:** 136, 140, 142, 146–147
Fire Screen, The (Merrill), **Supp. III Part 1:** 319, 325–329
"Fire Season" (Didion), **Supp. IV Part 1:** 199
"Fire Sequence" (Winters), **Supp. II Part 2:** 791, 796, 800
Fire Sermon (Morris), **III:** 238–239
"Fire Sermon, The" (Eliot), **Retro. Supp. I:** 60–61
Fireside Travels (Lowell), **Supp. I Part 2:** 407, 419–420
Firestarter (King), **Supp. V:** 140, 141, 144; **Supp. IX:** 114
"fire the bastards" (Green), **Supp. IV Part 1:** 285
"Fire-Truck, A" (Wilbur), **Supp. III Part 2:** 556
"Fireweed" (Clampitt), **Supp. IX:** **44–45**
"Firewood" (Banks), **Supp. V:** 15
"Fireworks" (Ford), **Supp. V:** 69
"Fireworks" (Shapiro), **Supp. II Part 2:** 707
Fir-Flower Tablets (Lowell), **II:** 512, 526–527
Firkins, Oscar W., **II:** 271
"Firmament, The" (Bryant), **Supp. I Part 1:** 162
Firmat, Gustavo Pérez, **Supp. VIII:** 76, 77, 79; **Supp. XI:** 184
"First American, The" (Toomer), **Supp. III Part 2:** 480, 487
"First Birth" (Olds), **Supp. X:** 212
First Book of Africa, The (Hughes), **Supp. I Part 1:** 344–345
First Book of Jazz, The (Hughes), **Supp. I Part 1:** 345
First Book of Negroes, The (Hughes), **Supp. I Part 1:** 345
First Book of Rhythms, The (Hughes), **Supp. I Part 1:** 345
First Book of the West Indies, The (Hughes), **Supp. I Part 1:** 345
Firstborn (Glück), **Supp. V:** 80, 81, 82, 84
"Firstborn" (Wright), **Supp. V:** 340
"First Chaldaic Oracle" (Carson), **Supp. XII:** 111

"First Communion" (Fante), **Supp. XI:** 160
"First Day of School, The" (Gibbons), **Supp. X:** 41, 42
"First Death in Nova Scotia" (Bishop), **Supp. I Part 1:** 73
"First Formal" (Olds), **Supp. X:** 212
First Four Books of Poems, The (Glück), **Supp. V:** 81, 83
"First Grade" (Stafford), **Supp. XI:** 328
"First Hawaiian Bank" (Nye), **Supp. XIII:** 278
"First Heat" (Taylor), **Supp. V:** 323
"First Job, The" (Cisneros), **Supp. VII:** 62
"1st Letter on Georges" (Olson), **Supp. II Part 2:** 578
First Light (Wagoner), **Supp. IX:** 330
"First Love" (Welty), **IV:** 264; **Retro. Supp. I:** 347
First Man, The (O'Neill), **III:** 390
First Manifesto (McGrath), **Supp. X:** 115
"First Meditation" (Roethke), **III:** 545–546
"First Noni Daylight, The" (Harjo), **Supp. XII:** 219
"First Passover" (Longfellow), **II:** 500–501
"First Person Female" (Harrison), **Supp. VIII:** 40, 41, 48
"First Place, The" (Wagoner), **Supp. IX:** 328
First Poems (Buechner), **Supp. XII:** 45
First Poems (Merrill), **Supp. III Part 1:** 318–321, 323
First Poems 1946–1954 (Kinnell), **Supp. III Part 1:** 235, 238–239
"First Praise" (W. C. Williams), **Retro. Supp. I:** 413
First Principles (Spencer), **Supp. I Part 1:** 368
"First Ride and First Walk" (Goldbarth), **Supp. XII:** 182–183
"First Seven Years, The" (Malamud), **Supp. I Part 2:** 431
"First Sex" (Olds), **Supp. X:** 208
"First Snow in Alsace" (Wilbur), **Supp. III Part 2:** 545, 546, 559
"First Song" (Kinnell), **Supp. III Part 1:** 239
"First Spade in the West, The" (Fiedler), **Supp. XIII:** 103
"First Steps" (McClatchy), **Supp. XII:** 256
"First Things First" (Auden), **Supp. II Part 1:** 13
"First Thought, Best Thought"

(Ginsberg), **Supp. II Part 1:** 327
"First Time I Saw Paris, The" (Fante), **Supp. XI:** 174
"First Travels of Max" (Ransom), **III:** 490–491
"First Tycoon of Teen, The" (Wolfe), **Supp. III Part 2:** 572
"First Views of the Enemy" (Oates), **Supp. II Part 2:** 508
"First Wife, The" (Buck), **Supp. II Part 1:** 127
"First World War" (White), **Supp. I Part 2:** 665
"Fish" (F. Barthelme), **Supp. XI:** 26
"Fish" (Levis), **Supp. XI:** 259–260
Fish, Stanley, **Supp. IV Part 1:** 48
"Fish, The" (Moore), **III:** 195, 197, 209, 211, 213–214
"Fish, The" (Oliver), **Supp. VII:** 236
"Fish and Shadow" (Pound), **III:** 466
Fishburne, Laurence, **Supp. VIII:** 345
"Fish Cannery" (Fante), **Supp. XI:** 167
Fisher, Alexander Metcalf, **Supp. I Part 2:** 582
Fisher, Alfred, **Retro. Supp. II:** 243
Fisher, Craig, **Supp. V:** 125
Fisher, Dorothy Canfield, **Retro. Supp. I:** 21, 133; **Supp. II Part 1:** 117. *See also* Canfield, Dorothy
Fisher, Mary, **Supp. I Part 2:** 455
Fisher, Phillip, **Retro. Supp. I:** 39
Fisher, Rudolph, **Retro. Supp. I:** 200; **Supp. I Part 1:** 325; **Supp. X:** 139
Fisher, Vardis, **Supp. IV Part 2:** 598
Fisher King, The (Marshall), **Supp. XI:** 275–276, **288–290**
"Fisherman, The" (Merwin), **Supp. II Part 1:** 346
"Fisherman and His Wife, The" (Welty), **IV:** 266
"Fishing" (Harjo), **Supp. XII:** 227–228
"Fish in the Stone, The" (Dove), **Supp. IV Part 1:** 245, 257
"Fish in the unruffled lakes" (Auden), **Supp. II Part 1:** 8–9
"Fish R Us" (Doty), **Supp. XI:** 135
Fisk, James, **I:** 4, 474
Fiske, John, **Supp. I Part 1:** 314; **Supp. I Part 2:** 493
"Fit Against the Country, A" (Wright), **Supp. III Part 2:** 591–592, 601
Fitch, Clyde, **Supp. IV Part 2:** 573
Fitch, Elizabeth. *See* Taylor, Mrs. Edward (Elizabeth Fitch)
Fitch, James, **IV:** 147
Fitch, Noël Riley, **Supp. X:** 186, 187
Fitts, Dudley, **I:** 169, 173; **Supp. I Part 1:** 342, 345; **Supp. XIII:** 346
FitzGerald, Edward, **Supp. I Part 2:** 416; **Supp. III Part 2:** 610

Fitzgerald, Ella, **Supp. XIII:** 132
Fitzgerald, F. Scott, **I:** 107, 117, 118, 123, 188, 221, 288, 289, 358, 367, 374–375, 382, 423, 476, 482, 487, 495, 509, 511; **II: 77–100,** 257, 263, 272, 283, 415, 416, 417–418, 420, 425, 427, 430, 431, 432, 433, 434, 436, 437, 450, 458–459, 482, 560; **III:** 2, 26, 35, 36, 37, 40, 44, 45, 69, 106, 244, 284, 334, 350–351, 453, 454, 471, 551, 552, 572; **IV:** 27, 49, 97, 101, 126, 140, 191, 222, 223, 287, 297, 427, 471; **Retro. Supp. I:** 1, 74, **97–120,** 178, 180, 186, 215, 359, 381; **Retro. Supp. II:** 257, 293, 339, 344, 346; **Supp. I Part 1:** 196, 197; **Supp. I Part 2:** 622; **Supp. III Part 2:** 409, 411, 585; **Supp. IV Part 1:** 123, 197, 200, 203, 341; **Supp. IV Part 2:** 463, 468, 607, 689; **Supp. V:** 23, 95, 226, 251, 262, 276, 313; **Supp. VIII:** 101, 103, 106, 137; **Supp. IX:** 15, 20, 55, 57–63, 199; **Supp. X:** 225; **Supp. XI:** 65, 221, 334; **Supp. XII:** 42, 173, 295; **Supp. XIII:** 170, 263
Fitzgerald, Robert, **I:** 27–28; **III:** 338, 348; **Retro. Supp. II:** 179, 221, 222, 223, 228, 229; **Supp. IV Part 2:** 631
"Fitzgerald: The Romance of Money" (Cowley), **Supp. II Part 1:** 143
Fitzgerald, Zelda (Zelda Sayre), **I:** 482; **II:** 77, 79, 82–85, 88, 90–91, 93, 95; **Supp. IV Part 1:** 310; **Supp. IX: 55–73; Supp. X:** 172. *See also* Sayre, Zelda
"Fitzgerald's Tragic Sense" (Schorer), **Retro. Supp. I:** 115
Five Came Back (West), **IV:** 287
5 Detroits (Levine), **Supp. V:** 178
"Five Dollar Guy, The" (W. C. Williams), **Retro. Supp. I:** 423
Five Easy Pieces (film), **Supp. V:** 26
"Five Elephants" (Dove), **Supp. IV Part 1:** 244–245
Five Hundred Scorpions (Hearon), **Supp. VIII:** 57, 65, **66**
Five Indiscretions (Ríos), **Supp. IV Part 2:** 545–547
Five Men and Pompey (Benét), **Supp. XI:** 43, 44
Five Plays (Hughes), **Retro. Supp. I:** 197, 209
Five Temperaments (Kalstone), **Retro. Supp. II:** 40
Five Young American Poets, **I:** 170; **II:** 367
Fixer, The (Malamud), **Supp. I Part 2:**

428, 435, 445, 446–448, 450, 451
Flaccus, Kimball, **Retro. Supp. I:** 136
Flacius, Matthias, **IV:** 163
Flag for Sunrise, A (Stone), **Supp. V:** 301–304
Flag of Childhood, The: Poems from the Middle East (Nye, ed.), **Supp. XIII:** 280
"Flag of Summer" (Swenson), **Supp. IV Part 2:** 645
Flagons and Apples (Jeffers), **Supp. II Part 2:** 413, 414, 417–418
Flags in the Dust (Faulkner), **Retro. Supp. I:** 81, 82, 83, 86, 88
Flamel, Nicolas, **Supp. XII:** 178
Flaming Corsage, The (Kennedy), **Supp. VII:** 133, 153–156
Flammarion, Camille, **Supp. I Part 1:** 260
Flanagan, John T., **Supp. I Part 2:** 464, 465, 468
"Flannery O'Connor: Poet to the Outcast" (Sister Rose Alice), **III:** 348
Flappers and Philosophers (Fitzgerald), **II:** 88; **Retro. Supp. I:** 103; **Supp. IX:** 56
Flash and Filigree (Southern), **Supp. XI:** 295, **296–297**
"Flashcards" (Dove), **Supp. IV Part 1:** 250
Flatt, Lester, **Supp. V:** 335
Flaubert, Gustave, **I:** 66, 123, 130, 272, 312, 314, 315, 477, 504, 506, 513, 514; **II:** 182, 185, 194, 198–199, 205, 209, 230, 289, 311, 316, 319, 325, 337, 392, 401, 577, 594; **III:** 196, 207, 251, 315, 461, 467, 511, 564; **IV:** 4, 29, 31, 37, 40, 134, 285, 428; **Retro. Supp. I:** 5, 215, 218, 222, 225, 235, 287; **Supp. III Part 2:** 411, 412; **Supp. XI:** 334
"Flavia and Her Artists" (Cather), **Retro. Supp. I:** 5
Flavoring of New England, The (Brooks), **I:** 253, 256
Flavor of Man, The (Toomer), **Supp. III Part 2:** 487
Flaxman, Josiah, **Supp. I Part 2:** 716
"Flèche d'Or" (Merrill), **Supp. III Part 1:** 328
Flecker, James Elroy, **Supp. I Part 1:** 257
"Flee on Your Donkey" (Sexton), **Supp. II Part 2:** 683, 685
Fleming, Ian, **Supp. XI:** 307
Fleming, Rene, **Supp. XII:** 321
"Fleshbody" (Ammons), **Supp. VII:** 27
Fletcher, H. D., **II:** 517, 529
Fletcher, John, **Supp. IV Part 2:** 621

Fletcher, John Gould, **I:** 243; **II:** 517, 529; **III:** 458; **Supp. I Part 1:** 263; **Supp. I Part 2:** 422
Fletcher, Phineas, **Supp. I Part 1:** 369
Fletcher, Virginia. *See* Caldwell, Mrs. Erskine (Virginia Fletcher)
Fleurs du mal, Les (Baudelaire), **Retro. Supp. II:** 282
Fleurs du mal, Les (Beaudelaire; Millay and Dillon, trans.), **III:** 141–142
"Flight" (Updike), **IV:** 218, 222, 224; **Retro. Supp. I:** 318
"Flight, The" (Haines), **Supp. XII:** 204–205
"Flight, The" (Roethke), **III:** 537–538
Flight among the Tombs (Hecht), **Supp. X:** 58, **71–74**
"Flight for Freedom" (McCoy), **Supp. XIII:** 170
"Flight from Byzantium" (Brodsky), **Supp. VIII:** 30–31
"Flight of Besey Lane, The" (Jewett), **Retro. Supp. II:** 139
Flight of the Rocket, The (Fitzgerald), **II:** 89
Flight to Canada (Reed), **Supp. X:** 240, **249–252**
Flint, F. S., **II:** 517; **III:** 459, 464, 465; **Retro. Supp. I:** 127; **Supp. I Part 1:** 261, 262
Flivver King, The (Sinclair), **Supp. V:** 290
Floating Opera, The (Barth), **I:** 121, 122–126, 127, 129, 130, 131
"Floating Poem, Unnumbered, The" (Rich), **Supp. I Part 2:** 572–573
Flood (Matthews), **Supp. IX:** 154, **160–161**
Flood (Warren), **IV:** 252, 256–257
"Flood of Years, The" (Bryant), **Supp. I Part 1:** 159, 170, 171; **Supp. I Part 2:** 416
"Floor and the Ceiling, The" (W. J. Smith), **Supp. XIII:** 345, 346
"Floor Plans" (Komunyakaa), **Supp. XIII:** 114
"Floral Decorations for Bananas" (Stevens), **IV:** 8
Florida (Acker), **Supp. XII:** 5
"Florida" (Bishop), **Retro. Supp. II:** 43
"Florida Road Workers" (Hughes), **Retro. Supp. I:** 203
"Florida Sunday, A" (Lanier), **Supp. I Part 1:** 364, 366
"Flossie Cabanis" (Masters), **Supp. I Part 2:** 461–462
Flow Chart (Ashbery), **Supp. VIII:** 275

"Flowchart" (Ashbery), **Supp. III Part 1:** 26
Flower-de-Luce (Longfellow), **II:** 490
Flower Fables (Alcott), **Supp. I Part 1:** 33
"Flower-Fed Buffaloes, The" (Lindsay), **Supp. I Part 2:** 398
"Flower Garden" (Jackson), **Supp. IX:** 119
"Flower-gathering" (Frost), **II:** 153
Flower Herding on Mount Monadnock (Kinnell), **Supp. III Part 1:** 235, 239, 241–244
"Flower Herding on Mount Monadnock" (Kinnell), **Supp. III Part 1:** 242
"Flowering Death" (Ashbery), **Supp. III Part 1:** 22
"Flowering Dream, The" (McCullers), **II:** 591
"Flowering Judas" (Porter), **III:** 434, 435–436, 438, 441, 445, 446, 450–451
Flowering Judas and Other Stories (Porter), **III:** 433, 434
Flowering of New England, The (Brooks), **IV:** 171–172; **Supp. VIII:** 101
Flowering of the Rod (Doolittle), **Supp. I Part 1:** 272
Flowering Peach, The (Odets), **Supp. II Part 2:** 533, 547, 549–550
"Flowering Plum" (Glück), **Supp. V:** 82
"Flowers for Marjorie" (Welty), **IV:** 262
"Flowers of the Fallow" (Larcom), **Supp. XIII:** 143, 145–146
"Flowers Well if anybody" (Dickinson), **Retro. Supp. I:** 30
"Fly, The" (Kinnell), **Supp. III Part 1:** 249
"Fly, The" (Shapiro), **Supp. II Part 2:** 705
"Fly, The" (Simic), **Supp. VIII:** 278
Flye, Father James Harold, **I:** 25, 26, 35–36, 37, 42, 46; **IV:** 215
"Fly in Buttermilk, A" (Baldwin), **Retro. Supp. II:** 8
"Flying High" (Levertov), **Supp. III Part 1:** 284
"Flying Home" (Ellison), **Retro. Supp. II:** 117, **125–126**; **Supp. II Part 1:** 235, 238–239
"Flying Home" (Kinnell), **Supp. III Part 1:** 250
"Flying Home" and Other Stories (Ellison), **Retro. Supp. II:** 119, 124
"Flying Home from Utah" (Swenson), **Supp. IV Part 2:** 645

"Flying to Hanoi" (Rukeyser), **Supp. VI:** 279
Foata, Anne, **Supp. XI:** 104
Focillon, Henri, **IV:** 90
Focus (A. Miller), **III:** 150–151, 156
Foer, Jonathan Safran, **Supp. XII:** 169
Foerster, Norman, **I:** 222; **Supp. I Part 2:** 423, 424; **Supp. IV Part 2:** 598
"Fog" (Sandburg), **III:** 586
"Fog Galleon" (Komunyakaa), **Supp. XIII:** 127
"Foggy Lane, The" (Simpson), **Supp. IX:** 274
Folded Leaf, The (Maxwell), **Supp. III Part 1:** 62; **Supp. VIII: 159–162**
Folding Star, The (Hollinghurst), **Supp. XIII:** 52
Foley, Jack, **Supp. X:** 125
Foley, Martha, **II:** 587
Folks from Dixie (Dunbar), **Supp. II Part 1:** 211–212
Folkways (Sumner), **III:** 102
Follain, Jean, **Supp. IX:** 152, 154
Follett, Wilson, **I:** 405; **Supp. XIII:** 173
Follower of Dusk (Salinas), **Supp. XIII:** 326
Following the Equator (Twain), **II:** 434; **IV:** 208
Folly (Minot), **Supp. VI:** 205, 208, **210–213**
Folsom, Charles, **Supp. I Part 1:** 156
Folsom, Ed, **Retro. Supp. I:** 392
Folson, Marcia McClintock, **Retro. Supp. II:** 139
Fonda, Henry, **Supp. I Part 1:** 67; **Supp. IV Part 1:** 236
Fonda, Jane, **III:** 284; **Supp. XI:** 307
Fonda, Peter, **Supp. VIII:** 42; **Supp. XI:** 293, 308
Foner, Eric, **Supp. I Part 2:** 523
Fong and the Indians (Theroux), **Supp. VIII:** 314, 315, **316–317**
Fontanne, Lynn, **III:** 397
Fool for Love (Shepard), **Supp. III Part 2:** 433, 447, 448
Fools (Simon), **Supp. IV Part 2:** 584–585
Fool's Progress, The: An Honest Novel (Abbey), **Supp. XIII:** 4, **13–15**
Foote, Horton, **Supp. I Part 1:** 281; **Supp. VIII:** 128, 129
Foote, Mary Hallock, **Retro. Supp. II:** 72; **Supp. IV Part 2:** 611
Foote, Roxanna. *See* Beecher, Mrs. Lyman (Roxanna Foote)
Foote, Samuel, **Supp. I Part 2:** 584
Foote, Stephanie, **Retro. Supp. II:** 139
"Foot Fault" (pseudonym). *See* Thurber, James

"Footing up a Total" (Lowell), **II:** 528
"Footnote to Howl" (Ginsberg), **Supp. II Part 1:** 316–317
"Footnote to Weather Forecasts, A" (Brodsky), **Supp. VIII:** 32
Footprints (Hearon), **Supp. VIII: 69–70**
Footprints (Levertov), **Supp. III Part 1:** 272, 281
"Footsteps of Angels" (Longfellow), **II:** 496
For a Bitter Season: New and Selected Poems (Garrett), **Supp. VII:** 99–100
"For a Dead Lady" (Robinson), **III:** 508, 513, 517
"For a Ghost Who Once Placed Bets in the Park" (Levis), **Supp. XI:** 265
"For a Lamb" (Eberhart), **I:** 523, 530, 531
"For All" (Snyder), **Supp. VIII:** 304
"For All Tuesday Travelers" (Cisneros), **Supp. VII:** 67–68
"For a Lost Child" (Stafford), **Supp. XI:** 329
"For a Marriage" (Bogan), **Supp. III Part 1:** 52
"For an Emigrant" (Jarrell), **II:** 371
"For Anna Akmatova" (Lowell), **II:** 544
"For Anna Mae Pictou Aquash, Whose Spirit Is Present Here and in the Dappled Stars" (Harjo), **Supp. XII:** 225
"For Anne, at a Little Distance" (Haines), **Supp. XII:** 207
"For Annie" (Poe), **III:** 427; **Retro. Supp. II:** 263
"For a Southern Man" (Cisneros), **Supp. VII:** 67
"For Bailey" (Angelou), **Supp. IV Part 1:** 15
Forbes, Malcolm, **Supp. IV Part 1:** 94
For Bread Alone (Choukri), **Supp. IV Part 1:** 92
Forché, Carolyn, **Supp. IV Part 1:** 208
Ford, Arthur, **Supp. IV Part 1:** 140
Ford, Ford Madox, **I:** 288, 405, 409, 417, 421, 423; **II:** 58, 144, 198, 257, 263, 265, 517, 536; **III:** 458, 464–465, 470–471, 472, 476; **IV:** 27, 126, 261; **Retro. Supp. I:** 127, 177, 178, 186, 231, 286–287, 418; **Supp. II Part 1:** 107; **Supp. III Part 2:** 617; **Supp. VIII:** 107
Ford, Harrison, **Supp. VIII:** 323
Ford, Harry, **Supp. V:** 179; **Supp. XIII:** 76
Ford, Henry, **I:** 295, 480–481; **III:** 292, 293; **Supp. I Part 1:** 21; **Supp. I Part 2:** 644; **Supp. III Part 2:** 612, 613; **Supp. IV Part 1:** 223; **Supp. V:** 290
Ford, John, **Supp. I Part 2:** 422; **Supp. III Part 2:** 619
Ford, Richard, **Supp. IV Part 1:** 342; **Supp. V:** 22, **57–75**
Ford, Webster (pseudonym). *See* Masters, Edgar Lee
"Fording and Dread" (Harrison), **Supp. VIII:** 41
"Ford Madox Ford" (Lowell), **II:** 547; **Retro. Supp. II:** 188
"For Dudley" (Wilbur), **Supp. III Part 2:** 558
Fordyce, David, **II:** 113
Foregone Conclusion, A (Howells), **II:** 278–279, 282
"Foreign Affairs" (Kunitz), **Supp. III Part 1:** 265
"Foreigner, The" (Jewett), **II:** 409–410; **Retro. Supp. II:** 133, 142
"Foreign Shores" (Salter), **Supp. IX:** 260
Forensic and the Navigators (Shepard), **Supp. III Part 2:** 439
Foreseeable Future, The (Price), **Supp. VI:** 265
Foreseeable Futures (Matthews), **Supp. IX:** 155, **163,** 169
"For Esmé with Love and Squalor" (Salinger), **III:** 560
"Forest" (Simic), **Supp. VIII:** 273
Forest, Jean-Claude, **Supp. XI:** 307
Forester's Letters (Paine), **Supp. I Part 2:** 508
"Forest Hymn, A" (Bryant), **Supp. I Part 1:** 156, 162, 163, 164, 165, 170
"Forest in the Seeds, The" (Kingsolver), **Supp. VII:** 203
Forest of the South, The (Gordon), **II:** 197
"Forest of the South, The" (Gordon), **II:** 199, 201
Forest without Leaves (Adams and Haines), **Supp. XII:** 209
"Forever and the Earth" (Bradbury), **Supp. IV Part 1:** 102
"For Fathers of Girls" (Dunn), **Supp. XI:** 146
"For/From Lew" (Snyder), **Supp. VIII:** 303
"For George Santayana" (Lowell), **II:** 547
Forgotten Helper, The: A Story for Children (Moore), **Supp. X:** 175
Forgotten Village, The (Steinbeck), **IV:** 51
Forgue, Guy J., **III:** 118, 119
"FOR HETTIE" (Baraka), **Supp. II Part 1:** 32
"FOR HETTIE IN HER FIFTH MONTH" (Baraka), **Supp. II Part 1:** 32, 38
"For Homer" (Corso), **Supp. XII:** 135
"For I'm the Boy" (Barthelme), **Supp. IV Part 1:** 47
"For Jessica, My Daughter" (Strand), **Supp. IV Part 2:** 629
"For John, Who Begs Me not to Enquire Further" (Sexton), **Supp. II Part 2:** 676
"For Johnny Pole on the Forgotten Beach" (Sexton), **Supp. II Part 2:** 675
"For Joy to Leave Upon" (Ortiz), **Supp. IV Part 2:** 508
"Fork" (Simic), **Supp. VIII:** 275
For Lancelot Andrewes (Eliot), **Retro. Supp. I:** 64
For Lizzie and Harriet (Lowell), **Retro. Supp. II:** 183, 186, 190
"Forlorn Hope of Sidney Lanier, The" (Leary), **Supp. I Part 1:** 373
For Love (Creeley), **Supp. IV Part 1:** 139, 140, 142–145, 147–149, 150, 154
"For Love" (Creeley), **Supp. IV Part 1:** 145
For Love (S. Miller), **Supp. XII: 297–299,** 299
"Formal Elegy" (Berryman), **I:** 170
"Formalist Criticism: Its Principles and Limits" (Burke), **I:** 282
Forman, Milos, **Supp. IV Part 1:** 236
"Form and Function of the Novel, The" (Goldbarth), **Supp. XII:** 183
"For Marse Chouchoute" (Chopin), **Retro. Supp. II:** 60
"Formation of a Separatist, I" (Howe), **Supp. IV Part 2:** 427
"Form Is Emptiness" (Baraka), **Supp. II Part 1:** 51
"For Mr. Death Who Stands with His Door Open" (Sexton), **Supp. II Part 2:** 695
Forms of Discovery (Winters), **Supp. II Part 2:** 812, 813
Forms of Fiction, The (Gardner and Dunlap), **Supp. VI:** 64
"For My Children" (Karr), **Supp. XI:** 254
"For My Daughter" (Olds), **Supp. X:** 206
"For My Lover, Returning to His Wife" (Sexton), **Supp. II Part 2:** 688
"For Night to Come" (Stern), **Supp. IX:** 292
"For Once, Then, Something" (Frost), **II:** 156–157; **Retro. Supp. I:** 126, 133, 134

"For Radicals" (Bourne), **I:** 221
"For Rainer Gerhardt" (Creeley), **Supp. IV Part 1:** 142–143, 147
Forrestal, James, **I:** 491; **Supp. I Part 2:** 489
"For Richard After All" (Kingsolver), **Supp. VII:** 208
"For Sacco and Vanzetti" (Kingsolver), **Supp. VII:** 208
"Forsaken Merman" (Arnold), **Supp. I Part 2:** 529
For Spacious Skies (Buck), **Supp. II Part 1:** 131
Forster, E. M., **I:** 292; **IV:** 201; **Retro. Supp. I:** 59, 232; **Supp. III Part 2:** 503; **Supp. V:** 258; **Supp. VIII:** 155, 171; **Supp. IX:** 128; **Supp. XII:** 79, 81
Forster, John, **II:** 315
Fort, Paul, **II:** 518, 528, 529; **Retro. Supp. I:** 55
"For the Ahkoond" (Bierce), **I:** 209
For the Century's End: Poems 1990–1999 (Haines), **Supp. XII: 211–213**
"For the Dedication of the New City Library, Boston" (Holmes), **Supp. I Part 1:** 308
"For the Fallen" (Levine), **Supp. V:** 188
"For the Last Wolverine" (Dickey), **Supp. IV Part 1:** 182
"For the Lovers of the Absolute" (Simic), **Supp. VIII:** 278–279
"For the Man Cutting the Grass" (Oliver), **Supp. VII:** 235
"For the Marriage of Faustus and Helen" (H. Crane), **I:** 395–396, 399, 402; **Retro. Supp. II:** 78–79, 82
"For the Meeting of the National Sanitary Association, 1860" (Holmes), **Supp. I Part 1:** 307
For the New Intellectual (Rand), **Supp. IV Part 2:** 521, 526–527, 527, 532
"For the New Railway Station in Rome" (Wilbur), **Supp. III Part 2:** 554
"For the Night" (Kenyon), **Supp. VII:** 163
"For Theodore Roethke: 1908–1963" (Lowell), **II:** 554
"For the Poem *Patterson*" (W. C. Williams), **Retro. Supp. I:** 424
"For the Poets of Chile" (Levine), **Supp. V:** 188
"FOR THE REVOLUTIONARY OUTBURST BY BLACK PEOPLE" (Baraka), **Supp. II Part 1:** 55
"For the Sleepless" (Dunn), **Supp. XI:** 145
For the Time Being (Auden), **Supp. II Part 1:** 2, 17, 18
For the Time Being (Dillard), **Supp. VI:** 23, 27, 29, 32, **34–35**
For the Union Dead (Lowell), **II:** 543, 550–551, 554, 555; **Retro. Supp. II:** 181, 182, 186, 189; **Supp. X:** 53
"For the Union Dead" (Lowell), **II:** 551; **Retro. Supp. II:** 189
"For the Walking Dead" (Komunyakaa), **Supp. XIII:** 121
"For the West" (Snyder), **Supp. VIII:** 299
"For the Word Is Flesh" (Kunitz), **Supp. III Part 1:** 262–264
"For This" (Rich), **Retro. Supp. II:** 293
"Fortress, The" (Glück), **Supp. V:** 82
"Fortress, The" (Sexton), **Supp. II Part 2:** 682
Fortune, T. Thomas, **Supp. II Part 1:** 159
Fortune's Daughter (Hoffman), **Supp. X:** 77, 85
45 Mercy Street (Sexton), **Supp. II Part 2:** 694, 695, 697
Forty Poems Touching on Recent American History (Bly, ed.), **Supp. IV Part 1:** 61
42nd Parallel, The (Dos Passos), **I:** 482, 484–485
Forty Stories (Barthelme), **Supp. IV Part 1:** 47, 49, 53, 54
For Whom the Bell Tolls (Hemingway), **II:** 249, 254–255, 261; **III:** 18, 363; **Retro. Supp. I:** 115, 176–177, 178, **184,** 187
Foscolo, Ugo, **II:** 543
Foss, Sam Walter, **Supp. II Part 1:** 197
"Fossils, The" (Kinnell), **Supp. III Part 1:** 244
Foster, Edward, **Supp. IV Part 2:** 431, 434
Foster, Edward Halsey, **Supp. XII:** 120, 129, 130, 135
Foster, Emily, **II:** 309
Foster, John Wilson, **Supp. XIII:** 32–33
Foster, Phil, **Supp. IV Part 2:** 574
Foster, Stephen, **Supp. I Part 1:** 100–101; **Supp. I Part 2:** 699
Foucault, Michel, **Supp. VIII:** 5; **Supp. XII:** 98
"Founder, The" (Stern), **Supp. IX:** 297
Founding of Harvard College, The (Morison), **Supp. I Part 2:** 485
"Fountain, The" (Bryant), **Supp. I Part 1:** 157, 165, 166, 168
Fountain, The (O'Neill), **III:** 391
Fountain and Other Poems, The (Bryant), **Supp. I Part 1:** 157
Fountainhead, The (film), **Supp. IV Part 2:** 524
Fountainhead, The (Rand), **Supp. IV Part 2:** 517, 521–523, 525, 531
Fountainhead, The: A Fiftieth Anniversary Celebration (Cox), **Supp. IV Part 2:** 523
"Fountain Piece" (Swenson), **Supp. IV Part 2:** 641
"Four Ages of Man, The" (Bradstreet), **Supp. I Part 1:** 111, 115
Four American Indian Literary Masters (Velie), **Supp. IV Part 2:** 486
"Four Beasts in One; the Homo Cameleopard" (Poe), **III:** 425
Four Black Revolutionary Plays (Baraka), **Supp. II Part 1:** 45; **Supp. VIII:** 330
"Four Brothers, The" (Sandburg), **III:** 585
"Four Evangelists, The" (Komunyakaa), **Supp. XIII:** 131
"Four for Sir John Davies" (Roethke), **III:** 540, 541
"Four Girls, The" (Alvarez), **Supp. VII:** 7
4-H Club (Shepard), **Supp. III Part 2:** 439
"Four Horse Songs" (Harjo), **Supp. XII:** 220
"400-Meter Free Style" (Kumin), **Supp. IV Part 2:** 442
Fourier, Charles, **II:** 342
"Four in a Family" (Rukeyser), **Supp. VI:** 272
Four in Hand: A Quartet of Novels (Warner), **Supp. VIII:** 164
"Four Lakes' Days" (Eberhart), **I:** 525
"Four Meetings" (James), **II:** 327
Four Million, The (O. Henry), **Supp. II Part 1:** 394, 408
"Four Monarchyes" (Bradstreet), **Supp. I Part 1:** 105, 106, 116
"Four Mountain Wolves" (Silko), **Supp. IV Part 2:** 561
Four of a Kind (Marquand), **III:** 54, 55
"Four of the Horsemen (Hypertense and Stroke, Coronary Occlusion and Cerebral Insult)" (Karr), **Supp. XI:** 250
"Four Poems" (Bishop), **Supp. I Part 1:** 92
"Four Preludes on Playthings of the Wind" (Sandburg), **III:** 586
Four Quartets (Eliot), **I:** 570, 576, 580–582, 585, 587; **II:** 537; **III:** 539; **Retro. Supp. I:** 66, 67; **Supp. II Part 1:** 1; **Supp. IV Part 1:** 284;

Supp. V: 343, 344; **Supp. VIII:** 182, 195; **Supp. XIII:** 344
Four Saints in Three Acts (Stein), **IV:** 30, 31, 33, 43, 44–45
"Four Seasons" (Bradstreet), **Supp. I Part 1:** 112–113
"Four Sides of One Story" (Updike), **Retro. Supp. I:** 328
"Four Skinny Trees" (Cisneros), **Supp. VII:** 64
"14: In A Dark Wood: Wood Thrushes" (Oliver), **Supp. VII:** 244
Fourteen Hundred Thousand (Shepard), **Supp. III Part 2:** 439
"14 Men Stage Head Winter 1624/ 25" (Olson), **Supp. II Part 2:** 574
Fourteen Sisters of Emilio Montez O'Brien, The (Hijuelos), **Supp. VIII: 82–85**
Fourteen Stories (Buck), **Supp. II Part 1:** 126
14 Stories (Dixon), **Supp. XII:** 141, **145–147**
"Fourteenth Ward, The" (H. Miller), **III:** 175
Fourth Book of Peace, The (Kingston), **Supp. V:** 173
"Fourth Down" (Marquand), **III:** 56
"Fourth of July in Maine" (Lowell), **II:** 535, 552–553
Fourth Wall, The (Gurney), **Supp. V:** 109–110
Fowler, Douglas, **Supp. IV Part 1:** 226, 227
Fowler, Gene, **Supp. VIII:** 290
Fowler, Henry Watson, **Supp. I Part 2:** 660
Fowler, Singrid, **Supp. VIII:** 249, 258
Fowler, Virginia C., **Supp. VIII:** 224
Fox, Alan, **Supp. XIII:** 120
Fox, Dixon Ryan, **I:** 337
Fox, Joe, **Supp. IX:** 259, 261
Fox, John, **Supp. XIII:** 166
Fox, Linda C., **Supp. XIII:** 217–218
Fox: Poems, 1998–2000 (Rich), **Retro. Supp. II:** 293
Fox, Ruth, **Supp. I Part 2:** 619
"Fox, The" (Levine), **Supp. V:** 181, 189
Fox-Genovese, Elizabeth, **Supp. IV Part 1:** 286
Fox of Peapack, The (White), **Supp. I Part 2:** 676, 677–678
"Fox of Peapack, The" (White), **Supp. I Part 2:** 677
Fraenkel, Michael, **III:** 178, 183
"Fragging" (Komunyakaa), **Supp. XIII:** 123
Fragile Beauty, A: John Nichols' Milagro Country: Text and Photographs from His Life and Work (Nichols), **Supp. XIII:** 268
"Fragility" (Shields), **Supp. VII:** 318
"Fragment" (Ashbery), **Supp. III Part 1:** 11, 13, 14, 19, 20
"Fragment" (Lowell), **II:** 516
"Fragment" (Ortiz), **Supp. IV Part 2:** 507
"Fragment of a Meditation" (Tate), **IV:** 129
"Fragment of an Agon" (Eliot), **I:** 579–580
"Fragment of a Prologue" (Eliot), **I:** 579–580
"Fragment of New York, 1929" (Eberhart), **I:** 536–537
"Fragments" (Emerson), **II:** 19
"Fragments for Fall" (Salinas), **Supp. XIII:** 320–321
"Fragments of a Liquidation" (Howe), **Supp. IV Part 2:** 426
Fragonard, Jean Honoré, **III:** 275; **IV:** 79
Fraiman, Susan, **Supp. IV Part 1:** 324
"Frame for Poetry, A" (W. J. Smith), **Supp. XIII:** 333
France, Anatole, **IV:** 444; **Supp. I Part 2:** 631
France and England in North America (Parkman), **Supp. II Part 2:** 596, 600–605, 607, 613–614
Franchere, Hoyt C., **II:** 131
Franchiser, The (Elkin), **Supp. VI:** 51–**52**, 58
Francis, Lee, **Supp. IV Part 2:** 499
Francis, Robert, **Supp. IX: 75–92**
Francis of Assisi, Saint, **III:** 543; **IV:** 69, 375, 410; **Supp. I Part 2:** 394, 397, 441, 442, 443
Franco, Francisco, **II:** 261
Franconia (Fraser), **Retro. Supp. I:** 136
"Franconia" tales (Abbott), **Supp. I Part 1:** 38
Frank, Anne, **Supp. X:** 149
Frank, Frederick S., **Retro. Supp. II:** 273
Frank, Jerome, **Supp. I Part 2:** 645
Frank, Joseph, **II:** 587
Frank, Mary, **Supp. X:** 213
Frank, Robert, **Supp. XI:** 295; **Supp. XII:** 127
Frank, Waldo, **I:** 106, 109, 117, 229, 236, 245, 259, 400; **Retro. Supp. II:** 77, 79, 83; **Supp. IX:** 308, 309, 311, 320
Frankel, Charles, **III:** 291
Frankel, Haskel, **Supp. I Part 2:** 448
Frankenberg, Lloyd, **I:** 436, 437, 445, 446; **III:** 194
Frankenheimer, John, **Supp. XI:** 343
Frankenstein (film), **Supp. IV Part 1:** 104
Frankenstein (Gardner), **Supp. VI:** 72
Frankenstein (Shelley), **Supp. XII:** 79
Frankfurter, Felix, **I:** 489
Frankie and Johnny (film), **Supp. XIII:** 206
Frankie and Johnny in the Clair de Lune (McNally), **Supp. XIII: 200,** 201
Franklin, Benjamin, **II:** 6, 8, 92, **101–125**, 127, 295, 296, 302, 306; **III:** 74, 90; **IV:** 73, 193; **Supp. I Part 1:** 306; **Supp. I Part 2:** 411, 503, 504, 506, 507, 510, 516, 518, 522, 524, 579, 639; **Supp. VIII:** 202, 205; **Supp. XIII:** 150
Franklin, Cynthia, **Supp. IV Part 1:** 332
Franklin, R. W., **Retro. Supp. I:** 29, 41, 43, 47
Franklin, Sarah, **II:** 122
Franklin, Temple, **II:** 122
Franklin, William, **II:** 122; **Supp. I Part 2:** 504
Franklin Evans (Whitman), **Retro. Supp. I:** 393
"Frank O'Connor and *The New Yorker*" (Maxwell), **Supp. VIII:** 172
Franks, Lucinda, **Supp. XIII:** 12
"Franny" (Salinger), **III:** 564, 565–566
Franny and Zooey (Salinger), **III:** 552, 564–567; **IV:** 216; **Supp. XIII:** 263
Franzen, Jonathan, **Retro. Supp. II:** 297
Fraser, G. S., **Supp. XII:** 128
Fraser, Joe, **III:** 46
Fraser, Marjorie Frost, **Retro. Supp. I:** 136
Frayn, Michael, **Supp. IV Part 2:** 582
Frazee, E. S., **Supp. I Part 2:** 381
Frazee, Esther Catherine. *See* Lindsay, Mrs. Vachel Thomas (Esther Catherine Frazee)
Frazer, Sir James G., **I:** 135; **II:** 204; **III:** 6–7; **IV:** 70; **Retro. Supp. I:** 80; **Supp. I Part 1:** 18; **Supp. I Part 2:** 541
Frazier, Ian, **Supp. VIII:** 272
Freaks: Myths and Images of the Secret Self (Fiedler), **Supp. XIII:** 106, 107
"Freak Show, The" (Sexton), **Supp. II Part 2:** 695
Freddy's Book (Gardner), **Supp. VI: 72**
Frederic, Harold, **I:** 409; **II: 126–149,** 175, 276, 289; **Retro. Supp. I:** 325
"Frederick Douglass" (Dunbar), **Supp. II Part 1:** 197, 199

"Frederick Douglass" (Hayden), **Supp. II Part 1:** 363
Frederick the Great, **II:** 103; **Supp. I Part 2:** 433
Fredrickson, George M., **Supp. I Part 2:** 589
"Free" (O'Hara), **III:** 369
Free, and Other Stories (Dreiser), **Retro. Supp. II:** 104
Free Air (Lewis), **II:** 441
Freedman, Monroe H., **Supp. VIII:** 127
Freedman, Richard, **Supp. V:** 244
"Freedom" (White), **Supp. I Part 2:** 659
"Freedom, New Hampshire" (Kinnell), **Supp. III Part 1:** 238, 239, 251
Freedom Is the Right to Choose: An Inquiry into the Battle for the American Future (MacLeish), **III:** 3
"Freedom's a Hard-Bought Thing" (Benét), **Supp. XI:** 47, 48
"Freedom's Plow" (Hughes), **Supp. I Part 1:** 346
"Free Fantasia: Tiger Flowers" (Hayden), **Supp. II Part 1:** 363, 366
Freeing of the Dust, The (Levertov), **Supp. III Part 1:** 281–282
"Free Lance, The" (Mencken), **III:** 104, 105
Free-Lance Pallbearers, The (Reed), **Supp. X:** 240, **242–243**, 244
"Free Man" (Hughes), **Supp. I Part 1:** 333
Freeman, Douglas Southall, **Supp. I Part 2:** 486, 493
Freeman, Joseph, **II:** 26; **Supp. I Part 2:** 610
Freeman, Mary E. Wilkins, **II:** 401; **Supp. IX:** 79
Freeman, Mary Wilkins, **Retro. Supp. II:** 51, 136, 138
Freeman, Morgan, **Supp. XII:** 317
Freeman, Suzanne, **Supp. X:** 83
"Free Man's Worship, A" (Russell), **Supp. I Part 2:** 522
Freinman, Dorothy, **Supp. IX:** 94
Frémont, John Charles, **Supp. I Part 2:** 486
Fremont-Smith, Eliot, **Supp. XIII:** 263
Fremstad, Olive, **I:** 319; **Retro. Supp. I:** 10
French, Warren, **Supp. XII:** 118–119
French Connection, The (film), **Supp. V:** 226
French Poets and Novelists (James), **II:** 336; **Retro. Supp. I:** 220
"French Scarecrow, The" (Maxwell), **Supp. VIII:** 169, 170
French Ways and Their Meaning (Wharton), **IV:** 319; **Retro. Supp. I:** 378
Freneau, Eleanor Forman (Mrs. Philip Freneau), **Supp. II Part 1:** 266
Freneau, Philip M., **I:** 335; **II:** 295; **Supp. I Part 1:** 124, 125, 127, 145; **Supp. II Part 1:** 65, **253–277**
Frescoes for Mr. Rockefeller's City (MacLeish), **III:** 14–15
Fresh Air Fiend: Travel Writings, 1985–2000 (Theroux), **Supp. VIII:** 325
Freud, Sigmund, **I:** 55, 58, 59, 66, 67, 135, 241, 242, 244, 247, 248, 283; **II:** 27, 370, 546–547; **III:** 134, 390, 400, 418, 488; **IV:** 7, 70, 138, 295; **Retro. Supp. I:** 80, 176, 253; **Retro. Supp. II:** 104; **Supp. I Part 1:** 13, 43, 253, 254, 259, 260, 265, 270, 315; **Supp. I Part 2:** 493, 527, 616, 643, 647, 649; **Supp. IV Part 2:** 450; **Supp. VIII:** 103, 196; **Supp. IX:** 102, 155, 161, 308; **Supp. X:** 193, 194; **Supp. XII:** 14–15; **Supp. XIII:** 75
Freud: The Mind of the Moralist (Sontag and Rieff), **Supp. III Part 2:** 455
"Freud: Within and Beyond Culture" (Trilling), **Supp. III Part 2:** 508
"Freud and Literature" (Trilling), **Supp. III Part 2:** 502–503
Freudian Psychology and Veblen's Social Theory, The (Schneider), **Supp. I Part 2:** 650
Freudian Wish and Its Place in Ethics, The (Holt), **I:** 59
"Freud's Room" (Ozick), **Supp. V:** 268
"Friday Morning Trial of Mrs. Solano, The" (Ríos), **Supp. IV Part 2:** 538, 548
Frieburger, William, **Supp. XIII:** 239
Friedenberg, Edgar Z., **Supp. VIII:** 240
Friedman, Bruce Jay, **I:** 161; **Supp. IV Part 1:** 379
Friedman, Lawrence S., **Supp. V:** 273
Friedman, Milton, **Supp. I Part 2:** 648
Friedman, Norman, **I:** 431–432, 435, 439
Friedman, Stan, **Supp. XII:** 186
Friedmann, Georges, **Supp. I Part 2:** 645
"Fried Sausage" (Simic), **Supp. VIII:** 270
Friend, Julius, **Retro. Supp. I:** 80
Friend, The (Coleridge), **II:** 10
"Friend Husband's Latest" (Sayre), **Retro. Supp. I:** 104
"Friendly Debate between a Conformist and a Non-Conformist, A" (Wild), **IV:** 155
Friend of the Earth (Boyle), **Supp. VIII:** 12, 16
"Friend of the Fourth Decade, The" (Merrill), **Supp. III Part 1:** 327
"Friends" (Beattie), **Supp. V:** 23, 27
"Friends" (Paley), **Supp. VI:** 219, 226
"Friends" (Sexton), **Supp. II Part 2:** 693
Friends: More Will and Magna Stories (Dixon), **Supp. XII:** 148, 149
Friend's Delight, The (Bierce), **I:** 195
"Friends from Philadelphia" (Updike), **Retro. Supp. I:** 319
"Friendship" (Emerson), **Supp. II Part 1:** 290
"Friends of Heraclitus, The" (Simic), **Supp. VIII:** 284
"Friends of Kafka, The" (Singer), **Retro. Supp. II:** 326
"Friends of the Family, The" (McCarthy), **II:** 566
"Friend to Alexander, A" (Thurber), **Supp. I Part 2:** 616
"Frigate Pelican, The" (Moore), **III:** 208, 210–211, 215
Frobenius, Leo, **III:** 475; **Supp. III Part 2:** 620
Frog (Dixon), **Supp. XII:** 151
"Frog Dances" (Dixon), **Supp. XII:** 151
"Frog Pond, The" (Kinnell), **Supp. III Part 1:** 254
"Frog Takes a Swim" (Dixon), **Supp. XII:** 152
Frohock, W. M., **I:** 34, 42
Frolic of His Own, A (Gaddis), **Supp. IV Part 1:** 279, 291, 292–294
"From a Mournful Village" (Jewett), **Retro. Supp. II:** 146
"From an Old House in America" (Rich), **Supp. I Part 2:** 551, 565–567
"From a Survivor" (Rich), **Supp. I Part 2:** 563
From a Writer's Notebook (Brooks), **I:** 254
From Bauhaus to Our House (Wolfe), **Supp. III Part 2:** 580, 581, 584
From Bondage (H. Roth), **Supp. IX:** 236, **238–240**
"From *Chants* to *Borders* to *Communion*" (Fox), **Supp. XIII:** 217–218
"From Chicago" (Anderson), **I:** 108–109
From Death to Morning (Wolfe), **IV:** 450, 456, 458
"From Feathers to Iron" (Kunitz),

Supp. III Part 1: 261
"From Fifth Avenue Up" (Barnes), **Supp. III Part 1:** 33, 44
"From Gorbunov and Gorchakov" (Brodsky), **Supp. VIII:** 26
"From Grand Canyon to Burbank" (H. Miller), **III:** 186
"From Hell to Breakfast," **Supp. IX:** 326–327
From Here to Eternity (film), **Supp. XI:** 221
From Here to Eternity (Jones), **I:** 477; **Supp. XI:** 215, 216, 217, 218, **219–221,** 223, 224, 226, 229, 230, 231, 232, 234
From Here to Eternity (miniseries), **Supp. XI:** 234
From Jordan's Delight (Blackmur), **Supp. II Part 1:** 91
Fromm, Erich, **I:** 58; **Supp. VIII:** 196
From Morn to Midnight (Kaiser), **I:** 479
"From Native Son to Invisible Man" (Locke), **Supp. IX:** 306
"From Pico, the Women: A Life" (Creeley), **Supp. IV Part 1:** 149
From Ritual to Romance (Weston), **II:** 540; **III:** 12; **Supp. I Part 2:** 439
From Room to Room (Kenyon), **Supp. VII:** 163–165, 166, 167
"From Room to Room" (Kenyon), **Supp. VII:** 159, 163–165
From Sand Creek: Rising in this Heart Which Is Our America (Ortiz), **Supp. IV Part 2:** 512–513
"From Sea Cliff, March" (Swenson), **Supp. IV Part 2:** 649
"From the Antigone" (Yeats), **III:** 459
From the Barrio: A Chicano Anthology (Salinas and Faderman, eds.), **Supp. XIII:** 313
"From the Childhood of Jesus" (Pinsky), **Supp. VI:** 244–245, 247
"From the Corpse Woodpiles, From the Ashes" (Hayden), **Supp. II Part 1:** 370
"From the Country to the City" (Bishop), **Supp. I Part 1:** 85, 86
"From the Cupola" (Merrill), **Supp. III Part 1:** 324–325, 331
"From the Dark Side of the Earth" (Oates), **Supp. II Part 2:** 510
"From the Diary of a New York Lady" (Parker), **Supp. IX:** 201
"From the Diary of One Not Born" (Singer), **IV:** 9
"From the East, Light" (Carver), **Supp. III Part 1:** 138
From the First Nine: Poems 1946–1976 (Merrill), **Supp. III Part 1:** 336
"From the Flats" (Lanier), **Supp. I Part 1:** 364
From the Heart of Europe (Matthiessen), **III:** 310
"From the Memoirs of a Private Detective" (Hammett), **Supp. IV Part 1:** 343
"From the Nursery" (Kenyon), **Supp. VII:** 171
"From the Poets in the Kitchen" (Marshall), **Supp. XI:** 277
From the Terrace (O'Hara), **III:** 362
"From the Thirties: Tillie Olsen and the Radical Tradition" (Rosenfelt), **Supp. XIII:** 296, 304
"From Trollope's Journal" (Bishop), **Retro. Supp. II:** 47
"Front, A" (Jarrell), **II:** 374
Front, The (film), **Supp. I Part 1:** 295
"Front and the Back Parts of the House, The" (Maxwell), **Supp. VIII:** 169
Frontier Eden (Bigelow), **Supp. X:** 227
"Front Lines" (Snyder), **Supp. VIII:** 301
Frost, A. B., **Retro. Supp. II:** 72
"Frost: A Dissenting Opinion" (Cowley), **Supp. II Part 1:** 143
Frost: A Time to Talk (Francis), **Supp. IX:** 76, **85–86**
"Frost: He Is Sometimes a Poet and Sometimes a Stump-Speaker" (News-Week), **Retro. Supp. I:** 137
Frost, Isabelle Moodie, **II:** 150, 151
Frost, Jeanie, **II:** 151
Frost, Robert, **I:** 26, 27, 60, 63, 64, 171, 229, 303, 326, 418; **II:** 55, 58, **150–172,** 276, 289, 388, 391, 471, 523, 527, 529, 535; **III:** 5, 23, 67, 269, 271, 272, 275, 287, 453, 510, 523, 536, 575, 581, 591; **IV:** 140, 190, 415; **Retro. Supp. I:** 67, **121–144,** 276, 287, 292, 298, 299, 311, 413; **Retro. Supp. II:** 40, 47, 50, 146, 178, 181, 280; **Supp. I Part 1:** 80, 242, 263, 264; **Supp. I Part 2:** 387, 461, 699; **Supp. II Part 1:** 4, 19, 26, 103; **Supp. III Part 1:** 63, 74–75, 239, 253; **Supp. III Part 2:** 546, 592, 593; **Supp. IV Part 1:** 15; **Supp. IV Part 2:** 439, 445, 447, 448, 599, 601; **Supp. VIII:** 20, 30, 32, 98, 100, 104, 259, 292; **Supp. IX:** 41, 42, 75, 76, 80, 87, 90, 266, 308; **Supp. X:** 64, 65, 66, 74, 120, 172; **Supp. XI:** 43, 123, 150, 153, 312; **Supp. XII:** 130, 241, 303, 307; **Supp. XIII:** 143, 147, 334–335
Frost, William Prescott, **II:** 150–151
"Frost at Midnight" (Coleridge), **Supp. X:** 71
"Frost Flowers" (Kenyon), **Supp. VII:** 168
Frothingham, Nathaniel, **I:** 3
Frothingham, Octavius B., **IV:** 173
"Frozen City, The" (Nemerov), **III:** 270
"Frozen Fields, The" (Bowles), **Supp. IV Part 1:** 80
"Fruit Garden Path, The" (Lowell), **II:** 516
"Fruit of the Flower" (Cullen), **Supp. IV Part 1:** 167
Fruit of the Tree, The (Wharton), **IV:** 314–315; **Retro. Supp. I:** 367, **370–371,** 373
"Fruit of Travel Long Ago" (Melville), **III:** 93
Fruits and Vegetables (Jong), **Supp. V:** 113, 115, 117, 118, 119
Frumkes, Lewis Burke, **Supp. XII:** 335–336
Fry, Christopher, **Supp. I Part 1:** 270
Frye, Joanne, **Supp. XIII:** 292, 296, 298, 302
Frye, Northrop, **Supp. I Part 2:** 530; **Supp. II Part 1:** 101; **Supp. X:** 80; **Supp. XIII:** 19
Fryer, Judith, **Retro. Supp. I:** 379
Fuchs, Daniel, **Supp. XIII:** 106
Fuchs, Miriam, **Supp. IV Part 1:** 284
Fuehrer Bunker, The (Snodgrass), **Supp. VI:** 314, 315–317, 319–321
Fuel (Nye), **Supp. XIII:** 277, **282–284**
"Fuel" (Nye), **Supp. XIII:** 283
Fuertes, Gloria, **Supp. V:** 178
Fugard, Athol, **Supp. VIII:** 330; **Supp. XIII:** 205
Fugitive Group, The (Cowan), **IV:** 120
Fugitive Kind, The (T. Williams), **IV:** 381, 383
Fugitives, The (group), **IV:** 122, 124, 125, 131, 237, 238
Fugitives, The: A Critical Account (Bradbury), **IV:** 130
"Fugitive Slave Law, The" (Emerson), **II:** 13
Fugitive's Return (Glaspell), **Supp. III Part 1:** 182–184
Fuller, B. A. G., **III:** 605
Fuller, Margaret, **I:** 261; **II:** 7, 276; **IV:** 172; **Retro. Supp. I:** 155–156, 163; **Retro. Supp. II:** 46; **Supp. I Part 2:** 524; **Supp. II Part 1:** **279–306;** **Supp. IX:** 37
Fuller, Thomas, **II:** 111, 112
Fullerton Street (Wilson), **Supp. VIII:** 331

"Full Fathom Five" (Plath), **Supp. I Part 2:** 538
Full Monty, The (musical, McNally), **Supp. XIII:** 207
"Full Moon" (Hayden), **Supp. II Part 1:** 370
"Full Moon: New Guinea" (Shapiro), **Supp. II Part 2:** 707
Full Moon and Other Plays (Price), **Supp. VI:** 266
"Full Moon and You're Not Here" (Cisneros), **Supp. VII:** 71–72
"Fullness of Life, The" (Wharton), **Retro. Supp. I:** 363
Full of Life (Fante), **Supp. XI:** 160
Full of Life (film), **Supp. XI:** 170
Full of Lust and Good Usage (Dunn), **Supp. XI: 145–147**
"Full Summer" (Olds), **Supp. X:** 212
Fulton, Robert, **Supp. I Part 2:** 519; **Supp. II Part 1:** 73
Function of Criticism, The (Winters), **Supp. II Part 2:** 812, 813
"Fundamentalism" (Tate), **IV:** 125
"Fundamental Project of Technology, The" (Kinnell), **Supp. III Part 1:** 253
"Funeral of Bobò, The" (Brodsky), **Supp. VIII:** 27, 28
"Funnel" (Sexton), **Supp. II Part 2:** 675
"Furious Seasons, The" (Carver), **Supp. III Part 1:** 137
Furious Seasons and Other Stories (Carver), **Supp. III Part 1:** 142, 143, 146
"Furnished Room, The" (Hayden), **Supp. II Part 1:** 386–387, 394, 397, 399, 406, 408
"Furor Scribendi" (O. Butler), **Supp. XIII:** 70
Fur Person, The (Sarton), **Supp. VIII: 264–265**
Further Fables for Our Time (Thurber), **Supp. I Part 2:** 612
"Further in Summer than the Birds" (Dickinson), **I:** 471
Further Poems of Emily Dickinson (Bianchi and Hampson, ed.), **Retro. Supp. I:** 35
Further Range, A (Frost), **II:** 155; **Retro. Supp. I:** 132, 136, 137, 138, 139
"Fury of Aerial Bombardment, The" (Eberhart), **I:** 535–536
"Fury of Flowers and Worms, The" (Sexton), **Supp. II Part 2:** 694
"Fury of Rain Storms, The" (Sexton), **Supp. II Part 2:** 695

Fury of the Jungle (film), **Supp. XIII:** 163
Fussell, Paul, **Supp. V:** 241
"Future, if Any, of Comedy, The" (Thurber), **Supp. I Part 2:** 620
Future is Ours, Comrade, The: Conversations with the Russians (Kosinski), **Supp. VII:** 215
Futureland: Nine Stories of an Imminent World (Mosley), **Supp. XIII: 247–249**
"Future Life, The" (Bryant), **Supp. I Part 1:** 170
Future Punishment of the Wicked, The (Edwards), **I:** 546
"Gabriel" (Rich), **Supp. I Part 2:** 557
Gabriel, Ralph H., **Supp. I Part 1:** 251
Gabriel, Trip, **Supp. V:** 212
Gabriel Conroy (Harte), **Supp. II Part 1:** 354
"Gabriel's Truth" (Kenyon), **Supp. VII:** 166
Gaddis, William, **Supp. IV Part 1: 279–296; Supp. IV Part 2:** 484; **Supp. V:** 52; **Supp. IX:** 208; **Supp. X:** 301, 302
Gadiot, Pud, **Supp. XI:** 295
Gain (Powers), **Supp. IX:** 212, **220–221**
Gaines, Ernest, **Supp. X:** 250
Gaines, Ernest J., **Supp. X:** 24
Gaines, James R., **Supp. IX:** 190
Galamain, Ivan, **Supp. III Part 2:** 624
Galatea 2.2 (Powers), **Supp. IX:** 212, **219–220**
"Galatea Encore" (Brodsky), **Supp. VIII:** 31
Galbraith, John Kenneth, **Supp. I Part 2:** 645, 650
Galdós, Benito Pérez. *See* Pérez Galdós, Benito
Gale, Zona, **Supp. I Part 2:** 613; **Supp. X:** 155
"Gale in April" (Jeffers), **Supp. II Part 2:** 423
Galignani, Giovanni Antonio, **II:** 315
Galileo Galilei, **I:** 480–481; **Supp. XII:** 180; **Supp. XIII:** 75
Gallant, Mavis, **Supp. VIII:** 151
Gallatin, Albert, **I:** 5
"Gallery" (Goldbarth), **Supp. XII:** 188
"Gallery of Real Creatures, A" (Thurber), **Supp. I Part 2:** 619
Gallows Songs (Snodgrass), **Supp. VI:** 317
Gallup, Donald, **III:** 404, 478
Galsworthy, John, **III:** 70, 153, 382
Galton Case, The (Macdonald), **Supp. IV Part 2:** 463, 473, 474

"Gal Young 'Un" (Rawlings), **Supp. X:** 228
"Gambler, the Nun, and the Radio, The" (Hemingway), **II:** 250
"Gambler's Wife, The" (Dunbar), **Supp. II Part 1:** 196
Gambone, Philip, **Supp. XII:** 81
"Gambrel Roof, A" (Larcom), **Supp. XIII:** 144
"Game at Salzburg, A" (Jarrell), **II:** 384, 389
"Game of Catch, A" (Wilbur), **Supp. III Part 2:** 552
"Games Two" (Wilbur), **Supp. III Part 2:** 550
"Gamut, The" (Angelou), **Supp. IV Part 1:** 15
Gandhi, Indira, **Supp. X:** 108
Gandhi, Mahatma, **III:** 179, 296–297; **IV:** 170, 185, 367; **Supp. VIII:** 203, 204; **Supp. X:** 27
Gandhi on Non-Violence (Merton, ed.), **Supp. VIII:** 204–205
"Gang of Mirrors, The" (Simic), **Supp. VIII:** 283
Gansevoort, Guert, **III:** 94
Gansevoort, Peter, **III:** 92
Garabedian, Michael, **Supp. XIII:** 115
Garbage (Ammons), **Supp. VII:** 24, 35–36
Garbage (Dixon), **Supp. XII:** 147, 148
Garbage Man, The (Dos Passos), **I:** 478, 479, 481, 493
Garber, Frederick, **Supp. IX:** 294–295
Garbo, Greta, **Supp. I Part 2:** 616
García, Cristina, **Supp. VIII:** 74; **Supp. XI: 177–192**
"García Lorca: A Photograph of the Granada Cemetery, 1966" (Levis), **Supp. XI:** 264
García Lorca, Federico. *See* Lorca, Federico García
García Márquez, Gabriel, **Supp. V:** 244; **Supp. VIII:** 81, 82, 84, 85; **Supp. XII:** 147, 310, 316, 322; **Supp. XIII:** 226
"Garden" (Marvell), **IV:** 161
"Garden, The" (Glück), **Supp. V:** 83
"Garden, The" (Strand), **Supp. IV Part 2:** 629
"Garden by Moonlight, The" (Lowell), **II:** 524
Gardener's Son, The (McCarthy), **Supp. VIII:** 187
"Gardenias" (Doty), **Supp. XI:** 122
"Gardenias" (Monette), **Supp. X:** 159
"Garden Lodge, The" (Cather), **I:** 316, 317
Garden of Adonis, The (Gordon), **II:** 196, 204–205, 209

INDEX / 435

Garden of Earthly Delights, A (Oates), **Supp. II Part 2:** 504, 507–509
"Garden of Eden" (Hemingway), **II:** 259
Garden of Eden, The (Hemingway), **Retro. Supp. I:** 186, **187–188**
"Garden of the Moon, The" (Doty), **Supp. XI:** 122
"Gardens, The" (Oliver), **Supp. VII:** 236
"Gardens of Mont-Saint-Michel, The" (Maxwell), **Supp. VIII:** 169
"Gardens of the Villa D'Este, The" (Hecht), **Supp. X:** 59
"Gardens of Zuñi, The" (Merwin), **Supp. III Part 1:** 351
Gardiner, Judith Kegan, **Supp. IV Part 1:** 205
Gardner, Erle Stanley, **Supp. IV Part 1:** 121, 345
Gardner, Isabella, **IV:** 127
Gardner, John, **Supp. I Part 1:** 193, 195, 196; **Supp. III Part 1:** 136, 142, 146; **Supp. VI: 61–76**
Gardons, S. S. *See* Snodgrass, W. D.
Garfield, John, **Supp. XII:** 160
Garibaldi, Giuseppe, **I:** 4; **II:** 284
Garland, Hamlin, **I:** 407; **II:** 276, 289; **III:** 576; **Retro. Supp. I:** 133; **Retro. Supp. II:** 72; **Supp. I Part 1:** 217; **Supp. IV Part 2:** 502
Garland Companion, The (Zverev), **Retro. Supp. I:** 278
Garments the Living Wear (Purdy), **Supp. VII:** 278–279, 280–281
Garner, Dwight, **Supp. X:** 202
Garnett, Edward, **I:** 405, 409, 417; **III:** 27
Garrett, George P., **Supp. I Part 1:** 196; **Supp. VII: 95–113; Supp. X:** 3, 7; **Supp. XI:** 218
Garrigue, Jean, **Supp. XII:** 260
Garrison, Deborah, **Supp. IX:** 299
Garrison, Fielding, **III:** 105
Garrison, William Lloyd, **Supp. I Part 2:** 524, 588, 683, 685, 686, 687
"Garrison of Cape Ann, The" (Whittier), **Supp. I Part 2:** 691, 694
Garry Moore Show (television show), **Supp. IV Part 2:** 575
"Garter Motif" (White), **Supp. I Part 2:** 673
Gartner, Zsuzsi, **Supp. X:** 276
Garvey, Marcus, **Supp. III Part 1:** 175, 180; **Supp. IV Part 1:** 168; **Supp. X:** 135, 136
Gas (Kaiser), **I:** 479
Gas-House McGinty (Farrell), **II:** 41–42

Gaskell, Elizabeth, A., **Supp. I Part 2:** 580
Gasoline (Corso), **Supp. XII:** 118, **121–123,** 134
Gass, William H., **Supp. V:** 44, 52, 238; **Supp. VI: 77–96; Supp. IX:** 208; **Supp. XII:** 152
Gassner, John, **IV:** 381; **Supp. I Part 1:** 284, 292
Gates, David, **Supp. V:** 24; **Supp. XIII:** 93
Gates, Elmer, **I:** 515–516
Gates, Henry Louis, **Retro. Supp. I:** 194, 195, 203; **Supp. X:** 242, 243, 245, 247
Gates, Lewis E., **III:** 315, 330
Gates, The (Rukeyser), **Supp. VI:** 271, 274, 281
"Gates, The" (Rukeyser), **Supp. VI:** 286
Gates, Tudor, **Supp. XI:** 307
Gates of Ivory, the Gates of Horn, The (McGrath), **Supp. X:** 118
Gates of Wrath, The; Rhymed Poems (Ginsberg), **Supp. II Part 1:** 311, 319
Gathering of Fugitives, A (Trilling), **Supp. III Part 2:** 506, 512
Gathering of Zion, The: The Story of the Mormon Trail (Stegner), **Supp. IV Part 2:** 599, 602–603
Gather Together in My Name (Angelou), **Supp. IV Part 1:** 2, 3, 4–6, 11
Gaudier-Brzeska, Henri, **III:** 459, 464, 465, 477
Gauguin, Paul, **I:** 34; **IV:** 290; **Supp. IV Part 1:** 81; **Supp. XII:** 128
"Gauley Bridge" (Rukeyser), **Supp. VI:** 278
Gauss, Christian, **II:** 82; **IV:** 427, 439–440, 444
Gautier, Théophile, **II:** 543; **III:** 466, 467; **Supp. I Part 1:** 277
Gay, John, **II:** 111; **Supp. I Part 2:** 523
Gay, Peter, **I:** 560
Gay, Sydney Howard, **Supp. I Part 1:** 158
Gay, Walter, **IV:** 317
Gayatri Prayer, The, **III:** 572
"Gay Chaps at the Bar" (Brooks), **Supp. III Part 1:** 74, 75
Gaylord, Winfield R., **III:** 579–580
"Gazebo" (Carver), **Supp. III Part 1:** 138, 144, 145
Gazer Within, The, and Other Essays by Larry Levis, **Supp. XI:** 270
Gazzara, Ben, **Supp. VIII:** 319
Gazzo, Michael V., **III:** 155

"Geese Gone Beyond" (Snyder), **Supp. VIII:** 304
"Gegenwart" (Goethe), **Supp. II Part 1:** 26
Geisel, Theodor Seuss (Dr. Seuss), **Supp. X:** 56
Geismar, Maxwell, **II:** 178, 431; **III:** 71; **Supp. IX:** 15; **Supp. XI:** 223
Gelb, Arthur, **IV:** 380
Gelbart, Larry, **Supp. IV Part 2:** 591
Gelder, Robert Van, **Supp. XIII:** 166
Gelfant, Blanche H., **II:** 27, 41
Gelfman, Jean, **Supp. X:** 3
Gellhorn, Martha. *See* Hemingway, Mrs. Ernest (Martha Gellhorn)
Gelpi, Albert, **Supp. I Part 2:** 552, 554, 560
Gelpi, Barbara, **Supp. I Part 2:** 560
Gemini: an extended autobiographical statement on my first twenty-five years of being a black poet (Giovanni), **Supp. IV Part 1:** 11
"Gen" (Snyder), **Supp. VIII:** 302
"Gender of Sound, The" (Carson), **Supp. XII:** 106
"Genealogy" (Komunyakaa), **Supp. XIII:** 129
"General Aims and Theories" (Crane), **I:** 389
General Died at Dawn, The (Odets), **Supp. II Part 2:** 546
"General Gage's Confession" (Freneau), **Supp. II Part 1:** 257
"General Gage's Soliloquy" (Freneau), **Supp. II Part 1:** 257
General History of the Robberies and Murders of the Most Notorious Pyrates from Their First Rise and Settlement in the Island of New Providence to the Present Year, A (Johnson), **Supp. V:** 128
"General William Booth Enters into Heaven" (Lindsay), **Supp. I Part 2:** 374, 382, 384, 385–388, 389, 392, 399
General William Booth Enters into Heaven and Other Poems (Lindsay), **Supp. I Part 2:** 379, 381, 382, 387–388, 391
"Generations of Men, The" (Frost), **Retro. Supp. I:** 128; **Supp. XIII:** 147
Generous Man, A (Price), **Supp. VI:** 259, 260, 261
Genesis (biblical book), **I:** 279; **II:** 540; **Retro. Supp. I:** 250, 256; **Supp. XII:** 54
"Genesis" (Stegner), **Supp. IV Part 2:** 604
Genesis: Book One (Schwartz), **Supp.**

II Part 2: 640, 651–655
Genet, Jean, I: 71, 82, 83, 84; **Supp. IV Part 1:** 8; **Supp. XI:** 308; **Supp. XII:** 1; **Supp. XIII:** 74
"Genetic Expedition" (Dove), **Supp. IV Part 1:** 249, 257
"Genetics of Justice" (Alvarez), **Supp. VII:** 19
"Genial Host, The" (McCarthy), **II:** 564
"Genie in the Bottle, The" (Wilbur), **Supp. III Part 2:** 542
"Genius, The" (MacLeish), **III:** 19
Genius and Lust: A Journey through the Major Writings of Henry Miller (Mailer), **Retro. Supp. II:** 208
"Genius Child" (Hughes), **Retro. Supp. I:** 203
"Genius," The (Dreiser), **I:** 497, 501, 509–511, 519; **Retro. Supp. II:** 94–95, **102–103**, 104, 105
"Genteel Tradition in American Philosophy, The" (Santayana), **I:** 222
"Gentle Communion" (Mora), **Supp. XIII:** 218–219
Gentle Crafter, The (O. Henry), **Supp. II Part 1:** 410
"Gentle Lena, The" (Stein), **IV:** 37, 40
Gentleman Caller, The (T. Williams), **IV:** 383
"Gentleman from Cracow, The" (Singer), **IV:** 9
"Gentleman of Bayou Têche, A" (Chopin), **Supp. I Part 1:** 211–212
"Gentleman of Shalott, The" (Bishop), **Supp. I Part 1:** 85, 86
Gentleman's Agreement (Hobson), **III:** 151
Gentry, Marshall Bruce, **Supp. IV Part 1:** 236
"Genuine Man, The" (Emerson), **II:** 10
Geo-Bestiary (Harrison), **Supp. VIII:** 53
"Geode" (Frost), **II:** 161
Geographical History of America, The (Stein), **IV:** 31, 45
Geography and Plays (Stein), **IV:** 29–30, 32, 43, 44
Geography III (Bishop), **Retro. Supp. II:** 50; **Supp. I Part 1:** 72, 73, 76, 82, 93, 94, 95
Geography of a Horse Dreamer (Shepard), **Supp. III Part 2:** 432
Geography of Home, The: California's Poetry of Place (Bluckey and Young, eds.), **Supp. XIII:** 313
Geography of Loigraire, The (Merton), **Supp. VIII:** 208
Geography of the Heart (Johnson), **Supp. XI:** 129

"Geometric Poem, The" (Corso), **Supp. XII:** 132, 133–134
George, Diana Hume, **Supp. IV Part 2:** 447, 449, 450
George, Henry, **II:** 276; **Supp. I Part 2:** 518
George, Jan, **Supp. IV Part 1:** 268
George, Lynell, **Supp. XIII:** 234–235, 237, 249
George, Peter, **Supp. XI:** 302, 303, 304
George Bernard Shaw: His Plays (Mencken), **III:** 102
George Mills (Elkin), **Supp. VI:** 53–54
"George Robinson: Blues" (Rukeyser), **Supp. VI:** 279
George's Mother (Crane), **I:** 408
"George Thurston" (Bierce), **I:** 202
"Georgia: Invisible Empire State" (Du Bois), **Supp. II Part 1:** 179
Georgia Boy (Caldwell), **I:** 288, 305–306, 308, 309, 310
"Georgia Dusk" (Toomer), **Supp. IX:** 309
"Georgia Night" (Toomer), **Supp. III Part 2:** 481
Georgia Scenes (Longstreet), **II:** 70, 313; **Supp. I Part 1:** 352
Georgics (Virgil), **Retro. Supp. I:** 135
Georgoudaki, Ekaterini, **Supp. IV Part 1:** 12
"Geraldo No Last Name" (Cisneros), **Supp. VII:** 60–61
Gerald's Game (King), **Supp. V:** 141, 148–150, 151, 152
Gerald's Party (Coover), **Supp. V:** 49–50, 51, 52
Gérando, Joseph Marie de, **II:** 10
"Geranium" (O'Connor), **Retro. Supp. II:** 221, 236
Gerber, Dan, **Supp. VIII:** 39
Gerhardt, Rainer, **Supp. IV Part 1:** 142
"German Girls! The German Girls!, The" (MacLeish), **III:** 16
"German Refugee, The" (Malamud), **Supp. I Part 2:** 436, 437
"Germany's Reichswehr" (Agee), **I:** 35
Germinal (Zola), **III:** 318, 322
Gernsback, Hugo, **Supp. IV Part 1:** 101
"Gerontion" (Eliot), **I:** 569, 574, 577, 578, 585, 588; **III:** 9, 435, 436; **Retro. Supp. I:** 290
Gerry, Elbridge, **Supp. I Part 2:** 486
"Gerry's Jazz" (Komunyakaa), **Supp. XIII:** 125
Gershwin, Ira, **Supp. I Part 1:** 281
"Gert" (Monette), **Supp. X:** 158
Gertrude of Stony Island Avenue (Purdy), **Supp. VII:** 281–282

Gertrude Stein (Sprigge), **IV:** 31
Gertrude Stein: A Biography of Her Work (Sutherland), **IV:** 38
"Gertrude Stein and the Geography of the Sentence" (Gass), **Supp. VI:** 87
Gesell, Silvio, **III:** 473
"Gestalt at Sixty" (Sarton), **Supp. VIII:** 260
"Gesture toward an Unfound Renaissance, A" (Stafford), **Supp. XI:** 323
Getlin, Josh, **Supp. V:** 22; **Supp. VIII:** 75, 76, 78, 79
"Getting Along" (Larcom), **Supp. XIII:** 144
"Getting Along with Nature" (Berry), **Supp. X:** 31–32
"Getting Away from Already Pretty Much Being Away from It All" (Wallace), **Supp. X:** 314–315
"Getting Born" (Shields), **Supp. VII:** 311
"Getting Out of Jail on Monday" (Wagoner), **Supp. IX:** 327
"Getting There" (Plath), **Supp. I Part 2:** 539, 542
"Getting to the Poem" (Corso), **Supp. XII:** 135
Getty, J. Paul, **Supp. X:** 108
"Gettysburg: July 1, 1863" (Kenyon), **Supp. VII:** 172
Gettysburg, Manila, Acoma (Masters), **Supp. I Part 2:** 471
Ghachem, Malick, **Supp. X:** 17
"Ghazals: Homage to Ghalib" (Rich), **Supp. I Part 2:** 557
Ghost, The (Crane), **I:** 409, 421
"Ghost Chant, et alii" (Komunyakaa), **Supp. XIII:** 114
Ghost in the Music, A (Nichols), **Supp. XIII:** 267
"Ghostlier Demarcations, Keener Sounds" (Vendler), **Supp. I Part 2:** 565
"Ghostly Father, I Confess" (McCarthy), **II:** 565–566
Ghostly Lover, The (Hardwick), **Supp. III Part 1:** 194–196, 208, 209
"Ghost of the Buffaloes, The" (Lindsay), **Supp. I Part 2:** 393
Ghosts (Auster), **Supp. XII:** 22, **24, 26–27**
Ghosts (Ibsen), **III:** 152
Ghosts (Wharton), **IV:** 316, 327
Ghost Town (Coover), **Supp. V:** 52–53
Ghost Writer, The (Roth), **Retro. Supp. II:** 22, 308, 309; **Supp. III Part 2:** 420–421
"G.I. Graves in Tuscany" (Hugo), **Supp. VI:** 138
Giachetti, Fosco, **Supp. IV Part 2:** 520

"Giacometti" (Wilbur), **Supp. III Part 2:** 551
Giacometti, Alberto, **Supp. VIII:** 168, 169
Giacomo, Padre, **II:** 278–279
Giant's House, The: A Romance (McCracken), **Supp. X:** 86
"Giant Snail" (Bishop), **Retro. Supp. II:** 49
Giant Weapon, The (Winters), **Supp. II Part 2:** 810
"Giant Woman, The" (Oates), **Supp. II Part 2:** 523
Gibbon, Edward, **I:** 4, 378; **IV:** 126; **Supp. I Part 2:** 503; **Supp. III Part 2:** 629; **Supp. XIII:** 75
Gibbons, Kaye, **Supp. X: 41–54; Supp. XII:** 311
Gibbons, Reginald, **Supp. X:** 113, 124, 127
Gibbons, Richard, **Supp. I Part 1:** 107
"Gibbs" (Rukeyser), **Supp. VI:** 273
Gibbs, Barbara, **Supp. IV Part 2:** 644
Gibbs, Wolcott, **Supp. I Part 2:** 604, 618; **Supp. VIII:** 151
"GIBSON" (Baraka), **Supp. II Part 1:** 54
Gibson, Charles Dana, **Supp. X:** 184
Gibson, Graeme, **Supp. XIII:** 20
Gibson, Wilfrid W., **Retro. Supp. I:** 128
Giddins, Gary, **Supp. XIII:** 245
Gide, André, **I:** 271, 290; **II:** 581; **III:** 210; **IV:** 53, 289; **Supp. I Part 1:** 51; **Supp. IV Part 1:** 80, 284, 347; **Supp. IV Part 2:** 681, 682; **Supp. VIII:** 40; **Supp. X:** 187
Gideon Planish (Lewis), **II:** 455
Gielgud, John, **I:** 82; **Supp. XI:** 305
Gierow, Dr. Karl Ragnar, **III:** 404
Gifford, Bill, **Supp. XI:** 38
"Gift, The" (Creeley), **Supp. IV Part 1:** 153
"Gift, The" (Doolittle), **Supp. I Part 1:** 267
Gift, The (Nabokov), **III:** 246, 255, 261–263; **Retro. Supp. I:** 264, 266, 268–270, 273, 274–275, 278
"Gift from the City, A" (Updike), **Retro. Supp. I:** 320
"Gift of God, The" (Robinson), **III:** 512, 517, 518–521, 524
Gift of the Black Folk, The: The Negroes in the Making of America (Du Bois), **Supp. II Part 1:** 179
"Gift of the Magi, The" (O. Henry), **Supp. II Part 1:** 394, 406, 408
"Gift of the *Osuo,* The" (Johnson), **Supp. VI:** 194
"Gift of the Prodigal, The" (Taylor),
Supp. V: 314, 326
"Gift Outright, The" (Frost), **II:** 152; **Supp. IV Part 1:** 15
"Gigolo" (Plath), **Retro. Supp. II:** 257
"Gila Bend" (Dickey), **Supp. IV Part 1:** 185–186
Gilbert, Jack, **Supp. IX:** 287
Gilbert, Peter, **Supp. IX:** 291, 300
Gilbert, Roger, **Supp. XI:** 124
Gilbert, Sandra M., **Retro. Supp. I:** 42; **Retro. Supp. II:** 342; **Supp. IX:** 66
Gilbert, Susan. *See* Dickinson, Mrs. William A.
Gilbert and Sullivan, **Supp. IV Part 1:** 389
Gil Blas (Le Sage), **II:** 290
Gilded Age, The (Twain), **III:** 504; **IV:** 198
"Gilded Six-Bits, The" (Hurston), **Supp. VI:** 154–155
Gilder, R. W., **Retro. Supp. II:** 66; **Supp. I Part 2:** 418
Gildersleeve, Basil, **Supp. I Part 1:** 369
Giles, H. A., **Retro. Supp. I:** 289
Giles, James R., **Supp. IX:** 11, 15; **Supp. XI:** 219, 223–224, 228, 234
"Giles Corey of the Salem Farms" (Longfellow), **II:** 505, 506; **Retro. Supp. II:** 166, 167
Giles Goat-Boy (Barth), **I:** 121, 122–123, 129, 130, 134, 135–138; **Supp. V:** 39
Gill, Brendan, **Supp. I Part 2:** 659, 660
Gillette, Chester, **I:** 512
Gilligan, Carol, **Supp. XIII:** 216
Gillis, Jim, **IV:** 196
Gillis, Steve, **IV:** 195
Gilman, Charlotte Perkins, **Supp. I Part 2:** 637; **Supp. V:** 121, 284, 285; **Supp. XI: 193–211; Supp. XIII:** 295, 306
Gilman, Daniel Coit, **Supp. I Part 1:** 361, 368, 370
Gilman, Richard, **IV:** 115; **Supp. IV Part 2:** 577; **Supp. XIII:** 100
Gilmore, Eddy, **Supp. I Part 2:** 618
Gilpin, Charles, **III:** 392
Gilpin, Laura, **Retro. Supp. I:** 7
Gilpin, Sam, **Supp. V:** 213
Gilpin, William, **Supp. IV Part 2:** 603
"Gil's Furniture Bought & Sold" (Cisneros), **Supp. VII:** 61–62, 64
"Gimpel the Fool" (Singer), **IV:** 14; **Retro. Supp. II:** 22, 325
Gimpel the Fool and Other Stories (Singer), **IV:** 1, 7–9, 10, 12
"Gin" (Levine), **Supp. V:** 193

"Gingerbread House, The" (Coover), **Supp. V:** 42–43
Gingerbread Lady, The (Simon), **Supp. IV Part 2:** 580, 583–584, 588
Gingerich, Willard, **Supp. IV Part 2:** 510
Gingertown (McKay), **Supp. X:** 132, 139
Gingrich, Arnold, **Retro. Supp. I:** 113
Ginna, Robert, **Supp. IX:** 259
Ginsberg, Allen, **I:** 183; **Retro. Supp. I:** 411, 426, 427; **Retro. Supp. II:** 298; **Supp. II Part 1:** 30, 32, 58, **307–333; Supp. III Part 1:** 2, 91, 96, 98, 100, 222, 226; **Supp. III Part 2:** 541, 627; **Supp. IV Part 1:** 79, 90, 322; **Supp. IV Part 2:** 502; **Supp. V:** 168, 336; **Supp. VIII:** 239, 242–243, 289; **Supp. IX:** 299; **Supp. X:** 120, 204; **Supp. XI:** 135, 297; **Supp. XII:** 118–119, 121–122, 124, 126, 130–131, 136, 182
Gioia, Dana, **Supp. IX:** 279; **Supp. XII:** 209; **Supp. XIII:** 337
Giotto di Bondone, **Supp. I Part 2:** 438; **Supp. XI:** 126
Giovanni, Nikki, **Supp. I Part 1:** 66; **Supp. II Part 1:** 54; **Supp. IV Part 1:** 11; **Supp. VIII:** 214
Giovanni's Room (Baldwin), **Retro. Supp. II:** 5, 6, **6–7,** 8, 10; **Supp. I Part 1:** 51, 52, 55–56, 57, 60, 63, 67; **Supp. III Part 1:** 125
Giovannitti, Arturo, **I:** 476
"Giraffe" (Swenson), **Supp. IV Part 2:** 651
Giraldi, Giovanni Battista. *See* Cinthio
"Girl" (Kincaid), **Supp. VII:** 182–183
"Girl, The" (Olds), **Supp. X:** 207
"Girl from Red Lion, P.A., A" (Mencken), **III:** 111
Girl in Glass, The: Love Poems (W. J. Smith), **Supp. XIII:** 335
"Girl in the Grave, The" (McCoy), **Supp. XIII:** 170
"Girl of the Golden West" (Didion), **Supp. IV Part 1:** 195, 208, 211
Girl of the Golden West, The (Puccini), **III:** 139
"Girl on the Baggage Truck, The" (O'Hara), **III:** 371–372
Girls at Play (Theroux), **Supp. VIII:** 314, 315, 316, **317**
"Girls at the Sphinx, The" (Farrell), **II:** 45
Girl Sleuth, The: A Feminist Guide (Mason), **Supp. VIII:** 133, 135, **139,** 142
"Girl's Story, A" (Bambara), **Supp. XI:** 10–11

"Girl the Prince Liked, The" (Z. Fitzgerald), **Supp. IX:** 71
Girl Who Loved Tom Gordon, The (King), **Supp. V:** 138, 152
Girl with Curious Hair (Wallace), **Supp. X:** 301, **305–308**
"Girl with Curious Hair" (Wallace), **Supp. X:** 306
"Girl with Silver Eyes, The" (Hammett), **Supp. IV Part 1:** 344, 345
"Girl with Talent, The" (Z. Fitzgerald), **Supp. IX:** 71
Girodias, Maurice, **III:** 171; **Supp. XI:** 297
Giroux, Robert, **Retro. Supp. II:** 177, 229, 235; **Supp. IV Part 1:** 280; **Supp. VIII:** 195
Gish, Dorothy, **Retro. Supp. I:** 103
Gissing, George, **II:** 138, 144
Gittings, Robert, **II:** 531
"Give Us Back Our Country" (Masters), **Supp. I Part 2:** 472
"Give Way, Ye Gates" (Roethke), **III:** 536
"Give Your Heart to the Hawks" (Jeffers), **Supp. II Part 2:** 433
"Giving Blood" (Updike), **IV:** 226; **Retro. Supp. I:** 332
Giving Good Weight (McPhee), **Supp. III Part 1:** 307
"Giving Myself Up" (Strand), **Supp. IV Part 2:** 627
Glackens, William, **Retro. Supp. II:** 103
Gladden, Washington, **III:** 293; **Supp. I Part 1:** 5
Gladstone, William Ewart, **Supp. I Part 2:** 419
"Gladys Poem, The" (Alvarez), **Supp. VII:** 10
"Glance at German 'Kultur,' A" (Bourne), **I:** 228
Glance Away, A (Wideman), **Supp. X:** 320
"Glance from the Bridge, A" (Wilbur), **Supp. III Part 2:** 551
Glanville-Hicks, Peggy, **Supp. IV Part 1:** 84
Glare (Ammons), **Supp. VII:** 35–36
Glasgow, Cary, **II:** 173, 182
Glasgow, Ellen, **II:** 173–195; **IV:** 328; **Supp. X:** 228, 234
Glasmon, Kubec, **Supp. XIII:** 166
Glaspell, Susan, **Supp. III Part 1:** 175–191; **Supp. X:** 46
"Glass" (Francis), **Supp. IX:** 80
Glass, Irony, and God (Carson), **Supp. XII:** 97, **104–106**
"Glass Ark, The" (Komunyakaa), **Supp. XIII:** 129
Glass Bees, The (Jünger; Bogan and Mayer, trans.), **Supp. III Part 1:** 63
"Glass Blower of Venice" (Malamud), **Supp. I Part 2:** 450
"Glass Essay, The" (Carson), **Supp. XII: 104–105**
"Glass Face in the Rain, A: New Poems" (Stafford), **Supp. XI: 327–328**
Glass Key, The (Hammett), **Supp. IV Part 1:** 351–353
"Glass Meadows" (Bausch), **Supp. VII:** 53–54
Glass Menagerie, The (T. Williams), **I:** 81; **IV:** 378, 379, 380, 382, 383, 385, 386, 387, 388, 389, 390, 391, 392, 393–394, 395, 398; **Supp. IV Part 1:** 84
"Glass Mountain, The" (Barthelme), **Supp. IV Part 1:** 47
Glatstein, Jacob, **Supp. X:** 70
Glazer, Nathan, **Supp. VIII:** 93, 243
"Gleaners, The" (Merwin), **Supp. III Part 1:** 346
Gleanings in Europe (Cooper), **I:** 346
Gleason, Ralph J., **Supp. IX:** 16
Glenday, Michael, **Retro. Supp. II:** 210
Glimcher, Arne, **Supp. VIII:** 73
"Glimpses" (Jones), **Supp. XI:** 218
Glimpses of the Moon, The (Wharton), **II:** 189–190; **IV:** 322–323; **Retro. Supp. I:** 381
"Glimpses of Vietnamese Life" (Levertov), **Supp. III Part 1:** 282
Glisson, J. T., **Supp. X:** 234
Gloria Mundi (Frederic), **II:** 144–145
Gloria Naylor (Fowler), **Supp. VIII:** 224
Glory of Hera, The (Gordon), **II:** 196–197, 198, 199, 217–220
Glory of the Conquered, The (Glaspell), **Supp. III Part 1:** 176
Glotfelty, Cheryll, **Supp. IX:** 25
Gluck, Christoph Willibald, **II:** 210, 211
Glück, Louise, **Supp. V: 77–94; Supp. VIII:** 272; **Supp. X:** 209
"Glutton, The" (Shapiro), **Supp. II Part 2:** 705
"Glutton for Punishment, A" (Yates), **Supp. XI:** 341
Gnädiges Fräulein, The (T. Williams), **IV:** 382, 395, 398
Gnomes and Occasions (Nemerov), **III:** 269
Gnomologia (Fuller), **II:** 111
"Gnothis Seauton" (Emerson), **II:** 11, 18–19
"Goal of Intellectual Men, The" (Eberhart), **I:** 529–530
Go-Between, The (Hartley), **Supp. I Part 1:** 293
God and the American Writer (Kazin), **Supp. VIII: 108–109**
Godard, Jean-Luc, **Supp. I Part 2:** 558
Godbey (Masters), **Supp. I Part 2:** 472
God Bless You, Mr. Rosewater (Vonnegut), **Supp. II Part 2:** 758, 767, 768–769, 771, 772
Goddess Abides, The (Buck), **Supp. II Part 1:** 129, 131–132
Gödel, Kurt, **Supp. IV Part 1:** 43
Godfather (Puzo), **Supp. IV Part 1:** 390
"God in the Doorway" (Dillard), **Supp. VI:** 28
"God is a distant-stately Lover" (Dickinson), **I:** 471
Godkin, E. L., **II:** 274
God Knows (Heller), **Supp. IV Part 1:** 386, 388–389
God Made Alaska for the Indians (Reed), **Supp. X:** 241
God of His Fathers, The (London), **II:** 469
God of Vengeance (Asch), **IV:** 11
Go Down, Moses (Faulkner), **Retro. Supp. I:** 75, 82, 85, 86, 88, 89, 90, 92
"Go Down, Moses" (Faulkner), **II:** 71–72
Go Down, Moses (Hayden), **Supp. II Part 1:** 365
Go Down, Moses and Other Stories (Faulkner), **II:** 71; **Supp. X:** 52
"Go Down Death A Funeral Sermon" (Johnson), **Supp. IV Part 1:** 7
"God Rest Ye Merry, Gentlemen" (Hemingway), **IV:** 122
Godric (Buechner), **Supp. XII:** 53
Gods, The (Goldbarth), **Supp. XII:** 189, 190
Gods Arrive, The (Wharton), **IV:** 326–327; **Retro. Supp. I:** 382
"God Save the Rights of Man" (Freneau), **Supp. II Part 1:** 268
"Godsildren" (Swenson), **Supp. IV Part 2:** 645
"God's Christ Theory" (Carson), **Supp. XII:** 106
God's Country and My People (Morris), **III:** 238
Gods Determinations touching his Elect: and the Elects Combat in their Conversion, and Coming up to God in Christ together with the Comfortable Effects thereof (Taylor), **IV:** 155–160, 165
God-Seeker, The (Lewis), **II:** 456

God's Favorite (Simon), **Supp. IV Part 2:** 575, 586, 588, 590
God's Little Acre (Caldwell), **I:** 288, 289, 290, 297, 298–302, 305–306, 309, 310
God's Man: A Novel in Wood Cuts (Ward), **I:** 31
"God's Peace in November" (Jeffers), **Supp. II Part 2:** 420
"God Stiff" (Carson), **Supp. XII:** 106
God's Trombones (Johnson), **Supp. II Part 1:** 201
Godwin, William, **II:** 304; **III:** 415; **Supp. I Part 1:** 126, 146; **Supp. I Part 2:** 512, 513–514, 522, 709, 719
God without Thunder (Ransom), **III:** 495–496, 499
Goebbels, Josef, **III:** 560
Goebel, Irma, **Supp. X:** 95
Goen, C. C., **I:** 560
Goethe, Johann Wolfgang von, **I:** 181, 396, 587–588; **II:** 5, 6, 320, 344, 488, 489, 492, 502, 556; **III:** 395, 453, 607, 612, 616; **IV:** 50, 64, 173, 326; **Retro. Supp. I:** 360; **Retro. Supp. II:** 94; **Supp. I Part 2:** 423, 457; **Supp. II Part 1:** 26; **Supp. III Part 1:** 63; **Supp. IX:** 131, 308; **Supp. X:** 60; **Supp. XI:** 169
Gogol, Nikolai, **I:** 296; **IV:** 1, 4; **Retro. Supp. I:** 266, 269; **Supp. VIII:** 14
Going, William T., **Supp. VIII:** 126
Going After Cacciato (O'Brien), **Supp. V:** 237, 238, 239, 244–246, 248, 249
Going All the Way (Wakefield), **Supp. VIII:** 43
"Going Critical" (Bambara), **Supp. XI:** 14
Going for the Rain (Ortiz), **Supp. IV Part 2:** 499, 505–508, 509, 514
"Going Home by Last Night" (Kinnell), **Supp. III Part 1:** 244
"Going Home in America" (Hardwick), **Supp. III Part 1:** 205
"Going North" (Salinas), **Supp. XIII:** 316
Going South (Lardner and Buck), **II:** 427
Going to Meet the Man (Baldwin), **Supp. I Part 1:** 60, 62–63
"Going to Meet the Man" (Baldwin), **Retro. Supp. II:** 8, 9; **Supp. I Part 1:** 62–63
"Going to Naples" (Welty), **IV:** 278; **Retro. Supp. I:** 352, 353
"Going to Shrewsbury" (Jewett), **II:** 393
"Going to the Bakery" (Bishop), **Supp. I Part 1:** 93
Going-to-the-Stars (Lindsay), **Supp. I Part 2:** 398
Going-to-the-Sun (Lindsay), **Supp. I Part 2:** 397–398
Going to the Territory (Ellison), **Retro. Supp. II:** 119, 123–124
"Going towards Pojoaque, A December Full Moon/72" (Harjo), **Supp. XII:** 218
"Going Under" (Dubus), **Supp. VII:** 83
"Gold" (Francis), **Supp. IX:** 82
Gold (O'Neill), **III:** 391
Gold, Michael, **II:** 26; **IV:** 363, 364, 365; **Retro. Supp. II:** 341; **Supp. I Part 1:** 331; **Supp. I Part 2:** 609
Goldbarth, Albert, **Supp. XII:** 175–195
Goldbarth's Book of Occult Phenomena (Goldbarth), **Supp. XII:** 181
Goldberg, S. L., **Supp. VIII:** 238
"Gold Bug, The" (Poe), **III:** 410, 413, 419, 420
Gold Bug Variations, The (Powers), **Supp. IX:** 210, 212, **216–217**, 219
Gold Cell, The (Olds), **Supp. X: 206–209**
Gold Diggers, The (Monette), **Supp. X:** 153
Golde, Miss (Mencken's Secretary), **III:** 104, 107
Golden, Harry, **III:** 579, 581; **Supp. VIII:** 244
Golden, Mike, **Supp. XI:** 294, 295, 297, 299, 303
Golden Age, The (Gurney), **Supp. V:** 101–103
Golden Apples (Rawlings), **Supp. X: 228–229,** 230, 234
Golden Apples, The (Welty), **IV:** 261, 271–274, 281, 293; **Retro. Supp. I:** 341, 342, 343, **350–351,** 352, 355
Golden Apples of the Sun, The (Bradbury), **Supp. IV Part 1:** 102, 103
Golden Book of Springfield, The (Lindsay), **Supp. I Part 2:** 376, 379, 395, 396
Golden Bough, The (Frazer), **II:** 204, 549; **III:** 6–7; **Supp. I Part 1:** 18; **Supp. IX:** 123; **Supp. X:** 124
Golden Bowl, The (James), **II:** 320, 333, 335; **Retro. Supp. I:** 215, 216, 218–219, 232, **234–235,** 374
Golden Boy (Odets), **Supp. II Part 2:** 538, 539, 540–541, 546, 551
Golden Calves, The (Auchincloss), **Supp. IV Part 1:** 35
Golden Day, The (Mumford), **Supp. II Part 2:** 471, 475, 477, 483, 484, 488–489, 493
Golden Fleece, The (Gurney), **Supp. V:** 97
"Golden Heifer, The" (Wylie), **Supp. I Part 2:** 707
"Golden Honeymoon, The" (Lardner), **II:** 429–430, 431
Golden Journey, The (W. J. Smith and Bogan, comps.), **Supp. XIII:** 347
"Golden Lads" (Marquand), **III:** 56
Golden Legend, The (Longfellow), **II:** 489, 490, 495, 505, 506, 507; **Retro. Supp. II:** 159, 165, 166
Golden Mean and Other Poems, The (Tate and Wills), **IV:** 122
"Golden Retrievals" (Doty), **Supp. XI:** 132
Goldensohn, Lorrie, **Retro. Supp. II:** 51
Golden Treasury of Best Songs and Lyrical Poems in the English Language (Palgrave), **Retro. Supp. I:** 124
Golden Whales of California and Other Rhymes in the American Language, The (Lindsay), **Supp. I Part 2:** 394–395, 396
"Goldfish Bowl, The" (Francis), **Supp. IX:** 78
Golding, Arthur, **III:** 467, 468
Golding, William, **Supp. IV Part 1:** 297
Goldini, Carlo, **II:** 274
Goldkorn Tales (Epstein), **Supp. XII: 163–164**
Goldman, Albert, **Supp. XI:** 299
Goldman, Emma, **III:** 176, 177; **Supp. I Part 2:** 524
Goldman, William, **Supp. IV Part 2:** 474
"Gold Mountain Stories" project (Kingston), **Supp. V:** 164
Goldring, Douglas, **III:** 458
Goldsmith, Oliver, **II:** 273, 282, 299, 304, 308, 314, 315, 514; **Retro. Supp. I:** 335; **Supp. I Part 1:** 310; **Supp. I Part 2:** 503, 714, 716
Gold Standard and the Logic of Naturalism, The (Michaels), **Retro. Supp. I:** 369
Goldwater, Barry, **I:** 376; **III:** 38
Goldwyn, Samuel, **Retro. Supp. II:** 199; **Supp. I Part 1:** 281
Golem, The (Leivick), **IV:** 6
"Goliardic Song" (Hecht), **Supp. X:** 63
"Go Like This" (Moore), **Supp. X:** 165
Goll, Ivan, **Supp. III Part 1:** 235, 243–244; **Supp. III Part 2:** 621
Goncharova, Natalya, **Supp. IX:** 66
Goncourt, Edmond de, **II:** 325, 328;

III: 315, 317–318, 321; **Retro. Supp. I:** 226
Goncourt, Jules de, **II:** 328; **III:** 315, 317–318, 321
Gone Fishin' (Mosley), **Supp. XIII:** 235–236, 240
Gone with the Wind (film), **Retro. Supp. I:** 113
Gone with the Wind (Mitchell), **II:** 177; **Retro. Supp. I:** 340
Gongora y Argote, Luis de, **II:** 552
Gonzalez, David, **Supp. VIII:** 85
Gooch, Brad, **Supp. XII:** 121
Good, George, **Supp. XI:** 306
"Good and Not So Good, The" (Dunn), **Supp. XI:** 141
"Good Anna, The" (Stein), **IV:** 37, 40, 43
Good As Gold (Heller), **Supp. IV Part 1:** 386, 388, 394
Good Boys and Dead Girls and Other Essays (Gordon), **Supp. IV Part 1:** 309–310
"Good-by and Keep Cold" (Frost), **Retro. Supp. I:** 135
"Good-bye" (Emerson), **II:** 19
"Goodbye, Christ" (Hughes), **Retro. Supp. I:** 202, 203
Goodbye, Columbus (Roth), **Retro. Supp. II:** 298, 299, 308; **Supp. III Part 2:** 403–406
"Goodbye, Columbus" (Roth), **Supp. III Part 2:** 401, 404, 408–409, 411
Goodbye, Columbus and Five Short Stories (Roth), **Retro. Supp. II:** 297
"Goodbye, Goldeneye" (Swenson), **Supp. IV Part 2:** 651
"Goodbye, My Brother" (Cheever), **Supp. I Part 1:** 175, 177, 193
"Goodbye and Good Luck" (Paley), **Supp. VI:** 219, 223
Goodbye Girl, The (film), **Supp. IV Part 2:** 589
Goodbye Girl, The (musical), **Supp. IV Part 2:** 576, 588
Goodbye Girl, The (Simon), **Supp. IV Part 2:** 575
Goodbye Look, The (Macdonald), **Supp. IV Part 2:** 473, 474
"Good-Bye My Fancy" (Whitman), **IV:** 348
"Goodbye to All That" (Didion), **Supp. IV Part 1:** 197
Goodbye to All That (Graves), **I:** 477
"Good-Bye to the Mezzogiorno" (Auden), **Supp. II Part 1:** 19
"Goodbye to the Poetry of Calcium" (Wright), **Supp. III Part 2:** 599
"Good Company" (Matthews), **Supp. IX:** 160

"Good Country People" (O'Connor), **III:** 343, 350, 351, 352, 358; **Retro. Supp. II:** 229, 232
Good Day to Die, A (Harrison), **Supp. VIII:** 42–44, 45, 47
Good Doctor, The (Simon), **Supp. IV Part 2:** 575, 585
Good Earth, The (Buck), **Supp. I Part 1:** 49; **Supp. II Part 1:** 115–175, 118, 125, 132
Good European, The (Blackmur), **Supp. II Part 1:** 91
Good Evening Mr. & Mrs. America, and All the Ships at Sea (Bausch), **Supp. VII:** 41, 47, 52
Good Gray Poet, The (O'Connor), **Retro. Supp. I:** 407
Good Health and How We Won It (Sinclair), **Supp. V:** 285–286
Good Hearts (Price), **Supp. VI:** 259, 265
"Good Job Gone, A" (Hughes), **Retro. Supp. I:** 204
Good Journey, A (Ortiz), **Supp. IV Part 2:** 497, 499, 503, 505, 509–510, 514
Good Luck in Cracked Italian (Hugo), **Supp. VI:** 133, 137–138
Goodman, Allegra, **Supp. XII:** 159
Goodman, Paul, **I:** 218, 261; **III:** 39; **Supp. I Part 2:** 524; **Supp. VIII:** 239–240
Goodman, Philip, **III:** 105, 108
Goodman, Walter, **Supp. IV Part 2:** 532
Good Man Is Hard to Find, A (O'Connor), **III:** 339, 343–345
"Good Man Is Hard to Find, A" (O'Connor), **III:** 339, 344, 353; **Retro. Supp. II:** 230–231
Good Man Is Hard to Find and Other Stories, A (O'Connor), **Retro. Supp. II:** 229, 230–232
Good Morning, America (Sandburg), **III:** 592–593
"Good Morning, Major" (Marquand), **III:** 56
Good Morning, Midnight (Rhys), **Supp. III Part 1:** 43
"Good Morning, Revolution" (Hughes), **Retro. Supp. I:** 201, 203
Good Morning Revolution: Uncollected Writings of Social Protest (Hughes), **Retro. Supp. I:** 194, 201, 202, 209
Good Mother, The (S. Miller), **Supp. XII:** 289, 290–294, 299, 301
Good News (Abbey), **Supp. XIII:** 11–12
"Good News from New-England"

(Johnson), **Supp. I Part 1:** 115
Good News of Death and Other Poems (Simpson), **Supp. IX:** 265, 268–269
Good Night, Willie Lee, I'll See You in the Morning (Walker), **Supp. III Part 2:** 520, 531
Goodrich, Samuel G., **Supp. I Part 1:** 38
Good Scent from a Strange Mountain, A (R. O. Butler), **Supp. XII:** 62, 70–72
Good School, A (Yates), **Supp. XI:** 334, 346–347, 348, 349
"*Good Shepherdess, The*/La Buena Pastora" (Mora), **Supp. XIII:** 228–229
Good Will (Smiley), **Supp. VI:** 292, 299–300
Goodwin, K. L., **III:** 478
Goodwin, Stephen, **Supp. V:** 314, 316, 322, 323, 325
"Good Word for Winter, A" (Lowell), **Supp. I Part 2:** 420
Goodwyn, Janet, **Retro. Supp. I:** 370
"Goose Fish, The" (Nemerov), **III:** 272, 284
"Goose Pond" (Kunitz), **Supp. III Part 1:** 262
Goose-Step, The (Sinclair), **Supp. V:** 276
Gordon, A. R., **III:** 199
Gordon, Caroline, **II:** 196–222, 536, 537; **III:** 454, 482; **IV:** 123, 126–127, 139, 282; **Retro. Supp. II:** 177, 222, 229, 233, 235; **Supp. II Part 1:** 139
Gordon, Charles G., **I:** 454
Gordon, Don, **Supp. X:** 119
Gordon, Eugene, **Supp. II Part 1:** 170
Gordon, Fran, **Supp. XIII:** 111
Gordon, James Morris, **II:** 197
Gordon, Lois, **Supp. IV Part 1:** 48; **Supp. V:** 46
Gordon, Lyndall, **Retro. Supp. I:** 55
Gordon, Mary, **Supp. IV Part 1:** 297–317
Gordon, Peter, **Supp. XII:** 3–4, 4–5, 8
Gordon, Ruth, **IV:** 357
Gore, Thomas Pryor, **Supp. IV Part 2:** 679
Gorey, Edward, **IV:** 430, 436
Gorilla, My Love (Bambara), **Supp. XI:** 1, 2–7
"Gorilla, My Love" (Bambara), **Supp. XI:** 2, 3–4
Gorki, Maxim, **I:** 478; **II:** 49; **III:** 402; **IV:** 299; **Supp. I Part 1:** 5, 51
Gorra, Michael, **Supp. V:** 71
Goslings, The (Sinclair), **Supp. V:** 276, 281

Gospel According to Joe, The (Gurney), **Supp. V:** 99
"Gospel According to Saint Mark, The" (Gordon), **Supp. IV Part 1:** 310
Gospel according to the Son (Mailer), **Retro. Supp. II:** 213
"Gospel of Beauty, The" (Lindsay), **Supp. I Part 2:** 380, 382, 384, 385, 391, 396
Gospel Singer, The (Crews), **Supp. XI:** 102, **109**
Gosse, Edmund, **II:** 538; **IV:** 350; **Supp. VIII:** 157
Gossips, Gorgons, and Crones: The Fates of the Earth (Caputi), **Supp. IV Part 1:** 335
Go Tell It on the Mountain (Baldwin), **Retro. Supp. II:** 1, 2, 3, **4–5**, 7, 14; **Supp. I Part 1:** 48, 49, 50, 51, 52, 53–54, 55, 56, 57, 59, 61, 63, 64, 67; **Supp. II Part 1:** 170
Gotera, Vince, **Supp. XIII:** 115, 116, 119, 121, 127
Gothic Writers (Thomson, Voller, and Frank, eds.), **Retro. Supp. II:** 273
"Go to the Devil and Shake Yourself" (song), **Supp. I Part 2:** 580
"Go to the Shine That's on a Tree" (Eberhart), **I:** 523
Go to the Widow-Maker (Jones), **Supp. XI:** 214, **225–226**, 227, 229, 233
Gottfried, Martin, **Supp. IV Part 2:** 584
Gotthelf, Allan, **Supp. IV Part 2:** 528
Gottlieb, Robert, **Supp. IV Part 2:** 474
Gottschalk and the Grande Tarantelle (Brooks), **Supp. III Part 1:** 86
"Gottschalk and the Grande Tarantelle" (Brooks), **Supp. III Part 1:** 86–87
Gould (Dixon), **Supp. XII:** 152, **153**
Gould, Edward Sherman, **I:** 346
Gould, Janice, **Supp. IV Part 1:** 322, 327; **Supp. XII:** 229
Gould, Jay, **I:** 4
Gourd Dancer, The (Momaday), **Supp. IV Part 2:** 481, 487, 491, 493
Gourmont, Remy de, **I:** 270, 272; **II:** 528, 529; **III:** 457, 467–468, 477; **Retro. Supp. I:** 55
Gouverneurs de la Rosée (Roumain), **Supp. IV Part 1:** 360, 367
"Governors of Wyoming, The" (Proulx), **Supp. VII:** 264
Goyen, William, **Supp. V:** 220
"Grace" (Dubus), **Supp. VII:** 91
"Grace" (Harjo), **Supp. XII:** 224
Grace Notes (Dove), **Supp. IV Part 1:** 248–250, 252
"Graduation" (Dubus), **Supp. VII:** 84

Grady, Henry W., **Supp. I Part 1:** 370
Graeber, Laurel, **Supp. V:** 15
Graham, Billy, **I:** 308
Graham, Don, **Supp. XI:** 252, 254
Graham, Jorie, **Supp. IX:** 38, 52; **Supp. X:** 73; **Supp. XII:** 209; **Supp. XIII:** 85
Graham, Martha, **Supp. XI:** 152
Graham, Maryemma, **Retro. Supp. I:** 201, 204
Graham, Nan, **Supp. XII:** 272
Graham, Sheilah, **II:** 94; **Retro. Supp. I:** 97, 113–114, 115; **Supp. IX:** 63
Graham, Shirley, **Supp. I Part 1:** 51
Graham, Stephen, **Supp. I Part 2:** 397
Graham, Tom (pseudonym). *See* Lewis, Sinclair
Grahn, Judy, **Supp. IV Part 1:** 325, 330
Grainger, Percy, **Supp. I Part 2:** 386
Grain of Mustard Seed, A (Sarton), **Supp. VIII: 259–260,** 263
Gramar (Lowth), **II:** 8
Grammar of Motives, A (Burke), **I:** 272, 275, 276–278, 283, 284
Granberry, Edwin, **I:** 288
Grand Design, The (Dos Passos), **I:** 489–490
"Grande Malade, The" (Barnes), **Supp. III Part 1:** 36
"Grandfather" (Dunn), **Supp. XI:** 147
"Grandfather and Grandson" (Singer), **Retro. Supp. II:** 325
"Grandfather's Blessing" (Alvarez), **Supp. VII:** 2
"Grand Forks" (Simpson), **Supp. IX:** 280–281
"Grand Inquisitor" (Dostoyevsky), **IV:** 106
Grandissimes (Cable), **II:** 291
"Grand-Master Nabokov" (Updike), **Retro. Supp. I:** 317
"Grand Miracle, The" (Karr), **Supp. XI:** 251
"Grandmother" (Gunn Allen), **Supp. IV Part 1:** 320, 325
"Grandmother in Heaven" (Levine), **Supp. V:** 186
"Grandmother of the Sun: Ritual Gynocracy in Native America" (Gunn Allen), **Supp. IV Part 1:** 328
"Grandmothers" (Rich), **Retro. Supp. II:** 291
Grandmothers of the Light: A Medicine Woman's Sourcebook (Gunn Allen, ed.), **Supp. IV Part 1:** 332, 333–334
"Grandmother Songs, The" (Hogan), **Supp. IV Part 1:** 413

"Grandpa and the Statue" (A. Miller), **III:** 147
"Grandparents" (Lowell), **II:** 550
"Grandstand Complex, The" (McCoy), **Supp. XIII:** 166
Grange, Red, **II:** 416
Granger's Index to Poetry (anthology), **Retro. Supp. I:** 37, 39
Grant, Lee, **Supp. XIII:** 295
Grant, Madison, **Supp. II Part 1:** 170
Grant, Richard, **Supp. X:** 282
Grant, Ulysses S., **I:** 4, 15; **II:** 542; **III:** 506, 584; **IV:** 348, 446; **Supp. I Part 2:** 418
Grantwood, **Retro. Supp. I:** 416, 417
"Grapes, The" (Hecht), **Supp. X:** 65–66
"Grape Sherbet" (Dove), **Supp. IV Part 1:** 246
Grapes of Wrath, The (Steinbeck), **I:** 301; **III:** 589; **IV:** 51, 53–55, 59, 63, 65, 67, 68, 69; **Supp. V:** 290; **Supp. XI:** 169
"Grapevine, The" (Ashbery), **Supp. III Part 1:** 4
"Grass" (Sandburg), **III:** 584
Grass, Günter, **Supp. VIII:** 40
"Grasse: The Olive Trees" (Wilbur), **Supp. III Part 2:** 550
Grass Harp, The (Capote), **Supp. III Part 1:** 114–117, 123
Grass Still Grows, The (A. Miller), **III:** 146
Gratitude to Old Teachers (Bly), **Supp. IV Part 1:** 73
"Grave, A" (Moore), **III:** 195, 202, 208, 213
Grave, The (Blair), **Supp. I Part 1:** 150
"Grave, The" (Porter), **III:** 433, 443, 445–446
"Grave, The" (Winters), **Supp. II Part 2:** 795, 796
"Graven Image" (O'Hara), **III:** 320
Grave of the Right Hand, The (Wright), **Supp. V:** 332, 338, 339
"Grave Piece" (Eberhart), **I:** 533
Graves, Billy, **Supp. I Part 2:** 607
Graves, John, **Supp. V:** 220
Graves, Morris, **Supp. X:** 264
Graves, Peter, **Supp. IV Part 2:** 474
Graves, Rean, **Supp. I Part 1:** 326
Graves, Robert, **I:** 437, 477, 523; **Supp. I Part 2:** 541; **Supp. IV Part 1:** 280, 348; **Supp. IV Part 2:** 685
Graveyard for Lunatics, A (Bradbury), **Supp. IV Part 1:** 102, 114–116
Gravity's Rainbow (Pynchon), **Supp. II Part 2:** 617, 618–619, 621–625, 627, 630, 633–636; **Supp. IV Part**

I: 279; **Supp. V:** 44
Gray, Cecil, **Supp. I Part 1:** 258
Gray, Francine Du Plessix, **Supp. V:** 169
Gray, James, **III:** 207; **Supp. I Part 2:** 410
Gray, Paul, **Supp. IV Part 1:** 305; **Supp. IV Part 2:** 639
Gray, Thomas, **I:** 68; **Supp. I Part 1:** 150; **Supp. I Part 2:** 422, 716
Gray, Thomas A., **Supp. I Part 2:** 710
"Gray Heron, The" (Kinnell), **Supp. III Part 1:** 250
"Gray Mills of Farley, The" (Jewett), **Retro. Supp. II:** 132, 144
Grayson, Charles, **Supp. XIII:** 171
"Gray Squirrel" (Francis), **Supp. IX:** 90
Grealy, Lucy, **Supp. XII:** 310
Greasy Lake (Boyle), **Supp. VIII:** 14–15
"Greasy Lake" (Boyle), **Supp. VIII:** 15
"Great Adventure of Max Breuck, The" (Lowell), **II:** 522
Great American Novel, The (Roth), **Retro. Supp. II:** 301, 306–307; **Supp. III Part 2:** 414–416
Great American Short Novels (Phillips, ed.), **Supp. VIII:** 156
Great Battles of the World (Crane), **I:** 415
Great Christian Doctrine of Original Sin Defended, The . . . (Edwards), **I:** 549, 557, 559
Great Circle (Aiken), **I:** 53, 55, 57
"Great Class-Reunion Bazaar, The" (Theroux), **Supp. VIII:** 312
Great Day, The (Hurston), **Supp. VI:** 154
Great Days (Barthelme), **Supp. IV Part 1:** 39
Great Days, The (Dos Passos), **I:** 491
Great Digest (Pound, trans.), **III:** 472
"Great Elegy for John Donne" (Brodsky), **Supp. VIII:** 21, 23
Greater Inclination, The (Wharton), **Retro. Supp. I:** 363, **364–365**, 366
"Greater Torment, The" (Blackmur), **Supp. II Part 1:** 92
Greatest Hits 1969–1996 (Salinas), **Supp. XIII:** 311
"Greatest Thing in the World, The" (Mailer), **Retro. Supp. II:** 196
Great Expectations (Acker), **Supp. XII:** 5, **9–11**
Great Expectations (Dickens), **III:** 247; **Retro. Supp. II:** 282; **Supp. I Part 1:** 35

"Great Figure, The" (W. C. Williams), **IV:** 414
"Great Fillmore Street Buffalo Drive, The" (Momaday), **Supp. IV Part 2:** 493
Great Gatsby, The (Fitzgerald), **I:** 107, 375, 514; **II:** 77, 79, 83, 84, 85, 87, 91–93, 94, 96, 98; **III:** 244, 260, 372, 572; **IV:** 124, 297; **Retro. Supp. I:** 98, 105, **105–108**, 110, 114, 115, 335, 359; **Retro. Supp. II:** 107, 201; **Supp. II Part 2:** 626; **Supp. III Part 2:** 585; **Supp. IV Part 2:** 468, 475; **Supp. IX:** 57, 58; **Supp. X:** 175; **Supp. XI:** 65, 69, 334
Great Gatsby, The (Fitzgerald) (Modern Library), **Retro. Supp. I:** 113
Great God Brown, The (O'Neill), **III:** 165, 391, 394–395
Great Goodness of Life: A Coon Show (Baraka), **Supp. II Part 1:** 47
Great Inclination, The (Wharton), **IV:** 310
"Great Infirmities" (Simic), **Supp. VIII:** 277
Great Jones Street (DeLillo), **Supp. VI:** 2, 3, 8–9, 11, 12
"Great Lawsuit, The: Man *versus* Men: Woman *versus* Women" (Fuller), **Retro. Supp. I:** 156; **Supp. II Part 1:** 292
"Great Men and Their Environment" (James), **II:** 347
"Great Mississippi Bubble, The" (Irving), **II:** 314
Great Railway Bazaar, The: By Train through Asia (Theroux), **Supp. VIII:** 318, 319, **320–321**, 322
Great Stories of Suspense (Millar, ed.), **Supp. IV Part 2:** 474
Great Topics of the World (Goldbarth), **Supp. XII:** 187, 189, 191
Great Valley, The (Masters), **Supp. I Part 2:** 465
Great World and Timothy Colt, The (Auchincloss), **Supp. IV Part 1:** 25, 31, 32
"Greek Boy, The" (Bryant), **Supp. I Part 1:** 168
Greek Mind/Jewish Soul: The Conflicted Art of Cynthia Ozick (Strandberg), **Supp. V:** 273
"Greek Partisan, The" (Bryant), **Supp. I Part 1:** 168
Greeley, Horace, **II:** 7; **IV:** 197, 286–287
Green, Ashbel, **Supp. IV Part 2:** 474
Green, Henry, **IV:** 279; **Retro. Supp.**

I: 354; **Supp. III Part 1:** 3; **Supp. XI:** 294–295, 296, 297; **Supp. XII:** 315
Green, Jack, **Supp. IV Part 1:** 284–285
Green, Martin, **Supp. I Part 1:** 299
Green, Michelle, **Supp. IV Part 1:** 95
"Green Automobile, The" (Ginsberg), **Supp. II Part 1:** 322
Greenberg, Eliezer, **Supp. I Part 2:** 432
Greenberg, Jonathan, **Supp. XII:** 285
Greenberg, Samuel, **I:** 393
Green Bough, A (Faulkner), **Retro. Supp. I:** 84
Green Centuries (Gordon), **II:** 196, 197–207, 209
"Green Crab's Shell, A" (Doty), **Supp. XI:** 126
"Green Door, The" (O. Henry), **Supp. II Part 1:** 395
Greene, A. C., **Supp. V:** 223, 225
Greene, Graham, **I:** 480; **II:** 62, 320; **III:** 57, 556; **Retro. Supp. I:** 215; **Supp. I Part 1:** 280; **Supp. IV Part 1:** 341; **Supp. V:** 298; **Supp. IX:** 261; **Supp. XI:** 99, **Supp. XI:** 104; **Supp. XIII:** 233
Greene, Helga, **Supp. IV Part 1:** 134, 135
Greene, J. Lee, **Retro. Supp. II:** 121
Greene, Nathanael, **Supp. I Part 2:** 508
Greene, Richard Tobias, **III:** 76
"Greene-ing of the Portables, The" (Cowley), **Supp. II Part 1:** 140
"Greenest Continent, The" (Stevens), **Retro. Supp. I:** 304
Greenfeld, Josh, **III:** 364
Green Hills of Africa (Hemingway), **II:** 253; **Retro. Supp. I:** 182, 186
"Green Lampshade" (Simic), **Supp. VIII:** 283
Greenlanders, The (Smiley), **Supp. VI:** 292, **296–298**, 299, 305, 307
Greenlaw, Edwin A., **IV:** 453
"Greenleaf" (O'Connor), **III:** 350, 351; **Retro. Supp. II:** 233, 237
Greenman, Walter F., **I:** 217, 222
Green Memories (Mumford), **Supp. II Part 2:** 474, 475, 479, 480–481
Green Pastures, The (Connelly), **Supp. II Part 1:** 223
"Green Red Brown and White" (Swenson), **Supp. IV Part 2:** 639
"Green River" (Bryant), **Supp. I Part 1:** 155, 164
Green Shadows, White Whale (Bradbury), **Supp. IV Part 1:** 102, 103, 116

"Green Shirt, The" (Olds), **Supp. X:** 209
Greenslet, Ferris, **I:** 19; **Retro. Supp. I:** 9, 10, 11, 13; **Retro. Supp. II:** 41
Greenspan, Alan, **Supp. IV Part 2:** 526
Greenstreet, Sydney, **Supp. IV Part 1:** 356
Greenwald, Ted, **Supp. IV Part 2:** 423
Green Wall, The (Wright), **Supp. III Part 2:** 591, 593, 595
Green Wave, The (Rukeyser), **Supp. VI:** 273, 280
"Green Ways" (Kunitz), **Supp. III Part 1:** 265
Green with Beasts (Merwin), **Supp. III Part 1:** 340, 344–346
Greenwood, Grace, **Supp. XIII:** 141
Gregerson, Linda, **Supp. IV Part 2:** 651; **Supp. X:** 204–205; **Supp. XI:** 142
"Gregorio Valdes" (Bishop), **Retro. Supp. II:** 51
Gregory, Alyse, **I:** 221, 226, 227, 231
Gregory, Horace, **II:** 512; **Supp. III Part 2:** 614, 615; **Supp. IX:** 229
Gregory, Lady Isabella Augusta, **III:** 458
Gregory, Sinda, **Supp. X:** 260, 268
Grendel (Gardner), **Supp. VI:** 63, **67,** 68, 74
"Gretel in Darkness" (Glück), **Supp. V:** 82
Gretta (Caldwell), **I:** 301, 302
Greuze, Jean Baptiste, **Supp. I Part 2:** 714
Grey, Zane, **Supp. XIII:** 5
Griffin, Bartholomew, **Supp. I Part 1:** 369
Griffin, John Howard, **Supp. VIII:** 208
Griffin, Merv, **Supp. IV Part 2:** 526
Griffith, Albert J., **Supp. V:** 325
Griffith, D. W., **I:** 31, 481–482; **Retro. Supp. I:** 103, 325; **Supp. XI:** 45
Griffiths, Clyde, **I:** 511
Grile, Dod (pseudonym). *See* Bierce, Ambrose
Grimm, Herman, **II:** 17
Grimm brothers, **II:** 378; **III:** 101, 491, 492; **IV:** 266; **Supp. I Part 2:** 596, 622; **Supp. X:** 78, 84, 86
Gris, Juan, **I:** 442; **Retro. Supp. I:** 430
Griswold, Rufus Wilmot, **III:** 409, 429; **Retro. Supp. II:** 261, 262
Grogg, Sam, Jr., **Supp. IV Part 2:** 468, 471
Gromer, Crystal, **Supp. XII:** 297
Gronlund, Laurence, **II:** 276
"Groping for Trouts" (Gass), **Supp. VI:** 87

Grosholz, Emily, **Supp. XII:** 185
"Grosse Fuge" (Doty), **Supp. XI:** 126–127
Grossman, Allen, **Retro. Supp. II:** 83
Grosz, George, **III:** 172; **IV:** 438; **Retro. Supp. II:** 339; **Supp. X:** 137
"Groundhog, The" (Eberhart), **I:** 523, 530–532, 533
"Ground on Which I Stand, The" (Wilson), **Supp. VIII:** 331
Group, The (McCarthy), **II:** 570, 574–578
"Group of Two, A" (Jarrell), **II:** 368
Group Therapy (Hearon), **Supp. VIII: 64–65**
"Grove" (Goldbarth), **Supp. XII:** 176
Groves of Academe, The (McCarthy), **II:** 568–571
"Growing Season, The" (Caldwell), **I:** 309
Growing Up Gay: A Literary Anthology (Singer, ed.), **Supp. IV Part 1:** 330
"Growing Up Good in Maycomb" (Shaffer), **Supp. VIII:** 128
"Grown-Up" (Jewett), **Retro. Supp. II:** 134
"Growth" (Lowell), **II:** 554
Growth of the American Republic, The (Morison and Commager), **Supp. I Part 2:** 484
"Growtown Buggle, The" (Jewett), **Retro. Supp. II:** 132
Gruenberg, Louis, **III:** 392
Grumbach, Doris, **II:** 560
Guardian Angel, The (Holmes), **Supp. I Part 1:** 315–316
Guard of Honor (Cozzens), **I:** 370–372, 375, 376–377, 378, 379
Guare, John, **Supp. XIII:** 196, 207
Gubar, Susan, **Retro. Supp. I:** 42; **Retro. Supp. II:** 342; **Supp. IX:** 66
Guerard, Albert, Jr., **Supp. X:** 79; **Supp. XIII:** 172
Guérin, Maurice de, **I:** 241
"Guerrilla Handbook, A" (Baraka), **Supp. II Part 1:** 36
Guess and Spell Coloring Book, The (Swenson), **Supp. IV Part 2:** 648
Guess Who's Coming to Dinner (film), **Supp. I Part 1:** 67
Guest, Val, **Supp. XI:** 307
"Guests of Mrs. Timms, The" (Jewett), **II:** 408; **Retro. Supp. II:** 135
"Guevara . . . Guevara" (Salinas), **Supp. XIII:** 312–313, 315
Guevara, Martha, **Supp. VIII:** 74
Guide in the Wilderness, A (Cooper), **I:** 337
"Guide to Dungeness Spit, A" (Wagoner), **Supp. IX:** 325–326, 329
Guide to Ezra Pound's Selected Cantos' (Kearns), **Retro. Supp. I:** 292
Guide to Kulchur (Pound), **III:** 475
Guide to the Ruins (Nemerov), **III:** 269, 270–271, 272
Guillén, Nicolás, **Retro. Supp. I:** 202; **Supp. I Part 1:** 345
Guillevic, Eugene, **Supp. III Part 1:** 283
"Guilty Man, The" (Kunitz), **Supp. II Part 1:** 263
Guilty Pleasures (Barthelme), **Supp. IV Part 1:** 44, 45, 53
Guinness, Alec, **Retro. Supp. I:** 65
"Gulf, The" (Dunn), **Supp. XI:** 149
Gulistan (Saadi), **II:** 19
Gullible's Travels (Lardner), **II:** 426, 427
Gulliver's Travels (Swift), **I:** 209, 348, 366; **II:** 301; **Supp. I Part 2:** 656; **Supp. XI:** 209
"Gulls" (Hayden), **Supp. II Part 1:** 367
"Gulls, The" (Nemerov), **III:** 272
"Gun, The" (Dobyns), **Supp. XIII:** 88
Günderode: A Translation from the German (Fuller), **Supp. II Part 1:** 293
Gundy, Jeff, **Supp. XI:** 315
Gunn, Thom, **Supp. IX:** 269
Gunn, Thomas, **Supp. V:** 178
Gunn Allen, Paula, **Supp. IV Part 1: 319–340,** 404; **Supp. IV Part 2:** 499, 502, 557, 568; **Supp. XII:** 218
"Guns as Keys; and the Great Gate Swings" (Lowell), **II:** 524
Gurdjieff, Georges, **Supp. V:** 199; **Supp. IX:** 320
Gurganus, Allan, **Supp. XII:** 308–309, 310
Gurko, Leo, **III:** 62
Gurney, A. R., **Supp. V: 95–112; Supp. IX:** 261
Gurney, Mary (Molly) Goodyear, **Supp. V:** 95
Gussow, Mel, **Supp. IX:** 93; **Supp. XII:** 325, 328, 341
Gustavus Vassa, the African (Vassa), **Supp. IV Part 1:** 11
Gusto, Thy Name Was Mrs. Hopkins: A Prose Rhapsody (Francis), **Supp. IX:** 89
Gute Mensch von Sezuan, Der (Brecht), **Supp. IX:** 138
Gutenberg, Johann, **Supp. I Part 2:** 392
Guthrie, A. B., **Supp. X:** 103
Gutman, Herbert, **Supp. I Part 1:** 47

Guttenplan, D. D., **Supp. XI:** 38
"Gutting of Couffignal, The" (Hammett), **Supp. IV Part 1:** 345
Guy Domville (James), **II:** 331; **Retro. Supp. I:** 228
"Gwendolyn" (Bishop), **Retro. Supp. II:** 51
Gypsy Ballads (Hughes, trans.), **Supp. I Part 1:** 345
Gypsy's Curse, The (Crews), **Supp. XI:** 110
"Gyroscope, The" (Rukeyser), **Supp. VI:** 271
Gysin, Brion, **Supp. XII:** 129
H. L. Mencken, a Portrait from Memory (Angoff), **III:** 107
H. L. Mencken: The American Scene (Cairns), **III:** 119
"H. L. Mencken Meets a Poet in the West Side Y.M.C.A." (White), **Supp. I Part 2:** 677
H. M. Pulham, Esquire (Marquand), **II:** 482–483; **III:** 58, 59, 65, 68–69
Haardt, Sara. *See* Mencken, Mrs. H. L. (Sara Haardt)
Habakkuk (biblical book), **III:** 200, 347
Habibi (Nye), **Supp. XIII:** 273, **279**
"Habit" (James), **II:** 351
Habitations of the Word (Gass), **Supp. VI:** 88
Hackett, David, **Supp. XII:** 236
Hadda, Janet, **Retro. Supp. II:** 335
Haeckel, Ernst Heinrich, **II:** 480
Hafif, Marcia, **Supp. IV Part 2:** 423
Hagedorn, Jessica, **Supp. X:** 292
Hagen, Beulah, **Supp. I Part 2:** 679
Haggard, Rider, **III:** 189
Hagoromo (play), **III:** 466
"Hail Mary" (Fante), **Supp. XI:** 160, 164
Haines, George, IV, **I:** 444
Haines, John, **Supp. XII: 197–214**
"Hair" (Corso), **Supp. XII:** 117, 126, 127
"Hair, The" (Carver), **Supp. III Part 1:** 137
"Haircut" (Lardner), **II:** 430, 436
Hairpiece: A Film for Nappy-Headed People (Chenzira; film), **Supp. XI:** 19–20
"Hairs" (Cisneros), **Supp. VII:** 59
Hairs/Pelitos (Cisneros), **Supp. VII:** 58
Hairy Ape, The (O'Neill), **III:** 391, 392, 393
"Haïta the Shepherd" (Bierce), **I:** 203
Haldeman, Anna, **Supp. I Part 1:** 2
Hale, Edward Everett, **Supp. I Part 2:** 584; **Supp. XI:** 193, 200

Hale, John Parker, **Supp. I Part 2:** 685
Hale, Nancy, **Supp. VIII:** 151, 171
Haley, Alex, **Supp. I Part 1:** 47, 66
Haley, J. Evetts, **Supp. V:** 226
"Half a Century Gone" (Lowell), **II:** 554
Half-a-Hundred: Tales by Great American Writers (Grayson, ed.), **Supp. XIII:** 171
Half Asleep in Frog Pajamas (Robbins), **Supp. X:** 259, **279–282**
Half-Century of Conflict, A (Parkman), **Supp. II Part 2:** 600, 607, 610
"Half Deity" (Moore), **III:** 210, 214, 215
"Half Hour of August" (Ríos), **Supp. IV Part 2:** 552
Half-Lives (Jong), **Supp. V:** 115, 119
Half Moon Street: Two Short Novels (Theroux), **Supp. VIII:** 322, 323
Half-Past Nation Time (Johnson), **Supp. VI:** 187
"Half-Skinned Steer, The" (Proulx), **Supp. VII:** 261–262
Half Sun Half Sleep (Swenson), **Supp. IV Part 2:** 645–646
Halfway (Kumin), **Supp. IV Part 2:** 441–442
"Halfway" (Rich), **Supp. I Part 2:** 553
Halfway Home (Monette), **Supp. X:** 154
Halfway to Silence (Sarton), **Supp. VIII:** 261
Half You Don't Know, The: Selected Stories (Cameron), **Supp. XII:** 79, 80, 81
Haliburton, Thomas Chandler, **II:** 301; **IV:** 193; **Supp. I Part 2:** 411
Halifax, Lord, **II:** 111
Hall, Daniel, **Supp. XII:** 258
Hall, Donald, **I:** 567; **III:** 194; **Retro. Supp. II:** 279; **Supp. IV Part 1:** 63, 72; **Supp. IV Part 2:** 621; **Supp. IX:** 269
Hall, James, **II:** 313; **Supp. I Part 2:** 584, 585
Hall, James Baker, **Supp. X:** 24
Hall, Timothy L., **Supp. VIII:** 127, 128
Halleck, Fitz-Greene, **Supp. I Part 1:** 156, 158
"Hallelujah: A Sestina" (Francis), **Supp. IX:** 82
"Hallelujah on the Bum" (Abbey), **Supp. XIII:** 2
"Haller's Second Home" (Maxwell), **Supp. VIII:** 169
Hallock, Rev. Moses, **Supp. I Part 1:** 153
Hall of Mirrors, A (Stone), **Supp. V:** 295, 296–299, 300, 301

"Halloween Party, The" (Chabon), **Supp. XI:** 72
Halloween Tree, The (Bradbury), **Supp. IV Part 1:** 102, 112–113
Hallwas, John E., **Supp. I Part 2:** 454
Halpern, Daniel, **Supp. IV Part 1:** 94–95, 95
Halsey, Theresa, **Supp. IV Part 1:** 330, 331
"Halt in the Desert, A" (Brodsky), **Supp. VIII:** 24
"Halves" (Dunn), **Supp. XI:** 149
Hamerik, Asger, **Supp. I Part 1:** 356
Hamill, Sam, **Supp. X:** 112, 125, 126, 127
Hamilton, Alexander, **I:** 485; **Supp. I Part 2:** 456, 483, 509
Hamilton, Alice, **Supp. I Part 1:** 5
Hamilton, David, **Supp. IX:** 296
Hamilton, Lady Emma, **II:** 524
Hamilton, Hamish, **Supp. I Part 2:** 617
Hamilton, Walton, **Supp. I Part 2:** 632
Hamilton Stark (Banks), **Supp. V:** 8, 9–10, 11
"Hamlen Brook" (Wilbur), **Supp. III Part 2:** 564
"Hamlet" (Laforgue), **I:** 573; **III:** 11
Hamlet (Miller and Fraenkel), **III:** 178, 183
Hamlet (Shakespeare), **I:** 53, 183, 205, 377, 586–587; **II:** 158, 531; **III:** 7, 11, 12, 183; **IV:** 116, 131, 227; **Supp. I Part 1:** 369; **Supp. I Part 2:** 422, 457, 471; **Supp. IV Part 2:** 612; **Supp. IX:** 14
Hamlet, The (Faulkner), **II:** 69–71, 73, 74; **IV:** 131; **Retro. Supp. I:** 82, 91, 92; **Supp. VIII:** 178; **Supp. IX:** 103; **Supp. XI:** 247
"Hamlet and His Problems" (Eliot), **I:** 586–587
Hamlet of A. MacLeish, The (MacLeish), **III:** 11–12, 14, 15, 18
Hamlin, Eva, **Retro. Supp. II:** 115
Hammer, Adam, **Supp. XIII:** 112
Hammer, Langdon, **Retro. Supp. II:** 45, 53; **Supp. X:** 65
"Hammer Man, The" (Bambara), **Supp. XI:** 4–5
Hammett, Dashiell, **IV:** 286; **Retro. Supp. II:** 345; **Supp. I Part 1:** 286, 289, 291, 292, 293, 294, 295; **Supp. III Part 1:** 91; **Supp. IV Part 1:** 120, 121, **341–357**; **Supp. IV Part 2:** 461, 464, 468, 469, 472, 473; **Supp. IX:** 200; **Supp. XI:** 228; **Supp. XIII:** 159
Hammond, Karla, **Supp. IV Part 2:** 439, 442, 448, 637, 640, 644, 648

Hampl, Patricia, **Supp. IX:** 291; **Supp. XI:** 126
Hampson, Alfred Leete, **Retro. Supp. I:** 35–36, 38
"Hamrick's Polar Bear" (Caldwell), **I:** 309–310
Hamsun, Knut, **Supp. VIII:** 40; **Supp. XI:** 161, 167; **Supp. XII:** 21, 128
Hancock, John, **Supp. I Part 2:** 524
Handbook of North American Indians (Sando), **Supp. IV Part 2:** 510
Handcarved Coffins: A Nonfiction Account of an American Crime (Capote), **Supp. III Part 1:** 131
Handel, Georg Friedrich, **III:** 210; **IV:** 369
"Handfuls" (Sandburg), **III:** 584
"Handle with Care" (Fitzgerald), **Retro. Supp. I:** 114
Handmaid's Tale, The (Atwood), **Supp. XIII:** 19, 20, **27–29**
"Hand of Emmagene, The" (Taylor), **Supp. V:** 314, 325–326
Hand of the Potter, The: A Tragedy in Four Acts (Dreiser), **Retro. Supp. II:** 104
"Hands" (Anderson), **I:** 106, 107
"Hands" (Mora), **Supp. XIII:** 215
Hand to Mouth (Auster), **Supp. XII:** 21
"Hand to Mouth" (Auster), **Supp. XII:** 31
Handy, Lowney, **Supp. XI:** 217, 220, 221, 225
Handy, W. C., **Supp. VIII:** 337
Handy Guide for Beggars, A (Lindsay), **Supp. I Part 2:** 376–378, 380, 382, 399
Hanging Garden, The (Wagoner), **Supp. IX: 338–339**
"Hanging Gardens of Tyburn, The" (Hecht), **Supp. X:** 58
"Hanging of the Crane, The" (Longfellow), **Retro. Supp. II:** 169, 171
"Hanging Pictures in Nanny's Room" (Kenyon), **Supp. VII:** 164
"Hanging the Wash" (Alvarez), **Supp. VII:** 4
"Hangman, The" (Sexton), **Supp. II Part 2:** 680, 691
Hangsaman (Jackson), **Supp. IX:** 116, 123, **124**
Hanh, Thich Nhat, **Supp. V:** 199
Hanks, Lucy, **III:** 587
Hanks, Nancy. *See* Lincoln, Mrs. Thomas (Nancy Hanks)
Hanley, Lynne T., **Supp. IV Part 1:** 208
Hanna, Mark, **Supp. I Part 2:** 395

Hannah, Barry, **Supp. X:** 285
"Hannah Armstrong" (Masters), **Supp. I Part 2:** 461
"Hannah Binding Shoes" (Larcom), **Supp. XIII:** 141, 143
Hannah's House (Hearon), **Supp. VIII:** 58, **60–61**
Hanneman, Audre, **II:** 259
Hannibal Lecter, My Father (Acker), **Supp. XII:** 6
Hanoi (McCarthy), **II:** 579
Hansberry, Lorraine, **Supp. IV Part 1: 359–377**; **Supp. VIII:** 329
Hanscom, Leslie, **Supp. XI:** 229
Hansen, Erik, **Supp. V:** 241
Hansen, Harry, **IV:** 366
Han-shan, **Supp. VIII:** 292
Hanson, Curtis, **Supp. XI:** 67
Han Suyin, **Supp. X:** 291
"Happenings: An Art of Radical Juxtaposition" (Sontag), **Supp. III Part 2:** 456
"Happenstance" (Komunyakaa), **Supp. XIII:** 130
Happenstance (Shields), **Supp. VII:** 315–318, 320, 323, 324, 326
Happersberger, Lucien, **Supp. I Part 1:** 51
"Happiest I've Been, The" (Updike), **IV:** 219
"Happiness" (Oliver), **Supp. VII:** 236
"Happiness" (Sandburg), **III:** 582–583
Happiness of Getting It Down Right, The (Steinman, ed.), **Supp. VIII:** 172
"Happy Birthday" (Bambara), **Supp. XI:** 4
Happy Birthday, Wanda June (Vonnegut), **Supp. II Part 2:** 759, 776–777
Happy Birthday of Death, The (Corso), **Supp. XII: 127–129**
Happy Childhood, A (Matthews), **Supp. IX:** 155, 160, **161–163**
Happy Days (Beckett), **Retro. Supp. I:** 206
Happy Days, 1880–1892 (Mencken), **III:** 100, 111, 120
"Happy End" (Simic), **Supp. VIII:** 276–277
"Happy Failure, The" (Melville), **III:** 90
Happy Families Are All Alike (Taylor), **Supp. V:** 322–323, 325
Happy Isles of Oceania, The: Paddling the Pacific (Theroux), **Supp. VIII:** 324
"Happy Journey to Trenton and Camden, The" (Wilder), **IV:** 366
"Happy Marriage, The" (MacLeish), **III:** 15–16
Happy Marriage and Other Poems, The (MacLeish), **III:** 4
"Hapworth 16, 1924" (Salinger), **III:** 552, 571–572
"Harbor Lights" (Doty), **Supp. XI:** 122
Harcourt, Alfred, **II:** 191, 451–452; **III:** 587; **Retro. Supp. I:** 131
Harcourt, Brace, **Retro. Supp. I:** 83
Harcourt, T. A., **I:** 196
Hard Candy, a Book of Stories (T. Williams), **IV:** 383
"Hardcastle Crags" (Plath), **Supp. I Part 2:** 537
"Hard Daddy" (Hughes), **Retro. Supp. I:** 200
Hard Facts (Baraka), **Supp. II Part 1:** 54, 55, 58
Hard Freight (Wright), **Supp. V:** 332, 339–340
Hard Hours, The (Hecht), **Supp. X:** 57, **59–62,** 63, 64
Hardie, Kier, **Supp. I Part 1:** 5
Harding, Walter, **IV:** 177, 178
Harding, Warren G., **I:** 486; **II:** 253, 433; **Supp. I Part 1:** 24
"Hard Kind of Courage, The" (Baldwin), **Supp. I Part 1:** 52
"Hard Time Keeping Up, A" (Ellison), **Retro. Supp. II:** 124
Hard Times (Dickens), **Supp. I Part 2:** 675
"Hard Times in Elfland, The" (Lanier), **Supp. I Part 1:** 365
Hardwick, Elizabeth, **II:** 543, 554, 566; **Retro. Supp. II:** 179, 180, 183, 184, 190, 221, 228–229, 245; **Supp. I Part 1:** 196; **Supp. III Part 1: 193–215**; **Supp. IV Part 1:** 299; **Supp. V,** 319; **Supp. X,** 171; **Supp. XII:** 209
"Hard Work 1956" (Dunn), **Supp. XI:** 147
Hardy, Barbara, **Supp. I Part 2:** 527
Hardy, Oliver, **Supp. I Part 2:** 607; **Supp. IV Part 2:** 574
Hardy, René, **Supp. III Part 1:** 235
Hardy, Thomas, **I:** 59, 103, 292, 317, 377; **II:** 181, 184–185, 186, 191–192, 271, 275, 372, 523, 542; **III:** 32, 453, 485, 508, 524; **IV:** 83, 135, 136; **Retro. Supp. I:** 141, 377–378; **Supp. I Part 1:** 217; **Supp. I Part 2:** 429, 512; **Supp. II Part 1:** 4, 26; **Supp. VIII:** 32; **Supp. IX:** 40, 78, 85, 108, 211; **Supp. X:** 228; **Supp. XI:** 311; **Supp. XIII:** 294, **Supp. XIII:** 130
Harjo, Joy, **Supp. IV Part 1:** 325, 404; **Supp. IV Part 2:** 499, 507; **Supp.**

XII: 215–234
"Harlem" (Hughes), **Retro. Supp. I:** 194, 204; **Supp. I Part 1:** 340; **Supp. VIII:** 213
Harlem: Negro Metropolis (McKay), **Supp. X:** 132, 141, 142
"Harlem Dancer, The" (McKay), **Supp. X:** 134
Harlem Gallery (Tolson), **Retro. Supp. I:** 208, 209, 210
Harlem Glory: A Fragment of Aframerican Life (McKay), **Supp. X:** 132, **141–142**
"Harlem Runs Wild" (McKay), **Supp. X:** 140
Harlem Shadows (McKay), **Supp. X:** 131–132, 136
"Harlequin of Dreams, The" (Lanier), **Supp. I Part 1:** 365
Harlot's Ghost (Mailer), **Retro. Supp. II:** 211–212
Harlow, Jean, **IV:** 256; **Retro. Supp. I:** 110
Harmon, William, **Retro. Supp. I:** 37; **Supp. XI:** 248
"Harmonic" (F. Barthelme), **Supp. XI:** 26
Harmonium (Stevens), **III:** 196; **IV:** 76, 77, 78, 82, 87, 89, 92; **Retro. Supp. I:** 296, 297, 299, **300–302,** 301, 302
"Harmony of the Gospels" (Taylor), **IV:** 149
Harper (film), **Supp. IV Part 2:** 473
Harper, Donna, **Retro. Supp. I:** 194, 195, 209
Harper, Frances E. Watkins, **Supp. II Part 1:** 201–202
Harper, Gordon Lloyd, **Retro. Supp. II:** 23
Harper, Michael S., **Retro. Supp. II:** 116, 123
Harper, William Rainey, **Supp. I Part 2:** 631
Harper's Anthology of 20th Century Native American Poetry (Niatum, ed.), **Supp. IV Part 1:** 331
"Harriet" (Lowell), **II:** 554
Harrigan, Edward, **II:** 276; **III:** 14
Harrington, Michael, **I:** 306
Harris, Celia, **Retro. Supp. I:** 9
Harris, George, **II:** 70
Harris, Joel Chandler, **III:** 338; **Supp. I Part 1:** 352; **Supp. II Part 1:** 192, 201
Harris, Julie, **II:** 587, 601; **Supp. IX:** 125
Harris, MacDonald, **Supp. XI:** 65
Harris, Marie, **Supp. IX:** 153
Harris, Peter, **Supp. X:** 206, 207

Harris, Victoria Frenkel, **Supp. IV Part 1:** 68, 69
Harrison, Hazel, **Retro. Supp. II:** 115
Harrison, Jim, **Supp. VIII: 37–56**
Harrison, Kathryn, **Supp. X:** 191
Harrison, Ken, **Supp. IX:** 101
Harrison, Oliver (pseudonym). *See* Smith, Harrison
Harryhausen, Ray, **Supp. IV Part 1:** 115
"Harry of Nothingham" (Hugo), **Supp. VI:** 146–147
"Harry's Death" (Carver), **Supp. III Part 1:** 146
"Harsh Judgment, The" (Kunitz), **Supp. III Part 1:** 264
Hart, Albert Bushnell, **Supp. I Part 2:** 479, 480, 481
Hart, Bernard, **I:** 241, 242, 248–250, 256
Hart, Henry, **Retro. Supp. II:** 187
Hart, Lorenz, **III:** 361
Hart, Moss, **Supp. IV Part 2:** 574
Hart, Pearl, **Supp. X:** 103
"Hart Crane" (Tate), **I:** 381
"Hart Crane and Poetry: A Consideration of Crane's Intense Poetics with Reference to 'The Return'" (Grossman), **Retro. Supp. II:** 83
Harte, Anna Griswold, **Supp. II Part 1:** 341
Harte, Bret, **I:** 193, 195, 203; **II:** 289; **IV:** 196; **Retro. Supp. II:** 72; **Supp. II Part 1: 335–359,** 399
Harte, Walter Blackburn, **I:** 199
Harter, Carol C., **Supp. IV Part 1:** 217
Hartley, David, **III:** 77
Hartley, L. P., **Supp. I Part 1:** 293
Hartley, Lois, **Supp. I Part 2:** 459, 464–465
Hartley, Marsden, **IV:** 409, 413; **Retro. Supp. I:** 430; **Supp. X:** 137
Hartman, Geoffrey, **Supp. IV Part 1:** 119; **Supp. XII:** 130, 253
Harum, David, **II:** 102
"Harvard" (Lowell), **II:** 554
Harvard College in the Seventeenth Century (Morison), **Supp. I Part 2:** 485
"Harvesters of Night and Water" (Hogan), **Supp. IV Part 1:** 412
"Harvest Song" (Toomer), **Supp. III Part 2:** 483
Harvill Book of 20th Century Poetry in English, **Supp. X:** 55
"Harv Is Plowing Now" (Updike), **Retro. Supp. I:** 318
Haselden, Elizabeth Lee, **Supp. VIII:** 125
Hass, Robert, **Supp. VI: 97–111;**

Supp. VIII: 24, 28; **Supp. XI:** 142, 270
Hassam, Childe, **Retro. Supp. II:** 136
Hassan, Ihab, **IV:** 99–100, 115; **Supp. XI:** 221
Hasse, Henry, **Supp. IV Part 1:** 102
Hasty-Pudding, The (Barlow), **Supp. II Part 1:** 74, 77–80
Hatful of Rain, A (Gazzo), **III:** 155
Hatlen, Burton, **Supp. V:** 138, 139–140
"Hattie Bloom" (Oliver), **Supp. VII:** 232
"Hattie Rice Rich" (Rich), **Retro. Supp. II:** 291
Haunch, Paunch, and Jowl (Ornitz), **Supp. IX:** 227
"Haunted Landscape" (Ashbery), **Supp. III Part 1:** 22
"Haunted Mind" (Simic), **Supp. VIII:** 282
"Haunted Mind, The" (Hawthorne), **II:** 230–231
"Haunted Oak, The" (Dunbar), **Supp. II Part 1:** 207, 208
"Haunted Palace, The" (Poe), **III:** 421
"Haunted Valley, The" (Bierce), **I:** 200
Haunting, The (film), **Supp. IX:** 125
Haunting of Hill House, The (Jackson), **Supp. IX:** 117, 121, 126
Hauptmann, Gerhart, **III:** 472
Haussmann, Sonja, **Supp. XIII:** 331, **Supp. XIII:** 347
"Havanna vanities come to dust in Miami" (Didion), **Supp. IV Part 1:** 210
Haven's End (Marquand), **III:** 55, 56, 63, 68
"Have You Ever Tried to Enter the Long Black Branches" (Oliver), **Supp. VII:** 247
"Having Been Interstellar" (Ammons), **Supp. VII:** 25
"Having It Out With Melancholy" (Kenyon), **Supp. VII:** 171
"Having Lost My Sons, I Confront the Wreckage of the Moon: Christmas, 1960" (Wright), **Supp. III Part 2:** 600
"Having Snow" (Schwartz), **Supp. II Part 2:** 652
Hawai'i One Summer (Kingston), **Supp. V:** 157, 160, 166, 169–170
"Hawk, The" (Francis), **Supp. IX:** 81
Hawke, David Freeman, **Supp. I Part 2:** 511, 516
Hawkes, John, **I:** 113; **Retro. Supp. II:** 234; **Supp. III Part 1:** 2; **Supp. V:** 40; **Supp. IX:** 212
Hawkins, William, **II:** 587

Hawk in the Rain, The (Hughes), **Retro. Supp. II:** 244; **Supp. I Part 2:** 537, 540
Hawk Is Dying, The (Crews), **Supp. XI:** 111
Hawk Moon (Shepard), **Supp. III Part 2:** 445
Hawks, Howard, **Supp. IV Part 1:** 130
"Hawk's Cry in Autumn, The" (Brodsky), **Supp. VIII:** 29
"Hawk's Shadow" (Glück), **Supp. V:** 85
Hawk's Well, The (Yeats), **III:** 459–460
Hawley, Joseph, **I:** 546
Hawthorne (James), **II:** 372–378; **Retro. Supp. I:** 220, **223–224**
"Hawthorne" (Longfellow), **Retro. Supp. II:** 169
"Hawthorne" (Lowell), **II:** 550
Hawthorne, Julian, **II:** 225; **Supp. I Part 1:** 38
Hawthorne, Mrs. Nathaniel (Sophia Peabody), **II:** 224, 244; **III:** 75, 86
Hawthorne, Nathaniel, **I:** 106, 204, 211, 340, 355, 363, 384, 413, 458, 561–562; **II:** 7, 8, 40, 60, 63, 74, 89, 127–128, 138, 142, 198, **223–246**, 255, 259, 264, 267, 272, 274, 277, 281, 282, 295, 307, 309, 311, 313, 322, 324, 326, 402, 408, 446, 501, 545; **III:** 51, 81–82, 83, 84, 85, 87, 88, 91, 92, 113, 316, 359, 412, 415, 421, 438, 453, 454, 507, 565, 572; **IV:** 2, 4, 167, 172, 179, 194, 333, 345, 453; **Retro. Supp. I:** 1, 53, 59, 62, 63, 91, **145–167**, 215, 218, 220, 223, 248–249, 252, 257, 258, 330, 331, 365; **Retro. Supp. II:** 136, 142, 153, 156–157, 158, 159, 187, 221; **Supp. I Part 1:** 38, 188, 197, 317, 372; **Supp. I Part 2:** 420, 421, 545, 579, 580, 582, 587, 595, 596; **Supp. III Part 2:** 501; **Supp. IV Part 1:** 80, 127, 297; **Supp. IV Part 2:** 463, 596; **Supp. V:** 152; **Supp. VIII:** 103, 105, 108, 153, 201; **Supp. IX:** 114; **Supp. X:** 78; **Supp. XI:** 51, 78; **Supp. XII:** 26; **Supp. XIII:** 102
Hawthorne, Rose, **II:** 225
Hawthorne, Una, **II:** 225
"Hawthorne and His Mosses" (Melville), **Retro. Supp. I:** 254
"Hawthorne Aspect [of Henry James], The" (Eliot), **Retro. Supp. I:** 63
"Hawthorne in Solitude" (Cowley), **Supp. II Part 1:** 143
Hay, John, **I:** 1, 10, 12, 14–15; **Supp. I Part 1:** 352
Hay, Mrs. John, **I:** 14

Hayakawa, S. I., **I:** 448; **Supp. I Part 1:** 315
Hayden, Robert, **Supp. II Part 1: 361–383**; **Supp. IV Part 1:** 169; **Supp. XIII:** 115, 127
Hayden, Sterling, **Supp. XI:** 304
Haydn, Hiram, **IV:** 100, 358
Hayduke Lives! (Abbey), **Supp. XIII:** 16
Hayek, Friedrich A. von, **Supp. IV Part 2:** 524
Hayes, Ira, **Supp. IV Part 1:** 326
Hayes, Richard, **Supp. V:** 320
Hayes, Rutherford B., **Supp. I Part 2:** 419
Haygood, Wil, **Supp. VIII:** 79
Hayne, Paul Hamilton, **Supp. I Part 1:** 352, 354, 355, 360, 372
Hayward, Florence, **Retro. Supp. II:** 65
Hayward, John, **Retro. Supp. I:** 67
Haywood, "Big" Bill, **I:** 483; **Supp. V:** 286
Hazard, Grace, **II:** 530
Hazard of Fortunes, A (Howells), **Retro. Supp. II:** 306
Hazard of New Fortunes, A (Howells), **II:** 275, 276, 286–297, 290
Hazel, Robert, **Supp. VIII:** 137, 138
Hazen, General W. B., **I:** 192, 193
Hazlitt, Henry, **Supp. IV Part 2:** 524
Hazlitt, William, **I:** 58, 378; **II:** 315
Hazmat (McClatchy), **Supp. XII: 265–270**
Hazo, Samuel, **I:** 386
Hazzard, Shirley, **Supp. VIII:** 151
H.D. *See* Doolittle, Hilda
"He" (Porter), **III:** 434, 435
"Head and Shoulders" (Fitzgerald), **Retro. Supp. I:** 101
"Head-Hunter, The" (O. Henry), **Supp. II Part 1:** 403
"Headless Hawk, The" (Capote), **Supp. III Part 1:** 124
Headlines (T. Williams), **IV:** 381
Headlong Hall (Peacock), **Supp. I Part 1:** 307
Headmaster, The (McPhee), **Supp. III Part 1:** 291, 294, 298
Headsman, The (Cooper), **I:** 345–346
"Headwaters" (Momaday), **Supp. IV Part 2:** 486
Healy, Eloise Klein, **Supp. XI:** 121, 124, 126, 127, 129, 137
Healy, Tim, **II:** 129, 137
Heaney, Seamus, **Retro. Supp. II:** 245; **Supp. IX:** 41, 42; **Supp. X:** 67, 122; **Supp. XI:** 249
Hearn, Lafcadio, **I:** 211; **II:** 311
Hearon, Shelby, **Supp. VIII: 57–72**

Hearst, Patty, **Supp. IV Part 1:** 195
Hearst, William Randolph, **I:** 198, 207, 208; **IV:** 298
"Heart and the Lyre, The" (Bogan), **Supp. III Part 1:** 65
"Heartbeat" (Harjo), **Supp. XII:** 221–222
Heartbreak Kid, The (film), **Supp. IV Part 2:** 575, 589
Heart for the Gods of Mexico, A (Aiken), **I:** 54
"Hear the Nightingale Sing" (Gordon), **II:** 200
Heart is a Lonely Hunter, The (McCullers), **II:** 586, 588–593, 604, 605
Heart of a Woman, The (Angelou), **Supp. IV Part 1:** 2, 5, 7–9, 9, 14, 17
Heart of Darkness (Conrad), **Retro. Supp. II:** 310; **Supp. V:** 249, 311; **Supp. VIII:** 4, 316
"Heart of Darkness" (Conrad), **I:** 575, 578; **II:** 595
Heart of Darkness (Didion), **Supp. IV Part 1:** 207
Heart of Happy Hollow, The (Dunbar), **Supp. II Part 1:** 214
Heart of Knowledge, The: American Indians on the Bomb (Gunn Allen and Caputi, eds.), **Supp. IV Part 1:** 334–335
"Heart of Knowledge, The: Nuclear Themes in Native American Thought and Literature" (Caputi), **Supp. IV Part 1:** 335
"Heart of the Park, The" (O'Connor), **Retro. Supp. II:** 225
Heart of the West (O. Henry), **Supp. II Part 1:** 410
"Hearts, The" (Pinsky), **Supp. VI:** 245–247, 248
"'Hearts and Flowers'" (MacLeish), **III:** 8
"Hearts and Heads" (Ransom), **Supp. I Part 1:** 373
"Heart's Graveyard Shift, The" (Komunyakaa), **Supp. XIII:** 120
Heart-Shape in the Dust (Hayden), **Supp. II Part 1:** 365, 366
"Heart's Needle" (Snodgrass), **Supp. VI: 311–313**, 320
Heart's Needle (Snodgrass), **I:** 400
"Heart Songs" (Proulx), **Supp. VII:** 254
Heart Songs and Other Stories (Proulx), **Supp. VII:** 252–256, 261
Heart to Artemis, The (Bryher), **Supp. I Part 1:** 259
Heath Anthology of American Litera-

ture, The, **Supp. IX:** 4
Heathcote, Anne. *See* De Lancey, Mrs. James
"Heathen Chinee, The" (Harte), **Supp. II Part 1:** 350–351, 352
Heathen Days, 1890–1936 (Mencken), **III:** 100, 111
"Heaven" (Dunn), **Supp. XI:** 154
"Heaven" (Levine), **Supp. V:** 182
"Heaven" (Patchett), **Supp. XII:** 309
Heaven and Earth: A Cosmology (Goldbarth), **Supp. XII: 187**
"Heaven and Earth in Jest" (Dillard), **Supp. VI:** 24, 28
"Heaven as Anus" (Kumin), **Supp. IV Part 2:** 448
Heavenly Conversation, The (Mather), **Supp. II Part 2:** 460
Heavens and Earth (Benét), **Supp. XI:** 44
Heaven's Coast (Doty), **Supp. XI:** 119, 121, **129–130,** 134
"Heavy Bear Who Goes with Me, The" (Schwartz), **Supp. II Part 2:** 646
"He Came Also Still" (Zukofsky), **Supp. III Part 2:** 612
Hecht, Anthony, **IV:** 138; **Supp. III Part 2:** 541, 561; **Supp. X: 55–75; Supp. XII:** 269–270
Hecht, Ben, **I:** 103; **II:** 42; **Supp. I Part 2:** 646; **Supp. XI:** 307; **Supp. XIII:** 106
Hecht, S. Theodore, **Supp. III Part 2:** 614
Heckewelder, John, **II:** 503
"Hedge Island" (Lowell), **II:** 524
Hedges, William I., **II:** 311–312
"He 'Digesteth Harde Yron'" (Moore), **Supp. IV Part 2:** 454
Hedin, Robert, **Supp. XII:** 200, 202
Hedylus (Doolittle), **Supp. I Part 1:** 259, 270
"Heel & Toe To the End" (W. C. Williams), **Retro. Supp. I:** 430
Heffernan, Michael, **Supp. XII:** 177
"HEGEL" (Baraka), **Supp. II Part 1:** 53
Hegel, Georg Wilhelm Friedrich, **I:** 265; **II:** 358; **III:** 262, 308–309, 480, 481, 487, 607; **IV:** 86, 333, 453; **Supp. I Part 2:** 633, 635, 640, 645
"Hegemony of Race, The" (Du Bois), **Supp. II Part 1:** 181
Hegger, Grace Livingston. *See* Lewis, Mrs. Sinclair (Grace Livingston Hegger)
"He Had Spent His Youth Dreaming" (Dobyns), **Supp. XIII:** 90
Heidegger, Martin, **II:** 362, 363; **III:** 292; **IV:** 491; **Retro. Supp. II:** 87; **Supp. V:** 267; **Supp. VIII:** 9
Heidenmauer, The (Cooper), **I:** 345–346
Heidi Chronicles, The (Wasserstein), **Supp. IV Part 2:** 309
"Height of the Ridiculous, The" (Holmes), **Supp. I Part 1:** 302
Heilbroner, Robert, **Supp. I Part 2:** 644, 648, 650
Heilbrun, Carolyn G., **Supp. IX:** 66; **Supp. XI:** 208
Heim, Michael, **Supp. V:** 209
Heine, Heinrich, **II:** 272, 273, 277, 281, 282, 387, 544; **IV:** 5
Heineman, Frank, **Supp. III Part 2:** 619
Heinlein, Robert, **Supp. IV Part 1:** 102
Heinz, Helen. *See* Tate, Mrs. Allen (Helen Heinz)
Heiress, The (film), **Retro. Supp. I:** 222
"Heirs" (Nye), **Supp. XIII:** 284
"Helas" (Creeley), **Supp. IV Part 1:** 150, 158
Helburn, Theresa, **IV:** 381
Heldreth, Leonard, **Supp. V:** 151
"Helen" (Lowell), **II:** 544
"Helen: A Courtship" (Faulkner), **Retro. Supp. I:** 81
"Helen, Thy Beauty Is to Me" (Fante), **Supp. XI:** 169
"Helen I Love You" (Farrell), **II:** 28, 45
Helen in Egypt (Doolittle), **Supp. I Part 1:** 260, 272, 273, 274
Helen Keller: Sketch for a Portrait (Brooks), **I:** 254
"Helen of Tyre" (Longfellow), **II:** 496
Heliodora (Doolittle), **Supp. I Part 1:** 266
Hellbox (O'Hara), **III:** 361
Heller, Joseph, **III:** 2, 258; **IV:** 98; **Retro. Supp. II:** 342; **Supp. I Part 1:** 196; **Supp. IV Part 1: 379–396; Supp. V:** 244; **Supp. VIII:** 245; **Supp. XI:** 307; **Supp. XII:** 167–168
Hellman, Lillian, **I:** 28; **II:** 28; **Supp. I Part 1: 276–298; Supp. IV Part 1:** 1, 12, 83, 353, 355, 356; **Supp. VIII:** 243; **Supp. IX:** 196, 198, 200–201, 204
Hellmann, Lillian, **Retro. Supp. II:** 345
Hello (Creeley), **Supp. IV Part 1:** 155, 157
"Hello, Hello Henry" (Kumin), **Supp. IV Part 2:** 446
"Hello, Stranger" (Capote), **Supp. III Part 1:** 120
Hello Dolly! (musical play), **IV:** 357
Hellyer, John, **Supp. I Part 2:** 468
Helmets (Dickey), **Supp. IV Part 1:** 175, 178, 180
"Helmsman, The" (Doolittle), **Supp. I Part 1:** 266
"Help" (Barth), **I:** 139
"Help Her to Believe" (Olsen). *See* "I Stand There Ironing" (Olsen)
"Helsinki Window" (Creeley), **Supp. IV Part 1:** 158
Hemenway, Robert E., **Supp. IV Part 1:** 6
Hemingway, Dr. Clarence Edwards, **II:** 248, 259
Hemingway, Ernest, **I:** 28, 64, 97, 99, 105, 107, 117, 150, 162, 190, 211, 221, 288, 289, 295, 367, 374, 378, 421, 423, 445, 476, 477, 478, 482, 484–485, 487, 488, 489, 491, 495, 504, 517; **II:** 27, 44, 51, 58, 68–69, 78, 90, 97, 127, 206, **247–270,** 289, 424, 431, 456, 457, 458–459, 482, 560, 600; **III:** 2, 18, 20, 35, 36, 37, 40, 61, 108, 220, 334, 363, 364, 382, 453, 454, 471–472, 476, 551, 575, 576, 584; **IV:** 27, 28, 33, 34, 35, 42, 49, 97, 108, 122, 126, 138, 190, 191, 201, 216, 217, 257, 297, 363, 404, 427, 433, 451; **Retro. Supp. I:** 74, 98, 108, 111, 112, 113, 115, **169–191,** 215, 292, 359, 418; **Retro. Supp. II:** 19, 24, 30, 68, 115, 123; **Supp. I Part 2:** 621, 658, 678; **Supp. II Part 1:** 221; **Supp. III Part 1:** 146; **Supp. III Part 2:** 617; **Supp. IV Part 1:** 48, 102, 123, 197, 236, 342, 343, 344, 348, 350, 352, 380–381, 383; **Supp. IV Part 2:** 463, 468, 502, 607, 679, 680, 681, 689, 692; **Supp. V:** 237, 240, 244, 250, 336; **Supp. VIII:** 40, 101, 105, 179, 182, 183, 188, 189, 196; **Supp. IX:** 16, 57, 58, 94, 106, 260, 262; **Supp. X:** 137, 167, 223, 225; **Supp. XI:** 214, 221; **Supp. XIII:** 96, 255, 270
Hemingway, Mrs. Ernest (Hadley Richardson), **II:** 257, 260, 263
Hemingway, Mrs. Ernest (Martha Gellhorn), **II:** 260
Hemingway, Mrs. Ernest (Mary Welsh), **II:** 257, 260
Hemingway, Mrs. Ernest (Pauline Pfeiffer), **II:** 260
"Hemingway: The Old Lion" (Cowley), **Supp. II Part 1:** 143
"Hemingway in Paris" (Cowley), **Supp. II Part 1:** 144

"Hemingway Story, A" (Dubus), **Supp. VII:** 91
"Hemp, The" (Benét), **Supp. XI:** 44
"Henchman, The" (Whittier), **Supp. I Part 2:** 696
Henderson, Alice Corbin, **Supp. I Part 2:** 387
Henderson, Darwin L., **Supp. XIII:** 213, 221–222
Henderson, Jane, **Supp. VIII:** 87
Henderson, Katherine, **Supp. IV Part 1:** 203, 207
Henderson, Linda. *See* Hogan, Linda
Henderson, Robert W., **Supp. VIII:** 124
Henderson, Stephen, **Supp. IV Part 1:** 365
Henderson, the Rain King (Bellow), **I:** 144, 147, 148, 152, 153, 154, 155, 158, 160, 161, 162–163; **Retro. Supp. II:** 19, **24–25,** 30
"Hen Flower, The" (Kinnell), **Supp. III Part 1:** 247–248
Henie, Sonja, **Supp. XII:** 165
Henle, James, **II:** 26, 30, 38, 41; **Supp. IX:** 2
Henri, Robert, **IV:** 411; **Supp. I Part 2:** 376
Henry, Arthur, **I:** 515; **Retro. Supp. II:** 97
Henry, DeWitt, **Supp. XI:** 342
Henry, O., **I:** 201; **III:** 5; **Supp. I Part 2:** 390, 462; **Supp. II Part 1: 385–412**
Henry, Robert, **Retro. Supp. II:** 103
Henry, William A., III, **Supp. IV Part 2:** 574
Henry and June (film), **Supp. X:** 186
Henry and June: From the Unexpurgated Diary of Anaïs Nin, **Supp. X:** 184, 185, 187, 194
Henry Holt and Company, **Retro. Supp. I:** 121, 131, 133, 136
Henry IV (Shakespeare), **III:** 166; **Supp. VIII:** 164
"Henry James, Jr." (Howells), **II:** 289; **Retro. Supp. I:** 220
"Henry James and the Art of Teaching" (Rowe), **Retro. Supp. I:** 216
"Henry Manley, Living Alone, Keeps Time" (Kumin), **Supp. IV Part 2:** 451
"Henry Manley Looks Back" (Kumin), **Supp. IV Part 2:** 451
"Henry Manley" poems (Kumin), **Supp. IV Part 2:** 446
Henry Miller Reader, The (Durrell, ed.), **III:** 175, 190
"Henry's Confession" (Berryman), **I:** 186

Henry VIII (Shakespeare), **Supp. IX:** 235
Henslee, **Supp. IV Part 1:** 217
Henson, Josiah, **Supp. I Part 2:** 589
Hentoff, Margot, **Supp. IV Part 1:** 205
Hentz, Caroline Lee, **Supp. I Part 2:** 584
Henze, Hans Werner, **Supp. II Part 1:** 24
"He of the Assembly" (Bowles), **Supp. IV Part 1:** 90
Hepburn, Katharine, **Supp. IX:** 189; **Supp. XI:** 17
Heraclitus, **II:** 1, 163; **IV:** 86
Herakles: A Play in Verse (MacLeish), **III:** 21, 22
Herald of the Autochthonic Spirit (Corso), **Supp. XII:** 134–136
Herberg, Will, **III:** 291
Herbert, Edward, **II:** 11
Herbert, Francis (pseudonym). *See* Bryant, William Cullen
Herbert, George, **II:** 12; **IV:** 141, 145, 146, 151, 153, 156, 165; **Retro. Supp. II:** 40; **Supp. I Part 1:** 80, 107, 108, 122; **Supp. IV Part 2:** 646
Herbert, Zbigniew, **Supp. VIII:** 20
Herbert of Cherbury, Lord, **II:** 108
Herbst, Josephine, **Retro. Supp. II:** 343, 346; **Supp. XIII:** 295
"Her Choice" (Larcom), **Supp. XIII:** 144
"Her Dead Brother" (Lowell), **Retro. Supp. II:** 188
"Her Dream Is of the Sea" (Ríos), **Supp. IV Part 2:** 546
"Here" (Kenyon), **Supp. VII:** 164
Here and Beyond (Wharton), **Retro. Supp. I:** 382
Here and Now (Levertov), **Supp. III Part 1:** 275, 276
"Here and There" (Wallace), **Supp. X:** 305–306
Heredia, Juanita, **Supp. XI:** 185, 190
Heredity and Variation (Lock), **Retro. Supp. I:** 375
Here Lies (Parker), **Supp. IX:** 192
Here on Earth (Hoffman), **Supp. X:** 77, 89
Heresy and the Ideal: On Contemporary Poetry (Baker), **Supp. XI:** 142
"Here to Learn" (Bowles), **Supp. IV Part 1:** 93
"Here to Yonder" (Hughes), **Retro. Supp. I:** 205
"Her Father's Letters" (Milburn), **Supp. XI:** 242
Herford, Reverend Brooke, **I:** 471

Hergesheimer, Joseph, **Supp. I Part 2:** 620
"Heritage" (Cullen), **Supp. IV Part 1:** 164–165, 168, 170, 171
"Heritage" (Hogan), **Supp. IV Part 1:** 413
"Her Kind" (Sexton), **Supp. II Part 2:** 687
Herland (Gilman), **Supp. XI:** 208–209
Herman, Florence. *See* Williams, Mrs. William Carlos (Florence Herman)
Herman, William (pseudonym). *See* Bierce, Ambrose
"Her Management" (Swenson), **Supp. IV Part 2:** 642
"Herman Melville" (Auden), **Supp. II Part 1:** 14
Herman Melville (Mumford), **Supp. II Part 2:** 471, 476, 489–491
"Hermes of the Ways" (Doolittle), **Supp. I Part 1:** 266
Hermetic Definition (Doolittle), **Supp. I Part 1:** 271, 272, 273, 274
"Hermitage, The" (Haines), **Supp. XII:** 205–206
Hermit and the Wild Woman, The (Wharton), **IV:** 315; **Retro. Supp. I:** 371
"Hermit and the Wild Woman, The" (Wharton), **Retro. Supp. I:** 372
"Hermit Meets the Skunk, The" (Kumin), **Supp. IV Part 2:** 447
"Hermit of Saba, The" (Freneau), **Supp. II Part 1:** 259
Hermit of 69th Street, The: The Working Papers or Norbert Kosky (Kosinski), **Supp. VII:** 215, 216, 223, 226–227
"Hermit Picks Berries, The" (Kumin), **Supp. IV Part 2:** 447
"Hermit Thrush, A" (Clampitt), **Supp. IX:** 40
Hernández, Miguel, **Supp. V:** 194; **Supp. XIII:** 315, 323
Herne, James A., **II:** 276; **Supp. II Part 1:** 198
Hernton, Calvin, **Supp. X:** 240
"Hero, The" (Moore), **III:** 200, 211, 212
Hero, The (Raglan), **I:** 135
Hérodiade (Mallarmé), **I:** 66
Herodotus, **Supp. I Part 2:** 405
Heroes, The (Ashbery), **Supp. III Part 1:** 3
Hero in America, The (Van Doren), **II:** 103
"Heroines" (Rich), **Retro. Supp. II:** 291
"Heroines of Nature: Four Women Respond to the American Land-

scape" (Norwood), **Supp. IX:** 24
"Heron, The" (Roethke), **III:** 540–541
"Her One Bad Eye" (Karr), **Supp. XI:** 244
"Her Own People" (Warren), **IV:** 253
"Her Quaint Honour" (Gordon), **II:** 196, 199, 200
Herr, Michael, **Supp. XI:** 245
Herrick, Robert, **II:** 11, 18, 444; **III:** 463, 592; **IV:** 453; **Retro. Supp. I:** 319; **Retro. Supp. II:** 101; **Supp. I Part 2:** 646; **Supp. XIII:** 334
Herrmann, John, **Retro. Supp. II:** 346
Herron, George, **Supp. I Part 1:** 7
Herschel, Sir John, **Supp. I Part 1:** 314
"Her Sense of Timing" (Elkin), **Supp. VI:** 56, 58
Hersey, John, **IV:** 4; **Supp. I Part 1:** 196
"Her Sweet turn to leave the Homestead" (Dickinson), **Retro. Supp. I:** 44
Herzog (Bellow), **I:** 144, 147, 149, 150, 152, 153, 154, 155, 156, 157, 158, 159–160; **Retro. Supp. II:** 19, 26–27; **Supp. IV Part 1:** 30
"He/She" (Dunn), **Supp. XI:** 149
"Hesitation Blues" (Hughes), **Retro. Supp. I:** 211
Hesse, Hermann, **Supp. V:** 208
"Hetch Hetchy Valley" (Muir), **Supp. IX:** 185
He Who Gets Slapped (Andreyev), **II:** 425
"He Who Spits at the Sky" (Stegner), **Supp. IV Part 2:** 605
"He Will Not Leave a Note" (Ríos), **Supp. IV Part 2:** 548
Hewlett, Maurice, **I:** 359
Heyen, William, **Supp. XIII:** 285, 344
"Hey! Hey!" (Hughes), **Supp. I Part 1:** 327–328
Hey Rub-a-Dub-Dub (Dreiser), **I:** 515; **II:** 26; **Retro. Supp. II:** 104, 105, 108
"Hey Sailor, What Ship?" (Olsen), **Supp. XIII:** 293, 294, 298, **299**
Hiawatha (Longfellow), **Supp. I Part 1:** 79; **Supp. III Part 2:** 609, 610
"Hibernaculum" (Ammons), **Supp. VII:** 26–27
Hichborn, Mrs. Philip. *See* Wylie, Elinor
Hichborn, Philip, **Supp. I Part 2:** 707, 708
"Hic Jacet" (W. C. Williams), **Retro. Supp. I:** 414
Hickok, James Butler ("Wild Bill"), **Supp. V:** 229, 230

Hicks, Granville, **I:** 254, 259, 374; **II:** 26; **III:** 342, 355, 452; **Supp. I Part 1:** 361; **Supp. I Part 2:** 609; **Supp. IV Part 1:** 22; **Supp. IV Part 2:** 526; **Supp. VIII:** 96, 124; **Supp. XII:** 250; **Supp. XIII:** 263
Hicok, Bethany, **Retro. Supp. II:** 39
"Hidden" (Nye), **Supp. XIII:** 283
"Hidden Gardens" (Capote), **Supp. III Part 1:** 125
Hidden Law, The (Hecht), **Supp. X:** 58
"Hidden Name and Complex Fate" (Ellison), **Supp. II Part 1:** 245
Hidden Wound, The (Berry), **Supp. X:** 23, 25, 26–27, 29, 34, 35
"Hide-and-Seek" (Francis), **Supp. IX:** 81
"Hiding" (Minot), **Supp. VI:** 203, 206
Hiding Place (Wideman), **Supp. X:** 320, 321, 327, 329, 331–332, 333
Hienger, Jorg, **Supp. IV Part 1:** 106
Higgins, George, **Supp. IV Part 1:** 356
Higginson, Thomas Wentworth, **I:** 451–452, 453, 454, 456, 458, 459, 463, 464, 465, 470; **Retro. Supp. I:** 26, 31, 33, 35, 39, 40; **Supp. I Part 1:** 307, 371; **Supp. IV Part 2:** 430
"High Bridge above the Tagus River at Toledo, The" (W. C. Williams), **Retro. Supp. I:** 429
"High Dive: A Variant" (Kumin), **Supp. IV Part 2:** 442
"High Diver" (Francis), **Supp. IX:** 82
"Higher Keys, The" (Merrill), **Supp. III Part 1:** 335–336
Higher Learning in America, The (Veblen), **Supp. I Part 2:** 630, 631, 641, 642
Highet, Gilbert, **Supp. I Part 1:** 268
High Noon (film), **Supp. V:** 46
"High on Sadness" (Komunyakaa), **Supp. XIII:** 114
"High School Senior" (Olds), **Supp. X:** 212
Highsmith, Patricia, **Supp. IV Part 1:** 79, 94, 132
"High Tide" (Marquand), **III:** 56
High Tide in Tucson: Essays from Now or Never (Kingsolver), **Supp. VII:** 198, 201, 209
"High-Toned Old Christian Woman, A" (Stevens), **Retro. Supp. I:** 301
"Highway, The" (Merwin), **Supp. III Part 1:** 346
"Highway 99E from Chico" (Carver), **Supp. III Part 1:** 136
High Window, The (Chandler), **Supp. IV Part 1:** 127–129, 130, 131
Hijuelos, Oscar, **Supp. IV Part 1:** 54; **Supp. VIII:** 73–91

Hike and the Aeroplane (Lewis), **II:** 440–441
Hilberg, Raul, **Supp. V:** 267
Hildebrand, Al, **III:** 118
Hiler, Hilaire, **Retro. Supp. II:** 345; **Supp. III Part 2:** 617
"Hill, A" (Hecht), **Supp. X:** 59–60, 63
Hill, Hamlin, **Retro. Supp. II:** 304
Hill, James J., **Supp. I Part 2:** 644
Hill, Joe, **I:** 493
Hill, Lee, **Supp. XI:** 293, 294, 297, 299, 301, 305, 307
Hill, Patti, **I:** 289
Hill, Peggy, **Supp. XIII:** 163
"Hill, The" (Strand), **Supp. IV Part 2:** 627
"Hill, The" (Toomer), **Supp. III Part 2:** 486
Hill, Vernon, **Supp. I Part 2:** 397
"Hillcrest" (Robinson), **III:** 504
Hill-Lubin, Mildred A., **Supp. IV Part 1:** 13
Hillman, Sidney, **Supp. I Part 1:** 5
Hillringhouse, Mark, **Supp. IX:** 286, 288, 299
Hills Beyond, The (Wolfe), **IV:** 450, 451, 460, 461
"Hills Beyond, The" (Wolfe), **IV:** 460
Hillside and Seaside in Poetry (Larcom, ed.), **Supp. XIII:** 142
"Hillside Thaw, A" (Frost), **Retro. Supp. I:** 133
"Hills Like White Elephants" (Hemingway), **Retro. Supp. I:** 170
"Hill-Top View, A" (Jeffers), **Supp. II Part 2:** 417
"Hill Wife, The" (Frost), **II:** 154; **Retro. Supp. I:** 131
Hillyer, Robert, **I:** 475; **Supp. IX:** 75
Hilton, James, **Supp. XIII:** 166
"Hiltons' Holiday, The" (Jewett), **II:** 391; **Retro. Supp. II:** 134
Him (Cummings), **I:** 429, 434–435
Himes, Chester, **Retro. Supp. II:** 117; **Supp. I Part 1:** 51, 325; **Supp. XIII:** 233
Himes, Norman, **Supp. V:** 128
"Him with His Foot in His Mouth" (Bellow), **Retro. Supp. II:** 34
Him with His Foot in His Mouth and Other Stories (Bellow), **Retro. Supp. II:** 31
Hinchman, Sandra K., **Supp. IV Part 1:** 210
Hindemith, Paul, **IV:** 357; **Supp. IV Part 1:** 81
Hindsell, Oliver, **Supp. XIII:** 162
Hinge Picture (Howe), **Supp. IV Part 2:** 423–424
"Hippies: Slouching towards Bethle-

hem" (Didion), **Supp. IV Part 1:** 200
Hippolytus (Euripides), **II:** 543; **Supp. I Part 1:** 270
Hippolytus Temporizes (Doolittle), **Supp. I Part 1:** 270
"Hips" (Cisneros), **Supp. VII:** 61, 62
Hirsch, Edward, **Supp. V:** 177; **Supp. IX:** 262
Hirsch, Sidney. *See* Mttron-Hirsch, Sidney
Hirschorn, Clive, **Supp. IV Part 2:** 577, 579
Hirson, Roger, **Supp. XI:** 343
"His Bride of the Tomb" (Dunbar), **Supp. II Part 1:** 196
"His Chest of Drawers" (Anderson), **I:** 113, 114
"His Lover" (Dubus), **Supp. VII:** 86
"His Music" (Dunn), **Supp. XI:** 149
"His Own Key" (Ríos), **Supp. IV Part 2:** 543
His Religion and Hers (Gilman), **Supp. XI:** 209
"Hiss, Chambers, and the Age of Innocence" (Fiedler), **Supp. XIII:** 99
"His Shield" (Moore), **III:** 211
"His Story" (Cisneros), **Supp. VII:** 67
His Thought Made Pockets & the Plane Buckt (Berryman), **I:** 170
Histoire comparée des systèmes de philosophie (Gérando), **II:** 10
Historical and Moral View of the Origin and Progress of the French Revolution (Wollstonecraft), **Supp. I Part 1:** 126
"Historical Conceptualization" (Huizinga), **I:** 255
"Historical Interpretation of Literature, The" (Wilson), **IV:** 431, 433, 445
Historical Jesus, The: The Life of a Mediterranean Jewish Peasant (Crossan), **Supp. V:** 251
"Historical Value of Crèvecoeur's *Voyage* . . .," (Adams), **Supp. I Part 1:** 251
"History" (Emerson), **II:** 13, 15
"History" (Hughes), **Supp. I Part 1:** 344
History (Lowell), **Retro. Supp. II:** 183, 190
"History" (Simic), **Supp. VIII:** 279
"History, Myth, and the Western Writer" (Stegner), **Supp. IV Part 2:** 596, 601
"History among the Rocks" (Warren), **IV:** 252
History as a Literary Art (Morison), **Supp. I Part 2:** 493
"History as Fate in E. L. Doctorow's Tale of a Western Town" (Arnold), **Supp. IV Part 1:** 220
"History Is the Memory of Time" (Olson), **Supp. II Part 2:** 574
"History Lessons" (Komunyakaa), **Supp. XIII:** 126
"History of a Literary Movement" (Nemerov), **III:** 270
"History of a Literary Radical, The" (Bourne), **I:** 215, 235, 236
History of a Radical: Essays by Randolph Bourne (Brooks), **I:** 245
"History of Buttons, The" (Goldbarth), **Supp. XII:** 187
History of English Literature (Taine), **III:** 323
History of Fortus, The (Emerson), **II:** 8
History of Henry Esmond, The (Thackeray), **II:** 91, 130
History of Modern Poetry, A (Perkins), **Supp. I Part 2:** 475
History of My Heart (Pinsky), **Supp. VI:** 243, 244, 245
History of New York, from the Beginning of the World to the End of the Dutch Dynasty, A (Irving), **II:** 300–303, 304, 310
History of Pendennis, The (Thackeray), **II:** 291
"History of Red, The" (Hogan), **Supp. IV Part 1:** 411
History of Roxbury Town (Ellis), **Supp. I Part 1:** 99
History of the Conquest of Mexico (Prescott), **Retro. Supp. I:** 123
History of the Conquest of Peru (Morison, ed.), **Supp. I Part 2:** 494
History of the Dividing Line betwixt Virginia and North Carolina (Byrd), **Supp. IV Part 2:** 425
History of the Life and Voyages of Christopher Columbus, A (Irving), **II:** 310, 314
History of the Navy of the United States of America (Cooper), **I:** 347
History of the United States of America during the Administrations of Thomas Jefferson and James Madison (Adams), **I:** 6–9, 10, 20, 21
History of the Work of Redemption, A (Edwards), **I:** 560
History of United States Naval Operations in World War II (Morison), **Supp. I Part 2:** 490–492
History of Womankind in Western Europe, The, **Supp. XI:** 197
"History Through a Beard" (Morison), **Supp. I Part 2:** 490
His Toy, His Dream, His Rest (Berryman), **I:** 169, 170, 183, 184–186
"His Words" (Roethke), **III:** 544
Hitchcock, Ada. *See* MacLeish, Mrs. Archibald (Ada Hitchcock)
Hitchcock, Alfred, **IV:** 357; **Supp. IV Part 1:** 132; **Supp. VIII:** 177
Hitchcock, George, **Supp. X:** 127
"Hitch Haiku" (Snyder), **Supp. VIII:** 297
"Hitch-Hikers, The" (Welty), **IV:** 262
Hitchins, Christopher, **Supp. VIII:** 241
Hitler, Adolf, **I:** 261, 290, 492; **II:** 146, 454, 561, 565, 592; **III:** 2, 3, 110, 115, 140, 156, 246, 298, 446; **IV:** 5, 17, 18, 298, 372; **Supp. I Part 2:** 431, 436, 446, 664; **Supp. V:** 290
Hitler, Wendy, **III:** 404
Hnizdovsky, Jacques, **Supp. XIII:** 346
"Hoarder, The" (Sexton), **Supp. II Part 2:** 692
Hobb, Gormley, **I:** 203
Hobbes, Thomas, **I:** 277; **II:** 9, 10, 540; **III:** 306; **IV:** 88; **Supp. XII:** 33
Hobson, Geary, **Supp. IV Part 1:** 321; **Supp. IV Part 2:** 502
Hobson, J. A., **I:** 232
Hobson, John A., **Supp. I Part 2:** 650
Hobson, Laura Z., **III:** 151
Hocking, Agnes, **Supp. VIII:** 251
Hocking, William Ernest, **III:** 303
Hodgson, Captain Joseph, **III:** 328
Hoffa, Jimmy, **I:** 493
Hoffenberg, Mason, **Supp. XI:** 294, 297, 299, 305
Hoffer, Eric, **Supp. VIII:** 188
Hoffman, Alice, **Supp. X: 77–94; Supp. XIII:** 13
Hoffman, Daniel, **Retro. Supp. II:** 265
Hoffman, Daniel G., **I:** 405; **II:** 307; **Supp. XI:** 152
Hoffman, Dustin, **Supp. IV Part 1:** 236
Hoffman, Frederick J., **I:** 60, 67; **II:** 443; **IV:** 113
Hoffman, Josiah Ogden, **II:** 297, 300
Hoffman, Matilda, **II:** 300, 314
Hoffman, William M., **Supp. X:** 153
Hoffmann, E. T. A., **III:** 415
Ho for a Hat (W. J. Smith), **Supp. XIII:** 346
Hofstadter, Richard, **Supp. VIII:** 98, 99, 108
Hogan, Linda, **Supp. IV Part 1:** 324, 325, **397–418**
Hogarth, William, **Supp. XII:** 44
Hogg, James, **I:** 53; **Supp. I Part 1:** 349; **Supp. IX:** 275
Hohne, Karen, **Supp. V:** 147

Hojoki (Chomei), **IV:** 170
Holbrook, David, **Supp. I Part 2:** 526–527, 546
Holcroft, Thomas, **Supp. I Part 2:** 514
Holden, Jonathan, **Supp. XI:** 143
Holden, William, **Supp. XI:** 307
"Holding On" (Levine), **Supp. V:** 184
Holding the Line: Women in the Great Arizona Mine Strike of 1983 (Kingsolver), **Supp. VII:** 197, 201–202, 204
"Holding the Mirror Up to Nature" (Nemerov), **III:** 275, 276
"Hold Me" (Levine), **Supp. V:** 186
Hold the Press (film), **Supp. XIII:** 163
"Hole in the Floor, A" (Wilbur), **Supp. III Part 2:** 556–557
Holiday (Barry), **Retro. Supp. I:** 104
"Holiday" (Porter), **III:** 454
Holiday, Billie, **Supp. I Part 1:** 80; **Supp. IV Part 1:** 2, 7
Holinshed, Raphael, **IV:** 370
Holland, Josiah, **Supp. I Part 2:** 420
Holland, Laurence Bedwell, **Retro. Supp. I:** 216
Holland, Mrs. Theodore, **I:** 453, 455, 465
Holland, Theodore, **I:** 453
Holland, William, **IV:** 381
Hollander, John, **Supp. III Part 2:** 541; **Supp. IV Part 2:** 642; **Supp. IX:** 50, 153, 155; **Supp. XII:** 254, 255, 260
Holley, Marietta, **Supp. XIII:** 152
Hollinghurst, Alan, **Supp. XIII:** 52
Hollis, Thomas Brand, **Supp. I Part 2:** 514
Hollow Men, The (Eliot), **I:** 574, 575, 578–579, 580, 585; **III:** 586; **Retro. Supp. I:** 63, 64
"Hollow Tree, A" (Bly), **Supp. IV Part 1:** 64, 66
Hollyberrys at the Shore, The, **Supp. X:** 42
"Hollywood!" (Vidal), **Supp. IV Part 2:** 688
Hollywood: American Movie-City (Rand, unauthorized), **Supp. IV Part 2:** 519
Hollywood: A Novel of America in the 1920s (Vidal), **Supp. IV Part 2:** 677, 684, 686, 688, 690, 691
Hollywood on Trial (film), **Supp. I Part 1:** 295
Holmes, Abiel, **Supp. I Part 1:** 300, 301, 302, 310
Holmes, John, **I:** 169; **Supp. II Part 1:** 87; **Supp. IV Part 2:** 440–441
Holmes, John Clellon, **Supp. XII:** 118
Holmes, Mrs. Abiel (Sarah Wendell), **Supp. I Part 1:** 300
Holmes, Mrs. Oliver Wendell (Amelia Jackson), **Supp. I Part 1:** 303
Holmes, Oliver Wendell, **I:** 487; **II:** 225, 273–274, 402, 403; **III:** 81–82, 590, 591–592; **IV:** 429, 436; **Retro. Supp. II:** 155; **Supp. I Part 1:** 103, 243, 254, **299–319**; **Supp. I Part 2:** 405, 414, 415, 420, 593, 704, 705; **Supp. XI:** 194
Holmes, Oliver Wendell, Jr., **I:** 3, 19; **Supp. IV Part 2:** 422
Holmes, Steven J., **Supp. IX:** 172, 177
Holmes, Ted, **Supp. V:** 180
Holmes, William Henry, **Supp. IV Part 2:** 603–604
Holt, Edwin E., **I:** 59
Holt, Felix, **II:** 179
Holt, Henry, **II:** 348; **III:** 587
Holtby, Winifred, **Supp. I Part 2:** 720
Holy Ghostly, The (Shepard), **Supp. III Part 2:** 437–438, 447
"Holy Innocents, The" (Lowell), **II:** 539
Holy Sonnets (Donne), **IV:** 145; **Supp. I Part 1:** 367; **Supp. III Part 2:** 619; **Supp. XIII:** 130–131
"Holy Terror, A" (Bierce), **I:** 203
"Holy Terror, The" (Maxwell), **Supp. VIII:** 169
Holy the Firm (Dillard), **Supp. VI:** 23, **29,** 30, 31, 32
Holy War, The (Bunyan), **IV:** 156
"Homage to Arthur Rimbaud" (Wright), **Supp. V:** 339
"Homage to Che Guevara" (Banks), **Supp. V:** 5
Homage to Clio (Auden), **Supp. II Part 1:** 24
"Homage to Elizabeth Bishop" (Ivask, ed.), **Supp. I Part 1:** 96
"Homage to Ezra Pound" (Wright), **Supp. V:** 339
Homage to Frank O'Hara (Ashbery), **Supp. III Part 1:** 2–3
"Homage to Franz Joseph Haydn" (Hecht), **Supp. X:** 69
"Homage to Hemingway" (Bishop), **IV:** 35
Homage to Mistress Bradstreet (Berryman), **I:** 168, 169, 170–171, 172, 174, 175, 178–183, 184, 186
"Homage to Paul Cézanne" (Wright), **Supp. V:** 341–342
Homage to Sextus Propertius (Pound), **Retro. Supp. I:** 290
"Homage to Sextus Propertius" (Pound), **III:** 462, 476; **Supp. III Part 2:** 622
"Homage to Shakespeare" (Cheever), **Supp. I Part 1:** 180
"Homage to the Empress of the Blues" (Hayden), **Supp. II Part 1:** 379
"Homage to the Memory of Wallace Stevens" (Justice), **Supp. VII:** 126
Homage to Theodore Dreiser (Warren), **I:** 517
Homans, Margaret, **Supp. X:** 229
"Home" (Hughes), **Supp. I Part 1:** 329, 330
"Home" (Mora), **Supp. XIII:** 217
Home (Updike), **Retro. Supp. I:** 320
Home: Social Essays (Baraka), **Supp. II Part 1:** 45, 61
"Home, Sweet Home" (Fante), **Supp. XI:** 164, 165
Home, The (Gilman), **Supp. XI:** 206–207
"Home after Three Months Away" (Lowell), **II:** 547
Home and Colonial Library (Murray), **Retro. Supp. I:** 246
Home as Found (Cooper), **I:** 348, 349, 350, 351
"Home Away from Home, A" (Humphrey), **Supp. IX:** 101
"Home Burial" (Frost), **Retro. Supp. I:** 124, 125, 128, **129–130**; **Supp. VIII:** 31
Homecoming (Alvarez), **Supp. VII:** 1, 3–5, 9
"Homecoming" (McGrath), **Supp. X:** 116
Homecoming, The (Wilson), **Supp. VIII:** 330
Homecoming Game, The (Nemerov), **III:** 268, 282, 284–285
"Home during a Tropical Snowstorm I Feed My Father Lunch" (Karr), **Supp. XI:** 241–242, 248
Home Economics (Berry), **Supp. X:** 28, 31–32, 35, 36, 37
Home from the Hill (film), **Supp. IX:** 95
Home from the Hill (Humphrey), **Supp. IX:** 93, 95, **96–98,** 104, 106, 109
"Homeland" (Merwin), **Supp. III Part 1:** 351
Homeland and Other Stories (Kingsolver), **Supp. VII:** 199, 202–204, 207
Home on the Range (Baraka), **Supp. II Part 1:** 47
Home Place, The (Morris), **III:** 221, 222, 232
Homer, **I:** 312, 433; **II:** 6, 8, 133, 302, 543, 544, 552; **III:** 14, 21, 278, 453, 457, 473, 567; **IV:** 54, 371; **Retro. Supp. I:** 59; **Supp. I Part 1:** 158, 283; **Supp. I Part 2:** 494; **Supp. X:**

36, 120, 122
Homer, Louise, **Retro. Supp. I:** 10
"Homesick Blues" (Hughes), **Supp. I Part 1:** 327
Home to Harlem (McKay), **Supp. X:** 132, 137–138, **138–139**
Homeward Bound (Cooper), **I:** 348
Homewood trilogy (Wideman), **Supp. X:** 319
"Homework" (Cameron), **Supp. XII:** 80, **83,** 84
"Homily" (Tate), **IV:** 121–122
"Homme Moyen Sensuel, L'" (Pound), **III:** 462
Homme révolté, L' (Camus), **III:** 306
"Homoeopathy and Its Kindred Delusions" (Holmes), **Supp. I Part 1:** 303–304, 305
Homo Ludens (Huizinga), **II:** 416–417, 425
"Homosexual Villain, The" (Mailer), **III:** 36
"Homo Will Not Inherit" (Doty), **Supp. XI:** 128
Hone and Strong Diaries of Old Manhattan, The (Auchincloss, ed.), **Supp. IV Part 1:** 23
"Honey" (Beattie), **Supp. V:** 33
"Honey" (Wright), **Supp. III Part 2:** 589
"Honey, We'll Be Brave" (Farrell), **II:** 45
Honey and Salt (Sandburg), **III:** 594–596
"Honey and Salt" (Sandburg), **III:** 594
"Honey Babe" (Hughes), **Supp. I Part 1:** 334
"Honey Tree, The" (Oliver), **Supp. VII:** 236
Hong, Maxine. *See* Kingston, Maxine Hong
Hongo, Garrett, **Supp. X:** 292; **Supp. XIII:** 114
"Honkytonk" (Shapiro), **Supp. II Part 2:** 705
"Honky Tonk in Cleveland, Ohio" (Sandburg), **III:** 585
Honorable Men (Auchincloss), **Supp. IV Part 1:** 23
Hood, Tom, **I:** 195
"Hoodoo in America" (Hurston), **Supp. VI:** 153–154
"Hook" (Wright), **Supp. III Part 2:** 604
Hook, Sidney, **I:** 265; **Supp. IV Part 2:** 527; **Supp. VIII:** 96, 100
Hooker, Adelaide. *See* Marquand, Mrs. John P. (Adelaide Hooker)
Hooker, Isabella Beecher, **Supp. XI:** 193

Hooker, Samuel, **IV:** 162, 165
Hooker, Thomas, **II:** 15–16; **IV:** 162
Hooper, Marian. *See* Adams, Mrs. Henry (Marian Hooper)
Hoosier Holiday, A (Dreiser), **Retro. Supp. II:** 104
Hoover, Herbert, **Supp. I Part 2:** 638
Hoover, J. Edgar, **Supp. XIII:** 170
"Hope" (Jarrell), **II:** 389
"Hope" (Matthews), **Supp. IX:** 163
Hope, A. D., **Supp. XIII:** 347
Hope, Lynn, **Supp. II Part 1:** 38
"Hope Atherton's Wanderings" (Howe), **Supp. IV Part 2:** 432
Hope of Heaven (O'Hara), **III:** 361
"Hop-Frog" (Poe), **Retro. Supp. II:** 264, 268, 269
Hopkins, Anne Yale, **Supp. I Part 1:** 100, 102, 113
Hopkins, Gerard Manley, **I:** 171, 179, 397, 401, 522, 525, 533; **II:** 537; **III:** 197, 209, 523; **IV:** 129, 135, 141, 421; **Retro. Supp. II:** 40; **Supp. I Part 1:** 79, 81, 94; **Supp. III Part 2:** 551; **Supp. IV Part 1:** 178; **Supp. IV Part 2:** 637, 638, 639, 641, 643; **Supp. V:** 337; **Supp. IX:** 39, 42; **Supp. X:** 61, 115; **Supp. XIII:** 294
Hopkins, L. A., **I:** 502
Hopkins, Lemuel, **Supp. II Part 1:** 70
Hopkins, Miriam, **IV:** 381; **Supp. I Part 1:** 281
Hopkins, Samuel, **I:** 547, 549
Hopkins, Vivian, **II:** 20
Hopkinson, Francis, **Supp. I Part 2:** 504
Hopper (Strand), **Supp. IV Part 2:** 632
Hopper, Dennis, **Supp. XI:** 293, 308
Hopper, Edward, **IV:** 411, 413; **Supp. IV Part 2:** 619, 623, 631, 634
Hopwood, Avery, **Supp. IV Part 2:** 573
Horace, **II:** 8, 154, 169, 543, 552, 568; **III:** 15; **IV:** 89; **Supp. I Part 2:** 423; **Supp. IX:** 152; **Supp. X:** 65; **Supp. XII:** 258, 260, 262
Horae Canonicae (Auden), **Supp. II Part 1:** 21
"Horatian Ode" (Marvell), **IV:** 135
Horkheimer, Max, **Supp. I Part 2:** 645; **Supp. IV Part 1:** 301
Horn, Mother, **Supp. I Part 1:** 49, 54
Hornby, Nick, **Supp. XII:** 286
"Horn of Plenty" (Hughes), **Retro. Supp. I:** 210; **Supp. I Part 1:** 342
Horowitz, James. *See* Salter, James
Horowitz, Mark, **Supp. V:** 219, 231
"Horse, The" (Levine), **Supp. V:** 182
"Horse, The" (Wright), **Supp. III Part

2:** 592, 601
Horse Eats Hay (play), **Supp. IV Part 1:** 82
Horse Feathers (film), **Supp. IV Part 1:** 384
Horse Has Six Legs, The (Simic), **Supp. VIII:** 272
"Horselaugh on Dibber Lannon" (Fante), **Supp. XI:** 164
Horseman, Pass By (McMurtry), **Supp. V:** 220–221, 224
"Horses" (Doty), **Supp. XI:** 122
Horses and Men (Anderson), **I:** 112–113, 114
"Horses and Men in Rain" (Sandburg), **III:** 584
"Horse Show, The" (W. C. Williams), **Retro. Supp. I:** 423
Horses Make a Landscape More Beautiful (Walker), **Supp. III Part 2:** 521, 533
"Horse Thief" (Caldwell), **I:** 310
"Horsie" (Parker), **Supp. IX:** 193
Horton, Philip, **I:** 383, 386, 387, 393, 441
Hosea (biblical book), **II:** 166
Hospers, John, **Supp. IV Part 2:** 528
Hospital, Janette Turner, **Supp. IV Part 1:** 311–302
Hospital Sketches (Alcott), **Supp. I Part 1:** 34, 35
Hostages to Fortune (Humphrey), **Supp. IX:** 96, **104–106,** 109
"Hot Dog" (Stern), **Supp. IX:** 298–299
"Hotel Bar" (McClatchy), **Supp. XII:** 269
Hotel Insomnia (Simic), **Supp. VIII:** 280, **281–282**
Hotel New Hampshire, The (Irving), **Supp. VI:** 163, 164, **172–173,** 177, 179
"Hot Night on Water Street" (Simpson), **Supp. IX:** 269, 270
"Hot Time, A" (Gunn Allen), **Supp. IV Part 1:** 333
Houdini, Harry, **IV:** 437
Houghton Mifflin, **Retro. Supp. I:** 7, 9, 13, 35
"Hound of Heaven" (Thompson), **Retro. Supp. I:** 55
"Hour in Chartres, An" (Bourne), **I:** 228
Hours, The (Cunningham), **Supp. XII:** 80
"Hours before Eternity" (Caldwell), **I:** 291
House, Bridge, Fountain, Gate (Kumin), **Supp. IV Part 2:** 448, 449, 451, 454
House, Edward, **Supp. I Part 2:** 643

"House, The" (Merrill), **Supp. III Part 1:** 323

House at Pooh Corner, The (Milne), **Supp. IX:** 189

Houseboat Days (Ashbery), **Supp. III Part 1:** 18–20

Housebreaker of Shady Hill and Other Stories, The (Cheever), **Supp. I Part 1:** 184

House by the Sea, The (Sarton), **Supp. VIII:** 264

House Divided, A (Buck), **Supp. II Part 1:** 118

"House Divided, The/La Casa Divida" (Kingsolver), **Supp. VII:** 207

"House Guest" (Bishop), **Retro. Supp. II:** 49; **Supp. I Part 1:** 93

"House in Athens, The" (Merrill), **Supp. III Part 1:** 323

House in the Uplands, A (Caldwell), **I:** 297, 301, 306

"House in Turk Street, The" (Hammett), **Supp. IV Part 1:** 344

"House in Winter, The" (Sarton), **Supp. VIII:** 259

"Housekeeping" (Alvarez), **Supp. VII:** 3–5, 10

"Housekeeping for Men" (Bourne), **I:** 231

House Made of Dawn (Momaday), **Supp. IV Part 1:** 274, 323, 326; **Supp. IV Part 2:** 479, 480, 481–484, 485, 486, 504, 562

Houseman, John, **Supp. IV Part 1:** 173

House of Dust, The: A Symphony (Aiken), **I:** 50

House of Earth trilogy (Buck), **Supp. II Part 1:** 118, 123

House of Five Talents, The (Auchincloss), **Supp. IV Part 1:** 21, 25–27

"House of Flowers" (Capote), **Supp. III Part 1:** 123

House of Houses (Mora), **Supp. XIII:** 213, 215, 218, 219, 223–224, **225–227,** 228, 229

House of Incest (Nin), **Supp. III Part 1:** 43; **Supp. X:** 187, 190, 193

House of Life, The: Rachel Carson at Work (Brooks), **Supp. IX:** 26

House of Light (Oliver), **Supp. VII:** 238–240

House of Mirth, The (Wharton), **II:** 180, 193; **IV:** 311–313, 314, 316, 318, 323, 327; **Retro. Supp. I:** 360, 366, 367, **367–370,** 373, 380

"House of Mist, The" (Rand), **Supp. IV Part 2:** 524

"House of My Own, A" (Cisneros), **Supp. VII:** 64

"House of Night, The" (Freneau), **Supp. II Part 1:** 259, 260

House of the Far and Lost, The (Wolfe), **IV:** 456

"House of the Injured, The" (Haines), **Supp. XII:** 203

House of the Prophet, The (Auchincloss), **Supp. IV Part 1:** 31

House of the Seven Gables (Hawthorne), **I:** 106; **II:** 60, 224, 225, 231, 237, 239, 240–241, 243, 244; **Retro. Supp. I:** 63, 149, **160–162,** 163, 164; **Supp. I Part 2:** 579

House of the Solitary Maggot, The (Purdy), **Supp. VII:** 274–275

House on Mango Street, The (Cisneros), **Supp. VII:** 58, 59–64, 65, 66, 67, 68, 72

"House on Mango Street, The" (Cisneros), **Supp. VII:** 59

House on Marshland, The (Glück), **Supp. V:** 81–83, 84

"House on the Heights, A" (Capote), **Supp. III Part 1:** 120

"House on the Hill, The" (Robinson), **III:** 505, 524

"House on 15th S.W., The" (Hugo), **Supp. VI:** 140

"Houses" (Hogan), **Supp. IV Part 1:** 402

"Houses, The" (Merwin), **Supp. III Part 1:** 354

"Houses of the Spirit" (Karr), **Supp. XI:** 250

"House Sparrows" (Hecht), **Supp. X:** 68

House That Tai Maing Built, The (Lee), **Supp. X:** 291

"House Unroofed by the Gale" (Tu Fu), **II:** 526

"House Where Mark Twain Was Born, The" (Masters), **Supp. I Part 2:** 472

"Housewife" (Sexton), **Supp. II Part 2:** 682

Housman, A. E., **III:** 15, 136, 606; **Supp. II Part 1:** 4; **Supp. IV Part 1:** 165

Houston Trilogy (McMurtry), **Supp. V:** 223–225

"How" (Moore), **Supp. X:** 167

"How About This?" (Carver), **Supp. III Part 1:** 141

"How Annandale Went Out" (Robinson), **III:** 513

Howard, Gerald, **Supp. XII:** 21

Howard, Jane, **Retro. Supp. I:** 334

Howard, June, **Retro. Supp. II:** 139

Howard, Leon, **Supp. I Part 2:** 408, 422, 423

Howard, Maureen, **Supp. XII:** 285

Howard, Richard, **Retro. Supp. II:** 43; **Supp. IV Part 2:** 624, 626, 640; **Supp. VIII:** 273; **Supp. IX:** 324, 326; **Supp. X:** 152; **Supp. XI:** 317; **Supp. XII:** 254; **Supp. XIII:** 76

Howard, Vilma, **Retro. Supp. II:** 111, 112

Howards, J. Z., **Supp. VIII:** 178

Howards End (Forster), **Supp. XII:** 87

Howarth, Cora, **I:** 408, 409

Howbah Indians (Ortiz), **Supp. IV Part 2:** 513

"How Black Sees Green and Red" (McKay), **Supp. X:** 136

"How David Did Not Care" (Bly), **Supp. IV Part 1:** 73

Howe, E.W., **I:** 106

Howe, Florence, **Supp. XIII:** 295, 306

Howe, Harriet, **Supp. XI:** 200, 201

Howe, Irving, **IV:** 10; **Retro. Supp. I:** 369; **Retro. Supp. II:** 112, 304; **Supp. I Part 2:** 432; **Supp. II Part 1:** 99; **Supp. VI: 113–129; Supp. VIII:** 93, 232; **Supp. IX:** 227; **Supp. X:** 203, 245; **Supp. XII:** 160; **Supp. XIII:** 98

Howe, James Wong, **Supp. I Part 1:** 281; **Supp. V:** 223

Howe, Julia Ward, **III:** 505; **Retro. Supp. II:** 135

Howe, M. A. De Wolfe, **I:** 258; **II:** 406

Howe, Mary Manning, **Supp. IV Part 2:** 422

Howe, Samuel, **Supp. I Part 1:** 153

Howe, Susan, **Retro. Supp. I:** 33, 43; **Supp. IV Part 2: 419–438**

Howell, Chris, **Supp. XIII:** 112

Howell, James, **II:** 111

Howells: His Life and World (Brooks), **I:** 254

Howells, Margaret, **II:** 271

Howells, Mrs. William Dean (Elinor Mead), **II:** 273

Howells, William C., **II:** 273

Howells, William Dean, **I:** 109, 192, 204, 210, 211, 254, 355, 407, 411, 418, 459, 469; **II:** 127–128, 130, 131, 136, 137, 138, 140, **271–294,** 322, 331–332, 338, 397–398, 400, 415, 444, 451, 556; **III:** 51, 118, 314, 327–328, 461, 576, 607; **IV:** 192, 202, 342, 349; **Retro. Supp. I:** 220, 334, 362, 378; **Retro. Supp. II:** 93, 101, 135, 306; **Supp. I Part 1:** 306, 318, 357, 360, 368; **Supp. I Part 2:** 414, 420, 645–646; **Supp. II Part 1:** 198, 352; **Supp. IV Part 2:** 678; **Supp. VIII:** 98, 101, 102; **Supp. XI:** 198, 200

Howells, Winifred, **II:** 271
"Howells as Anti-Novelist" (Updike), **Retro. Supp. I:** 334
Hower, Edward, **Supp. XII:** 330, 343
Howes, Barbara, **Supp. XIII:** 331
"How I Became a Shadow" (Purdy), **Supp. VII:** 269
"How I Learned to Sweep" (Alvarez), **Supp. VII:** 4
"How It Began" (Stafford), **Supp. XI:** 327
"How It Feels to Be Colored Me" (Hurston), **Supp. VI:** 152
"How I Told My Child About Race" (Brooks), **Supp. III Part 1:** 78
"How I Went to the Mines" (Harte), **Supp. II Part 1:** 336
"How I Write" (Welty), **IV:** 279, 280
"How Jonah Did Not Care" (Bly), **Supp. IV Part 1:** 73
Howl (Ginsberg), **Retro. Supp. I:** 426; **Supp. III Part 1:** 92; **Supp. IV Part 1:** 90; **Supp. V:** 336; **Supp. VIII:** 290
Howl and Other Poems (Ginsberg), **Supp. II Part 1:** 308, 317–318, 319; **Supp. X:** 123
Howlett, William, **Retro. Supp. I:** 17
"How Many Midnights" (Bowles), **Supp. IV Part 1:** 86–87
"How Many Nights" (Kinnell), **Supp. III Part 1:** 245–246
How Much? (Blechman), **Supp. I Part 1:** 290
"How Much Are You Worth" (Salinas), **Supp. XIII:** 325–326
"How Much Earth" (Levine), **Supp. V:** 184
How Much Earth: The Fresno Poets (Buckley, Oliveira, and Williams, eds.), **Supp. XIII:** 313
"How Poetry Comes to Me" (Corso), **Supp. XII:** 122
"How Poetry Comes to Me" (Snyder), **Supp. VIII:** 305
"How She Came By Her Name: An Interview with Louis Massiah" (Bambara), **Supp. XI:** 20
"How Soon Hath Time" (Ransom), **IV:** 123
How Stella Got Her Groove Back (McMillan), **Supp. XIII:** 185, **190–191**
How the Alligator Missed Breakfast (Kinney), **Supp. III Part 1:** 235, 253
"How the Devil Came Down Division Street" (Algren), **Supp. IX:** 3
How the García Girls Lost Their Accents (Alvarez), **Supp. VII:** 3, 5–9, 11, 15, 17, 18
How the Other Half Lives (Riis), **I:** 293
"How the Saint Did Not Care" (Bly), **Supp. IV Part 1:** 73
"How the Women Went from Dover" (Whittier), **Supp. I Part 2:** 694, 696, 697
"How to Be an Other Woman" (Moore), **Supp. X:** 165, 167, 168
"How to Become a Writer" (Moore), **Supp. X:** 167, 168
"How to Be Happy: Another Memo to Myself" (Dunn), **Supp. XI:** 145
How to Develop Your Personality (Shellow), **Supp. I Part 2:** 608
"How To Like It" (Dobyns), **Supp. XIII:** **85–86**
"How to Live. What to Do" (Stevens), **Retro. Supp. I:** 302
"How to Live on $36,000 a Year" (Fitzgerald), **Retro. Supp. I:** 105
How to Read (Pound), **Supp. VIII:** 291
How to Read a Novel (Gordon), **II:** 198
How to Save Your Own Life (Jong), **Supp. V:** 115, 123–125, 130
"How to Study Poetry" (Pound), **III:** 474
"How to Talk to Your Mother" (Moore), **Supp. X:** 167, 172
How to Win Friends and Influence People (Carnegie), **Supp. I Part 2:** 608
How to Worry Successfully (Seabury), **Supp. I Part 2:** 608
How to Write (Stein), **IV:** 32, 34, 35
"How to Write a Blackwood Article" (Poe), **III:** 425; **Retro. Supp. II:** 273
"How to Write a Memoir Like This" (Oates), **Supp. III Part 2:** 509
"How to Write Like Somebody Else" (Roethke), **III:** 540
How to Write Short Stories (Lardner), **II:** 430, 431
"How Vincentine Did Not Care" (Bly), **Supp. IV Part 1:** 73
How We Became Human: New and Selected Poems (Harjo), **Supp. XII:** **230–232**
"How We Danced" (Sexton), **Supp. II Part 2:** 692
"How You Sound??" (Baraka), **Supp. II Part 1:** 30
Hoy, Philip, **Supp. X:** 56, 58
Hoyer, Linda Grace (pseudonym). *See* Updike, Mrs. Wesley
Hoyt, Constance, **Supp. I Part 2:** 707
Hoyt, Elinor Morton. *See* Wylie, Elinor
Hoyt, Henry (father), **Supp. I Part 2:** 707
Hoyt, Henry (son), **Supp. I Part 2:** 708
Hoyt, Henry Martyn, **Supp. I Part 2:** 707
Hsu, Kai-yu, **Supp. X:** 292
Hubba City (Reed), **Supp. X:** 241
Hubbard, Elbert, **I:** 98, 383
Hubbell, Jay B., **Supp. I Part 1:** 372
"Hubbub, The" (Ammons), **Supp. VII:** 35
Huber, François, **II:** 6
Huckins, Olga, **Supp. IX:** 32
Huckleberry Finn (Twain). *See Adventures of Huckleberry Finn, The* (Twain)
Hud (film), **Supp. V:** 223, 226
Hudgins, Andrew, **Supp. X:** 206
Hudson, Henry, **I:** 230
"Hudsonian Curlew, The" (Snyder), **Supp. VIII:** 302
Hudson River Bracketed (Wharton), **IV:** 326–327; **Retro. Supp. I:** 382
Huebsch, B. W., **III:** 110
Hueffer, Ford Madox, **Supp. I Part 1:** 257, 262. *See also* Ford, Ford Madox
Hug Dancing (Hearon), **Supp. VIII:** **67–68**
Huge Season, The (Morris), **III:** 225–226, 227, 230, 232, 233, 238
Hugging the Jukebox (Nye), **Supp. XIII:** **275–276**, 277
"Hugging the Jukebox" (Nye), **Supp. XIII:** 276
Hughes, Carolyn, **Supp. XII:** 272, 285
Hughes, Frieda, **Supp. I Part 2:** 540, 541
Hughes, Glenn, **Supp. I Part 1:** 255
Hughes, H. Stuart, **Supp. VIII:** 240
Hughes, James Nathaniel, **Supp. I Part 1:** 321, 332
Hughes, Ken, **Supp. XI:** 307
Hughes, Langston, **Retro. Supp. I:** **193–214**; **Retro. Supp. II:** 114, 115, 117, 120; **Supp. I Part 1:** **320–348**; **Supp. II Part 1:** 31, 33, 61, 170, 173, 181, 227, 228, 233, 361; **Supp. III Part 1:** 72–77; **Supp. IV Part 1:** 15, 16, 164, 168, 169, 173, 243, 368; **Supp. VIII:** 213; **Supp. IX:** 306, 316; **Supp. X:** 131, 136, 139, 324; **Supp. XI:** 1; **Supp. XIII:** 75, 111, 132, 233
Hughes, Nicholas, **Supp. I Part 2:** 541
Hughes, Robert, **Supp. X:** 73
Hughes, Ted, **IV:** 3; **Retro. Supp. II:** 244, 245, 247, 257; **Supp. I Part 2:** 536, 537, 538, 539, 540, 541
Hughes, Thomas, **Supp. I Part 2:** 406
"Hugh Harper" (Bowles), **Supp. IV Part 1:** 94

Hughie (O'Neill), **III:** 385, 401, 405
Hugh Selwyn Mauberley (Pound), **I:** 66, 476; **III:** 9, 462–463, 465, 468; **Retro. Supp. I: 289–290,** 291, 299
Hugo, Richard, **Supp. VI: 131–148; Supp. IX:** 296, 323, 324, 330; **Supp. XI:** 315, 317; **Supp. XII:** 178; **Supp. XIII:** 112, 113, 133
Hugo, Victor, **II:** 290, 490, 543; **Supp. IV Part 2:** 518; **Supp. IX:** 308
Hui-neng, **III:** 567
Huis Clos (Sartre), **Supp. IV Part 1:** 84
Huizinga, Johan, **I:** 225; **II:** 416–417, 418, 425
Hulbert, Ann, **Supp. XI:** 38–39
Hull, Gloria T., **Retro. Supp. II:** 292
Hull, Lynda, **Supp. XI:** 131
Hulme, Thomas E., **I:** 68, 69, 475; **III:** 196, 209, 463–464, 465; **IV:** 122; **Supp. I Part 1:** 261, 262
Human, All Too Human (Nietzsche), **Supp. X:** 48
"Human Culture" (Emerson), **II:** 11–12
Human Factor, The (Greene), **Supp. V:** 298
"Human Figures" (Doty), **Supp. XI:** 123–124
"Human Immortality" (James), **II:** 353–354
"Human Life" (Emerson), **II:** 11–12
Human Stain, The (Roth), **Retro. Supp. II:** 297, 307, 312–313
"Human Things" (Nemerov), **III:** 279
Human Universe (Olson), **Supp. II Part 2:** 571
"Human Universe" (Olson), **Supp. II Part 2:** 565, 567
Human Wishes (Hass), **Supp. VI:** 105–106, 107
Human Work (Gilman), **Supp. XI:** 206
Humbert, Humbert, **Supp. X:** 283
Humble Inquiry into the Rules of the Word of God, An, Concerning the Qualifications Requisite to a Complete Standing and Full Communion in the Visible Christian Church (Edwards), **I:** 548
Humboldt, Alexander von, **III:** 428
Humboldt's Gift (Bellow), **Retro. Supp. II:** 19, 28–29, 34; **Supp. XIII:** 320
Hume, David, **I:** 125; **II:** 349, 357, 480; **III:** 618
Humes, H. L. "Doc," **Supp. XI:** 294
Humes, Harold, **Supp. V:** 201
"Hummingbirds, The" (Welty), **IV:** 273
Humphrey, William, **Supp. IX: 93–112**
Humphreys, Christmas, **Supp. V:** 267
Humphreys, David, **Supp. II Part 1:** 65, 69, 70, 268
Humphreys, Josephine, **Supp. XII:** 311
Humphries, Rolfe, **III:** 124; **Retro. Supp. I:** 137
Hunchback of Notre Dame, The (film), **Supp. IV Part 1:** 101
Huncke, Herbert, **Supp. XII:** 118
Hundred Camels in the Courtyard, A (Bowles), **Supp. IV Part 1:** 90
"Hundred Collars, A" (Frost), **Retro. Supp. I:** 128; **Supp. XIII:** 147
Hundred Secret Senses, The (Tan), **Supp. X:** 289, 293, 295, 297, 298, 299
Hundred White Daffodils, A: Essays, Interviews, Newspaper Columns, and One Poem (Kenyon), **Supp. VII:** 160–162, 165, 166, 167, 174
Huneker, James, **III:** 102
Hunger (Hamsun), **Supp. XI:** 167
"Hunger" (Hogan), **Supp. IV Part 1:** 411
"Hunger . . ." (Rich), **Supp. I Part 2:** 571
"Hungerfield" (Jeffers), **Supp. II Part 2:** 416–417, 436
Hungerfield and Other Poems (Jeffers), **Supp. II Part 2:** 422
Hungry Ghosts, The (Oates), **Supp. II Part 2:** 504, 510
Hunnewell, Susannah, **Supp. VIII:** 83
Hunt, Harriot K., **Retro. Supp. II:** 146
Hunt, Leigh, **II:** 515–516
Hunt, Richard Morris, **IV:** 312
Hunt, William, **II:** 343
Hunter, Dr. Joseph, **II:** 217
Hunter, J. Paul, **Supp. IV Part 1:** 332
Hunter, Kim, **Supp. I Part 1:** 286
"Hunter of Doves" (Herbst), **Retro. Supp. II:** 343
"Hunter of the West, The" (Bryant), **Supp. I Part 1:** 155
Hunters, The (film), **Supp. IX:** 250
Hunters, The (Salter), **Supp. IX:** 246, **249–250**
"Hunters in the Snow" (Brueghel), **I:** 174; **Retro. Supp. I:** 430
"Hunters in the Snow" (Wolff), **Supp. VII:** 339–340
"Hunter's Moon—Eating the Bear" (Oliver), **Supp. VII:** 234
"Hunter's Vision, The" (Bryant), **Supp. I Part 1:** 160
"Hunting Is Not Those Heads on the Wall" (Baraka), **Supp. II Part 1:** 45
Huntington, Collis P., **I:** 198, 207
"Hunt in the Black Forest, The" (Jarrell), **II:** 379–380
Huntley, Jobe, **Supp. I Part 1:** 339
Hurray Home (Wideman), **Supp. X:** 320
"Hurricane, The" (Crane), **I:** 401
"Hurricane, The" (Freneau), **Supp. II Part 1:** 262
"Hurry Kane" (Lardner), **II:** 425, 426, 427
"Hurry up Please It's Time" (Sexton), **Supp. II Part 2:** 694, 695
Hurston, Zora Neale, **Retro. Supp. I:** 194, 198, 200, 201, 203; **Supp. I Part 1:** 325, 326, 332; **Supp. II Part 1:** 33; **Supp. IV Part 1:** 5, 11, 12, 164, 257; **Supp. VI: 149–161; Supp. VIII:** 214; **Supp. X:** 131, 139, 232, 242; **Supp. XI:** 85; **Supp. XIII:** 185, 233, 236, 295, 306
Hurt, John, **Supp. XIII:** 132
"Husband-Right and Father-Right" (Rich), **Retro. Supp. II:** 285
Husband's Story, The (Shields), **Supp. VII:** 316. *See also* "Happenstance" (Shields)
Husserl, Edmund, **II:** 362, 363; **IV:** 491; **Supp. IV Part 1:** 42, 43
Hussey, Jo Ella, **Supp. XII:** 201
Hustler, The (film), **Supp. XI:** 306
Huston, John, **I:** 30, 31, 33, 35; **II:** 588; **III:** 161; **Supp. IV Part 1:** 102, 116, 355; **Supp. XI:** 307; **Supp. XIII:** 174
"Huswifery" (Taylor), **IV:** 161; **Supp. I Part 2:** 386
Hutchens, John K., **Supp. IX:** 276
Hutcheson, Francis, **I:** 559
Hutchins, Patricia, **III:** 478
Hutchinson, Abigail, **I:** 562
Hutchinson, Anne, **Supp. I Part 1:** 100, 101, 113; **Supp. IV Part 2:** 434; **Supp. VIII:** 202, 205
Hutton, James, **Supp. IX:** 180
Huxley, Aldous, **II:** 454; **III:** 281, 428, 429–430; **IV:** 77, 435; **Supp. I Part 2:** 714
Huxley, Julian, **Supp. VIII:** 251; **Supp. X:** 108
Huxley, Juliette, **Supp. VIII:** 251, 265
Huxley, Thomas, **III:** 102, 108, 113, 281; **Retro. Supp. II:** 60, 65, 93
Huxley, Thomas Henry, **Supp. I Part 1:** 368
Huysmans, Joris Karl (Charles Marie Georges), **I:** 66; **III:** 315; **IV:** 286; **Retro. Supp. II:** 344
"*Hwame, Koshkalaka,* and the Rest: Lesbians in American Indian Cultures" (Gunn Allen), **Supp. IV Part 1:** 330
Hwang, David Henry, **Supp. X:** 292

"Hyacinth Drift" (Rawlings), **Supp. X: 226–227**

"Hydras, The" (Merwin), **Supp. III Part 1:** 349

"Hydriotaphia; or, Urne-Buriall" (Browne), **Supp. IX:** 136–137

Hydriotaphia, The; or, Death of Dr. Browne: An Epic Farce about Death and Primitive Capital Accumulation (Kushner), **Supp. IX:** 133, **136–138**

Hyman, Stanley Edgar, **I:** 129, 264, 363, 377, 379; **Retro. Supp. II:** 118; **Supp. IX:** 113, 114, 117, 118, 121, 122, 128

Hymen (Doolittle), **Supp. I Part 1:** 266

"Hymie's Bull" (Ellison), **Retro. Supp. II:** 124; **Supp. II Part 1:** 229

"Hymn Books" (Emerson), **II:** 10

"HYMN FOR LANIE POO" (Baraka), **Supp. II Part 1:** 31, 37

"Hymn from a Watermelon Pavilion" (Stevens), **IV:** 81

"Hymn of the Sea, A" (Bryant), **Supp. I Part 1:** 157, 163, 165

"Hymns of the Marshes" (Lanier), **Supp. I Part 1:** 364

"Hymn to Death" (Bryant), **Supp. I Part 1:** 169, 170

"Hymn to Earth" (Wylie), **Supp. I Part 2:** 727–729

"Hymn to the Night" (Longfellow), **Supp. I Part 2:** 409

Hyperion (Longfellow), **II:** 488, 489, 491–492, 496; **Retro. Supp. II:** 58, 155–156

"Hypocrite Auteur" (MacLeish), **III:** 19

"Hypocrite Swift" (Bogan), **Supp. III Part 1:** 55

"Hysteria" (Eliot), **I:** 570

I (Dixon), **Supp. XII:** 141, 155, **156–157**

I, etcetera (Sontag), **Supp. III Part 2:** 451–452, 469

I, Governor of California and How I Ended Poverty (Sinclair), **Supp. V:** 289

I: Six Nonlectures (Cummings), **I:** 430, 433, 434

"I, Too" (Hughes), **Retro. Supp. I:** 193, 199; **Supp. I Part 1:** 320

I Accuse! (film), **Supp. IV Part 2:** 683

"I Almost Remember" (Angelou), **Supp. IV Part 1:** 15

"'I Always Wanted You to Admire My Fasting'; or, Looking at Kafka" (Roth), **Retro. Supp. II:** 300

"I am a cowboy in the boat of Ra" (Reed), **Supp. X:** 242

"I Am a Dangerous Woman" (Harjo), **Supp. XII:** 216, 219

"I Am Alive" (Momaday), **Supp. IV Part 2:** 489

I Am a Sonnet (Goldbarth), **Supp. XII:** 181

"I Am a Writer of Truth" (Fante), **Supp. XI:** 167

"'I Am Cherry Alive,' the Little Girl Sang" (Schwartz), **Supp. II Part 2:** 663

"I Am Dying, Meester?" (Burroughs), **Supp. III Part 1:** 98

I Am Elijah Thrush (Purdy), **Supp. VII:** 274

"I Am in Love" (Stern), **Supp. IX:** 295

"I Am Not Flattered" (Francis), **Supp. IX:** 78

I Am! Says the Lamb (Roethke), **III:** 545

"I and My Chimney" (Melville), **III:** 91

I and Thou (Buber), **III:** 308

"I Apologize" (Komunyakaa), **Supp. XIII:** 120, 121

I Apologize for the Eyes in My Head (Komunyakaa), **Supp. XIII: 119–121,** 126

Ibsen, Henrik, **II:** 27, 276, 280, 291–292; **III:** 118, 145, 148, 149, 150, 151, 152, 154–155, 156, 161, 162, 165, 511, 523; **IV:** 397; **Retro. Supp. I:** 228; **Retro. Supp. II:** 94; **Supp. IV Part 2:** 522

"I Came Out of the Mother Naked" (Bly), **Supp. IV Part 1:** 62–63, 68

"I Cannot Forget with What Fervid Devotion" (Bryant), **Supp. I Part 1:** 154

"I Can't Stand Your Books: A Writer Goes Home" (Gordon), **Supp. IV Part 1:** 314

"Icarium Mare" (Wilbur), **Supp. III Part 2:** 563

Icarus's Mother (Shepard), **Supp. III Part 2:** 446

"Ice" (Bambara), **Supp. XI:** 16

"Iceberg, The" (Merwin), **Supp. III Part 1:** 345

Ice-Cream Headache, The, and Other Stories (Jones), **Supp. XI:** 215, 227

Ice Fire Water: A Leib Goldkorn Cocktail (Epstein), **Supp. XII: 164–166**

"Ice House, The" (Gordon), **II:** 201

Iceman Cometh, The (O'Neill), **I:** 81; **III:** 151, 385, 386, 401, 402–403; **Supp. VIII:** 345

"Ice Palace, The" (Fitzgerald), **II:** 83, 88; **Retro. Supp. I:** 103

"Ice Storm, The" (Ashbery), **Supp. III Part 1:** 26

"Ice-Storm, The" (Pinsky), **Supp. VI:** 247–248

"Ichabod" (Whittier), **Supp. I Part 2:** 687, 689–690; **Supp. XI:** 50

"Icicles" (Francis), **Supp. IX:** 83

"Icicles" (Gass), **Supp. VI:** 83

Ickes, Harold, **Supp. I Part 1:** 5

Iconographs (Swenson), **Supp. IV Part 2:** 638, 646–648, 651

"Icosaphere, The" (Moore), **III:** 213

"I Could Believe" (Levine), **Supp. V:** 189

"I Cry, Love! Love!" (Roethke), **III:** 539–540

Ida (Stein), **IV:** 43, 45

"Idea, The" (Carver), **Supp. III Part 1:** 143

"Idea, The" (Strand), **Supp. IV Part 2:** 631

Ideal Husband (Wilde), **II:** 515

Idea of Florida in the American Literary Imagination, The (Rowe), **Supp. X:** 223

"Idea of Order at Key West, The" (Stevens), **IV:** 89–90; **Retro. Supp. I:** 302, 303, 313

Ideas of Order (Stevens), **Retro. Supp. I:** 296, 298, **302–303**, 303, 305

"Ideographs" (Olds), **Supp. X:** 205

Ides of March, The (Wilder), **IV:** 357, 372

"I Did Not Learn Their Names" (Ellison), **Retro. Supp. II:** 124

"I Died with the First Blow & Was Reborn Wrong" (Coleman), **Supp. XI:** 91

"Idiom of a Self, The" (Pinsky), **Supp. VI:** 240

"Idiot, The" (Crane), **I:** 401

Idiot, The (Dostoyevsky), **I:** 468

"Idiots First" (Malamud), **Supp. I Part 2:** 434–435, 437, 440–441

I Don't Need You Any More (A. Miller), **III:** 165

"I Dream I'm the Death of Orpheus" (Rich), **Supp. I Part 2:** 557–558

I Dreamt I Became a Nymphomaniac! Imagining (Acker), **Supp. XII:** 4, 6, **8,** 11

Idylls of the King (Tennyson), **III:** 487; **Supp. I Part 2:** 410; **Supp. XIII:** 146

Idyl of Work, An (Larcom), **Supp. XIII:** 139, 142, 146–147, 150

"If" (Creeley), **Supp. IV Part 1:** 158

If Beale Street Could Talk (Baldwin), **Retro. Supp. II:** 13–14; **Supp. I Part 1:** 48, 59–60, 67

If Blessing Comes (Bambara), **Supp. XI:** 1

I Feel a Little Jumpy around You (Nye and Janeczko, eds.), **Supp. XIII:** 280
"I felt a Funeral, in my Brain" (Dickinson), **Retro. Supp. I:** 38
"If I Could Be Like Wallace Stevens" (Stafford), **Supp. XI:** 327
"If I Could Only Live at the Pitch That Is Near Madness" (Eberhart), **I:** 523, 526–527
If I Die in a Combat Zone (O'Brien), **Supp. V:** 238, 239, 240, 245
"If I Had My Way" (Creeley), **Supp. IV Part 1:** 157
"*If I Might Be*" (Chopin), **Retro. Supp. II:** 61
"I Find the Real American Tragedy" (Dreiser), **Retro. Supp. II:** 105
If It Die (Gide), **I:** 290
"If I Were a Man" (Gilman), **Supp. XI:** 207
If Morning Ever Comes (Tyler), **Supp. IV Part 2:** 658–659
If Mountains Die: A New Mexico Memoir (Nichols), **Supp. XIII:** 255, 257, 267
I Forgot to Go to Spain (Harrison), **Supp. VIII:** 39, **52–53**
If the River Was Whiskey (Boyle), **Supp. VIII: 15–16**
"If They Knew Yvonne" (Dubus), **Supp. VII:** 81
"If We Had Bacon" (H. Roth), **Supp. IX:** 232, 234
"If We Had Known" (Francis), **Supp. IX:** 78
"If We Must Die" (McKay), **Supp. IV Part 1:** 3; **Supp. X:** 132, 134
"If We Take All Gold" (Bogan), **Supp. III Part 1:** 52
I Gaspiri (Lardner), **II:** 435
"I Gather the Limbs of Osiris" (Pound), **Retro. Supp. I:** 287
"I Give You Back" (Harjo), **Supp. XII:** 223
Ignatius of Loyola, **IV:** 151; **Supp. XI:** 162
Ignatow, David, **Supp. XIII:** 275
"Ignis Fatuus" (Tate), **IV:** 128
"I Go Back to May 1937" (Olds), **Supp. X:** 207
I Go Dreaming Serenades (Salinas), **Supp. XIII:** 316
I Got the Blues (Odets), **Supp. II Part 2:** 530
Iguana Killer, The (Ríos), **Supp. IV Part 2:** 542–544
"I Had Eight Birds Hatch in One Nest" (Bradstreet), **Supp. I Part 1:** 102, 115, 117, 119

"I had no time to Hate" (Dickinson), **Retro. Supp. I:** 44–45, 46
"I Have a Rendezvous with Life" (Cullen), **Supp. IV Part 1:** 168
"I Have Increased Power" (Ginsberg), **Supp. II Part 1:** 313
"I Have Seen Black Hands" (Wright), **Supp. II Part 1:** 228
"I Hear an Army" (Joyce), **Supp. I Part 1:** 262
"I heard a Fly buzz when I died" (Dickinson), **Retro. Supp. I:** 38
"I Heard Immanuel Singing" (Lindsay), **Supp. I Part 2:** 379
"I Hear It Was Charged against Me" (Whitman), **IV:** 343
"I Held a Shelley Manuscript" (Corso), **Supp. XII:** 128
"I Held His Name" (Ríos), **Supp. IV Part 2:** 547
I Knew a Phoenix (Sarton), **Supp. VIII:** 249, 251–252
"I Know a Man" (Creeley), **Supp. IV Part 1:** 147–148, 149
I Know Some Things: Stories about Childhood by Contemporary Writers (Moore, ed.), **Supp. X:** 175
I Know Why the Caged Bird Sings (Angelou), **Supp. IV Part 1:** 2–4, 5, 7, 11, 12, 13, 14, 15, 17
"Ikon: The Harrowing of Hell" (Levertov), **Supp. III Part 1:** 284
Ile (O'Neill), **III:** 388
"I Let Him Take Me" (Cisneros), **Supp. VII:** 71
Iliad (Bryant, trans.), **Supp. I Part 1:** 158
Iliad (Homer), **II:** 470; **Supp. IV Part 2:** 631; **Supp. IX:** 211; **Supp. X:** 114
Iliad (Pope, trans.), **Supp. I Part 1:** 152
"I like to see it lap the Miles" (Dickinson), **Retro. Supp. I:** 37
"I Live Up Here" (Merwin), **Supp. III Part 1:** 349
"Illegal Alien" (Mora), **Supp. XIII:** 215
"Illegal Days, The" (Paley), **Supp. VI:** 222
Illig, Joyce, **Retro. Supp. II:** 20
"Illinois" (Masters), **Supp. I Part 2:** 458
Illinois Poems (Masters), **Supp. I Part 2:** 472
"Illinois Village, The" (Lindsay), **Supp. I Part 2:** 381
Illness as Metaphor (Sontag), **Supp. III Part 2:** 452, 461, 466
I'll Take My Stand ("Twelve Southerners"), **II:** 196; **III:** 496; **IV:** 125, 237; **Supp. X:** 25, 52–53
Illumination (Frederic), **II:** 141
Illumination Night (Hoffman), **Supp. X:** 85, **86**, 88, 89
Illusion comique, L' (Corneille), **Supp. IX:** 138
"Illusion of Eternity, The" (Eberhart), **I:** 541
Illusions (Dash; film), **Supp. XI:** 20
"Illusions" (Emerson), **II:** 2, 5, 14, 16
Illustrated Man, The (Bradbury), **Supp. IV Part 1:** 102, 103, 113
Illustrations of Political Economy (Martineau), **Supp. II Part 1:** 288
"I Look at My Hand" (Swenson), **Supp. IV Part 2:** 638, 647
I Love Myself When I Am Laughing . . . : A Zora Neale Hurston Reader (Walker), **Supp. III Part 2:** 531, 532
"I'm a Fool" (Anderson), **I:** 113, 114, 116; **Supp. I Part 2:** 430
Image and Idea (Rahv), **Supp. II Part 1:** 146
Image and the Law, The (Nemerov), **III:** 268, 269–271, 272
"Images" (Hass), **Supp. VI:** 103
"Images, The" (Rich), **Retro. Supp. II:** 291
"Images and 'Images'" (Simic), **Supp. VIII:** 274
"Images for Godard" (Rich), **Supp. I Part 2:** 558
"Images of Walt Whitman" (Fiedler), **IV:** 352
"Imaginary Friendships of Tom McGrath, The" (Cohen), **Supp. X:** 112
"Imaginary Iceberg, The" (Bishop), **Retro. Supp. II:** 42; **Supp. I Part 1:** 86, 88
"Imaginary Jew, The" (Berryman), **I:** 174–175
Imaginary Letters (Pound), **III:** 473–474
Imagination and Fancy; or, Selections from the English Poets, illustrative of those first requisites of their art; with markings of the best passages, critical notices of the writers, and an essay in answer to the question 'What is Poetry?' (Hunt), **II:** 515–516
"Imagination as Value" (Stevens), **Retro. Supp. I:** 298
"Imagination of Disaster, The" (Gordon), **Supp. IV Part 1:** 306
"Imagine a Day at the End of Your Life" (Beattie), **Supp. V:** 33

"Imagine Kissing Pete" (O'Hara), **III:** 372; **Supp. VIII:** 156
"Imagining How It Would Be to Be Dead" (Eberhart), **I:** 533
Imagining Los Angeles: A City in Fiction (Fine), **Supp. XI:** 160
Imagining the Worst: Stephen King and the Representations of Women (Lant and Thompson), **Supp. V:** 141
"Imagisme" (Pound), **Retro. Supp. I:** 288
Imagistes, Des: An Anthology of the Imagists (Pound, ed.), **III:** 465, 471; **Retro. Supp. I:** 288
Imago (O. Butler), **Supp. XIII:** 63, **65–66**
"Imago" (Stevens), **IV:** 74, 89
Imagoes (Coleman), **Supp. XI:** 89–90
I Married a Communist (Roth), **Retro. Supp. II:** 307, 311–312
"I May, I Might, I Must" (Moore), **III:** 215
"I'm Crazy" (Salinger), **III:** 553
"I'm Here" (Roethke), **III:** 547
Imitations (Lowell), **II:** 543, 544–545, 550, 555; **Retro. Supp. II:** 181, 187
"Imitations of Drowning" (Sexton), **Supp. II Part 2:** 684, 686
"Immaculate Man" (Gordon), **Supp. IV Part 1:** 311
"Immanence of Dostoevsky, The" (Bourne), **I:** 235
"Immigrants" (Mora), **Supp. XIII:** 216
"Immigrant Story, The" (Paley), **Supp. VI:** 230
Immobile Wind, The (Winters), **Supp. II Part 2:** 786
"Immobile Wind, The" (Winters), **Supp. II Part 2:** 788, 811
"Immolatus" (Komunyakaa), **Supp. XIII:** 126
"Immoral Proposition, The" (Creeley), **Supp. IV Part 1:** 144
"Immortal Autumn" (MacLeish), **III:** 13
"Immortality Ode" (Nemerov), **III:** 87
Immortality Ode (Wordsworth), **II:** 17; **Supp. I Part 2:** 673
"Immortal Woman, The" (Tate), **IV:** 130, 131, 137
"I'm Not Ready to Die Yet" (Harjo), **Supp. XII:** 231
"I'm on My Way" (Salinas), **Supp. XIII:** 320
"Impasse" (Hughes), **Supp. I Part 1:** 343
Imperative Duty, An, a Novel (Howells), **II:** 286
Imperial Eyes: Travel Writing and Transculturation (Pratt), **Retro. Supp. II:** 48
Imperial Germany and the Industrial Revolution (Veblen), **Supp. I Part 2:** 642, 643
Imperial Way, The: By Rail from Peshawar to Chittagong (Theroux), **Supp. VIII:** 323
"Implosions" (Rich), **Supp. I Part 2:** 556
"Imp of the Perverse, The" (Poe), **III:** 414–415; **Retro. Supp. II:** 267
Impolite Interviews, **Supp. XI:** 293
"Importance of Artists' Biographies, The" (Goldbarth), **Supp. XII:** 183, 184, 191
"Important Houses, The" (Gordon), **Supp. IV Part 1:** 315
"Impossible to Tell" (Pinsky), **Supp. VI:** 247, 248
"Imposter, The" (West), **Retro. Supp. II:** 340, 345
"Impressionism and Symbolism in *Heart of Darkness*" (Watt), **Supp. VIII:** 4
"Impressions of a European Tour" (Bourne), **I:** 225
"Impressions of a Plumber" (H. Roth), **Supp. IX:** 228, 234
"Impressions of Europe, 1913–1914" (Bourne), **I:** 225
"I'm Walking behind the Spanish" (Salinas), **Supp. XIII:** 323–324
"I/Myself" (Shields), **Supp. VII:** 311
"In Absence" (Lanier), **Supp. I Part 1:** 364
"In Absentia" (Bowles), **Supp. IV Part 1:** 94
Inada, Lawson Fusao, **Supp. V:** 180
"In a Dark Room, Furniture" (Nye), **Supp. XIII:** 274
"In a Dark Time" (Roethke), **III:** 539, 547, 548
"In a Disused Graveyard" (Frost), **Retro. Supp. I:** 126, 133
In a Dusty Light (Haines), **Supp. XII:** 207
"In a Garden" (Lowell), **II:** 513
"In a Hard Intellectual Light" (Eberhart), **I:** 523
"In a Hollow of the Hills" (Harte), **Supp. II Part 1:** 354
"In Amicitia" (Ransom), **IV:** 141
In a Narrow Grave: Essays on Texas (McMurtry), **Supp. V:** 220, 223
"In Another Country" (Hemingway), **I:** 484–485; **II:** 249
In April Once (Percy), **Retro. Supp. I:** 341
In A Shallow Grave (Purdy), **Supp. VII:** 272
"In a Station of the Metro" (Pound), **Retro. Supp. I:** 288; **Supp. I Part 1:** 265
"In a Strange Town" (Anderson), **I:** 114, 115
In Battle for Peace: The Story of My 83rd Birthday (Du Bois), **Supp. II Part 1:** 185
In Bed One Night & Other Brief Encounters (Coover), **Supp. V:** 49, 50
"In Bertram's Garden" (Justice), **Supp. VII:** 117
"In Blackwater Woods" (Oliver), **Supp. VII:** 244, 246
In Broken Country (Wagoner), **Supp. IX:** 330
"In California" (Simpson), **Supp. IX:** 271
"In Camp" (Stafford), **Supp. XI:** 329
"Incant against Suicide" (Karr), **Supp. XI:** 249
"In Celebration of My Uterus" (Sexton), **Supp. II Part 2:** 689
"In Certain Places and Certain Times There Can Be More of You" (Dunn), **Supp. XI:** 144
Incest: From "A Journal of Love," the Unexpurgated Diary of Anaïs Nin, 1932–1934 (Nin), **Supp. X:** 182, 184, 185, 187, 191
Inchbald, Elizabeth, **II:** 8
Inchiquin, the Jesuit's Letters (Ingersoll), **I:** 344
"Incident" (Cullen), **Supp. IV Part 1:** 165, 166
Incidental Numbers (Wylie), **Supp. I Part 2:** 708
Incidentals (Sandburg), **III:** 579
Incident at Vichy (A. Miller), **III:** 165, 166
Incidents in the Life of a Slave Girl (Brent), **Supp. IV Part 1:** 13
"Incipience" (Rich), **Supp. I Part 2:** 559
In Cold Blood: A True Account of a Multiple Murder and Its Consequences (Capote), **Retro. Supp. II:** 107–108; **Supp. I Part 1:** 292; **Supp. III Part 1:** 111, 117, 119, 122, 123, 125–131; **Supp. III Part 2:** 574; **Supp. IV Part 1:** 220
In Cold Hell, in Thicket (Olson), **Supp. II Part 2:** 571
"In Cold Hell, in Thicket" (Olson), **Supp. II Part 2:** 558, 563–564, 566, 572, 580
"Incomparable Light, The" (Eberhart), **I:** 541
*Incorporative Consciousness of Robert

Bly, The (Harris), **Supp. IV Part 1:** 68
In Country (Mason), **Supp. VIII:** 133, **142–143**, 146
"Incredible Survival of Coyote, The" (Snyder), **Supp. VIII:** 297
"Increment" (Ammons), **Supp. VII:** 28
In Defense of Ignorance (Shapiro), **Supp. II Part 2:** 703, 704, 713–714
In Defense of Reason (Winters), **Supp. I Part 1:** 268
In Defense of Women (Mencken), **III:** 109
Independence Day (Ford), **Supp. V:** 57, 62–63, 67–68
Independence Day (film), **Supp. X:** 80
"Independent Candidate, The, a Story of Today" (Howells), **II:** 277
"Indestructible Mr. Gore, The" (Vidal), **Supp. IV Part 2:** 679
Index of American Design, **Supp. III Part 2:** 618
"Indian at the Burial-Place of His Fathers, An" (Bryant), **Supp. I Part 1:** 155–156, 167–168
"Indian Burying Ground, The" (Freneau), **Supp. II Part 1:** 264, 266
"Indian Camp" (Hemingway), **II:** 247–248, 263; **Retro. Supp. I:** 174–175, 176, 177, 181
Indian Country (Matthiessen), **Supp. V:** 211
"Indian Country" (Simpson), **Supp. IX:** 274
"Indian Manifesto" (Deloria), **Supp. IV Part 1:** 323
"Indian Names" (Sigourney), **Retro. Supp. II:** 47
"Indian Student, The" (Freneau), **Supp. II Part 1:** 264
"Indian Student, The" (Simpson), **Supp. IX:** 280
Indian Summer (Howells), **II:** 275, 279–281, 282
Indian Summer (Knowles), **Supp. XII:** 249, 250
"Indian Uprising, The" (Barthelme), **Supp. IV Part 1:** 44
Indifferent Children, The (Auchincloss), **Supp. IV Part 1:** 25
Indiscretions (Pound), **Retro. Supp. I:** 284
"Indispensability of the Eyes, The" (Olds), **Supp. X:** 202
"In Distrust of Merits" (Moore), **III:** 201, 214
"Individual and the State, The" (Emerson), **II:** 10
Individualism, Old and New (Dewey), **Supp. I Part 2:** 677

In Dreams Begin Responsibilities (Schwartz), **Supp. II Part 2:** 642, 645–650
"In Dreams Begin Responsibilities" (Schwartz), **Supp. II Part 2:** 641, 649, 654
In Dubious Battle (Steinbeck), **IV:** 51, 55–56, 59, 63
"In Durance" (Pound), **Retro. Supp. I:** 285
"Industry of Hard Kissing, The" (Ríos), **Supp. IV Part 2:** 547
"In Duty Bound" (Gilman), **Supp. XI:** 196–197
"I Need, I Need" (Roethke), **III:** 535–536
"I Need Help" (Stern), **Supp. IX:** 290
"Inés in the Kitchen" (García), **Supp. XI:** 190
"I never saw a Moor" (Dickinson), **Retro. Supp. I:** 37
Inevitable Exiles (Kielsky), **Supp. V:** 273
"Inevitable Trial, The" (Holmes), **Supp. I Part 1:** 318
"Inexhaustible Hat, The" (Wagoner), **Supp. IX:** 327
"In Extremis" (Berry), **Supp. X:** 23
"Infancy" (Wilder), **IV:** 375
"Infant Boy at Midcentury" (Warren), **IV:** 244–245, 252
Infante, Guillermo Cabrera, **Retro. Supp. I:** 278
Inferno (Dante), **IV:** 139; **Supp. V:** 338; **Supp. VIII:** 219–221
Inferno of Dante, The (Pinsky), **Supp. VI:** 235, 248
"Infidelity" (Komunyakaa), **Supp. XIII:** 130
"Infiltration of the Universe" (MacLeish), **III:** 19
Infinite Jest: A Novel (Wallace), **Supp. X:** 301, **310–314**
"Infinite Reason, The" (MacLeish), **III:** 19
"Infirmity" (Lowell), **II:** 554
"Infirmity" (Roethke), **III:** 548
In Five Years Time (Haines), **Supp. XII:** 206
"In Flower" (Snodgrass), **Supp. VI:** 325
"Influence of Landscape upon the Poet, The" (Eliot), **Retro. Supp. I:** 67
"In Football Season" (Updike), **IV:** 219
Informer, The (film), **Supp. III Part 2:** 619
Ingersoll, Charles J., **I:** 344
Ingersoll, Robert Green, **Supp. II Part 1:** 198

Ingster, Boris, **Retro. Supp. II:** 348
Inhabitants, The (Morris), **III:** 221–222
Inheritors (Glaspell), **Supp. III Part 1:** 175, 179–181, 186, 189
"In Honor of David Anderson Brooks, My Father" (Brooks), **Supp. III Part 1:** 79
"Inhumanist, The" (Jeffers), **Supp. II Part 2:** 423, 426
"In Illo Tempore" (Karr), **Supp. XI:** 242
"In Interims: Outlyer" (Harrison), **Supp. VIII:** 38
"Injudicious Gardening" (Moore), **III:** 198
"Injustice" (Paley), **Supp. VI:** 220
Injustice Collectors, The (Auchincloss), **Supp. IV Part 1:** 25
Ink, Blood, Semen (Goldbarth), **Supp. XII:** 181, 183
Ink Truck, The (Kennedy), **Supp. VII:** 132, 133–138, 140, 141, 149, 152
"In Limbo" (Wilbur), **Supp. III Part 2:** 544, 561
In Love and Trouble: Stories of Black Women (Walker), **Supp. III Part 2:** 520, 521, 530, 531, 532
In Mad Love and War (Harjo), **Supp. XII: 224–226**
"In Memoriam" (Emerson), **II:** 13
"In Memoriam" (Tennyson), **Retro. Supp. I:** 325; **Supp. I Part 2:** 416
In Memoriam to Identity (Acker), **Supp. XII:** 5, **16–18**
"In Memory of Arthur Winslow" (Lowell), **II:** 541, 547, 550; **Retro. Supp. II:** 187
"In Memory of Congresswoman Barbara Jordan" (Pinsky), **Supp. VI:** 250
"In Memory of W. B. Yeats" (Auden), **Supp. VIII:** 19, 30; **Supp. XI:** 243, 244
"In Memory of W. H. Auden" (Stern), **Supp. IX:** 288
"In Mercy on Broadway" (Doty), **Supp. XI:** 132
In Morocco (Wharton), **Retro. Supp. I:** 380; **Supp. IV Part 1:** 81
Inmost Leaf, The: A Selection of Essays (Kazin), **Supp. VIII:** 102, 103
In Motley (Bierce), **I:** 209
In My Father's Court (Singer), **IV:** 16–17; **Retro. Supp. II:** 319–320
"In My Life" (Dubus), **Supp. VII:** 81
Inner Landscape (Sarton), **Supp. VIII:** 259
Inner Room, The (Merrill), **Supp. III Part 1:** 336

"In Nine Sleep Valley" (Merrill), **Supp. III Part 1:** 328

Innocents, The: A Story for Lovers (Lewis), **II:** 441

Innocents Abroad, The; or, The New Pilgrim's Progress (Twain), **II:** 275, 434; **IV:** 191, 196, 197–198

Innocents at Cedro, The: A Memoir of Thorstein Veblen and Some Others (Duffus), **Supp. I Part 2:** 650

In Old Plantation Days (Dunbar), **Supp. II Part 1:** 214

In Ole Virginia (Page), **Supp. II Part 1:** 201

In Orbit (Morris), **III:** 236

In Other Words (Swenson), **Supp. IV Part 2:** 650–652

In Our Terribleness (Some elements and meaning in black style) (Baraka), **Supp. II Part 1:** 52, 53

In Our Time (Hemingway), **I:** 117; **II:** 68, 247, 252, 263; **IV:** 42; **Retro. Supp. I:** 170, 173, 174, 178, 180; **Supp. IX:** 106

"In Our Time" (Wolfe), **Supp. III Part 2:** 584

"Inpatient" (Kenyon), **Supp. VII:** 169

In Pharaoh's Army: Memories of the Lost War (Wolff), **Supp. VII:** 331–334, 335, 338

"In Plaster" (Plath), **Supp. I Part 2:** 540

"In Praise of Johnny Appleseed" (Lindsay), **Supp. I Part 2:** 397

"In Praise of Limestone" (Auden), **Supp. II Part 1:** 20–21; **Supp. VIII:** 23

In Quest of the Ordinary (Cavell), **Retro. Supp. I:** 307

Inquiry into the Nature of Peace, An (Veblen), **Supp. I Part 2:** 642

In Radical Pursuit (Snodgrass), **Supp. VI:** 312, 316, 318

In Reckless Ecstasy (Sandburg), **III:** 579

In Recognition of William Gaddis (Kuehl and Moore), **Supp. IV Part 1:** 279

"In Retirement" (Malamud), **Supp. I Part 2:** 437

"In Retrospect" (Angelou), **Supp. IV Part 1:** 15

In Russia (A. Miller), **III:** 165

"In Sabine" (Chopin), **Supp. I Part 1:** 213

"In School-Days" (Whittier), **Supp. I Part 2:** 699–700

"Inscription for the Entrance to a Wood" (Bryant), **Supp. I Part 1:** 154, 155, 161–162

In Search of Bisco (Caldwell), **I:** 296

"In Search of Our Mothers' Gardens" (Walker), **Supp. III Part 2:** 520–532, 524, 525, 527, 529, 532–533, 535, 536; **Supp. IX:** 306

"In Search of Thomas Merton" (Griffin), **Supp. VIII:** 208

"In Search of Yage" (Burroughs), **Supp. III Part 1:** 98

"In Shadow" (Crane), **I:** 386

"In Sickness and in Health" (Auden), **Supp. II Part 1:** 15

"In Sickness and in Health" (Humphrey), **Supp. IX:** 94

Inside His Mind (A. Miller), **III:** 154

"Insider Baseball" (Didion), **Supp. IV Part 1:** 211

Inside Sports magazine, **Supp. V:** 58, 61

"In So Many Dark Rooms" (Hogan), **Supp. IV Part 1:** 400

"Insomnia" (Bishop), **Supp. I Part 1:** 92

"Insomniac" (Plath), **Supp. I Part 2:** 539

"Inspiration for Greatness" (Caldwell), **I:** 291

"Installation #6" (Beattie), **Supp. V:** 33

Instinct of Workmanship and the State of the Industrial Arts, The (Veblen), **Supp. I Part 2:** 642

Instincts of the Herd in Peace and War, The (Trotter), **I:** 249

Institute (Calvin), **IV:** 158, 160

"Instruction Manual, The" (Ashbery), **Supp. III Part 1:** 6–7, 10, 12

"Instruction to Myself" (Brooks), **Supp. III Part 1:** 87

Instrument, The (O'Hara), **III:** 362, 364

"In Such Times, Ties Must Bind" (Nye), **Supp. XIII:** 286

"Insurance and Social Change" (Stevens), **Retro. Supp. I:** 297

Insurgent Mexico (Reed), **I:** 476

In Suspect Terrain (McPhee), **Supp. III Part 1:** 309, 310

"In Tall Grass" (Sandburg), **III:** 585

Intellectual History, An (Senghor), **Supp. X:** 139

"Intellectual Pre-Eminence of Jews in Modern Europe, The" (Veblen), **Supp. I Part 2:** 643–644

Intellectual Things (Kunitz), **Supp. III Part 1:** 260, 262–264

Intellectual versus the City, The (White), **I:** 258

Intentions (Wilde), **Retro. Supp. I:** 56

"Interest in Life, An" (Paley), **Supp. VI:** 222, 224–225

Interest of Great Britain Considered, with Regard to Her Colonies and the Acquisition of Canada and Guadeloupe, The (Franklin), **II:** 119

Interior Landscapes (Vizenor), **Supp. IV Part 1:** 262

Interiors (film), **Supp. IV Part 1:** 205

"Interlude" (A. Lowell), **Retro. Supp. II:** 46

Interlunar (Atwood), **Supp. XIII:** 35

"In Terms of the Toenail: Fiction and the Figures of Life" (Gass), **Supp. VI:** 85

"International Episode, An" (James), **II:** 327

International Workers Order, **Retro. Supp. I:** 202

Interpretation of Christian Ethics, An (Niebuhr), **III:** 298–300, 301, 302

"Interpretation of Dreams, The" (Matthews), **Supp. IX:** 162–163

Interpretation of Music of the XVIIth and XVIIIth Centuries, The (Dolmetsch), **III:** 464

Interpretations and Forecasts: 1922–1972 (Mumford), **Supp. II Part 2:** 481

Interpretations of Poetry and Religion (Santayana), **III:** 611

Interpreters and Interpretations (Van Vechten), **Supp. II Part 2:** 729, 733–734

"Interrogate the Stones" (MacLeish), **III:** 9

"Interrupted Conversation, An" (Van Vechten), **Supp. II Part 2:** 735

Intersect: Poems (Shields), **Supp. VII:** 310–311

Interstate (Dixon), **Supp. XII:** 140, 152–153, 153, 156

"Interview, The" (Thurber), **Supp. I Part 2:** 616

"Interview With a Lemming" (Thurber), **Supp. I Part 2:** 603

Interview with the Vampire (Rice), **Supp. VII:** 287, 288–291, 297–298, 303

"Interview with the Vampire" (Rice), **Supp. VII:** 288

Interzone (Burroughs), **Supp. IV Part 1:** 90

"In the Absence of Bliss" (Kumin), **Supp. IV Part 2:** 453

"In the Afternoon" (Dunn), **Supp. XI:** 146

"In the Alley" (Elkin), **Supp. VI:** 46–47

In the American Grain (W. C. Williams), **Retro. Supp. I:** 420–421

In the American Tree (Silliman), **Supp. IV Part 2:** 426
In the Bar of a Tokyo Hotel (T. Williams), **IV:** 382, 386, 387, 391, 393
In the Beauty of the Lilies (Updike), **Retro. Supp. I:** 322, 325, 326, 327, 333
"In the Beginning . . ." (Simic), **Supp. VIII:** 270, 271
In the Belly of the Beast: Letters from Prison (Abbott), **Retro. Supp. II:** 210
"In the Black Museum" (Nemerov), **III:** 275
"In the Bodies of Words" (Swenson), **Supp. IV Part 2:** 651
"In the Cage" (Gass), **Supp. VI:** 85
In the Cage (James), **Retro. Supp. I:** 229
"In the Cage" (James), **II:** 332; **Retro. Supp. I:** 231
"In the Cage" (Lowell), **Retro. Supp. II:** 187
"In the Cave at Lone Tree Meadow" (Haines), **Supp. XII:** 212
"In the City Ringed with Giants" (Kingsolver), **Supp. VII:** 209
"In the Clearing" (Brodsky), **Supp. VIII:** 32
In the Clearing (Frost), **II:** 153, 155, 164; **Retro. Supp. I:** 121, 122, 141
"In the Closet of the Soul" (Walker), **Supp. III Part 2:** 526
"In the Confidence of a Story-Writer" (Chopin), **Retro. Supp. II:** 66–67; **Supp. I Part 1:** 217
In the Country of Last Things (Auster), **Supp. XII:** 23, 29–30, 31, 32
"In the Courtyard of the Isleta Missions" (Bly), **Supp. IV Part 1:** 71
"In the Dark" (Levine), **Supp. V:** 194
"In the Dark New England Days" (Jewett), **Retro. Supp. II:** 139
"In the Days of Prismatic Colour" (Moore), **III:** 205, 213
"In the Evening" (Rich), **Retro. Supp. II:** 284
"In the Field" (Wilbur), **Supp. III Part 2:** 558
"In the Fleeting Hand of Time" (Corso), **Supp. XII:** 122–123
"In the Footsteps of Gutenberg" (Mencken), **III:** 101
"In the Forest" (Simpson), **Supp. IX:** 270
"In the Forties" (Lowell), **II:** 554
In the Garden of the North American Martyrs (Wolff), **Supp. VII:** 341–342

In the Garret (Van Vechten), **Supp. II Part 2:** 735
"In the Grove: The Poet at Ten" (Kenyon), **Supp. VII:** 160
"In the Hall of Mirrors" (Merrill), **Supp. III Part 1:** 322
In the Harbor (Longfellow), **II:** 491
In the Heart of the Heart of the Country (Gass), **Supp. VI:** 82–83, 84, 85, 93
In the Heat of the Night (film), **Supp. I Part 1:** 67
In the Hollow of His Hand (Purdy), **Supp. VII:** 278–280
In the Lake of the Woods (O'Brien), **Supp. V:** 240, 243, 250–252
In the Mecca (Brooks), **Supp. III Part 1:** 74
"In the Mecca" (Brooks), **Supp. III Part 1:** 70, 83–84
In the Midst of Life (Bierce), **I:** 200–203, 204, 206, 208, 212
"In the Miro District" (Taylor), **Supp. V:** 323
In the Miro District and Other Stories (Taylor), **Supp. V:** 325–326
In the Money (W. C. Williams), **Retro. Supp. I:** 423
"In the Naked Bed, in Plato's Cave" (Schwartz), **Supp. II Part 2:** 646–649
"In the Night" (Kincaid), **Supp. VII:** 183
In the Night Season: A Novel (Bausch), **Supp. VII:** 52–53
"In the Old Neighborhood" (Dove), **Supp. IV Part 1:** 241, 257
"In the Old World" (Oates), **Supp. II Part 2:** 503, 504
"In the Pit" (Proulx), **Supp. VII:** 255, 261
In the Presence of the Sun (Momaday), **Supp. IV Part 2:** 489, 490, 491–493, 493
"In the Realm of the Fisher King" (Didion), **Supp. IV Part 1:** 211
"In the Red Room" (Bowles), **Supp. IV Part 1:** 93
"In the Region of Ice" (Oates), **Supp. II Part 2:** 520
In the Room We Share (Simpson), **Supp. IX:** 279
"In These Dissenting Times" (Walker), **Supp. III Part 2:** 522
"In the Shadow of Gabriel, A.D.1550" (Frederic), **II:** 139
In the Spirit of Crazy Horse (Matthiessen), **Supp. V:** 211
In the Summer House (Jane Bowles), **Supp. IV Part 1:** 83, 89
In the Tennessee Country (Taylor), **Supp. V:** 328
"In the Thick of Darkness" (Salinas), **Supp. XIII:** 325
"In the Time of the Blossoms" (Mervin), **Supp. III Part 1:** 352
In the Time of the Butterflies (Alvarez), **Supp. VII:** 1, 12–15, 18
"In the Tunnel Bone of Cambridge" (Corso), **Supp. XII:** 120–121
"In the Upper Pastures" (Kumin), **Supp. IV Part 2:** 453
In the Valley (Frederic), **II:** 133–134, 136, 137
"In the Village" (Bishop), **Retro. Supp. II:** 38; **Supp. I Part 1:** 73, 74–75, 76, 77, 78, 88
"In the Waiting Room" (Bishop), **Retro. Supp. II:** 50; **Supp. I Part 1:** 81, 94, 95; **Supp. IV Part 1:** 249
"In the Ward: The Sacred Wood" (Jarrell), **II:** 376, 377
"In the White Night" (Beattie), **Supp. V:** 30–31
"In the Wind My Rescue Is" (Ammons), **Supp. VII:** 25
In the Winter of Cities (T. Williams), **IV:** 383
"In the X-Ray of the Sarcophagus of Ta-pero" (Goldbarth), **Supp. XII:** 191
"In the Yard" (Swenson), **Supp. IV Part 2:** 647
In the Zone (O'Neill), **III:** 388
In This, Our Life (film), **Supp. I Part 1:** 67
"In This Country, but in Another Language, My Aunt Refuses to Marry the Men Everyone Wants Her To" (Paley), **Supp. VI:** 225
In This Hung-up Age (Corso), **Supp. XII:** 119–120, 129
In This Our Life (Glasgow), **II:** 175, 178, 189
In This Our World (Gilman), **Supp. XI:** 196, 200, 202
"In Those Days" (Jarrell), **II:** 387–388
"In Time of War" (Auden), **Supp. II Part 1:** 8, 13
"Into Egypt" (Benét), **Supp. XI:** 56, 57–58
"Into My Own" (Frost), **II:** 153; **Retro. Supp. I:** 127
"Into the Night Life . . ." (H. Miller), **III:** 180, 184
"Into the Nowhere" (Rawlings), **Supp. X:** 220
Into the Stone (Dickey), **Supp. IV Part 1:** 178
"Into the Stone" (Dickey), **Supp. IV Part 1:** 179

Into the Stone and Other Poems (Dickey), **Supp. IV Part 1:** 176
In Touch: The Letters of Paul Bowles (J. Miller, ed.), **Supp. IV Part 1:** 95
"Intoxicated, The" (Jackson), **Supp. IX:** 116
"Intrigue" (Crane), **I:** 419
"Introducing the Fathers" (Kumin), **Supp. IV Part 2:** 452
Introductio ad Prudentiam (Fuller), **II:** 111
"Introduction to a Haggadah" (Paley), **Supp. VI:** 219
Introduction to Objectivist Epistemology (Rand), **Supp. IV Part 2:** 527, 528–529
Introduction to Objectivist Epistemology 2nd ed. (Rand), **Supp. IV Part 2:** 529
"Introduction to Some Poems, An" (Stafford), **Supp. XI:** 311, 324
Introduction to the Geography of Iowa, The (Doty), **Supp. XI:** 120
"Introduction to the Hoh" (Hugo), **Supp. VI:** 136–137
"Introduction to *The New Writing in the USA*" (Creeley), **Supp. IV Part 1:** 153–154
"Introduction to William Blake, An" (Kazin), **Supp. VIII:** 103
Introitus (Longfellow), **II:** 505, 506–507
"Intruder, The" (Dubus), **Supp. VII:** 76–78, 91
Intruder, The (Maeterlinck), **I:** 91
Intruder in the Dust (Faulkner), **II:** 71, 72
"Invaders, The" (Haines), **Supp. XII:** 205
Invasion of Privacy: The Cross Creek Trial of Marjorie Kinnan Rawlings (Acton), **Supp. X:** 233
Inventing Memory: A Novel of Mothers and Daughters (Jong), **Supp. V:** 115, 129
Inventing the Abbotts (S. Miller), **Supp. XII: 294–295**
"Invention of God in a Mouthful of Milk, The" (Karr), **Supp. XI:** 250
Invention of Solitude, The (Auster), **Supp. XII:** 21–22
Inventions of the March Hare (Eliot), **Retro. Supp. I:** 55–56, 58
"Inventions of the March Hare" (Eliot), **Retro. Supp. I:** 55
"Inventory" (Parker), **Supp. IX:** 192
"Inverted Forest, The" (Salinger), **III:** 552, 572
"Investigations of a Dog" (Kafka), **IV:** 438

"Investiture, The" (Banks), **Supp. V:** 7
"Investiture at Cecconi's" (Merrill), **Supp. III Part 1:** 336
Invisible: Poems (Nye), **Supp. XIII:** 277
Invisible Man (Ellison), **IV:** 493; **Retro. Supp. II:** 3, 12, 111, 112, 113, 117, 119, **120–123,** 125; **Supp. II Part 1:** 40, 170, 221, 224, 226, 227, 230, 231–232, 235, 236, 241–245; **Supp. IX:** 306; **Supp. X:** 242; **Supp. XI:** 18, 92
Invisible Spectator, An (Sawyer-Lauçanno), **Supp. IV Part 1:** 95
Invisible Swords (Farrell), **II:** 27, 46, 48–49
Invisible Worm, The (Millar), **Supp. IV Part 2:** 465
Invitation to a Beheading (Nabokov), **III:** 252–253, 254, 257–258; **Retro. Supp. I:** 265, 270, 273
"Invitation to the Country, An" (Bryant), **Supp. I Part 1:** 160
"Invocation" (McKay), **Supp. X:** 134
"Invocation to Kali" (Sarton), **Supp. VIII:** 260
"Invocation to the Social Muse" (MacLeish), **III:** 15
"In Weather" (Hass), **Supp. VI: 102–103**
"In Your Fugitive Dream" (Hugo), **Supp. VI:** 143
"In Your Good Dream" (Hugo), **Supp. VI:** 143–144
"Iola, Kansas" (Clampitt), **Supp. IX: 45–46**
Ion (Doolittle, trans.), **Supp. I Part 1:** 269, 274
Ion (Plato), **I:** 523
"Ione" (Dunbar), **Supp. II Part 1:** 199
Ionesco, Eugène, **I:** 71, 74, 75, 84, 295; **II:** 435; **Supp. VIII:** 201
"I Only Am Escaped Alone to Tell Thee" (Nemerov), **III:** 272, 273–274
"I Opened All the Portals Wide" (Chopin), **Retro. Supp. II:** 71
I Ought to Be in Pictures (Simon), **Supp. IV Part 2:** 584
I Promessi Sposi (Manzoni), **II:** 291
"I Remember" (Sexton), **Supp. II Part 2:** 680
"Irenicon" (Shapiro), **Supp. II Part 2:** 704
Irigaray, Luce, **Supp. XII:** 6
"Iris by Night" (Frost), **Retro. Supp. I:** 132
Irish Stories of Sarah Orne Jewett, The (Jewett), **Retro. Supp. II:** 142
Irish Triangle, An (Barnes), **Supp. III Part 1:** 34

"Iron Characters, The" (Nemerov), **III:** 279, 282
"Iron Hans" (Sexton), **Supp. II Part 2:** 691
Iron Heel, The (London), **II:** 466, 480
Iron John: A Book about Men (Bly), **Supp. IV Part 1:** 59, 67
"Iron Table, The" (Jane Bowles), **Supp. IV Part 1:** 82–83
"Iron Throat, The" (Olsen), **Supp. XIII:** 292, 297, 299
Ironweed (Kennedy), **Supp. VII:** 132, 133, 134, 135, 142, 144, 145–147, 148, 150, 153
"Irony as Art: The Short Fiction of William Humphrey" (Tebeaux), **Supp. IX:** 109
"Irony Is Not Enough: Essay on My Life as Catherine Deneuve" (Carson), **Supp. XII:** 112–113
Irony of American History, The (Niebuhr), **III:** 292, 306–307, 308
"Irrational Element in Poetry, The" (Stevens), **Retro. Supp. I:** 298, 301
"Irrevocable Diameter, An" (Paley), **Supp. VI:** 231–232
Irvine, Lorna, **Supp. XIII:** 26
Irving, Ebenezer, **II:** 296
Irving, John, **Supp. VI: 163–183;** **Supp. X:** 77, 85
Irving, John Treat, **II:** 296
Irving, Peter, **II:** 296, 297, 298, 299, 300, 303
Irving, Sir Henry, **IV:** 350
Irving, Washington, **I:** 211, 335, 336, 339, 343; **II: 295–318,** 488, 495; **III:** 113; **IV:** 309; **Retro. Supp. I:** 246; **Supp. I Part 1:** 155, 157, 158, 317; **Supp. I Part 2:** 377, 487, 585; **Supp. II Part 1:** 335; **Supp. IV Part 1:** 380
Irving, William, **II:** 296
Irving, William, Jr., **II:** 296, 297, 298, 299, 303
Irwin, Mark, **Supp. XII:** 21, 22, 24, 29
Irwin, William Henry, **Supp. II Part 1:** 192
Is 5 (Cummings), **I:** 429, 430, 434, 435, 440, 445, 446, 447
"Isaac and Abraham" (Brodsky), **Supp. VIII:** 21
"Isaac and Archibald" (Robinson), **III:** 511, 521, 523
"Isabel Sparrow" (Oliver), **Supp. VII:** 232
Isaiah (biblical book), **Supp. I Part 1:** 236; **Supp. I Part 2:** 516
"Isaiah Beethoven" (Masters), **Supp. I Part 2:** 461

"I Saw in Louisiana a Live-Oak Growing" (Whitman), **I:** 220
I Shall Spit on Your Graves (film), **Supp. I Part 1:** 67
Isherwood, Christopher, **II:** 586; **Supp. II Part 1:** 10, 11, 13; **Supp. IV Part 1:** 79, 82, 102; **Supp. XI:** 305
Ishiguro, Kazuo, **Supp. VIII:** 15
Ishi Means Man (Merton), **Supp. VIII:** 208
"Ishmael's Dream" (Stern), **Supp. IX:** 287
I Should Have Stayed Home (McCoy), **Supp. XIII:** 167, **168–170,** 171
"I Sigh in the Afternoon" (Salinas), **Supp. XIII:** 318
"I Sing the Body Electric" (Whitman), **Retro. Supp. I:** 394, 395
"Isis: Dorothy Eady, 1924" (Doty), **Supp. XI:** 122
"Is It True?" (Hughes), **Supp. I Part 1:** 342
"Island" (Hughes), **Supp. I Part 1:** 340
Island Garden, An (Thaxter), **Retro. Supp. II:** 136; **Supp. XIII:** 152
Island Holiday, An (Henry), **I:** 515
"Island of the Fay, The" (Poe), **III:** 412, 417
"Islands, The" (Hayden), **Supp. II Part 1:** 373
"Island Sheaf, An" (Doty), **Supp. XI:** 136
Islands in the Stream (Hemingway), **II:** 258; **Retro. Supp. I:** 186
Is Objectivism a Religion? (Ellis), **Supp. IV Part 2:** 527
"Isolation of Modern Poetry, The" (Schwartz), **Supp. II Part 2:** 644
Israel Potter, or Fifty Years of Exile (Melville), **III:** 90
"Israfel" (Poe), **III:** 411
Is Sex Necessary? (Thurber and White), **Supp. I Part 2:** 607, 612, 614, 653
"Issues, The" (Olds), **Supp. X:** 205
"I Stand Here Ironing" (Olsen), **Supp. XIII:** 292, 294, 296, 298, 300, 305
I Stole a Million (West), **IV:** 287
"Is Verse a Dying Technique?" (Wilson), **IV:** 431
It (Creeley), **Supp. IV Part 1:** 157, 158
IT (King), **Supp. V:** 139, 140, 141, 146–147, 151, 152
"It" (Olds), **Supp. X:** 208
Italian Backgrounds (Wharton), **Retro. Supp. I:** 370
Italian Hours (James), **I:** 12; **II:** 337; **Retro. Supp. I:** 235
Italian Journeys (Howells), **II:** 274
"Italian Morning" (Bogan), **Supp. III Part 1:** 58
Italian Villas and Their Gardens (Wharton), **IV:** 308; **Retro. Supp. I:** 361, 367
It All Adds Up: From the Dim Past to the Uncertain Future (Bellow), **Retro. Supp. II:** 32
"It Always Breaks Out" (Ellison), **Retro. Supp. II:** 126; **Supp. II Part 1:** 248
Itard, Jean-Marc Gaspard, **Supp. I Part 2:** 564
"I taste a liquor never brewed" (Dickinson), **Retro. Supp. I:** 30, 37
It Came from Outer Space (film), **Supp. IV Part 1:** 102
It Can't Happen Here (Lewis), **II:** 454
"It Don't Mean a Thing If It Ain't Got That Swing" (Matthews), **Supp. IX: 164–165**
I Tell You Now (Ortiz), **Supp. IV Part 2:** 500
"Ithaca" (Glück), **Supp. V:** 89
It Has Come to Pass (Farrell), **II:** 26
"I think to live May be a Bliss" (Dickinson), **Retro. Supp. I:** 44
I Thought of Daisy (Wilson), **IV:** 428, 434, 435
"Itinerary of an Obsession" (Kumin), **Supp. IV Part 2:** 450
"It Is a Strange Country" (Ellison), **Supp. II Part 1:** 238
"It Is Dangerous to Read Newspapers" (Atwood), **Supp. XIII:** 33
"It Must Be Abstract" (Stevens), **IV:** 95; **Retro. Supp. I:** 307
"It Must Change" (Stevens), **Retro. Supp. I:** 300, 307, 308
"It Must Give Pleasure" (Stevens), **Retro. Supp. I:** 307, 308, 309
"'It Out-Herods Herod. Pray You, Avoid It'" (Hecht), **Supp. X:** 62, 64
It's Loaded, Mr. Bauer (Marquand), **III:** 59
"It's Nation Time" (Baraka), **Supp. II Part 1:** 53
It's Nation Time (Baraka), **Supp. II Part 1:** 52, 53
It's Only a Play (McNally), **Supp. XIII:** 198
It Was (Zukofsky), **Supp. III Part 2:** 630
It Was the Nightingale (Ford), **III:** 470–471
"It Was When" (Snyder), **Supp. VIII:** 300
Ivanhoe (Scott), **I:** 216; **Supp. I Part 2:** 410
Ivens, Joris, **I:** 488; **Retro. Supp. I:** 184
"Iverson Boy, The" (Simpson), **Supp. IX:** 280
"Ives" (Rukeyser), **Supp. VI:** 273, 283
Ives, George H., **Supp. I Part 1:** 153
Ivory Grin, The (Macdonald), **Supp. IV Part 2:** 471, 472
Ivory Tower, The (James), **II:** 337–338
"Ivy Winding" (Ammons), **Supp. VII:** 33
"I Wandered Lonely as a Cloud" (Wordsworth), **Retro. Supp. I:** 121–122; **Supp. X:** 73
"I want, I want" (Plath), **Retro. Supp. II:** 246
"I Wanted to Be There When My Father Died" (Olds), **Supp. X:** 210
"I Want to Be a Father Like the Men" (Cisneros), **Supp. VII:** 71
"I Want to Be Miss America" (Alvarez), **Supp. VII:** 18
"I Want to Know Why" (Anderson), **I:** 114, 115, 116; **II:** 263
"I Want You Women Up North To Know" (Olsen), **Supp. XIII:** 292, 297
"I Was Born in Lucerne" (Levine), **Supp. V:** 181, 189
"I Went into the Maverick Bar" (Snyder), **Supp. VIII:** 301
"I Will Lie Down" (Swenson), **Supp. IV Part 2:** 640
I Wonder As I Wander (Hughes), **Retro. Supp. I:** 196, 203; **Supp. I Part 1:** 329, 332–333
"Iyani: It goes this Way" (Gunn Allen), **Supp. IV Part 1:** 321
"I years had been from home" (Dickinson), **I:** 471
Iyer, Pico, **Supp. V:** 215
J. B.: A Play in Verse (MacLeish), **II:** 163, 228; **III:** 3, 21–22, 23; **Supp. IV Part 2:** 586
"Jachid and Jechidah" (Singer), **IV:** 15
Jack and Jill (Alcott), **Supp. I Part 1:** 42
Jack Kelso (Masters), **Supp. I Part 2:** 456, 471–472
Jacklight (Erdrich), **Supp. IV Part 1:** 259, 270
Jack London, Hemingway, and the Constitution (Doctorow), **Supp. IV Part 1:** 220, 222, 224, 232, 235
Jackpot (Caldwell), **I:** 304
Jackson, Amelia. *See* Holmes, Mrs. Oliver Wendell (Amelia Jackson)
Jackson, Andrew, **I:** 7, 20; **III:** 473; **IV:** 192, 248, 298, 334, 348; **Supp. I Part 2:** 456, 461, 473, 474, 493, 695
Jackson, Blyden, **Supp. I Part 1:** 337

Jackson, Charles, **Supp. I Part 1:** 303
Jackson, George, **Supp. I Part 1:** 66
Jackson, Helen Hunt, **I:** 459, 470; **Retro. Supp. I:** 26, 27, 30–31, 32, 33
Jackson, J. O., **III:** 213
Jackson, James, **Supp. I Part 1:** 302, 303
Jackson, Joe, **Supp. I Part 2:** 441
Jackson, Katherine Gauss, **Supp. VIII:** 124
Jackson, Lawrence, **Retro. Supp. II:** 113, 115
Jackson, Melanie, **Supp. X:** 166
Jackson, Michael, **Supp. VIII:** 146
Jackson, Richard, **II:** 119; **Supp. IX:** 165
Jackson, Shirley, **Supp. IX: 113–130**
Jackson, Thomas J. ("Stonewall"), **IV:** 125, 126
"Jackson Square" (Levertov), **Supp. III Part 1:** 276
Jackstraws (Simic), **Supp. VIII:** 280, 282–283
"Jackstraws" (Simic), **Supp. VIII: 283**
Jack Tier (Cooper), **I:** 354, 355
"Jacob" (Garrett), **Supp. VII:** 109–110
"Jacob" (Schwartz), **Supp. II Part 2:** 663
"Jacob and the Indians" (Benét), **Supp. XI:** 47–48
Jacobs, Rita D., **Supp. XII:** 339
Jacobsen, Josephine, **Supp. XIII:** 346
"Jacob's Ladder" (Rawlings), **Supp. X:** 224, 228
"Jacob's Ladder, The" (Levertov), **Supp. III Part 1:** 278
Jacob's Ladder, The (Levertov), **Supp. III Part 1:** 272, 276–278, 281
Jacobson, Dale, **Supp. X:** 112
Jacoby, Russell, **Supp. IV Part 2:** 692
"Jacquerie, The" (Lanier), **Supp. I Part 1:** 355, 356, 360, 364, 370
Jade Mountain, The (Bynner), **II:** 527
Jaguar Totem (LaBastille), **Supp. X:** 99, 106, **107–109**
Jailbird (Vonnegut), **Supp. II Part 2:** 760, 779–780
Jaimes, M. Annette, **Supp. IV Part 1:** 330, 331
Jain, Manju, **Retro. Supp. I:** 53, 58
Jake's Women (Simon), **Supp. IV Part 2:** 576, 588
"Jakie's Mother" (Fante), **Supp. XI:** 164
Jakobson, Roman, **Supp. IV Part 1:** 155
"Jamaica Kincaid's New York" (Kincaid), **Supp. VII:** 181

James, Alice, **I:** 454; **Retro. Supp. I:** 228, 235
James, Caryn, **Supp. X:** 302, 303
James, Etta, **Supp. X:** 242
James, Henry, **I:** 4, 5, 9, 10, 12, 15, 16, 20, 52, 93, 109, 211, 226, 228, 244, 246, 251, 255, 258, 259, 336, 363, 374, 375, 379, 384, 409, 429, 436, 439, 452, 454, 459, 461–462, 463, 464, 485, 500, 504, 513, 514, 517–518, 571; **II:** 38, 58, 60, 73, 74, 95, 138, 140, 144, 147, 196, 198, 199, 228, 230, 234, 243, 259, 267, 271, 272, 275, 276, 278, 281, 282, 283, 284, 285, 286, 287, 288, 290, 306, 309, 316, **319–341,** 398, 404, 410, 415, 427, 444, 542, 544, 547–548, 556, 600; **III:** 44, 51, 136, 194–195, 199, 206, 208, 218, 228–229, 237, 281, 319, 325, 326, 334, 409, 453, 454, 457, 460, 461, 464, 511, 522, 576, 607; **IV:** 8, 27, 34, 37, 40, 53, 58, 73, 74, 134, 168, 172, 182, 198, 202, 285, 308, 309, 310, 311, 314, 316, 317, 318, 319, 321, 322, 323, 324, 328, 347, 352, 359, 433, 439, 476; **Retro. Supp. I:** 1, 8, 53, 56, 59, 108, 112, **215–242,** 272, 283, 284, 362, 366, 367, 368, 371, 373, 374, 375, 376, 377, 378, 379; **Retro. Supp. II:** 93, 135, 136, 203, 223; **Supp. I Part 1:** 35, 38, 43; **Supp. I Part 2:** 414, 454, 608, 609, 612–613, 618, 620, 646; **Supp. II Part 1:** 94–95; **Supp. III Part 1:** 14, 200; **Supp. III Part 2:** 410, 412; **Supp. IV Part 1:** 31, 35, 80, 127, 197, 349, 353; **Supp. IV Part 2:** 613, 677, 678, 682, 689, 693; **Supp. V:** 97, 101, 103, 258, 261, 263, 313; **Supp. VIII:** 98, 102, 156, 166, 168; **Supp. IX:** 121; **Supp. XI:** 153; **Supp. XIII:** 102
James, Henry (father), **II:** 7, 275, 321, 337, 342–344, 364; **IV:** 174; **Supp. I Part 1:** 300
James, Henry (nephew), **II:** 360
James, William, **I:** 104, 220, 224, 227, 228, 255, 454; **II:** 20, 27, 165, 166, 276, 321, 337, **342–366,** 411; **III:** 303, 309, 509, 599, 600, 605, 606, 612; **IV:** 26, 27, 28–29, 31, 32, 34, 36, 37, 43, 46, 291, 486; **Retro. Supp. I:** 57, 216, 227, 228, 235, 295, 300, 306; **Supp. I Part 1:** 3, 7, 11, 20
James, William (grandfather), **II:** 342
James Baldwin: The Legacy (Troupe, ed.), **Retro. Supp. II:** 15
James Baldwin—The Price of the Ticket (film), **Retro. Supp. II:** 2
James Dickey and the Politics of Canon (Suarez), **Supp. IV Part 1:** 175
"James Dickey on Yeats: An Interview" (Dickey), **Supp. IV Part 1:** 177
James Hogg: A Critical Study (Simpson), **Supp. IX:** 269, 276
James Jones: A Friendship (Morris), **Supp. XI:** 234
James Jones: An American Literary Orientalist Master (Carter), **Supp. XI:** 220
James Jones: Reveille to Taps (television documentary), **Supp. XI:** 234
"James Jones and Jack Kerouac: Novelists of Disjunction" (Stevenson), **Supp. XI:** 230
Jameson, F. R., **Supp. IV Part 1:** 119
Jameson, Sir Leander Starr, **III:** 327
James Shore's Daughter (Benét), **Supp. XI:** 48
"James Thurber" (Pollard), **Supp. I Part 2:** 468
"James Whitcomb Riley (From a Westerner's Point of View)" (Dunbar), **Supp. II Part 1:** 198
Jammes, Francis, **II:** 528; **Retro. Supp. I:** 55
Jan. 31 (Goldbarth), **Supp. XII:** 177, **178–179,** 180
"Jan, the Son of Thomas" (Sandburg), **III:** 593–594
Janeczko, Paul, **Supp. XIII:** 280
Janet, Pierre, **I:** 248, 249, 252; **Retro. Supp. I:** 55, 57
Jane Talbot: A Novel (Brown), **Supp. I Part 1:** 145–146
"Janet Waking" (Ransom), **III:** 490, 491
"Janice" (Jackson), **Supp. IX:** 117
Janowitz, Tama, **Supp. X:** 7
Jantz, Harold S., **Supp. I Part 1:** 112
"January" (Barthelme), **Supp. IV Part 1:** 54
"Janus" (Beattie), **Supp. V:** 31
Janzen, Jean, **Supp. V:** 180
Japanese by Spring (Reed), **Supp. X:** 241, **253–255**
Jara, Victor, **Supp. IV Part 2:** 549
Jarman, Mark, **Supp. IV Part 1:** 68; **Supp. IX:** 266, 270, 276; **Supp. XII:** 209
Jarrell, Mrs. Randall (Mary von Schrader), **II:** 368, 385
Jarrell, Randall, **I:** 167, 169, 173, 180; **II: 367–390,** 539–540; **III:** 134, 194, 213, 268, 527; **IV:** 352, 411, 422; **Retro. Supp. I:** 52, 121, 135, 140; **Retro. Supp. II:** 44, 177, 178,

182, 280; **Supp. I Part 1:** 89; **Supp. I Part 2:** 552; **Supp. II Part 1:** 109, 135; **Supp. III Part 1:** 64; **Supp. III Part 2:** 541, 550; **Supp. IV Part 2:** 440; **Supp. V:** 315, 318, 323; **Supp. VIII:** 31, 100, 271; **Supp. IX:** 94, 268; **Supp. XI:** 311, 315; **Supp. XII:** 121, 260, 297
Jarry, Alfred, **Retro. Supp. II:** 344
Jarvis, John Wesley, **Supp. I Part 2:** 501, 520
Jaskoski, Helen, **Supp. IV Part 1:** 325
"Jasmine" (Komunyakaa), **Supp. XIII:** 132
"Jason" (Hecht), **Supp. X:** 62
"Jason" (MacLeish), **III:** 4
Jason and Medeia (Gardner), **Supp. VI:** 63, **68–69**
Jaspers, Karl, **III:** 292; **IV:** 491
Jay, William, **I:** 338
Jayber Crow (Berry), **Supp. X:** 28, 34
"Jaz Fantasia" (Sandburg), **III:** 585
"Jazz Age Clerk, A" (Farrell), **II:** 45
Jazz Country: Ralph Ellison in America (Porter), **Retro. Supp. II:** 127
"Jazzonia" (Hughes), **Supp. I Part 1:** 324
Jazz Poetry Anthology, The (Komunyakaa and Feinstein, eds.), **Supp. XIII:** 125
"Jazztet Muted" (Hughes), **Supp. I Part 1:** 342
"Jealous" (Ford), **Supp. V:** 71
Jealousies, The: A Faery Tale, by Lucy Vaughan Lloyd of China Walk, Lambeth (Keats), **Supp. XII:** 113
Jean Huguenot (Benét), **Supp. XI:** 44
"Jeff Briggs's Love Story" (Harte), **Supp. II Part 1:** 355
Jeffers, Robinson, **I:** 66; **III:** 134; **Retro. Supp. I:** 202; **Supp. II Part 2: 413–440; Supp. VIII:** 33, 292; **Supp. IX:** 77; **Supp. X:** 112; **Supp. XI:** 312
Jeffers, Una Call Kuster (Mrs. Robinson Jeffers), **Supp. II Part 2:** 414
Jefferson, Blind Lemon, **Supp. VIII:** 349
Jefferson, Thomas, **I:** 1, 2, 5, 6–8, 14, 485; **II:** 5, 6, 34, 217, 300, 301, 437; **III:** 3, 17, 18, 294–295, 306, 310, 473, 608; **IV:** 133, 243, 249, 334, 348; **Supp. I Part 1:** 146, 152, 153, 229, 230, 234, 235; **Supp. I Part 2:** 389, 399, 456, 474, 475, 482, 507, 509, 510, 511, 516, 518–519, 520, 522; **Supp. X:** 26
Jefferson and/or Mussolini (Pound), **Retro. Supp. I:** 292
"Jefferson Davis as a Representative American" (Du Bois), **Supp. II Part 1:** 161
J-E-L-L-O (Baraka), **Supp. II Part 1:** 47
"Jelly-Bean, The" (Fitzgerald), **II:** 88
"Jellyfish, A" (Moore), **III:** 215
Jemie, Onwuchekwa, **Supp. I Part 1:** 343
Jenkins, J. L., **I:** 456
Jenkins, Kathleen, **III:** 403
Jenkins, Susan, **IV:** 123
Jenks, Deneen, **Supp. IV Part 2:** 550, 554
Jennie Gerhardt (Dreiser), **I:** 497, 499, 500, 501, 504–505, 506, 507, 519; **Retro. Supp. II:** 94, **99–101**
"Jennie M'Grew" (Masters), **Supp. I Part 2:** 468
Jennifer Lorn (Wylie), **Supp. I Part 2:** 709, 714–717, 718, 721, 724
"Jenny Garrow's Lover" (Jewett), **II:** 397
"Jerboa, The" (Moore), **III:** 203, 207, 209, 211–212
Jeremiah, **Supp. X:** 35
Jeremy's Version (Purdy), **Supp. VII:** 274
"Jericho" (Lowell), **II:** 536
"Jersey City Gendarmerie, Je T'aime" (Lardner), **II:** 433
Jersey Rain (Pinsky), **Supp. VI:** 235, **247–250**
"Jerusalem" (Nye), **Supp. XIII:** 287
Jessup, Richard, **Supp. XI:** 306
"*Je Suis Perdu*" (Taylor), **Supp. V:** 314, 321–322
Jesuits in North America in the Seventeenth Century, The (Parkman), **Supp. II Part 2:** 597, 603–605
Jesus, **I:** 27, 34, 68, 89, 136, 552, 560; **II:** 1, 16, 197, 198, 214, 215, 216, 218, 219, 239, 373, 377, 379, 537, 538, 539, 549, 569, 585, 591, 592; **III:** 39, 173, 179, 270, 291, 296–297, 300, 303, 305, 307, 311, 339, 340, 341, 342, 344, 345, 346, 347, 348, 352, 353, 354, 355, 436, 451, 489, 534, 564, 566, 567, 582; **IV:** 51, 69, 86, 107, 109, 117, 137, 138, 141, 144, 147, 149, 150, 151, 152, 155, 156, 157, 158, 159, 163, 164, 232, 241, 289, 293, 294, 296, 331, 364, 392, 396, 418, 430; **Supp. I Part 1:** 2, 54, 104, 107, 108, 109, 121, 267, 371; **Supp. I Part 2:** 379, 386, 458, 515, 580, 582, 583, 587, 588, 683; **Supp. V:** 280
"Jesus Asleep" (Sexton), **Supp. II Part 2:** 693
"Jesus of Nazareth, Then and Now" (Price), **Supp. VI:** 268
"Jesus Papers, The" (Sexton), **Supp. II Part 2:** 693
"Jesus Raises Up the Harlot" (Sexton), **Supp. II Part 2:** 693
Jetée, La (film), **Supp. IV Part 2:** 436
"Jeune Parque, La" (Valéry), **IV:** 92
"Jewbird, The" (Malamud), **Supp. I Part 2:** 435
"Jewboy, The" (Roth), **Supp. III Part 2:** 412
Jewett, Caroline, **II:** 396
Jewett, Dr. Theodore Herman, **II:** 396–397, 402
Jewett, Katharine, **Retro. Supp. II:** 46
Jewett, Mary, **II:** 396, 403
Jewett, Rutger, **Retro. Supp. I:** 381
Jewett, Sarah Orne, **I:** 313; **II: 391–414; Retro. Supp. I:** 6, 7, 19; **Retro. Supp. II:** 51, 52, **131–151,** 156; **Supp. I Part 2:** 495; **Supp. VIII:** 126; **Supp. IX:** 79; **Supp. XIII:** 153
Jewett, Theodore Furber, **II:** 395
Jew in the American Novel, The (Fiedler), **Supp. XIII:** 106
"Jewish Graveyards, Italy" (Levine), **Supp. V:** 190
"Jewish Hunter, The" (Moore), **Supp. X:** 163, 165, **174**
Jewison, Norman, **Supp. XI:** 306
Jews of Shklov (Schneour), **IV:** 11
Jig of Forslin, The: A Symphony (Aiken), **I:** 50, 51, 57, 62, 66
"Jig Tune: Not for Love" (McGrath), **Supp. X:** 116
"Jihad" (McClatchy), **Supp. XII:** 266
"Jilting of Granny Weatherall, The" (Porter), **III:** 434, 435, 438
Jim Crow's Last Stand (Hughes), **Retro. Supp. I:** 205
Jiménez, Juan Ramón, **Supp. XIII:** 315, 323
Jimmie Higgins (Sinclair), **Supp. V:** 288
Jimmy's Blues (Baldwin), **Retro. Supp. II:** 8, 9, 15
Jim's Book: A Collection of Poems and Short Stories (Merrill), **Supp. III Part 1:** 319
Jitney (Wilson), **Supp. VIII:** 330, 331, 351
Jitterbug Perfume (Robbins), **Supp. X:** 273, **274–276,** 279
Joachim, Harold, **Retro. Supp. I:** 58
Joan, Pope, **IV:** 165
Joanna and Ulysses (Sarton), **Supp. VIII: 254–255**
Joan of Arc, **IV:** 241; **Supp. I Part 1:** 286–288; **Supp. I Part 2:** 469

Joans, Ted, **Supp. IV Part 1:** 169
Job (biblical book), **II:** 165, 166–167, 168; **III:** 21, 199, 512; **IV:** 13, 158; **Supp. I Part 1:** 125
Job, The (Burroughs and Odier), **Supp. III Part 1:** 97, 103
Job, The: An American Novel (Lewis), **II:** 441
"Job History" (Proulx), **Supp. VII:** 262
Jobim, Antonio Carlos, **Supp. IV Part 2:** 549
"Job of the Plains, A" (Humphrey), **Supp. IX:** 101
"Jody Rolled the Bones" (Yates), **Supp. XI:** 335, 341
"Joe" (Alvarez), **Supp. VII:** 7–8
Joe Hill: A Biographical Novel (Stegner), **Supp. IV Part 2:** 599
Joe Turner's Come and Gone (Wilson), **Supp. VIII:** 334, **337–342,** 345
Johannes in Eremo (Mather), **Supp. II Part 2:** 453
John (biblical book), **I:** 68
"John" (Shields), **Supp. VII:** 310–311
"John, John Chinaman" (Buck), **Supp. II Part 1:** 128
John Addington Symonds: A Biographical Study (Brooks), **I:** 240, 241
John Barleycorn (London), **II:** 467, 481
John Brown (Du Bois), **Supp. II Part 1:** 171–172
"John Brown" (Emerson), **II:** 13
"John Brown" (Lindsay), **Supp. I Part 2:** 393
John Brown: The Making of a Martyr (Warren), **IV:** 236
John Brown's Body (Benét), **II:** 177; **Supp. XI:** 45, 46, 47, **56–57**
John Bull in America; or, The New Munchausen (Paulding), **I:** 344
"John Burke" (Olson), **Supp. II Part 2:** 579, 580
"John Burns of Gettysburg" (Harte), **Supp. II Part 1:** 343
"John Carter" (Agee), **I:** 27
"John Coltrane: Where Does Art Come From?" (Baraka), **Supp. II Part 1:** 60
John Deth: A Metaphysical Legend and Other Poems (Aiken), **I:** 61
"John Endicott" (Longfellow), **II:** 505, 506; **Retro. Supp. II:** 165–166, 167
"John Evereldown" (Robinson), **III:** 524
John Fante: Selected Letters, 1932–1981 (Cooney, ed.), **Supp. XI:** 170
John Fante Reader, The (Cooper, ed.), **Supp. XI:** 174
"John Gardner: The Writer As Teacher" (Carver), **Supp. III Part 1:** 136, 146–147
John Keats (Lowell), **II:** 530–531
"John L. Sullivan" (Lindsay), **Supp. I Part 2:** 394, 395
John Lane, **Retro. Supp. I:** 59
"John Marr" (Melville), **III:** 93
John Marr and Other Sailors (Melville), **III:** 93; **Retro. Supp. I:** 257
John Muir: A Reading Bibliography (Kimes and Kimes), **Supp. IX:** 178
Johnny Appleseed and Other Poems (Lindsay), **Supp. I Part 2:** 397
"Johnny Bear" (Steinbeck), **IV:** 67
"Johnny Panic and the Bible of Dreams" (Plath), **Retro. Supp. II:** 245
"Johnny Ray" (Ríos), **Supp. IV Part 2:** 543
John of the Cross (Saint), **I:** 585; **Supp. IV Part 1:** 284
John Paul Jones: A Sailor's Biography (Morison), **Supp. I Part 2:** 494–495
"John Redding Goes to Sea" (Hurston), **Supp. VI:** 150
Johns, George Sibley, **Retro. Supp. II:** 65
Johns, Orrick, **Retro. Supp. II:** 71
John Sloan: A Painter's Life (Brooks), **I:** 254
"John Smith Liberator" (Bierce), **I:** 209
Johnson, Alexandra, **Supp. X:** 86
Johnson, Alvin, **I:** 236
Johnson, Ben, **Retro. Supp. I:** 56
Johnson, Buffie, **Supp. IV Part 1:** 94
Johnson, Charles, **Supp. I Part 1:** 325; **Supp. V:** 128; **Supp. VI: 185–201;** **Supp. X:** 239; **Supp. XIII:** 182
Johnson, Charles S., **Supp. IX:** 309
Johnson, Claudia Durst, **Supp. VIII:** 126–127
Johnson, Diane, **Supp. XIII:** 127
Johnson, Dianne, **Retro. Supp. I:** 196
Johnson, Eastman, **IV:** 321
Johnson, Edward, **IV:** 157; **Supp. I Part 1:** 110, 115
Johnson, Fenton, **Supp. XI:** 129
Johnson, Georgia Douglas, **Supp. IV Part 1:** 164
Johnson, James Weldon, **Retro. Supp. II:** 114; **Supp. I Part 1:** 324, 325; **Supp. II Part 1:** 33, 194, 200, 202–203, 206–207; **Supp. III Part 1:** 73; **Supp. IV Part 1:** 7, 11, 15, 16, 164, 165, 166, 169; **Supp. X:** 42, 136, **246**
Johnson, Lady Bird, **Supp. IV Part 1:** 22
Johnson, Lyndon B., **I:** 254; **II:** 553, 582; **Retro. Supp. II:** 27
Johnson, Marguerite. *See* Angelou, Maya
Johnson, Nunnally, **Supp. IV Part 1:** 355
Johnson, Pamela Hansford, **IV:** 469
Johnson, Rafer, **Supp. I Part 1:** 271
Johnson, Reed, **Supp. IV Part 2:** 589
Johnson, Richard, **Supp. XIII:** 132
Johnson, Robert, **Supp. IV Part 1:** 146; **Supp. VIII:** 15, 134
Johnson, Robert K., **Supp. IV Part 2:** 573, 584
Johnson, Robert Underwood, **Supp. IX:** 182, 184, 185
Johnson, Samuel, **II:** 295; **III:** 491, 503; **IV:** 452; **Retro. Supp. I:** 56, 65; **Retro. Supp. II:** 281; **Supp. I Part 1:** 33; **Supp. I Part 2:** 422, 498, 503, 523, 656; **Supp. IV Part 1:** 34, 124; **Supp. XI:** 209; **Supp. XII:** 159; **Supp. XIII:** 55, 347
Johnson, Thomas H., **I:** 470–471; **IV:** 144, 158; **Retro. Supp. I:** 26, 28, 36, 39, 40, 41, 43
Johnson, Walter, **II:** 422
"Johnson Girls, The" (Bambara), **Supp. XI:** 7
Johnsrud, Harold, **II:** 562
Johnston, Basil, **Supp. IV Part 1:** 269
Johnston, Mary, **II:** 194
Johnston, Robert M., **Supp. I Part 1:** 369
"John Sutter" (Winters), **Supp. II Part 2:** 810
John's Wife (Coover), **Supp. V:** 51–52
John the Baptist, **I:** 389; **II:** 537, 591
John XXIII, Pope, **Supp. I Part 2:** 492
Jolas, Eugène, **Retro. Supp. II:** 85, 346; **Supp. IV Part 1:** 80
"Jolly Corner, The" (James), **I:** 571; **Retro. Supp. I:** 235
"Jonah" (Lowell), **II:** 536
Jonah's Gourd Vine (Hurston), **Supp. VI:** 149, 155
"Jonathan Edwards" (Holmes), **Supp. I Part 1:** 302, 315
"Jonathan Edwards in Western Massachusetts" (Lowell), **II:** 550
Jonathan Troy (Abbey), **Supp. XIII:** 4, 13
Jones, Anne, **Supp. X:** 8
Jones, Carolyn, **Supp. VIII:** 128
Jones, E. Stanley, **III:** 297
Jones, Edith Newbold. *See* Wharton, Edith
Jones, Everett LeRoi. *See* Baraka, Imamu Amiri
Jones, George Frederic, **IV:** 309
Jones, Grover, **Supp. XIII:** 166

Jones, Harry, **Supp. I Part 1:** 337
Jones, Howard Mumford, **I:** 353; **Supp. IV Part 2:** 606
Jones, James, **III:** 40; **IV:** 98; **Supp. XI:** 213–237
Jones, James Earl, **Supp. VIII:** 334; **Supp. XI:** 309
Jones, Jennifer, **Supp. IV Part 2:** 524
Jones, John Paul, **II:** 405–406; **Supp. I Part 2:** 479, 480, 494–495
Jones, LeRoi. *See* Baraka, Imamu Amiri
Jones, Lucretia Stevens Rhinelander, **IV:** 309
Jones, Madison, **Retro. Supp. II:** 235; **Supp. X:** 1
Jones, Major (pseudonym). *See* Thompson, William T.
Jones, Malcolm, **Supp. V:** 219
Jones, Robert Edmond, **III:** 387, 391, 394, 399
Jones, Tommy Lee, **Supp. V:** 227
"Jones's Private Argyment" (Lanier), **Supp. I Part 1:** 352
"Jones's *The Thin Red Line:* The End of Innocence" (Michel-Michot), **Supp. XI:** 224–225
Jong, Allan, **Supp. V:** 115
Jong, Erica, **Supp. V:** 113–135
Jong-Fast, Molly Miranda, **Supp. V:** 115
Jonson, Ben, **I:** 58, 358; **II:** 11, 16, 17, 18, 436, 556; **III:** 3, 463, 575–576; **IV:** 395, 453; **Retro. Supp. II:** 76; **Supp. I Part 2:** 423; **Supp. IV Part 2:** 585
Jonsson, Thorsten, **Retro. Supp. I:** 73
Joplin, Janis, **Supp. IV Part 1:** 206; **Supp. XI:** 239
Joplin, Scott, **Supp. IV Part 1:** 223
Jordan, Barbara, **Supp. VIII:** 63; **Supp. XI:** 249
Jordan, June, **Supp. XII:** 217
Jo's Boys (Alcott), **Supp. I Part 1:** 32, 35, 40–41, 42
Joseph Heller (Ruderman), **Supp. IV Part 1:** 380
"Josephine Has Her Day" (Thurber), **Supp. I Part 2:** 606
Josephine Stories, The (Fitzgerald), **Retro. Supp. I:** 109
"Joseph Pockets" (Stern), **Supp. IX:** 292
Josephson, Matthew, **I:** 259
"José's Country" (Winters), **Supp. II Part 2:** 789, 790
Joshua (biblical book), **Supp. I Part 2:** 515
Joslin, Katherine, **Retro. Supp. I:** 376

Journal (Emerson), **Supp. I Part 1:** 309
Journal (Thoreau), **IV:** 175
Journal (Woolman), **Supp. VIII:** 202
"Journal for My Daughter" (Kunitz), **Supp. III Part 1:** 268
Journal of Arthur Stirling, The (Sinclair), **Supp. V:** 280
"Journal of a Solitary Man, The" (Hawthorne), **II:** 226
Journal of a Solitude (Sarton), **Supp. VIII:** 256, 262–263
Journal of My Other Self (Rilke), **Retro. Supp. II:** 20
Journal of the Fictive Life (Nemerov), **III:** 267, 268, 269, 272, 273, 274, 280–281, 284–285, 286, 287
Journal of the Plague Year, A (Defoe), **III:** 423
"Journal of the Year of the Ox, A" (Wright), **Supp. V:** 343
Journals (Thoreau), **Supp. I Part 1:** 299
Journals and Other Documents on the Life and Voyages of Christopher Columbus (Morison, ed.), **Supp. I Part 2:** 494
Journals of Ralph Waldo Emerson, The (Emerson), **II:** 8, 17, 21
Journals of Susanna Moodie, The: Poems (Atwood), **Supp. XIII:** 33
"Journey, A" (Wharton), **Retro. Supp. I:** 364
"Journey, The" (Winters), **Supp. II Part 2:** 795
"Journey, The" (Wright), **Supp. III Part 2:** 605–606
"Journey, The: For Jane at Thirteen" (Kumin), **Supp. IV Part 2:** 442
Journey and Other Poems, The (Winters), **Supp. II Part 2:** 786, 794, 795, 796, 799, 800, 801
Journey Around My Room: The Autobiography of Louise Bogan—A Mosaic (Bogan), **Supp. III Part 1:** 47, 48, 52, 53
Journey Down, The (Bernstein), **IV:** 455
Journey Home, The (Abbey), **Supp. XIII:** 2, 12
Journeyman (Caldwell), **I:** 297, 302–304, 307, 309
Journey of Tai-me, The (Momaday), **Supp. IV Part 2:** 485
"Journey of the Magi" (Eliot), **Retro. Supp. I:** 64
Journey to a War (Auden and Isherwood), **Supp. II Part 1:** 13
Journey to Love (W. C. Williams), **IV:** 422; **Retro. Supp. I:** 429

Journey to My Father; Isaac Bashevis Singer (Zamir), **Retro. Supp. II:** 335
"Journey to Nine Miles" (Walker), **Supp. III Part 2:** 527
"Journey to the Interior" (W. J. Smith), **Supp. XIII:** 339, 340
"Joy" (Moore), **Supp. X:** 174
"Joy" (Singer), **IV:** 9; **Retro. Supp. II:** 325
Joyce, Cynthia, **Supp. X:** 194, 195, 196
Joyce, James, **I:** 53, 105, 108, 130, 174, 256, 285, 377, 395, 475–476, 478, 480, 483, 576; **II:** 27, 42, 58, 73, 74, 198, 209, 264, 320, 569; **III:** 7, 16, 26–27, 45, 174, 181, 184, 261, 273, 277, 343, 396, 398, 465, 471, 474; **IV:** 32, 73, 85, 95, 103, 171, 182, 211, 286, 370, 412, 418, 419, 428, 434, 456; **Retro. Supp. I:** 59, 63, 75, 80, 89, 91, 108, 109, 127, 287, 290, 292, 334, 335, 420; **Retro. Supp. II:** 221, 344; **Supp. I Part 1:** 257, 262, 270; **Supp. I Part 2:** 437, 546, 613, 620; **Supp. II Part 1:** 136; **Supp. III Part 1:** 35, 36, 65, 225, 229; **Supp. III Part 2:** 611, 617, 618; **Supp. IV Part 1:** 40, 47, 80, 227, 300, 310; **Supp. IV Part 2:** 424, 677; **Supp. V:** 261, 331; **Supp. VIII:** 14, 40, 103; **Supp. IX:** 211, 229, 235, 308; **Supp. X:** 115, 137, 194, 324; **Supp. XI:** 66; **Supp. XII:** 139, 151, 165, 191, 289
Joy Luck Club, The (Tan), **Supp. X:** 289, 291, 293, 294, 296, 297, 298, 299
"Joy of Sales Resistance, The" (Berry), **Supp. X:** 36
J R (Gaddis), **Supp. IV Part 1:** 279, 280, 285–289, 291, 294; **Supp. IV Part 2:** 484
"Juan's Song" (Bogan), **Supp. III Part 1:** 50
Jubilate Agno (Smart), **Supp. IV Part 2:** 626
Judah, Hettie, **Supp. XIII:** 246
"Judas Maccabaeus" (Longfellow), **II:** 506; **Retro. Supp. II:** 165, 167
Judd, Sylvester, **II:** 290; **Supp. I Part 2:** 420
Judd Rankin's Daughter (Glaspell), **Supp. III Part 1:** 186–188
Jude the Obscure (Hardy), **Supp. I Part 1:** 217
"Judgement Day" (O'Connor), **III:** 349, 350; **Retro. Supp. II:** 236
Judgment Day (Farrell), **II:** 29, 31, 32, 34, 39

"Judgment of Paris, The" (Merwin), **Supp. III Part 1:** 350
Judgment of Paris, The (Vidal), **Supp. IV Part 2:** 680, 682
"Judgment of the Sage, The" (Crane), **I:** 420
Judith (Farrell), **II:** 46, 48
"Judith" (Garrett), **Supp. VII:** 109–110
"Jug of Sirup, A" (Bierce), **I:** 206
"Jugurtha" (Longfellow), **II:** 499
"Juice or Gravy" (Roth), **Retro. Supp. II:** 297
"Juke Box Love Song" (Hughes), **Retro. Supp. I:** 209
"Julia" (Hellman), **Supp. I Part 1:** 280, 293
"Julia Miller" (Masters), **Supp. I Part 2:** 461
Julian (Vidal), **Supp. IV Part 2:** 677, 684–685, 685, 689
Julian the Apostate, **Retro. Supp. I:** 247
"Julian Vreden" (Bowles), **Supp. IV Part 1:** 94
Julie and Romeo (Ray), **Supp. XII:** 308, 310
Julien, Isaac, **Supp. XI:** 19
Julier, Laura, **Supp. IV Part 1:** 211
Julip (Harrison), **Supp. VIII:** 51
Julius Caesar (Shakespeare), **I:** 284
"July Midnight" (Lowell), **II:** 521
Jumel, Madame, **Supp. I Part 2:** 461
Jumping Out of Bed (Bly), **Supp. IV Part 1:** 71
"Jump-Up Day" (Kingsolver), **Supp. VII:** 203
"June Light" (Wilbur), **Supp. III Part 2:** 545
June Moon (Lardner and Kaufman), **II:** 427
"June Recital" (Welty), **IV:** 272–273
Juneteenth (Ellison), **Retro. Supp. II:** 119, 124, **126–128**
"Juneteenth" (Ellison), **Retro. Supp. II:** 119, 126; **Supp. II Part 1:** 248
Jung, Carl, **I:** 58, 135, 241, 248, 252, 402; **III:** 400, 534, 543; **Supp. I Part 2:** 439; **Supp. IV Part 1:** 68, 69; **Supp. VIII:** 45; **Supp. X:** 193
Junger, Ernst, **Supp. III Part 1:** 63
Jungle, The (Sinclair), **III:** 580; **Supp. V:** 281–284, 285, 289
Jungle Lovers (Theroux), **Supp. VIII:** 314, 315, 316, **317**
"Junior Addict" (Hughes), **Supp. I Part 1:** 343
"Juniper" (Francis), **Supp. IX:** 79
"Junk" (Wilbur), **Supp. III Part 2:** 556
Junkie: Confessions of an Unredeemed Drug Addict (Burroughs), **Supp. III Part 1:** 92, 94–96, 101
Juno and the Paycock (O'Casey), **Supp. IV Part 1:** 361
"Jupiter Doke, Brigadier General" (Bierce), **I:** 204
Jurgen (Cabell), **III:** 394; **IV:** 286; **Retro. Supp. I:** 80; **Supp. I Part 2:** 718
Jusserand, Jules, **II:** 338
Just above My Head (Baldwin), **Retro. Supp. II:** 14–15
"Just a Little One" (Parker), **Supp. IX:** 191
Just and the Unjust, The (Cozzens), **I:** 367–370, 372, 375, 377, 378, 379
Just an Ordinary Day (Jackson), **Supp. IX:** 120
Just Before Dark: Collected Nonfiction (Harrison), **Supp. VIII:** 41, 45, 46, 53
"Just Before the War with the Eskimos" (Salinger), **III:** 559
"Just Boys" (Farrell), **II:** 45
"Just for the Thrill: An Essay on the Difference Between Women and Men" (Carson), **Supp. XII: 103–104**
"Justice" (Hughes), **Supp. I Part 1:** 331
"Justice, A" (Faulkner), **Retro. Supp. I:** 83
Justice, Donald, **Retro. Supp. I:** 313; **Supp. III Part 2:** 541; **Supp. V:** 180, 337, 338, 341; **Supp. VII: 115–130**; **Supp. XI:** 141, 315; **Supp. XIII:** 76, 312
Justice and Expediency (Whitter), **Supp. I Part 2:** 686
"Justice Denied in Massachusetts" (Millay), **III:** 140
Justice of Gold in the Damnation of Sinners, The (Edwards), **I:** 559
"Justice to Feminism" (Ozick), **Supp. V:** 272
"Just Like Job" (Angelou), **Supp. IV Part 1:** 15
Just Wild About Harry (H. Miller), **III:** 190
Juvenal, **II:** 8, 169, 552
"K, The" (Olson), **Supp. II Part 2:** 558, 563, 569
Kabir, **Supp. IV Part 1:** 74
"Kabnis" (Toomer), **Supp. III Part 2:** 481, 484; **Supp. IX:** 309, 310, **319–320**
Kachel, Elsie. *See* Stevens, Mrs. Wallace (Elsie Kachel)
"Kaddish" (Ginsberg), **Supp. II Part 1:** 319, 327
Kaddish and Other Poems, 1958–1960 (Ginsberg), **Supp. II Part 1:** 309, 319–320
Kael, Pauline, **Supp. IX:** 253
Kafka, Franz, **II:** 244, 565, 569; **III:** 51, 253, 418, 566, 572; **IV:** 2, 113, 218, 437–439, 442; **Retro. Supp. II:** 20, 221, 300; **Supp. I Part 1:** 197; **Supp. III Part 1:** 105; **Supp. III Part 2:** 413; **Supp. IV Part 1:** 379; **Supp. IV Part 2:** 623; **Supp. VIII:** 14, 15, 103; **Supp. XII:** 21, 37, 98, 168; **Supp. XIII:** 305
Kaganoff, Penny, **Supp. XI:** 122
Kahane, Jack, **III:** 171, 178
Kahn, Otto, **I:** 385; **IV:** 123; **Retro. Supp. II:** 81, 84, 85
Kahn, R. T., **Supp. XI:** 216
"Kai, Today" (Snyder), **Supp. VIII:** 300
Kaiser, Georg, **I:** 479
Kaiser, Henry, **Supp. I Part 2:** 644
Kakutani, Michiko, **Supp. IV Part 1:** 196, 201, 205, 211, 212; **Supp. V:** 63; **Supp. VIII:** 81, 84, 86, 88, 141; **Supp. X:** 171, 301, 302, 310, 314; **Supp. XI:** 38, 179; **Supp. XII:** 165, 171, 172, 299
Kalem, T. E., **Supp. IV Part 2:** 585
Kalevala (Finnish epic), **II:** 503, 504; **Retro. Supp. II:** 155
Kalevala (Lönnrot), **Retro. Supp. II:** 159, 160
Kalki: A Novel (Vidal), **Supp. IV Part 2:** 677, 682, 685, 691, 692
Kallen, Horace, **I:** 229; **Supp. I Part 2:** 643
Kallman, Chester, **II:** 586; **Supp. II Part 1:** 15, 17, 24, 26
"Kallundborg Church" (Whittier), **Supp. I Part 2:** 696
Kalstone, David, **Retro. Supp. II:** 40
Kamel, Rose, **Supp. XIII:** 306
Kamera Obskura (Nabokov), **III:** 255
Kamhi, Michelle Moarder, **Supp. IV Part 2:** 529, 530
Kandy-Kolored Tangerine-Flake Streamline Baby, The (Wolfe), **Supp. III Part 2:** 569, 573–576, 580, 581
Kanellos, Nicolás, **Supp. VIII:** 82; **Supp. XIII:** 213
Kanin, Garson, **Supp. IV Part 2:** 574
"Kansas City Coyote" (Harjo), **Supp. XII:** 219, 222
"Kansas Emigrants, The" (Whittier), **Supp. I Part 2:** 687
Kant, Immanuel, **I:** 61, 277, 278; **II:** 10–11, 362, 480, 580–581, 582, 583; **III:** 300, 480, 481, 488, 612; **IV:** 90; **Supp. I Part 2:** 640; **Supp. IV Part 2:** 527

Kanter, Hal, **IV:** 383
Kapital, Das (Marx), **III:** 580
Kaplan, Abraham, **I:** 277
Kaplan, Justin, **I:** 247–248; **Retro. Supp. I:** 392
Kaplan, Steven, **Supp. V:** 238, 241, 243, 248
Karate Is a Thing of the Spirit (Crews), **Supp. XI:** 112–113
Karbo, Karen, **Supp. X:** 259, 262
"Karintha" (Toomer), **Supp. IX:** 311
Karl, Frederick R., **Supp. IV Part 1:** 384
Karl Shapiro's America (film), **Supp. II Part 2:** 703
Karr, Mary, **Supp. XI:** 239–256; **Supp. XIII:** 285
Kasabian, Linda, **Supp. IV Part 1:** 206
Kate Chopin (Toth), **Retro. Supp. II:** 71
Kate Chopin: A Critical Biography (Seyersted), **Retro. Supp. II:** 65; **Supp. I Part 1:** 225
Kate Chopin and Edith Wharton: An Annotated Bibliographical Guide to Secondary Sources (Springer), **Supp. I Part 1:** 225
Kate Chopin and Her Creole Stories (Rankin), **Retro. Supp. II:** 57; **Supp. I Part 1:** 200, 225
"Kate Chopin's *The Awakening* in the Perspective of Her Literary Career" (Arms), **Supp. I Part 1:** 225
Kate Vaiden (Price), **Supp. VI:** 264, 265
"Käthe Kollwitz" (Rukeyser), **Supp. VI:** 283, 284
Katherine and Jean (Rice), **Supp. VII:** 288
"Kathleen" (Whittier), **Supp. I Part 2:** 693
Kathy Goes to Haiti (Acker), **Supp. XII:** 5
Katz, Jonathan, **Supp. XII:** 179
Katz, Steve, **Supp. V:** 44
Kauffman, Carol, **Supp. XI:** 295
Kauffmann, Stanley, **III:** 452; **Supp. I Part 2:** 391
Kaufman, George S., **II:** 427, 435, 437; **III:** 62, 71–72, 394; **Retro. Supp. II:** 345; **Supp. IV Part 2:** 574; **Supp. IX:** 190
Kaufmann, James, **Supp. XI:** 39
Kauvar, Elaine M., **Supp. V:** 273
Kavanaugh (Longfellow), **I:** 458; **II:** 489, 491; **Retro. Supp. II:** 156; **Supp. I Part 2:** 420
Kaveney, Roz, **Supp. XI:** 39
Kazan, Elia, **III:** 153, 163; **IV:** 383; **Supp. I Part 1:** 66, 295

Kazin, Alfred, **I:** 248, 417, 419, 517; **II:** 177, 459; **IV:** 236; **Retro. Supp. II:** 206, 243, 246, 304; **Supp. I Part 1:** 195, 196, 294, 295, 296; **Supp. I Part 2:** 536, 631, 647, 650, 678, 679, 719; **Supp. II Part 1:** 143; **Supp. IV Part 1:** 200, 382; **Supp. V:** 122; **Supp. VIII:** 93–111; **Supp. IX:** 3, 227; **Supp. XIII:** 98, 106
Keach, Stacey, **Supp. XI:** 309
Keane, Sarah, **Supp. I Part 1:** 100
Kearns, Cleo McNelly, **Retro. Supp. I:** 57
Kearns, George, **Retro. Supp. I:** 292
Keating, AnnLouise, **Supp. IV Part 1:** 330
Keaton, Buster, **I:** 31; **Supp. I Part 2:** 607; **Supp. IV Part 2:** 574
Keats, John, **I:** 34, 103, 284, 314, 317–318, 385, 401, 448; **II:** 82, 88, 97, 214, 368, 512, 516, 530–531, 540, 593; **III:** 4, 10, 45, 122, 133–134, 179, 214, 237, 272, 275, 469, 485, 523; **IV:** 360, 405, 416; **Retro. Supp. I:** 91, 301, 313, 360, 395, 412; **Supp. I Part 1:** 82, 183, 266, 267, 312, 349, 362, 363, 365; **Supp. I Part 2:** 410, 422, 424, 539, 552, 675, 719, 720; **Supp. III Part 1:** 73; **Supp. IV Part 1:** 123, 168, 325; **Supp. IV Part 2:** 455; **Supp. VIII:** 41, 273; **Supp. IX:** 38, 39, 45; **Supp. XI:** 43, 320; **Supp. XII:** 9, 113, 255; **Supp. XIII:** 131, 281
Keats, John (other), **Supp. IX:** 190, 195, 200
"Keela, the Outcast Indian Maiden" (Welty), **IV:** 263
"Keen Scalpel on Racial Ills" (Bruell), **Supp. VIII:** 126
"Keep A-Inchin' Along" (Van Vechten), **Supp. III Part 2:** 744
Keeping (Goldbarth), **Supp. XII:** 179–180, 180
"Keeping Informed in D.C." (Nemerov), **III:** 287
Keeping Slug Woman Alive: A Holistic Approach to American Indian Texts (Sarris), **Supp. IV Part 1:** 329
"'Keeping Their World Large'" (Moore), **III:** 201–202
"Keeping Things Whole" (Strand), **Supp. IV Part 2:** 624
Keep It Simple: A Defense of the Earth (Nichols), **Supp. XIII:** 268
Kees, Weldon, **Supp. X:** 118; **Supp. XII:** 198
Keillor, Garrison, **Supp. XII:** 343; **Supp. XIII:** 274
Keith, Brian, **Supp. IV Part 2:** 474

Keith, Minor C., **I:** 483
Keller, A. G., **III:** 108
Keller, Helen, **I:** 254, 258
Keller, Lynn, **Supp. IV Part 2:** 423; **Supp. V:** 78, 80
Kelley, David, **Supp. IV Part 2:** 528, 529
Kelley, Florence, **Supp. I Part 1:** 5, 7
Kellogg, Paul U., **Supp. I Part 1:** 5, 7, 12
Kellogg, Reverend Edwin H., **III:** 200
Kelly, **II:** 464
Kelly, Emmett, **Supp. XI:** 99, 106
Kelly, Walt, **Supp. XI:** 105
Kemble, Fanny, **Retro. Supp. I:** 228
Kemble, Gouverneur, **II:** 298
Kemble, Peter, **II:** 298
Kempton, Murray, **Supp. VIII:** 104
Kempton-Wace Letters, The (London and Strunsky), **II:** 465
Kennan, George F., **Supp. VIII:** 241
Kennedy, Albert J., **Supp. I Part 1:** 19
Kennedy, Arthur, **III:** 153
Kennedy, Burt, **Supp. IV Part 1:** 236
Kennedy, J. Gerald, **Retro. Supp. II:** 271
Kennedy, John F., **I:** 136, 170; **II:** 49, 152–153; **III:** 38, 41, 42, 234, 411, 415, 581; **IV:** 229; **Supp. I Part 1:** 291; **Supp. I Part 2:** 496; **Supp. VIII:** 98, 104, 203; **Supp. XII:** 132
Kennedy, John Pendleton, **II:** 313
Kennedy, Mrs. John F., **I:** 136
Kennedy, Robert, **Supp. V:** 291
Kennedy, Robert F., **I:** 294; **Supp. I Part 1:** 52; **Supp. XI:** 343
Kennedy, William, **Supp. VII:** 131–157
Kennedy, X. J., **Supp. V:** 178, 182
Kenner, Hugh, **III:** 475, 478; **IV:** 412; **Supp. I Part 1:** 255; **Supp. IV Part 2:** 474
Kenneth Millar/Ross Macdonald: A Checklist (Bruccoli), **Supp. IV Part 2:** 464, 469, 471
Kenny, Maurice, **Supp. IV Part 2:** 502
Kent, George, **Supp. IV Part 1:** 11
Kenton, Maxwell. *See* Burnett, David; Hoffenberg, Mason; Southern, Terry
"Kent State, May 1970" (Haines), **Supp. XII:** 211
Kenyatta, Jomo, **Supp. X:** 135
Kenyon, Jane, **Supp. VII:** 159–177; **Supp. VIII:** 272
Kepler, Johannes, **III:** 484; **IV:** 18
Keppel, Frederick P., **I:** 214
"Kéramos" (Longfellow), **II:** 494; **Retro. Supp. II:** 167, 169
Kéramos and Other Poems (Longfellow), **II:** 490

Kerim, Ussin, **Supp. IX:** 152
Kermode, Frank, **IV:** 133; **Retro. Supp. I:** 301
Kern, Jerome, **II:** 427
Kerouac, Jack, **III:** 174; **Retro. Supp. I:** 102; **Supp. II Part 1:** 31, 307, 309, 318, 328; **Supp. III Part 1:** 91–94, 96, 100, **217–234; Supp. IV Part 1:** 90, 146; **Supp. V:** 336; **Supp. VIII:** 42, 138, 289, 305; **Supp. IX:** 246; **Supp. XII:** 118, 121, 122, 123, 126, 131, 132; **Supp. XIII:** 275, 284
Kerr, Deborah, **Supp. XI:** 307
Kerr, Orpheus C. (pseudonym). *See* Newell, Henry
Kerr, Walter, **Supp. IV Part 2:** 575, 579
Kesey, Ken, **III:** 558; **Supp. III Part 1:** 217; **Supp. V:** 220, 295; **Supp. X:** 24, 265; **Supp. XI:** 104
Kesten, Stephen, **Supp. XI:** 309
Kevane, Bridget, **Supp. XI:** 185, 190
"Key, The" (Welty), **IV:** 262
"Keys" (Nye), **Supp. XIII:** 281
Key to Uncle Tom's Cabin, A (Stowe), **Supp. I Part 2:** 580
Key West (H. Crane), **Retro. Supp. II:** 84
"Key West" (H. Crane), **I:** 400
Key West: An Island Sheaf (Crane), **I:** 385, 399–402
Khrushchev, Nikita, **I:** 136
Kid, The (Aiken), **I:** 61
Kid, The (Chaplin), **I:** 386
Kidder, Tracy, **Supp. III Part 1:** 302
Kidman, Nicole, **Supp. X:** 80
"Kidnapping in the Family, A" (Fante), **Supp. XI:** 164
"Kid's Guide to Divorce, The" (Moore), **Supp. X:** 167, 172
Kidwell, Clara Sue, **Supp. IV Part 1:** 333
Kielsky, Vera Emuma, **Supp. V:** 273
Kieran, John, **II:** 417
Kierkegaard, Søren Aabye, **II:** 229; **III:** 292, 305, 309, 572; **IV:** 438, 491; **Retro. Supp. I:** 326; **Retro. Supp. II:** 222; **Supp. V:** 9; **Supp. VIII:** 7–8
Kiernan, Robert F., **Supp. IV Part 2:** 684
Kieseritsky, L., **III:** 252
"Kilim" (McClatchy), **Supp. XII:** 258
"Killed at Resaca" (Bierce), **I:** 202
"Killed at the Ford" (Longfellow), **Retro. Supp. II:** 170–171
Killens, John Oliver, **Supp. IV Part 1:** 8, 369
"Killer in the Rain" (Chandler), **Supp. IV Part 1:** 122
"Killers, The" (Hemingway), **II:** 249; **Retro. Supp. I:** 188, 189
Killing Mister Watson (Matthiessen), **Supp. V:** 212, 214
"Killing of a State Cop, The" (Ortiz), **Supp. IV Part 2:** 499
Killing of Sister George, The (Marcus), **Supp. I Part 1:** 277
"Killings" (Dubus), **Supp. VII:** 85–86
"Killing the Plants" (Kenyon), **Supp. VII:** 167, 168
Kilmer, Joyce, **Supp. I Part 2:** 387
Kilpatrick, James K., **Supp. X:** 145
Kilvert, Francis, **Supp. VIII:** 172
Kim (Kipling), **Supp. X:** 230
Kim, Alfred, **Supp. XI:** 140
Kimball, J. Golden, **Supp. IV Part 2:** 602
Kimbrough, Mary Craig. *See* Sinclair, Mary Craig (Mary Craig Kimbrough)
Kimes, Maymie B., **Supp. IX:** 178
Kimes, William F., **Supp. IX:** 178
"Kin" (Welty), **IV:** 277; **Retro. Supp. I:** 353
Kincaid, Jamaica, **Supp. VII: 179–196**
"Kindness" (Dunn), **Supp. XI:** 149, 150
"Kindness" (Nye), **Supp. XIII:** 285
"Kindness" (Plath), **Retro. Supp. II:** 256
Kind of Order, A Kind of Folly, A: Essays and Conversations (Kunitz), **Supp. III Part 1:** 262, 268
Kindred (O. Butler), **Supp. XIII: 59–60,** 69
"Kind Sir: These Woods" (Sexton), **Supp. II Part 2:** 673
Kinds of Love (Sarton), **Supp. VIII: 253–254,** 256
Kinfolk (Buck), **Supp. II Part 1:** 126
King, Alexander, **IV:** 287
King, Carole, **Supp. XII:** 308
King, Clarence, **I:** 1
King, Ernest, **Supp. I Part 2:** 491
King, Fisher, **II:** 425
King, Grace, **Retro. Supp. II:** 136
King, Martin Luther, Jr., **Retro. Supp. II:** 12, 13
King, Michael, **Supp. XII:** 182
King, Queen, Knave (Nabokov), **III:** 251; **Retro. Supp. I:** 270
King, Starr, **Supp. II Part 1:** 341, 342
King, Stephen, **Supp. IV Part 1:** 102, 104; **Supp. IV Part 2:** 467; **Supp. V: 137–155; Supp. IX:** 114; **Supp. XIII:** 53
King, Tabitha (Mrs. Stephen King), **Supp. V:** 137
King, The (Barthelme), **Supp. IV Part 1:** 47, 52
King Coffin (Aiken), **I:** 53–54, 57
"King David" (Benét), **Supp. XI:** 44
Kingdom by the Sea, The: A Journey around Great Britain (Theroux), **Supp. VIII:** 323
Kingdom of Earth (T. Williams), **IV:** 382, 386, 387, 388, 391, 393, 398
"Kingdom of Earth, The" (T. Williams), **IV:** 384
Kingfisher, The (Clampitt), **Supp. IX:** 38
"Kingfishers, The" (Olson), **Supp. II Part 2:** 557, 558–563, 582
King Jasper (Robinson), **III:** 523
King Kong (film), **Supp. IV Part 1:** 104
King Lear (Shakespeare), **I:** 538; **II:** 540, 551; **Retro. Supp. I:** 248; **Supp. IV Part 1:** 31, 36; **Supp. IX:** 14; **Supp. XI:** 172
King Leopold's Soliloquy (Twain), **IV:** 208
King My Father's Wreck, The (Simpson), **Supp. IX:** 266, 267, 270, 275, 276
King of Babylon Shall Not Come Against You, The (Garrett), **Supp. VII:** 110–111; **Supp. X:** 3
"King of Folly Island, The" (Jewett), **II:** 394; **Retro. Supp. II:** 132, 133
King of Kings (film), **Supp. IV Part 2:** 520
"King of the Bingo Game" (Ellison), **Retro. Supp. II:** 117, 125; **Supp. II Part 1:** 235, 238, 240–241
"King of the Cats, The" (Benét), **Supp. XI:** 49–50
"King of the Clock Tower" (Yeats), **III:** 473
"King of the Desert, The" (O'Hara), **III:** 369
King of the Fields, The (Singer), **Retro. Supp. II:** 335
King of the Jews (Epstein), **Supp. XII:** 161, **166–170,** 172
King of the Mountain (Garrett), **Supp. VII:** 96, 97
"King of the River" (Kunitz), **Supp. III Part 1:** 263, 267–268
"King of the Sea" (Marquand), **III:** 60
"King over the Water" (Blackmur), **Supp. II Part 1:** 107
"King Pandar" (Blackmur), **Supp. II Part 1:** 92, 102
"King Pest" (Poe), **Retro. Supp. II:** 273
Kingsblood Royal (Lewis), **II:** 456
Kingsbury, John, **Supp. I Part 1:** 8

King's Henchman, The (Millay), **III:** 138–139
Kingsley, Sidney, **Supp. I Part 1:** 277, 281
"King's Missive, The" (Whittier), **Supp. I Part 2:** 694
Kingsolver, Barbara, **Supp. VII: 197–214; Supp. XIII:** 16
Kingston, Earll, **Supp. V:** 160
Kingston, Maxine Hong, **Supp. IV Part 1:** 1, 12; **Supp. V: 157–175,** 250; **Supp. X:** 291–292; **Supp. XI:** 18, 245
"King Volmer and Elsie" (Whittier), **Supp. I Part 2:** 696
Kinmont, Alexander, **Supp. I Part 2:** 588–589
Kinnaird, John, **Retro. Supp. I:** 399
Kinnell, Galway, **Retro. Supp. II:** 281; **Supp. III Part 1: 235–256; Supp. III Part 2:** 541; **Supp. IV Part 2:** 623; **Supp. V:** 332; **Supp. VIII:** 39; **Supp. XI:** 139; **Supp. XII:** 241
Kinsey, Alfred, **IV:** 230
Kinzie, Mary, **Supp. XII:** 181
"Kipling" (Trilling), **Supp. III Part 2:** 495
Kipling, Rudyard, **I:** 421, 587–588; **II:** 271, 338, 404, 439; **III:** 55, 328, 508, 511, 521, 524, 579; **IV:** 429; **Supp. IV Part 2:** 603; **Supp. X:** 255
Kirby, David, **Supp. XIII:** 89
Kirkland, Jack, **I:** 297
Kirkpatrick, Jeane, **Supp. VIII:** 241
Kirkwood, Cynthia A., **Supp. XI:** 177, 178, 179
Kirp, David L., **Supp. XI:** 129
Kirstein, Lincoln, **Supp. II Part 1:** 90, 97; **Supp. IV Part 1:** 82, 83
Kiss, The (Harrison), **Supp. X:** 191
"Kiss, The" (Sexton), **Supp. II Part 2:** 687
Kissel, Howard, **Supp. IV Part 2:** 580
Kissinger, Henry, **Supp. IV Part 1:** 388; **Supp. XII:** 9, 14
Kiss of the Spider Woman, the Musical (McNally), **Supp. XIII:** 207, 208
Kiss Tomorrow Good-bye (McCoy), **Supp. XIII:** 170, **172–173,** 174
"Kit and Caboodle" (Komunyakaa), **Supp. XIII:** 115
Kit Brandon: A Portrait (Anderson), **I:** 111
Kitchen, Judith, **Supp. IV Part 1:** 242, 245, 252; **Supp. IX:** 163; **Supp. XI:** 312, 313, 315, 317, 319, 320, 326, 329
"Kitchenette" (Brooks), **Retro. Supp. I:** 208

Kitchen God's Wife, The (Tan), **Supp. X:** 289, 292, 293, 294–295, 296–297, 298–299
Kit O'Brien (Masters), **Supp. I Part 2:** 471
Kittel, Frederick August. *See* Wilson, August
Kittredge, Charmian. *See* London, Mrs. Jack (Charmian Kittredge)
Kittredge, William, **Supp. VIII:** 39; **Supp. XI:** 316; **Supp. XII:** 209; **Supp. XIII:** 16
"Kitty Hawk" (Frost), **II:** 164; **Retro. Supp. I:** 124, 141
Klein, Joe, **Supp. XII:** 67–68
Klein, Marcus, **Supp. I Part 2:** 432; **Supp. XI:** 233
Kleist, Heinrich von, **Supp. IV Part 1:** 224
Klepfisz, Irena, **Retro. Supp. II:** 292
Kline, Franz, **Supp. XII:** 198
Kline, George, **Supp. VIII:** 22, 28
Klinkowitz, Jerome, **Supp. IV Part 1:** 40; **Supp. X:** 263; **Supp. XI:** 347
Knapp, Adeline, **Supp. XI:** 200
Knapp, Friedrich, **III:** 100
Knapp, Samuel, **I:** 336
Kneel to the Rising Sun (Caldwell), **I:** 304, 309
"Knees/Dura-Europos" (Goldbarth), **Supp. XII:** 185
"Knife" (Simic), **Supp. VIII:** 275
Knight, Etheridge, **Supp. XI:** 239
"Knight in Disguise, The" (Lindsay), **Supp. I Part 2:** 390
Knightly Quest, The (T. Williams), **IV:** 383
Knight's Gambit (Faulkner), **II:** 72
"Knock" (Dickey), **Supp. IV Part 1:** 182
"Knocking Around" (Ashbery), **Supp. III Part 1:** 22
Knockout Artist, The (Crews), **Supp. XI: 113–114**
Knopf, **Retro. Supp. I:** 13–14, 18, 20, 59, 199, 201, 202, 317, 320
Knopf, Alfred A., **III:** 99, 105, 106, 107; **Retro. Supp. I:** 13, 19, 317; **Supp. I Part 1:** 324, 325, 327; **Supp. IV Part 1:** 125, 354; **Supp. XIII:** 172
Knopf, Blanche, **Supp. I Part 1:** 324, 325, 327, 328, 332, 341; **Supp. IV Part 1:** 128, 346, 348; **Supp. XIII:** 169
"Knot, The" (Rich), **Supp. I Part 2:** 555
Knotts, Kristina, **Supp. XIII:** 238
"Knowing, The" (Olds), **Supp. X:** 215
"Knowledge Forwards and Backwards"

(Stern), **Supp. IX:** 296
Knowles, John, **Supp. IV Part 2:** 679; **Supp. XII: 235–250**
Knox, Frank, **Supp. I Part 2:** 488, 489
Knox, Israel, **Supp. X:** 70
Knox, Vicesimus, **II:** 8
Knoxville: Summer of 1915 (Agee), **I:** 42–46
Knudson, R. Rozanne, **Supp. IV Part 2:** 648
Kober, Arthur, **Supp. I Part 1:** 292
Koch, Frederick, **IV:** 453
Koch, John, **Supp. VIII:** 88
Koch, Vivienne, **III:** 194; **IV:** 136, 140; **Retro. Supp. I:** 428, 430
"Kochinnenako in Academe: Three Approaches to Interpreting a Keres Indian Tale" (Gunn Allen), **Supp. IV Part 1:** 329
"Kodachromes of the Island" (Hayden), **Supp. II Part 1:** 367, 380
Koestler, Arthur, **I:** 258; **Supp. I Part 2:** 671
Kolbenheyer, Dr. Frederick, **Supp. I Part 1:** 207
Kolodny, Annette, **Supp. X:** 97, 103, 229
Komunyakaa, Yusef, **Supp. XIII: 111–136**
Kon-Tiki (Heyerdahl), **II:** 477
Koopman, Harry Lyman, **Retro. Supp. I:** 40
Kora and Ka (Doolittle), **Supp. I Part 1:** 270
Kora in Hell (W. C. Williams), **Retro. Supp. I:** 416, **417–418,** 419, 430, 431
Korb, Rena, **Supp. XI:** 2
Korczak, Janosz, **Supp. X:** 70
Kort, Amy, **Supp. XIII:** 148
Kosinski, Jerzy, **Supp. VII: 215–228; Supp. XII:** 21
"Kostas Tympakianakis" (Merrill), **Supp. III Part 1:** 326
Koteliansky, S. S., **Supp. VIII:** 251, 265
Kowloon Tong (Theroux), **Supp. VIII:** 325
Kozlenko, William, **IV:** 378, 381
Kramer, Dale, **Supp. I Part 2:** 669
Kramer, Hilton, **III:** 537; **Supp. I Part 1:** 295, 296; **Supp. VIII:** 239
Kramer, Lawrence, **Supp. IV Part 1:** 61, 65, 66; **Supp. IX:** 291
Kramer, Stanley, **II:** 421, 587
Krapp's Last Tape (Beckett), **I:** 71; **III:** 387; **Retro. Supp. I:** 206
Krassner, Paul, **Supp. IV Part 1:** 385; **Supp. XI:** 293
Kreitman, Esther, **IV:** 2

Kreymborg, Alfred, **II:** 530; **III:** 465; **IV:** 76; **Retro. Supp. I:** 417
Kristeva, Julia, **Supp. XII:** 6
Kristofferson, Kris, **Supp. XIII:** 119
Kristol, Irving, **Supp. VIII:** 93, 244; **Supp. XIII:** 98
Kroll, Jack, **Supp. IV Part 2:** 590
Kroll, Judith, **Supp. I Part 2:** 541–543, 544, 546
Kroll Ring, Frances. *See* Ring, Frances Kroll
Krook, Dorothea, **Retro. Supp. II:** 243
Kropotkin, Peter, **I:** 493; **Supp. I Part 1:** 5; **Supp. IV Part 2:** 521
Kruif, Paul de, **II:** 446
Krupat, Arnold, **Supp. IV Part 2:** 500
Krutch, Joseph Wood, **II:** 459; **III:** 425; **IV:** 70, 175
Kublai Khan, **III:** 395
"Kubla Khan" (Coleridge), **Supp. XIII:** 131, 283
Kubrick, Stanley, **Supp. IV Part 1:** 392; **Supp. XI:** 293,**Supp. XI:** 301, 302–303
Kuehl, John, **Supp. IV Part 1:** 279, 284, 285, 287
Kuehl, Linda, **Supp. IV Part 1:** 199
Kukachin, Princess, **III:** 395
"Ku Klux" (Hughes), **Retro. Supp. I:** 205
Kulshrestha, Chirantan, **Retro. Supp. II:** 21
Kumin, Maxine, **Supp. IV Part 2:** 439–457; **Supp. XIII:** 294
Kundera, Milan, **Supp. VIII:** 241
Kunitz, Stanley, **I:** 179, 180, 181, 182, 521; **II:** 545; **Supp. III Part 1:** 257–270; **Supp. V:** 79; **Supp. XI:** 259; **Supp. XIII:** 341
Kuo, Helena, **Supp. X:** 291
Kuropatkin, General Aleksei Nikolaevich, **III:** 247–248
Kurzy of the Sea (Barnes), **Supp. III Part 1:** 34
Kushner, Tony, **Supp. IX:** 131–149
Kussy, Bella, **IV:** 468
Kuttner, Henry, **Supp. IV Part 1:** 102
LaBastille, Anne, **Supp. X:** 95–110
"Labours of Hercules, The" (Moore), **III:** 201
La Bruyère, Jean de, **I:** 58
La Bufera e Altro (Montale), **Supp. V:** 337
Labyrinth of Solitude, The (Paz), **Supp. XIII:** 223
Lacan, Jacques, **Supp. IV Part 1:** 45; **Supp. VIII:** 5; **Supp. XII:** 98
La Casa en Mango Street (Cisneros), **Supp. VII:** 58–59
Lachaise, Gaston, **I:** 434

"Lackawanna" (Merwin), **Supp. III Part 1:** 350
Lackawanna Elegy (Goll; Kinnell, trans.), **Supp. III Part 1:** 235, 243–244
Laclède, Pierre, **Supp. I Part 1:** 205
"Lacquer Prints" (Lowell), **II:** 524–525
Ladder of Years (Tyler), **Supp. IV Part 2:** 657, 671–672
Ladders to Fire (Nin), **Supp. X:** 185
"Ladies" (Coleman), **Supp. XI:** 93
Ladies Almanack (Barnes), **Supp. III Part 1:** 37–39, 42
"Ladies in Spring" (Welty), **IV:** 276–277; **Retro. Supp. I:** 353
Lady Audley's Secret (Braddon), **Supp. I Part 1:** 35, 36
"Lady Barberina" (James), **Retro. Supp. I:** 227
"Lady Bates" (Jarrell), **II:** 380–381
Lady Chatterley's Lover (Lawrence), **III:** 170; **IV:** 434
"Lady from Redhorse, A" (Bierce), **I:** 203
Lady in Kicking Horse Reservoir, The (Hugo), **Supp. VI:** 134, 138–139
Lady in the Lake, The (Chandler), **Supp. IV Part 1:** 127, 129–130
"Lady in the Lake, The" (Chandler), **Supp. IV Part 1:** 129
Lady in the Lake, The (film), **Supp. IV Part 1:** 130
"Lady in the Pink Mustang, The" (Erdrich), **Supp. IV Part 1:** 270
"Lady Is Civilized, The" (Taylor), **Supp. V:** 315
Lady Is Cold, The (White), **Supp. I Part 2:** 653
"Lady Lazarus" (Plath), **Retro. Supp. II:** 250, 251, 255; **Supp. I Part 2:** 529, 535, 542, 545
Lady of Aroostook, The (Howells), **II:** 280
"Lady of Bayou St. John, A" (Chopin), **Retro. Supp. II:** 58
"Lady of the Lake, The" (Malamud), **Supp. I Part 2:** 437
Lady Oracle (Atwood), **Supp. XIII:** 21, 23–24
Lady Sings the Blues (film), **Supp. I Part 1:** 67
"Lady's Maid's Bell, The" (Wharton), **IV:** 316
"Lady Wentworth" (Longfellow), **II:** 505
"Lady with a Lamp" (Parker), **Supp. IX:** 193
"Lady with the Heron, The" (Merwin), **Supp. III Part 1:** 343
La Farge, John, **I:** 1, 2, 20; **II:** 322,

338; **Retro. Supp. I:** 217
La Farge, Oliver, **Supp. IV Part 2:** 503
Lafayette, Marquis de, **I:** 344, 345; **II:** 405–406; **Supp. I Part 2:** 510, 511, 683
"La Figlia che Piange" (Eliot), **Retro. Supp. I:** 63
La Follette, Robert, **I:** 483, 485, 492; **III:** 580
La Fontaine, Jean de, **II:** 154; **III:** 194; **IV:** 80
Laforgue, Jules, **I:** 386, 569, 570, 572–573, 575, 576; **II:** 528; **III:** 8, 11, 466; **IV:** 37, 79, 80, 122; **Retro. Supp. I:** 55, 56; **Supp. XIII:** 332, 335, 346
La Gallienne, Eva, **Supp. VIII:** 251
"Lager Beer" (Dunbar), **Supp. II Part 1:** 193
"La Gringuita: On Losing a Native Language" (Alvarez), **Supp. VII:** 18
Laguna Woman (Silko), **Supp. IV Part 2:** 557, 560–561
Laing, R. D., **Supp. I Part 2:** 527
La kabbale pratique (Ambelain), **Supp. I Part 1:** 273
"Lake, The" (Bradbury), **Supp. IV Part 1:** 101
Lake, The (play), **Supp. IX:** 189
"Lake Chelan" (Stafford), **Supp. XI:** 321
Lake Effect Country (Ammons), **Supp. VII:** 34, 35
"Lake Isle of Innisfree" (Yeats), **Retro. Supp. I:** 413
Lalic, Ivan V., **Supp. VIII:** 272
L'Alouette (Anouilh), **Supp. I Part 1:** 286–288
Lamantia, Philip, **Supp. VIII:** 289
Lamb, Charles, **III:** 111, 207; **Supp. VIII:** 125
Lamb, Wendy, **Supp. IV Part 2:** 658
Lambardi, Marilyn May, **Retro. Supp. II:** 45–46
"Lament" (Wilbur), **Supp. III Part 2:** 550
"Lamentations" (Glück), **Supp. V:** 83, 84
"Lament for Dark Peoples" (Hughes), **Retro. Supp. I:** 199
"Lament for Saul and Jonathan" (Bradstreet), **Supp. I Part 1:** 111
"Lament-Heaven" (Doty), **Supp. XI:** 125
"Lament of a New England Mother, The" (Eberhart), **I:** 539
Laments for the Living (Parker), **Supp. IX:** 192
"Lame Shall Enter First, The" (O'Connor), **III:** 348, 351, 352, 355,

356–357, 358; **Retro. Supp. II:** 237
Lamia (Keats), **II:** 512; **III:** 523
La Motte-Fouqué, Friedrich Heinrich Karl, **III:** 77, 78
L'Amour, Louis, **Supp. XIII:** 5
Lamp for Nightfall, A (Caldwell), **I:** 297
"Lance" (Nabokov), **Retro. Supp. I:** 266
Lancelot (Percy), **Supp. III Part 1:** 384, 395–396
Lancelot (Robinson), **III:** 513, 522
Lanchester, John, **Retro. Supp. I:** 278
"Land" (Emerson), **II:** 6
Landau, Deborah, **Supp. XI:** 122, 123
"Land beyond the Blow, The" (Bierce), **I:** 209
Landfall (Wagoner), **Supp. IX:** 330
"Landing in Luck" (Faulkner), **Retro. Supp. I:** 85
"Landing on the Moon" (Swenson), **Supp. IV Part 2:** 643
Landlord at Lion's Head, The (Howells), **II:** 276, 287–288
Landmarks of Healing: A Study of House Made of Dawn (Scarberry-García), **Supp. IV Part 2:** 486
Land of Little Rain, The (Dillard), **Supp. VI:** 27–28
Land of the Free U.S.A. (MacLeish), **I:** 293; **III:** 16–17
Land of Unlikeness (Lowell), **II:** 537–538, 539, 547; **Retro. Supp. II:** 177, 178, **184–185**
Landor, Walter Savage, **III:** 15, 469; **Supp. I Part 2:** 422
"Landscape" (Sarton), **Supp. VIII:** 259
"Landscape: The Eastern Shore" (Barth), **I:** 122
"Landscape as a Nude" (MacLeish), **III:** 14
Landscape at the End of the Century (Dunn), **Supp. XI:** 139, 143, **150–151**
"Landscape Chamber, The" (Jewett), **II:** 408–409
"Landscape for the Disappeared" (Komunyakaa), **Supp. XIII:** 120, 126
Landscape in American Poetry (Larcom), **Supp. XIII:** 142
"Landscape Painter, A" (James), **II:** 322; **Retro. Supp. I:** 219
"Landscape Symbolism in Kate Chopin's *At Fault*" (Arner), **Retro. Supp. II:** 62
"Landscape with Boat" (Stevens), **Retro. Supp. I:** 306
"Landscape with the Fall of Icarus" (Brueghel), **Retro. Supp. I:** 430

"Land Where There Is No Death, The" (Benét), **Supp. XI:** 56
Lane, Ann, **Supp. XI:** 195, 208
Lane, Cornelia. *See* Anderson, Mrs. Sherwood
Lane, Homer, **Supp. II Part 1:** 6
Lane, Nathan, **Supp. XIII:** 207
Lane, Rose Wilder, **Supp. IV Part 2:** 524
Lang, Andrew, **Retro. Supp. I:** 127
Lang, Violet, **Supp. XII:** 119
Langdon, Olivia. *See* Clemens, Mrs. Samuel Langhorne (Olivia Langdon)
Lange, Carl Georg, **II:** 350
Lange, Dorothy, **I:** 293
Langland, Joseph, **III:** 542
Langston Hughes, American Poet (Walker), **Supp. III Part 2:** 530–531
Langston Hughes: Modern Critical Views (Bloom, ed.), **Retro. Supp. I:** 193
Langston Hughes: The Poet and His Critics (Barksdale), **Retro. Supp. I:** 202
Langston Hughes and the "Chicago Defender": Essays on Race, Politics, and Culture (De Santis, ed.), **Retro. Supp. I:** 194
Langston Hughes Reader, The (Hughes), **Retro. Supp. I:** 202; **Supp. I Part 1:** 345
"Language, Visualization and the Inner Library" (Shepard), **Supp. III Part 2:** 436, 438, 449
"Language and the Writer" (Bambara), **Supp. XI:** 18
Language As Gesture (Blackmur), **Supp. II Part 1:** 108
Language as Symbolic Action (Burke), **I:** 275, 282, 285
Language Book, The (Andrews and Bernstein), **Supp. IV Part 2:** 426
Language in Thought and Action (Hayakawa), **I:** 448
"Language of Being and Dying, The" (Gass), **Supp. VI:** 91
"Language of Home, The" (Wideman), **Supp. X:** 320, 323–324
Language of Life, The (Moyers, television series), **Supp. XIII:** 274, 276
"Language of the Brag, The" (Olds), **Supp. X:** 204
"Language We Know, The" (Ortiz), **Supp. IV Part 2:** 500
Lanier, Clifford, **Supp. I Part 1:** 349, 350, 353, 355, 356, 371
Lanier, James F. D., **Supp. I Part 1:** 350
Lanier, Lyle H., **Supp. X:** 25

Lanier, Mrs. Robert Sampson (Mary Jane Anderson), **Supp. I Part 1:** 349
Lanier, Mrs. Sidney (Mary Day), **Supp. I Part 1:** 351, 355, 357, 361, 362, 364, 370, 371
Lanier, Robert Sampson, **Supp. I Part 1:** 349, 351, 355, 356, 361
Lanier, Sidney, **IV:** 444; **Supp. I Part 1:** 349–373; **Supp. I Part 2:** 416; **Supp. IV Part 1:** 165
"Lanier as Poet" (Parks), **Supp. I Part 1:** 373
"Lanier's Reading" (Graham), **Supp. I Part 1:** 373
"Lanier's Use of Science for Poetic Imagery" (Beaver), **Supp. I Part 1:** 373
Lannegan, Helen. *See* Caldwell, Mrs. Erskine
Lannin, Paul, **II:** 427
Lanny Budd novels (Sinclair), **Supp. V:** 290
Lant, Kathleen Margaret, **Supp. V:** 141
Lanthenas, François, **Supp. I Part 2:** 515
Lao-tse, **III:** 173, 189, 567
"Lapis Lazuli" (Yeats), **I:** 532; **III:** 40
Laplace, Pierre Simon de, **III:** 428
Lapouge, M. G., **Supp. I Part 2:** 633
Larbaud, Valery, **IV:** 404; **Supp. XIII:** 332
Larcom, Lucy, **Retro. Supp. II:** 145; **Supp. XIII: 137–157**
Larcom's Poetical Works (Larcom), **Supp. XIII:** 142
Lardner, John, **II:** 437
Lardner, Ring, **I:** 487; **II:** 44, 91, 259, 263, **415–438**; **III:** 566, 572; **IV:** 433; **Retro. Supp. I:** 105; **Retro. Supp. II:** 222; **Supp. I Part 2:** 609; **Supp. IX:** 200
Lardner, Ring, Jr., **Supp. XI:** 306
"Lardner, Shakespeare and Chekhov" (Matthews), **II:** 430
"Large Bad Picture" (Bishop), **Retro. Supp. II:** 43; **Supp. I Part 1:** 73, 80–82, 85, 86, 89, 90
"Large Coffee" (Lardner), **II:** 437
Large Glass, or The Bride Stripped Bare by Her Bachelors, Even (Duchamp), **Supp. IV Part 2:** 423, 424
Largo (Handel), **IV:** 369
Lark, The (Hellman), **Supp. I Part 1:** 286–288, 297
Larkin, Philip, **Supp. I Part 2:** 536; **Supp. XI:** 243, 249; **Supp. XIII:** 76, 85
Larkin, Sharon Alile, **Supp. XI:** 20
Larmore, Phoebe, **Supp. X:** 266

La Rochefoucauld, François de, **I:** 279; **II:** 111
"La Rose des Vents" (Wilbur), **Supp. III Part 2:** 550
Larry's Party (Shields), **Supp. VII:** 324, 326–327
Larsen, Nella, **Supp. I Part 1:** 325, 326; **Supp. IV Part 1:** 164
Larson, Charles, **Supp. IV Part 1:** 331
Larson, Clinton, **Supp. XI:** 328
"Larval Stage of a Bookworm" (Mencken), **III:** 101
La Salle and the Discovery of the Great West (Parkman), **Supp. II Part 2:** 595, 598, 605–607
Lasch, Christopher, **I:** 259
Lasher (Rice), **Supp. VII:** 299–300
Lask, Thomas, **III:** 576
Laski, Harold, **Supp. I Part 2:** 632, 643
Lassalle, Ferdinand, **IV:** 429
"Last Acts" (Olds), **Supp. X:** 210
Last Adam, The (Cozzens), **I:** 362–363, 364, 368, 375, 377, 378, 379
Last Analysis, The (Bellow), **I:** 152, 160, 161; **Retro. Supp. II:** 26
Last and Lost Poems of Delmore Schwartz (Phillips, ed.), **Supp. II Part 2:** 661, 665
Last Beautiful Days of Autumn, The (Nichols), **Supp. XIII:** 254, 255, 267, 269
Last Blue (Stern), **Supp. IX: 299–300**
Last Carousel, The (Algren), **Supp. IX:** 16
"Last Day in the Field, The" (Gordon), **II:** 200
"Last Day of the Last Furlough" (Salinger), **III:** 552–553
"Last Days of Alice" (Tate), **IV:** 129
"Last Days of August, The" (Nye), **Supp. XIII:** 284
"Last Days of John Brown, The" (Thoreau), **IV:** 185
Last Days of Louisiana Red, The (Reed), **Supp. X:** 240, **248–249**
Last Decade, The (Trilling), **Supp. III Part 2:** 493, 499
"Last Demon, The" (Singer), **IV:** 15, 21
Last Exit to Brooklyn (Selby), **Supp. III Part 1:** 125
Last Flower, The (Thurber), **Supp. I Part 2:** 610
Last Gentleman, The (Percy), **Supp. III Part 1:** 383–388, 392–393
"Last Good Country, The" (Hemingway), **II:** 258–259
Last Good Time, The (Bausch), **Supp. VII:** 45–46

"Last Hiding Places of Snow, The" (Kinnell), **Supp. III Part 1:** 252
"Last Hours, The" (Dunn), **Supp. XI:** 141
Last Husband and Other Stories, The (Humphrey), **Supp. IX:** 94
Last Jew in America, The (Fiedler), **Supp. XIII:** 103
"Last Jew in America, The" (Fiedler), **Supp. XIII:** 103
Last Laugh, Mr. Moto (Marquand), **III:** 57
"Last Leaf, The" (Holmes), **Supp. I Part 1:** 302, 309
"Last Leaf, The" (Porter), **III:** 444
"Last Look at the Lilacs" (Stevens), **IV:** 74
"Last May" (Dixon), **Supp. XII: 143**
"Last Mohican, The" (Malamud), **Supp. I Part 2:** 437–438, 450, 451
"Lastness" (Kinnell), **Supp. III Part 1:** 248–249
"Last Night" (Olds), **Supp. X:** 212
"Last Night at Tía's" (Alvarez), **Supp. VII:** 5
Last Night of Summer, The (Caldwell), **I:** 292–293
"Last of the Brooding Miserables, The" (Karr), **Supp. XI:** 250
"Last of the Caddoes, The" (Humphrey), **Supp. IX:** 101
"Last of the Legions, The" (Benét), **Supp. XI:** 56, 57
Last of the Mohicans, The (Cooper), **I:** 341, 342, 349
Last of the Red Hot Lovers (Simon), **Supp. IV Part 2:** 575, 583, 589
"Last of the Valerii, The" (James), **II:** 327; **Retro. Supp. I:** 218
"Last One, The" (Merwin), **Supp. III Part 1:** 355
Last Picture Show, The (film), **Supp. V:** 223, 226
Last Picture Show, The (McMurtry), **Supp. V:** 220, 222–223, 233
Last Puritan, The (Santayana), **III:** 64, 600, 604, 607, 612, 615–617
"Last Ride Together, The" (Browning), **I:** 468
"Last River, The" (Kinnell), **Supp. III Part 1:** 236
Last Song, The (Harjo), **Supp. XII:** 218
"Last Song for the Mend-It Shop" (Nye), **Supp. XIII:** 283
"Last Tango in Fresno" (Salinas), **Supp. XIII:** 318
Last Tycoon, The: An Unfinished Novel (Fitzgerald), **II:** 84, 98; **Retro. Supp. I:** 109, 114, **114–115**; **Retro.**

Supp. II: 355; **Supp. IV Part 1:** 203; **Supp. IX:** 63; **Supp. XII:** 173; **Supp. XIII:** 170
"Last WASP in the World, The" (Fiedler), **Supp. XIII:** 103
Last Watch of the Night: Essays Too Personal and Otherwise (Monette), **Supp. X:** 147, 148, 153, **157–159**
Last Word, The: Letters between Marcia Nardi and William Carlos Williams (O'Neil, ed.), **Retro. Supp. I:** 427
"Last Words" (Levine), **Supp. V:** 190
"Last Words" (Olds), **Supp. X:** 210
Last Worthless Evening, The (Dubus), **Supp. VII:** 87–88
"Las Vegas (What?) Las Vegas (Can't Hear You! Too Noisy) Las Vegas! ! ! !" (Wolfe), **Supp. III Part 2:** 572
"Late" (Bogan), **Supp. III Part 1:** 53
"Late Air" (Bishop), **Supp. I Part 1:** 89
"Late Autumn" (Sarton), **Supp. VIII:** 261
Late Child, The (McMurtry), **Supp. V:** 231
"Late Conversation" (Doty), **Supp. XI:** 122
"Late Encounter with the Enemy, A" (O'Connor), **III:** 345; **Retro. Supp. II:** 232
Late Fire, Late Snow (Francis), **Supp. IX: 89–90**
Late George Apley, The (Marquand), **II:** 482–483; **III:** 50, 51, 52, 56–57, 58, 62–64, 65, 66
Late George Apley, The (Marquand and Kaufman), **III:** 62
Late Hour, The (Strand), **Supp. IV Part 2:** 620, 629–630
"Lately, at Night" (Kumin), **Supp. IV Part 2:** 442
"Late Moon" (Levine), **Supp. V:** 186
"Late Night Ode" (McClatchy), **Supp. XII:** 262–263
Later (Creeley), **Supp. IV Part 1:** 153, 156, 157
Later Life (Gurney), **Supp. V:** 103, 105
La Terre (Zola), **III:** 316, 322
Later the Same Day (Paley), **Supp. VI:** 218
Late Settings (Merrill), **Supp. III Part 1:** 336
"Late Sidney Lanier, The" (Stedman), **Supp. I Part 1:** 373
"Late Snow & Lumber Strike of the Summer of Fifty-Four, The" (Snyder), **Supp. VIII:** 294
"Latest Freed Man, The" (Stevens), **Retro. Supp. I:** 306

"Latest Injury, The" (Olds), **Supp. X:** 209

Latest Literary Essays and Addresses (Lowell), **Supp. I Part 2:** 407

"Late Subterfuge" (Warren), **IV:** 257

"Late Supper, A" (Jewett), **Retro. Supp. II:** 137

"Late Walk, A" (Frost), **II:** 153; **Retro. Supp. I:** 127

Latham, Edyth, **I:** 289

Lathrop, George Parsons, **Supp. I Part 1:** 365

Lathrop, H. B., **Supp. III Part 2:** 612

Lathrop, Julia, **Supp. I Part 1:** 5

Latière de Trianon, La (Wekerlin), **II:** 515

"La Tigresse" (Van Vechten), **Supp. II Part 2:** 735, 738

Latimer, Hugh, **II:** 15

Latimer, Margery, **Supp. IX:** 320

La Traviata (Verdi), **III:** 139

"Latter-Day Warnings" (Holmes), **Supp. I Part 1:** 307

La Turista (Shepard), **Supp. III Part 2:** 440

Lauber, John, **Supp. XIII:** 21

Laud, Archbishop, **II:** 158

"Lauds" (Auden), **Supp. II Part 1:** 23

"Laughing Man, The" (Salinger), **III:** 559

Laughing to Keep From Crying (Hughes), **Supp. I Part 1:** 329–330

Laughlin, J. Laurence, **Supp. I Part 2:** 641

Laughlin, James, **III:** 171; **Retro. Supp. I:** 423, 424, 428, 430, 431; **Supp. VIII:** 195

Laughlin, Jay, **Supp. II Part 1:** 94

Laughter in the Dark (Nabokov), **III:** 255–258; **Retro. Supp. I:** 270

Laughter on the 23rd Floor (Simon), **Supp. IV Part 2:** 575, 576, 588, 591–592

"Launcelot" (Lewis), **II:** 439–440

"Laura Dailey's Story" (Bogan), **Supp. III Part 1:** 52

Laurel, Stan, **Supp. I Part 2:** 607; **Supp. IV Part 2:** 574

Laurel and Hardy Go to Heaven (Auster), **Supp. XII:** 21

Laurence, Dan H., **II:** 338–339

Laurens, John, **Supp. I Part 2:** 509

Lautréamont, Comte de, **III:** 174

Law, John, **Supp. XI:** 307

Lawd Today (Wright), **IV:** 478, 492

Law for the Lion, A (Auchincloss), **Supp. IV Part 1:** 25

"Law Lane" (Jewett), **II:** 407

"Law of Nature and the Dream of Man, The: Ruminations of the Art of Fiction" (Stegner), **Supp. IV Part 2:** 604

Lawrence, D. H., **I:** 291, 336, 377, 522, 523; **II:** 78, 84, 98, 102, 264, 517, 523, 532, 594, 595; **III:** 27, 33, 40, 44, 46, 172, 173, 174, 178, 184, 229, 261, 423, 429, 458, 546–547; **IV:** 138, 339, 342, 351, 380; **Retro. Supp. I:** 7, 18, 203, 204, 421; **Retro. Supp. II:** 68; **Supp. I Part 1:** 227, 230, 243, 255, 257, 258, 263, 329; **Supp. I Part 2:** 546, 613, 728; **Supp. II Part 1:** 1, 9, 20, 89; **Supp. IV Part 1:** 81; **Supp. VIII:** 237; **Supp. X:** 137, 193, 194; **Supp. XII:** 172

Lawrence, Rhoda, **Supp. I Part 1:** 45

Lawrence, Seymour, **Supp. IX:** 107; **Supp. XI:** 335, 346, 348

Lawrence of Arabia (Aldington), **Supp. I Part 1:** 259

Lawrence of Arabia (film), **Supp. I Part 1:** 67

Laws (Plato), **Supp. IV Part 1:** 391

Laws of Ice, The (Price), **Supp. VI:** 264

Lawson, John Howard, **I:** 479, 482

Lawton Girl, The (Frederic), **II:** 132–133, 144

Layachi, Larbi (Driss ben Hamed Charhadi), **Supp. IV Part 1:** 92, 93

"Layers, The" (Kunitz), **Supp. III Part 1:** 260, 266–267

"Layers, The: Some Notes on 'The Abduction'" (Kunitz), **Supp. III Part 1:** 266

"Lay-mans Lamentation, The" (Taylor), **IV:** 162–163

Lay of the Land, The: Metaphor as Experience and History in American Life and Letters (Kolodny), **Supp. X:** 97

"Layover" (Hass), **Supp. VI:** 109

"Lay Preacher" (Dennie), **Supp. I Part 1:** 125

Layton, Irving, **Supp. XII:** 121

Lazarillo de Tormes (Mendoza), **III:** 182

Lazarus Laughed (O'Neill), **III:** 391, 395–396

Lazer, Hank, **Supp. IX:** 265

Lea, Luke, **IV:** 248

Leacock, Stephen, **Supp. IV Part 2:** 464

"LEADBELLY GIVES AN AUTOGRAPH" (Baraka), **Supp. II Part 1:** 49

Leaflets: Poems, 1965–1968 (Rich), **Retro. Supp. II:** 284; **Supp. I Part 2:** 551, 556–557

"League of American Writers, The: Communist Organizational Activity among American Writers 1929–1942" (Wolfe), **Supp. III Part 2:** 568

League of Brightened Philistines and Other Papers, The (Farrell), **II:** 49

Leaning Forward (Paley), **Supp. VI:** 221

"Leaning Tower, The" (Porter), **III:** 442, 443, 446–447

Leaning Tower and Other Stories, The (Porter), **III:** 433, 442, 443–447

"Leap, The" (Dickey), **Supp. IV Part 1:** 182

"Leaping Up into Political Poetry" (Bly), **Supp. IV Part 1:** 61, 63

Leap Year (Cameron), **Supp. XII:** 79–80, 81, **85–86**, 88

Lear, Edward, **III:** 428, 536

Lear, Linda, **Supp. IX:** 19, 22, 25, 26

Learned Ladies, The (Molière; Wilbur, trans.), **Supp. III Part 2:** 560

"Learning a Dead Language" (Merwin), **Supp. III Part 1:** 345

Learning a Trade: A Craftsman's Notebooks, 1955–1997 (Price), **Supp. VI:** 254, 255, 267

Learning to Love: Exploring Solitude and Freedom (Merton), **Supp. VIII:** 200

"Learning to Read" (Harper), **Supp. II Part 1:** 201–202

Leary, Lewis, **III:** 478

Leary, Paris, **Supp. IV Part 1:** 176

Leary, Timothy, **Supp. X:** 265

Least Heat Moon, William, **Supp. V:** 169

Leather-Stocking Tales, The (Cooper), **I:** 335

Leatherwood God, The (Howells), **II:** 276, 277, 288

"Leaves" (Updike), **Retro. Supp. I:** 323, 329, 335

Leaves and Ashes (Haines), **Supp. XII:** 206

Leaves from the Notebook of a Tamed Cynic (Niebuhr), **III:** 293

Leaves of Grass (Whitman), **II:** 8; **IV:** 331, 332, 333, 334, 335, 336, 340, 341–342, 348, 350, 405, 464; **Retro. Supp. I:** 387, 388, 389, 390, **392–395**, 406, 407, 408; **Retro. Supp. II:** 93; **Supp. I Part 1:** 365; **Supp. I Part 2:** 416, 579; **Supp. III Part 1:** 156; **Supp. V:** 170; **Supp. VIII:** 275; **Supp. IX:** 265; **Supp. X:** 120

"Leaves of Grass" (Whitman), **IV:** 463

Leaves of Grass (1856) (Whitman), **Retro. Supp. I:** 399–402

Leaves of Grass (1860) (Whitman), **Retro. Supp. I:** 402–405
Leaves of the Tree, The (Masters), **Supp. I Part 2:** 460
"Leaving" (Hogan), **Supp. IV Part 1:** 400
"Leaving" (Wilbur), **Supp. III Part 2:** 563
Leaving a Doll's House: A Memoir (C. Bloom), **Retro. Supp. II:** 299
Leaving Another Kingdom: Selected Poems (Stern), **Supp. IX:** 296
Leaving Cheyenne (McMurtry), **Supp. V:** 220, 221–222, 224, 229
"Leaving the Island" (Olds), **Supp. X:** 214
"Leaving the Yellow House" (Bellow), **Retro. Supp. II:** 27, 32
"Leaving Town" (Kenyon), **Supp. VII:** 163
Leavis, F. R., **I:** 522; **III:** 462–463, 475, 478; **Retro. Supp. I:** 67; **Retro. Supp. II:** 243; **Supp. I Part 2:** 536; **Supp. VIII:** 234, 236, 245
"Leavis-Snow Controversy, The" (Trilling), **Supp. III Part 2:** 512
Leavitt, David, **Supp. VIII:** 88
Le Braz, Anatole, **Supp. XIII:** 253
Lecker, Robert, **Supp. XIII:** 21
LeClair, Thomas, **Supp. IV Part 1:** 286
LeClair, Tom, **Supp. V:** 53; **Supp. XII:** 152
Le Conte, Joseph, **II:** 479; **III:** 227–228
"Lecture, The" (Singer), **IV:** 21
"LECTURE PAST DEAD CATS" (Baraka), **Supp. II Part 1:** 52
Lectures in America (Stein), **IV:** 27, 32, 33, 35, 36, 41, 42
"Lectures on Poetry" (Bryant), **Supp. I Part 1:** 159, 161
Lectures on Rhetoric (Blair), **II:** 8
"Leda and the Swan" (Yeats), **III:** 347; **Supp. IX:** 52
Ledger (Fitzgerald), **Retro. Supp. I:** 109, 110
Lee (Masters), **Supp. I Part 2:** 471
Lee, Don, **Supp. XII:** 295
Lee, Don L. *See* Madhubuti, Haki R.
Lee, Gypsy Rose, **II:** 586; **III:** 161; **Supp. IV Part 1:** 84
Lee, Harper, **Supp. VIII: 113–131**
Lee, James W., **Supp. IX:** 94, 97, 109
Lee, James Ward, **Supp. VIII:** 57
Lee, Robert E., **II:** 150, 206; **IV:** 126; **Supp. I Part 2:** 471, 486
Lee, Samuel, **IV:** 158
Lee, Spike, **Retro. Supp. II:** 12; **Supp. XI:** 19; **Supp. XIII:** 179, 186

Lee, Virginia Chin-lan, **Supp. X:** 291
Leeds, Barry, **Retro. Supp. II:** 204
Leeds, Daniel, **II:** 110
Leeds, Titan, **II:** 110, 111
Leeming, David, **Retro. Supp. II:** 4, 10
"Lees of Happiness, The" (Fitzgerald), **II:** 88
Left Out in the Rain: New Poems 1947–1985 (Snyder), **Supp. VIII:** 305
"Legacy" (Dunn), **Supp. XI:** 148
"Legacy" (Komunyakaa), **Supp. XIII:** 132
Legacy of Fear, A (Farrell), **II:** 39
Legacy of the Civil War, The: Meditations on the Centennial (Warren), **IV:** 236
"Legal Alien" (Mora), **Supp. XIII:** 215
Legal Kidnapping (Demeter), **Retro. Supp. II:** 285
"Legal Tender Act, The" (Adams), **I:** 5
Légende de la mort, La (Le Braz), **Supp. XIII:** 253
"Legend of Duluoz, The" (Kerouac), **Supp. III Part 1:** 218, 226, 227, 229
"Legend of Lillian Hellman, The" (Kazin), **Supp. I Part 1:** 297
"Legend of Monte del Diablo, The" (Harte), **Supp. II Part 1:** 339
"Legend of Paper Plates, The" (Haines), **Supp. XII:** 204
"Legend of Sammtstadt, A" (Harte), **Supp. II Part 1:** 355
"Legend of Sleepy Hollow, The" (Irving), **II:** 306–308
Legends (Lowell), **II:** 525–526
Legends of New England (Whittier), **Supp. I Part 2:** 684, 692
Legends of the Fall (Harrison), **Supp. VIII:** 38, 39, **45–46**, 48
Legends of the West (Hall), **II:** 313
Léger, Fernand, **Retro. Supp. I:** 292
Legge, James, **III:** 472
Leggett, William, **Supp. I Part 1:** 157
"Legion, The" (Karr), **Supp. XI:** 243
Legs (Kennedy), **Supp. VII:** 133, 134, 138–142, 143, 151
Le Guin, Ursula K., **Supp. IV Part 1:** 333
Lehan, Richard, **Retro. Supp. II:** 104
Lehman, David, **Supp. IX:** 161; **Supp. XIII:** 130
Lehmann, John, **Retro. Supp. II:** 243
Lehmann, Paul, **III:** 311
Lehmann-Haupt, Christopher, **Retro. Supp. II:** 309; **Supp. IV Part 1:** 205, 209, 306; **Supp. IX:** 95, 103
Leibniz, Gottfried Wilhelm von, **II:** 103; **III:** 428

Leibowitz, Herbert A., **I:** 386
Leithauser, Brad, **Retro. Supp. I:** 133
Leivick, H., **IV:** 6
Lekachman, Robert, **Supp. I Part 2:** 648
Leland, Charles, **Supp. II Part 1:** 193
Leland, Charles Godfrey, **I:** 257
Lem, Stanislaw, **Supp. IV Part 1:** 103
"Le marais du cygne" (Whittier), **Supp. I Part 2:** 687
Lemay, Harding, **Supp. VIII:** 125; **Supp. IX:** 98
Lemercier, Eugène, **Retro. Supp. I:** 299
Le Morte D'Arthur Notes (Gardner), **Supp. VI:** 65, 66
Lenin, V. I., **I:** 366, 439, 440; **III:** 14–15, 262, 475; **IV:** 429, 436, 443–444; **Supp. I Part 2:** 647
"Lenore" (Poe), **III:** 411
"Lenox Avenue: Midnight" (Hughes), **Retro. Supp. I:** 198
Leonard, Elmore, **Supp. IV Part 1:** 356; **Supp. X:** 5
Leonard, John, **Supp. IV Part 1:** 24; **Supp. IV Part 2:** 474; **Supp. V:** 164, 223–224; **Supp. XI:** 13
Leonardo da Vinci, **Supp. XII:** 44
Leopard, The (Lampedusa), **Supp. XII:** 13–14
Leopardi, Giacomo, **II:** 543
"Leopard Man's Story, The" (London), **II:** 475
Leopard's Mouth Is Dry and Cold Inside, The (Levis), **Supp. XI:** 258
Leopold, Aldo, **Supp. V:** 202; **Supp. X:** 108
"Leper's Bell, the" (Komunyakaa), **Supp. XIII:** 118
Lerman, Leo, **Supp. X:** 188
Lerner, Max, **III:** 60; **Supp. I Part 2:** 629, 630, 631, 647, 650, 654
"Lesbos" (Plath), **Retro. Supp. II:** 254
Lesesne, Teri, **Supp. XIII:** 277
Leskov, Nikolai, **IV:** 299
Leslie, Alfred, **Supp. XII:** 127
Les Misérables (Hugo), **II:** 179; **Supp. I Part 1:** 280
Lesser, Wendy, **Supp. IV Part 2:** 453; **Supp. XII:** 297
Lessing, Gotthold, **Supp. I Part 2:** 422
"Lesson, The" (Bambara), **Supp. XI:** 5–6
"Lesson, The" (Dunbar), **Supp. II Part 1:** 199
"Lesson, The" (Olsen), **Supp. XIII:** 297
"Lesson of the Master, The" (James), **Retro. Supp. I:** 227
Lesson of the Masters: An Anthology

of the Novel from Cervantes to Hemingway (Cowley-Hugo, ed.), **Supp. II Part 1:** 140
"Lesson on Concealment, A" (Brown), **Supp. I Part 1:** 133
"Lessons" (Epstein), **Supp. XII:** 163
"Lessons of the Body" (Simpson), **Supp. IX:** 267
Less than One (Brodsky), **Supp. VIII:** 22, 29–31
Lester, Jerry, **Supp. IV Part 2:** 574
Le Style Apollinaire (Zukofsky), **Supp. III Part 2:** 616
Le Sueur, Meridel, **Supp. V:** 113, 130; **Supp. XII:** 217
"Let America Be America Again" (Hughes), **Retro. Supp. I:** 202; **Supp. I Part 1:** 331
Let Evening Come (Kenyon), **Supp. VII:** 160, 169–171
Lethem, Jonathan, **Supp. IX:** 122
Let It Come Down (Bowles), **Supp. IV Part 1:** 87
"Let Me Be" (Levine), **Supp. V:** 181, 189
"Let Me Begin Again" (Levine), **Supp. V:** 181, 189
"Let No Charitable Hope" (Wylie), **Supp. I Part 2:** 713–714, 729
"Let one Eye his watches keep/While the Other Eye doth sleep" (Fletcher), **Supp. IV Part 2:** 621
"Letter . . ." (Whittier), **Supp. I Part 2:** 687
"Letter, A" (Bogan), **Supp. III Part 1:** 54
"Letter, May 2, 1959" (Olson), **Supp. II Part 2:** 579, 580
"Letter, Much Too Late" (Stegner), **Supp. IV Part 2:** 613
"Letter, The" (Malamud), **Supp. I Part 2:** 435–436
"Letter about Money, Love, or Other Comfort, If Any, The" (Warren), **IV:** 245
Letter Addressed to the People of Piedmont, on the Advantages of the French Revolution, and the Necessity of Adopting Its Principles in Italy, A (Barlow), **Supp. II Part 1:** 80, 81
"Letter for Marion, A" (McGrath), **Supp. X:** 116
"Letter from Aldermaston" (Merwin), **Supp. III Part 1:** 347
"Letter from a Region in My Mind" (Baldwin). *See* "Down at the Cross"
Letter from Li Po, A (Aiken), **I:** 68
"Letter from 'Manhattan'" (Didion), **Supp. IV Part 1:** 205

Letter from the End of the Twentieth Century (Harjo), **Supp. XII:** 223
"Letter from the End of the Twentieth Century" (Harjo), **Supp. XII:** 227
"Letter on Céline" (Kerouac), **Supp. III Part 1:** 232
Letters (Cato), **II:** 114
Letters (Landor), **Supp. I Part 2:** 422
Letters (White), **Supp. I Part 2:** 651, 653, 675, 680
Letters (Wolfe), **IV:** 462
Letters and Leadership (Brooks), **I:** 228, 240, 245, 246
"Letters for the Dead" (Levine), **Supp. V:** 186
Letters from an American Farmer (Crèvecoeur), **Supp. I Part 1:** 227–251
Letters from Maine (Sarton), **Supp. VIII:** 261
"Letters from Maine" (Sarton), **Supp. VIII:** 261
"Letters from My Father" (R. O. Butler), **Supp. XII:** 71
Letters from the Earth (Twain), **IV:** 209
Letters from the East (Bryant), **Supp. I Part 1:** 158
"Letters from the Ming Dynasty" (Brodsky), **Supp. VIII:** 28
"Letters in the Family" (Rich), **Retro. Supp. II:** 292
Letters of a Traveller (Bryant), **Supp. I Part 1:** 158
Letters of a Traveller, Second Series (Bryant), **Supp. I Part 1:** 158
Letters of Emily Dickinson, The (Johnson and Ward, eds.), **I:** 470; **Retro. Supp. I:** 28
Letters of Rosa Luxemburg (Bronner, trans.), **Retro. Supp. II:** 293
Letters of William James (Henry James, ed.), **II:** 362
Letters on Various Interesting and Important Subjects . . . (Freneau), **Supp. II Part 1:** 272
Letters to a Niece (Adams), **I:** 22
Letters to a Young Poet (Rilke), **Supp. XIII:** 74
"Letters to Dead Imagists" (Sandburg), **I:** 421
"Letters Written on a Ferry While Crossing Long Island Sound" (Sexton), **Supp. II Part 2:** 683
"Letter to Abbé Raynal" (Paine), **Supp. I Part 2:** 510
Letter to a Man in the Fire: Does God Exist or Does He Care? (Price), **Supp. VI:** 267–268
"Letter to American Teachers of History, A" (Adams), **I:** 19

Letter to an Imaginary Friend (McGrath), **Supp. X:** 111, 112–113, 116, **119–125**
"Letter to a Young Contributor" (Higginson), **Retro. Supp. I:** 31
"Letter to a Young Writer" (Price), **Supp. VI:** 267
"Letter to Bell from Missoula" (Hugo), **Supp. VI:** 142–143
"Letter to E. Franklin Frazier" (Baraka), **Supp. II Part 1:** 49
"Letter to Elaine Feinstein" (Olson), **Supp. II Part 2:** 561
"Letter to Freddy" (music) (Bowles), **Supp. IV Part 1:** 82
"Letter to Garber from Skye" (Hugo), **Supp. VI:** 146
"Letter to George Washington" (Paine), **Supp. I Part 2:** 517
"Letter to His Brother" (Berryman), **I:** 172, 173
Letter to His Countrymen, A (Cooper), **I:** 346, 347, 349
"Letter to Kizer from Seattle" (Hugo), **Supp. VI:** 142
Letter to Lord Byron (Auden), **Supp. II Part 1:** 11
"Letter to Lord Byron" (Mumford), **Supp. II Part 2:** 494
"Letter to Matthews from Barton Street Flats" (Hugo), **Supp. VI:** 133
"Letter to Minnesota" (Dunn), **Supp. XI:** 146
"Letter to Mr." (Poe), **III:** 411
"Letter Too Late to Vallejo" (Salinas), **Supp. XIII:** 313, 324
"Letter to Sister Madeline from Iowa City" (Hugo), **Supp. VI:** 142–143
"Letter to Soto" (Salinas), **Supp. XIII:** 325
"Letter to the Lady of the House" (Bausch), **Supp. VII:** 48
"Letter to the Rising Generation, A" (Comer), **I:** 214
"Letter to Walt Whitman" (Doty), **Supp. XI:** 135–136
"Letter to Wendell Berry, A" (Stegner), **Supp. IV Part 2:** 600
"Letter Writer, The" (Singer), **IV:** 20–21
"Let the Air Circulate" (Clampitt), **Supp. IX:** 45
"Letting Down of the Hair, The" (Sexton), **Supp. II Part 2:** 692
Letting Go (Roth), **Retro. Supp. II:** 300, 301; **Supp. III Part 2:** 403, 404, 409–412
"Letting the Puma Go" (Dunn), **Supp. XI:** 149
"Lettres d'un Soldat" (Stevens), **Retro.**

Supp. I: 299
Let Us Now Praise Famous Men (Agee and Evans), **I:** 25, 27, 35, 36–39, 42, 45, 293
Let Your Mind Alone! (Thurber), **Supp. I Part 2:** 608
Leutze, Emanuel, **Supp. X:** 307
Levels of the Game (McPhee), **Supp. III Part 1:** 292, 294, 301
Levertov, Denise, **Retro. Supp. I:** 411; **Supp. III Part 1: 271–287; Supp. III Part 2:** 541; **Supp. IV Part 1:** 325; **Supp. VIII:** 38, 39
Levi, Primo, **Supp. X:** 149
Leviathan (Auster), **Supp. XII:** 27, **33–34**
"Leviathan" (Lowell), **II:** 537, 538
"Leviathan" (Merwin), **Supp. III Part 1:** 345
Levin, Harry, **Supp. I Part 2:** 647
Levin, Jennifer, **Supp. X:** 305
Levine, Ellen, **Supp. V:** 4; **Supp. XI:** 178
Levine, Paul, **Supp. IV Part 1:** 221, 224
Levine, Philip, **Supp. III Part 2:** 541; **Supp. V: 177–197,** 337; **Supp. IX:** 293; **Supp. XI:** 123, 257, 259, 267, 271, 315; **Supp. XIII:** 312
Levine, Rosalind, **Supp. XII:** 123
Levine, Sherry, **Supp. XII:** 4
Le Violde Lucréce (Obey), **IV:** 356
Levis, Larry, **Supp. V:** 180; **Supp. IX:** 299; **Supp. XI: 257–274; Supp. XIII:** 312
Lévi-Strauss, Claude, **Supp. I Part 2:** 636; **Supp. IV Part 1:** 45; **Supp. IV Part 2:** 490
Levitation: Five Fictions (Ozick), **Supp. V:** 268–270
Levy, Alan, **Supp. IV Part 2:** 574, 589
Levy, G. Rachel, **Supp. I Part 2:** 567
Lévy-Bruhl, Lucien, **Retro. Supp. I:** 57
Levy Mayer and the New Industrial Era (Masters), **Supp. I Part 2:** 473
Lewes, George Henry, **II:** 569
Lewis, C. Day, **III:** 527
Lewis, Dr. Claude, **II:** 442
Lewis, Edith, **I:** 313; **Retro. Supp. I:** 19, 21, 22
Lewis, Edwin, J., **II:** 439, 442
Lewis, Jerry, **Supp. IV Part 2:** 575; **Supp. X:** 172
Lewis, John L., **I:** 493
Lewis, Lilburn, **IV:** 243
Lewis, Lorene, **Supp. IV Part 2:** 596, 597
Lewis, Lucy, **IV:** 243
Lewis, Maggie, **Supp. V:** 23

Lewis, Meriwether, **II:** 217; **III:** 14; **IV:** 179, 243, 283
Lewis, Merrill, **Supp. IV Part 2:** 596, 597
Lewis, Michael, **II:** 451, 452
Lewis, Mrs. Sinclair (Dorothy Thompson), **II:** 449–450, 451, 453
Lewis, Mrs. Sinclair (Grace Livingston Hegger), **II:** 441
Lewis, R. W. B., **I:** 386, 561; **II:** 457–458; **Retro. Supp. I:** 362, 367; **Supp. I Part 1:** 233; **Supp. XIII:** 93
Lewis, Robert Q., **Supp. IV Part 2:** 574
Lewis, Sinclair, **I:** 116, 212, 348, 355, 362, 374, 378, 487, 495; **II:** 27, 34, 74, 79, 271, 277, 306, **439–461,** 474; **III:** 28, 40, 51, 60, 61, 63–64, 66, 70, 71, 106, 394, 462, 572, 606; **IV:** 53, 326, 366, 455, 468, 475, 482; **Retro. Supp. I:** 332; **Retro. Supp. II:** 95, 108, 197, 340; **Supp. I Part 2:** 378, 613, 709; **Supp. IV Part 2:** 678; **Supp. V:** 278; **Supp. IX:** 308; **Supp. X:** 137
Lewis, Wyndham, **III:** 458, 462, 465, 470; **Retro. Supp. I:** 59, 170, 292; **Supp. III Part 2:** 617
Lexicon Tetraglotton (Howell), **II:** 111
"Leyenda" (Mora), **Supp. XIII:** 214
Leyte (Morison), **Supp. I Part 2:** 491
"Liar, The" (Baraka), **Supp. II Part 1:** 36
"Liars, The" (Sandburg), **III:** 586
Liars' Club, The: A Memoir (Karr), **Supp. XI:** 239, 240, 241, 242, **244–248,** 252, 254
Liars in Love (Yates), **Supp. XI:** 348, 349
Libation Bearers, The (Aeschylus), **III:** 398; **Supp. IX:** 103
Libby, Anthony, **Supp. XIII:** 87
Libera, Padre, **II:** 278
Liberal Imagination, The (Trilling), **III:** 308; **Retro. Supp. I:** 97, 216; **Supp. II Part 1:** 146; **Supp. III Part 2:** 495, 498, 501–504
"Liberation" (Winters), **Supp. II Part 2:** 791
Liber Brunensis (yearbook), **IV:** 286
Liberties, The (Howe), **Supp. IV Part 2:** 426–428, 430, 432
Liberty Jones (play), **Supp. IV Part 1:** 83
"Liberty Tree" (Paine), **Supp. I Part 2:** 505
Libra (DeLillo), **Supp. VI:** 2, **4, 5, 6, 7,** 9, 10, 12, 13, 14, 16
Library for Juana, A (Mora), **Supp. XIII:** 218
Library of America, **Retro. Supp. I:** 2
"Library of Law, A" (MacLeish), **III:** 4
Lice, The (Merwin), **Supp. III Part 1:** 339, 341–342, 346, 348, 349, 355
Lichtenstein, Roy, **Supp. I Part 2:** 665
"Liddy's Orange" (Olds), **Supp. X:** 209
Lieberman, Laurence, **Supp. XI:** 323–324
Liebestod (Wagner), **I:** 284, 395
Liebling, A. J., **IV:** 290; **Supp. VIII:** 151
Lie Down in Darkness (Styron), **IV:** 98, 99, 100–104, 105, 111; **Supp. XI:** 343
Lie of the Mind, A (Shepard), **Supp. III Part 2:** 433, 435, 441, 447–449
"Lies" (Haines), **Supp. XII:** 204
Lies Like Truth (Clurman), **IV:** 385
Lieutenant, The (Dubus), **Supp. VII:** 78
"Life" (Wharton), **Retro. Supp. I:** 372
Life along the Passaic River (W. C. Williams), **Retro. Supp. I:** 423
Life Among the Savages (Jackson), **Supp. IX:** 115, **125**
Life and Gabriella (Glasgow), **II:** 175, 176, 182–183, 184, 189
"Life and I" (Wharton), **Retro. Supp. I:** 360, 361, 362
Life and Letters of Harrison Gray Otis, Federalist, 1765–1848, The (Morison), **Supp. I Part 2:** 480–481
Life and Times of Frederick Douglass, Written by Himself, The (Douglass), **Supp. III Part 1:** 155, 159–163
Life and Writings of Horace McCoy, The (Wolfson), **Supp. XIII:** 172, 174
"Life as a Visionary Spirit" (Eberhart), **I:** 540, 541
"Life at Angelo's, A" (Benét), **Supp. XI:** 53
Life at Happy Knoll (Marquand), **III:** 50, 61
Life Before Man (Atwood), **Supp. XIII: 24–25**
"Life Cycle of Common Man" (Nemerov), **III:** 278
"Lifecycle Stairmaster" (Karr), **Supp. XI:** 250
Life Estates (Hearon), **Supp. VIII: 68–69**
Life for Life's Sake (Aldington), **Supp. I Part 1:** 256
Life Full of Holes, A (Layachi), **Supp. IV Part 1:** 92
"Lifeguard" (Updike), **IV:** 226; **Retro.**

Supp. I: 325
"Lifeguard, The" (Dickey), **Supp. IV Part 1:** 179–180
Life in the Clearings (Shields), **Supp. VII:** 313
"Life in the Country: A City Friend Asks, 'Is It Boring?'" (Paley), **Supp. VI:** 231
Life in the Forest (Levertov), **Supp. III Part 1:** 282–283
Life in the Iron Mills (Davis), **Supp. XIII:** 292, 295, 299, 305
Life Is a Miracle: An Essay Against Modern Superstition (Berry), **Supp. X:** 35
"Life Is Fine" (Hughes), **Supp. I Part 1:** 334, 338
"Life Is Motion" (Stevens), **IV:** 74
Life of Albert Gallatin, The (Adams), **I:** 6, 14
Life of Dryden (Johnson), **Retro. Supp. II:** 223
Life of Emily Dickinson, The (Sewall), **Retro. Supp. I:** 25
Life of Forms, The (Focillon), **IV:** 90
Life of Franklin Pierce (Hawthorne), **Retro. Supp. I:** 163
Life of George Cabot Lodge, The (Adams), **I:** 21
Life of George Washington (Irving), **II:** 314, 315–316
Life of Henry James (Edel), **Retro. Supp. I:** 224
"Life of Irony, The" (Bourne), **I:** 219
"Life of Lincoln West, The" (Brooks), **Supp. III Part 1:** 86
Life of Michelangelo (Grimm), **II:** 17
"Life of Nancy, The" (Jewett), **Retro. Supp. II:** 133, 144
Life of Oliver Goldsmith, The, with Selections from His Writings (Irving), **II:** 315
Life of Phips (Mather), **Supp. II Part 2:** 451, 452, 459
Life of Poetry, The (Rukeyser), **Supp. VI:** 271, 273, 275–276, 282, 283, 286
Life of Samuel Johnson (Boswell), **Supp. I Part 2:** 656
Life of Savage (Johnson), **Supp. I Part 2:** 523
Life of the Drama, The (Bentley), **IV:** 396
Life of the Right Reverend Joseph P. Machebeuf, The (Howlett), **Retro. Supp. I:** 17
Life of Thomas Paine, author of Rights of Men, With a Defence of his Writings (Chalmers), **Supp. I Part 2:** 514

Life of Thomas Paine, The (Cobbett), **Supp. I Part 2:** 517
"Life of Towne, The" (Carson), **Supp. XII:** 102
"Life on Beekman Place, A" (Naylor), **Supp. VIII:** 214
Life on the Hyphen: The Cuban-American Way (Firmat), **Supp. VIII:** 76; **Supp. XI:** 184
Life on the Mississippi (Twain), **I:** 209; **IV:** 198, 199; **Supp. I Part 2:** 440
"Life on the Rocks: The Galápagos" (Dillard), **Supp. VI:** 32
Life Story (Baker), **II:** 259
Life Studies (Lowell), **I:** 400; **II:** 384, 386, 543, 546–550, 551, 555; **Retro. Supp. II:** 180, 185, 186, 188, 189, 191; **Supp. I Part 2:** 543; **Supp. XI:** 240, 244, 250, 317; **Supp. XII:** 255
"Life Studies" (Lowell), **Retro. Supp. II:** 188
"Life Styles in the Golden Land" (Didion), **Supp. IV Part 1:** 200
"Life That Is, The" (Bryant), **Supp. I Part 1:** 169
"Life Work" (Stafford), **Supp. XI:** 329–330
"Life You Save May Be Your Own, The" (O'Connor), **III:** 344, 350, 354; **Retro. Supp. II:** 229, 230, 233
"Lifting, The" (Olds), **Supp. X:** 210
"Ligeia" (Poe), **III:** 412, 414; **Retro. Supp. II:** 261, 270, 271, 275
Liggett, Walter W., **Supp. XIII:** 168
Light, James F., **IV:** 290; **Retro. Supp. II:** 343
Light around the Body, The (Bly), **Supp. IV Part 1:** 61–62, 62
"Light Comes Brighter, The" (Roethke), **III:** 529–530
"Light from Above" (Eberhart), **I:** 541
Light in August (Faulkner), **II:** 63–64, 65, 74; **IV:** 207; **Retro. Supp. I:** 82, 84, 85, 86, 89, 92
"Light Man, A" (James), **II:** 322; **Retro. Supp. I:** 219
"Lightning" (Barthelme), **Supp. IV Part 1:** 53
"Lightning" (Oliver), **Supp. VII:** 235
"Lightning, The" (Swenson), **Supp. IV Part 2:** 645
"Lightning Rod Man, The" (Melville), **III:** 90
"Light of the World, The" (Hemingway), **II:** 249
"Lights in the Windows" (Nye), **Supp. XIII:** 280
Light Years (Salter), **Supp. IX:** 257–259
"LIKE, THIS IS WHAT I MEANT!"

(Baraka), **Supp. II Part 1:** 59
"Like All the Other Nations" (Paley), **Supp. VI:** 220
"Like Decorations in a Nigger Cemetery" (Stevens), **IV:** 74, 79; **Retro. Supp. I:** 305
Like Ghosts of Eagles (Francis), **Supp. IX:** 86
"Like Life" (Moore), **Supp. X:** 163, 165, **172–173**
Like Life: Stories (Moore), **Supp. X:** 163, **171–175**, 177, 178
"Like Talk" (Mills), **Supp. XI:** 311
"Like the New Moon I Will Live My Life" (Bly), **Supp. IV Part 1:** 71
Li'l Abner (Capp), **IV:** 198
"Lilacs" (Lowell), **II:** 527
"Lilacs, The" (Wilbur), **Supp. III Part 2:** 557–558
"Lilacs for Ginsberg" (Stern), **Supp. IX:** 299
Lilith's Brood (O. Butler), **Supp. XIII:** 63
Lillabulero Press, **Supp. V:** 4, 5
Lillian Hellman (Adler), **Supp. I Part 1:** 297
Lillian Hellman (Falk), **Supp. I Part 1:** 297
Lillian Hellman: Playwright (Moody), **Supp. I Part 1:** 280
Lillo, George, **II:** 111, 112
"Lily Daw and the Three Ladies" (Welty), **IV:** 262
Lima, Agnes de, **I:** 231, 232
"Limbo: Altered States" (Karr), **Supp. XI:** 249–250
Lime Orchard Woman, The (Ríos), **Supp. IV Part 2:** 538, 547–550, 553
"Lime Orchard Woman, The" (Ríos), **Supp. IV Part 2:** 548
"Limits" (Emerson), **II:** 19
Lincoln, Abraham, **I:** 1, 4, 30; **II:** 8, 13, 135, 273, 555, 576; **III:** 576, 577, 580, 584, 587–590, 591; **IV:** 192, 195, 298, 347, 350, 444; **Supp. I Part 1:** 2, 8, 26, 309, 321; **Supp. I Part 2:** 379, 380, 382, 385, 390, 397, 399, 418, 424, 454, 456, 471, 472, 473, 474, 483, 579, 687; **Supp. VIII:** 108; **Supp. IX:** 15
Lincoln: A Novel (Vidal), **Supp. IV Part 2:** 677, 684, 685, 688, 689–690, 691, 692
Lincoln, Kenneth, **Supp. IV Part 1:** 329; **Supp. IV Part 2:** 507
Lincoln, Mrs. Thomas (Nancy Hanks), **III:** 587
Lincoln: The Man (Masters), **Supp. I Part 2:** 471, 473–474
Lincoln, Thomas, **III:** 587

"Lincoln Relics, The" (Kunitz), **Supp. III Part 1:** 269
Lindbergh, Charles A., **I:** 482
"Linden Branch, The" (MacLeish), **III:** 19, 20
Linden Hills (Naylor), **Supp. VIII:** 214, 218, **219–223**
Linderman, Lawrence, **Supp. IV Part 2:** 579, 583, 585, 589
Lindsay, Howard, **III:** 284
Lindsay, John, **Supp. I Part 2:** 374
Lindsay, Mrs. Vachel (Elizabeth Connors), **Supp. I Part 2:** 398, 399, 473
Lindsay, Mrs. Vachel Thomas (Esther Catherine Frazee), **Supp. I Part 2:** 374, 375, 384–385, 398
Lindsay, Olive, **Supp. I Part 2:** 374, 375, 392
Lindsay, Vachel, **I:** 384; **II:** 263, 276, 530; **III:** 5, 505; **Retro. Supp. I:** 133; **Supp. I Part 1:** 324; **Supp. I Part 2:** 374–403, 454, 473, 474; **Supp. III Part 1:** 63, 71
Lindsay, Vachel Thomas, **Supp. I Part 2:** 374, 375
"Line, The" (Olds), **Supp. X:** 206
Lineage of Ragpickers, Songpluckers, Elegiasts, and Jewelers, A (Goldbarth), **Supp. XII:** 191
"Line of Least Resistance, The" (Wharton), **Retro. Supp. I:** 366
"Liner Notes for the Poetically Unhep" (Hughes), **Retro. Supp. I:** 210
"Lines After Rereading T. S. Eliot" (Wright), **Supp. V:** 343
"Lines Composed a Few Miles Above Tintern Abbey" (Wordsworth), **Supp. III Part 1:** 12
"Lines for an Interment" (MacLeish), **III:** 15
"Lines for My Father" (Cullen), **Supp. IV Part 1:** 167
"Lines from Israel" (Lowell), **II:** 554
"Lines on Revisiting the Country" (Bryant), **Supp. I Part 1:** 164
"Lines Suggested by a Tennessee Song" (Agee), **I:** 28
"Line-Storm Song, A" (Frost), **Retro. Supp. I:** 127
"Lines Written at Port Royal" (Freneau), **Supp. II Part 1:** 264
Lingeman, Richard, **Supp. X:** 82
Linn, Elizabeth. *See* Brown, Mrs. Charles Brockden (Elizabeth Linn)
Linn, John Blair, **Supp. I Part 1:** 145
Linnaeus, Carolus, **II:** 6; **Supp. I Part 1:** 245
"Linnets" (Levis), **Supp. XI:** 260, 261
"Linoleum Roses" (Cisneros), **Supp. VII:** 63, 66
Linotte: 1914–1920 (Nin), **Supp. X:** 193, 196, 197
Linschoten, Hans, **II:** 362, 363, 364
"Lion and Honeycomb" (Nemerov), **III:** 275, 278, 280
Lion and the Archer, The (Hayden), **Supp. II Part 1:** 366, 367
Lion and the Honeycomb, The (Blackmur), **Supp. II Part 1:** 91
Lion Country (Buechner), **Supp. XII:** 52, 53
Lionel Lincoln (Cooper), **I:** 339, 342
"Lion for Real, The" (Ginsberg), **Supp. II Part 1:** 320
Lion in the Garden (Meriweather and Millgate), **Retro. Supp. I:** 91
"Lionizing" (Poe), **III:** 411, 425
"Lions, Harts, and Leaping Does" (Powers), **III:** 356
"Lions in Sweden" (Stevens), **IV:** 79–80
Lipman, William R., **Supp. XIII:** 170
Li Po, **Supp. XI:** 241; **Supp. XII:** 218
Lippmann, Walter, **I:** 48, 222–223, 225; **III:** 291, 600; **IV:** 429; **Supp. I Part 2:** 609, 643; **Supp. VIII:** 104
Lips Together, Teeth Apart (McNally), **Supp. XIII: 201–202,** 208, 209
Lipton, James, **Supp. IV Part 2:** 576, 577, 579, 583, 586, 588
Lipton, Lawrence, **Supp. IX:** 3
Lisbon Traviata, The (McNally), **Supp. XIII:** 198, **199–200,** 201, 204, 208
Lisicky, Paul, **Supp. XI:** 120, 131, 135
"Lisp, The" (Olds), **Supp. X:** 211
"Listeners and Readers: The Unforgetting of Vachel Lindsay" (Trombly), **Supp. I Part 2:** 403
"Listening" (Paley), **Supp. VI:** 218, 231, 232
"Listening" (Stafford), **Supp. XI:** 321, 322
"Listening to the Desert" (Henderson), **Supp. XIII:** 221–222
"Listening to the Mockingbird" (Woodard), **Supp. VIII:** 128
Listening to Your Life: Daily Meditations with Frederick Buechner (Buechner), **Supp. XII:** 53
Listen to the Desert/Oye al desierto (Mora), **Supp. XIII:** 221
"Listen to the People" (Benét), **Supp. XI:** 51–52
Liston, Sonny, **III:** 38, 42
Li T'ai-po, **II:** 526
"Litany" (Ashbery), **Supp. III Part 1:** 21–22, 25, 26
"Litany" (Sandburg), **III:** 593
"Litany for Dictatorships" (Benét), **Supp. XI:** 46, 58
"Litany for Survival, A" (Lorde), **Supp. XII:** 220
"Litany of the Dark People, The" (Cullen), **Supp. IV Part 1:** 170, 171
"Litany of the Heroes" (Lindsay), **Supp. I Part 2:** 397
"Litany of Washington Street, The" (Lindsay), **Supp. I Part 2:** 376, 398–399
Literary Anthropology (Trumpener and Nyce), **Retro. Supp. I:** 380
"Literary Blacks and Jews" (Ozick), **Supp. V:** 272
"Literary Criticism of Georg Lukács, The" (Sontag), **Supp. III Part 2:** 453
Literary Essays of Thomas Merton, The, **Supp. VIII:** 207
Literary Friends and Acquaintance (Howells), **Supp. I Part 1:** 318
Literary History of the United States (Spiller et al., ed.), **Supp. I Part 1:** 104; **Supp. II Part 1:** 95
"Literary Importation" (Freneau), **Supp. II Part 1:** 264
"Literary Life of America, The" (Brooks), **I:** 245
Literary Situation, The (Cowley), **Supp. II Part 1:** 135, 140, 144, 146, 147, 148
"Literary Worker's Polonius, The" (Wilson), **IV:** 431, 432
"Literature" (Emerson), **II:** 6
Literature and American Life (Boynton), **Supp. I Part 2:** 415
Literature and Morality (Farrell), **II:** 49
"Literature and Place: Varieties of Regional Experience" (Erisman), **Supp. VIII:** 126
"Literature as a Symptom" (Warren), **IV:** 237
"Literature of Exhaustion, The" (Barth), **Supp. IV Part 1:** 48
"Lithuanian Nocturne" (Brodsky), **Supp. VIII:** 29
"Lit Instructor" (Stafford), **Supp. XI:** 321
Littauer, Kenneth, **Retro. Supp. I:** 114
Little Big Man (Berger), **Supp. XII:** 171
Little Big Man (film), **Supp. X:** 124
Littlebird, Harold, **Supp. IV Part 2:** 499
Littlebird, Larry, **Supp. IV Part 2:** 499, 505
Little Birds: Erotica (Nin), **Supp. X:** 192, 195
"Little Brown Baby" (Dunbar), **Supp.**

II Part 1: 206
"Little Brown Jug" (Baraka), **Supp. II Part 1:** 51
"Little Clown, My Heart" (Cisneros), **Supp. VII:** 71
"Little Cosmic Dust Poem" (Haines), **Supp. XII:** 209–210
"Little Country Girl, A" (Chopin), **Retro. Supp. II:** 71
"Little Curtis" (Parker), **Supp. IX:** 193
Little Disturbances of Man, The (Paley), **Supp. VI:** 218
"Little Dog" (Hughes), **Supp. I Part 1:** 329
Little Dorrit (Dickens), **Supp. I Part 1:** 35
"Little Edward" (Stowe), **Supp. I Part 2:** 587
"Little Expressionless Animals" (Wallace), **Supp. X:** 305
Littlefield, Catherine, **Supp. IX:** 58
Little Foxes, The (Hellman), **Supp. I Part 1:** 276, 278–279, 281, 283, 297
"Little Fred, the Canal Boy" (Stowe), **Supp. I Part 2:** 587
"Little French Mary" (Jewett), **II:** 400
Little Friend, Little Friend (Jarrell), **II:** 367, 372, 375–376
"Little Gidding" (Eliot), **I:** 582, 588; **II:** 539; **Retro. Supp. I:** 66
"Little Girl, My Stringbean, My Lovely Woman" (Sexton), **Supp. II Part 2:** 686
"Little Girl, The" (Paley), **Supp. VI:** 222, **228–229**
"Little Girl Tells a Story to a Lady, A" (Barnes), **Supp. III Part 1:** 36
"Little Goose Girl, The" (Grimm), **IV:** 266
Little Ham (Hughes), **Retro. Supp. I:** 203; **Supp. I Part 1:** 328, 339
Little Lady of the Big House, The (London), **II:** 481–482
"Little Lion Face" (Swenson), **Supp. IV Part 2:** 651
"Little Lobelia's Song" (Bogan), **Supp. III Part 1:** 66
"Little Local Color, A" (Henry), **Supp. II Part 1:** 399
Little Lord Fauntleroy (Burnett), **Retro. Supp. I:** 188
"Little Lyric" (Hughes), **Supp. I Part 1:** 334
Little Man, Little Man (Baldwin), **Supp. I Part 1:** 67
"Little Man at Chehaw Station, The" (Ellison), **Retro. Supp. II:** 123
Little Me (musical), **Supp. IV Part 2:** 575
Little Men (Alcott), **Supp. I Part 1:** 32, 39, 40
"Little Morning Music, A" (Schwartz), **Supp. II Part 2:** 662–663
Little Ocean (Shepard), **Supp. III Part 2:** 447
"Little Old Girl, A" (Larcom), **Supp. XIII:** 144
"Little Old Spy" (Hughes), **Supp. I Part 1:** 329
"Little Owl Who Lives in the Orchard" (Oliver), **Supp. VII:** 239
"Little Peasant, The" (Sexton), **Supp. II Part 2:** 690
"Little Rapids, The" (Swenson), **Supp. IV Part 2:** 645
Little Regiment and Other Episodes of the American Civil War, The (Crane), **I:** 408
"Little Road not made of Man , A" (Dickinson), **Retro. Supp. I:** 44
Little Sister, The (Chandler), **Supp. IV Part 1:** 122, 130, 131–132
"Little Sleep's-Head Sprouting Hair in the Moonlight" (Kinnell), **Supp. III Part 1:** 247
"Little Snow White" (Grimm), **IV:** 266
"Little Testament of Bernard Martin, Aet. 30" (Mumford), **Supp. II Part 2:** 472, 473, 474
"Little Things" (Olds), **Supp. X:** 208
Little Tour in France (James), **II:** 337
Little Women (Alcott), **Supp. I Part 1:** 28, 29, 32, 35, 37, 38, 39–40, 41, 43, 44; **Supp. IX:** 128
Little Yellow Dog, A (Mosley), **Supp. XIII:** 237, 241
"Liturgy and Spiritual Personalism" (Merton), **Supp. VIII:** 199
Litz, A. Walton, **Retro. Supp. I:** 306
"Liu Ch'e" (Pound), **III:** 466
"Live" (Sexton), **Supp. II Part 2:** 684, 686
Live from Golgotha (Vidal), **Supp. IV Part 2:** 677, 682, 691, 692
Live Now and Pay Later (Garrett), **Supp. VII:** 111
"Live-Oak with Moss" (Whitman), **Retro. Supp. I:** 403
Live or Die (Sexton), **Supp. II Part 2:** 670, 683–687
Liveright, Horace, **Retro. Supp. I:** 80, 81, 83; **Supp. I Part 2:** 464
Lives (Plutarch), **II:** 5, 104
Lives of a Cell, The (L. Thomas), **Retro. Supp. I:** 322, 323
Lives of Distinguished American Naval Officers (Cooper), **I:** 347
"Lives of Gulls and Children, The" (Nemerov), **III:** 271, 272
Lives of the Artists (Vasari), **Supp. I Part 2:** 450
Lives of the Poets (Doctorow), **Supp. IV Part 1:** 234
"Lives of the Poets" (Doctorow), **Supp. IV Part 1:** 234
"Lives of the—Wha'?, The" (Goldbarth), **Supp. XII:** 191
Living, The (Dillard), **Supp. VI:** 23
"Living at Home" (Gordon), **Supp. IV Part 1:** 311
Living by Fiction (Dillard), **Supp. VI:** 23, 31, **32,** 33
Living by the Word (Walker), **Supp. III Part 2:** 521, 522, 526, 527, 535
Living End, The (Elkin), **Supp. VI: 54,** 58
"Living in Sin" (Rich), **Retro. Supp. II:** 280–281
"Living Like Weasels" (Dillard), **Supp. VI:** 26, 33
Living Novel, The (Hicks), **III:** 342
Living of Charlotte Perkins Gilman, The (Gilman), **Supp. XI:** 193, 209
Living off the Country: Essays on Poetry and Place (Haines), **Supp. XII:** 199, 203, 207
Living Reed, The (Buck), **Supp. II Part 1:** 129–130
Living Theater, **Retro. Supp. I:** 424
"Living There" (Dickey), **Supp. IV Part 1:** 182–183
Living the Spirit: A Gay American Indian Anthology (Roscoe, ed.), **Supp. IV Part 1:** 330
"Living with a Peacock" (O'Connor), **III:** 350
"Livvie" (Welty), **IV:** 265; **Retro. Supp. I:** 348–349
"Livvie Is Back" (Welty), **Retro. Supp. I:** 351
Livy, **II:** 8
Lizzie (film), **Supp. IX:** 125
"Llantos de La Llorona: Warnings from the Wailer" (Mora), **Supp. XIII:** 217, 224
"L'Lapse" (Barthelme), **Supp. IV Part 1:** 45–47, 48
Lloyd, Henry Demarest, **Supp. I Part 1:** 5
Lloyd George, Harold, **I:** 490
"LMFBR" (Snyder), **Supp. VIII:** 302
"Loam" (Sandburg), **III:** 584–585
"Loan, The" (Malamud), **Supp. I Part 2:** 427, 428, 431, 437
Local Color (Capote), **Supp. III Part 1:** 120
"Local Color" (London), **II:** 475
Local Girls (Hoffman), **Supp. X:** 77, **90–91,** 92
"Local Girls" (Hoffman), **Supp. X:** 90

INDEX / 483

Local Time (Dunn), **Supp. XI:** 143, **148–149**
Lock, Helen, **Supp. XIII:** 233, 237–238
Lock, Robert H., **IV:** 319; **Retro. Supp. I:** 375
Locke, Alain, **Retro. Supp. II:** 115; **Supp. I Part 1:** 323, 325, 341; **Supp. II Part 1:** 53, 176, 182, 228, 247; **Supp. IV Part 1:** 170; **Supp. IX:** 306, 309; **Supp. X:** 134, 137, 139
Locke, Duane, **Supp. IX:** 273
Locke, John, **I:** 554–555, 557; **II:** 15–16, 113–114, 348–349, 480; **III:** 294–295; **IV:** 149; **Supp. I Part 1:** 130, 229, 230; **Supp. I Part 2:** 523
Locke, Sondra, **II:** 588
"Locked House, A" (Snodgrass), **Supp. VI:** 323
Locked Room, The (Auster), **Supp. XII:** 22, 24, **27–28**
Locket, The (Masters), **Supp. I Part 2:** 460
"Locksley Hall" (Tennyson), **Supp. IX:** 19
Lockwood Concern, The (O'Hara), **III:** 362, 364, 377–382
"Locus" (Ammons), **Supp. VII:** 28
"Locus" (Hayden), **Supp. II Part 1:** 361–362, 381
Loden, Barbara, **III:** 163
Lodge, Henry Cabot, **I:** 11–12, 21
Lodge, Mrs. Henry Cabot, **I:** 11–12, 19
Lodge, Thomas, **IV:** 370
Loeb, Gerald, **Supp. IV Part 2:** 523
Loeb, Jacques, **I:** 513; **Retro. Supp. II:** 104; **Supp. I Part 2:** 641
Loeffler, Jack, **Supp. XIII:** 1, 3, 12, 14, 16
"Log" (Merrlll), **Supp. III Part 1:** 328
Logan, Rayford W., **Supp. II Part 1:** 171, 194
Logan, William, **Supp. X:** 201, 213; **Supp. XI:** 131, 132; **Supp. XII:** 98, 107, 113, 184
Log Book of "The Loved One," The, **Supp. XI:** 306
Lohengrin (Wagner), **I:** 216
Lohrfinck, Rosalind, **III:** 107, 117
Lolita (Nabokov), **III:** 246, 247, 255, 258–261; **Retro. Supp. I:** 263, 264, 265, 266, 269, 270, **272–274**, 275; **Supp. V:** 127, 252; **Supp. VIII:** 133
"Lolita" (Parker), **Supp. IX:** 193
Lombardi, Marilyn May, **Retro. Supp. II:** 40
London, Eliza, **II:** 465
London, Jack, **I:** 209; **II:** 264, 440, 444, 451, **462–485**; **III:** 314, 580; **Supp. IV Part 1:** 236; **Supp. V:** 281; **Supp. IX:** 1, 14; **Supp. XIII:** 312
London, John, **II:** 464, 465
London, Mrs. Jack (Bessie Maddern), **II:** 465, 466, 473, 478
London, Mrs. Jack (Charmian Kittredge), **II:** 466, 468, 473, 476, 478, 481
London Embassy, The (Theroux), **Supp. VIII:** 323
London Fields (Amis), **Retro. Supp. I:** 278
London Magazine (Plath), **Supp. I Part 2:** 541
London Snow: A Christmas Story (Theroux), **Supp. VIII:** 322
London Suite (Simon), **Supp. IV Part 2:** 576, 581, 582, 588
Lonely Are the Brave (film), **Supp. XIII:** 6
"Lonely Coast, A" (Proulx), **Supp. VII:** 264
Lonely for the Future (Farrell), **II:** 46, 47
"Lonely Street, The" (W. C. Williams), **IV:** 413
"Lonely Worker, A" (Jewett), **Retro. Supp. II:** 132
Lonergan, Wayne, **Supp. I Part 1:** 51
Lonesome Dove (McMurtry), **Supp. V:** 226–228, 231, 232, 233
Lonesome Traveler (Kerouac), **Supp. III Part 1:** 219, 225
"Lone Striker, A" (Frost), **Retro. Supp. I:** 136, 137
Long, Ada, **Supp. V:** 178
Long, Huey, **I:** 489; **II:** 454; **IV:** 249; **Supp. IV Part 2:** 679
Long, Ray, **II:** 430; **III:** 54
Long after Midnight (Bradbury), **Supp. IV Part 1:** 102
Long and Happy Life, A (Price), **Supp. VI:** 258, **259–260**, 262, 264, 265
Long Approach, The (Kumin), **Supp. IV Part 2:** 452–453, 453
Long Christmas Dinner, The (Wilder), **IV:** 357, 365; **Supp. V:** 105
Long Christmas Dinner and Other Plays (Wilder), **IV:** 365–366
Long Day's Dying, A (Buechner), **Supp. XII:** **45–47**
Long Day's Journey into Night (O'Neill), **III:** 385, 401, 403–404; **Supp. IV Part 1:** 359
"Long Distance" (Stafford), **Supp. XI:** 329
"Long-Distance Runner, The" (Paley), **Supp. VI:** 221–222, 228, 230
Long Dream, The (Wright), **IV:** 478, 488, 494
"Long Embrace, The" (Levine), **Supp. V:** 187
"Long Enough" (Rukeyser), **Supp. VI:** 274
"Longest Night of My Life, The " (Nichols), **Supp. XIII:** 269
Longfellow, Henry Wadsworth, **I:** 458, 471; **II:** 274, 277, 295–296, 310, 313, 402, **486–510**; **III:** 269, 412, 421, 422, 577; **IV:** 309, 371; **Retro. Supp. I:** 54, 123, 150, 155, 362; **Retro. Supp. II:** **153–174**; **Supp. I Part 1:** 158, 299, 306, 317, 362, 368; **Supp. I Part 2:** 405, 406, 408, 409, 414, 416, 420, 586, 587, 602, 699, 704; **Supp. II Part 1:** 291, 353; **Supp. III Part 2:** 609; **Supp. IV Part 1:** 165; **Supp. IV Part 2:** 503; **Supp. XII:** 260; **Supp. XIII:** 141
"Long Fourth, A" (Taylor), **Supp. V:** 313
Long Fourth and Other Stories, A (Taylor), **Supp. V:** 318–319
Long Gay Book, A (Stein), **IV:** 42
Long Goodbye, The (Chandler), **Supp. IV Part 1:** 120, 122, 132–134, 135
Long Goodbye, The (T. Williams), **IV:** 381
"Long Hair" (Snyder), **Supp. VIII:** 300
Longing for Home, The: Recollections and Reflections (Buechner), **Supp. XII:** 53
Longinus, Dionysius Cassius, **I:** 279
"Long-Legged House, The" (Berry), **Supp. X:** 21, 24–25, 27, 31
Long Live Man (Corso), **Supp. XII:** 129–130, 132
Long Love, The (Sedges), **Supp. II Part 1:** 125
Long Made Short (Dixon), **Supp. XII:** 152
Long March, The (Styron), **IV:** 97, 99, 104–107, 111, 113, 117
"Long Night, The" (Bambara), **Supp. XI:** 9
"Long Novel, A" (Ashbery), **Supp. III Part 1:** 6
Long Patrol, The (Mailer), **III:** 46
"Long Point Light" (Doty), **Supp. XI:** 127
Long Road of Woman's Memory, The (Addams), **Supp. I Part 1:** 17–18
"Long Run, The" (Wharton), **IV:** 314
Long Season, The (Brosnan), **II:** 424, 425
"Long Shadow of Lincoln, The: A

Litany" (Sandburg), **III:** 591, 593
Longshot O'Leary (McGrath), **Supp. X:** 117
"Long Shower, The" (Francis), **Supp. IX:** 90
Longstreet, Augustus B., **II:** 70, 313; **Supp. I Part 1:** 352; **Supp. V:** 44; **Supp. X:** 227
"Long Summer" (Lowell), **II:** 553–554
"Long Term" (Dunn), **Supp. XI:** 149
Longtime Companion (film), **Supp. X:** 146, 152
Long Valley, The (Steinbeck), **IV:** 51
Long Voyage Home, The (O'Neill), **III:** 388
"Long Wail, A" (Crews), **Supp. XI:** 101
"Long Walk, The" (Bogan), **Supp. III Part 1:** 61
Long Walks and Intimate Talks (Paley), **Supp. VI:** 221
Long Way from Home, A (McKay), **Supp. X:** 132, 140
Lönnrot, Elias, **Retro. Supp. II:** 159
Looby, Christopher, **Supp. XIII:** 96
Look, Stranger! (Auden), **Supp. II Part 1:** 11
"Look, The" (Olds), **Supp. X:** 210
Look at the Harlequins (Nabokov), **Retro. Supp. I:** 266, 270
"Look for My White Self" (Ammons), **Supp. VII:** 25
Look Homeward, Angel (Wolfe), **II:** 457; **IV:** 450, 452, 453, 454, 455–456, 461, 462, 463, 464, 468, 471; **Supp. XI:** 216
"Looking a Mad Dog Dead in the Eyes" (Komunyakaa), **Supp. XIII:** 114
"Looking at Each Other" (Rukeyser), **Supp. VI:** 280, 285–286
"Looking at Kafka" (Roth), **Supp. III Part 2:** 402
"Looking Back" (Harjo), **Supp. XII:** 218
"Looking Back" (Merwin), **Supp. III Part 1:** 352
"Looking Back at Girlhood" (Jewett), **Retro. Supp. II:** 131, 133
Looking Backward (Bellamy), **II:** 276; **Supp. I Part 2:** 641; **Supp. XI:** 200
"Looking for a Ship" (McPhee), **Supp. III Part 1:** 312–313
"Looking for Dragon Smoke" (Bly), **Supp. IV Part 1:** 60
Looking for Holes in the Ceiling (Dunn), **Supp. XI:** 139, 143–145
Looking for Langston (Julien; film), **Supp. XI:** 19, 20
Looking for Luck (Kumin), **Supp. IV Part 2:** 453, 454–455
"Looking for Mr. Green" (Bellow), **Retro. Supp. II:** 27
"Looking for the Buckhead Boys" (Dickey), **Supp. IV Part 1:** 182, 183
"Looking Forward to Age" (Harrison), **Supp. VIII:** 49
"Looking from Inside My Body" (Bly), **Supp. IV Part 1:** 71
"Looking Glass, The" (Wharton), **Retro. Supp. I:** 382
"Lookout's Journal" (Snyder), **Supp. VIII:** 291
"Looks Like They'll Never Learn" (McCoy), **Supp. XIII:** 166
Loon Lake (Doctorow), **Supp. IV Part 1:** 219, 222, 224–227, 230, 231, 232, 233
"Loon Point" (O'Brien), **Supp. V:** 237
Loosestrife (Dunn), **Supp. XI:** 152–154
"Loosestrife" (Dunn), **Supp. XI:** 154
Loose Woman: Poems (Cisneros), **Supp. VII:** 58, 71–72
Lopate, Philip, **Supp. XII:** 184; **Supp. XIII:** 280–281
Lopez, Barry, **Supp. IV Part 1:** 416; **Supp. V:** 211; **Supp. X:** 29, 31; **Supp. XIII:** 16
Lopez, Rafael, **Supp. IV Part 2:** 602
Lorca, Federico García, **IV:** 380; **Supp. I Part 1:** 345; **Supp. IV Part 1:** 83; **Supp. VIII:** 38, 39; **Supp. XIII:** 315, 323, 324
Lord, Judge Otis P., **I:** 454, 457, 458, 470
Lorde, Audre, **Supp. I Part 2:** 550, 571; **Supp. IV Part 1:** 325; **Supp. XI:** 20; **Supp. XII:** 217, 220; **Supp. XIII:** 295
Lord Jim (Conrad), **I:** 422; **II:** 26; **Retro. Supp. II:** 310; **Supp. I Part 2:** 623; **Supp. IV Part 2:** 680; **Supp. V:** 251
"Lord of Hosts" (Pinsky), **Supp. VI:** 244
Lord of the Rings (Tolkien), **Supp. V:** 140
Lords of the Housetops (Van Vechten), **Supp. II Part 2:** 736
Lord's Prayer, **I:** 579
Lord Timothy Dexter of Newburyport, Mass. (Marquand), **III:** 55
Lord Weary's Castle (Lowell), **II:** 538, 542–551; **Retro. Supp. II:** 178, **186–187,** 188
"Lorelei" (Plath), **Retro. Supp. II:** 246; **Supp. I Part 2:** 538
Lorimer, George Horace, **II:** 430; **Retro. Supp. I:** 101, 113
Lorre, Peter, **Supp. IV Part 1:** 356
"Los Alamos" (Momaday), **Supp. IV Part 2:** 482
"Los Angeles, 1980" (Gunn Allen), **Supp. IV Part 1:** 325
"Los Angeles Days" (Didion), **Supp. IV Part 1:** 211
Losey, Joseph, **IV:** 383
"Losing a Language" (Merwin), **Supp. III Part 1:** 356
Losing Battles (Welty), **IV:** 261, 281–282; **Retro. Supp. I:** 341, 352, **353–354**
"Losing the Marbles" (Merrill), **Supp. III Part 1:** 337
"Losing Track of Language" (Clampitt), **Supp. IX:** 38, 40
Losses (Jarrell), **II:** 367, 372, 373–375, 376, 377, 380–381
"Losses" (Jarrell), **II:** 375–376
Lossky, N. O., **Supp. IV Part 2:** 519
"Loss of Breath" (Poe), **III:** 425–426
"Loss of My Arms and Legs, The" (Kingsolver), **Supp. VII:** 208
"Loss of the Creature, The" (Percy), **Supp. III Part 1:** 387
"Lost" (Wagoner), **Supp. IX:** 328
"Lost, The/Los Perdidos" (Kingsolver), **Supp. VII:** 208
"Lost and Found" (Levine), **Supp. V:** 188
"Lost Bodies" (Wright), **Supp. V:** 342
"Lost Boy, The" (Wolfe), **IV:** 451, 460, 466–467
"Lost Decade, The" (Fitzgerald), **II:** 98
Lost Galleon and Other Tales, The (Harte), **Supp. II Part 1:** 344
"Lost Girls, The" (Hogan), **Supp. IV Part 1:** 406–407
Lost Highway (film), **Supp. X:** 314
Lost Illusions (Balzac), **I:** 500
Lost in the Bonewheel Factory (Komunyakaa), **Supp. XIII: 114–115,** 116
Lost in the Cosmos: The Last Self-Help Book (Percy), **Supp. III Part 1:** 397
Lost in the Funhouse (Barth), **I:** 122, 135, 139; **Supp. X:** 307
"Lost in the Whichy Thicket" (Wolfe), **Supp. III Part 2:** 573, 574
"Lost in Translation" (Hass), **Supp. VIII:** 28
"Lost in Translation" (Merrill), **Supp. III Part 1:** 324, 329–330
Lost in Yonkers (film), **Supp. IV Part 2:** 588
Lost in Yonkers (Simon), **Supp. IV**

Part 2: 576, 577, 584, 587–588, 590–591
Lost Lady, A (Cather), **I:** 323–325, 327; **Retro. Supp. I:** 15–16, 20, 21, 382
"Lost Lover, A" (Jewett), **II:** 400–401, 402; **Retro. Supp. II:** 137
"Lost Loves" (Kinnell), **Supp. III Part 1:** 237, 245
Lost Man's River (Matthiessen), **Supp. V:** 212, 213, 214, 215
"Lost on September Trail, 1967" (Ríos), **Supp. IV Part 2:** 540
Lost Puritan (Mariani), **Retro. Supp. II:** 189
"Lost Sailor, The" (Freneau), **Supp. II Part 1:** 264
Lost Son, The (Roethke), **III:** 529, 530–532, 533
"Lost Son, The" (Roethke), **III:** 536, 537–539, 542
"Lost Sons" (Salter), **Supp. IX:** 260
Lost Souls (Singer). See *Meshugah* (Singer)
Lost Weekend, The (Jackson), **Supp. XIII:** 262
"Lost World, A" (Ashbery), **Supp. III Part 1:** 9
"Lost World, The" (Chabon), **Supp. XI:** 72–73
Lost World, The (Jarrell), **II:** 367, 368, 371, 379–380, 386, 387
"Lost World, The" cycle (Chabon), **Supp. XI: 71–73**
"Lost World of Richard Yates, The: How the Great Writer of the Age of Anxiety Disappeared from Print" (O'Nan), **Supp. XI:** 348
"Lost Young Intellectual, The" (Howe), **Supp. VI:** 113, **115–116**
Lost Zoo, The: (A Rhyme for the Young, But Not Too Young) (Cullen), **Supp. IV Part 1:** 173
Loti, Pierre, **II:** 311, 325; **Supp. IV Part 1:** 81
"Lot of People Bathing in a Stream, A" (Stevens), **IV:** 93
Lotringer, Sylvère, **Supp. XII:** 4
"Lot's Wife" (Nemerov), **III:** 270
"Lottery, The" (Jackson), **Supp. IX:** 113, 114, 118, 120, **122–123**
Lottery, The; or, The Adventures of James Harris (Jackson), **Supp. IX:** 113, 115, 116, 124, 125
Lotze, Hermann, **III:** 600
"Louie, His Cousin & His Other Cousin" (Cisneros), **Supp. VII:** 60
Louis, Joe, **II:** 589; **Supp. IV Part 1:** 360
Louis, Pierre Charles Alexandre, **Supp. I Part 1:** 302, 303

"Louisa, Please Come Home" (Jackson), **Supp. IX:** 122
Louis Lambert (Balzac), **I:** 499
"Louis Simpson and Walt Whitman: Destroying the Teacher" (Lazer), **Supp. IX:** 265
"Louis Zukofsky: *All: The Collected Short Poems, 1923–1958*" (Creeley), **Supp. IV Part 1:** 154
"Lounge" (Francis), **Supp. IX:** 83
Lounsbury, Thomas R., **I:** 335
Louter, Jan, **Supp. XI:** 173
"Love" (Olson), **Supp. II Part 2:** 571
"Love" (Paley), **Supp. VI:** 219, 222, 230
Love, Deborah, **Supp. V:** 208, 210
Love Alone: 18 Elegies for Rog (Monette), **Supp. X:** 146, 154
Love Always (Beattie), **Supp. V:** 29, 30, 35
Love among the Cannibals (Morris), **III:** 228, 230–231
"Love Among the Ruins" (Mosley), **Supp. XIII:** 247
Love and Death in the American Novel (Fiedler), **Supp. XIII:** 93, 96, **99–101**, 104
Love and Exile (Singer), **Retro. Supp. II: 320–322**, 333
Love and Fame (Berryman), **I:** 170
Love and Friendship (Bloom), **Retro. Supp. II:** 31, 33–34
"Love and How to Cure It" (Wilder), **IV:** 365
"Love and the Hate, The" (Jeffers), **Supp. II Part 2:** 434–435
Love and Will (Dixon), **Supp. XII:** 148, 149
Love and Work (Price), **Supp. VI:** 261
"Love Calls Us to the Things of This World" (Wilbur), **Supp. III Part 2:** 544, 552–553
Love Course, The (Gurney), **Supp. V:** 98
Loved One, The (film), **Supp. XI: 305–306**, 307
Loved One, The (Waugh), **Supp. XI:** 305
Love Feast (Buechner), **Supp. XII:** 52
"Love Fossil" (Olds), **Supp. X:** 203
Love in Buffalo (Gurney), **Supp. V:** 96
"Love—In Other Words" (Lee), **Supp. VIII:** 113
"Love in the Morning" (Dubus), **Supp. VII:** 91
Love in the Ruins: The Adventures of a Bad Catholic at a Time near the End of the World (Percy), **Supp. III Part 1:** 385, 387, 393–394, 397–398
Love in the Western World (de

Rougemont), **Retro. Supp. I:** 328
"Love Is a Deep and a Dark and a Lonely" (Sandburg), **III:** 595
Lovejoy, Elijah P., **Supp. I Part 2:** 588
Lovejoy, Owen R., **Supp. I Part 1:** 8
Lovejoy, Thomas, **Supp. X:** 108
Lovelace, Richard, **II:** 590
Love Letters (film), **Supp. IV Part 2:** 524
Love Letters (Gurney), **Supp. V:** 105, 108–109
Love Letters, The (Massie), **Supp. IV Part 2:** 524
Love Letters and Two Other Plays: The Golden Age and What I Did Last Summer (Gurney), **Supp. V:** 100
"Love Lies Sleeping" (Bishop), **Retro. Supp. II:** 42
Love Life (Mason), **Supp. VIII:** 145–146
"Love Life" (Mason), **Supp. VIII: 145–146**
Lovely Lady, The (Lawrence), **Retro. Supp. I:** 203
"Lovely Lady, The" (Lawrence), **Supp. I Part 1:** 329
Love Medicine (Erdrich), **Supp. IV Part 1:** 259, 260, 261, 263, 265, 266, 267–268, 270, 271, 274–275; **Supp. X:** 290
Love Medicine (expanded version) (Erdrich), **Supp. IV Part 1:** 263, 273, 274, 275
"Love Nest, The" (Lardner), **II:** 427, 429
Love Nest, The, and Other Stories (Lardner), **II:** 430–431, 436
Lovenheim, Barbara, **Supp. X:** 169
"Love of Elsie Barton: A Chronicle, The" (Warren), **IV:** 253
Love of Landry, The (Dunbar), **Supp. II Part 1:** 212
"Love of Morning, The" (Levertov), **Supp. III Part 1:** 284
Love of the Last Tycoon, The: A Western. See *Last Tycoon, The*
"Love on the Bon Dieu" (Chopin), **Supp. I Part 1:** 213
Love Poems (Sexton), **Supp. II Part 2:** 687–689
Love Poems of May Swenson, The (Swenson), **Supp. IV Part 2:** 652, 653
"Love Poet" (Agee), **I:** 28
"Love Ritual" (Mora), **Supp. XIII:** 215
Loveroot (Jong), **Supp. V:** 115, 130
"Lovers, The" (Berryman), **I:** 174
"Lovers, The" (Buck), **Supp. II Part 1:** 128
"Lover's Garden, A" (Ginsberg), **Supp.**

II Part 1: 311
"Lovers of the Poor, The" (Brooks), **Supp. III Part 1:** 81, 85
Lovers Should Marry (Martin), **Supp. IV Part 1:** 351
"Lover's Song" (Yeats), **Supp. I Part 1:** 80
"Love Rushes By" (Salinas), **Supp. XIII:** 326–327
Lovesick (Stern), **Supp. IX: 295–296**
Love's Labour's Lost (Shakespeare), **III:** 263
Love's Old Sweet Song (Saroyan), **Supp. IV Part 1:** 83
"Love Song of J. Alfred Prufrock, The" (Eliot), **I:** 52, 66, 569–570; **III:** 460; **Retro. Supp. I:** 55, 56, 57, 60; **Supp. II Part 1:** 5; **Supp. XIII:** 346
"Love Song of St. Sebastian" (Eliot), **Retro. Supp. I:** 57
Love's Pilgrimage (Sinclair), **Supp. V:** 286
"Love the Wild Swan" (Jeffers), **Supp. VIII:** 33
Love to Mamá: A Tribute to Mothers (Mora, ed.), **Supp. XIII:** 221
Lovett, Robert Morss, **II:** 43
"Love-Unknown" (Herbert), **Supp. I Part 1:** 80
Love! Valor! Compassion! (film), **Supp. XIII:** 206
Love! Valour! Compassion! (McNally), **Supp. XIII:** 199, **203–204**, 208, 209
"Love *versus* Law" (Stowe), **Supp. I Part 2:** 585–586
Love with a Few Hairs (Mrabet), **Supp. IV Part 1:** 92
Loving a Woman in Two Worlds (Bly), **Supp. IV Part 1:** 66, 67, 68–69, 71, 72
"Loving Shepherdess, The" (Jeffers), **Supp. II Part 2:** 432
"Loving the Killer" (Sexton), **Supp. II Part 2:** 688
Lovin' Molly (film), **Supp. V:** 223, 226
Lowe, John, **Supp. XIII:** 238
Lowe, Pardee, **Supp. X:** 291
Lowell, Abbott Lawrence, **I:** 487; **II:** 513; **Supp. I Part 2:** 483
Lowell, Amy, **I:** 231, 384, 405, 475, 487; **II:** 174, **511–533**, 534; **III:** 465, 581, 586; **Retro. Supp. I:** 131, 133, 288; **Retro. Supp. II:** 46, 175; **Supp. I Part 1:** 257–259, 261–263, 265, 266; **Supp. I Part 2:** 465, 466, 707, 714, 729
Lowell, Blanche, **Supp. I Part 2:** 409
Lowell, Harriet, **II:** 553, 554
Lowell, James Russell, **I:** 216, 458; **II:** 273, 274, 289, 302, 320, 402, 529, 530, 532, 534, 551; **III:** 409; **IV:** 129, 171, 175, 180, 182–183, 186; **Retro. Supp. I:** 228; **Retro. Supp. II:** 155, 175, 344; **Supp. I Part 1:** 168, 299, 300, 303, 306, 311, 312, 317, 318, 362; **Supp. I Part 2: 404–426**; **Supp. II Part 1:** 197, 291, 352
Lowell, Mrs. James Russell (Maria White), **Supp. I Part 2:** 405, 406, 414, 424
Lowell, Percival, **II:** 513, 525, 534
Lowell, Robert, **I:** 172, 381, 382, 400, 442, 521, 544–545, 550; **II:** 371, 376, 377, 384, 386–387, 532, **534–557**; **III:** 39, 44, 142, 508, 527, 528–529, 606; **IV:** 120, 138, 402, 430; **Retro. Supp. I:** 67, 140, 411; **Retro. Supp. II:** 27, 40, 44, 46, 48, 50, **175–193**, 221, 228–229, 235, 245; **Supp. I Part 1:** 89; **Supp. I Part 2:** 538, 543, 554; **Supp. III Part 1:** 6, 64, 84, 138, 147, 193, 194, 197–202, 205–208; **Supp. III Part 2:** 541, 543, 555, 561, 599; **Supp. IV Part 2:** 439, 620, 637; **Supp. V:** 81, 179, 180, 315–316, 337, 344; **Supp. VIII:** 27, 100, 271; **Supp. IX:** 325; **Supp. X:** 53, 58; **Supp. XI:** 146, 240, 244, 250, 317; **Supp. XII:** 253–254, 255; **Supp. XIII:** 76
Lowell, Rose, **Supp. I Part 2:** 409
"Lowell in the Classroom" (Vendler), **Retro. Supp. II:** 191
Lowenthal, Michael, **Supp. XII:** 82
Lower Depths, The (Gorki), **III:** 402
"Lower the Standard" (Shapiro), **Supp. II Part 2:** 715
Lowes, John Livingston, **II:** 512, 516, 532; **IV:** 453, 455
Lowin, Joseph, **Supp. V:** 273
"Low-Lands" (Pynchon), **Supp. II Part 2:** 620, 624
Lowle, Percival, **Supp. I Part 2:** 404
Lownsbrough, John, **Supp. IV Part 1:** 209, 211
Lowth, Richard, **II:** 8
Loy, Mina, **III:** 194
Loy, Myrna, **Supp. IV Part 1:** 355
"Loyal Woman's No, A" (Larcom), **Supp. XIII:** 142, 143–144
"Luani of the Jungle" (Hughes), **Supp. I Part 1:** 328
Lubbock, Percy, **I:** 504; **II:** 337; **IV:** 308, 314, 319, 322; **Retro. Supp. I:** 366, 367, 373; **Supp. VIII:** 165
Lubin, Isidor, **Supp. I Part 2:** 632
Lubow, Arthur, **Supp. VIII:** 310
Lucas, Victoria (pseudonym). See Plath, Sylvia
Luce, Dianne C., **Supp. VIII:** 189
Lucid, Robert F., **Retro. Supp. II:** 195, 204
"Lucid Eye in Silver Town, The" (Updike), **IV:** 218
"Lucinda Matlock" (Masters), **Supp. I Part 2:** 461, 465
"Luck" (Dunn), **Supp. XI:** 149
Luck of Barry Lyndon, The (Thackeray), **II:** 290
"Luck of Roaring Camp, The" (Harte), **Supp. II Part 1:** 335, 344, 345–347
"Luck of the Bogans, The" (Jewett), **Retro. Supp. II:** 142
Lucky Life (Stern), **Supp. IX: 290–291**
Lucretius, **I:** 59; **II:** 162, 163; **III:** 600, 610–611, 612; **Supp. I Part 1:** 363
Lucy (Kincaid), **Supp. VII:** 180, 185, 186, 187–188, 194
Lucy, Saint, **II:** 211
Lucy Gayheart (Cather), **I:** 331; **Retro. Supp. I:** 19
Ludvigson, Susan, **Supp. IV Part 2:** 442, 446, 447, 448, 451
Luhan, Mabel Dodge, **Retro. Supp. I:** 7
Lu Ji, **Supp. VIII:** 303
Luke (biblical book), **III:** 606
"Luke Havergal" (Robinson), **III:** 524
Luks, George, **IV:** 411; **Retro. Supp. II:** 103
"Lullaby" (Auden), **Supp. II Part 1:** 9
"Lullaby" (Bishop), **Supp. I Part 1:** 85
"Lullaby" (Silko), **Supp. IV Part 2:** 560, 568–569
Lullaby: The Comforting of Cock Robin (Snodgrass), **Supp. VI:** 324
"Lullaby of Cape Cod" (Brodsky), **Supp. VIII:** 27–28
Lullaby Raft (Nye), **Supp. XIII:** 278
Lullaby Raft (Nye, album), **Supp. XIII:** 274
"Lulls" (Walker), **Supp. III Part 2:** 525
"Lulu" (Wedekind), **Supp. XII:** 14
Lulu on the Bridge (film), **Supp. XII:** 21
Lulu's Library (Alcott), **Supp. I Part 1:** 43
"Lumber" (Baker), **Supp. XIII:** 55, 56
"Lumens, The" (Olds), **Supp. X:** 209
Lume Spento, A (Pound), **III:** 470
Lumet, Sidney, **Supp. IV Part 1:** 236; **Supp. IX:** 253
"Lumumba's Grave" (Hughes), **Supp. I Part 1:** 344
"Luna, Luna" (Mora), **Supp. XIII:** 217
Lupercal (Hughes), **Retro. Supp. II:** 245; **Supp. I Part 2:** 540

Lupton, Mary Jane, **Supp. IV Part 1:** 7
Luria, Isaac, **IV:** 7
Lurie, Alison, **Supp. X:** 166
Lust and Other Stories (Minot), **Supp. VI:** 205
Lustgarten, Edith, **III:** 107
Lustra (Pound), **Retro. Supp. I:** 289, 290
Luther, Martin, **II:** 11–12, 506; **III:** 306, 607; **IV:** 490
"Luther on Sweet Auburn" (Bambara), **Supp. XI:** 16–17
Lux, Thomas, **Supp. XI:** 270
Luxury Girl, The (McCoy), **Supp. XIII:** 163
Lyall, Sarah, **Supp. XIII:** 247
Lycidas (Milton), **II:** 540; **IV:** 347; **Retro. Supp. I:** 60; **Retro. Supp. II:** 186, 291; **Supp. I Part 1:** 370; **Supp. IX:** 41
Lydon, Susan, **Supp. XII:** 170
Lyell, Charles, **Supp. IX:** 180
Lyell, Frank H., **Supp. VIII:** 125
Lyford, Harry, **Supp. I Part 2:** 679
"Lying" (Wilbur), **Supp. III Part 2:** 547, 562
"Lying and Looking" (Swenson), **Supp. IV Part 2:** 652
"Lying in a Hammock at William Duffy's Farm in Pine Island, Minnesota" (Wright), **Supp. III Part 2:** 589, 599, 600
Lyles, Lois F., **Supp. XI:** 7, 8
Lyly, John, **III:** 536; **Supp. I Part 1:** 369
"Lynched Man, The" (Karr), **Supp. XI:** 241
Lynchers, The (Wideman), **Supp. X:** 320
"Lynching, The" (McKay), **Supp. I Part 1:** 63
"Lynching of Jube Benson, The" (Dunbar), **Supp. II Part 1:** 214
"Lynching Song" (Hughes), **Supp. I Part 1:** 331
Lynd, Staughton, **Supp. VIII:** 240
Lynn, Kenneth, **Supp. XIII:** 96–97
Lynn, Vera, **Supp. XI:** 304
Lyon, Kate, **I:** 409; **II:** 138, 143, 144
Lyon, Thomas, **Supp. IX:** 175
"Lyonnesse" (Plath), **Supp. I Part 2:** 541
Lyons, Bonnie, **Supp. V:** 58; **Supp. VIII:** 138
Lyotard, Jean-François, **Supp. IV Part 1:** 54
Lyrical Ballads (Wordsworth), **III:** 583; **IV:** 120; **Supp. IX:** 274; **Supp. XI:** 243

Lyrics of Love and Laughter (Dunbar), **Supp. II Part 1:** 207
Lyrics of Lowly Life (Dunbar), **Supp. II Part 1:** 197, 199, 200, 207
Lyrics of the Hearthside (Dunbar), **Supp. II Part 1:** 206
Lytal, Tammy, **Supp. XI:** 102
Lytle, Andrew, **IV:** 125; **Retro. Supp. II:** 220, 221, 235; **Supp. II Part 1:** 139; **Supp. X:** 1, 25; **Supp. XI:** 101
Lytton of Knebworth. *See* Bulwer-Lytton, Edward George
"M. Degas Teaches Art & Science at Durfee Intermediate School, Detroit, 1942" (Levine), **Supp. V:** 181, 193
McAlexander, Hubert H., **Supp. V:** 314, 319, 320, 323
McAlmon, Mrs. Robert (Winifred Ellerman), **III:** 194. *See also* Ellerman, Winifred
McAlmon, Robert, **IV:** 404; **Retro. Supp. I:** 418, 419, 420; **Retro. Supp. II:** 346; **Supp. I Part 1:** 259; **Supp. III Part 2:** 614
McAninch, Jerry, **Supp. XI:** 297, 298
Macaulay, Catherine, **Supp. I Part 2:** 522
Macaulay, Rose, **Supp. XII:** 88
Macaulay, Thomas, **II:** 15–16; **III:** 113, 591–592
Macauley, Robie, **Retro. Supp. II:** 228; **Supp. X:** 56
Macbeth (Shakespeare), **I:** 271; **IV:** 227; **Retro. Supp. I:** 131; **Supp. I Part 1:** 67; **Supp. I Part 2:** 457; **Supp. IV Part 1:** 87
MacBeth, George, **Retro. Supp. II:** 250
McCaffery, Larry, **Supp. IV Part 1:** 217, 227, 234; **Supp. V:** 53, 238; **Supp. VIII:** 13, 14; **Supp. X:** 260, 268, 301, 303, 307
McCarriston, Linda, **Supp. X:** 204
McCarthy, Charles Joseph, Jr. *See* McCarthy, Cormac
McCarthy, Cormac, **Supp. VIII: 175–192**; **Supp. XII:** 310
McCarthy, Eugene, **Retro. Supp. II:** 182
McCarthy, Joseph, **I:** 31, 492; **II:** 562, 568; **Supp. I Part 1:** 294, 295; **Supp. I Part 2:** 444, 611, 612, 620
McCarthy, Mary, **II: 558–584**; **Supp. I Part 1:** 84; **Supp. IV Part 1:** 209, 297, 310; **Supp. VIII:** 96, 99, 100; **Supp. X:** 177; **Supp. XI:** 246
McCay, Maura, **Supp. XII:** 271, 276
McClanahan, Ed, **Supp. X:** 24
McClanahan, Thomas, **Supp. XII:** 125–126

McClatchy, J. D., **Supp. XII: 253–270**
McClellan, John L., **I:** 493
McClung, Isabelle, **Retro. Supp. I:** 5
McClure, John, **Retro. Supp. I:** 80
McClure, Michael, **Supp. II Part 1:** 32; **Supp. VIII:** 289
McClure, S. S., **I:** 313; **II:** 465; **III:** 327; **Retro. Supp. I:** 5, 6, 9
McCombs, Judith, **Supp. XIII:** 33
McConnell, Frank, **Supp. X:** 260, 274
McCorkle, Jill, **Supp. X:** 6
McCourt, Frank, **Supp. XII: 271–287**
McCoy, Horace, **Supp. XIII: 159–177**
McCracken, Elizabeth, **Supp. X:** 86; **Supp. XII:** 310, 315–316, 321
McCullers, Carson, **I:** 113, 190, 211; **II: 585–608**; **IV:** 282, 384, 385, 386; **Retro. Supp. II:** 342; **Supp. II Part 1:** 17; **Supp. IV Part 1:** 31, 84; **Supp. IV Part 2:** 502; **Supp. VIII:** 124; **Supp. XII:** 309
McCullers, Reeves, **III:** 585, 586, 587
McDavid, Raven I., **III:** 120
McDermott, Alice, **Supp. XII:** 311
McDermott, John J., **II:** 364
MacDiarmid, Hugh, **Supp. X:** 112
Macdonald, Dwight, **I:** 233, 372, 379; **III:** 39; **Supp. V:** 265
McDonald, E. J., **Supp. I Part 2:** 670
Macdonald, George, **Supp. XIII:** 75
MacDonald, Jeanette, **II:** 589
Macdonald, Ross, **Supp. IV Part 1:** 116, 136; **Supp. IV Part 2: 459–477**; **Supp. XIII:** 233
MacDowell, Edward, **I:** 228; **III:** 504, 508, 524
McDowell, Frederick P. W., **II:** 194
McDowell, Mary, **Supp. I Part 1:** 5
McDowell, Robert, **Supp. IX:** 266, 270, 276, 279
MacDowell, Robert, **Supp. XI:** 249
McElroy, Joseph, **Supp. IV Part 1:** 279, 285
McEuen, Kathryn, **II:** 20
McEwen, Arthur, **I:** 206
McFarland, Ron, **Supp. IX:** 323, 327, 328, 333
McGann, Jerome, **Retro. Supp. I:** 47
McGovern, Edythe M., **Supp. IV Part 2:** 573, 582, 585
McGovern, George, **III:** 46
MacGowan, Christopher, **Retro. Supp. I:** 430
MacGowan, Kenneth, **III:** 387, 391
McGrath, Joseph, **Supp. XI:** 307, 309
McGrath, Patrick, **Supp. IX:** 113
McGrath, Thomas, **Supp. X: 111–130**
"McGrath on McGrath" (McGrath), **Supp. X:** 119, 120
McGuane, Thomas, **Supp. V:** 53, 220;

Supp. VIII: 39, 40, 42, 43
MacGuffin, The (Elkin), **Supp. VI: 55–56**
Machado y Ruiz, Antonio, **Supp. XIII:** 315, 323
Machan, Tibor, **Supp. IV Part 2:** 528
Machen, Arthur, **IV:** 286
Machiavelli, Niccolò, **I:** 485
"Machine-Gun, The" (Jarrell), **II:** 371
"Machine Song" (Anderson), **I:** 114
McInerney, Jay, **Supp. X:** 7, 166; **Supp. XI:** 65; **Supp. XII:** 81
"Mac in Love" (Dixon), **Supp. XII:** 142
McIntire, Holly, **Supp. V:** 338
McIntosh, Maria, **Retro. Supp. I:** 246
Mackail, John William, **Supp. I Part 1:** 268; **Supp. I Part 2:** 461
McKay, Claude, **Supp. I Part 1:** 63; **Supp. III Part 1:** 75, 76; **Supp. IV Part 1:** 3, 79, 164; **Supp. IX:** 306; **Supp. X: 131–144; Supp. XI:** 91
McKay, Donald, **Supp. I Part 2:** 482
McKee, Elizabeth, **Retro. Supp. II:** 221, 222
McKee, Ellen, **Retro. Supp. II:** 67
McKenney, Eileen, **IV:** 288; **Retro. Supp. II:** 339, 348
McKenney, Ruth, **IV:** 288; **Retro. Supp. II:** 339
MacKenzie, Agnes, **I:** 199
Mackenzie, Captain Alexander, **III:** 94
Mackenzie, Compton, **II:** 82; **Retro. Supp. I:** 100, 102
McKenzie, Geraldine, **Supp. XII:** 107
MacKenzie, Margaret, **I:** 199
McKinley, William, **I:** 474; **III:** 506; **Supp. I Part 2:** 395–396, 707
MacKinnon, Catharine, **Supp. XII:** 6
MacLachlan, Suzanne L., **Supp. XII:** 300,**Supp. XII:** 299
McLaverty, Michael, **Supp. X:** 67
McLay, Catherine, **Supp. XIII:** 21
Maclean, Alasdair, **Supp. V:** 244
MacLeish, Archibald, **I:** 283, 293, 429; **II:** 165, 228; **III: 1–25,** 427; **Supp. I Part 1:** 261; **Supp. I Part 2:** 654; **Supp. IV Part 1:** 359; **Supp. IV Part 2:** 586; **Supp. X:** 120
MacLeish, Kenneth, **III:** 1
MacLeish, Mrs. Archibald (Ada Hitchcock), **III:** 1
McLennan, Gordon Lawson, **Supp. IX:** 89
McLeod, A. W., **Supp. I Part 1:** 257
McLuhan, Marshall, **Supp. IV Part 2:** 474
Macmahon, Arthur, **I:** 226
McMahon, Helen, **Supp. IV Part 2:** 579

McMichael, George, **Supp. VIII:** 124
McMichael, Morton, **Supp. I Part 2:** 707
McMichaels, James, **Supp. XIII:** 114
McMillan, James B., **Supp. VIII:** 124
McMillan, Terry, **Supp. XIII: 179–193**
McMurtry, Josephine, **Supp. V:** 220
McMurtry, Larry, **Supp. V: 219–235; Supp. X:** 24; **Supp. XI:** 172
McNally, Terrence, **Supp. XIII: 195–211**
McNamer, Deirdre, **Supp. XI:** 190
McNeese, Gretchen, **Supp. V:** 123
MacNeice, Louis, **II:** 586; **III:** 527; **Supp. II Part 1:** 17, 24; **Supp. IV Part 2:** 440; **Supp. X:** 116; **Supp. XIII:** 347
McNeil, Claudia, **Supp. IV Part 1:** 360, 362
McPhee, John, **Supp. III Part 1: 289–316; Supp. X:** 29, 30
MacPherson, Aimee Semple, **Supp. V:** 278
McPherson, Dolly, **Supp. IV Part 1:** 2, 3, 4, 6, 8, 11, 12
McPherson, James Allen, **Retro. Supp. II:** 126
Macpherson, Jay, **Supp. XIII:** 19
MacPherson, Kenneth, **Supp. I Part 1:** 259
McQuade, Molly, **Supp. VIII:** 277, 281; **Supp. IX:** 151, 163
McQueen, Steve, **Supp. XI:** 306
Macrae, John, **I:** 252–253
McRobbie, Angela, **Supp. IV Part 2:** 691
MacShane, Frank, **Supp. IV Part 2:** 557; **Supp. XI:** 214, 216
"MacSwiggen" (Freneau), **Supp. II Part 1:** 259
McTaggart, John, **I:** 59
McTeague (Norris), **III:** 314, 315, 316–320, 322, 325, 327–328, 330, 331, 333, 335; **Retro. Supp. II:** 96; **Supp. IX:** 332
McWilliams, Carey, **Supp. XI:** 169
Madama Butterfly (Puccini), **III:** 139
"Madam and the Minister" (Hughes), **Supp. I Part 1:** 335
"Madam and the Wrong Visitor" (Hughes), **Supp. I Part 1:** 335
"Madame and Ahmad" (Bowles), **Supp. IV Part 1:** 93
"Madame Bai and the Taking of Stone Mountain" (Bambara), **Supp. XI:** 14–15
Madame Bovary (Flaubert), **II:** 185; **Retro. Supp. I:** 225; **Retro. Supp. II:** 70; **Supp. XI:** 334
"Madame Célestin's Divorce"
(Chopin), **Supp. I Part 1:** 213
Madame Curie (film), **Retro. Supp. I:** 113
"Madame de Mauves" (James), **II:** 327; **Retro. Supp. I:** 218, 220
Madame de Treymes (Wharton), **IV:** 314, 323; **Retro. Supp. I:** 376
"Madam's Calling Cards" (Hughes), **Retro. Supp. I:** 206
Madden, David, **Supp. IV Part 1:** 285
Maddern, Bessie. *See* London, Mrs. Jack (Bessie Maddern)
Mad Dog Black Lady (Coleman), **Supp. XI: 85–89,** 90
Mad Dog Blues (Shepard), **Supp. III Part 2:** 437, 438, 441
Maddox, Lucy, **Supp. IV Part 1:** 323, 325
Mademoiselle Coeur-Brisé (Sibon, trans.), **IV:** 288
Mademoiselle de Maupin (Gautier), **Supp. I Part 1:** 277
"Mad Farmer, Flying the Flag of Rough Branch, Secedes from the Union, The" (Berry), **Supp. X:** 35
"Mad Farmer Manifesto, The: The First Amendment" (Berry), **Supp. X:** 35
"Mad Farmer's Love Song, The" (Berry), **Supp. X:** 35
Madheart (Baraka), **Supp. II Part 1:** 47
Madhouse, The (Farrell), **II:** 41
Madhubuti, Haki R. (Don L. Lee), **Supp. II Part 1:** 34, 247; **Supp. IV Part 1:** 244
Madison, Dolley, **II:** 303
Madison, James, **I:** 1, 2, 6–9; **II:** 301; **Supp. I Part 2:** 509, 524
"Madison Smartt Bell: *The Year of Silence*" (Garrett), **Supp. X:** 7
"Madman, A" (Updike), **Retro. Supp. I:** 320
"Madman's Song" (Wylie), **Supp. I Part 2:** 711, 729
"Madonna" (Lowell), **II:** 535–536
"Madonna of the Evening Flowers" (Lowell), **II:** 524
"Madonna of the Future, The" (James), **Retro. Supp. I:** 219
Madwoman in the Attic, The (Gilbert and Gubar), **Retro. Supp. I:** 42; **Supp. IX:** 66
"Maelzel's Chess-Player" (Poe), **III:** 419, 420
"Maestria" (Nemerov), **III:** 275, 278–279
Maeterlinck, Maurice, **I:** 91, 220
"Magazine-Writing Peter Snook" (Poe), **III:** 421

Magdeburg Centuries (Flacius), **IV:** 163
Magellan, Ferdinand, **Supp. I Part 2:** 497
Maggie: A Girl of the Streets (S. Crane), **I:** 407, 408, 410–411, 416; **IV:** 208; **Retro. Supp. II:** 97, 107
Maggie Cassidy (Kerouac), **Supp. III Part 1:** 220–221, 225, 227, 229, 232
"Maggie of the Green Bottles" (Bambara), **Supp. XI:** 2–3
"Magi" (Plath), **Supp. I Part 2:** 544–545
"Magi, The" (Garrett), **Supp. VII:** 97
"Magic" (Porter), **III:** 434, 435
Magic Barrel, The (Malamud), **Supp. I Part 2:** 427, 428, 430–434
"Magic Barrel, The" (Malamud), **Supp. I Part 2:** 427, 428, 431, 432–433
Magic Christian, The (film), **Supp. XI:** 309
Magic Christian, The (Southern), **Supp. XI:** 297, 299–301, 309
Magic City (Komunyakaa), **Supp. XIII: 125–127,** 128, 131
"Magic Flute, The" (Epstein), **Supp. XII:** 165
Magic Flute, The (Mozart), **III:** 164
Magician of Lublin, The (Singer), **IV:** 6, 9–10; **Retro. Supp. II: 326–327**
Magician's Assistant, The (Patchett), **Supp. XII:** 307, 310, **317–320,** 322
"Magician's Wife, The" (Gordon), **Supp. IV Part 1:** 306
Magic Journey, The (Nichols), **Supp. XIII:** 266–267
Magic Kingdom, The (Elkin), **Supp. VI:** 42, **54–55,** 56, 58
"Magic Mirror, The: A Study of the Double in Two of Doestoevsky's Novels" (Plath), **Supp. I Part 2:** 536
Magic Mountain, The (Mann), **III:** 281–282; **Supp. IV Part 2:** 522; **Supp. XII:** 321
Magic Tower, The (Willams), **IV:** 380
Magnalia Christi Americana (Mather), **II:** 302; **Supp. I Part 1:** 102; **Supp. I Part 2:** 584; **Supp. II Part 2:** 441, 442, 452–455, 460, 467, 468; **Supp. IV Part 2:** 434
"Magnificent Little Gift" (Salinas), **Supp. XIII:** 318
"Magnifying Mirror" (Karr), **Supp. XI:** 240
Magpie, The (Baldwin, ed.), **Supp. I Part 1:** 49
Magpie's Shadow, The (Winters), **Supp. II Part 2:** 786, 788
"Magpie's Song" (Snyder), **Supp. VIII:** 302
Magritte, René, **Supp. IV Part 2:** 623
Mahan, Albert Thayer, **Supp. I Part 2:** 491
Mahomet and His Successors (Irving), **II:** 314
Mahoney, Jeremiah, **IV:** 285
"Maiden in a Tower" (Stegner), **Supp. IV Part 2:** 613
"Maiden Without Hands" (Sexton), **Supp. II Part 2:** 691
"Maid of St. Philippe, The" (Chopin), **Retro. Supp. II:** 63
"Maid's Shoes, The" (Malamud), **Supp. I Part 2:** 437
Mailer, Fanny, **III:** 28
Mailer, Isaac, **III:** 28
Mailer, Norman, **I:** 261, 292, 477; **III: 26–49,** 174; **IV:** 98, 216; **Retro. Supp. II:** 182, **195–217,** 297; **Supp. I Part 1:** 291, 294; **Supp. III Part 1:** 302; **Supp. IV Part 1:** 90, 198, 207, 236, 284, 381; **Supp. IV Part 2:** 689; **Supp. VIII:** 236; **Supp. XI:** 104, 218, 222, 229
"Maimed Man, The" (Tate), **IV:** 136
Main Currents in American Thought: The Colonial Mind, 1625–1800 (Parrington), **I:** 517; **Supp. I Part 2:** 484
"Maine Roustabout, A" (Eberhart), **I:** 539
"Maine Speech" (White), **Supp. I Part 2:** 669–670
Maine Woods, The (Thoreau), **IV:** 188
Main Street (Lewis), **I:** 362; **II:** 271, 440, 441–442, 447, 449, 453; **III:** 394
"Majorat, Das" (Hoffman), **III:** 415
Major Barbara (Shaw), **III:** 69
"Major Chord, The" (Bourne), **I:** 221
Majors and Minors (Dunbar), **Supp. II Part 1:** 197, 198
"Major's Tale, The" (Bierce), **I:** 205
Make It New (Pound), **III:** 470
Makers and Finders (Brooks), **I:** 253, 254, 255, 257, 258
"Making a Change" (Gilman), **Supp. XI:** 207
"Making a Living" (Sexton), **Supp. II Part 2:** 695
"Making Do" (Hogan), **Supp. IV Part 1:** 406
Making Face, Making Soul: Haciendo Caras, Creative and Critical Perspectives by Feminists of Color (Anzaldúa, ed.), **Supp. IV Part 1:** 330
Making It (Podhoretz), **Supp. VIII:** 231, 232, 233, **237–238,** 239, 244
"Making of a Marginal Farm, The" (Berry), **Supp. X:** 22
Making of Americans, The (Stein), **IV:** 35, 37, 40–42, 45, 46; **Supp. III Part 1:** 37
"Making of Ashenden, The" (Elkin), **Supp. VI:** 49, 50
"Making of a Soldier USA, The" (Simpson), **Supp. IX:** 270
"Making of Paths, The" (Stegner), **Supp. IV Part 2:** 614
"Making of Poems, The" (W. J. Smith), **Supp. XIII:** 348
Making of the Modern Mind (Randall), **III:** 605
Making the Light Come: The Poetry of Gerald Stern (Somerville), **Supp. IX:** 296–297
"Making Up Stories" (Didion), **Supp. IV Part 1:** 196, 203, 205
Malady of the Ideal, The: Oberman, Maurice de Guérin, and Amiel (Brooks), **I:** 240, 241, 242
Malamud, Bernard, **I:** 144, 375; **II:** 424, 425; **III:** 40, 272; **IV:** 216; **Retro. Supp. II:** 22, 297, 299; **Supp. I Part 2: 427–453; Supp. IV Part 1:** 297, 382; **Supp. V:** 257, 266; **Supp. IX:** 114, 227; **Supp. XIII:** 106, 264, 265, 294
Malamud, Mrs. Bernard (Ann de Chiara), **Supp. I Part 2:** 451
Malanga, Gerard, **Supp. III Part 2:** 629
Malaquais, Jean, **Retro. Supp. II:** 199
Malatesta, Sigismondo de, **III:** 472, 473
Malcolm (Purdy), **Supp. VII:** 270–273, 277
"Malcolm Cowley and the American Writer" (Simpson), **Supp. II Part 1:** 147
"MALCOLM REMEMBERED (FEB. 77)" (Baraka), **Supp. II Part 1:** 60
Malcolm X, **Retro. Supp. II:** 12, 13; **Supp. I Part 1:** 52, 63, 65, 66; **Supp. IV Part 1:** 2, 10; **Supp. VIII:** 330, 345; **Supp. X:** 240
Malcolm X (film), **Retro. Supp. II:** 12
"Maldrove" (Jeffers), **Supp. II Part 2:** 418
Male, Roy, **II:** 239
Male Animal, The (Thurber), **Supp. I Part 2:** 605, 606, 610–611
"Malediction upon Myself" (Wylie), **Supp. I Part 2:** 722
Malefactors, The (Gordon), **II:** 186, 199, 213–216; **IV:** 139
"Malest Cornifici Tuo Catullo" (Ginsberg), **Supp. II Part 1:** 315

Malick, Terrence, **Supp. XI:** 234
Malin, Irving, **I:** 147
"Malinche's Tips: Pique from Mexico's Mother" (Mora), **Supp. XIII:** 223
Mallarmé, Stéphane, **I:** 66, 569; **II:** 529, 543; **III:** 8, 409, 428; **IV:** 80, 86; **Retro. Supp. I:** 56; **Supp. I Part 1:** 261; **Supp. II Part 1:** 1; **Supp. III Part 1:** 319–320; **Supp. III Part 2:** 630; **Supp. XIII:** 114
Mallia, Joseph, **Supp. XII:** 26, 29, 37
Mallon, Thomas, **Supp. IV Part 1:** 200, 209
Maloff, Saul, **Supp. VIII:** 238
Malory, Thomas, **II:** 302; **III:** 486; **IV:** 50, 61; **Supp. IV Part 1:** 47
"Mal Paso Bridge" (Jeffers), **Supp. II Part 2:** 415, 420
Malraux, André, **I:** 33–34, 127, 509; **II:** 57, 376; **III:** 35, 310; **IV:** 236, 247, 434; **Retro. Supp. I:** 73; **Retro. Supp. II:** 115–116, 119; **Supp. II Part 1:** 221, 232
Maltese Falcon, The (film), **Supp. IV Part 1:** 342, 353, 355
Maltese Falcon, The (Hammett), **IV:** 286; **Supp. IV Part 1:** 345, 348–351
Mama (McMillan), **Supp. XIII:** 182, **187–188**
"Mama and Daughter" (Hughes), **Supp. I Part 1:** 334
Mama Day (Naylor), **Supp. VIII: 223–226,** 230
Mama Poc: An Ecologist's Account of the Extinction of a Species (LaBastille), **Supp. X:** 99, **104–105,** 106
"Mama Still Loves You" (Naylor), **Supp. VIII:** 214
Mambo Hips and Make Believe (Coleman), **Supp. XI: 94–96**
Mambo Kings, The (film), **Supp. VIII:** 73, 74
Mambo Kings Play Songs of Love, The (Hijuelos), **Supp. VIII:** 73–74, **79–82**
"Ma'me Pélagie" (Chopin), **Retro. Supp. II:** 64
"Mamie" (Sandburg), **III:** 582
Mammedaty, Novarro Scott. *See* Momaday, N. Scott
"Mammon and the Archer" (O. Henry), **Supp. II Part 1:** 394, 408
Mammonart (Sinclair), **Supp. V:** 276–277
"Mamouche" (Chopin), **Retro. Supp. II:** 66
"Man" (Corso), **Supp. XII:** 130
"Man" (Herbert), **II:** 12

"Man Against the Sky, The" (Robinson), **III:** 509, 523
"Man and a Woman Sit Near Each Other, A" (Bly), **Supp. IV Part 1:** 71
Man and Boy (Morris), **III:** 223, 224, 225
"Man and the Snake, The" (Bierce), **I:** 203
"Man and Woman" (Caldwell), **I:** 310
Manassas (Sinclair), **Supp. V:** 280, 281, 285
"Man Bring This Up Road" (T. Williams), **IV:** 383–384
"Man Carrying Thing" (Stevens), **IV:** 90
Manchester, William, **III:** 103
"Man Child, The" (Baldwin), **Supp. I Part 1:** 63
Man Could Stand Up, A (Ford), **I:** 423
"Mandarin's Jade" (Chandler), **Supp. IV Part 1:** 125
Mandelbaum, Maurice, **I:** 61
Mandelstam, Osip, **Retro. Supp. I:** 278; **Supp. III Part 1:** 268; **Supp. VIII:** 21, 22, 23, 27; **Supp. XIII:** 77
"Mandelstam: The Poem as Event" (Dobyns), **Supp. XIII:** 78
"Mandolin" (Dove), **Supp. IV Part 1:** 247
"Mandoline" (Verlaine), **IV:** 79
"Man Eating" (Kenyon), **Supp. VII:** 173
"Man Feeding Pigeons" (Clampitt), **Supp. IX: 49–50,** 52
Manfred, Frederick, **Supp. X:** 126
"Mango Says Goodbye Sometimes" (Cisneros), **Supp. VII:** 64
Manhattan (film), **Supp. IV Part 1:** 205
"Manhattan: Luminism" (Doty), **Supp. XI:** 135
"Manhattan Dawn" (Justice), **Supp. VII:** 117
Manhattan Transfer (Dos Passos), **I:** 26, 475, 478, 479, 480, 481, 482–484, 487; **II:** 286; **Supp. I Part 1:** 57
"Mania" (Lowell), **II:** 554
"Manic in the Moon, The" (Thurber), **Supp. I Part 2:** 620
"Man in Black" (Plath), **Supp. I Part 2:** 538
Man in Prehistory (Chard), **Supp. XII:** 177–178
Man in the Black Coat Turns, The (Bly), **Supp. IV Part 1:** 66–68, 71, 73
"Man in the Brooks Brothers Shirt, The" (McCarthy), **II:** 563–564
"Man in the Drawer, The" (Malamud), **Supp. I Part 2:** 437
Man in the Gray Flannel Suit, The (Wilson), **Supp. IV Part 1:** 387
Man in the Middle, The (Wagoner), **Supp. IX:** 324, **332–333**
Mankiewicz, Joseph, **Retro. Supp. I:** 113
Mankowitz, Wolf, **Supp. XI:** 307
"Man Made of Words, The" (Momaday), **Supp. IV Part 2:** 481, 484–485, 486, 487, 488
Man-Made World, The (Gilman), **Supp. XI:** 207
"Man-Moth, The" (Bishop), **Retro. Supp. II:** 42; **Supp. I Part 1:** 85–87, 88
Mann, Charles, **Retro. Supp. II:** 40
Mann, Erika, **Supp. II Part 1:** 11
Mann, Seymour (Samuel Weisman), **Supp. V:** 113
Mann, Thomas, **I:** 271, 490; **II:** 42, 539; **III:** 231, 281–282, 283; **IV:** 70, 73, 85; **Supp. IV Part 1:** 392; **Supp. IV Part 2:** 522; **Supp. V:** 51; **Supp. IX:** 21; **Supp. XI:** 275; **Supp. XII:** 173, 310, 321
Mannerhouse (Wolfe), **IV:** 460
"Manners" (Bishop), **Supp. I Part 1:** 73
"Manners" (Emerson), **II:** 4, 6
"Manners, Morals, and the Novel" (Trilling), **Supp. III Part 2:** 502, 503
Mannheim, Karl, **I:** 279; **Supp. I Part 2:** 644
Manning, Frederic, **III:** 459
Manning, Robert, **Supp. IX:** 236
Mannix, Daniel P., **Supp. II Part 1:** 140
Man Nobody Knows, The (B. Barton), **Retro. Supp. I:** 179
"Man of No Account, The" (Harte), **Supp. II Part 1:** 339
"Man of the Crowd, The" (Poe), **III:** 412, 417; **Retro. Supp. I:** 154
Man on Spikes (Asinof), **II:** 424
Man on Stage (Dixon), **Supp. XII:** 141, **154–155**
"Man on the Dump, The" (Stevens), **IV:** 74; **Retro. Supp. I:** 306
"Man on the Train, The" (Percy), **Supp. III Part 1:** 387
Manor, The (Singer), **IV:** 6, 17–19
Manrique, Jorge, **Retro. Supp. II:** 154
Mansart Builds a School (Du Bois), **Supp. II Part 1:** 185–186
Man's Fate (Malraux), **I:** 127; **Retro. Supp. II:** 121

"Man's Fate A Film Treatment of the Malraux Novel" (Agee), **I:** 33–34
Mansfield, June, **Supp. X:** 183, 194
Mansfield, Katherine, **III:** 362, 453
Mansfield, Stephanie, **Supp. IV Part 1:** 227
Man's Hope (Malraux), **IV:** 247
Mansion, The (Faulkner), **II:** 73; **Retro. Supp. I:** 74, 82
Man's Nature and His Communities (Niebuhr), **III:** 308
Manson, Charles, **Supp. IV Part 1:** 205
"Man Splitting Wood in the Daybreak, The" (Kinnell), **Supp. III Part 1:** 254
"Man's Pride" (Jeffers), **Supp. II Part 2:** 417
"Man's Story, The" (Anderson), **I:** 114
Man's Woman, A (Norris), **III:** 314, 322, 328, 329, 330, 332, 333
Man That Corrupted Hadleyburg, The (Twain), **I:** 204; **IV:** 208
"Man That Was Used Up, The" (Poe), **III:** 412, 425
"Mantis" (Zukofsky), **Supp. III Part 2:** 617
"'Mantis': An Interpretation" (Zukofsky), **Supp. III Part 2:** 617–618
Man to Send Rain Clouds, The (Rosen, ed.), **Supp. IV Part 2:** 499, 505, 513
"Man to Send Rain Clouds, The" (Silko), **Supp. IV Part 2:** 559
Mantrap (Lewis), **II:** 447
Manuductio Ad Ministerium (Mather), **Supp. II Part 2:** 465–467
"Manuelzinho" (Bishop), **Retro. Supp. II:** 47–48
Manuscript Books of Emily Dickinson, The (Franklin, ed.), **Retro. Supp. I:** 29, 41
"Man Waiting for It to Stop, A" (Dunn), **Supp. XI:** 144
"Man Who Became a Woman, The" (Anderson), **I:** 114
"Man Who Carries the Desert Around Inside Himself, The: For Wally" (Komunyakaa), **Supp. XIII:** 125
"Man Who Closed Shop, The" (Dunn), **Supp. XI:** 149
Man Who Gave Up His Name, The (Harrison), **Supp. VIII:** 45, 52
Man Who Had All the Luck, The (A. Miller), **III:** 148, 149, 164, 166
"Man Who Knew Belle Star, The" (Bausch), **Supp. VII:** 46
"Man Who Knew Coolidge, The" (Lewis), **II:** 449

Man Who Knew Coolidge, The: Being the Soul of Lowell Schmaltz, Constructive and Nordic Citizen (Lewis), **II:** 450
Man Who Lived Underground, The (Wright), **Supp. II Part 1:** 40
"Man Who Lived Underground, The" (Wright), **IV:** 479, 485–487, 492; **Retro. Supp. II:** 121
"Man Who Makes Brooms, The" (Nye), **Supp. XIII:** 276
"Man Who Studied Yoga, The" (Mailer), **III:** 35–36; **Retro. Supp. II:** 200
"Man Who Wanted to Win, The" (McCoy), **Supp. XIII:** 161
Man Who Was There, The (Morris), **III:** 220–221
"Man Who Writes Ants, The" (Merwin), **Supp. III Part 1:** 348
"Man with a Family" (Humphrey), **Supp. IX:** 94
Man without a Country, The (Hale), **I:** 488
"Man with the Blue Guitar, The" (Stevens), **I:** 266; **IV:** 85–87; **Retro. Supp. I:** 303–305, 306, 307, 309
Man with the Blue Guitar and Other Poems, The (Stevens), **IV:** 76; **Retro. Supp. I:** 303, 422
Man with the Golden Arm, The (Algren), **Supp. V:** 4; **Supp. IX:** 1, 3, 9–11, 14, 15
Man with the Golden Arm, The (film), **Supp. IX:** 3
"Man with the Golden Beef, The" (Podhoretz), **Supp. IX:** 3
Manyan Letters (Olson), **Supp. II Part 2:** 571
Many Circles (Goldbarth), **Supp. XII:** 193
"Many Handles" (Sandburg), **III:** 594
"Many Happy Returns" (Auden), **Supp. II Part 1:** 15
Many Loves (W. C. Williams), **Retro. Supp. I:** 424
"Many Mansions" (H. Roth), **Supp. IX:** 233, 234
Many Marriages (Anderson), **I:** 104, 111, 113
"Many of Our Waters: Variations on a Poem by a Black Child" (Wright), **Supp. III Part 2:** 602
"Many Swans" (Lowell), **II:** 526
"Many Thousands Gone" (Baldwin), **Retro. Supp. II:** 4; **Supp. I Part 1:** 51
"Many Wagons Ago" (Ashbery), **Supp. III Part 1:** 22
"Many-Windowed House, A"

(Cowley), **Supp. II Part 1:** 137
Many-Windowed House, A (Cowley), **Supp. II Part 1:** 141, 143
Mao II (DeLillo), **Supp. VI:** 2, 4, **5,** 6, **7,** 8, 9, 14, 16
"Map, The" (Bishop), **Retro. Supp. II:** 41; **Supp. I Part 1:** 72, 82, 85–88, 93
"Map, The" (Strand), **Supp. IV Part 2:** 623–624
"Maple Leaf, The" (Joplin), **Supp. IV Part 1:** 223
"Map of Montana in Italy, A" (Hugo), **Supp. VI:** 139
"Maps" (Hass), **Supp. VI:** 103–104
Mapson, Jo-Ann, **Supp. IV Part 2:** 440, 454
Map to the Next World, A: Poems and Tales (Harjo), **Supp. XII: 228–230**
"Mara" (Jeffers), **Supp. II Part 2:** 434
Ma Rainey's Black Bottom (Wilson), **Supp. VIII:** 331, **332–334,** 346, 349, 350
Marat, Jean Paul, **IV:** 117; **Supp. I Part 2:** 514, 515, 521
"Marathon" (Glück), **Supp. V:** 85
Marble Faun, The (Faulkner), **II:** 55, 56; **Retro. Supp. I:** 79
Marble Faun, The; or, The Romance of Monte Beni (Hawthorne), **II:** 225, 239, 242–243, 290, 324; **IV:** 167; **Retro. Supp. I:** 63, 149, 163, **164–165; Supp. I Part 1:** 38; **Supp. I Part 2:** 421, 596; **Supp. XIII:** 102
Marbles (Brodsky), **Supp. VIII:** 26–27
"March" (W. C. Williams), **Retro. Supp. I:** 418
March, Fredric, **III:** 154, 403; **IV:** 357; **Supp. X:** 220
Marchalonis, Shirley, **Supp. XIII:** 138, 140, 141, 143, 147–148
"Marché aux Oiseaux" (Wilbur), **Supp. III Part 2:** 550
"Märchen, The" (Jarrell), **II:** 378–379
March Hares (Frederic), **II:** 143–144
Marching Men (Anderson), **I:** 99, 101, 103–105, 111
"Marching Music" (Simic), **Supp. VIII:** 281
Marco Millions (O'Neill), **III:** 391, 395
Marcosson, Isaac, **III:** 322
Marcus, Steven, **Retro. Supp. II:** 196, 200
Marcus Aurelius, **II:** 1; **III:** 566
Marcuse, Herbert, **Supp. I Part 2:** 645; **Supp. VIII:** 196; **Supp. XII:** 2
Mardi and a Voyage Thither (Melville), **I:** 384; **II:** 281; **III:** 77–79, 84, 87, 89; **Retro. Supp. I:** 247, 254, 256

Margaret (Judd), **II:** 290
"Margaret Fuller, 1847" (Clampitt), **Supp. IX:** 43
"Marginalia" (Wilbur), **Supp. III Part 2:** 544
Margin of Hope, A: An Intellectual Autobiography (Howe), **Supp. VI:** 113–114, 117, 125, 128
"Margins of Maycomb, The: A Rereading of *To Kill a Mockingbird*" (Phelps), **Supp. VIII:** 128
Margoshes, Samuel, **Supp. X:** 70
"Margrave" (Jeffers), **Supp. II Part 2:** 426
"Maria Concepción" (Porter), **III:** 434–435, 451
Mariani, Paul L., **Retro. Supp. I:** 412, 419; **Retro. Supp. II:** 189
Marianne Moore Reader, (Moore), **III:** 199
Marie Antoinette (film), **Retro. Supp. I:** 113
Mariella Gable, Sister, **III:** 339, 355
"Marijuana Notation" (Ginsberg), **Supp. II Part 1:** 313
Marilyn: A Biography (Mailer), **Retro. Supp. II:** 208
"Marin" (Cisneros), **Supp. VII:** 60, 61
Marin, Jay, **Retro. Supp. II:** 343
"Marina" (Eliot), **I:** 584, 585; **Retro. Supp. I:** 64
"Marine Surface, Low Overcast" (Clampitt), **Supp. IX: 47–48**
Marinetti, Tommaso, **Retro. Supp. I:** 59
Marionettes, The (Faulkner), **Retro. Supp. I:** 79
Maritain, Jacques, **I:** 402
Maritime Compact (Paine), **Supp. I Part 2:** 519
Maritime History of Massachusetts, 1783–1860, The (Morison), **Supp. I Part 2:** 481–483
Marjolin, Jean-Nicolas, **Supp. I Part 1:** 302
Marjorie Kinnan Rawlings: Sojourner at Cross Creek (Silverthorne), **Supp. X:** 220, 234
"Mark, The" (Bogan), **Supp. III Part 1:** 52
Marker, Chris, **Supp. IV Part 2:** 434, 436
"Market" (Hayden), **Supp. II Part 1:** 368, 369
Marketplace, The (Frederic), **II:** 145–146
Markham, Edwin, **I:** 199, 207
Markings (Hammarskjold), **Supp. II Part 1:** 26
Markopoulos, Gregory, **Supp. XII:** 2

Markowick-Olczakova, Hanna, **Supp. X:** 70
Marks, Alison, **Supp. I Part 2:** 660
Marks, Barry A., **I:** 435, 438, 442, 446
Mark Twain in Eruption (Twain), **IV:** 209
Mark Twain's America (De Voto), **I:** 248
Mark Twain's Autobiography (Twain), **IV:** 209
Marley, Bob, **Supp. IX:** 152
Marlowe, Christopher, **I:** 68, 368, 384; **II:** 590; **III:** 259, 491; **Retro. Supp. I:** 127; **Retro. Supp. II:** 76; **Supp. I Part 2:** 422
"Marlowe Takes on the Syndicate" (Chandler), **Supp. IV Part 1:** 135
Marne, The (Wharton), **IV:** 319, 320; **Retro. Supp. I:** 378
Marquand, J. P., **I:** 362, 375; **II:** 459, 482–483; **III: 50–73,** 383; **Supp. I Part 1:** 196; **Supp. IV Part 1:** 31; **Supp. V:** 95
Marquand, John, **Supp. XI:** 301
Marquand, Mrs. John P. (Adelaide Hooker), **III:** 57, 61
Marquand, Mrs. John P. (Christina Sedgwick), **III:** 54, 57
Marquand, Philip, **III:** 52
Marquis, Don, **Supp. I Part 2:** 668
"Marriage" (Corso), **Supp. XII:** 117, 124, **127–128**
Marriage (Moore), **III:** 194
"Marriage" (Moore), **III:** 198–199, 213
Marriage A-la-Mode (Dryden), **Supp. IX:** 68
Marriage and Other Science Fiction (Goldbarth), **Supp. XII:** 189, 190
"Marriage in the Sixties, A" (Rich), **Supp. I Part 2:** 554
"Marriage of Heaven and Hell, The" (Blake), **III:** 544–545; **Supp. VIII:** 99
"Marriage of Phaedra, The" (Cather), **Retro. Supp. I:** 5
Marryat, Captain Frederick, **III:** 423
"Marrying Absurd" (Didion), **Supp. IV Part 1:** 200
"Marrying Iseult?" (Updike), **Retro. Supp. I:** 329
Marrying Man (Simon), **Supp. IV Part 2:** 588
"Marrying the Hangman" (Atwood), **Supp. XIII:** 34
Marry Me: A Romance (Updike), **Retro. Supp. I:** 329, 330, 332
"Mars and Hymen" (Freneau), **Supp. II Part 1:** 258
Marsden, Dora, **III:** 471; **Retro. Supp. I:** 416

Marsena (Frederic), **II:** 135, 136–137
Marsh, Edward, **Supp. I Part 1:** 257, 263
Marsh, Fred T., **Supp. IX:** 232
Marsh, Mae, **Supp. I Part 2:** 391
Marshall, George, **III:** 3
Marshall, John, **Supp. I Part 2:** 455
Marshall, Paule, **Supp. IV Part 1:** 8, 14, 369; **Supp. XI:** 18, **275–292;** **Supp. XIII:** 295
"Marshall Carpenter" (Masters), **Supp. I Part 2:** 463
"Marshes of Glynn, The" (Lanier), **Supp. I Part 1:** 364, 365–368, 370, 373
"&lsquoMarshes of Glynn, The': A Study in Symbolic Obscurity" (Ross), **Supp. I Part 1:** 373
Marsh Island, A (Jewett), **II:** 405; **Retro. Supp. II:** 134
"Mars Is Heaven!" (Bradbury), **Supp. IV Part 1:** 103, 106
Marsman, Henrik, **Supp. IV Part 1:** 183
Marston, Ed, **Supp. IV Part 2:** 492
Marta y Maria (Valdes), **II:** 290
"Martha's Lady" (Jewett), **Retro. Supp. II:** 140, 143
Marthe, Saint, **II:** 213
Martial, **II:** 1, 169; **Supp. IX:** 152
Martian Chronicles, The (Bradbury), **Supp. IV Part 1:** 102, 103, 106–107
Martin, Benjamin, **Supp. I Part 2:** 503
Martin, Dick, **Supp. XII:** 44
Martin, Jay, **I:** 55, 58, 60, 61, 67; **III:** 307; **Retro. Supp. II:** 344, 345, 347; **Supp. XI:** 162
Martin, John, **Supp. XI:** 172
Martin, Judith, **Supp. V:** 128
Martin, Nell, **Supp. IV Part 1:** 351, 353
Martin, Reginald, **Supp. X:** 247, 249
Martin, Stephen-Paul, **Supp. IV Part 2:** 430
Martin, Tom, **Supp. X:** 79
Martin du Gard, Roger, **Supp. I Part 1:** 51
Martineau, Harriet, **Supp. II Part 1:** 282, 288, 294
Martin Eden (London), **II:** 466, 477–481
Martinelli, Sheri, **Supp. IV Part 1:** 280
Martínez, Guillermo, **Supp. XIII:** 313
Mart'nez, Rafael, **Retro. Supp. I:** 423
Martone, John, **Supp. V:** 179
"Martyr, The" (Porter), **III:** 454
Martz, Louis L., **IV:** 151, 156, 165; **Supp. I Part 1:** 107
Marvell, Andrew, **IV:** 135, 151, 156,

161, 253; **Retro. Supp. I:** 62, 127; **Retro. Supp. II:** 186, 189; **Supp. I Part 1:** 80; **Supp. XII:** 159
"Marvella, for Borrowing" (Ríos), **Supp. IV Part 2:** 551
Marx, Karl, **I:** 60, 267, 279, 283, 588; **II:** 376, 462, 463, 483, 577; **IV:** 429, 436, 443–444, 469; **Retro. Supp. I:** 254; **Supp. I Part 2:** 518, 628, 632, 633, 634, 635, 639, 643, 645, 646; **Supp. III Part 2:** 619; **Supp. IV Part 1:** 355; **Supp. VIII:** 196; **Supp. IX:** 133; **Supp. X:** 119, 134; **Supp. XIII:** 75
Marx, Leo, **Supp. I Part 1:** 233
"Marxism and Monastic Perpectives" (Merton), **Supp. VIII:** 196
Mary (Nabokov), **Retro. Supp. I:** 267–268, 270, 277
"Mary Karr, Mary Karr, Mary Karr, Mary Karr" (Harmon), **Supp. XI:** 248
Maryles, Daisy, **Supp. XII:** 271
Mary Magdalene, **I:** 303
"Mary O'Reilly" (Anderson), **II:** 44
"Mary Osaka, I Love You" (Fante), **Supp. XI:** 169
"Mary's Song" (Plath), **Supp. I Part 2:** 541
"Mary Winslow" (Lowell), **Retro. Supp. II:** 187
Masefield, John, **II:** 552; **III:** 523
Mask for Janus, A (Merwin), **Supp. III Part 1:** 339, 341, 342
Maslow, Abraham, **Supp. I Part 2:** 540
Mason, Bobbie Ann, **Supp. VIII: 133–149; Supp. XI:** 26; **Supp. XII:** 294, 298, 311
Mason, David, **Supp. V:** 344
Mason, Lowell, **I:** 458
Mason, Marsha, **Supp. IV Part 2:** 575, 586
Mason, Otis Tufton, **Supp. I Part 1:** 18
"Mason Jars by the Window" (Ríos), **Supp. IV Part 2:** 548
Masque of Mercy, A (Frost), **II:** 155, 165, 167–168; **Retro. Supp. I:** 131, 140
"Masque of Mummers, The" (MacLeish), **III:** 18
"Masque of Pandora, The" (Longfellow), **Retro. Supp. II:** 167
Masque of Pandora, The, and Other Poems (Longfellow), **II:** 490, 494, 506; **Retro. Supp. II:** 169
Masque of Poets, A (Lathrop, ed.), **Retro. Supp. I:** 31; **Supp. I Part 1:** 365, 368

Masque of Reason, A (Frost), **II:** 155, 162, 165–167; **Retro. Supp. I:** 131, 140; **Retro. Supp. II:** 42
"Masque of the Red Death, The" (Poe), **III:** 412, 419, 424; **Retro. Supp. II:** 262, 268–269
"Masquerade" (Banks), **Supp. V:** 7
"Massachusetts 1932" (Bowles), **Supp. IV Part 1:** 94
Massachusetts, Its Historians and Its History (Adams), **Supp. I Part 2:** 484
"Massachusetts to Virginia" (Whittier), **Supp. I Part 2:** 688–689
"Massacre and the Mastermind, The" (Bausch), **Supp. VII:** 49
"Massacre at Scio, The" (Bryant), **Supp. I Part 1:** 168
"Massacre of the Innocents, The" (Simic), **Supp. VIII:** 282
Masses and Man (Toller), **I:** 479
"Masseur de Ma Soeur, Le" (Hecht), **Supp. X:** 58
Massey, Raymond, **Supp. IV Part 2:** 524
"Mass Eye and Ear: The Ward" (Karr), **Supp. XI:** 244
"Mass for the Day of St. Thomas Didymus" (Levertov), **Supp. III Part 1:** 283
Massie, Chris, **Supp. IV Part 2:** 524
Massing, Michael, **Supp. IV Part 1:** 208
Massinger, Philip, **Supp. I Part 2:** 422
Master Builder, The (Ibsen), **Supp. IV Part 2:** 522
Master Class (McNally), **Supp. XIII: 204–205,** 208
"Masterful" (Matthews), **Supp. IX: 161–162**
"Master Misery" (Capote), **Supp. III Part 1:** 117
Master of Dreams: A Memoir of Isaac Bashevis Singer (Telushkin), **Retro. Supp. II:** 335
"Master of Secret Revenges, The" (Gass), **Supp. VI:** 93
Master of the Crossroads (Bell), **Supp. X: 16–17**
"'Masterpiece of Filth, A': Portrait of Knoxville Forgets to Be Fair" (Howards), **Supp. VIII:** 178
Masterpieces of American Fiction, **Supp. XI:** 198
"Master Player, The" (Dunbar), **Supp. II Part 1:** 200
Masters, Edgar Lee, **I:** 106, 384, 475, 480, 518; **II:** 276, 529; **III:** 505, 576, 579; **IV:** 352; **Retro. Supp. I:** 131; **Supp. I Part 2:** 378, 386, 387,

454–478; **Supp. III Part 1:** 63, 71, 73, 75; **Supp. IV Part 2:** 502; **Supp. IX:** 308
Masters, Hardin W., **Supp. I Part 2:** 468
Masters, Hilary, **Supp. IX:** 96
Masters of Sociological Thought (Coser), **Supp. I Part 2:** 650
Masters of the Dew (Roumain), **Supp. IV Part 1:** 367
Matchmaker, The (Wilder), **IV:** 357, 369, 370, 374
Mate of the Daylight, The, and Friends Ashore (Jewett), **II:** 404; **Retro. Supp. II:** 146–147
Materassi, Mario, **Supp. IX:** 233
Mather, Cotton, **II:** 10, 104, 302, 506, 536; **III:** 442; **IV:** 144, 152–153, 157; **Supp. I Part 1:** 102, 117, 174, 271; **Supp. I Part 2:** 584, 599, 698; **Supp. II Part 2: 441–470; Supp. IV Part 2:** 430, 434
Mather, Increase, **II:** 10; **IV:** 147, 157; **Supp. I Part 1:** 100
Mathews, Cornelius, **III:** 81; **Supp. I Part 1:** 317
Mathews, Shailer, **III:** 293
"Matinees" (Merrill), **Supp. III Part 1:** 319, 327
"Matins" (Glück), **Supp. V:** 88
"Matisse: Blue Interior with Two Girls–1947" (Hecht), **Supp. X: 73–74**
Matisse, Henri, **III:** 180; **IV:** 90, 407; **Supp. I Part 2:** 619; **Supp. VIII:** 168; **Supp. IX:** 66; **Supp. X:** 73, 74
"Matisse: The Red Studio" (Snodgrass), **Supp. VI:** 316–317
Matlock, Lucinda, **Supp. I Part 2:** 462
Matson, Harold, **Supp. XIII:** 164, 166, 167, 169, 172
Matson, Peter, **Supp. IV Part 1:** 299
Matson, Suzanne, **Supp. VIII:** 281
Matters of Fact and Fiction: Essays 1973–1976 (Vidal), **Supp. IV Part 2:** 687
Matthew (biblical book), **IV:** 164
Matthew Arnold (Trilling), **Supp. III Part 2:** 500–501
Matthews, T. S., **II:** 430
Matthews, William, **Supp. V:** 4, 5; **Supp. IX: 151–170; Supp. XIII:** 112
Matthiessen, F. O., **I:** 254, 259–260, 517; **II:** 41, 554; **III:** 310, 453; **IV:** 181; **Retro. Supp. I:** 40, 217; **Retro. Supp. II:** 137; **Supp. IV Part 2:** 422; **Supp. XIII:** 93
Matthiessen, Peter, **Supp. V: 199–217,** 332; **Supp. XI:** 231, 294

Mattingly, Garrett, **Supp. IV Part 2:** 601
"Maud Island" (Caldwell), **I:** 310
Maud Martha (Brooks), **Supp. III Part 1:** 74, 78–79, 87; **Supp. XI:** 278
"Maud Muller" (Whittier), **Supp. I Part 2:** 698
Maugham, W. Somerset, **III:** 57, 64; **Supp. IV Part 1:** 209; **Supp. X:** 58
Maule's Curse: Seven Studies in the History of American Obscurantism (Winters), **Supp. II Part 2:** 807–808, 812
"Mau-mauing the Flak Catchers" (Wolfe), **Supp. III Part 2:** 577
Maupassant, Guy de, **I:** 309, 421; **II:** 191–192, 291, 325, 591; **IV:** 17; **Retro. Supp. II:** 65, 66, 67, 317; **Supp. I Part 1:** 207, 217, 223, 320
"Maurice Barrès and the Youth of France" (Bourne), **I:** 228
Maurier, George du, **II:** 338
Maurras, Charles, **Retro. Supp. I:** 55
Mauve Gloves & Madmen, Clutter & Vine (Wolfe), **Supp. III Part 2:** 581
Maverick in Mauve (Auchincloss), **Supp. IV Part 1:** 26
"Mavericks, The" (play) (Auchincloss), **Supp. IV Part 1:** 34
"Mavericks, The" (story) (Auchincloss), **Supp. IV Part 1:** 32
"Max" (H. Miller), **III:** 183
Max and the White Phagocytes (H. Miller), **III:** 178, 183–184
Maximilian (emperor of Mexico), **Supp. I Part 2:** 457–458
Maximilian: A Play in Five Acts (Masters), **Supp. I Part 2:** 456, 457–458
"Maximus, to Gloucester" (Olson), **Supp. II Part 2:** 574
"Maximus, to himself" (Olson), **Supp. II Part 2:** 565, 566, 567, 569, 570, 572
Maximus Poems, The (Olson), **Retro. Supp. I:** 209; **Supp. II Part 2:** 555, 556, 563, 564–580, 584; **Supp. VIII:** 305
Maximus Poems 1–10, The (Olson), **Supp. II Part 2:** 571
Maximus Poems IV, V, VI (Olson), **Supp. II Part 2:** 555, 580, 582–584
Maximus Poems Volume Three, The (Olson), **Supp. II Part 2:** 555, 582, 584–585
"Maximus to Gloucester, Letter 19 (A Pastoral Letter)" (Olson), **Supp. II Part 2:** 567
"Maximus to Gloucester, Sunday July 19" (Olson), **Supp. II Part 2:** 580

"Maximus to himself June 1964" (Olson), **Supp. II Part 2:** 584
Maxwell, William, **Supp. I Part 1:** 175; **Supp. III Part 1:** 62; **Supp. VIII:** 151–174
"May 1968" (Olds), **Supp. X:** 211–212
May, Abigail (Abba). *See* Alcott, Mrs. Amos Bronson (Abigail May)
May, Jill, **Supp. VIII:** 126
"May 24, 1980" (Brodsky), **Supp. VIII:** 28
"Mayan Warning" (Mora), **Supp. XIII:** 214
Maybe (Hellman), **Supp. IV Part 1:** 12
"Maybe" (Oliver), **Supp. VII:** 239
"Maybe, Someday" (Ritsos), **Supp. XIII:** 78
"Mayday" (Faulkner), **Retro. Supp. I:** 80
"May Day" (Fitzgerald), **II:** 88–89; **Retro. Supp. I:** 103
"May Day Dancing, The" (Nemerov), **III:** 275
"May Day Sermon to the Women of Gilmer County, Georgia, by a Woman Preacher Leaving the Baptist Church" (Dickey), **Supp. IV Part 1:** 182
Mayer, Elizabeth, **Supp. II Part 1:** 16; **Supp. III Part 1:** 63
Mayer, John, **Retro. Supp. I:** 58
Mayer, Louis B., **Supp. XII:** 160
Mayes, Wendell, **Supp. IX:** 250
Mayfield, Sara, **Supp. IX:** 65
Mayflower, The (Stowe), **Supp. I Part 2:** 585, 586
Maynard, Joyce, **Supp. V:** 23
Maynard, Tony, **Supp. I Part 1:** 65
Mayo, Robert, **III:** 478
Mayorga, Margaret, **IV:** 381
"Maypole of Merrymount, The" (Hawthorne), **II:** 229
May Sarton: Selected Letters 1916–1954, **Supp. VIII:** 265
"May Sun Sheds an Amber Light, The" (Bryant), **Supp. I Part 1:** 170
"May Swenson: The Art of Perceiving" (Stanford), **Supp. IV Part 2:** 637
"Maze" (Eberhart), **I:** 523, 525–526, 527
Mazurkiewicz, Margaret, **Supp. XI:** 2
Mazzini, Giuseppe, **Supp. I Part 1:** 2, 8; **Supp. II Part 1:** 299
M Butterfly (Hwang), **Supp. X:** 292
Mc. Names starting with Mc are alphabetized as if spelled Mac.
"Me, Boy Scout" (Lardner), **II:** 433
Me, Vashya! (T. Williams), **IV:** 381

Mead, Elinor. *See* Howells, Mrs. William Dean (Elinor Mead)
Mead, George Herbert, **II:** 27, 34; **Supp. I Part 1:** 5; **Supp. I Part 2:** 641
Mead, Margaret, **Supp. I Part 1:** 49, 52, 66; **Supp. IX:** 229
Meade, Frank, **Retro. Supp. II:** 114
Meade, Marion, **Supp. IX:** 191, 193, 194, 195
Meadow, Lynne, **Supp. XIII:** 198
Meadowlands (Glück), **Supp. V:** 88–90
"Mean, Mrs." (Gass), **Supp. VI:** 83
"Me and the Mule" (Hughes), **Supp. I Part 1:** 334
"Meaningless Institution, A" (Ginsberg), **Supp. II Part 1:** 313
"Meaning of a Literary Idea, The" (Trilling), **Supp. III Part 2:** 498
"Meaning of Birds, The" (C. Smith), **Supp. X:** 177
"Meaning of Death, The, An After Dinner Speech" (Tate), **IV:** 128, 129
"Meaning of Life, The" (Tate), **IV:** 137
"Meaning of Simplicity, The" (Ritsos), **Supp. XIII:** 78
Mean Spirit (Hogan), **Supp. IV Part 1:** 397, 404, 407–410, 415, 416–417
Mearns, Hughes, **III:** 220
"Measure" (Hass), **Supp. VI:** 99–100, 101
"Measuring My Blood" (Vizenor), **Supp. IV Part 1:** 262
Meatyard, Gene, **Supp. X:** 30
"Mechanism" (Ammons), **Supp. VII:** 28
"Mechanism in Thought and Morals" (Holmes), **Supp. I Part 1:** 314
Mecom, Mrs. Jane, **II:** 122
"Meddlesome Jack" (Caldwell), **I:** 309
Medea (Jeffers), **Supp. II Part 2:** 435
Medea and Some Poems, The (Cullen), **Supp. IV Part 1:** 169, 173
"Me Decade and the Third Great Awakening, The" (Wolfe), **Supp. III Part 2:** 581
"Médecin Malgré Lui, Le" (W. C. Williams), **IV:** 407–408
"Medfield" (Bryant), **Supp. I Part 1:** 157
Medical History of Contraception, A (Himes), **Supp. V:** 128
"Medicine Song" (Gunn Allen), **Supp. IV Part 1:** 326
Médicis, Marie de, **II:** 548
Medina (McCarthy), **II:** 579
"Meditation 1.6" (Taylor), **IV:** 165
"Meditation 1.20" (Taylor), **IV:** 165
"Meditation 2.102" (Taylor), **IV:** 150
"Meditation 2.112" (Taylor), **IV:** 165

"Meditation 20" (Taylor), **IV:** 154–155
"Meditation 40" (Second Series) (Taylor), **IV:** 147
"Meditation, A" (Eberhart), **I:** 533–535
"Meditation 2.68A" (Taylor), **IV:** 165
"Meditation at Lagunitas" (Hass), **Supp. VI:** 104–105
"Meditation at Oyster River" (Roethke), **III:** 537, 549
Meditations (Descartes), **III:** 618
"Meditations for a Savage Child" (Rich), **Supp. I Part 2:** 564–565
Meditations from a Movable Chair (Dubus), **Supp. VII:** 91
"Meditations in a Swine Yard" (Komunyakaa), **Supp. XIII:** 131
"Meditations of an Old Woman" (Roethke), **III:** 529, 540, 542, 543, 545–547, 548
Meditations on the Insatiable Soul (Bly), **Supp. IV Part 1:** 72–73
Meditative Poems, The (Martz), **IV:** 151
"Mediterranean, The" (Tate), **IV:** 129
"Medium of Fiction, The" (Gass), **Supp. VI:** 85–86
"Medley" (Bambara), **Supp. XI:** 9
"Medusa" (Bogan), **Supp. III Part 1:** 50, 51
Meehan, Thomas, **Supp. IV Part 2:** 577–578, 586, 590
Meek, Martha, **Supp. IV Part 2:** 439, 440, 441, 442, 445, 447, 448
Meeker, Richard K., **II:** 190
Meese, Elizabeth, **Supp. XIII:** 297
"Meeting and Greeting Area, The" (Cameron), **Supp. XII: 84–85**
"Meeting-House Hill" (Lowell), **II:** 522, 527
"Meeting South, A" (Anderson), **I:** 115
"Meeting the Mountains" (Snyder), **Supp. VIII:** 300
Meet Me at the Morgue (Macdonald), **Supp. IV Part 2:** 472
Mehta, Sonny, **Supp. XI:** 178
Meiners, R. K., **IV:** 136, 137, 138, 140
Meister, Charles W., **II:** 112
"Melancholia" (Dunbar), **Supp. II Part 1:** 194
"Melanctha" (Stein), **IV:** 30, 34, 35, 37, 38–40, 45
"Melancthon" (Moore), **III:** 212, 215
Meliboeus Hipponax (Lowell). *See Bigelow Papers, The* (Lowell)
Mellaart, James, **Supp. I Part 2:** 567
Mellard, James, **Supp. IV Part 1:** 387
Mellon, Andrew, **III:** 14
Mellor, Oscar, **Retro. Supp. II:** 279
Melnick, Jeffrey, **Supp. X:** 252

Melnyczuk, Askold, **Supp. IV Part 1:** 70
Melodrama Play (Shepard), **Supp. III Part 2:** 440–441, 443, 445
Melodramatists, The (Nemerov), **III:** 268, 281–283, 284
Melting-Pot, The (Zangwill), **I:** 229
Melville, Allan, **III:** 74, 77
Melville, Gansevoort, **III:** 76
Melville, Herman, **I:** 104, 106, 211, 288, 340, 343, 348, 354, 355, 561–562; **II:** 27, 74, 224–225, 228, 230, 232, 236, 255, 259, 271, 272, 277, 281, 295, 307, 311, 319, 320, 321, 418, 477, 497, 539–540, 545; **III:** 29, 45, 70, **74–98,** 359, 438, 453, 454, 507, 562–563, 572, 576; **IV:** 57, 105, 194, 199, 202, 250, 309, 333, 345, 350, 380, 444, 453; **Retro. Supp. I:** 54, 91, 160, 215, 220, **243–262; Retro. Supp. II:** 76; **Supp. I Part 1:** 147, 238, 242, 249, 309, 317, 372; **Supp. I Part 2:** 383, 495, 579, 580, 582, 602; **Supp. IV Part 2:** 463, 613; **Supp. V:** 279, 281, 298, 308; **Supp. VIII:** 48, 103, 104, 105, 106, 108, 156, 175, 181, 188; **Supp. XI:** 83; **Supp. XII:** 282; **Supp. XIII:** 294, 305
Melville, Maria Gansevoort, **III:** 74, 77, 85
Melville, Mrs. Herman (Elizabeth Shaw), **III:** 77, 91, 92
Melville, Thomas, **III:** 77, 79, 92; **Supp. I Part 1:** 309
Melville, Whyte, **IV:** 309
Melville Goodwin, USA (Marquand), **III:** 60, 65–66
Melville's Marginalia (Cowen), **Supp. IV Part 2:** 435
"Melville's Marginalia" (Howe), **Supp. IV Part 2:** 435
Member of the Wedding, The (McCullers), **II:** 587, 592, 600–604, 605, 606; **Supp. VIII:** 124
"Meme Ortiz" (Cisneros), **Supp. VII:** 60
Memnon (song cycle) (Bowles), **Supp. IV Part 1:** 82
Memnoch the Devil (Rice), **Supp. VII:** 289, 290, 294, 296–299
"Memoir" (Untermeyer), **II:** 516–517
"Memoirist's Apology, A" (Karr), **Supp. XI:** 245, 246
Memoir of Mary Ann, A (O'Connor), **III:** 357
Memoir of Thomas McGrath, A (Beeching), **Supp. X:** 114, 118
Memoirs of Arii Taimai (Adams), **I:** 2–3

"Memoirs of Carwin, the Biloquist" (Brown), **Supp. I Part 1:** 132
Memoirs of Hecate County (Wilson), **IV:** 429
Memoirs of Margaret Fuller Ossoli (Fuller), **Supp. II Part 1:** 280, 283, 285
"Memoirs of Stephen Calvert" (Brown), **Supp. I Part 1:** 133, 144
Memorabilia (Xenophon), **II:** 105
Memorable Providences (Mather), **Supp. II Part 2:** 458
"Memorial Day" (Cameron), **Supp. XII:** 80, **82–83**
"Memorial for the City" (Auden), **Supp. II Part 1:** 20
"Memorial Rain" (MacLeish), **III:** 15
"Memorial to Ed Bland" (Brooks), **Supp. III Part 1:** 77
"Memorial Tribute" (Wilbur), **Supp. IV Part 2:** 642
"Memories" (Whittier), **Supp. I Part 2:** 699
Memories of a Catholic Girlhood (McCarthy), **II:** 560–561, 566; **Supp. XI:** 246
"Memories of East Texas" (Karr), **Supp. XI:** 239
"Memories of Uncle Neddy" (Bishop), **Retro. Supp. II:** 38; **Supp. I Part 1:** 73, 93
"Memories of West Street and Lepke" (Lowell), **II:** 550
"Memory" (Epstein), **Supp. XII:** 163
"Memory, A" (Welty), **IV:** 261–262; **Retro. Supp. I:** 344–345
Memory Gardens (Creeley), **Supp. IV Part 1:** 141, 157
Memory of Murder, A (Bradbury), **Supp. IV Part 1:** 103
Memory of Old Jack, The (Berry), **Supp. X:** 34
Memory of Two Mondays, A (A. Miller), **III:** 153, 156, 158–159, 160, 166
"Memo to Non-White Peoples" (Hughes), **Retro. Supp. I:** 209
Men, Women and Ghosts (Lowell), **II:** 523–524
Menaker, Daniel, **Supp. VIII:** 151
Men and Angels (Gordon), **Supp. IV Part 1:** 304–305, 306, 308
Men and Brethen (Cozzens), **I:** 363–365, 368, 375, 378, 379
"Men and Women" (Bly), **Supp. IV Part 1:** 72
"Men at Forty" (Justice), **Supp. VII:** 126–127
Mencius (Meng-tzu), **IV:** 183
Mencken, August, **III:** 100, 108

Mencken, August, Jr., **III:** 99, 109, 118–119
Mencken, Burkhardt, **III:** 100, 108
Mencken, Charles, **III:** 99
Mencken, Gertrude, **III:** 99
Mencken, H. L., **I:** 199, 210, 212, 235, 245, 261, 405, 514, 515, 517; **II:** 25, 27, 42, 89, 90, 91, 271, 289, 430, 443, 449; **III:** 99–121, 394, 482; **IV:** 76, 432, 440, 475, 482; **Retro. Supp. I:** 1, 101; **Retro. Supp. II:** 97, 98, 102, 265; **Supp. I Part 2:** 484, 629–630, 631, 647, 651, 653, 659, 673; **Supp. II Part 1:** 136; **Supp. IV Part 1:** 201, 314, 343; **Supp. IV Part 2:** 521, 692, 693; **Supp. XI:** 163–164, 166; **Supp. XIII:** 161
Mencken, Mrs. August (Anna Abhau), **III:** 100, 109
Mencken, Mrs. H. L. (Sara Haardt), **III:** 109, 111
"Men Deified Because of Their Cruelty" (Simic), **Supp. VIII:** 282
Mendelbaum, Paul, **Supp. V:** 159
Mendele, **IV:** 3, 10
Mendelief, Dmitri Ivanovich, **IV:** 421
Mendelsohn, Daniel, **Supp. X:** 153, 154
"Mending Wall" (Frost), **II:** 153–154; **Retro. Supp. I:** 128, 130; **Supp. X:** 64
Men in the Off Hours (Carson), **Supp. XII:** 111–113
"Men in the Storm, The" (Crane), **I:** 411
"Men Loved Wholly Beyond Wisdom" (Bogan), **Supp. III Part 1:** 50
"Men Made Out of Words" (Stevens), **IV:** 88
Men Must Act (Mumford), **Supp. II Part 2:** 479
Mennes, John, **II:** 111
Mennoti, Gian Carlo, **Supp. IV Part 1:** 84
Men of Brewster Place, The (Naylor), **Supp. VIII:** 213, 228–230
"Men of Color, to Arms!" (Douglass), **Supp. III Part 1:** 171
Men of Good Hope: A Story of American Progressives (Aaron), **Supp. I Part 2:** 650
"Menstruation at Forty" (Sexton), **Supp. II Part 2:** 686
"Mental Hospital Garden, The" (W. C. Williams), **Retro. Supp. I:** 428
Mental Radio (Sinclair), **Supp. V:** 289
Men Who Made the Nation, The (Dos Passos), **I:** 485
Men Without Women (Hemingway), **II:** 249; **Retro. Supp. I:** 170, 176; **Supp. IX:** 202
"Merced" (Rich), **Supp. I Part 2:** 563
"Mercedes Hospital" (Bishop), **Retro. Supp. II:** 51
"Mercenary, A" (Ozick), **Supp. V:** 267
Merchant of Venice, The (Shakespeare), **IV:** 227
Mercury Theatre, **Retro. Supp. I:** 65
Mercy, Pity, Peace, and Love (Ozick), **Supp. V:** 257, 258
Mercy, The (Levine), **Supp. V:** 194–195
Mercy of a Rude Stream (H. Roth), **Supp. IX:** 231, 234, 235–242
Mercy Philbrick's Choice (Jackson), **Retro. Supp. I:** 26, 27, 33
Mercy Street (Sexton), **Supp. II Part 2:** 683, 689
Meredith, George, **II:** 175, 186; **Supp. IV Part 1:** 300
Meredith, Mary. *See* Webb, Mary
Meredith, William, **II:** 545; **Retro. Supp. II:** 181
"Merely to Know" (Rich), **Supp. I Part 2:** 554
"Mère Pochette" (Jewett), **II:** 400
"Merger II, The" (Auchincloss), **Supp. IV Part 1:** 34
"Mericans" (Cisneros), **Supp. VII:** 69
"Merida, 1969" (Matthews), **Supp. IX:** 151
"Meridian" (Clampitt), **Supp. IX:** 48–49
Meridian (Walker), **Supp. III Part 2:** 520, 524, 527, 528, 531–537
Mérimée, Prosper, **II:** 322
Meriweather, James B., **Retro. Supp. I:** 77, 91
Meriwether, James B., **Retro Supp. I:** 77, 91
"Meriwether Connection, The" (Cowley), **Supp. II Part 1:** 142
Merker, K. K., **Supp. XI:** 261
"Merlin" (Emerson), **II:** 19, 20
Merlin (Robinson), **III:** 522
"Merlin Enthralled" (Wilbur), **Supp. III Part 2:** 544, 554
Merrill, Christopher, **Supp. XI:** 329
Merrill, James, **Retro. Supp. I:** 296; **Retro. Supp. II:** 53; **Supp. III Part 1:** 317–338; **Supp. III Part 2:** 541, 561; **Supp. IX:** 40, 42, 48, 52; **Supp. X:** 73; **Supp. XI:** 123, 131, 249; **Supp. XII:** 44, 254, 255, 256, 261–262, 269–270; **Supp. XIII:** 76, 85
Merrill, Robert, **Retro. Supp. II:** 201
Merrill, Ronald, **Supp. IV Part 2:** 521
Merritt, Theresa, **Supp. VIII:** 332
"Merry-Go-Round" (Hughes), **Retro. Supp. I:** 194, 205; **Supp. I Part 1:** 333
Merry-Go-Round, The (Van Vechten), **Supp. II Part 2:** 734, 735
Merry Month of May, The (Jones), **Supp. XI:** 227–228
Merry Widow, The (Lehar), **III:** 183
Merton, Thomas, **III:** 357; **Supp. VIII:** 193–212
Merwin, W. S., **Supp. III Part 1:** 339–360; **Supp. III Part 2:** 541; **Supp. IV Part 2:** 620, 623, 626; **Supp. V:** 332; **Supp. IX:** 152, 155, 290; **Supp. XIII:** 274, 277
Meryman, Richard, **Supp. IV Part 2:** 579, 583
Meshugah (Singer), **Retro. Supp. II:** 333–334
Mesic, Michael, **Supp. IV Part 1:** 175
Mesic, Penelope, **Supp. X:** 15
Message in the Bottle, The (Percy), **Supp. III Part 1:** 387–388, 393, 397
"Message in the Bottle, The" (Percy), **Supp. III Part 1:** 388
"Message of Flowers and Fire and Flowers, The" (Brooks), **Supp. III Part 1:** 69
Messengers Will Come No More, The (Fiedler), **Supp. XIII:** 103
Messiah (Vidal), **Supp. IV Part 2:** 677, 680, 681–682, 685, 691, 692
Messiah of Stockholm, The (Ozick), **Supp. V:** 270–271
Metamorphic Tradition in Modern Poetry (Quinn), **IV:** 421
Metamorphoses (Ovid), **II:** 542–543; **III:** 467, 468
Metamorphoses (Pound, trans.), **III:** 468–469
Metamorphosis, The (Kafka), **IV:** 438; **Retro. Supp. II:** 305–306; **Supp. VIII:** 3
"Metamorphosis and Survival" (Woodcock), **Supp. XIII:** 33
"Metaphor as Mistake" (Percy), **Supp. III Part 1:** 387–388
Metaphor & Memory: Essays (Ozick), **Supp. V:** 272
"Metaphors of a Magnifico" (Stevens), **IV:** 92
"Metaphysical Poets, The" (Eliot), **I:** 527, 586
"Metaphysics" (Ginsberg), **Supp. II Part 1:** 313
"Meteor, The" (Bradbury), **Supp. IV Part 1:** 102
Metress, Christopher P., **Supp. V:** 314
Metrical History of Christianity, The

(Taylor), **IV:** 163
Metropolis, The (Sinclair), **Supp. V:** 285
"Metzengerstein" (Poe), **III:** 411, 417
Mew, Charlotte, **Retro. Supp. II:** 247
Mewshaw, Michael, **Supp. V:** 57; **Supp. X:** 82
"Mexico" (Lowell), **II:** 553, 554
"Mexico, Age Four" (Salinas), **Supp. XIII:** 315
Mexico City Blues (Kerouac), **Supp. III Part 1:** 225, 229
"Mexico Is a Foreign Country: Five Studies in Naturalism" (Warren), **IV:** 241, 252
Meyer, Donald B., **III:** 298
Meyer, Ellen Hope, **Supp. V:** 123
Meyers, Jeffrey, **Retro. Supp. I:** 124, 138; **Retro. Supp. II:** 191
Meynell, Alice, **Supp. I Part 1:** 220
Mezey, Robert, **Supp. IV Part 1:** 60; **Supp. V:** 180; **Supp. XIII:** 312
Mezzanine, The (Baker), **Supp. XIII:** 41–43, 44, 45, 48, 55
"Mezzo Cammin" (Longfellow), **II:** 490
"Mi Abuelo" (Ríos), **Supp. IV Part 2:** 541
Miami (Didion), **Supp. IV Part 1:** 199, 210
Miami and the Siege of Chicago (Mailer), **Retro. Supp. II:** 206
"Michael" (Wordsworth), **III:** 523
Michael, Magali Cornier, **Supp. XIII:** 32
"Michael Angelo: A Fragment" (Longfellow), **II:** 490, 494, 495, 506; **Retro. Supp. II:** 167
"Michael Egerton" (Price), **Supp. VI:** 257–258, 260
Michael Kohlhaas (Kleist), **Supp. IV Part 1:** 224
Michaels, Walter Benn, **Retro. Supp. I:** 115, 369, 379
Michael Scarlett (Cozens), **I:** 358–359, 378
Michelangelo, **I:** 18; **II:** 11–12; **III:** 124; **Supp. I Part 1:** 363
Michel-Michot, Paulette, **Supp. XI:** 224–225
Michelson, Albert, **IV:** 27
Mickelsson's Ghosts (Gardner), **Supp. VI:** 63, **73–74**
Mickiewicz, Adam, **Supp. II Part 1:** 299
Mid-American Chants (Anderson), **I:** 109, 114
"Midas" (Winters), **Supp. II Part 2:** 801
"Mid-August at Sourdough Mountain Lookout" (Snyder), **Supp. VIII:** 292–293
Midcentury (Dos Passos), **I:** 474, 475, 478, 490, 492–494; **Supp. I Part 2:** 646
Mid-Century American Poets, **III:** 532
"Mid-Day" (Doolittle), **Supp. I Part 1:** 266–267
"Middle Age" (Lowell), **II:** 550
"Middleaged Man, The" (Simpson), **Supp. IX:** 274–275
Middle Ages, The (Gurney), **Supp. V:** 96, 105, 108
Middlebrook, Diane Wood, **Supp. IV Part 2:** 444, 451
"Middle Daughter, The" (Kingsolver), **Supp. VII:** 209
Middlemarch (Eliot), **I:** 457, 459; **II:** 290, 291; **Retro. Supp. I:** 225; **Supp. I Part 1:** 174; **Supp. IX:** 43; **Supp. XI:** 68; **Supp. XII:** 335
"Middle of Nowhere, The" (Wagoner), **Supp. IX:** 327–328
Middle of the Journey, The (Trilling), **Supp. III Part 2:** 495, 504–506
"Middle of the Way" (Kinnell), **Supp. III Part 1:** 242
"Middle Passage" (Hayden), **Supp. II Part 1:** 363, 375–376
Middle Passage (Johnson), **Supp. VI:** **194–196,** 198, 199; **Supp. XIII:** 182
"Middle Toe of the Right Foot, The" (Bierce), **I:** 203
Middleton, Thomas, **Retro. Supp. I:** 62
Middle Years, The (James), **II:** 337–338; **Retro. Supp. I:** 235
"Middle Years, The" (James), **Retro. Supp. I:** 228, 272
"Midnight" (Dunn), **Supp. XI:** 147
"Midnight Consultations, The" (Freneau), **Supp. II Part 1:** 257
Midnight Cry, A (Mather), **Supp. II Part 2:** 460
"Midnight Gladness" (Levertov), **Supp. III Part 1:** 284–285
"Midnight Magic" (Mason), **Supp. VIII:** 146
Midnight Magic: Selected Stories of Bobbie Ann Mason (Mason), **Supp. VIII:** 148
Midnight Mass (Bowles), **Supp. IV Part 1:** 93
Midnight Salvage: Poems, 1995–1998 (Rich), **Retro. Supp. II:** 293
"Midnight Show" (Shapiro), **Supp. II Part 2:** 705
"Midpoint" (Updike), **Retro. Supp. I:** 321, 323, 327, 330, 335
Midpoint and Other Poems (Updike), **IV:** 214
"Midrash on Happiness" (Paley), **Supp. VI:** 217
"Midsummer in the Blueberry Barrens" (Clampitt), **Supp. IX:** 40–41
Midsummer Night's Dream, A (Shakespeare), **Supp. I Part 1:** 369–370; **Supp. X:** 69
"Midwest" (Stafford), **Supp. XI:** 317
Mies van der Rohe, Ludwig, **Supp. IV Part 1:** 40
"Migration, The" (Tate), **IV:** 130
Mihailovitch, Bata, **Supp. VIII:** 272
Miklitsch, Robert, **Supp. IV Part 2:** 628, 629
Mila 18 (Uris), **Supp. IV Part 1:** 379
Milagro Beanfield War, The (film), **Supp. XIII:** 267
Milagro Beanfield War, The (Nichols), **Supp. XIII:** 253, **265–266**
Milburn, Michael, **Supp. XI:** 239, 242
Milch, David, **Supp. XI:** 348
Miles, Barry, **Supp. XII:** 123
Miles, Jack, **Supp. VIII:** 86
Miles, Josephine, **Supp. XIII:** 275
Miles, Julie, **I:** 199
Miles, Kitty, **I:** 199
Milestone, Lewis, **Supp. I Part 1:** 281
Miles Wallingford (Cooper). See *Afloat and Ashore* (Cooper)
Milford, Nancy, **II:** 83; **Supp. IX:** 60
Milhaud, Darius, **Supp. IV Part 1:** 81
Miligate, Michael, **IV:** 123, 130, 132
"Militant Nudes" (Hardwick), **Supp. III Part 1:** 210–211
"Milk Bottles" (Anderson), **I:** 114
Milk Train Doesn't Stop Here Anymore, The (T. Williams), **IV:** 382, 383, 384, 386, 390, 391, 392, 393, 394, 395, 398
Mill, James, **II:** 357
Mill, John Stuart, **III:** 294–295; **Supp. XI:** 196
Millar, Kenneth. See Macdonald, Ross
Millar, Margaret (Margaret Sturm), **Supp. IV Part 2:** 464, 465
Millay, Cora, **III:** 123, 133–134, 135–136
Millay, Edna St. Vincent, **I:** 482; **II:** 530; **III:** **122–144;** **IV:** 433, 436; **Retro. Supp. II:** 48; **Supp. I Part 2:** 707, 714, 726; **Supp. IV Part 1:** 168; **Supp. IV Part 2:** 607; **Supp. V:** 113; **Supp. IX:** 20
Millennium Approaches (Kushner), **Supp. IX:** 141, 142, 145
Miller, Arthur, **I:** 81, 94; **III:** **145–169;** **Supp. IV Part 1:** 359; **Supp. IV Part 2:** 574; **Supp. VIII:** 334;

Supp. XIII: 127
Miller, Brown, **Supp. IV Part 1:** 67
Miller, Carol, **Supp. IV Part 1:** 400, 405, 409, 410, 411
Miller, Henry, **I:** 97, 157; **III:** 40, **170–192**; **IV:** 138; **Retro. Supp. II:** 345; **Supp. I Part 2:** 546; **Supp. V:** 119, 131; **Supp. X:** 183, 185, 187, 194, 195; **Supp. XIII:** 1, 17
Miller, Herman, **Supp. I Part 2:** 614, 617
Miller, J. Hillis, **Supp. IV Part 1:** 387
Miller, James E., Jr., **IV:** 352
Miller, Jeffrey, **Supp. IV Part 1:** 95
Miller, Joaquin, **I:** 193, 195, 459; **Supp. II Part 1:** 351
Miller, John Duncan, **Supp. I Part 2:** 604
Miller, Jonathan, **Retro. Supp. II:** 181
Miller, Laura, **Supp. XIII:** 48
Miller, Mrs. Arthur (Ingeborg Morath), **III:** 162–163
Miller, Mrs. Arthur (Marilyn Monroe), **III:** 161, 162–163
Miller, Mrs. Arthur (Mary Grace Slattery), **III:** 146, 161
Miller, Orilla, **Supp. I Part 1:** 48
Miller, Perry, **I:** 546, 547, 549, 550, 560; **IV:** 186; **Supp. I Part 1:** 31, 104; **Supp. I Part 2:** 484; **Supp. IV Part 2:** 422; **Supp. VIII:** 101
Miller, R. Baxter, **Retro. Supp. I:** 195, 207
Miller, Robert Ellis, **II:** 588
Miller, Ruth, **Supp. X:** 324
Miller, Sue, **Supp. X:** 77, 85; **Supp. XI:** 190; **Supp. XII: 289–305**
Miller of Old Church, The (Glasgow), **II:** 175, 181
"Miller's Tale" (Chaucer), **III:** 283
Millett, Kate, **Supp. X:** 193, 196
Millgate, Michael, **Retro. Supp. I:** 91
Mill Hand's Lunch Bucket (Bearden), **Supp. VIII:** 337
Millier, Brett C., **Retro. Supp. II:** 39
Milligan, Bryce, **Supp. XIII:** 274, 275, 277
Millions of Strange Shadows (Hecht), **Supp. X:** 57, **62–65**
"Million Young Workmen, 1915, A" (Sandburg), **III:** 585
Millroy the Magician (Theroux), **Supp. VIII:** 325
Mills, Alice, **Supp. XIII:** 233
Mills, Benjamin Fay, **III:** 176
Mills, C. Wright, **Supp. I Part 2:** 648, 650
Mills, Florence, **Supp. I Part 1:** 322
Mills, Ralph J., Jr., **III:** 530; **Supp. IV Part 1:** 64; **Supp. XI:** 311

Mills of the Kavanaughs, The (Lowell), **II:** 542–543, 546, 550; **III:** 508; **Retro. Supp. II:** 178, 179, 188
"Mills of the Kavanaughs, The" (Lowell), **II:** 542–543
Milne, A. A., **Supp. IX:** 189
Milne, A. J. M., **I:** 278
Milosz, Czeslaw, **Supp. III Part 2:** 630; **Supp. VIII:** 20, 22; **Supp. XI:** 267, 312
Miltner, Robert, **Supp. XI:** 142
Milton, Edith, **Supp. VIII:** 79; **Supp. X:** 82
Milton, John, **I:** 6, 138, 273, 587–588; **II:** 11, 15, 113, 130, 411, 540, 542; **III:** 40, 124, 201, 225, 274, 468, 471, 486, 487, 503, 511; **IV:** 50, 82, 126, 137, 155, 157, 241, 279, 347, 422, 461, 494; **Retro. Supp. I:** 60, 67, 127, 360; **Retro. Supp. II:** 161, 313; **Supp. I Part 1:** 124, 150, 370; **Supp. I Part 2:** 412, 422, 491, 501, 522, 622, 722, 724; **Supp. IV Part 2:** 430, 634; **Supp. VIII:** 294; **Supp. X:** 22, 23, 36; **Supp. XII:** 180
Milton, John R., **Supp. IV Part 2:** 503
"Milton by Firelight" (Snyder), **Supp. II Part 1:** 314; **Supp. VIII:** 294
"Miltonic Sonnet, A" (Wilbur), **Supp. III Part 2:** 558
Mimesis (Auerbach), **III:** 453
"Mimnermos and the Motions of Hedonism" (Carson), **Supp. XII: 99–100**
"Mimnermos Interviews, The" (Carson), **Supp. XII: 100–101**
Mims, Edwin, **Supp. I Part 1:** 362, 364, 365, 371
"Mind" (Wilbur), **Supp. III Part 2:** 554
"Mind, The" (Kinnell), **Supp. III Part 1:** 245
Mind Breaths: Poems 1972–1977 (Ginsberg), **Supp. II Part 1:** 326
Mindfield: New and Selected Poems (Corso), **Supp. XII: 136**
"Mind in the Modern World" (Trilling), **Supp. III Part 2:** 512
"Mind Is Shapely, Art Is Shapely" (Ginsberg), **Supp. II Part 1:** 327
Mindlin, Henrique, **Supp. I Part 1:** 92
Mind of My Mind (O. Butler), **Supp. XIII:** 62, 63
"Mind-Reader, The" (Wilbur), **Supp. III Part 2:** 561–562
Mind-Reader, The (Wilbur), **Supp. III Part 2:** 560–562
Mindwheel (Pinsky), **Supp. VI:** 235
"Mined Country" (Wilbur), **Supp. III Part 2:** 546–548
"Mine Own John Berryman" (Levine),

Supp. V: 179–180
Miner, Bob, **Supp. V:** 23
Miner, Earl, **III:** 466, 479
Miner, Madonne, **Supp. XIII:** 29
"Minerva Writes Poems" (Cisneros), **Supp. VII:** 63–64, 66
Mingus, Charles, **Supp. IX:** 152
"Mingus in Diaspora" (Matthews), **Supp. IX:** 166
"Mingus in Shadow" (Matthews), **Supp. IX:** 168–169
Ming Yellow (Marquand), **III:** 56
"Minimal, The" (Roethke), **III:** 531–532
"Mini-novela: *Rosa y sus espinas*" (Mora), **Supp. XIII:** 218
"Minions of Midas, The" (London), **II:** 474–475
Minister's Charge, The, or The Apprenticeship of Lemuel Barber (Howells), **II:** 285–286, 287
"Minister's Wooing, The" (Stowe), **Supp. I Part 2:** 592–595
Minister's Wooing, The (Stowe), **II:** 541
"Ministration of Our Departed Friends, The" (Stowe), **Supp. I Part 2:** 586–587
"Minneapolis Poem, The" (Wright), **Supp. III Part 2:** 601–602
"Minnesota Transcendentalist" (Peseroff), **Supp. IV Part 1:** 71
Minnie, Temple, **II:** 344
Minority Report: H. L. Mencken's Notebooks (Mencken), **III:** 112
"Minor Poems" (Eliot), **I:** 579
"Minor Topics" (Howells), **II:** 274
Minot, Susan, **Supp. VI: 203–215**
"Minotaur Loves His Labyrinth, The" (Simic), **Supp. VIII:** 270, 279, 281
"Minstrel Man" (Hughes), **Supp. I Part 1:** 325
Mint (Nye), **Supp. XIII:** 277
"Minting Time" (Sarton), **Supp. VIII:** 259
Mint Snowball (Nye), **Supp. XIII:** 277–278, **284–285**
"Mint Snowball" (Nye), **Supp. XIII:** 278, 284
"Mint Snowball II" (Nye), **Supp. XIII:** 284, 285
Minutes to Go (Corso, Gysin, Beiles and Burroughs), **Supp. XII:** 129
Mirabell: Books of Number (Merrill), **Supp. III Part 1:** 332–334
"Miracle" (Carver), **Supp. III Part 1:** 139–140
"Miracle for Breakfast, A" (Bishop), **Retro. Supp. II:** 43
"Miracle of Lava Canyon, The"

(Henry), **Supp. II Part 1:** 389, 390
Miracle of Mindfulness, The: A Manual on Meditation (Thich Nhat Hanh), **Supp. V:** 199–200
Mirage (Masters), **Supp. I Part 2:** 459, 470, 471
"Mirages, The" (Hayden), **Supp. II Part 1:** 373
"Miranda" (Buck), **Supp. II Part 1:** 128
Miranda, Carmen, **Supp. XII:** 165
Miranda, Francisco de, **Supp. I Part 2:** 522
"Miranda Over the Valley" (Dubus), **Supp. VII:** 81–83
"Miriam" (Capote), **Supp. III Part 1:** 117, 120, 122
"Miriam" (Whittier), **Supp. I Part 2:** 691, 703
"Miriam Tazewell" (Ransom), **Supp. X:** 58
"Mirror" (Merrill), **Supp. III Part 1:** 322
"Mirror" (Plath), **Retro. Supp. II:** 248–249, 257
"Mirror, The" (Glück), **Supp. V:** 83
"Mirroring Evil: Nazi Images/Recent Art" (Epstein), **Supp. XII:** 166
Mirrors (Creeley), **Supp. IV Part 1:** 156
Mirrors and Windows (Nemerov), **III:** 269, 275–277
"Mirrors of Chartres Street" (Faulkner), **II:** 56
Misanthrope, The (Molière; Wilbur, trans.), **Supp. III Part 2:** 552, 560
Miscellaneous Works of Mr. Philip Freneau, Containing His Essays and Additional Poems (Freneau), **Supp. II Part 1:** 263, 264, 266
Misery (King), **Supp. V:** 140, 141, 142, 147–148, 151, 152
Mises, Ludwig von, **Supp. IV Part 2:** 524
Misfits, The (A. Miller), **III:** 147, 149, 156, 161–162, 163
"Misogamist, The" (Dubus), **Supp. VII:** 86–87
Misrepresentations Corrected, and Truth Vindicated, in a Reply to the Rev. Mr. Solomon Williams's Book (Edwards), **I:** 549
"Miss Ella" (Z. Fitzgerald), **Supp. IX:** 57, 59, **71–72**
"Miss Emily and the Bibliographer" (Tate), **Supp. II Part 1:** 103
"Miss Furr and Miss Skeene" (Stein), **IV:** 29–30
"Missing Child" (Simic), **Supp. VIII:** 282

"Missing in Action" (Komunyakaa), **Supp. XIII:** 123, 124
"Mission of Jane, The" (Wharton), **Retro. Supp. I:** 367
Mission to Moscow (film), **Supp. I Part 1:** 281
"Mississippi" (Faulkner), **Retro. Supp. I:** 77
"Mississippi" (Simpson), **Supp. IX:** 271
"Miss Kate in H-1" (Twain), **IV:** 193
Miss Leonora When Last Seen (Taylor), **Supp. V:** 323
Miss Lonelyhearts (West), **I:** 107; **II:** 436; **III:** 357; **IV:** 287, 288, 290–297, 300, 301, 305, 306; **Retro. Supp. II:** 339, 340, 343, 346, **350–353**
Miss Mamma Aimee (Caldwell), **I:** 308, 309, 310
"Miss Mary Pask" (Wharton), **IV:** 316; **Retro. Supp. I:** 382
"Miss McEnders" (Chopin), **Retro. Supp. II:** 67
"Missoula Softball Tournament" (Hugo), **Supp. VI:** 132
Miss Ravenel's Conversion from Secession to Loyalty (De Forest), **IV:** 350
"Miss Tempy's Watchers" (Jewett), **II:** 401; **Retro. Supp. II:** 139
"Miss Terriberry to Wed in Suburbs" (Updike), **Retro. Supp. I:** 335
"Mist, The" (King), **Supp. V:** 144
"Mistaken Charity, A" (Freeman), **Retro. Supp. II:** 138
"Mister Toussan" (Ellison), **Retro. Supp. II:** 124–125; **Supp. II Part 1:** 238
"Mistress of Sydenham Plantation, The" (Jewett), **Retro. Supp. II:** 141
Mitchell, Burroughs, **Supp. XI:** 218, 222, 227
Mitchell, Dr. S. Weir, **IV:** 310
Mitchell, Margaret, **II:** 177
Mitchell, Roger, **Supp. IV Part 1:** 70
Mitchell, Tennessee. *See* Anderson, Mrs. Sherwood (Tennessee Mitchell)
Mitchell, Wesley C., **Supp. I Part 2:** 632, 643
Mitch Miller (Masters), **Supp. I Part 2:** 456, 466, 469–471, 474, 475, 476
Mitchum, Robert, **Supp. IX:** 95, 250
Mitgang, Herbert, **Supp. IV Part 1:** 220, 226, 307; **Supp. VIII:** 124
"Mixed Sequence" (Roethke), **III:** 547
Miyazawa Kenji, **Supp. VIII:** 292
Mizener, Arthur, **II:** 77, 81, 84, 94; **IV:** 132
Mladenoff, Nancy, **Supp. X:** 176
"M'liss: An Idyl of Red Mountain"

(Harte), **Supp. II Part 1:** 339
"Mnemonic Devices" (Goldbarth), **Supp. XII:** 183
"Mobile in Back of the Smithsonian, The" (Swenson), **Supp. IV Part 2:** 646
Mobilio, Albert, **Supp. VIII:** 3
Moby Dick (film), **Supp. IV Part 1:** 102, 116
Moby Dick; or, The Whale (Melville), **I:** 106, 354; **II:** 33, 224–225, 236, 539–540; **III:** 28–29, 74, 75, 77, 81, 82, 83–86, 87, 89, 90, 91, 93, 94, 95, 359, 453, 556; **IV:** 57, 199, 201, 202; **Retro. Supp. I:** 160, 220, 243, 244, 248, **249–253**, 254, 256, 257, 335; **Retro. Supp. II:** 121, 186, 275; **Supp. I Part 1:** 249; **Supp. I Part 2:** 579; **Supp. IV Part 2:** 613; **Supp. V:** 281; **Supp. VIII:** 106, 188, 198
Mock, John, **Supp. XIII:** 174
"Mocking-Bird, The" (Bierce), **I:** 202
"Mock Orange" (Glück), **Supp. V:** 84–85
Modarressi, Mitra, **Supp. IV Part 2:** 657
Models of Misrepresentation: On the Fiction of E. L. Doctorow (Morris), **Supp. IV Part 1:** 231
Model World and Other Stories, A (Chabon), **Supp. XI:** 66
Modern Brazilian Architecture (Bishop, trans.), **Supp. I Part 1:** 92
Modern Fiction Studies, **Supp. V:** 238
Modern Instance a Novel, A (Howells), **II:** 275, 279, 282–283, 285
Modern Library, The, **Retro. Supp. I:** 112, 113
Modern Mephistopheles, A (Alcott), **Supp. I Part 1:** 37–38
Modern Poetic Sequence, The (Rosenthal), **Supp. V:** 333
"Modern Poetry" (Crane), **I:** 390
"Modern Sorcery" (Simic), **Supp. VIII:** 283
"Modern Times" (Zukofsky), **Supp. III Part 2:** 624
Modern Writer, The (Anderson), **I:** 117
Modersohn, Mrs. Otto (Paula Becker), **Supp. I Part 2:** 573–574
Modersohn, Otto, **Supp. I Part 2:** 573
"Modes of Being" (Levertov), **Supp. III Part 1:** 282
Modest Enquiry into the Nature and Necessity of a Paper-Currency, A (Franklin), **II:** 108–109
"Modest Proposal, A" (Swift), **I:** 295; **Retro. Supp. II:** 305

"Modest Self-Tribute, A" (Wilson), **IV:** 431, 432
Moeller, Philip, **III:** 398, 399
"Moench von Berchtesgaden, Der" (Voss), **I:** 199–200
Moers, Ellen, **Retro. Supp. II:** 99
Moe's Villa and Other Stories (Purdy), **Supp. VII:** 270, 280
Mogen, David, **Supp. IV Part 1:** 106
Mohammed, **I:** 480; **II:** 1
Mohawk (Russo), **Supp. XII: 326–328**
Moir, William Wilmerding, **Supp. V:** 279
"Moles" (Oliver), **Supp. VII:** 235
Molesworth, Charles, **Supp. IV Part 1:** 39; **Supp. VIII:** 292, 306
Molière (Jean-Baptiste Poquelin), **III:** 113; **Supp. I Part 2:** 406; **Supp. III Part 2:** 552, 560; **Supp. IV Part 2:** 585; **Supp. V:** 101
"Molino Rojo, El" (Ríos), **Supp. IV Part 2:** 544
Moll Flanders (Defoe), **Supp. V:** 127; **Supp. XIII:** 43
"Molloch in State Street" (Whittier), **Supp. I Part 2:** 687
"Moll Pitcher" (Whittier), **Supp. I Part 2:** 684
"Molly Brant, Iroquois Matron" (Gunn Allen), **Supp. IV Part 1:** 331
"Moloch" (H. Miller), **III:** 177
Momaday, N. Scott, **Supp. IV Part 1:** 274, 323, 324, 404; **Supp. IV Part 2: 479–496**, 504, 557, 562; **Supp. XII:** 209
Moments of the Italian Summer (Wright), **Supp. III Part 2:** 602
"Momus" (Robinson), **III:** 508
Monaghan, Pat, **Supp. XI:** 121
"Mon Ami" (Bourne), **I:** 227
Monet, Claude, **Retro. Supp. I:** 378
"Monet's 'Waterlilies'" (Hayden), **Supp. II Part 1:** 361–362
Monette, Paul, **Supp. X: 145–161**
Money (Amis), **Retro. Supp. I:** 278
"Money" (Matthews), **Supp. IX:** 166
"Money" (Nemerov), **III:** 287
Money, Money, Money (Wagoner), **Supp. IX:** 324, **333–334**
Moneychangers, The (Sinclair), **Supp. V:** 285
Money Writes! (Sinclair), **Supp. V:** 277
Monica, Saint, **IV:** 140
Monikins, The (Cooper), **I:** 348, 354
Monk and the Hangman's Daughter, The (Bierce), **I:** 199–200, 209
"Monkey Garden, The" (Cisneros), **Supp. VII:** 63
"Monkey Puzzle, The" (Moore), **III:** 194, 207, 211

Monkeys (Minot), **Supp. VI:** 203–205, **206–210**
"Monkeys, The" (Moore), **III:** 201, 202
Monkey Wrench Gang, The (Abbey), **Supp. VIII:** 42; **Supp. XIII: 9–11**, 16
"Monk of Casal-Maggiore, The" (Longfellow), **II:** 505
"Monocle de Mon Oncle, Le" (Stevens), **IV:** 78, 84; **Retro. Supp. I:** 301; **Supp. III Part 1:** 20; **Supp. X:** 58
Monro, Harold, **III:** 465; **Retro. Supp. I:** 127
Monroe, Harriet, **I:** 235, 384, 390, 393; **III:** 458, 581, 586; **IV:** 74; **Retro. Supp. I:** 58, 131; **Retro. Supp. II:** 82, 83; **Supp. I Part 1:** 256, 257, 258, 262, 263, 267; **Supp. I Part 2:** 374, 387, 388, 464, 610, 611, 613, 614, 615, 616
Monroe, James, **Supp. I Part 2:** 515, 517
Monroe, Lucy, **Retro. Supp. II:** 70
Monroe, Marilyn, **III:** 161, 162–163
Monroe's Embassy; or, the Conduct of the Government in Relation to Our Claims to the Navigation of the Mississippi (Brown), **Supp. I Part 1:** 146
"Monsoon Season" (Komunyakaa), **Supp. XIII:** 122
"Monster, The" (Crane), **I:** 418
Monster, The, and Other Stories (Crane), **I:** 409
Montage of a Dream Deferred (Hughes), **Retro. Supp. I:** 194, **208–209**; **Supp. I Part 1:** 333, 339–341
Montagu, Ashley, **Supp. I Part 1:** 314
"Montaigne" (Emerson), **II:** 6
Montaigne, Michel de, **II:** 1, 5, 6, 8, 14–15, 16, 535; **III:** 600; **Retro. Supp. I:** 247
Montale, Eugenio, **Supp. III Part 1:** 320; **Supp. V:** 337–338; **Supp. VIII:** 30
"Montana; or the End of Jean-Jacques Rousseau" (Fiedler), **Supp. XIII: 97–98**
"Montana Ranch Abandoned" (Hugo), **Supp. VI:** 139
"Mont Blanc" (Shelley), **Supp. IX:** 52
Montcalm, Louis Joseph de, **Supp. I Part 2:** 498
Montcalm and Wolfe (Parkman), **Supp. II Part 2:** 596, 609, 610, 611–613
Montgomery, Benilde, **Supp. XIII:** 202
Montgomery, Robert, **Supp. I Part 2:**

611; **Supp. IV Part 1:** 130
Month of Sundays, A (Updike), **Retro. Supp. I:** 325, 327, 329, 330, 331, 333, 335
Monti, Luigi, **II:** 504
Montoya, José, **Supp. IV Part 2:** 545
"Montrachet-le-Jardin" (Stevens), **IV:** 82
Mont-Saint-Michel and Chartres (Adams), **I:** 1, 9, 12–14, 18, 19, 21; **Supp. I Part 2:** 417
Montserrat (Hellman), **Supp. I Part 1:** 283–285
Montserrat (Robles), **Supp. I Part 1:** 283–285
"Monument, The" (Bishop), **Supp. I Part 1:** 89
Monument, The (Strand), **Supp. IV Part 2:** 629, 630
"Monument Mountain" (Bryant), **Supp. I Part 1:** 156, 162
"Monument to After-Thought Unveiled, A" (Frost), **Retro. Supp. I:** 124
Moo (Smiley), **Supp. VI:** 292, **303–305**
Moods (Alcott), **Supp. I Part 1:** 33, 34–35, 43
Moody, Anne, **Supp. IV Part 1:** 11
Moody, Mrs. William Vaughn, **I:** 384; **Supp. I Part 2:** 394
Moody, Richard, **Supp. I Part 1:** 280
Moody, William Vaughn, **III:** 507; **IV:** 26
"Moon and the Night and the Men, The" (Berryman), **I:** 172
"Moon Deluxe" (F. Barthelme), **Supp. XI:** 26, 27, 33, 36
Mooney, Tom, **I:** 505
"Moon-Face" (London), **II:** 475
Moon-Face and Other Stories (London), **II:** 483
"Moon Flock" (Dickey), **Supp. IV Part 1:** 186
Moon for the Misbegotten, A (O'Neill), **III:** 385, 401, 403, 404
Moon Is a Gong, The (Dos Passos). *See Garbage Man, The* (Dos Passos)
Moon Is Down, The (Steinbeck), **IV:** 51
Moon Lady, The (Tan), **Supp. X:** 289
"Moonlight Alert" (Winters), **Supp. II Part 2:** 801, 811, 815
Moon of the Caribbees, The (O'Neill), **III:** 388
Moon Palace (Auster), **Supp. XII:** 22, 27, **30–32**
"Moonshine" (Komunyakaa), **Supp. XIII:** 127, 128

"Moon Solo" (Laforgue), **Supp. XIII:** 346

"Moon upon her fluent Route, The" (Dickinson), **I:** 471

Moony's Kid Don't Cry (T. Williams), **IV:** 381

Moore, Arthur, **Supp. I Part 1:** 49

Moore, Dr. Merrill, **III:** 506

Moore, George, **I:** 103

Moore, John Milton, **III:** 193

Moore, Lorrie, **Supp. VIII:** 145; **Supp. X: 163–180**

Moore, Marianne, **I:** 58, 285, 401, 428; **III: 193–217,** 514, 592–593; **IV:** 74, 75, 76, 91, 402; **Retro. Supp. I:** 416, 417; **Retro. Supp. II:** 39, 44, 48, 50, 82, 178, 179, 243, 244; **Supp. I Part 1:** 84, 89, 255, 257; **Supp. I Part 2:** 707; **Supp. II Part 1:** 21; **Supp. III Part 1:** 58, 60, 63; **Supp. III Part 2:** 612, 626, 627; **Supp. IV Part 1:** 242, 246, 257; **Supp. IV Part 2:** 454, 640, 641

Moore, Marie Lorena. See Moore, Lorrie

Moore, Mary Tyler, **Supp. V:** 107

Moore, Mary Warner, **III:** 193

Moore, Steven, **Supp. IV Part 1:** 279, 283, 284, 285, 287; **Supp. XII:** 151

Moore, Sturge, **III:** 459

Moore, Thomas, **II:** 296, 299, 303; **Supp. IX:** 104; **Supp. X:** 114

Moos, Malcolm, **III:** 116, 119

"Moose, The" (Bishop), **Retro. Supp. II:** 50; **Supp. I Part 1:** 73, 93, 94, 95; **Supp. IX:** 45, 46

"Moose Wallow, The" (Hayden), **Supp. II Part 1:** 367

Mora, Pat, **Supp. XIII: 213–232**

"Moral Bully, The" (Holmes), **Supp. I Part 1:** 302

"Moral Character, the Practice of Law, and Legal Education" (Hall), **Supp. VIII:** 127

"Moral Equivalent for Military Service, A" (Bourne), **I:** 230

"Moral Equivalent of War, The" (James), **II:** 361; **Supp. I Part 1:** 20

Moralités Légendaires (Laforgue), **I:** 573

"Morality and Mercy in Vienna" (Pynchon), **Supp. II Part 2:** 620, 624

"Morality of Indian Hating, The" (Momaday), **Supp. IV Part 2:** 484

"Morality of Poetry, The" (Wright), **Supp. III Part 2:** 596–597, 599

Moral Man and Immoral Society (Niebuhr), **III:** 292, 295–297

"Morals Is Her Middle Name" (Hughes), **Supp. I Part 1:** 338

"Morals of Chess, The" (Franklin), **II:** 121

"Moral Substitute for War, A" (Addams), **Supp. I Part 1:** 20

"Moral Theology of Atticus Finch, The" (Shaffer), **Supp. VIII:** 127

"Moral Thought, A" (Freneau), **Supp. II Part 1:** 262

Moran, Thomas, **Supp. IV Part 2:** 603–604

Moran of the Lady Letty (Norris), **II:** 264; **III:** 314, 322, 327, 328, 329, 330, 331, 332, 333

Morath, Ingeborg. See Miller, Mrs. Arthur (Ingeborg Morath)

Moravia, Alberto, **I:** 301

Moré, Gonzalo, **Supp. X:** 185

More, Henry, **I:** 132

More, Paul Elmer, **I:** 223–224, 247; **Supp. I Part 2:** 423

Moreau, Gustave, **I:** 66

More Conversations with Eudora Welty (Prenshaw, ed.), **Retro. Supp. I:** 340, 341, 342, 343, 344, 352, 353, 354

More Die of Heartbreak (Bellow), **Retro. Supp. II:** 31, 33, 34

"More Girl Than Boy" (Komunyakaa), **Supp. XIII:** 117

"More Light! More Light! (Hecht), **Supp. X:** 60

"Morella" (Poe), **III:** 412; **Retro. Supp. II:** 270

"More Love in the Western World" (Updike), **Retro. Supp. I:** 327–328, 329

"Morels" (W. J. Smith), **Supp. XIII: 336–339**

"More of a Corpse Than a Woman" (Rukeyser), **Supp. VI:** 280

"More Pleasant Adventures" (Ashbery), **Supp. III Part 1:** 1

More Poems to Solve (Swenson), **Supp. IV Part 2:** 640, 642, 648

More Stately Mansions (O'Neill), **III:** 385, 401, 404–405

"More Than Human" (Chabon), **Supp. XI:** 71–72

Morgan, Edmund S., **IV:** 149; **Supp. I Part 1:** 101, 102; **Supp. I Part 2:** 484

Morgan, Edwin, **Supp. IV Part 2:** 688

Morgan, Henry, **II:** 432; **IV:** 63

Morgan, J. P., **I:** 494; **III:** 14, 15

Morgan, Jack, **Retro. Supp. II:** 142

Morgan, Robert, **Supp. V:** 5

Morgan, Robin, **Supp. I Part 2:** 569

Morgan's Passing (Tyler), **Supp. IV Part 2:** 666–667, 668, 669

Morgenthau, Hans, **III:** 291, 309

Moricand, Conrad, **III:** 190

Morison, Mrs. Samuel Eliot (Elizabeth Shaw Greene), **Supp. I Part 2:** 483

Morison, Mrs. Samuel Eliot (Priscilla Barton), **Supp. I Part 2:** 493, 496, 497

Morison, Samuel Eliot, **Supp. I Part 2: 479–500**

"Morituri Salutamus" (Longfellow), **II:** 499, 500; **Retro. Supp. II:** 169; **Supp. I Part 2:** 416

"Moriturus" (Millay), **III:** 126, 131–132

Morley, Christopher, **III:** 481, 483, 484; **Supp. I Part 2:** 653; **Supp. IX:** 124

Morley, Edward, **IV:** 27

Morley, Lord John, **I:** 7

Mormon Country (Stegner), **Supp. IV Part 2:** 598, 601–602

"Morning, The" (Updike), **Retro. Supp. I:** 329

"Morning after My Death, The" (Levis), **Supp. XI:** 260, 263–264

"Morning Glory" (Merrill), **Supp. III Part 1:** 337

Morning Glory, The (Bly), **Supp. IV Part 1:** 63–65, 66, 71

"Morning Imagination of Russia, A" (W. C. Williams), **Retro. Supp. I:** 428

Morning in Antibes (Knowles), **Supp. XII:** 249

Morning in the Burned House (Atwood), **Supp. XIII:** 20, 35

Morning Is Near Us, The (Glaspell), **Supp. III Part 1:** 184–185

Morning Noon and Night (Cozzens), **I:** 374, 375, 376, 377, 379, 380

"Morning of the Day They Did It, The" (White), **Supp. I Part 2:** 663

"Morning Prayers" (Harjo), **Supp. XII:** 231

"Morning Roll Call" (Anderson), **I:** 116

"Mornings in a New House" (Merrill), **Supp. III Part 1:** 327

Mornings Like This (Dillard), **Supp. VI:** 23, 34

"Morning Song" (Plath), **Retro. Supp. II:** 252

Morning Watch, The (Agee), **I:** 25, 39–42

"Morning with Broken Window" (Hogan), **Supp. IV Part 1:** 405

Morrell, Ottoline, **Retro. Supp. I:** 60

Morris, Christopher D., **Supp. IV Part 1:** 231, 236

Morris, George Sylvester, **Supp. I Part 2:** 640
Morris, Gouverneur, **Supp. I Part 2:** 512, 517, 518
Morris, Lloyd, **III:** 458
Morris, Robert, **Supp. I Part 2:** 510
Morris, Timothy, **Retro. Supp. I:** 40
Morris, William, **II:** 323, 338, 523; **IV:** 349; **Supp. I Part 1:** 260, 356; **Supp. XI:** 202
Morris, Willie, **Supp. XI:** 216, 231, 234
Morris, Wright, **I:** 305; **III: 218–243,** 558, 572; **IV:** 211
Morrison, Charles Clayton, **III:** 297
Morrison, Jim, **Supp. IV Part 1:** 206
Morrison, Toni, **Retro. Supp. II:** 15, 118; **Supp. III Part 1: 361–381; Supp. IV Part 1:** 2, 13, 14, 250, 253, 257; **Supp. V:** 169, 259; **Supp. VIII:** 213, 214; **Supp. X:** 85, 239, 250, 325; **Supp. XI:** 4, 14, 20, 91; **Supp. XII:** 289, 310; **Supp. XIII:** 60, 185
"Morro Bay" (Jeffers), **Supp. II Part 2:** 422
Morrow, W. C., **I:** 199
Morse, Robert, **Supp. XI:** 305
Morse, Samuel F. B., **Supp. I Part 1:** 156
Mortal Acts, Mortal Words (Kinnell), **Supp. III Part 1:** 235, 236, 237, 249–254
Mortal Antipathy, A (Holmes), **Supp. I Part 1:** 315–316
"Mortal Enemies" (Humphrey), **Supp. IX:** 109
"Mortal Eternal" (Olds), **Supp. X:** 214
Mortal No, The (Hoffman), **IV:** 113
Morte D'Arthur, Le (Malory), **Supp. IV Part 1:** 47
Morton, David, **Supp. IX:** 76
Morton, Jelly Roll, **Supp. X:** 242
"Mosaic of the Nativity: Serbia, Winter 1993" (Kenyon), **Supp. VII:** 173
Mosby's Memoirs and Other Stories (Bellow), **Retro. Supp. II:** 27
Moscow under Fire (Caldwell), **I:** 296
Moses, Man of the Mountain (Hurston), **Supp. VI:** 149, 158, 160
Mosle, Sara, **Supp. XI:** 254
Mosley, Walter, **Supp. XIII: 233–252**
Mosquito Coast, The (film), **Supp. VIII:** 323
Mosquito Coast, The (Theroux), **Supp. VIII:** 321, **322–323**
Mosquitos (Faulkner), **II:** 56; **Retro. Supp. I:** 79, 81
Moss, Howard, **III:** 452; **Supp. IV Part 2:** 642; **Supp. IX:** 39; **Supp. XIII:** 114
Moss, Stanley, **Supp. XI:** 321
Moss, Thylias, **Supp. XI:** 248
Mosses from an Old Manse (Hawthorne), **I:** 562; **II:** 224; **III:** 82, 83; **Retro. Supp. I:** 157, 248
"Moss of His Skin" (Sexton), **Supp. II Part 2:** 676
"Most Extraordinary Case, A" (James), **II:** 322; **Retro. Supp. I:** 218
Most Likely to Succeed (Dos Passos), **I:** 491
"Most of It, The" (Frost), **Retro. Supp. I:** 121, 125, 129, 139
Motel Chronicles (Shepard), **Supp. III Part 2:** 445
"Mother" (Paley), **Supp. VI: 222–223**
"Mother" (Snyder), **Supp. VIII:** 298
Mother (Whistler), **IV:** 369
Mother, The (Buck), **Supp. II Part 1:** 118–119
"Mother and Jack and the Rain" (Sexton), **Supp. II Part 2:** 686
"Mother and Son" (Tate), **IV:** 128, 137–138
Mother Courage and Her Children (Brecht), **III:** 160; **Supp. IX:** 140; **Supp. XII:** 249
"Mother Earth: Her Whales" (Snyder), **Supp. VIII:** 302
"Motherhood" (Swenson), **Supp. IV Part 2:** 645
Mother Hubbard (Reed), **Supp. X:** 241
"Mother-in-Law" (Rich), **Retro. Supp. II:** 291
Mother Love (Dove), **Supp. IV Part 1:** 250–251, 254
"Mother Marie Therese" (Lowell), **Retro. Supp. II:** 188
Mother Night (Vonnegut), **Supp. II Part 2:** 757, 758, 767, 770, 771
"Mother Rosarine" (Kumin), **Supp. IV Part 2:** 442
Mother's Recompense, The (Wharton), **IV:** 321, 324; **Retro. Supp. I:** 382
"Mother's Tale, A" (Agee), **I:** 29–30
"Mother's Things" (Creeley), **Supp. IV Part 1:** 141
"Mother's Voice" (Creeley), **Supp. IV Part 1:** 156
Mother to Daughter, Daughter to Mother (Olsen, ed.), **Supp. XIII:** 295
"Mother Tongue" (Simic), **Supp. VIII:** 283
"Mother to Son" (Hughes), **Retro. Supp. I:** 199, 203; **Supp. I Part 1:** 321–322, 323
"Mother Writes to the Murderer, The: A Letter" (Nye), **Supp. XIII:** 276
"Moth Hour" (Rich), **Retro. Supp. II:** 283
"Motion, The" (Olson), **Supp. II Part 2:** 571
Motion of History, The (Baraka), **Supp. II Part 1:** 55, 56
"Motive for Metaphor, The" (Stevens), **IV:** 89; **Retro. Supp. I:** 310
Motiveless Malignity (Auchincloss), **Supp. IV Part 1:** 31
Motley, John Lothrop, **Supp. I Part 1:** 299; **Supp. I Part 2:** 479
"Motor Car, The" (White), **Supp. I Part 2:** 661
Motor-Flight Through France (Wharton), **I:** 12; **Retro. Supp. I:** 372
Mott, Michael, **Supp. VIII:** 204, 208
"Mountain, The" (Frost), **Retro. Supp. I:** 121
"Mountain Hermitage, The: Pages from a Japanese Notebook" (Passin), **Supp. XIII:** 337
Mountain Interval (Frost), **II:** 154; **Retro. Supp. I:** 131, 132, 133
"Mountain Lion" (Hogan), **Supp. IV Part 1:** 412
Mountainous Journey, A (Tuqan), **Supp. XIII:** 278
Mountains, The (Wolfe), **IV:** 461
Mountains and Rivers without End (Snyder), **Supp. VIII:** 295, **305–306**
"Mountains grow unnoticed, The" (Dickinson), **Retro. Supp. I:** 46
Mountains of California, The (Muir), **Supp. IX:** 183
"Mountain Whippoorwill, The" (Benét), **Supp. XI:** 44–45, 46, 47
"Mount-Joy: or Some Passages Out of the Life of a Castle-Builder" (Irving), **II:** 314
"Mourners, The" (Malamud), **Supp. I Part 2:** 431, 435, 436–437
Mourners Below (Purdy), **Supp. VII:** 274, 280
"Mourning and Melancholia" (Freud), **Supp. IV Part 2:** 450
Mourning Becomes Electra (O'Neill), **III:** 391, 394, 398–400
"Mourning Poem for the Queen of Sunday" (Hayden), **Supp. II Part 1:** 379–380
"Mouse Elegy" (Olds), **Supp. X:** 209
"Mouth of Brass" (Humphrey), **Supp. IX:** 101
Moveable Feast, A (Hemingway), **II:** 257; **Retro. Supp. I:** 108, 171, **186–187**
Movement, The: Documentary of a Struggle for Equality (Student Non-

violent Coordinating Committee), **Supp. IV Part 1:** 369
"Move over Macho, Here Comes Feminismo" (Robbins), **Supp. X:** 272
"Move to California, The" (Stafford), **Supp. XI:** 318, 321
"Movie" (Shapiro), **Supp. II Part 2:** 707
Movie at the End of the World, The (McGrath), **Supp. X:** 127
Moviegoer, The (Percy), **Supp. III Part 1:** 383–385, 387, 389–392, 394, 397
"Movie Magazine, The: A Low 'Slick'" (Percy), **Supp. III Part 1:** 385
Movies (Dixon), **Supp. XII:** 147
"Moving Around" (Matthews), **Supp. IX:** 155
"Moving Finger, The" (Wharton), **Retro. Supp. I:** 365
Moving On (McMurtry), **Supp. V:** 223–224
Moving Target, The (Macdonald), **Supp. IV Part 2:** 462, 463, 467, 470, 471, 473, 474
Moving Target, The (Merwin), **Supp. III Part 1:** 346, 347–348, 352, 357
"Mowbray Family, The" (Farrell and Alden), **II:** 45
"Mowing" (Frost), **II:** 169–170; **Retro. Supp. I:** 127, 128
"Moxan's Master" (Bierce), **I:** 206
Moyers, Bill, **Supp. IV Part 1:** 267; **Supp. VIII:** 331; **Supp. XI:** 126, 132; **Supp. XII:** 217; **Supp. XIII:** 274, 276
Moynihan, Daniel Patrick, **Retro. Supp. II:** 123; **Supp. VIII:** 241
Mozart, Wolfgang Amadeus, **I:** 479, 588; **IV:** 74, 358; **Supp. IV Part 1:** 284
"Mozart and the Gray Steward" (Wilder), **IV:** 358
Mr. and Mrs. Baby and Other Stories (Strand), **Supp. IV Part 2:** 631
"Mr. and Mrs. Fix-It" (Lardner), **II:** 431
Mr. Arcularis (Aiken), **I:** 54, 56
"Mr. Bruce" (Jewett), **II:** 397; **Retro. Supp. II:** 134, 143
"Mr. Burnshaw and the Statue" (Stevens), **Retro. Supp. I:** 298, 303
"Mr. Carson Death on His Nights Out" (McGrath), **Supp. X:** 118
Mr. Clemens and Mark Twain (Kaplan), **I:** 247–248
"Mr. Coffee and Mr. Fixit" (Carver), **Supp. III Part 1:** 145
"Mr. Cornelius Johnson, Office-Seeker" (Dunbar), **Supp. II Part 1:** 211, 213

"Mr. Costyve Duditch" (Toomer), **Supp. III Part 2:** 486
"Mr. Dajani, Calling from Jericho" (Nye), **Supp. XIII:** 286–287
"Mr. Edwards and the Spider" (Lowell), **I:** 544; **II:** 550; **Retro. Supp. II:** 187
Mr. Field's Daughter (Bausch), **Supp. VII:** 47–48, 51–52
"Mr. Flood's Party" (Robinson), **III:** 512
"Mr. Forster's Pageant" (Maxwell), **Supp. VIII:** 172
"Mr. Frost's Chickens" (Oliver), **Supp. VII:** 232–233
Mr. Hodge and Mr. Hazard (Wylie), **Supp. I Part 2:** 708, 709, 714, 721–724
"Mr. Hueffer and the Prose Tradition" (Pound), **III:** 465
Mr. Ives' Christmas (Hijuelos), **Supp. VIII:** 85–86
"Mr. Longfellow and His Boy" (Sandburg), **III:** 591
"Mr. Luna and History" (Ríos), **Supp. IV Part 2:** 551
Mr. Moto Is So Sorry (Marquand), **III:** 57, 58
"Mr. Preble Gets Rid of His Wife" (Thurber), **Supp. I Part 2:** 615
"Mr. Rolfe" (Wilson), **IV:** 436
Mr. Sammler's Planet (Bellow), **I:** 144, 147, 150, 151, 152, 158; **Retro. Supp. II:** 19, 28, 30
"Mr. Shelley Speaking" (Wylie), **Supp. I Part 2:** 719
Mr. Spaceman (R. O. Butler), **Supp. XII:** 62, **74–75**
"Mr. Thompson's Prodigal" (Harte), **Supp. II Part 1:** 354
Mr. Vertigo (Auster), **Supp. XII: 34–35,** 36
"Mr. Whittier" (Scott), **Supp. I Part 2:** 705
Mr. Wilson's War (Dos Passos), **I:** 485
Mrabet, Mohammed, **Supp. IV Part 1:** 92, 93
Mrs. Albert Grundy: Observations in Philistia (Frederic), **II:** 138–139
"Mrs. Bilingsby's Wine" (Taylor), **Supp. V:** 323
"Mrs. Cassidy's Last Year" (Gordon), **Supp. IV Part 1:** 306
Mrs. Dalloway (Woolf), **Supp. IV Part 1:** 299; **Supp. VIII:** 5
"Mrs. Krikorian" (Olds), **Supp. X:** 211
"Mrs. Maecenas" (Burke), **I:** 271
"Mrs. Mandrill" (Nemerov), **III:** 278
"Mrs. Manstey's View" (Wharton), **Retro. Supp. I:** 362, 363

"Mrs. Mobry's Reason" (Chopin), **Retro. Supp. II:** 61
Mrs. Reynolds (Stein), **IV:** 43
Mrs. Stevens Hears the Mermaids Singing (Sarton), **Supp. VIII:** 252–253, **256–257**
Mrs. Ted Bliss (Elkin), **Supp. VI:** 56, 58
"Mrs. Turner Cutting the Grass" (Shields), **Supp. VII:** 319–320
"Mrs. Walpurga" (Rukeyser), **Supp. VI:** 273
"MS. Found in a Bottle" (Poe), **III:** 411, 416; **Retro. Supp. II:** 274
"Ms. Lot" (Rukeyser), **Supp. VI:** 281
Ms. Magazine, **Supp. V:** 259
Mttron-Hirsch, Sidney, **III:** 484–485
"Muchas Gracias Por Todo" (Nye), **Supp. XIII:** 282–283
"Much Madness is divinest Sense" (Dickinson), **Retro. Supp. I:** 37–38
"Muck-A-Muck" (Harte), **Supp. II Part 1:** 342
"Mud Below, The" (Proulx), **Supp. VII:** 262
Mudrick, Marvin, **Retro. Supp. II:** 307
"Mud Season" (Kenyon), **Supp. VII:** 167–168
Mueller, Lisel, **Supp. I Part 1:** 83, 88
Muggli, Mark, **Supp. IV Part 1:** 207
Muhammad, Elijah, **Supp. I Part 1:** 60
Muir, Edwin, **I:** 527; **II:** 368; **III:** 20
Muir, John, **Supp. VIII:** 296; **Supp. IX:** 33, **171–188;** **Supp. X:** 29
Mujica, Barbara, **Supp. VIII:** 89
Mulatto (Hughes), **Retro. Supp. I:** 197, 203; **Supp. I Part 1:** 328, 339
Mulching of America, The (Crews), **Supp. XI:** 107
Muldoon, William, **I:** 500–501
Mule Bone (Hughes and Hurston), **Retro. Supp. I:** 194, 203; **Supp. VI:** 154
Mules and Men (Hurston), **Supp. VI:** 149, 153, 154, 160
Mulford, Prentice, **I:** 193
Mulligan, Robert, **Supp. VIII:** 128, 129
Mulligan Stew (Sorrentino), **Supp. XII:** 139
Mullins, Eustace, **III:** 479
Mullins, Priscilla, **II:** 502–503
Multitudes, Multitudes (Clampitt), **Supp. IX:** 39
Mumbo Jumbo (Reed), **Supp. X:** 240, 242, **245–248,** 251
Mumford, Lewis, **I:** 245, 250, 251, 252, 259, 261; **II:** 271, 473–474; **Supp. I Part 2:** 632, 638; **Supp. II**

Part 2: 471–501
Mumford, Sophia Wittenberg (Mrs. Lewis Mumford), **Supp. II Part 2:** 474, 475
Mummy, The (film), **Supp. IV Part 1:** 104
"Mundus et Infans" (Auden), **Supp. II Part 1:** 15
"Munich, 1938" (Lowell), **II:** 554
"Munich Mannequins, The" (Plath), **Retro. Supp. II:** 256
"Municipal Report, A" (Henry), **Supp. II Part 1:** 406–407
Munro, Alice, **Supp. IX:** 212; **Supp. X:** 290; **Supp. XII:** 289–290, 310
Munsey, Frank, **I:** 501
Munson, Gorham, **I:** 252, 388, 432; **Retro. Supp. II:** 77, 78, 79, 82, 83; **Supp. I Part 2:** 454
"Murano" (Doty), **Supp. XI:** 131
Murasaki, Lady, **II:** 577
Muray, Nicholas, **Supp. I Part 2:** 708
Murder, My Sweet (film), **Supp. IV Part 1:** 130
"Murderer Guest, The" (Gordon), **Supp. IV Part 1:** 306
Murder in Mount Holly (Theroux), **Supp. VIII:** 315–316
Murder in the Cathedral (Eliot), **I:** 571, 573, 580, 581; **II:** 20; **Retro. Supp. I:** 65; **Retro. Supp. II:** 222
Murder of Lidice, The (Millay), **III:** 140
"Murders in the Rue Morgue, The" (Poe), **III:** 412, 416, 419–420; **Retro. Supp. II:** 271, 272
Murdoch, Iris, **Supp. VIII:** 167
Murphy, Jacqueline Shea, **Retro. Supp. II:** 143
Murphy, Patrick, **Supp. XIII:** 214
Murphy, Richard, **Retro. Supp. II:** 250
Murray, Albert, **Retro. Supp. II:** 119, 120
Murray, Edward, **I:** 229
Murray, G. E., **Supp. X:** 201; **Supp. XI:** 143, 155
Murray, Gilbert, **III:** 468–469
Murray, Jan, **Supp. IV Part 2:** 574
Murray, John, **II:** 304; **III:** 76, 79; **Retro. Supp. I:** 246
Murray, Margaret A., **Supp. V:** 128
Murrell, John A., **IV:** 265
Mursell, James L., **Supp. I Part 2:** 608
"Muse" (Ammons), **Supp. VII:** 29
"Muse, Postmodern and Homeless, The" (Ozick), **Supp. V:** 272
"Musée des Beaux Arts" (Auden), **Retro. Supp. I:** 430; **Supp. II Part 1:** 14
Muses Are Heard, The (Capote), **Supp. III Part 1:** 126
"Muses of Terrence McNally, The" (Zinman), **Supp. XIII:** 207–208
"Muse's Tragedy, The" (Wharton), **Retro. Supp. I:** 364
Museum (Dove), **Supp. IV Part 1:** 245–247, 248
"Museum" (Hass), **Supp. VI:** 107
Museums and Women (Updike), **Retro. Supp. I:** 321
"Museum Vase" (Francis), **Supp. IX:** 83
"Mushrooms" (Plath), **Retro. Supp. II:** 246; **Supp. I Part 2:** 539
"Music" (Oliver), **Supp. VII:** 236
Music After the Great War (Van Vechten), **Supp. II Part 2:** 732
Music and Bad Manners (Van Vechten), **Supp. II Part 2:** 733
"Music for a Farce" (Bowles), **Supp. IV Part 1:** 83
Music for Chameleons (Capote), **Supp. III Part 1:** 120, 125–127, 131, 132
"Music for Museums?" (Van Vechten), **Supp. II Part 2:** 732
"Music for the Movies" (Van Vechten), **Supp. II Part 2:** 733
"Music from Spain" (Welty), **IV:** 272
Music of Chance, The (Auster), **Supp. XII:** 21, 23, **32–33**
"Music of Prose, The" (Gass), **Supp. VI:** 92
Music of Spain, The (Van Vechten), **Supp. II Part 2:** 734, 735
"Music of the Spheres" (Epstein), **Supp. XII:** 165
Music School, The (Updike), **IV:** 214, 215, 219, 226, 227; **Retro. Supp. I:** 320, 328, 329, 330
"Music School, The" (Updike), **Retro. Supp. I:** 326, 329, 335
"Music Swims Back to Me" (Sexton), **Supp. II Part 2:** 673
Muske, Carol, **Supp. IV Part 2:** 453–454
"Mussel Hunter at Rock Harbor" (Plath), **Supp. I Part 2:** 529, 537
Musset, Alfred de, **I:** 474; **II:** 543
Mussolini, Benito, **III:** 115, 473, 608; **IV:** 372, 373; **Supp. I Part 1:** 281, 282; **Supp. I Part 2:** 618; **Supp. V:** 290
"Must the Novelist Crusade?" (Welty), **IV:** 280
"Mutability of Literature, The" (Irving), **II:** 308
"Mutation of the Spirit" (Corso), **Supp. XII:** 132, 133
Mute, The (McCullers), **II:** 586
Mutilated, The (T. Williams), **IV:** 382, 386, 393
Mutiny of the Elsinore, The (London), **II:** 467
"My Adventures as a Social Poet" (Hughes), **Retro. Supp. I:** 194, 207
"My Alba" (Ginsberg), **Supp. II Part 1:** 320, 321
My Alexandria (Doty), **Supp. XI:** 119, 120, 121, **123–125**, 130
My Ántonia (Cather), **I:** 321–322; **Retro. Supp. I:** 1, 3, 4, **11–13**, 14, 17, 18, 22; **Supp. IV Part 2:** 608
"My Appearance" (Wallace), **Supp. X:** 306–307
My Argument with the Gestapo: A Macaronic Journal (Merton), **Supp. VIII:** 207
"My Arkansas" (Angelou), **Supp. IV Part 1:** 15
"My Aunt" (Holmes), **Supp. I Part 1:** 302, 310
"My Beginnings" (Simpson), **Supp. IX:** 273
My Bondage and My Freedom (Douglass), **Supp. III Part 1:** 155, 173
My Brother (Kincaid), **Supp. VII:** 191–193
"My Brother Paul" (Dreiser), **Retro. Supp. II:** 94
"My Brothers the Silent" (Merwin), **Supp. III Part 1:** 349–350
"My Brother's Work" (Dunn), **Supp. XI:** 147
"My Butterfly" (Frost), **II:** 151; **Retro. Supp. I:** 124
"My Children, and a Prayer for Us" (Ortiz), **Supp. IV Part 2:** 507
"My Confession" (McCarthy), **II:** 562
My Country and My People (Yutang), **Supp. X:** 291
"My Country 'Tis of Thee" (Reznikoff), **Supp. III Part 2:** 616
My Days of Anger (Farrell), **II:** 34, 35–36, 43
My Death My Life by Pier Paolo Pasolini (Acker), **Supp. XII:** 7
My Dog Stupid (Fante), **Supp. XI:** 160, **170–171**
My Emily Dickinson (Howe), **Retro. Supp. I:** 33, 43; **Supp. IV Part 2:** 430–431
"My English" (Alvarez), **Supp. VII:** 2
Myers, Linda A., **Supp. IV Part 1:** 10
"My Extended Family" (Theroux), **Supp. VIII:** 311
"My Father" (Sterne), **IV:** 466
"My Father: October 1942" (Stafford), **Supp. XI:** 323

"My Father at Eighty-Five" (Bly), **Supp. IV Part 1:** 73
"My Father Is a Simple Man" (Salinas), **Supp. XIII:** 324
"My Fathers Came From Kentucky" (Lindsay), **Supp. I Part 2:** 395
"My Father's Friends" (Maxwell), **Supp. VIII:** 171
"My Father's Ghost" (Wagoner), **Supp. IX:** 330
"My Father's God" (Fante), **Supp. XI:** 160, 174
"My Father's Love Letters" (Komunyakaa), **Supp. XIII:** 127
"My Father Speaks to me from the Dead" (Olds), **Supp. X:** 210
"My Father's Telescope" (Dove), **Supp. IV Part 1:** 246, 248
"My Father with Cigarette Twelve Years Before the Nazis Could Break His Heart" (Levine), **Supp. V:** 194
"My Favorite Murder" (Bierce), **I:** 205
My Favorite Plant: Writers and Gardeners on the Plants They Love (Kincaid), **Supp. VII:** 193–194
"My Fifty-Plus Years Celebrate Spring" (Salinas), **Supp. XIII:** 327
"My First Book" (Harte), **Supp. II Part 1:** 343
My First Summer in the Sierra (Muir), **Supp. IX:** 172, 173, **178–181**, 183, 185
"My Fountain Pen" (McClatchy), **Supp. XII:** 254, 260
My Friend, Henry Miller (Perlès), **III:** 189
My Friend, Julia Lathrop (Addams), **Supp. I Part 1:** 25
"My Friend, Walt Whitman" (Oliver), **Supp. VII:** 245
"My Garden Acquaintance" (Lowell), **Supp. I Part 2:** 420
My Garden [Book]: (Kincaid), **Supp. VII:** 193–194
"My Grandfather" (Lowell), **II:** 554
"My Grandmother's Love Letters" (H. Crane), **Retro. Supp. II:** 78
"My Grandson, Home at Last" (Angelou), **Supp. IV Part 1:** 13
My Green Hills of Jamaica (McKay), **Supp. X:** 132, 142
My Heart's in the Highlands (Saroyan), **Supp. IV Part 1:** 83
"My High School Reunion" (Kingston), **Supp. V:** 169
"My Kinsman, Major Molineux" (Hawthorne), **II:** 228, 229, 237–239, 243; **Retro. Supp. I:** 153–154, 158, 160, 161; **Retro. Supp. II:** 181, 187
My Kinsman, Major Molineux (Lowell), **II:** 545–546
"My Last Afternoon with Uncle Devereux Winslow" (Lowell), **II:** 547–548; **Retro. Supp. II:** 189
"My Last Drive" (Hardy), **Supp. VIII:** 32
"My Life" (Strand), **Supp. IV Part 2:** 627
My Life, Starring Dara Falcon (Beattie), **Supp. V:** 31, 34–35
My Life a Loaded Gun: Dickinson, Plath, Rich, and Female Creativity (Bennett), **Retro. Supp. I:** 29
My Life and Hard Times (Thurber), **Supp. I Part 2:** 607, 609
My Life as a Man (Roth), **Retro. Supp. II:** 299, 304, 307; **Supp. III Part 2:** 401, 404, 405, 417–418
"My Life as a P.I.G., or the True Adventures of Smokey the Cop" (Abbey), **Supp. XIII:** 3
"My life closed twice before its close" (Dickinson), **Retro. Supp. I:** 38
"My Life had stood a Loaded Gun" (Dickinson), **Retro. Supp. I:** 42, 43, 45, 46; **Supp. IV Part 2:** 430
"My Life with Medicine" (Nye), **Supp. XIII:** 282
"My Life with R. H. Macy" (Jackson), **Supp. IX:** 118
"My Little Utopia" (Simic), **Supp. VIII:** 283
My Lives and How I Lost Them (Cullen), **Supp. IV Part 1:** 173
"My Lost City" (Fitzgerald), **Retro. Supp. I:** 102
"My Lost Youth" (Longfellow), **II:** 487, 499; **Retro. Supp. II:** 168
My Love Affair with America: The Cautionary Tale of a Cheerful Conservative (Podhoretz), **Supp. VIII:** 232, 233, 237, **244–246**
"My Lover Has Dirty Fingernails" (Updike), **Retro. Supp. I:** 332, 333
"My Lucy Friend Who Smells Like Corn" (Cisneros), **Supp. VII:** 68–69
"My Mammogram" (McClatchy), **Supp. XII:** 263–264
"My Man Bovanne" (Bambara), **Supp. XI:** 2
"My Mariner" (Larcom), **Supp. XIII:** 147
My Mark Twain (Howells), **II:** 276
"My Metamorphosis" (Harte), **Supp. II Part 1:** 339
"My Moby Dick" (Humphrey), **Supp. IX:** 95
My Mortal Enemy (Cather), **I:** 327–328; **Retro. Supp. I:** 16–17; **Supp. I Part 2:** 719
My Mother: Demonology (Acker), **Supp. XII:** 6
My Mother, My Father and Me (Hellman), **Supp. I Part 1:** 290–291
"My Mother and My Sisters" (Ortiz), **Supp. IV Part 2:** 499
"My Mother Is Speaking from the Desert" (Gordon), **Supp. IV Part 1:** 309, 314
"My Mother's Goofy Song" (Fante), **Supp. XI:** 164
"My Mother's Memoirs, My Father's Lie, and Other True Stories" (Banks), **Supp. V:** 15
"My Mother's Nipples" (Hass), **Supp. VI:** 109
"My Mother's Story" (Kunitz), **Supp. III Part 1:** 259
"My Mother with Purse the Summer They Murdered the Spanish Poet" (Levine), **Supp. V:** 194
My Movie Business: A Memoir (Irving), **Supp. VI:** 164
"My Name" (Cisneros), **Supp. VII:** 60
"My Negro Problem—And Ours" (Podhoretz), **Supp. VIII: 234–236**
"My New Diet" (Karr), **Supp. XI:** 241
"My Old Man" (Hemingway), **II:** 263
My Other Life (Theroux), **Supp. VIII:** 310, 324
My Own True Name: New and Selected Poems for Young Adults, 1984–1999 (Mora), **Supp. XIII:** 222
"My Passion for Ferries" (Whitman), **IV:** 350
"My People" (Hughes), **Retro. Supp. I:** 197; **Supp. I Part 1:** 321–322, 323
"My Playmate" (Whittier), **Supp. I Part 2:** 699–700
"My Priests" (Monette), **Supp. X:** 159
Myra Breckinridge (Vidal), **Supp. IV Part 2:** 677, 685–686, 689, 691
"My Recollections of S. B. Fairchild" (Jackson), **Supp. IX:** 118–119
"My Religion" (Carson), **Supp. XII: 105–106**
"My Road to Hell Was Paved" (Patchett), **Supp. XII:** 310–311
Myron (Vidal), **Supp. IV Part 2:** 677, 685, 686, 691
"My Roomy" (Lardner), **II:** 420, 421, 428, 430
"My Sad Self" (Ginsberg), **Supp. II Part 1:** 320
My Secret History (Theroux), **Supp. VIII:** 310, 324
"My Shoes" (Simic), **Supp. VIII:** 275
"My Side of the Matter" (Capote), **Supp. III Part 1:** 114, 115

My Silk Purse and Yours: The Publishing Scene and American Literary Art (Garrett), **Supp. VII:** 111; **Supp. X:** 7

My Sister Eileen (McKenney), **IV:** 288; **Retro. Supp. II:** 339

My Sister's Hand in Mine: The Collected Works of Jane Bowles, **Supp. IV Part 1:** 82–83

"My Son" (Strand), **Supp. IV Part 2:** 629

My Son, John (film), **Supp. I Part 1:** 67

"My Son, the Murderer" (Malamud), **Supp. I Part 2:** 437

"My Son the Man" (Olds), **Supp. X:** 212

"Mysteries of Caesar, The" (Hecht), **Supp. X:** 73

"Mysteries of Eleusis, The" (Hardwick), **Supp. III Part 1:** 195

Mysteries of Pittsburgh, The (Chabon), **Supp. XI:** 65, 68, **69–71**

Mysterious Stranger, The (Twain), **IV:** 190–191, 210

Mystery, A (Shields). *See Swann* (Shields)

"Mystery, The" (Dunbar), **Supp. II Part 1:** 199, 210

"Mystery, The" (Glück), **Supp. V:** 91

Mystery and Manners (O'Connor), **Retro. Supp. II:** 230

"'Mystery Boy' Looks for Kin in Nashville" (Hayden), **Supp. II Part 1:** 366, 372

"Mystery of Heroism, A" (Crane), **I:** 414

"Mystery of Marie Rogêt, The" (Poe), **III:** 413, 419; **Retro. Supp. II:** 271

"Mystic" (Plath), **Retro. Supp. II:** 257; **Supp. I Part 2:** 539, 541

"Mystical Poet, A" (Bogan), **Retro. Supp. I:** 36

"Mystic of Sex, The—A First Look at D. H. Lawrence" (Nin), **Supp. X:** 188

"Mystic Vision in 'The Marshes of Glynn'" (Warfel), **Supp. I Part 1:** 366, 373

"Mystification" (Poe), **III:** 425

My Study Windows (Lowell), **Supp. I Part 2:** 407

"Myth" (Rukeyser), **Supp. VI:** 281–282

Myth of Sisyphus, The (Camus), **I:** 294; **Supp. XIII:** 165

"Myth of the Isolated Artist, The" (Oates), **Supp. II Part 2:** 520

Myth of the Machine, The (Mumford), **Supp. II Part 2:** 476, 478, 482, 483, 493, 497

Mythology and the Romantic Tradition in English Poetry (Bush), **Supp. I Part 1:** 268

Myths and Texts (Snyder), **Supp. VIII: 295–296**

"My *Tocaya*" (Cisneros), **Supp. VII:** 69

My Uncle Dudley (Morris), **I:** 305; **III:** 219–220

"My Uncle's Favorite Coffee Shop" (Nye), **Supp. XIII:** 283

"My Weariness of Epic Proportions" (Simic), **Supp. VIII:** 276

My Wicked Wicked Ways (Cisneros), **Supp. VII:** 58, 64–68, 71

"My Wicked Wicked Ways" (Cisneros), **Supp. VII:** 58, 64–66

"My Word-house" (Mora), **Supp. XIII:** 219, 225

My Works and Days (Mumford), **Supp. II Part 2:** 475, 477, 481

My World and Welcome to It (Thurber), **Supp. I Part 2:** 610

Nabokov, Peter, **Supp. IV Part 2:** 490

Nabokov, Véra, **Retro. Supp. I:** 266, 270

Nabokov, Vladimir, **I:** 135; **III: 244–266**, 283, 286; **Retro. Supp. I: 263–281**, 317, 335; **Supp. I Part 1:** 196; **Supp. II Part 1:** 2; **Supp. IV Part 1:** 135; **Supp. V:** 127, 237, 251, 252, 253; **Supp. VIII:** 105, 133, 138; **Supp. IX:** 152, 212, 261; **Supp. X:** 283; **Supp. XI:** 66; **Supp. XII:** 310; **Supp. XIII:** 46, 52

Nabokov's Dozen (Nabokov), **Retro. Supp. I:** 266

Nabokov's Garden: A Guide to Ada (Mason), **Supp. VIII:** 138

Naca, Kristin, **Supp. XIII:** 133

Nadeau, Robert, **Supp. X:** 261, 270

Nadel, Alan, **Supp. IV Part 1:** 209

Naipaul, V. S., **Supp. IV Part 1:** 297; **Supp. VIII:** 314; **Supp. X:** 131

Naked and the Dead, The (Mailer), **I:** 477; **III:** 26, 27, 28–30, 31, 33, 35, 36, 44; **Retro. Supp. II: 197–199; Supp. IV Part 1:** 381; **Supp. XI:** 218

Naked in Garden Hills (Crews), **Supp. XI:** 102, **110**

Naked Lunch (Burroughs), **Supp. III Part 1:** 92–95, 97–105; **Supp. IV Part 1:** 90

"Naked Nude" (Malamud), **Supp. I Part 2:** 450

Naked Poetry (Berg and Mezey, eds.), **Supp. IV Part 1:** 60

Naked Poetry (Levine), **Supp. V:** 180

Namedropping: Mostly Literary Memoirs (Coover), **Supp. V:** 40

"Name in the Papers" (Hughes), **Supp. I Part 1:** 330

Name Is Archer, The (Macdonald, under Millar), **Supp. IV Part 2:** 466

"Name Is Burroughs, The" (Burroughs), **Supp. III Part 1:** 93

Name Is Fogarty, The: Private Papers on Public Matters (Farrell), **II:** 49

Names, The (DeLillo), **Supp. VI:** 3, 10, 13, 14

Names, The (Momaday), **Supp. IV Part 2:** 479, 480, 483, 486, 487, 488, 489

Names and Faces of Heroes, The (Price), **Supp. VI:** 258, 260

Names of the Lost, The (Levine), **Supp. V:** 177–178, 179, 187–188

"Naming Myself" (Kingsolver), **Supp. VII:** 208

Naming of the Beasts, The (Stern). *See Rejoicings: Selected Poems, 1966–1972* (Stern)

Nana (Zola), **III:** 321

"Nancy Culpepper" (Mason), **Supp. VIII:** 141

Nancy Drew stories, **Supp. VIII:** 133, 135, 137, 142

"Nancy Knapp" (Masters), **Supp. I Part 2:** 461

"Naomi Shihab Nye: U.S. Mideast-History a Harbinger of 9-11?" (Nye), **Supp. XIII:** 286

"Nap, The" (Banks), **Supp. V:** 7

"Napoleon" (Emerson), **II:** 6

Napoleon I, **I:** 6, 7, 8, 474; **II:** 5, 309, 315, 321, 523; **Supp. I Part 1:** 153; **Supp. I Part 2:** 518, 519

Narcissa and Other Fables (Auchincloss), **Supp. IV Part 1:** 21, 34

"Narcissus as Narcissus" (Tate), **IV:** 124

Nardal, Paulette, **Supp. X:** 139

Nardi, Marcia, **Retro. Supp. I:** 426, 427

Narration (Stein), **IV:** 27, 30, 32, 33, 36

Narrative of a Four Months' Residence among the Natives of a Valley of the Marquesas Islands (Melville), **III:** 76

Narrative of Arthur Gordon Pym, The (Poe), **III:** 412, 416; **Retro. Supp. II:** 265, **273–275**; **Supp. XI:** 293

Narrative of the Life of Frederick Douglass, an American Slave, Written by Himself (Douglass), **Supp. III**

Part 1: 154–159, 162, 165; **Supp. IV Part 1:** 13; **Supp. VIII:** 202
Narrenschiff, Das (Brant), **III:** 447
"Narrow Fellow in the Grass, A" (Dickinson), **Retro. Supp. I:** 30, 37
Narrow Heart, A: Portrait of a Woman (Gordon), **II:** 197, 217
Narrow Rooms (Purdy), **Supp. VII:** 274
Nash, Roderick, **Supp. IX:** 185
Nash, Thomas, **Supp. III Part 1:** 387–388
Nashe, Thomas, **I:** 358
Nashville (film), **Supp. IX:** 143
Nasser, Gamal Abdel, **IV:** 490
Natalie Mann (Toomer), **Supp. III Part 2:** 484–486
Nathan, George Jean, **II:** 91; **III:** 103, 104, 106, 107; **IV:** 432; **Supp. IV Part 1:** 343; **Supp. IX:** 56–57; **Supp. XIII:** 161
"Nathanael West" (Herbst), **Retro. Supp. II:** 343
Nathanael West: The Art of His Life (Martin), **Retro. Supp. II:** 343
Nathan Coulter (Berry), **Supp. X:** 24, 33
"Nationalist, The" (Anderson), **I:** 115
"Nation Is Like Ourselves, The" (Baraka), **Supp. II Part 1:** 53
"Native, The" (Olds), **Supp. X:** 215
"Native American Attitudes to the Environment" (Momaday), **Supp. IV Part 2:** 481, 491
Native American Renaissance (Lincoln), **Supp. IV Part 2:** 507
Native American Testimony (Nabokov, ed.), **Supp. IV Part 2:** 490
"Native Hill, A" (Berry), **Supp. X:** 21
Native in a Strange Land: Trials & Tremors (Coleman), **Supp. XI:** 84–85, 87
Native of Winby and Other Tales, A (Jewett), **II:** 396; **Retro. Supp. II:** 138
Native Son (Wright), **IV:** 476, 477, 478, 479, 481, 482–484, 485, 487, 488, 491, 495; **Retro. Supp. II:** 107, 116; **Supp. I Part 1:** 51, 64, 67, 337; **Supp. II Part 1:** 170, 235–236; **Supp. IX:** 306
"Native Trees" (Merwin), **Supp. III Part 1:** 355
Natural, The (Malamud), **II:** 424, 425; **Retro. Supp. II:** 306; **Supp. I Part 2:** 438–441, 443
"*Natural, The:* Malamud's World Ceres" (Wasserman), **Supp. I Part 2:** 439

"Natural History" (Olds), **Supp. X:** 210
"Natural History of Some Poems, A" (Harrison), **Supp. VIII:** 53
"Natural History of the Dead" (Hemingway), **II:** 206; **Retro. Supp. I:** 176
"Naturally Superior School, A" (Knowles), **Supp. XII:** 235, 240–241
"Natural Method of Mental Philosophy" (Emerson), **II:** 14
"Natural Resources" (Rich), **Supp. I Part 2:** 575
Natural Selection (F. Barthelme), **Supp. XI:** 2, 28, 32, 33
Nature (Emerson), **I:** 463; **II:** 1, 8, 12, 16; **IV:** 171, 172–173
"Nature" (Emerson), **Retro. Supp. I:** 250; **Supp. I Part 2:** 383; **Supp. III Part 1:** 387; **Supp. IX:** 178
"Nature, Inc." (Lewis), **II:** 441
Nature: Poems Old and New (Swenson), **Supp. IV Part 2:** 652
Nature and Destiny of Man, The (Niebuhr), **III:** 292, 303–306, 310
"Nature and Life" (Emerson), **II:** 19
"Nature and Nurture: When It Comes to Twins, Sometimes It's Hard to Tell the Two Apart" (Bausch), **Supp. VII:** 40
"Nature-Metaphors" (Lanier), **Supp. I Part 1:** 352
Nature Morte (Brodsky), **Supp. VIII:** 25
Nature of Evil, The (James), **II:** 343
Nature of Peace, The (Veblen), **Supp. I Part 2:** 642
Nature of True Virtue, The (Edwards), **I:** 549, 557–558, 559
Nature's Economy: A History of Ecological Ideas (Worster), **Supp. IX:** 19
Nausea (Sartre), **Supp. VIII:** 7
"Navajo Blanket, A" (Swenson), **Supp. IV Part 2:** 649
Navarette, Don Martín de, **II:** 310
Navarro, Ramon, **Supp. IV Part 1:** 206
Navigator, The (film), **I:** 31
Naylor, Gloria, **Supp. VIII:** 213–230
Naylor, Paul Kenneth, **Supp. IV Part 2:** 420
Nazimova, **III:** 399
Neal, Larry, **Retro. Supp. II:** 112, 128; **Supp. X:** 324, 328
Neal, Lawrence P., **Supp. II Part 1:** 53
Neal, Patricia, **Supp. I Part 1:** 286; **Supp. IV Part 2:** 524; **Supp. V:** 223

Neale, Walter, **I:** 192, 208
Nearer the Moon: From "A Journal of Love," the Unexpurgated Diary of Anaïs Nin, 1937–1939, **Supp. X:** 184, 185
Near-Johannesburg Boy and Other Poems, The (Brooks), **Supp. III Part 1:** 86
Near Klamath (Carver), **Supp. III Part 1:** 137
"Near Perigord" (Pound), **Retro. Supp. I:** 289, 290
Near the Ocean (Lowell), **II:** 543, 550, 551–553, 554, 555; **Retro. Supp. II:** 182, 186, 189–190
"Near View of the High Sierra, A" (Muir), **Supp. IX:** 183
Nebeker, Helen, **Supp. IX:** 122
Necessary Angel, The (Stevens), **IV:** 76, 79, 89, 90
Necessities of Life: Poems, 1962–1965 (Rich), **Retro. Supp. II:** 283; **Supp. I Part 2:** 553, 555
"Necrological" (Ransom), **III:** 486–489, 490, 492
Ned Christie's War (Conley), **Supp. V:** 232
"Need for a Cultural Base to Civil Rites & Bpower Mooments, The" (Baraka), **Supp. II Part 1:** 48
"Need for Christian Preaching, The" (Buechner), **Supp. XII:** 49
Needful Things (King), **Supp. V:** 139, 146
"Needle" (Simic), **Supp. VIII:** 275
"Need of Being Versed in Country Things, The" (Frost), **II:** 154; **Retro. Supp. I:** 133, 135
"Negative Capability" (Komunyakaa), **Supp. XIII:** 131
Negligible Tales (Bierce), **I:** 209
"Negotiating the Darkness, Fortified by Poets' Strength" (Karr), **Supp. XI:** 254; **Supp. XIII:** 285
Negotiating with the Dead (Atwood), **Supp. XIII:** 20, 35
Negritude movement, **Supp. X:** 131, 139
"Negro" (Hughes), **Supp. I Part 1:** 321–322
Negro, The (Du Bois), **Supp. II Part 1:** 178, 179, 185
Negro, The: The Southerner's Problem (Page), **Supp. II Part 1:** 168
"Negro Artisan, The" (Du Bois), **Supp. II Part 1:** 166
"Negro Artist and the Racial Mountain, The" (Hughes), **Retro. Supp. I:** 200, 207; **Supp. I Part 1:** 323, 325; **Supp. IV Part 1:** 169

"Negro Assays the Negro Mood, A" (Baldwin), **Supp. I Part 1:** 52
"Negro Citizen, The" (Du Bois), **Supp. II Part 1:** 179
"Negro Dancers" (Hughes), **Retro. Supp. I:** 199; **Supp. I Part 1:** 324
Negroes in America, The (McKay), **Supp. X:** 132, 136
"Negroes of Farmville, Virginia, The: A Social Study" (Du Bois), **Supp. II Part 1:** 166
Negro Family, The: The Case for National Action (Moynihan), **Retro. Supp. II:** 123
"Negro Farmer, The" (Du Bois), **Supp. II Part 1:** 167
"Negro Ghetto" (Hughes), **Supp. I Part 1:** 331
Negro in American Civilization, The (Du Bois), **Supp. II Part 1:** 179
"Negro in Large Cities, The" (Du Bois), **Supp. II Part 1:** 169
"Negro in Literature and Art, The" (Du Bois), **Supp. II Part 1:** 174
Negro in New York, The (Ellison), **Supp. II Part 1:** 230
"Negro in the Black Belt, The: Some Social Sketches" (Du Bois), **Supp. II Part 1:** 166
"Negro in the Well, The" (Caldwell), **I:** 309
"Negro Love Song, A" (Dunbar), **Supp. II Part 1:** 204
Negro Mother, The (Hughes), **Supp. I Part 1:** 328
Negro Mother and Other Dramatic Recitations, The (Hughes), **Retro. Supp. I:** 203
Negro Novel in America, The (Bone), **Supp. IX:** 318–319
Negro Publication Society of America, **Retro. Supp. I:** 205
"Negro Renaissance, The: Jean Toomer and the Harlem of the 1920s" (Bontemps), **Supp. IX:** 306
"Negro Schoolmaster in the New South, A" (Du Bois), **Supp. II Part 1:** 168
"Negro Sermon, A: Simon Legree" (Lindsay), **Supp. I Part 2:** 393
"Negro Sings of Rivers, The" (Hughes), **Supp. IV Part 1:** 16
"Negro Speaks of Rivers, The" (Hughes), **Retro. Supp. I:** 199; **Supp. I Part 1:** 321
"Negro Takes Stock, The" (Du Bois), **Supp. II Part 1:** 180
"Negro Theatre, The" (Van Vechten), **Supp. II Part 2:** 735
"Negro Voter Sizes Up Taft, A" (Hurston), **Supp. VI:** 160
"Negro Writer and His Roots, The: Toward a New Romanticism" (Hansberry), **Supp. IV Part 1:** 364
"Nehemias Americanus" (Mather), **Supp. II Part 2:** 453
Nehru, Jawaharlal, **IV:** 490
"Neighbor" (Hugo), **Supp. VI:** 135–136
"Neighbors" (Carver), **Supp. III Part 1:** 135, 139, 141; **Supp. XI:** 153
"Neighbors" (Hogan), **Supp. IV Part 1:** 405
"Neighbour Rosicky" (Cather), **I:** 331–332
Neil Simon (Johnson), **Supp. IV Part 2:** 573
"Neil Simon: Toward Act III?" (Walden), **Supp. IV Part 2:** 591
"Neil Simon's Jewish-Style Comedies" (Walden), **Supp. IV Part 2:** 584, 591
Neilson, Heather, **Supp. IV Part 2:** 681
"Neither Out Far Nor In Deep" (Frost), **I:** 303; **Retro. Supp. I:** 121, 138
"Nellie Clark" (Masters), **Supp. I Part 2:** 461
Nelson, Ernest, **I:** 388
Nelson, Howard, **Supp. IV Part 1:** 66, 68
Nelson, Lord Horatio, **II:** 524
Nelson, Shirley, **Supp. XII:** 293
Nelson Algren (Cox and Chatterton), **Supp. IX:** 11–12
Nelson Algren: A Life on the Wild Side (Drew), **Supp. IX:** 2
Nemerov, David, **II:** 268
Nemerov, Howard, **III:** 267–289; **IV:** 137, 140; **Supp. III Part 2:** 541; **Supp. IV Part 2:** 455, 650; **Supp. IX:** 114
Nemiroff, Robert Barron, **Supp. IV Part 1:** 360, 361, 365, 369, 370, 374
Neoconservative Criticism: Norman Podhoretz, Kenneth S. Lynn, and Joseph Epstein (Winchell), **Supp. VIII:** 241
"Neo-Hoodoo Manifesto, The" (Reed), **Supp. X:** 242
Neon Vernacular (Komunyakaa), **Supp. XIII:** 121, **127–128**, 131
Neon Wilderness, The (Algren), **Supp. IX:** 3, 4
Neo-Slave Narratives (Rushdy), **Supp. X:** 250
Nepantla: Essays from the Land in the Middle (Mora), **Supp. XIII:** 213, **219–221**, 227
Nephew, The (Purdy), **Supp. VII:** 271, 273, 282
"Nereids of Seriphos, The" (Clampitt), **Supp. IX:** 41
Neruda, Pablo, **Supp. I Part 1:** 89; **Supp. IV Part 2:** 537; **Supp. V:** 332; **Supp. VIII:** 272, 274; **Supp. IX:** 157, 271; **Supp. X:** 112; **Supp. XI:** 191; **Supp. XII:** 217; **Supp. XIII:** 114, 315, 323
Nesbit, Edith, **Supp. VIII:** 171
Nesbitt, Robin, **Supp. VIII:** 89
Nesting Ground, The (Wagoner), **Supp. IX:** 324, **325–326**
Nest of Ninnies, A (Ashbery and Schuyler), **Supp. III Part 1:** 3
Nets to Catch the Wind (Wylie), **Supp. I Part 2:** 709, 710–712, 714
Nettleton, Asahel, **I:** 458
"Net to Snare the Moonlight, A" (Lindsay), **Supp. I Part 2:** 387
Neubauer, Carol E., **Supp. IV Part 1:** 9
Neugroschel, Joachim, **Supp. IX:** 138
Neuhaus, Richard John, **Supp. VIII:** 245
Neumann, Erich, **Supp. I Part 2:** 567; **Supp. IV Part 1:** 68, 69
Neuromancer (Gibson), **Supp. XII:** 15
"Neurotic America and the Sex Impulse" (Dreiser), **Retro. Supp. II:** 105
"Never Bet the Devil Your Head" (Poe), **III:** 425; **Retro. Supp. II:** 273
Never Come Morning (Algren), **Supp. IX:** 3, **7–9**
Never in a Hurry: Essays on People and Places (Nye), **Supp. XIII:** 273, **280–282**, 286
"Never Marry a Mexican" (Cisneros), **Supp. VII:** 70
"Never Room with a Couple" (Hughes), **Supp. I Part 1:** 330
"Nevertheless" (Moore), **III:** 214
Nevins, Allan, **I:** 253; **Supp. I Part 2:** 486, 493
"Nevsky Prospekt" (Olds), **Supp. X:** 205
"New Age of the Rhetoricians, The" (Cowley), **Supp. II Part 1:** 135
New American Literature, The (Pattee), **II:** 456
New American Novel of Manners, The (Klinkowitz), **Supp. XI:** 347
New American Poetry, 1945–1960 (Allen, ed.), **Supp. XIII:** 112
New American Poetry, The (Allen, ed.), **Supp. VIII:** 291, 292
"New American Writer, A" (W. C.

Williams), **Retro. Supp. II:** 353
New and Collected Poems (Reed), **Supp. X:** 241
New and Collected Poems (Wilbur), **Supp. III Part 2:** 562–564
New and Selected Poems (Nemerov), **III:** 269, 275, 277–279
New and Selected Poems (Oliver), **Supp. VII:** 240–241, 245
New and Selected Poems (Wagoner), **Supp. IX:** 326–327
New and Selected Poems (W. J. Smith), **Supp. XIII:** 332
New and Selected Poems: 1974–1994 (Dunn), **Supp. XI: 151–152**
New and Selected Things Taking Place (Swenson), **Supp. IV Part 2:** 648–650, 651
"New Art Gallery Society, The" (Wolfe), **Supp. III Part 2:** 580
Newcomb, Ralph, **Supp. XIII:** 12
Newcomb, Robert, **II:** 111
New Conscience and an Ancient Evil, A (Addams), **Supp. I Part 1:** 14–15, 16
New Criticism, The (Ransom), **III:** 497–498, 499, 501
"New Day, A" (Levine), **Supp. V:** 182
Newdick, Robert Spangler, **Retro. Supp. I:** 138
Newdick's Season of Frost (Newdick), **Retro. Supp. I:** 138
New Dictionary of Quotations, A (Mencken), **III:** 111
"New Directions in Poetry" (D. Locke), **Supp. IX:** 273
Newell, Henry, **IV:** 193
"New England" (Lowell), **II:** 536
"New England" (Robinson), **III:** 510, 524
New England: Indian Summer (Brooks), **I:** 253, 256
"New England Bachelor, A" (Eberhart), **I:** 539
"New Englander, The" (Anderson), **I:** 114
New England Girlhood, A (Larcom), **Supp. XIII:** 137, 142, 143, 144, **147–154**
New England Local Color Literature (Donovan), **Retro. Supp. II:** 138
"New England Sabbath-Day Chace, The" (Freneau), **Supp. II Part 1:** 273
New-England Tale, A (Sedgwick), **I:** 341
New England Tragedies, The (Longfellow), **II:** 490, 505, 506; **Retro. Supp. II:** 165, 167
Newer Ideals of Peace (Addams), **Supp. I Part 1:** 11–12, 15, 16–17, 19, 20–21
New Feminist Criticism, The: Essays on Women, Literature, and Theory (Showalter), **Supp. X:** 97
"New Folsom Prison" (Matthews), **Supp. IX:** 165
New Found Land: Fourteen Poems (MacLeish), **III:** 12–13
New Hampshire: A Poem with Notes and Grace Notes (Frost), **II:** 154–155; **Retro. Supp. I:** 132, 133, 135
"New Hampshire, February" (Eberhart), **I:** 536
New Industrial State, The (Galbraith), **Supp. I Part 2:** 648
"New Journalism, The" (Wolfe), **Supp. III Part 2:** 571
New Journalism, The (Wolfe and Johnson, eds.), **Supp. III Part 2:** 570, 579–581, 583, 586
New Left, The: The Anti-Industrial Revolution (Rand), **Supp. IV Part 2:** 527
"New Letters from Thomas Jefferson" (Stafford), **Supp. XI:** 324
New Letters on the Air: Contemporary Writers on Radio, **Supp. X:** 165, 169, 173
"New Life" (Glück), **Supp. V:** 90
New Life, A (Malamud), **Supp. I Part 2:** 429–466
"New Life at Kyerefaso" (Sutherland), **Supp. IV Part 1:** 9
"New Light on Veblen" (Dorfman), **Supp. I Part 2:** 650
Newman, Charles, **Supp. I Part 2:** 527, 546–548
Newman, Edwin, **Supp. IV Part 2:** 526
Newman, Judie, **Supp. IV Part 1:** 304, 305
Newman, Paul, **Supp. IV Part 2:** 473, 474
New Man, The (Merton), **Supp. VIII:** 208
"New Medea, The" (Howells), **II:** 282
New Mexico trilogy (Nichols), **Supp. XIII:** 269
"New Mother" (Olds), **Supp. X:** 206
"New Mothers, The" (Shields), **Supp. VII:** 310
New Music (Price), **Supp. VI:** 264, 265
"New Mutants, The" (Fiedler), **Supp. XIII:** 104
"New Name for Some Old Ways of Thinking, A" (James), **II:** 353
New Native American Novel, The: Works in Progress (Bartlett), **Supp. IV Part 1:** 335
"New Natural History, A" (Thurber), **Supp. I Part 2:** 619
New Negro, The (Locke, ed.), **Supp. II Part 1:** 176; **Supp. IX:** 309; **Supp. X:** 137
New Negro, The: An Interpretation (Locke, ed.), **Retro. Supp. I:** 199; **Supp. IV Part 1:** 170
New Orleans Sketches (Faulkner), **Retro. Supp. I:** 80
New Path to the Waterfall, A (Carver), **Supp. III Part 1:** 138–140, 147, 149
"New Poem, The" (Wright), **Supp. V:** 339, 340
"New Poems" (MacLeish), **III:** 19
"New Poems" (Oliver), **Supp. VII:** 240
New Poems: 1980–88 (Haines), **Supp. XII: 209–210**
New Poetry, The (Monroe and Henderson, eds.), **Supp. I Part 2:** 387
"New Poetry Handbook, The" (Strand), **Supp. IV Part 2:** 626
New Poetry of Mexico (Strand, trans.), **Supp. IV Part 2:** 630
New Poets of England and America (Hall, Pack, and Simpson, eds.), **Supp. IV Part 2:** 621
"Newport of Anchuria" (Henry), **Supp. II Part 1:** 409
"*New Republic* Moves Uptown, The" (Cowley), **Supp. II Part 1:** 142
"News, The" (McClatchy), **Supp. XII:** 269
"New Season" (Levine), **Supp. V:** 188
New Seeds of Contemplation (Merton), **Supp. VIII:** 200, 208
News from the Glacier: Selected Poems 1960–1980 (Haines), **Supp. XII:** 207, 208–209
"News Item" (Parker), **Supp. IX:** 190
New Song, A (Hughes), **Retro. Supp. I:** 202; **Supp. I Part 1:** 328, 331–332
"New South, The" (Lanier), **Supp. I Part 1:** 352, 354, 370
Newspaper Days, 1899–1906 (Mencken), **III:** 100, 102, 120
"New Spirit, The" (Ashbery), **Supp. III Part 1:** 14, 15
New Spoon River, The (Masters), **Supp. I Part 2:** 461–465, 473
New Star Chamber and Other Essays, The (Masters), **Supp. I Part 2:** 455–456, 459
New Tales of the Vampires (Rice), **Supp. VII:** 290
New Testament, **I:** 303, 457, 458; **II:** 167; **III:** 305; **IV:** 114, 134, 152;

Retro. Supp. I: 58, 140, 360; **Supp. I Part 1:** 104, 106; **Supp. I Part 2:** 516. *See also* names of New Testament books
New Testament, A (Anderson), **I:** 101, 114
"New Theory of Thorstein Veblen, A" (Galbraith), **Supp. I Part 2:** 650
Newton, Benjamin Franklin, **I:** 454
Newton, Huey P., **Supp. I Part 1:** 66; **Supp. IV Part 1:** 206
Newton, Isaac, **I:** 132, 557; **II:** 6, 103, 348–349; **III:** 428; **IV:** 18, 149
"New-Wave Format, A" (Mason), **Supp. VIII:** 141, 143, 147
New West of Edward Abbey, The (Ronald), **Supp. XIII:** 4
New Woman's Survival Sourcebook, The (Rennie and Grimstead, eds.), **Supp. I Part 2:** 569
New World, The: Tales (Banks), **Supp. V:** 8, 9, 10
New World Naked, A (Mariani), **Retro. Supp. I:** 419
New Worlds of Literature (Beaty and Hunter, eds.), **Supp. IV Part 1:** 331
New World Writing (Updike), **IV:** 217
New Year Letter (Auden), **Supp. II Part 1:** 14, 16
"New Year's Day" (Wharton), **Retro. Supp. I:** 381
"New Year's Eve" (Schwartz), **Supp. II Part 2:** 640, 656–657
New Year's Eve/1929 (Farrell), **II:** 43
"New Year's Eve 1968" (Lowell), **II:** 554
"New Year's Gift, The" (Stowe), **Supp. I Part 2:** 587
"New York" (Capote), **Supp. III Part 1:** 122
"New York" (Moore), **III:** 196, 198, 202, 206
"New York 1965" (Bowles), **Supp. IV Part 1:** 94
New York City Arts Project, **Supp. III Part 2:** 618
"New York City in 1979" (Acker), **Supp. XII:** 5
New York Edition, **Retro. Supp. I:** 235
"New York Edition" (James), **II:** 336, 337
"New York Gold Conspiracy, The" (Adams), **I:** 4
New York Intellectuals, **Supp. VIII:** 93
"New York Intellectuals, The" (Howe), **Supp. VI:** 120
New York Jew (Kazin), **Supp. VIII:** 95, **97–100**
New York Trilogy, The (Auster), **Supp. XII:** 21, **24–28**
Next (McNally), **Supp. XIII:** 197
"Next in Line, The" (Bradbury), **Supp. IV Part 1:** 102
Next Room of the Dream, The (Nemerov), **III:** 269, 275, 278, 279–280, 284
Next-to-Last Things: New Poems and Essays (Kunitz), **Supp. III Part 1:** 257–259, 261, 262, 265, 266, 268
"'Next to Reading Matter'" (Henry), **Supp. II Part 1:** 399
Nexus (H. Miller), **III:** 170, 187, 188, 189
Niatum, Duane, **Supp. IV Part 1:** 331; **Supp. IV Part 2:** 505
Nice Jewish Boy, The (Roth), **Supp. III Part 2:** 412
Nicholas II, Tsar, **Supp. I Part 2:** 447
Nichols, Charles, **Retro. Supp. I:** 194
Nichols, John, **Supp. XIII:** 253–272
Nichols, Luther, **Supp. X:** 265
Nichols, Mike, **Supp. IV Part 1:** 234; **Supp. IV Part 2:** 577
Nicholson, Colin, **Supp. VIII:** 129
Nicholson, Jack, **Supp. V:** 26; **Supp. VIII:** 45; **Supp. XI:** 308
Nick Adams Stories, The (Hemingway), **II:** 258; **Retro. Supp. I:** 174
"Nick and the Candlestick" (Plath), **Supp. I Part 2:** 544
Nickel Mountain: A Pastoral Novel (Gardner), **Supp. VI:** 63, 64, 68, **69**
Nicoll, Allardyce, **III:** 400
Nicoloff, Philip, **II:** 7
Niebuhr, Gustav, **III:** 292
Niebuhr, H. Richard, **I:** 494
Niebuhr, Lydia, **III:** 292
Niebuhr, Reinhold, **III: 290–313;** **Supp. I Part 2:** 654
Niedecker, Lorine, **Supp. III Part 2:** 616, 623
Nielsen, Ed, **Supp. IX:** 254
Nielson, Dorothy, **Supp. I Part 2:** 659
Nietzsche, Friedrich Wilhelm, **I:** 227, 283, 383, 389, 396, 397, 402, 509; **II:** 7, 20, 27, 42, 90, 145, 262, 462, 463, 577, 583, 585; **III:** 102–103, 113, 156, 176; **IV:** 286, 491; **Supp. I Part 1:** 254, 299, 320; **Supp. I Part 2:** 646; **Supp. IV Part 1:** 104, 105–106, 107, 110, 284; **Supp. IV Part 2:** 519; **Supp. V:** 277, 280; **Supp. VIII:** 11, 181, 189; **Supp. X:** 48; **Supp. XII:** 98
Niflis, N. Michael, **Supp. IV Part 1:** 175
Nigger Heaven (Van Vechten), **Supp. II Part 2:** 739, 744–746

"Nigger Jeff" (Dreiser), **Retro. Supp. II:** 97
Nigger of the "Narcissus," The (Conrad), **II:** 91; **Retro. Supp. I:** 106
"NIGGY THE HO" (Baraka), **Supp. II Part 1:** 54
"Night, Death, Mississippi" (Hayden), **Supp. II Part 1:** 369
'Night, Mother (Norman), **Supp. VIII:** 141
"Night above the Avenue" (Merwin), **Supp. III Part 1:** 355
"Night among the Horses, A" (Barnes), **Supp. III Part 1:** 33–34, 39, 44
Night at the Movies, A, or, You Must Remember This: Fictions (Coover), **Supp. V:** 50–51
"Night at the Opera, A" (Matthews), **Supp. IX:** 167
"Nightbird" (Komunyakaa), **Supp. XIII:** 132
"Night-Blooming Cereus, The" (Hayden), **Supp. II Part 1:** 367
Night-Blooming Cereus, The (Hayden), **Supp. II Part 1:** 367, 373
Night-Born, The (London), **II:** 467
"Nightbreak" (Rich), **Supp. I Part 2:** 556
Night Dance (Price), **Supp. VI:** 264
"Night Dances, The" (Plath), **Supp. I Part 2:** 544
"Night Dream, The" (MacLeish), **III:** 15
"Night Ferry" (Doty), **Supp. XI:** 124
Night in Acadie, A (Chopin), **Retro. Supp. II:** 66–67, 73; **Supp. I Part 1:** 200, 219, 220, 224
"Night in Acadie, A" (Chopin), **Retro. Supp. II:** 66
"Night in June, A" (W. C. Williams), **Retro. Supp. I:** 424
"Night in New Arabia, A" (Henry), **Supp. II Part 1:** 402
Night in Question, The: Stories (Wolff), **Supp. VII:** 342–344
"Night Journey" (Roethke), **Supp. III Part 1:** 260
Night Light (Justice), **Supp. VII:** 126–127
"Nightmare" (Kumin), **Supp. IV Part 2:** 442
Nightmare Factory, The (Kumin), **Supp. IV Part 2:** 444–447, 451
"Nightmare Factory, The" (Kumin), **Supp. IV Part 2:** 445, 453
Nightmare on Main Street (Poe), **Retro. Supp. II:** 262
"Nightmare" poems (Benét), **Supp. XI:** 46, 58

Night Music (Odets), **Supp. II Part 2:** 541, 543, 544
"Night of First Snow" (Bly), **Supp. IV Part 1:** 71
Night of January 16th (Rand), **Supp. IV Part 2:** 527
Night of the Iguana, The (T. Williams), **IV:** 382, 383, 384, 385, 386, 387, 388, 391, 392, 393, 394, 395, 397, 398
"Night of the Iguana, The" (T. Williams), **IV:** 384
"Night of the Living Beanfield: How an Unsuccessful Cult Novel Became an Unsuccessful Cult Film in Only Fourteen Years, Eleven Nervous Breakdowns, and $20 Million" (Nichols), **Supp. XIII:** 267
Night Rider (Warren), **IV:** 243, 246–247
Nights (Doolittle), **Supp. I Part 1:** 270, 271
Nights and Days (Merrill), **Supp. III Part 1:** 319, 320, 322–325
"Nights and Days" (Rich), **Supp. I Part 2:** 574
"Night Shift" (Plath), **Supp. I Part 2:** 538
"Night-Side" (Oates), **Supp. II Part 2:** 523
Night-Side (Oates), **Supp. II Part 2:** 522
"Night Sketches: Beneath an Umbrella" (Hawthorne), **II:** 235–237, 238, 239, 242
"Night-Sweat" (Lowell), **II:** 554
"Night-Talk" (Ellison), **Retro. Supp. II:** 126; **Supp. II Part 1:** 248
Night Thoughts (Young), **III:** 415
Night Traveler, The (Oliver), **Supp. VII:** 233
"Night Watch, The" (Wright), **Supp. V:** 339
"Night We All Had Grippe, The" (Jackson), **Supp. IX:** 118
Nightwood (Barnes), **Supp. III Part 1:** 31, 32, 35–37, 39–43
"Nihilist as Hero, The" (Lowell), **II:** 554; **Retro. Supp. II:** 190
Nikolai Gogol (Nabokov), **Retro. Supp. I:** 266
Niles, Thomas, **Retro. Supp. I:** 35
Niles, Thomas, Jr., **Supp. I Part 1:** 39
Nilsson, Christine, **Supp. I Part 1:** 355
Nilsson, Harry, **Supp. XI:** 309
Nimitz, Chester, **Supp. I Part 2:** 491
"Nimram" (Gardner), **Supp. VI:** 73
Nims, John Frederick, **III:** 527
Nin, Anaïs, **III:** 182, 184, 190; **Supp. III Part 1:** 43; **Supp. IV Part 2:** 680; **Supp. X:** 181–200
"9" (Oliver), **Supp. VII:** 244
"Nine from Eight" (Lanier), **Supp. I Part 1:** 352–354
Nine Headed Dragon River: Zen Journals 1969–1982 (Matthiessen), **Supp. V:** 199
"Nine Nectarines" (Moore), **III:** 203, 209, 215
"Nine Poems for the Unborn Child" (Rukeyser), **Supp. VI:** 280–281, 284
Nine Stories (Nabokov), **Retro. Supp. I:** 266
Nine Stories (Salinger), **III:** 552, 558–564
1984 (Orwell), **Supp. XIII:** 29
"1940" (Stafford), **Supp. XI:** 328–329
"1945–1985: Poem for the Anniversary" (Oliver), **Supp. VII:** 237
19 Necromancers from Now (Reed), **Supp. X:** 240
1919 (Dos Passos), **I:** 482, 485–486, 487, 489, 490, 492
"1975" (Wright), **Supp. V:** 341
"1910" (Mora), **Supp. XIII:** 215
"1938" (Komunyakaa), **Supp. XIII:** 114
"1939" (Taylor), **Supp. V:** 316
1933 (Levine), **Supp. V:** 185–187
"1933" (Levine), **Supp. V:** 188
"Nineteenth New York, The" (Doctorow), **Supp. IV Part 1:** 232
"1929" (Auden), **Supp. II Part 1:** 6
19 Varieties of Gazelle (Nye), **Supp. XIII:** 275, **286–288**
"19 Varieties of Gazelle" (Nye), **Supp. XIII:** 286
95 Poems (Cummings), **I:** 430, 433, 435, 439, 446, 447
"90 North" (Jarrell), **II:** 370, 371
"91 Revere Street" (Lowell), **II:** 547; **Retro. Supp. II:** 188; **Supp. XI:** 240
90 Trees (Zukofsky), **Supp. III Part 2:** 631
"Nine Years Later" (Brodsky), **Supp. VIII:** 32
"Nirvana" (Lanier), **Supp. I Part 1:** 352
Nirvana Blues, The (Nichols), **Supp. XIII:** 266, 267
Nishikigi (play), **III:** 466
Niven, David, **Supp. XI:** 307
Nixon, Richard M., **I:** 376; **III:** 38, 46; **Supp. I Part 1:** 294, 295; **Supp. V:** 45, 46, 51; **Supp. XII:** 14
"NJ Transit" (Komunyakaa), **Supp. XIII:** 132
Nketia, J. H., **Supp. IV Part 1:** 10

Nketsia, Nana, **Supp. IV Part 1:** 2, 10
Nkize, Julius, **Supp. IV Part 1:** 361
Nkrumah, Kwame, **I:** 490, 494; **Supp. IV Part 1:** 361; **Supp. X:** 135
Noailles, Anna de, **IV:** 328
Noa Noa (Gauguin), **I:** 34
Nobel Lecture (Singer), **Retro. Supp. II:** 318
"No Better Than a 'Withered Daffodil'" (Moore), **III:** 216
Noble, David W., **Supp. I Part 2:** 650
"Noble Rider and the Sound of Words, The" (Stevens), **Retro. Supp. I:** 299
Noble Savage, The (Coover), **Supp. V:** 40
"No Bobolink reverse His Singing" (Dickinson), **Retro. Supp. I:** 45
Nobodaddy (MacLeish), **III:** 5–6, 8, 10, 11, 18, 19, 20
"Nobody in Hollywood" (Bausch), **Supp. VII:** 54
Nobody Knows My Name (Baldwin), **Supp. XIII:** 111
"Nobody Knows My Name" (Baldwin), **Retro. Supp. II:** 8; **Supp. I Part 1:** 52
Nobody Knows My Name: More Notes of a Native Son (Baldwin), **Retro. Supp. II:** 6, 8; **Supp. I Part 1:** 47, 52, 55
"Nobody knows this little Rose" (Dickinson), **Retro. Supp. I:** 30
"Nobody Said Anything" (Carver), **Supp. III Part 1:** 141
Nobody's Fool (Russo), **Supp. XII:** 326, **331–335,** 340
"No Change of Place" (Auden), **Supp. II Part 1:** 5
"Noche Triste, La" (Frost), **Retro. Supp. I:** 123
Nock, Albert Jay, **I:** 245; **Supp. IV Part 2:** 521, 524
"No Coward Soul Is Mine" (Brontë), **I:** 458
"No Crime in the Mountains" (Chandler), **Supp. IV Part 1:** 129
"Nocturne" (Komunyakaa), **Supp. XIII:** 126
"Nocturne" (MacLeish), **III:** 8
"Nocturne in a Deserted Brickyard" (Sandburg), **III:** 586
Nocturne of Remembered Spring (Aiken), **I:** 50
No Door (Wolfe), **IV:** 451–452, 456
"No Door" (Wolfe), **IV:** 456
"No Epitaph" (Carson), **Supp. XII:** 111
No Exit (Sartre), **I:** 82, 130
No Exit (Sartre; Bowles, trans.), **Supp. IV Part 1:** 84
No Gifts from Chance (Benstock),

Retro. Supp. I: 361
"No-Good Blues" (Komunyakaa), **Supp. XIII:** 130
No Hero (Marquand), **III:** 57
No! In Thunder (Fiedler), **Supp. XIII:** 101
"Noiseless Patient Spider" (Whitman), **III:** 555; **IV:** 348; **Supp. IV Part 1:** 325
Noises Off (Frayn), **Supp. IV Part 2:** 582
Noi vivi. See *We the Living* (film)
"No Lamp Has Ever Shown Us Where to Look" (MacLeish), **III:** 9
Nolan, Sidney, **Retro. Supp. II:** 189
No Laughing Matter (Heller and Vogel), **Supp. IV Part 1:** 384, 389
No Love Lost, a Romance of Travel (Howells), **II:** 277
No Man Is an Island (Merton), **Supp. VIII:** 207
No Name in the Street (Baldwin), **Retro. Supp. II:** 13, 14; **Supp. I Part 1:** 47, 48, 52, 65–66, 67
No Nature: New and Selected Poems (Snyder), **Supp. VIII: 305**
Nonconformist's Memorial, The (Howe), **Supp. IV Part 2:** 434, 435–436
Nonconformity (Algren), **Supp. IX:** 15
None but the Lonely Heart (film), **Supp. II Part 2:** 546
Nones (Auden), **Supp. II Part 1:** 21
"Nones" (Auden), **Supp. II Part 1:** 22–23
None Shall Look Back (Gordon), **II:** 205–207, 208
"Noon" (Bryant), **Supp. I Part 1:** 157
"No One Remembers" (Levine), **Supp. V:** 187
"Noon Walk on the Asylum Lawn" (Sexton), **Supp. II Part 2:** 673
"Noon Wine" (Porter), **III:** 436, 437–438, 442, 446
"No Pain Whatsoever" (Yates), **Supp. XI:** 341
"No Place for You, My Love" (Welty), **IV:** 278, 279; **Retro. Supp. I:** 353
No Plays of Japan, The (Waley), **III:** 466
No Pockets in a Shroud (McCoy), **Supp. XIII: 166–168,** 171, 172, 173, 174
"No Poem So Fine" (Francis), **Supp. IX:** 83
Norcross, Frances, **I:** 456, 462
Norcross, Louise, **I:** 456, 462
Nordyke, Lewis, **Supp. XIII:** 5
No Relief (Dixon), **Supp. XII:** 139, **142–143**

No Resting Place (Humphrey), **Supp. IX:** 94, **106–108**
Norma (Bellini), **IV:** 309
Norma Ashe (Glaspell), **Supp. III Part 1:** 175, 186–187
"Normal Motor Adjustments" (Stein and Solomons), **IV:** 26
Norman, Charles, **III:** 479
Norman, Gurney, **Supp. X:** 24
Norman, Marsha, **Supp. VIII:** 141
Norman Mailer (Poirier), **Retro. Supp. II:** 207–208
Norman Mailer: Modern Critical Views (Bloom), **Retro. Supp. II:** 205
Norman Mailer Revisited (Merrill), **Retro. Supp. II:** 201
Norna; or, The Witch's Curse (Alcott), **Supp. I Part 1:** 33
Norris, Charles, **III:** 320; **Retro. Supp. I:** 100
Norris, Frank, **I:** 211, 355, 500, 506, 517, 518, 519; **II:** 89, 264, 276, 289, 307; **III:** 227, **314–336,** 596; **IV:** 29; **Retro. Supp. I:** 100, 325; **Retro. Supp. II:** 96, 101; **Supp. III Part 2:** 412; **Supp. VIII:** 101, 102; **Supp. IX:** 14, 15
"North" (Hugo), **Supp. VI:** 135
North, Milou (pseudonym), **Supp. IV Part 1:** 260. See also Dorris, Michael; Erdrich, Louise
North, Sir Thomas, **IV:** 370
"North American Sequence" (Roethke), **I:** 171–172, 183; **III:** 529, 545, 547, 548
"North Beach" (Snyder), **Supp. VIII:** 289
"North Country Sketches" (McClatchy), **Supp. XII:** 256
"Northeast Playground" (Paley), **Supp. VI:** 226–227, 229
Northern Lights (O'Brien), **Supp. V:** 237, 239, 241–244, 250
"Northern Motive" (Levine), **Supp. V:** 195
Northfield Poems (Ammons), **Supp. VII:** 29
"Northhanger Ridge" (Wright), **Supp. V:** 335, 340
"North Haven" (Bishop), **Retro. Supp. II:** 50
"North Labrador" (Crane), **I:** 386
North of Boston (Frost), **II:** 152, 153–154, 527; **Retro. Supp. I:** 121, 125, 127, **128–130,** 131; **Supp. I Part 1:** 263; **Supp. XIII:** 146
North of Jamaica (Simpson), **Supp. IV Part 2:** 448; **Supp. IX:** 275, 276
North of the Danube (Caldwell), **I:** 288, 290, 293, 294, 309, 310

Northrup, Cyrus, **Supp. I Part 1:** 350
"North Sea Undertaker's Complaint, The" (Lowell), **II:** 550
North & South (Bishop), **Retro. Supp. II: 41–43; Supp. I Part 1:** 72, 84, 85, 89
North Star, The (Hellman), **Supp. I Part 1:** 281
Norton, Charles Eliot, **I:** 223, 568; **II:** 279, 322–323, 338; **Retro. Supp. I:** 371; **Retro. Supp. II:** 135; **Supp. I Part 1:** 103; **Supp. I Part 2:** 406, 479
Norton, Jody, **Supp. VIII:** 297
Norton, John, **Supp. I Part 1:** 99, 110, 112, 114
Norton Anthology of African American Literature, The, **Supp. X:** 325
Norton Anthology of American Literature, **Supp. X:** 325
Norton Anthology of Modern Poetry, The, **Supp. XI:** 259
Norton Anthology of Short Fiction, The, **Supp. IX:** 4
Norton Lectures, **Retro. Supp. I:** 65
Norwood, Vera, **Supp. IX:** 24
No Safe Harbour (Porter), **III:** 447
"No Speak English" (Cisneros), **Supp. VII:** 63
"Nostalgia of the Lakefronts" (Justice), **Supp. VII:** 118, 119, 120
"Nostalgic Mood" (Farrell), **II:** 45
No Star Is Lost (Farrell), **II:** 34, 35, 44
Nostromo (Conrad), **II:** 600; **IV:** 245
"Nosty Fright, A" (Swenson), **Supp. IV Part 2:** 651
Not about Nightingales (T. Williams), **IV:** 381
Not Dancing (Dunn), **Supp. XI:** 143, **148**
"Note about *Iconographs,* A" (Swenson), **Supp. IV Part 2:** 646
Notebook (Lowell), **Retro. Supp. II:** 186, 190; **Supp. V:** 343
Notebook 1967–68 (Lowell), **II:** 553–555; **Retro. Supp. II:** 182, 186, 190
Notebook of Malte Laurids Brigge, The (Rilke), **III:** 571
Notebooks (Fitzgerald), **Retro. Supp. I:** 110
"Note on Abraham Lincoln" (Vidal), **Supp. IV Part 2:** 688
"Note on Commercial Theatre" (Hughes), **Retro. Supp. I:** 207
"Note on Ezra Pound, A" (Eliot), **Retro. Supp. I:** 290
"Note on Lanier's Music, A" (Graham), **Supp. I Part 1:** 373
Note on Literary Criticism, A (Farrell), **II:** 26, 49

"Note on Poetry, A" (Doolittle), **Supp. I Part 1:** 254, 267–268
"Note on Realism, A" (Anderson), **I:** 110
"Notes" (Dove), **Supp. IV Part 1:** 246
"Notes for a Moving Picture: The House" (Agee), **I:** 33, 34
"Notes for an Autobiography" (Van Vechten), **Supp. II Part 2:** 749
"Notes for a Novel About the End of the World" (Percy), **Supp. III Part 1:** 393
"Notes for a Preface" (Sandburg), **III:** 591, 596–597
"NOTES FOR A SPEECH" (Baraka), **Supp. II Part 1:** 33
Notes for the Green Box (Duchamp), **Supp. IV Part 2:** 423
Notes from a Sea Diary: Hemingway All the Way (Algren), **Supp. IX:** 16
"Notes from the Childhood and Girlhood" (Brooks), **Supp. III Part 1:** 77
"Notes from the River" (Stern), **Supp. IX:** 285, 287, 294, 295
Notes from Underground (Dostoyevsky), **III:** 571; **IV:** 485; **Retro. Supp. II:** 121
"Notes of a Faculty Wife" (Jackson), **Supp. IX:** 126
"Notes of a Native Daughter" (Didion), **Supp. IV Part 1:** 196, 197, 200, 201
Notes of a Native Son (Baldwin), **Retro. Supp. II:** 1, 2, 3, 5, 6; **Supp. I Part 1:** 50, 52, 54; **Supp. IV Part 1:** 163
"Notes of a Native Son" (Baldwin), **Supp. I Part 1:** 50, 54
Notes of a Son and Brother (James), **II:** 337; **Retro. Supp. I:** 235
"Notes on a Departure" (Trilling), **Supp. III Part 2:** 498
"Notes on Babbitt and More" (Wilson), **IV:** 435
"Notes on 'Camp'" (Sontag), **Supp. III Part 2:** 455–456
Notes on Democracy (Mencken), **III:** 104, 107–108, 109, 116, 119
"Notes on Free Verse" (Dobyns), **Supp. XIII:** 77
"Notes on 'Layover'" (Hass), **Supp. VI:** 109
Notes on Novelists (James), **II:** 336, 337; **Retro. Supp. I:** 235
"Notes on Nukes, Nookie, and Neo-Romanticism" (Robbins), **Supp. X:** 272
"Notes on Poetry" (Eberhart), **I:** 524, 527–528, 529

"Notes on the Craft of Poetry" (Strand), **Supp. IV Part 2:** 626
"Notes on the Decline of Outrage" (Dickey), **Supp. IV Part 1:** 181
"Notes to Be Left in a Cornerstone" (Benét), **Supp. XI:** 46, 58
"Notes toward a Supreme Fiction" (Stevens), **IV:** 87–89; **Retro. Supp. I:** 300, 306, **306–309**, 311; **Supp. I Part 1:** 80
"Notes towards a Poem That Can Never Be Written" (Atwood), **Supp. XIII:** 34–35
No Thanks (Cummings), **I:** 430, 431, 432, 436, 437, 441, 443, 446
"Nothing Big" (Komunyakaa), **Supp. XIII:** 121
"Nothing Gold Can Stay" (Frost), **Retro. Supp. I:** 133
"Nothing Missing" (O'Hara), **III:** 369
Nothing Personal (Baldwin), **Supp. I Part 1:** 58, 60
"Nothing Song, The" (Snodgrass), **Supp. VI:** 326
"Nothing Stays Put" (Clampitt), **Supp. IX:** 42
"Nothing Will Yield" (Nemerov), **III:** 279
No Third Path (Kosinski), **Supp. VII:** 215
"Not Ideas About the Thing but the Thing Itself" (Stevens), **IV:** 87
Notions of the Americans: Picked up by a Travelling Bachelor (Cooper), **I:** 343–345, 346
"Not-Knowing" (Barthelme), **Supp. IV Part 1:** 48
"Not Leaving the House" (Snyder), **Supp. VIII:** 300
"'Not Marble nor the Gilded Monument'" (MacLeish), **III:** 12
"Not Quite Social" (Frost), **II:** 156
"Not Sappho, Sacco" (Rukeyser), **Supp. VI:** 277
"Not Sixteen" (Anderson), **I:** 114
"Not Slightly" (Stein), **IV:** 44
Not So Deep as a Well (Parker), **Supp. IX:** 192
"Not Somewhere Else, but Here" (Rich), **Supp. I Part 2:** 552, 573
Not So Simple: The "Simple" Stories by Langston Hughes (Harper), **Retro. Supp. I:** 194, 209
Not-So-Simple Neil Simon (McGovern), **Supp. IV Part 2:** 573
"Not the Point" (Cameron), **Supp. XII:** 83
"Not They Who Soar" (Dunbar), **Supp. II Part 1:** 199
Not This Pig (Levine), **Supp. V:** 178,

181, 182–183
Not to Eat; Not for Love (Weller), **III:** 322
Not Without Laughter (Hughes), **Retro. Supp. I:** 197, 198, 201; **Supp. I Part 1:** 328, 332
Nova Express (Burroughs), **Supp. III Part 1:** 93, 103, 104
Novel, The (Bulwer), **Retro. Supp. II:** 58
"Novel as a Function of American Democracy, The" (Ellison), **Retro. Supp. II:** 124
"Novel Démeublé, The" (Cather), **Retro. Supp. I:** 15
Novel History: Historians and Novelists Confront America's Past (and Each Other) (Carnes), **Supp. X:** 14
Novella (Goethe; Bogan and Mayer, trans.), **Supp. III Part 1:** 63
"Novella" (Rich), **Retro. Supp. II:** 283
Novellas and Other Writings (Wharton), **Retro. Supp. I:** 360
"Novel of the Thirties, A" (Trilling), **Supp. III Part 2:** 499
Novels and Other Writings (Bercovitch), **Retro. Supp. II:** 343
Novels and Tales of Henry James, The (James), **Retro. Supp. I:** 232
"Novel-Writing and Novel-Reading" (Howells), **II:** 276, 290
"November" (Larcom), **Supp. XIII:** 143
"November Cotton Flower" (Toomer), **Supp. IX:** 312
November Twenty Six Nineteen Sixty Three (Berry), **Supp. X:** 24
"Novices" (Moore), **III:** 200–201, 202, 213
"Novogodnee" ("New Year's Greetings") (Tsvetayeva), **Supp. VIII:** 30
"Novotny's Pain" (Roth), **Supp. III Part 2:** 403
"No Voyage" (Oliver), **Supp. VII:** 231
No Voyage and Other Poems (Oliver), **Supp. VII:** 230–231, 232
Now and Another Time (Hearon), **Supp. VIII:** 58, **61–62**
Now and Then (Buechner), **Supp. XII:** 49, 53
"Now and Then, America" (Mora), **Supp. XIII:** 217
Nowhere Is a Place: Travels in Patagonia (Theroux and Chatwin), **Supp. VIII:** 322
"Now I Am Married" (Gordon), **Supp. IV Part 1:** 299
"Now I Lay Me" (Hemingway), **II:** 249; **Retro. Supp. I:** 175

"Now I Lay Me" (Olds), **Supp. X:** 208
"Now Is the Air Made of Chiming Balls" (Eberhart), **I:** 523
"No Word" (Kunitz), **Supp. III Part 1:** 263
Now Sheba Sings the Song (Angelou), **Supp. IV Part 1:** 16
"Now That We Live" (Kenyon), **Supp. VII:** 165
"Now the Servant's Name Was Malchus" (Wilder), **IV:** 358
"Now We Know" (O'Hara), **III:** 368–369
NOW with Bill Moyers (television), **Supp. XIII:** 286
Noyes, Alfred, **IV:** 434
Nuamah, Grace, **Supp. IV Part 1:** 10
"Nuances of a Theme by Williams" (Stevens), **Retro. Supp. I:** 422
Nuclear Age, The (O'Brien), **Supp. V:** 238, 243, 244, 246–248, 249, 251
Nude Croquet (Fiedler), **Supp. XIII:** 103
"Nude Descending a Staircase" (Duchamp), **IV:** 408; **Retro. Supp. I:** 416
Nugent, Bruce, **Retro. Supp. I:** 200
Nugent, Elliot, **Supp. I Part 2:** 606, 611, 613
Nuggets and Dust (Bierce), **I:** 195
"Nullipara" (Olds), **Supp. X:** 209
Number One (Dos Passos), **I:** 489
"Numbers, Letters" (Baraka), **Supp. II Part 1:** 50
Nunc Dimittis (Brodsky), **Supp. VIII:** 25–26, 28
"Nun No More, A" (Fante), **Supp. XI:** 160
"Nun's Priest's Tale" (Chaucer), **III:** 492
Nunzio, Nanzia, **IV:** 89
Nuptial Flight, The (Masters), **Supp. I Part 2:** 460, 471
"Nuptials" (Tate), **IV:** 122
"Nurse Whitman" (Olds), **Supp. X:** 203
Nurture (Kumin), **Supp. IV Part 2:** 453–454, 455
Nussbaum, Emily, **Supp. XI:** 143
Nussbaum, Felicity A., **Supp. X:** 189
Nutcracker, The (Tchaikovsky), **Retro. Supp. I:** 196
"Nux Postcoenatica" (Holmes), **Supp. I Part 1:** 303
Nyce, James M., **Retro. Supp. I:** 380
Nye, Naomi Shihab, **Supp. XI:** 316; **Supp. XIII: 273–290**
Nyerere, Julius, **Supp. X:** 135
"Nympholepsy" (Faulkner), **Retro. Supp. I:** 81

"Ö" (Dove), **Supp. IV Part 1:** 245
O. Henry Biography (C. A. Smith), **Supp. II Part 1:** 395
Oak and Ivy (Dunbar), **Supp. II Part 1:** 98
Oak Openings, The (Cooper), **I:** 354, 355
Oandasan, Bill, **Supp. IV Part 2:** 499
Oasis, The (McCarthy), **II:** 566–568
Oates, Joyce Carol, **Supp. II Part 2: 503–527; Supp. IV Part 1:** 205; **Supp. IV Part 2:** 447, 689; **Supp. V:** 323; **Supp. XI:** 239; **Supp. XII:** 343; **Supp. XIII:** 306
"Oath, The" (Tate), **IV:** 127
Obbligati (Hecht), **Supp. X:** 57
Ober, Harold, **Retro. Supp. I:** 101, 103, 105, 110, 113
Oberndorf, Clarence P., **Supp. I Part 1:** 315
Obey, André, **IV:** 356, 375
"Obit" (Lowell), **II:** 554
"Objective Value of a Social Settlement, The" (Addams), **Supp. I Part 1:** 4
"Objective Woman, The" (Jong), **Supp. V:** 119
"Objectivist Ethics, The" (Rand), **Supp. IV Part 2:** 530–532
"Objectivists" Anthology, An (Zukofsky), **Supp. III Part 2:** 613, 615
"Objects" (Wilbur), **Supp. III Part 2:** 545–547
Oblique Prayers (Levertov), **Supp. III Part 1:** 283
"Oblivion" (Justice), **Supp. VII:** 121
Oblivion Seekers, The (Eberhardt), **Supp. IV Part 1:** 92
"Oblong Box, The" (Poe), **III:** 416
Obregon, Maurice, **Supp. I Part 2:** 488
O'Briant, Don, **Supp. X:** 8
O'Brien, Edward J., **I:** 289; **III:** 56
O'Brien, Fitzjames, **I:** 211
O'Brien, Geoffrey, **Supp. IV Part 2:** 471, 473
O'Brien, John, **Supp. V:** 48, 49; **Supp. X:** 239, 244
O'Brien, Tim, **Supp. V: 237–255; Supp. XI:** 234
"Obscene Poem, An" (Creeley), **Supp. IV Part 1:** 150
Obscure Destinies (Cather), **I:** 331–332; **Retro. Supp. I:** 19
"Observation Relative to the Intentions of the Original Founders of the Academy in Philadelphia" (Franklin), **II:** 114

"Observations" (Dillard), **Supp. VI:** 34
Observations (Moore), **III:** 194, 195–196, 197, 199, 203, 205, 215
Observations: Photographs by Richard Avedon: Comments by Truman Capote, **Supp. III Part 1:** 125–126
O Canada: An American's Notes on Canadian Culture (Wilson), **IV:** 429–430
"O Carib Isle!" (Crane), **I:** 400–401
O'Casey, Sean, **III:** 145; **Supp. IV Part 1:** 359, 361, 364
"Occidentals" (Ford), **Supp. V:** 71–72
"Occultation of Orion, The" (Longfellow), **Retro. Supp. II:** 168
"Occurrence at Owl Creek Bridge, An" (Bierce), **I:** 200–201; **II:** 264
"Ocean 1212-W" (Plath), **Supp. I Part 2:** 528
O'Connell, Nicholas, **Supp. IX:** 323, 325, 334
O'Connor, Edward F., Jr., **III:** 337
O'Connor, Flannery, **I:** 113, 190, 211, 298; **II:** 606; **III: 337–360; IV:** 4, 217, 282; **Retro. Supp. II:** 179, **219–239,** 272, 342; **Supp. I Part 1:** 290; **Supp. III Part 1:** 146; **Supp. V:** 59, 337; **Supp. VIII:** 13, 14, 158; **Supp. X:** 1, 26, 69, 228, 290; **Supp. XI:** 104; **Supp. XIII:** 294
O'Connor, Frank, **III:** 158; **Retro. Supp. II:** 242; **Supp. I Part 2:** 531; **Supp. VIII:** 151, 157, 165, 167, 171
O'Connor, Richard, **II:** 467
O'Connor, T. P., **II:** 129
O'Connor, William, **IV:** 346; **Retro. Supp. I:** 392, 407
O'Connor, William Van, **III:** 479; **Supp. I Part 1:** 195
"Octascope" (Beattie), **Supp. V:** 27, 28
"Octaves" (Robinson), **Supp. III Part 2:** 593
"Octet" (Wallace), **Supp. X:** 309
"October" (Oliver), **Supp. VII:** 241
"October" (Swenson), **Supp. IV Part 2:** 649
"October, 1866" (Bryant), **Supp. I Part 1:** 169
"October and November" (Lowell), **II:** 554
"October in the Railroad Earth" (Kerouac), **Supp. III Part 1:** 225, 227, 229
October Light (Gardner), **Supp. VI:** 63, **69–71,** 72
"October Maples, Portland" (Wilbur), **Supp. III Part 2:** 556
"Octopus, An" (Moore), **III:** 202, 207–208, 214

"Octopus, The" (Merrill), **Supp. III Part 1:** 321
Octopus, The (Norris), **I:** 518; **III:** 314, 316, 322–326, 327, 331–333, 334, 335
"O Daedalus, Fly Away Home" (Hayden), **Supp. II Part 1:** 377–378
"OD and Hepatitis Railroad or Bust, The" (Boyle), **Supp. VIII:** 1
Odd Couple, The (film), **Supp. IV Part 2:** 589
Odd Couple, The (Simon), **Supp. IV Part 2:** 575, 579–580, 585, 586
Odd Couple, The (1985 version, Simon), **Supp. IV Part 2:** 580
Odd Jobs (Updike), **Retro. Supp. I:** 334
Odd Mercy (Stern), **Supp. IX:** 298–299
"Odds, The" (Hecht), **Supp. X:** 64–65
"Odds, The" (Salinas), **Supp. XIII:** 321
"Ode" (Emerson), **II:** 13
"Ode (Intimations of Immortality)" (Matthews), **Supp. IX:** 162
"Ode: Intimations of Immortality" (Wordsworth), **Supp. I Part 2:** 729; **Supp. III Part 1:** 12
"Ode: My 24th Year" (Ginsberg), **Supp. II Part 1:** 312
"Ode for Memorial Day" (Dunbar), **Supp. II Part 1:** 199
"Ode for the American Dead in Asia" (McGrath), **Supp. X:** 119
"Ode on a Grecian Urn" (Keats), **I:** 284; **III:** 472; **Supp. XII:** 113
"Ode on Human Destinies" (Jeffers), **Supp. II Part 2:** 419
"Ode on Indolence" (Keats), **Supp. XII:** 113
"Ode on Melancholy" (Keats), **Retro. Supp. I:** 301
Ode Recited at the Harvard Commemoration (Lowell), **Supp. I Part 2:** 416–418, 424
"Ode Recited at the Harvard Commemoration" (Lowell), **II:** 551
"Ode Secrète" (Valéry), **III:** 609
"Odes to Natural Processes" (Updike), **Retro. Supp. I:** 323
"Ode to a Nightingale" (Keats), **II:** 368; **Retro. Supp. II:** 261; **Supp. IX:** 52
"Ode to Autumn" (Masters), **Supp. I Part 2:** 458
"Ode to Cervantes" (Salinas), **Supp. XIII:** 324
"Ode to Coit Tower" (Corso), **Supp. XII:** 122
"Ode to Ethiopia" (Dunbar), **Supp. II Part 1:** 199, 207, 208, 209
"Ode to Fear" (Tate), **IV:** 128
"Ode to Meaning" (Pinsky), **Supp. VI:** 249–250, 251
"Ode to Night" (Masters), **Supp. I Part 2:** 458
"Ode to Our Young Pro-Consuls of the Air" (Tate), **IV:** 135
"Ode to the Austrian Socialists" (Benét), **Supp. XI:** 46, 58
"Ode to the Confederate Dead" (Tate), **II:** 551; **IV:** 124, 133, 137; **Supp. X:** 52
"Ode to the Johns Hopkins University" (Lanier), **Supp. I Part 1:** 370
"Ode to the Maggot" (Komunyakaa), **Supp. XIII:** 130
"Ode to the Mexican Experience" (Salinas), **Supp. XIII:** 316–317
"Ode to the Virginian Voyage" (Drayton), **IV:** 135
"Ode to the West Wind" (Shelley), **Retro. Supp. I:** 308; **Supp. I Part 2:** 728; **Supp. IX:** 52; **Supp. XII:** 117
"Ode to Walt Whitman" (Benét), **Supp. XI:** 52
Odets, Clifford, **Supp. I Part 1:** 277, 295; **Supp. I Part 2:** 679; **Supp. IV Part 2:** 529–554; **Supp. IV Part 2:** 587; **Supp. V:** 109; **Supp. VIII:** 96
Odier, Daniel, **Supp. III Part 1:** 97
O'Donnell, George Marion, **II:** 67
O'Donnell, Thomas F., **II:** 131
"Odor of Verbena" (Faulkner), **II:** 66
O'Doul, Lefty, **II:** 425
"Odysseus to Telemachus" (Brodsky), **Supp. VIII:** 25
Odyssey (Bryant, trans.), **Supp. I Part 1:** 158
Odyssey (Homer), **III:** 14, 470; **Retro. Supp. I:** 286, 290; **Retro. Supp. II:** 121; **Supp. I Part 1:** 185; **Supp. IV Part 2:** 631; **Supp. IX:** 211; **Supp. X:** 114
"Odyssey of a Wop, The" (Fante), **Supp. XI:** 164, 165
Oedipus Rex (Sophocles), **I:** 137; **III:** 145, 151, 152, 332; **Supp. I Part 2:** 428
Oedipus Tyrannus (Sophocles), **II:** 203
Oehlschlaeger, Fritz, **Supp. IX:** 123
"Of Alexander Crummell" (Du Bois), **Supp. II Part 1:** 170
O'Faoláin, Seán, **Supp. II Part 1:** 101
Of a World That Is No More (Singer), **IV:** 16
"Of Booker T. Washington and Others" (Du Bois), **Supp. II Part 1:** 168
"Of Bright & Blue Birds & the Gala Sun" (Stevens), **IV:** 93
"Of Christian Heroism" (Ozick), **Supp. V:** 272
"Of Dying Beauty" (Zukofsky), **Supp. III Part 2:** 610
"Of 'Father and Son'" (Kunitz), **Supp. III Part 1:** 262
Offenbach, Jacques, **II:** 427
"Offering for Mr. Bluehart, An" (Wright), **Supp. III Part 2:** 596, 601
"Offerings" (Mason), **Supp. VIII:** 141
"Official Piety" (Whittier), **Supp. I Part 2:** 687
"Off-Shore Pirates, The" (Fitzgerald), **II:** 88
Off the Beaten Path (Proulx), **Supp. VII:** 261
"Off the Cuff" (Simpson), **Supp. IX:** 278
Off the Map (Levine), **Supp. V:** 178
O'Flaherty, George, **Supp. I Part 1:** 202, 205–206
O'Flaherty, Kate. *See* Chopin, Kate
O'Flaherty, Thomas, **Supp. I Part 1:** 202, 203–204, 205
O'Flaherty, Thomas, Jr., **Supp. I Part 1:** 202
"Of Maids and Other Muses" (Alvarez), **Supp. VII:** 11
"Of Margaret" (Ransom), **III:** 491
Of Mice and Men (Steinbeck), **IV:** 51, 57–58
"Of Modern Poetry" (Stevens), **IV:** 92
Of Plymouth Plantation (Bradford), **Retro. Supp. II:** 161, 162
Of Plymouth Plantation (Morison, ed.), **Supp. I Part 2:** 494
"Ofrenda for Lobo" (Mora), **Supp. XIII:** 224
"Often" (Kenyon), **Supp. VII:** 171
"Often, in Dreams, He Moved through a City" (Dobyns), **Supp. XIII:** 90
"Of the Coming of John" (Du Bois), **Supp. II Part 1:** 170
"Of the Culture of White Folk" (Du Bois), **Supp. II Part 1:** 175
Of the Farm (Updike), **IV:** 214, 217, 223–225, 233; **Retro. Supp. I:** 318, 329, 332
"Of the Passing of the First-Born" (Du Bois), **Supp. II Part 1:** 170
"Of the Sorrow Songs" (Du Bois), **Supp. II Part 1:** 170
"Of the Wings of Atlanta" (Du Bois), **Supp. II Part 1:** 170
Of This Time, Of This Place (Trilling), **Supp. III Part 2:** 498, 504
Of Time and the River (Wolfe), **IV:** 450, 451, 452, 455, 456, 457, 458,

459, 462, 464–465, 467, 468, 469
Of Woman Born: Motherhood as Experience and Institution (Rich), **Retro. Supp. II:** 284–285, 291; **Supp. I Part 2:** 554, 567–569
Of Women and Their Elegance (Mailer), **Retro. Supp. II:** 209
Ogden, Archie, **Supp. XIII:** 174
Ogden, Henry, **II:** 298
Ogden, Uzal, **Supp. I Part 2:** 516
"Oh, Fairest of the Rural Maids" (Bryant), **Supp. I Part 1:** 169
"Oh, Immobility, Death's Vast Associate" (Dobyns), **Supp. XIII:** 89
"Oh, Joseph, I'm So Tired" (Yates), **Supp. XI:** 348
"O'Halloran's Luck" (Benét), **Supp. XI:** 47
O'Hara, Frank, **Supp. XII:** 121
O'Hara, J. D., **Supp. IV Part 1:** 43; **Supp. V:** 22
O'Hara, John, **I:** 375, 495; **II:** 444, 459; **III:** 66, **361–384**; **IV:** 59; **Retro. Supp. I:** 99, 112; **Supp. I Part 1:** 196; **Supp. II Part 1:** 109; **Supp. IV Part 1:** 31, 383; **Supp. IV Part 2:** 678; **Supp. V:** 95; **Supp. VIII:** 151, 156; **Supp. IX:** 208
O'Hehir, Andrew, **Supp. XII:** 280
"Ohio Pagan, An" (Anderson), **I:** 112, 113
Oil! (Sinclair), **Supp. V:** 276, 277–279, 282, 288, 289
"Oil Painting of the Artist as the Artist" (MacLeish), **III:** 14
O'Keeffe, Georgia, **Supp. IX:** 62, 66
"Oklahoma" (Levis), **Supp. XI:** 267
"Old, Old, Old, Old Andrew Jackson" (Lindsay), **Supp. I Part 2:** 398
"Old Amusement Park, An" (Moore), **III:** 216
"Old Angel Midnight" (Kerouac), **Supp. III Part 1:** 229–230
"Old Apple Dealer, The" (Hawthorne), **II:** 227, 233–235, 237, 238
"Old Apple-Tree, The" (Dunbar), **Supp. II Part 1:** 198
"Old Army Game, The" (Garrett), **Supp. VII:** 100–101
"Old Aunt Peggy" (Chopin), **Retro. Supp. II:** 64
"Old Barn at the Bottom of the Fogs, The" (Frost), **Retro. Supp. I:** 138
Old Beauty and Others, The (Cather), **I:** 331
Old Bruin: Commodore Matthew C. Perry, 1794–1858 (Morison), **Supp. I Part 2:** 494–495
"Old Cracked Tune, An" (Kunitz), **Supp. III Part 1:** 264

Old Curiosity Shop, The (Dickens), **I:** 458; **Supp. I Part 2:** 409
"Old Farmer, The" (Jeffers), **Supp. II Part 2:** 418
Old-Fashioned Girl, An (Alcott), **Supp. I Part 1:** 29, 41, 42
"Old Father Morris" (Stowe), **Supp. I Part 2:** 586
"Old Flame, The" (Lowell), **II:** 550
"Old Florist" (Roethke), **III:** 531
"Old Folsom Prison" (Matthews), **Supp. IX:** 165
Old Forest, The (Taylor), **Supp. V:** 320, 321, 326, 327
"Old Forest, The" (Taylor), **Supp. V:** 313, 321, 323, 326
Old Forest and Other Stories (Taylor), **Supp. V:** 326
Old Friends and New (Jewett), **II:** 402; **Retro. Supp. II:** 137, 140
Old Glory, The (Lowell), **II:** 543, 545–546, 555; **Retro. Supp. II:** 188
"Old Homestead, The" (Dunbar), **Supp. II Part 1:** 198
"Old Iron" (Nye), **Supp. XIII:** 276
"Old Ironsides" (Holmes), **Supp. I Part 1:** 302
"Old Lady We Saw, An" (Shields), **Supp. VII:** 310–311
"Old Love" (Singer), **Retro. Supp. II:** 325
"Old McGrath Place, The" (McGrath), **Supp. X:** 114
"Old Maid, The" (Wharton), **Retro. Supp. I:** 381, 382
"Old Man" (Faulkner), **II:** 68, 69
Old Man and the Sea, The (Hemingway), **II:** 250, 256–257, 258, 265; **III:** 40; **Retro. Supp. I:** 180, **185**, 186
"Old Man Drunk" (Wright), **Supp. III Part 2:** 595
"Old Man Feeding Hens" (Francis), **Supp. IX:** 78
"Old Man on the Hospital Porch" (Ríos), **Supp. IV Part 2:** 546–547
Old Man Rubbing His Eyes (Bly), **Supp. IV Part 1:** 65
"Old Manse, The" (Hawthorne), **II:** 224
"Old Man's Winter Night, An" (Frost), **Retro. Supp. I:** 126, 131
"Old Meeting House, The" (Stowe), **Supp. I Part 2:** 586
"Old Memory, An" (Dunbar), **Supp. II Part 1:** 198
"Old Men, The" (McCarthy), **II:** 566
"Old Mortality" (Porter), **III:** 436, 438–441, 442, 445, 446
"Old Mrs. Harris" (Cather), **I:** 332;

Retro. Supp. I: 19
Old New York (Wharton), **IV:** 322; **Retro. Supp. I:** 381
"Ol' Doc Hyar" (Campbell), **Supp. II Part 1:** 202
"Old One-Two, The" (Gurney), **Supp. V:** 98
"Old Order, The" (Porter), **III:** 443, 444–445, 451
"Old Osawatomie" (Sandburg), **III:** 584
Old Patagonia Express, The: By Train through the Americas (Theroux), **Supp. VIII:** 322
"Old People, The" (Faulkner), **II:** 71–72
"Old Poet Moves to a New Apartment 14 Times, The" (Zukofsky), **Supp. III Part 2:** 628
Old Possum's Book of Practical Cats (Eliot), **Supp. XIII:** 228, 344
"Old Red" (Gordon), **II:** 199, 200, 203
Old Red and Other Stories (Gordon), **II:** 157
Old Régime in Canada, The (Parkman), **Supp. II Part 2:** 600, 607, 608–609, 612
Olds, Sharon, **Supp. X:** **201–217**; **Supp. XI:** 139, 142, 244; **Supp. XII:** 229
"Old Saws" (Garrett), **Supp. VII:** 96–97
Old Testament, **I:** 109, 181, 300, 328, 401, 410, 419, 431, 457, 458; **II:** 166, 167, 219; **III:** 270, 272, 348, 390, 396; **IV:** 41, 114, 152, 309; **Retro. Supp. I:** 122, 140, 249, 311, 360; **Retro. Supp. II:** 317; **Supp. I Part 1:** 60, 104, 106, 151; **Supp. I Part 2:** 427, 515, 516; **Supp. IX:** 14. *See also* names of Old Testament books
"Old Things, The" (James), **Retro. Supp. I:** 229
"Old Times on the Mississippi" (Twain), **IV:** 199
Oldtown Folks (Stowe), **Supp. I Part 2:** 587, 596–598
"Old Town of Berwick, The" (Jewett), **Retro. Supp. II:** 132
"Old Trails" (Robinson), **III:** 513, 517
"Old Tyrannies" (Bourne), **I:** 233
"Old West" (Bausch), **Supp. VII:** 48
"Old Whorehouse, An" (Oliver), **Supp. VII:** 235
"Old Woman" (Pinsky), **Supp. VI:** 238
"Old Word, The" (Simic), **Supp. VIII:** 282
Oldys, Francis. *See* Chalmers, George

Olendorf, Donna, **Supp. IV Part 1:** 196
"Olga Poems, The" (Levertov), **Supp. III Part 1:** 279–281
"Olive Groves of Thasos, The" (Clampitt), **Supp. IX: 51–52**
Oliver, Bill, **Supp. VIII:** 138
Oliver, Mary, **Supp. VII: 229–248; Supp. X:** 31
Oliver, Sydney, **I:** 409
Oliver Goldsmith: A Biography (Irving), **II:** 315
Oliver Twist (Dickens), **I:** 354; **Supp. IV Part 2:** 464
"Olivia" (Salinas), **Supp. XIII:** 316
Olivieri, David (pseudonym), **Retro. Supp. I:** 361. *See also* Wharton, Edith
Ollive, Samuel, **Supp. I Part 2:** 503
Olmsted, Frederick Law, **Supp. I Part 1:** 355
Olsen, Lance, **Supp. IV Part 1:** 54; **Supp. IV Part 2:** 623
Olsen, Tillie, **Supp. V:** 114, 220; **Supp. XIII: 291–309**
Olson, Charles, **Retro. Supp. I:** 209; **Supp. II Part 1:** 30, 328; **Supp. II Part 2: 555–587; Supp. III Part 1:** 9, 271; **Supp. III Part 2:** 542, 624; **Supp. IV Part 1:** 139, 144, 146, 153, 154, 322; **Supp. IV Part 2:** 420, 421, 423, 426; **Supp. VIII:** 290, 291; **Supp. XII:** 2, 198; **Supp. XIII:** 104
"Ol' Tunes, The" (Dunbar), **Supp. II Part 1:** 197
"O Lull Me, Lull Me" (Roethke), **III:** 536–537
Omar Khayyam, **Supp. I Part 1:** 363
O'Meally, Robert, **Retro. Supp. II:** 112
"Omen" (Komunyakaa), **Supp. XIII:** 126, 127
Omensetter's Luck (Gass), **Supp. VI: 80–82,** 87
"Ominous Baby, An" (Crane), **I:** 411
Ommateum, with Doxology (Ammons), **Supp. VII: 24–26,** 27, 28, 36
"Omnibus Jaunts and Drivers" (Whitman), **IV:** 350
Omoo: A Narrative of Adventures in the South Seas (Melville), **III:** 76–77, 79, 84; **Retro. Supp. I:** 247
O My Land, My Friends (H. Crane), **Retro. Supp. II:** 76
"On a Certain Condescension in Foreigners" (Lowell), **Supp. I Part 2:** 419
"On Acquiring Riches" (Banks), **Supp. V:** 5

On a Darkling Plain (Stegner), **Supp. IV Part 2:** 598, 607
On a Fire on the Moon (Mailer), **Retro. Supp. II:** 206
"On a Hill Far Away" (Dillard), **Supp. VI:** 28
"On a Honey Bee, Drinking from a Glass and Drowned Therein" (Freneau), **Supp. II Part 1:** 273
"On a Mountainside" (Wagoner), **Supp. IX:** 332
O'Nan, Stewart, **Supp. XI:** 348
"On an Old Photograph of My Son" (Carver), **Supp. III Part 1:** 140
"On a Proposed Trip South" (W. C. Williams), **Retro. Supp. I:** 413
"On a Tree Fallen across the Road" (Frost), **Retro. Supp. I:** 134
"On a View of Pasadena from the Hills" (Winters), **Supp. II Part 2:** 795, 796–799, 814
"On a Visit to a Halfway House after a Long Absence" (Salinas), **Supp. XIII:** 325
"On a Windy Night" (Dixon), **Supp. XII:** 155
On Becoming a Novelist (Gardner), **Supp. VI:** 64
"On Being an American" (Toomer), **Supp. III Part 2:** 479
"On Being a Woman" (Parker), **Supp. IX:** 201
On Being Blue (Gass), **Supp. VI:** 77, 78, 86, 94
"On Burroughs' Work" (Ginsberg), **Supp. II Part 1:** 320
Once (Walker), **Supp. III Part 2:** 519, 522, 530
Once at Antietam (Gaddis), **Supp. IV Part 1:** 285
"Once by the Pacific" (Frost), **II:** 155; **Retro. Supp. I:** 122, 137
"Once More, the Round" (Roethke), **III:** 529
"Once More to the Lake" (White), **Supp. I Part 2:** 658, 668, 673–675
"On Certain Political Measures Proposed to Their Consideration" (Barlow), **Supp. II Part 1:** 82
"Once There Was Light" (Kenyon), **Supp. VII:** 171–172
Ondaatje, Michael, **Supp. IV Part 1:** 252
On Distant Ground (R. O. Butler), **Supp. XII:** 62, **66–68,** 69, 74
O'Neale, Sondra, **Supp. IV Part 1:** 2
"One Arm" (T. Williams), **IV:** 383
One Arm, and Other Stories (T. Williams), **IV:** 383
"One Art" (Bell), **Supp. X:** 2

One Art (Bishop), **Retro. Supp. II:** 51
"One Art" (Bishop), **Retro. Supp. II:** 50; **Supp. I Part 1:** 72, 73, 82, 93, 94–95, 96
"One Art: The Poetry of Elizabeth Bishop, 1971–1976" (Schwartz), **Supp. I Part 1:** 81
"One Blessing had I than the rest" (Dickinson), **Retro. Supp. I:** 45
"One Body" (Hass), **Supp. VI:** 106
One Boy's Boston, 1887–1901 (Morison), **Supp. I Part 2:** 494
"One Coat of Paint" (Ashbery), **Supp. III Part 1:** 26
"One Dash-Horses" (Crane), **I:** 416
One Day (Morris), **III:** 233–236
One Day, When I Was Lost (Baldwin), **Retro. Supp. II:** 13; **Supp. I Part 1:** 48, 66, 67
"One Dead Friend" (Kumin), **Supp. IV Part 2:** 441
One Flew Over the Cuckoo's Nest (Kesey), **III:** 558
One for the Rose (Levine), **Supp. V:** 178, 179, 181, 187, 189–191
"One for the Rose" (Levine), **Supp. V:** 181, 190
"One Friday Morning" (Hughes), **Supp. I Part 1:** 330
"One Holy Night" (Cisneros), **Supp. VII:** 69–70
"One Home" (Stafford), **Supp. XI:** 321
"$106,000 Blood Money" (Hammett), **Supp. IV Part 1:** 345, 346
$106,000 Blood Money (Hammett), **Supp. IV Part 1:** 345
One Hundred Days in Europe (Holmes), **Supp. I Part 1:** 317
100 Faces of Death, The, Part IV (Boyle), **Supp. VIII:** 16
158-Pound Marriage, The (Irving), **Supp. VI:** 163, 164, **167–170**
O'Neil, Elizabeth Murrie, **Retro. Supp. I:** 427
O'Neill, Brendan, **Supp. XII:** 286
O'Neill, Eugene, **I:** 66, 71, 81, 94, 393, 445; **II:** 278, 391, 427, 585; **III:** 151, 165, **385–408; IV:** 61, 383; **Retro. Supp. II:** 82, 104; **Supp. III Part 1:** 177–180, 189; **Supp. IV Part 1:** 359; **Supp. IV Part 2:** 587, 607; **Supp. V:** 277; **Supp. VIII:** 332, 334
"One Is a Wanderer" (Thurber), **Supp. I Part 2:** 616
"1 January 1965" (Brodsky), **Supp. VIII:** 23–24
"One Last Look at the Adige: Verona in the Rain" (Wright), **Supp. III Part 2:** 603

One Life (Rukeyser), **Supp. VI:** 273, 281, 283
One Life at a Time, Please (Abbey), **Supp. XIII:** 13
One Man in His Time (Glasgow), **II:** 178, 184
"One Man's Fortunes" (Dunbar), **Supp. II Part 1:** 211, 212–213
One Man's Initiation (Dos Passos), **I:** 476–477, 479, 488
"One Man's Meat" (White), **Supp. I Part 2:** 655
One Man's Meat (White), **Supp. I Part 2:** 654, 669, 676
"One Moment on Top of the Earth" (Nye), **Supp. XIII:** 282
"One More Song" (Lindsay), **Supp. I Part 2:** 400–401
"One More Thing" (Carver), **Supp. III Part 1:** 138, 144
"One More Time" (Gordon), **II:** 200
One Nation (Stegner), **Supp. IV Part 2:** 599, 608
"ONE NIGHT STAND" (Baraka), **Supp. II Part 1:** 32
"One of Our Conquerors" (Bourne), **I:** 223
One of Ours (Cather), **I:** 322–323; **Retro. Supp. I:** 1, 3, **13–15,** 20
"One of the Missing" (Bierce), **I:** 201–202
"One of the Rooming Houses of Heaven" (Doty), **Supp. XI:** 131
"One of the Smallest" (Stern), **Supp. IX:** 299–300
"One of Us" (Fante), **Supp. XI:** 165
"One Out of Twelve: Writers Who Are Women in Our Century" (Olsen), **Supp. XIII:** 294
"One Part Humor, 2 Parts Whining" (Kakutani), **Supp. XI:** 38
"One Person" (Wylie), **Supp. I Part 2:** 709, 724–727
"One Sister have I in our house" (Dickinson), **Retro. Supp. I:** 34
"One Song, The" (Strand), **Supp. IV Part 2:** 619
"One Summer in Spain" (Coover), **Supp. V:** 40
One Time, One Place: Mississippi in the Depression, a Snapshot Album (Welty), **Retro. Supp. I:** 339, 343, 344
1 x 1 (One Times One) (Cummings), **I:** 430, 436, 438–439, 441, 446, 447, 448
"One Touch of Nature" (McCarthy), **II:** 580
"One Trip Abroad" (Fitzgerald), **II:** 95
"One Way" (Creeley), **Supp. IV Part 1:** 150–151
One Way or Another (Cameron), **Supp. XII:** 81
One-Way Ticket (Hughes), **Retro. Supp. I:** 206, 207, 208; **Supp. I Part 1:** 333–334
One Way to Heaven (Cullen), **Supp. IV Part 1:** 170, 172
One Way to Spell Man (Stegner), **Supp. IV Part 2:** 595, 598, 601, 609
"One Way to Spell Man" (Stegner), **Supp. IV Part 2:** 601
"One Who Skins Cats, The" (Gunn Allen), **Supp. IV Part 1:** 331
"One Who Went Forth to Feel Fear" (Grimms), **Supp. X:** 86
"One Winter I Devise a Plan of My Own" (Ríos), **Supp. IV Part 2:** 549
One Writer's Beginnings (Welty), **Retro. Supp. I:** 339, 340, 341, 343, 344, 355–356
"One Year" (Olds), **Supp. X:** 210
"On First Looking Out through Juan de la Cosa's Eyes" (Olson), **Supp. II Part 2:** 565, 566, 570, 579
"On First Opening *The Lyric Year*" (W. C. Williams), **Retro. Supp. I:** 414
"On Freedom's Ground" (Wilbur), **Supp. III Part 2:** 562
On Glory's Course (Purdy), **Supp. VII:** 275–276, 279, 280
On Grief and Reason (Brodsky), **Supp. VIII: 31–32**
"On Hearing a Symphony of Beethoven" (Millay), **III:** 132–133
"On Hearing the Airlines Will Use a Psychological Profile to Catch Potential Skyjackers" (Dunn), **Supp. XI:** 144–145
On Human Finery (Bell), **Supp. I Part 2:** 636
On Liberty (Mill), **Supp. XI:** 196
On Lies, Secrets, and Silence: Selected Prose, 1966–1978 (Rich), **Retro. Supp. II:** 282, 285–286
"On Looking at a Copy of Alice Meynell's Poems, Given Me, Years Ago, by a Friend" (Lowell), **II:** 527–528
"On Lookout Mountain" (Hayden), **Supp. II Part 1:** 380
Only a Few of Us Left (Marquand), **III:** 55
"Only Bar in Dixon, The" (Hugo), **Supp. VI:** 140, 141
Only Dark Spot in the Sky, The (Dove), **Supp. IV Part 1:** 244
"Only Good Indian, The" (Humphrey), **Supp. IX:** 101
Only in America (Golden), **Supp. VIII:** 244
"Only in the Dream" (Eberhart), **I:** 523
"Only Path to Tomorrow, The" (Rand), **Supp. IV Part 2:** 524
"Only Rose, The" (Jewett), **II:** 408
"Only Son of the Doctor, The" (Gordon), **Supp. IV Part 1:** 305, 306
"Only the Cat Escapes," **Supp. XII:** 150–151
"Only the Dead Know Brooklyn" (Wolfe), **IV:** 451
Only When I Laugh (Simon), **Supp. IV Part 2:** 575
On Moral Fiction (Gardner), **Supp. VI:** 61, **71,** 72, 73
"On Morality" (Didion), **Supp. IV Part 1:** 196
"On My Own" (Levine), **Supp. V:** 181, 189–190
"On My Own Work" (Wilbur), **Supp. III Part 2:** 541–542
On Native Grounds: An Interpretation of Modern American Prose Literature (Kazin), **I:** 517; **Supp. I Part 2:** 650; **Supp. VIII:** 93, 96–97, 98, **100–102**
"On Not Being a Dove" (Updike), **Retro. Supp. I:** 323
"On Open Form" (Merwin), **Supp. III Part 1:** 347–348, 353
On Photography (Sontag), **Supp. III Part 2:** 451, 458, 462–465
"On Political Poetry" (Bly), **Supp. IV Part 1:** 61
On Politics: A Carnival of Buncombe (Moos, ed.), **III:** 116
"On Pretentiousness" (Kushner), **Supp. IX:** 131–132
"On Quitting a Little College" (Stafford), **Supp. XI:** 321
"On Reading Eckerman's Conversations with Goethe" (Masters), **Supp. I Part 2:** 458
"On Reading to Oneself" (Gass), **Supp. VI:** 88, 89
On Revolution (Arendt), **Retro. Supp. I:** 87
"On Seeing Red" (Walker), **Supp. III Part 2:** 527
"On Social Plays" (A. Miller), **III:** 147, 148, 159
"On Steinbeck's Story 'Flight'" (Stegner), **Supp. IV Part 2:** 596
"On Style" (Sontag), **Supp. III Part 2:** 456–459, 465–466
"On the Antler" (Proulx), **Supp. VII:** 252–253
"On the Banks of the Wabash" (Paul

Dresser), **Retro. Supp. II:** 94
"On the Beach, at Night" (Whitman), **IV:** 348
On the Boundary (Tillich), **Retro. Supp. I:** 326
"On the Building of Springfield" (Lindsay), **Supp. I Part 2:** 381
"On the Coast of Maine" (Hayden), **Supp. II Part 1:** 381
On the Contrary: Articles of Belief (McCarthy), **II:** 559, 562
"On the Death of a Friend's Child" (Lowell), **Supp. I Part 2:** 409
"On the Death of Senator Thomas J. Walsh" (Winters), **Supp. II Part 2:** 802, 806
"On the Death of Yeats" (Bogan), **Supp. III Part 1:** 59
"On the Death of Zhukov" (Brodsky), **Supp. VIII:** 27
"On the Disadvantages of Central Heating" (Clampitt), **Supp. IX:** 41, 47, 52
"On the Edge" (Levine), **Supp. V:** 181–182
On the Edge and Over (Levine), **Supp. V:** 178, 180–182, 186
On the Edge of the Great Rift: Three Novels of Africa (Theroux), **Supp. VIII:** 316
"On the Eve of the Feast of the Immaculate Conception, 1942" (Lowell), **II:** 538; **Retro. Supp. II:** 185
"On the Eyes of an SS Officer" (Wilbur), **Supp. III Part 2:** 548
"On the Fall of General Earl Cornwallis" (Freneau), **Supp. II Part 1:** 261
"On the Folly of Writing Poetry" (Freneau), **Supp. II Part 1:** 263
On the Frontier (Auden and Isherwood), **Supp. II Part 1:** 13
"On the Island" (Stern), **Supp. IX:** 290
"On the Late Eclipse" (Bryant), **Supp. I Part 1:** 152
On the Laws of the Poetic Art (Hecht), **Supp. X:** 58
"On the Marginal Way" (Wilbur), **Supp. III Part 2:** 558, 559
On the Mesa (Nichols), **Supp. XIII:** 268
"On the Moon and Matriarchal Consciousness" (Neumann), **Supp. IV Part 1:** 68
"On the Morning after the Sixties" (Didion), **Supp. IV Part 1:** 205, 206
On the Motion and Immobility of Douve (Bonnefoy; Kinnell, trans.), **Supp. III Part 1:** 235
"On the Murder of Lieutenant José del Castillo by the Falangist Bravo Martinez, July 12, 1936" (Levine), **Supp. V:** 187
"On the Night of a Friend's Wedding" (Robinson), **III:** 524
"On the Occasion of a Poem: Richard Hugo" (Wright), **Supp. III Part 2:** 596
On the Occasion of My Last Afternoon (Gibbons), **Supp. X:** 46, 50–53
"On the Parapet" (Tanner), **Retro. Supp. II:** 205
"On the Platform" (Nemerov), **III:** 287
On the Poetry of Philip Levine: Stranger to Nothing (Levis), **Supp. XI:** 257
"On the Powers of the Human Understanding" (Freneau), **Supp. II Part 1:** 274
"On the Pulse of Morning" (Angelou), **Supp. IV Part 1:** 15–17
"On the Railway Platform" (Jarrell), **II:** 370
"On the Rainy River" (O'Brien), **Supp. V:** 250
On the Rebound: A Story and Nine Poems (Purdy), **Supp. VII:** 276–277
"On the Religion of Nature" (Freneau), **Supp. II Part 1:** 275
"On the River" (Dunbar), **Supp. II Part 1:** 193
"On the River" (Levine), **Supp. V:** 193
On the River Styx and Other Stories (Matthiessen), **Supp. V:** 212
On the Road (Kerouac), **Retro. Supp. I:** 102; **Supp. III Part 1:** 92, 218, 222–224, 226, 230–231; **Supp. V:** 336; **Supp. X:** 269; **Supp. XIII:** 275
"On the Road Home" (Stevens), **Retro. Supp. I:** 306
On the Road with the Archangel (Buechner), **Supp. XII:** 54
On These I Stand: An Anthology of the Best Poems of Countee Cullen (Cullen), **Supp. IV Part 1:** 173
"On the Skeleton of a Hound" (Wright), **Supp. III Part 2:** 593
"On the Street: Monument" (Gunn Allen), **Supp. IV Part 1:** 326
"On the Subway" (Olds), **Supp. X:** 207
"On the System of Policy Hitherto Pursued by Their Government" (Barlow), **Supp. II Part 1:** 82
"On the Teaching of Modern Literature" (Trilling), **Supp. III Part 2:** 509–510
"On the Uniformity and Perfection of Nature" (Freneau), **Supp. II Part 1:** 275
"On the Universality and Other Attributes of the God of Nature" (Freneau), **Supp. II Part 1:** 275
"On the Use of Trisyllabic Feet in Iambic Verse" (Bryant), **Supp. I Part 1:** 156
On the Way toward a Phenomenological Psychology: The Psychology of William James (Linschoten), **II:** 362
"On the Way to Work" (Dunn), **Supp. XI:** 149–150
"On the Wide Heath" (Millay), **III:** 130
"On the Writing of Novels" (Buck), **Supp. II Part 1:** 121
On This Island (Auden), **Supp. II Part 1:** 11
"On Time" (O'Hara), **III:** 369–370
"Ontology of the Sentence, The" (Gass), **Supp. VI:** 77
"On Top" (Snyder), **Supp. VIII:** 304
"On Translating Akhmatova" (Kunitz), **Supp. III Part 1:** 268
On William Stafford: The Worth of Local Things (Andrews, ed.), **Supp. XI:** 311, 312, 317, 321, 324, 326
"On Writing" (Carver), **Supp. III Part 1:** 142–143
"On Writing" (Nin), **Supp. X:** 182
Opatoshu, Joseph, **IV:** 9
"Open Boat, The" (Crane), **I:** 408, 415, 416–417, 423; **Retro. Supp. I:** 325
Open Boat and Other Stories (Crane), **I:** 408
Open House (Roethke), **III:** 529–530, 540
"Open House" (Roethke), **III:** 529
"Opening, An" (Swenson), **Supp. IV Part 2:** 639
Opening of the Field, The (Duncan), **Supp. III Part 2:** 625
Opening the Hand (Merwin), **Supp. III Part 1:** 341, 353, 355
"Open Letter" (Roethke), **III:** 532, 534
"Open Letter to Surrealists Everywhere, An" (H. Miller), **III:** 184
Open Meeting, The (Gurney), **Supp. V:** 98
"Open Road, The" (Dreiser), **II:** 44
Open Sea, The (Masters), **Supp. I Part 2:** 471
Open Season: Sporting Adventures (Humphrey), **Supp. IX:** 95
"Open the Gates" (Kunitz), **Supp. III Part 1:** 264–265, 267
"Opera Company, The" (Merrill), **Supp. III Part 1:** 326
"Operation, The" (Sexton), **Supp. II Part 2:** 675, 679
Operation Shylock: A Confession

(Roth), **Retro. Supp. II:** 297, 298, 309
Operation Sidewinder (Shepard), **Supp. III Part 2:** 434–435, 439, 446–447
Operations in North African Waters (Morison), **Supp. I Part 2:** 490
Operation Wandering Soul (Powers), **Supp. IX:** 212, **217–219**
Opffer, Emil, **Retro. Supp. II:** 80
"Opinion" (Du Bois), **Supp. II Part 1:** 173
Opinionator, The (Bierce), **I:** 209
Opinions of Oliver Allston (Brooks), **I:** 254, 255, 256
O Pioneers! (Cather), **I:** 314, 317–319, 320; **Retro. Supp. I:** 1, 5, 6, **7–9**, 10, 13, 20; **Retro. Supp. II:** 136
Oppen, George, **IV:** 415; **Supp. III Part 2:** 614, 615, 616, 626, 628
Oppenheim, James, **I:** 106, 109, 239, 245
Oppenheimer, J. Robert, **I:** 137, 492
Oppenheimer, Judy, **Supp. IX:** 115, 116, 118, 120, 126
"Opportunity for American Fiction, An" (Howells), **Supp. I Part 2:** 645–646
Opposing Self, The (Trilling), **Supp. III Part 2:** 506–507
"Opposition" (Lanier), **Supp. I Part 1:** 368, 373
Opticks: A Poem in Seven Sections (Goldbarth), **Supp. XII:** 177, **178**
"Optimist's Daughter, The" (Welty), **IV:** 280–281
Optimist's Daughter, The (Welty), **IV:** 261, 280; **Retro. Supp. I:** 339, 355
Options (O. Henry), **Supp. II Part 1:** 410
Opus Posthumous (Stevens), **IV:** 76, 78
Oracle at Stoneleigh Court, The (Taylor), **Supp. V:** 328
Orage, Alfred, **III:** 473
Orange, Max (pseudonym). *See* Heller, Joseph
Orange Fish, The (Shields), **Supp. VII:** 318, 320, 323, 328
Oranges (McPhee), **Supp. III Part 1:** 298–299, 301, 309
Oration Delivered at Washington, July Fourth, 1809 (Barlow), **Supp. II Part 1:** 80, 83
Orations and Addresses (Bryant), **Supp. I Part 1:** 158
Orators, The (Auden), **Supp. II Part 1:** 6, 7, 11, 18–19
Orb Weaver, The (Francis), **Supp. IX: 81–82**

"Orchard" (Doolittle), **Supp. I Part 1:** 263–264, 265, 266
"Orchard" (Eberhart), **I:** 539
Orchard Keeper, The (McCarthy), **Supp. VIII: 175–176**
Orchestra (Davies), **III:** 541
"Orchids" (Roethke), **III:** 530–531
"Or Consider Prometheus" (Clampitt), **Supp. IX:** 44
Ordeal of Mansart, The (Du Bois), **Supp. II Part 1:** 185–186
Ordeal of Mark Twain, The (Brooks), **I:** 240, 247, 248; **II:** 482
"Order of Insects" (Gass), **Supp. VI:** 83
Order Out of Chaos (McPherson), **Supp. IV Part 1:** 2, 12
"Ordinary Afternoon in Charlottesville, An" (Wright), **Supp. V:** 344
"Ordinary Days" (Dunn), **Supp. XI:** 151
"Ordinary Evening in New Haven, An" (Stevens), **IV:** 91–92; **Retro. Supp. I:** 297, 300, 311, 312
Ordinary Love (Smiley), **Supp. VI:** 292, **299–300**
Ordinary Love; and Good Will: Two Novellas (Smiley), **Supp. VI:** 292, **299–300**
Ordinary Miracles (Jong), **Supp. V:** 115, 130–131
"Ordinary Time: Virginia Woolf and Thucydides on War" (Carson), **Supp. XII:** 111
"Ordinary Women, The" (Stevens), **IV:** 81
Ordways, The (Humphrey), **Supp. IX:** 95, **98–100,** 109
"Oread" (Doolittle), **II:** 520–521; **Supp. I Part 1:** 265–266
Oregon Message, An (Stafford), **Supp. XI: 328–329**
Oregon Trail, The (Parkman), **II:** 312; **Supp. II Part 2:** 592, 595–596, 598, 606
Oresteia (Aeschylus), **Supp. IX:** 103
"Orestes at Tauris" (Jarrell), **II:** 376, 377
Orfalea, Gregory, **Supp. XIII:** 278
Orfeo ed Euridice (Gluck), **II:** 210, 211
Orff, Carl, **Supp. X:** 63
"Organizer's Wife, The" (Bambara), **Supp. XI:** 8–9
"Orgy" (Rukeyser), **Supp. VI:** 280
Orgy, The (Rukeyser), **Supp. VI:** 274, 283
Orient Express (Dos Passos), **I:** 480
"Orient Express, The" (Jarrell), **II:** 382, 383–384
Origen, Adamantius, **IV:** 153

"Origin" (Harjo), **Supp. XII:** 219
Original Child Bomb: Points for Meditation to Be Scratched on the Walls of a Cave (Merton), **Supp. VIII:** 203
Original Essays on the Poetry of Anne Sexton (George), **Supp. IV Part 2:** 450
"Original Follies Girl, The" (Z. Fitzgerald), **Supp. IX:** 71
Original Light (Goldbarth), **Supp. XII:** 181, **183–184,** 188
Original of Laura, The (Nabokov), **Retro. Supp. I:** 266
"Original Sin" (Jeffers), **Supp. II Part 2:** 426
"Original Sin" (Warren), **IV:** 245
"Origin of Extermination in the Imagination, The" (Gass), **Supp. VI:** 89
Origin of Species, The (Darwin), **II:** 173, 462
Origin of the Brunists, The (Coover), **Supp. V:** 39, 41, 52
"Origins and History of Consciousness" (Rich), **Supp. I Part 2:** 570
"Origins of a Poem" (Levertov), **Supp. III Part 1:** 273
"Origins of the Beat Generation, The" (Kerouac), **Supp. III Part 1:** 231
Origo, Iris, **IV:** 328
"Orion" (Rich), **Retro. Supp. II:** 284; **Supp. I Part 2:** 557
O'Riordan, Conal Holmes O'Connell, **III:** 465
Orlando (Woolf), **Supp. I Part 2:** 718; **Supp. VIII:** 263; **Supp. XII:** 9
Orlovsky, Peter, **Supp. XII:** 121, 126
Ormond; or, The Secret Witness (Brown), **Supp. I Part 1:** 133–137
Ormonde, Czenzi, **Supp. IV Part 1:** 132
Orne, Sarah. *See* Jewett, Sarah Orne
Ornitz, Samuel, **Supp. IX:** 227; **Supp. XIII:** 166
Orphan Angel, The (Wylie), **Supp. I Part 2:** 707, 709, 714, 717, 719–721, 722, 724
Orpheus (Rukeyser), **Supp. VI:** 273
"Orpheus" (Winters), **Supp. II Part 2:** 801
"Orpheus (1)" (Atwood), **Supp. XIII:** 35
"Orpheus (2)" (Atwood), **Supp. XIII:** 35
"Orpheus, Eurydice, Hermes" (Rilke), **Supp. VIII:** 31, 32
"Orpheus Alone" (Strand), **Supp. IV Part 2:** 632
Orpheus Descending (T. Williams), **IV:** 380, 381, 382, 385, 386, 387, 389,

391–392, 395, 396, 398
Orr, Peter, **Supp. I Part 2:** 538, 540, 543
Ortega y Gasset, José, **I:** 218, 222; **Supp. IV Part 2:** 521
Ortiz, Simon J., **Supp. IV Part 1:** 319, 404; **Supp. IV Part 2: 497–515,** 557; **Supp. XII:** 217, 218
O'Ruddy, The (Crane), **I:** 409, 424
Orwell, George, **I:** 489; **II:** 454, 580; **Supp. I Part 2:** 523, 620; **Supp. II Part 1:** 143; **Supp. IV Part 1:** 236; **Supp. V:** 250; **Supp. VIII:** 241
Osborn, Dwight, **III:** 218–219, 223
"Osborn Look, The" (Morris), **III:** 221
Osgood, J. R., **II:** 283
O'Shea, Kitty, **II:** 137
O'Shea, Milo, **Supp. XI:** 308
"Oshkikwe's Baby" (traditional Chippewa story), **Supp. IV Part 1:** 333
Oshogay, Delia, **Supp. IV Part 1:** 333
Ossana, Diana, **Supp. V:** 230–231, 232
Ossian, **Supp. I Part 2:** 491
Ossip, Kathleen, **Supp. X:** 201
Ostanovka v Pustyne (A halt in the wilderness) (Brodsky), **Supp. VIII:** 21
Ostriker, Alicia, **Supp. I Part 2:** 540; **Supp. IV Part 2:** 439, 447, 449; **Supp. X:** 207, 208; **Supp. XI:** 143
Ostrom, Hans, **Retro. Supp. I:** 195
Oswald, Lee Harvey, **III:** 234, 235
Oswald II (DeLillo), **Supp. VI:** 16
Oswald's Tale (Mailer), **Retro. Supp. II:** 212–213
O Taste and See (Levertov), **Supp. III Part 1:** 278–279, 281
Othello (Shakespeare), **I:** 284–285
"Other, The" (Sexton), **Supp. II Part 2:** 692
Other America, The (Harrington), **I:** 306
Other Destinies: Understanding the American Indian Novel (Owens), **Supp. IV Part 1:** 404
"Other Frost, The" (Jarrell), **Retro. Supp. I:** 121
Other Gods: An American Legend (Buck), **Supp. II Part 1:** 123, 130–131
Other House, The (James), **Retro. Supp. I:** 229
"Other League of Nations, The" (Ríos), **Supp. IV Part 2:** 552
"Other Margaret, The" (Trilling), **Supp. III Part 2:** 504–505
"Other Miller, The" (Wolff), **Supp. VII:** 343–344

"Other Mothers" (Paley), **Supp. VI:** 225
"Other Night at Columbia, The" (Trilling), **Supp. XII:** 126
"Other Robert Frost, The" (Jarrell), **Retro. Supp. I:** 135
Others (Shields), **Supp. VII:** 310
Other Side, The (Gordon), **Supp. IV Part 1:** 299, 306, 307–309, 310–311
Other Side, The/El Otro Lado (Alvarez), **Supp. VII:** 9–12
Other Side of the River, The (Wright), **Supp. V:** 332–333, 342
"Other Side of the River, The" (Wright), **Supp. V:** 335
"Other Tradition, The" (Ashbery), **Supp. III Part 1:** 15, 18
"Other Two, The" (Wharton), **Retro. Supp. I:** 367
Other Voices, Other Rooms (Capote), **Supp. III Part 1:** 113–118, 121, 123–124
"Other War, The" (Cowley), **Supp. II Part 1:** 144
"Otherwise" (Kenyon), **Supp. VII:** 172, 174
Otherwise: New and Selected Poems (Kenyon), **Supp. VII:** 167, 172–174
"Other Woman, The" (Anderson), **I:** 114
Otho the Great: A Tragedy in Five Acts (Keats), **Supp. XII:** 113
Otis, Harrison Gray, **Supp. I Part 2:** 479–481, 483, 486, 488
Otis, James, **III:** 577; **Supp. I Part 2:** 486
O to Be a Dragon (Moore), **III:** 215
"Ouija" (McClatchy), **Supp. XII:** 269–270
Our America (Frank), **I:** 229; **Supp. IX:** 308
Our America (Michaels), **Retro. Supp. I:** 379
"Our Assistant's Column" (Twain), **IV:** 193
"Our Bourgeois Literature" (Sinclair), **Supp. V:** 281
Our Brains and What Ails Them (Gilman), **Supp. XI:** 207
Our Century (Wilder), **IV:** 374
"Our Countrymen in Chains!" (Whittier), **Supp. I Part 2:** 688
"Our Cultural Humility" (Bourne), **I:** 223, 228
Our Depleted Society (Seymour), **Supp. XIII:** 264
"Our Father Who Drowns the Birds" (Kingsolver), **Supp. VII:** 208–209
"Our First House" (Kingston), **Supp. V:** 169

Our Gang (Roth), **Retro. Supp. II:** 305; **Supp. III Part 2:** 414; **Supp. IV Part 1:** 388
"Our Good Day" (Cisneros), **Supp. VII:** 60
Our Ground Time Here Will Be Brief (Kumin), **Supp. IV Part 2:** 450–452
Our House in the Last World (Hijuelos), **Supp. VIII:** 73, **76–79,** 87, 88
"Our Lady of the Annunciation/Nuestra Señora de la Anunciación" (Mora), **Supp. XIII:** 217, 224, 228
"Our Lady of Troy" (MacLeish), **III:** 3, 20
"Our Limitations" (Holmes), **Supp. I Part 1:** 314
"Our Martyred Soldiers" (Dunbar), **Supp. II Part 1:** 193
"Our Master" (Whittier), **Supp. I Part 2:** 704
"Our Mother Pocahontas" (Lindsay), **Supp. I Part 2:** 393
Our Mr. Wrenn: The Romantic Adventures of a Gentle Man (Lewis), **II:** 441
Our National Parks (Muir), **Supp. IX:** 181, 184
Our New York: A Personal Vision in Words and Photographs (Kazin), **Supp. VIII: 106–107**
"Our Old Aunt Who Is Now in a Retirement Home" (Shields), **Supp. VII:** 310
Our Old Home: A Series of English Sketches (Hawthorne), **II:** 225; **Retro. Supp. I:** 163
"Our Own Movie Queen" (Z. Fitzgerald), **Supp. IX:** 71
Ourselves to Know (O'Hara), **III:** 362, 365
"Our Story Begins" (Wolff), **Supp. VII:** 345
Our Town (Wilder), **IV:** 357, 364, 365, 366, 368–369
"Our Unplanned Cities" (Bourne), **I:** 229, 230
Our Wonder World, **Retro. Supp. I:** 341
Ouspensky, P. D., **I:** 383
"Out" (Harjo), **Supp. XII:** 219
"'Out, Out'" (Frost), **Retro. Supp. I:** 131
"Outcast" (McKay), **Supp. X:** 135
"Outcasts of Poker Flats, The" (Harte), **Supp. II Part 1:** 345, 347–348
Outcroppings (Harte), **Supp. II Part 1:** 343
Out Cry (T. Williams), **IV:** 383, 393

Outcry, The (James), **Retro. Supp. I:** 235
"Outdoor Shower" (Olds), **Supp. X:** 214
Outerbridge Reach (Stone), **Supp. V:** 306–308
Outer Dark (McCarthy), **Supp. VIII: 176–177**
Outermost Dream, The: Essays and Reviews (Maxwell), **Supp. VIII: 171–172**
"Outing, The" (Baldwin), **Supp. I Part 1:** 63
"Out Like a Lamb" (Dubus), **Supp. VII:** 91
"Outline of an Autobiography" (Toomer), **Supp. III Part 2:** 478
Outlyer and Ghazals (Harrison), **Supp. VIII:** 41
"Out of Business" (Mora), **Supp. XIII:** 217
"Out of Nowhere into Nothing" (Anderson), **I:** 113
"Out of Season" (Hemingway), **II:** 263
"Out of the Cradle Endlessly Rocking" (Whitman), **IV:** 342, 343–345, 346, 351; **Retro. Supp. I:** 404, 406
"Out of the Hospital and Under the Bar" (Ellison), **Retro. Supp. II:** 118–119; **Supp. II Part 1:** 246
"Out of the Rainbow End" (Sandburg), **III:** 594–595
"Out of the Sea, Early" (Swenson), **Supp. IV Part 2:** 645
"Out of the Snow" (Dubus), **Supp. VII:** 91
Out of the Stars (Purdy), **Supp. VII:** 281–282
Outre-Mer: A Pilgrimage beyond the Sea (Longfellow), **II:** 313, 491; **Retro. Supp. II:** 155, 165
"Outside" (Stafford), **Supp. XI:** 318
Outside, The (Glaspell), **Supp. III Part 1:** 179, 187
Outsider, The (Wright), **IV:** 478, 481, 488, 491–494, 495
"Out with the Old" (Yates), **Supp. XI:** 342
"Ouzo for Robin" (Merrill), **Supp. III Part 1:** 326
"Oval Portrait, The" (Poe), **III:** 412, 415; **Retro. Supp. II:** 270
"Oven Bird, The" (Frost), **Retro. Supp. I:** 131; **Supp. XI:** 153
"Over by the River" (Maxwell), **Supp. VIII:** 169, 170
"Overgrown Pasture, The" (Lowell), **II:** 523
"Over 2,000 Illustrations and a Complete Concordance" (Bishop), **Retro. Supp. II:** 45; **Supp. I Part 1:** 90–91
"Over Kansas" (Ginsberg), **Supp. II Part 1:** 320
Overland to the Islands (Levertov), **Supp. III Part 1:** 275, 276
"Over-Soul, The" (Emerson), **II:** 7
"Over the Hill" (Dubus), **Supp. VII:** 76, 79–80
Overtime (Gurney), **Supp. V:** 104
"Overwhelming Question, An" (Taylor), **Supp. V:** 323
Ovid, **I:** 62; **II:** 542–543; **III:** 457, 467, 468, 470; **Retro. Supp. I:** 63; **Supp. IV Part 2:** 634; **Supp. XII:** 264
"Ovid's Farewell" (McClatchy), **Supp. XII:** 257–258
Owen, David, **II:** 34
Owen, Maureen, **Supp. IV Part 2:** 423
Owen, Wilfred, **II:** 367, 372; **III:** 524; **Supp. X:** 146
Owens, Hamilton, **III:** 99, 109
Owens, Louis, **Supp. IV Part 1:** 404
"O Where Are You Going?" (Auden), **Supp. X:** 116
Owl in the Attic, The (Thurber), **Supp. I Part 2:** 614
Owl in the Mask of the Dreamer, The: Collected Poems (Haines), **Supp. XII:** 211
"Owl in the Sarcophagus, The" (Stevens), **Retro. Supp. I:** 300
"Owl's Clover" (Stevens), **IV:** 75
Owl's Clover (Stevens), **Retro. Supp. I:** 298, **303–304**
Owl's Insomnia, Poems by Rafael Alberti, The (Strand, trans.), **Supp. IV Part 2:** 630
"Owl Who Was God, The" (Thurber), **Supp. I Part 2:** 610
Owning Jolene (Hearon), **Supp. VIII: 66–67**
Oxford Anthology of American Literature, The, **III:** 197; **Supp. I Part 1:** 254
Oxford Book of American Verse (Matthiessen, ed.), **Retro. Supp. I:** 40
Oxford History of the American People, The (Morison), **Supp. I Part 2:** 495–496
Oxford History of the United States, 1783–1917, The (Morison), **Supp. I Part 2:** 483–484
Oxherding Tale (Johnson), **Supp. VI: 190–192,** 193, 194, 196
"O Yes" (Olsen), **Supp. XIII:** 294, 298, **299–300,** 301
"O Youth and Beauty!" (Cheever), **Retro. Supp. I:** 335

"Oysters" (Sexton), **Supp. II Part 2:** 692
Ozick, Cynthia, **Supp. V: 257–274; Supp. VIII:** 141; **Supp. X:** 192
O-Zone (Theroux), **Supp. VIII:** 323–324
P. D. Kimerakov (Epstein), **Supp. XII:** 160, **162**
Pace, Patricia, **Supp. XI:** 245
Pacernik, Gary, **Supp. IX:** 287, 291
"Pacific Distances" (Didion), **Supp. IV Part 1:** 211
Pack, Robert, **Supp. IV Part 2:** 621
"Packed Dirt, Churchgoing, a Dying Cat, a Traded Cat" (Updike), **IV:** 219
Padel, Ruth, **Supp. XII:** 107
Pafko at the Wall (DeLillo), **Supp. VI:** 4
"Pagan Prayer" (Cullen), **Supp. IV Part 1:** 170
"Pagan Rabbi, The" (Ozick), **Supp. V:** 262, 264, 265
Pagan Rabbi and Other Stories, The (Ozick), **Supp. V:** 260, 261, 263–265
Pagan Spain (Wright), **IV:** 478, 488, 495
Page, Kirby, **III:** 297
Page, Thomas Nelson, **II:** 174, 176, 194
Page, Walter Hines, **II:** 174, 175; **Supp. I Part 1:** 370
"Pages from Cold Point" (Bowles), **Supp. IV Part 1:** 85, 86, 87
Paid on Both Sides: A Charade (Auden), **Supp. II Part 1:** 6, 18–19
Paige, Satchel, **Supp. I Part 1:** 234
Paige, T. D. D., **III:** 475
Pain, Joseph, **Supp. I Part 2:** 502
Paine, Albert Bigelow, **I:** 249
Paine, Thomas, **I:** 490; **II:** 117, 302; **III:** 17, 148, 219; **Retro. Supp. I:** 390; **Supp. I Part 1:** 231; **Supp. I Part 2: 501–525; Supp. XI:** 55
"Pain has an Element of Blank" (Dickinson), **Retro. Supp. I:** 44
"Paint and Powder" (Z. Fitzgerald), **Supp. IX:** 71
Painted Bird, The (Kosinski), **Supp. VII:** 215–217, 219–221, 222, 227
Painted Desert (F. Barthelme), **Supp. XI:** 28–29, 32
Painted Dresses (Hearon), **Supp. VIII:** 63
"Painted Head" (Ransom), **III:** 491, 494; **Supp. II Part 1:** 103, 314
Painted Word, The (Wolfe), **Supp. III Part 2:** 580–581, 584
"Painter, The" (Ashbery), **Supp. III**

Part 1: 5–6, 13
Painter Dreaming in the Scholar's House, The (Nemerov), **III:** 269
"Painters" (Rukeyser), **Supp. VI:** 281
"Painting a Mountain Stream" (Nemerov), **III:** 275
"Pair a Spurs" (Proulx), **Supp. VII:** 263–264
"Pair of Bright Blue Eyes, A" (Taylor), **Supp. V:** 321
"Pajamas" (Olds), **Supp. X:** 206
Pakula, Alan, **Supp. XIII:** 264
Palace at 4 A.M. (Giacometti), **Supp. VIII:** 169
"Palantine, The" (Whittier), **Supp. I Part 2:** 694, 696
Palatella, John, **Retro. Supp. II:** 48
Pale Fire (Nabokov), **III:** 244, 246, 252, 263–265; **Retro. Supp. I:** 264, 265, 266, 270, 271, 272, 276, 278, 335; **Supp. V:** 251, 253
"Pale Horse, Pale Rider" (Porter), **III:** 436, 437, 441–442, 445, 446, 449
Pale Horse, Pale Rider: Three Short Novels (Porter), **III:** 433, 436–442; **Supp. VIII:** 157
"Pale Pink Roast, The" (Paley), **Supp. VI:** 217
Paley, Grace, **Supp. VI: 217–233**; **Supp. IX:** 212; **Supp. X:** 79, 164; **Supp. XII:** 309
Paley, William, **II:** 9
Palgrave, Francis Turner, **Retro. Supp. I:** 124
Palgrave's Golden Treasury (Palgrave), **IV:** 405
Palimpsest (Doolittle), **Supp. I Part 1:** 259, 268, 269, 270–271
Palimpsest (Vidal), **Supp. X:** 186
"Palingenesis" (Longfellow), **II:** 498
Pal Joey (O'Hara), **III:** 361, 367–368
"Pal Joey" stories (O'Hara), **III:** 361
Pallbearers Envying the One Who Rides (Dobyns), **Supp. XIII:** 89
"Palm, The" (Merwin), **Supp. III Part 1:** 355
Palmer, Charles, **II:** 111
Palmer, Elihu, **Supp. I Part 2:** 520
Palmer, Michael, **Supp. IV Part 2:** 421
Palmerston, Lord, **I:** 15
"Palo Alto: The Marshes" (Hass), **Supp. VI:** 100
Palpable God, A: Thirty Stories Translated from the Bible with an Essay on the Origins and Life of Narrative (Price), **Supp. VI:** 262, 267
Palubinskas, Helen, **Supp. X:** 292
Pamela (Richardson), **Supp. V:** 127
Panache de bouquets (Komunyakaa; Cadieux, trans.), **Supp. XIII:** 127

Pan-African movement, **Supp. II Part 1:** 172, 175
Pandaemonium (Epstein), **Supp. XII:** 161, **172–173**
"Pandora" (Adams), **I:** 5
Pandora: New Tales of Vampires (Rice), **Supp. VII:** 295
"Pangolin, The" (Moore), **III:** 210
Panic: A Play in Verse (MacLeish), **III:** 2, 20
Panic in Needle Park (film), **Supp. IV Part 1:** 198
Pantagruel (Rabelais), **II:** 112
"Pantaloon in Black" (Faulkner), **II:** 71
Panther and the Lash, The (Hughes), **Retro. Supp. I:** 204, 211; **Supp. I Part 1:** 342–344, 345–346
"Panthers, The" (Southern), **Supp. XI:** 295
"Pan versus Moses" (Ozick), **Supp. V:** 262
"Papa and Mama Dance, The" (Sexton), **Supp. II Part 2:** 688
"Papa Who Wakes Up Tired in the Dark" (Cisneros), **Supp. VII:** 62
Pape, Greg, **Supp. V:** 180; **Supp. XIII:** 312
"Paper Dolls Cut Out of a Newspaper" (Simic), **Supp. VIII:** 282
"Paper House, The" (Mailer), **III:** 42–43
Papers on Literature and Art (Fuller), **Supp. II Part 1:** 292, 299
Papp, Joseph, **Supp. IV Part 1:** 234
"Paprika Johnson" (Barnes), **Supp. III Part 1:** 33
"Par" (Bausch), **Supp. VII:** 54
"Parable in the Later Novels of Henry James" (Ozick), **Supp. V:** 257
"Parable of the Gift" (Glück), **Supp. V:** 89
"Parable of the Hostages" (Glück), **Supp. V:** 89
"Parable of the King" (Glück), **Supp. V:** 89
Parable of the Sower (O. Butler), **Supp. XIII: 66–67**, 69
Parable of the Talents (O. Butler), **Supp. XIII:** 61, 66, **67–69**
"Parable of the Trellis" (Glück), **Supp. V:** 89
Parachutes & Kisses (Jong), **Supp. V:** 115, 123, 125–126, 129
"Parade of Painters" (Swenson), **Supp. IV Part 2:** 645
"Paradigm, The" (Tate), **IV:** 128
Paradise (Barthelme), **Supp. IV Part 1:** 52
"Paradise" (Doty), **Supp. XI:** 123

Paradise Lost (Milton), **I:** 137; **II:** 168, 549; **IV:** 126; **Supp. XII:** 173, 297
Paradise Lost (Odets), **Supp. II Part 2:** 530, 531, 538–539, 550
"Paradise of Bachelors and the Tartarus of Maids, The" (Melville), **III:** 91
Paradise Poems (Stern), **Supp. IX: 293–294**, 295
Paradiso (Dante), **Supp. IX:** 50
"Paradoxes and Oxymorons" (Ashbery), **Supp. III Part 1:** 23–24
Paradox of Progressive Thought, The (Noble), **Supp. I Part 2:** 650
Paragon, The (Knowles), **Supp. XII:** 249
"Parameters" (Dunn), **Supp. XI:** 154
"Paraphrase" (Crane), **I:** 391–392, 393
"Pardon, The" (Wilbur), **Supp. III Part 2:** 544, 550
Paredes, Américo, **Supp. XIII:** 225
Paredes, Raymund A., **Supp. XIII:** 320, 321
"Parentage" (Stafford), **Supp. XI:** 321, 322
"Parents" (F. Barthelme), **Supp. XI:** 34
"Parents Taking Shape" (Karr), **Supp. XI:** 243
"Parents' Weekend: Camp Kenwood" (Kenyon), **Supp. VII:** 169
Pareto, Vilfredo, **II:** 577
Paretsky, Sarah, **Supp. IV Part 2:** 462
Parini, Jay, **Supp. X:** 17
"Paris" (Stern), **Supp. IX:** 300
"Paris, 7 A.M." (Bishop), **Retro. Supp. II:** 41, 42; **Supp. I Part 1:** 85, 89
Paris France (Stein), **IV:** 45
Park, Robert, **IV:** 475
"Park Bench" (Hughes), **Supp. I Part 1:** 331–332
Park City (Beattie), **Supp. V:** 24, 35–36
"Park City" (Beattie), **Supp. V:** 35
Parker, Charlie, **Supp. I Part 1:** 59; **Supp. X:** 240, 242, 246; **Supp. XIII:** 129
Parker, Dorothy, **Retro. Supp. II:** 345; **Supp. IV Part 1:** 353; **Supp. IX:** 62, 114, **189–206**; **Supp. X:** 164; **Supp. XI:** 28
Parker, Idella, **Supp. X:** 232, 234–235
Parker, Muriel, **Supp. IX:** 232
Parker, Robert B., **Supp. IV Part 1:** 135, 136
Parker, Theodore, **Supp. I Part 1:** 38; **Supp. I Part 2:** 518
Parker, Thomas, **Supp. I Part 1:** 102
"Parker's Back" (O'Connor), **III:** 348, 352, 358

Parkes, Henry Bamford, **Supp. I Part 2:** 617
Park-Fuller, Linda, **Supp. XIII:** 297
Parkman, Francis, **II:** 278, 310, 312; **IV:** 179, 309; **Supp. I Part 2:** 420, 479, 481–482, 486, 487, 493, 498; **Supp. II Part 2: 589–616**
Parkman Reader, The (Morison, ed.), **Supp. I Part 2:** 494
Parks, Gordon, Sr., **Supp. XI:** 17
Parks, Larry, **Supp. I Part 1:** 295
Parks, Rosa, **Supp. I Part 1:** 342
"Park Street Cemetery, The" (Lowell), **II:** 537, 538
Par le Détroit (cantata) (Bowles), **Supp. IV Part 1:** 82
Parliament of Fowls, The (Chaucer), **III:** 492
Parmenides (Plato), **II:** 10
Parnassus (Emerson), **II:** 8, 18
Parnell, Charles Stewart, **II:** 129, 137
Parole (film), **Supp. XIII:** 166
Parole Fixer (film), **Supp. XIII:** 170
Parrington, Vernon Louis, **I:** 254, 517, 561; **III:** 335, 606; **IV:** 173; **Supp. I Part 2:** 484, 640
Parrish, Robert, **Supp. XI:** 307
"Parrot, The" (Merrill), **Supp. III Part 1:** 320
"Parsley" (Dove), **Supp. IV Part 1:** 245, 246
Parson, Annie, **Supp. I Part 2:** 655
Parsons, Elsie Clews, **I:** 231, 235
Parsons, Ian, **Supp. IX:** 95
Parsons, Louella, **Supp. XII:** 173
Parsons, Talcott, **Supp. I Part 2:** 648
Parsons, Theophilus, **II:** 396, 504; **Retro. Supp. II:** 134; **Supp. I Part 1:** 155
"Parthian Shot, The" (Hammett), **Supp. IV Part 1:** 343
Partial Portraits (James), **II:** 336
Parties (Van Vechten), **Supp. II Part 2:** 739, 747–749
"Parting" (Kunitz), **Supp. III Part 1:** 263
"Parting Gift" (Wylie), **Supp. I Part 2:** 714
"Parting Glass, The" (Freneau), **Supp. II Part 1:** 273
"Partings" (Hogan), **Supp. IV Part 1:** 413
Partington, Blanche, **I:** 199
Partisans (Matthiessen), **Supp. V:** 201
"Partner, The" (Roethke), **III:** 541–542
Partners, The (Auchincloss), **Supp. IV Part 1:** 31, 34
"Part of a Letter" (Wilbur), **Supp. III Part 2:** 551

Part of Speech, A (Brodsky), **Supp. VIII:** 22
"Part of the Story" (Dobyns), **Supp. XIII:** 79
Parton, Sara, **Retro. Supp. I:** 246
Partridge, John, **II:** 110, 111
"Parts of a Journal" (Gordon), **Supp. IV Part 1:** 310
Parts of a World (Stevens), **Retro. Supp. I:** 305–306, 307, 309, 313
"Party, The" (Dunbar), **Supp. II Part 1:** 198, 205–206
"Party, The" (Taylor), **Supp. V:** 315
Party at Jack's, The (Wolfe), **IV:** 451–452, 469
"Party Down at the Square, A" (Ellison), **Retro. Supp. II:** 124
Pascal, Blaise, **II:** 8, 159; **III:** 292, 301, 304, 428; **Retro. Supp. I:** 326, 330
"Passage" (Crane), **I:** 391
"Passage in the Life of Mr. John Oakhurst, A" (Harte), **Supp. II Part 1:** 353–354
"Passages from a Relinquished Work" (Hawthorne), **Retro. Supp. I:** 150
Passages toward the Dark (McGrath), **Supp. X:** 126, 127
"Passage to India" (Whitman), **IV:** 348
Passage to India, A (Forster), **II:** 600
Passaro, Vince, **Supp. X:** 167, 302, 309, 310
"Passenger Pigeons" (Jeffers), **Supp. II Part 2:** 437
Passin, Herbert, **Supp. XIII:** 337
"Passing of Sister Barsett, The" (Jewett), **Retro. Supp. II:** 138–139, 143
"Passing Show, The" (Bierce), **I:** 208
"Passing Through" (Kunitz), **Supp. III Part 1:** 265
"Passion, The" (Barnes), **Supp. III Part 1:** 36
"Passion, The" (Merwin), **Supp. III Part 1:** 343
Passionate Pilgrim, A (James), **II:** 324; **Retro. Supp. I:** 219
"Passionate Pilgrim, A" (James), **II:** 322, 323–324; **Retro. Supp. I:** 218
Passion Play (Kosinski), **Supp. VII:** 215, 225–226
Passions of Uxport, The (Kumin), **Supp. IV Part 2:** 444
"Passive Resistance" (McKay), **Supp. X:** 133
Passport to the War (Kunitz), **Supp. III Part 1:** 261–264
Passwords (Stafford), **Supp. XI:** 329–330

"Past, The" (Bryant), **Supp. I Part 1:** 157, 170
Past, The (Kinnell), **Supp. III Part 1:** 235, 253–254
"Past, The" (Kinnell), **Supp. III Part 1:** 254
Past and Present (Carlyle), **Supp. I Part 2:** 410
Pasternak, Boris, **II:** 544
"Pastiches et Pistaches" (Van Vechten), **Supp. II Part 2:** 732
"Past Is the Present, The" (Moore), **III:** 199–200
"Pastoral" (Carver), **Supp. III Part 1:** 137, 146
"Pastoral" (Dove), **Supp. IV Part 1:** 249
"Pastoral Hat, A" (Stevens), **IV:** 91
"Pastor Dowe at Tacaté" (Bowles), **Supp. IV Part 1:** 87
Pastorela (ballet) (Kirstein), **Supp. IV Part 1:** 83
Pastorius, Francis Daniel, **Supp. I Part 2:** 700
"Pasture Poems" (Kumin), **Supp. IV Part 2:** 446
Pastures of Heaven, The (Steinbeck), **IV:** 51
Patchen, Kenneth, **Supp. III Part 2:** 625
Patchett, Ann, **Supp. XII: 307–324**
Pater, Walter, **I:** 51, 272, 476; **II:** 27, 338; **III:** 604; **IV:** 74; **Retro. Supp. I:** 56, 79; **Retro. Supp. II:** 344; **Supp. I Part 2:** 552; **Supp. IX:** 66
Paterna (Mather), **Supp. II Part 2:** 451
"Paterson" (Ginsberg), **Supp. II Part 1:** 314–315, 321, 329
Paterson (W. C. Williams), **I:** 62, 446; **IV:** 418–423; **Retro. Supp. I:** 209, 284, 413, 419, 421, **424–428**, 428, 429, 430; **Retro. Supp. II:** 339, 346; **Supp. II Part 2:** 557, 564, 625; **Supp. VIII:** 275, 305
Paterson, Book Five (W. C. Williams), **IV:** 422–423
Paterson, Book One (W. C. Williams), **IV:** 421–422
Paterson, Isabel, **Supp. IV Part 2:** 524
Paterson, Part Three (W. C. Williams), **IV:** 420–421
"Path, The" (Bryant), **Supp. I Part 1:** 169
Pathfinder, The (Cooper), **I:** 349, 350, 355
Pat Hobby Stories, The (Fitzgerald), **Retro. Supp. I:** 114
"Patience of a Saint, The" (Humphrey), **Supp. IX:** 106

Patinkin, Mandy, **Supp. IV Part 1:** 236
Paton, Alan, **Supp. VIII:** 126
Patria Mia (Pound), **III:** 460–461; **Retro. Supp. I:** 284
"Patria Mia" (Pound), **Retro. Supp. I:** 284
"Patriarch, The" (Alvares), **Supp. V:** 11
Patrimony: A True Story (Roth), **Retro. Supp. II:** 297, 298, 309; **Supp. III Part 2:** 427
Patriot, The (Buck), **Supp. II Part 1:** 122–123
Patriotic Gore: Studies in the Literature of the American Civil War (Wilson), **III:** 588; **IV:** 430, 438, 443, 445–445, 446; **Supp. VIII:** 100
"Patriots, The/Los Patriotas" (Kingsolver), **Supp. VII:** 209
Patron Saint of Liars, The (Patchett), **Supp. XII:** 307, 310, **311–314,** 317
Pattee, Fred L., **II:** 456
Patten, Gilbert, **II:** 423
Patten, Simon, **Supp. I Part 2:** 640
Patternmaster (O. Butler), **Supp. XIII:** 61, 62, 63
Patternmaster Series (O. Butler), **Supp. XIII: 62–63**
"Patterns" (Lowell), **II:** 524
Patterson, Floyd, **III:** 38
Patterson, William M., **Supp. I Part 1:** 265
Patton, General George, **III:** 575; **Supp. I Part 2:** 664
Paul, Saint, **I:** 365; **II:** 15, 494; **IV:** 122, 154, 164, 335; **Retro. Supp. I:** 247; **Supp. I Part 1:** 188
Paul, Sherman, **I:** 244; **IV:** 179
"Paula Becker to Clara Westhoff" (Rich), **Supp. I Part 2:** 573–574
"Paula Gunn Allen" (Ruppert), **Supp. IV Part 1:** 321
Paul Bowles: Romantic Savage (Caponi), **Supp. IV Part 1:** 95
Paulding, James Kirke, **I:** 344; **II:** 298, 299, 303; **Supp. I Part 1:** 157
"Paul Monette: The Brink of Summer's End" (film), **Supp. X:** 152
"Paul Revere" (Longfellow), **II:** 489, 501
"Paul Revere's Ride" (Longfellow), **Retro. Supp. II:** 163
"Paul's Case" (Cather), **I:** 314–315; **Retro. Supp. I:** 3, 5
Paulsen, Friedrich, **III:** 600
"Pauper Witch of Grafton, The" (Frost), **Retro. Supp. II:** 42
"Pause by the Water, A" (Merwin), **Supp. III Part 1:** 354
"Pavane for the Nursery, A" (W. J. Smith), **Supp. XIII:** 335
"Pavement, The" (Olson), **Supp. II Part 2:** 571
Pavilion of Women (Buck), **Supp. II Part 1:** 125–126
"Pawnbroker, The" (Kumin), **Supp. IV Part 2:** 442, 443–444, 451
Payne, Daniel, **Supp. V:** 202
Payne, John Howard, **II:** 309
Paz, Octavio, **Supp. III Part 2:** 630; **Supp. VIII:** 272; **Supp. XI:** 191; **Supp. XIII:** 223
Peabody, Elizabeth, **Retro. Supp. I:** 155–156, 225
Peabody, Francis G., **III:** 293; **Supp. I Part 1:** 5
Peabody, Josephine Preston, **III:** 507
Peace and Bread in Time of War (Addams), **Supp. I Part 1:** 21, 22–23
Peace Breaks Out (Knowles), **Supp. XII:** 249
"Peace March, The" (Simpson), **Supp. IX:** 279
"Peace of Cities, The" (Wilbur), **Supp. III Part 2:** 545
"Peaches—Six in a Tin Box, Sarajevo" (Cisneros), **Supp. VII:** 67
Peacock, Doug, **Supp. VIII:** 38; **Supp. XIII:** 12
Peacock, Gibson, **Supp. I Part 1:** 360
"Peacock, The" (Merrill), **Supp. III Part 1:** 320
Peacock, Thomas Love, **Supp. I Part 1:** 307; **Supp. VIII:** 125
"Peacock Room, The" (Hayden), **Supp. II Part 1:** 374–375
Pearce, Richard, **Supp. IX:** 254
Pearce, Roy Harvey, **II:** 244; **Supp. I Part 1:** 111, 114; **Supp. I Part 2:** 475
Pearl, The (Steinbeck), **IV:** 51, 62–63
Pearlman, Daniel, **III:** 479
Pearlman, Mickey, **Supp. XIII:** 293, 306
Pearl of Orr's Island, The (Stowe), **Supp. I Part 2:** 592–593, 595
Pears, Peter, **II:** 586; **Supp. IV Part 1:** 84
Pearson, Norman Holmes, **Supp. I Part 1:** 259, 260, 273
"Peasants' Way O' Thinkin'" (McKay), **Supp. X:** 133
Pease, Donald E., **Supp. IV Part 2:** 687
Peck, Gregory, **Supp. VIII:** 128, 129; **Supp. XII:** 160, 173
Peckinpah, Sam, **Supp. XI:** 306
"Peck of Gold, A" (Frost), **II:** 155
Peculiar Treasures: A Biblical Who's Who (Buechner), **Supp. XII:** 53
"Pedal Point" (Francis), **Supp. IX:** 87
"Pedersen Kid, The" (Gass), **Supp. VI:** 83
"Pedigree, The" (Creeley), **Supp. IV Part 1:** 150
Peebles, Melvin Van, **Supp. XI:** 17
"Peed Onk" (Moore). See "People Like That Are the Only People Here: Canonical Babbling in Peed Onk" (Moore)
"Peeler, The" (O'Connor), **Retro. Supp. II:** 225
Peikoff, Leonard, **Supp. IV Part 2:** 520, 526, 529
Peirce, Charles Sanders, **II:** 20, 352–353; **III:** 599; **Supp. I Part 2:** 640; **Supp. III Part 2:** 626
Pelagius, **III:** 295
"Pelican, The" (Merrill), **Supp. III Part 1:** 320
"Pelican, The" (Wharton), **IV:** 310; **Retro. Supp. I:** 364
Pellacchia, Michael, **Supp. XIII:** 16
Peltier, Leonard, **Supp. V:** 212
"Pen and Paper and a Breath of Air" (Oliver), **Supp. VII:** 245
"Pencil, The" (Chandler), **Supp. IV Part 1:** 135
Pencillings by the Way (Willis), **II:** 313
"Pencils" (Sandburg), **III:** 592
"Pendulum" (Bradbury and Hasse), **Supp. IV Part 1:** 102
"Penelope's Song" (Glück), **Supp. V:** 89
Penhally (Gordon), **II:** 197, 199, 201–203, 204
"Penis" (McClatchy), **Supp. XII:** 266–267
Penitent, The (Singer), **Retro. Supp. II: 327–328,** 331
Penn, Robert, **I:** 489
Penn, Sean, **Supp. XI:** 107
Penn, Thomas, **II:** 118
Penn, William, **Supp. I Part 2:** 683
"Pennsylvania Pilgrim, The" (Whittier), **Supp. I Part 2:** 700
"Pennsylvania Planter, The" (Freneau), **Supp. II Part 1:** 268
Penny, Rob, **Supp. VIII:** 330
Penrod (Tarkington), **III:** 223
Pentagon of Power, The (Mumford), **Supp. II Part 2:** 498
Pentimento (Hellman), **Supp. I Part 1:** 280, 292–294, 296; **Supp. IV Part 1:** 12; **Supp. VIII:** 243
"Peonies at Dusk" (Kenyon), **Supp. VII:** 171
People, The (Glaspell), **Supp. III Part 1:** 179

People, Yes, The (Sandburg), **III:** 575, 589, 590, 591
"PEOPLE BURNING, THE" (Baraka), **Supp. II Part 1:** 49
"People in Hell Just Want a Drink of Water" (Proulx), **Supp. VII:** 263
"People Like That Are the Only People Here: Canonical Babbling in Peed Onk" (Moore), **Supp. X:** 168, **178–179**
People Live Here: Selected Poems 1949–1983 (Simpson), **Supp. IX:** 269, 277
"People Next Door, The" (Simpson), **Supp. IX:** 279
People of the Abyss, The (London), **II:** 465–466
"People on the Roller Coaster, The" (Hardwick), **Supp. III Part 1:** 196
People Shall Continue, The (Ortiz), **Supp. IV Part 2:** 510
"People's Surroundings" (Moore), **III:** 201, 202, 203
"People v. Abe Lathan, Colored, The" (Caldwell), **I:** 309
"Peppermint Lounge Revisited, The" (Wolfe), **Supp. III Part 2:** 571
Pepys, Samuel, **Supp. I Part 2:** 653
"Perch'io non spero di tornar giammai" (Cavalcanti), **Supp. III Part 2:** 623
Percy, Walker, **Supp. III Part 1: 383–400; Supp. IV Part 1:** 297; **Supp. V:** 334; **Supp. X:** 42
Percy, William, **Supp. V:** 334
Percy, William Alexander, **Retro. Supp. I:** 341
"Peregrine" (Wylie), **Supp. I Part 2:** 712–713, 714
Perelman, Bob, **Supp. XII:** 23
Perelman, S. J., **IV:** 286; **Retro. Supp. I:** 342; **Retro. Supp. II:** 339, 340, 343, 344, 345, 354; **Supp. IV Part 1:** 353; **Supp. XI:** 66
"Perennial Answer, The" (Rich), **Retro. Supp. II:** 280
Perestroika (Kushner), **Supp. IX:** 141, 142, 145
Péret, Benjamin, **Supp. VIII:** 272
Peretz, Isaac Loeb, **IV:** 1, 3; **Retro. Supp. II:** 317
Pérez Galdós, Benito, **II:** 275
Perfect Analysis Given by a Parrot, A (T. Williams), **IV:** 395
"Perfect Day for Bananafish, A" (Salinger), **III:** 563–564, 571
Perfect Ganesh, A (McNally), **Supp. XIII: 202–203,** 208, 209
"Perfect Knight, The" (Chandler), **Supp. IV Part 1:** 120
Perfect Party, The (Gurney), **Supp. V:** 100, 105, 106–107
"Perfect Things" (F. Barthelme), **Supp. XI:** 30, 33–34
"Performance, The" (Dickey), **Supp. IV Part 1:** 178–179, 181
"Perfume" (Mora), **Supp. XIII:** 218
"Perhaps the World Ends Here" (Harjo), **Supp. XII:** 228, 231
Perhaps Women (Anderson), **I:** 114
Pericles (Shakespeare), **I:** 585; **Supp. III Part 2:** 624, 627, 629
Period of Adjustment (T. Williams), **IV:** 382, 386, 387, 388, 389, 390, 392, 393, 394, 397
"Period Pieces from the Mid-Thirties" (Agee), **I:** 28
"Periphery" (Ammons), **Supp. VII:** 28
Perkins, David, **Supp. I Part 2:** 459, 475
Perkins, Maxwell, **I:** 252, 289, 290; **II:** 87, 93, 95, 252; **IV:** 452, 455, 457, 458, 461, 462, 463, 469; **Retro. Supp. I:** 101, 105, 108, 109, 110, 113, 114, 178; **Supp. IX:** 57, 58, 60, 232; **Supp. X:** 219, 224, 225, 229, 230, 233; **Supp. XI:** 218, 227
Perlès, Alfred, **III:** 177, 183, 187, 189
Perloff, Marjorie, **Supp. I Part 2:** 539, 542; **Supp. IV Part 1:** 68; **Supp. IV Part 2:** 420, 424, 432
Permanence and Change (Burke), **I:** 274
Permanent Errors (Price), **Supp. VI:** 261
"Permanent Traits of the English National Genius" (Emerson), **II:** 18
Permit Me Voyage (Agee), **I:** 25, 27
Perrault, Charles, **IV:** 266; **Supp. I Part 2:** 622
Perry, Anne, **Supp. V:** 335
Perry, Bliss, **I:** 243
Perry, Donna, **Supp. IV Part 1:** 322, 327, 335
Perry, Dr. William, **II:** 395, 396
Perry, Edgar A., **III:** 410
Perry, Lincoln, **Supp. V:** 24, 33
Perry, Matthew C., **Supp. I Part 2:** 494–495
Perry, Patsy Brewington, **Supp. I Part 1:** 66
Perry, Ralph Barton, **I:** 224; **II:** 356, 362, 364
Perse, St.-John, **III:** 12, 13, 14, 17; **Supp. III Part 1:** 14; **Supp. IV Part 1:** 82; **Supp. XIII:** 344
"Persephone in Hell" (Dove), **Supp. IV Part 1:** 250, 251
"Persistence of Desire, The" (Updike), **IV:** 222–223, 228
"Persistences" (Hecht), **Supp. X: 68–69**
Person, Place, and Thing (Shapiro), **Supp. II Part 2:** 702, 705
Personae: The Collected Poems (Pound), **Retro. Supp. I:** 285, 286; **Supp. I Part 1:** 255
Personae of Ezra Pound (Pound), **III:** 458
"Personal" (Stern), **Supp. IX:** 299
"Personal and Occasional Pieces" (Welty), **Retro. Supp. I:** 355
Personal Narrative (Edwards), **I:** 545, 552, 553, 561, 562; **Supp. I Part 2:** 700
Personal Recollection of Joan of Arc (Twain), **IV:** 208
"Personals" (Didion), **Supp. IV Part 1:** 200
Persons and Places (Santayana), **III:** 615
Persons in Hiding (film), **Supp. XIII:** 170
Persons in Hiding (Hoover), **Supp. XIII:** 170
Person Sitting in Darkness, A (Twain), **IV:** 208
"Perspective" (Francis), **Supp. IX:** 78
"Perspective: Anniversary D-Day" (Karr), **Supp. XI:** 241
"Perspectives: Is It Out of Control?" (Gleason), **Supp. IX:** 16
Perspectives by Incongruity (Burke), **I:** 284–285
Perspectives on Cormac McCarthy (Arnold and Luce, eds.), **Supp. VIII:** 189
Pertes et Fracas (McCoy), **Supp. XIII:** 175
"Peruvian Child" (Mora), **Supp. XIII:** 218
Peseroff, Joyce, **Supp. IV Part 1:** 71
"Peter" (Cather), **Retro. Supp. I:** 4
"Peter" (Moore), **III:** 210, 212
Peter, Saint, **III:** 341, 346; **IV:** 86, 294
Peterkin, Julia, **Supp. I Part 1:** 328
"Peter Klaus" (German tale), **II:** 306
"Peter Parley" works (Goodrich), **Supp. I Part 1:** 38
"Peter Pendulum" (Poe), **III:** 425
"Peter Quince at the Clavier" (Stevens), **IV:** 81, 82
Peter Rabbit tales, **Retro. Supp. I:** 335
Peters, Cora, **Supp. I Part 2:** 468
Peters, Jacqueline, **Supp. XII:** 225
Peters, Margot, **Supp. VIII:** 252
Peters, Robert, **Supp. XIII:** 114
Peters, S. H. (pseudonym). *See* Henry, O.
Peters, Timothy, **Supp. XI:** 39

Petersen, David, **Supp. XIII:** 2
Petersen, Donald, **Supp. V:** 180
Peterson, Houston, **I:** 60
Peterson, Roger Tory, **Supp. V:** 202
Peterson, Virgilia, **Supp. IV Part 1:** 30
Peter Whiffle: His Life and Works (Van Vechten), **Supp. II Part 2:** 728–729, 731, 735, 738–741, 749
"Petey and Yotsee and Mario" (H. Roth), **Supp. IX:** 234
"Petition, A" (Winters), **Supp. II Part 2:** 785
"'Pet Negro' System, The" (Hurston), **Supp. VI:** 159
"Petra and Its Surroundings" (Frost), **Retro. Supp. I:** 124
Petrarch, **I:** 176; **II:** 590; **III:** 4
"Petrified Man" (Welty), **IV:** 262; **Retro. Supp. I:** 345, 351
"Petrified Man, The" (Twain), **IV:** 195
"Petrified Woman, The" (Gordon), **II:** 199
Petronius, **III:** 174, 179
Petry, Ann, **Supp. VIII:** 214; **Supp. XI:** 6, 85
Pet Sematary (King), **Supp. V:** 138, 143, 152
Pettengill, Richard, **Supp. VIII:** 341, 345, 348
Pettis, Joyce, **Supp. XI:** 276, 277, 278, 281
Pfaff, Timothy, **Supp. V:** 166
Pfister, Karin, **IV:** 467, 475
Phaedo (Plato), **II:** 10
Phaedra (Lowell and Barzun, trans.), **II:** 543–544
"Phantasia for Elvira Shatayev" (Rich), **Supp. I Part 2:** 570
Phantasms of War (Lowell), **II:** 512
"Phantom of the Movie Palace, The" (Coover), **Supp. V:** 50–51
"Pharaoh, The" (Kenyon), **Supp. VII:** 172
Pharr, Mary, **Supp. V:** 147
"Phases" (Stevens), **Retro. Supp. I:** 299
Phases of an Inferior Planet (Glasgow), **II:** 174–175
"Pheasant, The" (Carver), **Supp. III Part 1:** 146
Pheloung, Grant, **Supp. XI:** 39
Phelps, Elizabeth Stuart, **Retro. Supp. II:** 146; **Supp. XIII:** 141
Phelps, Teresa Godwin, **Supp. VIII:** 128
"Phenomenology of Anger, The" (Rich), **Supp. I Part 2:** 562–563, 571
Phenomenology of Moral Experience, The (Mandelbaum), **I:** 61
"Phenomenology of *On Moral Fiction*" (Johnson), **Supp. VI:** 188
Phidias, **Supp. I Part 2:** 482
Philadelphia Fire (Wideman), **Supp. X:** 320, 334
Philadelphia Negro, The (Du Bois), **Supp. II Part 1:** 158, 163–164, 166
Philbrick, Thomas, **I:** 343
Philip, Jim, **Supp. XII:** 136
Philip, Prince, **Supp. X:** 108
"Philip of Pokanoket" (Irving), **II:** 303
Philippians (biblical book), **IV:** 154
"Philippine Conquest, The" (Masters), **Supp. I Part 2:** 456
"Philip Roth Reconsidered" (Howe), **Retro. Supp. II:** 304
"Philistinism and the Negro Writer" (Baraka), **Supp. II Part 1:** 39, 44
Phillips, Adam, **Supp. XII:** 97–98
Phillips, David Graham, **II:** 444; **Retro. Supp. II:** 101
Phillips, Gene D., **Supp. XI:** 306
Phillips, J. O. C., **Supp. I Part 1:** 19
Phillips, Robert, **Supp. XIII:** 335, 344
Phillips, Wendell, **Supp. I Part 1:** 103; **Supp. I Part 2:** 524
Phillips, Willard, **Supp. I Part 1:** 154, 155
Phillips, William, **Supp. VIII:** 156
Phillips, William L., **I:** 106
"Philosopher, The" (Farrell), **II:** 45
Philosopher of the Forest (pseudonym). *See* Freneau, Philip
Philosophes classiques, Les (Taine), **III:** 323
"Philosophical Concepts and Practical Results" (James), **II:** 352
"Philosophical Investigation of Metaphor, A" (Gass), **Supp. VI:** 79
Philosophical Transactions (Watson), **II:** 114
"Philosophy, Or Something Like That" (Roth), **Supp. III Part 2:** 403
Philosophy: Who Needs It (Rand), **Supp. IV Part 2:** 517, 518, 527, 533
"Philosophy and Its Critics" (James), **II:** 360
"Philosophy and the Form of Fiction" (Gass), **Supp. VI:** 85
"Philosophy for People" (Emerson), **II:** 14
"Philosophy in Warm Weather" (Kenyon), **Supp. VII:** 168
"Philosophy Lesson" (Levine), **Supp. V:** 195
"Philosophy of Composition, The" (Poe), **III:** 416, 421; **Retro. Supp. II:** 266, 267, 271
Philosophy of Friedrich Nietzsche, The (Mencken), **III:** 102–103
"Philosophy of Handicap, A" (Bourne), **I:** 216, 218
"Philosophy of History" (Emerson), **II:** 11–12
Philosophy of Literary Form, The (Burke), **I:** 275, 281, 283, 291
Philosophy of the Human Mind, The (Stewart), **II:** 8
Philoxenes, **Supp. VIII:** 201
"Phineas" (Knowles), **Supp. XII:** 238–240
Phineas: Six Stories (Knowles), **Supp. XII:** 249
"Phocion" (Lowell), **II:** 536
Phoenix and the Turtle, The (Shakespeare), **I:** 284
"Phoenix Lyrics" (Schwartz), **Supp. II Part 2:** 665
"Phony War Films" (Jones), **Supp. XI:** 217, 232
"Photograph: Migrant Worker, Parlier, California, 1967" (Levis), **Supp. XI:** 272
"Photograph of a Child on a Vermont Hillside" (Kenyon), **Supp. VII:** 168
"Photograph of the Girl" (Olds), **Supp. X:** 205
"Photograph of the Unmade Bed" (Rich), **Supp. I Part 2:** 558
Photographs (Welty), **Retro. Supp. I:** 343
"Photographs, The" (Barthelme), **Supp. IV Part 1:** 53
"Photography" (Levine), **Supp. V:** 194
Phyrrho, **Retro. Supp. I:** 247
"Physical Universe" (Simpson), **Supp. IX:** 278
"Physicist We Know, A" (Shields), **Supp. VII:** 310
"Physics and Cosmology in the Fiction of Tom Robbins" (Nadeau), **Supp. X:** 270
"Physiology of Versification, The: Harmonies of Organic and Animal Life" (Holmes), **Supp. I Part 1:** 311
Physique de l'Amour (Gourmont), **III:** 467–468
Piaf, Edith, **Supp. IV Part 2:** 549
Piaget, Jean, **Supp. XIII:** 75
"Piano Fingers" (Mason), **Supp. VIII:** 146
Piano Lesson, The (Bearden), **Supp. VIII:** 342
Piano Lesson, The (Wilson), **Supp. VIII:** 342–345
Piatt, James, **Supp. I Part 2:** 420
Piatt, John J., **II:** 273
Piazza, Ben, **Supp. XIII:** 163

"Piazza de Spagna, Early Morning" (Wilbur), **Supp. III Part 2:** 553
Piazza Tales (Melville), **III:** 91
Picabia, Francis, **Retro. Supp. I:** 416; **Retro. Supp. II:** 349
Picasso (Stein), **IV:** 28, 32, 45
Picasso, Pablo, **I:** 429, 432, 440, 442, 445; **II:** 602; **III:** 197, 201, 470; **IV:** 26, 31, 32, 46, 87, 407, 436; **Retro. Supp. I:** 55, 63; **Supp. IV Part 1:** 81; **Supp. IX:** 66
"Piccola Comedia" (Wilbur), **Supp. III Part 2:** 561
Pickard, Samuel T., **Supp. I Part 2:** 682
Picked-Up Pieces (Updike), **Retro. Supp. I:** 320, 322, 323, 335
Picker, Lauren, **Supp. VIII:** 78, 83
Picker, Tobias, **Supp. XII:** 253
Pickford, Mary, **Retro. Supp. I:** 325; **Supp. I Part 2:** 391
"Picking and Choosing" (Moore), **III:** 205
Picnic Cantata (music) (Bowles), **Supp. IV Part 1:** 89
"Picnic Remembered" (Warren), **IV:** 240
Pictorial History of the Negro in America, A (Hughes), **Supp. I Part 1:** 345
"Picture, The" (Olson), **Supp. II Part 2:** 574
Picture Bride (Son), **Supp. X:** 292
"Picture I Want, The" (Olds), **Supp. X:** 209
Picture of Dorian Gray, The (Wilde), **Supp. IX:** 105
"Picture of Little J. A. in a Prospect of Flowers, A" (Ashbery), **Supp. III Part 1:** 3
Picture Palace (Theroux), **Supp. VIII:** 322
"Pictures at an Extermination" (Epstein), **Supp. XII:** 161
"Pictures from an Expedition" (Duffy), **Supp. IV Part 1:** 207
Pictures from an Institution (Jarrell), **II:** 367, 385
Pictures from Brueghel (W. C. Williams), **Retro. Supp. I:** 429–431
"Pictures from Brueghel" (W. C. Williams), **Retro. Supp. I:** 419
"Pictures of Columbus, the Genoese, The" (Freneau), **Supp. II Part 1:** 258
Pictures of Fidelman: An Exhibition (Malamud), **Supp. I Part 2:** 450–451
"Pictures of the Artist" (Malamud), **Supp. I Part 2:** 450

Pictures of the Floating World (Lowell), **II:** 521, 524–525
Pictures of Travel (Heine), **II:** 281
"Picturesque: San Cristóbal de las Casas" (Mora), **Supp. XIII:** 218
Picturesque America; or, the Land We Live In (Bryant, ed.), **Supp. I Part 1:** 158
Picture This (Heller), **Supp. IV Part 1:** 386, 388, 390–391
Picturing Will (Beattie), **Supp. V:** 29, 31–32, 34
"Piece, A" (Creeley), **Supp. IV Part 1:** 155, 156
"Piece of Moon, A" (Hogan), **Supp. IV Part 1:** 407
Piece of My Heart, A (Ford), **Supp. V:** 57, 58–61, 62
Piece of My Mind, A: Reflections at Sixty (Wilson), **IV:** 426, 430, 438, 441
"Piece of News, A" (Welty), **IV:** 263; **Retro. Supp. I:** 345, 346
Pieces (Creeley), **Supp. IV Part 1:** 155
Pieces and Pontifications (Mailer), **Retro. Supp. II:** 209–210
Pieces of the Frame (McPhee), **Supp. III Part 1:** 293
Pierce, Franklin, **II:** 225, 226, 227; **III:** 88; **Retro. Supp. I:** 150, 163, 164, 165
Pierce, Frederick, **Retro. Supp. I:** 136
Piercy, Josephine K., **Supp. I Part 1:** 103
Pierpont, Claudia Roth, **Supp. X:** 192, 193, 196
Pierre: or The Ambiguities (Melville), **III:** 86–88, 89; **IV:** 194; **Retro. Supp. I:** 249, 253–254, 256; **Supp. I Part 2:** 579
Pierre et Jean (Maupassant), **I:** 421
Pierrepont, Sarah. *See* Edwards, Sarah
Pierrot Qui Pleure et Pierrot Qui Rit (Rostand), **II:** 515
Pig Cookies (Ríos), **Supp. IV Part 2:** 537, 550, 552–554
Pigeon Feathers (Updike), **IV:** 214, 218, 219, 221–223, 226
"Pigeon Feathers" (Updike), **Retro. Supp. I:** 318, 322, 323
"Pigeons" (Rilke), **II:** 544
"Pigeon Woman" (Swenson), **Supp. IV Part 2:** 644
Pigs in Heaven (Kingsolver), **Supp. VII:** 197, 199, 209–210
Pike County Ballads, The (Hay), **Supp. I Part 1:** 352
Piket, Vincent, **Supp. IV Part 1:** 24

Pilar San-Mallafre, Maria del, **Supp. V:** 40
"Pilgrim" (Freneau), **Supp. I Part 1:** 125
"Pilgrimage" (Sontag), **Supp. III Part 2:** 454–455
"Pilgrimage, The" (Maxwell), **Supp. VIII:** 169, 171
Pilgrimage of Festus, The (Aiken), **I:** 50, 55, 57
Pilgrimage of Henry James, The (Brooks), **I:** 240, 248, 250; **IV:** 433
Pilgrim at Tinker Creek (Dillard), **Supp. VI:** 22, **23–26**, 28, 29, **30–31**, 34
"Pilgrim Makers" (Lowell), **II:** 541
Pilgrim's Progress (Bunyan), **I:** 92; **II:** 15, 168, 572; **Supp. I Part 1:** 32, 38; **Supp. I Part 2:** 599
Pili's Wall (Levine), **Supp. V:** 178, 183–184
"Pillar of Fire" (Bradbury), **Supp. IV Part 1:** 113–114
Pillars of Hercules, The: A Grand Tour of the Mediterranean (Theroux), **Supp. VIII:** 325
Pilot, The (Cooper), **I:** 335, 337, 339, 342–343, 350
"Pilot from the Carrier, A" (Jarrell), **II:** 374
"Pilots, Man Your Planes" (Jarrell), **II:** 374–375
"Pilots, The" (Levertov), **Supp. III Part 1:** 282
"Pimp's Revenge, A" (Malamud), **Supp. I Part 2:** 435, 450, 451
Pinball (Kosinski), **Supp. VII:** 215, 226
Pinchot, Gifford, **Supp. IX:** 184
Pindar, **I:** 381; **II:** 543; **III:** 610
"Pine" (Dickey), **Supp. IV Part 1:** 183
Pine Barrens, The (McPhee), **Supp. III Part 1:** 298–301, 309
"Pineys, The" (Stern), **Supp. IX:** 288, 296
Pinget, Robert, **Supp. V:** 39
"Pink Dog" (Bishop), **Retro. Supp. II:** 48
Pinker, James B., **I:** 409; **Retro. Supp. I:** 231
Pinkerton, Jan, **Supp. V:** 323–324
"Pink Moon—The Pond" (Oliver), **Supp. VII:** 234
Pinocchio in Venice (Coover), **Supp. V:** 40, 51
Pinsker, Sanford, **Retro. Supp. II:** 23; **Supp. V:** 272; **Supp. IX:** 293, 327; **Supp. XI:** 251, 254, 317
Pinsky, Robert, **Retro. Supp. II:** 50; **Supp. VI: 235–251**; **Supp. IX:** 155,

158; **Supp. XIII:** 277, 285
Pinter, Harold, **I:** 71; **Supp. XIII:** 20, 196
Pinto and Sons (Epstein), **Supp. XII:** 170, **171–172**
Pioneers, The (Cooper), **I:** 336, 337, 339, 340–341, 342, 348; **II:** 313
Pioneers of France in the New World (Parkman), **Supp. III Part 2:** 599, 602
"Pioneers! O Pioneers!" (Whitman), **Retro. Supp. I:** 8
"Pioneer's Vision, The" (Larcom), **Supp. XIII:** 140
Pious and Secular America (Niebuhr), **III:** 308
Pipe Night (O'Hara), **III:** 361, 368
Piper, Dan, **Supp. IX:** 65
"Piper's Rocks" (Olson), **Supp. IV Part 1:** 153
Pippa Passes (Browning), **IV:** 128
Piquion, René, **Supp. I Part 1:** 346
Pirandello, Luigi, **Supp. IV Part 2:** 576, 588
Pirate, The (Robbins), **Supp. XII:** 6
Pirate, The (Scott), **I:** 339
Pirates of Penzance, The (Gilbert and Sullivan), **IV:** 386
Pisan Cantos, The (Pound), **III:** 476; **Retro. Supp. I:** 140, 283, 285, 293; **Supp. III Part 1:** 63; **Supp. V:** 331, 337
Piscator, Erwin, **IV:** 394
Pissarro, Camille, **I:** 478
"Pissing off the Back of the Boat into the Nevernais Canal" (Matthews), **Supp. IX:** 160–161
Pistol, The (Jones), **Supp. XI:** 219, **223–224**, 227, 234
Pit, The (Norris), **III:** 314, 322, 326–327, 333, 334
"Pit, The" (Roethke), **III:** 538
"Pit and the Pendulum, The" (Poe), **III:** 413, 416; **Retro. Supp. II:** 264, 269–270, 273
"Pitcher" (Francis), **Supp. IX:** 82
"Pitcher, The" (Dubus), **Supp. VII:** 87
Pitchford, Nicola, **Supp. XII:** 13
"Pits, The" (Graham), **Supp. XI:** 252, 254
Pitt, William, **Supp. I Part 2:** 510, 518
"Pity Me" (Wylie), **Supp. I Part 2:** 729
Pity the Monsters (Williamson), **Retro. Supp. II:** 185
Pius II, Pope, **III:** 472
Pius IX, Pope, **II:** 79
"Piute Creek" (Snyder), **Supp. VIII:** 293
Pixley, Frank, **I:** 196

Pizer, Donald, **III:** 321; **Retro. Supp. II:** 100, 199
"Place at the Outskirts" (Simic), **Supp. VIII:** 282
Place Called Estherville, A (Caldwell), **I:** 297, 307
"Place in Fiction" (Welty), **IV:** 260, 279
Place of Dead Roads, The (Burroughs), **Supp. III Part 1:** 196
Place of Love, The (Shapiro), **Supp. II Part 2:** 702, 706
"Place of Poetry, The" (Stevens), **Retro. Supp. I:** 304
Place of Science in Modern Civilization and Other Essays, The (Veblen), **Supp. I Part 2:** 629, 642
Place on Earth, A (Berry), **Supp. X:** 33–34, 36
Places Left Unfinished at the Time of Creation (Santos), **Supp. XIII:** 274
"Places to Look for Your Mind" (Moore), **Supp. X:** 174–175
"Place to Live, A" (Levertov), **Supp. III Part 1:** 281
"Place to Stand, A" (Price), **Supp. VI:** 258
Place to Stand, A (Wagoner), **Supp. IX:** 324
"Place (Any Place) to Transcend All Places, A" (W. C. Williams), **Retro. Supp. I:** 422
Placi, Carlo, **IV:** 328
"Plagiarist, The" (Singer), **IV:** 19
"Plain Language from Truthful James" (Harte). See "Heathen Chinee, The"
"Plain Sense of Things, The" (Stevens), **Retro. Supp. I:** 298, 299, 307, 312
Plain Song (Harrison), **Supp. VIII:** **38–39**
"Plain Song for Comadre, A" (Wilbur), **Supp. III Part 2:** 554
"Plain Talk." See *Common Sense* (Paine)
Plaint of a Rose, The (Sandburg), **III:** 579
Plain Truth: Or, Serious Considerations on the Present State of the City of Philadelphia, and Province of Pennsylvania (Franklin), **II:** 117–119
Plainwater: Essays and Poetry (Carson), **Supp. XII:** 97, **99–104**
"Planchette" (London), **II:** 475–476
"Planetarium" (Rich), **Retro. Supp. II:** 284; **Supp. I Part 2:** 557
Planet News: 1961–1967 (Ginsberg), **Supp. II Part 1:** 321
"Plantation a beginning, a" (Olson), **Supp. II Part 2:** 573

Plant Dreaming Deep (Sarton), **Supp. VIII:** 250, 263
Plante, David, **Supp. IV Part 1:** 310
Plarr, Victor, **III:** 459, 477
Plath, James, **Retro. Supp. I:** 334
Plath, Sylvia, **Retro. Supp. II:** 181, **241–260,** 281; **Supp. I Part 2: 526–549,** 554, 571; **Supp. III Part 2:** 543, 561; **Supp. IV Part 2:** 439; **Supp. V:** 79, 81, 113, 117, 118, 119, 344; **Supp. X:** 201, 202, **203,** 215; **Supp. XI:** 146, 240, 241, 317; **Supp. XII:** 217, 308; **Supp. XIII:** 35, 76, 312
Plath, Warren, **Supp. I Part 2:** 528
Plato, **I:** 224, 279, 383, 389, 485, 523; **II:** 5, 8, 10, 15, 233, 346, 391–392, 591; **III:** 115, 480, 600, 606, 609, 619–620; **IV:** 74, 140, 333, 363, 364; **Retro. Supp. I:** 247; **Retro. Supp. II:** 31; **Supp. I Part 2:** 595, 631; **Supp. IV Part 1:** 391; **Supp. IV Part 2:** 526; **Supp. X:** 78
"Plato" (Emerson), **II:** 6
"Platonic Relationship, A" (Beattie), **Supp. V:** 22
Platonic Scripts (Justice), **Supp. VII:** 115
Platonov, Dmitri, **Supp. VIII:** 30
Platt, Anthony M., **Supp. I Part 1:** 13–14
Plautus, Titus Maccius, **IV:** 155; **Supp. III Part 2:** 630
Play and Other Stories, The (Dixon), **Supp. XII:** 148, 149
Playback (Chandler), **Supp. IV Part 1:** 134–135
Playback (script) (Chandler), **Supp. IV Part 1:** 131
"Play Ball!" (Francis), **Supp. IX:** 89
Playboy of the Western World, The (Synge), **Supp. III Part 1:** 34
Play Days (Jewett), **Retro. Supp. II:** 135
Play Days: A Book of Stories for Children (Jewett), **II:** 401–402
Player Piano (Vonnegut), **Supp. II Part 2:** 756, 757, 760–765
Players (DeLillo), **Supp. VI:** 3, 6, 8, 14
"Players, The" (W. J. Smith), **Supp. XIII:** 340, 343
"Playground, The" (Bradbury), **Supp. IV Part 1:** 104
Playing in the Dark (Morrison), **Retro. Supp. II:** 118; **Supp. XIII:** 185–186
"Playin with Punjab" (Bambara), **Supp. XI:** 6
Play It as It Lays (Didion), **Supp. IV Part 1:** 198, 201–203, 203, 211

Play It as It Lays (film), **Supp. IV Part 1:** 198
Plays: Winesburg and Others (Anderson), **I:** 113
"Plays and Operas Too" (Whitman), **IV:** 350
"Playthings" (Komunyakaa), **Supp. XIII:** 126
Playwright's Voice, The (Savran), **Supp. XIII:** 209
Plaza Suite (Simon), **Supp. IV Part 2:** 575, 581–582, 583, 589
"Plea for Captain Brown, A" (Thoreau), **IV:** 185
"Please" (Komunyakaa), **Supp. XIII:** 122
"Please Don't Kill Anything" (A. Miller), **III:** 161
Pleasure Dome (Frankenberg), **I:** 436
Pleasure Dome (Komunyakaa), **Supp. XIII:** 113, 121, **131–133**
Pleasure of Hope, The (Emerson), **II:** 8
"Pleasure of Ruins, The" (McClatchy), **Supp. XII:** 256
"Pleasures of Formal Poetry, The" (Bogan), **Supp. III Part 1:** 51
Plimpton, George, **Supp. IV Part 1:** 386; **Supp. V:** 201; **Supp. VIII:** 82, 157; **Supp. IX:** 256; **Supp. XI:** 294
Pliny the Younger, **II:** 113
"Plot against the Giant, The" (Stevens), **IV:** 81
Plough and the Stars, The (O'Casey), **III:** 159
"Ploughing on Sunday" (Stevens), **IV:** 74
Plowing the Dark (Powers), **Supp. IX:** 212–213, **221–224**
"Plumet Basilisk, The" (Moore), **III:** 203, 208, 215
Plumly, Stanley, **Supp. IV Part 2:** 625
Plummer, Amanda, **Supp. IV Part 1:** 236
Plunder (serial movie), **Supp. IV Part 2:** 464
"Plunkville Patriot" (O'Henry), **Supp. II Part 1:** 389
Pluralistic Universe, A (James), **II:** 342, 348, 357–358
Plutarch, **II:** 5, 8, 16, 555; **Retro. Supp. I:** 360
Pnin (Nabokov), **III:** 246; **Retro. Supp. I:** 263, 265, 266, 275, 335
"Po' Boy Blues" (Hughes), **Supp. I Part 1:** 327
Pocahontas, **I:** 4; **II:** 296; **III:** 584
"Pocahontas to Her English Husband, John Rolfe" (Gunn Allen), **Supp. IV Part 1:** 331

Podhoretz, Norman, **IV:** 441; **Retro. Supp. II:** 341; **Supp. IV Part 1:** 382; **Supp. VIII:** 93, **231–247;** **Supp. IX:** 3
Podnieks, Elizabeth, **Supp. X:** 189, 190, 191, 192
"Pod of the Milkweed" (Frost), **Retro. Supp. I:** 141
Poe, Edgar Allan, **I:** 48, 53, 103, 190, 194, 200, 210, 211, 261, 340, 459; **II:** 74, 77, 194, 255, 273, 295, 308, 311, 313, 421, 475, 482, 530, 595; **III:** 259, **409–432,** 485, 507, 593; **IV:** 123, 129, 133, 141, 187, 261, 345, 350, 432, 438, 439, 453; **Retro. Supp. I:** 41, 273, 365, 421; **Retro. Supp. II:** 102, 104, 160, 164, 220, **261–277,** 340; **Supp. I Part 1:** 36, 309; **Supp. I Part 2:** 376, 384, 385, 388, 393, 405, 413, 421, 474, 682; **Supp. II Part 1:** 385, 410; **Supp. III Part 2:** 544, 549–550; **Supp. IV Part 1:** 80, 81, 101, 128, 341, 349; **Supp. IV Part 2:** 464, 469; **Supp. VIII:** 105; **Supp. IX:** 115; **Supp. X:** 42, 78; **Supp. XI:** 85, 293; **Supp. XIII:** 100, 111
Poe Abroad: Influence, Reputation, Affinities (Vines), **Retro. Supp. II:** 261
"Poem" (Bishop), **Retro. Supp. II:** 40; **Supp. I Part 1:** 73, 76–79, 82, 95
"Poem" (Harrison), **Supp. VIII:** 38
"Poem" (Justice), **Supp. VII:** 125
"Poem" (Kunitz), **Supp. III Part 1:** 263
"Poem" (Wright), **Supp. III Part 2:** 590
"Poem About George Doty in the Death House, A" (Wright), **Supp. III Part 2:** 594–595, 597–598
"Poem about People" (Pinsky), **Supp. VI:** **240–241,** 244, 248
"Poem as Mask, The" (Rukeyser), **Supp. VI:** 281, 285
"Poem Beginning 'The'" (Zukofsky), **Supp. III Part 2:** 610, 611, 614
"Poem for a Birthday" (Plath), **Supp. I Part 2:** 539
"POEM FOR ANNA RUSS AND FANNY JONES, A" (Baraka), **Supp. II Part 1:** 58
"Poem for Black Hearts, A" (Baraka), **Supp. II Part 1:** 50
"Poem for D. H. Lawrence" (Creeley), **Supp. IV Part 1:** 141
"POEM FOR DEEP THINKERS, A" (Baraka), **Supp. II Part 1:** 55
"Poem for Dorothy, A" (Merwin), **Supp. III Part 1:** 342

"Poem for Hemingway and W. C. Williams" (Carver), **Supp. III Part 1:** 147
"Poem for my Son" (Kumin), **Supp. IV Part 2:** 442
"Poem for People Who Are Understandably Too Busy to Read Poetry" (Dunn), **Supp. XI:** 147
"Poem for Someone Killed in Spain, A" (Jarrell), **II:** 371
"Poem for the Blue Heron, A" (Oliver), **Supp. VII:** 235–236
"Poem For Willie Best, A" (Baraka), **Supp. II Part 1:** 36
"Poem in Prose" (Bogan), **Supp. III Part 1:** 58
"Poem in Which I Refuse Contemplation" (Dove), **Supp. IV Part 1:** 249
"Poem Is a Walk, A" (Ammons), **Supp. VII:** 36
"Poem Like a Grenade, A" (Haines), **Supp. XII:** 204
"Poem of Flight, The" (Levine), **Supp. V:** 189
"Poem of Liberation, The" (Stern), **Supp. IX:** 292
Poem of the Cid (Merwin, trans.), **Supp. III Part 1:** 347
"Poem of the Forgotten" (Haines), **Supp. XII:** 202–203
"Poem on the Memorable Victory Obtained by the Gallant Captain Paul Jones" (Freneau), **Supp. II Part 1:** 261
"Poem out of Childhood" (Rukeyser), **Supp. VI:** 272, 277
"Poem Read at the Dinner Given to the Author by the Medical Profession" (Holmes), **Supp. I Part 1:** 310–311
Poems (Auden), **Supp. II Part 1:** 6
Poems (Berryman), **I:** 170
Poems (Bryant), **II:** 311; **Supp. I Part 1:** 155, 157
Poems (Cummings), **I:** 430, 447
Poems (Eliot), **I:** 580, 588; **IV:** 122; **Retro. Supp. I:** 59, 291
Poems (Emerson), **II:** 7, 8, 12–13, 17
Poems (Holmes), **Supp. I Part 1:** 303
Poems (Lowell), **Supp. I Part 2:** 405
Poems (Moore), **III:** 194, 205, 215
Poems (Poe), **III:** 411
Poems (Tate), **IV:** 121
Poems (Winters), **Supp. II Part 2:** 809, 810
Poems (Wordsworth), **I:** 468
Poems (W. C. Williams), **Retro. Supp. I:** 412–413, 416, 424
Poems (W. J. Smith), **Supp. XIII:** 332
Poems 1940–1953 (Shapiro), **Supp. II**

Part 2: 703, 711
Poems 1957–1967 (Dickey), **Supp. IV Part 1:** 178, 181
Poems, 1909–1925 (Eliot), **Retro. Supp. I:** 64
Poems, 1924–1933 (MacLeish), **III:** 7, 15
Poems, 1943–1956 (Wilbur), **Supp. III Part 2:** 554
Poems: 1947–1957 (W. J. Smith), **Supp. XIII:** 333
Poems: North & South–A Cold Spring, (Bishop), **Supp. I Part 1:** 83, 89
Poems, The (Freneau), **Supp. II Part 1:** 263
Poems about God (Ransom), **III:** 484, 486, 491; **IV:** 121
"Poems about Painting" (Snodgrass), **Supp. VI:** 316
Poems and Essays (Ransom), **III:** 486, 490, 492
Poems and New Poems (Bogan), **Supp. III Part 1:** 60–62
"Poems and Places" (Haines), **Supp. XII:** 203
Poems and Poetry of Europe, The (Longfellow, ed.), **Retro. Supp. II:** 155
Poems by Emily Dickinson (Todd and Higginson, eds.), **I:** 469, 470; **Retro. Supp. I:** 35, 39
Poems by Emily Dickinson, Second Series (Todd and Higginson, eds.), **I:** 454; **Retro. Supp. I:** 35
Poems by Emily Dickinson, The (Bianchi and Hampson, eds.), **Retro. Supp. I:** 35
Poems by Emily Dickinson, Third Series (Todd, ed.), **Retro. Supp. I:** 35
Poems by James Russell Lowell, Second Series (Lowell), **Supp. I Part 2:** 406, 409
Poems by Sidney Lanier, (Lanier), **Supp. I Part 1:** 364
Poems from Black Africa (Hughes, ed.), **Supp. I Part 1:** 344
"Poems I Have Lost, The" (Ortiz), **Supp. IV Part 2:** 507
Poems of a Jew (Shapiro), **Supp. II Part 2:** 703, 712–713
Poems of Anna Akhmatova, The (Kunitz and Hayward, trans.), **Supp. III Part 1:** 269
Poems of Emily Dickinson, The (Bianchi and Hampson, eds.), **Retro. Supp. I:** 35
Poems of Emily Dickinson, The (Johnson, ed.), **I:** 470
Poems of François Villon (Kinnell, trans.), **Supp. III Part 1:** 235, 243, 249
"Poems of Our Climate, The" (Stevens), **Retro. Supp. I:** 313
Poems of Philip Freneau, Written Chiefly during the Late War (Freneau), **Supp. II Part 1:** 261
Poems of Places (Longfellow, ed.), **II:** 490; **Retro. Supp. II:** 155; **Supp. I Part 1:** 368
Poems of Stanley Kunitz, The (Kunitz), **Supp. III Part 1:** 258, 263, 264, 266, 268
"Poems of These States" (Ginsberg), **Supp. II Part 1:** 323, 325
Poems of Two Friends (Howells and Piatt), **II:** 273, 277
"POEM SOME PEOPLE WILL HAVE TO UNDERSTAND, A" (Baraka), **Supp. II Part 1:** 49
Poems on Slavery (Longfellow), **II:** 489; **Retro. Supp. II:** 157, 168; **Supp. I Part 2:** 406
Poem Spoken at the Public Commencement at Yale College, in New Haven; September 1, 1781, A (Barlow), **Supp. II Part 1:** 67–68, 74, 75
Poems to Solve (Swenson), **Supp. IV Part 2:** 642
Poems Written and Published during the American Revolutionary War (Freneau), **Supp. II Part 1:** 273, 274
Poems Written between the Years 1768 and 1794 (Freneau), **Supp. II Part 1:** 269
"Poem That Took the Place of a Mountain" (Olson), **Supp. II Part 2:** 582
"Poem to My First Lover" (Olds), **Supp. X:** 206
"Poem to the Reader" (Olds), **Supp. X:** 213
"Poem with No Ending, A" (Levine), **Supp. V:** 186, 190
"Poem You Asked For, The" (Levis), **Supp. XI:** 259–260
Poe Poe Poe Poe Poe Poe Poe (Hoffman), **Retro. Supp. II:** 265
Poésies 1917–1920 (Cocteau), **Retro. Supp. I:** 82
"Poet, The" (Dunbar), **Supp. II Part 1:** 207, 209–210
"Poet, The" (Emerson), **II:** 13, 19, 20, 170
"Poet, The" (Ortiz), **Supp. IV Part 2:** 505
"Poet and His Book, The" (Millay), **III:** 126, 138
"Poet and His Public, The" (Jarrell), **Supp. I Part 1:** 96
"Poet and His Song, The" (Dunbar), **Supp. II Part 1:** 199
"Poet and the World, The" (Cowley), **Supp. II Part 1:** 145
"Poet as Anti-Specialist, The" (Swenson), **Supp. IV Part 2:** 638, 643
"Poet as *Curandera*" (Mora), **Supp. XIII:** 214, 220
"Poet as Hero, The: Keats in His Letters" (Trilling), **Supp. III Part 2:** 506–507
"Poet as Religious Moralist, The" (Larson), **Supp. XI:** 328
"Poet at Seven, The" (Rimbaud), **II:** 545
Poet at the Breakfast-Table, The (Holmes), **Supp. I Part 1:** 313–314
"Poète contumace, Le" (Corbiere), **II:** 384–385
"Poet for President, A" (Mora), **Supp. XIII:** 220–221
Poetic Achievement of Ezra Pound, The (Alexander), **Retro. Supp. I:** 293
Poetic Diction: A Study in Meaning (Barfield), **III:** 274, 279
"Poetic Principle, The" (Poe), **III:** 421, 426; **Retro. Supp. II:** 266
"Poetics" (Ammons), **Supp. VII:** 29–30
Poetics (Aristotle), **III:** 422; **Supp. XI:** 249; **Supp. XIII:** 75
Poetics of Space, The (Bachelard), **Supp. XIII:** 225
"Poetics of the Periphery: Literary Experimentalism in Kathy Acker's *In Memoriam to Identity*" (Acker), **Supp. XII:** 17
"Poetics of the Physical World, The" (Kinnell), **Supp. III Part 1:** 239
Poet in the World, The (Levertov), **Supp. III Part 1:** 271, 273, 278, 282
"Poet or the Growth of a Lit'ry Figure" (White), **Supp. I Part 2:** 676
Poetry (Barber), **Supp. IV Part 2:** 550
"Poetry" (Moore), **III:** 204–205, 215
"Poetry" (Nye), **Supp. XIII:** 282
"Poetry: A Metrical Essay" (Holmes), **Supp. I Part 1:** 310
"Poetry, Community and Climax" (Snyder), **Supp. VIII:** 290
"Poetry and Belief in Thomas Hardy" (Schwartz), **Supp. II Part 2:** 666
Poetry and Criticism (Nemerov, ed.), **III:** 269
"Poetry and Drama" (Eliot), **I:** 588
Poetry and Fiction: Essays (Nemerov), **III:** 269, 281
"Poetry and Place" (Berry), **Supp. X:**

22, 28, 31, 32
Poetry and Poets (Lowell), **II:** 512
Poetry and the Age (Jarrell), **IV:** 352; **Retro. Supp. I:** 121; **Supp. II Part 1:** 135
"Poetry and the Primitive: Notes on Poetry as an Ecological Survival Technique" (Snyder), **Supp. VIII:** 291, 292, 299, 300
"Poetry and the Public World" (MacLeish), **III:** 11
Poetry and the World (Pinsky), **Supp. VI:** 236, 239, 244, 247
Poetry and Truth (Olson), **Supp. II Part 2:** 583
"Poetry As a Way of Life" (Bishop interview), **Retro. Supp. II:** 53
"Poetry as Survival" (Harrison), **Supp. VIII:** 45
"Poetry for the Advanced" (Baraka), **Supp. II Part 1:** 58
Poetry Handbook, A (Oliver), **Supp. VII:** 229, 245
"Poetry of Barbarism, The" (Santayana), **IV:** 353
Poetry of Chaucer, The (Gardner), **Supp. VI:** 63
Poetry of Meditation, The (Martz), **IV:** 151; **Supp. I Part 1:** 107
Poetry of Mourning: The Modern Elegy from Hardy to Heaney (Ramazani), **Supp. IV Part 2:** 450
Poetry of Stephen Crane, The (Hoffman), **I:** 405
Poetry of the Negro 1746–1949, The (Hughes, ed.), **Supp. I Part 1:** 345
Poetry Reading against the Vietnam War, A (Bly and Ray, eds.), **Supp. IV Part 1:** 61, 63
"Poetry Wreck, The" (Shapiro), **Supp. II Part 2:** 717
Poetry Wreck, The: Selected Essays (Shapiro), **Supp. II Part 2:** 703, 704, 717
Poet's Alphabet, A: Reflections on the Literary Art and Vocation (Bogan), **Supp. III Part 1:** 55, 64
Poet's Choice (Engle and Langland, eds.), **III:** 277, 542
Poets of the Old Testament, The (Gordon), **III:** 199
Poets of Today (Wheelock, ed.), **Supp. IV Part 2:** 639
Poets on Poetry (Nemerov, ed.), **III:** 269
"Poet's View, A" (Levertov), **Supp. III Part 1:** 284
"Poet's Voice, The" (Oliver), **Supp. VII:** 245
"Poet Turns on Himself, The" (Dickey), **Supp. IV Part 1:** 177, 181, 185
Poganuc People (Stowe), **Supp. I Part 2:** 581, 596, 599–600
Pogo (comic strip), **Supp. XI:** 105
Poincaré, Raymond, **IV:** 320
"Point, The" (Hayden), **Supp. II Part 1:** 373
"Point at Issue!, A" (Chopin), **Retro. Supp. II:** 61; **Supp. I Part 1:** 208
"Point of Age, A" (Berryman), **I:** 173
Point of No Return (Marquand), **III:** 56, 59–60, 65, 67, 69
Point Reyes Poems (Bly), **Supp. IV Part 1:** 71
"Point Shirley" (Plath), **Supp. I Part 2:** 529, 538
Points in Time (Bowles), **Supp. IV Part 1:** 93
"Points West" (column), **Supp. IV Part 1:** 198
Poirier, Richard, **I:** 136, 239; **III:** 34; **Retro. Supp. I:** 134; **Retro. Supp. II:** 207–208; **Supp. I Part 2:** 660, 665; **Supp. IV Part 2:** 690
Poison Pen (Garrett), **Supp. VII:** 111
Poisonwood Bible, The (Kingsolver), **Supp. VII:** 197–198, 202, 210–213
Poitier, Sidney, **Supp. IV Part 1:** 360, 362
"Polar Bear" (Heller), **Supp. IV Part 1:** 383
Pole, Rupert, **Supp. X:** 185
"Pole Star" (MacLeish), **III:** 16
Po Li, **Supp. I Part 1:** 262
Police (Baraka), **Supp. II Part 1:** 47
"Police" (Corso), **Supp. XII:** 117, 127
"Police Dreams" (Bausch), **Supp. VII:** 47
Politian (Poe), **III:** 412
Political Essays (Lowell), **Supp. I Part 2:** 407
Political Fable, A (Coover), **Supp. V:** 44, 46, 47, 49, 51
"Political Fables" (Mather), **Supp. II Part 2:** 450
"Political Interests" (Stevens), **Retro. Supp. I:** 295
"Political Litany, A" (Freneau), **Supp. II Part 1:** 257
"Political Pastoral" (Frost), **Retro. Supp. I:** 139
"Political Poem" (Baraka), **Supp. II Part 1:** 36
Politics (Acker), **Supp. XII:** 3, 4
Politics (Macdonald), **I:** 233–234
"Politics" (Paley), **Supp. VI:** 217
"Politics, Structure, and Poetic Development" (McCombs), **Supp. XIII:** 33
"Politics and the English Language" (Orwell), **Retro. Supp. II:** 305; **Supp. I Part 2:** 620
Politics and the Novel (Howe), **Supp. VI:** 113
"Politics of Silence, The" (Monette), **Supp. X:** 148
Politt, Katha, **Supp. XII:** 159
Polk, James, **Supp. XIII:** 20
Polk, James K., **I:** 17; **II:** 433–434
Pollack, Sydney, **Supp. XIII:** 159
"Pollen" (Nye), **Supp. XIII:** 284
Pollitt, Katha, **Supp. X:** 186, 191, 193
Pollock, Jackson, **IV:** 411, 420
"Polly" (Chopin), **Retro. Supp. II:** 72
Polo, Marco, **III:** 395
Polybius, **Supp. I Part 2:** 491
"Polydore" (Chopin), **Retro. Supp. II:** 66
"Pomegranate" (Glück), **Supp. V:** 82
"Pomegranate Seed" (Wharton), **IV:** 316; **Retro. Supp. I:** 382
Ponce de Leon, Luis, **III:** 391
"Pond, The" (Nemerov), **III:** 272
"Pond at Dusk, The" (Kenyon), **Supp. VII:** 168
Ponder Heart, The (Welty), **IV:** 261, 274–275, 281; **Retro. Supp. I:** 351–352
Poodle Springs (Parker and Chandler), **Supp. IV Part 1:** 135
Poodle Springs Story, The (Chandler), **Supp. IV Part 1:** 135
"Pool, The" (Doolittle), **Supp. I Part 1:** 264–265
Poole, Ernest, **II:** 444
"Pool Lights" (F. Barthelme), **Supp. XI:** 25, 26–27, 36
"Pool Room in the Lions Club" (Merwin), **Supp. III Part 1:** 346
"Poor Black Fellow" (Hughes), **Retro. Supp. I:** 204
"Poor Bustard, The" (Corso), **Supp. XII:** 134
Poore, Charles, **III:** 364
Poor Fool (Caldwell), **I:** 291, 292, 308
Poorhouse Fair, The (Updike), **IV:** 214, 228–229, 232; **Retro. Supp. I:** 317, 320
"Poor Joanna" (Jewett), **II:** 394
"Poor Man's Pudding and Rich Man's Crumbs" (Melville), **III:** 89–90
"Poor Richard" (James), **II:** 322
Poor Richard's Almanac (undated) (Franklin), **II:** 112
Poor Richard's Almanac for 1733 (Franklin), **II:** 108, 110
Poor Richard's Almanac for 1739 (Franklin), **II:** 112
Poor Richard's Almanac for 1758

(Franklin), **II:** 101
Poor White (Anderson), **I:** 110–111
"Poor Working Girl" (Z. Fitzgerald), **Supp. IX:** 71
Popa, Vasko, **Supp. VIII:** 272
Pope, Alexander, **I:** 198, 204; **II:** 17, 114; **III:** 263, 267, 288, 517; **IV:** 145; **Retro. Supp. I:** 335; **Supp. I Part 1:** 150, 152, 310; **Supp. I Part 2:** 407, 422, 516, 714; **Supp. II Part 1:** 70, 71; **Supp. X:** 32, 36; **Supp. XII:** 260
"Pope's Penis, The" (Olds), **Supp. X:** 207
"Poplar, Sycamore" (Wilbur), **Supp. III Part 2:** 549
Popo and Fifina (Hughes and Bontemps), **Retro. Supp. I:** 203
"Poppies" (Oliver), **Supp. VII:** 240
"Poppies in July" (Plath), **Supp. I Part 2:** 544
"Poppies in October" (Plath), **Supp. I Part 2:** 544
"Poppycock" (Francis), **Supp. IX:** 87
"Poppy Seed" (Lowell), **II:** 523
Popular Culture (Goldbarth), **Supp. XII: 186**
Popular History of the United States (Gay), **Supp. I Part 1:** 158
"Popular Songs" (Ashbery), **Supp. III Part 1:** 6
"Populist Manifesto" (Ferlinghetti), **Supp. VIII:** 290
"Porcelain Bowl" (Glück), **Supp. V:** 83
Porcher, Frances, **Retro. Supp. II:** 71
"Porcupine, The" (Kinnell), **Supp. III Part 1:** 244
Porcupine's Kiss, The (Dobyns), **Supp. XIII: 89–90**
Porgy and Bess (film), **Supp. I Part 1:** 66
Porgy and Bess (play), **Supp. IV Part 1:** 6
"Porphyria's Lover" (Browning), **II:** 522
Portable Blake, The (Kazin, ed.), **Supp. VIII:** 103
Portable Faulkner, The (Cowley, ed.), **II:** 57, 59; **Retro. Supp. I:** 73
Portable Paul and Jane Bowles, The (Dillon), **Supp. IV Part 1:** 95
Portable Veblen, The (Veblen), **Supp. I Part 2:** 630, 650
"Porte-Cochere" (Taylor), **Supp. V:** 320
"Porter" (Hughes), **Supp. I Part 1:** 327
Porter, Bern, **III:** 171
Porter, Cole, **Supp. IX:** 189
Porter, Eliot, **Supp. IV Part 2:** 599

Porter, Herman W., **Supp. I Part 1:** 49
Porter, Horace, **Retro. Supp. II:** 4, 127
Porter, Jacob, **Supp. I Part 1:** 153
Porter, Katherine Anne, **I:** 97, 385; **II:** 194, 606; **III: 433–455,** 482; **IV:** 26, 138, 246, 261, 279, 280, 282; **Retro. Supp. I:** 354; **Retro. Supp. II:** 233, 235; **Supp. IV Part 1:** 31, 310; **Supp. V:** 225; **Supp. VIII:** 156, 157; **Supp. IX:** 93, 94, 95, 98, 128; **Supp. X:** 50; **Supp. XIII:** 294
Porter, Noah, **Supp. I Part 2:** 640
Porter, William Sydney. *See* Henry, O.
Porteus, Beilby, **Supp. I Part 1:** 150
"Portland Going Out, The" (Merwin), **Supp. III Part 1:** 345
Portnoy's Complaint (Roth), **Retro. Supp. II: 300–304,** 309; **Supp. III Part 2:** 401, 404, 405, 407, 412–414, 426; **Supp. V:** 119, 122; **Supp. XI:** 140
Port of Saints (Burroughs), **Supp. III Part 1:** 106
"Portrait" (Dixon), **Supp. XII:** 154
"Portrait, A" (Parker), **Supp. IX:** 192–193
"Portrait, The" (Kunitz), **Supp. III Part 1:** 263
"Portrait, The" (Wharton), **Retro. Supp. I:** 364
"Portrait d'une Femme" (Pound), **Retro. Supp. I:** 288
Portrait in Brownstone (Auchincloss), **Supp. IV Part 1:** 21, 23, 27, 31
"Portrait in Georgia" (Toomer), **Supp. IX:** 314
"Portrait in Greys, A" (W. C. Williams), **Retro. Supp. I:** 416
"Portrait of a Girl in Glass" (T. Williams), **IV:** 383
"Portrait of a Lady" (Eliot), **I:** 569, 570, 571, 584; **III:** 4; **Retro. Supp. I:** 55, 56, 62
Portrait of a Lady, The (James), **I:** 10, 258, 461–462, 464; **II:** 323, 325, 327, 328–329, 334; **Retro. Supp. I:** 215, 216, 217, 219, 220, 223, **224–225,** 232, 233, 381
"Portrait of an Artist" (Roth), **Supp. III Part 2:** 412
Portrait of an Eye: Three Novels (Acker), **Supp. XII:** 6, **7–9**
"Portrait of an Invisible Man" (Auster), **Supp. XII:** 21
Portrait of Bascom Hawkes, A (Wolfe), **IV:** 451–452, 456
Portrait of Edith Wharton (Lubbock), **Retro. Supp. I:** 366
Portrait of Picasso as a Young Man (Mailer), **Retro. Supp. II:** 213

"Portrait of the Artist as an Old Man, A" (Humphrey), **Supp. IX:** 109
Portrait of the Artist as a Young Man, A (Joyce), **I:** 475–476; **III:** 471, 561; **Retro. Supp. I:** 127; **Retro. Supp. II:** 4, 349; **Supp. IX:** 236; **Supp. XIII:** 53, 95
"Portrait of the Artist with Hart Crane" (Wright), **Supp. V:** 342
"Portrait of the Intellectual as a Yale Man" (McCarthy), **II:** 563, 564–565
"Port Town" (Hughes), **Retro. Supp. I:** 199
Portuguese Voyages to America in the Fifteenth Century (Morison), **Supp. I Part 2:** 488
Poseidon Adventure, The (film), **Supp. XII:** 321
"Poseidon and Company" (Carver), **Supp. III Part 1:** 137
"Positive Obsession" (O. Butler), **Supp. XIII:** 70
"Possessions" (H. Crane), **I:** 392–393; **Retro. Supp. II:** 78
Postal Inspector (film), **Supp. XIII:** 166
Postcards (Proulx), **Supp. VII:** 249, 256–258, 262
"Postcolonial Tale, A" (Harjo), **Supp. XII:** 227
"Posthumous Letter to Gilbert White" (Auden), **Supp. II Part 1:** 26
"Post-Larkin Triste" (Karr), **Supp. XI:** 242–243
Postlethwaite, Diana, **Supp. XII:** 317–318
"Postlude" (W. C. Williams), **Retro. Supp. I:** 415
Postman, Neil, **Supp. XI:** 275
Postman Always Rings Twice, The (Cain), **Supp. XIII:** 165–166
"Postmortem Guide, A" (Dunn), **Supp. XI:** 155
"Postscript" (Du Bois), **Supp. II Part 1:** 173
"Postscript" (Nye), **Supp. XIII:** 287
"Potato" (Wilbur), **Supp. III Part 2:** 545
"Potatoes' Dance, The" (Lindsay), **Supp. I Part 2:** 394
Pot of Earth, The (MacLeish), **III:** 5, 6–8, 10, 12, 18
"Pot Roast" (Strand), **Supp. IV Part 2:** 629
Pot Shots at Poetry (Francis), **Supp. IX: 83–84**
Potter, Beatrix, **Supp. I Part 2:** 656
Potter, Stephen, **IV:** 430
Potter's House, The (Stegner), **Supp. IV Part 2:** 598, 606

Poulenc, Francis, **Supp. IV Part 1:** 81
Poulin, Al, Jr., **Supp. IX:** 272; **Supp. XI:** 259
Pound, Ezra, **I:** 49, 58, 60, 66, 68, 69, 105, 236, 243, 256, 384, 403, 428, 429, 475, 476, 482, 487, 521, 578; **II:** 26, 55, 168, 263, 316, 371, 376, 513, 517, 520, 526, 528, 529, 530; **III:** 2, 5, 8, 9, 13–14, 17, 174, 194, 196, 278, 430, 453, **456–479,** 492, 504, 511, 523, 524, 527, 575–576, 586, 590; **IV:** 27, 28, 407, 415, 416, 433, 446; **Retro. Supp. I:** 51, 52, 55, 58, 59, 63, 82, 89, 127, 140, 171, 177, 178, 198, 216, **283–294,** 298, 299, 359, 411, 412, 413, 414, 417, 418, 419, 420, 423, 426, 427, 430, 431; **Retro. Supp. II:** 178, 183, 189, 344; **Supp. I Part 1:** 253, 255–258, 261–268, 272, 274; **Supp. I Part 2:** 387, 721; **Supp. II Part 1:** 1, 8, 20, 30, 91, 136; **Supp. III Part 1:** 48, 63, 64, 73, 105, 146, 225, 271; **Supp. III Part 2:** 542, **609–617,** 619, 620, 622, 625, 626, 628, 631; **Supp. IV Part 1:** 153, 314; **Supp. V:** 331, 338, 340, 343, 345; **Supp. VIII:** 39, 105, 195, 205, 271, 290, 291, 292, 303; **Supp. IX:** 291; **Supp. X:** 24, 36, 112, 120, 122; **Supp. XII:** 97
Pound, Louise, **Retro. Supp. I:** 4
Pound, T. S., **I:** 428
"Pound Reweighed" (Cowley), **Supp. II Part 1:** 143
Powell, Betty, **Retro. Supp. II:** 140
Powell, Dawn, **Supp. IV Part 2:** 678, 682
Powell, Dick, **Supp. IX:** 250
Powell, John Wesley, **Supp. IV Part 2:** 598, 604, 611
Powell, Lawrence Clark, **III:** 189
Powell, William, **Supp. IV Part 1:** 355
"Power" (Corso), **Supp. XII:** 117, 126, 127, **128**
"Power" (Emerson), **II:** 2, 3
"Power" (Rich), **Supp. I Part 2:** 569
"Power and Light" (Dickey), **Supp. IV Part 1:** 182
Power and the Glory, The (Greene), **III:** 556
"Powerhouse" (Welty), **Retro. Supp. I:** 343, 346
"Power Never Dominion" (Rukeyser), **Supp. VI:** 281
"Power of Fancy, The" (Freneau), **Supp. II Part 1:** 255
Power of Myth, The (Campbell), **Supp. IX:** 245
"Power of Prayer, The" (Lanier), **Supp. I Part 1:** 357
"Power of Suggestion" (Auchincloss), **Supp. IV Part 1:** 33
Power of Sympathy, The (Brown), **Supp. II Part 1:** 74
Power Politics (Atwood), **Supp. XIII:** 20, 33–34, 35
Powers, J. F., **Supp. V:** 319
Powers, Kim, **Supp. VIII:** 329, 340
Powers, Richard, **Supp. IX: 207–225**
Powers of Attorney (Auchincloss), **Supp. IV Part 1:** 31, 32, 33
"Powers of Darkness" (Wharton), **Retro. Supp. I:** 379
Powys, John Cowper, **Supp. I Part 2:** 454, 476; **Supp. IX:** 135
Practical Magic (film), **Supp. X:** 80
Practical Magic (Hoffman), **Supp. X:** 78, 82, **88–89**
"Practical Methods of Meditation, The" (Dawson), **IV:** 151
Practical Navigator, The (Bowditch), **Supp. I Part 2:** 482
Practice of Perspective, The (Dubreuil), **Supp. IV Part 2:** 425
Practice of Reading, The (Donoghue), **Supp. VIII:** 189
Pragmatism: A New Name for Some Old Ways of Thinking (James), **II:** 352
Prague Orgy, The (Roth), **Retro. Supp. II:** 298
"Praire, The" (Clampitt), **Supp. IX:** 42
"Prairie" (Sandburg), **III:** 583, 584
Prairie, The (Cooper), **I:** 339, 342
Prairie Home Companion, A (Keillor, radio program), **Supp. XIII:** 274
"Prairie Life, A Citizen Speaks" (Dunn), **Supp. XI:** 145
"Prairies, The" (Bryant), **Supp. I Part 1:** 157, 162, 163, 166
Praise (Hass), **Supp. VI:** 104–105, 106
"Praise for an Urn" (Crane), **I:** 388
"Praise for Sick Women" (Snyder), **Supp. VIII:** 294
"Praise in Summer" (Wilbur), **Supp. III Part 2:** 546–548, 560, 562
"Praise of a Palmtree" (Levertov), **Supp. III Part 1:** 284
"Praise of the Committee" (Rukeyser), **Supp. VI:** 278
"Praises, The" (Goldbarth), **Supp. XII:** 185
"Praises, The" (Olson), **Supp. II Part 2:** 558, 560, 563, 564
Praises and Dispraises (Des Pres), **Supp. X:** 120
Praisesong for the Widow (Marshall), **Supp. IV Part 1:** 14; **Supp. XI:** 18, 276, 278, **284–286,** 287
"Praise to the End!" (Roethke), **III:** 529, 532, 539
Prajadhipok, King of Siam, **I:** 522
Pratt, Anna (Anna Alcott), **Supp. I Part 1:** 33
Pratt, Louis H., **Retro. Supp. II:** 6
Pratt, Mary Louise, **Retro. Supp. II:** 48
Pratt, Parley, **Supp. IV Part 2:** 603
"Prattler" (newspaper column), **I:** 207
"Prattler, The" (Bierce), **I:** 196
"Prayer" (Olds), **Supp. X:** 204
"Prayer" (Toomer), **Supp. IX:** 318
"Prayer, A" (Kushner), **Supp. IX: 134**
"Prayer for Columbus" (Whitman), **IV:** 348
"Prayer for My Daughter" (Yeats), **II:** 598
"Prayer for My Grandfather to Our Lady, A" (Lowell), **II:** 541–542
Prayer for Owen Meany, A (Irving), **Supp. VI:** 164, 165, 166, **175–176**
"PRAYER FOR SAVING" (Baraka), **Supp. II Part 1:** 52–53
"Prayer in Spring, A" (Frost), **II:** 153, 164
"Prayer on All Saint's Day" (Cowley), **Supp. II Part 1:** 138, 153
Prayers for Dark People (Du Bois), **Supp. II Part 1:** 186
"Prayer to Hermes" (Creeley), **Supp. IV Part 1:** 156, 157
"Prayer to Masks" (Senghor), **Supp. IV Part 1:** 16
"Prayer to the Child of Prague" (Salinas), **Supp. XIII:** 327
"Prayer to the Good Poet" (Wright), **Supp. III Part 2:** 603
"Prayer to the Pacific" (Silko), **Supp. IV Part 2:** 560
"Pray without Ceasing" (Emerson), **II:** 9–10
Praz, Mario, **IV:** 430
"Preacher, The" (Whittier), **Supp. I Part 2:** 698–699
Preacher and the Slave, The (Stegner), **Supp. IV Part 2:** 599, 608, 609
Precaution (Cooper), **I:** 337, 339
"Preconceptions of Economic Science, The" (Veblen), **Supp. I Part 2:** 634
Predecessors, Et Cetera (Clampitt), **Supp. IX:** 37
"Predicament, A" (Poe), **Retro. Supp. II:** 273
Predilections (Moore), **III:** 194
Prefaces and Prejudices (Mencken), **III:** 99, 104, 106, 119
Preface to a Twenty Volume Suicide Note. . . . (Baraka), **Supp. II Part 1:** 31, 33–34, 51, 61

"Preference" (Wylie), **Supp. I Part 2:** 713
"Prejudice against the Past, The" (Moore), **IV:** 91
Prejudices (Mencken), **Supp. I Part 2:** 630
Prejudices: A Selection (Farrell, ed.), **III:** 116
Prejudices: First Series (Mencken), **III:** 105
Prelude, A: Landscapes, Characters and Conversations from the Earlier Years of My Life (Wilson), **IV:** 426, 427, 430, 434, 445
Prelude, The (Wordsworth), **III:** 528; **IV:** 331, 343; **Supp. I Part 2:** 416, 676; **Supp. XI:** 248
Prelude and Liebestod (McNally), **Supp. XIII:** 201
"Preludes" (Eliot), **I:** 573, 576, 577; **Retro. Supp. I:** 55; **Supp. IV Part 2:** 436
Preludes for Memnon (Aiken), **I:** 59, 65
Preludes from Memnon (Aiken), **Supp. X:** 50
"Prelude to an Evening" (Ransom), **III:** 491, 492–493
Prelude to Darkness (Salinas), **Supp. XIII:** 311, **318–319**, 320
"Prelude to the Present" (Mumford), **Supp. II Part 2:** 471
"Premature Burial, The" (Poe), **III:** 415, 416, 418; **Retro. Supp. II:** 270
Preminger, Otto, **Supp. IX:** 3, 9
"Premonitions of the Bread Line" (Komunyakaa), **Supp. XIII:** 114, 115
Prenshaw, Peggy Whitman, **Supp. X:** 229
"Preparations" (Silko), **Supp. IV Part 2:** 560
Preparatory Meditations (Taylor), **IV:** 145, 148, 149, 150, 152, 153, 154–155, 164, 165
Prepositions: The Collected Critical Essays of Louis Zukofsky (Zukofsky), **Supp. III Part 2:** 630
Prescott, Anne, **Supp. IV Part 1:** 299
Prescott, Orville, **Supp. IV Part 2:** 680; **Supp. XI:** 340
Prescott, Peter, **Supp. X:** 83
Prescott, William, **Retro. Supp. I:** 123
Prescott, William Hickling, **II:** 9, 310, 313–314; **IV:** 309; **Supp. I Part 2:** 414, 479, 493, 494
"Prescription of Painful Ends" (Jeffers), **Supp. II Part 2:** 424
"Presence, The" (Gordon), **II:** 199, 200
"Presence, The" (Kumin), **Supp. IV Part 2:** 445, 455
"Presence of Others, The" (Kenyon), **Supp. VII:** 164
Presences (Taylor), **Supp. V:** 325
"Present Age, The" (Emerson), **II:** 11–12
Present Danger, The: Do We Have the Will to Reverse the Decline of American Power? (Podhoretz), **Supp. VIII:** 241
"Present Hour" (Sandburg), **III:** 593–594
Present Philosophical Tendencies (Perry), **I:** 224
"Present State of Ethical Philosophy, The" (Emerson), **II:** 9
"Present State of Poetry, The" (Schwartz), **Supp. II Part 2:** 666
"Preservation of Innocence" (Baldwin), **Supp. I Part 1:** 51
"Preserving Wildness" (Berry), **Supp. X:** 28, 29, 32
"President and Other Intellectuals, The" (Kazin), **Supp. VIII:** 104
Presidential Papers, The (Mailer), **III:** 35, 37–38, 42, 45; **Retro. Supp. II:** 203, 204, 206
"Presidents" (Merwin), **Supp. III Part 1:** 351
Presnell, Robert, Sr., **Supp. XIII:** 166
"PRES SPOKE IN A LANGUAGE" (Baraka), **Supp. II Part 1:** 60
"Pretext, The" (Wharton), **Retro. Supp. I:** 371
Pretty Boy Floyd (McMurtry), **Supp. V:** 231
"Pretty Girl, The" (Dubus), **Supp. VII:** 87–88
"Pretty Mouth and Green My Eyes" (Salinger), **III:** 560
"Previous Condition" (Baldwin), **Supp. I Part 1:** 51, 55, 63
"Previous Tenant, The" (Simpson), **Supp. IX:** 278–279
Priaulx, Allan, **Supp. XI:** 228
Price, Alan, **Retro. Supp. I:** 377
Price, Reynolds, **Supp. VI: 253–270;** **Supp. IX:** 256, 257
Price, Richard, **II:** 9; **Supp. I Part 2:** 522
Price, The (A. Miller), **III:** 165–166
"Price of the Harness, The" (Crane), **I:** 414
Pricksongs & Descants; Fictions (Coover), **Supp. V:** 39, 42, 43, 49, 50
"Pride" (Hughes), **Supp. I Part 1:** 331
Pride and Prejudice (Austen), **II:** 290
Prideaux, Tom, **Supp. IV Part 2:** 574, 590
"Priesthood, The" (Winters), **Supp. II Part 2:** 786
Priestly, Joseph, **Supp. I Part 2:** 522
Primary Colors, The (A. Theroux), **Supp. VIII:** 312
"Primary Ground, A" (Rich), **Supp. I Part 2:** 563
"Prime" (Auden), **Supp. II Part 1:** 22
"Primer Class" (Bishop), **Retro. Supp. II:** 38, 51
Primer for Blacks (Brooks), **Supp. III Part 1:** 85
"Primer for the Nuclear Age" (Dove), **Supp. IV Part 1:** 246
Primer of Ignorance, A (Blackmur), **Supp. II Part 1:** 91
"Primitive Black Man, The" (Du Bois), **Supp. II Part 1:** 176
"Primitive Like an Orb, A" (Stevens), **IV:** 89; **Retro. Supp. I:** 309
"Primitive Singing" (Lindsay), **Supp. I Part 2:** 389–390
Primitivism and Decadence (Winters), **Supp. II Part 2:** 786, 803–807, 812
Prince, Richard, **Supp. XII:** 4
"Prince, The" (Jarrell), **II:** 379
"Prince, The" (Winters), **Supp. II Part 2:** 802
Prince and the Pauper, The (Twain), **IV:** 200–201, 206
Prince Hagen (Sinclair), **Supp. V:** 280
Prince of a Fellow, A (Hearon), **Supp. VIII:** 58, **62–63**
Princess, The (Tennyson), **Supp. I Part 2:** 410
Princess and the Goblins, The (Macdonald), **Supp. XIII:** 75
Princess Casamassima, The (James), **II:** 276, 291; **IV:** 202; **Retro. Supp. I:** 216, 221, 222, 225, **226–227**
"Princess Casamassima, The" (Trilling), **Supp. III Part 2:** 502, 503
Princess of Arcady, A (Henry), **Retro. Supp. II:** 97
"Principles" (Du Bois), **Supp. II Part 1:** 172
Principles of Literary Criticism (Richards), **I:** 274; **Supp. I Part 1:** 264
Principles of Psychology, The (James), **II:** 321, 350–352, 353, 354, 357, 362, 363–364; **IV:** 28, 29, 32, 37
Principles of Zoölogy (Agassiz), **Supp. I Part 1:** 312
Prior, Matthew, **II:** 111; **III:** 521
Prior, Sir James, **II:** 315
"Prison, The" (Malamud), **Supp. I Part 2:** 431, 437
Prisoner of Second Avenue, The

(Simon), **Supp. IV Part 2:** 583, 584
Prisoner of Sex, The (Mailer), **III:** 46; **Retro. Supp. II:** 206
Prisoner of Zenda, The (film), **Supp. I Part 2:** 615
Prisoner's Dilemma (Powers), **Supp. IX:** 212, **214–216,** 221
Pritchard, William H., **Retro. Supp. I:** 131, 141; **Supp. IV Part 1:** 285; **Supp. IV Part 2:** 642; **Supp. XI:** 326
Pritchett, V. S., **II:** 587; **Supp. II Part 1:** 143; **Supp. VIII:** 171; **Supp. XIII:** 168
"Privatation and Publication" (Cowley), **Supp. II Part 1:** 149
Private Contentment (Price), **Supp. VI:** 263
"Private History of a Campaign That Failed" (Twain), **IV:** 195
Private Life of Axie Reed, The (Knowles), **Supp. XII:** 249
"Private Man Confronts His Vulgarities at Dawn, A" (Dunn), **Supp. XI:** 146
Private Memoirs and Confessions of a Justified Sinner, The (Hogg), **Supp. IX:** 276
"Private Property and the Common Wealth" (Berry), **Supp. X:** 25
"Private Theatricals" (Howells), **II:** 280
Privilege, The (Kumin), **Supp. IV Part 2:** 442–444, 451
"Probing the Dark" (Komunyakaa), **Supp. XIII:** 131
"Problem from Milton, A" (Wilbur), **Supp. III Part 2:** 550
"Problem of Being, The" (James), **II:** 360
"Problem of Housing the Negro, The" (Du Bois), **Supp. II Part 1:** 168
Problems and Other Stories (Updike), **Retro. Supp. I:** 322, 329
"Problem Solving" (Goldbarth), **Supp. XII:** 185
Procedures for Underground (Atwood), **Supp. XIII:** 33
"Procedures for Underground" (Atwood), **Supp. XIII:** 33
Processional (Lawson), **I:** 479
"Procession at Candlemas, A" (Clampitt), **Supp. IX:** 41
Proclus, **Retro. Supp. I:** 247
"Prodigal" (Ammons), **Supp. VII:** 29
"Prodigal, The" (Bishop), **Supp. I Part 1:** 90, 92
Prodigal Parents, The (Lewis), **II:** 454–455
"Prodigy" (Simic), **Supp. VIII:** 278

"Proem" (Crane), **I:** 397
"Proem, The: By the Carpenter" (O. Henry), **Supp. II Part 1:** 409
"Professions for Women" (Woolf), **Supp. XIII:** 305
"Professor" (Hughes), **Supp. I Part 1:** 330
"Professor, The" (Bourne), **I:** 223
Professor at the Breakfast Table, The (Holmes), **Supp. I Part 1:** 313, 316
"Professor Clark's Economics" (Veblen), **Supp. I Part 2:** 634
Professor of Desire, The (Roth), **Retro. Supp. II:** 306; **Supp. III Part 2:** 403, 418–420
Professor's House, The (Cather), **I:** 325–336; **Retro. Supp. I:** 16
"Professor Veblen" (Mencken), **Supp. I Part 2:** 630
Proffer, Carl R., **Supp. VIII:** 22
Profits of Religion, The (Sinclair), **Supp. V:** 276
"Prognosis" (Warren), **IV:** 245
"Progress Report" (Simic), **Supp. VIII:** 278
"Project for a Trip to China" (Sontag), **Supp. II Part 2:** 454, 469
"Project for *The Ambassadors*" (James), **Retro. Supp. I:** 229
"Projection" (Nemerov), **III:** 275
"Projective Verse" (Olson), **Supp. III Part 1:** 30; **Supp. III Part 2:** 555, 556, 557, 624; **Supp. IV Part 1:** 139, 153; **Supp. VIII:** 290
"Projector, The" (Baker), **Supp. XIII:** 53, 55
Prokofiev, Sergey Sergeyevich, **Supp. IV Part 1:** 81
"Prolegomena, Section 1" (Pound), **Supp. III Part 2:** 615–616
"Prolegomena, Section 2" (Pound), **Supp. III Part 2:** 616
"Prolegomenon to a Biography of Mailer" (Lucid), **Retro. Supp. II:** 195
Proletarian Literature in the United States (Hicks), **Supp. I Part 2:** 609–610
"Prologue" (MacLeish), **III:** 8, 14
"Prologue to Our Time" (Mumford), **Supp. III Part 2:** 473
"Prometheus" (Longfellow), **II:** 494
Prometheus Bound (Lowell), **II:** 543, 544, 545, 555
Promise, The (Buck), **Supp. II Part 1:** 124
"Promise, The" (Olds), **Supp. X:** 213
Promised Land, The (Antin), **Supp. IX:** 227
Promised Land, The (Porter), **III:** 447

Promised Lands (Sontag), **Supp. III Part 2:** 452
Promise of American Life, The (Croly), **I:** 229
"Promise of Blue Horses, The" (Harjo), **Supp. XII:** 228
Promise of Rest, The (Price), **Supp. VI:** 262, 266
Promises: Poems 1954–1956 (Warren), **IV:** 244–245, 249, 252
Promises, Promises (musical), **Supp. IV Part 2:** 575
"Promise This When You Be Dying" (Dickinson), **Retro. Supp. I:** 44, 46
Proof, The (Winters), **Supp. II Part 2:** 786, 791, 792–794
Proofs and Theories: Essays on Poetry (Glück), **Supp. V:** 77, 79, 92
"Propaganda of History, The" (Du Bois), **Supp. II Part 1:** 182
Propertius, Sextus, **III:** 467; **Retro. Supp. II:** 187; **Supp. XII:** 2
Property Of: A Novel (Hoffman), **Supp. X:** 77, 79, **80–82**
"Prophecy of Samuel Sewall, The" (Whittier), **Supp. I Part 2:** 699
"Prophetic Pictures, The" (Hawthorne), **II:** 227
"Proportion" (Lowell), **II:** 525
"Proposal" (Carver), **Supp. III Part 1:** 149
Proposals Relating to the Education of Youth in Pensilvania (Franklin), **II:** 113
"Proposed New Version of the Bible" (Franklin), **II:** 110
Prose, Francine, **Supp. XII:** 333
"Prose for Departure" (Merrill), **Supp. III Part 1:** 336
"Prose Poem as an Evolving Form, The" (Bly), **Supp. IV Part 1:** 64
"Proserpina and the Devil" (Wilder), **IV:** 358
"Prosody" (Shapiro), **Supp. II Part 2:** 710
Prospect before Us, The (Dos Passos), **I:** 491
"Prospective Immigrants Please Note" (Rich), **Supp. I Part 2:** 555
Prospect of Peace, The (Barlow), **Supp. II Part 1:** 67, 68, 75
Prospects on the Rubicon (Paine), **Supp. I Part 2:** 510–511
Prospectus of a National Institution, to Be Established in the United States (Barlow), **Supp. II Part 1:** 80, 82
Prospice (Browning), **IV:** 366
"Protestant Easter" (Sexton), **Supp. II Part 2:** 684
"Prothalamion" (Schwartz), **Supp. II**

INDEX / 537

Part 2: 649, 652
"Prothalamion" (Spenser), **Retro. Supp. I:** 62
Proud, Robert, **Supp. I Part 1:** 125
"Proud Farmer, The" (Lindsay), **Supp. I Part 2:** 381
Proud Flesh (Humphrey), **Supp. IX:** 94, 95, 96, **102–103**, 104, 105, 109
"Proud Flesh" (Warren), **IV:** 243
"Proud Lady" (Wylie), **Supp. I Part 2:** 711–712
Proulx, Annie, **Supp. VII: 249–267**
Proust, Marcel, **I:** 89, 319, 327, 377, 461; **II:** 377, 514, 606; **III:** 174, 181, 184, 244–245, 259, 471; **IV:** 32, 201, 237, 301, 312, 328, 359, 428, 431, 434, 439, 443, 466, 467; **Retro. Supp. I:** 75, 89, 169, 335; **Supp. III Part 1:** 10, 12, 14, 15; **Supp. IV Part 2:** 600; **Supp. VIII:** 103; **Supp. IX:** 211; **Supp. X:** 193, 194; **Supp. XII:** 289
Proverbs, **Supp. X:** 45
"Providence" (Komunyakaa), **Supp. XIII:** 132
"Provincia deserta" (Pound), **Retro. Supp. I:** 289
Pruette, Lorine, **Supp. IV Part 2:** 522
Prufrock and Other Observations (Eliot), **I:** 569–570, 571, 573, 574, 576–577, 583, 584, 585; **Retro. Supp. I:** 59, 62
"Prufrock's Perivigilium" (Eliot), **Retro. Supp. I:** 57
Pryor, Richard, **Supp. XIII:** 343
Pryse, Marjorie, **Retro. Supp. II:** 139, 146
"Psalm" (Ginsberg), **Supp. II Part 1:** 312
"Psalm" (Simic), **Supp. VIII:** 282
"Psalm: Our Fathers" (Merwin), **Supp. III Part 1:** 350
"Psalm and Lament" (Justice), **Supp. VII:** 116, 117–118, 120–122, 124
"Psalm of Life, A" (Longfellow), **II:** 489, 496; **Retro. Supp. II:** 164, 168, 169; **Supp. I Part 2:** 409
"Psalm of the West" (Lanier), **Supp. I Part 1:** 362, 364
Psalms (biblical book), **I:** 83; **II:** 168, 232; **Retro. Supp. I:** 62; **Supp. I Part 1:** 125
Psalms, Hymns, and Spiritual Songs of the Rev. Isaac Watts, The (Worcester, ed.), **I:** 458
Psychiatric Novels of Oliver Wendell Holmes, The (Oberndorf), **Supp. I Part 1:** 315
Psychology: Briefer Course (James), **II:** 351–352

"Psychology and Form" (Burke), **I:** 270
Psychology of Art (Malraux), **IV:** 434
Psychology of Insanity, The (Hart), **I:** 241–242, 248–250
Psychophysiks (Fechner), **II:** 358
"Publication is the Auction" (Dickinson), **Retro. Supp. I:** 31
"Public Bath, The" (Snyder), **Supp. VIII:** 298
Public Burning, The (Coover), **Supp. IV Part 1:** 388; **Supp. V:** 44, 45, 46–47, 48, 51, 52
"Public Burning of Julius and Ethel Rosenberg, The: An Historical Romance" (Coover), **Supp. V:** 44
"Public Garden, The" (Lowell), **II:** 550
Public Good (Paine), **Supp. I Part 2:** 509–510
Public Poetry of Robert Lowell, The (Cosgrave), **Retro. Supp. II:** 185
Public Speech: Poems (MacLeish), **III:** 15–16
Public Spirit (Savage), **II:** 111
"Puck" (Monette), **Supp. X:** 157–158
Pudd'nhead Wilson (Twain), **I:** 197
"Pudd'nhead Wilson's Calendar" (Twain), **I:** 197
"Pueblo Revolt, The" (Sando), **Supp. IV Part 2:** 510
Puella (Dickey), **Supp. IV Part 1:** 178, 185
Pulitzer, Alfred, **Retro. Supp. I:** 257
Pull Down Vanity (Fiedler), **Supp. XIII:** 103
Pullman, George, **Supp. I Part 1:** 9
"Pullman Car Hiawatha" (Wilder), **IV:** 365–366
Pull My Daisy (film), **Supp. XII:** 126–127
"Pulpit and the Pew, The" (Holmes), **Supp. I Part 1:** 302
"Pulse-Beats and Pen-Strokes" (Sandburg), **III:** 579
"Pump, The" (Humphrey), **Supp. IX:** 101
Pump House Gang, The (Wolfe), **Supp. III Part 2:** 575, 578, 580, 581
Punch, Brothers, Punch and Other Sketches (Twain), **IV:** 200
Punch: The Immortal Liar, Documents in His History (Aiken), **I:** 57, 61
Punishment Without Vengeance (Vega; Merwin, trans.), **Supp. III Part 1:** 341, 347
"Pupil" (F. Barthelme), **Supp. XI:** 26
"Pupil, The" (James), **II:** 331; **Retro. Supp. I:** 217, 219, 228
"Purchase" (Banks), **Supp. V:** 6
"Purchase of Some Golf Clubs, A"

(O'Hara), **III:** 369
"Purdah" (Plath), **Supp. I Part 2:** 602
Purdy, Charles, **Supp. VIII:** 330
Purdy, James, **Supp. VII: 269–285**
Purdy, Theodore, **Supp. VIII:** 153
"Pure Good of Theory, The" (Stevens), **Retro. Supp. I:** 310
Purgatorio (Dante), **III:** 182
Puritan Family (Morgan), **Supp. I Part 1:** 101
"Puritanical Pleasures" (Hardwick), **Supp. III Part 1:** 213–214
Puritan Origins of the American Self, The (Bercovitch), **Supp. I Part 1:** 99
Puritan Pronaos, The: Studies in the Intellectual Life of New England in the Seventeenth Century (Morison), **Supp. I Part 2:** 485
Puritans, The (P. Miller), **Supp. VIII:** 101
"Puritan's Ballad, The" (Wylie), **Supp. I Part 2:** 723
"Purloined Letter, The" (Poe), **Retro. Supp. II:** 271, 272
Purple Decades, The (Wolfe), **Supp. III Part 2:** 584
"Purple Hat, The" (Welty), **IV:** 264
"Pursuit of Happiness" (Simpson), **Supp. IX:** 279
"Pursuit of Happiness, The" (Ashbery), **Supp. III Part 1:** 23
Pursuit of the Prodigal, The (Auchincloss), **Supp. IV Part 1:** 25
Pushcart at the Curb, A (Dos Passos), **I:** 478, 479
"Pushcart Man" (Hughes), **Supp. I Part 1:** 330
Pushcart Prize, XIII, The (Ford), **Supp. V:** 58
"Pushing 100" (Mora), **Supp. XIII:** 215
Pushkin, Aleksander, **III:** 246, 261, 262; **Retro. Supp. I:** 266, 269
Pussy, King of the Pirates (Acker), **Supp. XII:** 6–7
"Pussycat and the Expert Plumber Who Was a Man, The" (A. Miller), **III:** 146–147
Pussycat Fever (Acker), **Supp. XII:** 6
Putnam, George P., **II:** 314
Putnam, Phelps, **I:** 288
Putnam, Samuel, **II:** 26; **III:** 479; **Supp. III Part 2:** 615
"Put Off the Wedding Five Times and Nobody Comes to It" (Sandburg), **III:** 586–587
Puttenham, George, **Supp. I Part 1:** 113
Puttermesser Papers, The (Ozick),

Supp. V: 269
"Putting on *Visit to a Small Planet*" (Vidal), **Supp. IV Part 2:** 683
Put Yourself in My Shoes (Carver), **Supp. III Part 1:** 139
"Put Yourself in My Shoes" (Carver), **Supp. III Part 1:** 139, 141
Puzo, Mario, **Supp. IV Part 1:** 390
"Puzzle of Modern Society, The" (Kazin), **Supp. VIII:** 103
Pygmalion (Shaw), **Supp. XII:** 14
Pyle, Ernie, **III:** 148; **Supp. V:** 240
Pylon (Faulkner), **II:** 64–65, 73; **Retro. Supp. I:** 84, 85
Pynchon, Thomas, **III:** 258; **Retro. Supp. I:** 278; **Retro. Supp. II:** 297, 342; **Supp. II Part 2:** 557, **617–638**; **Supp. III Part 1:** 217; **Supp. IV Part 1:** 53, 279; **Supp. IV Part 2:** 570; **Supp. V:** 40, 44, 52; **Supp. VIII:** 14; **Supp. IX:** 207, 208, 212; **Supp. X:** 260, 301, 302; **Supp. XI:** 103; **Supp. XII:** 289
Pyrah, Gill, **Supp. V:** 126
"Pyramid Club, The" (Doctorow), **Supp. IV Part 1:** 234
"Pyrography" (Ashbery), **Supp. III Part 1:** 18
Pythagoras, **I:** 332
Pythagorean Silence (Howe), **Supp. IV Part 2:** 426, 428–429
"Qebehseneuf" (Goldbarth), **Supp. XII:** 186
"Quai d'Orléans" (Bishop), **Supp. I Part 1:** 89
"Quail for Mr. Forester" (Humphrey), **Supp. IX:** 94
"Quail in Autumn" (W. J. Smith), **Supp. XIII:** 334–335, 339
"Quaker Graveyard in Nantucket, The" (Lowell), **II:** 54, 550; **Retro. Supp. II:** 178, 186–187
"Quake Theory" (Olds), **Supp. X:** 203
Qualey, Carlton C., **Supp. I Part 2:** 650
"Quality Time" (Kingsolver), **Supp. VII:** 203
Quang-Ngau-chè, **III:** 473
Quarles, Francis, **I:** 178, 179
"Quarry, The" (Nemerov), **III:** 272
Quarry, The: New Poems (Eberhart), **I:** 532, 539
Quartermain, Peter, **Supp. IV Part 2:** 423, 434
"Quaternions, The" (Bradstreet), **Supp. I Part 1:** 104–106, 114, 122
"Quatrains for Ishi" (Komunyakaa), **Supp. XIII:** 129
"Queen of the Blues" (Brooks), **Supp. III Part 1:** 75

Queen of the Damned, The (Rice), **Supp. VII:** 290, 292–293, 297, 299
Queen of the Mob (film), **Supp. XIII:** 170
"Queens of France" (Wilder), **IV:** 365
"Queen's Twin, The" (Jewett), **Retro. Supp. II:** 138
Queen's Twin, The, and Other Stories (Jewett), **Retro. Supp. II:** 140
Queen Victoria (Strachey), **Supp. I Part 2:** 485, 494
Queer (Burroughs), **Supp. III Part 1:** 93–102
"Queer Beer" (Hansberry), **Supp. IV Part 1:** 374
"Quelques considérations sur la méthode subjective" (James), **II:** 345–346
"Question" (Swenson), **Supp. IV Part 2:** 640
"Question and Answer" (Hughes), **Retro. Supp. I:** 211
"Questioning Faces" (Frost), **Retro. Supp. I:** 141
"Question Mark in the Circle, The" (Stegner), **Supp. IV Part 2:** 597
"Questionnaire, The" (Snodgrass), **Supp. VI:** 313
"Question of Fidelity, A" (Beauvoir), **Supp. IX:** 4
"Question of Our Speech, The" (Ozick), **Supp. V:** 272
"Question of Simone de Beauvoir, The" (Algren), **Supp. IX:** 4
"Questions of Geography" (Hollander), **Supp. I Part 1:** 96
Questions of Travel (Bishop), **Retro. Supp. II:** 46–48; **Supp. I Part 1:** 72, 83, 92, 94
"Questions of Travel" (Bishop), **Retro. Supp. II:** 47
"Questions to Tourists Stopped by a Pineapple Field" (Merwin), **Supp. III Part 1:** 355
"Questions without Answers" (T. Williams), **IV:** 384
"Quest of the Purple-Fringed, The" (Frost), **Retro. Supp. I:** 139
Quest of the Silver Fleece, The (Du Bois), **Supp. II Part 1:** 176–178
Quevedo y Villegas, Francisco Gómez, **Retro. Supp. I:** 423
Quickly: A Column for Slow Readers (Mailer), **Retro. Supp. II:** 202
"Quies," (Pound), **Retro. Supp. I:** 413
Quiet Days in Clichy (H. Miller), **III:** 170, 178, 183–184, 187
"Quiet Desperation" (Simpson), **Supp. IX:** 277–278
"Quiet of the Mind" (Nye), **Supp.**

XIII: 284
Quinlan, Kathleen, **Supp. X:** 80
Quinn, John, **III:** 471
Quinn, Paul, **Supp. V:** 71
Quinn, Sister M. Bernetta, **III:** 479; **IV:** 421
Quinn, Vincent, **I:** 386, 401, 402; **Supp. I Part 1:** 270
"Quinnapoxet" (Kunitz), **Supp. III Part 1:** 263
Quinn's Book (Kennedy), **Supp. VII:** 133, 148–150, 153
Quintero, José, **III:** 403
Quintilian, **IV:** 123
Quinzaine for This Yule, A (Pound), **Retro. Supp. I:** 285
Quite Contrary: The Mary and Newt Story (Dixon), **Supp. XII: 144,** 153
Quod Erat Demonstrandum (Stein), **IV:** 34
Quo Vadis? (Sienkiewicz), **Supp. IV Part 2:** 518
Raab, Max, **Supp. XI:** 309
"Rabbi, The" (Hayden), **Supp. II Part 1:** 363, 369
Rabbit, Run (Updike), **IV:** 214, 223, 230–234; **Retro. Supp. I:** 320, 325, 326, 327, 331, 333, 335; **Supp. XI:** 140; **Supp. XII:** 298
"Rabbit, The" (Barnes), **Supp. III Part 1:** 34
Rabbit at Rest (Updike), **Retro. Supp. I:** 334
Rabbit Is Rich (Updike), **Retro. Supp. I:** 334
Rabbit novels (Updike), **Supp. V:** 269
Rabbit Redux (Updike), **IV:** 214; **Retro. Supp. I:** 332, 333
"Rabbits Who Caused All the Trouble, The" (Thurber), **Supp. I Part 2:** 610
Rabelais, and His World (Bakhtin), **Retro. Supp. II:** 273
Rabelais, François, **I:** 130; **II:** 111, 112, 302, 535; **III:** 77, 78, 174, 182; **IV:** 68; **Supp. I Part 2:** 461
Rabelais and His World (Bakhtin), **Supp. X:** 120
Rabinbach, Anson, **Supp. XII:** 166
Rabinowitz, Paula, **Supp. V:** 161
"Race" (Emerson), **II:** 6
"'RACE LINE' IS A PRODUCT OF CAPITALISM, THE" (Baraka), **Supp. II Part 1:** 61
"Race of Life, The" (Thurber), **Supp. I Part 2:** 614
"Race Problems and Modern Society" (Toomer), **Supp. III Part 2:** 486
"Race Riot, Tulsa, 1921" (Olds), **Supp. X:** 205
Race Rock (Matthiessen), **Supp. V:** 201

"Races, The" (Lowell), **II:** 554
Rachel Carson: Witness for Nature (Lear), **Supp. IX:** 19
Racine, Jean Baptiste, **II:** 543, 573; **III:** 145, 151, 152, 160; **IV:** 317, 368, 370; **Supp. I Part 2:** 716
"Radical" (Moore), **III:** 211
"Radical Chic" (Wolfe), **Supp. III Part 2:** 577–578, 584, 585
Radical Chic & Mau-mauing the Flak Catchers (Wolfe), **Supp. III Part 2:** 577–578
Radical Empiricism of William James, The (Wild), **II:** 362, 363–364
Radicalism in America, The (Lasch), **I:** 259
"Radical Jewish Humanism: The Vision of E. L. Doctorow" (Clayton), **Supp. IV Part 1:** 238
"Radically Condensed History of Postindustrial Life, A" (Wallace), **Supp. X:** 309
"Radio" (O'Hara), **III:** 369
"Radio Pope" (Goldbarth), **Supp. XII:** 188, 192
Raditzer (Matthiessen), **Supp. V:** 201
Radkin, Paul, **Supp. I Part 2:** 539
"Rafaela Who Drinks Coconut & Papaya Juice on Tuesdays" (Cisneros), **Supp. VII:** 63
"Raft, The" (Lindsay), **Supp. I Part 2:** 393
Rag and Bone Shop of the Heart, The: Poems for Men (Bly, Hillman, and Meade, eds.), **Supp. IV Part 1:** 67
Rage to Live, A (O'Hara), **III:** 361
Raglan, Lord, **I:** 135
Rago, Henry, **Supp. III Part 2:** 624, 628, 629
Ragtime (Doctorow), **Retro. Supp. II:** 108; **Supp. IV Part 1:** 217, 222–224, 231, 232, 233, 234, 237, 238; **Supp. V:** 45
"Ragtime" (Doctorow), **Supp. IV Part 1:** 234
Ragtime (film), **Supp. IV Part 1:** 236
Ragtime (musical, McNally), **Supp. XIII:** 207
Rahv, Philip, **Retro. Supp. I:** 112; **Supp. II Part 1:** 136; **Supp. VIII:** 96; **Supp. IX:** 8
"Raid" (Hughes), **Retro. Supp. I:** 208
Raids on the Unspeakable (Merton), **Supp. VIII:** 201, 208
Rail, DeWayne, **Supp. XIII:** 312
"Rain and the Rhinoceros" (Merton), **Supp. VIII:** 201
Rainbow, The (Lawrence), **III:** 27
"Rainbows" (Marquand), **III:** 56
Rainbow Tulip, The (Mora), **Supp. XIII:** 221
"Rain Country" (Haines), **Supp. XII:** 210
"Rain-Dream, A" (Bryant), **Supp. I Part 1:** 164
Raine, Kathleen, **I:** 522, 527
"Rain Falling Now, The" (Dunn), **Supp. XI:** 147
"Rain in the Heart" (Taylor), **Supp. V:** 317, 319
Rain in the Trees, The (Merwin), **Supp. III Part 1:** 340, 342, 345, 349, 354–356
"Rainmaker, The" (Humphrey), **Supp. IX:** 101
Rainwater, Catherine, **Supp. V:** 272
"Rainy Day" (Longfellow), **II:** 498
"Rainy Day, The" (Buck), **Supp. II Part 1:** 127
"Rainy Mountain Cemetery" (Momaday), **Supp. IV Part 2:** 486
Rainy Mountain Christmas Doll (painting) (Momaday), **Supp. IV Part 2:** 493
"Rainy Season: Sub-Tropics" (Bishop), **Supp. I Part 1:** 93
"Raise High the Roof Beam, Carpenters" (Salinger), **III:** 567–569, 571
Raise High the Roof Beam, Carpenters; and Seymour: An Introduction (Salinger), **III:** 552, 567–571, 572
Raise Race Rays Raze: Essays Since 1965 (Baraka), **Supp. II Part 1:** 47, 52, 55
Raisin (musical), **Supp. IV Part 1:** 374
Raising Demons (Jackson), **Supp. IX:** 125–126
Raisin in the Sun, A (film: Columbia Pictures), **Supp. IV Part 1:** 360, 367
Raisin in the Sun, A (Hansberry), **Supp. IV Part 1:** 359, 360, 361, 362–364; **Supp. VIII:** 343
Raisin in the Sun, A (television film: American Playhouse), **Supp. IV Part 1:** 367, 374
Raisin in the Sun, A (unproduced screenplay) (Hansberry), **Supp. IV Part 1:** 360
Rajan, R., **I:** 390
Rake's Progress, The (opera), **Supp. II Part 1:** 24
Rakosi, Carl, **Supp. III Part 2:** 614, 615, 616, 617, 618, 621, 629
Ralegh, Sir Walter, **Supp. I Part 1:** 98
Raleigh, John Henry, **IV:** 366
Ramakrishna, Sri, **III:** 567
Ramazani, Jahan, **Supp. IV Part 2:** 450
"Ramble of Aphasia, A" (O. Henry), **Supp. II Part 1:** 410
Ramey, Phillip, **Supp. IV Part 1:** 94
Rampersad, Arnold, **Retro. Supp. I:** 196, 200, 201, 204; **Supp. IV Part 1:** 244, 250
Rampling, Anne, **Supp. VII:** 201. *See also* Rice, Anne
Rampling, Charlotte, **Supp. IX:** 253
Ramsey, Priscilla R., **Supp. IV Part 1:** 15
Ramus, Petrus, **Supp. I Part 1:** 104
Rand, Ayn, **Supp. I Part 1:** 294; **Supp. IV Part 2: 517–535**
Randall, Jarrell, 1914–1965 (Lowell, Taylor, and Warren, eds.), **II:** 368, 385
Randall, John H., **III:** 605
Randolph, John, **I:** 5–6
"Range-Finding" (Frost), **Retro. Supp. I:** 131
Rangoon (F. Barthelme), **Supp. XI:** 25
Rank, Otto, **I:** 135; **Supp. IX:** 105; **Supp. X:** 183, 185, 193
Ranke, Leopold von, **Supp. I Part 2:** 492
Rankin, Daniel, **Retro. Supp. II:** 57, 72; **Supp. I Part 1:** 200, 203, 225
Ransohoff, Martin, **Supp. XI:** 305, 306
Ransom, John Crowe, **I:** 265, 301; **II:** 34, 367, 385, 389, 536–537, 542; **III:** 454, **480–502,** 549; **IV:** 121, 122, 123, 124, 125, 127, 134, 140, 141, 236, 237, 433; **Retro. Supp. I:** 90; **Retro. Supp. II:** 176, 177, 178, 183, 220, 228, 246; **Supp. I Part 1:** 80, 361; **Supp. I Part 2:** 423; **Supp. II Part 1:** 90, 91, 136, 137, 139, 318; **Supp. II Part 2:** 639; **Supp. III Part 1:** 318; **Supp. III Part 2:** 542, 591; **Supp. IV Part 1:** 217; **Supp. V:** 315, 331, 337; **Supp. X:** 25, 56, 58
"Rape" (Coleman), **Supp. XI:** 89–90
"Rape, The" (Baraka), **Supp. II Part 1:** 40
Rape of Bunny Stuntz, The (Gurney), **Supp. V:** 109
"Rape of Philomel, The" (Shapiro), **Supp. II Part 2:** 720
Raphael, **I:** 15; **III:** 505, 521, 524; **Supp. I Part 1:** 363
"Rapist" (Dunn), **Supp. XI:** 144
Rap on Race, A (Baldwin and Mead), **Supp. I Part 1:** 66
"Rappaccini's Daughter" (Hawthorne), **II:** 229
"Rapunzel" (Sexton), **Supp. II Part 2:** 691
Rare & Endangered Species: A Novella & Short Stories (Bausch), **Supp.**

VII: 51, 54
"Raree Show" (MacLeish), **III:** 9
Rascoe, Burton, **III:** 106, 115
"Raskolnikov" (Simic), **Supp. VIII:** 282
Rasmussen, Douglas, **Supp. IV Part 2:** 528, 530
Rasselas (Johnson), **Supp. XI:** 209
"Ration" (Baraka), **Supp. II Part 1:** 50
"Rationale of Verse, The" (Poe), **III:** 427–428; **Retro. Supp. II:** 266
Ratner's Star (DeLillo), **Supp. VI:** 1, 2, 3, 4, 10, 12, 14
"Rat of Faith, The" (Levine), **Supp. V:** 192
Rattigan, Terence, **III:** 152
Raugh, Joseph, **Supp. I Part 1:** 286
Rauschenbusch, Walter, **III:** 293; **Supp. I Part 1:** 7
Ravelstein (Bellow), **Retro. Supp. II:** 19, **33–34**
Raven, Simon, **Supp. XII:** 241
"Raven, The" (Poe), **III:** 413, 421–422, 426; **Retro. Supp. II:** 265, 266–267
Raven, The, and Other Poems (Poe), **III:** 413
Ravenal, Shannon, **Supp. IV Part 1:** 93
"Raven Days, The" (Lanier), **Supp. I Part 1:** 351
Ravenna, Michael. *See* Welty, Eudora
Raven's Road (Gunn Allen), **Supp. IV Part 1:** 330, 335
Rawlings, Marjorie Kinnan, **Supp. X: 219–237**
Ray, David, **Supp. IV Part 1:** 61
Ray, Jeanne Wilkinson, **Supp. XII:** 308, 310
Ray, John, **II:** 111, 112
Ray, Man, **IV:** 404; **Retro. Supp. I:** 416; **Supp. XII:** 124
Ray Bradbury Theatre, The (television show), **Supp. IV Part 1:** 103
Reactionary Essays on Poetry and Ideas (Tate), **Supp. II Part 1:** 106, 146
Read, Deborah, **II:** 122
Read, Forrest, **III:** 478
Read, Herbert, **I:** 523; **II:** 372–373, 377–378; **Retro. Supp. I:** 54; **Supp. III Part 1:** 273; **Supp. III Part 2:** 624, 626
Reade, Charles, **Supp. I Part 2:** 580
Reader, Constant. *See* Parker, Dorothy
Reader, Dennis J., **Supp. I Part 2:** 454
Reader's Encyclopedia, The: An Encyclopedia of World Literature and the Arts (W. Benét), **Supp. XI:** 44
Reader's Guide to William Gaddis's The Recognitions, A (Moore), **Supp. IV Part 1:** 283
"Reader's Tale, A" (Doty), **Supp. XI:** 119, 120, 128, 129
"Reading" (Auden), **Supp. VIII:** 155
"Reading Group Guide," **Supp. XI:** 244–245
"Reading Lao Tzu Again in the New Year" (Wright), **Supp. V:** 343
"Reading Late of the Death of Keats" (Kenyon), **Supp. VII:** 169
"Reading Myself" (Lowell), **II:** 555
Reading Myself and Others (Roth), **Retro. Supp. II:** 300; **Supp. V:** 45
"Reading of the Psalm, The" (Francis), **Supp. IX:** 79
"Reading Philosophy at Night" (Simic), **Supp. VIII:** 272
Reading Rilke: Reflections on the Problems of Translation (Gass), **Supp. VI:** 92, **93–94**
"Reading Rorty and Paul Celan One Morning in Early June" (Wright), **Supp. V:** 343
"Readings of History" (Rich), **Supp. I Part 2:** 554
"Reading the Signs, Empowering the Eye" (Bambara), **Supp. XI:** 17–18
Reading the Spirit (Eberhart), **I:** 525, 527, 530
"Ready Or Not" (Baraka), **Supp. II Part 1:** 50
Reagan, Ronald, **Supp. IV Part 1:** 224–225
"Real Class" (Vidal), **Supp. IV Part 1:** 35
Real Dope, The (Lardner), **II:** 422–423
"Real Estate" (Moore), **Supp. X:** 178
"Real Gone Guy, A" (McGrath), **Supp. X:** 117
"Real Horatio Alger Story, The" (Cowley), **Supp. II Part 1:** 143
"Realities" (MacLeish), **III:** 4
"Reality in America" (Trilling), **Supp. III Part 2:** 495, 502
"Reality! Reality! What Is It?" (Eberhart), **I:** 536
Reality Sandwiches, 1953–60 (Ginsberg), **Supp. II Part 1:** 315, 320
Real Life of Sebastian Knight, The (Nabokov), **III:** 246; **Retro. Supp. I:** 266, 269, 270, 274
"Really Good Jazz Piano, A" (Yates), **Supp. XI:** 342
Real Presence: A Novel (Bausch), **Supp. VII:** 42–43, 50
"Real Revolution Is Love, The" (Harjo), **Supp. XII:** 224, 225–226
"Real Thing, The" (H. James), **Retro. Supp. I:** 228; **Retro. Supp. II:** 223
"Real Two-Party System" (Vidal), **Supp. IV Part 2:** 679
Real West Marginal Way, The (Hugo), **Supp. VI:** 132, 134
"Real World around Us, The" (Carson), **Supp. IX:** 21
Reaper Essays, The (Jarman and McDowell), **Supp. IX:** 270
"Reapers" (Toomer), **Supp. III Part 2:** 481; **Supp. IX:** 312
"Reason for Moving, A" (Strand), **Supp. IV Part 2:** 624
"Reason for Stories, The: Toward a Moral Fiction" (Stone), **Supp. V:** 298, 300
Reasons for Moving (Strand), **Supp. IV Part 2:** 624–626, 626
"Reasons for Music" (MacLeish), **III:** 19
"Rebellion" (Lowell), **Retro. Supp. II:** 187
Rebel Powers (Bausch), **Supp. VII:** 41, 45–46, 49–51
Rebel without a Cause (film), **Supp. XII:** 9
"Rebirth of God and the Death of Man, The " (Fiedler), **Supp. XIII:** 108
Rebolledo, Tey Diana, **Supp. XIII:** 214
Recapitulation (Stegner), **Supp. IV Part 2:** 598, 600, 612–613
"Recapitulation, The" (Eberhart), **I:** 522
"Recapitulations" (Shapiro), **Supp. II Part 2:** 701, 702, 708, 710–711
"Recencies in Poetry" (Zukofsky), **Supp. III Part 2:** 615
Recent Killing, A (Baraka), **Supp. II Part 1:** 55
"Recent Negro Fiction" (Ellison), **Supp. II Part 1:** 233, 235
"Recital, The" (Ashbery), **Supp. III Part 1:** 14
"Recitative" (H. Crane), **I:** 390; **Retro. Supp. II:** 78
Reckless Eyeballing (Reed), **Supp. X:** 241
Recognitions, The (Gaddis), **Supp. IV Part 1:** 279, 280–285, 286, 287, 288, 289, 291, 292, 294
"Reconciliation" (Whitman), **IV:** 347
"Reconstructed but Unregenerate" (Ransom), **III:** 496
"Reconstruction and Its Benefits" (Du Bois), **Supp. II Part 1:** 171
Recovering (Sarton), **Supp. VIII:** 264
Recovering the U.S. Hispanic Literary Heritage (Paredes), **Supp. XIII:** 320
"Recovery" (Dove), **Supp. IV Part 1:** 248

INDEX / 541

Rector of Justin, The (Auchincloss), **Supp. IV Part 1:** 21, 23, 27–30, 36
"RED AUTUMN" (Baraka), **Supp. II Part 1:** 55
Red Badge of Courage, The (Crane), **I:** 201, 207, 212, 405, 406, 407, 408, 412–416, 419, 421, 422, 423, 477, 506; **II:** 264; **III:** 317; **IV:** 350; **Retro. Supp. II:** 108; **Supp. IV Part 1:** 380
"Redbreast in Tampa" (Lanier), **Supp. I Part 1:** 364
"Red Brocade" (Nye), **Supp. XIII:** 288
Redburn: His First Voyage (Melville), **III:** 79–80, 84; **Retro. Supp. I:** 245, 247–248, 249
"Red Carpet for Shelley, A" (Wylie), **Supp. I Part 2:** 724
"Red Clowns" (Cisneros), **Supp. VII:** 63
Red Coal, The (Stern), **Supp. IX:** 291–292
"Red Cross" (Hughes), **Retro. Supp. I:** 205
Red Cross (Shepard), **Supp. III Part 2:** 440, 446
Red Death, A (Mosley), **Supp. XIII:** 237, 239, 240
Redding, Saunders, **Supp. I Part 1:** 332, 333
Reddings, J. Saunders, **Supp. IV Part 1:** 164
Red Dust (Levine), **Supp. V:** 178, 183–184, 188
"Red Dust" (Levine), **Supp. V:** 184
"Redemption" (Gardner), **Supp. VI:** 72
"Redeployment" (Nemerov), **III:** 267, 272
Redfield, Robert, **IV:** 475
Redford, Robert, **Supp. IX:** 253, 259; **Supp. XIII:** 267
Redgrave, Lynn, **Supp. V:** 107
Red Harvest (Hammett), **Supp. IV Part 1:** 346–348, 348; **Supp. IV Part 2:** 468
Red-headed Woman (film), **Retro. Supp. I:** 110
"Red Horse Wind over Albuquerque" (Harjo), **Supp. XII:** 219
Red Hot Vacuum, The (Solotaroff), **Retro. Supp. II:** 299
"Red Leaves" (Faulkner), **II:** 72
"Red Meat: What Difference Did Stesichoros Make?" (Carson), **Supp. XII:** 107
"Red Pawn" (Rand), **Supp. IV Part 2:** 520
Red Pony, The (Steinbeck), **IV:** 50, 51, 58, 70

Redrawing the Boundaries (Fisher), **Retro. Supp. I:** 39
Red Roses for Bronze (Doolittle), **Supp. I Part 1:** 253, 268, 271
Red Rover, The (Cooper), **I:** 342–343, 355
"Red Silk Stockings" (Hughes), **Retro. Supp. I:** 200
Redskins, The (Cooper), **I:** 351, 353
Red Suitcase (Nye), **Supp. XIII:** 277, 278, 287
"Red Wheelbarrow, The" (W. C. Williams), **IV:** 411–412; **Retro. Supp. I:** 419, 430
"Red Wind" (Chandler), **Supp. IV Part 1:** 122
"Redwings" (Wright), **Supp. III Part 2:** 603
Reed, Ishmael, **Retro. Supp. II:** 111, 342–343; **Supp. II Part 1:** 34; **Supp. X:** 239–257, 331; **Supp. XIII:** 181, 182
Reed, John, **I:** 48, 476, 483; **Supp. X:** 136
Reed, Lou, **Retro. Supp. II:** 266
"Reedbeds of the Hackensack, The" (Clampitt), **Supp. IX:** 41
"Reed of Pan, A" (McCullers), **II:** 585
Reedy, Billy, **Retro. Supp. II:** 65, 67, 71, 73
Reedy, William Marion, **Supp. I Part 2:** 456, 461, 465
Reef, The (Wharton), **IV:** 317–318, 322; **Retro. Supp. I:** 372, 373–374
Reena and Other Stories (Marshall), **Supp. XI:** 275, 277, 278
Reeve's Tale (Chaucer), **I:** 131
"Reflections" (Komunyakaa), **Supp. XIII:** 117
Reflections: Thinking Part I (Arendt), **Supp. I Part 2:** 570
Reflections at Fifty and Other Essays (Farrell), **II:** 49
"Reflections by a Fire" (Sarton), **Supp. VIII:** 259
Reflections in a Golden Eye (McCullers), **II:** 586, 588, 593–596, 604; **IV:** 384, 396
Reflections of a Jacobite (Auchincloss), **Supp. IV Part 1:** 31
Reflections on Poetry and Poetics (Nemerov), **III:** 269
"Reflections on the Constitution of Nature" (Freneau), **Supp. II Part 1:** 274
"Reflections on the Death of the Reader" (Morris), **III:** 237
Reflections on the End of an Era (Niebuhr), **III:** 297–298
"Reflections on the Life and Death of Lord Clive" (Paine), **Supp. I Part 2:** 505
Reflections on the Revolution in France (Burke), **Supp. I Part 2:** 511, 512
"Reflex Action and Theism" (James), **II:** 345, 363
"Refrains/Remains/Reminders" (Goldbarth), **Supp. XII:** 180–181, 181
"Refuge" (Kingsolver), **Supp. VII:** 208
"Refuge, A" (Goldbarth), **Supp. XII:** 190
Refugee Children: Theory, Research, and Services (Ahearn and Athey, eds.), **Supp. XI:** 184
"Refugees, The" (Jarrell), **II:** 371
Regarding Wave (Snyder), **Supp. VIII:** 299–300
Regina (Epstein), **Supp. XII:** 170–171
"Regional Literature of the South" (Rawlings), **Supp. X:** 228
"Regional Writer, The" (O'Connor), **Retro. Supp. II:** 223, 225
Régnier, Henri de, **II:** 528–529
Regulators, The (King), **Supp. V:** 141
Rehder, Robert, **Supp. IV Part 1:** 69
Reichel, Hans, **III:** 183
Reichl, Ruth, **Supp. X:** 79, 85
Reid, B. L., **II:** 41, 47
Reid, Thomas, **II:** 9; **Supp. I Part 1:** 151
Reign of Wonder, The (Tanner), **I:** 260
Rein, Yevgeny, **Supp. VIII:** 22
"Reincarnation" (Dickey), **Supp. IV Part 1:** 181–182
Reiner, Carl, **Supp. IV Part 2:** 591
Reinfeld, Linda, **Supp. IV Part 2:** 421
Reinventing the Enemy's Language: Contemporary Native Women's Writing of North America (Bird and Harjo, eds.), **Supp. XII:** 216, 217
Reisman, Jerry, **Supp. III Part 2:** 618
Reitlinger, Gerald, **Supp. XII:** 161
Reivers, The: A Reminiscence (Faulkner), **I:** 305; **II:** 57, 73; **Retro. Supp. I:** 74, 82, 91
"Rejoicings" (Stern), **Supp. IX:** 289–290
Rejoicings: Selected Poems, 1966–1972 (Stern), **Supp. IX:** 289–290
Relation of My Imprisonment, The (Banks), **Supp. V:** 8, 12–13
"Relations between Poetry and Painting, The" (Stevens), **Retro. Supp. I:** 312
"Relativity of Beauty, The" (Rawlings), **Supp. X:** 226
Relearning the Alphabet (Levertov), **Supp. III Part 1:** 280, 281
"Release, The" (MacLeish), **III:** 16

Reles, Abe ("Kid Twist"), **Supp. IV Part 1:** 382
"Relevance of an Impossible Ethical Ideal, The" (Niebuhr), **III:** 298
"Religion" (Dunbar), **Supp. II Part 1:** 199
"Religion" (Emerson), **II:** 6
Religion of Nature Delineated, The (Wollaston), **II:** 108
"Reluctance" (Frost), **II:** 153
Remains (Snodgrass), **Supp. VI:** 311, **313–314**
"Remains, The" (Strand), **Supp. IV Part 2:** 627
"Remarks on Spencer's *Definition of Mind as Correspondence*" (James), **II:** 345
Remarque, Erich Maria, **Retro. Supp. I:** 113; **Supp. IV Part 1:** 380
Rembrandt, **II:** 536; **IV:** 310; **Supp. IV Part 1:** 390, 391
"Rembrandt, The" (Wharton), **IV:** 310
"Rembrandt's Hat" (Malamud), **Supp. I Part 2:** 435, 437
Rembrandt Takes a Walk (Strand), **Supp. IV Part 2:** 631
"Rembrandt to Rembrandt" (Robinson), **III:** 521–522
Remembered Earth, The: An Anthology of Contemporary Native American Literature (Hobson, ed.), **Supp. IV Part 1:** 321
Remembered Yesterdays (Johnson), **Supp. IX:** 184
"Remembering" (Angelou), **Supp. IV Part 1:** 15
"Remembering Allen Tate" (Cowley), **Supp. II Part 1:** 153
"Remembering Barthes" (Sontag), **Supp. III Part 2:** 451, 471
"Remembering Guston" (Kunitz), **Supp. III Part 1:** 257
"Remembering James Laughlin" (Karr), **Supp. XI:** 242
Remembering Laughter (Stegner), **Supp. IV Part 2:** 598, 606, 607, 608, 611, 614
"Remembering Lobo" (Mora), **Supp. XIII:** 220, 227
"Remembering My Father" (Berry), **Supp. X:** 23
"Remembering that Island" (McGrath), **Supp. X:** 116
"Remembering the Children of Auschwitz" (McGrath), **Supp. X:** 127
"Remembering the Lost World" (Jarrell), **II:** 388
"Remembering the Sixties" (Simpson), **Supp. IX:** 279
Remember Me to Tom (T. Williams), **IV:** 379–380
"Remember the Moon Survives" (Kingsolver), **Supp. VII:** 209
Remember to Remember (H. Miller), **III:** 186
Remembrance of Things Past (Proust), **Supp. IV Part 2:** 600; **Supp. XII:** 9; **Supp. XIII:** 44
Remembrance Rock (Sandburg), **III:** 590
Reminiscence, A (Ashbery), **Supp. III Part 1:** 2
"Remora" (Merrill), **Supp. III Part 1:** 326
"Removal" (White), **Supp. I Part 2:** 664–665
"Removal, The" (Merwin), **Supp. III Part 1:** 350, 351
Removed from Time (Matthews and Feeney), **Supp. IX:** 154
Remsen, Ira, **Supp. I Part 1:** 369
"Rémy de Gourmont, A Distinction" (Pound), **III:** 467
Renaissance in the South (Bradbury), **I:** 288–289
"Renaming the Kings" (Levine), **Supp. V:** 184
Renan, Joseph Ernest, **II:** 86; **IV:** 440, 444
Renard, Jules, **IV:** 79
"Renascence" (Millay), **III:** 123, 125–126, 128
Renault, Mary, **Supp. IV Part 2:** 685
"Rendezvous, The" (Kumin), **Supp. IV Part 2:** 455
René, Norman, **Supp. X:** 146, 152
"Renegade, The" (Jackson), **Supp. IX:** 120
Renewal of Life series (Mumford), **Supp. II Part 2:** 476, 479, 481, 482, 485, 495, 497
Renoir, Jean, **Supp. XII:** 259
Renouvrier, Charles, **II:** 344–345, 346
"Renunciation" (Banks), **Supp. V:** 10
Renza, Louis A., **Retro. Supp. II:** 142
Repent in Haste (Marquand), **III:** 59
"Repetitive Heart, The: Eleven Poems in Imitation of the Fugue Form" (Schwartz), **Supp. II Part 2:** 645–646
"Replacing Regionalism" (Murphy), **Retro. Supp. II:** 143
Replansky, Naomi, **Supp. X:** 119
"Reply to Mr. Wordsworth" (MacLeish), **III:** 19
"Report from a Forest Logged by the Weyhaeuser Company" (Wagoner), **Supp. IX:** 328
"Report from North Vietnam" (Paley), **Supp. VI:** 227

Report from Part One (Brooks), **Supp. III Part 1:** 70, 72, 80, 82–85
Report from Part Two (Brooks), **Supp. III Part 1:** 87
"Report on the Barnhouse Effect" (Vonnegut), **Supp. II Part 2:** 756
"Report to Crazy Horse" (Stafford), **Supp. XI: 324–325**
"Repose of Rivers" (H. Crane), **I:** 393; **Retro. Supp. II:** 78, 81
"Representation and the War for Reality" (Gass), **Supp. VI:** 88
Representative Men (Emerson), **II:** 1, 5–6, 8
"Representing Far Places" (Stafford), **Supp. XI:** 321
"REPRISE OF ONE OF A. G.'S BEST POEMS" (Baraka), **Supp. II Part 1:** 59
Republic (Plato), **I:** 485
"Republican Manifesto, A" (Paine), **Supp. I Part 2:** 511
Republic of Love, The (Shields), **Supp. VII:** 323–324, 326, 327
"Requa" (Olsen), **Supp. XIII:** 294, **302–303**, 304
Requa, Kenneth A., **Supp. I Part 1:** 107
"Requa I" (Olsen). *See* "Requa" (Olsen)
"Request for Offering" (Eberhart), **I:** 526
"Requiem" (Akhmatova), **Supp. VIII:** 20
"Requiem" (LaBastille), **Supp. X:** 105
Requiem for a Nun (Faulkner), **II:** 57, 72–73
Requiem for Harlem (H. Roth), **Supp. IX:** 235, 236, **240–242**
"Rescue, The" (Updike), **IV:** 214
Rescued Year, The (Stafford), **Supp. XI: 321–322**
"Rescued Year, The" (Stafford), **Supp. XI:** 322, 323
"Rescue with Yul Brynner" (Moore), **III:** 215
"Resemblance" (Bishop), **Supp. I Part 1:** 86
"Resemblance between a Violin Case and a Coffin, A" (T. Williams), **IV:** 378–379
"Reservations" (Taylor), **Supp. V:** 323
"Reserved Memorials" (Mather), **Supp. II Part 2:** 446, 449
"Resistance to Civil Government" (Thoreau), **Supp. X:** 27, 28
Resist Much, Obey Little (Berry), **Supp. XIII:** 2
Resources of Hope (R. Williams), **Supp. IX:** 146

"Respectable Place, A" (O'Hara), **III:** 369

"Respectable Woman, A" (Chopin), **Retro. Supp. II:** 66

Responses (Wilbur), **Supp. III Part 2:** 541

"Response to a Rumor that the Oldest Whorehouse in Wheeling, West Virginia, Has Been Condemned" (Wright), **Supp. III Part 2:** 602

Restif de La Bretonne, Nicolas, **III:** 175

"Rest of Life, The" (Gordon), **Supp. IV Part 1:** 311

Rest of Life, The: Three Novellas (Gordon), **Supp. IV Part 1:** 310–312

Rest of the Way, The (McClatchy), **Supp. XII:** 255, **258–259**

Restoration comedy, **Supp. I Part 2:** 617

"Restraint" (F. Barthelme), **Supp. XI:** 26

"Result" (Emerson), **II:** 6

"Résumé" (Parker), **Supp. IX:** 189

"Resurrection" (Harjo), **Supp. XII:** 224

Resurrection, The (Gardner), **Supp. VI:** 61, 63, **64–65**, 68, 69, 73, 74

Retrieval System, The (Kumin), **Supp. IV Part 2:** 449, 451, 452

"Retrievers in Translation" (Doty), **Supp. XI:** 132

"Retroduction to American History" (Tate), **IV:** 129

"Retrospects and Prospects" (Lanier), **Supp. I Part 1:** 352

"Return" (Corso), **Supp. XII:** 135

"Return" (Creeley), **Supp. IV Part 1:** 141, 145

"Return" (MacLeish), **III:** 12

"Return: An Elegy, The" (Warren), **IV:** 239

"Return: Buffalo" (Hogan), **Supp. IV Part 1:** 411

"Return, The" (Pound), **Retro. Supp. I:** 288

"Return, The" (Roethke), **III:** 533

"Return, The: Orihuela, 1965" (Levine), **Supp. V:** 194

"Returning" (Komunyakaa), **Supp. XIII:** 122

"Returning a Lost Child" (Glück), **Supp. V:** 81

"Returning from the Enemy" (Harjo), **Supp. XII:** 229–230

"Returning the Borrowed Road" (Komunyakaa), **Supp. XIII:** 113, 133

"Return of Alcibiade, The" (Chopin), **Retro. Supp. II:** 58, 64

Return of Ansel Gibbs, The (Buechner), **III:** 310; **Supp. XII:** 48

"Return of Spring" (Winters), **Supp. II Part 2:** 791

Return of the Native, The (Hardy), **II:** 184–185, 186

Return of the Vanishing American, The (Fiedler), **Supp. XIII:** 103

Return to a Place Lit by a Glass of Milk (Simic), **Supp. VIII:** 274, 276, 283

"Return to Lavinia" (Caldwell), **I:** 310

Reuben (Wideman), **Supp. X:** 320

"Reunion in Brooklyn" (H. Miller), **III:** 175, 184

Reuther brothers, **I:** 493

"Rev. Freemont Deadman" (Masters), **Supp. I Part 2:** 463

"Reveille" (Kingsolver), **Supp. VII:** 208

"Reveille, The" (Harte), **Supp. II Part 1:** 342–343

Revelation (biblical book), **II:** 541; **IV:** 104, 153, 154; **Supp. I Part 1:** 105, 273

"Revelation" (O'Connor), **III:** 349, 353–354; **Retro. Supp. II:** 237

"Revelation" (Warren), **III:** 490

Revenge (Harrison), **Supp. VIII:** 39, 45

"Revenge of Hamish, The" (Lanier), **Supp. I Part 1:** 365

"Revenge of Hannah Kemhuff, The" (Walker), **Supp. III Part 2:** 521

"Revenge of Rain-in-the-Face, The" (Longfellow), **Retro. Supp. II:** 170

Reverberator, The (James), **Retro. Supp. I:** 227

"Reverdure" (Berry), **Supp. X:** 22

"Reverend Father Gilhooley" (Farrell), **II:** 45

Reverse Transcription (Kushner), **Supp. IX:** 138

Reviewer's ABC, A (Aiken), **I:** 58

"Revolt, against the Crepuscular Spirit in Modern Poetry" (Pound), **Retro. Supp. I:** 286

Revolutionary Petunias (Walker), **Supp. III Part 2:** 520, 522, 530

Revolutionary Road (Yates), **Supp. XI:** 334, **335–340**

"Revolutionary Symbolism in America" (Burke), **I:** 272

"Revolutionary Theatre, The" (Baraka), **Supp. II Part 1:** 42

Revolution in Taste, A: Studies of Dylan Thomas, Allen Ginsberg, Sylvia Plath, and Robert Lowell (Simpson), **Supp. IX:** 276

"Revolution in the Revolution in the Revolution" (Snyder), **Supp. VIII:** 300

Revon, Marcel, **II:** 525

"Rewaking, The" (W. C. Williams), **Retro. Supp. I:** 430

"Rewrite" (Dunn), **Supp. XI:** 147

Rexroth, Kenneth, **II:** 526; **Supp. II Part 1:** 307; **Supp. II Part 2:** 436; **Supp. III Part 2:** 625, 626; **Supp. IV Part 1:** 145–146; **Supp. VIII:** 289; **Supp. XIII:** 75

Reynolds, Clay, **Supp. XI:** 254

Reynolds, Quentin, **IV:** 286

Reynolds, Sir Joshua, **Supp. I Part 2:** 716

Reznikoff, Charles, **IV:** 415; **Retro. Supp. I:** 422; **Supp. III Part 2:** 615, 616, 617, 628

"Rhapsodist, The" (Brown), **Supp. I Part 1:** 125–126

"Rhapsody on a Windy Night" (Eliot), **Retro. Supp. I:** 55

Rhetoric of Motives, A (Burke), **I:** 272, 275, 278, 279

Rhetoric of Religion, The (Burke), **I:** 275, 279

"Rhobert" (Toomer), **Supp. IX:** 316–317

"Rhododendrons" (Levis), **Supp. XI:** 260, 263

"Rhyme of Sir Christopher, The" (Longfellow), **II:** 501

Rhymes to Be Traded for Bread (Lindsay), **Supp. I Part 2:** 380, 381–382

Rhys, Ernest, **III:** 458

Rhys, Jean, **Supp. III Part 1:** 42, 43

"Rhythm & Blues" (Baraka), **Supp. II Part 1:** 37–38

Ribalow, Harold, **Supp. IX:** 236

Ribbentrop, Joachim von, **IV:** 249

Ribicoff, Abraham, **Supp. IX:** 33

Ricardo, David, **Supp. I Part 2:** 628, 634

Rice, Allen Thorndike, **Retro. Supp. I:** 362

Rice, Anne, **Supp. VII:** **287–306**

Rice, Elmer, **I:** 479; **III:** 145, 160–161

Rice, Mrs. Grantland, **II:** 435

Rice, Philip Blair, **IV:** 141

Rice, Stan, **Supp. XII:** 2

Rich, Adrienne, **Retro. Supp. I:** 8, 36, 42, 47, 404; **Retro. Supp. II:** 43, 191, 245, **279–296**; **Supp. I Part 2:** 546–547, **550–578**; **Supp. III Part 1:** 84, 354; **Supp. III Part 2:** 541, 599; **Supp. IV Part 1:** 257, 325; **Supp. V:** 82; **Supp. VIII:** 272; **Supp. XII:** 217, 229, 255; **Supp. XIII:** 294

Rich, Arnold, **Supp. I Part 2:** 552
Rich, Frank, **Supp. IV Part 2:** 585, 586; **Supp. V:** 106
Richard Cory (Gurney), **Supp. V:** 99–100, 105
"Richard Hunt's 'Arachne'" (Hayden), **Supp. II Part 1:** 374
Richard III (Shakespeare), **Supp. I Part 2:** 422
Richards, David, **Supp. IV Part 2:** 576
Richards, Grant, **I:** 515
Richards, I. A., **I:** 26, 273–274, 279, 522; **III:** 498; **IV:** 92; **Supp. I Part 1:** 264, 265; **Supp. I Part 2:** 647
Richards, Laura E., **II:** 396; **III:** 505–506, 507
Richards, Lloyd, **Supp. IV Part 1:** 362; **Supp. VIII:** 331
Richards, Rosalind, **III:** 506
Richardson, Alan, **III:** 295
Richardson, Dorothy, **I:** 53; **II:** 320; **Supp. III Part 1:** 65
Richardson, Helen Patges, **Retro. Supp. II:** 95
Richardson, Henry Hobson, **I:** 3, 10
Richardson, Maurice, **Supp. XII:** 241
Richardson, Samuel, **I:** 134; **II:** 104, 111, 322; **Supp. V:** 127; **Supp. IX:** 128
Richardson, Tony, **Supp. XI:** 305, 306
"Richard Wright and Recent Negro Fiction" (Ellison), **Retro. Supp. II:** 116
"Richard Wright's Blues" (Ellison), **Retro. Supp. II:** 117, 124
"Richard Yates: A Requiem" (Lawrence), **Supp. XI:** 335
"Rich Boy, The" (Fitzgerald), **II:** 94; **Retro. Supp. I:** 98, 108
"Riches" (Bausch), **Supp. VII:** 54
Richler, Mordecai, **Supp. XI:** 294, 297
Richman, Robert, **Supp. XI:** 249
Richmond (Masters), **Supp. I Part 2:** 471
Richter, Conrad, **Supp. X:** 103
Richter, Jean Paul, **II:** 489, 492
Rickman, Clio, **Supp. I Part 2:** 519
Ricks, Christopher, **Retro. Supp. I:** 56
Riddel, Joseph N., **IV:** 95
"Riders to the Blood-Red Wrath" (Brooks), **Supp. III Part 1:** 82–83
Riders to the Sea (Synge), **III:** 157
Ridge, Lola, **Supp. IX:** 308
Riding, Laura, **I:** 437
Riding the Iron Rooster: By Train through China (Theroux), **Supp. VIII:** 324
Riesenberg, Felix, **I:** 360, 361
Riesman, David, **Supp. I Part 2:** 649, 650

"Rif, to Music, The" (Bowles), **Supp. IV Part 1:** 89
Riffs & Reciprocities (Dunn), **Supp. XI:** 154–155
Riggs, Marlon, **Supp. XI:** 19
Right Madness on Skye, The (Hugo), **Supp. VI:** 145–147
Rights of Man (Paine), **Supp. I Part 2:** 508, 511, 512–514, 516, 519, 523
"Rights of Women, The" (Brown). *See Alcuin: A Dialogue* (Brown)
Right Stuff, The (Wolfe), **Supp. III Part 2:** 581–584
Right Thoughts in Sad Hours (Mather), **IV:** 144
Rigney, Barbara Hill, **Supp. VIII:** 215
"Rigorists" (Moore), **III:** 198
Riis, Jacob A., **I:** 293; **Supp. I Part 1:** 13
Riley, James Whitcomb, **I:** 205; **Supp. II Part 1:** 192, 193, 196, 197
Rilke, Rainer Maria, **I:** 445, 523; **II:** 367, 381, 382–383, 389, 543, 544; **III:** 552, 558, 563, 571, 572; **IV:** 380, 443; **Retro. Supp. II:** 20, 187; **Supp. I Part 1:** 264; **Supp. I Part 2:** 573; **Supp. III Part 1:** 239, 242, 246, 283, 319–320; **Supp. IV Part 1:** 284; **Supp. V:** 208, 343; **Supp. VIII:** 30, 40; **Supp. X:** 164; **Supp. XI:** 126; **Supp. XIII:** 74, 88
Rilke on Love and Other Difficulties (Rilke), **Supp. X:** 164
"Rilke's Growth as a Poet" (Dobyns), **Supp. XIII:** 77
"Rimbaud" (Kerouac), **Supp. III Part 1:** 232
Rimbaud, Arthur, **I:** 381, 383, 389, 391, 526; **II:** 528, 543, 545; **III:** 23, 174, 189; **IV:** 286, 380, 443; **Retro. Supp. I:** 56; **Retro. Supp. II:** 187, 344; **Supp. III Part 1:** 14, 195; **Supp. IV Part 2:** 624; **Supp. VIII:** 39, 40; **Supp. XII:** 1, 16, 128, 255; **Supp. XIII:** 284
Rinehart, Stanley, **III:** 36
Ring, Frances Kroll, **Supp. IX:** 63, 64
Ring and the Book, The (Browning), **Supp. I Part 2:** 416, 468
Ring cycle (Wagner), **Supp. IV Part 1:** 392
Ringe, Donald, **I:** 339, 343; **Retro. Supp. II:** 270
"Ringing the Bells" (Sexton), **Supp. II Part 2:** 672, 687
Ringle, Ken, **Supp. X:** 15
Ring of Heaven: Poems (Hongo), **Supp. X:** 292
Rink, The (musical, McNally), **Supp. XIII:** 207

Ríos, Alberto Alvaro, **Supp. IV Part 2: 537–556**
"Riot" (Brooks), **Supp. III Part 1:** 71, 84–85
Ripley, Ezra, **II:** 8; **IV:** 172
Rip-off Red, Girl Detective (Acker), **Supp. XII:** 3–4
Ripostes (Pound), **Retro. Supp. I:** 287–288, 413
Ripostes of Ezra Pound, The, Whereunto Are Appended the Complete Poetical Works of T. E. Hulme, with Prefatory Note (Pound), **III:** 458, 464, 465
Riprap (Snyder), **Supp. VIII: 292–294,** 295
"Riprap" (Snyder), **Supp. VIII:** 293–294
"Rip Van Winkle" (Irving), **II:** 304–306; **Supp. I Part 1:** 185
Risco-Lozado, Eliezar, **Supp. XIII:** 313
Rise of David Levinsky, The (Cahan), **Supp. IX:** 227; **Supp. XIII:** 106
Rise of Silas Lapham, The (Howells), **II:** 275, 279, 283–285; **IV:** 202; **Retro. Supp. II:** 93, 101
"Rise of the Middle Class" (Banks), **Supp. V:** 10
Rising and Falling (Matthews), **Supp. IX:** 154, **160**
"Rising Daughter, The" (Olds), **Supp. X:** 204
Rising from the Plains (McPhee), **Supp. III Part 1:** 309–310
Rising Glory of America, The (Brackenridge and Freneau), **Supp. I Part 1:** 124; **Supp. II Part 1:** 67, 253, 256, 263
"Rising of the Storm, The" (Dunbar), **Supp. II Part 1:** 199
Rising Sun in the Pacific, The (Morison), **Supp. I Part 2:** 490
Risk Pool, The (Russo), **Supp. XII: 328–331**
Ristovic, Aleksandar, **Supp. VIII:** 272
"Rita Dove: Identity Markers" (Vendler), **Supp. IV Part 1:** 247, 257
"Rite of Passage" (Olds), **Supp. X:** 206
"Rites and Ceremonies" (Hecht), **Supp. X:** 61
"Rites of Spring, The" (Morris), **III:** 223
Ritschl, Albrecht, **III:** 309, 604
Ritsos, Yannis, **Supp. X:** 112
"Ritsos and the Metaphysical Moment" (Dobyns), **Supp. XIII:** 78
Rittenhouse, David, **Supp. I Part 2:** 507

"Ritual and Renewal: Keres Traditions in the Short Fiction of Leslie Silko" (Ruoff), **Supp. IV Part 2:** 559
Ritz, The (film), **Supp. XIII:** 206
Ritz, The (McNally), **Supp. XIII:** 198
"Rival, The" (Plath), **Retro. Supp. II:** 254
Riven Rock (Boyle), **Supp. VIII:** 5–6
"River" (Ammons), **Supp. VII:** 28
"River, The" (O'Connor), **III:** 344, 352, 353, 354, 356; **Retro. Supp. II:** 229, 231–232
Rivera, Tomás, **Supp. XIII:** 216, 221
Riverbed (Wagoner), **Supp. IX:** 327–328
"River Driftwood" (Jewett), **Retro. Supp. II:** 132, 133, 147
"River Jordan, The" (DeLillo), **Supp. VI:** 3, 4
River King, The (Hoffman), **Supp. X:** 78, 85, 90, **91–92**
"River Merchant's Wife: A Letter, The" (Pound), **III:** 463
"River Now, The" (Hugo), **Supp. VI:** 144
"River of Rivers in Connecticut, The" (Stevens), **Retro. Supp. I:** 313
"River Profile" (Auden), **Supp. II Part 1:** 26
"River Road" (Kunitz), **Supp. III Part 1:** 260
Rivers, Larry, **Supp. III Part 1:** 3
Rivers and Mountains (Ashbery), **Supp. III Part 1:** 10, 26
Riverside Drive (Simpson), **Supp. IX:** 275–276
River Styx, Ohio, and Other Poems, The (Oliver), **Supp. VII:** 231, 232
"River That Is East, The" (Kinnell), **Supp. III Part 1:** 241–242
"River Towns" (Masters), **Supp. I Part 2:** 473
Rives, Amélie, **II:** 194
Rivière, Jacques, **Retro. Supp. I:** 63
"Rivington's Last Will and Testament" (Freneau), **Supp. II Part 1:** 261
"Rivulet, The" (Bryant), **Supp. I Part 1:** 155, 162
Rix, Alice, **I:** 199
RL's Dream (Mosley), **Supp. XIII:** 234, **244–245**, 249
Roach, Max, **Supp. X:** 239
Road Between, The (Farrell), **II:** 29, 38, 39–40
"Road Between Here and There, The" (Kinnell), **Supp. III Part 1:** 254
"Road Home, The" (Hammett), **Supp. IV Part 1:** 343
Road Home, The (Harrison), **Supp. VIII:** 37, 45, 48, **49–50**, 53

"Road Not Taken, The" (Frost), **II:** 154; **Retro. Supp. I:** 131; **Supp. XI:** 150
Roadside Poems for Summer Travellers (Larcom, ed.), **Supp. XIII:** 142
Roads of Destiny (O. Henry), **Supp. II Part 1:** 410
Road through the Wall, The (Jackson), **Supp. IX:** 115, 118, 120, 123–124
"Road to Avignon, The" (Lowell), **II:** 516
"Road to Hell, The" (Fante), **Supp. XI:** 160
Road to Los Angeles, The (Fante), **Supp. XI:** 160, 166, 167, **168**, 172
Road to Many a Wonder, The (Wagoner), **Supp. IX:** 327, **336**
Road to the Temple, The (Glaspell), **Supp. III Part 1:** 175, 182, 186
Road to Wellville, The (Boyle), **Supp. VIII:** 6–8
Road to Xanadu, The (Lowes), **IV:** 453
"Roan Stallion" (Jeffers), **Supp. II Part 2:** 428–429
"Roast-beef" (Stein), **IV:** 43
"Roast Possum" (Dove), **Supp. IV Part 1:** 247, 248
Robards, Jason, Jr., **III:** 163, 403
Robbe-Grillet, Alain, **I:** 123; **IV:** 95; **Supp. IV Part 1:** 42; **Supp. V:** 47, 48
Robber Bride, The (Atwood), **Supp. XIII:** **30–31**
Robber Bridegroom, The (Welty), **IV:** 261, 266–268, 271, 274; **Retro. Supp. I:** 347
Robbins, Harold, **Supp. XII:** 6
Robbins, Henry, **Supp. IV Part 1:** 198, 201, 210, 211
Robbins, Katherine Robinson, **Supp. X:** 264
Robbins, Tom, **Supp. IV Part 1:** 227; **Supp. VIII:** 14; **Supp. X:** **259–288**; **Supp. XIII:** 11
"Robe, The" (Douglas), **IV:** 434
"Robert Bly" (Davis), **Supp. IV Part 1:** 70
Robert Bly (Sugg), **Supp. IV Part 1:** 68
Robert Bly: An Introduction to the Poetry (Nelson), **Supp. IV Part 1:** 66
Robert Bly: The Poet and His Critics (Davis), **Supp. IV Part 1:** 63
"Robert Bly and the Trouble with America" (Mitchell), **Supp. IV Part 1:** 70
Robert Coover: The Universal Fictionmaking Process (Gordon), **Supp. V:** 46

Robert Creeley (Ford), **Supp. IV Part 1:** 140
Robert Creeley and the Genius of the American Common Place (Clark), **Supp. IV Part 1:** 140
Robert Creeley's Poetry: A Critical Introduction (Edelberg), **Supp. IV Part 1:** 155
Robert Frost (Meyers), **Retro. Supp. I:** 138
Robert Lowell (Meyers), **Retro. Supp. II:** 191
Robert Lowell: The First Twenty years (Staples), **Retro. Supp. II:** 187
Robert Lowell and the Sublime (Hart), **Retro. Supp. II:** 187
Robert Lowell's Shifting Colors (Doreski), **Retro. Supp. II:** 185
Roberts, Diane, **Supp. X:** 15
Roberts, J. M., **IV:** 454
Roberts, Leo, **II:** 449
Roberts, Margaret, **II:** 449; **IV:** 453, 454
Roberts, Matthew, **Retro. Supp. II:** 342
Roberts, Meade, **IV:** 383
Roberts, Michael, **I:** 527, 536
Roberts, Richard, **III:** 297
Roberts, Wally, **Supp. XI:** 119, 120, 126
Roberts, William, **Supp. XI:** 343
Roberts Brothers, **Retro. Supp. I:** 31, 35
Robertson, D. B., **III:** 311
Robertson, David, **Supp. VIII:** 305
Robertson, Nan, **Supp. IV Part 1:** 300
Robertson, William, **II:** 8
Robert the Devil (Merwin, trans.), **Supp. III Part 1:** 341, 346
Robeson, Paul, **III:** 392; **Supp. IV Part 1:** 360, 361; **Supp. X:** 137
Robespierre, Maximilien, **Supp. I Part 2:** 514, 515, 517
Robinson, Christopher L., **Supp. XII:** 13, 14
Robinson, Dean, **III:** 506
Robinson, Edward, **III:** 505
Robinson, Edward G., **Supp. XI:** 306
Robinson, Edwin Arlington, **I:** 480; **II:** 388, 391, 529, 542; **III:** 5, **503–526,** 576; **Supp. I Part 2:** 699; **Supp. II Part 1:** 191; **Supp. III Part 1:** 63, 75; **Supp. III Part 2:** 592, 593; **Supp. IX:** 77, 266, 276, 308
Robinson, Forrest G., **Supp. IV Part 2:** 597, 601, 604
Robinson, H. M., **IV:** 369, 370
Robinson, Herman, **III:** 506–507
Robinson, Jackie, **Supp. I Part 1:** 338
Robinson, James Harvey, **I:** 214; **Supp.**

I Part 2: 492
Robinson, James K., **Supp. IX:** 328
Robinson, Margaret G., **Supp. IV Part 2:** 597, 601, 604
Robinson, Mary, **Supp. XI:** 26
Robinson, Sugar Ray, **Supp. IV Part 1:** 167
Robinson, Ted, **Supp. XIII:** 166
Robinson Crusoe (Defoe), **II:** 159; **III:** 113, 423; **IV:** 369; **Retro. Supp. II:** 274; **Supp. I Part 2:** 714; **Supp. IV Part 2:** 502
Robison, Mary, **Supp. V:** 22
Roblès, Emmanuel, **Supp. I Part 1:** 283
"Robstown" (Salinas), **Supp. XIII:** 315
Rochefoucauld, Louis Alexandre, **Supp. I Part 2:** 510
"Rock" (Nye), **Supp. XIII:** 287
Rock (Wagoner), **Supp. IX:** 324, **334,** 335
Rock, Catherine, **Supp. XII:** 17
Rock, The (Eliot), **Retro. Supp. I:** 65
Rock, The (Stevens), **Retro. Supp. I:** 309, 312
"Rock, The" (Stevens), **Retro. Supp. I:** 312
"Rock Climbers, The" (Francis), **Supp. IX:** 82
Rock-Drill (Pound), **Retro. Supp. I:** 293
Rockefeller, John D., **I:** 273; **III:** 580; **Supp. I Part 2:** 486; **Supp. V:** 286
Rockefeller, Nelson, **III:** 14, 15
Rocket to the Moon (Odets), **Supp. II Part 2:** 541–543, 544
Rock Garden, The (Shepard), **Supp. III Part 2:** 432, 447
"Rocking Horse Winner, The" (Lawrence), **Supp. I Part 1:** 329
Rocking the Boat (Vidal), **Supp. IV Part 2:** 683
"Rockpile, The" (Baldwin), **Supp. I Part 1:** 63
Rock Springs (Ford), **Supp. V:** 57, 58–59, 68–69
Rocky Mountains, The: or, Scenes, Incidents, and Adventures in the Far West; Digested from the Journal of Captain E. L. E Bonneville, of the Army of the United States, and Illustrated from Various Other Sources (Irving), **II:** 312
Roderick Hudson (James), **II:** 284, 290, 324, 326, 328; **Retro. Supp. I:** 219, **220–221,** 221, 226; **Supp. IX:** 142
Rodgers, Richard, **III:** 361

Rodgers, Ronald, **Supp. IV Part 2:** 503
Rodker, John, **III:** 470
Rodman, Selden, **Supp. I Part 1:** 83; **Supp. X:** 115
"Rodrigo Returns to the Land and Linen Celebrates" (Cisneros), **Supp. VII:** 68
Roethke, Charles, **III:** 531
Roethke, Theodore, **I:** 167, 171–172, 183, 254, 285, 521; **III:** 273, **527–550; IV:** 138, 402; **Retro. Supp. II:** 178, 181, 246; **Supp. I Part 2:** 539; **Supp. III Part 1:** 47, 54, 56, 239, 253, 260–261, 350; **Supp. IV Part 2:** 626; **Supp. IX:** 323
"Roger Malvin's Burial" (Hawthorne), **II:** 243; **Retro. Supp. I:** 153
Rogers, Michael, **Supp. X:** 265, 266
Rogers, Samuel, **II:** 303; **Supp. I Part 1:** 157
Rogers, Will, **I:** 261; **IV:** 388
Roger's Version (Updike), **Retro. Supp. I:** 325, 327, 330
Roget, Peter Mark, **Supp. I Part 1:** 312
"Rogue River Jet-Board Trip, Gold Beach, Oregon, July 4, 1977" (Carver), **Supp. III Part 1:** 140
"Rogue's Gallery" (McCarthy), **II:** 563
Roland de La Platière, Jean Marie, **II:** 554
"Role of Society in the Artist, The" (Ammons), **Supp. VII:** 34
Rolfe, Alfred, **IV:** 427
"Roll, Jordan, Roll" (spiritual), **Supp. IV Part 1:** 16
"Roll Call" (Komunyakaa), **Supp. XIII:** 123
Rolle, Esther, **Supp. IV Part 1:** 367
Rollin, Charles, **II:** 113
Rolling Stones (O. Henry), **Supp. II Part 1:** 410
Rolling Thunder Logbook (Shepard), **Supp. III Part 2:** 433
"Rolling Up" (Simpson), **Supp. IX:** 265, 274, 280
Rollins, Howard E., Jr., **Supp. IV Part 1:** 236
Rollins, Hyder E., **Supp. IV Part 1:** 168
Rollins, Sonny, **Supp. V:** 195
"Rollo" tales (Abbott), **Supp. I Part 1:** 38
"Roma I" (Wright), **Supp. V:** 338
"Roma II" (Wright), **Supp. V:** 338
Romains, Jules, **I:** 227
Román, David, **Supp. XIII:** 208
"Romance and a Reading List" (Fitzgerald), **Retro. Supp. I:** 101

Romance of a Plain Man, The (Glasgow), **II:** 175, 180–181
"Romance of Certain Old Clothes, The" (James), **II:** 322; **Retro. Supp. I:** 218
"Roman Elegies" (Brodsky), **Supp. VIII:** 29
"Roman Fever" (Wharton), **Retro. Supp. I:** 382
"Roman Fountain" (Bogan), **Supp. III Part 1:** 56
"*Romanitas* of Gore Vidal, The" (Tatum), **Supp. IV Part 2:** 684
"Roman Sarcophagus, A" (Lowell), **II:** 544
Roman Spring of Mrs. Stone, The (T. Williams), **IV:** 383, 385
"Romantic, The" (Bogan), **Supp. III Part 1:** 50
Romantic Comedians, The (Glasgow), **II:** 175, 186, 190, 194
Romantic Egoists, The (Auchincloss), **Supp. IV Part 1:** 25
Romantic Egotist, The (Fitzgerald), **II:** 82
"Romantic Egotist, The" (Fitzgerald), **Retro. Supp. I:** 100
"Romanticism and Classicism" (Hulme), **III:** 196
"Romanticism Comes Home" (Shapiro), **Supp. II Part 2:** 713
Romantic Manifesto, The: A Philosophy of Literature (Rand), **Supp. IV Part 2:** 521, 523, 527, 529–530
"Romantic Regionalism of Harper Lee, The" (Erisman), **Supp. VIII:** 126
"Rome" (W. C. Williams), **Retro. Supp. I:** 420
Rome Brothers, **Retro. Supp. I:** 393
Romeo and Juliet (Shakespeare), **Supp. V:** 252; **Supp. VIII:** 223
Romola (Eliot), **II:** 291; **IV:** 311
Romulus: A New Comedy (Vidal), **Supp. IV Part 2:** 683
Romulus der Grosse (Dürrenmatt), **Supp. IV Part 2:** 683
Ronald, Ann, **Supp. XIII:** 4, 5, 6, 7, 9, 11
"Rondel for a September Day" (White), **Supp. I Part 2:** 676
"Ron Narrative Reconstructions, The" (Coleman), **Supp. XI:** 83
Ronsard, Pierre de, **Supp. X:** 65
Rood, John, **IV:** 261
"Roof, the Steeple, and the People, The" (Ellison), **Retro. Supp. II:** 118, 126; **Supp. II Part 1:** 248
"Room" (Levertov), **Supp. III Part 1:** 282
"Room at the Heart of Things, A"

(Merrill), **Supp. III Part 1:** 337
Room Called Remember, A: Uncollected Pieces (Buechner), **Supp. XII:** 53
"Roomful of Hovings, A" (McPhee), **Supp. III Part 1:** 291, 294
Room of One's Own, A (Woolf), **Supp. V:** 127; **Supp. IX:** 19; **Supp. XIII:** 305
Room Temperature (Baker), **Supp. XIII:** 41, **43–45,** 48, 50
Roosevelt, Eleanor, **IV:** 371; **Supp. IV Part 2:** 679
Roosevelt, Franklin, **Supp. V:** 290
Roosevelt, Franklin Delano, **I:** 482, 485, 490; **II:** 553, 575; **III:** 2, 18, 69, 110, 297, 321, 376, 476, 580, 581; **Supp. I Part 2:** 488, 489, 490, 491, 645, 654, 655
Roosevelt, Kermit, **III:** 508
Roosevelt, Theodore, **I:** 14, 62; **II:** 130; **III:** 508; **IV:** 321; **Retro. Supp. I:** 377; **Supp. I Part 1:** 1, 21; **Supp. I Part 2:** 455, 456, 502, 707; **Supp. V:** 280, 282; **Supp. IX:** 184
Roosevelt After Inauguration And Other Atrocities (Burroughs), **Supp. III Part 1:** 98
"Roosters" (Bishop), **Retro. Supp. II:** 39, 43, 250; **Supp. I Part 1:** 89
Root, Abiah, **I:** 456
Root, Elihu, **Supp. IV Part 1:** 33
Root, Simeon, **I:** 548
Root, Timothy, **I:** 548
Rootabaga Stories (Sandburg), **III:** 583, 587
"Rootedness: The Ancestor as Foundation" (Morrison), **Supp. III Part 1:** 361
Roots in the Soil (film), **Supp. IV Part 1:** 83
"Rope" (Porter), **III:** 451
Rope, The (O'Neill), **III:** 388
Ropemakers of Plymouth, The (Morison), **Supp. I Part 2:** 494
"Ropes" (Nye), **Supp. XIII:** 276
"Rope's End, The" (Nemerov), **III:** 282
Roquelaure, A. N., **Supp. VII:** 301. *See also* Rice, Anne
Rorem, Ned, **Supp. IV Part 1:** 79, 84
"Rosa" (Ozick), **Supp. V:** 271
Rosa, Rodrigo Rey, **Supp. IV Part 1:** 92
Rosaldo, Renato, **Supp. IV Part 2:** 544
"Rosalia" (Simic), **Supp. VIII:** 278
Roscoe, Will, **Supp. IV Part 1:** 330
"Rose" (Dubus), **Supp. VII:** 88
Rose, Alice, Sister, **III:** 348
Rose, Philip, **Supp. IV Part 1:** 362

"Rose, The" (Roethke), **III:** 537
"Rose, The" (W. C. Williams), **Retro. Supp. I:** 419
"Rose for Emily, A" (Faulkner), **II:** 72; **Supp. IX:** 96
Rose in Bloom (Alcott), **Supp. I Part 1:** 42
"Rose-Johnny" (Kingsolver), **Supp. VII:** 203
Rose Madder (King), **Supp. V:** 141, 148, 150, 152
"Rose-Morals" (Lanier), **Supp. I Part 1:** 364
Rosen, Kenneth, **Supp. IV Part 2:** 499, 505, 513
Rosenbaum, Alissa Zinovievna. *See* Rand, Ayn
Rosenberg, Bernard, **Supp. I Part 2:** 650
Rosenberg, Julius and Ethel, **Supp. I Part 1:** 295; **Supp. I Part 2:** 532; **Supp. V:** 45
Rosenbloom, Joel, **Supp. IV Part 2:** 527
Rosenfeld, Alvin H., **Supp. I Part 1:** 120
Rosenfeld, Isaac, **Supp. XII:** 160
Rosenfeld, Paul, **I:** 116, 117, 231, 245
Rosenfelt, Deborah, **Supp. XIII:** 296, 304
Rosenfield, Isaac, **IV:** 3
Rosenthal, Lois, **Supp. VIII:** 258
Rosenthal, M. L., **II:** 550; **III:** 276, 479; **Supp. V:** 333
"Rose Pogonias" (Frost), **Retro. Supp. I:** 127
"Rose Red and Snow White" (Grimms), **Supp. X:** 82
"Roses" (Dove), **Supp. IV Part 1:** 246
"Roses and Skulls" (Goldbarth), **Supp. XII:** 192
"Roses for Lubbock" (Nye), **Supp. XIII:** 281
"Roses Only" (Moore), **III:** 195, 198, 200, 202, 215
Rose Tattoo, The (T. Williams), **IV:** 382, 383, 387, 388, 389, 392–393, 394, 397, 398
"Rosewood, Ohio" (Matthews), **Supp. IX:** 160
Rosinante to the Road Again (Dos Passos), **I:** 478
Rosmersholm (Ibsen), **III:** 152
Rosmond, Babette, **II:** 432
Ross, Eleanor. *See* Taylor, Eleanor Ross
Ross, Harold, **Supp. I Part 1:** 174; **Supp. I Part 2:** 607, 617, 653, 654, 655, 660; **Supp. VIII:** 151, 170; **Supp. IX:** 190

Ross, John F., **II:** 110
Ross, Lillilan, **Retro. Supp. II:** 198
Ross, Mitchell S., **Supp. IV Part 2:** 692; **Supp. X:** 260
Rossen, Robert, **Supp. XI:** 306
Rosset, Barney, **III:** 171
Rossetti, Dante Gabriel, **I:** 433; **II:** 323; **Retro. Supp. I:** 128, 286; **Supp. I Part 2:** 552
Rossetti, William Michael, **Retro. Supp. I:** 407
Rosskam, Edwin, **IV:** 477
Ross Macdonald (Bruccoli), **Supp. IV Part 2:** 468, 470
Rostand, Edmond, **II:** 515; **Supp. IV Part 2:** 518
Rosy Crucifixion, The (H. Miller), **III:** 170, 187, 188–189, 190
Roth, Henry, **Supp. IV Part 1:** 314; **Supp. VIII:** 233; **Supp. IX: 227–243; Supp. XIII:** 106
Roth, Philip, **I:** 144, 161; **II:** 591; **Retro. Supp. II:** 22, **297–315; Supp. I Part 1:** 186, 192; **Supp. I Part 2:** 431, 441, 443; **Supp. II Part 1:** 99; **Supp. III Part 2: 401–429; Supp. IV Part 1:** 236, 379, 388; **Supp. V:** 45, 119, 122, 257, 258; **Supp. VIII:** 88, 236, 245; **Supp. IX:** 227; **Supp. XI:** 64, 68, 99, 140; **Supp. XII:** 190, 310
Rothenberg, Jerome, **Supp. VIII:** 292; **Supp. XII:** 3
Rothermere, Lady Mary, **Retro. Supp. I:** 63
Rothstein, Mervyn, **Supp. VIII:** 142
"Rouge High" (Hughes), **Supp. I Part 1:** 330
Rougemont, Denis de, **II:** 586; **IV:** 216; **Retro. Supp. I:** 328, 329, 330, 331
Roughing It (Twain), **II:** 312; **IV:** 195, 197, 198
Roughing It in the Bush (Shields), **Supp. VII:** 313
"Rough Outline" (Simic), **Supp. VIII:** 276
Rougon-Macquart, Les (Zola), **II:** 175–176
Roumain, Jacques, **Retro. Supp. I:** 202; **Supp. IV Part 1:** 360, 367
"Round, The" (Kunitz), **Supp. III Part 1:** 268
"Round Trip" (Dunn), **Supp. XI:** 148–149
Round Up (Lardner), **II:** 426, 430, 431
Rourke, Constance, **I:** 258; **IV:** 339, 352
Rourke, Milton, **Retro. Supp. II:** 89
Rousseau, Jean-Jacques, **I:** 226; **II:** 8,

343; **III:** 170, 178, 259; **IV:** 80, 173, 440; **Supp. I Part 1:** 126; **Supp. I Part 2:** 637, 659; **Supp. IV Part 1:** 171; **Supp. XI:** 245
Roussel, Raymond, **Supp. III Part 1:** 6, 7, 10, 15, 16, 21
"Route Six" (Kunitz), **Supp. III Part 1:** 258
Route Two (Erdrich and Dorris), **Supp. IV Part 1:** 260
"Routine Things Around the House, The" (Dunn), **Supp. XI:** 148
Rover Boys (Winfield), **III:** 146
Rovit, Earl, **IV:** 102
Rowe, Anne E., **Supp. X:** 223
Rowe, John Carlos, **Retro. Supp. I:** 216
"Rowing" (Sexton), **Supp. II Part 2:** 696
"Rowing Endeth, The" (Sexton), **Supp. II Part 2:** 696
Rowlandson, Mary, **Supp. IV Part 2:** 430, 431
"Rows of Cold Trees, The" (Winters), **Supp. II Part 2:** 790–791, 800
Rowson, Susanna, **Supp. I Part 1:** 128
Roxanna Slade (Price), **Supp. VI:** 267
"Royal Palm" (Crane), **I:** 401
Royce, Josiah, **I:** 443; **III:** 303, 600; **IV:** 26; **Retro. Supp. I:** 57
Royster, Sarah Elmira, **III:** 410, 429
Różewicz, Tadeusz, **Supp. X:** 60
Ruas, Charles, **Supp. IV Part 1:** 383
Rubáiyát (Khayyám), **I:** 568
Rubaiyat of Omar Khayyam (Fitzgerald), **Supp. I Part 2:** 416; **Supp. III Part 2:** 610
Rubin, Louis, **Supp. I Part 2:** 672, 673, 679; **Supp. X:** 42
Rubin, Louis D., Jr., **IV:** 116, 462–463
Rubin, Stan Sanvel, **Supp. IV Part 1:** 242, 245, 252
"Ruby Brown" (Hughes), **Supp. I Part 1:** 327
"Ruby Daggett" (Eberhart), **I:** 539
Rucker, Rudy, **Supp. X:** 302
Rudd, Hughes, **Supp. XII:** 141
"Rude Awakening, A" (Chopin), **Retro. Supp. II:** 64
Rudens (Plautus), **Supp. III Part 2:** 630
Ruderman, Judith, **Supp. IV Part 1:** 380
Rudge, Olga, **Supp. V:** 338
Rueckert, William, **I:** 264
Rugby Chapel (Arnold), **Supp. I Part 2:** 416
"Rugby Road" (Garrett), **Supp. VII:** 100
Ruining the New Road (Matthews), **Supp. IX:** 154, **155–157**
"Ruins of Italica, The" (Bryant, trans.), **Supp. I Part 1:** 166
Rukeyser, Muriel, **Retro. Supp. II:** 48; **Supp. VI: 271–289**
"Rule of Phase Applied to History, The" (Adams), **I:** 19
Rule of the Bone (Banks), **Supp. V:** 16
"Rules by Which a Great Empire May Be Reduced to a Small One" (Franklin), **II:** 120
Rules For the Dance: A Handbook for Reading and Writing Metrical Verse (Oliver), **Supp. VII:** 229, 247
Rules of the Game, The (film), **Supp. XII:** 259
Rulfo, Juan, **Supp. IV Part 2:** 549
Rumbaut, Rubén, **Supp. XI:** 184
Rumens, Carol, **Supp. XI:** 14
Rumkowski, Chaim, **Supp. XII:** 168
Rummel, Mary Kay, **Supp. XIII:** 280
"Rumor and a Ladder" (Bowles), **Supp. IV Part 1:** 93
Rumors (Simon), **Supp. IV Part 2:** 582–583, 591
Rumpelstiltskin (Gardner), **Supp. VI:** 72
"Rumpelstiltskin" (Grimm), **IV:** 266
"Rumpelstiltskin" (Sexton), **Supp. II Part 2:** 690
"Runagate Runagate" (Hayden), **Supp. II Part 1:** 377
"Runes" (Nemerov), **III:** 267, 277–278
"Running" (Wilbur), **Supp. III Part 2:** 558–559
Running Dog (DeLillo), **Supp. VI:** 3, 6, 8, 14
"Run of Bad Luck, A" (Proulx), **Supp. VII:** 253–254
Run of Jacks, A (Hugo), **Supp. VI:** 131, 133, 134, 135, 136
Run River (Didion), **Supp. IV Part 1:** 197, 199–200, 201
Ruoff, A. LaVonne Brown, **Supp. IV Part 1:** 324, 327; **Supp. IV Part 2:** 559
Rupert, Jim, **Supp. XII:** 215
Ruppert, James, **Supp. IV Part 1:** 321
Rural Hours (Cooper), **Supp. XIII:** 152
"Rural Reflections" (Rich), **Retro. Supp. II:** 283
"Rural Route" (Wright), **Supp. V:** 340
"Rural South, The" (Du Bois), **Supp. II Part 1:** 174
Rush, Benjamin, **Supp. I Part 2:** 505, 507
Rushdie, Salman, **Supp. IV Part 1:** 234, 297
Rushdy, Ashraf, **Supp. X:** 250
Rushing, Jimmy, **Retro. Supp. II:** 113
Rusk, Dean, **II:** 579
Ruskin, John, **II:** 323, 338; **IV:** 349; **Retro. Supp. I:** 56, 360; **Supp. I Part 1:** 2, 10, 87, 349; **Supp. I Part 2:** 410
Russell, Ada Dwyer, **II:** 513, 527
Russell, Bertrand, **II:** 27; **III:** 605, 606; **Retro. Supp. I:** 57, 58, 59, 60; **Supp. I Part 2:** 522; **Supp. V:** 290; **Supp. XII:** 45
Russell, Diarmuid, **Retro. Supp. I:** 342, 345, 346–347, 349–350
Russell, George, **Retro. Supp. I:** 342
Russell, Herb, **Supp. I Part 2:** 465–466
Russell, Peter, **III:** 479
Russell, Richard, **Supp. XI:** 102
Russell, Sue, **Supp. IV Part 2:** 653
Russert, Tim, **Supp. XII:** 272
Russia at War (Caldwell), **I:** 296
Russian Journal, A (Steinbeck), **IV:** 52, 63
Russo, Richard, **Supp. XI:** 349; **Supp. XII: 325–344**
"Rusty Autumn" (Swenson), **Supp. IV Part 2:** 640
Rutabaga-Roo: I've Got a Song and It's for You (Nye, album), **Supp. XIII:** 274
Ruth (biblical book), **Supp. I Part 2:** 516
Ruth, George Herman ("Babe"), **II:** 423; **Supp. I Part 2:** 438, 440
Ruth Hall (Fern), **Supp. V:** 122
Rutledge, Ann, **III:** 588; **Supp. I Part 2:** 471
Ruwe, Donelle R., **Supp. XII:** 215
Ryder (Barnes), **Supp. III Part 1:** 31, 36–38, 42, 43
"Ryder" (Rukeyser), **Supp. VI:** 273, 283
Rymer, Thomas, **IV:** 122
S-1 (Baraka), **Supp. II Part 1:** 55, 57
S. (Updike), **Retro. Supp. I:** 330, 331, 332, 333
Saadi, **II:** 19
"Sabbath, The" (Stowe), **Supp. I Part 2:** 587
"Sabbath Mom" (White), **Supp. I Part 2:** 671–672
Sabbaths (Berry), **Supp. X:** 31
Sabbath's Theater (Roth), **Retro. Supp. II:** 297, 306
Sabines, Jaime, **Supp. V:** 178
"Sabotage" (Baraka), **Supp. II Part 1:** 49, 53
Sacco, Nicola, **I:** 482, 486, 490, 494; **II:** 38–39, 426; **III:** 139–140; **Supp. I Part 2:** 446; **Supp. V:** 288–289;

INDEX / 549

Supp. IX: 199
Sachs, Hanns, Supp. I Part 1: 259; Supp. X: 186
"Sacks" (Carver), Supp. III Part 1: 143–144
Sacks, Peter, Supp. IV Part 2: 450
Sackville-West, Vita, Supp. VIII: 263
"Sacrament of Divorce, The" (Patchett), Supp. XII: 309
"Sacraments" (Dubus), Supp. VII: 91
Sacred and Profane Memories (Van Vechten), Supp. II Part 2: 735, 749
"Sacred Chant for the Return of Black Spirit and Power" (Baraka), Supp. II Part 1: 51
"Sacred Factory, The" (Toomer), Supp. IX: 320
Sacred Fount, The (James), II: 332–333; Retro. Supp. I: 219, 228, 232
"Sacred Hoop, The: A Contemporary Perspective" (Gunn Allen), Supp. IV Part 1: 324
Sacred Hoop, The: Recovering the Feminine in American Indian Traditions (Gunn Allen), Supp. IV Part 1: 319, 320, 322, 324, 325, 328–330, 331, 333, 334
Sacred Journey, The (Buechner), Supp. XII: 42, 53
Sacred Wood, The (Eliot), IV: 431; Retro. Supp. I: 59, 60; Supp. I Part 1: 268; Supp. II Part 1: 136, 146
"Sacrifice, The" (Oates), Supp. II Part 2: 523
Sacrilege of Alan Kent, The (Caldwell), I: 291–292
"Sad Brazil" (Hardwick), Supp. III Part 1: 210
"Sad Dust Glories" (Ginsberg), Supp. II Part 1: 376
Sad Dust Glories: Poems Written Work Summer in Sierra Woods (Ginsberg), Supp. II Part 1: 326
Sade, Marquis de, III: 259; IV: 437, 442; Supp. XII: 1, 14–15
Sad Flower in the Sand, A (film), Supp. XI: 173
Sad Heart at the Supermarket, A (Jarrell), II: 386
"Sadie" (Matthiessen), Supp. V: 201
Sadness and Happiness (Pinsky), Supp. VI: 235, 237–241
"Sadness of Brothers, The" (Kinnell), Supp. III Part 1: 237, 251
"Sadness of Days, The" (Salinas), Supp. XIII: 325
Sadness of Days, The: Selected and New Poems (Salinas), Supp. XIII: 311, 324–326

"Sadness of Lemons, The" (Levine), Supp. V: 184
"Sad Rite" (Karr), Supp. XI: 243
"Sad Strains of a Gay Waltz" (Stevens), Retro. Supp. I: 302
"Safe" (Gordon), Supp. IV Part 1: 299, 306
"Safe in their Alabaster Chambers" (Dickinson), Retro. Supp. I: 30
"Safe Subjects" (Komunyakaa), Supp. XIII: 118
"Safeway" (F. Barthelme), Supp. XI: 26, 27, 36
Saffin, John, Supp. I Part 1: 115
Saffy, Edna, Supp. X: 227
"Saga of Arturo Bandini" (Fante), Supp. XI: 159, 166–169
"Saga of King Olaf, The" (Longfellow), II: 489, 505; Retro. Supp. II: 154, 155, 164
"Sage of Stupidity and Wonder, The" (Goldbarth), Supp. XII: 191
Sahl, Mort, II: 435–436
"Said" (Dixon), Supp. XII: 149–150
"Sailing after Lunch" (Stevens), IV: 73
"Sailing Home from Rapallo" (Lowell), Retro. Supp. II: 189
Sailing through China (Theroux), Supp. VIII: 323
"Sailing to Byzantium" (Yeats), III: 263; Supp. VIII: 30; Supp. X: 74; Supp. XI: 281
"Sail Made of Rags, The" (Nye), Supp. XIII: 277
"Sailors Lost at Sea" (Shields), Supp. VII: 318
"St. Augustine and the Bullfights" (Porter), III: 454
St. Elmo (Wilson), Retro. Supp. I: 351–352
"St. Francis Einstein of the Daffodils" (W. C. Williams), IV: 409–411
"St. George, the Dragon, and the Virgin" (Bly), Supp. IV Part 1: 73
St. George and the Godfather (Mailer), III: 46; Retro. Supp. II: 206, 208
St. John, David, Supp. V: 180; Supp. XI: 270, 272; Supp. XIII: 312
St. John, Edward B., Supp. IV Part 2: 490
St. John, James Hector. See Crèvecoeur, Michel-Guillaume Jean de
St. Louis Woman (Bontemps and Cullen), Supp. IV Part 1: 170
St. Mawr (Lawrence), II: 595
St. Petersburg (Biely), Supp. XII: 13
"St. Roach" (Rukeyser), Supp. VI: 286
"St. Thomas Aquinas" (Simic), Supp. VIII: 281
"*St Anne*/Santa Ana" (Mora), Supp.

XIII: 229
"*Saint Anthony of Padua*/San Antonio de Padua" (Mora), Supp. XIII: 228
Sainte-Beuve, Charles Augustin, IV: 432
Sainte Vierge, La (Picabia), Retro. Supp. II: 349
Saint-Exupéry, Antoine de, Supp. IX: 247
Saint-Gaudens, Augustus, I: 18, 228; II: 551
Saint Jack (Theroux), Supp. VIII: 319
"Saint John and the Back-Ache" (Stevens), Retro. Supp. I: 310
Saint Judas (Wright), Supp. III Part 2: 595–599
"Saint Judas" (Wright), Supp. III Part 2: 598–599
Saint Maybe (Tyler), Supp. IV Part 2: 670–671
"Saint Nicholas" (Moore), III: 215
"Saint Robert" (Dacey), Supp. IV Part 1: 70
Saintsbury, George, IV: 440
Saints' Everlasting Rest, The (Baxter), III: 199; IV: 151, 153
Saint-Simon, Claude Henri, Supp. I Part 2: 648
Saks, Gene, Supp. IV Part 2: 577, 588
Salamun, Tomaz, Supp. VIII: 272
Salazar, Dixie, Supp. V: 180
Saldívar, José David, Supp. IV Part 2: 544, 545
Sale, Richard, Supp. IV Part 1: 379
Sale, Roger, Supp. V: 244
Saleh, Dennis, Supp. V: 182, 186
"Salem" (Lowell), II: 550
Salemi, Joseph, Supp. IV Part 1: 284
Salem's Lot (King), Supp. V: 139, 144, 146, 151
"Sale of the Hessians, The" (Franklin), II: 120
Salinas, Luis Omar, Supp. IV Part 2: 545; Supp. V: 180; Supp. XIII: 311–330
"Salinas Is on His Way" (Salinas), Supp. XIII: 317
"Salinas Sends Messengers to the Stars" (Salinas), Supp. XIII: 317
"Salinas Summering at the Caspian and Thinking of Hamlet" (Salinas), Supp. XIII: 320
"Salinas Wakes Early and Goes to the Park to Lecture Sparrows" (Salinas), Supp. XIII: 320
Salinger, Doris, III: 551
Salinger, J. D., II: 255; III: 551–574; IV: 190, 216, 217; Retro. Supp. I: 102, 116, 335; Supp. IV Part 2: 502; Supp. V: 23, 119; Supp. VIII:

151; **Supp. XI:** 2, 66
Salisbury, Harrison, **Supp. I Part 2:** 664
Salle, David, **Supp. XII:** 4
"Sally" (Cisneros), **Supp. VII:** 63
Salmagundi; or, The Whim-Whams and Opinions of Launcelot Langstaff Esq., and Others (Irving), **II:** 299, 300, 304
Salome (Strauss), **IV:** 316
Salon (online magazine), **Supp. VIII:** 310; **Supp. X:** 202
Salt Eaters, The (Bambara), **Supp. XI:** 1, **12–14**
Salt Ecstasies, The (White), **Supp. XI:** 123
Salter, James, **Supp. IX: 245–263**
Salter, Mary Jo, **Supp. IV Part 2:** 653; **Supp. IX:** 37, 292
Salt Garden, The (Nemerov), **III:** 269, 272–275, 277
"Salt Garden, The" (Nemerov), **III:** 267–268
Salting the Ocean (Nye, ed.), **Supp. XIII:** 280
"Salts and Oils" (Levine), **Supp. V:** 190
Saltzman, Arthur, **Supp. XIII:** 48
Saltzman, Harry, **Supp. XI:** 307
"Salut au Monde!" (Whitman), **Retro. Supp. I:** 387, 396, 400
"Salute" (MacLeish), **III:** 13
"Salute to Mister Yates, A" (Dubus), **Supp. XI:** 347, 349
Salvador (Didion), **Supp. IV Part 1:** 198, 207–208, 210
"Salvage" (Clampitt), **Supp. IX:** 41
Samain, Albert, **II:** 528
Same Door, The (Updike), **IV:** 214, 219, 226; **Retro. Supp. I:** 320
"Same in Blues" (Hughes), **Retro. Supp. I:** 208
Sam Lawson's Oldtown Fireside Stories (Stowe), **Supp. I Part 2:** 587, 596, 598–599
"Sa'm Pèdi" (Bell), **Supp. X:** 17
"Sampler, A" (MacLeish), **III:** 4
Sampoli, Maria, **Supp. V:** 338
Sampson, Edward, **Supp. I Part 2:** 664, 673
Sampson, Martin, **Supp. I Part 2:** 652
Samson Agonistes (Milton), **III:** 274
"Samson and Delilah" (Masters), **Supp. I Part 2:** 459
Samuel de Champlain: Father of New France (Morison), **Supp. I Part 2:** 496–497
Samuels, Charles Thomas, **Retro. Supp. I:** 334
"Samuel Sewall" (Hecht), **Supp. X:** 58

Sanborn, Franklin B., **IV:** 171, 172, 178
Sanborn, Kate, **Supp. XIII:** 152
Sanchez, Carol Anne, **Supp. IV Part 1:** 335
Sanchez, Carol Lee, **Supp. IV Part 2:** 499, 557
Sanchez, Sonia, **Supp. II Part 1:** 34
Sanctified Church, The (Hurston), **Supp. VI:** 150
"Sanction of the Victims, The" (Rand), **Supp. IV Part 2:** 528
Sanctuary (Faulkner), **II:** 57, 61–63, 72, 73, 74, 174; **Retro. Supp. I:** 73, 84, 86–87, 87; **Supp. I Part 2:** 614; **Supp. XII:** 16
Sanctuary (Wharton), **IV:** 311
"Sanctuary" (Wylie), **Supp. I Part 2:** 711
"Sanctuary, The" (Nemerov), **III:** 272, 274
Sand, George, **II:** 322; **Retro. Supp. I:** 235, 372
"Sandalphon" (Longfellow), **II:** 498
Sandbox, The (Albee), **I:** 74–75, 89
Sandburg, Carl, **I:** 103, 109, 384, 421; **II:** 529; **III:** 3, 20, **575–598**; **Retro. Supp. I:** 133, 194; **Supp. I Part 1:** 257, 320; **Supp. I Part 2:** 387, 389, 454, 461, 653; **Supp. III Part 1:** 63, 71, 73, 75; **Supp. IV Part 1:** 169; **Supp. IV Part 2:** 502; **Supp. IX:** 1, 15, 308; **Supp. XIII:** 274, 277
Sandburg, Helga, **III:** 583
Sandburg, Janet, **III:** 583, 584
Sandburg, Margaret, **III:** 583, 584
Sandburg, Mrs. Carl (Lillian Steichen), **III:** 580
"Sand Dabs" (Oliver), **Supp. VII:** 245
"Sand Dunes" (Frost), **Retro. Supp. I:** 137; **Retro. Supp. II:** 41
Sander, August, **Supp. IX:** 211
"Sandman, The" (Barthelme), **Supp. IV Part 1:** 47
Sando, Joe S., **Supp. IV Part 2:** 510
Sandoe, James, **Supp. IV Part 1:** 131; **Supp. IV Part 2:** 470
Sandperl, Ira, **Supp. VIII:** 200
"Sand-Quarry and Moving Figures" (Rukeyser), **Supp. VI:** 271, 278
Sand Rivers (Matthiessen), **Supp. V:** 203
"Sand Roses, The" (Hogan), **Supp. IV Part 1:** 401
Sands, Diana, **Supp. IV Part 1:** 362
Sands, Robert, **Supp. I Part 1:** 156, 157
"Sands at Seventy" (Whitman), **IV:** 348

"Sandstone Farmhouse, A" (Updike), **Retro. Supp. I:** 318
Sanford, John, **IV:** 286, 287
"San Francisco Blues" (Kerouac), **Supp. III Part 1:** 225
Sangamon County Peace Advocate, The (Lindsay), **Supp. I Part 2:** 379
Sanger, Margaret, **Supp. I Part 1:** 19
Sansom, William, **IV:** 279
Sans Soleil (film), **Supp. IV Part 2:** 436
"Santa" (Sexton), **Supp. II Part 2:** 693
Santa Claus: A Morality (Cummings), **I:** 430, 441
"Santa Fé Trail, The" (Lindsay), **Supp. I Part 2:** 389
"Santa Lucia" (Hass), **Supp. VI:** 105–106
"Santa Lucia II" (Hass), **Supp. VI:** 105–106
Santayana, George, **I:** 222, 224, 236, 243, 253, 460; **II:** 20, 542; **III:** 64, **599–622**; **IV:** 26, 339, 351, 353, 441; **Retro. Supp. I:** 55, 57, 67, 295; **Retro. Supp. II:** 179; **Supp. I Part 2:** 428; **Supp. II Part 1:** 107; **Supp. X:** 58
Santiago, Esmeralda, **Supp. XI:** 177
"Santorini: Stopping the Leak" (Merrill), **Supp. III Part 1:** 336
Santos, John Phillip, **Supp. XIII:** 274
Santos, Sherod, **Supp. VIII:** 270
Sapir, Edward, **Supp. VIII:** 295
Sapphira and the Slave Girl (Cather), **I:** 331; **Retro. Supp. I:** 2, **19–20**
Sappho, **II:** 544; **III:** 142; **Supp. I Part 1:** 261, 269; **Supp. I Part 2:** 458; **Supp. XII:** 98, 99
"Sappho" (Wright), **Supp. III Part 2:** 595, 604
"Sarah" (Schwartz), **Supp. II Part 2:** 663
"Saratoga" mysteries (Dobyns), **Supp. XIII:** 79–80
Sargent, John Singer, **II:** 337, 338
Saroyan, William, **III:** 146–147; **IV:** 393; **Supp. I Part 2:** 679; **Supp. IV Part 1:** 83; **Supp. IV Part 2:** 502; **Supp. XIII:** 280
Sarris, Greg, **Supp. IV Part 1:** 329, 330
Sarton, George, **Supp. VIII:** 249
Sarton, May, **Supp. III Part 1:** 62, 63; **Supp. VIII: 249–268**; **Supp. XIII:** 296
Sartoris (Faulkner), **II:** 55, 56–57, 58, 62; **Retro. Supp. I:** 77, 81, 82, 83, 88
Sartor Resartus (Carlyle), **II:** 26; **III:** 82

Sartre, Jean-Paul, **I:** 82, 494; **II:** 57, 244; **III:** 51, 204, 292, 453, 619; **IV:** 6, 223, 236, 477, 487, 493; **Retro. Supp. I:** 73; **Supp. I Part 1:** 51; **Supp. IV Part 1:** 42, 84; **Supp. VIII:** 11; **Supp. IX:** 4; **Supp. XIII:** 74, 171
Sassone, Ralph, **Supp. X:** 171
Sassoon, Siegfried, **II:** 367
Satan in Goray (Singer), **IV:** 1, 6–7, 12; **Retro. Supp. II:** 321, **322–323**
Satan Says (Olds), **Supp. X:** 201, 202, **202–204**, 215
"Satan Says" (Olds), **Supp. X:** 202
Satanstoe (Cooper), **I:** 351–352, 355
"Sather Gate Illumination" (Ginsberg), **Supp. II Part 1:** 329
"Satire as a Way of Seeing" (Dos Passos), **III:** 172
Satires of Persius, The (Merwin, trans.), **Supp. III Part 1:** 347
Satirical Rogue on Poetry, The (Francis). *See Pot Shots at Poetry* (Francis)
Satori in Paris (Kerouac), **Supp. III Part 1:** 231
"Saturday" (Salinas), **Supp. XIII:** 315
"Saturday Route, The" (Wolfe), **Supp. III Part 2:** 580
Satyagraha (Gandhi), **IV:** 185
Saunders, Richard, **II:** 110
Savage, Augusta, **Retro. Supp. II:** 115
Savage, James, **II:** 111
Savage Holiday (Wright), **IV:** 478, 488
Savage Love (Shepard and Chaikin), **Supp. III Part 2:** 433
Savage Wilds (Reed), **Supp. X:** 241
Save Me, Joe Louis (Bell), **Supp. X:** 7, 10, **11–12**
Save Me the Waltz (Z. Fitzgerald), **II:** 95; **Retro. Supp. I:** 110; **Supp. IX:** 58, 59, 65, **66–68**
Savers, Michael, **Supp. XI:** 307
Saving Lives (Goldbarth), **Supp. XII:** 192
Saving Private Ryan (film), **Supp. V:** 249; **Supp. XI:** 234
Savings (Hogan), **Supp. IV Part 1:** 397, 404, 405, 406, 410
Savo, Jimmy, **I:** 440
Savran, David, **Supp. IX:** 145; **Supp. XIII:** 209
Sawyer-Lauçanno, Christopher, **Supp. IV Part 1:** 95
Saxon, Lyle, **Retro. Supp. I:** 80
Saye and Sele, Lord, **Supp. I Part 1:** 98
Sayer, Mandy, **Supp. XIII:** 118
Sayers, Dorothy, **Supp. IV Part 1:** 341; **Supp. IV Part 2:** 464

Sayers, Valerie, **Supp. XI:** 253
"Sayings/For Luck" (Goldbarth), **Supp. XII:** 176
Say! Is This the U.S.A.? (Caldwell), **I:** 293, 294–295, 304, 309, 310
Saylor, Bruce, **Supp. XII:** 253
Sayre, Joel, **Supp. XIII:** 166
Sayre, Nora, **Supp. XII:** 119
Sayre, Zelda, **Retro. Supp. I:** 101, 102–103, 104, 105, 108, 109, 110, 113, 114. *See also* Fitzgerald, Zelda (Zelda Sayre)
"Say Yes" (Wolff), **Supp. VII:** 344
"Scales of the Eyes, The" (Nemerov), **III:** 272, 273, 277
Scalpel (McCoy), **Supp. XIII: 174–175**
Scalpel (screen treatment, McCoy), **Supp. XIII:** 174
Scandalabra (Zelda Fitzgerald), **Supp. IX:** 60, 61, 65, 67, **68–70**
"Scandal Detectives, The" (Fitzgerald), **II:** 80–81; **Retro. Supp. I:** 99
Scarberry-García, Susan, **Supp. IV Part 2:** 486
"Scarecrow, The" (Farrell), **II:** 45
"Scarf, A" (Shields), **Supp. VII:** 328
Scarlet Letter, The (Hawthorne), **II:** 63, 223, 224, 231, 233, 239–240, 241, 243, 244, 255, 264, 286, 290, 291, 550; **Retro. Supp. I:** 63, 145, 147, 152, **157–159**, 160, 163, 165, 220, 248, 330, 335; **Retro. Supp. II:** 100; **Supp. I Part 1:** 38; **Supp. II Part 1:** 386; **Supp. VIII:** 108, 198; **Supp. XII:** 11
Scarlet Plague, The (London), **II:** 467
Scar Lover (Crews), **Supp. XI:** 103, 107, **114–115**
"Scarred Girl, The" (Dickey), **Supp. IV Part 1:** 180
"Scenario" (H. Miller), **III:** 184
"Scene" (Howells), **II:** 274
"Scene in Jerusalem, A" (Stowe), **Supp. I Part 2:** 587
"Scenes" (Shields), **Supp. VII:** 318
Scènes d'Anabase (chamber music) (Bowles), **Supp. IV Part 1:** 82
Scenes from American Life (Gurney), **Supp. V:** 95, 96, 105, 108
Scenes from Another Life (McClatchy), **Supp. XII: 255–256**
"Scenes of Childhood" (Merrill), **Supp. III Part 1:** 322, 323, 327
"Scented Herbage of My Breast" (Whitman), **IV:** 342–343
"Scent of Unbought Flowers, The" (Ríos), **Supp. IV Part 2:** 547
Scepticisms (Aiken), **I:** 58
Scève, Maurice, **Supp. III Part 1:** 11

Schad, Christian, **Supp. IV Part 1:** 247
Schaller, George, **Supp. V:** 208, 210–211
Schapiro, Meyer, **II:** 30
Scharmann, Hermann Balthazar, **Supp. XII:** 41
Schary, Dore, **Supp. IV Part 1:** 365; **Supp. XIII:** 163
Schaumbergh, Count de, **II:** 120
Scheffauer, G. H., **I:** 199
"Scheherazade" (Ashbery), **Supp. III Part 1:** 18
Scheick, William, **Supp. V:** 272
Scheler, Max, **I:** 58
Schelling, Friedrich, **Supp. I Part 2:** 422
Schenk, Margaret, **I:** 199
Scheponik, Peter, **Supp. X:** 210
Scherer, Loline, **Supp. XIII:** 161
Schevill, James, **I:** 116
Schilder, Paul, **Supp. I Part 2:** 622
Schiller, Andrew, **II:** 20
Schiller, Frederick, **Supp. V:** 290
Schiller, Johann Christoph Friedrich von, **I:** 224; **Supp. IV Part 2:** 519
Schiller, Lawrence, **Retro. Supp. II:** 208, 212, 214
Schimmel, Harold, **Supp. V:** 336
Schlegel, Augustus Wilhelm, **III:** 422, 424
Schlegell, David von, **Supp. IV Part 2:** 423
Schleiermacher, Friedrich, **III:** 290–291, 309
Schlesinger, Arthur, Jr., **III:** 291, 297–298, 309
Schmidt, Jon Zlotnik, **Supp. IV Part 1:** 2
Schmidt, Kaspar. *See* Stirner, Max
Schmidt, Michael, **Supp. X:** 55
Schmitt, Carl, **I:** 386–387
Schmitz, Neil, **Supp. X:** 243
Schneider, Alan, **I:** 87
Schneider, Louis, **Supp. I Part 2:** 650
Schneider, Romy, **Supp. IV Part 2:** 549
Schneider, Steven, **Supp. IX:** 271, 274
Schnellock, Emil, **III:** 177
Schneour, Zalman, **IV:** 11
"Scholar Gypsy, The" (Arnold), **II:** 541
"Scholastic and Bedside Teaching" (Holmes), **Supp. I Part 1:** 305
Schöler, Bo, **Supp. IV Part 1:** 399, 400, 403, 407, 409; **Supp. IV Part 2:** 499
Scholes, Robert, **Supp. V:** 40, 42
Schomburg, Arthur, **Supp. X:** 134
Schoolcraft, Henry Rowe, **II:** 503; **Retro. Supp. II:** 160

"School Daze" (Bambara), **Supp. XI:** 19

School Daze (film), **Supp. XI:** 19, 20

"Schoolhouse" (Levis), **Supp. XI:** 258

"School of Giorgione, The" (Pater), **I:** 51

"School Play, The" (Merrill), **Supp. III Part 1:** 336

"Schooner Fairchild's Class" (Benét), **Supp. XI:** 55

Schopenhauer, Arthur, **III:** 600, 604; **IV:** 7; **Retro. Supp. I:** 256; **Retro. Supp. II:** 94; **Supp. I Part 1:** 320; **Supp. I Part 2:** 457; **Supp. X:** 187

Schorer, Mark, **II:** 28; **III:** 71; **Retro. Supp. I:** 115; **Supp. IV Part 1:** 197, 203, 211

Schott, Webster, **Supp. IX:** 257

Schotts, Jeffrey, **Supp. XII:** 193

Schrader, Mary von. *See* Jarrell, Mrs. Randall (Mary von Schrader)

Schreiner, Olive, **I:** 419; **Supp. XI:** 203

Schroeder, Eric James, **Supp. V:** 238, 244

Schubert, Franz Peter, **Supp. I Part 1:** 363

Schubnell, Matthias, **Supp. IV Part 2:** 486

Schulberg, Budd, **II:** 98; **Retro. Supp. I:** 113; **Supp. XIII:** 170

Schulz, Bruno, **Supp. IV Part 2:** 623

Schuman, William, **Supp. XII:** 253

Schumann, Dr. Alanson Tucker, **III:** 505

Schuster, Edgar H., **Supp. VIII:** 126

Schuyler, George S., **III:** 110

Schuyler, William, **Supp. I Part 1:** 211

Schwartz, Delmore, **I:** 67, 168, 188, 288; **IV:** 128, 129, 437; **Retro. Supp. II:** 29, 178; **Supp. II Part 1:** 102, 109; **Supp. II Part 2: 639–668; Supp. VIII:** 98; **Supp. IX:** 299; **Supp. XIII:** 320

Schwartz, Lloyd, **Supp. I Part 1:** 81

Schwartz, Marilyn, **Supp. XII:** 126, 128, 130, 132

Schweitzer, Albert, **Supp. IV Part 1:** 373

Schweitzer, Harold, **Supp. X:** 210

Schwitters, Kurt, **III:** 197; **Retro. Supp. II:** 340, 349, 354; **Supp. IV Part 1:** 79

"Science" (Jeffers), **Supp. II Part 2:** 426

Science and Health with Key to the Scriptures (Eddy), **I:** 383

"Science Favorable to Virtue" (Freneau), **Supp. II Part 1:** 274

Science of English Verse, The (Lanier), **Supp. I Part 1:** 368, 369

"Science of the Night, The" (Kunitz), **Supp. III Part 1:** 258, 265

Sciolino, Martina, **Supp. XII:** 9

Scopes, John T., **III:** 105, 495

"Scorched Face, The" (Hammett), **Supp. IV Part 1:** 344

"Scorpion, The" (Bowles), **Supp. IV Part 1:** 84, 86

Scorsese, Martin, **Supp. IV Part 1:** 356

Scott, A. O., **Supp. X:** 301, 302; **Supp. XII:** 343

Scott, Anne Firor, **Supp. I Part 1:** 19

Scott, Evelyn, **Retro. Supp. I:** 73

Scott, George C., **III:** 165–166; **Supp. XI:** 304

Scott, George Lewis, **Supp. I Part 2:** 503, 504

Scott, Herbert, **Supp. V:** 180

Scott, Howard, **Supp. I Part 2:** 645

Scott, Lizabeth, **Supp. IV Part 2:** 524

Scott, Lynn Orilla, **Retro. Supp. II:** 12

Scott, Mark, **Retro. Supp. I:** 127

Scott, Nathan A., Jr., **II:** 27

Scott, Paul, **Supp. IV Part 2:** 690

Scott, Ridley, **Supp. XIII:** 268

Scott, Sir Walter, **I:** 204, 339, 341, 343, 354; **II:** 8, 17, 18, 217, 296, 301, 303, 304, 308; **III:** 415, 482; **IV:** 204, 453; **Retro. Supp. I:** 99; **Supp. I Part 2:** 579, 580, 685, 692; **Supp. IV Part 2:** 690; **Supp. IX:** 175; **Supp. X:** 51, 114

Scott, Winfield Townley, **II:** 512; **Supp. I Part 2:** 705

Scottsboro boys, **I:** 505; **Supp. I Part 1:** 330

Scottsboro Limited (Hughes), **Retro. Supp. I:** 203; **Supp. I Part 1:** 328, 330–331, 332

Scoundrel Time (Hellman), **Supp. I Part 1:** 294–297; **Supp. IV Part 1:** 12; **Supp. VIII:** 243

Scratch (MacLeish), **III:** 22–23

"Scream, The" (Lowell), **II:** 550

"Screamer, The" (Coleman), **Supp. XI:** 92–93

"Screamers, The" (Baraka), **Supp. II Part 1:** 38

"Screen Guide for Americans" (Rand), **Supp. IV Part 2:** 524

"Screeno" (Schwartz), **Supp. II Part 2:** 660

Screens, The (Genet), **Supp. XII:** 12

Scripts for the Pageant (Merrill), **Supp. III Part 1:** 332, 333, 335

Scrolls from the Dead Sea, The (Wilson), **IV:** 429

Scruggs, Earl, **Supp. V:** 335

Scudder, Horace Elisha, **II:** 400, 401; **Retro. Supp. II:** 67; **Supp. I Part 1:** 220; **Supp. I Part 2:** 410, 414

Scully, James, **Supp. XII:** 131

"Sculpting the Whistle" (Ríos), **Supp. IV Part 2:** 549

"Sculptor" (Plath), **Supp. I Part 2:** 538

"Sculptor's Funeral, The" (Cather), **I:** 315–316; **Retro. Supp. I:** 5, 6

Scum (Singer), **Retro. Supp. II:** 334–335

Scupoli, Lorenzo, **IV:** 156

"Scythe Song" (Lang), **Retro. Supp. I:** 128

Sea and the Mirror, The: A Commentary on Shakespeare's "The Tempest" (Auden), **Supp. II Part 1:** 2, 18

Sea around Us, The (Carson), **Supp. IX:** 19, 23–25

Sea around Us, The (film), **Supp. IX:** 25

Sea Birds Are Still Alive, The (Bambara), **Supp. XI:** 1, 4, 7–12

"Sea Birds Are Still Alive, The" (Bambara), **Supp. XI:** 8

"Sea-Blue and Blood-Red" (Lowell), **II:** 524

Seabrook, John, **Supp. VIII:** 157

"Sea Burial from the Cruiser Reve" (Eberhart), **I:** 532–533

Seabury, David, **Supp. I Part 2:** 608

"Sea Calm" (Hughes), **Retro. Supp. I:** 199

"Sea Chanty" (Corso), **Supp. XII:** 118

"Sea Dream, A" (Whitter), **Supp. I Part 2:** 699

"Seafarer, The" (Pound, trans.), **Retro. Supp. I:** 287

Seagall, Harry, **Supp. XIII:** 166

Sea Garden (Doolittle), **Supp. I Part 1:** 257, 259, 266, 269, 272

Seager, Allan, **IV:** 305

"Sea Lily" (Doolittle), **Supp. I Part 1:** 266

Sea Lions, The (Cooper), **I:** 354, 355

Sealts, Merton M., Jr., **Retro. Supp. I:** 257

Seaman, Donna, **Supp. VIII:** 86; **Supp. X:** 1, 4, 12, 16, 213

"Séance, The" (Singer), **IV:** 20

Séance and Other Stories, The (Singer), **IV:** 19–21

Sea of Cortez (Steinbeck), **IV:** 52, 54, 62, 69

"Sea Pieces" (Melville), **III:** 93

Searches and Seizures (Elkin), **Supp. VI:** 49

"Search for Southern Identity, The" (Woodward), **Retro. Supp. I:** 75

Search for the King, A: A Twelfth-Century Legend (Vidal), **Supp. IV Part 2:** 681
Searching for Caleb (Tyler), **Supp. IV Part 2:** 663–665, 671
"Searching for Poetry: Real *vs.* Fake" (B. Miller), **Supp. IV Part 1:** 67
Searching for Survivors (Banks), **Supp. V:** 7
"Searching for Survivors (I)" (Banks), **Supp. V:** 8
"Searching for Survivors (II)" (Banks), **Supp. V:** 7, 8
Searching for the Ox (Simpson), **Supp. IX:** 266, **274–275**
"Searching for the Ox" (Simpson), **Supp. IX:** 275, 280
"Searching in the Britannia Tavern" (Wagoner), **Supp. IX:** 327
Searching Wing, The, (Hellman), **Supp. I Part 1:** 277, 278, 281–282, 283, 292, 297
"Search Party, The" (Matthews), **Supp. IX: 156**
Searle, Ronald, **Supp. I Part 2:** 604, 605
"Seascape" (Bishop), **Retro. Supp. II:** 42–43
"Sea's Green Sameness, The" (Updike), **IV:** 217
Seaside and the Fireside, The (Longfellow), **II:** 489; **Retro. Supp. II:** 159, 168
Season in Hell, A (Rimbaud), **III:** 189
Seasons, The (Thomson), **II:** 304; **Supp. I Part 1:** 151
Seasons' Difference, The (Buechner), **Supp. XII:** 47
Seasons of Celebration (Merton), **Supp. VIII:** 199, 208
"Seasons of the Soul" (Tate), **IV:** 136–140
"Sea Surface Full of Clouds" (Stevens), **IV:** 82
"Sea Unicorns and Land Unicorns" (Moore), **III:** 202–203
Seaver, Richard, **Supp. XI:** 301
"Seaweed" (Longfellow), **II:** 498
Sea-Wolf, The (London), **II:** 264, 466, 472–473
Seckler, David, **Supp. I Part 2:** 650
Second American Revolution and Other Essays (1976–1982), The (Vidal), **Supp. IV Part 2:** 679, 687, 688
Secondary Colors, The (A. Theroux), **Supp. VIII:** 312
Second Chance (Auchincloss), **Supp. IV Part 1:** 33
"Second Chances" (Hugo), **Supp. VI:** 144, 145

Second Coming, The (Percy), **Supp. III Part 1:** 383, 384, 387, 388, 396–397
"Second Coming, The" (Yeats), **III:** 294; **Retro. Supp. I:** 290, 311; **Supp. VIII:** 24
Second Decade, The. See *Stephen King, The Second Decade: "Danse Macabre" to "The Dark Half"* (Magistrale)
Second Dune, The (Hearon), **Supp. VIII:** 58, **59–60**
Second Flowering, A: Works and Days of the Lost Generation (Cowley), **Retro. Supp. II:** 77; **Supp. II Part 1:** 135, 141, 143, 144, 147, 149
Second Growth (Stegner), **Supp. IV Part 2:** 599, 608
Second Marriage (F. Barthelme), **Supp. XI:** 32, 33
Second Nature (Hoffman), **Supp. X:** 88, 89
"2nd Air Force" (Jarrell), **II:** 375
Second Set, The (Komunyakaa and Feinstein, eds.), **Supp. XIII:** 125
Second Sex, The (Beauvoir), **Retro. Supp. II:** 283; **Supp. IV Part 1:** 360
Second Stone, The (Fiedler), **Supp. XIII:** 102
"Second Swimming, The" (Boyle), **Supp. VIII:** 13, 14
Second Tree from the Corner (White), **Supp. I Part 2:** 654
"Second Tree from the Corner" (White), **Supp. I Part 2:** 651
Second Twenty Years at Hull-House, The: September 1909 to September 1929, with a Record of a Growing World Consciousness (Addams), **Supp. I Part 1:** 24–25
Second Voyage of Columbus, The (Morison), **Supp. I Part 2:** 488
Second Words, (Atwood), **Supp. XIII:** 35
Second World, The (Blackmur), **Supp. II Part 1:** 91
"Secret, The" (Levine), **Supp. V:** 195
Secret Agent, The (Conrad), **Supp. IV Part 1:** 341
Secret Agent X-9 (Hammett), **Supp. IV Part 1:** 355
"Secret Courts of Men's Hearts, The: Code and Law in Harper Lee's *To Kill a Mockingbird*" (Johnson), **Supp. VIII:** 126
"Secret Dog, The" (Cameron), **Supp. XII: 83–84**
Secret Garden, The (Burnett), **Supp. I Part 1:** 44

Secret Historie (J. Smith), **I:** 131
Secret History of the Dividing Line (Howe), **Supp. IV Part 2:** 424, 425–426
"Secret Integration, The" (Pynchon), **Supp. II Part 2:** 624
"Secret Life of Walter Mitty, The" (Thurber), **Supp. I Part 2:** 623
"Secret Lion, The" (Ríos), **Supp. IV Part 2:** 543, 544
"Secret of the Russian Ballet, The" (Van Vechten), **Supp. II Part 2:** 732
"Secret Prune" (Ríos), **Supp. IV Part 2:** 549
Secret River, The (Rawlings), **Supp. X:** 233
Secrets and Surprises (Beattie), **Supp. V:** 23, 27, 29
Secrets from the Center of the World (Harjo), **Supp. XII: 223–224**
"Secret Sharer, The" (Conrad), **Supp. IX:** 105
"Secret Society, A" (Nemerov), **III:** 282
Secular Journal of Thomas Merton, The, **Supp. VIII:** 206
"Security" (Stafford), **Supp. XI:** 329
Sedges, John (pseudonym). See Buck, Pearl S.
Sedgwick, Catherine Maria, **I:** 341; **Supp. I Part 1:** 155, 157
Sedgwick, Christina. See Marquand, Mrs. John P. (Christina Sedgwick)
Sedgwick, Ellery, **I:** 217, 229, 231; **III:** 54–55
Sedgwick, Henry, **Supp. I Part 1:** 156
Sedgwick, Robert, **Supp. I Part 1:** 156
"Seduction and Betrayal" (Hardwick), **Supp. III Part 1:** 207
Seduction and Betrayal: Women and Literature (Hardwick), **Supp. III Part 1:** 194, 204, 206–208, 212, 213
Seed, David, **Supp. IV Part 1:** 391
"Seed Eaters, The" (Francis), **Supp. IX:** 82
"Seed Leaves" (Wilbur), **Supp. III Part 2:** 558
"Seeds" (Anderson), **I:** 106, 114
Seeds of Contemplation (Merton), **Supp. VIII:** 199, 200, 207, 208
Seeds of Destruction (Merton), **Supp. VIII:** 202, 203, 204, 208
Seeing through the Sun (Hogan), **Supp. IV Part 1:** 397, 400, 401–402, 402, 413
"See in the Midst of Fair Leaves" (Moore), **III:** 215
"Seekers, The" (McGrath), **Supp. X:** 117

"Seele im Raum" (Jarrell), **II:** 382–383
"Seele im Raum" (Rilke), **II:** 382–383
"See Naples and Die" (Hecht), **Supp. X:** 69, 70
"Seen from the 'L'" (Barnes), **Supp. III Part 1:** 33
"See the Moon?" (Barthelme), **Supp. IV Part 1:** 42, 49–50, 50
Segal, D. (pseudonym). *See* Singer, Isaac Bashevis
Segal, George, **Supp. XI:** 343
Segregation: The Inner Conflict in the South (Warren), **IV:** 237, 238, 246, 252
Segrest, Mab, **Retro. Supp. II:** 292
Seidel, Frederick, **I:** 185
Seize the Day (Bellow), **I:** 144, 147, 148, 150, 151, 152, 153, 155, 158, 162; **Retro. Supp. II:** 19, 23–24, 27, 32, 34; **Supp. I Part 2:** 428
Selby, Hubert, **Supp. III Part 1:** 125
Selby, John, **Retro. Supp. II:** 221, 222
Seldes, Gilbert, **II:** 437, 445; **Retro. Supp. I:** 108
Selected Criticism: Prose, Poetry (Bogan), **Supp. III Part 1:** 64
Selected Essays (Eliot), **I:** 572
Selected Letters (W. C. Williams), **Retro. Supp. I:** 430
Selected Letters of Robert Frost (Thompson, ed.), **Retro. Supp. I:** 125
Selected Levis, The (Levis), **Supp. XI:** 257, 272
Selected Poems (Aiken), **I:** 69
Selected Poems (Ashbery), **Supp. III Part 1:** 25–26
Selected Poems (Bly), **Supp. IV Part 1:** 60, 62, 65, 66, 68, 69–71
Selected Poems (Brodsky), **Supp. VIII:** 22
Selected Poems (Brooks), **Supp. III Part 1:** 82–83
Selected Poems (Corso), **Supp. XII:** 129
Selected Poems (Dove), **Supp. IV Part 1:** 241, 243, 250
Selected Poems (Frost), **Retro. Supp. I:** 133, 136
Selected Poems (Guillevic; Levertov, trans.), **Supp. III Part 1:** 283
Selected Poems (Hayden), **Supp. II Part 1:** 363, 364, 367
Selected Poems (Hughes), **Retro. Supp. I:** 202; **Supp. I Part 1:** 341, 345, 346
Selected Poems (Hugo), **Supp. VI:** 143
Selected Poems (Jarrell), **II:** 367, 370, 371, 374, 377, 379, 380, 381, 382, 384
Selected Poems (Justice), **Supp. VII:** 115
Selected Poems (Kinnell), **Supp. III Part 1:** 235, 253
Selected Poems (Levine, 1984), **Supp. V:** 178, 179
Selected Poems (Lowell), **II:** 512, 516; **Retro. Supp. II:** 184, 186, 188, 190
Selected Poems (Merton), **Supp. VIII:** 207, 208
Selected Poems (Moore), **III:** 193, 194, 205–206, 208, 215
Selected Poems (Pound), **Retro. Supp. I:** 289, 291
Selected Poems (Ransom), **III:** 490, 492
Selected Poems (Rukeyser), **Supp. VI:** 274
Selected Poems (Sexton), **Supp. IV Part 2:** 449
Selected Poems (Strand), **Supp. IV Part 2:** 630
Selected Poems 1936–1965 (Eberhart), **I:** 541
Selected Poems 1965–1975 (Atwood), **Supp. XIII:** 32–34
Selected Poems, 1923–1943 (Warren), **IV:** 241–242, 243
Selected Poems, 1928–1958 (Kunitz), **Supp. III Part 1:** 261, 263–265
Selected Poems, 1938–1988 (McGrath), **Supp. X:** 127
Selected Poems: 1957–1987 (Snodgrass), **Supp. VI:** 314–315, 323, 324
Selected Poems, 1963–1983 (Simic), **Supp. VIII:** 275
Selected Poems II: Poems Selected and New, 1976–1986 (Atwood), **Supp. XIII:** 20, 34–35
Selected Poems of Ezra Pound (Pound), **Supp. V:** 336
Selected Poems of Gabriela Mistral (Hughes, trans.), **Supp. I Part 1:** 345
Selected Poetry of Amiri Baraka/LeRoi Jones (Baraka), **Supp. II Part 1:** 58
Selected Stories (Dubus), **Supp. VII:** 88–89
Selected Stories of Richard Bausch, The (Bausch), **Supp. VII:** 42
Selected Translations (Snodgrass), **Supp. VI:** 318, 324, 325–326
Selected Works of Djuna Barnes, The (Barnes), **Supp. III Part 1:** 44
Selected Writings 1950–1990 (Howe), **Supp. VI:** 116–117, 118, 120
Select Epigrams from the Greek Anthology (Mackail), **Supp. I Part 2:** 461
"Selene Afterwards" (MacLeish), **III:** 8
"Self" (James), **II:** 351
Self and the Dramas of History, The (Niebuhr), **III:** 308
Self-Consciousness (Updike), **Retro. Supp. I:** 318, 319, 320, 322, 323, 324
Self-Help: Stories (Moore), **Supp. X:** 163, 166, **167–169,** 174, 175
Self-Interviews (Dickey), **Supp. IV Part 1:** 179
"Self-Made Man, A" (Crane), **I:** 420
"Self-Portrait" (Creeley), **Supp. IV Part 1:** 156
"Self-Portrait" (Mumford), **Supp. II Part 2:** 471
"Self-Portrait" (Wylie), **Supp. I Part 2:** 729
Self-Portrait: Ceaselessly into the Past (Millar, ed. Sipper), **Supp. IV Part 2:** 464, 469, 472, 475
"Self-Portrait in a Convex Mirror" (Ashbery), **Supp. III Part 1:** 5, 7, 9, 16–19, 22, 24, 26
"Self-Reliance" (Emerson), **II:** 7, 15, 17; **Retro. Supp. I:** 159; **Retro. Supp. II:** 155; **Supp. X:** 42, 45
Sélincourt, Ernest de, **Supp. I Part 2:** 676
Selinger, Eric Murphy, **Supp. XI:** 248
Sellers, Isaiah, **IV:** 194–195
Sellers, Peter, **Supp. XI:** 301, 304, 306, 307, 309
Sellers, William, **IV:** 208
Seltzer, Mark, **Retro. Supp. I:** 227
Selznick, David O., **Retro. Supp. I:** 105, 113; **Supp. IV Part 1:** 353
"Semi-Lunatics of Kilmuir, The" (Hugo), **Supp. VI:** 145
"Semiotics/The Doctor's Doll" (Goldbarth), **Supp. XII:** 183–184
Semmelweiss, Ignaz, **Supp. I Part 1:** 304
Senancour, Étienne Divert de, **I:** 241
Sendak, Maurice, **Supp. IX:** 207, 208, 213, 214
Seneca, **II:** 14–15; **III:** 77
Senghor, Leopold Sédar, **Supp. IV Part 1:** 16; **Supp. X:** 132, 139
Senier, Siobhan, **Supp. IV Part 1:** 330
"Senility" (Anderson), **I:** 114
"Senior Partner's Ethics, The" (Auchincloss), **Supp. IV Part 1:** 33
Senlin: A Biography (Aiken), **I:** 48, 49, 50, 52, 56, 57, 64
Sennett, Mack, **III:** 442
"Señora X No More" (Mora), **Supp. XIII:** 218

INDEX / 555

"Señor Ong and Señor Ha" (Bowles), **Supp. IV Part 1:** 87
Sense of Beauty, The (Santayana), **III:** 600
Sense of Life in the Modern Novel, The (Mizener), **IV:** 132
"Sense of Shelter, A" (Updike), **Retro. Supp. I:** 318
Sense of the Past, The (James), **II:** 337–338
"Sense of the Past, The" (Trilling), **Supp. III Part 2:** 503
"Sense of the Present, The" (Hardwick), **Supp. III Part 1:** 210
"Sense of the Sleight-of-Hand Man, The" (Stevens), **IV:** 93
"Sense of Where You Are, A" (McPhee), **Supp. III Part 1:** 291, 296–298
"Sensibility! O La!" (Roethke), **III:** 536
"Sensible Emptiness, A" (Kramer), **Supp. IV Part 1:** 61, 66
"Sensuality Plunging Barefoot Into Thorns" (Cisneros), **Supp. VII:** 68
"Sentence" (Barthelme), **Supp. IV Part 1:** 47
Sent for You Yesterday (Wideman), **Supp. X:** 320, 321
"Sentimental Education, A" (Banks), **Supp. V:** 10
"Sentimental Journey" (Oates), **Supp. II Part 2:** 522, 523
"Sentimental Journey, A" (Anderson), **I:** 114
Sentimental Journey, A (Sterne), **Supp. I Part 2:** 714
"Sentimental Journeys" (Didion), **Supp. IV Part 1:** 211
"Sentiment of Rationality, The" (James), **II:** 346–347
Separate Flights (Dubus), **Supp. VII:** 78–83
"Separate Flights" (Dubus), **Supp. VII:** 83
Separate Peace, A (Knowles), **Supp. IV Part 2:** 679; **Supp. XII:** 241–249
"Separating" (Updike), **Retro. Supp. I:** 321
"Separation, The" (Kunitz), **Supp. III Part 1:** 263
"Sepia High Stepper" (Hayden), **Supp. II Part 1:** 379
"September" (Komunyakaa), **Supp. XIII:** 130
"September 1, 1939" (Auden), **Supp. II Part 1:** 13; **Supp. IV Part 1:** 225; **Supp. VIII:** 30, 32
September 11, 2001: American Writers Respond (Heyen), **Supp. XIII:** 285
September Song (Humphrey), **Supp. IX:** 101, 102, **108–109**
"Sept Vieillards, Les" (Millay, trans.), **III:** 142
Sequel to Drum-Taps (Whitman), **Retro. Supp. I:** 406
"Sequence, Sometimes Metaphysical" (Roethke), **III:** 547, 548
Sequence of Seven Plays with a Drawing by Ron Slaughter, A (Nemerov), **III:** 269
Sequoya, Jana, **Supp. IV Part 1:** 334
Seraglio, The (Merrill), **Supp. III Part 1:** 331
Seraphita (Balzac), **I:** 499
Seraph on the Suwanee (Hurston), **Supp. VI:** 149, 159–160
Sergeant, Elizabeth Shepley, **I:** 231, 236, 312, 319, 323, 328
Sergeant Bilko (television show), **Supp. IV Part 2:** 575
"Serious Talk, A" (Carver), **Supp. III Part 1:** 138, 144
Serly, Tibor, **Supp. III Part 2:** 617, 619
"Sermon by Doctor Pep" (Bellow), **I:** 151
Sermones (Horace), **II:** 154
"Sermon for Our Maturity" (Baraka), **Supp. II Part 1:** 53
Sermons and Soda Water (O'Hara), **III:** 362, 364, 371–373, 382
"Sermons on the Warpland" (Brooks), **Supp. III Part 1:** 84
"Serpent in the Wilderness, The" (Masters), **Supp. I Part 2:** 458
Servant of the Bones (Rice), **Supp. VII:** 298, 302
"Servant to Servants, A" (Frost), **Retro. Supp. I:** 125, 128; **Supp. X:** 66
Seshachari, Neila, **Supp. V:** 22
"Session, The" (Adams), **I:** 5
"Sestina" (Bishop), **Supp. I Part 1:** 73, 88
Set-angya, **Supp. IV Part 2:** 493
Seth's Brother's Wife (Frederic), **II:** 131–132, 137, 144
Set This House on Fire (Styron), **IV:** 98, 99, 105, 107–113, 114, 115, 117
Setting Free the Bears (Irving), **Supp. VI:** 163, **166–167**, 169–170
Setting the Tone (Rorem), **Supp. IV Part 1:** 79
Settle, Mary Lee, **Supp. IX:** 96
Settlement Horizon, The: A National Estimate (Woods and Kennedy), **Supp. I Part 1:** 19
"Settling the Colonel's Hash" (McCarthy), **II:** 559, 562
Setzer, Helen, **Supp. IV Part 1:** 217
"Seurat's Sunday Afternoon along the Seine" (Schwartz), **Supp. II Part 2:** 663–665
Seven against Thebes (Aeschylus; Bacon and Hecht, trans.), **Supp. X:** 57
Seven Ages of Man, The (Wilder), **IV:** 357, 374–375
Seven Deadly Sins, The (Wilder), **IV:** 357, 374–375
Seven Descents of Myrtle, The (T. Williams), **IV:** 382
Seven Guitars (Wilson), **Supp. VIII:** 331, **348–351**
Seven-League Crutches, The (Jarrell), **II:** 367, 372, 381, 382, 383–384, 389
Seven Mountains of Thomas Merton, The (Mott), **Supp. VIII:** 208
Seven-Ounce Man, The (Harrison), **Supp. VIII:** 51
"Seven Places of the Mind" (Didion), **Supp. IV Part 1:** 200, 210
Seven Plays (Shepard), **Supp. III Part 2:** 434
"Seven Stanzas at Easter" (Updike), **IV:** 215
Seven Storey Mountain, The (Merton), **Supp. VIII:** 193, 195, 198, 200, 207, 208
Seventh Heaven (Hoffman), **Supp. X:** 87, 89
"Seventh of March" (Webster), **Supp. I Part 2:** 687
"7000 Romaine, Los Angeles 38" (Didion), **Supp. IV Part 1:** 200
"Seventh Street" (Toomer), **Supp. IX:** 316
Seven Types of Ambiguity (Empson), **II:** 536; **IV:** 431
77 Dream Songs (Berryman), **I:** 168, 169, 170, 171, 174, 175, 183–188
73 Poems (Cummings), **I:** 430, 431, 446, 447, 448
7 Years from Somewhere (Levine), **Supp. V:** 178, 181, 188–189
Sevier, Jack, **IV:** 378
Sévigné, Madame de, **IV:** 361
Sewall, Richard, **Retro. Supp. I:** 25
Sewall, Samuel, **IV:** 145, 146, 147, 149, 154, 164; **Supp. I Part 1:** 100, 110
Sewell, Elizabeth, **Supp. XIII:** 344
Sex, Economy, Freedom and Community (Berry), **Supp. X:** 30, 36
Sex & Character (Weininger), **Retro.**

Supp. I: 416
"Sext" (Auden), **Supp. II Part 1:** 22
Sexton, Anne, **Retro. Supp. II:** 245, 286; **Supp. I Part 2:** 538, 543, 546; **Supp. II Part 2: 669–700; Supp. III Part 2:** 599; **Supp. IV Part 1:** 245; **Supp. IV Part 2:** 439, 440–441, 442, 444, 447, 449, 451, 620; **Supp. V:** 113, 118, 124; **Supp. X:** 201, 202, 213; **Supp. XI:** 146, 240, 317; **Supp. XII:** 217, 253, 254, 256, 260, 261; **Supp. XIII:** 35, 76, 294, 312
Sexual Behavior in the American Male (Kinsey), **Supp. XIII:** 96–97
"Sexual Revolution, The" (Dunn), **Supp. XI:** 142
Sexus (H. Miller), **III:** 170, 171, 184, 187, 188
"Sex Without Love" (Olds), **Supp. X:** 206
Seyersted, Per E., **Retro. Supp. II:** 65; **Supp. I Part 1:** 201, 204, 211, 216, 225; **Supp. IV Part 2:** 558
Seyfried, Robin, **Supp. IX:** 324
"Seymour: An Introduction" (Salinger), **III:** 569–571, 572
Seymour, Miranda, **Supp. VIII:** 167
Shacochis, Bob, **Supp. VIII:** 80
"Shadow" (Creeley), **Supp. IV Part 1:** 158
"Shadow, The" (Lowell), **II:** 522
Shadow and Act (Ellison), **Retro. Supp. II:** 119; **Supp. II Part 1:** 245–246
"Shadow and Shade" (Tate), **IV:** 128
"Shadow and the Flesh, The" (London), **II:** 475
"Shadow A Parable" (Poe), **III:** 417–418
Shadow Country (Gunn Allen), **Supp. IV Part 1:** 322, 324, 325–326
Shadow Man, The (Gordon), **Supp. IV Part 1:** 297, 298, 299, 312–314, 315
Shadow of a Dream, The, a Story (Howells), **II:** 285, 286, 290
"Shadow of the Crime, The: A Word from the Author" (Mailer), **Retro. Supp. II:** 214
Shadow on the Dial, The (Bierce), **I:** 208, 209
"Shadow Passing" (Merwin), **Supp. III Part 1:** 355
Shadows (Gardner), **Supp. VI:** 74
Shadows by the Hudson (Singer), **IV:** 1
Shadows of Africa (Matthiessen), **Supp. V:** 203
Shadows on the Hudson (Singer), **Retro. Supp. II: 329–331**

Shadows on the Rock (Cather), **I:** 314, 330–331, 332; **Retro. Supp. I:** 18
Shadow Train (Ashbery), **Supp. III Part 1:** 23–24, 26
"Shad-Time" (Wilbur), **Supp. III Part 2:** 563
Shaffer, Thomas L., **Supp. VIII:** 127, 128
Shaft (Parks; film), **Supp. XI:** 17
Shaftesbury, Earl of, **I:** 559
Shahn, Ben, **Supp. X:** 24
Shakelford, Dean, **Supp. VIII:** 129
Shaker, Why Don't You Sing? (Angelou), **Supp. IV Part 1:** 16
Shakespear, Mrs. Olivia, **III:** 457; **Supp. I Part 1:** 257
"Shakespeare" (Emerson), **II:** 6
Shakespeare, William, **I:** 103, 271, 272, 284–285, 358, 378, 433, 441, 458, 461, 573, 585, 586; **II:** 5, 8, 11, 18, 72, 273, 297, 302, 309, 320, 411, 494, 577, 590; **III:** 3, 11, 12, 82, 83, 91, 124, 130, 134, 145, 153, 159, 183, 210, 263, 286, 468, 473, 492, 503, 511, 567, 575–576, 577, 610, 612, 613, 615; **IV:** 11, 50, 66, 127, 132, 156, 309, 313, 362, 368, 370, 373, 453; **Retro. Supp. I:** 43, 64, 91, 248; **Retro. Supp. II:** 114, 287–289, 317; **Supp. I Part 1:** 79, 150, 262, 310, 356, 363, 365, 368, 369, 370; **Supp. I Part 2:** 397, 421, 422, 470, 494, 622, 716, 720; **Supp. II Part 2:** 624, 626; **Supp. IV Part 1:** 31, 83, 87, 243; **Supp. IV Part 2:** 430, 463, 519, 688; **Supp. V:** 252, 280, 303; **Supp. VIII:** 160, 164; **Supp. IX:** 14, 133; **Supp. X:** 42, 62, 65, 78; **Supp. XII:** 54–57, 277, 281; **Supp. XIII:** 111, 115, 233
Shakespeare and His Forerunners (Lanier), **Supp. I Part 1:** 369
Shakespeare in Harlem (Hughes), **Retro. Supp. I:** 194, 202, 205, 206, 207, 208; **Supp. I Part 1:** 333, 334, 345
Shalit, Gene, **Supp. VIII:** 73
Shall We Gather at the River (Wright), **Supp. III Part 2:** 601–602
"Shame" (Oates), **Supp. II Part 2:** 520
"Shame" (Wilbur), **Supp. III Part 2:** 556
"Shameful Affair, A" (Chopin), **Retro. Supp. II:** 61
Shamela (Fielding), **Supp. V:** 127
"Shampoo, The" (Bishop), **Retro. Supp. II:** 46; **Supp. I Part 1:** 92
Shange, Ntozake, **Supp. VIII:** 214
Shank, Randy, **Supp. X:** 252
Shankaracharya, **III:** 567

Shannon, Sandra, **Supp. VIII:** 333, 348
"Shape of Flesh and Bone, The" (MacLeish), **III:** 18–19
Shape of the Journey, The (Harrison), **Supp. VIII:** 53
Shapes of Clay (Bierce), **I:** 208, 209
Shapiro, David, **Supp. XII:** 175, 185
Shapiro, Dorothy, **IV:** 380
Shapiro, Karl, **I:** 430, 521; **II:** 350; **III:** 527; **Supp. II Part 2: 701–724; Supp. III Part 2:** 623; **Supp. IV Part 2:** 645; **Supp. X:** 116; **Supp. XI:** 315
Shapiro, Laura, **Supp. IX:** 120
Sharif, Omar, **Supp. IX:** 253
"Shark Meat" (Snyder), **Supp. VIII:** 300
Shatayev, Elvira, **Supp. I Part 2:** 570
Shaviro, Steven, **Supp. VIII:** 189
Shaw, Colonel Robert Gould, **II:** 551
Shaw, Elizabeth. *See* Melville, Mrs. Herman (Elizabeth Shaw)
Shaw, George Bernard, **I:** 226; **II:** 82, 271, 276, 581; **III:** 69, 102, 113, 145, 155, 161, 162, 163, 373, 409; **IV:** 27, 64, 397, 432, 440; **Retro. Supp. I:** 100, 228; **Supp. IV Part 1:** 36; **Supp. IV Part 2:** 585, 683; **Supp. V:** 243–244, 290; **Supp. IX:** 68, 308; **Supp. XI:** 202; **Supp. XII:** 94
Shaw, Irwin, **IV:** 381; **Supp. IV Part 1:** 383; **Supp. IX:** 251; **Supp. XI:** 221, 229, 231
Shaw, Joseph Thompson ("Cap"), **Supp. IV Part 1:** 121, 345, 351; **Supp. XIII:** 161
Shaw, Judge Lemuel, **III:** 77, 88, 91
Shaw, Sarah Bryant, **Supp. I Part 1:** 169
Shaw, Wilbur, Jr., **Supp. XIII:** 162
Shawl, The (Ozick), **Supp. V:** 257, 260, 271
"Shawl, The" (Ozick), **Supp. V:** 271–272
Shawn, William, **Supp. VIII:** 151, 170
"Shawshank Redemption, The" (King), **Supp. V:** 148
She (Haggard), **III:** 189
Shearer, Flora, **I:** 199
"Sheaves, The" (Robinson), **III:** 510, 524
"She Came and Went" (Lowell), **Supp. I Part 2:** 409
Sheed, Wilfrid, **IV:** 230; **Supp. XI:** 233
Sheeler, Charles, **IV:** 409; **Retro. Supp. I:** 430
Sheffer, Jonathan, **Supp. IV Part 1:** 95
She Had Some Horses (Harjo), **Supp.**

XII: 220–223, 231
"She Had Some Horses" (Harjo), **Supp. XII:** 215, 222
"Shell, The" (Humphrey), **Supp. IX:** 94
Shelley, Percy Bysshe, **I:** 18, 68, 381, 476, 522, 577; **II:** 331, 516, 535, 540; **III:** 412, 426, 469; **IV:** 139; **Retro. Supp. I:** 308, 360; **Supp. I Part 1:** 79, 311, 349; **Supp. I Part 2:** 709, 718, 719, 720, 721, 722, 724, 728; **Supp. IV Part 1:** 235; **Supp. V:** 258, 280; **Supp. IX:** 51; **Supp. XII:** 117, 132, 136–137, 263
Shellow, Sadie Myers, **Supp. I Part 2:** 608
"Shelter" (Doty), **Supp. XI:** 132
Sheltered Life, The (Glasgow), **II:** 174, 175, 179, 186, 187–188
Sheltering Sky, The (Bowles), **Supp. IV Part 1:** 82, 84, 85–86, 87
Sheltering Sky, The (film), **Supp. IV Part 1:** 94, 95
Shelton, Frank, **Supp. IV Part 2:** 658
Shelton, Mrs. Sarah. *See* Royster, Sarah Elmira
Shelton, Richard, **Supp. XI:** 133; **Supp. XIII:** 7
Shenandoah (Schwartz), **Supp. II Part 2:** 640, 651–652
"Shenandoah" (Shapiro), **Supp. II Part 2:** 704
Shepard, Alice, **IV:** 287
Shepard, Odell, **II:** 508; **Supp. I Part 2:** 418
Shepard, Sam, **Supp. III Part 2:** 431–450
Shepard, Thomas, **I:** 554; **IV:** 158
Sheppard Lee (Bird), **III:** 423
"She Remembers the Future" (Harjo), **Supp. XII:** 222
Sheridan, Richard Brinsley, **Retro. Supp. I:** 127
Sherlock, William, **IV:** 152
Sherman, Sarah Way, **Retro. Supp. II:** 145
Sherman, Stuart Pratt, **I:** 222, 246–247; **Supp. I Part 2:** 423
Sherman, Susan, **Supp. VIII:** 265
Sherman, Tom, **IV:** 446
Sherman, William T., **IV:** 445, 446
Sherwood, Robert, **II:** 435; **Supp. IX:** 190
Sherwood Anderson & Other Famous Creoles (Faulkner), **I:** 117; **II:** 56
Sherwood Anderson Reader, The (Anderson), **I:** 114, 116
Sherwood Anderson's Memoirs (Anderson), **I:** 98, 101, 102, 103, 108, 112, 116

Sherwood Anderson's Notebook (Anderson), **I:** 108, 115, 117
She Stoops to Conquer (Goldsmith), **II:** 514
Shestov, Lev, **Supp. VIII:** 20, 24
Shetley, Vernon, **Supp. IX:** 292; **Supp. XI:** 123
"She Wept, She Railed" (Kunitz), **Supp. III Part 1:** 265
"Shiddah and Kuziba" (Singer), **IV:** 13, 15
Shield of Achilles, The (Auden), **Supp. II Part 1:** 21
"Shield of Achilles, The" (Auden), **Supp. II Part 1:** 21, 25
Shields, Carol, **Supp. VII:** 307–330
Shifting Landscape: A Composite, 1925–1987 (H. Roth), **Supp. IX:** 233–235
Shifts of Being (Eberhart), **I:** 525
Shigematsu, Soiko, **Supp. III Part 1:** 353
Shihab, Aziz, **Supp. XIII:** 273
Shih-hsiang Chen, **Supp. VIII:** 303
"Shiloh" (Mason), **Supp. VIII:** 140
Shiloh and Other Stories (Mason), **Supp. VIII:** 133, **139–141,** 143, 145
Shilts, Randy, **Supp. X:** 145
Shining, The (King), **Supp. V:** 139, 140, 141, 143–144, 146, 149, 151, 152
Shinn, Everett, **Retro. Supp. II:** 103
"Ship of Death" (Lawrence), **Supp. I Part 2:** 728
Ship of Fools (Porter), **III:** 433, 447, 453, 454; **IV:** 138
Shipping News, The (Proulx), **Supp. VII:** 249, 258–259
"Ships" (O. Henry), **Supp. II Part 1:** 409
Ships Going into the Blue: Essays and Notes on Poetry (Simpson), **Supp. IX:** 275
Ship to America, A (Singer), **IV:** 1
"Shipwreck, The" (Merwin), **Supp. III Part 1:** 346
"Shirt" (Pinsky), **Supp. VI:** 236–237, 239, 240, 241, 245, 247
"Shirt Poem, The" (Stern), **Supp. IX:** 292
"Shiva and Parvati Hiding in the Rain" (Pinsky), **Supp. VI:** 244
Shively, Charley, **Retro. Supp. I:** 391; **Supp. XII:** 181, 182
Shock of Recognition, The (Wilson), **II:** 530
Shock of the New, The (Hughes), **Supp. X:** 73
Shoe Bird, The (Welty), **IV:** 261; **Retro. Supp. I:** 353

"Shoes" (O. Henry), **Supp. II Part 1:** 409
"Shoes of Wandering, The" (Kinnell), **Supp. III Part 1:** 248
"Shooters, Inc." (Didion), **Supp. IV Part 1:** 207, 211
"Shooting, The" (Dubus), **Supp. VII:** 84, 85
"Shooting Niagara; and After?" (Carlyle), **Retro. Supp. I:** 408
"Shooting Script" (Rich), **Supp. I Part 2:** 558; **Supp. IV Part 1:** 257
Shooting Star, A (Stegner), **Supp. IV Part 2:** 599, 608–609
"Shooting Whales" (Strand), **Supp. IV Part 2:** 630
"Shopgirls" (F. Barthelme), **Supp. XI:** 26, 27, 33, 36
Shop Talk (Roth), **Retro. Supp. II:** 300
Shoptaw, John, **Supp. IV Part 1:** 247
Shore Acres (Herne), **Supp. II Part 1:** 198
Shorebirds of North America, The (Matthiessen), **Supp. V:** 204
"Shore House, The" (Jewett), **II:** 397
Shore Leave (Wakeman), **Supp. IX:** 247
"Shoreline Horses" (Ríos), **Supp. IV Part 2:** 553
Shores of Light, The: A Literary Chronicle of the Twenties and Thirties (Wilson), **IV:** 432, 433
Shorey, Paul, **III:** 606
Short Cuts (film), **Supp. IX:** 143
"Short End, The" (Hecht), **Supp. X:** 65
Short Fiction of Norman Mailer, The (Mailer), **Retro. Supp. II:** 205
Short Friday and Other Stories (Singer), **IV:** 14–16
"Short Happy Life of Francis Macomber, The" (Hemingway), **II:** 250, 263–264; **Retro. Supp. I:** 182; **Supp. IV Part 1:** 48; **Supp. IX:** 106
Short Novels of Thomas Wolfe, The (Wolfe), **IV:** 456
Short Poems (Berryman), **I:** 170
"SHORT SPEECH TO MY FRIENDS" (Baraka), **Supp. II Part 1:** 35
Short Stories (Rawlings), **Supp. X:** 224
"Short Story, The" (Welty), **IV:** 279
Short Story Masterpieces, **Supp. IX:** 4
Short Studies of American Authors (Higginson), **I:** 455
"Short-timer's Calendar" (Komunyakaa), **Supp. XIII:** 125
Shosha (Singer), **Retro. Supp. II:** 331–332
Shostakovich, Dimitri, **IV:** 75; **Supp. VIII:** 21

"Shots" (Ozick), **Supp. V:** 268
"Should Wizard Hit Mommy?" (Updike), **IV:** 221, 222, 224; **Retro. Supp. I:** 335
"Shovel Man, The" (Sandburg), **III:** 553
Showalter, Elaine, **Retro. Supp. I:** 368; **Supp. IV Part 2:** 440, 441, 444; **Supp. X:** 97
"Shower of Gold" (Welty), **IV:** 271–272
"Shrike and the Chipmunks, The" (Thurber), **Supp. I Part 2:** 617
Shrimp Girl (Hogarth), **Supp. XII:** 44
"Shrouded Stranger, The" (Ginsberg), **Supp. II Part 1:** 312
"Shroud of Color, The" (Cullen), **Supp. IV Part 1:** 166, 168, 170, 171
Shuffle Along (musical), **Supp. I Part 1:** 322; **Supp. X:** 136
Shultz, George, **Supp. IV Part 1:** 234
Shurr, William, **Retro. Supp. I:** 43
Shuster, Joel, **Supp. XI:** 67
Shusterman, Richard, **Retro. Supp. I:** 53
"Shut a Final Door" (Capote), **Supp. III Part 1:** 117, 120, 124
Shut Up, He Explained (Lardner), **II:** 432
Shylock's Daughter: A Novel of Love in Venice (Serenissima) (Jong), **Supp. V:** 115, 127, 128–129
Siberian Village, The (Dove), **Supp. IV Part 1:** 255, 256
Sibley, Mulford Q., **Supp. I Part 2:** 524
"Sibling Mysteries" (Rich), **Supp. I Part 2:** 574
Sibon, Marcelle, **IV:** 288
"Sicilian Emigrant's Song" (W. C. Williams), **Retro. Supp. I:** 413
"Sick Wife, The" (Kenyon), **Supp. VII:** 173, 174
"'Sic transit gloria mundi'" (Dickinson), **Retro. Supp. I:** 30
Sid Caesar Show (television show), **Supp. IV Part 2:** 575
Siddons, Sarah, **II:** 298
Side of Paradise, This (Fitgerald), **Supp. IX:** 56
Sidnee Poet Heroical, The (Baraka), **Supp. II Part 1:** 55
Sidney, Algernon, **II:** 114
Sidney, Mary, **Supp. I Part 1:** 98
Sidney, Philip, **II:** 470; **Supp. I Part 1:** 98, 111, 117–118, 122; **Supp. I Part 2:** 658; **Supp. II Part 1:** 104–105; **Supp. V:** 250; **Supp. XII:** 264
Sidney, Sylvia, **Supp. I Part 1:** 67
Sidney Lanier: A Bibliographical and Critical Study (Starke), **Supp. I Part 1:** 371
Sidney Lanier: A Biographical and Critical Study (Starke), **Supp. I Part 1:** 371
Siegel, Catherine, **Supp. XII:** 126
Siegel, Jerry, **Supp. XI:** 67
"Siege of London, The" (James), **Retro. Supp. I:** 227
Siegle, Robert, **Supp. XII:** 8
Sienkiewicz, Henryk, **Supp. IV Part 2:** 518
"Sierra Kid" (Levine), **Supp. V:** 180–181
Sigg, Eric, **Retro. Supp. I:** 53
"Sight" (Merwin), **Supp. III Part 1:** 356
"Sight in Camp in the Daybreak Gray and Dim, A" (Whitman), **II:** 373
Sights and Spectacles (McCarthy), **II:** 562
"Sights from a Steeple" (Hawthorne), **Retro. Supp. I:** 62
Sights Unseen (Gibbons), **Supp. X:** 49–50
"Signals" (Carver), **Supp. III Part 1:** 143
"Signature for Tempo" (MacLeish), **III:** 8–9
"Signed Confession of Crimes against the State" (Merton), **Supp. VIII:** 201
Signifying Monkey, The (Gates), **Supp. X:** 243
Signifying Monkey, The (Hughes), **Retro. Supp. I:** 195
"Signing, The (Dixon), **Supp. XII:** 146
Sign in Sidney Brustein's Window, The (Hansberry), **Supp. IV Part 1:** 359, 365, 369, 370–372
Sign of Jonas, The (Merton), **Supp. VIII:** 194–195, 195, 197, 200, 206, 207
"Sign of Saturn, The" (Olds), **Supp. X:** 206
Sigourney, Lydia, **Supp. I Part 2:** 684
Sikora, Malgorzata, **Retro. Supp. II:** 342
Silas Marner (Eliot), **II:** 26
"Silence" (Moore), **III:** 212
"Silence" (Poe), **III:** 416
"Silence, A" (Clampitt), **Supp. IX:** 53
"Silence—A Fable" (Poe), **III:** 416
"Silence Before Harvest, The" (Merwin), **Supp. III Part 1:** 352
Silence Dogood Papers, The (Franklin), **II:** 106–107
Silence in the Snowy Fields (Bly), **Supp. IV Part 1:** 60–61, 62, 63, 65, 66, 72

Silence of History, The (Farrell), **II:** 46–47
Silence Opens, A (Clampitt), **Supp. IX:** 53
Silences (Olsen), **Supp. XIII:** 293, 294, 295, 296, **304–306**
"Silences: When Writers Don't Write" (Olsen), **Supp. XIII:** 294
Silencing the Past: Power and the Production of History (Trouillot), **Supp. X:** 14
"Silent in America" (Levine), **Supp. V:** 183
Silent Life, The (Merton), **Supp. VIII:** 208
Silent Partner, The (Odets), **Supp. II Part 2:** 539
"Silent Poem" (Francis), **Supp. IX:** 86
"Silent Slain, The" (MacLeish), **III:** 9
"Silent Snow, Secret Snow" (Aiken), **I:** 52
Silent Spring (Carson), **Supp. V:** 202; **Supp. IX:** 19, 24, **31–34**
"Silken Tent, The" (Frost), **Retro. Supp. I:** 138–139; **Supp. IV Part 2:** 448
Silko, Leslie Marmon, **Supp. IV Part 1:** 274, 319, 325, 333–334, 335, 404; **Supp. IV Part 2:** 499, 505, **557–572**; **Supp. V:** 169; **Supp. XI:** 18; **Supp. XII:** 217
Silliman, Ron, **Supp. IV Part 2:** 426
Silman, Roberta, **Supp. X:** 6
"Silver Crown, The" (Malamud), **Supp. I Part 2:** 434–435, 437; **Supp. V:** 266
"Silver Dish, The" (Bellow), **Retro. Supp. II:** 30
"Silver Filigree" (Wylie), **Supp. I Part 2:** 707
Silvers, Phil, **Supp. IV Part 2:** 574
Silverthorne, Elizabeth, **Supp. X:** 220, 221, 222, 226, 234
"Silver To Have and to Hurl" (Didion), **Supp. IV Part 1:** 197
Simic, Charles, **Supp. V:** 5, 332; **Supp. VIII:** 39, **269–287**; **Supp. XI:** 317
"Similar Cases" (Gilman), **Supp. XI:** 200, 202
Similitudes, from the Ocean and Prairie (Larcom), **Supp. XIII:** 141
Simmel, Georg, **Supp. I Part 2:** 644
Simmons, Charles, **Supp. XI:** 230
Simmons, Maggie, **Retro. Supp. II:** 21
Simms, Michael, **Supp. XII:** 184
Simms, William Gilmore, **I:** 211
Simon, John, **Supp. IV Part 2:** 691
Simon, Neil, **Supp. IV Part 2: 573–594**

"Simon Gerty" (Wylie), **Supp. I Part 2:** 713
Simonides, **Supp. XII:** 110–111
"Simon Ortiz" (Gingerich), **Supp. IV Part 2:** 510
Simon Ortiz (Wiget), **Supp. IV Part 2:** 509
Simonson, Lee, **III:** 396
"Simple Art of Murder, The" (Chandler), **Supp. IV Part 1:** 121, 341
"Simple Autumnal" (Bogan), **Supp. III Part 1:** 52–53
Simple Heart (Flaubert), **I:** 504
Simple Speaks his Mind (Hughes), **Retro. Supp. I:** 209; **Supp. I Part 1:** 337
Simple Stakes a Claim (Hughes), **Retro. Supp. I:** 209; **Supp. I Part 1:** 337
Simple's Uncle Sam (Hughes), **Retro. Supp. I:** 209; **Supp. I Part 1:** 337
Simple Takes a Wife (Hughes), **Retro. Supp. I:** 209; **Supp. I Part 1:** 337
Simple Truth, The (Hardwick), **Supp. III Part 1:** 199, 200, 208
Simple Truth, The (Levine), **Supp. V:** 178, 179, 193–194
Simply Heavenly (Hughes), **Retro. Supp. I:** 209; **Supp. I Part 1:** 338, 339
Simpson, Louis, **Supp. III Part 2:** 541; **Supp. IV Part 2:** 448, 621; **Supp. VIII:** 39, 279; **Supp. IX:** 265–283, 290; **Supp. XI:** 317; **Supp. XII:** 130; **Supp. XIII:** 337
Sinatra, Frank, **Supp. IX:** 3; **Supp. X:** 119; **Supp. XI:** 213
Sincere Convert, The (Shepard), **IV:** 158
Sincerely, Willis Wayde (Marquand), **III:** 61, 63, 66, 67–68, 69
Sincerity and Authenticity (Trilling), **Supp. III Part 2:** 510–512
Sinclair, Mary Craig (Mary Craig Kimbrough), **Supp. V:** 275, 286, 287
Sinclair, Upton, **II:** 34, 440, 444, 451; **III:** 580; **Retro. Supp. II:** 95; **Supp. V:** 275–293; **Supp. VIII:** 11
Sinclair Lewis: An American Life (Schorer), **II:** 459
"Singapore" (Oliver), **Supp. VII:** 239, 240
Singer, Bennett L., **Supp. IV Part 1:** 330
Singer, Isaac Bashevis, **I:** 144; **IV:** 1–24; **Retro. Supp. II:** 22, 317–338; **Supp. IX:** 114
Singer, Israel Joshua, **IV:** 2, 16, 17; **Retro. Supp. II:** 320
Singer, Joshua, **IV:** 4
Singer, Rabbi Pinchos Menachem, **IV:** 16
Singin' and Swingin' and Gettin' Merry Like Christmas (Angelou), **Supp. IV Part 1:** 2, 5, 6–7, 9, 13, 14
"Singing & Doubling Together" (Ammons), **Supp. VII:** 34–35
Singing Jailbirds (Sinclair), **Supp. V:** 277
"Singing the Black Mother" (Lupton), **Supp. IV Part 1:** 7
Single Hound, The (Sarton), **Supp. VIII:** 251, 265
Single Hound, The: Poems of a Lifetime (Dickinson; Bianchi, ed.), **Retro. Supp. I:** 35
"Single Sonnet" (Bogan), **Supp. III Part 1:** 56–58
Singley, Carol, **Retro. Supp. I:** 373
Singular Family, A: Rosacoke and Her Kin (Price), **Supp. VI:** 258–259, 260
Singularities (Howe), **Supp. IV Part 2:** 431
"Sinister Adolescents, The" (Dos Passos), **I:** 493
Sinister Street (Mackenzie), **II:** 82
Sinners in the Hands of an Angry God (Edwards), **I:** 546, 552–553, 559, 562
Sinning with Annie, and Other Stories (Theroux), **Supp. VIII:** 318
"Sins of Kalamazoo, The" (Sandburg), **III:** 586
Sintram and His Companions (La Motte-Fouqué), **III:** 78
"Siope" (Poe), **III:** 411
"Sipapu: A Cultural Perspective" (Gunn Allen), **Supp. IV Part 1:** 323
Sipchen, Bob, **Supp. X:** 145
Sipper, Ralph B., **Supp. IV Part 2:** 475
"Sire" (Cisneros), **Supp. VII:** 62–63, 64
"Siren and Signal" (Zukofsky), **Supp. III Part 2:** 611, 612
Sirens of Titan, The (Vonnegut), **Supp. II Part 2:** 757, 758, 760, 765–767
"Sir Galahad" (Tennyson), **Supp. I Part 2:** 410
Sirin, V. (pseudonym), **Retro. Supp. I:** 266. *See also* Nabokov, Vladimir
Sir Vadia's Shadow: A Friendship across Five Continents (Theroux), **Supp. VIII:** 309, 314, 321, 325
"Sis" (F. Barthelme), **Supp. XI:** 26
Sisley, Alfred, **I:** 478
Sissman, L. E., **Supp. X:** 69

"Sister" (Hughes), **Retro. Supp. I:** 208
Sister Carrie (Dreiser), **I:** 482, 497, 499, 500, 501–502, 503–504, 505, 506, 515, 519; **III:** 327; **IV:** 208; **Retro. Supp. I:** 376; **Retro. Supp. II:** 93, 96–99
"Sister of the Minotaur" (Stevens), **IV:** 89; **Supp. IX:** 332
"Sisters, The" (Whittier), **Supp. I Part 2:** 696
Sister's Choice (Showalter), **Retro. Supp. I:** 368
"Sisyphus" (Kumin), **Supp. IV Part 2:** 443, 444, 451
"Sitalkas" (Doolittle), **Supp. I Part 1:** 266
Sitney, P. Adams, **Supp. XII:** 2
Sitting Bull, **Supp. IV Part 2:** 492
"Sitting in a Rocking Chair Going Blind" (Komunyakaa), **Supp. XIII:** 114
Sitti's Secrets (Nye), **Supp. XIII:** 278
Situation Normal (A. Miller), **III:** 148, 149, 156, 164
Situation of Poetry, The: Contemporary Poetry and Its Traditions (Pinsky), **Supp. VI:** 237–238, 239, 241, 242
Sitwell, Edith, **IV:** 77; **Supp. I Part 1:** 271
"Six Brothers" (Cisneros), **Supp. VII:** 67
Six Characters in Search of an Author (Pirandello), **Supp. IV Part 2:** 576
"Six Days: Some Rememberings" (Paley), **Supp. VI:** 226
Six French Poets (Lowell), **II:** 528–529
"Six Persons" (Baraka), **Supp. II Part 1:** 53
Six Sections from Mountains and Rivers without End (Snyder), **Supp. VIII:** 305
"Sixteen Months" (Sandburg), **III:** 584
1601, or Conversation as It Was by the Fireside in the Time of the Tudors (Twain), **IV:** 201
"Sixth-Month Song in the Foothills" (Snyder), **Supp. VIII:** 297
Sixties, The (magazine) (Bly), **Supp. IV Part 1:** 60; **Supp. IX:** 271
"Sixty" (Dunn), **Supp. XI:** 155
"Sixty Acres" (Carver), **Supp. III Part 1:** 141
Sixty Stories (Barthelme), **Supp. IV Part 1:** 41, 42, 44, 47, 49, 50
63: Dream Palace (Purdy), **Supp. VII:** 270–271
"Six Variations" (Levertov), **Supp. III Part 1:** 277–278

"Six-Year-Old Boy" (Olds), **Supp. X:** 206
"Six Years Later" (Brodsky), **Supp. VIII:** 26, 28
"Size and Sheer Will" (Olds), **Supp. X:** 206
Size of Thoughts, The: Essays and Other Lumber (Baker), **Supp. XIII: 52–53,** 55, 56
Sizwe Bansi Is Dead (Fugard), **Supp. VIII:** 330
"Skagway" (Haines), **Supp. XII:** 206
"Skaters, The" (Ashbery), **Supp. III Part 1:** 10, 12, 13, 18, 25
"Skaters, The" (Jarrell), **II:** 368–369
Skau, Michael, **Supp. XII:** 129, 130, 132, 134
Skeeters Kirby (Masters), **Supp. I Part 2:** 459, 470, 471
Skeleton Crew (King), **Supp. V:** 144
"Skeleton in Armor, The" (Longfellow), **Retro. Supp. II:** 168
"Skeleton's Cave, The" (Bryant), **Supp. I Part 1:** 157
Skelton, John, **III:** 521
Sketch Book of Geoffrey Crayon, Gent., The (Irving), **II:** 295, 303, 304–308, 309, 311, 491; **Supp. I Part 1:** 155
Sketches of Art (Jameson), **Retro. Supp. II:** 58
Sketches of Eighteenth Century America (Crèvecoeur), **Supp. I Part 1:** 233, 240–241, 250, 251
Sketches of Switzerland (Cooper), **I:** 346
Sketches Old and New (Twain), **IV:** 198
"Sketch for a Job-Application Blank" (Harrison), **Supp. VIII:** 38
Sketch of Old England, by a New England Man (Paulding), **I:** 344
"Skier and the Mountain, The" (Eberhart), **I:** 528–529
Skinker, Mary Scott, **Supp. IX:** 20
Skinny Island (Auchincloss), **Supp. IV Part 1:** 33
Skinny Legs and All (Robbins), **Supp. X:** 267, 273, **276–279**
Skin of Our Teeth, The (Wilder), **IV:** 357, 358, 369–372; **Supp. IV Part 2:** 586
"Skins" (Wright), **Supp. V:** 340
Skins and Bones: Poems 1979–1987 (Gunn Allen), **Supp. IV Part 1:** 321, 331
"Skipper Ireson's Ride" (Whittier), **Supp. I Part 2:** 691, 693–694
"Skirmish at Sartoris" (Faulkner), **II:** 67
Skow, John, **Supp. V:** 213

"Skunk Cabbage" (Oliver), **Supp. VII:** 235, 236
"Skunk Hour" (Lowell), **II:** 548–550; **Retro. Supp. II:** 188, 189
"Sky Line" (Taylor), **Supp. V:** 316
"Sky Line, The" (Mumford), **Supp. II Part 2:** 475
"Skyscraper" (Sandburg), **III:** 581–582
Sky's the Limit, The: A Defense of the Earth (Nichols), **Supp. XIII:** 268
"Sky Valley Rider" (Wright), **Supp. V:** 335, 340
Sky-Walk; or the Man Unknown to Himself (Brown), **Supp. I Part 1:** 127–128
"Slang in America" (Whitman), **IV:** 348
Slapstick (Vonnegut), **Supp. II Part 2:** 753, 754, 778
Slapstick Tragedy (T. Williams), **IV:** 382, 393
Slate, Lane, **Supp. IX:** 251, 253
Slattery, Mary Grace. *See* Miller, Mrs. Arthur (Mary Grace Slattery)
"Slaughterer, The" (Singer), **IV:** 19
Slaughterhouse-Five (Vonnegut), **Supp. II Part 2:** 755, 758–759, 760, 770, 772–776; **Supp. V:** 41, 244
Slave, The (Baraka), **Supp. II Part 1:** 42, 44, 56
Slave, The: A Novel (Singer), **IV:** 13; **Retro. Supp. II:** 323–325
"Slave Coffle" (Angelou), **Supp. IV Part 1:** 16
"Slave on the Block" (Hughes), **Supp. I Part 1:** 329
"Slave Quarters" (Dickey), **Supp. IV Part 1:** 181
"Slave's Dream, The" (Longfellow), **Supp. I Part 2:** 409
Slave Ship: A Historical Pageant (Baraka), **Supp. II Part 1:** 47–49, 53, 56–57
"Slave-Ships, The" (Whittier), **Supp. I Part 2:** 687–688
Slavs! Thinking about the Longstanding Problems of Virtue and Happiness (Kushner), **Supp. IX: 146**
Sledge, Eugene, **Supp. V:** 250
Sleek for the Long Flight (Matthews), **Supp. IX:** 154, 155, **157–158**
Sleep (Dixon), **Supp. XII:** 154
"Sleep, The" (Strand), **Supp. IV Part 2:** 627
"Sleeper, The" (Poe), **III:** 411
"Sleepers, The" (Whitman), **IV:** 336
"Sleepers in Jaipur" (Kenyon), **Supp. VII:** 172
Sleepers in Moon-Crowned Valleys (Purdy), **Supp. VII:** 274, 275

"Sleepers Joining Hands" (Bly), **Supp. IV Part 1:** 63, 73
Sleeping Beauty (Macdonald), **Supp. IV Part 2:** 474, 475
"Sleeping Fury, The" (Bogan), **Supp. III Part 1:** 58
Sleeping Fury, The: Poems (Bogan), **Supp. III Part 1:** 55–58
Sleeping Gypsy and Other Poems, The (Garrett), **Supp. VII:** 96–98
Sleeping in the Forest (Oliver), **Supp. VII:** 233
"Sleeping in the Forest" (Oliver), **Supp. VII:** 233–234
Sleeping in the Woods (Wagoner), **Supp. IX: 328**
Sleeping on Fists (Ríos), **Supp. IV Part 2:** 540
"Sleeping Standing Up" (Bishop), **Supp. I Part 1:** 85, 89, 93
"Sleeping with Animals" (Kumin), **Supp. IV Part 2:** 454
Sleeping with One Eye Open (Strand), **Supp. IV Part 2:** 621–624, 623, 628
"Sleepless at Crown Point" (Wilbur), **Supp. III Part 2:** 561
Sleepless Nights (Hardwick), **Supp. III Part 1:** 193, 208–211
Sleight, Ken, **Supp. XIII:** 12
Slick, Sam (pseudonym). *See* Haliburton, Thomas Chandler
"Slick Gonna Learn" (Ellison), **Retro. Supp. II:** 116; **Supp. II Part 1:** 237–238
"Slight Rebellion off Madison" (Salinger), **III:** 553
"Slight Sound at Evening, A" (White), **Supp. I Part 2:** 672
"Slim Greer" series (Hayden), **Supp. II Part 1:** 369
"Slim in Hell" (Hayden), **Supp. II Part 1:** 369
"Slim Man Canyon" (Silko), **Supp. IV Part 2:** 560
"Slippery Fingers" (Hammett), **Supp. IV Part 1:** 343
Slipping-Down Life, A (Tyler), **Supp. IV Part 2:** 660–661
Sloan, Jacob, **IV:** 3, 6
Sloan, John, **I:** 254; **IV:** 411; **Retro. Supp. II:** 103
"Slob" (Farrell), **II:** 25, 28, 31
Slocum, Joshua, **Supp. I Part 2:** 497
Slonim, Véra. *See* Nabokov, Véra
Slouching towards Bethlehem (Didion), **Supp. IV Part 1:** 196, 197, 200–201, 202, 206, 210
"Slow Child with a Book of Birds" (Levis), **Supp. XI:** 268
"Slow Down for Poetry" (Strand),

Supp. IV Part 2: 620
"Slow Pacific Swell, The" (Winters), **Supp. II Part 2:** 790, 793, 795, 796, 799
"Slumgullions" (Olsen), **Supp. IV Part 1:** 54
Slumgullion Stew: An Edward Abbey Reader (Abbey), **Supp. XIII:** 4
"S & M" (Komunyakaa), **Supp. XIII:** 114
Small, Albion, **Supp. I Part 1:** 5
"Small, Good Thing, A" (Carver), **Supp. III Part 1:** 145, 147
Small, Miriam Rossiter, **Supp. I Part 1:** 319
Small Boy and Others, A (James), **II:** 337, 547; **Retro. Supp. I:** 235
"Small but Urgent Request to the Unknowable" (Karr), **Supp. XI:** 243
Small Ceremonies (Shields), **Supp. VII:** 312–315, 320
Small Craft Warnings (T. Williams), **IV:** 382, 383, 384, 385, 386, 387, 392, 393, 396, 398
Small Place, A (Kincaid), **Supp. VII:** 186–187, 188, 191
"Small Rain, The" (Pynchon), **Supp. II Part 2:** 620
Small Room, The (Sarton), **Supp. VIII:** 252, **255–256**
Smalls, Bob, **II:** 128
Small Town, A (Hearon), **Supp. VIII: 65–66**
"Small Vases from Hebron, The" (Nye), **Supp. XIII:** 283
"Small Vision, The" (Goldbarth), **Supp. XII:** 180
"Small Wire" (Sexton), **Supp. II Part 2:** 696
Smart, Christopher, **III:** 534; **Supp. I Part 2:** 539; **Supp. IV Part 2:** 626
Smart, Joyce H., **Supp. XI:** 169
"Smart Cookie, A" (Cisneros), **Supp. VII:** 64
"Smashup" (Thurber), **Supp. I Part 2:** 616
Smedly, Agnes, **Supp. XIII:** 295
"Smelt Fishing" (Hayden), **Supp. II Part 1:** 367
"Smiles" (Dunn), **Supp. XI:** 151
Smiles, Samuel, **Supp. X:** 167
Smiley, Jane, **Supp. VI: 291–309; Supp. XII:** 73, 297; **Supp. XIII:** 127
Smith, Adam, **II:** 9; **Supp. I Part 2:** 633, 634, 639
Smith, Benjamin, **IV:** 148
Smith, Bernard, **I:** 260
Smith, Bessie, **Retro. Supp. I:** 343; **Supp. VIII:** 330

Smith, Charlie, **Supp. X:** 177
Smith, Dave, **Supp. V:** 333; **Supp. XI:** 152; **Supp. XII:** 178, 198
Smith, David, **Supp. XIII:** 246, 247
Smith, Dinitia, **Supp. VIII:** 74, 82, 83
Smith, Elihu Hubbard, **Supp. I Part 1:** 126, 127, 130
Smith, George Adam, **III:** 199
Smith, Harrison, **II:** 61
Smith, Henry Nash, **IV:** 210; **Supp. I Part 1:** 233
Smith, Herbert F., **Supp. I Part 2:** 423
Smith, James, **II:** 111
Smith, Jedediah Strong, **Supp. IV Part 2:** 602
Smith, Jerome, **Supp. IV Part 1:** 369
Smith, Joe, **Supp. IV Part 2:** 584
Smith, John, **I:** 4, 131; **II:** 296
Smith, John Allyn, **I:** 168
Smith, Johnston (pseudonym). See Crane, Stephen
Smith, Kellogg, **Supp. I Part 2:** 660
Smith, Lamar, **II:** 585
Smith, Lee, **Supp. XII:** 311
Smith, Lula Carson. See McCullers, Carson
Smith, Martha Nell, **Retro. Supp. I:** 33, 43, 46, 47
Smith, Mary Rozet, **Supp. I Part 1:** 5, 22
Smith, Mrs. Lamar (Marguerite Walters), **II:** 585, 587
Smith, Oliver, **II:** 586
Smith, Patricia Clark, **Supp. IV Part 1:** 397, 398, 402, 406, 408, 410; **Supp. IV Part 2:** 509; **Supp. XII:** 218
Smith, Patrick, **Supp. VIII:** 40, 41
Smith, Patti, **Supp. XII:** 136
Smith, Porter, **III:** 572
Smith, Red, **II:** 417, 424
Smith, Seba, **Supp. I Part 2:** 411
Smith, Sidonie Ann, **Supp. IV Part 1:** 11
Smith, Stevie, **Supp. V:** 84
Smith, Sydney, **II:** 295
Smith, Thorne, **Supp. IX:** 194
Smith, Wendy, **Supp. XII:** 330, 335
Smith, Wilford Bascom "Pitchfork," **Supp. XIII:** 168
Smith, William, **II:** 114
Smith, William Jay, **Supp. XIII: 331–350**
Smoke (film), **Supp. XII:** 21
Smoke and Steel (Sandburg), **III:** 585–587, 592
"Smokers" (Wolff), **Supp. VII:** 340–341
"Smoking My Prayers" (Ortiz), **Supp. IV Part 2:** 503

"Smoking Room, The" (Jackson), **Supp. IX:** 116
Smollett, Tobias G., **I:** 134, 339, 343; **II:** 304–305; **III:** 61
Smuggler's Bible, A (McElroy), **Supp. IV Part 1:** 285
Smuggler's Handbook, The (Goldbarth), **Supp. XII:** 181, 183
Smugglers of Lost Soul's Rock, The (Gardner), **Supp. VI:** 70
Smyth, Albert Henry, **II:** 123
"Snake, The" (Berry), **Supp. X:** 31
"Snake, The" (Crane), **I:** 420
"Snakecharmer" (Plath), **Supp. I Part 2:** 538
"Snakes, Mongooses" (Moore), **III:** 207
"Snakes of September, The" (Kunitz), **Supp. III Part 1:** 258
"Snapshot of 15th S.W., A" (Hugo), **Supp. VI:** 141
"Snapshots of a Daughter-in-Law" (Rich), **Retro. Supp. II:** 281–283; **Supp. I Part 2:** 553–554
Snapshots of a Daughter-in-Law: Poems, 1954–1962 (Rich), **Retro. Supp. II:** 281; **Supp. I Part 2:** 550–551, 553–554; **Supp. XII:** 255
"Sneeze, The" (Chekhov), **Supp. IV Part 2:** 585
Snell, Ebenezer, **Supp. I Part 1:** 151
Snell, Thomas, **Supp. I Part 1:** 153
"Snob, The" (Shapiro), **Supp. II Part 2:** 705
Snodgrass, W. D., **I:** 400; **Retro. Supp. II:** 179; **Supp. III Part 2:** 541; **Supp. V:** 337; **Supp. VI: 311–328; Supp. XI:** 141, 315; **Supp. XIII:** 312
"Snow" (Frost), **Retro. Supp. I:** 133
"Snow" (Haines), **Supp. XII:** 212
"Snow" (Sexton), **Supp. II Part 2:** 696
Snow, C. P., **Supp. I Part 2:** 536
Snow, Hank, **Supp. V:** 335
Snow: Meditations of a Cautious Man in Winter (Banks), **Supp. V:** 6
Snow Ball, The (Gurney), **Supp. V:** 99
"Snow-Bound" (Whittier), **Supp. I Part 2:** 700–703
"Snow Bound at Eagle's" (Harte), **Supp. II Part 1:** 356
"Snowflakes" (Longfellow), **II:** 498
Snow-Image and Other Twice Told Tales, The (Hawthorne), **II:** 237; **Retro. Supp. I:** 160
"Snowing in Greenwich Village" (Updike), **IV:** 226; **Retro. Supp. I:** 321
"Snow in New York" (Swenson), **Supp. IV Part 2:** 644

Snow Leopard, The (Matthiessen), **Supp. V:** 199, 207–211
"Snow Man, The" (Stevens), **IV:** 82–83; **Retro. Supp. I:** 299, 300, 302, 306, 307, 312
"Snowmass Cycle, The" (Dunn), **Supp. XI:** 152
Snow Poems, The (Ammons), **Supp. VII:** 32–34
"Snows of Kilimanjaro, The" (Hemingway), **II:** 78, 257, 263, 264; **Retro. Supp. I:** 98, 182; **Supp. XII:** 249
"Snow Songs" (Snodgrass), **Supp. VI:** 324
"Snowstorm, The" (Oates), **Supp. II Part 2:** 523
"Snowstorm as It Affects the American Farmer, A" (Crèvecoeur), **Supp. I Part 1:** 251
Snow White (Barthelme), **Supp. IV Part 1:** 40, 47, 48–49, 50, 52; **Supp. V:** 39
"Snowy Mountain Song, A" (Ortiz), **Supp. IV Part 2:** 506
Snyder, Gary, **Supp. III Part 1:** 350; **Supp. IV Part 2:** 502; **Supp. V:** 168–169; **Supp. VIII:** 39, **289–307**
"So-and-So Reclining on Her Couch" (Stevens), **IV:** 90
"Soapland" (Thurber), **Supp. I Part 2:** 619
Soares, Lota de Macedo, **Retro. Supp. II:** 44; **Supp. I Part 1:** 89, 94
"Sobbin' Women, The" (Benét), **Supp. XI:** 47
Social Ethics (Gilman), **Supp. XI:** 207
"Socialism and the Negro" (McKay), **Supp. X:** 135
"Socialism of the Skin, A (Liberation, Honey!)" (Kushner), **Supp. IX:** 135
Social Thought in America: The Revolt against Formalism (White), **Supp. I Part 2:** 648, 650
"Society, Morality, and the Novel" (Ellison), **Retro. Supp. II:** 118, 123–124
"Sociological Habit Patterns in Linguistic Transmogrification" (Cowley), **Supp. II Part 1:** 143
"Sociological Poet, A" (Bourne), **I:** 228
Socrates, **I:** 136, 265; **II:** 8–9, 105, 106; **III:** 281, 419, 606; **Supp. I Part 2:** 458; **Supp. XII:** 98
Socrates Fortlow stories (Mosley), **Supp. XIII: 242–243**
So Forth (Brodsky), **Supp. VIII:** 32–33
"So Forth" (Brodsky), **Supp. VIII:** 33
Soft Machine, The (Burroughs), **Supp. III Part 1:** 93, 103, 104
"Soft Mask" (Karr), **Supp. XI:** 243
Soft Side, The (James), **II:** 335; **Retro. Supp. I:** 229
"Soft Spring Night in Shillington, A" (Updike), **Retro. Supp. I:** 318, 319
"Soft Wood" (Lowell), **II:** 550–551
"So Help Me" (Algren), **Supp. IX:** 2
"Soirée in Hollywood" (H. Miller), **III:** 186
Sojourner, The (Rawlings), **Supp. X:** 233–234
"Sojourn in a Whale" (Moore), **III:** 211, 213
"Sojourns" (Didion), **Supp. IV Part 1:** 205
Solar Storms (Hogan), **Supp. IV Part 1:** 397, 410, 414–415
"Soldier, The" (Frost), **II:** 155
Soldier Blue (film), **Supp. X:** 124
"Soldier's Home" (Hemingway), **Retro. Supp. I:** 189
Soldier's Joy (Bell), **Supp. X:** 7, **7–8,** 10, 11
Soldiers of the Storm (film), **Supp. XIII:** 163
Soldiers' Pay (Faulkner), **I:** 117; **II:** 56, 68; **Retro. Supp. I:** 80, 81
"Soldier's Testament, The" (Mumford), **Supp. II Part 2:** 473
"Soliloquy: Man Talking to a Mirror" (Komunyakaa), **Supp. XIII:** 116–117
"Solitary Pond, The" (Updike), **Retro. Supp. I:** 323
So Little Time (Marquand), **III:** 55, 59, 65, 67, 69
"Solitude" (Maupassant), **Supp. I Part 1:** 223
Solo Faces (Salter), **Supp. IX: 259–260**
Solomon, Andy, **Supp. X:** 11
Solomon, Charles, **Supp. VIII:** 82
Solomon, Henry, Jr., **Supp. I Part 2:** 490
Solomons, Leon, **IV:** 26
So Long, See You Tomorrow (Maxwell), **Supp. VIII:** 156, 160, 162, **167–169**
"So Long Ago" (Bausch), **Supp. VII:** 41–42
Solotaroff, Robert, **Retro. Supp. II:** 203
Solotaroff, Theodore, **III:** 452–453; **Retro. Supp. II:** 299; **Supp. I Part 2:** 440, 445; **Supp. X:** 79; **Supp. XI:** 340; **Supp. XII:** 291
"Solstice" (Jeffers), **Supp. II Part 2:** 433, 435
"Solstice, The" (Merwin), **Supp. III Part 1:** 356
"Solus Rex" (Nabokov), **Retro. Supp. I:** 274
"Solutions" (McCarthy), **II:** 578
"Solving the Puzzle" (Dunn), **Supp. XI:** 152
Solzhenitsyn, Alexandr, **Retro. Supp. I:** 278; **Supp. VIII:** 241
"Some Afternoon" (Creeley), **Supp. IV Part 1:** 150–151
Some American People (Caldwell), **I:** 292, 294, 295, 296, 304, 309
"Some Ashes Drifting above Piedra, California" (Levis), **Supp. XI:** 264–265
"Some Aspects of the Grotesque in Southern Fiction" (O'Connor), **Retro. Supp. II:** 223, 224
"Somebody Always Grabs the Purple" (H. Roth), **Supp. IX:** 234
Somebody in Boots (Algren), **Supp. IX:** 3, **5–7,** 12
Somebody's Darling (McMurtry), **Supp. V:** 225
Some Came Running (film), **Supp. XI:** 213
Some Came Running (Jones), **Supp. XI:** 214, 215, 220, **222–223,** 226, 227, 232
Some Can Whistle (McMurtry), **Supp. V:** 229
"Some Children of the Goddess" (Mailer), **Retro. Supp. II:** 204
Someday, Maybe (Stafford), **Supp. XI: 323–325; Supp. XIII:** 281
"Some Dreamers of the Golden Dream" (Didion), **Supp. IV Part 1:** 200
"Some Foreign Letters" (Sexton), **Supp. II Part 2:** 674
"Some Good News" (Olson), **Supp. II Part 2:** 575, 576, 577
"Some Grass along a Ditch Bank" (Levis), **Supp. XI:** 266
"Some Greek Writings" (Corso), **Supp. XII:** 130
Some Honorable Men: Political Conventions, 1960–1972 (Mailer), **Retro. Supp. II:** 208
Some Imagist Poets (Lowell), **III:** 511, 518, 520; **Supp. I Part 1:** 257, 261
"Some keep the Sabbath going to Church" (Dickinson), **Retro. Supp. I:** 30
"Some Like Indians Endure" (Gunn Allen), **Supp. IV Part 1:** 330
"Some Like Them Cold" (Lardner), **II:** 427–428, 430, 431; **Supp. IX:** 202
"Some Lines from Whitman" (Jarrell), **IV:** 352
"Some Negatives: X. at the Chateau"

(Merrill), **Supp. III Part 1:** 322
"Some Neglected Points in the Theory of Socialism" (Veblen), **Supp. I Part 2:** 635
"Some Notes for an Autobiographical Lecture" (Trilling), **Supp. III Part 2:** 493, 497, 500
"Some Notes on French Poetry" (Bly), **Supp. IV Part 1:** 61
"Some Notes on Miss L." (West), **IV:** 290–291, 295; **Retro. Supp. II:** 340
"Some Notes on Organic Form" (Levertov), **Supp. III Part 1:** 272, 279
"Some Notes on Teaching: Probably Spoken" (Paley), **Supp. VI:** 225
"Some Notes on the Gazer Within" (Levis), **Supp. XI:** 270
"Some Notes on Violence" (West), **IV:** 304; **Retro. Supp. II:** 340, 341
Some of the Dharma (Kerouac), **Supp. III Part 1:** 225
"Someone Is Buried" (Salinas), **Supp. XIII:** 324
"Someone Puts a Pineapple Together" (Stevens), **IV:** 90–91
"Someone's Blood" (Dove), **Supp. IV Part 1:** 245
"Someone Talking" (Harjo), **Supp. XII:** 219–220
"Someone Talking to Himself" (Wilbur), **Supp. III Part 2:** 557
"Someone to Watch Over Me" (Stern), **Supp. IX:** 300
Someone to Watch Over Me: Stories (Bausch), **Supp. VII:** 53
Some People, Places, & Things That Will Not Appear in My Next Novel (Cheever), **Supp. I Part 1:** 184–185
Some Problems of Philosophy: A Beginning of an Introduction to Philosophy (James), **II:** 360–361
"Some Questions You Might Ask" (Oliver), **Supp. VII:** 238–239
"Some Remarks on Humor" (White), **Supp. I Part 2:** 672
"Some Remarks on Rhythm" (Roethke), **III:** 548–549
Somers, Fred, **I:** 196
Somerville, Jane, **Supp. IX:** 289, 296–297
"Some Secrets" (Stern), **Supp. IX:** 286, 287, 288, 289, 295
Some Sort of Epic Grandeur (Bruccoli), **Retro. Supp. I:** 115, 359
"Something" (Oliver), **Supp. VII:** 236
Something Happened (Heller), **Supp. IV Part 1:** 383, 386–388, 389, 392
"Something Happened: The Imaginary, the Symbolic, and the Discourse of the Family" (Mellard), **Supp. IV Part 1:** 387
Something in Common (Hughes), **Supp. I Part 1:** 329–330
Something Inside: Conversations with Gay Fiction Writers (Gambone), **Supp. XII:** 81
"Something New" (Stern), **Supp. IX:** 290
"Something Spurious from the Mindinao Deep" (Stegner), **Supp. IV Part 2:** 605
Something to Declare (Alvarez), **Supp. VII:** 1, 2, 11, 17–19
Something to Remember Me By (Bellow), **Retro. Supp. II:** 32
"Something to Remember Me By" (Bellow), **Retro. Supp. II:** 32
Something Wicked This Way Comes (Bradbury), **Supp. IV Part 1:** 101, 110–111
"Something Wild . . ." (T. Williams), **IV:** 381
"Some Thoughts" (McNally), **Supp. XIII:** 207
"Some Thoughts on the Line" (Oliver), **Supp. VII:** 238
"Sometimes, Reading" (Stafford), **Supp. XI:** 314
"Sometimes I Wonder" (Hughes), **Supp. I Part 1:** 337
Sometimes Mysteriously (Salinas), **Supp. XIII:** 311, **326–328**
"Sometimes Mysteriously" (Salinas), **Supp. XIII:** 328
Some Trees (Ashbery), **Supp. III Part 1:** 3–7, 12
"Some Trees" (Ashbery), **Supp. III Part 1:** 2
"Some Views on the Reading and Writing of Short Stories" (Welty), **Retro. Supp. I:** 351
"Somewhere" (Nemerov), **III:** 279–280
"Somewhere Else" (Paley), **Supp. VI:** 227
"Somewhere in Africa" (Sexton), **Supp. II Part 2:** 684–685
"Somewhere Is Such a Kingdom" (Ransom), **III:** 492
"Somewhere near Phu Bai" (Komunyakaa), **Supp. XIII:** 123–124
"Some Words with a Mummy" (Poe), **III:** 425
"Some Yips and Barks in the Dark" (Snyder), **Supp. VIII:** 291
Sommers, Michael, **Supp. IV Part 2:** 581
Sommers, William, **I:** 387, 388
"Somnambulisma" (Stevens), **Retro. Supp. I:** 310
"So Much Summer" (Dickinson), **Retro. Supp. I:** 26, 44, 45
"So Much the Worse for Boston" (Lindsay), **Supp. I Part 2:** 398
"So Much Water So Close to Home" (Carver), **Supp. III Part 1:** 143, 146
Son, Cathy, **Supp. X:** 292
"Son, The" (Dove), **Supp. IV Part 1:** 245
"Sonata for the Invisible" (Harjo), **Supp. XII:** 228
Sonata for Two Pianos (Bowles), **Supp. IV Part 1:** 83
Son at the Front, A (Wharton), **II:** 183; **IV:** 320; **Retro. Supp. I:** 378
Sondheim, Stephen, **Supp. XII:** 260
Son Excellence Eugène Rougon (Zola), **III:** 322
"Song" (Bogan), **Supp. III Part 1:** 57
"Song" (Bryant). *See* "Hunter of the West, The"
"Song" (Dunbar), **Supp. II Part 1:** 199
"Song" (Ginsberg), **Supp. II Part 1:** 317
"Song" (Kenyon), **Supp. VII:** 169
"Song" (Rich), **Supp. I Part 2:** 560
"Song" (Wylie), **Supp. I Part 2:** 729
"Song, A" (Creeley), **Supp. IV Part 1:** 145
"Song: Love in Whose Rich Honor" (Rukeyser), **Supp. VI:** 285
"Song: 'Rough Winds Do Shake the Darling Buds of May'" (Simpson), **Supp. IX:** 268
Song and Idea (Eberhart), **I:** 526, 529, 533, 539
"Song for Myself and the Deer to Return On" (Harjo), **Supp. XII:** 225
"Song for Occupations, A" (Whitman), **Retro. Supp. I:** 394
"Song for Simeon, A" (Eliot), **Retro. Supp. I:** 64
"Song for the Coming of Smallpox" (Wagoner), **Supp. IX:** 329, 330
"Song for the First People" (Wagoner), **Supp. IX:** 328
"Song for the Last Act" (Bogan), **Supp. III Part 1:** 64
"Song for the Middle of the Night, A" (Wright), **Supp. III Part 2:** 594
"Song for the Rainy Season" (Bishop), **Supp. I Part 1:** 93–94, 96
"Song for the Romeos, A" (Stern), **Supp. IX:** 296
"Songline of Dawn" (Harjo), **Supp. XII:** 229
"Song of Advent, A" (Winters), **Supp. II Part 2:** 789

"Song of a Man Who Rushed at the Enemy" (Wagoner), **Supp. IX:** 329, 330
"Song of Courage, A" (Masters), **Supp. I Part 2:** 458
Song of Hiawatha, The (Longfellow), **II:** 501, 503–504; **Retro. Supp. II:** 155, **159–161,** 162, 163
"Song of Innocence, A" (Ellison), **Retro. Supp. II:** 126; **Supp. II Part 1:** 248
"Song of My Fiftieth Birthday, The" (Lindsay), **Supp. I Part 2:** 399
"Song of Myself" (Whitman), **II:** 544; **III:** 572, 584, 595; **IV:** 333, 334, 337–339, 340, 341, 342, 344, 348, 349, 351, 405; **Retro. Supp. I:** 388, 389, 395–399, 400; **Supp. V:** 122; **Supp. IX:** 131, 136, 143, 328, 331
Song of Russia (film), **Supp. I Part 1:** 281, 294
Song of Solomon (biblical book), **III:** 118; **IV:** 150
Song of Solomon (Morrison), **Supp. III Part 1:** 364, 368, 369, 372, 379
Song of Songs (biblical book), **II:** 538; **IV:** 153–154
"Song of the Answerer" (Whitman), **Retro. Supp. I:** 393, 399
"Song of the Chattahoochee, The" (Lanier), **Supp. I Part 1:** 365, 368
"Song of the Degrees, A" (Pound), **III:** 466
"Song of the Exposition" (Whitman), **IV:** 332
"Song of the Greek Amazon" (Bryant), **Supp. I Part 1:** 168
Song of the Lark, The (Cather), **I:** 312, 319–321, 323; **Retro. Supp. I:** 1, 3, 7, **9–11,** 13, 19, 20
"Song of the Open Road" (McGrath), **Supp. X:** 127
"Song of the Open Road" (Whitman), **IV:** 340–341; **Retro. Supp. I:** 400; **Supp. IX:** 265
"Song of the Redwood Tree" (Whitman), **IV:** 348
"Song of the Sky Loom" (traditional Tewa poem), **Supp. IV Part 1:** 325
"Song of the Son" (Toomer), **Supp. III Part 2:** 482–483; **Supp. IX:** 313
"Song of the Sower, The" (Bryant), **Supp. I Part 1:** 169
"Song of the Stars" (Bryant), **Supp. I Part 1:** 163
"Song of the Swamp-Robin, The" (Frederic), **II:** 138
"Song of the Vermonters, The" (Whittier), **Supp. I Part 2:** 692
"Song of Three Smiles" (Merwin), **Supp. III Part 1:** 344
"Song of Wandering Aengus, The" (Yeats), **IV:** 271; **Retro. Supp. I:** 342, 350
"Song of Welcome" (Brodsky), **Supp. VIII:** 32
"Song on Captain Barney's Victory" (Freneau), **Supp. II Part 1:** 261
"Song/Poetry and Language-Expression and Perception" (Ortiz), **Supp. IV Part 2:** 500, 508
Songs and Satires (Masters), **Supp. I Part 2:** 465–466
Songs and Sonnets (Masters), **Supp. I Part 2:** 455, 459, 461, 466
"Songs for a Colored Singer" (Bishop), **Supp. I Part 1:** 80, 85
Songs for a Summer's Day (A Sonnet Cycle) (MacLeish), **III:** 3
Songs for Eve (MacLeish), **III:** 3, 19
"Songs for Eve" (MacLeish), **III:** 19
"Songs for My Father" (Komunyakaa), **Supp. XIII:** 128
Songs from This Earth on Turtle's Back: Contemporary American Indian Poetry (Bruchac, ed.), **Supp. IV Part 1:** 320, 328
"Songs of a Housewife" (Rawlings), **Supp. X:** 221–222
"Songs of Billy Bathgate, The" (Doctorow), **Supp. IV Part 1:** 230
Songs of Innocence (Blake), **Supp. I Part 2:** 708
Songs of Jamaica (McKay), **Supp. X:** 131, 133
"Songs of Maximus, The" (Olson), **Supp. II Part 2:** 567
"Songs of Parting" (Whitman), **IV:** 348
Songs of the Sierras (J. Miller), **I:** 459
Songs of Three Centuries (Whittier and Larcom, eds.), **Supp. XIII:** 142
"Song to David" (Smart), **III:** 534
"Song to No Music, A" (Brodsky), **Supp. VIII:** 26
Sonneschein, Rosa, **Retro. Supp. II:** 65
"Sonnet" (Rukeyser), **Supp. VI:** 284
"Sonnets at Christmas" (Tate), **IV:** 135
"Sonnet-To Zante" (Poe), **III:** 421
"Sonny's Blues" (Baldwin), **Retro. Supp. II:** 7, 8, 10, 14; **Supp. I Part 1:** 58–59, 63, 67; **Supp. XI:** 288
Son of Laughter, The: A Novel (Buechner), **Supp. XII:** 54
Son of Perdition, The (Cozzens), **I:** 359–360, 377, 378, 379
Son of the Circus, A (Irving), **Supp. VI:** 165, 166, **176–179**
"Son of the Gods, A" (Bierce), **I:** 202
Son of the Morning (Oates), **Supp. II Part 2:** 518, 519, 520–522
"Son of the Romanovs, A" (Simpson), **Supp. IX:** 273–274
Son of the Wolf, The (London), **II:** 465, 469
"Son of the Wolfman" (Chabon), **Supp. XI:** 76
"Sonrisas" (Mora), **Supp. XIII:** 216, 219
Sons (Buck), **Supp. II Part 1:** 117–118
Sons and Lovers (Lawrence), **III:** 27
Sontag, Susan, **IV:** 13, 14; **Retro. Supp. II:** 297; **Supp. I Part 2:** 423; **Supp. III Part 2: 451–473; Supp. VIII:** 75
"Soonest Mended" (Ashbery), **Supp. III Part 1:** 1, 13
"Sootfall and Fallout" (White), **Supp. I Part 2:** 671
Sophocles, **I:** 274; **II:** 291, 385, 577; **III:** 145, 151, 152, 153, 159, 398, 476, 478, 609, 613; **IV:** 291, 363, 368, 370; **Supp. I Part 1:** 153, 284; **Supp. I Part 2:** 491; **Supp. V:** 97; **Supp. VIII:** 332
"Sophronsiba" (Bourne), **I:** 221
Sorcerer's Apprentice, The: Tales and Conjurations (Johnson), **Supp. VI: 192–193,** 194
"Sorcerer's Eye, The" (Nemerov), **III:** 283
Sordello (Browning), **III:** 467, 469, 470
"Sordid? Good God!" (W. C. Williams), **Retro. Supp. II:** 352
"Sorghum" (Mason), **Supp. VIII:** 146
Sorokin, Pitirim, **Supp. I Part 2:** 679
Sorrentino, Gilbert, **Retro. Supp. I:** 426; **Supp. IV Part 1:** 286; **Supp. XII:** 139
"Sorrow" (Komunyakaa), **Supp. XIII:** 119
Sorrow Dance, The (Levertov), **Supp. III Part 1:** 279–280, 283
"Sorrowful Guest, A" (Jewett), **Retro. Supp. II:** 137
Sorrows of Fat City, The: A Selection of Literary Essays and Reviews (Garrett), **Supp. VII:** 111
Sorrows of Young Werther, The (Goethe), **Supp. XI:** 169
Sorrows of Young Werther, The (Goethe; Bogan and Mayer, trans.), **Supp. III Part 1:** 63
"Sorting Facts; or, Nineteen Ways of Looking at Marker" (Howe), **Supp. IV Part 2:** 434, 436
"S O S" (Baraka), **Supp. II Part 1:** 50

"So Sassafras" (Olson), **Supp. II Part 2:** 574
"So There" (Creeley), **Supp. IV Part 1:** 157
Sotirov, Vasil, **Supp. IX:** 152
Soto, Gary, **Supp. IV Part 2:** 545; **Supp. V:** 180; **Supp. XI:** 270; **Supp. XIII:** 313, 315, 316, 320, 323
"Soto Thinking of the Ocean" (Salinas), **Supp. XIII:** 321
"Sotto Voce" (Kunitz), **Supp. III Part 1:** 265
Sot-Weed Factor, The (Barth), **I:** 122, 123, 125, 129, 130, 131–134, 135
Soul, The (Brooks), **I:** 244
Soul and Body of John Brown, The (Rukeyser), **Supp. VI:** 273
Soul Clap Hands and Sing (Marshall), **Supp. XI:** 276, 278, **280–282**
Soul Expeditions (Singer). *See Shosha* (Singer)
Soul Gone Home (Hughes), **Retro. Supp. I:** 203; **Supp. I Part 1:** 328
"Soul inside the Sentence, The" (Gass), **Supp. VI:** 88
Soul Is Here for Its Own Joy, The (Bly, ed.), **Supp. IV Part 1:** 74
Soul of Man under Socialism, The (Wilde), **Supp. IX:** 134–135
Soul of the Far East, The (Lowell), **II:** 513
Soul on Ice (Cleaver), **Retro. Supp. II:** 12, 13
"Souls Belated" (Wharton), **Retro. Supp. I:** 364
"Soul selects her own Society, The" (Dickinson), **Retro. Supp. I:** 37
Souls of Black Folk, The (Du Bois), **Supp. II Part 1:** 33, 40, 160, 168–170, 176, 183; **Supp. IV Part 1:** 164; **Supp. IX:** 305, 306; **Supp. X:** 133; **Supp. XIII:** 185, 238, 243
"Sound, The" (Olds), **Supp. X:** 214
"Sound and Fury" (O. Henry), **Supp. II Part 1:** 402
Sound and the Fury, The (Faulkner), **I:** 480; **II:** 55, 57, 58–60, 73; **III:** 237; **IV:** 100, 101, 104; **Retro. Supp. I:** 73, 75, 77, 82, **83–84,** 86, 88, 89, 90, 91, 92; **Supp. VIII:** 215; **Supp. IX:** 103; **Supp. X:** 44; **Supp. XII:** 33
"Sound Bites" (Alvarez), **Supp. VII:** 11
Sound I Listened For, The (Francis), **Supp. IX: 78–79,** 87
"Sound Mind, Sound Body" (Lowell), **II:** 554
"Sound of Distant Thunder, A" (Elkin), **Supp. VI: 42–43,** 44

"Sound of Light, The" (Merwin), **Supp. III Part 1:** 356
Sound of Mountain Water, The (Stegner), **Supp. IV Part 2:** 595, 596, 598, 600, 608
"Sound of Talking" (Purdy), **Supp. VII:** 270
Sounds of Poetry, The (Pinsky), **Supp. VI:** 236, 247, 248
Soupault, Philippe, **IV:** 288, 404; **Retro. Supp. II:** 85, 339, 342
Source (Doty), **Supp. XI:** 121, **134–137**
"Source" (Doty), **Supp. XI:** 136
"Source, The" (Olds), **Supp. X:** 211
"Source, The" (Porter), **III:** 443
Source of Light, The (Price), **Supp. VI:** 262, 266
"Sources of Soviet Conduct, The" (Kennan), **Supp. VIII:** 241
Sour Grapes (W. C. Williams), **Retro. Supp. I:** 418
"South" (Levis), **Supp. XI:** 266
"South, The" (Hughes), **Supp. I Part 1:** 321
"Southbound on the Freeway" (Swenson), **Supp. IV Part 2:** 643
Southern, Terry, **Supp. IV Part 1:** 379; **Supp. V:** 40, 201; **Supp. XI: 293–310**
Southern Cross, The (Wright), **Supp. V:** 332, 342
"Southern Cross, The" (Wright), **Supp. V:** 338
"Southerner's Problem, The" (Du Bois), **Supp. II Part 1:** 168
"Southern Girl" (Zelda Fitzgerald), **Supp. IX:** 71
"Southern Mode of the Imagination, A" (Tate), **IV:** 120
"Southern Romantic, A" (Tate), **Supp. I Part 1:** 373
Southey, Robert, **II:** 304, 502; **Supp. I Part 1:** 154
South Moon Under (Rawlings), **Supp. X: 225–226,** 229, 233
Southpaw, The (Harris), **II:** 424–425
"South Sangamon" (Cisneros), **Supp. VII:** 66
Southwell, Robert, **IV:** 151
Southwick, Marcia, **Supp. XI:** 259
Southworth, E. D. E. N, **Retro. Supp. I:** 246
Souvenir of the Ancient World, Selected Poems of Carlos Drummond de Andrade (Strand, trans.), **Supp. IV Part 2:** 630
"Sow" (Plath), **Supp. I Part 2:** 537
Space between Our Footsteps, The: Poems and Paintings from the Middle East (Nye, ed.), **Supp. XIII:** 280
"Space Quale, The" (James), **II:** 349
"Spaces Between, The" (Kingsolver), **Supp. VII:** 209
"Spain" (Auden), **Supp. II Part 1:** 12–13, 14
"Spain in Fifty-Ninth Street" (White), **Supp. I Part 2:** 677
"Spanish-American War Play" (Crane), **I:** 422
Spanish Ballads (Merwin, trans.), **Supp. III Part 1:** 347
Spanish Bayonet (Benét), **Supp. XI:** 45, 47
Spanish Earth, The (film), **Retro. Supp. I:** 184
Spanish Papers and Other Miscellanies (Irving), **II:** 314
"Spanish Revolution, The" (Bryant), **Supp. I Part 1:** 153, 168
Spanish Student, The (Longfellow), **II:** 489, 506; **Retro. Supp. II:** 165
Spanking the Maid (Coover), **Supp. V:** 47, 48, 49, 52
Spargo, John, **Supp. I Part 1:** 13
"Spark, The" (Wharton), **Retro. Supp. I:** 381
"Sparkles from the Wheel" (Whitman), **IV:** 348
Sparks, Debra, **Supp. X:** 177
Sparks, Jared, **Supp. I Part 1:** 156
"Sparrow" (Berry), **Supp. X:** 31
Sparrow, Henry, **III:** 587
Sparrow, Mrs. Henry, **III:** 587
"Spawning Run, The" (Humphrey), **Supp. IX:** 95
"Speak, Gay Memory" (Kirp), **Supp. XI:** 129
Speak, Memory (Nabokov), **III:** 247–250, 252; **Retro. Supp. I:** 264, 265, 266, 267, 268, 277
Speaking and Language (Shapiro), **Supp. II Part 2:** 721
Speaking for Nature: How Literary Naturalists from Henry Thoreau to Rachel Carson Have Shaped America (Brooks), **Supp. IX:** 31
Speaking for Ourselves: American Ethnic Writing (Faderman and Bradshaw, eds.), **Supp. XIII:** 313
"Speaking of Counterweights" (White), **Supp. I Part 2:** 669
Speaking of Literature and Society (Trilling), **Supp. III Part 2:** 494, 496, 499
Speaking on Stage (Kolin and Kullman, eds.), **Supp. IX:** 145
Speak What We Feel (Not What We Ought to Say): Reflections on Litera-

ture and Faith (Buechner), **Supp. XII:** 57
Spear, Roberta, **Supp. V:** 180
"Special Kind of Fantasy, A: James Dickey on the Razor's Edge" (Niflis), **Supp. IV Part 1:** 175
"Special Pleading" (Lanier), **Supp. I Part 1:** 364
"Special Problems in Teaching Leslie Marmon Silko's *Ceremony*" (Gunn Allen), **Supp. IV Part 1:** 333
Special Providence, A (Yates), **Supp. XI:** 342, **344–345**
"Special Time, a Special School, A" (Knowles), **Supp. XII:** 236
Special View of History, The (Olson), **Supp. II Part 2:** 566, 569, 572
Specimen Days (Whitman), **IV:** 338, 347, 348, 350; **Retro. Supp. I:** 408
Specimens of the American Poets, **Supp. I Part 1:** 155
"Spectacles, The" (Poe), **III:** 425
Spectator Bird, The (Stegner), **Supp. IV Part 2:** 599, 604, 606, 611–612
Spector, Robert, **Supp. XIII:** 87
"Spectre Bridegroom, The" (Irving), **II:** 304
"Spectre Pig, The" (Holmes), **Supp. I Part 1:** 302
"Speech Sounds" (O. Butler), **Supp. XIII:** 61, **70**
"Speech to a Crowd" (MacLeish), **III:** 16
"Speech to the Detractors" (MacLeish), **III:** 16
"Speech to the Young" (Brooks), **Supp. III Part 1:** 79, 86
"Speech to Those Who Say Comrade" (MacLeish), **III:** 16
Speedboat (Adler), **Supp. X:** 171
Speed of Darkness, The (Rukeyser), **Supp. VI:** 274, 281
Speilberg, Steven, **Supp. XI:** 234
"Spell" (Francis), **Supp. IX:** 87
Spence, Thomas, **Supp. I Part 2:** 518
Spence + Lila (Mason), **Supp. VIII:** 133, **143–145**
Spencer, Edward, **Supp. I Part 1:** 357, 360
Spencer, Herbert, **I:** 515; **II:** 345, 462–463, 480, 483, 536; **III:** 102, 315; **IV:** 135; **Retro. Supp. II:** 60, 65, 93, 98; **Supp. I Part 1:** 368; **Supp. I Part 2:** 635
Spencer, Sharon, **Supp. X:** 185, 186, 195, 196
Spencer, Theodore, **I:** 433; **Supp. III Part 1:** 2
Spender, Natasha, **Supp. IV Part 1:** 119, 127, 134

Spender, Stephen, **II:** 371; **III:** 504, 527; **Retro. Supp. I:** 216; **Retro. Supp. II:** 243, 244; **Supp. I Part 2:** 536; **Supp. II Part 1:** 11; **Supp. IV Part 1:** 82, 134; **Supp. IV Part 2:** 440; **Supp. X:** 116
Spengler, Oswald, **I:** 255, 270; **II:** 7, 577; **III:** 172, 176; **Retro. Supp. II:** 342; **Supp. I Part 2:** 647
Spens, Sir Patrick, **Supp. I Part 2:** 404
Spenser, Edmund, **I:** 62; **III:** 77, 78, 89; **IV:** 155, 453; **Retro. Supp. I:** 62; **Supp. I Part 1:** 98, 152, 369; **Supp. I Part 2:** 422, 719
"Spenser's Ireland" (Moore), **III:** 211, 212
Sperry, Margaret, **Supp. IV Part 1:** 169
Sphere: The Form of a Motion (Ammons), **Supp. VII:** 24, 32, 33, 35, 36
"Sphinx" (Hayden), **Supp. II Part 1:** 373
"Spiced Plums" (Ríos), **Supp. IV Part 2:** 553
"Spider and the Ghost of the Fly, The" (Lindsay), **Supp. I Part 2:** 375
Spider Bay (Van Vechten), **Supp. II Part 2:** 746
"Spiders" (Schwartz), **Supp. II Part 2:** 665
Spider's House, The (Bowles), **Supp. IV Part 1:** 87–89, 90, 91
Spider Woman's Granddaughters: Traditional Tales and Contemporary Writing by Native American Women (Gunn Allen, ed.), **Supp. IV Part 1:** 320, 326, 332–333; **Supp. IV Part 2:** 567
Spiegelman, Willard, **Supp. XI:** 126
Spillane, Mickey, **Supp. IV Part 2:** 469, 472
Spiller, Robert E., **I:** 241; **Supp. I Part 1:** 104
Spillway (Barnes), **Supp. III Part 1:** 44
Spingarn, Amy, **Supp. I Part 1:** 325, 326
Spingarn, Joel, **I:** 266; **Supp. I Part 1:** 325
Spinoza, Baruch, **I:** 493; **II:** 590, 593; **III:** 600; **IV:** 5, 7, 11, 12, 17; **Retro. Supp. II:** 318; **Supp. I Part 1:** 274; **Supp. I Part 2:** 643
"Spinoza of Market Street, The" (Singer), **IV:** 12–13; **Retro. Supp. II:** 325
"Spinster" (Plath), **Supp. I Part 2:** 536
"Spinster's Tale, A" (Taylor), **Supp. V:** 314–315, 316–317, 319, 323

Spiral of Memory, The: Interviews (Coltelli, ed.), **Supp. XII:** 215
Spires, Elizabeth, **Supp. X:** 8
"Spire Song" (Bowles), **Supp. IV Part 1:** 80
Spirit and the Flesh, The: Sexual Diversity in American Indian Culture (W. L. Williams), **Supp. IV Part 1:** 330
"Spirit Birth" (Cullen), **Supp. IV Part 1:** 168
Spirit in Man, The (Jung), **Supp. IV Part 1:** 68
Spirit of Culver (West), **IV:** 287
Spirit of Romance, The (Pound), **III:** 470; **Retro. Supp. I:** 286
Spirit of Youth and the City Streets, The (Addams), **Supp. I Part 1:** 6–7, 12–13, 16, 17, 19
"Spirits" (Bausch), **Supp. VII:** 46–47
Spirits, and Other Stories (Bausch), **Supp. VII:** 46–47, 54
"Spirit Says, You Are Nothing, The" (Levis), **Supp. XI:** 265–266
Spiritual Conflict, The (Scupoli), **IV:** 156
Spiritual Exercises, The (Loyola), **IV:** 151; **Supp. XI:** 162
"Spiritual Manifestation, A" (Whittier), **Supp. I Part 2:** 699
"Spirituals and Neo-Spirituals" (Hurston), **Supp. VI:** 152–153
Spits, Ellen Handler, **Supp. XII:** 166
"Spitzbergen Tales" (Crane), **I:** 409, 415, 423
"Spleen" (Eliot), **I:** 569, 573–574
Splendid Drunken Twenties, The (Van Vechten), **Supp. II Part 2:** 739–744
"Split at the Root" (Rich), **Retro. Supp. II:** 292
"Splittings" (Rich), **Supp. I Part 2:** 570–571
"Splitting Wood at Six Above" (Kumin), **Supp. IV Part 2:** 449
Spofford, Harriet Prescott, **Supp. XIII:** 143
Spoils of Poynton, The (James), **I:** 463; **Retro. Supp. I:** 229–230
Spoken Page, The (Nye), **Supp. XIII:** 274
"Spokes" (Auster), **Supp. XII:** 23
Spokesmen (Whipple), **II:** 456
Spook Sonata, The (Strindberg), **III:** 387, 392
Spooky Art, The: A Book about Writing (Mailer), **Retro. Supp. II:** 214
"Spoon, The" (Simic), **Supp. VIII:** 275
Spoon River Anthology (Masters), **I:** 106; **III:** 579; **Supp. I Part 2:** 454, 455, 456, 460–465, 466, 467, 471,

472, 473, 476; **Supp. IX:** 306
Sport and a Pastime, A (Salter), **Supp. IX: 254–257**
Sporting Club, The (McGuane), **Supp. VIII:** 43
Sport of the Gods, The (Dunbar), **Supp. II Part 1:** 193, 200, 207, 214–217
Sportsman's Sketches, A (Turgenev), **I:** 106; **IV:** 277
Sportswriter, The (Ford), **Supp. V:** 57, 58, 62–67
"Spotted Horses" (Faulkner), **IV:** 260
Sprague, Morteza, **Retro. Supp. II:** 115
Spratling, William, **II:** 56; **Retro. Supp. I:** 80
"Spray Paint King, The" (Dove), **Supp. IV Part 1:** 252–253
Spreading Fires (Knowles), **Supp. XII:** 249
Sprigge, Elizabeth, **IV:** 31
"Spring" (Millay), **III:** 126
"Spring" (Mora), **Supp. XIII:** 217
Spring and All (W. C. Williams), **Retro. Supp. I:** 412, 418, **418–420,** 427, 430, 431
"Spring and All" (W. C. Williams), **Retro. Supp. I:** 419
"Spring Evening" (Farrell), **II:** 45
"Spring Evening" (Kenyon), **Supp. VII:** 173
"Springfield Magical" (Lindsay), **Supp. I Part 2:** 379
Spring in New Hampshire and Other Poems (McKay), **Supp. X:** 131, 135
"Spring Pastoral" (Wylie), **Supp. I Part 2:** 707
"Spring Pools" (Frost), **II:** 155; **Retro. Supp. I:** 137
"Spring Snow" (Matthews), **Supp. IX:** 160
"SPRING SONG" (Baraka), **Supp. II Part 1:** 60
Springsteen, Bruce, **Supp. VIII:** 143
"Spring Strains" (W. C. Williams), **Retro. Supp. I:** 416
Spring Tides (Morison), **Supp. I Part 2:** 494
Springtime and Harvest (Sinclair), **Supp. V:** 280
Spruance, Raymond, **Supp. I Part 2:** 479, 491
"Spruce Has No Taproot, The" (Clampitt), **Supp. IX:** 41–42
"Spunk" (Hurston), **Supp. VI:** 150, 151–152
Spunk: The Selected Stories (Hurston), **Supp. VI:** 150
Spy, The (Cooper), **I:** 335, 336, 337, 339, 340; **Supp. I Part 1:** 155

"Spy, The" (Francis), **Supp. IX:** 81
Spy, The (Freneau), **Supp. II Part 1:** 260
Spy in the House of Love, A (Nin), **Supp. X:** 186
Squanto, **Supp. I Part 2:** 486
"Square Business" (Baraka), **Supp. II Part 1:** 49
Square Root of Wonderful, The (McCullers), **II:** 587–588
"Squash in Blossom" (Francis), **Supp. IX:** 81
"Squatter on Company Land, The" (Hugo), **Supp. VI:** 133
"Squatter's Children" (Bishop), **Retro. Supp. II:** 47
Squeeze Play (Auster), **Supp. XII:** 21
Squires, Radcliffe, **IV:** 127
S.S. Gliencairn (O'Neill), **III:** 387, 388, 405
S.S. San Pedro (Cozzens), **I:** 360–362, 370, 378, 379
"Ssshh" (Olds), **Supp. X:** 215
"Stacking the Straw" (Clampitt), **Supp. IX:** 41
Stade, George, **Supp. IV Part 1:** 286
Staël, Madame de, **II:** 298
"Staff of Life, The" (H. Miller), **III:** 187
Stafford, Jean, **II:** 537; **Retro. Supp. II:** 177; **Supp. V:** 316
Stafford, William, **Supp. IV Part 1:** 72; **Supp. IV Part 2:** 642; **Supp. IX:** 273; **Supp. XI: 311–332; Supp. XIII:** 76, 274, 276, 277, 281, 283
"Stage All Blood, The" (MacLeish), **III:** 18
"Staggerlee Wonders" (Baldwin), **Retro. Supp. II:** 15
Stalin, Joseph, **I:** 261, 490; **II:** 39, 40, 49, 564; **III:** 30, 298; **IV:** 372; **Supp. V:** 290
"Stalking the Billion-Footed Beast: A Literary Manifesto for the New Social Novel" (Wolfe), **Supp. III Part 2:** 586
Stallman, R. W., **I:** 405
Stamberg, Susan, **Supp. IV Part 1:** 201; **Supp. XII:** 193
Stamford, Anne Marie, **Supp. XII:** 162
Stanard, Mrs. Jane, **III:** 410, 413
Stand, The (King), **Supp. V:** 139, 140–141, 144–146, 148, 152
"Standard of Living, The" (Parker), **Supp. IX: 198–199**
Stander, Lionel, **Supp. I Part 1:** 289
Standing by Words (Berry), **Supp. X:** 22, 27, 28, 31, 32, 33, 35
"Standing Halfway Home" (Wagoner), **Supp. IX:** 324

Stand in the Mountains, A (Taylor), **Supp. V:** 324
Standish, Burt L. (pseudonym). *See* Patten, Gilbert
Standish, Miles, **I:** 471; **II:** 502–503
Standley, Fred L., **Retro. Supp. II:** 6
Stand Still Like the Hummingbird (H. Miller), **III:** 184
"Stand Up" (Salinas), **Supp. XIII:** 315
Stand with Me Here (Francis), **Supp. IX:** 76
Stanford, Ann, **Retro. Supp. I:** 41; **Supp. I Part 1:** 99, 100, 102, 103, 106, 108, 109, 113, 117; **Supp. IV Part 2:** 637
Stanford, Donald E., **II:** 217
Stanford, Leland, **I:** 196, 198
"Stanley Kunitz" (Oliver), **Supp. VII:** 237
Stanton, Frank L., **Supp. II Part 1:** 192
Stanton, Robert J., **Supp. IV Part 2:** 681
"Stanzas from the Grande Chartreuse" (Arnold), **Supp. I Part 2:** 417
Stanzas in Meditation (Stein), **Supp. III Part 1:** 13
Staples, Hugh, **Retro. Supp. II:** 187
Star, Alexander, **Supp. X:** 310
Starbuck, George, **Retro. Supp. II:** 53, 245; **Supp. I Part 2:** 538; **Supp. IV Part 2:** 440; **Supp. XIII:** 76
Star Child (Gunn Allen), **Supp. IV Part 1:** 324
"Stare, The" (Updike), **Retro. Supp. I:** 329
"Starfish, The" (Bly), **Supp. IV Part 1:** 72
"Staring at the Sea on the Day of the Death of Another" (Swenson), **Supp. IV Part 2:** 652
Star Is Born, A (film), **Supp. IV Part 1:** 198; **Supp. IX:** 198
Stark, David, **Supp. XII:** 202
"Stark Boughs on the Family Tree" (Oliver), **Supp. VII:** 232
Starke, Aubrey Harrison, **Supp. I Part 1:** 350, 352, 356, 360, 362, 365, 370, 371
Starkey, David, **Supp. XII:** 180, 181
"Starlight" (Levine), **Supp. V:** 188
"Starlight Scope Myopia" (Komunyakaa), **Supp. XIII:** 123, 124
"Star of the Nativity" (Brodsky), **Supp. VIII:** 33
Starr, Ellen Gates, **Supp. I Part 1:** 4, 5, 11
Starr, Ringo, **Supp. XI:** 309
Star Rover, The (London), **II:** 467

"Starry Night, The" (Sexton), **Supp. II Part 2:** 681
"Stars" (Frost), **II:** 153
Stars, the Snow, the Fire, The: Twenty-five Years in the Northern Wilderness (Haines), **Supp. XII: 199–201,** 206, 209
Star Shines over Mt. Morris Park, A (H. Roth), **Supp. IX:** 227, 236, **236–237**
"Stars of the Summer Night" (Longfellow), **II:** 493
"Stars over Harlem" (Hughes), **Retro. Supp. I:** 207
"Star-Spangled" (García), **Supp. XI:** 177, 178
Star-Spangled Girl, The (Simon), **Supp. IV Part 2:** 579
"Star-Splitter, The" (Frost), **Retro. Supp. I:** 123, 133
Stars Principal (McClatchy), **Supp. XII: 256–258**
"Starting from Paumanok" (Whitman), **IV:** 333
Starting Out in the Thirties (Kazin), **Supp. VIII: 95–97**
"Starved Lovers" (MacLeish), **III:** 19
Starved Rock (Masters), **Supp. I Part 2:** 465
"Starving Again" (Moore), **Supp. X:** 163, 172, 175
"State, The" (Bourne), **I:** 233
"Statement: Phillipa Allen" (Rukeyser), **Supp. VI:** 283–284
"Statement of Principles" (Ransom), **III:** 496
"Statements on Poetics" (Snyder), **Supp. VIII:** 291, 292
"State of the Art, The" (Elkin), **Supp. VI:** 52
State of the Nation (Dos Passos), **I:** 489
"State of the Union" (Vidal), **Supp. IV Part 2:** 678
"Statue, The" (Berryman), **I:** 173
"Statue and Birds" (Bogan), **Supp. III Part 1:** 50
"Statues, The" (Schwartz), **Supp. II Part 2:** 654, 659
"Status Rerum" (Pound), **Supp. I Part 1:** 257
Stavans, Ilan, **Supp. XI:** 190
"Staying Alive" (Levertov), **Supp. III Part 1:** 281
Staying Alive (Wagoner), **Supp. IX:** 324, **326**
"Staying at Ed's Place" (Swenson), **Supp. IV Part 2:** 648
Stayton, Richard, **Supp. IX:** 133
Steadman, Goodman, **IV:** 147

"Steak" (Snyder), **Supp. VIII:** 301
Stealing Beauty (Minot), **Supp. VI:** 205
Stealing Glimpses (McQuade), **Supp. IX:** 151
"Stealing the Thunder: Future Visions for American Indian Women, Tribes, and Literary Studies" (Gunn Allen), **Supp. IV Part 1:** 331
"Steam Shovel Cut" (Masters), **Supp. I Part 2:** 468
Stearns, Harold, **I:** 245
Stedman, Edmund Clarence, **Supp. I Part 1:** 372; **Supp. II Part 1:** 192
Steele, Sir Richard, **I:** 378; **II:** 105, 107, 300; **III:** 430
Steenburgen, Mary, **Supp. IV Part 1:** 236
Steeple Bush (Frost), **II:** 155; **Retro. Supp. I:** 140; **Retro. Supp. II:** 42
"Steeple-Jack, The" (Moore), **III:** 212, 213, 215
"Steerage" (Goldbarth), **Supp. XII:** 187
Steers, Nina, **Retro. Supp. II:** 25
Steffens, Lincoln, **II:** 577; **III:** 580; **Retro. Supp. I:** 202; **Retro. Supp. II:** 101; **Supp. I Part 1:** 7
Stegner, Page, **IV:** 114, 116; **Supp. IV Part 2:** 599
Stegner, Wallace, **Supp. IV Part 2: 595–618; Supp. V:** 220, 224, 296; **Supp. X:** 23, 24
"Stegner's Short Fiction" (Ahearn), **Supp. IV Part 2:** 604
Steichen, Edward, **III:** 580, 594–595
Steichen, Lillian. *See* Sandburg, Mrs. Carl (Lillian Steichen)
Steier, Rod, **Supp. VIII:** 269
Steiger, Rod, **Supp. XI:** 305
Stein, Gertrude, **I:** 103, 105, 476; **II:** 56, 251, 252, 257, 260, 262–263, 264, 289; **III:** 71, 454, 471–472, 600; **IV: 24–48,** 368, 375, 404, 415, 443, 477; **Retro. Supp. I:** 108, 170, 176, 177, 186, 418, 422; **Retro. Supp. II:** 85, 207, 344, 349; **Supp. I Part 1:** 292; **Supp. III Part 1:** 13, 37, 225, 226; **Supp. III Part 2:** 626; **Supp. IV Part 1:** 11, 79, 80, 81, 322; **Supp. IV Part 2:** 468; **Supp. V:** 53; **Supp. IX:** 55, 57, 62, 66; **Supp. XII:** 1, 139
Stein, Karen F., **Supp. XIII:** 29, 30
Stein, Leo, **IV:** 26
Stein, Lorin, **Supp. XII:** 254
Steinbeck, John, **I:** 107, 288, 301, 378, 495, 519; **II:** 272; **III:** 382, 453, 454, 589; **IV: 49–72; Retro. Supp. II:** 19, 196; **Supp. IV Part 1:** 102,

225; **Supp. IV Part 2:** 502; **Supp. V:** 290, 291; **Supp. VIII:** 10; **Supp. IX:** 33, 171; **Supp. XI:** 169; **Supp. XIII:** 1, 17
Steinbeck, Olive Hamilton, **IV:** 51
Steinberg, Saul, **Supp. VIII:** 272
Steinem, Gloria, **Supp. IV Part 1:** 203
Steiner, George, **Retro. Supp. I:** 327; **Supp. IV Part 1:** 286
Steiner, Nancy, **Supp. I Part 2:** 529
Steiner, Stan, **Supp. IV Part 2:** 505
Steinman, Michael, **Supp. VIII:** 172
Steinmetz, Charles Proteus, **I:** 483
Steinway Quintet Plus Four, The (Epstein), **Supp. XII:** 159, **162–166**
Stekel, Wilhelm, **III:** 554
Stella (Goethe), **Supp. IX:** 133, 138
Stella (Kushner), **Supp. IX:** 133
Stella, Joseph, **I:** 387
"Stellaria" (Francis), **Supp. IX:** 83
Stelligery and Other Essays (Wendell), **Supp. I Part 2:** 414
Stendhal, **I:** 316; **III:** 465, 467; **Supp. I Part 1:** 293; **Supp. I Part 2:** 445
Stepanchev, Stephen, **Supp. XI:** 312
Stephen, Leslie, **IV:** 440
Stephen, Saint, **II:** 539; **IV:** 228
Stephen, Sir Leslie, **IV:** 440; **Supp. I Part 1:** 306
Stephen Crane (Berryman), **I:** 169–170, 405
Stephen King: The Art of Darkness (Winter), **Supp. V:** 144
Stephen King, The Second Decade: "Danse Macabre" to "The Dark Half" (Magistrale), **Supp. V:** 138, 146, 151
Stephens, Jack, **Supp. X:** 11, 14, 15, 17
Stephenson, Gregory, **Supp. XII:** 120, 123
"Stepping Out" (Dunn), **Supp. XI:** 140, 141
Steps (Kosinski), **Supp. VII:** 215, 221–222, 225
"Steps" (Nye), **Supp. XIII:** 288
Steps to the Temple (Crashaw), **IV:** 145
"Steps Toward Poverty and Death" (Bly), **Supp. IV Part 1:** 60
Stepto, Robert B., **Retro. Supp. II:** 116, 120, 123
Sterile Cuckoo, The (Nichols), **Supp. XIII:** 258, **259–263,** 264
Sterling, George, **I:** 199, 207, 208, 209; **II:** 440; **Supp. V:** 286
Stern, Daniel, **Supp. VIII:** 238
Stern, Frederick C., **Supp. X:** 114, 115, 117
Stern, Gerald, **Supp. IX: 285–303; Supp. XI:** 139, 267

Stern, Madeleine B., **Supp. I Part 1:** 35
Stern, Maurice, **IV:** 285
Stern, Philip Van Doren, **Supp. XIII:** 164
Stern, Richard, **Retro. Supp. II:** 309
Stern, Richard G., **Retro. Supp. II:** 204
"Sterne" (Schwartz), **Supp. II Part 2:** 663
Sterne, Laurence, **II:** 302, 304–305, 308; **III:** 454; **IV:** 68, 211, 465; **Supp. I Part 2:** 714; **Supp. IV Part 1:** 299; **Supp. V:** 127; **Supp. X:** 324
Sterritt, David, **Supp. IV Part 2:** 574
Stetson, Caleb, **IV:** 178
Stetson, Charles Walter, **Supp. XI:** 195, 196, 197, 202, 204, 209
Stevens, Mrs. Wallace (Elsie Kachel), **IV:** 75
Stevens, Wallace, **I:** 60, 61, 266, 273, 462, 521, 528, 540–541; **II:** 56, 57, 530, 552, 556; **III:** 19, 23, 194, 216, 270–271, 272, 278, 279, 281, 453, 463, 493, 509, 521, 523, 600, 605, 613, 614; **IV: 73–96,** 140, 141, 332, 402, 415; **Retro. Supp. I:** 67, 89, 193, 284, 288, **295–315,** 335, 403, 411, 416, 417, 422; **Retro. Supp. II:** 40, 44, 344; **Supp. I Part 1:** 80, 82, 257; **Supp. II Part 1:** 9, 18; **Supp. III Part 1:** 2, 3, 12, 20, 48, 239, 318, 319, 344; **Supp. III Part 2:** 611; **Supp. IV Part 1:** 72, 393; **Supp. IV Part 2:** 619, 620, 621, 634; **Supp. V:** 337; **Supp. VIII:** 21, 102, 195, 271, 292; **Supp. IX:** 41; **Supp. X:** 58; **Supp. XI:** 123, 191, 312; **Supp. XIII:** 44, 45
"Stevens and the Idea of the Hero" (Bromwich), **Retro. Supp. I:** 305
Stevenson, Adlai, **II:** 49; **III:** 581
Stevenson, David, **Supp. XI:** 230
Stevenson, Robert Louis, **I:** 2, 53; **II:** 283, 290, 311, 338; **III:** 328; **IV:** 183–184, 186, 187; **Retro. Supp. I:** 224, 228; **Supp. I Part 1:** 49; **Supp. II Part 1:** 404–405; **Supp. IV Part 1:** 298, 314; **Supp. VIII:** 125; **Supp. XIII:** 75
Stevick, Robert D., **III:** 509
Stewart, Dugald, **II:** 8, 9; **Supp. I Part 1:** 151, 159; **Supp. I Part 2:** 422
Stewart, Randall, **II:** 244
Stewart, Robert E., **Supp. XI:** 216
Stickeen (Muir), **Supp. IX:** 182
Sticks and Stones (Mumford), **Supp. II Part 2:** 475, 483, 487–488
Sticks & Stones (Matthews), **Supp. IX:** 154, 155, 157, 158

Stieglitz, Alfred, **Retro. Supp. I:** 416; **Retro. Supp. II:** 103; **Supp. VIII:** 98
"Stigmata" (Oates), **Supp. II Part 2:** 520
Stiles, Ezra, **II:** 108, 122; **IV:** 144, 146, 148
Still, William Grant, **Retro. Supp. I:** 203
"Stillborn" (Plath), **Supp. I Part 2:** 544
"Still Here" (Hughes), **Retro. Supp. I:** 211
"Still Just Writing" (Tyler), **Supp. IV Part 2:** 658
"Still Life" (Hecht), **Supp. X:** 68
"Still Life" (Malamud), **Supp. I Part 2:** 450
"Still Life" (Sandburg), **III:** 584
"Still Life: Moonlight Striking up on a Chess-Board" (Lowell), **II:** 528
"Still Life Or" (Creeley), **Supp. IV Part 1:** 141, 150, 158
Still Life with Oysters and Lemon (Doty), **Supp. XI:** 119, 121, **133–134**
Still Life with Woodpecker (Robbins), **Supp. X:** 260, **271–274,** 282
"Still Moment, A" (Welty), **IV:** 265; **Retro. Supp. I:** 347
Stillness (Gardner), **Supp. VI:** 74
"Still Small Voices, The" (Fante), **Supp. XI:** 164
Still Such (Salter), **Supp. IX:** 246
"Still the Place Where Creation Does Some Work on Itself" (Davis), **Supp. IV Part 1:** 68
Stimpson, Catharine R., **Supp. IV Part 2:** 686
Stimson, Eleanor Kenyon. *See* Brooks, Mrs. Van Wyck
"Stings" (Plath), **Retro. Supp. II:** 255; **Supp. I Part 2:** 541
"Stirling Street September" (Baraka), **Supp. II Part 1:** 51
Stirner, Max, **II:** 27
"Stirrup-Cup, The" (Lanier), **Supp. I Part 1:** 364
Stitt, Peter, **Supp. IV Part 1:** 68; **Supp. IV Part 2:** 628; **Supp. IX:** 152, 163, 291, 299; **Supp. XI:** 311, 317; **Supp. XIII:** 87
Stivers, Valerie, **Supp. X:** 311
Stock, Noel, **III:** 479
Stockton, Frank R., **I:** 201
Stoddard, Charles Warren, **I:** 193, 195, 196; **Supp. II Part 1:** 192, 341, 351
Stoddard, Elizabeth, **II:** 275
Stoddard, Richard, **Supp. I Part 1:** 372

Stoddard, Solomon, **I:** 545, 548; **IV:** 145, 148
Stoic, The (Dreiser), **I:** 497, 502, 508, 516; **Retro. Supp. II:** 95, 96, 101, 108
"Stolen Calf, The" (Dunbar), **Supp. II Part 1:** 196
Stolen Past, A (Knowles), **Supp. XII:** 249
Stone, Edward, **III:** 479
Stone, Irving, **II:** 463, 466, 467
Stone, Phil, **II:** 55
Stone, Robert, **Supp. V: 295–312; Supp. X:** 1
Stone, Wilmer, **Supp. I Part 1:** 49
"Stone Bear, The" (Haines), **Supp. XII:** 206–207, 212
"Stone City" (Proulx), **Supp. VII:** 251–253
Stone Diaries, The (Shields), **Supp. VII:** 307, 315, **324–326,** 327
"Stone Dreams" (Kingsolver), **Supp. VII:** 203
Stone Harp, The (Haines), **Supp. XII: 204,** 205, 206, 207
Stonemason, The (McCarthy), **Supp. VIII:** 175, 187
"Stones" (Kumin), **Supp. IV Part 2:** 447
"Stones, The" (Plath), **Supp. I Part 2:** 535, 539
"Stones in My Passway, Hellhounds on My Trail" (Boyle), **Supp. VIII:** 15
Stones of Florence, The (McCarthy), **II:** 562
"Stone Walls" (Sarton), **Supp. VIII:** 259
"Stop" (Wilbur), **Supp. III Part 2:** 556
"Stop Me If You've Heard This One" (Lardner), **II:** 433
Stopover: Tokyo (Marquand), **III:** 53, 57, 61, 70
Stoppard, Tom, **Retro. Supp. I:** 189
"Stopping by Woods" (Frost), **II:** 154
"Stopping by Woods on a Snowy Evening" (Frost), **Retro. Supp. I:** 129, 133, 134, 135, 139
Stopping Westward (Richards), **II:** 396
"Stop Player. Joke No. 4" (Gaddis), **Supp. IV Part 1:** 280
Store, The (Stribling), **Supp. VIII:** 126
"*Store* and *Mockingbird:* Two Pulitzer Novels about Alabama" (Going), **Supp. VIII:** 126
Storer, Edward, **Supp. I Part 1:** 261, 262
Stories, Fables and Other Diversions (Nemerov), **III:** 268–269, 285
Stories for the Sixties (Yates, ed.),

Supp. XI: 343
Stories from World Literature, **Supp. IX:** 4
Stories of F. Scott Fitzgerald, The (Cowley, ed.), **Retro. Supp. I:** 115
Stories of F. Scott Fitzgerald, The (Fitzgerald), **II:** 94
Stories of Modern America, **Supp. IX:** 4
Stories of Stephen Dixon, The (Dixon), **Supp. XII:** 152
Stories of the Spanish Civil War (Hemingway), **II:** 258
Stories Revived (James), **II:** 322
Stories that Could Be True (Stafford), **Supp. XI: 325–327**
Storm, The (Buechner), **Supp. XII: 54–57**
"Storm, The" (Chopin), **Retro. Supp. II:** 60, 68; **Supp. I Part 1:** 218, 224
"Storm Fear" (Frost), **II:** 153; **Retro. Supp. I:** 127
"Storm Ship, The" (Irving), **II:** 309
"Storm Warnings" (Kingsolver), **Supp. VII:** 207–208
"Storm Warnings" (Rich), **Retro. Supp. II:** 279
"Stormy Weather" (Ellison), **Supp. II Part 1:** 233
"Story, A" (Jarrell), **II:** 371
Story, Richard David, **Supp. IV Part 2:** 575, 588
"Story about Chicken Soup, A" (Simpson), **Supp. IX:** 272–273
"Story about the Anteater, The" (Benét), **Supp. XI:** 53
"Story About the Body, A" (Hass), **Supp. VI: 107–108**
"Story Hearer, The" (Paley), **Supp. VI:** 230, 231
Story of a Country Town, The (Howe), **I:** 106
"Story of an Hour, The" (Chopin), **Retro. Supp. II:** 72; **Supp. I Part 1:** 212–213, 216
Story of a Novel, The (Wolfe), **IV:** 456, 458
"Story of a Proverb, The" (Lanier), **Supp. I Part 1:** 365
"Story of a Proverb, The: A Fairy Tale for Grown People" (Lanier), **Supp. I Part 1:** 365
Story of a Story and Other Stories, The: A Novel (Dixon), **Supp. XII:** 155
Story of a Wonder Man, The (Lardner), **II:** 433–434
"Story of a Year, The" (James), **Retro. Supp. I:** 218

"Story of Gus, The" (A. Miller), **III:** 147–148
"Story of How a Wall Stands, A" (Ortiz), **Supp. IV Part 2:** 499, 507
Story of Mount Desert Island, Maine, The (Morison), **Supp. I Part 2:** 494
Story of My Boyhood and Youth, The (Muir), **Supp. IX: 172–174,** 176
Story of My Father, The: A Memoir (S. Miller), **Supp. XII:** 301
Story of O, The (Réage), **Supp. XII:** 9, 10
Story of Our Lives, The (Strand), **Supp. IV Part 2:** 620, 628–629, 629
Story of the Normans, The, Told Chiefly in Relation to Their Conquest of England (Jewett), **II:** 406
"Story of Toby, The" (Melville), **III:** 76
Story of Utopias, The (Mumford), **Supp. II Part 2:** 475, 483–486, 495
Story on Page One, The (Odets), **Supp. II Part 2:** 546
Storyteller (Silko), **Supp. IV Part 2:** 558, 559, 560, 561, **566–570**
"Storyteller" (Silko), **Supp. IV Part 2:** 569
"*Storyteller:* Grandmother Spider's Web" (Danielson), **Supp. IV Part 2:** 569
"Storyteller's Notebook, A" (Carver), **Supp. III Part 1:** 142–143
Story Teller's Story, A: The Tale of an American Writer's Journey through His Own Imaginative World and through the World of Facts . . . (Anderson), **I:** 98, 101, 114, 117
"Story That Could Be True, A" (Stafford), **Supp. XI:** 326
"Stout Gentleman, The" (Irving), **II:** 309
Stover at Yale (Johnson), **III:** 321
Stowe, Calvin, **IV:** 445; **Supp. I Part 2:** 587, 588, 590, 596, 597
Stowe, Charles, **Supp. I Part 2:** 581, 582
Stowe, Eliza, **Supp. I Part 2:** 587
Stowe, Harriet Beecher, **II:** 274, 399, 403, 541; **Retro. Supp. I:** 34, 246; **Retro. Supp. II:** 4, 138, 156; **Supp. I Part 1:** 30, 206, 301; **Supp. I Part 2: 579–601; Supp. III Part 1:** 154, 168, 171; **Supp. IX:** 33; **Supp. X:** 223, 246, 249, 250; **Supp. XI:** 193; **Supp. XIII:** 141, 295
Stowe, Samuel Charles, **Supp. I Part 2:** 587
Stowe, William, **Supp. IV Part 1:** 129
Strachey, Lytton, **I:** 5; **IV:** 436; **Retro.**

Supp. I: 59; **Supp. I Part 2:** 485, 494
Straight Cut (Bell), **Supp. X:** 5, **6–7,** 10
Straight Man (Russo), **Supp. XII: 335–339,** 340
Strand, Mark, **Supp. IV Part 2: 619–636; Supp. V:** 92, 332, 337, 338, 343; **Supp. IX:** 155; **Supp. XI:** 139, 145; **Supp. XII:** 254; **Supp. XIII:** 76
Strand, Paul, **Supp. VIII:** 272
Strandberg, Victor, **Supp. V:** 273
Strange Case of Dr. Jekyll and Mr. Hyde, The (Stevenson), **II:** 290
Strange Children, The (Gordon), **II:** 196, 197, 199, 211–213
"Strange Fruit" (Harjo), **Supp. XII:** 224, 225
"Strange Fruit" (song), **Supp. I Part 1:** 80
Strange Interlude (O'Neill), **III:** 391, 397–398; **IV:** 61
Stranger, The (Camus), **I:** 53, 292; **Supp. VIII:** 11
"Stranger, The" (Rich), **Supp. I Part 2:** 555, 560
"Stranger, The" (Salinger), **III:** 552–553
"Stranger in My Own Life, A: Alienation in American Indian Poetry and Prose" (Gunn Allen), **Supp. IV Part 1:** 322
"Stranger in the Village" (Baldwin), **Retro. Supp. II:** 3; **Supp. I Part 1:** 54; **Supp. IV Part 1:** 10
"Stranger in Town" (Hughes), **Supp. I Part 1:** 334
"Strangers" (Howe), **Supp. VI:** 120
Strangers and Wayfarers (Jewett), **Retro. Supp. II:** 138
"Strangers from the Horizon" (Merwin), **Supp. III Part 1:** 356
Strangers on a Train (Highsmith), **Supp. IV Part 1:** 132
"Strange Story, A" (Taylor), **Supp. V:** 323
"Strange Story, A" (Wylie), **Supp. I Part 2:** 723
Strange Things (Atwood), **Supp. XIII:** 35
"Strato in Plaster" (Merrill), **Supp. III Part 1:** 328
Straus, Ralph, **Supp. XIII:** 168
Straus, Roger, **Supp. VIII:** 82
Strauss, Johann, **I:** 66
Strauss, Richard, **IV:** 316
Strauss, Robert, **Supp. XI:** 141, 142
Stravinsky (De Schloezer), **III:** 474
Stravinsky, Igor, **Retro. Supp. I:** 378;

Supp. IV Part 1: 81; **Supp. XI:** 133
"Stravinsky's Three Pieces 'Grotesques,' for String Quartet" (Lowell), **II:** 523
Straw, The (O'Neill), **III:** 390
"Stray Document, A" (Pound), **II:** 517
Streaks of the Tulip, The: Selected Criticism (W. J. Smith), **Supp. XIII:** 333, 334, 344, **347–348**
Streamline Your Mind (Mursell), **Supp. I Part 2:** 608
"Street, Cloud" (Ríos), **Supp. IV Part 2:** 549
Streetcar Named Desire, A (T. Williams), **IV:** 382, 383, 385, 386, 387, 389–390, 395, 398; **Supp. IV Part 1:** 359
Street in Bronzeville, A (Brooks), **Retro. Supp. I:** 208; **Supp. III Part 1:** 74–78
"Street Musicians" (Ashbery), **Supp. III Part 1:** 18
"Street off Sunset, A" (Jarrell), **II:** 387
"Streets" (Dixon), **Supp. XII:** **145–146**
Streets in the Moon (MacLeish), **III:** 5, 8–11, 15, 19
Streets of Laredo (McMurtry), **Supp. V:** 230
"Streets of Laredo" (screenplay) (McMurtry and Ossana), **Supp. V:** 226, 230
Streets of Night (Dos Passos), **I:** 478, 479–480, 481, 488
Streitfeld, David, **Supp. XIII:** 234
Strength of Fields, The (Dickey), **Supp. IV Part 1:** 178
"Strength of Fields, The" (Dickey), **Supp. IV Part 1:** 176, 184–185
"Strength of Gideon, The" (Dunbar), **Supp. II Part 1:** 212
Strength of Gideon and Other Stories, The (Dunbar), **Supp. II Part 1:** 211, 212
Strether, Lambert, **II:** 313
Stribling, T. S., **Supp. VIII:** 126
Strickland, Joe (pseudonym). *See* Arnold, George W.
"Strictly Bucolic" (Simic), **Supp. VIII:** 278
Strictly Business (O. Henry), **Supp. II Part 1:** 410
"Strike, The" (Olsen), **Supp. XIII:** 292, 297
Strindberg, August, **I:** 78; **III:** 145, 165, 387, 390, 391, 392, 393; **IV:** 17
"String, The" (Dickey), **Supp. IV Part 1:** 179
"Strivings of the Negro People" (Du Bois), **Supp. II Part 1:** 167

Strohbach, Hermann, **Supp. XI:** 242
"Stroke of Good Fortune, A" (O'Connor), **III:** 344; **Retro. Supp. II:** 229, 232
Strom, Stephen, **Supp. XII:** 223
Strong, George Templeton, **IV:** 321
"Strong Draughts of Their Refreshing Minds" (Dickinson), **Retro. Supp. I:** 46
Strong Opinions (Nabokov), **Retro. Supp. I:** 263, 266, 270, 276
"Strong Women" (Dorman), **Supp. XI:** 240
Strout, Elizabeth, **Supp. X:** 86
Structure of Nations and Empires, The (Niebuhr), **III:** 292, 308
"Strumpet Song" (Plath), **Retro. Supp. II:** 246; **Supp. I Part 2:** 536
Strunk, William, **Supp. I Part 2:** 652, 662, 670, 671, 672
Strunsky, Anna, **II:** 465
"Strut for Roethke, A" (Berryman), **I:** 188
Stuart, Gilbert, **I:** 16
Stuart, J. E. B., **III:** 56
Stuart Little (White), **Supp. I Part 2:** 655–658
"Student, The" (Moore), **III:** 212, 215
"Student of Salmanaca, The" (Irving), **II:** 309
"Student's Wife, The" (Carver), **Supp. III Part 1:** 141
Studies in American Indian Literature: Critical Essays and Course Designs (Gunn Allen), **Supp. IV Part 1:** 324, 333
Studies in Classic American Literature (Lawrence), **II:** 102; **III:** 33; **IV:** 333; **Retro. Supp. I:** 421
"Studs" (Farrell), **II:** 25, 28, 31
Studs Lonigan: A Trilogy (Farrell), **II:** 25, 26, 27, 31–34, 37, 38, 41–42
"Study of Images" (Stevens), **IV:** 79
"Study of Lanier's Poems, A" (Kent), **Supp. I Part 1:** 373
Study of Milton's Prosody (Bridges), **II:** 537
"Study of the Negro Problems, The" (Du Bois), **Supp. II Part 1:** 165
Stuewe, Paul, **Supp. IV Part 1:** 68
Stuhlmann, Gunther, **Supp. X:** 182, 184, 185, 187
Stultifera Navis (Brant), **III:** 447
Sturak, John Thomas, **Supp. XIII:** 162, 163, 165, 168
Sturgis, George, **III:** 600
Sturgis, Howard, **IV:** 319; **Retro. Supp. I:** 367, 373
Sturgis, Susan, **III:** 600
Sturm, Margaret. *See* Millar, Margaret

Stuttaford, Genevieve, **Supp. IX:** 279
Stuyvesant, Peter, **II:** 301
"Style" (Nemerov), **III:** 275
Styles of Radical Will (Sontag), **Supp. III Part 2:** 451, 459, 460–463
Styron, William, **III:** 40; **IV:** 4, **97–119**, 216; **Supp. V:** 201; **Supp. IX:** 208; **Supp. X:** 15–16, 250; **Supp. XI:** 229, 231, 343
Suares, J. C., **Supp. IV Part 1:** 234
Suarez, Ernest, **Supp. IV Part 1:** 175; **Supp. V:** 180
"Sub, The" (Dixon), **Supp. XII:** 146
Subjection of Women, The (Mill), **Supp. XI:** 196, 203
"Subjective Necessity for Social Settlements" (Addams), **Supp. I Part 1:** 4
"Subject of Childhood, A" (Paley), **Supp. VI:** 221
"Submarginalia" (Howe), **Supp. IV Part 2:** 422
Substance and Shadow (James), **II:** 344
Subterraneans, The (Kerouac), **Supp. III Part 1:** 225, 227–231
Subtreasury of American Humor, A (White and White), **Supp. I Part 2:** 668
"Suburban Culture, Imaginative Wonder: The Fiction of Frederick Barthelme" (Brinkmeyer), **Supp. XI:** 38
Suburban Sketches (Howells), **II:** 274, 277
"Subverted Flower, The" (Frost), **Retro. Supp. I:** 139
"Subway, The" (Tate), **IV:** 128
"Subway Singer, The" (Clampitt), **Supp. IX:** 45
"Success" (Mora), **Supp. XIII:** 217
Successful Love and Other Stories (Schwartz), **Supp. II Part 2:** 661, 665
Succession, The: A Novel of Elizabeth and James (Garrett), **Supp. VII:** 104–107, 108
"Success is counted sweetest" (Dickinson), **Retro. Supp. I:** 30, 31–32, 38
Success Stories (Banks), **Supp. V:** 14–15
"Success Story" (Banks), **Supp. V:** 15
"Such Counsels You Gave to Me" (Jeffers), **Supp. II Part 2:** 433
Such Silence (Milburn), **Supp. XI:** 242
"Such Things Happen Only in Books" (Wilder), **IV:** 365
Suddenly, Last Summer (film) (Vidal), **Supp. IV Part 2:** 683

Suddenly Last Summer (T. Williams), **I:** 73; **IV:** 382, 383, 385, 386, 387, 389, 390, 391, 392, 395–396, 397, 398
Sudermann, Hermann, **I:** 66
Sugg, Richard P., **Supp. IV Part 1:** 68
"Suggestion from a Friend" (Kenyon), **Supp. VII:** 171
"Suicide" (Barnes), **Supp. III Part 1:** 33
"Suicide off Egg Rock" (Plath), **Supp. I Part 2:** 529, 538
"Suicide's Note" (Hughes), **Retro. Supp. I:** 199
"Suitable Surroundings, The" (Bierce), **I:** 203
"Suitcase, The" (Ozick), **Supp. V:** 262, 264
"Suite for Augustus, A" (Dove), **Supp. IV Part 1:** 245
"Suite for Lord Timothy Dexter" (Rukeyser), **Supp. VI:** 283, 285
"Suite from the Firebird" (Stravinsky), **Supp. XI:** 133
"Suitor, The" (Kenyon), **Supp. VII:** 164–165
Sukarno, **IV:** 490
Sukenick, Ronald, **Supp. V:** 39, 44, 46; **Supp. XII:** 139
Sula (Morrison), **Supp. III Part 1:** 362, 364, 367, 368, 379; **Supp. VIII:** 219
Sullivan, Andrew, **Supp. IX:** 135
Sullivan, Frank, **Supp. IX:** 201
Sullivan, Harry Stack, **I:** 59
Sullivan, Jack, **Supp. X:** 86; **Supp. XII:** 331
Sullivan, Noel, **Retro. Supp. I:** 202; **Supp. I Part 1:** 329, 333
Sullivan, Richard, **Supp. VIII:** 124
Sullivan, Walter, **Supp. VIII:** 168
"Sullivan County Sketches" (Crane), **I:** 407, 421
"Sumach and Goldenrod: An American Idyll" (Mumford), **Supp. II Part 2:** 475
Suma Genji (Play), **III:** 466
Sumerian Vistas (Ammons), **Supp. VII:** 34, 35
"Summer" (Emerson), **II:** 10
"Summer" (Lowell), **II:** 554
Summer (Wharton), **IV:** 317; **Retro. Supp. I:** 360, 367, 374, **378–379,** 382
Summer, Bob, **Supp. X:** 1, 5, 6, 42
"Summer: West Side" (Updike), **Retro. Supp. I:** 320
Summer and Smoke (T. Williams), **IV:** 382, 384, 385, 386, 387, 395, 397, 398; **Supp. IV Part 1:** 84

Summer Anniversaries, The (Justice), **Supp. VII:** 115, 117
"Summer Commentary, A" (Winters), **Supp. II Part 2:** 808
"Summer Day" (O'Hara), **III:** 369
"Summer Days, The" (Oliver), **Supp. VII:** 239
"Summer Night" (Hughes), **Supp. I Part 1:** 325
"Summer Night, A" (Auden), **Supp. II Part 1:** 8
"Summer Noon: 1941" (Winters), **Supp. II Part 2:** 811
"Summer of '82" (Merwin), **Supp. III Part 1:** 355–356
Summer on the Lakes in 1843 (Fuller), **Supp. II Part 1:** 279, 295–296
"Summer People" (Hemingway), **II:** 258–259
"Summer People, The" (Jackson), **Supp. IX:** 120
"Summer People, The" (Merrill), **Supp. III Part 1:** 325–326
"Summer Ramble, A" (Bryant), **Supp. I Part 1:** 162, 164
Summers, Claude J., **Supp. IV Part 2:** 680–681
Summers, Robert, **Supp. IX:** 289
"Summer Solstice, New York City" (Olds), **Supp. X:** 207
"Summer's Reading, A" (Malamud), **Supp. I Part 2:** 430–431, 442
"Summer Storm" (Simpson), **Supp. IX:** 268
"'Summertime and the Living . . .'" (Hayden), **Supp. II Part 1:** 363, 366
Summertime Island (Caldwell), **I:** 307–308
"Summit Beach, 1921" (Dove), **Supp. IV Part 1:** 249
Summoning of Stones, A (Hecht), **Supp. X:** 57, 58, **58–59**
Summons to Memphis, A (Taylor), **Supp. V:** 313, 314, 327
Summons to the Free, A (Benét), **Supp. XI:** 47
Sumner, Charles, **I:** 3, 15; **Supp. I Part 2:** 685, 687
Sumner, John, **Retro. Supp. II:** 95
Sumner, John B., **I:** 511
Sumner, William Graham, **III:** 102, 108; **Supp. I Part 2:** 640
"Sumptuous Destination" (Wilbur), **Supp. III Part 2:** 553
"Sun" (Moore), **III:** 215
"Sun" (Swenson), **Supp. IV Part 2:** 640
"Sun, Sea, and Sand" (Marquand), **III:** 60
Sun Also Rises, The (Hemingway), **I:**

107; **II:** 68, 90, 249, 251–252, 260, 600; **III:** 36; **IV:** 35, 297; **Retro. Supp. I:** 171, **177–180,** 181, 189; **Supp. I Part 2:** 614; **Supp. XIII:** 263
"Sun and Moon" (Kenyon), **Supp. VII:** 168
"Sun and the Still-born Stars, The" (Southern), **Supp. XI:** 295
Sun at Midnight (Soseki; Merwin and Shigematsu, trans.), **Supp. III Part 1:** 353
"Sun Crosses Heaven from West to East Bringing Samson Back to the Womb, The" (Bly), **Supp. IV Part 1:** 73
"Sun Dance Shield" (Momaday), **Supp. IV Part 2:** 491
Sunday, Billy, **II:** 449
"Sunday Afternoons" (Komunyakaa), **Supp. XIII:** 127
Sunday after the War (H. Miller), **III:** 184
"Sunday at Home" (Hawthorne), **II:** 231–232
"Sunday Morning" (Stevens), **II:** 552; **III:** 278, 463, 509; **IV:** 92–93; **Retro. Supp. I:** 296, 300, 301, 304, 307, 313
"Sunday Morning Apples" (Crane), **I:** 387
"Sunday Morning Prophecy" (Hughes), **Supp. I Part 1:** 334
"Sundays" (Salter), **Supp. IX:** 257
"Sundays, They Sleep Late" (Rukeyser), **Supp. VI:** 278
"Sundays of Satin-Legs Smith, The" (Brooks), **Supp. III Part 1:** 74, 75
"Sundays Visiting" (Ríos), **Supp. IV Part 2:** 541
Sundial, The (Jackson), **Supp. IX:** **126–127**
Sundog (Harrison), **Supp. VIII:** **46–48**
Sun Dogs (R. O. Butler), **Supp. XII:** **64–65**
Sun Do Move, The (Hughes), **Supp. I Part 1:** 339
"Sunflower Sutra" (Ginsberg), **Supp. II Part 1:** 317, 321
Sunlight Dialogues, The (Gardner), **Supp. VI:** 63, **68,** 69, 70
"Sunlight Is Imagination" (Wilbur), **Supp. III Part 2:** 549
"Sunrise" (Lanier), **Supp. I Part 1:** 370
"Sunrise runs for Both, The" (Dickinson), **Retro. Supp. I:** 45
Sunrise with Seamonsters: Travels and Discoveries, 1964–1984 (Theroux), **Supp. VIII:** 311, 313, 323, 325

"Sun Rising" (Donne), **Supp. VIII:** 164

"Sunset" (Ransom), **III:** 484

"Sunset from Omaha Hotel Window" (Sandburg), **III:** 584

Sunset Gun (Parker), **Supp. IX:** 192

Sunset Limited (Harrison), **Supp. VIII:** 51

"Sunset Maker, The" (Justice), **Supp. VII:** 123

Sunset Maker, The: Poems, Stories, a Memoir (Justice), **Supp. VII:** 116, 118, 119, 123–124

Sunshine Boys, The (film), **Supp. IV Part 2:** 589

Sunshine Boys, The (Simon), **Supp. IV Part 2:** 575, 584–585

"Sunthin' in the Pastoral Line" (Lowell), **Supp. I Part 2:** 415–416

Sun to Sun (Hurston), **Supp. VI:** 154

Sun Tracks (Ortiz), **Supp. IV Part 2:** 499, 500

Sun Under Wood (Hass), **Supp. VI:** 103, 108–109

"Superb Lily, The" (Pinsky), **Supp. VI:** 250

"Superman Comes to the Supermarket" (Mailer), **Retro. Supp. II:** 204

"Supermarket in California, A" (Ginsberg), **Supp. XI:** 135

"Supper After the Last, The" (Kinnell), **Supp. III Part 1:** 239

"Supposedly Fun Thing I'll Never Do Again, A" (Wallace), **Supp. X:** 315

Supposedly Fun Thing I'll Never Do Again, A: Essays and Arguments (Wallace), **Supp. X:** 314–316

Suppressed Desires (Glaspell), **Supp. III Part 1:** 178

Suppression of the African Slave Trade to the United States of America, 1638–1870 (Du Bois), **Supp. II Part 1:** 157, 162

Sure Hand of God, The (Caldwell), **I:** 297, 302

"Surety and Fidelity Claims" (Stevens), **Retro. Supp. I:** 296, 309

Surface of Earth, The (Price), **Supp. VI:** 261–262

"Surfaces" (Ammons), **Supp. VII:** 36

Surfacing (Atwood), **Supp. XIII:** 20, 21, **22–23,** 24, 33, 35

"Surgeon at 2 A.M." (Plath), **Supp. I Part 2:** 545

Surmmer Knowledge (Schwartz), **Supp. II Part 2:** 662, 665

"Surprise" (Kenyon), **Supp. VII:** 173

"Surround, The Imagining Herself as the Environment,/She Speaks to James Wright at Sundow" (Dickey), **Supp. IV Part 1:** 185

"Survey of Literature" (Ransom), **III:** 480

"Surveyor, The" (H. Roth), **Supp. IX:** 233, 234

Survival (Atwood), **Supp. XIII:** 20, 22, 35

Survival of the Bark Canoe, The (McPhee), **Supp. III Part 1:** 301, 302, 308, 313

Survival This Way: Interviews with American Indian Poets (Bruchac), **Supp. IV Part 2:** 506

"Surviving Love" (Berryman), **I:** 173

Survivor (O. Butler), **Supp. XIII:** 62, 63

Susanna Moodie: Voice and Vision (Shields), **Supp. VII:** 313

Suspect in Poetry, The (Dickey), **Supp. IV Part 1:** 177

"Sustained by Fiction" (Hoffman), **Supp. X:** 90, 92

"Susto" (Ríos), **Supp. IV Part 2:** 553

Sutherland, Donald, **IV:** 38, 44; **Supp. IX:** 254

Sutherland, Efua, **Supp. IV Part 1:** 9, 16

Sutherland-Smith, James, **Supp. X:** 211, 212

Sut Lovingood's Yarns (Harris), **II:** 70

Sutton, Roger, **Supp. X:** 266

Sutton, Walter, **III:** 479

Suttree (McCarthy), **Supp. VIII: 178–180,** 189

Suvero, Mark di, **Supp. IX:** 251

Swados, Harvey, **Supp. XI:** 222

Swallow, Alan, **Supp. X:** 112, 115, 116, 120, 123

Swallow Barn (Kennedy), **II:** 313

Swan, Barbara, **Supp. IV Part 2:** 447

Swan, Jon, **Supp. IV Part 1:** 176

Swan Lake (Tchaikovsky), **Supp. IX:** 51

"Swan Legs" (Stern), **Supp. IX:** 299

Swann (Shields), **Supp. VII:** 315, 318–323, 326

Swann, Brian, **Supp. IV Part 2:** 500

Swanson, Gloria, **II:** 429

Swanton, John Reed, **Supp. VIII:** 295

"Swarm, The" (Plath), **Retro. Supp. II:** 255

"Sway" (Simpson), **Supp. IX:** 276

Sweat (Hurston), **Supp. VI:** 152

Swedenborg, Emanuel, **II:** 5, 10, 321, 342, 343–344, 396

Sweeney Agonistes (Eliot), **I:** 580; **Retro. Supp. I:** 64, 65; **Retro. Supp. II:** 247

"Sweeney Among the Nightingales" (Eliot), **III:** 4

Sweet, Blanche, **Supp. I Part 2:** 391

Sweet, Timothy, **Supp. IV Part 1:** 330

Sweet and Sour (O'Hara), **III:** 361

Sweet Bird of Youth (T. Williams), **IV:** 382, 383, 385, 386, 387, 388, 389, 390, 391, 392, 395, 396, 398; **Supp. IV Part 1:** 84, 89

Sweet Charity (musical), **Supp. IV Part 2:** 575

Sweet Flypaper of Life, The (Hughes), **Supp. I Part 1:** 335–336

"Sweetheart of the Song Tra Bong, The" (O'Brien), **Supp. V:** 243, 249

"Sweethearts" (Ford), **Supp. V:** 69

Sweet Hereafter, The (Banks), **Supp. V:** 15–16

Sweet Machine (Doty), **Supp. XI:** 121, **131–132,** 135

Sweet Sue (Gurney), **Supp. V:** 105, 107–108

Sweet Sweetback's Baadasss Song (Peebles; film), **Supp. XI:** 17

Sweet Thursday (Steinbeck), **IV:** 50, 52, 64–65

Sweet Will (Levine), **Supp. V:** 178, 187, 189, 190

"Sweet Will" (Levine), **Supp. V:** 190

"Sweet Words on Race" (Hughes), **Retro. Supp. I:** 211

Sweezy, Paul, **Supp. I Part 2:** 645

"Swell-Looking Girl, A" (Caldwell), **I:** 310

Swenson, May, **Retro. Supp. II:** 44; **Supp. IV Part 2: 637–655**

"Swift" (Schwartz), **Supp. II Part 2:** 663

Swift, Jonathan, **I:** 125, 194, 209, 441; **II:** 110, 302, 304–305, 577; **III:** 113; **IV:** 68; **Retro. Supp. I:** 66; **Supp. I Part 2:** 406, 523, 603, 656, 665, 708, 714; **Supp. IV Part 1:** 51; **Supp. IV Part 2:** 692; **Supp. XI:** 105, 209; **Supp. XII:** 276

"Swimmer" (Francis), **Supp. IX:** 82

"Swimmer, The" (Cheever), **Supp. I Part 1:** 185, 187

"Swimmer, The" (Glück), **Supp. V:** 82

"Swimmers, The" (Fitzgerald), **Retro. Supp. I:** 110, 111

"Swimmers, The" (Tate), **IV:** 136

"Swimming" (Harjo), **Supp. XII:** 218

Swinburne, Algernon C., **I:** 50, 384, 568; **II:** 3, 4, 129, 400, 524; **IV:** 135; **Retro. Supp. I:** 100; **Supp. I Part 1:** 79; **Supp. I Part 2:** 422, 552

"Swinburne as Poet" (Eliot), **I:** 576

Swinger of Birches, A: A Portrait of Robert Frost (Cox), **Retro. Supp. I:** 132

"Swinging on a Birch-Tree" (Larcom), **Supp. XIII:** 147
Switch, The (Dixon), **Supp. XII:** 141
Swope, D. B., **Supp. IX:** 95
Sword Blades and Poppy Seed (Lowell), **II:** 518, 520, 522, 532
Sybil (Auchincloss), **Supp. IV Part 1:** 25
"Sycamore" (Stern), **Supp. IX:** 294
"Sycamore, The" (Moore), **III:** 216
"Sycamores, The" (Whittier), **Supp. I Part 2:** 699
Sylvester, Johnny, **Supp. I Part 2:** 438
Sylvester, Joshua, **I:** 178, 179; **II:** 18; **III:** 157; **Supp. I Part 1:** 98, 104, 114, 116
Sylvia (Gurney), **Supp. V:** 105
"Sylvia" (Larcom), **Supp. XIII:** 144
"Sylvia" (Stern), **Supp. IX:** 297
Sylvia Plath: Method and Madness (Butscher), **Supp. I Part 2:** 526
Sylvia Plath: Poetry and Existence (Holbrook), **Supp. I Part 2:** 526–527
"Sylvia's Death" (Sexton), **Supp. II Part 2:** 671, 684, 685
"Symbol and Image in the Shorter Poems of Herman Melville" (Dickey), **Supp. IV Part 1:** 176
Symbolist Movement in Literature, The (Symons), **I:** 50, 569; **Retro. Supp. I:** 55
Symonds, John Addington, **I:** 241, 242, 251, 259; **IV:** 334
Symons, Arthur, **I:** 50, 569; **Retro. Supp. I:** 55
Symons, Julian, **Supp. IV Part 1:** 343, 351
"Sympathy" (Dunbar), **Supp. IV Part 1:** 15
Sympathy of Souls, A (Goldbarth), **Supp. XII:** 175, 176, **186–187**
"Symphony, The" (Lanier), **Supp. I Part 1:** 352, 360–361, 364; **Supp. I Part 2:** 416
Symposium (Plato), **Retro. Supp. II:** 31; **Supp. IV Part 1:** 391
Symposium: To Kill a Mockingbird (Alabama Law Review), **Supp. VIII:** 127, 128
Symptoms of Being 35 (Lardner), **II:** 434
Synge, John Millington, **I:** 434; **III:** 591–592; **Supp. III Part 1:** 34; **Supp. VIII:** 155
Synthetic Philosophy (Spencer), **II:** 462–463
"Syringa" (Ashbery), **Supp. III Part 1:** 19–21, 25
"Syrinx" (Clampitt), **Supp. IX:** 53

"Syrinx" (Merrill), **Supp. III Part 1:** 328
"System, The" (Ashbery), **Supp. III Part 1:** 14, 15, 18, 21–22
System of Dante's Hell, The (Baraka), **Supp. II Part 1:** 39–41, 55
"System of Dante's Inferno, The" (Baraka), **Supp. II Part 1:** 40
"System of Doctor Tarr and Professor Fether, The" (Poe), **III:** 419, 425
System of General Geography, A (Brown), **Supp. I Part 1:** 146
Sze, Mai-mai, **Supp. X:** 291
Szentgyorgyi, Tom, **Supp. IX:** 135, 136, 140, 141–142
Szymborka, Wislawa, **Supp. XI:** 267
T. S. Eliot and American Philosophy (Jain), **Retro. Supp. I:** 58
T. S. Eliot's Silent Voices (Mayer), **Retro. Supp. I:** 58
"Table of Delectable Contents, The" (Simic), **Supp. VIII:** 276
Tabloid Dreams (R. O. Butler), **Supp. XII: 70–72,** 74
Tacitus, Cornelius, **I:** 485; **II:** 113
Tadic, Novica, **Supp. VIII:** 272
Taft (Patchett), **Supp. XII:** 307, 312, **314–317**
"Tag" (Hughes), **Supp. I Part 1:** 341
Taggard, Genevieve, **IV:** 436
Taggart, John, **Supp. IV Part 2:** 421
Tagore, Rabindranath, **I:** 383
"Taibele and Her Demon" (Singer), **Retro. Supp. II:** 325
"Tailor Shop, The" (H. Miller), **III:** 175
"Tails" (Dixon), **Supp. XII:** 154
Taine, Hippolyte, **I:** 503; **II:** 271; **III:** 323; **IV:** 440, 444
"Tain't So" (Hughes), **Supp. I Part 1:** 330
Takasago (play), **III:** 466
Take Me Back: A Novel (Bausch), **Supp. VII:** 41, 43–45, 46, 49
"Take My Saddle from the Wall: A Valediction" (McMurtry), **Supp. V:** 219
"'Take No for an Answer'" (Didion), **Supp. IV Part 1:** 203
"Take Pity" (Malamud), **Supp. I Part 2:** 427, 428, 435, 436, 437
"Takers, The" (Olds), **Supp. X:** 205
"Take the I Out" (Olds), **Supp. X:** 213
"Taking Away the Name of a Nephew" (Ríos), **Supp. IV Part 2:** 545–546
Taking Care of Mrs. Carroll (Monette), **Supp. X:** 153
"Taking of Captain Ball, The" (Jewett), **Retro. Supp. II:** 134
"Taking Out the Lawn Chairs" (Karr), **Supp. XI:** 241

"Taking the Forest" (Howe), **Supp. IV Part 2:** 433
"Taking the Lambs to Market" (Kumin), **Supp. IV Part 2:** 455
"Taking Women Students Seriously" (Rich), **Retro. Supp. II:** 286
"Tale, A" (Bogan), **Supp. III Part 1:** 50, 51
Taleb-Khyar, Mohamed, **Supp. IV Part 1:** 242, 243, 244, 247, 257
"Tale of Jerusalem, A" (Poe), **III:** 411
Tale of Possessors Self-Dispossessed, A (O'Neill), **III:** 404
Tale of the Body Thief, The (Rice), **Supp. VII:** 290, 293–294, 297
Tale of Two Cities, A (film), **Supp. I Part 1:** 67
"Tale of Two Liars, A" (Singer), **IV:** 12
Tales (Baraka), **Supp. II Part 1:** 39, 55
Tales (Poe), **III:** 413
Tales and Stories for Black Folks (Bambara, ed.), **Supp. XI:** 1
Tales before Midnight (Benét), **Supp. XI:** 46, 53, 57
Tales of a Traveller (Irving), **II:** 309–310
Tales of a Wayside Inn (Longfellow), **II:** 489, 490, 501, 502, 504–505; **Retro. Supp. II:** 154, **162–165**
Tales of Glauber-Spa (Bryant, ed.), **Supp. I Part 1:** 157
Tales of Manhattan (Auchincloss), **Supp. IV Part 1:** 23
Tales of Men and Ghosts (Wharton), **IV:** 315; **Retro. Supp. I:** 372
Tales of Rhoda, The (Rice), **Supp. VII:** 288
Tales of Soldiers and Civilians (Bierce), **I:** 200–203, 204, 206, 208, 212
Tales of the Argonauts (Harte), **Supp. II Part 1:** 337, 348, 351
Tales of the Fish Patrol (London), **II:** 465
Tales of the Grotesque and Arabesque (Poe), **II:** 273; **III:** 412, 415; **Retro. Supp. II:** 270
Tales of the Jazz Age (Fitzgerald), **II:** 88; **Retro. Supp. I:** 105; **Supp. IX:** 57
"Talisman, A" (Moore), **III:** 195–196
Talisman, The (King), **Supp. V:** 140, 144, 152
"Talkin Bout Sonny" (Bambara), **Supp. XI:** 6–7
"Talking" (Merwin), **Supp. III Part 1:** 354

Talking All Morning (Bly), **Supp. IV Part 1:** 59, 60, 61, 62, 64, 65
Talking Dirty to the Gods (Komunyakaa), **Supp. XIII:** 130–131
"Talking Horse" (Malamud), **Supp. I Part 2:** 435
"Talking to Barr Creek" (Wagoner), **Supp. IX:** 328
"Talking to Sheep" (Sexton), **Supp. II Part 2:** 695
"Talk of the Town" (*The New Yorker* column), **IV:** 215; **Supp. IV Part 1:** 53, 54
"Talk with the Yellow Kid, A" (Bellow), **I:** 151
Tallent, Elizabeth, **Supp. IV Part 2:** 570
Tallman, Warren, **Supp. IV Part 1:** 154
TallMountain, Mary, **Supp. IV Part 1:** 324–325
Talma, Louise, **IV:** 357
Talmey, Allene, **Supp. IV Part 1:** 197; **Supp. XIII:** 172
Talmud, **IV:** 8, 17
Taltos: Lives of the Mayfair Witches (Rice), **Supp. VII:** 299–300
"Tamar" (Jeffers), **Supp. II Part 2:** 427–428, 436
Tamar and Other Poems (Jeffers), **Supp. II Part 2:** 416, 419
Tambourines to Glory (Hughes), **Supp. I Part 1:** 338–339
"Tame Indians" (Jewett), **Retro. Supp. II:** 141
"Tamerlane" (Poe), **III:** 426
Tamerlane and Other Poems (Poe), **III:** 410
"Tam O'Shanter" (Burns), **II:** 306
Tan, Amy, **Supp. X:** 289–300
Tangential Views (Bierce), **I:** 209
"Tangier 1975" (Bowles), **Supp. IV Part 1:** 94
"Tankas" (McClatchy), **Supp. XII:** 266
Tanner, Laura E., **Supp. X:** 209
Tanner, Tony, **I:** 260, 261; **Retro. Supp. II:** 205; **Supp. IV Part 1:** 285
Tannhäuser (Wagner), **I:** 315
"Tan Ta Ra, Cries Mars...," (Wagoner), **Supp. IX:** 325
Tao of Physics, The (Capra), **Supp. X:** 261
Tapahonso, Luci, **Supp. IV Part 1:** 404; **Supp. IV Part 2:** 499, 508
Tape for the Turn of the Year (Ammons), **Supp. VII:** 31–33, 35
"Tapestry" (Ashbery), **Supp. III Part 1:** 22–23

"Tapiama" (Bowles), **Supp. IV Part 1:** 89–90
"Tapiola" (W. C. Williams), **Retro. Supp. I:** 429
Tappan, Arthur, **Supp. I Part 2:** 588
Taps at Reveille (Fitzgerald), **II:** 94, 96; **Retro. Supp. I:** 113
Tar: A Midwest Childhood (Anderson), **I:** 98, 115; **II:** 27
Tarantino, Quentin, **Supp. IV Part 1:** 356
Tar Baby (Morrison), **Supp. III Part 1:** 364, 369–372, 379; **Supp. IV Part 1:** 13
Tarbell, Ida, **III:** 322, 580; **Retro. Supp. II:** 101
"Target Study" (Baraka), **Supp. II Part 1:** 49–50, 54
Tarkington, Booth, **II:** 444; **III:** 70; **Retro. Supp. I:** 100
Tarpon (film), **Supp. VIII:** 42
Tarr, Rodger L., **Supp. X:** 222, 224, 226
Tartuffe (Molière; Wilbur, trans.), **Supp. III Part 2:** 560
Tarumba, Selected Poems of Jaime Sabines (Levine and Trejo, trans.), **Supp. V:** 178
"Tarzan Is an Expatriate" (Theroux), **Supp. VIII:** 313
Task, The (Cowper), **II:** 304
Tasso, Torquato, **I:** 276
Taste of Palestine, A: Menus and Memories (Shihab), **Supp. XIII:** 273
Tate, Allen, **I:** 48, 49, 50, 67, 69, 381, 382, 386, 390, 396, 397, 399, 402, 441, 468; **II:** 197–198, 367, 536, 537, 542, 551, 554; **III:** 424, 428, 454, 482, 483, 485, 493, 495, 496, 497, 499, 500, 517; **IV:** 120–143, 236, 237, 433; **Retro. Supp. I:** 37, 41, 90; **Retro. Supp. II:** 77, 79, 82, 83, 89, 176, 178, 179; **Supp. I Part 1:** 364, 371; **Supp. I Part 2:** 423; **Supp. II Part 1:** 90–91, 96, 98, 103–104, 136, 139, 144, 150, 151, 318; **Supp. II Part 2:** 643; **Supp. III Part 2:** 542; **Supp. V:** 315, 331; **Supp. X:** 1, 52
Tate, Benjamin Lewis Bogan, **IV:** 127
Tate, Greg, **Supp. XIII:** 233, 237
Tate, James, **Supp. V:** 92, 338; **Supp. VIII:** 39, 279
Tate, John Allen, **IV:** 127
Tate, Michael Paul, **IV:** 127
Tate, Mrs. Allen (Caroline Gordon). *See* Gordon, Caroline
Tate, Mrs. Allen (Helen Heinz), **IV:** 127

Tate, Mrs. Allen (Isabella Gardner), **IV:** 127
Tate, Nancy, **II:** 197
Tattooed Countess, The (Van Vechten), **I:** 295; **Supp. II Part 2:** 726–728, 738, 742
Tattooed Feet (Nye), **Supp. XIII:** 274
"Tattoos" (McClatchy), **Supp. XII:** 266–267, 268
"Tattoos" (Wright), **Supp. V:** 335, 340
Tatum, Anna, **I:** 516
Tatum, James, **Supp. IV Part 2:** 684
Taupin, René, **II:** 528, 529; **Supp. III Part 2:** 614, 615, 617, 621
Tawney, Richard Henry, **Supp. I Part 2:** 481
Taylor, Bayard, **II:** 275; **Supp. I Part 1:** 350, 361, 362, 365, 366, 372
Taylor, Cora. *See* Howarth, Cora
Taylor, Deems, **III:** 138
Taylor, Edward, **III:** 493; **IV:** 144–166; **Supp. I Part 1:** 98; **Supp. I Part 2:** 375, 386, 546
Taylor, Eleanor Ross, **Supp. V:** 317, 318
Taylor, Elizabeth, **II:** 588
Taylor, Frank, **III:** 81
Taylor, Frederick Winslow, **Supp. I Part 2:** 644
Taylor, Graham, **Supp. I Part 1:** 5
Taylor, Henry, **Retro. Supp. I:** 212; **Supp. XI:** 317; **Supp. XIII:** 333
Taylor, Henry W., **IV:** 144
Taylor, Jeremy, **II:** 11; **III:** 487; **Supp. I Part 1:** 349; **Supp. XII:** 45
Taylor, John, **IV:** 149
Taylor, Katherine, **Supp. VIII:** 251
Taylor, Kezia, **IV:** 148
Taylor, Mrs. Edward (Elizabeth Fitch), **IV:** 147, 165
Taylor, Mrs. Edward (Ruth Wyllys), **IV:** 148
Taylor, Nathaniel W., **Supp. I Part 2:** 580
Taylor, Paul, **I:** 293
Taylor, Peter, **Retro. Supp. II:** 179; **Supp. V:** 313–329
Taylor, Richard, **IV:** 146
Taylor, Robert, **Supp. I Part 1:** 294
Taylor, Thomas, **II:** 10
Taylor, William, **IV:** 145–146
Taylor, Zachary, **I:** 3; **II:** 433–434
Tchelitchew, Peter, **II:** 586
Tea and Sympathy (Anderson), **Supp. I Part 1:** 277; **Supp. V:** 108
"Tea at the Palaz of Hoon" (Stevens), **Retro. Supp. I:** 300, 302, 306
"Teacher's Pet" (Thurber), **Supp. I Part 2:** 605–606
Teaching a Stone to Talk: Expeditions

and Encounters (Dillard), **Supp. VI:** 23, 26, 28, 32, 33, 34–35
Teachings of Don B., The (Barthelme), **Supp. IV Part 1:** 53
Teale, Edwin Way, **Supp. XIII:** 7
Teall, Dorothy, **I:** 221
Team Team Team (film), **Supp. IX:** 251
"Tea on the Mountain" (Bowles), **Supp. IV Part 1:** 90
"Tea Party, The" (MacLeish), **III:** 11
"Tears of the Pilgrims, The" (McClatchy), **Supp. XII:** 256
Teasdale, Sara, **Retro. Supp. I:** 133; **Supp. I Part 2:** 393, 707
Tebeaux, Elizabeth, **Supp. IX:** 109
Technics and Civilization (Mumford), **Supp. I Part 2:** 638; **Supp. II Part 2:** 479, 493, 497
Technics and Human Development (Mumford), **Supp. I Part 2:** 638; **Supp. II Part 2:** 497
"Teddy" (Salinger), **III:** 561–563, 571
Tedlock, Dennis, **Supp. IV Part 2:** 509
"Teeth Mother Naked at Last, The" (Bly), **Supp. IV Part 1:** 63, 68, 73
Teggart, Richard, **Supp. I Part 2:** 650
Tegnér, Esaias, **Retro. Supp. II:** 155
Teilhard de Chardin, Pierre, **Supp. I Part 1:** 314
Telephone, The (film), **Supp. XI:** 309
"Telephone Call, A" (Parker), **Supp. IX:** 202–203
"Telephone Number of the Muse, The" (Justice), **Supp. VII:** 124–125
Telephone Poles and Other Poems (Updike), **IV:** 214, 215
"Television" (Beattie), **Supp. V:** 33
Teller, Edward, **I:** 137
"Telling" (Ortiz), **Supp. IV Part 2:** 509
"Telling It in Black and White: The Importance of the Africanist Presence in *To Kill a Mockingbird*" (Baecker), **Supp. VIII:** 128
Telling Secrets (Buechner), **Supp. XII:** 53–54
Telling Stories (Didion), **Supp. IV Part 1:** 197
"Telling Stories" (Didion), **Supp. IV Part 1:** 197
"Telling the Bees" (Whittier), **Supp. I Part 2:** 694–695
Telling the Truth: The Gospel as Tragedy, Comedy, and Fairy Tale (Buechner), **Supp. XII:** 53
"Tell Me" (Hughes), **Supp. VIII:** 213
Tell Me, Tell Me (Moore), **III:** 215
Tell Me a Riddle (film), **Supp. XIII:** 295
Tell Me a Riddle (Olsen), **Supp. XIII:** 294, 296, **298–302,** 303, 305
"Tell Me a Riddle" (Olsen), **Supp. XIII:** 294, 297, 298, **300–302,** 305
Tell Me How Long the Train's Been Gone (Baldwin), **Retro. Supp. II:** 9, **11–12,** 14; **Supp. I Part 1:** 48, 52, 63–65, 67
"Tell Me My Fortune" (Epstein), **Supp. XII:** 163
Tell Me Your Answer True (Sexton), **Supp. II Part 2:** 683
Tell My Horse (Hurston), **Supp. VI:** 149, 156, 158
"Tell-Tale Heart, The" (Poe), **III:** 413, 414–415, 416; **Retro. Supp. II:** 267, 269, 270
"Tell the Women We're Going" (Carver), **Supp. III Part 1:** 138, 144
"Telluride Blues—A Hatchet Job" (Abbey), **Supp. XIII:** 10
Telushkin, Dvorah, **Retro. Supp. II:** 335
Temblor (Howe), **Supp. IV Part 2:** 431
"Temper of Steel, The" (Jones), **Supp. XI:** 218
Tempers, The (W. C. Williams), **Retro. Supp. I: 413–414,** 415, 416, 424
Tempest, The (Shakespeare), **I:** 394; **II:** 12; **III:** 40, 61, 263; **Retro. Supp. I:** 61; **Supp. IV Part 2:** 463; **Supp. V:** 302–303; **Supp. XII:** 54–57
Temple, Minnie, **II:** 323
Temple, The (Herbert), **IV:** 145, 153
Temple, William, **III:** 303
Temple of My Familiar, The (Walker), **Supp. III Part 2:** 521, 527, 529, 535, 537; **Supp. IV Part 1:** 14
"Temple of the Holy Ghost, A" (O'Connor), **III:** 344, 352; **Retro. Supp. II:** 232
Templin, Charlotte, **Supp. V:** 116
Temporary Shelter (Gordon), **Supp. IV Part 1:** 299, 305–307
"Temporary Shelter" (Gordon), **Supp. IV Part 1:** 306
Temptation Game, The (Gardner), **Supp. VI:** 72
"Temptation of St. Anthony, The" (Barthelme), **Supp. IV Part 1:** 47
Temptations, The, **Supp. X:** 242
"Tenancy, A" (Merrill), **Supp. III Part 1:** 322, 323
Tenants, The (Malamud), **Supp. I Part 2:** 448–450
Ten Commandments (McClatchy), **Supp. XII: 262–265**
Ten Days That Shook the World (Reed), **II:** 577; **Supp. X:** 136
Tendencies in Modern American Poetry (Lowell), **II:** 529
Tender Buttons (Stein), **I:** 103, 105; **IV:** 27, 42–43; **Retro. Supp. II:** 349
"Tenderfoot" (Haines), **Supp. XII:** 209
Tender Is the Night (Fitzgerald), **I:** 375; **II:** 79, 84, 91, 95–96, 97, 98, 420; **Retro. Supp. I:** 105, 108, 109, **110–112,** 114; **Supp. IX:** 59, 60, 61
"Tenderloin" (Crane), **I:** 408
"Tenderly" (Dobyns), **Supp. XIII:** 86–87
'Tender Man, A" (Bambara), **Supp. XI:** 9–10
"Tenderness" (Dunn), **Supp. XI:** 149, 150
"Tender Offer, The" (Auchincloss), **Supp. IV Part 1:** 34
"Tenebrae" (Komunyakaa), **Supp. XIII:** 132
"Ten Forty-Four" (Kingsolver), **Supp. VII:** 208
Ten Indians (Bell), **Supp. X:** 7, **12**
"Ten Neglected American Writers Who Deserve to Be Better Known" (Cantor), **Supp. IV Part 1:** 285
Tennent, Gilbert, **I:** 546
Tennessee Day in St. Louis (Taylor), **Supp. V:** 324
"Tennessee's Partner" (Harte), **Supp. II Part 1:** 345, 348–350
"Tennis" (Pinsky), **Supp. VI:** 241, 242
Tennis Court Oath, The (Ashbery), **Supp. III Part 1:** 7, 9, 12, 14, 26
Ten North Frederick (O'Hara), **III:** 361
Tennyson, Alfred, Lord, **I:** 587–588; **II:** 18, 82, 273, 338, 404, 439, 604; **III:** 5, 409, 469, 485, 511, 521, 523; **Retro. Supp. I:** 100, 325; **Retro. Supp. II:** 135; **Supp. I Part 1:** 349, 356; **Supp. I Part 2:** 410, 416, 552; **Supp. IX:** 19; **Supp. X:** 157; **Supp. XIII:** 111
"Ten O'Clock News" (Ortiz), **Supp. IV Part 2:** 503–504
Ten Poems (Dove), **Supp. IV Part 1:** 244
Ten Poems of Francis Ponge Translated by Robert Bly and Ten Poems of Robert Bly Inspired by the Poems by Francis Ponge (Bly), **Supp. IV Part 1:** 71
"Tension in Poetry" (Tate), **IV:** 128, 129, 135
Tenth Muse, The (Bradstreet), **Supp. I Part 1:** 102, 103, 114
"Tent on the Beach, The" (Whittier), **Supp. I Part 2:** 703
"Teodoro Luna Confesses after Years to His Brother, Anselmo the Priest, Who Is Required to Understand, But

Who Understands Anyway, More Than People Think" (Ríos), **Supp. IV Part 2:** 552
Teodoro Luna's Two Kisses (Ríos), **Supp. IV Part 2:** 550–552, 553
"Tepeyac" (Cisneros), **Supp. VII:** 69
"Terce" (Auden), **Supp. II Part 1:** 22
Terence, **IV:** 155, 363; **Supp. I Part 2:** 405
Terkel, Studs, **Supp. IV Part 1:** 364
"Term" (Merwin), **Supp. III Part 1:** 356–357
"Terminal Days at Beverly Farms" (Lowell), **Retro. Supp. II:** 189
Terminating, or Sonnet LXXV, or "Lass Meine Schmerzen nicht verloren sein, or Ambivalence" (Kushner), **Supp. IX:** 132
Terminations (James), **Retro. Supp. I:** 229
"Terminus" (Emerson), **II:** 13, 19
"Terminus" (Wharton), **Retro. Supp. I:** 371
"Terms in Which I Think of Reality, The" (Ginsberg), **Supp. II Part 1:** 311
Terms of Endearment (film), **Supp. V:** 226
Terms of Endearment (McMurtry), **Supp. V:** 224–225
"Terrace, The" (Wilbur), **Supp. III Part 2:** 550
"Terrence McNally" (Bryer), **Supp. XIII:** 200
"Terrence McNally" (Di Gaetani), **Supp. XIII:** 200
Terrence McNally: A Casebook (Zinman), **Supp. XIII:** 209
"Terrible Peacock, The" (Barnes), **Supp. III Part 1:** 33
Terrible Threes, The (Reed), **Supp. X:** 241, 253
Terrible Twos, The (Reed), **Supp. X:** 241, **252–253**
"Terrific Mother" (Moore), **Supp. X:** 178
Territory Ahead, The (Morris), **III:** 228–229, 236
Terry, Edward A., **II:** 128, 129
Terry, Rose, **Supp. I Part 2:** 420
Tertium Organum (Ouspensky), **I:** 383
"Terza Rima" (Rich), **Retro. Supp. II:** 293
Tess of the d'Urbervilles (Hardy), **II:** 181; **Retro. Supp. II:** 100
"Testament" (Berry), **Supp. X:** 36
"Testament (Or, Homage to Walt Whitman)" (Jong), **Supp. V:** 130
"Testament of Flood" (Warren), **IV:** 253

Testament of François Villon, The (Pound, opera), **Retro. Supp. I:** 287
"Testimonia on the Question of Stesichoros' Blinding by Helen" (Carson), **Supp. XII:** 107
"Testimony" (Komunyakaa), **Supp. XIII:** 129
"Testing-Tree, The" (Kunitz), **Supp. III Part 1:** 269
Testing-Tree, The (Kunitz), **Supp. III Part 1:** 260, 263, 264, 267, 268
Test of Poetry, A (Zukofsky), **Supp. III Part 2:** 618, 622
"Texas Moon, and Elsewhere, The" (McMurtry), **Supp. V:** 225
Texas Poets in Concert: A Quartet (Gwynn, ed.), **Supp. XIII:** 277
Texas Summer (Southern), **Supp. XI:** 309
Texasville (McMurtry), **Supp. V:** 228, 233
Thacher, Molly Day, **IV:** 381
Thackeray, William Makepeace, **I:** 194, 354; **II:** 182, 271, 282, 288, 316, 321, 322; **III:** 64, 70; **IV:** 326; **Retro. Supp. I:** 218; **Supp. I Part 1:** 307; **Supp. I Part 2:** 421, 495, 579; **Supp. IV Part 1:** 297; **Supp. IX:** 200; **Supp. XI:** 277
Thaddeus, Janice Farrar, **Supp. IV Part 1:** 299
"Thailand" (Barthelme), **Supp. IV Part 1:** 41
Thalberg, Irving, **Retro. Supp. I:** 109, 110, 114
Thales, **I:** 480–481
Thalia Trilogy (McMurtry), **Supp. V:** 220–223, 234
Tham, Claire, **Supp. VIII:** 79
"Thanatopsis" (Bryant), **Supp. I Part 1:** 150, 154, 155, 170
Thanatos Syndrome, The (Percy), **Supp. III Part 1:** 385, 397–399
"Thanksgiving" (Glück), **Supp. V:** 83
"Thanksgiving, A" (Auden), **Supp. II Part 1:** 26
"Thanksgiving for a Habitat" (Auden), **Supp. II Part 1:** 24
"Thanksgiving Spirit" (Farrell), **II:** 45
Thanksgiving Visitor, The (Capote), **Supp. III Part 1:** 116, 118, 119
Thank You, Fog (Auden), **Supp. II Part 1:** 24
"Thank You, Lord" (Angelou), **Supp. IV Part 1:** 15
Thank You, Mr. Moto (Marquand), **III:** 57, 58
"Thank You in Arabic" (Nye), **Supp. XIII:** 273, 281
"Thar's More in the Man Than Thar Is

in the Land" (Lanier), **Supp. I Part 1:** 352–353, 359–360
"That Evening Sun" (Faulkner), **II:** 72; **Retro. Supp. I:** 75, 83
That Horse (Hogan), **Supp. IV Part 1:** 397, 404, 405
"That I Had the Wings" (Ellison), **Supp. II Part 1:** 238
"That's the Place Indians Talk About" (Ortiz), **Supp. IV Part 2:** 511
"That the Soul May Wax Plump" (Swenson), **Supp. IV Part 2:** 650
"That Tree" (Porter), **III:** 434–435, 446, 451
"That Year" (Olds), **Supp. X:** 203
Thaxter, Celia, **Retro. Supp. II:** 136, 147; **Supp. XIII:** 143, 153
Thayer, Abbott, **I:** 231
Thayer, Scofield, **I:** 231; **Retro. Supp. I:** 58
Thayer and Eldridge, **Retro. Supp. I:** 403
"Theater" (Toomer), **Supp. IX:** 309, 317–318
"Theater Chronicle" (McCarthy), **II:** 562
Theatricals (James), **Retro. Supp. I:** 228
"Theft" (Porter), **III:** 434, 435
Theft, A (Bellow), **Retro. Supp. II:** 31–32, 34
Their Eyes Were Watching God (Hurston), **Supp. VI:** 149, 152, 156–157
Their Heads Are Green and Their Hands Are Blue: Scenes from the Non-Christian World (Bowles), **Supp. IV Part 1:** 89
"Their Losses" (Taylor), **Supp. V:** 320
Their Wedding Journey (Howells), **II:** 277–278; **Retro. Supp. I:** 334
them (Oates), **Supp. II Part 2:** 503, 511–514
Theme Is Freedom, The (Dos Passos), **I:** 488–489, 492, 494
"Theme with Variations" (Agee), **I:** 27
"Then" (Barthelme), **Supp. IV Part 1:** 48
"Then It All Came Down" (Capote), **Supp. III Part 1:** 125, 131
Theocritus, **II:** 169; **Retro. Supp. I:** 286
"Theodore the Poet" (Masters), **Supp. I Part 2:** 461
Theological Position, A (Coover), **Supp. V:** 44
Theophrastus, **I:** 58
Theory and Practice of Rivers and Other Poems, The (Harrison), **Supp. VIII:** 47, 49

Theory of Business Enterprise, The (Veblen), **Supp. I Part 2:** 638, 641, 644
Theory of Flight (Rukeyser), **Supp. VI:** 272, 275, **277–278**, 284
"Theory of Flight" (Rukeyser), **Supp. VI:** 277–278
Theory of Moral Sentiments, The (A. Smith), **Supp. I Part 2:** 634
Theory of the Leisure Class, The (Veblen), **I:** 475–476; **Supp. I Part 2:** 629, 633, 641, 645; **Supp. IV Part 1:** 22
"There" (Taylor), **Supp. V:** 323
"There Are No Such Trees in Alpine California" (Haines), **Supp. XII:** 207
"There Goes (Varoom! Varoom!) That Kandy-Kolored Tangerine-Flake Streamline Baby" (Wolfe), **Supp. III Part 2:** 569–571
"There Is a Lesson" (Olsen), **Supp. XIII:** 292, 297
"There Is Only One of Everything" (Atwood), **Supp. XIII:** 34
There Is Something Out There (McNally). See *And Things That Go Bump in the Night* (McNally)
"There's a certain Slant of light" (Dickinson), **Retro. Supp. I:** 38
Thérèse de Lisieux, Saint, **Supp. VIII:** 195
"There She Is She Is Taking Her Bath" (Anderson), **I:** 113, 114
"There Was a Child Went Forth" (Whitman), **IV:** 348
"There Was a Man, There Was a Woman" (Cisneros), **Supp. VII:** 70
"There Was an Old Woman She Had So Many Children She Didn't Know What to Do" (Cisneros), **Supp. VII:** 60
"There Was a Youth Whose Name Was Thomas Granger" (Olson), **Supp. II Part 2:** 558, 560, 563
There Were Giants in the Land (Benét), **Supp. XI:** 50
There You Are (Simpson), **Supp. IX: 279–280**
"There You Are" (Simpson), **Supp. IX:** 279
"Thermopylae" (Clampitt), **Supp. IX:** 43
Theroux, Alexander, **Supp. VIII:** 312
Theroux, Marcel, **Supp. VIII:** 325
Theroux, Paul, **Supp. V:** 122; **Supp. VIII: 309–327**
"These Are My People" (Hayden), **Supp. II Part 1:** 365
"These are the days when Birds come back" (Dickinson), **Retro. Supp. I:** 30
"These Days" (Olds), **Supp. X:** 215
"These Flames and Generosities of the Heart: Emily Dickinson and the Illogic of Sumptuary Values" (Howe), **Supp. IV Part 2:** 431
"These saw Visions" (Dickinson), **Retro. Supp. I:** 46
These Thirteen (Faulkner), **II:** 72
These Three (film), **Supp. I Part 1:** 281
"Thessalonica: A Roman Story" (Brown), **Supp. I Part 1:** 133
Thew, Harvey, **Supp. XIII:** 166
"They Ain't the Men They Used To Be" (Farrell), **II:** 45
"They Burned the Books" (Benét), **Supp. XI:** 46
They Came Like Swallows (Maxwell), **Supp. VIII: 155–159**, 168, 169
"They Can't Turn Back" (Baldwin), **Supp. I Part 1:** 52
They Feed They Lion (Levine), **Supp. V:** 178, 179, 181, 184–185, 186
"They Feed They Lion" (Levine), **Supp. V:** 188
"They Lion Grow" (Levine), **Supp. V:** 184–185
"They're Not Your Husband" (Carver), **Supp. III Part 1:** 141, 143
They're Playing Our Song (musical), **Supp. IV Part 2:** 589
They Shall Inherit the Laughter (Jones), **Supp. XI:** 217, 218, 232
They Shoot Horses (film), **Supp. XIII:** 159
They Shoot Horses, Don't They? (McCoy), **Supp. XIII:** 159, **164–166**, 168, 171, 172, 174
"They Sing, They Sing" (Roethke), **III:** 544
They Stooped to Folly (Glasgow), **II:** 175, 186–187
They Whisper (R. O. Butler), **Supp. XII: 72–73**
"Thieves" (Yates), **Supp. XI:** 349
Thieves of Paradise (Komunyakaa), **Supp. XIII:** 113, **128–130**, 132
"Thimble, The" (Kenyon), **Supp. VII:** 164
"Thing and Its Relations, The" (James), **II:** 357
"Things" (Haines), **Supp. XII:** 207
"Things" (Kenyon), **Supp. VII:** 169
"Things, The" (Kinnell), **Supp. III Part 1:** 246
Things As They Are (Stein), **IV:** 34, 37, 40
"Things Don't Stop" (Nye), **Supp. XIII:** 287
Things Gone and Things Still Here (Bowles), **Supp. IV Part 1:** 91
"Things of August" (Stevens), **Retro. Supp. I:** 309
Things of This World (Wilbur), **Supp. III Part 2:** 552–555
Things Themselves: Essays and Scenes (Price), **Supp. VI:** 261
Things They Carried, The (O'Brien), **Supp. V:** 238, 239, 240, 243, **248–250**
"Thing That Killed My Father Off, The" (Carver), **Supp. III Part 1:** 143
Think Back on Us . . . (Cowley), **Supp. II Part 1:** 139, 140, 142
Think Fast, Mr. Moto (Marquand), **III:** 57, 58
"Thinking about Barbara Deming" (Paley), **Supp. VI:** 227
"Thinking about Being Called Simple by a Critic" (Stafford), **Supp. XI:** 328
Thinking about the Longstanding Problems of Virtue and Happiness: Essays, a Play, Two Poems, and a Prayer (Kushner), **Supp. IX:** 131, 134, 135
"Thinking about the Past" (Justice), **Supp. VII:** 123–124
"Thinking about Western Thinking" (Didion), **Supp. IV Part 1:** 204, 206
"'Thinking against Oneself': Reflections on Cioran" (Sontag), **Supp. III Part 2:** 459–460
"Thinking Back Through Our Mothers: Traditions in Canadian Women's Writing" (Shields), **Supp. VII:** 307–308
"Thinking for Berky" (Stafford), **Supp. XI:** 320
"Thinking of the Lost World" (Jarrell), **II:** 338–389
Thin Man, The (film), **Supp. IV Part 1:** 342, 355
Thin Man, The (Hammett), **Supp. IV Part 1:** 354–355
"Thinnest Shadow, The" (Ashbery), **Supp. III Part 1:** 5
"Thin People, The" (Plath), **Supp. I Part 2:** 538, 547
Thin Red Line, The (film), **Supp. V:** 249
Thin Red Line, The (Jones), **Supp. XI:** 219, **224–225**, 229, 231, 232, 233, 234
"Thin Strips" (Sandburg), **III:** 587
"Third Avenue in Sunlight" (Hecht), **Supp. X:** 61

INDEX / 579

"Third Body, A" (Bly), **Supp. IV Part 1:** 71
Third Circle, The (Norris), **III:** 327
"Third Expedition, The" (Bradbury), **Supp. IV Part 1:** 103, 106
Third Life of Grange Copeland, The (Walker), **Supp. III Part 2:** 520, 527–536
Third Mind, The (Burroughs), **Supp. XII:** 3
Third Rose, The (Brinnin), **IV:** 26
"Third Sermon on the Warpland, The" (Brooks), **Supp. III Part 1:** 85
"Third Thing That Killed My Father Off, The" (Carver), **Supp. III Part 1:** 144
Third Violet, The (Crane), **I:** 408, 417–418
Thirlwall, John C., **Retro. Supp. I:** 430
"Thirst: Introduction to Kinds of Water" (Carson), **Supp. XII:** 103
Thirteen Hands: A Play in Two Acts (Shields), **Supp. VII:** 322–323
Thirteen O'Clock (Benét), **Supp. XI:** 46
Thirteen Other Stories (Purdy), **Supp. VII:** 278
"Thirteenth and Pennsylvania" (Stafford), **Supp. XI:** 324
"Thirteen Ways of Looking at a Blackbird" (Stevens), **IV:** 94; **Supp. IX:** 47
"30. Meditation. 2. Cor. 5.17. He Is a New Creature" (Taylor), **IV:** 144
30: Pieces of a Novel (Dixon), **Supp. XII:** 152, **153–154**
30/6 (poetry chapbook), **Supp. V:** 5, 6
"Thirty Bob a Week" (Davidson), **Retro. Supp. I:** 55
"Thirty Delft Tiles" (Doty), **Supp. XI:** 131
"35/10" (Olds), **Supp. X:** 206
"35,000 Feet—The Lanterns" (Goldbarth), **Supp. XII:** 182
31 Letters and 13 Dreams (Hugo), **Supp. VI:** 141–144
Thirty Poems (Bryant), **Supp. I Part 1:** 157, 158
Thirty-Six Poems (Warren), **IV:** 236, 239, 240
"33" (Alvarez), **Supp. VII:** 4
"3275" (Monette), **Supp. X:** 148, 159
Thirty Years (Marquand), **III:** 56, 60–61
Thirty Years of Treason (Bentley), **Supp. I Part 1:** 297
"This, That & the Other" (Nemerov), **III:** 269
This Body Is Made of Camphor and Gopherwood (Bly), **Supp. IV Part 1:** 63–65, 66, 71

This Boy's Life: A Memoir (T. Wolff), **Supp. VII:** 334–339, 340, 343; **Supp. XI:** 246, 247
"This Bright Dream" (Benét), **Supp. XI:** 55
This Coffin Has No Handles (McGrath), **Supp. X:** 117
"This Configuration" (Ashbery), **Supp. III Part 1:** 22
"This Corruptible" (Wylie), **Supp. I Part 2:** 727, 729
"This Crutch That I Love" (Nye), **Supp. XIII:** 288
"This Gentile World" (H. Miller), **III:** 177
"This Hand" (Wylie), **Supp. I Part 2:** 713
"This Hour" (Olds), **Supp. X:** 212
"This House I Cannot Leave" (Kingsolver), **Supp. VII:** 208
This Hunger (Nin), **Supp. X:** 185
"This Is a Photograph of Me" (Atwood), **Supp. XIII:** 33
"This Is It" (Stern), **Supp. IX:** 290
"This Is Just to Say" (W. C. Williams), **Supp. XI:** 328
"This Is My Heart" (Harjo), **Supp. XII:** 230
"This Is Not Who We Are" (Nye), **Supp. XIII:** 285, 286
"This Is What I Said" (Salinas), **Supp. XIII:** 322
This Journey (Wright), **Supp. III Part 2:** 605–606
This Man and This Woman (Farrell), **II:** 42
"This Morning" (Kenyon), **Supp. VII:** 164
"This Morning, This Evening, So Soon" (Baldwin), **Supp. I Part 1:** 63
"This Morning Again It Was in the Dusty Pines" (Oliver), **Supp. VII:** 240
This Music Crept by Me upon the Waters (MacLeish), **III:** 21
This People Israel: The Meaning of Jewish Existence (Baeck), **Supp. V:** 260
"This Personal Maze Is Not the Prize" (Selinger), **Supp. XI:** 248
"This Place in the Ways" (Rukeyser), **Supp. VI:** 273–274
This Property Is Condemned (T. Williams), **IV:** 378
This Proud Heart (Buck), **Supp. II Part 1:** 119–120
This Same Sky: A Collection of Poems from around the World (Nye, ed.),

Supp. XIII: 280
"This Sandwich Has No Mayonnaise" (Salinger), **III:** 552–553
This Side of Paradise (Fitzgerald), **I:** 358; **II:** 77, 80, 81, 82–83, 84, 85–87, 88; **Retro. Supp. I:** 99–100, **101–102**, 103, 105, 106, 110, 111
This Stubborn Self: Texas Autobiographies (Almon), **Supp. XIII:** 288
This Thing Don't Lead to Heaven (Crews), **Supp. XI:** 112
This Time: New and Selected Poems (Stern), **Supp. IX:** 290–291, **299**
"Thistle Seed in the Wind" (Francis), **Supp. IX:** 81
"Thistles in Sweden, The" (Maxwell), **Supp. VIII:** 169
"This Tokyo" (Snyder), **Supp. VIII:** 298
This Tree Will Be Here for a Thousand Years (Bly), **Supp. IV Part 1:** 65–66, 71, 72
This Tree Will Be Here for a Thousand Years (revised edition) (Bly), **Supp. IV Part 1:** 66
This Very Earth (Caldwell), **I:** 297, 302
Thoens, Karen, **Supp. V:** 147
Thomas, Brandon, **II:** 138
Thomas, D. M., **Supp. VIII:** 5
Thomas, Debra, **Supp. XIII:** 114
Thomas, Dylan, **I:** 49, 64, 382, 432, 526, 533; **III:** 21, 521, 528, 532, 534; **IV:** 89, 93, 136; **Supp. I Part 1:** 263; **Supp. III Part 1:** 42, 47; **Supp. V:** 344; **Supp. VIII:** 21; **Supp. IX:** 114; **Supp. X:** 115
Thomas, Edward, **II:** 154; **Retro. Supp. I:** 127, 131, 132; **Supp. I Part 1:** 263; **Supp. II Part 1:** 4
Thomas, J. Parnell, **Supp. I Part 1:** 286
Thomas, Lewis, **Retro. Supp. I:** 323
Thomas, William I., **Supp. I Part 2:** 641
Thomas-a-Kempis, **Retro. Supp. I:** 247
Thomas and Beulah (Dove), **Supp. IV Part 1:** 242, 247–248, 249
Thomas Aquinas (Saint), **I:** 13, 14, 265, 267; **III:** 270; **Retro. Supp. II:** 222; **Supp. IV Part 2:** 526
"Thomas at the Wheel" (Dove), **Supp. IV Part 1:** 248
"Thomas McGrath: Words for a Vanished Age" (Vinz), **Supp. X:** 117
Thomas Merton on Peace, **Supp. VIII:** 208
Thomas Merton Studies Center, The, **Supp. VIII:** 208
Thompson, Barbara, **Supp. V:** 322

Thompson, Cy, **I:** 538
Thompson, Dorothy, **II:** 449–450, 451, 453
Thompson, E. P., **Supp. X:** 112, 117
Thompson, Francis, **Retro. Supp. I:** 55
Thompson, Frank, **II:** 20
Thompson, George, **Supp. I Part 2:** 686
Thompson, Hunter S., **Supp. VIII:** 42; **Supp. XI:** 105; **Supp. XIII:** 1, 17
Thompson, James R., **Supp. IV Part 1:** 217
Thompson, John, **Supp. V:** 323
Thompson, Lawrance, **II:** 508
Thompson, Lawrance Roger, **Retro. Supp. I:** 138, 141
Thompson, Morton, **Supp. XIII:** 170
Thompson, Theresa, **Supp. V:** 141
Thompson, William T., **Supp. I Part 2:** 411
Thomson, James, **II:** 304; **Supp. I Part 1:** 150, 151
Thomson, Virgil, **IV:** 45; **Supp. IV Part 1:** 81, 83, 84, 173
"Thoreau" (Lowell), **Supp. I Part 2:** 420, 422
Thoreau, Henry David, **I:** 98, 104, 228, 236, 257, 258, 261, 305, 433; **II:** 7, 8, 13, 17, 101, 159, 224, 273–274, 295, 312–313, 321, 457–458, 540, 546–547; **III:** 171, 174, 186–187, 189, 208, 214–215, 453, 454, 507, 577; **IV:** 167–189, 191, 341; **Retro. Supp. I:** 51, 62, 122; **Retro. Supp. II:** 13, 96, 142, 158; **Supp. I Part 1:** 29, 34, 116, 188, 299, 358; **Supp. I Part 2:** 383, 400, 420, 421, 507, 540, 579, 580, 655, 659, 660, 664, 678; **Supp. III Part 1:** 340, 353; **Supp. IV Part 1:** 236, 392, 416; **Supp. IV Part 2:** 420, 430, 433, 439, 447; **Supp. V:** 200, 208; **Supp. VIII:** 40, 42, 103, 105, 198, 201, 204, 205, 292, 303; **Supp. IX:** 25, 90, 171; **Supp. X:** 21, 27, 28–29, 101, 102; **Supp. XI:** 155; **Supp. XIII:** 1, 17
Thoreau, John, **IV:** 171, 182
Thoreau, Mrs. John, **IV:** 172
"Thorn, The" (Gordon), **Supp. IV Part 1:** 314
Thorne, Francis, **Supp. XII:** 253
"Thorn Merchant, The" (Komunyakaa), **Supp. XIII:** 119–120
Thornton, Billy Bob, **Supp. VIII:** 175
Thornton, Lionel, **III:** 291
"Thorofare" (Minot), **Supp. VI:** 209–210
"Thorow" (Howe), **Supp. IV Part 2:** 419, 420, 421, 431, 433–434
Thorp, Willard, **Supp. XIII:** 101
Thorslev, Peter L., Jr., **I:** 524
Thorstein Veblen (Dowd), **Supp. I Part 2:** 650
Thorstein Veblen (Qualey, ed.), **Supp. I Part 2:** 650
Thorstein Veblen: A Chapter in American Economic Thought (Teggart), **Supp. I Part 2:** 650
Thorstein Veblen: A Critical Interpretation (Riesman), **Supp. I Part 2:** 649, 650
Thorstein Veblen: A Critical Reappraisal (Dowd, ed.), **Supp. I Part 2:** 650
Thorstein Veblen and His America (Dorfman), **Supp. I Part 2:** 631, 650
Thorstein Veblen and the Institutionalists: A Study in the Social Philosophy of Economics (Seckler), **Supp. I Part 2:** 650
"Those before Us" (Lowell), **II:** 550
"Those Being Eaten by America" (Bly), **Supp. IV Part 1:** 62
Those Bones Are Not My Child (Bambara), **Supp. XI:** 1, 14, **20–22**
Those Extraordinary Twins (Twain), **IV:** 205–206
"Those Graves in Rome" (Levis), **Supp. XI:** 266
"Those of Us Who Think We Know" (Dunn), **Supp. XI:** 146
"Those Times . . ." (Sexton), **Supp. II Part 2:** 670, 684
"Those Various Scalpels" (Moore), **III:** 202
"Those Were the Days" (Levine), **Supp. V:** 190
"Those Who Don't" (Cisneros), **Supp. VII:** 60
"Those Who Thunder" (Hogan), **Supp. IV Part 1:** 406
"Thought, A" (Sarton), **Supp. VIII:** 262
Thought and Character of William James (Perry), **II:** 362
Thoughtbook of Francis Scott Key Fitzgerald (Fitzgerald), **Retro. Supp. I:** 99
"Thoughtful Roisterer Declines the Gambit, The" (Hecht), **Supp. X:** 63
"Thought of Heaven, The" (Stern), **Supp. IX:** 297
"Thoughts after Lambeth" (Eliot), **I:** 587; **Retro. Supp. I:** 324
Thoughts and Reflections (Lord Halifax), **II:** 111
Thoughts in Solitude (Merton), **Supp. VIII:** 207
"Thoughts on Being Bibliographed" (Wilson), **IV:** 435
"Thoughts on the Establishment of a Mint in the United States" (Paine), **Supp. I Part 2:** 512
"Thoughts on the Gifts of Art" (Kenyon), **Supp. VII:** 167
Thousand Acres, A (Smiley), **Supp. VI:** 292, **301–303**
"Thousand and Second Night, The" (Merrill), **Supp. III Part 1:** 324
"Thousand Dollar Vagrant, The" (Olsen), **Supp. XIII:** 292, 297
"Thousand Faces of Danny Torrance, The" (Figliola), **Supp. V:** 143
Thousand-Mile Walk to the Gulf, A (Muir), **Supp. IX:** **177–178**
"Thou Shalt Not Steal" (McClatchy), **Supp. XII:** 264
"Thread, The" (Merwin), **Supp. III Part 1:** 351
Three (film), **Supp. IX:** 253
3-3-8 (Marquand), **III:** 58
"Three Academic Pieces" (Stevens), **IV:** 90
"Three Agee Wards, The" (Morris), **III:** 220–221
"Three American Singers" (Cather), **Retro. Supp. I:** 10
"Three Around the Old Gentleman" (Berryman), **I:** 188
"Three Avilas, The" (Jeffers), **Supp. II Part 2:** 418
Three Books of Song (Longfellow), **II:** 490
"Three Bushes" (Yeats), **Supp. I Part 1:** 80
Three Cantos (Pound), **Retro. Supp. I:** 290
Three Centuries of Harvard (Morison), **Supp. I Part 2:** 485
Three Comrades (Remarque), **Retro. Supp. I:** 113
"Three-Day Blow, The" (Hemingway), **II:** 248
Three Essays on America (Brooks), **I:** 246
Three Farmers on Their Way to a Dance (Powers), **Supp. IX:** 211–212, **213–214,** 222
"Three Fates, The" (Benét), **Supp. XI:** 48–49, 50
Three Gospels (Price), **Supp. VI:** 267
"Three Kings, The: Hemingway, Faulkner, and Fitzgerald" (Ford), **Supp. V:** 59
Three Lives (Auchincloss), **Supp. IV Part 1:** 25
Three Lives (Stein), **I:** 103; **IV:** 26, 27,

31, 35, 37–41, 42, 45, 46; **Supp. IX:** 306
"THREE MOVEMENTS AND A CODA" (Baraka), **Supp. II Part 1:** 50
Three on the Tower: The Lives and Works of Ezra Pound, T. S. Eliot, and William Carlos Williams (Simpson), **Supp. IX:** 276
Three Papers on Fiction (Welty), **IV:** 261
Three-Penny Opera (Brecht), **I:** 301
Three Philosophical Poets (Santayana), **III:** 610–612
"Three Players of a Summer Game" (T. Williams), **IV:** 383
Three Poems (Ashbery), **Supp. III Part 1:** 2, 3, 14, 15, 18, 24–26
"Three Pokes of a Thistle" (Nye), **Supp. XIII:** 281
Three Roads, The (Macdonald, under Millar), **Supp. IV Part 2:** 466, 467
"Three Silences of Molinos, The" (Longfellow), **Retro. Supp. II:** 169
"Three Sisters, The" (Cisneros), **Supp. VII:** 64
Three Soldiers (Dos Passos), **I:** 477–478, 480, 482, 488, 493–494
"Three Songs at the End of Summer" (Kenyon), **Supp. VII:** 169–170
"Three Steps to the Graveyard" (Wright), **Supp. III Part 2:** 593, 596
Three Stories and Ten Poems (Hemingway), **II:** 68, 263
Three Taverns, The (Robinson), **III:** 510
"Three Taverns, The" (Robinson), **III:** 521, 522
Three Tenant Families (Agee), **I:** 37–38
"Three Types of Poetry" (Tate), **IV:** 131
"Three Vagabonds of Trinidad" (Harte), **Supp. II Part 1:** 338
"Three Waterfalls, The" (Lanier), **Supp. I Part 1:** 350
"Three-Way Mirror" (Brooks), **Supp. III Part 1:** 69–70
"Three Women" (Plath), **Supp. I Part 2:** 539, 541, 544, 545, 546
Three Young Poets (Swallow, ed.), **Supp. X:** 116
Threnody (Emerson), **Supp. I Part 2:** 416
"Threnody" (Emerson), **II:** 7
"Threnody for a Brown Girl" (Cullen), **Supp. IV Part 1:** 166
"Threshing-Floor, The" (Baldwin), **Supp. I Part 1:** 50
Threshold (film), **Supp. IX:** 254

"Threshold" (Goldbarth), **Supp. XII:** 175
Threshold (Jackson), **Supp. IX:** 117
"Throat" (Goldbarth), **Supp. XII:** 177–178
Thrones (Pound), **Retro. Supp. I:** 293
Through Dooms of Love (Kumin), **Supp. IV Part 2:** 444
"Through the Black Curtain" (Kingston), **Supp. V:** 169
Through the Forest: New and Selected Poems, 1977–1987 (Wagoner), **Supp. IX: 330–331**
"Through the Hills of Spain" (Salinas), **Supp. XIII:** 315
"Through the Hole in the Mundane Millstone" (West), **Retro. Supp. II:** 339, 340
Through the Ivory Gate (Dove), **Supp. IV Part 1:** 242, 243, 251, 252, 253–254, 254
"Through the Kitchen Window, Chiapas" (Nye), **Supp. XIII:** 277
"Through the Smoke Hole" (Snyder), **Supp. VIII:** 299
Thucydides, **II:** 418; **IV:** 50; **Supp. I Part 2:** 488, 489, 492; **Supp. IV Part 1:** 391; **Supp. XIII:** 233
Thunderbolt and Lightfoot (film), **Supp. X:** 126
"Thunderhead" (MacLeish), **III:** 19
Thurber, James, **I:** 487; **II:** 432; **IV:** 396; **Supp. I Part 2: 602–627,** 653, 654, 668, 672, 673, 679; **Supp. II Part 1:** 143; **Supp. IV Part 1:** 349; **Supp. IX:** 118
Thurber, Mrs. James (Althea Adams), **Supp. I Part 2:** 613, 615, 617
Thurber, Mrs. James (Helen Muriel Wismer), **Supp. I Part 2:** 613, 617, 618
Thurber, Robert, **Supp. I Part 2:** 613, 617
Thurber, Rosemary, **Supp. I Part 2:** 616
Thurber, William, **Supp. I Part 2:** 602
Thurber Album, The (Thurber), **Supp. I Part 2:** 611, 619
Thurber Carnival, A (Thurber), **Supp. I Part 2:** 620
Thurman, Judith, **Supp. IV Part 1:** 309
Thurman, Wallace, **Retro. Supp. I:** 200; **Supp. I Part 1:** 325, 326, 328, 332; **Supp. IV Part 1:** 164; **Supp. X:** 136, 139
"Thursday" (Millay), **III:** 129
"Thurso's Landing" (Jeffers), **Supp. II Part 2:** 433
Thus Spake Zarathustra (Nietzsche), **II:** 463; **Supp. IV Part 1:** 110;

Supp. IV Part 2: 519
Thwaite, Lady Alicia. *See* Rawlings, Marjorie Kinnan
Thyrsis (Arnold), **Retro. Supp. II:** 291
"Tiara" (Doty), **Supp. XI:** 122
Ticket for a Seamstitch, A (Harris), **II:** 424–425
Tickets for a Prayer Wheel (Dillard), **Supp. VI:** 22, 34
Ticket That Exploded, The (Burroughs), **Supp. III Part 1:** 93, 103, 104
Tickless Time (Glaspell), **Supp. III Part 1:** 179
Ticknor, George, **II:** 488; **Supp. I Part 1:** 313
"Ti Démon" (Chopin), **Supp. I Part 1:** 225
Tide of Time, The (Masters), **Supp. I Part 2:** 471
"Tide Rises, the Tide Falls, The" (Longfellow), **I:** 498
Tidyman, Ernest, **Supp. V:** 226
"Tiger" (Blake), **Supp. I Part 1:** 80; **Supp. VIII:** 26
"Tiger, The" (Buechner), **Supp. XII:** 48
Tiger in the House, The (Van Vechten), **Supp. II Part 2:** 736
Tiger Joy (Benét), **Supp. XI:** 45
Tiger-Lilies (Lanier), **Supp. I Part 1:** 350–351, 357, 360, 371
Tiger Who Wore White Gloves, The: or, What You Are, You Are (Brooks), **Supp. III Part 1:** 86
Till, Emmett, **Supp. I Part 1:** 61
Tillich, Paul, **II:** 244; **III:** 291, 292, 303, 309; **IV:** 226; **Retro. Supp. I:** 325, 326, 327; **Supp. V:** 267; **Supp. XIII:** 74, 91
Tillie Olsen: A Study of the Short Fiction (Frye), **Supp. XIII:** 292, 296, 298, 299, 302
Tillman, Lynne, **Supp. XII:** 4
Tillotson, John, **II:** 114
Till the Day I Die (Odets), **Supp. II Part 2:** 530, 533–536, 552
Tilton, Eleanor, **Supp. I Part 1:** 317
Timaeus (Plato), **II:** 10; **III:** 609
Timber (Jonson), **II:** 16
Timbuktu (Auster), **Supp. XII:** 34, **35–36**
"Time" (Matthews), **Supp. IX: 165–166**
"Time" (Merrill), **Supp. III Part 1:** 325
Time and a Place, A (Humphrey), **Supp. IX:** 95, 98, **100–102**
"Time and the Garden" (Winters), **Supp. II Part 2:** 801, 809
"Time and the Liturgy" (Merton),

Supp. VIII: 199
Time in the Rock (Aiken), **I:** 65
Time Is Noon, The (Buck), **Supp. II Part 1:** 129, 130–131
Time & Money (Matthews), **Supp. IX:** 155, **165–167**
"Time of Friendship, The" (Bowles), **Supp. IV Part 1:** 90–91
"Time of Her Time, The" (Mailer), **III:** 37, 45; **Retro. Supp. II:** 200
Time of Our Time, The (Mailer), **Retro. Supp. II:** 213–214
Time of the Assassins, The: A Study of Rimbaud (H. Miller), **III:** 189
"Time Past" (Morris), **III:** 232
"Time Present" (Morris), **III:** 232
"Times" (Beattie), **Supp. V:** 31
"Times, The" (Emerson), **II:** 11–12
Times Are Never So Bad, The (Dubus), **Supp. VII:** 87–88
Time's Arrow (Amis), **Retro. Supp. I:** 278
"Time Shall Not Die" (Chandler), **Supp. IV Part 1:** 120
Times of Melville and Whitman, The (Brooks), **I:** 257
Time's Power: Poems, 1985–1988 (Rich), **Retro. Supp. II:** 292
"Timesweep" (Sandburg), **III:** 595–596
Time to Act, A (MacLeish), **III:** 3
Time to Go (Dixon), **Supp. XII:** 147
Time to Kill (film), **Supp. IV Part 1:** 130
Time to Speak, A (MacLeish), **III:** 3
Time Will Darken It (Maxwell), **Supp. VIII:** 159, **162–164**, 169
"Timing of Sin, The" (Dubus), **Supp. VII:** 91
Tim O'Brien (Herzog), **Supp. V:** 239
Timoleon (Melville), **III:** 93; **Retro. Supp. I:** 257
Timothy Dexter Revisited (Marquand), **III:** 55, 62, 63
Tin Can, The (W. J. Smith), **Supp. XIII:** 334, **Supp. XIII:** 336, 337
"Tin Can, The" (W. J. Smith), **Supp. XIII: 337–339**
Tin Can Tree, The (Tyler), **Supp. IV Part 2:** 659–660
Tintern Abbey (Wordsworth), **Supp. I Part 2:** 673, 675
Tiny Alice (Albee), **I:** 81–86, 87, 88, 94
"Tiny Mummies! The True Story of the Ruler of 43rd Street's Land of the Walking Dead" (Wolfe), **Supp. III Part 2:** 573, 574
"Tired" (Hughes), **Supp. I Part 1:** 331
"Tired and Unhappy, You Think of Houses" (Schwartz), **Supp. II Part 2:** 649
"Tiresias" (Garrett), **Supp. VII:** 96–97
'Tis (McCourt), **Supp. XII:** 271, **279–286**
Tisch (Dixon), **Supp. XII:** 141, **155–156**
Titan, The (Dreiser), **I:** 497, 501, 507–508, 509, 510; **Retro. Supp. II:** 94, 101, 102
Titian, **Supp. I Part 2:** 397, 714
"Tito's Goodbye" (García), **Supp. XI:** 190
To a Blossoming Pear Tree (Wright), **Supp. III Part 2:** 602–605
"To a Blossoming Pear Tree" (Wright), **Supp. III Part 2:** 604
"To Abolish Children" (Shapiro), **Supp. II Part 2:** 717
To Abolish Children and Other Essays (Shapiro), **Supp. II Part 2:** 703
"To a Caty-Did, the Precursor of Winter" (Freneau), **Supp. II Part 1:** 274–275
"To a Chameleon" (Moore), **III:** 195, 196, 215
"To a Conscript of 1940" (Read), **II:** 372–373, 377–378
"To a Contemporary Bunk Shooter" (Sandburg), **III:** 582
"To a Cough in the Street at Midnight" (Wylie), **Supp. I Part 2:** 727, 729–730
"To a Defeated Savior" (Wright), **Supp. III Part 2:** 593–594, 596
"To a Face in the Crowd" (Warren), **IV:** 239
"To a Fish Head Found on the Beach near Malaga" (Levine), **Supp. V:** 185
"To a Friend" (Nemerov), **III:** 272
"To a Friend Whose Work Has Come to Triumph" (Sexton), **Supp. II Part 2:** 683
To a God Unknown (Steinbeck), **I:** 107; **IV:** 51, 59–60, 67
"To a Greek Marble" (Aldington), **Supp. I Part 1:** 257
"To a Locomotive in Winter" (Whitman), **IV:** 348
"To a Military Rifle" (Winters), **Supp. II Part 2:** 810, 811, 815
"To a Mouse" (Burns), **Supp. IX:** 173
"To a Negro Jazz Band in a Parisian Cabaret" (Hughes), **Supp. I Part 1:** 325
"To an Old Philosopher in Rome" (Stevens), **III:** 605; **Retro. Supp. I:** 312
"To an Old Poet in Peru" (Ginsberg), **Supp. II Part 1:** 322
"To Any Would-Be Terrorists" (Nye), **Supp. XIII:** 285, 286
"To a Poet" (Rich), **Supp. I Part 2:** 571
"To a Prize Bird" (Moore), **III:** 215
"To a Republican, with Mr. Paine's Rights of Man" (Freneau), **Supp. II Part 1:** 267
"To a Shade" (Yeats), **III:** 18
"To a Skylark" (Shelley), **Supp. I Part 2:** 720; **Supp. X:** 31
"Toast to Harlem, A" (Hughes), **Supp. I Part 1:** 338
"To Aunt Rose" (Ginsberg), **Supp. II Part 1:** 320
"To Autumn" (Keats), **Supp. IX:** 50
"To a Waterfowl" (Bryant), **Supp. I Part 1:** 154, 155, 162, 171
"To a Young Writer" (Stegner), **Supp. X:** 24
Tobacco Road (Caldwell), **I:** 288, 289, 290, 295–296, 297, 298, 302, 307, 309, 310; **IV:** 198
"To Be a Monstrous Clever Fellow" (Fante), **Supp. XI:** 167
To Bedlam and Part Way Back (Sexton), **Retro. Supp. II:** 245; **Supp. II Part 2:** 672–678; **Supp. IV Part 2:** 441; **Supp. XI:** 317
"To Beethoven" (Lanier), **Supp. I Part 1:** 364
Tobey, Mark, **Supp. X:** 264
To Be Young, Gifted, and Black: Lorraine Hansberry in Her Own Words (Nemiroff), **Supp. IV Part 1:** 372, 374
"To Big Mary from an Ex-Catholic" (Mora), **Supp. XIII:** 217, 224, 228
"Tobin's Palm" (O. Henry), **Supp. II Part 1:** 408
Tobit (apocryphal book), **I:** 89
"To Build a Fire" (London), **II:** 468
Toby Tyler: or, Ten Weeks with a Circus (Otis), **III:** 577
"To Change in a Good Way" (Ortiz), **Supp. IV Part 2:** 511
"To Charlotte Cushman" (Lanier), **Supp. I Part 1:** 364
"To Cole, the Painter, Departing for Europe" (Bryant), **Supp. I Part 1:** 157, 161
Tocqueville, Alexis de, **III:** 261; **IV:** 349; **Retro. Supp. I:** 235; **Supp. I Part 1:** 137; **Supp. I Part 2:** 659, 660; **Supp. II Part 1:** 281, 282, 284
"To Crispin O'Conner" (Freneau), **Supp. II Part 1:** 268
"To Da-Duh, In Memoriam" (Marshall), **Supp. XI:** 276

"TODAY" (Baraka), **Supp. II Part 1:** 55
"Today" (Ginsberg), **Supp. II Part 1:** 328
"Today Is a Good Day To Die" (Bell), **Supp. X:** 7
Todd, Mabel Loomis, **I:** 454, 470; **Retro. Supp. I:** 33, 34, 35, 39, 47
"To Death" (Levertov), **Supp. III Part 1:** 274
"To Delmore Schwartz" (Lowell), **II:** 547; **Retro. Supp. II:** 188
"to disembark" (Brooks), **Supp. III Part 1:** 86
"To Dr. Thomas Shearer" (Lanier), **Supp. I Part 1:** 370
"To E. T." (Frost), **Retro. Supp. I:** 132
"To Earthward" (Frost), **II:** 154
"To Edwin V. McKenzie" (Winters), **Supp. II Part 2:** 801
"To Eleonora Duse" (Lowell), **II:** 528
"To Elizabeth Ward Perkins" (Lowell), **II:** 516
"To Elsie" (W. C. Williams), **Retro. Supp. I:** 419
"To Emily Dickinson" (H. Crane), **Retro. Supp. II:** 76
Toffler, Alvin, **Supp. IV Part 2:** 517
"To Fill" (Moore), **Supp. X:** 168, 169
"To Gabriela, a Young Writer" (Mora), **Supp. XIII:** 220
To Have and Have Not (Hemingway), **I:** 31; **II:** 253–254, 264; **Retro. Supp. I:** 182, **183**, 187
"To Helen" (Poe), **III:** 410, 411, 427; **Retro. Supp. II:** 102
"To Hell With Dying" (Walker), **Supp. III Part 2:** 523
"To His Father" (Jeffers), **Supp. II Part 2:** 415
Toilet, The (Baraka), **Supp. II Part 1:** 37, 40–42
"To James Russell Lowell" (Holmes), **Supp. I Part 1:** 311
To Jerusalem and Back (Bellow), **Retro. Supp. II:** 29
"To Jesus on His Birthday" (Millay), **III:** 136–137
"To John Keats" (Lowell), **II:** 516
"To Justify My Singing" (Wright), **Supp. III Part 2:** 590
To Kill a Mockingbird (film), **Supp. VIII:** 128–129
To Kill a Mockingbird (Lee), **Supp. VIII: 113–129**
"*To Kill a Mockingbird*: Harper Lee's Tragic Vision" (Dave), **Supp. VIII:** 126
To Kill a Mockingbird: Threatening Boundaries (Johnson), **Supp. VIII:** 126
Toklas, Alice B., **IV:** 27; **Supp. IV Part 1:** 81, 91
"To Light" (Hogan), **Supp. IV Part 1:** 402
Tolkien, J. R. R., **Supp. V:** 140
Tolkin, Michael, **Supp. XI:** 160
Toller, Ernst, **I:** 479
"To Lose the Earth" (Sexton), **Supp. II Part 2:** 684, 685
Tolson, Melvin, **Retro. Supp. I:** 208, 209, 210
Tolstoy, Leo, **I:** 6, 7, 58, 103, 312, 376; **II:** 191–192, 205, 271, 272, 275, 276, 281, 285, 286, 320, 407, 542, 559, 570, 579, 606; **III:** 37, 45, 61, 323, 467, 572; **IV:** 17, 21, 170, 285; **Retro. Supp. I:** 91, 225; **Retro. Supp. II:** 317; **Supp. I Part 1:** 2, 3, 6, 20; **Supp. IV Part 1:** 392; **Supp. V:** 277, 323; **Supp. IX:** 246; **Supp. XI:** 68; **Supp. XII:** 310, 322
"To Lu Chi" (Nemerov), **III:** 275
Tom (Cummings), **I:** 430
"Tom" (Oliver), **Supp. VII:** 232
"Tom, Tom, the Piper's Son" (Ransom), **Supp. X:** 58
"To M, with a Rose" (Lanier), **Supp. I Part 1:** 364
To Make a Prairie (Kumin), **Supp. IV Part 2:** 440, 441
"To Make Words Disappear" (Simpson), **Supp. IX:** 265–266
Tomás and the Library Lady (Mora), **Supp. XIII:** 216, 221
"Tomatoes" (Francis), **Supp. IX:** 82
"Tom Brown at Fisk" (Du Bois), **Supp. II Part 1:** 160
Tom Brown's School Days (Hughes), **Supp. I Part 2:** 406
"Tomb Stone" (Dickey), **Supp. IV Part 1:** 185
Tomcat in Love (O'Brien), **Supp. V:** 238, 240, 243, 252–254
"Tom Fool at Jamaica" (Moore), **III:** 215
To Mix with Time (Swenson), **Supp. IV Part 2:** 637, 643–645, 645
Tom Jones (Fielding), **I:** 131; **Supp. V:** 127
Tommy Gallagher's Crusade (Farrell), **II:** 44
Tommyknockers, The (King), **Supp. V:** 139, 144
"Tommy's Burglar" (Henry), **Supp. II Part 1:** 399, 401
Tomo Cheeki (pseudonym). *See* Freneau, Philip
"Tomorrow the Moon" (Dos Passos), **I:** 493
"Tom Outland's Story" (Cather), **I:** 325–326
Tompson, Benjamin, **Supp. I Part 1:** 110, 111
Tom Sawyer (musical) (Gurney), **Supp. V:** 96
Tom Sawyer (Twain). *See Adventures of Tom Sawyer, The* (Twain)
Tom Sawyer Abroad (Twain), **II:** 482; **IV:** 19, 204
Tom Sawyer Detective (Twain), **IV:** 204
"Tom's Husband" (Jewett), **Retro. Supp. II:** 132, 141
Tom Swift (Stratemeyer), **III:** 146
"Tom Wolfe's Guide to Etiquette" (Wolfe), **Supp. III Part 2:** 578
"To My Brother Killed: Haumont Wood: October, 1918" (Bogan), **Supp. III Part 1:** 58
"To My Class, on Certain Fruits and Flowers Sent Me in Sickness" (Lanier), **Supp. I Part 1:** 370
"To My Ghost Reflected in the Auxvasse River" (Levis), **Supp. XI:** 265
"To My Greek" (Merrill), **Supp. III Part 1:** 326
"To My Mother" (Berry), **Supp. X:** 23
"To Name is to Possess" (Kincaid), **Supp. VII:** 194
Tone, Aileen, **I:** 21–22
"Tongue Is, The" (Komunyakaa), **Supp. XIII:** 113
Tongues (Shepard and Chaikin), **Supp. III Part 2:** 433
Tongues of Angels, The (Price), **Supp. VI:** 265
Tongues Untied (Riggs; film), **Supp. XI:** 19, 20
"Tonight" (Lowell), **II:** 538
Tony Kushner in Conversation (Vorlicky, ed.), **Supp. IX:** 132
"Too Anxious for Rivers" (Frost), **II:** 162
"Too Blue" (Hughes), **Retro. Supp. I:** 207
"Too Early Spring" (Benét), **Supp. XI:** 53
"Too Far from Home" (Bowles), **Supp. IV Part 1:** 94–95
Too Far from Home: Selected Writings of Paul Bowles (Halpern, ed.), **Supp. IV Part 1:** 94, 95
Too Far to Go: The Maples Stories (Updike), **Retro. Supp. I:** 321
"*Too Good To Be True*": The Life and Art of Leslie Fiedler" (Winchell), **Supp. XIII:** 94, 98, 99, 101
Toohey, John Peter, **Supp. IX:** 190

Toolan, David, **Supp. IV Part 1:** 308
Too Late (Dixon), **Supp. XII:** 143–144
"Too-Late Born, The" (Hemingway), **III:** 9
Toomer, Jean, **Retro. Supp. II:** 79; **Supp. I Part 1:** 325, 332; **Supp. III Part 2:** 475–491; **Supp. IV Part 1:** 16, 164, 168; **Supp. IX:** 305–322; **Supp. XIII:** 305
Toomer, Nathan Eugene Pinchback. *See* Toomer, Jean
Too Much Johnson (film), **Supp. IV Part 1:** 83
"To One Who Said Me Nay" (Cullen), **Supp. IV Part 1:** 166
"Tooth, The" (Jackson), **Supp. IX:** 122
Tooth of Crime, The (Shepard), **Supp. III Part 2:** 432, 441–445, 447
"Too Young" (O'Hara), **III:** 369
"To P. L., 1916–1937" (Levine), **Supp. V:** 185
"Top Israeli Official Hints at 'Shared' Jerusalem" (Nye), **Supp. XIII:** 287
"To Please a Shadow" (Brodsky), **Supp. VIII:** 30
"Top of the Hill" (Jewett), **II:** 406
"Topography" (Olds), **Supp. X:** 208
Topper (T. Smith), **Supp. IX:** 194
Torah, **IV:** 19
"Torquemada" (Longfellow), **II:** 505; **Retro. Supp. II:** 164
Torrence, Ridgely, **III:** 507
Torrent and the Night Before, The (Robinson), **III:** 504
Torrents of Spring, The (Hemingway), **I:** 117; **II:** 250–251
Torres, Héctor A., **Supp. XIII:** 225
Torres, Louis, **Supp. IV Part 2:** 529, 530
Torsney, Cheryl, **Retro. Supp. I:** 224
Tortilla Curtain, The (Boyle), **Supp. VIII:** 9–10
Tortilla Flat (Steinbeck), **IV:** 50, 51, 61, 64
Tory Lover, The (Jewett), **II:** 406; **Retro. Supp. II:** 144–145
"Toscana" (Dixon), **Supp. XII:** 154
"To Sir Toby" (Freneau), **Supp. II Part 1:** 269
"To Sophy, Expectant" (Mumford), **Supp. II Part 2:** 475
"To Speak of Woe That Is in Marriage" (Lowell), **II:** 550
"To Statecraft Embalmed" (Moore), **III:** 197
To Stay Alive (Levertov), **Supp. III Part 1:** 280–282
"Total Eclipse" (Dillard), **Supp. VI:** 28
Toth, Emily, **Retro. Supp. II:** 71

Toth, Susan Allan, **Retro. Supp. II:** 138
"To the Americans of the United States" (Freneau), **Supp. II Part 1:** 271
"To the Apennines" (Bryant), **Supp. I Part 1:** 157, 164
"To the Bleeding Hearts Association of American Novelists" (Nemerov), **III:** 281
"To the Botequim & Back" (Bishop), **Retro. Supp. II:** 51
"To the Citizens of the United States" (Paine), **Supp. I Part 2:** 519–520
"To the Dandelion" (Lowell), **Supp. I Part 2:** 424
"To the Days" (Rich), **Retro. Supp. II:** 293
"To the End" (Haines), **Supp. XII:** 212–213
To the Ends of the Earth: The Selected Travels of Paul Theroux, **Supp. VIII:** 324
To the Finland Station: A Study in the Writing and Acting of History (Wilson), **IV:** 429, 436, 443–444, 446
"To the Governor & Legislature of Massachusetts" (Nemerov), **III:** 287
To the Holy Spirit (Winters), **Supp. II Part 2:** 810
"To the Keeper of the King's Water Works" (Freneau), **Supp. II Part 1:** 269
"To the Lacedemonians" (Tate), **IV:** 134
"To the Laodiceans" (Jarrell), **Retro. Supp. I:** 121, 140
To the Lighthouse (Woolf), **I:** 309; **II:** 600; **Retro. Supp. II:** 355; **Supp. VIII:** 155
"To the Man on Trail" (London), **II:** 466
"To the Memory of the Brave Americans Under General Greene" (Freneau), **Supp. II Part 1:** 262, 274
"To the Muse" (Wright), **Supp. III Part 2:** 601
"To the New World" (Jarrell), **II:** 371
"To the One of Fictive Music" (Stevens), **IV:** 89; **Retro. Supp. I:** 297, 300
"To the One Upstairs" (Simic), **Supp. VIII:** 283
"To the Peoples of the World" (Du Bois), **Supp. II Part 1:** 172
"To the Pliocene Skull" (Harte), **Supp. II Part 1:** 343–344

"To the Reader" (Baudelaire), **II:** 544–545
"To the Reader" (Levertov), **Supp. III Part 1:** 277
"To the River Arve" (Bryant), **Supp. I Part 1:** 163
"To the Snake" (Levertov), **Supp. III Part 1:** 277
"To the Stone-Cutters" (Jeffers), **Supp. II Part 2:** 420
"To the Unseeable Animal" (Berry), **Supp. X:** 31
"To the Western World" (Simpson), **Supp. IX:** 269, 270
To the White Sea (Dickey), **Supp. IV Part 1:** 186, 190–191
"To the Young Who Want to Die" (Brooks), **Supp. III Part 1:** 85–86
"To Train a Writer" (Bierce), **I:** 199
"Touch, The" (Sexton), **Supp. II Part 2:** 687
"Touching the Tree" (Merwin), **Supp. III Part 1:** 355
Touching the World (Eakin), **Supp. VIII:** 167
Touch of Danger, A (Jones), **Supp. XI:** 226, **228–229**
Touch of the Poet, A (O'Neill), **III:** 385, 401, 404
Touchstone, The (Wharton), **Retro. Supp. I:** 365
"Touch-up Man" (Komunyakaa), **Supp. XIII:** 119
Tough Guys Don't Dance (Mailer), **Retro. Supp. II:** 211
Toulet, Paul Jean, **IV:** 79
Tour (McNally), **Supp. XIII:** 197
"Tour 5" (Hayden), **Supp. II Part 1:** 381
To Urania (Brodsky), **Supp. VIII:** 22, 28–29
"Tour Guide" (Komunyakaa), **Supp. XIII:** 114
"Tourist Death" (MacLeish), **III:** 12
Tour of Duty (Dos Passos), **I:** 489
Tour on the Prairies, A (Irving), **II:** 312–313
To Walk a Crooked Mile (McGrath), **Supp. X:** 117
Toward a New Synthesis (Begiebing), **Retro. Supp. II:** 210
"Toward Nightfall" (Simic), **Supp. VIII:** 277
Towards a Better Life (Burke), **I:** 270
"Towards a Chicano Poetics: The Making of the Chicano Subject, 1969–1982" (Saldívar), **Supp. IV Part 2:** 544
Towards an Enduring Peace (Bourne), **I:** 232

Toward the Gulf (Masters), **Supp. I Part 2:** 465–466
"Toward the Solstice" (Rich), **Supp. I Part 2:** 575–576
Toward Wholeness in Paule Marshall's Fiction (Pettis), **Supp. XI:** 276
"Tower" (Merwin), **Supp. III Part 1:** 343
"Tower Beyond Tragedy, The" (Jeffers), **Supp. II Part 2:** 429–430
Tower of Ivory (MacLeish), **III:** 3–4
Towers, Robert, **Supp. IX:** 259
"To Whistler, American" (Pound), **III:** 465–466
"To Wine" (Bogan), **Supp. III Part 1:** 57, 58
Town, The (Faulkner), **II:** 57, 73; **Retro. Supp. I:** 74, 82
Town and the City, The (Kerouac), **Supp. III Part 1:** 222–224
"Town Crier" (Bierce), **I:** 193, 194, 195, 196
"*Town Crier* Exclusive, Confessions of a Princess Manqué: 'How Royals Found Me "Unsuitable" to Marry Their Larry'" (Elkin), **Supp. VI:** 56
Town Down the River, The (Robinson), **III:** 508
"Town Dump, The" (Nemerov), **III:** 272, 275, 281
Towne, Robert, **Supp. XI:** 159, 172, 174
"Townhouse Interior with Cat" (Clampitt), **Supp. IX:** 40
"Townies" (Dubus), **Supp. VII:** 86
"Town of the Sound of a Twig Breaking" (Carson), **Supp. XII:** 102
"Town Poor, The" (Jewett), **Retro. Supp. II:** 138, 139, 143
Townsend, Alison, **Supp. XIII:** 222
Townsend, Ann, **Supp. V:** 77
"Towns in Colour" (Lowell), **II:** 523–524
Townsman, The (Sedges), **Supp. II Part 1:** 124–125
Toys in a Field (Komunyakaa), **Supp. XIII: 121–122**
"Toys in a Field" (Komunyakaa), **Supp. XIII:** 122
Toys in the Attic (Hellman), **Supp. I Part 1:** 289–290
Tracer (F. Barthelme), **Supp. XI:** 31–32, 33
Traces of Thomas Hariot, The (Rukeyser), **Supp. VI:** 273, 274, 283
"Tracing Life with a Finger" (Caldwell), **I:** 291
Tracker (Wagoner), **Supp. IX:** 329, **336–337**

"Tracking" (Wagoner), **Supp. IX:** 329
"Track Meet, The" (Schwartz), **Supp. II Part 2:** 665
Tracks (Erdrich), **Supp. IV Part 1:** 259, 262–263, 269, 272, 273–274, 274, 275
"Tract" (W. C. Williams), **Retro. Supp. I:** 414
"Tract against Communism, A" (Twelve Southerners), **IV:** 125, 237
Tracy, Lee, **IV:** 287, 288
Tracy, Steven, **Retro. Supp. I:** 195
"Trade, The" (Levine), **Supp. V:** 193
Trading Twelves (Callahan and Murray, eds.), **Retro. Supp. II:** 119
"Tradition and Industrialization" (Wright), **IV:** 489–490
"Tradition and Mythology: Signatures of Landscape in Chicana Poetry" (Rebolledo), **Supp. XIII:** 214
"Tradition and the Individual Talent" (Eliot), **I:** 441, 574, 585; **Retro. Supp. I:** 59, 286
Tragedies, Life and Letters of James Gates Percival (Swinburne), **Supp. I Part 2:** 422
Tragedy of Don Ippolito, The (Howells), **II:** 279
"Tragedy of Error, A" (James), **II:** 322; **Retro. Supp. I:** 218
Tragedy of Pudd'nhead Wilson, The (Twain), **IV:** 206–207
Tragic America (Dreiser), **Retro. Supp. II:** 95
"Tragic Dialogue" (Wylie), **Supp. I Part 2:** 724
Tragic Ground (Caldwell), **I:** 297, 306
Tragic Muse, The (James), **Retro. Supp. I:** 227
Traherne, Thomas, **IV:** 151; **Supp. III Part 1:** 14; **Supp. V:** 208
"Trail, The" (W. J. Smith), **Supp. XIII:** 342
Trailerpark (Banks), **Supp. V:** 12
"Trailing Arbutus, The" (Whittier), **Supp. I Part 2:** 691
Trail of the Lonesome Pine, The (Fox), **Supp. XIII:** 166
"Train, The" (O'Connor), **Retro. Supp. II:** 225
"Train Rising Out of the Sea" (Ashbery), **Supp. III Part 1:** 22
"Trains" (Banks), **Supp. V:** 8
"Train Tune" (Bogan), **Supp. III Part 1:** 64
"Traits of Indian Character" (Irving), **II:** 303
Tramp Abroad, A (Twain), **IV:** 200
Tramping With a Poet in the Rockies (Graham), **Supp. I Part 2:** 397

Tramp's Excuse, The (Lindsay), **Supp. I Part 2:** 379, 380, 382
"Transatlantic" (Toomer), **Supp. III Part 2:** 486
Transatlantic Sketches (James), **II:** 324; **Retro. Supp. I:** 219
"Transcendental Etude" (Rich), **Supp. I Part 2:** 576
"Transcontinental Highway" (Cowley), **Supp. II Part 1:** 141
"Transducer" (Ammons), **Supp. VII:** 28
"Transfigured Bird" (Merrill), **Supp. III Part 1:** 320–321
"Transformations" (Harjo), **Supp. XII:** 226
Transformations (Sexton), **Supp. II Part 2:** 689–691; **Supp. IV Part 2:** 447
Transit to Narcissus, A (Mailer), **Retro. Supp. II:** 196
"Translation and Transposition" (Carne-Ross), **Supp. I Part 1:** 268–269
"Translation of a Fragment of Simonides" (Bryant), **Supp. I Part 1:** 153, 155
"Translations" (Rich), **Supp. I Part 2:** 563
Translations of Ezra Pound, The (Kenner, ed.), **III:** 463
"Trans-National America" (Bourne), **I:** 229, 230
Transparent Man, The (Hecht), **Supp. X:** 57, **69–71**
"Transparent Man, The" (Hecht), **Supp. X: 69–70**
Transparent Things (Nabokov), **Retro. Supp. I:** 266, 270, 277
"Transport" (Simic), **Supp. VIII:** 282
Transport to Summer (Stevens), **IV:** 76, 93; **Retro. Supp. I:** 309–312
Tranströmer, Thomas, **Supp. IV Part 2:** 648
"Traps for the Unwary" (Bourne), **I:** 235
Trash Trilogy (McMurtry), **Supp. V:** 225–226, 231
Traubel, Horace, **IV:** 350
"Travel: After a Death" (Kenyon), **Supp. VII:** 169
Travel Alarm (Nye), **Supp. XIII:** 277
"Traveler, The" (Haines), **Supp. XII:** 203–204, 210
"Traveler, The" (Stegner), **Supp. IV Part 2:** 605
Traveler at Forty, A (Dreiser), **I:** 515
Traveler from Altruria, a Romance A, (Howells), **II:** 285, 287
Traveler's Tree, The: New and Selected

Poems (W. J. Smith), **Supp. XIII:** 332, 347
"Traveling" (Paley), **Supp. VI:** 230
"Traveling Light" (Wagoner), **Supp. IX:** 329
"Traveling Onion, The" (Nye), **Supp. XIII:** 276
Traveling through the Dark (Stafford), **Supp. XI:** 311, 316, **318–321**
"Traveling through the Dark" (Stafford), **Supp. XI:** 318–320, 321, 323, 329
Travelling in Amherst: A Poet's Journal, 1931–1954, **Supp. IX: 88–89**
Travels in Alaska (Muir), **Supp. IX:** 182, 185–186
"Travels in Georgia" (McPhee), **Supp. III Part 1:** 293–294
Travels in the Congo (Gide), **III:** 210
"Travels in the South" (Ortiz), **Supp. IV Part 2:** 506
Travels with Charley (Steinbeck), **IV:** 52
"Travel Writing: Why I Bother" (Theroux), **Supp. VIII:** 310
Travis, Merle, **Supp. V:** 335
Travisano, Thomas, **Retro. Supp. II:** 40
Treasure Hunt (Buechner), **Supp. XII:** 52
Treasure Island (Stevenson), **Supp. X:** 230
"Treasure of the Redwoods, A" (Harte), **Supp. II Part 1:** 337
Treasury of Art Masterpieces, A: From the Renaissance to the Present Day (Craven), **Supp. XII:** 44
Treasury of the Theatre, A (Gassner), **Supp. I Part 1:** 292
Treasury of Yiddish Stories, A (Howe and Greenberg, eds.), **Supp. I Part 2:** 432
Treat 'Em Rough (Lardner), **II:** 422–423
Treatise Concerning Religious Affections (Edwards), **I:** 547, 552, 554, 555, 557, 558, 560, 562
Treatise Concerning the Lord's Supper (Doolittle), **IV:** 150
"Treatise on Poetry" (Milosz), **Supp. VIII:** 20
Treatise on Right and Wrong, A (Mencken), **III:** 110, 119
"Treatise on Tales of Horror, A" (Wilson), **IV:** 438
Treatise on the Gods, A (Mencken), **III:** 108–109, 119
Tre Croce (Tozzi), **Supp. III Part 2:** 616
"Tree, a Rock, a Cloud, A" (McCullers), **II:** 587
"Tree, The" (Pound), **Retro. Supp. I:** 286; **Supp. I Part 1:** 255
"Tree, the Bird, The" (Roethke), **III:** 548
"Tree at My Window" (Frost), **II:** 155
"Tree House at Night, The" (Dickey), **Supp. IV Part 1:** 179
Tree Is Older Than You Are, The (Nye, ed.), **Supp. XIII:** 280
"Tree of Laughing Bells, The" (Lindsay), **Supp. I Part 2:** 376
"Tree of Night, A" (Capote), **Supp. III Part 1:** 114, 120
Tree of Night and Other Stories, A (Capote), **Supp. III Part 1:** 114
"Trees, The" (Rich), **Supp. I Part 2:** 555
"Trees Listening to Bach" (Merrill), **Supp. III Part 1:** 336
Tree Where Man Was Born, The (Matthiessen), **Supp. V:** 199, 203, 204
Trejo, Ernesto, **Supp. V:** 178, 180; **Supp. XIII:** 313, 316
Trelawny, Edward John, **Supp. I Part 2:** 721
"Trellis for R., A" (Swenson), **Supp. IV Part 2:** 647
Tremblay, Bill, **Supp. XIII:** 112
"Trespass" (Frost), **Retro. Supp. I:** 139
"Tretitoli, Where the Bomb Group Was" (Hugo), **Supp. VI:** 138
Trial, The (Kafka), **IV:** 113; **Retro. Supp. II:** 20
"Trial, The" (Rukeyser), **Supp. VI:** 278
"Trial by Existence, The" (Frost), **II:** 166
Trial of a Poet, The (Shapiro), **Supp. II Part 2:** 710
Trial of the Hawk, The: A Comedy of the Seriousness of Life (Lewis), **II:** 441
Tribal Secrets: Recovering American Indian Intellectual Traditions (Warrior), **Supp. IV Part 1:** 329
"Tribute (To My Mother)" (Cullen), **Supp. IV Part 1:** 166
"Tribute, A" (Easton), **Supp. IV Part 2:** 461
"Tribute, The" (Doolittle), **Supp. I Part 1:** 267
Tribute to Freud (Doolittle), **Supp. I Part 1:** 253, 254, 258, 259, 260, 268
Tribute to the Angels (Doolittle), **Supp. I Part 1:** 272
"Trick on the World, A" (Ríos), **Supp. IV Part 2:** 553
"Tricks" (Olds), **Supp. X:** 203–204
"Trick Scenery" (F. Barthelme), **Supp. XI:** 26
Trifler, The (Masters), **Supp. I Part 2:** 459–460
Trifles (Glaspell), **Supp. III Part 1:** 175, 178, 179, 182, 186, 187; **Supp. X:** 46
Trifonov, Iurii V., **Retro. Supp. I:** 278
Triggering Town, The: Lectures and Essays on Poetry and Writing (Hugo), **Supp. VI:** 133, 140
Trilling, Diana, **II:** 587, 600; **Supp. I Part 1:** 297; **Supp. XII:** 126
Trilling, Lionel, **I:** 48; **II:** 579; **III:** 308, 310, 319, 327; **IV:** 201, 211; **Retro. Supp. I:** 19, 97, 121, 216, 227; **Supp. III Part 2: 493–515;** **Supp. V:** 259; **Supp. VIII:** 93, 98, 190, 231, 236, 243; **Supp. IX:** 266, 287; **Supp. XIII:** 100–101
Trilogy (Doolittle), **Supp. I Part 1:** 271, 272
Trilogy of Desire (Dreiser), **I:** 497, 508; **Retro. Supp. II:** 94, 96, **101–102**
Trimmed Lamp, The (O. Henry), **Supp. II Part 1:** 410
"Trinc" (McGrath), **Supp. X:** 127
Trio (Baker), **Supp. I Part 1:** 277
"Trip" (F. Barthelme), **Supp. XI:** 26
Triple Thinkers, The: Ten Essays on Literature (Wilson), **IV:** 428, 431; **Supp. II Part 1:** 146
"Triplex" (Doolittle), **Supp. I Part 1:** 271
Tripmaster Monkey: His Fake Book (Kingston), **Supp. V:** 157, 158, 169, 170–173
"Trip to Hanoi" (Sontag), **Supp. III Part 2:** 460–462
"Triptych" (Eberhart), **I:** 522, 539
Tristan and Iseult, **Retro. Supp. I:** 328, 329, 330, 331
Tristessa (Kerouac), **Supp. III Part 1:** 225, 227, 229
Tristram (Robinson), **III:** 521, 522, 523
Tristram Shandy (Sterne), **I:** 299; **IV:** 465–466; **Supp. V:** 127
"Triumphal March" (Eliot), **I:** 580; **III:** 17; **Retro. Supp. I:** 64
Triumph of Achilles, The (Glück), **Supp. V:** 79, 84–86, 92
"Triumph of a Modern, The, or, Send for the Lawyer" (Anderson), **I:** 113, 114
"Triumph of the Egg, The" (Anderson), **I:** 113
Triumph of the Egg, The: A Book of

Impressions from American Life in Tales and Poems (Anderson), **I:** 112, 114
Triumph of the Spider Monkey, The (Oates), **Supp. II Part 2:** 522
Triumphs of the Reformed Religion in America (Mather), **Supp. II Part 2:** 453
Trivial Breath (Wylie), **Supp. I Part 2:** 709, 722–724
Trocchi, Alexander, **Supp. XI:** 294, 295, 301
Troilus and Criseyde (Chaucer), **Retro. Supp. I:** 426
Trois contes (Flaubert), **IV:** 31, 37
Trojan Horse, The: A Play (MacLeish), **III:** 21
"Trojan Women, The" (Maxwell), **Supp. VIII:** 169
Troll Garden, The (Cather), **I:** 313, 314–316, 322; **Retro. Supp. I:** 5, 6, 8, 14
"Trolling for Blues" (Wilbur), **Supp. III Part 2:** 563–564
Trollope, Anthony, **I:** 10, 375; **II:** 192, 237; **III:** 51, 70, 281, 382; **Retro. Supp. I:** 361
Trombly, Albert Edmund, **Supp. I Part 2:** 403
"Troop Train" (Shapiro), **Supp. II Part 2:** 707
"Tropes of the Text" (Gass), **Supp. VI:** 88
Tropic of Cancer (H. Miller), **III:** 170, 171, 174, 177, 178–180, 181, 182, 183, 187, 190; **Supp. V:** 119; **Supp. X:** 187
Tropic of Capricorn (H. Miller), **III:** 170, 176–177, 178, 182, 183, 184, 187, 188–189, 190
Trotsky, Leon, **I:** 366; **II:** 562, 564; **IV:** 429
Trotter, W., **I:** 249
Troubled Island (opera; Hughes and Still), **Retro. Supp. I:** 203
Troubled Lovers in History (Goldbarth), **Supp. XII:** 176, 192–193
Trouble Follows Me (Macdonald, under Millar), **Supp. IV Part 2:** 466
Trouble in July (Caldwell), **I:** 297, 304–305, 306, 309
Trouble Island (Hughes), **Supp. I Part 1:** 328
"Trouble of Marcie Flint, The" (Cheever), **Supp. I Part 1:** 186
Trouble with Francis, The: An Autobiography (Francis), **Supp. IX:** 76, 77, 82, **84–85**

Trouble with God, The (Francis), **Supp. IX:** 88
"Trouble with the Stars and Stripes" (Nye), **Supp. XIII:** 277
Trouillot, Michel-Rolphe, **Supp. X:** 14–15
Troupe, Quincy, **Retro. Supp. II:** 15, 111; **Supp. X:** 242
"Trout" (Hugo), **Supp. VI:** 135
Trout Fishing in America (Brautigan), **Supp. VIII:** 43
"Trouvée" (Bishop), **Retro. Supp. II:** 49
"Truce of the Bishop, The" (Frederic), **II:** 139–140
"Truck Stop: Minnesota" (Dunn), **Supp. XI:** 145–146
Trueblood, Valerie, **Supp. XIII:** 306
True Confessions (Dunne), **Supp. IV Part 1:** 198
True Confessions (film), **Supp. IV Part 1:** 198
True History of the Conquest of New Spain, The (Castillo), **III:** 13
True Intellectual System of the Universe, The (Cuddleworth), **II:** 10
"True Love" (Olds), **Supp. X:** 212
Trueman, Matthew (pseudonym). *See* Lowell, James Russell
"True Morality" (Bell), **Supp. X:** 13
True Stories (Atwood), **Supp. XIII:** 34–35
"True Stories" (Atwood), **Supp. XIII:** 34
"Truest Sport, The: Jousting with Sam and Charlie" (Wolfe), **Supp. III Part 2:** 581–582
"True Vine" (Wylie), **Supp. I Part 2:** 723
True West (Shepard), **Supp. III Part 2:** 433, 441, 445, 447, 448
Truman, Harry, **III:** 3
Trumbo, Dalton, **Supp. I Part 1:** 295; **Supp. XIII:** 6
Trumbull, John, **Supp. II Part 1:** 65, 69, 70, 268
Trump, Donald, **Supp. IV Part 1:** 393
Trumpener, Katie, **Retro. Supp. I:** 380
"Trumpet Player" (Hughes), **Supp. I Part 1:** 333
Trumpet Shall Sound, The (Wilder), **IV:** 356
"Truro Bear, The" (Oliver), **Supp. VII:** 234
Truscott, Lucian K., **Supp. IV Part 2:** 683
Trust (Ozick), **Supp. V:** 257–258, 259, 260–263, 270, 272
Trust Me (Updike), **Retro. Supp. I:** 322

"Trust Yourself" (Emerson), **II:** 10
"Truth" (Emerson), **II:** 6
"Truth, The" (Jarrell), **II:** 381–382
"Truth about God, The" (Carson), **Supp. XII: 105–106**
"Truthful James" (Harte), **IV:** 196
"Truth Is, The" (Hogan), **Supp. IV Part 1:** 401–402
"Truth Is Forced, The" (Swenson), **Supp. IV Part 2:** 652
"Truth of the Matter, The" (Nemerov), **III:** 270
Truth Serum (Cooper), **Supp. XI:** 129
"Truth the Dead Know, The" (Sexton), **Supp. II Part 2:** 681
Trying to Save Piggy Sneed (Irving), **Supp. VI: 19–165**
"Trying to Talk with a Man" (Rich), **Supp. I Part 2:** 559
"Tryptich I" (Bell), **Supp. X:** 7
"Tryst, The" (Wharton), **Retro. Supp. I:** 378
"Try the Girl" (Chandler), **Supp. IV Part 1:** 125
"Ts'ai Chih" (Pound), **III:** 466
Tsvetayeva, Marina, **Supp. VIII:** 30
"T-2 Tanker Blues" (Snyder), **Supp. VIII:** 294
Tuckerman, Frederick Goddard, **IV:** 144
"Tuesday, November 5th, 1940" (Benét), **Supp. XI:** 46, 52
"Tuesday April 25th 1966" (Olson), **Supp. II Part 2:** 585
"Tuesday Night at the Savoy Ballroom" (Komunyakaa), **Supp. XIII:** 132
"Tuft of Flowers, The" (Frost), **II:** 153; **Retro. Supp. I:** 126, 127
Tufts, James Hayden, **Supp. I Part 2:** 632
Tu Fu, **II:** 526
Tu Fu (Ayscough), **II:** 527
Tugwell, Rexford Guy, **Supp. I Part 2:** 645
"Tulip" (Hammett), **Supp. IV Part 1:** 356
"Tulips" (Nye), **Supp. XIII:** 281
"Tulips" (Plath), **Retro. Supp. II:** 252–253; **Supp. I Part 2:** 540, 542, 544
"Tulips" (Snodgrass), **Supp. VI:** 325
Tulips and Chimneys (Cummings), **I:** 436, 437, 440, 445, 447
Tully, Jim, **III:** 103, 109
Tumble Tower (Modarressi and Tyler), **Supp. IV Part 2:** 657
"Tuned in Late One Night" (Stafford), **Supp. XI:** 327–328
Tunnel, The (Gass), **Supp. V:** 44; **Supp. VI: 89–91**, 94

"Tunnel, The" (Strand), **Supp. IV Part 2:** 622

"Tunnels" (Komunyakaa), **Supp. XIII:** 123

Tuqan, Fadwa, **Supp. XIII:** 278

Tura, Cosimo, **III:** 474–475

Turandot and Other Poems (Ashbery), **Supp. III Part 1:** 3

Turgenev, Ivan Sergeevich, **I:** 106; **II:** 263, 271, 275, 280, 281, 288, 319, 320, 324–325, 338, 407; **III:** 461; **IV:** 17, 277; **Retro. Supp. I:** 215, 222; **Supp. VIII:** 167

Turgot, Anne Robert Jacques, **II:** 103; **Supp. I Part 1:** 250

"Turkey and Bones and Eating and We Liked It" (Stein), **IV:** 44

Turman, Glynn, **Supp. IV Part 1:** 362

Turnbull, Dr. George, **II:** 113

Turnbull, Lawrence, **Supp. I Part 1:** 352

"Turned" (Gilman), **Supp. XI:** 207

Turner, Addie, **IV:** 123

Turner, Darwin, **Supp. I Part 1:** 339; **Supp. IV Part 1:** 165

Turner, Frederick Jackson, **Supp. I Part 2:** 480, 481, 632, 640; **Supp. IV Part 2:** 596

Turner, Nat, **IV:** 113–114, 115, 116, 117

Turner, Patricia, **Supp. XIII:** 237

Turner, Victor, **Supp. IV Part 1:** 304

"Turning Away Variations on Estrangement" (Dickey), **Supp. IV Part 1:** 183

Turning Point, The (McCoy), **Supp. XIII:** 175

"Turning Thirty, I Contemplate Students Bicycling Home" (Dove), **Supp. IV Part 1:** 250

Turning Wind, A (Rukeyser), **Supp. VI:** 272–273, 279–280

Turn of the Screw, The (James), **Retro. Supp. I:** 219, 231; **Supp. IV Part 2:** 682

"Turn of the Screw, The" (James), **II:** 331–332; **Retro. Supp. I:** 228, 229, 231, 232

Turns and Movies and Other Tales in Verse (Aiken), **I:** 65

"Turn with the Sun, A" (Knowles), **Supp. XII:** 237–238

Turow, Scott, **Supp. V:** 220

Turrinus, Lucius Mamilius, **IV:** 373

"Turtle" (Hogan), **Supp. IV Part 1:** 401

Turtle, Swan (Doty), **Supp. XI:** 121–122

"Turtle, Swan" (Doty), **Supp. XI:** 121–122

Turtle Island (Snyder), **Supp. VIII:** 300–303

Turtle Moon (Hoffman), **Supp. X:** 77, **87–88,** 89

"Turtle Shrine near Chittagong, The" (Nye), **Supp. XIII:** 277

Turturro, John, **Supp. XI:** 174

Tuscan Cities (Howells), **II:** 280

Tuskegee movement, **Supp. II Part 1:** 169, 172

Tuten, Frederic, **Supp. VIII:** 75, 76; **Supp. XIII:** 237, 249

Tuthill, Louisa Cavolne, **Supp. I Part 2:** 684

"Tutored Child, The" (Kunitz), **Supp. III Part 1:** 264

Tuttleton, James W., **Supp. IV Part 1:** 166, 168

"T.V.A." (Agee), **I:** 35

Tvedten, Brother Benet, **Supp. IV Part 2:** 505

"TV Men" (Carson), **Supp. XII:** 105, **112**

Twain, Mark, **I:** 57, 103, 107, 109, 190, 192, 193, 195, 197, 203, 209, 245, 246, 247–250, 255, 256, 257, 260, 261, 292, 342, 418, 469, 485; **II:** 70, 140, 259, 262, 266–268, 271, 272, 274–275, 276, 277, 280, 285–286, 287, 288, 289, 301, 304, 306, 307, 312, 415, 432, 434, 436, 446, 457, 467, 475, 476, 482; **III:** 65, 101, 102, 112–113, 114, 220, 347, 357, 409, 453, 454, 504, 507, 554, 558, 572, 575, 576; **IV:** 190–213, 333, 349, 451; **Retro. Supp. I:** 169, 194, 195; **Retro. Supp. II:** 123; **Supp. I Part 1:** 37, 39, 44, 247, 251, 313, 317; **Supp. I Part 2:** 377, 385, 393, 410, 455, 456, 457, 473, 475, 579, 602, 604, 618, 629, 651, 660; **Supp. II Part 1:** 193, 344, 354, 385; **Supp. IV Part 1:** 386, 388; **Supp. IV Part 2:** 463, 468, 603, 607, 693; **Supp. V:** 44, 113, 131; **Supp. VIII:** 40, 189; **Supp. IX:** 14, 171; **Supp. X:** 51, 227; **Supp. XII:** 343; **Supp. XIII:** 1, 17

"Twa Sisters, The" (ballad), **Supp. I Part 2:** 696

Twelfth Night (Shakespeare), **Supp. IV Part 1:** 83; **Supp. IX:** 14

Twelve Men (Dreiser), **Retro. Supp. II:** 94, 104

Twelve Moons (Oliver), **Supp. VII:** 231, 233–236, 238, 240

"12 O'Clock News" (Bishop), **Retro. Supp. II:** 48

Twelve Southerners, **IV:** 125; **Supp. X:** 25

Twentieth Century Authors, **I:** 376, 527

"Twentieth Century Fiction and the Black Mask of Humanity" (Ellison), **Retro. Supp. II:** 118

Twentieth Century Pleasures (Hass), **Supp. VI:** 103, 106, 109

"28" (Levine), **Supp. V:** 187, 191

"Twenty-Four Poems" (Schwartz), **Supp. II Part 2:** 646, 649

"2433 Agnes, First Home, Last House in Missoula" (Hugo), **Supp. VI:** 139–140

"Twenty Hill Hollow" (Muir), **Supp. IX:** 178

"Twenty Minutes" (Salter), **Supp. IX:** 260

"Twenty-One Love Poems" (Rich), **Supp. I Part 2:** 572–573

Twenty-one Love Poems (Rich), **Retro. Supp. II:** 287

"Twenty-One Poems" (MacLeish), **III:** 19

Twenty Poems (Haines), **Supp. XII:** 204, 205–206

Twenty Poems of Anna Akhmatova (Kenyon), **Supp. VII:** 165–166

Twenty Questions: (Posed by Poems) (McClatchy), **Supp. XII:** 254, **259–262**

27 Wagons Full of Cotton and Other One-Act Plays (T. Williams), **IV:** 381, 383

Twenty Thousand Leagues under the Sea (Verne), **I:** 480; **Supp. XI:** 63

"Twenty Years Ago" (Lindsay), **Supp. I Part 2:** 384, 399

Twenty Years at Hull-House (Addams), **Supp. I Part 1:** 3, 4, 11, 16

Twice-Told Tales (Hawthorne), **I:** 354; **II:** 224; **III:** 412, 421; **Retro. Supp. I:** 154–155, 160

Twichell, Chase, **Supp. V:** 16

Twilight (Frost), **II:** 151

"Twilight's Last Gleaming" (Burroughs and Elvins), **Supp. III Part 1:** 93, 94, 101

Twilight Sleep (Wharton), **IV:** 320–322, 324–325, 327, 328; **Retro. Supp. I:** 381

"Twin, The" (Olds), **Supp. X:** 207

"Twin Beds in Rome" (Updike), **Retro. Supp. I:** 332

"Twins of Table Mountain, The" (Harte), **Supp. II Part 1:** 355

"Twist, The" (Olson), **Supp. II Part 2:** 570

Two: Gertrude Stein and Her Brother (Stein), **IV:** 43

Two Admirals, The (Cooper), **I:** 350

Two against One (F. Barthelme), **Supp.**

XI: 32, 33, 36
"Two Boys" (Moore), **Supp. X:** 173
"Two Brothers, The" (Jewett), **Retro. Supp. II:** 132
Two-Character Play, The (T. Williams), **IV:** 382, 386, 393, 398
Two Citizens (Wright), **Supp. III Part 2:** 602–604
"Two Domains, The" (Goldbarth), **Supp. XII:** 192
"Two Environments, The" (Trilling), **Supp. III Part 2:** 510
"Two-Fisted Self Pity" (Broyard), **Supp. XI:** 348
"Two Friends" (Cather), **I:** 332
"Two Gardens in Linndale" (Robinson), **III:** 508
Two Gentlemen in Bonds (Ransom), **III:** 491–492
"Two Ghosts" (Francis), **Supp. IX:** 87
"Two Hangovers" (Wright), **Supp. III Part 2:** 596
Two-Headed Poems (Atwood), **Supp. XIII:** 34
Two Hours to Doom (Bryant), **Supp. XI:** 302
"Two Ladies in Retirement" (Taylor), **Supp. V:** 320
Two Letters to the Citizens of the United States, and One to General Washington (Barlow), **Supp. II Part 1:** 80
"Two Lives, The" (Hogan), **Supp. IV Part 1:** 400, 402, 403, 406, 411
Two Long Poems (Stern), **Supp. IX:** 296
"Two Lovers and a Beachcomber by the Real Sea" (Plath), **Supp. I Part 2:** 536
"Two Men" (McClatchy), **Supp. XII:** 269
Two Men of Sandy Bar (Harte), **Supp. II Part 1:** 354
"Two Moods of Love" (Cullen), **Supp. IV Part 1:** 166
"Two Morning Monologues" (Bellow), **I:** 150; **Retro. Supp. II:** 20
Two-Ocean War, The (Morison), **Supp. I Part 2:** 491
"Two of Hearts" (Hogan), **Supp. IV Part 1:** 410
"Two on a Party" (T. Williams), **IV:** 388
"Two Pendants: For the Ears" (W. C. Williams), **Retro. Supp. I:** 423
"Two Poems of Going Home" (Dickey), **Supp. IV Part 1:** 182–183
"Two Portraits" (Chopin), **Supp. I Part 1:** 218

"Two Presences, The" (Bly), **Supp. IV Part 1:** 65
"Two Rivers" (Stegner), **Supp. IV Part 2:** 605
Tworkov, Jack, **Supp. XII:** 198
"Two Scenes" (Ashbery), **Supp. III Part 1:** 4
Two Serious Ladies (Jane Bowles), **Supp. IV Part 1:** 82
"Two Sisters" (Farrell), **II:** 45
Two Sisters: A Memoir in the Form of a Novel (Vidal), **Supp. IV Part 2:** 679
"Two Sisters of Persephone" (Plath), **Retro. Supp. II:** 246
"Two Songs on the Economy of Abundance" (Agee), **I:** 28
"Two Temples, The" (Melville), **III:** 89–90
Two Thousand Seasons (Armah), **Supp. IV Part 1:** 373
Two Trains Running (Wilson), **Supp. VIII:** 345–348
"Two Tramps in Mudtime" (Frost), **II:** 164; **Retro. Supp. I:** 137; **Supp. IX:** 261
"Two Views of a Cadaver Room" (Plath), **Supp. I Part 2:** 538
"Two Villages" (Paley), **Supp. VI:** 227
"Two Voices in a Meadow" (Wilbur), **Supp. III Part 2:** 555
"Two Witches" (Frost), **Retro. Supp. I:** 135
"Two Words" (Francis), **Supp. IX:** 81
Two Years before the Mast (Dana), **I:** 351
Tyler, Anne, **Supp. IV Part 2:** 657–675; **Supp. V:** 227, 326; **Supp. VIII:** 141; **Supp. X:** 1, 77, 83, 85; **Supp. XII:** 307
Tyler, Royall, **I:** 344; **Retro. Supp. I:** 377
Tymms, Ralph, **Supp. IX:** 105
Tyndale, William, **II:** 15
Tyndall, John, **Retro. Supp. II:** 93
Typee: A Peep at Polynesian Life (Melville), **III:** 75–77, 79, 84; **Retro. Supp. I:** 245–246, 249, 252, 256
Typewriter Town (W. J. Smith), **Supp. XIII:** 332
"Typhus" (Simpson), **Supp. IX:** 277
Tyranny of the Normal (Fiedler), **Supp. XIII:** 107–108
"Tyranny of the Normal" (Fiedler), **Supp. XIII:** 107–108
"Tyrant of Syracuse" (MacLeish), **III:** 20
"Tyrian Businesses" (Olson), **Supp. II Part 2:** 567, 568, 569

Tzara, Tristan, **Supp. III Part 1:** 104, 105
U and I (Baker), **Supp. XIII:** 45–47, 48, 52, 55
Überdie Seelenfrage (Fechner), **II:** 358
"Ulalume" (Poe), **III:** 427; **Retro. Supp. II:** 264, 266
Ulin, David, **Supp. XIII:** 244
Ullman, Leslie, **Supp. IV Part 2:** 550
Ultimate Good Luck, The (Ford), **Supp. V:** 57, 61–62
Ultima Thule (Longfellow), **II:** 490; **Retro. Supp. II:** 169
"Ultima Thule" (Nabokov), **Retro. Supp. I:** 274
Ultramarine (Carver), **Supp. III Part 1:** 137, 138, 147, 148
Ulysses (Joyce), **I:** 395, 475–476, 478, 479, 481; **II:** 42, 264, 542; **III:** 170, 398; **IV:** 103, 418, 428, 455; **Retro. Supp. I:** 59, 63, 290, 291; **Retro. Supp. II:** 121; **Supp. I Part 1:** 57; **Supp. III Part 2:** 618, 619; **Supp. IV Part 1:** 285; **Supp. IV Part 2:** 424; **Supp. V:** 261; **Supp. IX:** 102; **Supp. X:** 114; **Supp. XIII:** 43, 191
"*Ulysses*, Order and Myth" (Eliot), **Retro. Supp. I:** 63
Unaccountable Worth of the World, The (Price), **Supp. VI:** 267
Unamuno y Jugo, Miguel de, **III:** 310
"Unattached Smile, The" (Crews), **Supp. XI:** 101
"Unbeliever, The" (Bishop), **Retro. Supp. II:** 43
"Unborn Song" (Rukeyser), **Supp. VI:** 274
Uncalled, The (Dunbar), **Supp. II Part 1:** 200, 211, 212
Uncertain Certainty, The: Interviews, Essays, and Notes on Poetry (Simic), **Supp. VIII:** 270, 273, 274
Uncertainty and Plenitude: Five Contemporary Poets (Stitt), **Supp. IX:** 299
"Uncle" (Levine), **Supp. V:** 186
"Uncle Christmas" (Ríos), **Supp. IV Part 2:** 552
"Uncle Jim's Baptist Revival Hymn" (Lanier and Lanier), **Supp. I Part 1:** 353
"Uncle Lot" (Stowe), **Supp. I Part 2:** 585–586
Uncle Remus Tales (Harris), **Supp. II Part 1:** 201
Uncle Tom's Cabin (Stowe), **II:** 291; **Supp. I Part 1:** 49; **Supp. I Part 2:** 410, 579, 582, 589–592; **Supp. II Part 1:** 170; **Supp. III Part 1:** 154, 171; **Supp. IX:** 19; **Supp. X:** 246,

249, 250; **Supp. XIII:** 95
Uncle Tom's Children (Wright), **IV:** 476, 478, 488; **Supp. II Part 1:** 228, 235
"Uncle Wiggily in Connecticut" (Salinger), **III:** 559–560, 563
"Unclouded Day, The" (Proulx), **Supp. VII:** 254–255
"Uncommon Visage" (Brodsky), **Supp. VIII:** 31
Uncompromising Fictions of Cynthia Ozick (Pinsker), **Supp. V:** 272
"Unconscious Came a Beauty" (Swenson), **Supp. IV Part 2:** 646
"Uncreation, The" (Pinsky), **Supp. VI:** 245
"Undead, The" (Wilbur), **Supp. III Part 2:** 556
"Undefeated, The" (Hemingway), **II:** 250; **Retro. Supp. I:** 180
Under a Glass Bell (Nin), **Supp. X:** 186
"Under Ben Bulben" (Yeats), **Supp. V:** 220
Undercliff: Poems 1946–1953 (Eberhart), **I:** 528, 536–537
Under Cover (Goldbarth), **Supp. XII:** 177, 180, 193
Undercover Doctor (film), **Supp. XIII:** 170
"Under Cygnus" (Wilbur), **Supp. III Part 2:** 558
"Under Forty" (Trilling), **Supp. III Part 2:** 494
Underground Man, The (film), **Supp. IV Part 2:** 474
Underground Man, The (Macdonald), **Supp. IV Part 2:** 474, 475
"Under Libra: Weights and Measures" (Merrill), **Supp. III Part 1:** 328
Under Milk Wood (D. Thomas), **III:** 21
"Undersea" (Carson), **Supp. IX:** 21
Understanding Cynthia Ozick (Friedman), **Supp. V:** 273
Understanding E. L. Doctorow (Fowler), **Supp. IV Part 1:** 226
Understanding Fiction (Brooks and Warren), **IV:** 279
Understanding Flannery O'Connor (Whitt), **Retro. Supp. II:** 226
Understanding Nicholson Baker (Saltzman), **Supp. XIII:** 48
Understanding Poetry (Brooks and Warren), **IV:** 236; **Retro. Supp. I:** 40, 41
Understanding Tim O'Brien (Kaplan), **Supp. V:** 241
Understanding To Kill a Mockingbird: A Student Casebook to Issues,

Sources, and Documents (Johnson), **Supp. VIII:** 127
Undertaker's Garland, The (Wilson and Bishop), **IV:** 427
"Under the Cedarcroft Chestnut" (Lanier), **Supp. I Part 1:** 364
"Under the Harbour Bridge" (Komunyakaa), **Supp. XIII:** 125
Under the Lilacs (Alcott), **Supp. I Part 1:** 42–43, 44
"Under the Maud Moon" (Kinnell), **Supp. III Part 1:** 246–247
Under the Mountain Wall: A Chronicle of Two Seasons in the Stone Age (Matthiessen), **Supp. V:** 202
"Under the Rose" (Pynchon), **Supp. II Part 2:** 620
Under the Sea-Wind: A Naturalist's Picture of Ocean Life (Carson), **Supp. IX:** 19, **22–23**
Under the Sign of Saturn (Sontag), **Supp. III Part 2:** 451, 452, 458, 470–471
"Under the Sign of Saturn" (Sontag), **Supp. III Part 2:** 470
"Under the Sky" (Bowles), **Supp. IV Part 1:** 87
"Under the Willows" (Lowell), **Supp. I Part 2:** 416
Under the Willows and Other Poems (Lowell), **Supp. I Part 2:** 424
Underwood, Wilbur, **Retro. Supp. II:** 79
Underworld (DeLillo), **Supp. VI:** 2, 4–5, 6–7, 8, 9, 10, 11, **13–15**; **Supp. XI:** 68
Undine (La Motte-Fouqué), **II:** 212; **III:** 78
Undiscovered Country, The (Howells), **II:** 282
Uneasy Chair, The (Stegner), **Supp. IV Part 2:** 599
"Unemployed, Disabled, and Insane, The" (Haines), **Supp. XII:** 211–212
Unending Blues (Simic), **Supp. VIII:** **278–279**
"Unexpressed" (Dunbar), **Supp. II Part 1:** 199
"Unfinished Bronx, The" (Paley), **Supp. VI:** 228
"Unfinished Poems" (Eliot), **I:** 579
Unfinished Woman, An (Hellman), **Supp. I Part 1:** 292, 293, 294; **Supp. IV Part 1:** 12, 353–354; **Supp. IX:** 196, 200–201
Unforeseen Wilderness, The: An Essay on Kentucky's Red River Gorge (Berry), **Supp. X:** 28, 29, 30, 36
"Unfortunate Coincidence" (Parker), **Supp. IX:** 190

Unframed Originals (Merwin), **Supp. III Part 1:** 341
Ungar, Sanford, **Supp. XI:** 228
Ungaretti, Giuseppe, **Supp. V:** 337
Unguided Tour (Sontag), **Supp. III Part 2:** 452
"Unidentified Flying Object" (Hayden), **Supp. II Part 1:** 368
"Unifying Principle, The" (Ammons), **Supp. VII:** 28
"Union" (Hughes), **Supp. I Part 1:** 331
"Union Street: San Francisco, Summer 1975" (Carver), **Supp. III Part 1:** 138
United States Army in World War II (Morison), **Supp. I Part 2:** 490
United States Constitution, **I:** 6, 283
United States Essays, 1951–1991 (Vidal), **Supp. IV Part 2:** 678, 687
United States of Poetry, The (television series), **Supp. XIII:** 274
Universal Baseball Asociation, Inc., J. Henry Waugh, Prop., The (Coover), **Supp. V:** 39, 41–42, 44, 46
Universal Passion (Young), **III:** 111
"Universe of Death, The" (H. Miller), **III:** 184
Universe of Time, A (Anderson), **II:** 27, 28, 45, 46, 48, 49
"Universities" (Emerson), **II:** 6
"Universities: A Mirage? " (Mora), **Supp. XIII:** 219
"University" (Shapiro), **Supp. II Part 2:** 704–705, 717
"University Avenue" (Mora), **Supp. XIII:** 216
"University Days" (Thurber), **Supp. I Part 2:** 605
"University Hospital, Boston" (Oliver), **Supp. VII:** 235
"Unknowable, The" (Levine), **Supp. V:** 195
"Unknown Girl in the Maternity Ward" (Sexton), **Supp. II Part 2:** 676
"Unknown Love, The" (Chandler), **Supp. IV Part 1:** 120
"Unknown War, The" (Sandburg), **III:** 594
Unleashed (anthology), **Supp. XI:** 132
"Unlighted Lamps" (Anderson), **I:** 112
Unloved Wife, The (Alcott), **Supp. I Part 1:** 33
Unmarried Woman, An (film), **Supp. IV Part 1:** 303
"Unnatural Mother, The" (Gilman), **Supp. XI:** 207
"Unnatural State of the Unicorn" (Komunyakaa), **Supp. XIII:** 119
"Unparalleled Adventure of One Hans

Pfaall, The" (Poe), **III:** 424
Unprecedented Era, The (Goebbels), **III:** 560
"Unprofitable Servant, The" (O. Henry), **Supp. II Part 1:** 403
Unpublished Poems of Emily Dickinson (Bianchi and Hampson, ed.), **Retro. Supp. I:** 35
Unpunished (Gilman), **Supp. XI:** 208
"Unseen, The" (Pinsky), **Supp. VI:** 243–244
"Unseen, The" (Singer), **Retro. Supp. II:** 325
Unseen Hand, The (Shepard), **Supp. III Part 2:** 439, 445–446
Unselected Poems (Levine), **Supp. V:** 179
Unsettling of America, The: Culture and Agriculture (Berry), **Supp. X:** 22, 26, 29, 32, 33, 35
Unspeakable Gentleman, The (Marquand), **III:** 53–54, 60, 63
Unspeakable Practices, Unnatural Acts (Barthelme), **Supp. IV Part 1:** 39
"Unspeakable Things Unspoken: The Afro-American Presence in American Literature" (Morrison), **Supp. III Part 1:** 375, 377–379
"Untelling, The" (Strand), **Supp. IV Part 2:** 629
Unterecker, John, **I:** 386
Untermeyer, Jean, **II:** 530
Untermeyer, Louis, **II:** 516–517, 530, 532; **III:** 268; **Retro. Supp. I:** 124, 133, 136; **Supp. III Part 1:** 2; **Supp. IX:** 76
Untimely Papers (Bourne), **I:** 218, 233
"Untitled Blues" (Komunyakaa), **Supp. XIII:** 117
"Untrustworthy Speaker, The" (Glück), **Supp. V:** 86
"Unused" (Anderson), **I:** 112, 113
Unvanquished, The (Faulkner), **II:** 55, 67–68, 71; **Retro. Supp. I:** 84; **Supp. I Part 2:** 450
"Unvexed Isles, The" (Warren), **IV:** 253
"Unwedded" (Larcom), **Supp. XIII:** 144
"Unweepables, The" (Karr), **Supp. XI:** 243
Unwelcome Words (Bowles), **Supp. IV Part 1:** 93, 94
"Unwelcome Words" (Bowles), **Supp. IV Part 1:** 94, 95
Unwin, T. Fisher, **Supp. XI:** 202
"Unwithered Garland, The" (Kunitz), **Supp. III Part 1:** 265
Unwobbling Pivot, The (Pound, trans.), **III:** 472

"Unwritten, The" (Merwin), **Supp. III Part 1:** 352
"Unwritten Law" (Glück), **Supp. V:** 91
Up (Sukenick), **Supp. V:** 39
Up Above the World (Bowles), **Supp. IV Part 1:** 82, 91, 92
"Up and Down" (Merrill), **Supp. III Part 1:** 328
Upanishads, **IV:** 183
Up Country: Poems of New England (Kumin), **Supp. IV Part 2:** 446, 447–448, 453
"Update" (Dunn), **Supp. XI:** 150–151
Updike, John, **I:** 54; **III:** 572; **IV:** 214–235; **Retro. Supp. I:** 116, 317–338; **Retro. Supp. II:** 213, 297, 298; **Supp. I Part 1:** 186, 196; **Supp. IV Part 2:** 657; **Supp. V:** 23, 43, 95, 119; **Supp. VIII:** 151, 167, 236; **Supp. IX:** 208; **Supp. XI:** 65, 66, 99, 140; **Supp. XII:** 140, 296, 298, 310; **Supp. XIII:** 45–46, 47, 52
Updike, Mrs. Wesley, **IV:** 218, 220
Up from Slavery (Washington), **Supp. II Part 1:** 169; **Supp. IX:** 19
Upham, Thomas Goggswell, **II:** 487
"Upholsterers, The" (Lardner), **II:** 435
"Up in Michigan" (Hemingway), **II:** 263
Upjohn, Richard, **IV:** 312
"Upon a Spider Catching a Fly" (Taylor), **IV:** 161
"Upon a Wasp Child with Cold" (Taylor), **IV:** 161
"Upon Meeting Don L. Lee, in a Dream" (Dove), **Supp. IV Part 1:** 244
"Upon My Dear and Loving Husband His Going into England, Jan. 16, 1661" (Bradstreet), **Supp. I Part 1:** 110
"Upon Returning to the Country Road" (Lindsay), **Supp. I Part 2:** 382
"Upon the Burning of Our House, July 10th, 1666" (Bradstreet), **Supp. I Part 1:** 107–108, 122
"Upon the Sweeping Flood" (Taylor), **IV:** 161
"Upon Wedlock, and Death of Children" (Taylor), **IV:** 144, 147, 161
"Upset, An" (Merrill), **Supp. III Part 1:** 336
Upstairs and Downstairs (Vonnegut), **Supp. II Part 2:** 757
Upstate (Wilson), **IV:** 447
Upton, Lee, **Supp. X:** 209
"Upturned Face" (Crane), **I:** 423
Upward, Allen, **Supp. I Part 1:** 262
"Upward Moon and the Downward Moon, The" (Bly), **Supp. IV Part 1:** 71
Urania: A Rhymed Lesson (Holmes), **Supp. I Part 1:** 300
"Urban Convalescence, An" (Merrill), **Supp. III Part 1:** 322–324
"Urban Renewal" (Komunyakaa), **Supp. XIII:** 113
Urich, Robert, **Supp. V:** 228
"Uriel" (Emerson), **II:** 19
Uris, Leon, **Supp. IV Part 1:** 285, 379
Uroff, Margaret D., **Supp. I Part 2:** 542
"Us" (Sexton), **Supp. II Part 2:** 687
U.S. 1 (Rukeyser), **Supp. VI:** 272, 278, 283, 285
"U.S. Commercial Orchid, The" (Agee), **I:** 35
U.S.A. (Dos Passos), **I:** 379, 475, 478, 482–488, 489, 490, 491, 492, 493, 494, 495; **Retro. Supp. II:** 197; **Supp. I Part 2:** 646; **Supp. III Part 1:** 104, 105
"U.S.A. School of Writing, The" (Bishop), **Retro. Supp. II:** 43
"Used-Boy Raisers, The" (Paley), **Supp. VI:** 218, 228
"Used Cars on Oahu" (Nye), **Supp. XIII:** 282
"Used Side of the Sofa, The" (Ríos), **Supp. IV Part 2:** 551
Use of Fire, The (Price), **Supp. VI:** 265
"Use of Force, The" (W. C. Williams), **Retro. Supp. I:** 424
Use of Poetry and the Use of Criticism, The (Eliot), **Retro. Supp. I:** 65
Uses of Enchantment, The: The Meaning and Importance of Fairy Tales (Bettleheim), **Supp. X:** 77
"Uses of Poetry, The" (W. C. Williams), **Retro. Supp. I:** 412
"Uses of the Blues, The" (Baldwin), **Retro. Supp. II:** 8
Ushant: An Essay (Aiken), **I:** 49, 54, 55, 56, 57
"Usher 11" (Bradbury), **Supp. I Part 2:** 622
"Using Parrots to Kill Mockingbirds: Yet Another Racial Prosecution and Wrongful Conviction in Maycomb" (Fair), **Supp. VIII:** 128
Usual Star, The (Doolittle), **Supp. I Part 1:** 270
"Usurpation (Other People's Stories)" (Ozick), **Supp. V:** 268, 271
Utopia 14 (Vonnegut), **Supp. II Part 2:** 757
V. (Pynchon), **Supp. II Part 2:** 618, 620–622, 627–630; **Supp. IV Part 1:** 279

V. S. Naipaul: An Introduction to His Work (Theroux), **Supp. VIII:** 314, 318
"V. S. Pritchett's Apprenticeship" (Maxwell), **Supp. VIII:** 172
"V. V." (Alcott), **Supp. I Part 1:** 37
"Vacation" (Stafford), **Supp. XI:** 321, 322
"Vacation Trip" (Stafford), **Supp. XI:** 322
Vachel Lindsay: A Poet in America (Masters), **Supp. I Part 2:** 473, 474
"Vachel Lindsay: The Midwest as Utopia" (Whitney), **Supp. I Part 2:** 403
"Vachel Lindsay Writes to Floyd Dell" (Tanselle), **Supp. I Part 2:** 403
Vadim, Roger, **Supp. XI:** 293, 307
"Vag" (Dos Passos), **I:** 487–488
Valentine, Jean, **Supp. V:** 92
Valentine, Saint, **IV:** 396
Valentino, Rudolph, **I:** 483
Valéry, Paul, **II:** 543, 544; **III:** 279, 409, 428, 609; **IV:** 79, 91, 92, 428, 443; **Retro. Supp. II:** 187
"Valhalla" (Francis), **Supp. IX:** 77
Valhalla and Other Poems (Francis), **Supp. IX:** 76
Valitsky, Ken, **Supp. XII:** 7
Vallejo, César, **Supp. V:** 332; **Supp. IX:** 271; **Supp. XIII:** 114, 315, 323
"Valley Between, The" (Marshall), **Supp. XI:** 278
Valley of Decision, The (Wharton), **IV:** 311, 315; **Retro. Supp. I:** 365–367
Valley of the Moon, The (London), **II:** 467, 481
"Valley of Unrest, The" (Poe), **III:** 411
Valli, Alida, **Supp. IV Part 2:** 520
"Valor" (Bausch), **Supp. VII:** 54
Valparaiso (DeLillo), **Supp. VI:** 4, 12
"Values and Fictions" (Toomer), **Supp. III Part 2:** 485–486
Values of Veblen, The: A Critical Appraisal (Rosenberg), **Supp. I Part 2:** 650
"Vampire" (Karr), **Supp. XI:** 241
Vampire Armand, The (Rice), **Supp. VII:** 290, 294–295
Vampire Chronicles, The (Rice), **Supp. VII:** 290
Vampire Lestat, The (Rice), **Supp. VII:** 290–292, 298, 299
Van Buren, Martin, **II:** 134, 312; **III:** 473
Vande Kieft, Ruth M., **IV:** 260
Vanderbilt, Cornelius, **III:** 14
Van Dine, S. S., **Supp. IV Part 1:** 341
Van Doren, Carl, **I:** 252–253, 423; **II:** 103, 111, 112; **Supp. I Part 2:** 474, 486, 707, 709, 717, 718, 727; **Supp. II Part 1:** 395; **Supp. VIII:** 96–97
Van Doren, Mark, **I:** 168; **III:** 4, 23, 589; **Supp. I Part 2:** 604; **Supp. III Part 2:** 626; **Supp. VIII:** 231; **Supp. IX:** 266, 268
Vandover and the Brute (Norris), **III:** 314, 315, 316, 320–322, 328, 333, 334
Van Duyn, Mona, **Supp. IX:** 269
Van Dyke, Annette, **Supp. IV Part 1:** 327
Van Dyke, Henry, **I:** 223; **II:** 456
Van Gogh, Vincent, **I:** 27; **IV:** 290; **Supp. I Part 2:** 451; **Supp. IV Part 1:** 284
Van Gogh's Room at Arles (Elkin), **Supp. VI:** 56
"Vanisher, The" (Whittier), **Supp. I Part 2:** 691
"Vanishing Red, The" (Frost), **Retro. Supp. II:** 47
"Vanity" (B. Diop), **Supp. IV Part 1:** 16
Vanity Fair (Thackeray), **I:** 354; **II:** 91; **III:** 70; **Supp. IX:** 200
"Vanity of All Wordly Things, The" (Bradstreet), **Supp. I Part 1:** 102, 119
Vanity of Duluoz (Kerouac), **Supp. III Part 1:** 221, 222
"Vanity of Existence, The" (Freneau), **Supp. II Part 1:** 262
Van Matre, Lynn, **Supp. V:** 126
Vanquished, The (Faulkner), **I:** 205
Van Rensselaer, Stephen, **I:** 351
Van Vechten, Carl, **I:** 295; **IV:** 76; **Supp. I Part 1:** 324, 327, 332; **Supp. I Part 2:** 715; **Supp. II Part 2:** 725–751; **Supp. X:** 247
Vanzetti, Bartolomeo, **I:** 482, 486, 490, 494; **II:** 38–39, 426; **III:** 139–140; **Supp. I Part 2:** 446, 610, 611; **Supp. V:** 288–289; **Supp. IX:** 199
"Vapor Trail Reflected in the Frog Pond" (Kinnell), **Supp. III Part 1:** 242–243
"Vapor Trails" (Snyder), **Supp. VIII:** 298
"Variation: Ode to Fear" (Warren), **IV:** 241
"Variation on a Sentence" (Bogan), **Supp. III Part 1:** 60
"Variation on Gaining a Son" (Dove), **Supp. IV Part 1:** 248
"Variation on Pain" (Dove), **Supp. IV Part 1:** 248
"Variations: The air is sweetest that a thistle guards" (Merrill), **Supp. III Part 1:** 321
"Variations: White Stag, Black Bear" (Merrill), **Supp. III Part 1:** 321
"Varick Street" (Bishop), **Supp. I Part 1:** 90, 92
Varieties of Metaphysical Poetry, The (Eliot), **Retro. Supp. I:** 65
Varieties of Religious Experience, The (William James), **II:** 344, 353, 354, 359–360, 362; **IV:** 28, 291; **Supp. IX:** 19
Variety (film), **Supp. XII:** 7
Variorum (Whitman), **Retro. Supp. I:** 406
Various Miracles (Shields), **Supp. VII:** 318–320, 323, 324
"Various Miracles" (Shields), **Supp. VII:** 318–319, 324
Vasari, Giorgio, **Supp. I Part 2:** 450; **Supp. III Part 1:** 5
Vasquez, Robert, **Supp. V:** 180
Vassall Morton (Parkman), **Supp. II Part 2:** 595, 597–598
Vasse, W. W., **III:** 478
Vaudeville for a Princess (Schwartz), **Supp. II Part 2:** 661–662
Vaughan, Henry, **IV:** 151
Vaughn, Robert, **Supp. XI:** 343
"Vaunting Oak" (Ransom), **III:** 490
Vazirani, Reetika, **Supp. XIII:** 133
Veblen (Hobson), **Supp. I Part 2:** 650
Veblen, Andrew, **Supp. I Part 2:** 640
Veblen, Mrs. Thorstein (Ellen Rolfe), **Supp. I Part 2:** 641
Veblen, Oswald, **Supp. I Part 2:** 640
Veblen, Thorstein, **I:** 104, 283, 475–476, 483, 498, 511; **II:** 27, 272, 276, 287; **Supp. I Part 2: 628–650**; **Supp. IV Part 1:** 22
Veblenism: A New Critique (Dobriansky), **Supp. I Part 2:** 648, 650
"Veblen's Attack on Culture" (Adorno), **Supp. I Part 2:** 650
Vechten, Carl Van, **Retro. Supp. I:** 199
Vedas, **IV:** 183
Vega, Lope de, **Retro. Supp. I:** 285; **Supp. III Part 1:** 341, 347
Vegetable, The (Fitzgerald), **Retro. Supp. I:** 105; **Supp. IX:** 57
Vegetable, The, or From President to Postman (Fitzgerald), **II:** 91
Veinberg, Jon, **Supp. V:** 180; **Supp. XIII:** 313
Vein of Iron (Glasgow), **II:** 175, 186, 188–189, 191, 192, 194
Vein of Riches, A (Knowles), **Supp. XII:** 249
Velie, Alan R., **Supp. IV Part 2:** 486
Velocities: New and Selected Poems, 1966–1992 (Dobyns), **Supp. XIII:**

86–87, 87, 88
"Velorio" (Cisneros), **Supp. VII:** 66
"Velvet Shoes" (Wylie), **Supp. I Part 2:** 711, 714
Venant, Elizabeth, **Supp. XI:** 343
Vencloca, Thomas, **Supp. VIII:** 29
Vendler, Helen H., **Retro. Supp. I:** 297; **Retro. Supp. II:** 184, 191; **Supp. I Part 1:** 77, 78, 92, 95; **Supp. I Part 2:** 565; **Supp. IV Part 1:** 245, 247, 249, 254, 257; **Supp. IV Part 2:** 448; **Supp. V:** 78, 82, 189, 343; **Supp. XII:** 187, 189
"Venetian Blind, The" (Jarrell), **II:** 382–383
Venetian Glass Nephew, The (Wylie), **Supp. I Part 2:** 707, 709, 714, 717–719, 721, 724
Venetian Life (Howells), **II:** 274, 277, 279
Venetian Vespers, The (Hecht), **Supp. X:** 57, **65–69**
"Venetian Vespers, The" (Hecht), **Supp. X:** 65, **66–67**
Venice Observed (McCarthy), **II:** 562
Ventadorn, Bernard de, **Supp. IV Part 1:** 146
"Ventriloquists' Conversations" (Gentry), **Supp. IV Part 1:** 236
"Venus, Cupid, Folly and Time" (Taylor), **Supp. V:** 322–323
Venus and Adonis (film), **Supp. IV Part 1:** 82
Venus in Sparta (Auchincloss), **Supp. IV Part 1:** 25
"Venus's-flytraps" (Komunyakaa), **Supp. XIII:** 126, 127
"Veracruz" (Hayden), **Supp. II Part 1:** 371, 373
Verga, Giovanni, **II:** 271, 275
Verghese, Abraham, **Supp. X:** 160
Verhaeren, Emile, **I:** 476; **II:** 528, 529
Verlaine, Paul, **II:** 529, 543; **III:** 466; **IV:** 79, 80, 86, 286; **Retro. Supp. I:** 56, 62; **Retro. Supp. II:** 344
"Vermeer" (Nemerov), **III:** 275, 278, 280
Vermeer, Jan, **Retro. Supp. I:** 335
Vermont Notebook, The (Ashbery), **Supp. III Part 1:** 1
"Vernal Ague, The" (Freneau), **Supp. II Part 1:** 258
Verne, Jules, **I:** 480; **Retro. Supp. I:** 270; **Supp. XI:** 63
Vernon, John, **Supp. X:** 15
Verplanck, Gulian C., **Supp. I Part 1:** 155, 156, 157, 158
Verrazano, Giovanni da, **Supp. I Part 2:** 496, 497
Verse (Zawacki), **Supp. VIII:** 272

"Verse for Urania" (Merrill), **Supp. III Part 1:** 329, 330
Verses (Wharton), **Retro. Supp. I:** 362
Verses, Printed for Her Friends (Jewett), **II:** 406
"Verses for Children" (Lowell), **II:** 516
"Verses Made at Sea in a Heavy Gale" (Freneau), **Supp. II Part 1:** 262
"Verses on the Death of T. S. Eliot" (Brodsky), **Supp. VIII:** 19
"Version of a Fragment of Simonides" (Bryant), **Supp. I Part 1:** 153, 155
Verulam, Baron. *See* Bacon, Francis
Very, Jones, **III:** 507
"Very Hot Sun in Bermuda, The" (Jackson), **Supp. IX:** 126
Very Old Bones (Kennedy), **Supp. VII:** 133, 148, 150–153
"Very Proper Gander, The" (Thurber), **Supp. I Part 2:** 610
"Very Short Story, A" (Hemingway), **II:** 252; **Retro. Supp. I:** 173
"Vesalius in Zante" (Wharton), **Retro. Supp. I:** 372
Vesey, Denmark, **Supp. I Part 2:** 592
"Vespers" (Auden), **Supp. II Part 1:** 23
"Vespers" (Glück), **Supp. V:** 88
Vestal Lady on Brattle, The (Corso), **Supp. XII:** 119, **120–121,** 134
Vested Interests and the Common Man, The (Veblen), **Supp. I Part 2:** 642
"Vesuvius at Home" (Rich), **Retro. Supp. I:** 42; **Retro. Supp. II:** 286
"Veteran, The" (Crane), **I:** 413
"Veterans Day" (Rich), **Retro. Supp. II:** 293
"Veteran Sirens" (Robinson), **III:** 512, 524
"Vetiver" (Ashbery), **Supp. III Part 1:** 26
"Via Dieppe-Newhaven" (H. Miller), **III:** 183
"Via Negativa" (Salter), **Supp. IX:** 257
Vicar of Wakefeld, The (Goldsmith), **I:** 216
"Vicissitudes of the Avant-Garde, The" (Gass), **Supp. VI:** 91
Victim, The (Bellow), **I:** 144, 145, 147, 149, 150, 151, 152, 153, 155, 156, 158, 159, 164; **IV:** 19; **Retro. Supp. II:** 21, 22, 34
"Victor" (Mumford), **Supp. II Part 2:** 476
"Victory at Sea" (television series), **Supp. I Part 2:** 490
"Victory comes late" (Dickinson), **Retro. Supp. I:** 45
"Victory of the Moon, The" (Crane), **I:** 420

Vidal, Gore, **II:** 587; **IV:** 383; **Supp. IV Part 1:** 22, 35, 92, 95, 198; **Supp. IV Part 2: 677–696; Supp. IX:** 96; **Supp. X:** 186, 195
Viebahn, Fred, **Supp. IV Part 1:** 248
Viera, Joseph M., **Supp. XI:** 178, 186
Viereck, Peter, **Supp. I Part 2:** 403
Viet Journal (Jones), **Supp. XI: 230–231**
Vietnam (McCarthy), **II:** 578–579
"Vietnam in Me, The" (O'Brien), **Supp. V:** 241, 252
Vie unanime, La (Romains), **I:** 227
"View, The" (Roussel), **Supp. III Part 1:** 15, 16, 21
View from 80, The (Cowley), **Supp. II Part 1:** 141, 144, 153
View from the Bridge, A (A. Miller), **III:** 147, 148, 156, 158, 159–160
View of My Own, A: Essays in Literature and Society (Hardwick), **Supp. III Part 1:** 194, 200
"View of the Capital from the Library of Congress" (Bishop), **Retro. Supp. II:** 45
View of the Soil and Climate of the United States, A (Brown, trans.), **Supp. I Part 1:** 146
"View of the Woods, A" (O'Connor), **III:** 349, 351, 358; **Retro. Supp. II:** 237
"Views of the Mysterious Hill: The Appearance of Parnassus in American Poetry" (Strand), **Supp. IV Part 2:** 631
"Vigil" (Karr), **Supp. XI:** 241
"Vigil, The" (Dante), **III:** 542
Vigny, Alfred Victor de, **II:** 543
Vile Bodies (Waugh), **Supp. I Part 2:** 607
Villa, Pancho, **I:** 210; **III:** 584
"Village Blacksmith, The" (Longfellow), **Retro. Supp. II:** 167, 168; **Supp. I Part 2:** 409
Village Hymns, a Supplement to Dr. Watts's Psalms and Hymns (Nettleton), **I:** 458
"Village Improvement Parade, The" (Lindsay), **Supp. I Part 2:** 388, 389
Village Magazine, The (Lindsay), **Supp. I Part 2:** 379–380, 382
Village Virus, The (Lewis), **II:** 440
"Villanelle at Sundown" (Justice), **Supp. VII:** 119, 122–123
"Villanelle of Change" (Robinson), **III:** 524
Villard, Oswald, **Supp. I Part 1:** 332
"Villa Selene" (Simpson), **Supp. IX:** 279
Villon, François, **II:** 544; **III:** 9, 174,

592; **Retro. Supp. I:** 286; **Supp. I Part 1:** 261; **Supp. III Part 1:** 235, 243, 249, 253; **Supp. III Part 2:** 560; **Supp. IX:** 116
"Villonaud for This Yule" (Pound), **Retro. Supp. I:** 286
Vindication of the Rights of Woman (Wollstonecraft), **Supp. I Part 1:** 126; **Supp. XI:** 203
Vines, Lois Davis, **Retro. Supp. II:** 261
"Vintage Thunderbird, A" (Beattie), **Supp. V:** 27
Vinz, Mark, **Supp. X:** 117
Violence (Bausch), **Supp. VII:** 48–49, 54
Violent Bear It Away, The (O'Connor), **III:** 339, 345–348, 350, 351, 354, 355, 356, 357; **Retro. Supp. II:** 233, **234–236**
"Violent Vet, The" (O'Brien), **Supp. V:** 238
Violin (Rice), **Supp. VII:** 302
Viorst, Judith, **Supp. X:** 153
Viper Run (Karr), **Supp. XI: 248–251**
Virgil, **I:** 312, 322, 587; **II:** 133, 542; **IV:** 137, 359; **Retro. Supp. I:** 135; **Supp. I Part 1:** 153; **Supp. I Part 2:** 494; **Supp. IV Part 2:** 631
"Virgin and the Dynamo" (Adams), **III:** 396
"Virgin Carrying a Lantern, The" (Stevens), **IV:** 80
Virginia (Glasgow), **II:** 175, 178, 181–182, 193, 194
"Virginia" (Lindsay), **Supp. I Part 2:** 398
"Virginia Britannia" (Moore), **III:** 198, 208–209
"Virginians Are Coming Again, The" (Lindsay), **Supp. I Part 2:** 399
"Virgin Violeta" (Porter), **III:** 454
"Virility" (Ozick), **Supp. V:** 262, 265
Virtue of Selfishness, The: A New Concept of Egoism (Rand), **Supp. IV Part 2:** 527, 530–532
"Virtuoso" (Francis), **Supp. IX:** 82
Virtuous Woman, A (Gibbons), **Supp. X: 44–45**, 46, 50
Visconti, Luchino, **Supp. V:** 51
Visible Saints: The History of a Puritan Idea (Morgan), **IV:** 149
"Vision, A" (Olds), **Supp. X:** 214
"Vision, A" (Winters), **Supp. II Part 2:** 785, 795
"Vision and Prayer" (D. Thomas), **I:** 432
"Visionary, The" (Poe), **III:** 411
Visionary Farms, The (Eberhart), **I:** 537–539

Visioning, The (Glaspell), **Supp. III Part 1:** 175–177, 180, 187, 188
Vision in Spring (Faulkner), **Retro. Supp. I:** 79
Vision of Columbus (Barlow), **Supp. I Part 1:** 124; **Supp. II Part 1:** 67, 68, 70–75, 77, 79
Vision of Sir Launfal, The (Lowell), **Supp. I Part 1:** 311; **Supp. I Part 2:** 406, 409, 410
"Vision of the World, A" (Cheever), **Supp. I Part 1:** 182, 192
Visions of Cody (Kerouac), **Supp. III Part 1:** 225–227
Visions of Gerard (Kerouac), **Supp. III Part 1:** 219–222, 225, 227, 229
"Visions of the Daughters of Albion" (Blake), **III:** 540
"Visit" (Ammons), **Supp. VII:** 28–29
"Visit, The" (Kenyon), **Supp. VII:** 169
"Visitant, The" (Dunn), **Supp. XI:** 147
"Visitation, The/La Visitación" (Mora), **Supp. XIII:** 217, 224, 228
"Visit Home, A" (Stafford), **Supp. XI:** 318
Visit in 2001, The (musical, McNally), **Supp. XIII:** 207
"Visiting My Own House in Iowa City" (Stern), **Supp. IX:** 300
"Visit of Charity, A" (Welty), **IV:** 262
"Visitors" (Salinas), **Supp. XIII:** 318
"Visitors, The/Los Visitantes" (Kingsolver), **Supp. VII:** 208
"Visits to St. Elizabeths" (Bishop), **Retro. Supp. II:** 47
"Visit to a Small Planet" (teleplay) (Vidal), **Supp. IV Part 2:** 682
Visit to a Small Planet: A Comedy Akin to Vaudeville (Vidal), **Supp. IV Part 2:** 682–683
"Visit to Avoyelles, A" (Chopin), **Supp. I Part 1:** 213
"Vissi d'Arte" (Moore), **Supp. X: 173–174**
Vistas of History (Morison), **Supp. I Part 2:** 492
"Vita" (Stafford), **Supp. XI:** 330
Vital Provisions (Price), **Supp. VI:** 262–263
"Vitamins" (Carver), **Supp. III Part 1:** 138
Vita Nova (Glück), **Supp. V:** 90–92
Vittorio, the Vampire (Rice), **Supp. VII:** 295–296
Viudas (Dorfman), **Supp. IX:** 138
Vizenor, Gerald, **Supp. IV Part 1:** 260, 262, 329, 404; **Supp. IV Part 2:** 502
Vladimir Nabokov: The American Years (Nabokov), **Retro. Supp. I:** 275

"Vlemk, the Box Painter" (Gardner), **Supp. VI:** 73
"V-Letter" (Shapiro), **Supp. II Part 2:** 707
V-Letter and Other Poems (Shapiro), **Supp. II Part 2:** 702, 706
"Vocabulary of Dearness" (Nye), **Supp. XIII:** 284
"Vocation" (Stafford), **Supp. XI:** 312, 321
Vocation and a Voice, A (Chopin), **Retro. Supp. II:** 67, 72
"Vocation and a Voice, A" (Chopin), **Retro. Supp. II:** 72; **Supp. I Part 1:** 200, 220, 224, 225
Vogel, Speed, **Supp. IV Part 1:** 390
"Voice, The" (Dunn), **Supp. XI:** 152
Voiced Connections of James Dickey, The (Dickey), **Supp. IV Part 1:** 177
"Voice from the Woods, A" (Humphrey), **Supp. IX:** 101
"Voice from Under the Table, A" (Wilbur), **Supp. III Part 2:** 553, 554
Voice of Reason, The: Essays in Objectivist Thought (Rand), **Supp. IV Part 2:** 527, 528, 532
"Voice of Rock, The" (Ginsberg), **Supp. II Part 1:** 313
Voice of the Butterfly, The (Nichols), **Supp. XIII:** 270
Voice of the City, The (O. Henry), **Supp. II Part 1:** 410
"Voice of the Mountain, The" (Crane), **I:** 420
Voice of the Negro (Barber), **Supp. II Part 1:** 168
Voice of the People, The (Glasgow), **II:** 175, 176
Voice of the Turtle: American Indian Literature 1900–1970 (Gunn Allen, ed.), **Supp. IV Part 1:** 332, 334
Voices from the Moon (Dubus), **Supp. VII:** 88–89
"Voices from the Other World" (Merrill), **Supp. III Part 1:** 331
Voices in the House (Sedges), **Supp. II Part 1:** 125
Voices of the Night (Longfellow), **II:** 489, 493; **Retro. Supp. II:** 154, 157, 168
"Voices of Village Square, The" (Wolfe), **Supp. III Part 2:** 571–572
Voice That Is Great within Us, The (Caruth, ed.), **Supp. XIII:** 112
Voigt, Ellen Bryan, **Supp. XIII:** 76
Volkening, Henry, **Retro. Supp. II:** 117
Volney, Constantin François de Chasseboeuf, **Supp. I Part 1:** 146

Voltaire, **I:** 194; **II:** 86, 103, 449; **III:** 420; **IV:** 18; **Retro. Supp. II:** 94; **Supp. I Part 1:** 288–289; **Supp. I Part 2:** 669, 717
Vonnegut, Kurt, **Retro. Supp. I:** 170; **Supp. II Part 2:** 557, 689, **753–784; Supp. IV Part 1:** 227, 392; **Supp. V:** 40, 42, 237, 244, 296; **Supp. X:** 260; **Supp. XI:** 104; **Supp. XII:** 139, 141
"Voracities and Verities" (Moore), **III:** 214
Vore, Nellie, **I:** 199
Vorlicky, Robert, **Supp. IX:** 132, 135, 136, 141, 144, 147
"Vorticism" (Pound), **Retro. Supp. I:** 288
Voss, Richard, **I:** 199–200
"Vow, The" (Hecht), **Supp. X:** 64
"Vowels 2" (Baraka), **Supp. II Part 1:** 51
Vow of Conversation, A: Journal, 1964–1965 (Merton), **Supp. VIII:** 206
Vox (Baker), **Supp. XIII: 47–49,** 50, 52, 53
"Voyage" (MacLeish), **III:** 15
"Voyage, The" (Irving), **II:** 304
Voyage, The, and Other Versions of Poems by Baudelaire (Lowell), **Retro. Supp. II:** 187
Voyage dans la Haute Pennsylvanie et dans l'état de New-York (Crèvecoeur), **Supp. I Part 1:** 250–251
Voyage of the Beagle (Darwin), **Supp. IX:** 211
"Voyages" (H. Crane), **I:** 393–395; **Retro. Supp. II:** 78, 80, 81
"Voyages" (Levine), **Supp. V:** 190
Voyages and Discoveries of the Companions of Columbus (Irving), **II:** 310
Voyage to Pagany, A (W. C. Williams), **IV:** 404; **Retro. Supp. I:** 418–419, **420–421,** 423
Voznesensky, Andrei, **II:** 553; **Supp. III Part 1:** 268; **Supp. III Part 2:** 560
Vrbovska, Anca, **Supp. IV Part 2:** 639
"Vulgarity in Literature" (Huxley), **III:** 429–430
"Vultures" (Oliver), **Supp. VII:** 235
W (Viva) (Cummings), **I:** 429, 433, 434, 436, 443, 444, 447
"W. D. Sees Himself Animated" (Snodgrass), **Supp. VI:** 327
"W. D. Sits in Kafka's Chair and Is Interrogated Concerning the Assumed Death of Cock Robin" (Snodgrass), **Supp. VI:** 319
"W. D. Tries to Warn Cock Robin" (Snodgrass), **Supp. VI:** 319
Wabash (R. O. Butler), **Supp. XII:** 61, **68–69**
Wade, Grace, **I:** 216
"Wading at Wellfleet" (Bishop), **Retro. Supp. II:** 42, 43; **Supp. I Part 1:** 80, 85, 86
Wadsworth, Charles, **I:** 454, 470; **Retro. Supp. I:** 32, 33
Wagenknecht, Edward, **II:** 508; **Supp. I Part 2:** 408, 584; **Supp. IV Part 2:** 681
Wagner, Jean, **Supp. I Part 1:** 341, 346; **Supp. IV Part 1:** 165, 167, 171
Wagner, Richard, **I:** 284, 395; **II:** 425; **III:** 396, 507; **Supp. IV Part 1:** 392
Wagner, Robert, **Supp. IX:** 250
"Wagnerians, The" (Auchincloss), **Supp. IV Part 1:** 23
"Wagner Matinee, A" (Cather), **I:** 315–316; **Retro. Supp. I:** 5, 8
Wagoner, David, **Supp. IX: 323–340; Supp. XII:** 178
Waid, Candace, **Retro. Supp. I:** 360, 372, 373
Waif, The (Longfellow, ed.), **Retro. Supp. II:** 155
"Waif of the Plains, A" (Harte), **Supp. II Part 1:** 354
"Wait" (Kinnell), **Supp. III Part 1:** 250
"Waiting" (Dubus), **Supp. VII:** 87
"Waiting" (W. C. Williams), **Retro. Supp. I:** 418
"Waiting, The" (Olds), **Supp. X:** 209
"Waiting between the Trees" (Tan), **Supp. X:** 290
"Waiting by the Gate" (Bryant), **Supp. I Part 1:** 171
Waiting for God (Weil), **I:** 298
Waiting for Godot (Beckett), **I:** 78, 91, 298; **Supp. IV Part 1:** 368–369
Waiting for Lefty (Odets), **Supp. I Part 1:** 277; **Supp. II Part 2:** 529, 530–533, 540; **Supp. V:** 109
Waiting for the End of the World (Bell), **Supp. X: 4–5,** 11
"Waiting in a Rain Forest" (Wagoner), **Supp. IX:** 329
Waiting to Exhale (McMillan), **Supp. XIII:** 184, 185, **189–190,** 191
"Waiting to Freeze" (Banks), **Supp. V:** 5, 6
Waiting to Freeze: Poems (Banks), **Supp. V:** 6, 8
Waits, Tom, **Supp. VIII:** 12
Wait until Spring, Bandini (Fante), **Supp. XI:** 160, 161, 164, 165, **166–167**
Wait until Spring, Bandini (film), **Supp. XI:** 173
"Wake, The" (Dove), **Supp. IV Part 1:** 250
"Wakefield" (Hawthorne), **Retro. Supp. I:** 154, 159
Wakefield, Dan, **Supp. VIII:** 43
Wakefield, Richard, **Supp. IX:** 323
"Wake Island" (Rukeyser), **Supp. VI:** 273
Wakeman, Frederic, **Supp. IX:** 247
Wake Up and Live! (Brande), **Supp. I Part 2:** 608
Waking, The (Roethke), **III:** 541
"Waking Early Sunday Morning" (Lowell), **II:** 552; **Retro. Supp. II:** 190
"Waking in the Blue" (Lowell), **II:** 547; **Retro. Supp. II:** 180
"Waking in the Dark" (Rich), **Supp. I Part 2:** 559
"Waking Up the Rake" (Hogan), **Supp. IV Part 1:** 415–416, 416
Wakoski, Diane, **Supp. V:** 79; **Supp. XII:** 184
Walcott, Charles C., **II:** 49
Walcott, Derek, **Supp. VIII:** 28; **Supp. X:** 122, 131
Walcott, Jersey Joe, **Supp. V:** 182
Wald, Lillian, **Supp. I Part 1:** 12
Walden, Daniel, **Supp. IV Part 2:** 584, 591; **Supp. V:** 272
Walden; or, Life in the Woods (Thoreau), **I:** 219, 305; **II:** 8, 142, 159, 312–313, 458; **IV:** 168, 169, 170, 176, 177–178, 179–182, 183, 187; **Retro. Supp. I:** 62; **Supp. I Part 2:** 579, 655, 664, 672; **Supp. VIII:** 296; **Supp. X:** 27, 101; **Supp. XIII:** 152
Waldmeir, Joseph, **III:** 45
Waldmeir, Joseph J., **Supp. I Part 2:** 476
Waldo (Theroux), **Supp. VIII:** 313, 314, **314–315**
Waley, Arthur, **II:** 526; **III:** 466; **Supp. V:** 340
"Walk, A" (Snyder), **Supp. VIII:** 297
"Walk at Sunset, A" (Bryant), **Supp. I Part 1:** 155
"Walk before Mass, A" (Agee), **I:** 28–29
Walker, Alice, **Retro. Supp. I:** 215; **Retro. Supp. II:** 292; **Supp. I Part 2:** 550; **Supp. III Part 2:** 488, **517–540; Supp. IV Part 1:** 14; **Supp. VIII:** 141, 214; **Supp. IX:** 306, 311; **Supp. X:** 85, 228, 252, 325, 330;

Supp. XIII: 179, 185, 291, 295
Walker, Cheryl, **Supp. XI:** 145
Walker, David, **Supp. V:** 189
Walker, Franklin D., **III:** 321
Walker, Gue, **Supp. XII:** 207
Walker, Marianne, **Supp. VIII:** 139
Walker, Obadiah, **II:** 113
Walker in the City, A (Kazin), **Supp. VIII: 93–95,** 99
"Walking" (Hogan), **Supp. IV Part 1:** 416
"Walking" (Thoreau), **Supp. IV Part 1:** 416; **Supp. IX:** 178
"Walking Along in Winter" (Kenyon), **Supp. VII:** 167
"Walking around the Block with a Three-Year-Old" (Wagoner), **Supp. IX:** 331–332
"Walking Backwards into the Future" (R. Williams), **Supp. IX:** 146
Walking Down the Stairs: Selections from Interviews (Kinnell), **Supp. III Part 1:** 235, 249
"Walking Home at Night" (Ginsberg), **Supp. II Part 1:** 313
Walking Light (Dunn), **Supp. XI:** 140, 141, 153
"Walking Man of Rodin, The" (Sandburg), **III:** 583
"Walking Sticks and Paperweights and Water Marks" (Moore), **III:** 215
Walking Tall (Dunn), **Supp. XI:** 140
Walking the Black Cat (Simic), **Supp. VIII:** 280, **282–284**
Walking to Sleep (Wilbur), **Supp. III Part 2:** 557–560
"Walking to Sleep" (Wilbur), **Supp. III Part 2:** 544, 557, 559, 561, 562
Walkin' the Dog (Mosley), **Supp. XIII:** 242
"Walk in the Moonlight, A" (Anderson), **I:** 114
Walk on the Wild Side, A (Algren), **Supp. V:** 4; **Supp. IX:** 3, **12–13,** 14
"Walks in Rome" (Merrill), **Supp. III Part 1:** 337
Walk with Tom Jefferson, A (Levine), **Supp. V:** 179, 187, 190–191
"Wall, The" (Brooks), **Supp. III Part 1:** 70, 71, 84
Wall, The (Hersey), **IV:** 4
"Wall, The" (Roethke), **III:** 544
"Wall, The" (Sexton), **Supp. II Part 2:** 696
Wallace, David Foster, **Retro. Supp. II:** 297; **Supp. X: 301–318**
Wallace, Henry, **I:** 489; **III:** 111, 475; **Supp. I Part 1:** 286; **Supp. I Part 2:** 645
Wallace, Mike, **Supp. IV Part 1:** 364; **Supp. IV Part 2:** 526
Wallace Stevens (Kermode), **Retro. Supp. I:** 301
Wallace Stevens: The Poems of our Climate (Bloom), **Retro. Supp. I:** 299
Wallace Stevens: Words Chosen out of Desire (Stevens), **Retro. Supp. I:** 297
Wallach, Eli, **III:** 161
Wallas, Graham, **Supp. I Part 2:** 643
"Walled City" (Oates), **Supp. II Part 2:** 524
Wallenstein, Anna. *See* Weinstein, Mrs. Max (Anna Wallenstein)
Waller, Edmund, **III:** 463
Waller, Fats, **IV:** 263
Walling, William English, **Supp. I Part 2:** 645
Walls Do Not Fall, The (Doolittle), **Supp. I Part 1:** 271, 272
"Wall Songs" (Hogan), **Supp. IV Part 1:** 413
Wall Writing (Auster), **Supp. XII:** 23–24
Walpole, Horace, **I:** 203; **Supp. I Part 2:** 410, 714
Walpole, Hugh, **Retro. Supp. I:** 231
Walpole, Robert, **IV:** 145
Walsh, Ed, **II:** 424
Walsh, George, **Supp. IV Part 2:** 528
Walsh, Raoul, **Supp. XIII:** 174
Walsh, Richard J., **Supp. II Part 1:** 119, 130
Walsh, William, **Supp. IV Part 1:** 242, 243, 246, 248, 252, 254, 257
Walter Benjamin at the Dairy Queen: Reflections at Sixty and Beyond (McMurtry), **Supp. V:** 232
Walters, Marguerite. *See* Smith, Mrs. Lamar (Marguerite Walters)
"Walter T. Carriman" (O'Hara), **III:** 368
Walton, Izaak, **Supp. I Part 2:** 422
"Walt Whitman" (Masters), **Supp. I Part 2:** 458
"Walt Whitman at Bear Mountain" (Simpson), **Supp. IX:** 265
Walt Whitman Bathing (Wagoner), **Supp. IX: 331–332**
Walt Whitman Handbook (Allen), **IV:** 352
Walt Whitman Reconsidered (Chase), **IV:** 352
"Waltz, The" (Parker), **Supp. IX:** 204
"Waltzer in the House, The" (Kunitz), **Supp. III Part 1:** 258
Walzer, Kevin, **Supp. XII:** 202
Wambaugh, Joseph, **Supp. X:** 5
Wampeters, Foma, & Granfalloons (Vonnegut), **Supp. II Part 2:** 758, 759–760, 776, 779
Wand, David Hsin-fu, **Supp. X:** 292
"Wanderer, The" (W. C. Williams), **Retro. Supp. I:** 414, 421
"Wanderers, The" (Welty), **IV:** 273–274
"Wandering Jew, The" (Robinson), **III:** 505, 516–517
Wanderings of Oisin (Yeats), **Supp. I Part 1:** 79
Wang, Dorothy, **Supp. X:** 289
Waniek, Marilyn Nelson, **Supp. IV Part 1:** 244
"Wan Lee, the Pagan" (Harte), **Supp. II Part 1:** 351
Want, The (Olds), **Supp. X:** 210
Want Bone, The (Pinsky), **Supp. VI:** 236–237, 244–245, 247
"Wanted: An Ontological Critic" (Ransom), **III:** 498
"Wanting to Die" (Sexton), **Supp. II Part 2:** 684, 686
"Wants" (Paley), **Supp. VI:** 219
Waples, Dorothy, **I:** 348
Wapshot Chronicle, The (Cheever), **Supp. I Part 1:** 174, 177–180, 181, 196
Wapshot Scandal, The (Cheever), **Supp. I Part 1:** 180–184, 187, 191, 196
"War" (Kingston), **Supp. V:** 169
"War" (Simic), **Supp. VIII:** 282
"War, Response, and Contradiction" (Burke), **I:** 283
War and Peace (Tolstoy), **I:** 6, 7; **II:** 191, 205, 291; **IV:** 446; **Supp. V:** 277; **Supp. XI:** 68
War and War (F. Barthelme), **Supp. XI:** 25
"War Between Men and Women, The" (Thurber), **Supp. I Part 2:** 615
War Bulletins (Lindsay), **Supp. I Part 2:** 378–379
Ward, Aileen, **II:** 531
Ward, Artemus (pseudonym). *See* Browne, Charles Farrar
Ward, Douglas Turner, **Supp. IV Part 1:** 362
Ward, Henry, **Supp. I Part 2:** 588
Ward, Leo R., **Supp. VIII:** 124
Ward, Lester F., **Supp. I Part 2:** 640; **Supp. XI:** 202, 203
Ward, Lynn, **I:** 31
Ward, Mrs. Humphry, **II:** 338
Ward, Nathaniel, **Supp. I Part 1:** 99, 102, 111, 116
Ward, Theodora, **I:** 470; **Retro. Supp. I:** 28

Ward, William Hayes, **Supp. I Part 1:** 371
"War Debt, A" (Jewett), **Retro. Supp. II:** 138, 141
"War Diary, A" (Bourne), **I:** 229
War Dispatches of Stephen Crane, The (Crane), **I:** 422
"Ward Line, The" (Morris), **III:** 220
Warfel, Harry R., **Supp. I Part 1:** 366
War Games (Morris), **III:** 238
War in Heaven, The (Shepard and Chaikin), **Supp. III Part 2:** 433
War Is Kind (Crane), **I:** 409; **III:** 585
"War Is Kind" (Crane), **I:** 419
Warlock (Harrison), **Supp. VIII:** 45, **46**
Warner, Charles Dudley, **II:** 405; **IV:** 198
Warner, Jack, **Supp. XII:** 160–161
Warner, John R., **III:** 193
Warner, Oliver, **I:** 548
Warner, Susan, **Retro. Supp. I:** 246
Warner, Sylvia Townsend, **Supp. VIII:** 151, 155, 164, 171
Warner, W. Lloyd, **III:** 60
"Warning" (Hughes), **Supp. I Part 1:** 343
"Warning" (Pound), **III:** 474
"Warning, The" (Creeley), **Supp. IV Part 1:** 150
"Warning, The" (Longfellow), **II:** 498
Warning Hill (Marquand), **III:** 55–56, 60, 68
"War of Eyes, A" (Coleman), **Supp. XI:** 93–94
War of Eyes and Other Stories, A (Coleman), **Supp. XI: 91–92**
War of the Classes (London), **II:** 466
"War of the Wall, The" (Bambara), **Supp. XI:** 15–16
"War Poems" (Sandburg), **III:** 581
Warren, Austin, **I:** 265, 268, 271; **Supp. I Part 2:** 423
Warren, Earl, **III:** 581
Warren, Gabriel, **IV:** 244
Warren, Mrs. Robert Penn (Eleanor Clark), **IV:** 244
Warren, Robert Penn, **I:** 190, 211, 517; **II:** 57, 217, 228, 253; **III:** 134, 310, 382–383, 454, 482, 485, 490, 496, 497; **IV:** 121, 122, 123, 125, 126, **236–259**, 261, 262, 279, 340–341, 458; **Retro. Supp. I:** 40, 41, 73, 90; **Retro. Supp. II:** 220, 235; **Supp. I Part 1:** 359, 371; **Supp. I Part 2:** 386, 423; **Supp. II Part 1:** 139; **Supp. III Part 2:** 542; **Supp. V:** 261, 316, 318, 319, 333; **Supp. VIII:** 126, 176; **Supp. IX:** 257; **Supp. X:** 1, 25, 26; **Supp. XI:** 315; **Supp. XII:** 254, 255
Warren, Rosanna, **IV:** 244
Warrington Poems, The (Ríos), **Supp. IV Part 2:** 540
Warrior, Robert Allen, **Supp. IV Part 1:** 329
"Warrior, The" (Gunn Allen), **Supp. IV Part 1:** 326
"Warrior: 5th Grade" (Olds), **Supp. X:** 214
"Warrior Road" (Harjo), **Supp. XII:** 217
Warshavsky, Isaac (pseudonym). *See* Singer, Isaac Bashevis
Warshow, Robert, **Supp. I Part 1:** 51
Wars I Have Seen (Stein), **IV:** 27, 36, 477
Wartime (Fussell), **Supp. V:** 241
"War Widow, The" (Frederic), **II:** 135–136
"Was" (Creeley), **Supp. IV Part 1:** 155
"Was" (Faulkner), **II:** 71
"Wash" (Faulkner), **II:** 72
Wash, Richard, **Supp. XII:** 14
"Washed in the Rain" (Fante), **Supp. XI:** 165
Washington, Booker T., **Supp. I Part 2:** 393; **Supp. II Part 1:** 157, 160, 167, 168, 171, 225
Washington, D.C. (Vidal), **Supp. IV Part 2:** 677, 684, 686–687, 690
Washington, George, **I:** 453; **II:** 313–314; **Supp. I Part 2:** 399, 485, 508, 509, 511, 513, 517, 518, 520, 599
Washington Post Book World (Lesser), **Supp. IV Part 2:** 453; **Supp. VIII:** 80, 84, 241; **Supp. X:** 282
Washington Square (James), **II:** 327, 328; **Retro. Supp. I:** 215, 220, **222–223**
"Washington Square, 1946" (Ozick), **Supp. V:** 272
Washington Square Ensemble, The (Bell), **Supp. X:** 1, **3–4**
"Was Lowell an Historical Critic?" (Altick), **Supp. I Part 2:** 423
Wasserman, Earl R., **Supp. I Part 2:** 439, 440
Wasserman, Jakob, **Supp. I Part 2:** 669
Wasserstein, Wendy, **Supp. IV Part 1:** 309
Wasson, Ben, **Retro. Supp. I:** 79, 83
"Waste Carpet, The" (Matthews), **Supp. IX: 158–159**
Waste Land, The (Eliot), **I:** 107, 266, 298, 395, 396, 482, 570–571, 572, 574–575, 577–578, 580, 581, 584, 585, 586, 587; **III:** 6–8, 12, 196, 277–278, 453, 471, 492, 586; **IV:** 122, 123, 124, 140, 418, 419, 420; **Retro. Supp. I:** 51, 60, **60–62**, 63, 64, 66, 210, 290, 291, 299, 311, 420, 427; **Retro. Supp. II:** 85, 121, 190, 282; **Supp. I Part 1:** 272; **Supp. I Part 2:** 439, 455, 614; **Supp. II Part 1:** 4, 5, 11, 96; **Supp. III Part 1:** 9, 10, 41, 63, 105; **Supp. IV Part 1:** 47, 284; **Supp. V:** 338; **Supp. IX:** 158, 305; **Supp. X:** 125; **Supp. XIII:** 341–342, 344, 346
"Waste Land, The": A Facsimile and Transcript of the Original Drafts Including the Annotations of Ezra Pound (Eliot, ed.), **Retro. Supp. I:** 58
Watch and Ward (James), **II:** 323; **Retro. Supp. I:** 218, **219**, 220
"Watcher, The" (Bly), **Supp. IV Part 1:** 71
"Watcher by the Dead, A" (Bierce), **I:** 203
Watchfires (Auchincloss), **Supp. IV Part 1:** 23
"Watching Crow, Looking toward the Manzano Mountains" (Harjo), **Supp. XII:** 219
"Watching the Sunset" (Coleman), **Supp. XI:** 92
Watch on the Rhine (Hellman), **Supp. I Part 1:** 276, 278, 279–281, 283–284; **Supp. IV Part 1:** 83
"Water" (Emerson), **II:** 19
"Water" (Komunyakaa), **Supp. XIII:** 132
"Water" (Lowell), **II:** 550
"Waterbird" (Swenson), **Supp. IV Part 2:** 651
"Water Borders" (Dillard), **Supp. VI:** 27
"Water Buffalo" (Komunyakaa), **Supp. XIII:** 122
"Watercolor of Grantchester Meadows" (Plath), **Supp. I Part 2:** 537
"Waterfall, The" (Clampitt), **Supp. IX:** 44
Waterhouse, Keith, **Supp. VIII:** 124
"Waterlily Fire" (Rukeyser), **Supp. VI:** 285, 286
Waterlily Fire: Poems 1935–1962 (Rukeyser), **Supp. VI:** 274, 283, 285
Watermark (Brodsky), **Supp. VIII:** 29
Water-Method Man, The (Irving), **Supp. VI:** 163, **167–179**, 180
Water Music (Boyle), **Supp. VIII:** 1, 3–5, 8, 14
"Water Music for the Progress of Love in a Life-Raft Down the Sammamish Slough" (Wagoner), **Supp. IX:** 326

"Water Picture" (Swenson), **Supp. IV Part 2:** 641
"Water Rising" (Hogan), **Supp. IV Part 1:** 400
Waters, Ethel, **II:** 587
Waters, Frank, **Supp. X:** 124
Waters, Muddy, **Supp. VIII:** 345
"Watershed" (Kingsolver), **Supp. VII:** 208
"Watershed" (Warren), **IV:** 239
"Watershed, The" (Auden), **Supp. II Part 1:** 5
Waters of Siloe, The (Merton), **Supp. VIII:** 196, 208
Waterston, Sam, **Supp. IX:** 253
Water Street (Merrill), **Supp. III Part 1:** 321–323
"Water Walker" (Wilbur), **Supp. III Part 2:** 548, 560
Water-Witch, The (Cooper), **I:** 342–343
Waterworks, The (Doctorow), **Supp. IV Part 1:** 218, 222, 223, 231–233, 234
"Water Works, The" (Doctorow), **Supp. IV Part 1:** 234
Watkin, E. I., **Retro. Supp. II:** 187
Watkins, Floyd C., **IV:** 452
Watkins, James T., **I:** 193, 194
Watkins, Mel, **Supp. X:** 330; **Supp. XIII:** 246
Watrous, Peter, **Supp. VIII:** 79
Watson, J. B., **II:** 361
Watson, James Sibley, Jr., **I:** 261
Watson, Richard, **Supp. I Part 2:** 516, 517
Watson, William, **II:** 114
Watt, Ian, **Supp. VIII:** 4
Watteau, Jean Antoine, **III:** 275; **IV:** 79
Watts, Emily Stipes, **Supp. I Part 1:** 115
Waugh, Evelyn, **I:** 480; **III:** 281; **Supp. I Part 2:** 607; **Supp. IV Part 2:** 688; **Supp. XI:** 305, 306
"Wave" (Snyder), **Supp. VIII:** 299
Wave, A (Ashbery), **Supp. III Part 1:** 1, 4, 24–26
"Wave, A" (Ashbery), **Supp. III Part 1:** 9, 19, 24–25
"Wave, The" (MacLeish), **III:** 19
"Waxwings" (Francis), **Supp. IX:** 82
Way, The (Steiner and Witt, eds.), **Supp. IV Part 2:** 505
"Way Down, The" (Kunitz), **Supp. III Part 1:** 263
"Way It Is, The" (Ellison), **Supp. II Part 1:** 245
"Way It Is, The" (Jones), **Supp. XI:** 229

Way It Is, The (Stafford), **Supp. XIII:** 274
"Way It Is, The" (Strand), **Supp. IV Part 2:** 627
Wayne, John, **Supp. IV Part 1:** 200
Way of Chuang-Tzu, The (Merton), **Supp. VIII:** 208
"Way of Exchange in James Dickey's Poetry, The" (Weatherby), **Supp. IV Part 1:** 175
Way Out, A (Frost), **Retro. Supp. I:** 133
Wayside Motor Inn, The (Gurney), **Supp. V:** 96, 105, 109
Ways of the Hour, The (Cooper), **I:** 354
Ways of White Folks, The (Hughes), **Retro. Supp. I:** 203, 204; **Supp. I Part 1:** 329, 330, 332
Way Some People Die, The (Macdonald), **Supp. IV Part 2:** 470, 471, 472, 474
Way Some People Live, The (Cheever), **Supp. I Part 1:** 175
"Way the Cards Fall, The" (Komunyakaa), **Supp. XIII:** 117
Way to Rainy Mountain, The (Momaday), **Supp. IV Part 2:** 485–486, 487–489, 491, 493
Way to Wealth, The (Franklin), **II:** 101–102, 110
Wayward and the Seeking, The: A Collection of Writings by Jean Toomer (Toomer), **Supp. III Part 2:** 478–481, 484, 487
Wayward Bus, The (Steinbeck), **IV:** 51, 64–65
"Way We Live Now, The" (Sontag), **Supp. III Part 2:** 467–468
"Way You'll Never Be, A" (Hemingway), **II:** 249
Weaks, Mary Louise, **Supp. X:** 5
Weales, Gerald, **II:** 602
"Wealth," from *Conduct of Life, The* (Emerson), **II:** 2, 3–4
"Wealth," from *English Traits* (Emerson), **II:** 6
Wealth of Nations, The (A. Smith), **II:** 109
"We Are Looking at You, Agnes" (Caldwell), **I:** 309
"We Are the Crazy Lady and Other Feisty Feminist Fables" (Ozick), **Supp. V:** 259
Weary Blues, The (Hughes), **Retro. Supp. I:** 195, 197, 198, 199, 200, 203, 205; **Supp. I Part 1:** 325
"Weary Blues, The" (Hughes), **Retro. Supp. I:** 198, 199; **Supp. I Part 1:** 324, 325

"Weary Kingdom" (Irving), **Supp. VI:** 163
Weatherby, H. L., **Supp. IV Part 1:** 175
"Weathering Out" (Dove), **Supp. IV Part 1:** 248
Weaver, Harriet, **III:** 471
Weaver, Mike, **Retro. Supp. I:** 430
"Weaving" (Larcom), **Supp. XIII:** 142, 144–145, 150, 151
"Web" (Oliver), **Supp. VII:** 236
Web and the Rock, The (Wolfe), **IV:** 451, 455, 457, 459–460, 462, 464, 467, 468
Webb, Beatrice, **Supp. I Part 1:** 5
Webb, Mary, **I:** 226
Webb, Sidney, **Supp. I Part 1:** 5
Webb, W. P., **Supp. V:** 225
Weber, Brom, **I:** 383, 386
Weber, Carl, **Supp. IX:** 133, 138, 141
Weber, Max, **I:** 498; **Supp. I Part 2:** 637, 648
Weber, Sarah, **Supp. I Part 1:** 2
Web of Earth, The (Wolfe), **IV:** 451–452, 456, 458, 464, 465
"Web of Life, The" (Nemerov), **III:** 282
Webster, Daniel, **II:** 5, 9; **Supp. I Part 2:** 659, 687, 689, 690
Webster, John, **I:** 384; **Supp. I Part 2:** 422
Webster, Noah, **Supp. I Part 2:** 660; **Supp. II Part 1:** 77
Wector, Dixon, **II:** 103
"Wedding Cake" (Nye), **Supp. XIII:** 283
"Wedding in Brownsville, A" (Singer), **IV:** 15
Wedding in Hell, A (Simic), **Supp. VIII:** 280, **282**
"Wedding of the Rose and Lotus, The" (Lindsay), **Supp. I Part 2:** 387
"Wedding Toast, A" (Wilbur), **Supp. III Part 2:** 561
Wedekind, Frank, **III:** 398
Wedge, The (W. C. Williams), **Retro. Supp. I:** 424
"Wednesday at the Waldorf" (Swenson), **Supp. IV Part 2:** 647
"We Don't Live Here Anymore" (Dubus), **Supp. VII:** 78–79, 85
"Weed, The" (Bishop), **Supp. I Part 1:** 80, 88–89
"Weeds, The" (McCarthy), **II:** 566
"Weekend" (Beattie), **Supp. V:** 27
Weekend, The (Cameron), **Supp. XII:** 80, 81, **86–88**
"Weekend at Ellerslie, A" (Wilson), **IV:** 431
Weekend Edition (National Public

Radio), **Supp. IX:** 299
Week on the Concord and Merrimack Rivers, A (Thoreau), **IV:** 168, 169, 177, 182–183; **Supp. I Part 2:** 420
Weeks, Edward, **III:** 64
Weeks, Jerome, **Supp. VIII:** 76
"Weeping Burgher" (Stevens), **IV:** 77
"Weeping Women" (Levertov), **Supp. III Part 1:** 282
We Fly Away (Francis), **Supp. IX:** 79–80, 84
We Have Always Lived in the Castle (Jackson), **Supp. IX:** 121, 126, **127–128**
"We Have Our Arts So We Won't Die of Truth" (Bradbury), **Supp. IV Part 1:** 105
Weich, Dave, **Supp. XII:** 321
"Weight" (Wideman), **Supp. X:** 321
Weigl, Bruce, **Supp. VIII:** 269, 274
Weil, Robert, **Supp. IX:** 236
Weil, Simone, **I:** 298
Weiland (C. B. Brown), **Supp. XIII:** 100
Weinberger, Eliot, **Supp. IV Part 1:** 66; **Supp. VIII:** 290, 292
Weininger, Otto, **Retro. Supp. I:** 416
Weinreb, Mindy, **Supp. X:** 24
Weinstein, Hinda, **IV:** 285
Weinstein, Max, **IV:** 285
Weinstein, Mrs. Max (Anna Wallenstein), **IV:** 285, 287
Weinstein, Nathan. *See* West, Nathanael
Weisheit, Rabbi, **IV:** 76
Weismuller, Johnny, **Supp. X:** 264
Weiss, Peter, **IV:** 117
Weiss, Theodore, **Supp. IV Part 2:** 440; **Supp. IX:** 96
Weist, Dianne, **Supp. X:** 80
Weithas, Art, **Supp. XI:** 231
Welch, James, **Supp. IV Part 1:** 404; **Supp. IV Part 2:** 503, 513, 557, 562
Welch, Lew, **Supp. V:** 170; **Supp. VIII:** 303
"Welcome from War" (Rukeyser), **Supp. VI:** 286
"Welcome Morning" (Sexton), **Supp. II Part 2:** 696
"Welcome the Wrath" (Kunitz), **Supp. III Part 1:** 261
Welcome to Hard Times (Doctorow), **Supp. IV Part 1:** 218, 219–220, 222, 224, 230, 238
Welcome to Hard Times (film), **Supp. IV Part 1:** 236
Welcome to Our City (Wolfe), **IV:** 461
Welcome to the Monkey House (Vonnegut), **Supp. II Part 2:** 758

Weld, Theodore, **Supp. I Part 2:** 587, 588
Weld, Tuesday, **Supp. XI:** 306
Welded (O'Neill), **III:** 390
"Well, The" (Momaday), **Supp. IV Part 2:** 483
"Well Dressed Man with a Beard, The" (Stevens), **Retro. Supp. I:** 297
Wellek, René, **I:** 253, 261, 282; **II:** 320
Weller, George, **III:** 322
Welles, Gideon, **Supp. I Part 2:** 484
Welles, Orson, **IV:** 476; **Supp. I Part 1:** 67; **Supp. IV Part 1:** 82, 83; **Supp. V:** 251; **Supp. VIII:** 46; **Supp. XI:** 169, 307
"Wellfleet Whale, The" (Kunitz), **Supp. III Part 1:** 263, 269
Wellfleet Whale and Companion Poems, The (Kunitz), **Supp. III Part 1:** 263
Wellman, Flora, **II:** 463–464, 465
"Well Rising, The" (Stafford), **Supp. XI:** 318
Wells, H. G., **I:** 103, 226, 241, 243, 253, 405, 409, 415; **II:** 82, 144, 276, 337, 338, 458; **III:** 456; **IV:** 340, 455; **Retro. Supp. I:** 100, 228, 231
Wellspring, The (Olds), **Supp. X:** 211–212
Welsh, Mary. *See* Hemingway, Mrs. Ernest (Mary Welsh)
Welty, Eudora, **II:** 194, 217, 606; **IV:** 260–284; **Retro. Supp. I:** 339–358; **Retro. Supp. II:** 235; **Supp. IV Part 2:** 474; **Supp. V:** 59, 315, 336; **Supp. VIII:** 94, 151, 171; **Supp. X:** 42, 290; **Supp. XII:** 310, 322
"We miss Her, not because We see—" (Dickinson), **Retro. Supp. I:** 46
We Must Dance My Darlings (Trilling), **Supp. I Part 1:** 297
Wendell, Barrett, **III:** 507; **Supp. I Part 2:** 414
Wendell, Sarah. *See* Holmes, Mrs. Abiel (Sarah Wendell)
Wept of Wish-ton-Wish, The (Cooper), **I:** 339, 342, 350
Werbe, Peter, **Supp. XIII:** 236
"We Real Cool" (Brooks), **Supp. III Part 1:** 80
"We're Friends Again" (O'Hara), **III:** 372–373
"Were the Whole Realm of Nature Mine" (Watts), **I:** 458
Werewolves in Their Youth (Chabon), **Supp. XI:** 66, **76–77**
Werlock, Abby, **Supp. XIII:** 293
Werthman, Michael, **Supp. V:** 115
"Wer-Trout, The" (Proulx), **Supp. VII:** 255–256

Wescott, Glenway, **I:** 288; **II:** 85; **III:** 448, 454; **Supp. VIII:** 156
"We Shall All Be Born Again But We Shall Not All Be Saved" (Matthews), **Supp. IX:** 162
West, Anthony, **Supp. IV Part 1:** 284
West, Benjamin, **Supp. I Part 2:** 511
West, Dorothy, **Supp. XIII:** 295
West, James, **II:** 562
West, Nathanael, **I:** 97, 107, 190, 211, 298; **II:** 436; **III:** 357, 425; **IV:** **285–307**; **Retro. Supp. II:** **339–359**; **Supp. IV Part 1:** 203; **Supp. VIII:** 97; **Supp. XI:** 85, 105, 159, 296; **Supp. XII:** 173, 310; **Supp. XIII:** 106, 170
West, Rebecca, **II:** 412, 445
Westall, Julia Elizabeth. *See* Wolfe, Mrs. William Oliver (Julia Elizabeth Westall)
"We Stand United" (Benét), **Supp. XI:** 46
"West Authentic, The: Willa Cather" (Stegner), **Supp. IV Part 2:** 608
"West Coast, The: Region with a View" (Stegner), **Supp. IV Part 2:** 608–609
Westcott, Edward N., **II:** 102
"Western Association of Writers" (Chopin), **Supp. I Part 1:** 217
"Western Ballad, A" (Ginsberg), **Supp. II Part 1:** 311
Western Borders, The (Howe), **Supp. IV Part 2:** 424–425
Western Canon: The Books and Schools of the Ages (Bloom), **Supp. IX:** 146
Western Lands, The (Burroughs), **Supp. III Part 1:** 106
Western Star (Benét), **Supp. XI:** 46, 47, 57
"West Marginal Way" (Hugo), **Supp. VI:** 131, 135
West of Yesterday, East of Summer: New and Selected Poems, 1973–1993 (Monette), **Supp. X:** 159
West of Your City (Stafford), **Supp. XI:** 316, **317–318,** 321, 322
Weston, Jessie L., **II:** 540; **III:** 12; **Supp. I Part 2:** 438
"West Real" (Ríos), **Supp. IV Part 2:** 539, 540
"West-running Brook" (Frost), **II:** 150, 162–164
West-running Brook (Frost), **II:** 155; **Retro. Supp. I:** 136, 137
"West Wall" (Merwin), **Supp. III Part 1:** 355
"Westward Beach, A" (Jeffers), **Supp. II Part 2:** 418

Westward Ho (Harrison), **Supp. VIII:** 51, **52**

Westward the Course of Empire (Leutze), **Supp. X:** 307

"Westward the Course of Empire Takes Its Way" (Wallace), **Supp. X: 307–308**

"West Wind" (Oliver), **Supp. VII:** 246

West Wind: Poems and Prose Poems (Oliver), **Supp. VII:** 243, 246–248

"West Wind, The" (Bryant), **Supp. I Part 1:** 155

"Wet Casements" (Ashbery), **Supp. III Part 1:** 18–20

We the Living (film), **Supp. IV Part 2:** 520

We the Living (Rand), **Supp. IV Part 2:** 520–521

Wet Parade (Sinclair), **Supp. V:** 289

"We've Adjusted Too Well" (O'Brien), **Supp. V:** 247

Wevill, David, **Retro. Supp. II:** 247, 249

"We Wear the Mask" (Dunbar), **Supp. II Part 1:** 199, 207, 209–210

Weybright, Victor, **Supp. XIII:** 172

Weyden, Rogier van der, **Supp. IV Part 1:** 284

Whalen, Marcella, **Supp. I Part 1:** 49

Whalen, Philip, **Supp. VIII:** 289

Whalen-Bridge, John, **Retro. Supp. II:** 211–212

Wharton, Edith, **I:** 12, 375; **II:** 96, 180, 183, 186, 189–190, 193, 283, 338, 444, 451; **III:** 69, 175, 576; **IV:** 8, 53, 58, **308–330; Retro. Supp. I:** 108, 232, **359–385; Supp. IV Part 1:** 23, 31, 35, 36, 80, 81, 310; **Supp. IX:** 57; **Supp. XII:** 308

Wharton, Edward Robbins, **IV:** 310, 313–314, 319

"What" (Dunn), **Supp. XI:** 144

What a Kingdom It Was (Kinnell), **Supp. III Part 1:** 235, 238, 239

"What America Would Be Like without Blacks" (Ellison), **Retro. Supp. II:** 123

What Are Masterpieces (Stein), **IV:** 30–31

What Are Years (Moore), **III:** 208–209, 210, 215

"What Are Years?" (Moore), **III:** 211, 213

What a Way to Go (Morris), **III:** 230–232

"What Became of the Flappers?" (Zelda Fitzgerald), **Supp. IX:** 71

"What Can I Tell My Bones?" (Roethke), **III:** 546, 549

"What Do We Have Here" (Carson), **Supp. XII: 101**

"What Do We See" (Rukeyser), **Supp. VI:** 282

What Do Women Want? Bread Roses Sex Power (Jong), **Supp. V:** 115, 117, 129, 130

"What Do You Do in San Francisco?" (Carver), **Supp. III Part 1:** 143

Whatever Happened to Gloomy Gus of the Chicago Bears? (Coover), **Supp. V:** 51, 52

Whatever Happened to Jacy Farrow? (Cleveland), **Supp. V:** 222

"What Every Boy Should Know" (Maxwell), **Supp. VIII:** 169

"What Feels Like the World" (Bausch), **Supp. VII:** 46

"What God Is Like to Him I Serve" (Bradstreet), **Supp. I Part 1:** 106–107

"What Happened Here Before" (Snyder), **Supp. VIII:** 302

What Have I Ever Lost by Dying? (Bly), **Supp. IV Part 1:** 71–72

What Have You Lost? (Nye, ed.), **Supp. XIII:** 280

"What I Believe" (Mumford), **Supp. II Part 2:** 479

"What I Call What They Call Onanism" (Goldbarth), **Supp. XII:** 175

What I Did Last Summer (Gurney), **Supp. V:** 96, 100, 107, 108

"What if God" (Olds), **Supp. X:** 208

"What I Have to Defend, What I Can't Bear Losing" (Stern), **Supp. IX:** 286, 287, 288, 298

"What I Know about Being a Playwright" (McNally), **Supp. XIII:** 195, 207

"What I Mean" (Ortiz), **Supp. IV Part 2:** 497

"What Is an Emotion" (James), **II:** 350

What Is Art? (Tolstoy), **I:** 58

"What Is Civilization? Africa's Answer" (Du Bois), **Supp. II Part 1:** 176

"What Is College For?" (Bourne), **I:** 216

"What Is Exploitation?" (Bourne), **I:** 216

What Is Found There: Notebooks on Poetry and Politics (Rich), **Retro. Supp. II:** 292

"What Is It?" (Carver), **Supp. III Part 1:** 139

What Is Man? (Twain), **II:** 434; **IV:** 209

"What Is Poetry" (Ashbery), **Supp. III Part 1:** 19

"What Is Seized" (Moore), **Supp. X:** 164, 168, 169, 172, 175

"What Is the Earth?" (Olds), **Supp. X:** 213

"What Is This Poet" (Stern), **Supp. IX:** 295

"What I Think" (Hogan), **Supp. IV Part 1:** 406

What Maisie Knew (James), **II:** 332; **Retro. Supp. I:** 229, **230**

What Makes Sammy Run? (Schulberg), **Supp. XIII:** 170

What Moon Drove Me to This? (Harjo), **Supp. XII: 218–220**

"What Must" (MacLeish), **III:** 18

"What Sally Said" (Cisneros), **Supp. VII:** 63

"What's Happening in America" (Sontag), **Supp. III Part 2:** 460–461

"What's in Alaska?" (Carver), **Supp. III Part 1:** 141, 143

What's New, Pussycat? (Allen; film), **Supp. XI:** 307

"What's New in American and Canadian Poetry" (Bly), **Supp. IV Part 1:** 67

What's O'Clock (Lowell), **II:** 511, 527, 528

"What the Arts Need Now" (Baraka), **Supp. II Part 1:** 47

"What the Brand New Freeway Won't Go By" (Hugo), **Supp. VI:** 132–133

"What the Gypsies Told My Grandmother While She Was Still a Young Girl" (Simic), **Supp. VIII:** 283

"What the Prose Poem Carries with It" (Bly), **Supp. IV Part 1:** 64

"What They Wanted" (Dunn), **Supp. XI:** 151

What Thou Lovest Well (Hugo), **Supp. VI:** 140, 141

"What Thou Lovest Well Remains American" (Hugo), **Supp. VI:** 140, 141

What Time Collects (Farrell), **II:** 46, 47–48

What to Do? (Chernyshevsky), **Retro. Supp. I:** 269

What Use Are Flowers? (Hansberry), **Supp. IV Part 1:** 359, 368–369, 374

What Was Literature? (Fiedler), **Supp. XIII:** 96–97, **105–106**

What Was Mine (Beattie), **Supp. V:** 33, 35

What Was the Relationship of the Lone Ranger to the Means of Production? (Baraka), **Supp. II Part 1:** 58

"What We Came Through" (Goldbarth), **Supp. XII:** 179–180

What We Talk About When We Talk

About Love (Carver), **Supp. III Part 1:** 142–146
What We Talk about When We Talk about Love (Carver), **Supp. XII:** 139
"What Why When How Who" (Pinsky), **Supp. VI:** 244
What Will Suffice: Contemporary American Poets on the Art of Poetry (Buckley and Young, eds.), **Supp. XIII:** 313
What Work Is (Levine), **Supp. V:** 181, 187, 192–193
"What You Hear from Em" (Taylor), **Supp. V:** 314, 320, 324
"What You Want" (O. Henry), **Supp. II Part 1:** 402
Wheatly, Phyllis, **Supp. XIII:** 111
Wheeler, John, **II:** 433
Wheelock, John Hall, **IV:** 461; **Supp. IX:** 268
Wheel of Life, The (Glasgow), **II:** 176, 178, 179, 183
"When" (Olds), **Supp. X:** 207
When Boyhood Dreams Come True (Farrell), **II:** 45
"When Death Came April Twelve 1945" (Sandburg), **III:** 591, 593
"When Death Comes" (Oliver), **Supp. VII:** 241
"When De Co'n Pone's Hot" (Dunbar), **Supp. II Part 1:** 202–203
"When Grandma Died—1942" (Shields), **Supp. VII:** 311
"When I Buy Pictures" (Moore), **III:** 205
"When I Came from Colchis" (Merwin), **Supp. III Part 1:** 343
"When I Left Business for Literature" (Anderson), **I:** 101
"When in Rome—Apologia" (Komunyakaa), **Supp. XIII:** 120
"When It Comes" (Olds), **Supp. X:** 213
"When I Was Seventeen" (Kincaid), **Supp. VII:** 181
When Knighthood Was in Flower (Major), **III:** 320
"[When] Let by rain" (Taylor), **IV:** 160–161
"When Lilacs Last in the Dooryard Bloom'd" (Whitman), **IV:** 347–348, 351; **Retro. Supp. I:** 406; **Supp. IV Part 1:** 16
"When Malindy Sings" (Dunbar), **Supp. II Part 1:** 200, 204–205
When She Was Good (Roth), **Retro. Supp. II:** 300, 301, 302; **Supp. III Part 2:** 403, 405, 410–413
"When Sue Wears Red" (Hughes), **Retro. Supp. I:** 195, 204
"When the Dead Ask My Father about Me" (Olds), **Supp. X:** 210
"When the Frost Is on the Punkin" (Riley), **Supp. II Part 1:** 202
When the Jack Hollers (Hughes), **Retro. Supp. I:** 203; **Supp. I Part 1:** 328
"When the Light Gets Green" (Warren), **IV:** 252
"When the Peace Corps Was Young" (Theroux), **Supp. VIII:** 314
"When the World Ended as We Knew It" (Harjo), **Supp. XII:** 231
When Time Was Born (Farrell), **II:** 46, 47
"When We Dead Awaken: Writing as Re-Vision" (Rich), **Supp. I Part 2:** 552–553, 560
"When We Gonna Rise" (Baraka), **Supp. II Part 1:** 48
"When We Have To" (Salinas), **Supp. XIII:** 322–323
"WHEN WE'LL WORSHIP JESUS" (Baraka), **Supp. II Part 1:** 54
"When Women Throw Down Bundles: Strong Women Make Strong Nations" (Gunn Allen), **Supp. IV Part 1:** 328
"'When You Finally See Them': The Unconquered Eye in *To Kill a Mockingbird*" (Champion), **Supp. VIII:** 128
"When You Lie Down, the Sea Stands Up" (Swenson), **Supp. IV Part 2:** 643
Where Does One Go When There's No Place Left to Go? (Crews), **Supp. XI:** 103
"Where I Come from Is Like This" (Gunn Allen), **Supp. IV Part 1:** 319
"Where I'm Calling From" (Carver), **Supp. III Part 1:** 145
Where I'm Calling From: New and Selected Stories (Carver), **Supp. III Part 1:** 138, 148
"Where I Ought to Be" (Erdrich), **Supp. IV Part 1:** 265
Where Is My Wandering Boy Tonight? (Wagoner), **Supp. IX:** 335–336
"Where Is the Island?" (Francis), **Supp. IX:** 78
"Where Is the Voice Coming From?" (Welty), **IV:** 280; **Retro. Supp. I:** 355
"Where Knock Is Open Wide" (Roethke), **III:** 533–535
"Where My Sympathy Lies" (H. Roth), **Supp. IX:** 234
Where the Bluebird Sings to the Lemonade Springs (Stegner), **Supp. IV Part 2:** 596, 597, 598, 600, 604, 606, 613
Where the Cross Is Made (O'Neill), **III:** 388, 391
"Where the Soft Air Lives" (Nye), **Supp. XIII:** 275
Where the Twilight Never Ends (Haines), **Supp. XII:** 211
Where the Wild Things Are (Sendak), **Supp. IX:** 207
"Wherever Home Is" (Wright), **Supp. III Part 2:** 605, 606
Where Water Comes Together With Other Water (Carver), **Supp. III Part 1:** 147, 148
"Where We Crashed" (Hugo), **Supp. VI:** 138
"Where You Are" (Doty), **Supp. XI:** 131
Where You'll Find Me, and Other Stories (Beattie), **Supp. V:** 30–31
Whicher, Stephen, **II:** 20
"Which Is More Than I Can Say for Some People" (Moore), **Supp. X:** 177, 178
Which Ones Are the Enemy? (Garrett), **Supp. VII:** 98
"Which Theatre Is the Absurd One?" (Albee), **I:** 71
"Which Way to the Future?" (Rehder), **Supp. IV Part 1:** 69
While I Was Gone (S. Miller), **Supp. XII:** 290, **301–303**
"While Seated in a Plane" (Swenson), **Supp. IV Part 2:** 645
Whilomville Stories (Crane), **I:** 414
"Whip, The" (Robinson), **III:** 513
Whipple, Thomas K., **II:** 456, 458; **IV:** 427
"Whippoorwill, The" (Francis), **Supp. IX:** 90
"Whip-poor-will, The" (Thurber), **Supp. I Part 2:** 616
"Whispering Gallery, The" (Komunyakaa), **Supp. XIII:** 132
"Whispering Leaves" (Glasgow), **II:** 190
Whispering to Fool the Wind (Ríos), **Supp. IV Part 2:** 540–541, 544, 545
"Whispers in the Next Room" (Simic), **Supp. VIII:** 278
"Whispers of Heavenly Death" (Whitman), **IV:** 348
"Whispers of Immortality" (Eliot), **Supp. XI:** 242
Whistle (Jones), **Supp. XI:** 219, 224, **231–234**
"Whistle, The" (Franklin), **II:** 121
"Whistle, The" (Komunyakaa), **Supp.**

XIII: 111, 126
"Whistle, The" (Welty), **IV:** 262
Whistler, James, **I:** 484; **III:** 461, 465, 466; **IV:** 77, 369
"Whistling Dick's Christmas Stocking" (O. Henry), **Supp. II Part 1:** 390, 392
Whistling in the Dark (Garrett), **Supp. VII:** 111
Whistling in the Dark: True Stories and Other Fables (Garrett), **Supp. VII:** 95
Whitcher, Frances Miriam Berry, **Supp. XIII:** 152
"White" (Simic), **Supp. VIII:** 275–276
White, Barbara, **Retro. Supp. I:** 379
White, E. B., **Retro. Supp. I:** 335; **Supp. I Part 2:** 602, 607, 608, 612, 619, 620, **651–681; Supp. II Part 1:** 143; **Supp. VIII:** 171; **Supp. IX:** 20, 32
White, Elizabeth Wade, **Supp. I Part 1:** 100, 103, 111
White, Henry Kirke, **Supp. I Part 1:** 150
White, James L., **Supp. XI:** 123
White, Joel, **Supp. I Part 2:** 654, 678
White, Katharine. (Katharine Sergeant Angell), **Supp. I Part 2:** 610, 653, 655, 656, 669; **Supp. VIII:** 151, 171
White, Lillian, **Supp. I Part 2:** 651
White, Lucia, **I:** 258
White, Maria. *See* Lowell, Mrs. James Russell (Maria White)
White, Morton, **I:** 258; **Supp. I Part 2:** 647, 648, 650
White, Roberta, **Supp. XII:** 293
White, Stanford, **Supp. IV Part 1:** 223
White, Stanley, **Supp. I Part 2:** 651, 655
White, T. H., **III:** 522
White, T. W., **III:** 411, 415
White, Walter, **Supp. I Part 1:** 345
White, William, **Retro. Supp. II:** 344
White, William A., **I:** 252
White Album, The (Didion), **Supp. IV Part 1:** 198, 202, 205–207, 210
"White Album, The" (Didion), **Supp. IV Part 1:** 205, 206
White Buildings (H. Crane), **I:** 385, 386, 390–395, 400; **Retro. Supp. II:** 77–78, **80–81,** 82, 83, 85
White Butterfly (Mosley), **Supp. XIII:** 237, 238, 240
White Center (Hugo), **Supp. VI:** 144–145
"White Center" (Hugo), **Supp. VI:** 144, 146
Whited, Stephen, **Supp. XI:** 135
White Deer, The (Thurber), **Supp. I Part 2:** 606
"White Eagle, The" (Chopin), **Retro. Supp. II:** 72
White Fang (London), **II:** 471–472, 481
Whitefield, George, **I:** 546
White-Footed Deer and Other Poems (Bryant), **Supp. I Part 1:** 157
White Goddess, The (Graves), **Supp. IV Part 1:** 280
White-Haired Lover (Shapiro), **Supp. II Part 2:** 703, 717
Whitehead, Alfred North, **III:** 605, 619, 620; **IV:** 88; **Supp. I Part 2:** 554, 647
Whitehead, Colson, **Supp. XIII:** 233, 241
Whitehead, Margaret, **IV:** 114, 115, 116
Whitehead, Mrs. Catherine, **IV:** 116
White Heat (Walsh), **Supp. XIII:** 174
"White Heron, A" (Jewett), **II:** 409; **Retro. Supp. II:** 17
White Heron and Other Stories, A (Jewett), **II:** 396
White Horses (Hoffman), **Supp. X:** 83–85, 90, 92
White House Diary, A (Lady Bird Johnson), **Supp. IV Part 1:** 22
White Jacket; or, The World in a Man-of-War (Melville), **III:** 80, 81, 84, 94; **Retro Supp. I:** 248, 249, 254
"White Lights, The" (Robinson), **III:** 524
"White Lilies, The" (Glück), **Supp. V:** 88
White Man, Listen! (Wright), **IV:** 478, 488, 489, 494
"White Mulberry Tree, The" (Cather), **I:** 319; **Retro. Supp. I:** 7, 9, 17
White Mule (W. C. Williams), **Retro. Supp. I:** 423
"White Negro, The" (Mailer), **III:** 36–37; **Retro. Supp. II:** 202
"Whiteness of the Whale, The" (Melville), **III:** 84, 86
"White Night" (Oliver), **Supp. VII:** 236
"White Nights" (Auster), **Supp. XII:** 23–24
White Noise (DeLillo), **Supp. VI:** 1, 3–4, 5–7, 10, 11–12, 16
White Oxen and Other Stories, The (Burke), **I:** 269, 271
White Paper on Contemporary American Poetry (McClatchy), **Supp. XII:** 253, **259–260**
"White Pine" (Oliver), **Supp. VII:** 244
White Pine: Poems and Prose Poems (Oliver), **Supp. VII:** 243–246
"White Silence, The" (London), **II:** 468
"White Silk" (Nye), **Supp. XIII:** 275
"White Snake, The" (Sexton), **Supp. II Part 2:** 691
"White Spot" (Anderson), **I:** 116
"White-Tailed Hornet, The" (Frost), **Retro. Supp. I:** 138
Whitfield, Raoul, **Supp. IV Part 1:** 345
Whitlock, Brand, **II:** 276
Whitman (Masters), **Supp. I Part 2:** 473, 475, 476
Whitman, George, **IV:** 346, 350
Whitman, Sarah Wyman, **Retro. Supp. II:** 136
"Whitman: The Poet and the Mask" (Cowley), **Supp. II Part 1:** 143
Whitman, Walt, **I:** 61, 68, 98, 103, 104, 109, 219, 220, 227, 228, 242, 246, 250, 251, 260, 261, 285, 381, 384, 386, 396, 397, 398, 402, 419, 430, 459, 460, 483, 485, 486, 577; **II:** 7, 8, 18, 127, 140, 273–274, 275, 289, 295, 301, 320, 321, 373, 445, 446, 451, 457, 494, 529, 530, 552; **III:** 171, 175, 177, 181–182, 189, 203, 234, 260, 426, 430, 453, 454, 461, 505, 507–508, 511, 528, 548, 552, 555, 559, 567, 572, 576, 577, 579, 584, 585, 595, 606, 609; **IV:** 74, 169, 191, 192, 202, **331–354,** 405, 409, 416, 444, 450–451, 457, 463, 464, 469, 470, 471; **Retro. Supp. I:** 8, 52, 194, 254, 283, 284, 333, **387–410,** 412, 417, 427; **Retro. Supp. II:** 40, 76, 93, 99, 155, 156, 158, 170, 262, 285; **Supp. I Part 1:** 6, 79, 167, 311, 314, 325, 365, 368, 372; **Supp. I Part 2:** 374, 384, 385, 387, 389, 391, 393, 399, 416, 436, 455, 456, 458, 473, 474, 475, 525, 540, 579, 580, 582, 682, 691; **Supp. III Part 1:** 6, 20, 156, 239–241, 253, 340; **Supp. III Part 2:** 596; **Supp. IV Part 1:** 16, 169, 325; **Supp. IV Part 2:** 597, 625; **Supp. V:** 113, 118, 122, 130, 170, 178, 183, 277, 279, 332; **Supp. VIII:** 42, 95, 105, 126, 198, 202, 269; **Supp. IX:** 8, 9, 15, 38, 41, 44, 48, 53, 131, 292, 298, 299, 308, 320; **Supp. X:** 36, 112, 203, 204; **Supp. XI:** 83, 123, 132, 135, 203, 321; **Supp. XII:** 132, 185, 190, 256; **Supp. XIII:** 1, 77, 115, 153, 221, 304, 335
Whitmarsh, Jason, **Supp. VIII:** 283
Whitmer, Peter, **Supp. X:** 264, 265
Whitney, Blair, **Supp. I Part 2:** 403
Whitney, Josiah, **Supp. IX:** 180, 181

Whitt, Margaret Earley, **Retro. Supp. II:** 226
Whittemore, Reed, **III:** 268; **Supp. XI:** 315
Whittier, Elizabeth, **Supp. I Part 2:** 700, 701, 703; **Supp. XIII:** 141, 142
Whittier, John Greenleaf, **I:** 216; **II:** 275; **III:** 52; **Retro. Supp. I:** 54; **Retro. Supp. II:** 155, 163, 169; **Supp. I Part 1:** 168, 299, 313, 317, 372; **Supp. I Part 2:** 420, 602, **682–707; Supp. VIII:** 202, 204; **Supp. XI:** 50; **Supp. XIII:** 140, 145
Whittier, Mary, **Supp. I Part 2:** 683
"Whittier Birthday Speech" (Twain), **Supp. I Part 1:** 313
"Who" (Kenyon), **Supp. VII:** 174
"Who Am I—Who I Am" (Corso), **Supp. XII:** 134
"Who Be Kind To" (Ginsberg), **Supp. II Part 1:** 323
"Whoever Was Using This Bed" (Carver), **Supp. III Part 1:** 148
"Whoever You Are Holding Me Now in Hand" (Whitman), **IV:** 342; **Retro. Supp. I:** 52
Who Gathered and Whispered behind Me (Goldbarth), **Supp. XII:** 181, 182
"Who in One Lifetime" (Rukeyser), **Supp. VI:** 276, 279
"Who Is Your Mother? Red Roots of White Feminism" (Gunn Allen), **Supp. IV Part 1:** 329
Whole Hog (Wagoner), **Supp. IX:** 337–338
"Whole Mess...Almost, The" (Corso), **Supp. XII:** 135
"Whole Moisty Night, The" (Bly), **Supp. IV Part 1:** 69
Whole New Life, A (Price), **Supp. VI:** 265, **266,** 267
"Whole Self, The" (Nye), **Supp. XIII:** 275
"Whole Soul, The" (Levine), **Supp. V:** 192
"Whole Story, The" (Strand), **Supp. IV Part 2:** 622
"Whole World Knows, The" (Welty), **IV:** 272; **Retro. Supp. I:** 343
Who'll Stop the Rain (film), **Supp. V:** 301
Who Lost an American? (Algren), **Supp. IX: 15–16**
"Who Puts Together" (Hogan), **Supp. IV Part 1:** 403, 405, 412–413
Who's Afraid of Virginia Woolf? (Albee), **I:** 71, 77–81, 83, 85, 86, 87, 94; **IV:** 230
Who Shall Be the Sun? Poems Based on the Lore, Legends, and Myths of the Northwest Coast and Plateau Indians (Wagoner), **Supp. IX:** 328, **329–330,** 337
"Whosis Kid, The" (Hammett), **Supp. IV Part 1:** 344
"Who's Passing for Who?" (Hughes), **Supp. I Part 1:** 330
Who Will Run the Frog Hospital?: A Novel (Moore), **Supp. X:** 163, 165, 169, **175–177**
Why Are We in Vietnam? (Mailer), **III:** 27, 29, 30, 33, 34–35, 39, 42, 44; **Retro. Supp. II:** 205–206
"Why Did the Balinese Chicken Cross the Road?" (Walker), **Supp. III Part 2:** 527
"Why Do the Heathens Rage?" (O'Connor), **III:** 351
"Why Do You Write About Russia?" (Simpson), **Supp. IX:** 277
"Why I Am a Danger to the Public" (Kingsolver), **Supp. VII:** 204
Why I Am Not a Christian (Russell), **Supp. I Part 2:** 522
"Why I Entered the Gurdjieff Work" (Toomer), **Supp. III Part 2:** 481
"Why I Like Laurel" (Patchett), **Supp. XII:** 309
"Why I Live at the P.O." (Welty), **IV:** 262; **Retro. Supp. I:** 345
"Why Is Economics Not an Evolutionary Science?" (Veblen), **Supp. I Part 2:** 634
"Why I Write" (Didion), **Supp. IV Part 1:** 201, 203
"Why Negro Women Leave Home" (Brooks), **Supp. III Part 1:** 75
"Why the Little Frenchman Wears His Hand in a Sling" (Poe), **III:** 425
Why We Behave Like Microbe Hunters (Thurber), **Supp. I Part 2:** 606
Why We Were in Vietnam (Podhoretz), **Supp. VIII:** 241
"Why Write?" (Updike), **Retro. Supp. I:** 317
"Wichita Vortex Sutra" (Ginsberg), **Supp. II Part 1:** 319, 321, 323–325, 327
Wickford Point (Marquand), **III:** 50, 58, 64–65, 69
Wicks, Robert Russell, **Supp. XII:** 49
"Wide Empty Landscape with a Death in the Foreground" (Momaday), **Supp. IV Part 2:** 492
Wideman, John Edgar, **Retro. Supp. II:** 123; **Supp. X:** 239, 250, **319–336; Supp. XI:** 245; **Supp. XIII:** 247
"Wide Net, The" (Welty), **IV:** 266
Wide Net and Other Stories, The (Welty), **IV:** 261, 264–266, 271; **Retro. Supp. I: 347–349,** 352, 355
Widening Spell of the Leaves, The (Levis), **Supp. XI:** 258, 259, 261, **268–269,** 271
"Wide Prospect, The" (Jarrell), **II:** 376–377
Widow for One Year, A (Irving), **Supp. VI:** 165, **179–181**
Widows of Thornton, The (Taylor), **Supp. V:** 320, 321
Wieland; or, The Transformation. An American Tale (Brown), **Supp. I Part 1:** 128–132, 133, 137, 140
Wiene, Robert, **Retro. Supp. I:** 268
Wiener, John, **Supp. IV Part 1:** 153
Wieners, John, **Supp. II Part 1:** 32
"Wife, Forty-five, Remembers Love, A" (Shields), **Supp. VII:** 310
"Wifebeater, The" (Sexton), **Supp. II Part 2:** 693
"Wife for Dino Rossi, A" (Fante), **Supp. XI:** 165
"Wife of Jesus Speaks, The" (Karr), **Supp. XI:** 250–251
"Wife of Nashville, A" (Taylor), **Supp. V:** 320
Wife's Story, The (Shields), **Supp. VII:** 316. *See also* Happenstance
"Wife-Wooing" (Updike), **IV:** 226
Wigan, Gareth, **Supp. XI:** 306
Wiget, Andrew, **Supp. IV Part 2:** 509
Wigglesworth, Michael, **IV:** 147, 156; **Supp. I Part 1:** 110, 111
Wilbur, Richard, **III:** 527; **Retro. Supp. II:** 50; **Supp. III Part 1:** 64; **Supp. III Part 2: 541–565; Supp. IV Part 2:** 626, 634, 642; **Supp. V:** 337; **Supp. VIII:** 28; **Supp. X:** 58, 120; **Supp. XII:** 258; **Supp. XIII:** 76, 336
Wilcocks, Alexander, **Supp. I Part 1:** 125
Wilcox, Ella Wheeler, **Supp. II Part 1:** 197
Wild 90 (film) (Mailer), **Retro. Supp. II:** 205
Wild, John, **II:** 362, 363–364
Wild, Peter, **Supp. V:** 5
Wild, Robert, **IV:** 155
"Wild, The" (Berry), **Supp. X:** 30
Wild Boy of Aveyron, The (Itard). *See* De l'éducation d'un homme sauvage
Wild Boys, The: A Book of the Dead (Burroughs), **Supp. III Part 1:** 106–107
Wilde, Oscar, **I:** 50, 66, 381, 384; **II:** 515; **IV:** 77, 350; **Retro. Supp. I:** 56, 102, 227; **Retro. Supp. II:** 76,

344; **Supp. IV Part 2:** 578, 679, 683; **Supp. V:** 106, 283; **Supp. IX:** 65, 66, 68, 189, 192; **Supp. X:** 148, 151, 188–189
Wilder, Amos Parker, **IV:** 356
Wilder, Billy, **Supp. IV Part 1:** 130; **Supp. XI:** 307
Wilder, Isabel, **IV:** 357, 366, 375
Wilder, Mrs. Amos Parker (Isabella Thornton Niven), **IV:** 356
Wilder, Thornton, **I:** 360, 482; **IV:** 355–377, 431; **Retro. Supp. I:** 109, 359; **Supp. I Part 2:** 609; **Supp. IV Part 2:** 586; **Supp. V:** 105; **Supp. IX:** 140; **Supp. XII:** 236–237
"Wilderness" (Sandburg), **III:** 584, 595
Wilderness (Warren), **IV:** 256
"Wilderness, The" (Merwin), **Supp. III Part 1:** 340, 345
"Wilderness, The" (Robinson), **III:** 524
Wilderness of Vision, The: On the Poetry of John Haines (Bezner and Walzer, eds.), **Supp. XII:** 202
Wilderness World of Anne LaBastille, The (LaBastille), **Supp. X:** 105, 106
Wild Flag, The (White), **Supp. I Part 2:** 654
"Wildflower, The" (W. C. Williams), **Retro. Supp. I:** 420
"Wild Flowers" (Caldwell), **I:** 310
"Wildflowers" (Minot), **Supp. VI:** 208
"Wild Geese" (Oliver), **Supp. VII:** 237
"Wild Honey Suckle, The" (Freneau), **Supp. II Part 1:** 253, 264, 266
Wild in the Country (Odets), **Supp. II Part 2:** 546
Wild Iris, The (Glück), **Supp. V:** 79, 87–89, 91
Wildlife (Ford), **Supp. V:** 57, 69–71
Wildlife in America (Matthiessen), **Supp. V:** 199, 201, 204
Wild Old Wicked Man, The (MacLeish), **III:** 3, 20
Wild Palms, The (Faulkner), **II:** 68–69; **Retro. Supp. I:** 85
"Wild Palms, The" (Faulkner), **II:** 68
Wild Patience Has Taken Me This Far, A: Poems, 1978–1981 (Rich), **Retro. Supp. II:** 291
"Wild Peaches" (Wylie), **Supp. I Part 2:** 707, 712
Wild Roses of Cape Ann and Other Poems (Larcom), **Supp. XIII:** 142, 147
Wild Seed (O. Butler), **Supp. XIII:** 62, 63
"Wildwest" (MacLeish), **III:** 14
Wiley, Craig, **Supp. VIII:** 313
Wilhelm Meister (Goethe), **II:** 291

Wilkes, John, **Supp. I Part 2:** 503, 519, 522
Wilkie, Curtis, **Supp. V:** 11
Wilkins, Roy, **Supp. I Part 1:** 345
Wilkinson, Alec, **Supp. VIII:** 164, 168, 171
Wilkinson, Max, **Supp. IX:** 251
Willard, Samuel, **IV:** 150
Willard Gibbs (Rukeyser), **Supp. VI:** 273, 283, 284
Willey, Basil, **Retro. Supp. II:** 243
William Carlos Williams (Koch), **Retro. Supp. I:** 428
William Carlos Williams: An American Artist (Breslin), **Retro. Supp. I:** 430
William Carlos Williams: The American Background (Weaver), **Retro. Supp. I:** 430
William Carlos Williams and Alterity (Ahearn), **Retro. Supp. I:** 415
William Carlos Williams and the Meanings of Measure (Cushman), **Retro. Supp. I:** 430
William Faulkner: A Critical Study (Howe), **Supp. VI:** 119–120, 125
William Faulkner: Early Prose and Poetry (Faulkner), **Retro. Supp. I:** 80
"William Faulkner: The Stillness of Light in August" (Kazin), **Supp. VIII:** 104
"William Faulkner's Legend of the South" (Cowley), **Supp. II Part 1:** 143
"William Humphrey, 73, Writer of Novels about Rural Texas" (Gussow), **Supp. IX:** 93
William Humphrey. Boise State University Western Writers Series (Winchell), **Supp. IX:** 109
William Humphrey, Destroyer of Myths (Almon), **Supp. IX:** 93
William Humphrey. Southwestern Series (Lee), **Supp. IX:** 109
"William Humphrey Remembered" (Masters), **Supp. IX:** 96
"William Ireland's Confession" (A. Miller), **III:** 147–148
William James and Phenomenology: A Study of the "Principles of Psychology" (Wilshire), **II:** 362
Williams, Annie Laurie, **Supp. IX:** 93
Williams, C. K., **Supp. XIII:** 114
Williams, Cecil, **II:** 508
Williams, Charles, **Supp. II Part 1:** 15, 16
Williams, Dakin, **IV:** 379
Williams, David Reichard, **Supp. XIII:** 162
Williams, Edward, **IV:** 404
Williams, Edwina Dakin, **IV:** 379

Williams, Esther, **Supp. XII:** 165
Williams, George, **Supp. V:** 220
Williams, Horace, **IV:** 453
Williams, Joan, **Supp. IX:** 95
Williams, John Sharp, **IV:** 378
Williams, Michael, **Supp. V:** 286
Williams, Mrs. William Carlos (Florence Herman), **IV:** 404
Williams, Paul, **IV:** 404
Williams, Raymond, **Supp. IX:** 146
Williams, Roger, **Supp. I Part 2:** 699
Williams, Rose, **IV:** 379
Williams, Sherley Anne, **Supp. V:** 180
Williams, Solomon, **I:** 549
Williams, Stanley T., **II:** 301, 316; **Supp. I Part 1:** 251
Williams, Stephen, **IV:** 148
Williams, Ted, **IV:** 216; **Supp. IX:** 162
Williams, Tennessee, **I:** 73, 81, 113, 211; **II:** 190, 194; **III:** 145, 147; **IV:** 4, **378–401**; **Supp. I Part 1:** 290, 291; **Supp. IV Part 1:** 79, 83, 84, 359; **Supp. IV Part 2:** 574, 682; **Supp. IX:** 133; **Supp. XI:** 103; **Supp. XIII:** 331
Williams, Terry Tempest, **Supp. XIII:** 16
Williams, Walter L., **Supp. IV Part 1:** 330, 331
Williams, William, **IV:** 404, 405
Williams, William Carlos, **I:** 61, 62, 229, 255, 256, 261, 285, 428, 438, 446, 539; **II:** 133, 536, 542, 543, 544, 545; **III:** 194, 196, 198, 214, 269, 409, 453, 457, 458, 464, 465, 591; **IV:** 30, 74, 75, 76, 94, 95, 286, 287, **402–425**; **Retro. Supp. I:** 51, 52, 62, 209, 284, 285, 288, 296, 298, **411–433**; **Retro. Supp. II:** 178, 181, 189, 250, 339, 340, 344, 345, 346, 352, 353; **Supp. I Part 1:** 254, 255, 259, 266; **Supp. II Part 1:** 9, 30, 308, 318; **Supp. II Part 2:** 421, 443; **Supp. III Part 1:** 9, 147, 239, 271, 275, 276, 278, 350; **Supp. III Part 2:** 542, 610, 613, 614, 615, 616, 617, 621, 622, 626, 628; **Supp. IV Part 1:** 151, 153, 246, 325; **Supp. V:** 180, 337; **Supp. VIII:** 195, 269, 272, 277, 292; **Supp. IX:** 38, 268, 291; **Supp. X:** 112, 120, 204; **Supp. XI:** 311, 328; **Supp. XII:** 198; **Supp. XIII:** 77, 90, 335
Williamson, Alan, **Retro. Supp. II:** 185
William Styron's Nat Turner: Ten Black Writers Respond (Clarke, ed.), **IV:** 115
Williams-Walsh, Mary Ellen, **Supp. IV Part 2:** 611

William the Conqueror, **Supp. I Part 2:** 507
William Wetmore Story and His Friends (James), **Retro. Supp. I:** 235
William Wilson (Gardner), **Supp. VI:** 72
"William Wilson" (Poe), **II:** 475; **III:** 410, 412; **Retro. Supp. II:** 269; **Supp. IX:** 105
"Willie" (Angelou), **Supp. IV Part 1:** 15
Willie Masters' Lonesome Wife (Gass), **Supp. VI:** 77, **84–85,** 86–87
"Willing" (Moore), **Supp. X:** 178
Willis, Bruce, **Supp. IV Part 1:** 236
Willis, Mary Hard, **Supp. V:** 290–291
Willis, Nathaniel Parker, **II:** 313; **Supp. I Part 2:** 405
Williwaw (Vidal), **Supp. IV Part 2:** 677, 680, 681
"Willow Woman" (Francis), **Supp. IX:** 78
Wills, Garry, **Supp. I Part 1:** 294; **Supp. IV Part 1:** 355
Wills, Ridley, **IV:** 122
Wills, Ross B., **Supp. XI:** 169
"Will to Believe, The" (James), **II:** 352
Will to Believe, The, and Other Essays in Popular Philosophy (James), **II:** 356; **IV:** 28
Will to Change, The: Poems, 1968–1970 (Rich), **Retro. Supp. II:** 284; **Supp. I Part 2:** 551, 557–559
"Will You Please Be Quiet, Please?" (Carver), **Supp. III Part 1:** 137, 141
Will You Please Be Quiet, Please? (Carver), **Supp. III Part 1:** 138, 140, 144
"Will You Tell Me?" (Barthelme), **Supp. IV Part 1:** 42, 47
Wilshire, Bruce, **II:** 362, 364
Wilshire, Gaylord, **Supp. V:** 280
Wilson, Angus, **IV:** 430, 435
Wilson, August, **Supp. VIII: 329–353**
Wilson, Augusta Jane Evans, **Retro. Supp. I:** 351
Wilson, E. O., **Supp. X:** 35
Wilson, Earl, **Supp. X:** 264
Wilson, Edmund, **I:** 67, 185, 236, 247, 260, 434, 482; **II:** 79, 80, 81, 86, 87, 91, 97, 98, 146, 276, 430, 530, 562, 587; **III:** 588; **IV:** 308, 310, **426–449; Retro. Supp. I:** 1, 97, 100, 101, 103, 104, 105, 115, 274; **Retro. Supp. II:** 339, 345, 347; **Supp. I Part 1:** 372; **Supp. I Part 2:** 407, 646, 678, 709; **Supp. II Part 1:** 19, 90, 106, 136, 137, 143; **Supp. III Part 2:** 612; **Supp. IV Part 2:** 693; **Supp. VIII:** 93, 95, 96, 97, 98–99, 100, 101, 103, 105, 162; **Supp. IX:** 55, 65, 190; **Supp. X:** 186; **Supp. XI:** 160; **Supp. XIII:** 170
Wilson, Edmund (father), **IV:** 441
Wilson, Reuel, **II:** 562
Wilson, Robert, **Supp. XI:** 144
Wilson, Sloan, **Supp. IV Part 1:** 387
Wilson, Thomas, **IV:** 153
Wilson, Victoria, **Supp. X:** 166
Wilson, Woodrow, **I:** 245, 246, 490; **II:** 183, 253; **III:** 105, 581; **Supp. I Part 1:** 21; **Supp. I Part 2:** 474, 643; **Supp. V:** 288
Wilton, David, **IV:** 147
Winchell, Mark, **Supp. VIII:** 176, 189
Winchell, Mark Royden, **Supp. VIII:** 241; **Supp. IX:** 97, 98, 109; **Supp. XIII:** 94, 98, 99, 101
Winckelmann, Johann Joachim, **Supp. XII:** 178
Wind, Sand, and Stars (Saint-Exupéry), **Supp. IX:** 247
Windham, Donald, **IV:** 382
"Windhover" (Hopkins), **I:** 397; **II:** 539; **Supp. IX:** 43
"Winding Street, The" (Petry), **Supp. XI:** 6
"Window" (Pinsky), **Supp. VI:** 237, 247
Windows (Creeley), **Supp. IV Part 1:** 157, 158
"Windows" (Jarrell), **II:** 388, 389
"Window Seat, A" (Goldbarth), **Supp. XII:** 185
Wind Remains, The (opera) (Bowles), **Supp. IV Part 1:** 83
"Winds, The" (Welty), **IV:** 265; **Retro. Supp. I:** 348, 350
"Wind up Sushi" (Goldbarth), **Supp. XII:** 186–187
"Windy Day at the Reservoir, A" (Beattie), **Supp. V:** 33
Windy McPherson's Son (Anderson), **I:** 101, 102–103, 105, 111
"Wine" (Carver), **Supp. III Part 1:** 138
"Wine Menagerie, The" (H. Crane), **I:** 389, 391; **Retro. Supp. II:** 82
Wine of the Puritans, The: A Study of Present-Day America (Brooks), **I:** 240
"Wine of Wizardry, A" (Sterling), **I:** 208
Winer, Linda, **Supp. IV Part 2:** 580
Winesburg, Ohio: A Group of Tales of Ohio Small Town Life (Anderson), **I:** 97, 102, 103, 104, 105–108; **III:** 112, 113, 114, 116, 224, 579; **Supp. V:** 12; **Supp. IX:** 306, 308; **Supp. XI:** 164

Wing-and-Wing, The (Cooper), **I:** 350, 355
Winged Words: American Indian Writers Speak (Coltelli), **Supp. IV Part 2:** 493, 497
"Wingfield" (Wolff), **Supp. VII:** 341–342
"Wings, The" (Doty), **Supp. XI:** 124
Wings of the Dove, The (James), **I:** 436; **II:** 320, 323, 333, 334–335; **Retro. Supp. I:** 215, 216, 217, 232, **233–234; Supp. II Part 1:** 94–95; **Supp. IV Part 1:** 349
Winner Take Nothing (Hemingway), **II:** 249; **Retro. Supp. I:** 170, 175, 176, 181
"Winnie" (Brooks), **Supp. III Part 1:** 86
Winokur, Maxine. *See* Kumin, Maxine
Winslow, Devereux, **II:** 547
Winslow, Harriet, **II:** 552–553
Winslow, Ola Elizabeth, **I:** 547
Winslow, Warren, **II:** 540
Winston, Andrew, **Supp. XII:** 189
Winter, Douglas, **Supp. V:** 144
Winter, Johnny and Edgar, **Supp. V:** 334
Winter, Kate, **Supp. X:** 104
"Winter Branch, A" (Irving), **Supp. VI:** 163
"Winter Burial, A" (Clampitt), **Supp. IX:** 48
Winter Carnival (film), **Retro. Supp. I:** 113
"Winter Daybreak at Vence, A" (Wright), **Supp. III Part 1:** 249–250
Winter Diary, A (Van Doren), **I:** 168
"Winter Dreams" (Fitzgerald), **II:** 80, 94; **Retro. Supp. I:** 108
"Winter Drive, A" (Jewett), **Retro. Supp. II:** 147
"Winter Eden, A" (Frost), **Retro. Supp. I:** 137
"Winter Father, The" (Dubus), **Supp. VII:** 83, 87
Winter Hours: Prose, Prose Poems, and Poems (Oliver), **Supp. VII:** 230, 247
"Winter in Dunbarton" (Lowell), **II:** 547; **Retro. Supp. II:** 187
"Wintering" (Plath), **Retro. Supp. II:** 255
Winter Insomnia (Carver), **Supp. III Part 1:** 138
Winter in the Blood (Welch), **Supp. IV Part 2:** 562
"Winter Landscape" (Berryman), **I:** 174; **Retro. Supp. I:** 430
Winter Lightning (Nemerov), **III:** 269

Winter News (Haines), **Supp. XII:** 199, **201–204,** 207–208, 208
Winternitz, Mary. *See* Cheever, Mrs. John (Mary Winternitz)
Winter of Our Discontent, The (Steinbeck), **IV:** 52, 65–66, 68
"Winter on Earth" (Toomer), **Supp. III Part 2:** 486
"Winter Piece, A" (Bryant), **Supp. I Part 1:** 150, 155
"Winter Rains, Cataluña" (Levine), **Supp. V:** 182
"Winter Remembered" (Ransom), **III:** 492–493
Winterrowd, Prudence, **I:** 217, 224
Winters, Jonathan, **Supp. XI:** 305
Winters, Yvor, **I:** 59, 63, 386, 393, 397, 398, 402, 471; **III:** 194, 498; **IV:** 153; **Retro. Supp. II:** 76, 77, 78, 82, 83, 85, 89; **Supp. I Part 1:** 268; **Supp. II Part 2:** 416, 666, **785–816; Supp. IV Part 2:** 480; **Supp. V:** 180, 191–192
"Winter Scenes" (Bryant). *See* "Winter Piece, A"
Winterset (Anderson), **III:** 159
"Winter Sleep" (Wylie), **Supp. I Part 2:** 711, 729
Winter's Tale, The (Shakespeare), **Supp. XIII:** 219
Winter Stars (Levis), **Supp. XI:** 259, **266–268**
"Winter Stars" (Levis), **Supp. XI:** 267–268
"Winter Swan" (Bogan), **Supp. III Part 1:** 52
Winter Trees (Plath), **Retro. Supp. II:** 257; **Supp. I Part 2:** 526, 539, 541
"Winter Weather Advisory" (Ashbery), **Supp. III Part 1:** 26
"Winter Words" (Levine), **Supp. V:** 192
Winthrop, John, **Supp. I Part 1:** 99, 100, 101, 102, 105; **Supp. I Part 2:** 484, 485
Winthrop Covenant, The (Auchincloss), **Supp. IV Part 1:** 23
Wirt, William, **I:** 232
Wirth, Louis, **IV:** 475
"Wisdom Cometh with the Years" (Cullen), **Supp. IV Part 1:** 166
Wisdom of the Desert, The: Sayings from the Desert Fathers of the Fourth Century (Merton), **Supp. VIII:** 201
Wisdom of the Heart, The (H. Miller), **III:** 178, 184
Wise Blood (O'Connor), **III:** 337, 338, 339–343, 344, 345, 346, 350, 354, 356, 357; **Retro. Supp. II:** 219, 221, 222, 223, **225–228**
Wise Men, The (Price), **Supp. VI:** 254
"Wiser Than a God" (Chopin), **Retro. Supp. II:** 61; **Supp. I Part 1:** 208
"Wish for a Young Wife" (Roethke), **III:** 548
Wishful Thinking: A Theological ABC (Buechner), **Supp. XII:** 53
Wismer, Helen Muriel. *See* Thurber, Mrs. James (Helen Muriel Wismer)
Wisse, Ruth, **Supp. XII:** 167, 168
Wister, Owen, **I:** 62; **Retro. Supp. II:** 72
"Witchbird" (Bambara), **Supp. XI:** 11
"Witch Burning" (Plath), **Supp. I Part 2:** 539
Witchcraft of Salem Village, The (Jackson), **Supp. IX:** 121
"Witch Doctor" (Hayden), **Supp. II Part 1:** 368, 380
Witches of Eastwick, The (Updike), **Retro. Supp. I:** 330, 331
Witching Hour, The (Rice), **Supp. VII:** 299–300
"Witch of Coös, The" (Frost), **II:** 154–155; **Retro. Supp. I:** 135; **Retro. Supp. II:** 42
"Witch of Owl Mountain Springs, The: An Account of Her Remarkable Powers" (Taylor), **Supp. V:** 328
"Witch of Wenham, The" (Whittier), **Supp. I Part 2:** 694, 696
"With a Little Help from My Friends" (Kushner), **Supp. IX:** 131
"With Che at Kitty Hawk" (Banks), **Supp. V:** 6
"With Che at the Plaza" (Banks), **Supp. V:** 7
"With Che in New Hampshire" (Banks), **Supp. V:** 6
"Withdrawal Symptoms" (Mora), **Supp. XIII:** 216
"Withered Skins of Berries" (Toomer), **Supp. III Part 2:** 485; **Supp. IX:** 320
Withers, Harry Clay, **Supp. XIII:** 161
Witherspoon, John, **Supp. I Part 2:** 504
With Eyes at the Back of Our Heads (Levertov), **Supp. III Part 1:** 276–277
With Her in Ourland (Gilman), **Supp. XI:** 208–209
With His Pistol in His Hand (Paredes), **Supp. XIII:** 225
"Within the Words: An Apprenticeship" (Haines), **Supp. XII:** 197
"With Kit, Age 7, at the Beach" (Stafford), **Supp. XI:** 323
"With Mercy for the Greedy" (Sexton), **Supp. II Part 2:** 680
Without a Hero (Boyle), **Supp. VIII:** 16
Without Stopping (Bowles), **Supp. IV Part 1:** 79, 81, 85, 90, 91, 92
"Without Tradition and within Reason: Judge Horton and Atticus Finch in Court" (Johnson), **Supp. VIII:** 127
With Shuddering Fall (Oates), **Supp. II Part 2:** 504–506
"With the Dog at Sunrise" (Kenyon), **Supp. VII:** 170
With the Empress Dowager of China (Carl), **III:** 475
With the Old Breed: At Peleliu and Okinawa (Sledge), **Supp. V:** 249–250
"With the Violin" (Chopin), **Retro. Supp. II:** 61
"Witness" (Clampitt), **Supp. IX:** 42–43, 45, 46
"Witness" (Dubus), **Supp. VII:** 89
"Witness" (Harjo), **Supp. XII:** 227–228
Witness (McNally), **Supp. XIII:** 197
"Witness, The" (Porter), **III:** 443–444
"Witness for Poetry, A" (Stafford), **Supp. XI:** 324
"Witnessing My Father's Will" (Karr), **Supp. XI:** 241
Witness to the Times! (McGrath), **Supp. X:** 118
Witness Tree, A (Frost), **II:** 155; **Retro. Supp. I:** 122, 137, 139
Wit's End: Days and Nights of the Algonquin Round Table (Gaines), **Supp. IX:** 190
Wits Recreations (Mennes and Smith), **II:** 111
Witt, Shirley Hill, **Supp. IV Part 2:** 505
Wittenberg, Judith Bryant, **Retro. Supp. II:** 146
Wittgenstein, Ludwig, **Retro. Supp. I:** 53; **Supp. III Part 2:** 626–627; **Supp. X:** 304; **Supp. XII:** 21
Wittliff, William, **Supp. V:** 227
"Witty War, A" (Simpson), **Supp. IX:** 268
"Wives and Mistresses" (Hardwick), **Supp. III Part 1:** 211–212
Wizard of Loneliness, The (Nichols), **Supp. XIII:** 259, 263, 264
Wizard of Oz, The (Baum), **Supp. IV Part 1:** 113
Wizard of Oz, The (film), **Supp. X:** 172, 214
Wizard's Tide, The: A Story (Buechner), **Supp. XII:** 54
Wodehouse, P. G., **Supp. IX:** 195

Woiwode, Larry, **Supp. VIII:** 151
Wojahn, David, **Supp. IX:** 161, 292, 293
Wolcott, James, **Supp. IX:** 259
Wolf: A False Memoir (Harrison), **Supp. VIII:** 40, **41–42,** 45
Wolf, Christa, **Supp. IV Part 1:** 310, 314
Wolf, Daniel, **Retro. Supp. II:** 202
Wolfe, Ben, **IV:** 454
Wolfe, James, **Supp. I Part 2:** 498
Wolfe, Linnie, **Supp. IX:** 176
Wolfe, Mabel, **IV:** 454
Wolfe, Mrs. William Oliver (Julia Elizabeth Westall), **IV:** 454
Wolfe, Thomas, **I:** 288, 289, 374, 478, 495; **II:** 457; **III:** 40, 108, 278, 334, 482; **IV:** 52, 97, 357, **450–473;** **Retro. Supp. I:** 382; **Supp. I Part 1:** 29; **Supp. IV Part 1:** 101; **Supp. IX:** 229; **Supp. X:** 225; **Supp. XI:** 213, 216, 217, 218; **Supp. XIII:** 17
Wolfe, Tom, **Supp. III Part 2: 567–588; Supp. IV Part 1:** 35, 198; **Supp. V:** 296; **Supp. X:** 264; **Supp. XI:** 239
Wolfe, William Oliver, **IV:** 454
"Wolfe Homo Scribens" (Cowley), **Supp. II Part 1:** 144
Wolfert's Roost (Irving), **II:** 314
Wolff, Cynthia Griffin, **Retro. Supp. I:** 379; **Supp. IV Part 1:** 203
Wolff, Donald, **Supp. XIII:** 316, 317, 326
Wolff, Geoffrey, **Supp. II Part 1:** 97; **Supp. XI:** 239, 245, 246
Wolff, Tobias, **Retro. Supp. I:** 190; **Supp. V:** 22; **Supp. VII: 331–346; Supp. X:** 1; **Supp. XI:** 26, 239, 245, 246, 247
Wolfson, P. J., **Supp. XIII:** 172
"Wolf Town" (Carson), **Supp. XII:** 102
Wolf Willow: A History, a Story, and a Memory of the Last Plains Frontier (Stegner), **Supp. IV Part 2:** 595, 596, 597, 598, 599, 600, 601, 604, 606, 611, 613, 614
Wollaston, William, **II:** 108
Wollstonecraft, Mary, **Retro. Supp. II:** 281; **Supp. I Part 1:** 126; **Supp. I Part 2:** 512, 554
"Woman" (Bogan), **Supp. X:** 102
"Woman, I Got the Blues" (Komunyakaa), **Supp. XIII:** 117
"Woman, Why Are You Weeping?" (Kenyon), **Supp. VII:** 174–175
"Woman, Young and Old, A" (Paley), **Supp. VI:** 222, 225
Woman at the Washington Zoo, The (Jarrell), **II:** 367, 386, 387, 389

"Woman Dead in Her Forties, A" (Rich), **Retro. Supp. II:** 290–291; **Supp. I Part 2:** 574–575
"Woman Hanging from the Thirteenth Floor Window, The" (Harjo), **Supp. XII:** 216, 221
"Woman Hollering Creek" (Cisneros), **Supp. VII:** 70
Woman Hollering Creek and Other Stories (Cisneros), **Supp. VII:** 58, 68–70
"Womanhood" (Brooks), **Supp. III Part 1:** 77
Woman in the Dark (Hammett), **Supp. IV Part 1:** 343
"Woman in the House, A" (Caldwell), **I:** 310
Woman in the Nineteenth Century (Fuller), **Retro. Supp. I:** 156; **Supp. II Part 1:** 279, 292, 294–296; **Supp. XI:** 197, 203
Woman in White, The (Collins), **Supp. I Part 1:** 35, 36
"Womanizer, The" (Ford), **Supp. V:** 71, 72
Woman Lit by Fireflies, The (Harrison), **Supp. VIII:** 50–51
"Woman Loses Cookie Bake-Off, Sets Self on Fire" (R. O. Butler), **Supp. XII:** 72
Woman of Andros, The (Wilder), **IV:** 356, 363–364, 367, 368, 374
Woman of Means, A (Taylor), **Supp. V:** 319–320
Woman on the Edge of Time (Piercy), **Supp. XIII:** 29
Woman on the Porch, The (Gordon), **II:** 199, 209–211
"Woman on the Stair, The" (MacLeish), **III:** 15–16
"Woman's Heartlessness" (Thaxter), **Retro. Supp. II:** 147
Woman's Honor (Glaspell), **Supp. III Part 1:** 179
"Woman Singing" (Ortiz), **Supp. IV Part 2:** 513
Woman's Share in Primitive Culture (Mason), **Supp. I Part 1:** 18
"Woman Struck by Car Turns into Nymphomaniac" (R. O. Butler), **Supp. XII:** 72
"Woman's Work" (Alvarez), **Supp. VII:** 4
"Woman Uses Glass Eye to Spy on Philandering Husband" (R. O. Butler), **Supp. XII:** 70, 72
Woman Warrior (Kingston), **Supp. IV Part 1:** 12; **Supp. V:** 157, 158, 159, 160–164, 166, 169; **Supp. X:** 291–292

Woman Who Fell from the Sky, The (Harjo), **Supp. XII: 226–228**
"Woman Who Fell From the Sky, The" (Iroquois creation story), **Supp. IV Part 1:** 327
Woman Who Owned the Shadows, The (Gunn Allen), **Supp. IV Part 1:** 320, 322, 326, 327–328
Woman Within, The (Glasgow), **II:** 183, 190–191
"Womanwork" (Gunn Allen), **Supp. IV Part 1:** 326
Women (Bukowski), **Supp. XI:** 172
"Women" (Didion), **Supp. IV Part 1:** 205
"Women" (Rich), **Retro. Supp. II:** 284
"Women" (Swenson), **Supp. IV Part 2:** 647
Women, The (film), **Retro. Supp. I:** 113
Women and Economics (Gilman), **Supp. I Part 2:** 637; **Supp. V:** 284; **Supp. XI:** 200, **203–204,** 206
Women and Thomas Harrow (Marquand), **III:** 50, 61, 62, 66, 68, 69–70, 71
Women and Wilderness (LaBastille), **Supp. X:** 97, **102–104**
Women at Point Sur, The (Jeffers), **Supp. II Part 2:** 430–431
Women in Love (Lawrence), **III:** 27, 34
Women of Brewster Place, The: A Novel in Seven Stories (Naylor), **Supp. VIII:** 213, **214–218**
"Women of My Color" (Coleman), **Supp. XI:** 88–89
Women of Trachis (Pound, trans.), **III:** 476
Women on the Wall, The (Stegner), **Supp. IV Part 2:** 599, 605, 606
Women Poets in English (Stanford, ed.), **Retro. Supp. I:** 41
"Women Reformers and American Culture, 1870–1930" (Conway), **Supp. I Part 1:** 19
"Women's Movement, The" (Didion), **Supp. IV Part 1:** 206
"Women Waiting" (Shields), **Supp. VII:** 320
"Women We Love Whom We Never See Again" (Bly), **Supp. IV Part 1:** 66
"Women We Never See Again" (Bly), **Supp. IV Part 1:** 66
Women with Men (Ford), **Supp. V:** 57, 71–72
"Wonder" (Olds), **Supp. X:** 210
Wonder Boys (Chabon), **Supp. XI:** 67, **73–75,Supp. XI:** 78

Wonder Boys (film), **Supp. XI:** 67
Wonderful O, The (Thurber), **Supp. I Part 2:** 612
"Wonderful Old Gentleman, The" (Parker), **Supp. IX:** 197
"Wonderful Pen, The" (Swenson), **Supp. IV Part 2:** 650
Wonderful Words, Silent Truth: Essays on Poetry and a Memoir (Simic), **Supp. VIII:** 270
Wonderland (Oates), **Supp. II Part 2:** 511, 512, 514–515
Wonders of the Invisible World, The (Mather), **Supp. II Part 2:** 456–459, 460, 467
Wonder-Working Providence (Johnson), **IV:** 157
Wong, Hertha, **Supp. IV Part 1:** 275
Wong, Jade Snow, **Supp. X:** 291
"Wood" (Nye), **Supp. XIII:** 276
Wood, Audrey, **IV:** 381
Wood, Clement Biddle, **Supp. XI:** 307
Wood, Mabel, **I:** 199
Wood, Michael, **Supp. IV Part 2:** 691
Wood, Mrs. Henry, **Supp. I Part 1:** 35
Woodard, Calvin, **Supp. VIII:** 128
Woodard, Charles L., **Supp. IV Part 2:** 484, 493
Woodard, Deborah, **Supp. XIII:** 114
Woodberry, George Edward, **III:** 508
Woodbridge, Frederick, **I:** 217, 224
Woodbridge, John, **Supp. I Part 1:** 101, 102, 114
"Wood-Choppers, The" (Chopin), **Retro. Supp. II:** 72
Woodcock, George, **Supp. XIII:** 33
"Wood Dove at Sandy Spring, The" (MacLeish), **III:** 19
"Wooden Spring" (Rukeyser), **Supp. VI:** 285
"Wooden Umbrella, The" (Porter), **IV:** 26
"Woodnotes" (Emerson), **II:** 7, 19
"Wood-Pile, The" (Frost), **Retro. Supp. I:** 128; **Supp. IV Part 2:** 445
Woodrow, James, **Supp. I Part 1:** 349, 366
Woods, Robert A., **Supp. I Part 1:** 19
Woodswoman (LaBastille), **Supp. X:** 95, **96–99**, 108
Woodswoman III: Book Three of the Woodswoman's Adventures (LaBastille), **Supp. X:** 95, **106–107**
"Wood Thrush" (Kenyon), **Supp. VII:** 172
Woodward, C. Vann, **IV:** 114, 470–471; **Retro. Supp. I:** 75, 76
"Wooing the Inanimate" (Brodsky), **Supp. VIII:** 32
Woolcott, Alexander, **Supp. IX:** 197

Wooley, Bryan, **Supp. V:** 225
Woolf, Leonard, **Supp. IX:** 95
Woolf, Virginia, **I:** 53, 79, 112, 309; **II:** 320, 415; **IV:** 59; **Retro. Supp. I:** 59, 75, 170, 215, 291, 359; **Supp. I Part 2:** 553, 714, 718; **Supp. IV Part 1:** 299; **Supp. V:** 127; **Supp. VIII:** 5, 155, 251, 252, 263, 265; **Supp. IX:** 66, 109; **Supp. XI:** 134, 193; **Supp. XII:** 81, 98, 289; **Supp. XIII:** 305
Woollcott, Alexander, **IV:** 432; **Retro. Supp. II:** 345; **Supp. I Part 2:** 664; **Supp. IX:** 190, 194
Woolman, John, **Supp. VIII:** 202, 204, 205
Woolson, Constance Fenimore, **Retro. Supp. I:** 224, 228
Worcester, Samuel, **I:** 458
Word of God and the Word of Man, The (Barth), **Retro. Supp. I:** 327
"Word out of the Sea, A" (Whitman), **IV:** 344
Words (Creeley), **Supp. IV Part 1:** 139, 150–153, 154, 155, 158
"Words" (Creeley), **Supp. IV Part 1:** 152
"Words" (Merwin), **Supp. III Part 1:** 352
"Words" (Plath), **Supp. I Part 2:** 547
"Words" (Shields), **Supp. VII:** 323
"Words, The" (Wagoner), **Supp. IX:** 326
"Words above a Narrow Entrance" (Wagoner), **Supp. IX:** 325
"Words for a Bike-Racing, Osprey-Chasing Wine-Drunk Squaw Man" (Gunn Allen), **Supp. IV Part 1:** 325
Words for Dr. Y (Sexton), **Supp. II Part 2:** 698
"Words for Hart Crane" (Lowell), **I:** 381; **II:** 547; **Retro. Supp. II:** 188
"Words for Maria" (Merrill), **Supp. III Part 1:** 327
"Words for the Unknown Makers" (Kunitz), **Supp. III Part 1:** 264
Words for the Wind (Roethke), **III:** 529, 533, 541, 543, 545
"Words for the Wind" (Roethke), **III:** 542–543
Words in the Mourning Time (Hayden), **Supp. II Part 1:** 361, 366, 367
"Words in the Mourning Time" (Hayden), **Supp. II Part 1:** 370–371
"Words into Fiction" (Welty), **IV:** 279
"Words Like Freedom" (Hughes), **Retro. Supp. I:** 207
"Words of a Young Girl" (Lowell), **II:** 554
Words under the Words: Selected Poems (Nye), **Supp. XIII:** 277
Wordsworth, Dorothy, **Supp. IX:** 38
Wordsworth, William, **I:** 283, 522, 524, 525, 588; **II:** 7, 11, 17, 18, 97, 169, 273, 303, 304, 532, 549, 552; **III:** 219, 263, 277, 278, 511, 521, 523, 528, 583; **IV:** 120, 331, 343, 453, 465; **Retro. Supp. I:** 121, 196; **Retro. Supp. II:** 292; **Supp. I Part 1:** 150, 151, 154, 161, 163, 312, 313, 349, 365; **Supp. I Part 2:** 375, 409, 416, 422, 607, 621, 622, 673, 674, 675, 676, 677, 710–711, 729; **Supp. II Part 1:** 4; **Supp. III Part 1:** 12, 15, 73, 279; **Supp. IV Part 2:** 597, 601; **Supp. V:** 258; **Supp. VIII:** 273; **Supp. IX:** 38, 41, 265, 274; **Supp. X:** 22, 23, 65, 120; **Supp. XI:** 248, 251, 312; **Supp. XIII:** 214
Work (Alcott), **Supp. I Part 1:** 32–33, 42
Work (Dixon), **Supp. XII:** 141, **143**
"Work" (Oliver), **Supp. VII:** 243
Work and Love (Dunn), **Supp. XI:** **147–148**
"Worker" (Coleman), **Supp. XI:** 89
"Working the Landscape" (Dunn), **Supp. XI:** 151
Workin' on the Chain Gang: Shaking Off the Dead Hand of History (Mosley), **Supp. XIII:** 247, 248
"Work Notes '66" (Baraka), **Supp. II Part 1:** 47
Work of Art (Lewis), **II:** 453–454
"Work of Shading, The" (Simic), **Supp. VIII:** 277–278
Work of Stephen Crane, The (Follett, ed.), **I:** 405
"Work on Red Mountain, The" (Harte), **Supp. II Part 1:** 339
Works of Love, The (Morris), **III:** 223–224, 225, 233
"World, The" (Simic), **Supp. VIII:** 282
World According to Garp, The (Irving), **Supp. VI:** 163, 164, **170–173**, 181
World and Africa, The: An Inquiry into the Part Which Africa Has Played in World History (Du Bois), **Supp. II Part 1:** 184–185
"World and All Its Teeth, The" (Nye), **Supp. XIII:** 282
"World and the Door, The" (O. Henry), **Supp. II Part 1:** 402
"World and the Jug, The" (Ellison), **Retro. Supp. II:** 112, 119, 123
World Authors 1950–1970, **Supp. XIII:** 102
World Below, The (S. Miller), **Supp. XII:** **303–304**

World Below the Window, The: Poems 1937–1997 (W. J. Smith), **Supp. XIII:** 332, 340, 345
World Doesn't End, The (Simic), **Supp. VIII:** 272, **279–280**
World Elsewhere, A: The Place of Style in American Literature (Poirier), **I:** 239
"World Ends Here, The" (Harjo), **Supp. XII:** 227–228
World Enough and Time (Warren), **IV:** 243, 253–254
"World I Live In, The" (T. Williams), **IV:** 388
World I Never Made, A (Farrell), **II:** 34, 35, 424
World in the Attic, The (Morris), **III:** 222–223, 224
World Is a Wedding, The (Schwartz), **Supp. II Part 2:** 643, 654–660
"World Is a Wedding, The" (Schwartz), **Supp. II Part 2:** 655–656, 657
"World Is Too Much with Us, The" (Wordsworth), **Supp. I Part 1:** 312
Worldly Hopes (Ammons), **Supp. VII:** 34
Worldly Philosophers, The (Heilbroner), **Supp. I Part 2:** 644, 650
World of Apples, The (Cheever), **Supp. I Part 1:** 191, 193
World of David Wagoner, The (McFarland), **Supp. IX:** 323
"World of Easy Rawlins, The" (Mosley), **Supp. XIII:** 234, 236
World of Gwendolyn Brooks, The (Brooks), **Supp. III Part 1:** 83, 84
World of H. G. Wells, The (Brooks), **I:** 240, 241, 242
World of Light, A: Portraits and Celebrations (Sarton), **Supp. III Part 1:** 62; **Supp. VIII:** 249, 253, 262
World of Our Fathers: The Journey of the Eastern European Jews to America and the Life They Found and Made (Howe), **Supp. VI:** 113, 114, 116, 118, 119, **120–125**
"World of Pure Experience, A" (James), **II:** 356–357
World of Raymond Chandler, The (Spender), **Supp. IV Part 1:** 119
World of Sex, The (H. Miller), **III:** 170, 178, 187
"World of the Perfect Tear, The" (McGrath), **Supp. X:** 116, 118
World of the Ten Thousand Things, The: Selected Poems (Wright), **Supp. V:** 333
"World of Tomorrow, The" (White), **Supp. I Part 2:** 663

World of Washington Irving, The (Brooks), **I:** 256–257
World Over, The (Wharton), **Retro. Supp. I:** 382
"Worlds" (Goldbarth), **Supp. XII:** 183, 189
World's Body, The (Ransom), **III:** 497, 499; **Supp. II Part 1:** 146
World's End (Boyle), **Supp. VIII:** 11–12
World's End and Other Stories (Theroux), **Supp. VIII:** 322
"World's Fair" (Berryman), **I:** 173
World's Fair (Doctorow), **Supp. IV Part 1:** 217, 224, 227–229, 234, 236–237
World's Fair, The (Fitzgerald), **II:** 93
Worlds of Color (Du Bois), **Supp. II Part 1:** 185–186
"Worlds of Color" (Du Bois), **Supp. II Part 1:** 175
World So Wide (Lewis), **II:** 456
"World-Telegram" (Berryman), **I:** 173
World within the Word, The (Gass), **Supp. VI:** 77
"World Without Objects Is a Sensible Place, A" (Wilbur), **Supp. III Part 2:** 550
"World Without Rodrigo, The" (Cisneros), **Supp. VII:** 68
"Worm Moon" (Oliver), **Supp. VII:** 234
"Worn Path, A" (Welty), **IV:** 262; **Retro. Supp. I:** 345–346
"Worsening Situation" (Ashbery), **Supp. III Part 1:** 17–18
"Worship" (Emerson), **II:** 2, 4–5
"Worship and Church Bells" (Paine), **Supp. I Part 2:** 521
Worster, Donald, **Supp. IX:** 19
Worthington, Marjorie, **Supp. XII:** 13
Wouldn't Take Nothing for My Journey Now (Angelou), **Supp. IV Part 1:** 10, 12, 14, 15, 16
Wound and the Bow, The: Seven Studies in Literature (Wilson), **IV:** 429
Wounds in the Rain (Crane), **I:** 409, 414, 423
Woven Stone (Ortiz), **Supp. IV Part 2:** 501, 514
Woven Stories (Ortiz), **Supp. IV Part 2:** 503
"Wraith, The" (Roethke), **III:** 542
"Wrath of God, The" (Fante), **Supp. XI:** 160, 164
"Wreath for a Bridal" (Plath), **Supp. I Part 2:** 537
Wreath for Garibaldi and Other Stories, A (Garrett), **Supp. VII:** 99–101

"Wreath of Women" (Rukeyser), **Supp. VI:** 280
Wreckage of Agathon, The (Gardner), **Supp. VI:** 63, **65–66**
Wrecking Crew (Levis), **Supp. XI:** **259–260**
"Wreck of Rivermouth, The" (Whittier), **Supp. I Part 2:** 694, 696–697
"Wreck of the Deutschland" (Hopkins), **Supp. X:** 61
"Wreck of the Hesperus, The" (Longfellow), **Retro. Supp. II:** 168, 169
Wrestler's Cruel Study, The (Dobyns), **Supp. XIII:** **82–83**
"Wrestler with Sharks, A" (Yates), **Supp. XI:** 341
Wright, Bernie, **I:** 191, 193
Wright, Charles, **Supp. V:** 92, **331–346**; **Supp. VIII:** 272; **Supp. XIII:** 114
Wright, Chauncey, **II:** 344
Wright, Frank Lloyd, **I:** 104, 483
Wright, George, **III:** 479
Wright, Harold Bell, **II:** 467–468
Wright, Holly, **Supp. VIII:** 272
Wright, James, **I:** 291; **Supp. III Part 1:** 249; **Supp. III Part 2:** 541, **589–607**; **Supp. IV Part 1:** 60, 72; **Supp. IV Part 2:** 557, 558, 561, 566, 571, 623; **Supp. V:** 332; **Supp. IX:** 152, 155, 159, 265, 271, 290, 293, 296; **Supp. X:** 69, 127; **Supp. XI:** 150; **Supp. XII:** 217; **Supp. XIII:** 76
Wright, Mrs. Richard (Ellen Poplar), **IV:** 476
Wright, Nathalia, **IV:** 155
Wright, Philip Green, **III:** 578, 579, 580
Wright, Richard, **II:** 586; **IV:** 40, **474–497**; **Retro. Supp. II:** 4, 111, 116, 120; **Supp. I Part 1:** 51, 52, 64, 332, 337; **Supp. II Part 1:** 17, 40, 221, 228, 235, 250; **Supp. IV Part 1:** 1, 11, 84, 374; **Supp. VIII:** 88; **Supp. IX:** 316; **Supp. X:** 131, 245, 254; **Supp. XI:** 85; **Supp. XII:** 316; **Supp. XIII:** 46, 233
Wright, Sarah, **Supp. IV Part 1:** 8; **Supp. XIII:** 295
Wright, William, **Retro. Supp. II:** 76, 77
"Writer, The" (Wilbur), **Supp. III Part 2:** 561, 562
"Writer as Alaskan, The" (Haines), **Supp. XII:** 199
Writer in America, The (Brooks), **I:** 253, 254, 257
Writer in America, The (Stegner),

Supp. IV Part 2: 597, 599, 607
"Writers" (Lowell), II: 554
Writer's Almanac, The (Keillor, radio program), Supp. XIII: 274
Writer's America, A: Landscape in Literature (Kazin), Supp. VIII: 106
Writer's Capital, A (Auchincloss), Supp. IV Part 1: 21, 23, 24, 31
"Writer's Credo, A" (Abbey), Supp. XIII: 1, 17
Writer's Eye, A: Collected Book Reviews (Welty), Retro. Supp. I: 339, 354, 356
Writers in Revolt (Southern, Seaver, and Trocchi, eds.), Supp. XI: 301
Writer's Notebook, A (Maugham), Supp. X: 58
Writers on America (U.S. Department of State, ed.), Supp. XIII: 288
Writers on the Left (Aaron), IV: 429; Supp. II Part 1: 137
"Writer's Prologue to a Play in Verse" (W. C. Williams), Retro. Supp. I: 424
"Writer's Quest for a Parnassus, A" (T. Williams), IV: 392
Writers' Workshop (University of Iowa), Supp. V: 42
"Writing" (Nemerov), III: 275
"Writing About the Universe" (Mosley), Supp. XIII: 247
"Writing American Fiction" (Roth), Retro. Supp. II: 297; Supp. I Part 1: 192; Supp. I Part 2: 431; Supp. III Part 2: 414, 420, 421; Supp. V: 45
"Writing and a Life Lived Well" (Patchett), Supp. XII: 308
Writing a Woman's Life (Heilbrun), Supp. IX: 66
Writing Chicago: Modernism, Ethnography, and the Novel (Cappetti), Supp. IX: 4, 8
"Writing from the Inside Out: Style Is Not the Frosting; It's the Cake" (Robbins), Supp. X: 266
"Writing here last autumn of my hopes of seeing a hoopoe" (Updike), Retro. Supp. I: 335
"Writing Lesson, The" (Gordon), Supp. IV Part 1: 306
Writing Life, The (Dillard), Supp. VI: 23, 31
"Writing of Apollinaire, The" (Zukofsky), Supp. III Part 2: 616, 617
"Writing of *Fearless Jones*, The" (Mosley), Supp. XIII: 242
Writing on the Wall, The, and Literary Essays (McCarthy), II: 579

Writings to an Unfinished Accompaniment (Merwin), Supp. III Part 1: 352
Writing the World (Stafford), Supp. XI: 314
"Writing to Save Our Lives" (Milligan), Supp. XIII: 274
Writin' Is Fightin' (Reed), Supp. X: 241
"Writ on the Eve of My 32nd Birthday" (Corso), Supp. XII: 129–130
"Written History as an Act of Faith" (Beard), Supp. I Part 2: 492
"Wunderkind" (McCullers), II: 585
Wunderlich, Mark, Supp. XI: 119, 132
Wundt, Wilhelm, II: 345
Wurster, William Wilson, Supp. IV Part 1: 197
WUSA (film), Supp. V: 301
Wuthering Heights (E. Brontë), Supp. V: 305; Supp. X: 89
WWII (Jones), Supp. XI: 219, 231
Wyandotté (Cooper), I: 350, 355
Wyatt, Robert B., Supp. V: 14
Wyatt, Thomas, Supp. I Part 1: 369
Wycherly Woman, The (Macdonald), Supp. IV Part 2: 473
Wylie, Elinor, IV: 436; Supp. I Part 2: 707–730; Supp. III Part 1: 2, 63, 318–319; Supp. XI: 44
Wylie, Horace, Supp. I Part 2: 708, 709
Wylie, Philip, III: 223
Wyllys, Ruth. *See* Taylor, Mrs. Edward (Ruth Wyllys)
"Wyoming Valley Tales" (Crane), I: 409
Xaipe (Cummings), I: 430, 432–433, 447
Xenogenesis trilogy (O. Butler), Supp. XIII: 63–66, 69
Xenophon, II: 105
Xingu and Other Stories (Wharton), IV: 314, 320; Retro. Supp. I: 378
Xionia (Wright), Supp. V: 333
XLI Poems (Cummings), I: 429, 432, 440, 443
Yacoubi, Ahmed, Supp. IV Part 1: 88, 92, 93
Yage Letters, The (Burroughs), Supp. III Part 1: 94, 98, 100
Yagoda, Ben, Supp. VIII: 151
Yamamoto, Isoroku, Supp. I Part 2: 491
Yankee City (Warner), III: 60
Yankee Clipper (ballet) (Kirstein), Supp. IV Part 1: 82
Yankee in Canada, A (Thoreau), IV: 188
Yankey in London (Tyler), I: 344

"Yánnina" (Merrill), Supp. III Part 1: 329
"Yanosz Korczak's Last Walk" (Markowick-Olczakova), Supp. X: 70
Yarboro, Chelsea Quinn, Supp. V: 147
Yardley, Jonathan, Supp. V: 326; Supp. XI: 67
"Yard Sale" (Kenyon), Supp. VII: 169
Yates, Richard, Supp. XI: 333–350
"Year, The" (Sandburg), III: 584
Yearling, The (Rawlings), Supp. X: 219, 230–231, 233, 234
Year of Happy, A (Goldbarth), Supp. XII: 180
"Year of Mourning, The" (Jeffers), Supp. II Part 2: 415
Year of Silence, The (Bell), Supp. X: 1, 5–6, 7
"Year of the Double Spring, The" (Swenson), Supp. IV Part 2: 647
Year's Life, A (Lowell), Supp. I Part 2: 405
"Years of Birth" (Cowley), Supp. II Part 1: 149
Years of My Youth (Howells), II: 276
"Years of Wonder" (White), Supp. I Part 2: 652, 653
Years With Ross, The (Thurber), Supp. I Part 2: 619
Yeats, John Butler, III: 458
Yeats, William Butler, I: 69, 172, 384, 389, 403, 434, 478, 494, 532; II: 168–169, 566, 598; III: 4, 5, 8, 18, 19, 20, 23, 29, 40, 205, 249, 269, 270–271, 272, 278, 279, 294, 347, 409, 457, 458–460, 472, 473, 476–477, 521, 523, 524, 527, 528, 533, 540, 541, 542, 543–544, 591–592; IV: 89, 93, 121, 126, 136, 140, 271, 394, 404; Retro. Supp. I: 59, 66, 127, 141, 270, 283, 285, 286, 288, 290, 311, 342, 350, 378, 413; Retro. Supp. II: 185, 349; Supp. I Part 1: 79, 80, 254, 257, 262; Supp. I Part 2: 388, 389; Supp. II Part 1: 1, 4, 9, 20, 26, 361; Supp. III Part 1: 59, 63, 236, 238, 253; Supp. IV Part 1: 81; Supp. IV Part 2: 634; Supp. V: 220; Supp. VIII: 19, 21, 30, 155, 156, 190, 239, 262, 292; Supp. IX: 43, 119; Supp. X: 35, 58, 119, 120; Supp. XI: 140; Supp. XII: 132, 198, 217, 266; Supp. XIII: 77, 87
Yellow Back Radio Broke-Down (Reed), Supp. X: 240, 242, 243–245
"Yellow Dog Café" (Komunyakaa), Supp. XIII: 126
"Yellow Girl" (Caldwell), I: 310

Yellow Glove (Nye), **Supp. XIII:** 275, **276–277**
"Yellow Glove" (Nye), **Supp. XIII:** 276
"Yellow Gown, The" (Anderson), **I:** 114
Yellow House on the Corner, The (Dove), **Supp. IV Part 1:** 244, 245, 246, 254
"Yellow River" (Tate), **IV:** 141
"Yellow Violet, The" (Bryant), **Supp. I Part 1:** 154, 155
"Yellow Wallpaper, The" (Gilman), **Supp. XI: 198–199,** 207
"Yellow Woman" (Keres stories), **Supp. IV Part 1:** 327
"Yellow Woman" (Silko), **Supp. IV Part 2:** 567–568
Yelverton, Theresa, **Supp. IX:** 181
Yenser, Stephen, **Supp. X:** 207, 208
"Yentl the Yeshiva Boy" (Singer), **IV:** 15, 20
Yerkes, Charles E., **I:** 507, 512
Yerma (opera) (Bowles), **Supp. IV Part 1:** 89
"Yes" (Stafford), **Supp. XI:** 329
Yes, Mrs. Williams (W. C. Williams), **Retro. Supp. I:** 423
Yes, Yes, No, No (Kushner), **Supp. IX:** 133
"Yes and It's Hopeless" (Ginsberg), **Supp. II Part 1:** 326
Yesenin, Sergey, **Supp. VIII:** 40
"Yes! No!" (Oliver), **Supp. VII:** 243–244
"Yet Another Example of the Porousness of Certain Borders" (Wallace), **Supp. X:** 309
"Yet Do I Marvel" (Cullen), **Supp. IV Part 1:** 165, 169
Yet Other Waters (Farrell), **II:** 29, 38, 39, 40
Yevtushenko, Yevgeny, **Supp. III Part 1:** 268
Yezzi, David, **Supp. XII:** 193
Y no se lo trago la tierra (And the Earth Did Not Cover Him) (Rivera), **Supp. XIII:** 216
[00a1]Yo! (Alvarez), **Supp. VII:** 1, 15–17
Yohannan, J. D., **II:** 20
Yonge, Charlotte, **II:** 174
"Yonnondio" (Whitman), **Supp. XIII:** 304
Yonnondio: From the Thirties (Olsen), **Supp. XIII:** 292, 295, 296, **303–304,** 305
"Yore" (Nemerov), **III:** 283
"York Beach" (Toomer), **Supp. III Part 2:** 486

Yorke, Dorothy, **Supp. I Part 1:** 258
Yorke, Henry Vincent. *See* Green, Henry
"York Garrison, 1640" (Jewett), **Retro. Supp. II:** 141
Yosemite, The (Muir), **Supp. IX:** 185
"Yosemite Glaciers: Ice Streams of the Great Valley" (Muir), **Supp. IX:** 181
Yoshe Kalb (Singer), **IV:** 2
"You, Andrew Marvell" (MacLeish), **III:** 12–13
"You, Dr. Martin" (Sexton), **Supp. II Part 2:** 673
You, Emperors, and Others: Poems 1957–1960 (Warren), **IV:** 245
"You, Genoese Mariner" (Merwin), **Supp. III Part 1:** 343
"You All Know the Story of the Other Woman" (Sexton), **Supp. II Part 2:** 688
You Are Happy (Atwood), **Supp. XIII:** 34
"You Are Happy" (Atwood), **Supp. XIII:** 34
"You Are in Bear Country" (Kumin), **Supp. IV Part 2:** 453, 455
"You Are Not I" (Bowles), **Supp. IV Part 1:** 87
"You Begin" (Atwood), **Supp. XIII:** 34
"You Bring Out the Mexican in Me" (Cisneros), **Supp. VII:** 71
You Came Along (film), **Supp. IV Part 2:** 524
"You Can Go Home Again" (TallMountain), **Supp. IV Part 1:** 324–325
"You Can Have It" (Levine), **Supp. V:** 188–189
You Can't Go Home Again (Wolfe), **IV:** 450, 451, 454, 456, 460, 462, 468, 469, 470
You Can't Keep a Good Woman Down (Walker), **Supp. III Part 2:** 520, 525, 531
"You Can't Tell a Man by the Song He Sings" (Roth), **Supp. III Part 2:** 406
"You Don't Know What Love Is" (Carver), **Supp. III Part 1:** 147
"You Have Left Your Lotus Pods on the Bus" (Bowles), **Supp. IV Part 1:** 91
You Have Seen Their Faces (Caldwell), **I:** 290, 293–294, 295, 304, 309
You Know Me Al (comic strip), **II:** 423
You Know Me Al (Lardner), **II:** 26, 415, 419, 422, 431
"You Know What" (Beattie), **Supp. V:** 33

"You Know Who You Are" (Nye), **Supp. XIII:** 275
You Might As Well Live: The Life and Times of Dorothy Parker (Keats), **Supp. IX:** 190
You Must Revise Your Life (Stafford), **Supp. XI:** 312–313, 313–314, 315
"Young" (Sexton), **Supp. II Part 2:** 680
Young, Al, **Supp. X:** 240
Young, Art, **IV:** 436
Young, Brigham, **Supp. IV Part 2:** 603
Young, Edward, **II:** 111; **III:** 415, 503
Young, Mary, **Supp. XIII:** 236, 238, 239, 240
Young, Philip, **II:** 306; **Retro. Supp. I:** 172
Young Adventure (Benét), **Supp. XI:** 44
"Young Child and His Pregnant Mother, A" (Schwartz), **Supp. II Part 2:** 650
Young Christian, The (Abbott), **Supp. I Part 1:** 38
"Young Dr. Gosse" (Chopin), **Supp. I Part 1:** 211, 216
"Young Folks, The" (Salinger), **III:** 551
Young Folk's Cyclopaedia of Persons and Places (Champlin), **III:** 577
"Young Goodman Brown" (Hawthorne), **II:** 229; **Retro. Supp. I:** 151–152, 153, 154; **Supp. XI:** 51
Young Hearts Crying (Yates), **Supp. XI:** 348
"Young Housewife, The" (W. C. Williams), **Retro. Supp. I:** 415
Young Immigrants, The (Lardner), **II:** 426
Young Lonigan: A Boyhood in Chicago Streets (Farrell), **II:** 31, 41
Young Manhood of Studs Lonigan, The (Farrell), **II:** 31, 34
Young People's Pride (Benét), **Supp. XI:** 44
Young Poet's Primer (Brooks), **Supp. III Part 1:** 86
"Young Sammy's First Wild Oats" (Santayana), **III:** 607, 615
"Young Sor Juana, The" (Mora), **Supp. XIII:** 218
"Your Death" (Dove), **Supp. IV Part 1:** 250
"You're Ugly, Too" (Moore), **Supp. X:** 171
"Your Face on the Dog's Neck" (Sexton), **Supp. II Part 2:** 686
"Your Life" (Stafford), **Supp. XI:** 329
"Your Mother's Eyes" (Kingsolver),

Supp. VII: 209
Your Native Land, Your Life: Poems (Rich), **Retro. Supp. II:** 291–292
"You Take a Train through a Foreign Country" (Dobyns), **Supp. XIII:** 90
"Youth" (Hughes), **Supp. I Part 1:** 321
Youth and Life (Bourne), **I:** 217–222, 232
Youth and the Bright Medusa (Cather), **I:** 322; **Retro. Supp. I:** 14
"Youthful Religious Experiences" (Corso), **Supp. XII:** 117
You Touched Me! (Williams and Windham), **IV:** 382, 385, 387, 390, 392–393
Yurka, Blanche, **Supp. I Part 1:** 67
Yutang, Adet, **Supp. X:** 291
Yutang, Anor, **Supp. X:** 291
Yutang, Lin, **Supp. X:** 291
Yutang, Mei-mei, **Supp. X:** 291
Yvernelle: A Legend of Feudal France (Norris), **III:** 314
Y & X (Olson), **Supp. II Part 2:** 556
Zabel, Morton Dauwen, **II:** 431; **III:** 194, 215; **Supp. I Part 2:** 721
Zagarell, Sandra A., **Retro. Supp. II:** 140, 143
"Zagrowsky Tells" (Paley), **Supp. VI:** 229
Zakrzewska, Marie, **Retro. Supp. II:** 146
Zaleski, Jeff, **Supp. XI:** 143
Zaltzberg, Charlotte, **Supp. IV Part 1:** 374
"Zambesi and Ranee" (Swenson), **Supp. IV Part 2:** 647
Zamir, Israel, **Retro. Supp. II:** 321, 335
Zamora, Bernice, **Supp. IV Part 2:** 545
Zangwill, Israel, **I:** 229
Zanita: A Tale of the Yosemite (Yelverton), **Supp. IX:** 181
Zanuck, Darryl F., **Supp. XI:** 170; **Supp. XII:** 165
Zapata, Emiliano, **Supp. XIII:** 324
"Zapatos" (Boyle), **Supp. VIII:** 15
Zarathustra, **III:** 602
Zawacki, Andrew, **Supp. VIII:** 272
"Zaydee" (Levine), **Supp. V:** 186
Zebra-Striped Hearse, The (Macdonald), **Supp. IV Part 2:** 473
Zechariah (biblical book), **IV:** 152
Zeidner, Lisa, **Supp. IV Part 2:** 453
"Zeitl and Rickel" (Singer), **IV:** 20
Zeke and Ned (McMurtry and Ossana), **Supp. V:** 232
Zeke Proctor, Cherokee Outlaw (Conley), **Supp. V:** 232
Zelda: A Biography (Milford), **Supp. IX:** 60
"Zelda and Scott: The Beautiful and Damned" (National Portrait Gallery exhibit), **Supp. IX:** 65
Zen and the Birds of Appetite (Merton), **Supp. VIII:** 205–206, 208
Zend-Avesta (Fechner), **II:** 358
Zeno, **Retro. Supp. I:** 247
Zero db and Other Stories (Bell), **Supp. X:** 1, 5, 6
"Zeus over Redeye" (Hayden), **Supp. II Part 1:** 380
Zevi, Sabbatai, **IV:** 6
Ziegfeld, Florenz, **II:** 427–428
Zigrosser, Carl, **I:** 226, 228, 231
Zimmerman, Paul D., **Supp. IV Part 2:** 583, 589, 590
Zinman, Toby Silverman, **Supp. XIII:** 207–208, 209
Zinn, Howard, **Supp. V:** 289
Zinsser, Hans, **I:** 251, 385
"Zizi's Lament" (Corso), **Supp. XII:** 123
Zodiac, The (Dickey), **Supp. IV Part 1:** 178, 183–184, 185
Zola, Émile, **I:** 211, 411, 474, 500, 502, 518; **II:** 174, 175–176, 182, 194, 275, 276, 281, 282, 319, 325, 337, 338; **III:** 315, 316, 317–318, 319–320, 321, 322, 323, 393, 511, 583; **IV:** 326; **Retro. Supp. I:** 226, 235; **Retro. Supp. II:** 93; **Supp. I Part 1:** 207; **Supp. II Part 1:** 117
Zolotow, Maurice, **III:** 161
"Zone" (Bogan), **Supp. III Part 1:** 60–61
Zone Journals (Wright), **Supp. V:** 332–333, 342–343
"Zooey" (Salinger), **III:** 564–565, 566, 567, 569, 572
"Zoo Revisited" (White), **Supp. I Part 2:** 654
Zoo Story, The (Albee), **I:** 71, 72–74, 75, 77, 84, 93, 94; **III:** 281
Zorach, William, **I:** 260
Zuckerman Bound: A Trilogy and Epilogue (Roth), **Supp. III Part 2:** 423
Zuckerman Unbound (Roth), **Retro. Supp. II:** 301; **Supp. III Part 2:** 421–422
Zueblin, Charles, **Supp. I Part 1:** 5
Zuger, Abigail, **Supp. X:** 160
Zukofsky, Celia (Mrs. Louis), **Supp. III Part 2:** 619–621, 623, 625, 626–629, 631
Zukofsky, Louis, **IV:** 415; **Retro. Supp. I:** 422; **Supp. III Part 2:** **619–636**; **Supp. IV Part 1:** 154
Zukofsky, Paul, **Supp. III Part 2:** 622, 623–626, 627, 628
Zuleika Dobson (Beerbohm), **Supp. I Part 2:** 714
Zverev, Aleksei, **Retro. Supp. I:** 278
Zwinger, Ann, **Supp. X:** 29
Zyda, Joan, **Retro. Supp. II:** 52

# A Complete Listing of Authors in *American Writers*

Abbey, Edward   Supp. XIII
Acker, Kathy   Supp. XII
Adams, Henry   Vol. I
Addams, Jane   Supp. I
Agee, James   Vol. I
Aiken, Conrad   Vol. I
Albee, Edward   Vol. I
Alcott, Louisa May   Supp. I
Algren, Nelson   Supp. IX
Alvarez, Julia   Supp. VII
Ammons, A. R.   Supp. VII
Anderson, Sherwood   Vol. I
Angelou, Maya   Supp. IV
Ashbery, John   Supp. III
Atwood, Margaret   Supp. XIII
Auchincloss, Louis   Supp. IV
Auden, W. H.   Supp. II
Auster, Paul   Supp. XII
Baker, Nicholson   Supp. XIII
Baldwin, James   Supp. I
Baldwin, James   Retro. Supp. II
Bambara, Toni Cade   Supp. XI
Banks, Russell   Supp. V
Baraka, Amiri   Supp. II
Barlow, Joel   Supp. II
Barnes, Djuna   Supp. III
Barth, John   Vol. I
Barthelme, Donald   Supp. IV
Barthelme, Frederick   Supp. XI
Bausch, Richard   Supp. VII
Beattie, Ann   Supp. V
Bell, Madison Smartt   Supp. X
Bellow, Saul   Vol. I
Bellow, Saul   Retro. Supp. II
Benét, Stephen Vincent   Supp. XI
Berry, Wendell   Supp. X
Berryman, John   Vol. I

Bierce, Ambrose   Vol. I
Bishop, Elizabeth   Supp. I
Bishop, Elizabeth   Retro. Supp. II
Blackmur, R. P.   Supp. II
Bly, Robert   Supp. IV
Bogan, Louise   Supp. III
Bourne, Randolph   Vol. I
Bowles, Paul   Supp. IV
Boyle, T. C.   Supp. VIII
Bradbury, Ray   Supp. IV
Bradstreet, Anne   Supp. I
Brodsky, Joseph   Supp. VIII
Brooks, Gwendolyn   Supp. III
Brooks, Van Wyck   Vol. I
Brown, Charles Brockden   Supp. I
Bryant, William Cullen   Supp. I
Buck, Pearl S.   Supp. II
Buechner, Frederick   Supp. XII
Burke, Kenneth   Vol. I
Burroughs, William S.   Supp. III
Butler, Octavia   Supp. XIII
Butler, Robert Olen   Supp. XII
Caldwell, Erskine   Vol. I
Cameron, Peter   Supp. XII
Capote, Truman   Supp. III
Carson, Anne   Supp. XII
Carson, Rachel   Supp. IX
Carver, Raymond   Supp. III
Cather, Willa   Vol. I
Cather, Willa   Retro. Supp. I
Chabon, Michael   Supp. XI
Chandler, Raymond   Supp. IV
Cheever, John   Supp. I
Chopin, Kate   Supp. I
Chopin, Kate   Retro. Supp. II
Cisneros, Sandra   Supp. VII
Clampitt, Amy   Supp. IX

613

Coleman, Wanda   Supp. XI
Cooper, James Fenimore   Vol. I
Coover, Robert   Supp. V
Corso, Gregory   Supp. XII
Cowley, Malcolm   Supp. II
Cozzens, James Gould   Vol. I
Crane, Hart   Vol. I
Crane, Hart   Retro. Supp. II
Crane, Stephen   Vol. I
Creeley, Robert   Supp. IV
Crèvecoeur, Michel-Guillaume Jean de   Supp. I
Crews, Harry   Supp. XI
Cullen, Countee   Supp. IV
Cummings, E. E.   Vol. I
DeLillo, Don   Supp. VI
Dickey, James   Supp. IV
Dickinson, Emily   Vol. I
Dickinson, Emily   Retro. Supp. I
Didion, Joan   Supp. IV
Dillard, Annie   Supp. VI
Dixon, Stephen   Supp. XII
Dobyns, Stephen   Supp. XIII
Doctorow, E. L.   Supp. IV
Doolittle, Hilda (H.D.)   Supp. I
Dos Passos, John   Vol. I
Doty, Mark   Supp. XI
Douglass, Frederick   Supp. III
Dove, Rita   Supp. IV
Dreiser, Theodore   Vol. I
Dreiser, Theodore   Retro. Supp. II
Du Bois, W. E. B.   Supp. II
Dubus, Andre   Supp. VII
Dunbar, Paul Laurence   Supp. II
Dunn, Stephen   Supp. XI
Eberhart, Richard   Vol. I
Edwards, Jonathan   Vol. I
Eliot, T. S.   Vol. I
Eliot, T. S.   Retro. Supp. I
Elkin, Stanley   Supp. VI
Ellison, Ralph   Supp. II
Ellison, Ralph   Retro. Supp. II
Emerson, Ralph Waldo   Vol. II
Epstein, Leslie   Supp. XII

Erdrich, Louise   Supp. IV
Fante, John   Supp. XI
Farrell, James T.   Vol. II
Faulkner, William   Vol. II
Faulkner, William   Retro. Supp. I
Fiedler, Leslie   Supp. XIII
Fitzgerald, F. Scott   Vol. II
Fitzgerald, F. Scott   Retro. Supp. I
Fitzgerald, Zelda   Supp. IX
Ford, Richard   Supp. V
Francis, Robert   Supp. IX
Franklin, Benjamin   Vol. II
Frederic, Harold   Vol. II
Freneau, Philip   Supp. II
Frost, Robert   Vol. II
Frost, Robert   Retro. Supp. I
Fuller, Margaret   Supp. II
Gaddis, William   Supp. IV
García, Cristina   Supp. XI
Gardner, John   Supp. VI
Garrett, George   Supp. VII
Gass, William   Supp. VI
Gibbons, Kaye   Supp. X
Gilman, Charlotte Perkins   Supp. XI
Ginsberg, Allen   Supp. II
Glasgow, Ellen   Vol. II
Glaspell, Susan   Supp. III
Goldbarth, Albert   Supp. XII
Glück, Louise   Supp. V
Gordon, Caroline   Vol. II
Gordon, Mary   Supp. IV
Gunn Allen, Paula   Supp. IV
Gurney, A. R.   Supp. V
Haines, John   Supp. XII
Hammett, Dashiell   Supp. IV
Hansberry, Lorraine   Supp. IV
Hardwick, Elizabeth   Supp. III
Harjo, Joy   Supp. XII
Harrison, Jim   Supp. VIII
Harte, Bret   Supp. II
Hass, Robert   Supp. VI
Hawthorne, Nathaniel   Vol. II
Hawthorne, Nathaniel   Retro. Supp. I
Hayden, Robert   Supp. II

Hearon, Shelby   Supp. VIII
Hecht, Anthony   Supp. X
Heller, Joseph   Supp. IV
Hellman, Lillian   Supp. I
Hemingway, Ernest   Vol. II
Hemingway, Ernest   Retro. Supp. I
Henry, O.   Supp. II
Hijuelos, Oscar   Supp. VIII
Hoffman, Alice   Supp. X
Hogan, Linda   Supp. IV
Holmes, Oliver Wendell   Supp. I
Howe, Irving   Supp. VI
Howe, Susan   Supp. IV
Howells, William Dean   Vol. II
Hughes, Langston   Supp. I
Hughes, Langston   Retro. Supp. I
Hugo, Richard   Supp. VI
Humphrey, William   Supp. IX
Hurston, Zora Neale   Supp. VI
Irving, John   Supp. VI
Irving, Washington   Vol. II
Jackson, Shirley   Supp. IX
James, Henry   Vol. II
James, Henry   Retro. Supp. I
James, William   Vol. II
Jarrell, Randall   Vol. II
Jeffers, Robinson   Supp. II
Jewett, Sarah Orne   Vol. II
Jewett, Sarah Orne   Retro. Supp. II
Johnson, Charles   Supp. VI
Jones, James   Supp. XI
Jong, Erica   Supp. V
Justice, Donald   Supp. VII
Karr, Mary   Supp. XI
Kazin, Alfred   Supp. VIII
Kennedy, William   Supp. VII
Kenyon, Jane   Supp. VII
Kerouac, Jack   Supp. III
Kincaid, Jamaica   Supp. VII
King, Stephen   Supp. V
Kingsolver, Barbara   Supp. VII
Kingston, Maxine Hong   Supp. V
Kinnell, Galway   Supp. III
Knowles, John   Supp. XII

Komunyakaa, Yusef   Supp. XIII
Kosinski, Jerzy   Supp. VII
Kumin, Maxine   Supp. IV
Kunitz, Stanley   Supp. III
Kushner, Tony   Supp. IX
LaBastille, Anne   Supp. X
Lanier, Sidney   Supp. I
Larcom, Lucy   Supp. XIII
Lardner, Ring   Vol. II
Lee, Harper   Supp. VIII
Levertov, Denise   Supp. III
Levine, Philip   Supp. V
Levis, Larry   Supp. XI
Lewis, Sinclair   Vol. II
Lindsay, Vachel   Supp. I
London, Jack   Vol. II
Longfellow, Henry Wadsworth   Vol. II
Longfellow, Henry Wadsworth   Retro. Supp. II
Lowell, Amy   Vol. II
Lowell, James Russell   Supp. I
Lowell, Robert   Vol. II
Lowell, Robert   Retro. Supp. II
McCarthy, Cormac   Supp. VIII
McCarthy, Mary   Vol. II
McClatchy, J. D.   Supp. XII
McCourt, Frank   Supp. XII
McCoy, Horace   Supp. XIII
McCullers, Carson   Vol. II
Macdonald, Ross   Supp. IV
McGrath, Thomas   Supp. X
McKay, Claude   Supp. X
MacLeish, Archibald   Vol. III
McMillan, Terry   Supp. XIII
McMurty, Larry   Supp. V
McNally, Terrence   Supp. XIII
McPhee, John   Supp. III
Mailer, Norman   Vol. III
Mailer, Norman   Retro. Supp. II
Malamud, Bernard   Supp. I
Marquand, John P.   Vol. III
Marshall, Paule   Supp. XI
Mason, Bobbie Ann   Supp. VIII
Masters, Edgar Lee   Supp. I

Mather, Cotton   Supp. II
Matthews, William   Supp. IX
Matthiessen, Peter   Supp. V
Maxwell, William   Supp. VIII
Melville, Herman   Vol. III
Melville, Herman   Retro. Supp. I
Mencken, H. L.   Vol. III
Merrill, James   Supp. III
Merton, Thomas   Supp. VIII
Merwin, W. S.   Supp. III
Millay, Edna St. Vincent   Vol. III
Miller, Arthur   Vol. III
Miller, Henry   Vol. III
Miller, Sue   Supp. XII
Minot, Susan   Supp. VI
Momaday, N. Scott   Supp. IV
Monette, Paul   Supp. X
Moore, Lorrie   Supp. X
Moore, Marianne   Vol. III
Mora, Pat   Supp. XIII
Morison, Samuel Eliot   Supp. I
Morris, Wright   Vol. III
Morrison, Toni   Supp. III
Mosley, Walter   Supp. XIII
Muir, John   Supp. IX
Mumford, Lewis   Supp. III
Nabokov, Vladimir   Vol. III
Nabokov, Vladimir   Retro. Supp. I
Naylor, Gloria   Supp. VIII
Nemerov, Howard   Vol. III
Nichols, John   Supp. XIII
Niebuhr, Reinhold   Vol. III
Nin, Anaïs   Supp. X
Norris, Frank   Vol. III
Nye, Naomi Shihab   Supp. XIII
Oates, Joyce Carol   Supp. II
O'Brien, Tim   Supp. V
O'Connor, Flannery   Vol. III
O'Connor, Flannery   Retro. Supp. II
Odets, Clifford   Supp. II
O'Hara, John   Vol. III
Olds, Sharon   Supp. X
Oliver, Mary   Supp. VII
Olsen, Tillie   Supp. XIII

Olson, Charles   Supp. II
O'Neill, Eugene   Vol. III
Ortiz, Simon J.   Supp. IV
Ozick, Cynthia   Supp. V
Paine, Thomas   Supp. I
Paley, Grace   Supp. VI
Parker, Dorothy   Supp. IX
Parkman, Francis   Supp. II
Patchett, Ann   Supp. XII
Percy, Walker   Supp. III
Pinsky, Robert   Supp. VI
Plath, Sylvia   Supp. I
Plath, Sylvia   Retro. Supp. II
Podhoretz, Norman   Supp. VIII
Poe, Edgar Allan   Vol. III
Poe, Edgar Allan   Retro. Supp. II
Porter, Katherine Anne   Vol. III
Pound, Ezra   Vol. III
Pound, Ezra   Retro. Supp. I
Powers, Richard   Supp. IX
Price, Reynolds   Supp. VI
Proulx, Annie   Supp. VII
Purdy, James   Supp. VII
Pynchon, Thomas   Supp. II
Rand, Ayn   Supp. IV
Ransom, John Crowe   Vol. III
Rawlings, Marjorie Kinnan   Supp. X
Reed, Ishmael   Supp. X
Rice, Anne   Supp. VII
Rich, Adrienne   Supp. I
Rich, Adrienne   Retro. Supp. II
Ríos, Alberto Álvaro   Supp. IV
Robbins, Tom   Supp. X
Robinson, Edwin Arlington   Vol. III
Roethke, Theodore   Vol. III
Roth, Henry   Supp. IX
Roth, Philip   Supp. III
Roth, Philip   Retro. Supp. II
Rukeyser, Muriel   Supp. VI
Russo, Richard   Supp. XII
Salinas, Luis Omar   Supp. XIII
Salinger, J. D.   Vol. III
Salter, James   Supp. IX
Sandburg, Carl   Vol. III

Santayana, George Vol. III	Twain, Mark Vol. IV
Sarton, May Supp. VIII	Tyler, Anne Supp. IV
Schwartz, Delmore Supp. II	Updike, John Vol. IV
Sexton, Anne Supp. II	Updike, John Retro. Supp. I
Shapiro, Karl Supp. II	Van Vechten, Carl Supp. II
Shepard, Sam Supp. III	Veblen, Thorstein Supp. I
Shields, Carol Supp. VII	Vidal, Gore Supp. IV
Silko, Leslie Marmon Supp. IV	Vonnegut, Kurt Supp. II
Simic, Charles Supp. VIII	Wagoner, David Supp. IX
Simon, Neil Supp. IV	Walker, Alice Supp. III
Simpson, Louis Supp. IX	Wallace, David Foster Supp. X
Sinclair, Upton Supp. V	Warren, Robert Penn Vol. IV
Singer, Isaac Bashevis Vol. IV	Welty, Eudora Vol. IV
Singer, Isaac Bashevis Retro. Supp. II	Welty, Eudora Retro. Supp. I
Smiley, Jane Supp. VI	West, Nathanael Vol. IV
Smith, William Jay Supp. XIII	West, Nathanael Retro. Supp. II
Snodgrass, W. D. Supp. VI	Wharton, Edith Vol. IV
Snyder, Gary Supp. VIII	Wharton, Edith Retro. Supp. I
Sontag, Susan Supp. III	White, E. B. Supp. I
Southern, Terry Supp. XI	Whitman, Walt Vol. IV
Stafford, William Supp. XI	Whitman, Walt Retro. Supp. I
Stegner, Wallace Supp. IV	Whittier, John Greenleaf Supp. I
Stein, Gertrude Vol. IV	Wilbur, Richard Supp. III
Steinbeck, John Vol. IV	Wideman, John Edgar Supp. X
Stern, Gerald Supp. IX	Wilder, Thornton Vol. IV
Stevens, Wallace Vol. IV	Williams, Tennessee Vol. IV
Stevens, Wallace Retro. Supp. I	Williams, William Carlos Vol. IV
Stone, Robert Supp. V	Williams, William Carlos Retro. Supp. I
Stowe, Harriet Beecher Supp. I	Wilson, August Supp. VIII
Strand, Mark Supp. IV	Wilson, Edmund Vol. IV
Styron, William Vol. IV	Winters, Yvor Supp. II
Swenson, May Supp. IV	Wolfe, Thomas Vol. IV
Tan, Amy Supp. X	Wolfe, Tom Supp. III
Tate, Allen Vol. IV	Wolff, Tobias Supp. VII
Taylor, Edward Vol. IV	Wright, Charles Supp. V
Taylor, Peter Supp. V	Wright, James Supp. III
Theroux, Paul Supp. VIII	Wright, Richard Vol. IV
Thoreau, Henry David Vol. IV	Wylie, Elinor Supp. I
Thurber, James Supp. I	Yates, Richard Supp. XI
Toomer, Jean Supp. IX	Zukofsky, Louis Supp. III
Trilling, Lionel Supp. III